The Law of
Higher Education

◆ ◆ ◆

William A. Kaplin

Barbara A. Lee

◆   ◆   ◆

The Law of Higher Education

◆ ◆ ◆

*A Comprehensive Guide
to Legal Implications
of Administrative Decision Making*

THIRD EDITION

Jossey-Bass Publishers • San Francisco

Substantial discounts on bulk quantities of Jossey-Bass books are available to corporations, professional associations, and other organizations. For details and discount information, contact the special sales department at Jossey-Bass Inc., Publishers. (415) 433-1740; Fax (800) 605-2665.

Jossey-Bass Web address: http://www.josseybass.com

Manufactured in the United States of America. Nearly all Jossey-Bass books and jackets are printed on recycled paper that contains at least 50 percent recycled waste, including 10 percent postconsumer waste. Many of our materials are also printed with vegetable-based inks; during the printing process these inks emit fewer volatile organic compounds (VOCs) than petroleum-based inks. VOCs contribute to the formation of smog.

Library of Congress Cataloging-in-Publication Data

Kaplin, William A., date.
    The law of higher education : a comprehensive guide to legal implications of administrative decision making / William A. Kaplin, Barbara A. Lee. — 3rd ed.
      p.   cm. — (The Jossey-Bass higher education series)
    Includes bibliographical references and index.
    ISBN 0-7879-0052-4
    1. Universities and colleges—Law and legislation—United States.
2. School management and organization—Law and legislation—United States. 3. Universities and colleges—United States—Administration. I. Lee, Barbara A. II. Title. III. Series.
KF4225.K36   1995
344.73′074—dc20
[347.30474]
                  94-38999
                  CIP

THIRD EDITION
HB Printing   10 9 8 7 6 5 4 3   *Code 9509*

The Jossey-Bass
Higher and Adult Education Series

◆   ◆   ◆

Instructional Guide for the Third Edition

A companion volume of instructional materials is available to users of *The Law of Higher Education* (3d ed.). This volume, *Cases, Problems, and Materials: An Instructional Supplement to* The Law of Higher Education, may be used by instructors of courses on the law of higher education, as well as by leaders of workshops in which higher education legal issues are addressed. Among other materials, the supplement contains an orientation to the study of education law, numerous questions and small problems designed to elicit discussion, a series of "large-scale" problems suitable for role-playing, and guidelines for answering and analyzing all the problems.

The authors of *The Law of Higher Education* have prepared this supplement under the sponsorship of Jossey-Bass Publishers and the National Association of College and University Attorneys (NACUA). NACUA, the supplement's publisher, is making review copies available without charge to instructors who have adopted or are considering adopting *The Law of Higher Education* (3d ed.) for classroom use. Workshop leaders may also request review copies. Instructors who use *The Law of Higher Education* as a required text may either order additional copies of the supplement for purchase by students or reproduce the review copy, or selected portions of it, for distribution to students in the course. No other reproduction or distribution is permitted.

Please address inquiries to:

Manager of Publications
National Association of College and University Attorneys
Suite 620, One Dupont Circle NW
Washington, D.C. 20036
(202) 833-8390; Fax (202) 296-8379

Individuals wishing a review copy of the supplement should so indicate on their institutional letterhead, including their title and the title of the course. For those ordering copies for purchase, please call NACUA before ordering to ascertain the per-copy price.

Contents

◆ ◆ ◆

Contents

Preface

◆ ◆ ◆

This book is the revised, updated, and expanded third edition of a volume that was first published in 1978. The first edition was supplemented with a companion volume in 1980 (*The Law of Higher Education 1980*). The second edition was published in 1985, and it was supplemented in 1991 with *The Law of Higher Education: 1985-1990 Update* (published by the National Association of College and University Attorneys). This new third edition is current to approximately August 1994.

Background and Scope

In the decade since publication of the second edition, many new and newly complex legal concerns have arisen on the campuses—from hate speech, to regulation of the use of animals in research, to conflicts of interest in research ventures, to increased governmental scrutiny of the information that colleges give to current and prospective students on everything from crime statistics to graduation rates to loan repayment requirements. Indeed, it is difficult to think of any other entities—including large corporations and government agencies—that are subject to as great an array of legal requirements as colleges and universities are. To serve the needs occasioned by this continual growth of the law, the third edition retains all material of continuing legal currency from the second edition and the 1991 update, reedited to maximize clarity and to accommodate the deletion and addition of materials. We have added considerable new material to this base: approximately half of the contents of the third edition did not appear in earlier editions or supplements. Specifically, we have extended the discussion of matters that (in hindsight) were given insufficient attention in earlier editions or have since acquired greater significance; integrated pertinent new developments regarding topics in the earlier editions; and introduced numerous new topics not covered in earlier editions.

Although considerable material from earlier editions has lost its legal currency as a result of later developments, we have nevertheless retained some of this material for its continuing historical significance. What has been retained, however, is often presented in a more compressed format than in earlier editions. Thus, for a more extended or complete history of particular developments, readers may wish to consult the first and second editions. Moreover, we have sometimes deleted or compressed material that still has legal currency, because later cases or developments provide more instructive illustrations; readers may thus also wish to consult the first and second editions for additional examples of particular legal issues.

Audience

The Law of Higher Education was originally written for administrative officers, trustees, and legal counsel who deal with the many challenges and complexities that arise from the law's presence on campus, and for students and observers of higher education and law who desire to explore the intersection of these two disciplines. The third edition continues to serve the ever-increasing needs of these groups. In addition, its materials and scope have been expanded to serve additional groups that are regularly encountering legal conflicts and challenges in their professional lives: deans, department chairs, student life staff, business managers, purchasing officers, grants and contracts officers, patent and copyright administrators, staff who work with disabled students or with foreign students, athletic directors, directors of campus security, and environmental compliance officers. Outside the university, officers and staff at higher education associations, executives and project officers of foundations serving academia, and state and federal government officials will also find the third edition useful.

Overview of the Contents

Even though we have broadened its scope, the third edition retains the basic organization, format, and objectives of the first two editions. Also, like the earlier editions, the third edition covers all of *postsecondary* education—from the large state university to the small private liberal arts college, from the graduate and professional school to the community college and vocational and technical institution, and from the traditional campus-based program to the innovative off-campus or multistate program. The third edition also reflects the same perspective on the intersection of law and education, as described in the preface to the first edition:

> The law has arrived on the campus. Sometimes it has been a beacon, other times a blanket of ground fog. But even in its murkiness, the law has not come "on little cat feet," like Carl Sandburg's "Fog"; nor has it sat silently on its haunches; nor will it soon move on. It has come noisily and sometimes has stumbled. And even in its imperfections, the law has spoken forcefully and meaningfully to the higher education community and will continue to do so.

To be equally usable by administrators and legal counsel, the text avoids legal jargon and technicalities when possible and explains them when they are used. Footnotes throughout the book are designed primarily to provide additional technical analysis and research resources for legal counsel.

In seeking to serve its audiences, this book organizes and conceptualizes the entire range of legal considerations pertinent to the operation of colleges and universities. It analyzes legal developments, identifies trends, and tracks their implications for academic institutions—sometimes pointing out how particular legal developments may clash with important academic practices or values. It also suggests preventive law measures and facilitates effective working relationships between counsel and administrators who must grapple with law's impact on their campuses.

This third edition contains nine chapters, each divided into numerous sections and subsections. Chapter One provides a framework for understanding and integrating what is presented in subsequent chapters and a perspective for dealing with future legal developments. Chapters Two, Three, and Four discuss legal concepts and issues affecting the internal relationships among the various members of the campus community and address the law's impact on particular roles, functions, and responsibilities of postsecondary administrators. Chapters Five, Six, and Seven are concerned with the postsecondary institution's external relationships with government at the local, state, and federal levels. These chapters examine broad questions of governmental power and process that cut across all the internal relationships and administrative functions considered in earlier chapters; they also discuss particular legal issues arising from the institution's dealings with government, and they point out connections between these issues and those explored in the earlier chapters. Chapter Eight and Chapter Nine also deal with the institution's external relationships, but the relationships are those with the private sector rather than with government. Chapter Eight covers the various national and regional education organizations with which the institution interacts; Chapter Nine covers the myriad relationships—many on the cutting edge—that institutions are increasingly entering with the commercial and industrial world.

Citations and References

Each chapter ends with a selected annotated bibliography. Readers can use the listed books, articles, reports, and other sources to extend the discussion of particular issues presented in the chapter, to explore issues not treated in the chapter, to obtain additional practical guidance in dealing with the chapter's issues, to keep abreast of later developments, and to discover resources for research. Other sources pertaining to particular questions are cited in the text, and footnotes contain additional legal resources (primarily for lawyers). Court decisions, statutes, and administrative regulations are cited throughout the text. In addition, the footnotes contain copious citations to *American Law Reports* (A.L.R.) annotations that collect additional court decisions on particular subjects and periodically update each collection. The citation form for the third edition generally follows *The Bluebook: A Uniform System of Citation* (15th ed., Columbia Law Review Association, Harvard Law Review Association, University of Pennsylvania Law Review, and Yale Law Journal, 1991). The legal sources that these citations refer to are described in Chapter One, Section 1.3.3, of the third edition.

What Is New in This Edition

In the light cast by recent developments, many new topics of concern have emerged on stage, and older topics that once were bit players have assumed major roles. To cover these topics, the third edition adds entirely new sections on the litigation process (Section 1.4); the college's staff (Section 2.2.3); captive and affiliated organizations (Section 2.2.5); contracts in religious institutions (Section 3.1.6); legal planning with contracts (Section 3.1.7); sexual orientation discrimination, including recent opinions involving the military (Section 3.3.8); the public faculty member's right to due process in matters other than contract renewal and tenure (Section 3.6.2.4); the private faculty member's procedural rights (Section 3.6.3); academic freedom in research and publication (Section 3.7.3); academic freedom in religious institutions (Section 3.7.5.2); minority scholarships, including the most recent policy guidance from the U.S. Department of Education (Section 4.3.4); disciplining students with psychiatric illnesses (Section 4.6.3); hate speech, including the U.S. Supreme Court's decision in *R.A.V. v. City of St. Paul* (Section 4.10); fraternities and sororities (Section 4.12); athletic scholarships (Section 4.15.2); drug testing of athletes (Section 4.15.5); tort liability for athletic injuries (Section 4.15.6); federal statutes related to campus security (Section 4.17.3); local zoning of off-campus student housing (Section 5.2.8); open-records laws (Section 6.5.2); laws regulating medical services and medical research (Section 6.5.6); laws governing animal research (Section 7.2.9); trademark laws (Section 7.2.12); environmental laws (Section 7.2.15); the Americans with Disabilities Act (Section 7.2.16); the Family and Medical Leave Act (Section 7.2.17); the Student Right-to-Know Act (Section 7.4.3.3); protecting institutional interests in disputes with funding agencies (Section 7.4.5.); overview of the education associations (Section 8.1); state statutes regulating NCAA enforcement activities (Section 8.4.2); and the American Association of University Professors (Section 8.5). The third edition also contains an entirely new chapter, Chapter Nine, on the college's relationships with the business/industrial community.

Other sections from the second edition have been reconceptualized and reorganized in the process of our updating and expanding them: Section 1.3 on the sources of postsecondary education law; Section 3.3 on nondiscrimination in employment; Section 4.7 on grades, credits, and degrees; Section 4.15 on athletics; and the entire Chapter Eight on the national and regional education associations.

Yet other sections from the second edition or the 1991 update have been extensively revised or expanded to account for important recent developments. Examples of new topics and materials include international law aspects of university affairs (Sections 1.2, 1.3.1.5, 9.1.1, and 9.4.2); *Corporation of Mercer University v. Smith,* on trustee authority to close an institution (Section 2.2.1); new cases on institutional liability for acts of others (Section 2.3); employee handbooks as contracts, and drug testing of employees (Section 3.1.1); *Curran v. Catholic University of America, Alicea v. New Brunswick Theological Seminary,* and *Welter v. Seton Hall University,* involving the interplay between contract law, canon or church law, and the First Amendment's Establishment Clause (Section 3.1.6); agency shops and the rights of dissenting bargaining unit members—including the U.S. Supreme Court's decision in *Lehnert v. Ferris Faculty Assn.* (Section 3.2.2); U.S. Supreme Court decisions regarding the right of dissenting bargaining unit members to withhold part of their agency fee on First Amendment grounds (*Chicago Teachers' Union v. Hudson, Communication Workers v. Beck*) (Section 3.2.2); the U.S. Supreme Court's opinion in *Franklin v. Gwinnett County Public Schools*, permitting plaintiffs to receive money damages in Title IX lawsuits (Sections 3.3.2.3 and 7.5.9); the impact of the employment discrimination provisions of the Americans with Disabilities Act (Section 3.3.2.5); sexual harassment of faculty, including the U.S. Supreme Court's decision in *Harris v. Forklift Systems* (Section 3.3.4.3); recent U.S. Supreme Court decisions on affirmative action in employment (Section 3.4); new cases on termination of tenure for cause, including *San Filippo v. Bongiovanni* (Section 3.5.2); *Bishop v. Aronov* and other new cases on academic freedom in the classroom (Section 3.7.2); the *Ayoub, Colburn, Dorsett,* and *Johnson* cases on academic freedom in institutional affairs (Section 3.7.4); *EEOC v. University of Pennsylvania*, the U.S. Supreme Court case on the academic freedom privilege (Section 3.7.7.1); the U.S. Supreme Court's decision in *United States v. Fordice* on desegregation of public higher education systems (Sections 4.2.4.1 and 7.5.2); *United States v. Commonwealth of Virginia* (the Virginia Military Institute case) and *Faulkner v. Jones* (the Citadel case) on gender discrimination in military academies (Section 4.2.4.2); various new issues regarding students with disabilities (Sections 4.2.4.3, 4.6.3, 4.7.4, and 4.14.1); *Podberesky v. Kirwan*, on the legality of minority-only scholarships (Section 4.3.4); sexual harassment of students (Sections 4.7.3 and 7.5.3); *Carroll v. Blinken* and *Smith v. Regents of California*, regarding the constitutionality of mandatory student fees (Section 4.11.2); Title IX's application to the funding of intercollegiate athletics (Section 4.15.3); recent amendments to FERPA (the Buckley Amendment) (Section 4.16.1); the Campus Security Act (Section 4.17.3); recent cases on students' right to vote where they attend college (Section 5.4.1); state court interpretations of the application of open-meetings and open-records laws to student disciplinary hearings (Sections 6.5.1 and 6.5.2); new statutes and regulations on immigration (Section 7.2.7); the Kinko's copyright litigation and its implications for the fair use doctrine (Section 7.2.10.2); new statutes and cases on federal income taxation (Section 7.3.1); accreditation cases implicating state action law and bankruptcy law (Sections 8.3.2.3 and 8.3.2.6); and a new federal statute and U.S. Department of Education rules on accrediting agencies (Section 8.3.3).

Recommendations for Using the Book and Keeping Up-to-Date

As with the first two editions, some precautions on using this third edition are in order:

> The legal analyses and suggestions, of necessity, are general; they are not adapted to the law of any particular state or to the circumstances prevailing at any particular postsecondary institution. Thus, the book is not a substitute for the advice of legal counsel, for further research into primary legal resources, or for individualized study of each legal problem's specific circumstances. Nor is the book necessarily the latest word on the law. There is a saying among lawyers that "the law must be stable and yet it cannot stand still" [R. Pound, *Interpretations of Legal History*, p. 1 (1923)], and the law is moving especially fast in its applications to postsecondary education. Thus, administrators and counsel will want to keep abreast of ongoing developments concerning the issues in this book. Various aids [described hereafter] exist for this purpose.

Keeping abreast of developments is just as much a necessity—and a challenge—as it was when the previous editions were published. To assist in this task,
we plan to update the third edition every other year in a paperback volume to
be published by the National Association of College and University Attorneys
(NACUA), Washington, D.C. Readers will also be helped by the annual review of
higher education cases ("The Law of Higher Education and the Courts") that is
published in NACUA's *Journal of College and University Law* (further described
later). In addition, there are now a number of publications designed for counsel,
administrators, or both that provide more immediate information and analysis. There
is also a legal reporter that reprints court opinions and provides commentary on
higher education law: *West's Education Law Reporter*, published biweekly by West
Publishing Company, St. Paul, Minnesota (included in the selected annotated bibliography for Chapter One (Section 1.1)).

Also helpful are various periodicals that provide information on current legal
developments. *Synthesis: Law and Policy in Higher Education*, published five times
a year by College Administration Publications, Asheville, North Carolina, provides
in-depth analysis and commentary on major contemporary issues. *Synfax Weekly
Report* and *Synfax Bulletin*, published by Synfax, Crofton, Maryland, are fax newsletters that digest and critique current legal and policy developments. These resources
are also included in the selected annotated bibliography for Chapter One (Sections
1.1 and 1.2). The *School Law News*—a biweekly publication of Capitol Publications,
Alexandria, Virginia—provides journalistic coverage of legal events. The *College
Law Digest*, published every four weeks for its members by NACUA in cooperation
with West Publishing Company, reports on recent court decisions (unpublished
as well as published), journal articles and other publications, and acquisitions by
NACUA's Exchange of Legal Information service; it also contains original commentary on current topics. *Perspective: The Campus Legal Monthly*, published by Magna
Publications, Madison, Wisconsin, provides analysis of recent cases and campus
issues, along with preventive law suggestions. *Lex Collegii*, a newsletter published
quarterly by College Legal Information, Nashville, Tennessee, analyzes selected legal
issues and provides preventive law suggestions, especially for private institutions.
Business Officer, a monthly magazine published for its members by the National
Association of College and University Business Officers, emphasizes developments in
Congress and the federal administrative agencies. And *CUPA News*, a semimonthly
newsletter published for its members by the College and University Personnel Association, covers current legislative, regulatory, and judicial developments and professional trends affecting campus personnel.

For news reporting of current events in higher education generally, but particularly for substantial coverage of legal developments, readers may wish to consult
the *Chronicle of Higher Education*, published weekly by Editorial Projects for Education, Washington, D.C.; or *Education Daily*, published every weekday by Capitol
Publications.

For keeping abreast of conference papers, journal articles, and pertinent government and association reports, *Higher Education Abstracts* would be helpful; it is
published four times a year by the Claremont Graduate School, Claremont, California. The ERIC (Educational Resources Information Center) database, sponsored by
the U.S. Department of Education, performs a similar service encompassing books,

monographs, research reports, conference papers and proceedings, bibliographies, legislative materials, dissertations, and journal articles on higher education.

For extended analytical commentary on recent developments, these two journals should be helpful: the *Journal of College and University Law*, published quarterly by NACUA and focusing exclusively on postsecondary education; and the *Journal of Law and Education*, covering elementary and secondary as well as postsecondary education and published quarterly by Jefferson Lawbook Company, Cincinnati, Ohio.

Many of the resources above are described, and their uses are examined, in R. Shaffer, *Legal Resources for Higher Education Law: A Review Essay*, Monograph 84-3 (Institute for Higher Education Law and Governance, University of Houston, 1984), reprinted in 7 *Review of Higher Education* 443 (1984) and in 12 *Journal of College and University Law* 83 (1985).

A final resource may be of interest to those who wish to use the third edition as a classroom or workshop text. We have developed an instructor's manual that includes edited versions of leading court opinions, illustrative statutes and regulations, notes and discussion questions, problems and sample examination questions (with outlines of suggested answers), and other useful materials. The manual, entitled *Cases, Problems, and Materials: An Instructional Supplement to* The Law of Higher Education, is available from the National Association of College and University Attorneys; for further information, see page viii.

Overall, the goal for this third edition is the same as for the first edition:

> The hope of this book is to provide a base for the debate concerning law's role on campus; for improved understanding between law and academia; and for effective relationships between administrators and counsel. The challenge of our age is not to get the law off the campus; it is there to stay. The challenge is to make law more a beacon and less a fog. The challenge is for law and higher education to accommodate one another, preserving the best values of each for the mutual benefit of both. Just as academia benefits from the understanding and respect of the legal community, so law benefits from the understanding and respect of academia.

March 1995   William A. Kaplin
                                                           Washington, D.C.

                                                             Barbara A. Lee
                                                        New Brunswick, N.J.

Acknowledgments

◆ ◆ ◆

Colleagues at the Catholic University of America reviewed portions of the third edition manuscript, providing helpful feedback on matters within their expertise and good wishes for the project: Lou Barracato, Cliff Fishman, Bill Fox, George Garvey, Roger Hartley, Kathy Kelly, David Kempler, Lisa Lerman, Veryl Miles, Benjamin Mintz, Michael Noone, Shira Perlmutter, George Smith, Bill Wagner, and Harvey Zuckman, all professors at the Columbus School of Law; and Craig Parker, university general counsel. Colleagues at Rutgers University also reviewed portions of the third edition manuscript, providing advice and encouragement: David Scott, Beckmann Rich, and Shirley Weitz of the University Counsel's office, and Frances Loren and John Wolf from the Employment and Labor Counsel's office.

Various colleagues from outside our institutions also reviewed sections of the manuscript and gave helpful advice: Claire M. Boccella, health, safety, and environment counsel for Rhone Poulenc; Ralph Brown, an emeritus professor at Yale University Law School; Peter Byrne, professor of law at Georgetown University; Sandra Mulay Casey, assistant counsel for the State University of New York; Richard B. Crockett, a private practitioner in New York; Rosalind Fink, a private practitioner in New York; Donald R. Fowler, former general counsel at the California Institute of Technology; Ann Franke, associate secretary and counsel, American Association of University Professors; John Garland, executive assistant to the president of the University of Virginia; Eileen Jennings, university counsel at Central Michigan University; Jordan Kurland, associate general secretary of the American Association of University Professors; Sandra McMullan, a consultant in Houston, Texas; Marcus Mills, immigration specialist at the University of Iowa; Michael Olivas, associate dean and professor of law at the University of Houston; Steven G. Olswang, vice provost at the University of Washington; Gary Pavela, director of judicial programs at the University of Maryland; Benjamin Rawlins, special assistant to the chancellor and legal counsel at North Carolina A&T University; Bonita Sindelar, a private practitioner in New Jersey; Ted Sky, senior counsel and former associate general counsel at the U.S. Department of Education; and Joan Van Tol, corporate counsel and executive assistant to the president at the Law School Admission Service.

Our research assistants provided valuable aid at every stage of this project. At Catholic University: Beth Andreozzi, George Hani, Lisa Mangan, Melanie Santos, and Vytas Vergeer; also T. K. Daniel and S. Dawn Robinson (summer research associates). At Wake Forest University: Barbara Allen, Jesse Bone, Kevin Lake, and Christopher Roshon. At the University of Houston: Albert Garcia. At Rutgers University: Celeste Campos and Norman Jimerson. Special thanks go to Lisa Mangan for a year of dedicated service at the crunch time when the final manuscript was being completed.

A number of persons performed critical word-processing and secretarial services during the years in which this manuscript was in process. At Catholic University: Katherine Hein, Debra Hopkins, Barbara Mitchell, Jean Singleton, Diana Wright; also Stephanie Michael, who oversaw these services. At Wake Forest University: Anne Church Bailey. At the University of Houston: Deborah Jones. Special thanks go to Debra Hopkins and Jean Singleton for dedicated service at critical periods of time when the bulk of the manuscript was being assembled.

The library staff at the Columbus School of Law, Catholic University, provided many important support functions. Mark Hammond provided general reference assistance. James Roscher checked the accuracy of all the book citations in the bibliographies. Diana Botluk ran a WestCheck for all the citations in the manuscript. Stephen Margeton, the library director, made arrangements for exclusive use of a research office in the new law library during the latter stages of this project. Patrick Petit, associate library director, coordinated all these services.

Barbara Kaplin assisted with proofreading and file organization for the entire length of this project.

Dorothy Conway, who had performed heroic service as manuscript editor for the second edition, reenlisted in the same capacity for the third edition and provided constructive suggestions and technical improvements with the same precision, commitment, and patience as she had displayed with the earlier edition.

Ralph Rohner, dean of the Columbus School of Law, Catholic University, provided continual encouragement for this project and gracious understanding when the pressures of book deadlines sometimes required that W.K. decline faculty administrative assignments. The Columbus School of Law also provided summer research grants to W.K. during the summers in which he was preparing this manuscript.

Robert Walsh, dean, Thomas Steele, library director, and Professor David Shores at Wake Forest University School of Law provided services and accommodations to W.K. during the summer of 1991, facilitating his work on the manuscript.

Michael Olivas, director of the Institute for Higher Education Law and Governance at the University of Houston, invited W.K. to spend a semester in residence at the institute during a critical formative stage in the development of the manuscript. Professor Olivas's encouragement and the support services he arranged for during that visit—research assistance, secretarial support, computer scanning services, and use of a specialized library of higher education materials—were invaluable to the progress of this project.

Cynthia Lester extended the use of her cabin in the West Virginia woods to W.K. and his family during summer 1992 as a quiet haven for writing sections of the manuscript. Rachel Callahan, Vivian Smith, and the IO's group of Grace Presbyterian Church provided special encouragement to W.K. through all the years of this project.

Phillip M. Grier and Linda Henderson at the National Association of College and University Attorneys arranged for publication of the supplement to the second edition (*The Law of Higher Education: 1985–1990 Update*) and laid plans for publishing similar updates of the third edition, as well as the instructional manual. Marcus Mills at NACUA made available various outlines of previous NACUA conferences.

Robert Bickel of Stetson University College of Law provided encouragement for this project by inviting the authors to serve as conference faculty for Stetson's Annual National Conference on Law and Higher Education.

The American Council on Education and the Borden Foundation provided stimulus for continuing work by recognizing the first edition as the outstanding book on higher education for 1978.

The students in a graduate course on higher education law at Rutgers University and a seminar on higher education law at Catholic University Law School, as well as colleagues from other institutions who have used the first and second editions as texts, provided suggestions that have enhanced the third edition.

Our spouses and families tolerated the years of intrusion that this third edition imposed on our personal lives, encouraged us when this project seemed too large and unending, and looked forward with us to the time when "the book" would finally be finished.

W.A.K.
B.A.L.

W.K.: To Robert M. Kiebala (1943–1991), my college roommate, fellow lawyer, and constant friend; and to Janet N. Gantt (1945–1994), my special friend in a couples covenant group—both of whom died during the time I was preparing this manuscript. "Kuby" 's sense of humor and fun-loving laughter and grin, and Janet's unwavering Christian faith, will always be shining examples for me.

B.L.: To my late parents, Robert and Keren Dalrymple Lee, whose love and encouragement have always inspired and motivated me, and to Jim and Robby, without whose patience and forbearance this project could not have been completed.

The Authors

◆ ◆ ◆

WILLIAM A. KAPLIN is professor of law at the Columbus School of Law, Catholic University of America, in Washington, D.C., where he is also special counsel to the university general counsel. He has been a visiting professor at Cornell Law School and at Wake Forest University School of Law; a distinguished visiting scholar at the Institute for Higher Education Law and Governance, University of Houston; and a visiting scholar at the Institute for Educational Leadership, George Washington University. A former editor of the *Journal of College and University Law* and a former member of the Education Appeal Board at the U.S. Department of Education, he is currently a contributing editor for *Synfax Weekly Report* and *Synfax Bulletin* and a member of the advisory board for *Synthesis: Law and Policy in Higher Education*.

Kaplin received the American Council on Education's Borden Award, in recognition of the first edition of *The Law of Higher Education*, and the Association for Student Judicial Affairs' D. Parker Young Award for research contributions. He has also been named a Fellow of the National Association of College and University Attorneys.

In addition to the various editions and updates of *The Law of Higher Education*, William Kaplin has also coauthored *State, School, and Family: Cases and Materials on Law and Education* (2d ed., 1979) and has written *The Concepts and Methods of Constitutional Law* (1992) as well as numerous articles, monographs, and reports on education law and policy and on constitutional law.

William Kaplin received his B.A. degree (1964) in political science from the University of Rochester and his J.D. degree (1967) from Cornell University, where he was editor-in-chief of the *Cornell Law Review*. He then worked with a Washington, D.C., law firm, served as a law clerk at the U.S. Court of Appeals for the District of

Columbia Circuit, and was an attorney in the education division of the U.S. Department of Health, Education and Welfare before joining the Catholic University law faculty.

BARBARA A. LEE is professor of human resource management at the School of Management and Labor Relations, Rutgers University, New Brunswick, New Jersey, where she directs the graduate program in human resource management and is acting associate provost for the social sciences as well. She is co-chair of the editorial board of the *Journal of College and University Law,* a former member of the board of directors of the National Association of College and University Attorneys, a member of the executive committee of the Human Resources Division of the Academy of Management, and a member of the executive committee of the Labor and Employment Law Section of the New Jersey Bar Association.

Lee is the author of numerous books, chapters, and articles focusing on the legal aspects of academic employment, including the book *Academics in Court* (1987, with George LaNoue). Her work in the area of employment discrimination and labor relations in corporate settings has also been published extensively.

Barbara Lee received her B.A. degree (1971) in English and French from the University of Vermont and both her M.A. degree (1972) in English and her Ph.D. degree (1977) in higher education administration from the Ohio State University. She received her J.D. degree (1982) from Georgetown University. She has held professional positions with the U.S. Department of Education and the Carnegie Foundation for the Advancement of Teaching and has taught at Rutgers University since 1982.

I

Overview of Postsecondary Education Law

◆ ◆ ◆

Sec. 1.1. How Far Does the Law Reach and How Loud Does It Speak?

Law's presence on the campus and its impact on the daily affairs of postsecondary institutions have grown continuously since publication of this text's first edition in 1978. Whether one is responding to campus disputes, planning to avoid future disputes, or charting the institution's policies and priorities, law remains an indispensable consideration. Legal issues arising on campuses across America also continue to be aired not only within the groves of academia but also in external forums. Students, faculty members, staff members, and their institutions, for example, are still frequently litigants in the courts (see Section 1.4). As this trend continues, more and more questions of educational policy become converted into legal questions as well. Litigation has extended into every corner of campus activity. In some of the more striking cases, students have sued their universities for damages after being accused of plagiarism; a student has sued after being barred from the campus computer network; student athletes have sought injunctions ordering their institutions or athletic conferences to grant or reinstate eligibility for intercollegiate sports; disabled students have filed suits against their institutions or state rehabilitation agencies, seeking sign-language interpreters or other auxiliary services to support their education; students who have been victims of violence have sued their institutions for alleged failures of campus security; and former students involved in bankruptcy proceedings have sought judicial discharge of student-loan debts owed to institutions. Disappointed students have sued over grades—and have even lodged challenges such as the remarkable 1980s lawsuit in which a student sued her institution for $125,000 after an instructor gave her a B+ grade, which she claimed should have been an A–. Women

1

and minority students have challenged the heavy reliance by scholarship selection panels and medical schools on standardized tests, and "truth-in-testing" proponents have sued to force disclosure of standardized test questions and answers. Students and others supporting animal rights have used lawsuits (and civil disobedience as well) to pressure research laboratories to reduce or eliminate the use of animals. And rejected female applicants have sued two all-male bastions, Virginia Military Institute and The Citadel, seeking increased opportunities for women.

Faculty members have been similarly active. Professors have sought legal redress after their institutions have changed their laboratory or office space or increased the size of their classes. One group of faculty members in the 1980s challenged their institution's plan to build a new basketball arena, because they feared that construction costs would create a drain on funds available for academic programs; another group sued their institution and the state higher education commission, challenging a salary structure that allegedly benefited more recently hired faculty members; and another group challenged their institution's decision to terminate several women's studies courses, alleging sex discrimination and violation of free speech. Female faculty members have increasingly brought sexual harassment claims to the courts. Across the country suits brought by faculty members who have been denied tenure— once one of the most closely guarded and sacrosanct of all institutional judgments— are now commonplace.

Outside parties also have been increasingly involved in postsecondary education litigation. In the student athlete cases above, athletic conferences were sometimes defendants. In the disabled student cases, state rehabilitation agencies were sometimes defendants. In the truth-in-testing litigation, testing organizations were defendants. Private student clubs have been in litigation regarding the exclusion or admission of women. Sporting goods companies have been sued by universities for trademark infringement because they allegedly appropriated university insignia and emblems for use on their products. Broadcasting companies have been in litigation over rights to control television broadcasts of intercollegiate athletic contests. Separate entities created by institutions, or with which institutions affiliate, have been involved in litigation with the institutions (see Section 2.2.5). Drug companies have sued and been sued in disputes over patent rights to discoveries. And increasingly, other commercial and industrial entities of various types have engaged in litigation with institutions regarding purchases, sales, and research ventures (see Chapter Nine). Community groups, environmental organizations, taxpayers, and other outsiders have also gotten into the act, suing institutions for a wide variety of reasons, from curriculum to land use. Recipients of university services have also resorted to the courts. In one late 1980s suit, a couple sued a state university veterinary hospital after their llama died while being examined by a veterinary student; and in another late 1980s suit, seed companies and potato farmers sued a state university for alleged negligence in certifying seed.

As such judicial business has expanded, so has the use of administrative agencies as alternative forums for airing legal disputes. Government regulations at federal, state, and local levels increasingly apply to the various aspects of institutional operations. Thus, postsecondary institutions may find themselves before the federal Equal Employment Opportunity Commission, the National Labor Relations Board, the administrative law judges of the U.S. Department of Education, contract-dispute boards of the U.S. Department of Defense, state licensing or approval boards, state public employment commissions and civil service commissions, state tax commissions, state or local human relations commissions, local zoning boards, and other quasi-judicial bodies at all levels of government. Proceedings can be complex, and the legal sanctions that these agencies may invoke (and the relief they may provide) can be substantial.

Paralleling these developments has been an increase in the internal forums created by postsecondary institutions for their own use in resolving disputes. Faculty and staff grievance committees, student judiciaries, honor boards, and grade appeals panels are common examples. In recent years mediation has begun to assume a promising role in some of these processes. In addition to such internal forums, private organizations and associations involved in postsecondary governance have given increased attention to their own dispute-resolution mechanisms. Thus, besides appearing before courts and administrative agencies, postsecondary institutions may become involved in grievance procedures of faculty and staff unions, hearings of accrediting agencies on the accreditation status of institutional programs, probation hearings of athletic conferences, and censure proceedings of the American Association of University Professors (see Sections 8.3, 8.4, and 8.5).

As the work of courts and other dispute-resolution forums continues to expand, so do the types of issues that are presented to these forums or dealt with more informally. The spread of AIDS has challenged institutions in numerous ways, for instance, and has raised a variety of new legal issues, from tort liability to privacy rights to nondiscrimination. Drug abuse problems have created other new issues—especially those concerning mandatory drug testing of employees or student athletes (see Section 4.15.5) and compliance with new "drug-free-campus" laws (see Section 7.4.3). Advances in computer technology have brought concomitant legal problems, such as liability for the spread of computer viruses, copyright infringement litigation for unauthorized copying of software, and debate about defamation-by-computer versus privacy and free speech. Outbreaks of racial, anti-Semitic, and homophobic tensions on campuses, and the attempts of colleges and universities to prohibit and punish such "hate speech," have created a range of new issues, most centering on freedom of speech (see Section 4.10). Sexual harassment, whether verbal or in other forms, also continues as a major concern affecting both employee relations and student-faculty relations. Alleged sex inequity in intercollegiate athletics has prompted suits by both female and male athletes whose teams have been eliminated and by women coaches claiming to have received lower pay and fewer benefits than men coaches. Date rape has also become a major sensitive issue affecting student heterosexual relationships. Hazing, alcohol use, and behavioral problems, implicating fraternities especially, have reemerged as major issues (see Section 4.12). The confidentiality of records and meetings has been pitted against claims for public access to information, engendering numerous disputes. Conflicts between civil law and canon law, and between religious mission and secular legal rights, have resulted in an increasing number and breadth of disputes concerning students and faculty at religiously affiliated institutions (see Section 3.1.6). And in the realm of research, numerous issues concerning scientific misconduct, research on human subjects, patent rights, and conflicts of interest have emerged (see Section 9.4).

The expansion of dispute forums and the generation of new issues, as well as the passage of new laws and regulations and the expanded interpretation of others, all influence the way in which faculty and administrators do their jobs. Institutions have responded by increasing the number of administrators in legally sensitive positions, by expanding or reorganizing their legal staffs and outside counsel relationships, by developing elaborate procedural requirements for decision making, by enhancing their risk management programs, by placing new emphasis on preventive legal planning, or by combinations of these strategies.

At the same time, administrators, counsel, public policy makers, and scholars have increasingly reflected on law's role on the campuses. Criticism of that role has been frequent. It is said that the law reaches too far and speaks too loudly. Especially because of the courts' and federal government's involvement, it is said that legal proceedings and compliance with legal requirements are too costly, in money, talents, and energies; that they divert higher education from its primary mission of teaching and scholarship; and that they erode the integrity of campus decision making by bending it to real or perceived legal technicalities that are not always in the campus community's best interests.

Such criticisms continue to highlight pressing issues for higher education's future, but they do not reveal all sides of these issues. We cannot evaluate the role of law on campus by looking only at dollars expended, hours of time logged, pages of compliance reports completed, or numbers of legal proceedings participated in. We must also consider a number of less quantifiable questions: Are legal claims made against institutions, faculty, or staff usually frivolous or unimportant, or are they often justified? Are institutions providing adequate mechanisms for dealing with claims and complaints internally, thus helping themselves avoid any negative effects of outside legal proceedings? Are courts and college counsel doing an adequate job of sorting out frivolous from justifiable claims, and of developing means for summary disposition of frivolous claims, where appropriate, and settlement of justifiable ones? Have administrators and counsel ensured that their legal houses are in order by engaging in effective preventive planning? Are courts being sensitive to the mission of higher education when they apply legal rules to campuses or devise remedies in suits lost by institutions? Do government regulations for the campus implement worthy policy goals, and are they adequately sensitive to higher education's mission? In situations where law's message has appeared to conflict with the best interests of the campus community, what have been education's responses: to kill the messenger, or to develop more positive remedies; to hide behind rhetoric, or to forthrightly document and defend its interests?

We still do not know all we should about these questions. But they are clearly a critical counterpoint to questions about dollars, time, and pages. We must have insight into *both* sets of questions before we can fully judge law's impact on the campus—before we can know, in particular situations, whether law is more a beacon or a blanket of ground fog.

Sec. 1.2. *Evolution of the Law Relating to Postsecondary Education*

Traditionally, the law's relationship to postsecondary (or higher) education was much different from what it is now. There were few legal requirements relating to the educational administrator's functions, and they were not a major factor in most administrative decisions. The higher education world, moreover, tended to think of itself as removed from and perhaps above the world of law and lawyers. The roots of this traditional separation between academia and law are several.

Higher education (particularly private education) was often viewed as a unique enterprise that could regulate itself through reliance on tradition and consensual agreement. It operated best by operating autonomously, and it thrived on the privacy afforded by autonomy. Academia, in short, was like a Victorian gentlemen's club whose sacred precincts were not to be profaned by the involvement of outside agents in its internal governance.

Not only was the academic environment perceived as private; it was also thought to be delicate and complex. An outsider would, almost by definition, be ignorant of the special arrangements and sensitivities underpinning this environment. And lawyers and judges as a group, at least in the early days, were clearly outsiders. Law schools did not become an established part of American higher education until the early twentieth century, and the older tradition of "reading law" (studying and working in a practitioner's office) persisted for many years afterward. Lawyers, moreover, were often perceived as representatives of the crass world of business and industry, or as representatives of the political world, or as mere pettifoggers scratching for a fee. Interference by such "outsiders" would destroy the understanding and mutual trust that must prevail in academia.

The special higher education environment was also thought to support a special virtue and ability in its personnel. The faculties and administrators (often themselves respected scholars) had knowledge and training far beyond that of the general populace, and they were charged with the guardianship of knowledge for future generations. Theirs was a special mission pursued with special expertise and often at a considerable financial sacrifice. The combination spawned the perception that ill will and personal bias were strangers to academia and that outside monitoring of its affairs was therefore largely unnecessary.

The law to a remarkable extent reflected and reinforced such attitudes. Federal and state governments generally avoided extensive regulation of higher education. Legislatures and administrative agencies imposed few legal obligations on institutions and provided few official channels through which their activities could be legally challenged. What legal oversight existed was generally centered in the courts.

The judiciary also was deferential to higher education. In matters concerning students, courts found refuge in the "in loco parentis" doctrine borrowed from early English common law. In placing the educational institution in the parents' shoes, the doctrine permitted the institution to exert almost untrammeled authority over students' lives:

> College authorities stand *in loco parentis* concerning the physical and moral welfare and mental training of the pupils, and we are unable to see why, to that end, they may not make any rule or regulation for the government or betterment of their pupils that a parent could for the same purpose. Whether the rules or regulations are wise or their aims worthy is a matter left solely to the discretion of the authorities or parents, as the case may be, and, in the exercise of that discretion, the courts are not disposed to interfere, unless the rules and aims are unlawful or against public policy [*Gott v. Berea College*, 161 S.W. 204, 206 (Ky. 1913)].

Nor could students lay claim to constitutional rights in the higher education environment. In private education the U.S. Constitution had no application; and in the public realm—in cases such as *Hamilton v. Regents of the University of California,* 293 U.S. 245 (1934), which upheld an order that student conscientious objectors must take military training as a condition of attending the institution—courts accepted the proposition that attendance at a public postsecondary institution was a privilege and not a right. Being a "privilege," attendance could constitutionally be extended and was subject to termination on whatever conditions the institution determined were in its and the students' best interests. Occasionally courts did hold that students have some contract rights under an express or implied contractual relationship with the institution. But—as in *Anthony v. Syracuse University,* 231 N.Y.S. 435 (N.Y. App. Div. 1928), where the institution was upheld in dismissing a student without assigning a reason but apparently because she was not "a typical Syracuse girl"—contract law provided little meaningful recourse for students. The institution was given virtually unlimited power to dictate the contract terms, and the contract, once made, was construed heavily in the institution's favor.

Similar judicial deference prevailed in the institution's relationship with faculty members. While an employment relationship substituted here for in loco parentis, it focused far more on judgments of senior faculty members and experienced administrators than on the formalities of written employment contracts. Courts considered academic judgments regarding appointment, promotion, and tenure to be expert judgments suitably governed by the complex traditions of the academic world. Judges did not possess the special skill needed to review such judgments, nor, without glaring evidence to the contrary, could they presume that nonacademic considerations might play a part in such processes. Furthermore, in private institutions faculty members, like students, could assert no constitutional rights against the institution, since the Constitution had no application to private activity. And in public institutions the judicial view was that employment, somewhat like student attendance, was a privilege and not a right. Thus, as far as the Constitution was concerned, employment could also be extended or terminated on whatever grounds the institution considered appropriate.

As further support for these judicial hands-off attitudes, higher education institutions also enjoyed immunity from a broad range of lawsuits alleging negligence or other torts. For public institutions this protection arose from the governmental immunity doctrine, which shielded state and local governments and their instrumentalities from legal liability for their sovereign acts. For private institutions a comparable result was reached under the charitable immunity doctrine, which shielded charitable organizations from legal liability that would divert their funds from the purposes for which they were intended.

Traditionally, then, the immunity doctrines substantially limited the range of suits maintainable against higher education institutions. And because of the judicial attitudes discussed above, the chances of victory in suits against either the institution or its officers and employees were slim. Reinforcing these legal limitations was a practical limitation on litigation: before free legal services were available, few of the likely plaintiffs—faculty members, administrators, and students—had enough money to sue.

Since the mid-twentieth century, however, events and changing circumstances have worked a revolution in the relationship between academia and the law. The federal government and state governments have become heavily involved in postsecondary education, creating many new legal requirements and new forums for raising legal challenges. (See generally Carnegie Foundation for the Advancement of Teaching, *The Control of the Campus: A Report on the Governance of Higher Education*

(Princeton University Press, 1982).) Students, faculty, other employees, and outsiders have become more willing and more able to sue postsecondary institutions and their officials. Courts have become more willing to entertain such suits on their merits and to offer relief from certain institutional actions. (See generally R. O'Neil, *The Courts, Government, and Higher Education,* Supplementary Paper no. 37 (Committee for Economic Development, 1972).)

The most obvious and perhaps most significant change to occur since World War II has been the dramatic increase in the number, size, and diversity of postsecondary institutions. But beyond the obvious point that more people and institutions produce more litigation is the crucial fact of the changed character of the academic population itself (see, for example, K. P. Cross, *Beyond the Open Door: New Students to Higher Education* (Jossey-Bass, 1971)). The GI Bill expansions of the late 1940s and early 1950s, and the "baby-boom" expansion of the 1960s, brought large numbers of new students, faculty members, and administrative personnel into the educational process. In 1940 there were approximately 1.5 million degree students enrolled in institutions of higher education; by 1955 the figure had grown to more than 2.5 million and by 1965 to more than 5.5 million. (In 1992 the number of students had increased to nearly 14.5 million.) The expanding pool of persons seeking postsecondary education prompted the growth of new educational institutions and programs, as well as new methods for delivering educational services. Great increases in federal aid for both students and institutions further stimulated these developments.

As new social, economic, and ethnic groups entered this broadened world of postsecondary education, the traditional processes of selection, admission, and academic acculturation began to break down. Because of the changed job opportunities and rapid promotion processes occasioned by rapid growth, many of the new academics did not have sufficient time to learn the old rules. Others were hostile to traditional attitudes and values because they perceived them as part of a process that had excluded their group or race or sex from access to academic success in earlier days. For others in new settings—such as junior and community colleges, technical institutes, and experiential learning programs—the traditional trappings of academia simply did not fit.

For many of the new students as well, older patterns of deference to tradition and authority became a thing of the past—perhaps an irrelevant or even consciously repudiated past. The emergence of the student veteran; the loosening of the "lockstep" pattern of educational preparation, which led students directly from high school to college to graduate work; and, finally, the lowered age of majority—all combined to make the in loco parentis relationship between institution and student less and less tenable. The notion that attendance was a privilege seemed an irrelevant nicety in an increasingly credentialized society. To many students higher education became an economic or professional necessity, and some, such as the GI Bill veterans, had cause to view it as an earned right.

As a broader and larger cross section of the world passed through postsecondary education's gates, institutions became more tied to the outside world. Government allocations and foundation support covered a larger share of institutional budgets, making it more difficult to maintain the autonomy and self-sufficiency afforded by large endowments. Competition for money, students, and outstanding faculty members focused institutional attentions outward. As institutions engaged increasingly in government research projects, as large state universities grew and became more dependent on annual state legislative appropriations, and as federal and state governments increasingly paid tuition bills through scholarship and loan programs, postsecondary education lost much of its isolation from the political process. Social and political movements—notably the civil rights movement and the movement against the Vietnam War—became a more integral part of campus life. And when these movements and other outside influences converged on postsecondary institutions, the law came also.

In the 1980s the development of higher education law continued to reflect, and be reflected in, social movements in higher education and in the world outside the campus. Various trends and movements begun in the 1970s and extended in the 1980s have altered higher education's relationship to the outside world and have carved new features into the face of higher education law.

One major trend is student (or educational) consumerism (see, for example, D. Riesman, *On Higher Education: The Academic Enterprise in an Era of Rising Student Consumerism* (Jossey-Bass, 1981)). A shift from a seller's to a buyer's market has spurred competition among institutions in the search for students and introduced marketing techniques and attitudes into postsecondary education. These developments, like many others in the post–World War II era, have helped turn institutional attentions outward—to competitor institutions, to the world of business, to government agencies concerned with regulating the education "marketplace." An increasing emphasis on students as consumers of education with attendant rights, to whom institutions owe corresponding responsibilities, has further undermined the traditional concept of education as a privilege. Student litigation on matters such as tuition and financial aid, course offerings, award of degrees, campus security, and support services has become more common, as have government consumer protection regulations, such as the required disclosure of graduation rates.

Institutional self-regulation, partly a response to student consumerism, is another important trend with continued significance (see, for example, Carnegie Council on Policy Studies in Higher Education, *Fair Practices in Higher Education: Rights and Responsibilities of Students and Their Colleges in a Period of Intensified Competition for Enrollments* (Jossey-Bass, 1979)). The movement is not back to the old days of "self-regulation," when institutions governed their cloistered worlds by tradition and consensus. Rather, the movement has spawned an increase in institutional guidelines and regulations on matters concerning students and faculty and in grievance processes for airing complaints. On the one hand, by creating new rights and responsibilities or making existing ones explicit, this movement can give members of campus communities more claims to press against one another. On the other hand, self-regulation can facilitate the internal and more collegial resolution of claims, forestalling the intervention of courts, legislatures, and administrative agencies in campus matters. For an analysis of the ethical issues facing colleges and universities, and their implications for self-regulation, see J. R. Wilcox & S. L. Ebbs, *The Leadership Compass: Values and Ethics in Higher Education*, ASHE-ERIC Report no. 1 (Association for the Study of Higher Education, 1992).

Both the state and federal governments have increased the scope and pervasiveness of regulation of postsecondary education over the 1980s and into the 1990s. At the state level, demands for assessment and accountability persist, and new pressures are placed on research universities to demonstrate their devotion to teaching and service. At the federal level, reformation of the federal student assistance programs and declining reliance on regional accrediting associations to certify the eligibility of institutions for participation in federal student aid programs have changed long-term relationships among these organizations and postsecondary institutions.

Closely related to government regulation of postsecondary education is the issue of government financial support. Where once the trend was toward increasing aid—both for students and institutions, at federal and state levels—now the trend is reversing. In the scramble for funds, postsecondary education is drawn even further into the political process. Issues arise concerning equitable allocation of funds among and within institutions and among various categories of needy students. As the burden of diminishing support is perceived to fall on minority and low-income students, whose numbers will decrease if government aid is not forthcoming, or on the minority and women faculty newcomers most subject to layoffs prompted by budget cuts, new civil rights issues are emerging.

Government budget cutting, in turn, adds new impetus to yet another prominent trend: institutional response to tighter financial times. Because of the combined pressures of inflation, new types of institutional costs (such as computer equipment), declining enrollments, and, now, government aid reduction, financial belt tightening has become a fact of life affecting many aspects of institutional operation. Many legal questions have arisen concerning standards and procedures for faculty and staff layoffs, termination of tenured faculty, and reduction or termination of programs. As some institutions are strained to their financial limits, other questions concerning closures, mergers, and bankruptcies have arisen. (See, for example, J. Martin, J. E. Samels, & Associates, *Merging Colleges for Mutual Growth* (Johns Hopkins University Press, 1994).) Moreover, there has been renewed attention to statewide planning for postsecondary education in financial hard times. Legal, as well as political and policy, issues have emerged concerning program review and elimination in state public systems and concerning state authority to issue or refuse licenses for new programs of private (particularly out-of-state) institutions.

In a different vein, the technological revolution on campus is yet another trend with critical legal ramifications. The use of computers creates new issues of privacy, potential copyright disputes, and free speech concerns. Biotechnological research raises issues concerning use of human subjects as well as patentability and licensing of discoveries. Devising and enforcing specifications for the lease or purchase of technology for office support, laboratories, or innovative learning systems may create complex problems involving contract or commercial law.

Similarly, as a result of private industry's interest in university research and the universities' interest in private funding of research efforts, a new alliance has been forged between the campus and the corporate world (see, for example, M. Bach & R. Thornton, "Academic-Industrial Partnerships in Biomedical Research: Inevitability and Desirability," 64 *Educ. Record* 26 (1983)). As new ties with the outside world are discussed, questions of institutional autonomy and academic freedom are being raised. The legal and policy implications for postsecondary education are enormous. There are complex problems concerning the structuring of research agreements, patent and licensing arrangements, and trade secrets (see D. Fowler, "University-Industry Research Relationships: The Research Agreement," 9 *J. Coll. & Univ. Law* 515 (1982–83), and B. D. Reams, Jr., *University-Industry Research Partnerships* (Greenwood Press, 1986)). The specter of conflicts of interest, for both faculty researchers and the institution as a corporate entity, arises (see Comment, "Ties That Bind: Conflicts of Interest in University-Industry Links," 17 *U. Cal. Davis L. Rev.* 895 (1984)). And federal government support for university-industrial cooperative research has become an issue, as has federal regulation in sensitive areas such as genetic engineering.

In addition to these new trends, the post–World War II movement toward diversity in postsecondary education has continued in important ways. Although the 1970s brought some moderation in the birth and growth of institutions and expansion of student bodies, the diversity of students and of special educational programs to serve their needs has nevertheless increased. The percentage of women enrolled as students is greater than ever before; women, in fact, have been a majority for over a decade (see R. Cowan, "Higher Education Has Obligations to a New Majority," *Chron. Higher Educ.*, June 23, 1980, A48). The proportion of blacks also increased in the 1970s, with black student enrollment increasing more rapidly than white student enrollment, especially in community colleges (see G. Thomas (ed.), *Black Students in Higher Education: Conditions and Experiences in the 1970s* (Greenwood Press, 1981)). Although blacks comprised approximately 10.2 percent of all undergraduate students in 1992, blacks received only 4 percent of the Ph.D. degrees awarded in 1991. Asians comprised approximately 4.9 percent of undergraduates, and Latinos 7 percent. For an overview of the status of minorities in higher education, see American Council on Education, *Tenth Annual Status Report on Minorities in Higher Education* (ACE, 1991). For a discussion of issues affecting Latino students, see M. A. Olivas (ed.), *Latino College Students* (Teachers College Press, 1986). In 1992 American Indians comprised less than 1 percent of U.S. undergraduates (see B. Wright & W. G. Tierny, "American Indians in Higher Education: A History of Cultural Conflict," *Change*, Mar./Apr. 1991, 11–18). Diversity and access to education continue to be significant issues on most campuses (see R. C. Richardson, Jr., & L. W. Bender, *Fostering Minority Access and Achievement in Higher Education: The Role of Urban Community Colleges and Universities* (Jossey-Bass, 1987)). For a discussion of the implications of an increasingly diverse student body upon American higher education, see A. Levine & Associates, *Shaping Higher Education's Future: Demographic Realities and Opportunities, 1990–2000* (Jossey-Bass, 1989).

The proportion of postsecondary students who are "adult learners," beyond the traditional college-age group of eighteen to twenty-four years old, has also increased markedly (see K. P. Cross, *Adults as Learners: Increasing Participation and Facilitating Learning* (Jossey-Bass, 1981)). The proportion of part-time students (many of whom are also women and/or adult learners) has similarly increased; part-time enrollments are rising much faster than full-time enrollments, to the point where, by 1992, public colleges enrolled roughly equal numbers of part- and full-time students, and one-third of the students at private colleges were attending part-time. The increase in part-time students has resulted in lengthening the number of years required to earn the baccalaureate degree; a 1992 study (M. C. Cage, "Fewer Students Get Bachelor's Degrees in 4 Years, Study Finds," *Chron. Higher Educ.*, July 15, 1992, A29) revealed that, even within six years, only 53 percent of students complete their baccalaureate degree. Military personnel also have become a significant component of the burgeoning adult learner and part-time populations.

One further category of students, standing apart from the interlocking categories above, has also begun substantial growth: foreign students. These students are making a particularly important contribution to campus diversity and are also having a direct impact on law. The application of immigration law to foreign students has become a major concern for federal officials, who must balance shifting political and educational concerns as they devise and enforce regulations; and for postsecondary administrators, who must work within these complex regulations on their own campuses (see Committee on Foreign Students and Institutional Policy, *Foreign Students and Institutional Policy: Toward an Agenda for Action* (American Council on Education, 1982)). Foreign students are also earning an increasing proportion of the graduate degrees awarded by U.S. universities, and their service as teaching assistants has motivated legislation and institutional policies on English-language fluency.

These changes in the student population have been reflected, as expected, in changes in the universe of postsecondary institutions and programs. Community colleges and private two-year institutions have become more prominent, as increases in their enrollments and in the numbers of new institutions have exceeded those at four-year and graduate levels (see A. M. Cohen & F. B. Brawer, *The American Community College* (2d ed., Jossey-Bass, 1989), and S. Brint & J. Karabel, *The Diverted Dream: Community Colleges and the Promise of Educational Opportunity in America, 1900–1985* (Oxford University Press, 1989)). Postsecondary education programs sponsored by private industry have increased, creating a new context for questions about state degree-granting authority and private accreditation, as well as academic freedom and other faculty/student rights and obligations (see N. Eurich, *Corporate Classrooms: The Learning Business* (Princeton University Press, 1986), and J. E. Bowsher, *Educating America: Lessons Learned in the Nation's Corporations* (Wiley, 1989)). Issues of academic credit and the transferability of industry-sponsored education have proliferated (see N. S. Nash & E. M. Hawthorne, *Formal Recognition of Employer-Sponsored Instruction: Conflict and Collegiality in Postsecondary Education*, ASHE-ERIC Higher Education Report no. 3 (Association for the Study of Higher Education, 1987)). Work-study programs, internships, and other forms of experiential education are increasing in numbers and importance (see M. T. Keeton & P. J. Tate (eds.), *Learning by Experience: What, Why, How*, New Directions for Experiential Learning no. 1 (Jossey-Bass, 1978)). The movement raises new questions on matters such as institutional liability for off-campus acts; the use of affiliation agreements with outside entities; and coverage of experiential learners under workers' compensation, unemployment compensation, and minimum wage laws.

Other initiatives have been fueled by the lifelong learning and "distance learning" movements, which have promoted diversity in delivery mechanisms and innovations in learning models (see R. E. Peterson & Associates, *Lifelong Learning in America: An Overview of Current Practices, Available Resources, and Future Prospects* (Jossey-Bass, 1979), and C. Knapper & A. J. Cropley, *Lifelong Learning in Higher Education* (Croom Helm, 1985)). Thus, continuing education programs; correspondence, television, and computer home-study courses; and off-campus and external degree programs, such as those on military bases and in foreign countries, have all grown in recent years and are having significant impact on postsecondary education.

An increasing number of legal questions concern the funding, conduct, and disclosure of research, as well as the regulation of research by the federal government. For example, research on both human and animal subjects is tightly controlled, through institutional committees, by federal regulations (see Sections 7.2.8 and 7.2.9). Research on embryos and fetuses has received considerable federal scrutiny, and federal policies on its lawfulness have shifted with changes in the political party controlling federal research policy. Questions about the ownership of human tissue have given rise to other questions—for instance, about informed consent and disclosure of the use to be made of the tissue. The patentability of living organisms and of human genes has also raised complex legal and policy questions. And problems related to conflict of interest and scientific misconduct continue to plague universities and the federal agencies that fund their research.

The internationalization of higher education continues to increase, through the establishment of U.S. programs in other countries and foreign entities establishing academic programs in the United States. For example, Japanese educational institutions and corporations have either purchased or invested funds in several U.S. colleges, which enroll both Japanese and American students. And although a few U.S. universities have had foreign-study programs for some time, the number of colleges establishing programs abroad has risen sharply in recent years; for example, in 1987 approximately 341,000 foreign students were attending classes in the United Kingdom alone. This trend has substantial implications in the areas of institutional autonomy, state coordination and control, tax liability (for both students and employees), student rights, negligence liability, and access to foreign-study programs for students with disabilities. (See Note, "Foreign Educational Programs in Britain: Legal Issues Associated with the Establishment and Taxation of Programs Abroad," 16 *J. Coll. & Univ. Law* 521 (1990), and R. B. Evans, Note, " 'A Stranger in a Strange Land': Responsibility for Students Enrolled in Foreign-Study Programs," 18 *J. Coll. & Univ. Law* 299 (1991).)

Since tenured faculty can no longer be required to retire at age seventy (see Section 3.3.2.6), increased attention will be given to the performance of tenured faculty. Post-tenure review, a developing trend on a few campuses, will very likely increase as funding sources (both public and private), students, and institutional leaders focus on faculty productivity and the quality of their teaching, scholarship, and service. Particularly in the current environment of financial pressures on postsecondary institutions, accountability demands will drive this scrutiny, and will undoubtedly lead to tensions between faculty, their colleagues, and the administration.

The late 1980s and early 1990s have witnessed increasing conflict on campus related to diversity of ideas, races and ethnic identities, sexual orientations, and gender concerns. These tensions have been played out in the debate over "hate speech" codes (see Section 4.10); curriculum revision to place greater emphasis on nonwhite, non-Western cultures and writers; gender equity in the classroom and in college athletics; acquaintance rape and sexual harassment; and a multitude of issues related to tolerance for alternative life-styles, including whether campus recruitment by representatives of the military is appropriate at a college whose policies forbid discrimination on the basis of sexual orientation.

Another form of diversity receiving increased attention and litigation involves the rights of people with disabilities. New laws directed at these individuals—giving them access to educational programs and accommodations, and requiring an institution to provide public access to its theaters, sports arenas, and other facilities and events to which the general public is invited—have both financial and legal implications for colleges and universities (see Sections 3.3.2.5 (employment), 4.2.4.3. and 4.4 (students), 7.2.16, and 7.5.4).

Campus security issues, and the degree to which colleges are responsible for protecting students from their own actions and the acts of others, have been high on the public agenda. Federal laws requiring the disclosure of crime statistics have spotlighted this issue, and the persistent problem of underage and excessive alcohol consumption continues to produce litigation and, occasionally, liability (Sections 2.3.1.1 and 4.17).

In all, while some individual institutions may have waned, postsecondary education as a whole has been a dynamic enterprise through the 1970s and 1980s and into the 1990s. The challenge for law is to keep pace with education by maintaining a dynamism of its own that is sensitive to education's evolving mission. And the challenge for higher education, of course, is to understand and respond to the rapid changes in the law while maintaining its focus on its multiple purposes and constituencies.

Sec. 1.3. Sources of Postsecondary Education Law

The modern law of postsecondary education is not simply a product of what the courts say, or refuse to say, about educational problems. The modern law comes from a variety of sources, some "external" to the postsecondary institution and some "internal." The internal law, as described in Section 1.3.2 below, is at the core or heart of the institution's operations. It is the law the institution creates for itself in its own exercise of institutional governance. The external law, as described in Section 1.3.1 below, is created and enforced by bodies external to the institution. It circumscribes the internal law, thus limiting the institution's options in the creation of internal law.

1.3.1. External sources of law

1.3.1.1. Federal and state constitutions. Constitutions are the fundamental source for determining the nature and extent of governmental powers. Constitutions are also the fundamental source of the individual rights guarantees that limit the powers of governments and protect citizens generally, including members of the academic community. The federal Constitution is by far the most prominent and important source of individual liberties. The First Amendment protections for speech, press, and religion are often litigated in major court cases involving postsecondary institutions, as are the Fourteenth Amendment guarantees of due process and equal protection. As explained in Section 1.5, these federal constitutional provisions apply differently to public and to private institutions.

The federal Constitution has no provision that specifically refers to education. State constitutions, however, often have specific provisions establishing state colleges and universities or state college and university systems, and occasionally community college systems (see Section 6.2.2). State constitutions may also have provisions establishing a state department of education or other governing authority with some responsibility for postsecondary education.

The federal Constitution is the highest legal authority that exists. No other law, either state or federal, may conflict with its provisions. Thus, although a state constitution is the highest state law authority, and all state statutes and other state laws must be consistent with it, any of its provisions that conflict with the federal Constitution will be subject to invalidation by the courts. It is not considered a conflict, however, if state constitutions establish more expansive individual rights than those guaranteed by parallel provisions of the federal Constitution (see the discussion of state constitutions in Section 1.5.3).

1.3.1.2. Statutes. Statutes are enacted both by states and by the federal government. Ordinances, which are in effect local statutes, are enacted by local legislative bodies, such as county and city councils. While laws at all three levels may refer specifically to postsecondary education or postsecondary institutions, the greatest amount of such specific legislation is written by the states. Examples include laws establishing and regulating state postsecondary institutions or systems, laws creating statewide coordinating councils for postsecondary education, and laws providing for the licensure of postsecondary institutions (see Sections 6.2.1 and 6.3). At the federal level, the major examples of such specific legislation are the federal grant-in-aid statutes, such as the Higher Education Act of 1965 (see Section 7.4). At all three levels, there is also a considerable amount of legislation that applies to postsecondary institutions in common with other entities in the jurisdiction. Examples are the federal tax laws and civil rights laws (see Sections 7.3 and 7.5), state unemployment compensation and workers' compensation laws (see Sections 6.5.4 and 6.5.5), and local zoning and tax laws (see Sections 5.2 and 5.3). All these state and federal statutes and local ordinances are subject to the higher constitutional authorities.

Federal statutes, for the most part, are collected and codified in the *United States Code* (U.S.C.) or *United States Code Annotated* (U.S.C.A.). State statutes are similarly gathered in state codifications, such as the *Minnesota Statutes Annotated* (Minn. Stat. Ann.) or the *Annotated Code of Maryland* (Md. Code Ann.). These codifications are available in many law libraries. Local ordinances are usually collected in local ordinance books, but those may be difficult to find and may not be organized as systematically as state and federal codifications are. Moreover, local ordinance books—and state codes as well—may be considerably out of date. In order to be sure that the statutory law on a particular point is up to date, one must check what are called the session or slip laws of the jurisdiction for the current year or sometimes the preceding year. These laws are usually issued by a designated state or local office in the order in which the laws are passed; many law libraries maintain current session laws of individual states in loose-leaf volumes and may maintain similar collections of current local ordinances for area jurisdictions.

1.3.1.3. Administrative rules and regulations. The most rapidly expanding sources of postsecondary education law are the directives of state and federal administrative agencies. The number and size of these bodies are increasing, and the number and complexity of their directives are easily keeping pace. In recent years the rules applicable to postsecondary institutions, especially those issued at the federal level, have often generated controversy in the education world, which must negotiate a substantial regulatory maze in order to receive federal grants or contracts or to comply with federal employment laws and other requirements in areas of federal concern (these regulations are discussed in Sections 7.2 through 7.5).

Administrative agency directives are often published as regulations that have the status of law and are as binding as a statute would be. But agency directives do not always have such status. Thus, in order to determine their exact status, administrators must check with legal counsel when problems arise. Every rule or regulation issued by an administrative agency, whether state or federal, must be within the scope of the authority delegated to that agency by its enabling statutes. Any rule or regulation that is not authorized by the relevant statutes is subject to invalidation by a court. And, like the statutes and ordinances referred to earlier, administrative rules and regulations must also comply with and be consistent with applicable state and federal constitutional provisions.

Federal administrative agencies publish both proposed regulations, which are issued to elicit public comment, and final regulations, which have the status of law. These agencies also publish other types of documents, such as policy interpretations of statutes or regulations, notices of meetings, and invitations to submit grant proposals. Such regulations and documents appear upon issuance in the *Federal Register* (Fed. Reg.), a daily government publication. Final regulations appearing in the *Federal Register* are eventually republished—without the agency's explanatory commentary, which sometimes accompanies the *Federal Register* version—in the *Code of Federal Regulations* (C.F.R.).

State administrative agencies have various ways of publicizing their rules and regulations, sometimes in government publications comparable to the *Federal Register* or the *Code of Federal Regulations*. Generally speaking, however, administrative rules and regulations are harder to find and less likely to be codified at the state level than at the federal level.

Besides promulgating rules and regulations (called rule making), administrative agencies often also have the authority to enforce their rules by applying them to particular parties and issuing decisions regarding these parties' compliance with the rules (called adjudication). The extent of an administrative agency's adjudicatory authority, as well as its rule-making powers, depends on the relevant statutes that establish and empower the agency. An agency's adjudicatory decisions must be consistent with its own rules and regulations and with any applicable statutory or constitutional provisions. Legal questions concerning the validity of an adjudicatory decision are usually reviewable in the courts. Examples of such decisions at the federal level would include a National Labor Relations Board decision on an unfair labor practice charge or, in another area, a Department of Education decision on whether to terminate funds to a federal grantee for noncompliance with statutory or administrative requirements. Examples at the state level would include the determination of a state human relations commission on a complaint charging violation of individual rights, or the decision of a state workers' compensation board in a case involving workers' compensation benefits. Administrative agencies may or may not officially publish compilations of their adjudicatory decisions. Agencies without official compilations may informally compile and issue their opinions; other agencies may simply file opinions in their internal files or distribute them in a limited way. It can often be a difficult problem for counsel to determine what all the relevant adjudicatory precedents are within an agency.

1.3.1.4. State common law. Sometimes courts issue opinions that interpret neither a statute, nor an administrative rule or regulation, nor a constitutional provision. In breach-of-contract disputes, for instance, the applicable precedents are typically those the courts have created themselves. These decisions create what is called American "common law." Common law, in short, is judge-made law rather than law that originates from constitutions or from legislatures or administrative agencies. Contract law (see, for example, Sections 3.1, 4.1.3, and 9.1) is a critical component of this common law. Tort law (Sections 2.3.1 and 2.4.1) and agency law (Sections 2.1 and 2.2) are comparably important. Such common law is developed primarily by the state courts and thus varies somewhat from state to state.

1.3.1.5. Foreign and international law. In addition to all the American or domestic sources of law noted above, the laws of other countries (foreign laws) and international law have become increasingly important to postsecondary education. This source of law may come into play, for instance, when the institution sends faculty members or students on trips to foreign countries, or engages in business transactions with companies or institutions in foreign countries (see Section 9.4.2), or seeks to establish educational programs in foreign countries (see, for example, Note, "Foreign Educational Programs in Britain: Legal Issues Associated with the Establishment and Taxation of Programs Abroad," 16 *J. Coll. & Univ. Law* 521 (1990)).

1.3.2. Internal sources of law

1.3.2.1. Institutional rules and regulations. The rules and regulations promulgated by individual institutions are also a source of postsecondary education law. These rules and regulations are subject to all the external sources of law listed in Section 1.3.1 and must be consistent with all the legal requirements of those sources that apply to the particular institution and to the subject matter of the internal rule or regulation. Courts may consider some institutional rules and regulations to be part of the faculty-institution contract or the student-institution contract (see Section 1.3.2.2), in which case these rules and regulations are enforceable by contract actions in the courts. Some rules and regulations of public institutions may also be legally enforceable as administrative regulations (see Section 1.3.1.3) of a government agency. Even where such rules are not legally enforceable by courts or outside agencies, a postsecondary institution will likely want to follow and enforce them internally, to achieve fairness and consistency in its dealings with the campus community.

Institutions may establish adjudicatory bodies with authority to interpret and enforce institutional rules and regulations (see, for example, Section 4.5). When such decision-making bodies operate within the scope of their authority under institutional rules and regulations, their decisions also become part of the governing law in the institution; and courts may regard these decisions as part of the faculty-institution or student-institution contract, at least in the sense that they become part of the applicable custom and usage (see Section 1.3.2.3) in the institution.

1.3.2.2. Institutional contracts. Postsecondary institutions have contractual relationships of various kinds with faculties (see Section 3.1); staffs; students (see Section 4.1.3); government agencies (see Section 7.4.1); and outside parties such as construction firms, suppliers, research sponsors from private industry, and other institutions (see Section 9.1). These contracts create binding legal arrangements between the contracting parties, enforceable by either party in case of the other's breach. In this sense a contract is a source of law governing a particular subject matter and relationship. When a question arises concerning a subject matter or relationship covered by a contract, the first legal source to consult is usually the contract terms.

Contracts, especially with faculty members and students, may incorporate some institutional rules and regulations (see Section 1.3.2.1), so that they become part of the contract terms. Contracts are interpreted and enforced according to the common law of contracts (Section 1.3.1.4) and any applicable statute or administrative rule or regulation (Sections 1.3.1.2 and 1.3.1.3). They may also be interpreted with reference to academic custom and usage.

1.3.2.3. Academic custom and usage. By far the most amorphous source of postsecondary education law, academic custom and usage comprises the particular established practices and understandings within particular institutions. It differs from institutional rules and regulations (Section 1.3.2.1) in that it is not necessarily a written source of law and, even if written, is far more informal; custom and usage may be found, for instance, in policy statements from speeches, internal memoranda, and other such documentation within the institution.

This source of postsecondary education law, sometimes called "campus common law," is important in particular institutions because it helps define what the various members of the academic community expect of each other as well as of the institution itself. Whenever the institution has internal decision-making processes, such as a faculty grievance process or a student disciplinary procedure, campus common law can be an important guide for decision making. In this sense campus common law does not displace formal institutional rules and regulations but supplements them, helping the decision maker and the parties in situations where rules and regulations are ambiguous or do not exist for the particular point at issue. Academic custom and usage is also important in another, and broader, sense: it can supplement contractual understandings between the institution and its faculty and between the institution and its students. Whenever the terms of such contractual relationship are unclear, courts may look to academic custom and usage in order to interpret the terms of the contract. In *Perry v. Sindermann*, 408 U.S. 593 (1972), the U.S. Supreme Court placed its imprimatur on this concept of academic custom and usage when it analyzed a professor's claim that he was entitled to tenure at Odessa College:

> The law of contracts in most, if not all, jurisdictions long has employed a process by which agreements, though not formalized in writing, may be "implied" (3 *Corbin on Contracts*, §§ 561–672A). Explicit contractual provisions may be supplemented by other agreements implied from "the promisor's words and conduct in the light of the surrounding circumstances" (§ 562). And "the meaning of [the promisor's] words and acts is found by relating them to the usage of the past" (§ 562).
>
> A teacher, like the respondent, who has held his position for a number of years might be able to show from the circumstances of this service—and from other relevant facts—that he has a legitimate claim of entitlement to job tenure. Just as this Court has found there to be a "common law of a particular industry or of a particular plant" that may supplement a collective bargaining agreement (*United Steelworkers v. Warrior & Gulf Nav. Co.*, 363 U.S. 574, 579 . . . (1960)), so there may be an unwritten "common law" in a particular university that certain employees shall have the equivalent of tenure [408 U.S. at 602].

Sindermann was a constitutional due process case, and academic custom and usage was relevant to determining whether the professor had a "property interest" in continued employment that would entitle him to a hearing prior to nonrenewal (see Section 3.6.2). Academic custom and usage is also important in contract cases where courts, arbitrators, or grievance committees must interpret provisions of the faculty-institution contract (see Sections 3.1 and 3.2) or the student-institution contract (see Section 4.1). In *Strank v. Mercy Hospital of Johnstown*, 117 A.2d 697 (Pa. 1955), a student nurse who had been dismissed from nursing school sought to require the school to award her transfer credits for the two years' work she had successfully completed. The student alleged that she had "oral arrangements with the school at the time she entered, later confirmed in part by writing and carried out by both parties for a period of two years, . . . [and] that these arrangements and understandings imposed upon defendant the legal duty to give her proper credits for work completed." When the school argued that the court had no jurisdiction over such a claim, the court responded: "[Courts] have jurisdiction . . . for the enforcement of obligations whether arising under express contracts, written or oral, or implied contracts, including those in which a duty may have resulted from long recognized and established customs and usages, as in this case, perhaps, between an educational institution and its students" (117 A.2d at 698).

Faculty members may make similar contract claims relying on academic custom and usage. For example, in *Lewis v. Salem Academy and College*, 208 S.E.2d 404 (N.C. Ct. App. 1974), the court considered but rejected the plaintiff's claim that, by campus custom and usage, the college's retirement age of sixty-five had been raised to seventy, thus entitling him to teach to that age. And in *Krotkoff v. Goucher College*, 585 F.2d 675 (4th Cir. 1978) (discussed in this volume, Section 3.8.1), the court rejected another professor's claim that "national" academic custom and usage protected her from termination of tenure due to financial exigency. Custom and usage is also relevant in implementing faculty collective bargaining agreements (see the *Sindermann* quotation above), and such agreements may explicitly provide that they are not intended to override "past practices" of the institution.

1.3.3. The role of case law. Every year, the state and federal courts reach decisions in hundreds of cases involving postsecondary education. Opinions are issued and published for many of these decisions. Many more decisions are reached and opinions rendered each year in cases that do not involve postsecondary education but do elucidate important established legal principles with potential application to postsecondary education. Judicial opinions (case law) may interpret federal, state, or local statutes. They may also interpret the rules and regulations of administrative agencies. Therefore, in order to understand the meaning of statutes, rules, and regulations, one must understand the case law that has construed them. Judicial opinions may also interpret federal or state constitutional provisions, and may sometimes determine the constitutionality of particular statutes or rules and regulations. A statute, rule, or regulation that is found to be unconstitutional because it conflicts with a particular provision of the federal or a state constitution is void and no longer enforceable by the courts. In addition to these functions, judicial opinions also frequently develop and apply the "common law" of the jurisdiction in which the court sits. And judicial opinions may interpret postsecondary institutions' "internal law" (Section 1.3.2) and measure its validity against the backdrop of the constitutional provisions, statutes, and regulations (the "external law"; Section 1.3.1) that binds institutions.

Besides their opinions in postsecondary education cases, courts issue numerous opinions each year in cases concerning elementary and secondary education (see, for example, the *Wood v. Strickland* case in Section 2.4.3 and the *Goss v. Lopez* case in Section 4.8.2). Insights and principles from these cases are often transferable to postsecondary education. But elementary or secondary precedents cannot be applied routinely or uncritically to postsecondary education. Differences in the structures, missions, and clienteles of these levels of education may make precedents from one level inapplicable to the other or may require that the precedent's application be modified to account for the differences. In *Lansdale v. Tyler Junior College*, 470 F.2d

659 (5th Cir. 1972), for instance, the court considered the applicability to postsecondary education of a prior precedent permitting high schools to regulate the length of students' hair. The court refused to extend the precedent. As one judge explained:

> The college campus marks the appropriate boundary where the public institution can no longer assert that the regulation of . . . [hair length] is reasonably related to the fostering or encouraging of education. . . .
>
> There are a number of factors which support the proposition that the point between high school and college is the place where the line should be drawn. . . . That place is the point in the student's process of maturity where he usually comes within the ambit of the Twenty-Sixth Amendment and the Selective Service Act, where he often leaves home for dormitory life, and where the educational institution ceases to deal with him through parents and guardians. . . .
>
> The majority holds today that as a matter of law the college campus is the line of demarcation where the weight of the student's maturity, as compared with the institution's modified role in his education, tips the scales in favor of the individual and marks the boundary of the area within which a student's hirsute adornment becomes constitutionally irrelevant to the pursuit of educational activities [470 F.2d at 662-64].

More recently, courts in various cases have debated whether secondary education precedents permitting regulation of vulgar and offensive speech would apply to faculty or student speech in postsecondary institutions (see, for example, *Martin v. Parrish*, 805 F.2d 583 at 585-86 (majority opin.) and 586-89 (concurring opin.) (5th Cir. 1986)). Conversely, other courts have considered whether academic freedom precedents from postsecondary education are applicable to high school education. In *Cary v. Adams-Arapahoe School Board*, 427 F. Supp. 945 (D. Colo. 1977), *affirmed on other grounds*, 598 F.2d 535 (10th Cir. 1979), for instance, after exploring "the role of elementary and secondary public education in the United States" and finding parallels between the missions of high school and postsecondary education, the trial court decided that "it would be inappropriate to conclude that academic freedom is required only in the colleges and universities."

A court's decision has the effect of binding precedent only within its own jurisdiction. Thus, at the state level, a particular decision may be binding either on the entire state or only on a subdivision of the state, depending on the court's jurisdiction. At the federal level, decisions by district courts and appellate courts are binding within a particular district or region of the country, while decisions of the U.S. Supreme Court are binding precedent throughout the country. Since the Supreme Court's decisions are the supreme law of the land, they bind all lower federal courts as well as all state courts, even the highest court of the state.

The important opinions of state and federal courts are published periodically and collected in bound volumes available in most law libraries. For state court decisions, besides each state's official reports, there is the National Reporter System, a series of regional case reports comprising the (1) *Atlantic Reporter* (cited A. or A.2d), (2) *Northeastern Reporter* (N.E. or N.E.2d), (3) *Northwestern Reporter* (N.W. or N.W.2d), (4) *Pacific Reporter* (P. or P.2d), (5) *Southeastern Reporter* (S.E. or S.E.2d), (6) *Southwestern Reporter* (S.W. or S.W.2d), and (7) *Southern Reporter* (So. or So. 2d). Each regional reporter publishes opinions of the courts in that particular region. There are also special reporters in the National Reporter System for the states of New

York (*New York Supplement,* cited N.Y.S. or N.Y.S.2d) and California (*California Reporter,* cited Cal. Rptr.).

In the federal system, U.S. Supreme Court opinions are published in the *United States Supreme Court Reports* (U.S.), the official reporter, as well as in two unofficial reporters, the *Supreme Court Reporter* (S. Ct.) and the *United States Supreme Court Reports—Lawyers' Edition* (L. Ed. or L. Ed. 2d). Supreme Court opinions are also available, shortly after issuance, in the loose-leaf format of *United States Law Week* (U.S.L.W.), which also contains digests of other recent selected opinions from federal and state courts. Opinions of the U.S. Courts of Appeals are published in the *Federal Reporter* (F., F.2d, or F.3d). U.S. District Court opinions are published in the *Federal Supplement* (F. Supp.) or, for decisions regarding federal rules of judicial procedure, in *Federal Rules Decisions* (F.R.D.). All of these sources, as well as those for state court decisions, are on-line in both the Westlaw and LEXIS legal research databases.

Sec. 1.4. Litigation in the Courts

This section provides an overview of the litigation process in federal and state courts. It covers matters of jurisdiction, procedure, evidence, and remedies that are particularly pertinent to higher education litigation. The material is addressed to institutions and their officers and employees both as potential defendants and as potential plaintiffs in lawsuits.

The section is written primarily for administrators; attorneys will already know (or once knew) most of what is here. For attorneys, however, this section does provide useful illustrations and citations regarding the application of general legal doctrines to the special circumstances of higher education. Moreover, for both attorneys and administrators, this section offers a common reference point from which to work together (see Section 1.7) on the major issues and strategic choices confronted in litigation planning.

1.4.1. The challenge of litigation. Of all the forums available for the resolution of higher education disputes (see Section 1.1), administrators are usually most concerned about court litigation. There is good reason for the concern. Courts are the most public and thus most visible of the various dispute-resolution forums. Courts are also the most formal, involving numerous technical matters that require extensive involvement of attorneys. In addition, courts may order the strongest and the widest range of remedies, including compensatory and punitive money damages. Court decrees and opinions also have the highest level of authoritativeness; not only do a court's judgments and orders bind the parties for the future regarding the issues litigated, subject to enforcement through judicial contempt powers and other mechanisms, but a court's written opinions may also create precedents binding litigants in other future disputes as well (see Section 1.3.3).

For these reasons and others, court litigation is the costliest means of dispute resolution that institutions engage in—costly in time and emotional drain as well as money—and the most risky. Thus, although lawsuits have become a regular occurrence in the lives of postsecondary institutions, involving a broad array of parties and situations (see Section 1.1), administrators should never trivialize the prospect of litigation. Involvement in a lawsuit is serious and often complex business that can create internal campus friction, drain institutional resources, and affect an institution's public image, even if the institution eventually emerges as the "winner." The following history of a protracted university case illustrates the problem.

In *Hildebrand v. Board of Trustees of Michigan State University*, 607 F.2d 705 (6th Cir. 1979) and 662 F.2d 439 (6th Cir. 1981), the defendant had denied the plaintiff tenure in 1968 and officially ended his employment in 1969. Initiating the first of a series of intrauniversity appeals, Hildebrand addressed the full faculty and presented reasons why he should be tenured, but he did not persuade the faculty to change its mind. He then pled his case to the Departmental Advisory Committee (DAC), an elected committee to which he himself had recently been elected, and which contained a majority of nontenured members for the first time in its history; although the DAC issued a resolution that there was no basis for denying Professor Hildebrand tenure, this resolution was ineffectual. Finally, he appealed to the University Faculty Tenure Committee, which denied his appeal.

Professor Hildebrand then began seeking forums outside the university. He complained to the AAUP (see Section 8.5). He filed two unfair labor practice charges (see generally Section 3.2) with the Michigan Employment Relations Commission, both of which failed. He petitioned the Michigan state courts, which denied him leave to appeal.

In 1971 Professor Hildebrand filed suit in federal court, requesting back pay and reinstatement. He claimed that the university had denied tenure in retaliation for his exercise of First Amendment rights (see Sections 3.5.1. and 3.7.4), and also that the university had violated his procedural due process rights (see Section 3.6.2.2). A five-day jury trial was held in 1974, but, literally moments before the judge was to instruct the jury, he belatedly decided that the plaintiff's claims were equitable in nature and should be decided by the judge rather than a jury. In 1977 the trial judge finally dismissed the professor's complaint. On appeal in 1979, the U.S. Court of Appeals held that the district judge had erred in taking the case from the jury and that "[t]he only fair solution to this tangled and protracted case is to reverse and remand for a prompt jury trial on all issues" (607 F.2d 705). The subsequent trial resulted in a jury verdict for the professor that included back pay, compensatory and punitive damages, and a directive that the university reinstate him as a professor. Ironically, however, the trial judge then entertained and granted the university's motion for a "judgment notwithstanding the verdict." This ruling, of course, precipitated yet another appeal by the professor. In 1981 the U.S. Court of Appeals upheld the trial court's decision in favor of the university (662 F.2d 439). At that point, thirteen years after the tenure denial, the case finally ended.

While the *Hildebrand* case is by no means the norm, even garden-variety litigation can become complex. It can involve extensive formal pretrial activities, such as depositions, interrogatories, subpoenas, conferences, and motion hearings, as well as various informal pretrial activities such as attorney-administrator conferences, witness interviews, document searches and document reviews, and negotiation sessions. If the case proceeds to trial, there are all the difficulties associated with presenting a case before a judge or jury: further preparatory meetings with the attorneys; preparation of trial exhibits; scheduling, travel, and preparation of witnesses; the actual trial time; and the possibility of appeals. In order for the institution to present its best case, administrators will need to be intimately involved with virtually every stage of the process.

Litigation, including the garden variety, is also monetarily expensive, since a large amount of employee time must be committed to it and various fees must be paid for outside attorneys, court reporters, and so forth. Federal litigation is generally more costly than state litigation. (See generally D. M. Trubek et al., "The Cost of Ordinary Litigation," 31 *UCLA L. Rev.* 73 (1983).)

Fortunately, lawsuits proceed to trial and judgment less often than most lay-people believe. The vast majority of disputes are resolved through settlement negotiations (see M. Galanter, "Reading the Landscape of Disputes: What We Know and Don't Know (and Think We Know) About Our Allegedly Contentious and Litigious Society," 31 *UCLA L. Rev.* 4 (1983)). Although administrators must also be involved in such negotiations, the process is less protracted, more informal, and more private than a trial.

Despite the potential costs and complexities, administrators should avoid over-reacting to the threat of litigation and, instead, develop a balanced view of the litigation process. Lawsuits can usually be made manageable with careful litigation planning, resulting from good working relationships between the institution's lawyers and its administrators. Often lawsuits can be avoided entirely with careful preventive planning (see Sections 1.4.6 and 1.7). And preventive planning, even when it does not deflect the lawsuit, will likely strengthen the institution's litigation position, narrow the range of viable issues in the case, and help ensure that the institution retains control of its institutional resources and maintains focus on its institutional mission. Particularly for administrators, sound understanding of the litigation process is predicate to both constructive litigation planning and constructive preventive planning.

1.4.2. Access to court. Courts will not hear every dispute that litigants seek to bring before them. Rather, under the constitutional provisions and statutes that apply to it, a court must have jurisdiction over both the subject matter of the suit ("subject matter jurisdiction") and the persons who are parties to the suit (personal, or "in personam," jurisdiction), and various other technical requirements must also be met. The jurisdictional and technical requirements for access to federal court differ from those for state courts, and variances exist among the state court systems as well. Skillful use of these requirements may enable institutions to stay out of court in certain circumstances when they are threatened with suit and also to gain access to courts when they seek to use them offensively.

1.4.2.1. Subject matter jurisdiction. The federal courts have only limited jurisdiction; they may hear only the types of cases listed in Article III of the federal Constitution, most especially cases that present issues of federal statutory or constitutional law ("federal question jurisdiction") or cases in which the plaintiff(s) and defendant(s) are citizens of different states ("diversity jurisdiction"). State courts, on the other hand, are courts of general jurisdiction and may, under the relevant state constitutional provisions, hear all or most types of disputes brought to them. (Often, however, there is more than one type of state trial-level court for the same geographical area—for example, a trial court for cases seeking damages below a certain amount and another for cases seeking damages above that amount.) State courts may also hear cases presenting federal law claims, except for certain federal statutory claims for which the statute gives the federal courts exclusive jurisdiction. It is the plaintiff's responsibility to meet these requirements of subject matter jurisdiction; if the plaintiff does not do so, the defendant may be able to escape from the suit altogether, especially in a federal court.

Jurisdictional issues are further complicated when a lawsuit filed in federal court also presents state law claims, or when a lawsuit filed in state court also presents federal law claims. As a means of determining whether a federal court is a proper forum for the state law claim as well, the doctrines of "pendant" and "ancillary" jurisdiction are applied. The principles of "concurrent jurisdiction" and "removal" are invoked to support a claim that the state court is not a proper forum for the federal law claims.

A foundational case concerning suits filed in federal court but also containing state claims is *United Mine Workers v. Gibbs,* 383 U.S. 715 (1966). In this case the U.S. Supreme Court determined that a federal court may in its discretion exercise jurisdiction over an entire case, including its state law claims, whenever the federal and state law claims "derive from a common nucleus of operative fact and are such that a plaintiff would ordinarily be expected to try them all in one proceeding." In 1990, building on *Gibbs* and later cases interpreting the scope of pendant and ancillary jurisdiction, Congress enacted a statute that codified the two judicial doctrines and renamed them "supplemental jurisdiction" (28 U.S.C. § 1367). The statute establishes a uniform standard for determining whether a federal court has jurisdiction to hear a state claim attached to a federal claim and provides guidance to the trial court in determining whether to assert that jurisdiction or decline it. The court may decline jurisdiction over the state claim if it raises a novel or complex issue of state law; if it substantially predominates over the federal claim; if the federal claim has been dismissed; or if there are other compelling reasons for declining jurisdiction.

Where the plaintiff files an action in state court containing both federal and state claims, the state court generally may hear the federal claims as well as the state claims, because the state courts have concurrent jurisdiction with the federal courts over federal claims. Sometimes, however (as noted above), a state court will not have jurisdiction over the federal claim because the federal statute under which the claim arises gives the federal courts exclusive jurisdiction. Moreover, a state court may be deprived of jurisdiction if a defendant files a removal petition to remove the federal claim (and attached state claims) to federal court. The defendant has the option of removing most claims that would fall within the federal court's subject matter jurisdiction (28 U.S.C. § 1441).

1.4.2.2. Personal jurisdiction. To entertain a lawsuit, a court must have jurisdiction not only over the subject matter but also over the parties involved (personal or "in personam" jurisdiction). This type of jurisdictional question may arise, for instance, when an institution is a defendant in a lawsuit in a state other than its home state. Generally, a court has jurisdiction over defendants who consent to being sued in the state, are physically present in the state, reside in the state, or commit torts or conduct business within the state. Most challenges to jurisdiction arise in the last of these categories. Typically, a state's "long-arm" statute determines whether a court can exercise personal jurisdiction over an out-of-state defendant who commits a tort or conducts business within the state. In addition, the federal Constitution's Fourteenth Amendment, through its Due Process Clause, has been found to limit the ability of state courts to exercise personal jurisdiction, since it prescribes the "minimum contacts" that a defendant must have with a state before that state's courts may exercise personal jurisdiction under a long-arm statute. If the contacts are both purposeful and substantial, so that maintenance of the suit would not offend traditional notions of fair play and substantial justice, the state may assert jurisdiction (see *Worldwide Volkswagen Corp. v. Woodson*, 444 U.S. 286 (1980)). In other words, an institution will not be compelled to bear the costs and inconvenience of a lawsuit out of state unless its activities in that state satisfy the state's long-arm statute *and* the statute is consistent with the Constitution's "minimum contacts" standard.

Brainerd v. Governors of the University of Alberta, 873 F.2d 1257 (9th Cir. 1989), illustrates the assertion of jurisdiction based on the commission of a tort within the state. The court held that Arizona could exercise personal jurisdiction over the vice president of a Canadian university who received two telephone calls from and responded to one letter from a University of Arizona administrator. The calls and letter were employment inquiries concerning the plaintiff, a former professor at the Canadian university, who was applying for an appointment at the University of Arizona. The plaintiff claimed that the vice president's remarks defamed him. The court found that the vice president intentionally directed his communications to Arizona, that the alleged defamation (a tort) would have taken place in the state (the communications were themselves the defamation), and that Arizona had a strong interest in protecting its citizens from torts that cause injury within the state. The court therefore could assert personal jurisdiction over the vice president under the state's long-arm statute.

Hahn v. Vermont Law School, 698 F.2d 48 (1st Cir. 1983), illustrates how personal jurisdiction may be obtained over a defendant who conducts business within the state. A Massachusetts resident sued his law school and one of his professors for breach of contract in a Massachusetts federal court. The student claimed that the law school breached its contract with him by hiring and not supervising the professor who gave Hahn an F on an examination. The court held that Massachusetts had personal jurisdiction over the law school because it had mailed application materials and an acceptance letter to the student in Massachusetts, and had done so as part of an overall effort "to serve the market for legal education in Massachusetts." According to the court, these were purposeful activities that satisfied the conducting-business requirement of the Massachusetts long-arm statute. The court could not exercise personal jurisdiction over the law professor, a citizen of Vermont, however, since the professor taught his courses in Vermont and did not participate in any recruiting activities in Massachusetts.

Despite the minimal nature of the contacts with the state that these cases require, it does not follow that all states and courts would be as permissive in accepting jurisdiction, or that any contact with the state will do. In *Gehling v. St. George's School of Medicine*, 773 F.2d 539 (3d Cir. 1985), for instance, parents sued in Pennsylvania for the wrongful death of their son, a Pennsylvania resident, who had attended the defendant school in the West Indies and had died after running in a school-sponsored race in Grenada. The court held that, even though the school placed recruiting information in New York newspapers that were circulated throughout Pennsylvania, sent officials to visit Pennsylvania and appear on talk shows there to gain exposure for the school, and was involved in a joint international program with a Pennsylvania university, it did not have sufficient contacts with the state to be subject to jurisdiction under the Pennsylvania long-arm statute for its alleged negligence and breach of contract in Grenada. None of the school's activities in Pennsylvania were continuous, or geared to recruiting students. Nor did the mere mailing of an acceptance letter and other information to the student in Pennsylvania constitute a contact sufficient to create jurisdiction. (However, the parents of the deceased student also claimed that, when school officials brought their son's body to Pennsylvania, they misrepresented the cause of his death. Since the misrepresentation constituted a tort actually committed within the state, the court did assert jurisdiction over the university for purposes of litigating the misrepresentation claim.)

1.4.2.3. Other technical doctrines. Even when a court has subject matter jurisdiction, other technical access doctrines may keep the court from hearing the case. Such doctrines—primarily the doctrines of abstention, mootness, and standing—work together to ensure that the case involves proper parties, is brought at a proper time, and presents issues appropriate for resolution by the court in which the case is filed. These considerations tend to pose greater problems in federal than in state courts.

In *Ivy Club v. Edwards*, 943 F.2d 270 (3d Cir. 1991), for instance, "eating clubs" at Princeton had sued New Jersey officials in federal court after the state civil rights agency had asserted authority over the clubs. Determining that there were relevant, unresolved issues of *state* law regarding the civil rights agency's authority, and invoking one of the "abstention" doctrines, the federal district court abstained from hearing the case so that the New Jersey state courts could themselves resolve the state law issues (*Tiger Inn v. Edwards*, 636 F. Supp. 787 (D.N.J. 1986)).[1] After extended state court proceedings, resulting in an order that the eating clubs admit women as members (this volume, Section 4.11.3), the clubs sought to revive their earlier federal court action, in order to assert that the order violated their federal constitutional rights. The federal appellate court ruled that the federal district court had improperly invoked *Pullman* abstention in the earlier federal action, that the clubs had explicitly reserved the right to return to federal court, and that the state courts had not litigated the federal constitutional issues. The clubs could therefore proceed in federal court with their federal claims.

In *People for the Ethical Treatment of Animals v. Institutional Animal Care and Use Committee of the University of Oregon*, 817 P.2d 1299 (Or. 1991), the question was whether the plaintiff (PETA) had "standing" to challenge (that is, was a proper party to challenge) the defendant's approval of a professor's proposal for research involving barn owls. The applicable requirements for obtaining state court standing were in a state statute governing challenges to state administrative agency actions (Or. Rev. Stat. § 183.480(1) (1993)). The court held that PETA was not "aggrieved," as required by this statute, because it had not suffered any injury to any substantial personal interest, did not seek to vindicate any interest that the state legislature had sought to protect, and did not have a "personal stake" in the outcome of the litigation. The court therefore dismissed the suit because PETA had no standing to bring it.

In *Cook v. Colgate University*, 992 F.2d 17 (2d Cir. 1993), the problem was "mootness," a problem concerning the timing of the lawsuit. Mootness doctrines generally require dismissal of a case if the controversy between the parties has expired as a result of the passage of time or changes in events. In the *Cook* case, this doctrine

---

[1] The abstention doctrine invoked by the court was "*Pullman* abstention," named after the case of *Railroad Commission of Texas v. Pullman*, 312 U.S. 496 (1941), to be contrasted with "*Younger* abstention," a doctrine named after *Younger v. Harris*, 401 U.S. 37 (1971). See *Ivy Club v. Edwards*, 943 F.2d at 276–84.

effectively negated a victory for the student plaintiffs, all of whom were members of the women's ice hockey club team of Colgate. They had sued in federal district court under Title IX, alleging that Colgate had failed to provide comparable programs for men's and women's ice hockey (see this volume, Section 4.15.3). The court issued an order requiring Colgate to upgrade the women's club team to varsity status starting with the 1993–94 season. However, three of the five plaintiffs had already graduated, and, by the time of the appeal, the other two had completed their college hockey careers and were scheduled to graduate in May of 1993. The appellate court held that, because "none of the plaintiffs [could] benefit from an order requiring equal athletic opportunities for women ice hockey players," the case must be dismissed as moot. Although the appellate court noted that "situations 'capable of repetition, yet evading review'" (*Southern Pacific Terminal Co. v. Interstate Commerce Commission*, 219 U.S. 498, 515 (1911)), are an exception to the mootness doctrine, it reasoned that this exception applies only if the same plaintiffs might reasonably be expected to be involved again with the same type of suit. Because the plaintiffs here had graduated or were graduating, they did not fall within the exception. Moreover, the plaintiffs might have avoided the mootness doctrine had they sued "in a 'representational capacity' as the leader of a student organization" (see generally Section 1.4.3.1), but this argument was not open to them because they had sued "individually, not as representatives of the women's ice hockey club team or other 'similarly situated' individuals."

1.4.2.4. Statutes of limitations. Another type of timing problem arises from the application of statutes of limitations. In order to maintain a lawsuit, a plaintiff must file the claim within a restricted time period. This time period is defined by the "statute of limitations" applicable to the particular type of claim being asserted. If it is a state law claim, the court will apply a state statute of limitations; if it is a federal law claim, the court will apply a federal statute of limitations. Federal laws, however, sometimes do not stipulate a time period for bringing particular claims. In such circumstances the court may "borrow" a state statute of limitations applicable to state claims most similar to the federal claim at issue.

Postsecondary institutions may confront two types of issues when complying with or challenging a particular statute of limitations. The first issue concerns which state statute to borrow when a federal limitations statute does not exist. This problem frequently arises, for example, in Section 1983 litigation (see Section 2.3.3 in this volume). In *Braden v. Texas A&M University System*, 636 F.2d 90 (5th Cir. 1981), a professor used Section 1983 to challenge his termination, claiming that the university had violated his property and reputational interests protected by the federal Constitution. Since the Section 1983 statute does not stipulate any period of limitation, the court had to borrow the state statute of limitations governing state claims most analogous to the federal claim at issue, as the U.S. Supreme Court had directed in *Board of Regents of the University of the State of New York v. Tomanio*, 446 U.S. 478 (1980). In compliance with *Tomanio*, the court considered the essential nature of the plaintiff's claim and compared it to similar state law claims. The court rejected the professor's suggestion that state contract claims were most analogous to his claim and instead analogized his claims to tort actions for trespass, conversion of property, and injury done to the person of another. The court thus borrowed the state statute of limitations for tort actions, providing that such claims must be filed within two years of the date upon which the claim arose, rather than the statute of limitations for contract actions, which was three years. Since the professor's claim had arisen more than two (but less than three) years before he filed his case, the court dismissed the lawsuit, thus releasing the university from all liability, simply because the professor had filed the case too late. (For a recent example of a similar borrowing problem regarding a claim of disability discrimination under the federal Section 504 statute (this volume, Section 7.5.4), see *Wolsky v. Medical College of Hampton Roads*, 1 F.3d 222 (4th Cir. 1993).)

The second type of issue concerns the determination of when the statute of limitations time period begins to "run." Generally that period begins when the plaintiff's claim first accrued, a technical question of some difficulty. *Pauk v. Board of Trustees of the City University of New York*, 654 F.2d 856 (2d Cir. 1981), another case in which the court dismissed a professor's Section 1983 claim against a university, is illustrative. The university had declined to reappoint the professor. The professor claimed that university officials had taken this action in retaliation for his active participation in the faculty union, thus violating his First Amendment rights. The federal court borrowed and applied a state statute of limitations of three years. The question before the court was whether that three-year time period commenced running in 1975, when the professor received final notification that he would not be reappointed, or in 1976, when his term appointment expired. Relying on the U.S. Supreme Court's decision in *Delaware State College v. Ricks*, 449 U.S. 250 (1980), the court determined that federal law defines when a claim accrues under Section 1983, and that the professor's claim had accrued when he received the notice in 1975. Because the professor had not filed his lawsuit within three years of the date he received notice, his claim was dismissed.

Other types of accrual issues arise in situations where a plaintiff attacks a general university policy, such as a retirement or seniority plan. In *Equal Employment Opportunity Commission v. City Colleges of Chicago*, 944 F.2d 339 (7th Cir. 1991), for example, the EEOC brought a claim based on the Age Discrimination in Employment Act of 1967 (this volume, Section 3.3.6), which has a two-year statute of limitations. The EEOC challenged the colleges' retirement plan on grounds that it had been adopted with an intent to discriminate against older workers. The question was whether the EEOC's claim accrued when the colleges first adopted the early-retirement plan rather than when the plan was later applied to harm particular older professors. Relying on the U.S. Supreme Court's decision in *Lorance v. AT&T Technologies, Inc.*, 490 U.S. 900 (1989), the court determined that "assessing when a statute of limitations begins to run" depends on a precise identification of the discriminatory act at issue and that, under the EEOC's complaint and the pertinent ADEA provisions and interpretive case law, "the relevant discriminatory act in this case . . . was the plan's adoption." The court thus held the claim to be time-barred because it was not filed until 1988, six years after the plan's adoption in 1982. Had the court instead held that the EEOC's claim accrued anew each time a faculty member was injured by the application of the plan, the suit would not have been time-barred, since the claim then would have accrued within two years of filing the suit.

1.4.2.5. Exhaustion of remedies. A prospective plaintiff may sometimes be prevented (or at least delayed) from bringing a court suit by the "exhaustion-of-remedies" doctrine. Simply put, the doctrine requires that a court not hear a plaintiff's claim until the plaintiff has exhausted any and all administrative remedies that may be available—for example, a hearing before an administrative agency or a grievance board. The doctrine is particularly important to a postsecondary institution that is threatened with suit but has an internal process available for resolving the problem. Thus, in *Florida Board of Regents v. Armesto*, 563 So. 2d 1080 (Fla. 1990), the court refused to consider a student's request to enjoin Florida State University Law School from formally charging her with cheating on her final exams. The school had adopted internal procedures for challenging such charges, but the student had not exercised her right to use them (including the availability of a full hearing on the charges). Although the court recognized that an exception to the exhaustion-of-remedies doctrine exists in situations where the available procedures would not provide an adequate or timely remedy, it found no basis for applying the exception in this instance. Further, the court rejected the student's argument that she could bypass the administrative remedies because the school's investigation of the charges violated her due process rights. The exhaustion doctrine applies even when a suit is based on constitutional deficiencies in the application of the administrative process to the plaintiff. Quoting the trial judge's opinion, the Florida Supreme Court held that in such instances the doctrine ensures that "the responsible agency 'has had a full opportunity to reach a sensitive, mature, and considered decision upon a complete record appropriate to the issue'" (563 So. 2d at 1081).[2]

Similarly, in *Pfaff v. Columbia-Greene Community College*, 472 N.Y.S.2d 480 (N.Y. App. Div. 1984), the court dismissed the complaint of a student who had sued her college, contesting a C grade entered in a course, because the college had an internal appeal process and the student "failed to show that pursuit of the available administrative appeal would have been fruitless." And in *Beck v. Board of Trustees of State Colleges*, 344 A.2d 273 (Conn. 1975), where faculty members sought to enjoin the defendant board from implementing proposed new personnel policies that allegedly threatened tenured faculty rights, the court dismissed the suit under the exhaustion doctrine because the state's administrative procedure act "provides a comprehensive, potentially inexpensive, and completely adequate method of resolving the issues raised in the present . . . [suit]."

Key to all these cases, as administrators and counsel should carefully note, is the court's determination that available administrative remedies could provide adequate relief to the complaining party, in a timely fashion, and would thus not be fruitless to pursue.

1.4.3. Pretrial and trial issues. After access to court has clearly been established, attention shifts to the numerous technical and strategic matters regarding the pretrial phase and the trial itself.

1.4.3.1. Class action suits. Sometimes defendants are sued by a group or class of plaintiffs, using the mechanism of the "class action suit," rather than by a single person. Such suits may involve extensive financial costs, time-absorbing procedures, complex legal issues, and potentially vast liability for the defendants. The plaintiffs must obtain a judicial ruling certifying the class, however, before such a suit may proceed. For state courts certification requirements are set out in state civil procedure statutes or rules, and for federal courts they are in Rule 23 of the Federal Rules of

---

[2]Plaintiffs filing civil rights claims under Section 1983, the federal civil rights statute, need not exhaust state administrative remedies; see *Patsy v. Board of Regents of the State of Florida*, 457 U.S. 496 (1982), discussed in Section 2.3.3.

Civil Procedure (28 U.S.C. Appendix). Rule 23(a) sets out four prerequisites for certification:

1. Numerosity. There must be a large enough number of plaintiffs that individual suits are impracticable.
2. Commonality. The members of the class must have claims that include common questions of fact or law.
3. Typicality. The claims of the class representatives who are named plaintiffs must be typical of the claims of other class members.
4. Adequacy of representation. The class representatives must fairly and adequately protect the interests of the entire class.

Once the plaintiff has satisfied these four requirements, Rule 23(b) then imposes certain other requirements, under which the lawsuit is classified into one of three types of permissible class actions. The federal trial judge has discretion to grant or deny certification and to modify the class certification during the course of the proceedings.

Lamphere v. Brown, 553 F.2d 714 (1st Cir. 1977), illustrates the application of Federal Rule 23. The federal appellate court refused to review the trial judge's decision to certify a class of women for a class action suit against Brown University alleging gender discrimination (71 F.R.D. 641 (D.R.I. 1976)). The certified class consisted of "[a]ll women who have been employed in faculty positions by Brown University at any time after March 24, 1972, or who have applied for but were denied employment by Brown in such positions after said date; all women who are now so employed; all women who may in the future be so employed or who may in the future apply for but be denied such employment"—a class that would cover an estimated 20,100 persons. The university argued that its academic decision making is decentralized into numerous departments and divisions, thus making a university-wide class and "broadside" approach to class actions inappropriate. Although the appellate court "decline[d] to intervene in what is essentially an exercise of discretion by the district court," it did caution the district court to "follow closely the developing evidence as to class-wide decision making" by the university, to consider "the implications of class-wide defense" on the university's pursuit of its institutional mission, and to "take seriously its power under [Federal Rule] 23(c)(1) to alter or amend its certification order before the decision on the merits."[3]

In contrast to *Lamphere*, in *Samuel v. University of Pittsburgh*, 538 F.2d 991 (3d Cir. 1976), the trial judge had refused to certify the plaintiff's proposed class (375 F. Supp. 1119 (W.D. Pa. 1974)), and the appellate court reviewed and reversed the trial judge's order. The class was defined as married female students at the university who were Pennsylvania residents but had been denied the lower tuition rate for state residents. The university had denied such rates because it assumed that the students'

[3]There is an exception to Rule 23 applicable to the Equal Employment Opportunity Commission (EEOC). If the EEOC brings an employment discrimination suit on behalf of a group of employees, those employees need not be certified as a class under Rule 23. In *General Telephone Company of the Northwest v. EEOC*, 446 U.S. 318 (1980), the U.S. Supreme Court concluded that, under the powers conferred on the EEOC by Section 706 of Title VII (see this volume, Section 3.3.2.1), the EEOC may bring a suit without satisfying Rule 23.

residences were the same as their husbands', and the husbands lived out of state. In reversing the trial court, the appellate court determined that the class's damages could be calculated easily and that the trial judge's decision had been based on sympathy for the university's financial constraints rather than on legal precedent.

Although both *Lamphere* and *Samuel* illustrate the institution's plight as defendant in a class action suit, institutions can also use the class action mechanism to their own benefit as prospective plaintiffs in litigation. In *Central Wesleyan College v. W. R. Grace & Co.*, 143 F.R.D. 628 (D.S.C. 1992), for example, a federal district judge certified a class of virtually all colleges and universities in the nation in a property damage suit against asbestos companies. In certifying the class under Federal Rule 23(b)(3), the court noted that (1) there was little interest among the nation's colleges in individually suing asbestos companies; (2) there was little preexisting litigation between colleges and the asbestos companies; (3) the South Carolina district court was a desirable forum and not unfair to the defendants; and (4) if the issues certified were limited to discrete, factual inquiries, the large size of the class would not pose undue problems. The appellate court affirmed (6 F.3d 177 (4th Cir. 1993)). Under this ruling, the individual colleges can save many thousands of dollars in legal fees and still have their claims adequately heard.

1.4.3.2. Pretrial discovery. One of the most important aspects of the pretrial process is "discovery." A prescribed period of discovery—which may include depositions, interrogatories, and requests for the production of documents, among other things—affords all parties the opportunity to request information to clarify the facts and legal issues in the case. Although the discovery process may be time-consuming, expensive, and sometimes anxiety-provoking, it is essential to the trial as well as to prospects for pretrial settlement. Many tactical issues will arise as the parties seek to confine the scope of discovery in order to protect confidential records or sensitive information, or to save money and time, or to broaden the scope of discovery in order to obtain more information from the opposing party.

The Federal Rules of Civil Procedure, generally Rules 26–37 (28 U.S.C. Appendix), define the permissible scope and methods of discovery in the federal courts. Most states have similar rules. The trial judge usually has broad discretion in applying such rules. In general, under the Federal Rules, the "[parties] may obtain discovery regarding any matter, not privileged, which is relevant to the subject matter in the pending action" (Rule 26(b)(1)). In making decisions concerning the propriety of particular discovery requests, the trial judge may consider whether the discovery is "unreasonably cumulative or duplicative, or is obtainable from some other source that is more convenient, less burdensome, or less expensive" and may also consider other matters, such as undue expense and burden of filling the request (Rule 26(b)(1)). A party seeking to confine the scope of discovery may make any of these objections or may contend that the information sought is irrelevant or privileged.

The opinion in *Zahorik v. Cornell University*, 98 F.R.D. 27 (N.D.N.Y. 1983), illustrates the federal courts' preference for full disclosure of information within the scope of Rule 26. The plaintiffs filed an employment discrimination suit against Cornell University. When the plaintiffs requested a class certification (see Section 1.4.3.1 above), the district court denied the request but suggested that the plaintiffs consider reapplying at a later date if they obtained proof that they fulfilled the class certification requirements under Rule 23(a) of the Federal Rules. In an effort to meet the numerosity requirement, the plaintiffs sought broad discovery of university records, requesting information on past internal complaints of sex discrimination and the results of investigations of those complaints, copies of university affirmative action plans, copies of university reports on various aspects of campus life, information about the capabilities of and data stored in university computers, and biographical and statistical data on tenure-track employees. The university opposed these discovery requests on grounds that they were oppressive, burdensome, and irrelevant to the lawsuit. Although the court disagreed, it did refine the scope and method of discovery. It determined that the discovery requests for reports on university campus life and for computer information were too broad and denied these requests subject to their reformulation and narrowing by the plaintiffs. It then approved all of the plaintiffs' other requests. As to the method of discovery, the court ruled that the university must either give the plaintiffs and their attorneys access to the records for review and copying, or produce the specific records requested on a college-by-college list that the plaintiffs would develop.[4]

1.4.3.3. Issues regarding evidence. During pretrial discovery as well as the trial itself, various issues concerning evidence are likely to arise. During discovery, for instance, each party may object to various discovery requests of the other party on grounds that the information sought is privileged or irrelevant (see Section 1.4.3.2 above); in pretrial motions, each party may seek to limit the evidence to be admitted at trial; and during presentation of each party's case at trial, one party may object on a variety of grounds to the introduction of information that the other party seeks to present.[5] In addition, parties may seek and courts may issue summonses and subpoenas directly to the other party or to witnesses. Such matters are governed by the rules of civil procedure, the rules of evidence, and the common law of the jurisdiction in which suit is brought.

Questions about obtaining and using privileged information are among the most important and difficult of these pretrial and trial issues (see, for example, the attempts to create new privileges, discussed in Section 3.7.7). All jurisdictions apparently agree that a party cannot obtain privileged information through discovery. Rule 26(b)(1) of the Federal Rules of Civil Procedure, for instance, states that the scope of discovery is confined to information that is "not privileged" (28 U.S.C. Appendix). Privileged matter is information that is protected under the formal evidentiary privileges recognized under the rules of evidence of each particular jurisdiction. For federal courts Section 501 of the Federal Rules of Evidence leaves the definition and implementation of privileges entirely to the "principles of common law." (See generally 8 *Wigmore on Evidence* § 2196 (McNaughton rev.) (4th ed., Little, Brown, 1961).) Section 501 also provides that, in federal court actions based on state law (diversity actions), state law will determine whether a privilege applies. Privileged communi-

---

[4]At times a discovery request may include student educational records. Typically, an educational institution must receive consent from either a parent or a student prior to disclosing the records. According to the Buckley Amendment, 34 C.F.R. § 99.31(9) (see this volume, Section 4.16.1), an institution may disclose the information without consent if it does so in compliance with a judicial order or subpoena, but it must make a reasonable effort to notify the parent or student before disclosure.

[5]See, for example, Annot., "Admissibility of School Records Under Hearsay Exceptions," 57 A.L.R.4th 1111 (1993 and periodic supp.).

cations are immune from discovery because protecting and preserving the confidentiality of certain relationships—including attorney-client, doctor-patient, priest-penitent, and husband-wife—are considered more important than permitting full disclosure for litigation purposes.

The privilege that postsecondary institutions are most likely to struggle with in litigation is the attorney-client privilege. Confidential communications between an attorney and the attorney's client may be both immune from discovery and inadmissible at trial (see *Wigmore,* above, at § 2290). As the U.S. Supreme Court explained in *Upjohn Co. v. United States,* 449 U.S. 383 (1981), the purpose of this attorney-client privilege is

> to encourage full and frank communication between attorneys and their clients and thereby promote broader public interests in the observance of law and administration of justice. The privilege recognizes that sound legal advice or advocacy serves public ends and that such advice or advocacy depends upon the lawyer's being fully informed by the client.
> . . . [T]he privilege exists to protect not only the giving of professional advice to those who can act on it but also the giving of information to the lawyer to enable him to give sound informed advice [449 U.S. at 389, 390].

In *Upjohn* the Court reaffirmed that the attorney-client privilege applies to corporations as clients as well as to individuals, and may extend in certain situations to communications between a corporation's in-house general counsel and the corporation's employees. Corporate officers had sought legal advice from in-house counsel concerning the corporation's compliance with federal securities and tax laws. To gather information about compliance issues, counsel had interviewed corporate employees (not officers). In determining that counsel's communications with the employees were protected from disclosure, the Court considered that counsel had interviewed the employees about matters that were within their corporate duties and that the employees were aware that the interviews would assist the corporation in obtaining legal advice from its counsel. Under these circumstances, said the Court, the application of the privilege in this case would serve the purpose of the privilege. The result is thus broadly hospitable to the assertion of privilege by corporations (including private postsecondary institutions) for their attorneys' confidential communications with managers, staff, and other employees. Similar protection would apparently be available to public institutions as well.

An important corollary to the attorney-client privilege is the attorney work-product doctrine, established (at least for the federal courts) in *Hickman v. Taylor,* 329 U.S. 495 (1947), and subsequently codified in Rule 26(b)(3) of the Federal Rules of Civil Procedure. The doctrine protects from disclosure memos, notes, and other materials prepared by an attorney "in anticipation of litigation or for trial," subject to some exceptions where the other party can make a strong showing of need and unavailability of equivalent information from any other source (Rule 26(b)(3)). In *Upjohn* the Court, relying on both *Hickman* and Rule 26, used the work-product doctrine as a supplement to the attorney-client privilege so that counsel's notes and memos, which "reveal[ed] the attorneys' mental processes in evaluating" their interviews with corporate employees, would be protected.

1.4.3.4. Ethical issues. Attorneys, in litigation and otherwise, are subject to ethical standards in their professional dealings with clients. These standards are embodied in the ethics codes and rules of court of the various states. There are ethical rules, for instance, concerning attorney conflicts of interest. In the litigation context, these rules have particular applicability in situations where counsel represents more than one party and these parties' legal claims or objectives may be opposed to one another. For example, a university and several of its administrators may be joined as defendants in the same lawsuit, or may all be likely defendants in a potential lawsuit, and the defenses that one administrator may seek to assert are in conflict with those of another. Counsel for the university then must decide whether the situation presents an actual or a potential conflict of interest, requiring that other attorneys not associated with the original counsel represent one or more of the individual defendants.

Similarly, there are ethical rules that prohibit an attorney representing a party in litigation from contacting opposing parties who are themselves represented by counsel. Rule 4.2 of the *Model Rules of Professional Conduct* (promulgated by the American Bar Association) states that "[i]n representing a client, a lawyer shall not communicate about the subject of the representation with a party the lawyer knows to be represented by another lawyer in the matter, unless the lawyer has the consent of the other lawyer or is authorized by law to do so." If an attorney violates this ethical rule, he or she may be disqualified from the case and any evidence obtained may be inadmissible at trial; in addition, he or she may be subject to discipline by the state bar.

In *University Patents, Inc. v. Kligman,* 737 F. Supp. 325 (E.D. Pa. 1990) (more fully discussed in Section 9.4.3), the plaintiffs attempted to have the defendant's attorney removed from the case because he had made "ex parte" contacts, allegedly in violation of Rule 4.2, with current and former employees of one of the plaintiffs, the University of Pennsylvania. The attorney had contacted two current professors, one current department chair (and professor), one current trustee, and two former professors of the university. In ruling that the attorney's actions were improper, the court noted that Rule 4.2 "was intended to forbid ex parte communications with all institutional employees whose acts or omissions could bind or impute liability to the organization or whose statements could be used as admissions against the organization, presumably pursuant to Federal Rule of Evidence 801(d)(2)(D)" (otherwise known as the "control group"). The court ascertained that at least the current employees contacted by the defendant's attorney could fall within that category and thus be considered parties to the litigation. The attorney's actions thus violated the rule. Although the court decided it would not sanction the attorney by disqualifying him from the case, it did preclude the defendants "from introducing any information obtained through [the attorney's] ex parte contacts with persons whose statements could bind the University."

A different result obtained in *Morrison v. Brandeis University,* 125 F.R.D. 14 (D. Mass. 1989). The plaintiff was a faculty member who had sued Brandeis for discrimination after being denied tenure. Her attorney sought to interview Brandeis employees who had been directly involved in the tenure decision but were not named as defendants in the lawsuit, and to do so without giving prior notice to or gaining consent of the university's attorney. The state bar's disciplinary rules included a provision similar to Rule 4.2, which was applied in *Kligman* above. Nevertheless, the court granted the plaintiff's attorney permission to interview. Declining to use the "control group" test, the court applied a "case-by-case balancing test," focusing on "a plaintiff's need to gather information on an informal basis on the one hand and the defendant's need for effective representation on the other. . . ." Since the employees to be interviewed would have information on the alleged nondiscriminatory reasons for the tenure denial, a key issue in the case (see generally Section 3.3), and since some of these employees voted in favor of tenure and would likely be called as witnesses for the plaintiff, the plaintiff's interests outweighed those of the defendant.

1.4.3.5. Summary judgments and motions to dismiss. Both federal courts and the state courts have procedures for streamlining litigation by summarily disposing of lawsuits on the merits—that is, for a judicial determination prior to trial as to whether the plaintiff's legal claim is valid and sustainable by the facts. The most basic procedure is the defendant's motion to dismiss. Although this type of motion is frequently used to raise jurisdictional and other access issues (Section 1.4.2), it may also be used to dismiss a case on the merits if the defendant can demonstrate that the facts pleaded in the plaintiff's complaint, even if true, do not state a valid claim that would entitle the plaintiff to relief. In the federal courts, this motion is provided for by Rule 12(b)(6) of the Federal Rules of Civil Procedure.

Another procedure, potentially more important and usually utilized at a later stage of the pretrial proceedings than the motion to dismiss, is the summary judgment. In the federal courts, motions for summary judgment are governed by Federal Rule 56. Under this rule and similar state laws, either the plaintiff or the defendant may make such a motion. The moving party must demonstrate that no genuine issue of material fact remains in the lawsuit and that the governing law, as applied to the undisputed facts, indicates that the moving party is entitled to judgment as a matter of law. If the party makes such a showing, the court will enter a judgment (a "summary judgment") in that party's favor. Successfully employed, then, this procedure can allow either party to avoid many of the costs of litigation (see Section 1.4.1 above) while still obtaining the benefits of a judgment that is binding on the parties (see Section 1.4.4) and may fully resolve the dispute.

1.4.3.6. Standards of judicial review and burdens of proof. Postsecondary institutions have numerous processes for making internal decisions regarding the status of faculty, students, and staff, and for internally resolving disputes among members of the campus community. Whenever a disappointed party seeks judicial review of an institution's internal decision, the reviewing court must determine what "standard of review" it will apply in deciding the case. This standard of review establishes the degree of scrutiny the court will give to the institution's decision, the reasons behind it, and the evidence supporting it. Put another way, the standard of review helps establish the extent to which the court will defer to the institution's decision and the value and fact judgments undergirding it. The more deference the court is willing to accord the decision, the less scrutiny it will give to the decision and the greater is the likelihood the court will uphold it. Issues regarding standards of review are thus crucial in most litigation.

In turn, standards of review are related to the "burdens of proof" for the litigation. After a court determines which party is responsible for demonstrating that the institution's decision does or does not meet the standard of review, the court allocates the burden of proof to that party. This burden can shift during the course of the litigation (see, for example, Section 3.3.2.1). Burdens of proof also elucidate the elements or type of proof each party must submit to meet its burden on each claim or defense presented. Such issues are also critical to the outcome of litigation and can become very complicated (see, for example, Section 3.3.2.1).

There are many possible standards of review (and likewise many variations of burdens of proof). The standard that applies in any particular litigation will depend on numerous factors: the type of institution subject to the review (whether public or private); the type of claim that the plaintiff makes; the institution's internal rules for reviewing decisions of the type being challenged; the character of the contractual relationship between the institution and the party seeking court review; and the common law and statutory administrative law of the particular state (see this volume, Section 1.3.1), insofar as it prescribes standards of review for particular situations. At a subtler level, the court's selection of a standard of review may also depend on comparative competence—the court's sense of its own competence, compared with that of the institution, to explore and resolve the types of issues presented by the case.

If a court is reviewing the substance of a decision (whether the institution is right or wrong on the merits), it may be more deferential than it would be if it were reviewing the adequacy of the procedures the institution followed in making its decision—the difference being attributable to the court's expertise regarding procedural matters and relative lack of expertise regarding substantive judgments (such as whether a faculty member's credentials are sufficient to warrant a grant of tenure).

There are three basic types of standards of review. The "substantial evidence" standard is a gauge of whether the institution's decision-making body carefully considered the evidence and had a substantial body of evidence on which to base its decision. The "arbitrary and capricious" standard gauges whether the deciding body acted without reason or irrationally. The "de novo" standard authorizes the court to consider the case from scratch, giving virtually no deference to the decision-making body's decision, and requiring all evidence to be submitted and considered anew.

Of the three types, the de novo standard provides for the highest level of judicial scrutiny of, and the least amount of deference to, the institution's decision; the arbitrary and capricious standard calls for the least scrutiny and the greatest deference; and the substantial evidence standard is somewhere in between. In constitutional rights litigation, there is also sometimes a fourth type of standard, associated with de novo review, called a "strict scrutiny" standard, which is the most stringent of all review standards.

The following two cases illustrate the operation of standards of review in the context of court challenges to institutional decisions to deny tenure and also illustrate the controversy that such issues may create.

In *Riggin v. Board of Trustees of Ball State University*, 489 N.E.2d 616 (Ind. 1986), the defendant, a public institution, had discharged a tenured professor, for cause. At an internal hearing, the university adduced evidence that the professor had attended virtually no faculty meetings, rescheduled and canceled a large number of classes, wasted a great deal of class time with irrelevant films and discussions, failed to cover the course material, and produced no research, among other things. The board of trustees affirmed the hearing committee's recommendation to terminate. In reviewing the professor's claim that the board of trustees' decision constituted a breach of contract, the trial court applied the "arbitrary and capricious" standard of review and upheld the board's decision. The appellate court affirmed both the trial court's decision and its selection of a standard of review. As a state institution, the university was considered to be an administrative agency under Indiana law and subject to the standard of review applicable to court review of agency decisions:

> [A] court of review will not interfere with the acts of an administrative agency which are within the agency's allowable scope of responsible discretion unless it found that the administrative act was arbitrary, capricious, an abuse of discretion or unsupported by substantial evidence. . . . The court may not substitute its own opinions for that of the Board of Trustees, but must give deference to its expertise. . . . A court may not reweigh the evidence or determine the credibility of witnesses. . . . The burden of proving that the administrative action was arbitrary and capricious or an abuse of discretion falls on the party attempting to vacate the administrative order. . . . An arbitrary and capricious act is one that is willful and unreasonable and done without regard to the facts and circumstances of the case; an act without some basis which would lead a reasonable and honest person to the same conclusion. . . .
>
> The court's review of the decisions of the committee and the Board of Trustees was not a hearing de novo. Rather, its sole function was to determine whether the action was illegal, or arbitrary and capricious. In doing so it must accept the evidence most favorable to support the administrative decision [489 N.E.2d at 625].

Because the court adopted this deferential standard of review, and because the university had foresight to present extensive evidence to the ad hoc hearing committee, the university easily prevailed in court.

An altogether different approach was taken by the court in *McConnell v. Howard University*, 818 F.2d 58 (D.C. Cir. 1987) (also discussed in Section 3.5.2). Again the defendant had discharged a tenured professor who thereupon sued for breach of contract. But in this case the university was a private institution, and the contract issues presented were different from those in *Riggin*. The professor refused to continue teaching one of his courses after a student had called him a racist and refused to apologize. The professor continued to teach his other courses and otherwise perform his professorial duties. After exhausting his internal university appeals, the professor went to federal court, and the court entered summary judgment for the university. The U.S. Court of Appeals then vacated the district court's ruling, noting that the district court had erred in using the lenient "arbitrary and capricious" standard to review the university's actions. The appellate court viewed the case as a standard contract claim and found no reason to accord the university any special deference in such a situation. Rejecting the trial court's choice of standard, the appellate court noted:

> In other words, according to the trial court, any Trustees' decision to fire a tenured faculty member is largely unreviewable, with judicial scrutiny limited to a modest inquiry as to whether the Trustees' decision was "arbitrary," "irrational" or infected by improper motivation. Such a reading of the contract renders tenure a virtual nullity. Faculty members like Dr. McConnell would have no real *substantive* right to continued employment, but only certain *procedural* rights that must be followed before their appointment may be terminated. We find this to be an astonishing concept, and one not compelled by a literal reading of the Faculty Handbook [818 F.2d at 67].

Thus, the court determined that "[o]n remand, the trial court must consider *de novo* the appellant's breach of contract claims; no special deference is due the Board of Trustees once the case is properly before the court for resolution of the contract dispute." The court also rejected an administrative agency model such as the *Riggin* court had used:

> [T]he theory of deference to administrative action flows from prudential concepts of separation of powers, as well as statutory proscriptions on the scope of judicial review. Obviously, none of those factors apply here. The notion of treating a private university as if it were a state or federal administrative agency is simply unsupported where a contract claim is involved [818 F.2d at 69; footnote omitted].

Further, the court explained:

> [W]e do not understand why university affairs are more deserving of judicial deference than the affairs of any other business or profession. Arguably, there might be matters unique to education on which courts are relatively ill equipped to pass judgment. However, this is true in many areas of the law, including, for example, technical, scientific and medical issues. Yet, this lack of expertise does not compel courts to defer to the view of one of the parties in such cases. The parties can supply such specialized knowledge through the use of expert testimony. Moreover, even if there are issues on which courts are ill equipped to rule, the interpretation of a contract is not one of them [818 F.2d at 69].

One additional circumstance will influence a court's standard of review: if the institution's decision was subject to arbitration before the filing of the court suit, the court will accord great deference to the arbitrator's decision, because the parties have usually agreed ahead of time to abide by it. In *Samaan v. Trustees of California State University and Colleges,* 197 Cal. Rptr. 856 (Cal. 1983), the plaintiff, another terminated tenured professor, had lost his case in arbitration. When he proceeded to court, the court indicated that his only remedy was a motion to vacate the arbitrator's award. An applicable statute set out five narrow grounds—each essentially a standard of review—for vacating an arbitration award (Cal. Civ. Proc. Code § 1286.2). The professor had not alleged or demonstrated any of these grounds but instead sought a more stringent standard of review. In response, the court conducted an independent review of the record and determined that the professor could not prevail even if a more stringent standard of review were available. It therefore upheld the university's dismissal decision, and the appellate court affirmed.

1.4.4. Final judgments. If a court proceeds to the merits of a plaintiff's claim, and if the parties do not in the meantime enter a voluntary settlement or consent decree disposing of the litigation, the court will decide the dispute and enter judgment for one of the parties. Judgment may be entered either after trial; before (or during) trial, by way of a motion for summary judgment or a motion to dismiss (Section 1.4.3.5 above); or—if the defendant does not contest the plaintiff's claim—by "default judgment." When the losing party's rights to appeal have been exhausted, the court's judgment becomes final.

After entry of judgment, issues may still arise concerning the judgment's enforcement, the award of attorney's fees, and related matters, which are discussed in Section 1.4.5. Other issues may arise concerning the binding effect of the judgment in later litigation, as discussed below.

In general, the law forbids relitigation of claims disposed of in prior litigation, even if that litigation was in a different court system. The technical rules that preclude relitigation of claims are often cumulatively referred to as the doctrine of "res judicata" (a Latin term meaning "things which have been decided") or as "claim preclusion."[6] These rules become important when a party is involved in multiple lawsuits against the same party or related parties, either simultaneously or seriatim. A postsecondary institution, for example, may successfully defend itself against a lawsuit in state court, only to find itself sued again by the same plaintiff in federal court; or it may successfully defend itself against a suit seeking damages, only to find itself again in the same court in a second suit by the same plaintiff seeking a different remedy. In such circumstances the institution will generally be able to use res judicata to preclude the second suit if it challenges any part of the same institutional action that was challenged and fully litigated to final judgment in the first suit. The doctrine thus promotes defendants' interests in finality and society's interests in judicial economy while still according plaintiffs a full opportunity to press their claims.

Pauk v. Board of Trustees of the City University of New York, 488 N.Y.S.2d 685 (N.Y. App. Div. 1985), *affirmed*, 497 N.E.2d 675 (N.Y. 1986), illustrates the res judicata doctrine at work, in particular the manner in which a court analyzes the scope of the initial claim and determines whether the same transactions are challenged in the second claim and thus barred. The plaintiff, a professor at Queens College, challenged a denial of reappointment and tenure. He alleged that he had already acquired tenure de facto as an assistant professor because he had been employed for five years and reappointed for a sixth year. In 1976, in a state court proceeding, he had sought to compel the defendant to rescind the letter of termination and to declare him a tenured assistant professor. A dismissal of his claim on the merits was affirmed by the highest state court (401 N.E.2d 214 (N.Y. 1979)). The professor was persistent, however, and in 1981 brought another suit against the defendant, alleging three different claims. (In 1979, between this suit and the first suit, the professor had filed yet another lawsuit against the defendant in federal court. That suit was dismissed because it was filed after the statute of limitations had expired; see Section 1.4.2.4.) In the first claim in the 1981 suit, the professor alleged that the refusal to renew his employment contract violated the implied terms of that contract; in the second claim, he separately alleged that the defendant had violated his rights under an article of the state constitution and a section of the state education law; and in the third claim, he alleged that the defendant's policy of maintaining the secrecy of the personnel committee's votes was unconstitutional. The defendant argued that the court should dismiss the first two claims because they were based on transactions already challenged in the claim that was adjudicated and dismissed in the earlier state court proceeding. (The court dismissed the third claim on other unrelated grounds.) The trial court held that the second claim but not the first was barred under the res judicata doctrine. The appellate court affirmed as to the second claim and reversed

---

[6]Related rules, called "issue preclusion" or "collateral estoppel," also preclude relitigation of particular issues of fact or law. They are beyond the scope of this discussion.

as to the first, concluding that it, like the second claim, arose from the same transactions as the earlier claim adjudicated in the earlier state court proceeding. Although the second claim relied on a different legal theory of recovery than the earlier state court claim, the plaintiff could have used that legal theory in the earlier proceeding to obtain relief comparable to that sought in the later proceeding. Res judicata therefore applied.

The result in *Pauk* should be no different if the second action had been filed in a different jurisdiction—that is, in the courts of another state or in federal rather than state court. Generally, the Full Faith and Credit Clause of the federal Constitution (Article IV, Section 1) compels the courts in every state to give a judgment rendered in a different state the same full faith and credit as a judgment rendered in its own state; and a federal statute, 28 U.S.C. § 1738, compels the federal courts to give full faith and credit to the judgments of state courts in state matters. Additional complications arise, however, when the initial claim is not filed in a state court but rather with a state administrative agency. Neither the Full Faith and Credit Clause nor the federal statute applies to this situation, and the binding effect of an administrative determination will depend on the rules of the particular state or, in the federal courts, on federal common law. *University of Tennessee v. Elliott*, 478 U.S. 788 (1986), illustrates the problem in the federal courts, where the difficulties concern "issue preclusion" rather than res judicata as such (see note 6 above, this section).

In *Elliott* a black employee of the university's Agricultural Extension Service challenged his termination on grounds that it was racially motivated. He first petitioned for administrative review of his termination under the state administrative procedure act. While his administrative proceeding was pending, he filed suit in federal court, alleging employment discrimination violative of both Title VII (this volume, Section 3.3.2.1) and Section 1983 (this volume, Section 2.3.3). Subsequently, the state administrative law judge ruled that the employee's termination was not racially motivated. Instead of appealing this decision to the state courts, he persevered with the federal court suit. The federal courts then had to determine whether they were bound by the administrative law judge's *fact-finding* that the termination was not racially motivated—that is, "whether this finding is entitled to preclusive effect in federal court." In a complicated analysis set against the backdrop of the federal common law of preclusion, the U.S. Supreme Court concluded that in passing Title VII Congress expressed an intent to allow plaintiffs to relitigate the fact determinations of state agencies in federal court but that, in passing Section 1983, Congress expressed no such intent. Thus, the state administrative fact-findings had a preclusive effect as to the Section 1983 claim but not as to the Title VII claim.

1.4.5. Judicial remedies. If the defendant prevails in a lawsuit, the only needed remedy is dismissal of the action and perhaps an award of attorney's fees or court costs. If the plaintiff prevails, however, that party is entitled to one or more types of affirmative remedies, most prominent of which are money damages and injunctive relief, and may be entitled to attorney's fees and costs as well. If the plaintiff does not comply with the court's remedial orders, the court may also use its contempt powers to enforce compliance.

1.4.5.1. Money damages. Depending on the character of the plaintiff's claim and proof, a court may award compensatory damages and, less often, punitive damages as well (see, for example, Sections 2.3.3 and 2.4.3 regarding damages under

Section 1983). Occasionally, even treble damages may be available (see, for example, Section 7.2.12 regarding federal antitrust laws). Money damages, however, are not necessarily a permissible remedy in all types of cases where the plaintiff sustains quantifiable injury. For example, in cases under the federal Age Discrimination Act, plaintiffs are entitled only to injunctive relief (see this volume, Section 7.5.9). But the trend appears to be to permit the award of money damages in an increasing range of cases. In Section 102 of the Civil Rights Act of 1991 (Pub. L. No. 102-166, 105 Stat. 1071, 1072 (1991)), for example, Congress amended Title VII so that it expressly authorizes the award of money damages in intentional discrimination actions under that statute (see this volume, Section 3.3.2.1); and in *Franklin v. Gwinnett County Public Schools,* 112 S. Ct. 1028 (1992), the U.S. Supreme Court construed Title IX to permit money damage awards in private causes of action under that statute (see this volume, Section 7.5.9).

When money damage awards are available, there may be caps on the amount of damages the court may award, or there may be questions about the measurement of the amount of damages. In *Memphis School District v. Stachura,* 477 U.S. 299 (1986), for example, the U.S. Supreme Court held that money damages based on the abstract "value" of the constitutional rights that had been infringed was not a proper component of compensatory damages in a Section 1983 suit. The plaintiff, a public school teacher, was fired because of certain teaching techniques he used for a course on human reproduction. The trial judge instructed the jury that, in addition to any other compensatory and punitive damages they might award to the plaintiff, they could also award damages based on the importance of the constitutional rights that were violated. The jury returned with a verdict for the plaintiff resulting in compensatory damages of $266,750 and punitive damages of $36,000, allocated among the school board and various individual defendants. The Supreme Court held that compensatory money damages are awarded on the basis of actual, provable injury, not on the basis of subjective valuation. If the jury were permitted to consider the "value" of the rights involved in determining the amount of compensatory damages, juries might "use their unbounded discretion to punish unpopular defendants." The court therefore remanded the case for a new trial on the issue of compensatory damages.

1.4.5.2. Injunctions. Injunctions are a type of specific nonmonetary, or equitable, relief. An injunction may be either permanent or temporary and may be either prohibitory (prohibiting the defendant from taking certain actions) or mandatory (requiring the defendant to take certain specified actions). A court may issue an injunction as a final remedy after adjudication of the merits of the lawsuit, or it may issue a "preliminary injunction" prior to trial in order to preserve the status quo or otherwise protect the plaintiff's rights during the pendency of the lawsuit.

Preliminary injunctions raise a host of important tactical questions for both plaintiffs and defendants. In determining whether to grant a motion for such an injunction, the court will commonly balance the plaintiff's likelihood of success on the merits of the lawsuit, the likelihood that the plaintiff will suffer irreparable harm absent the injunction, the injury that the defendant would sustain as a result of the injunction, and the general public interest in the matter. In *Jones v. University of North Carolina,* 704 F.2d 713 (4th Cir. 1983), the court applied such a balancing test and granted the plaintiff's request for a preliminary injunction. The plaintiff was a nursing student who had been accused of cheating on an examination, found guilty after somewhat contorted proceedings on campus, and barred from taking courses during the spring semester. She then filed a Section 1983 suit (this volume, Section 2.3.3), alleging that the university's disciplinary action violated her procedural due process rights. She requested and the court granted a preliminary injunction ordering the university to reinstate her as a student in good standing pending resolution of the suit. The university appealed the court's order, claiming it was an abuse of the court's discretion. The appellate court considered the hardships to both parties and the seriousness of the issues the plaintiff had raised. Regarding hardships, the court noted that, without the injunction, the plaintiff would have been barred from taking courses and delayed from graduating, denied the opportunity to graduate with her classmates, and forced to explain this educational gap throughout her professional career. On the other hand, according to the court, issuance of the injunction would not significantly harm the university's asserted interests:

> While we recognize the University's institutional interest in speedy reso-
> lution of disciplinary charges and in maintaining public confidence in the in-
> tegrity of its processes, Jones will suffer far more substantial, concrete injury if
> the injunction is dissolved and she is ultimately vindicated than will the Univer-
> sity if the injunction stands and its position is finally upheld [704 F.2d at 716].

Similarly, in *Cohen v. Brown University*, 991 F.2d 888 (1st Cir. 1993), a U.S. Court of Appeals upheld a district court's preliminary injunction ordering Brown University to reinstate its women's gymnastics and women's volleyball programs to full varsity status pending the trial of a Title IX claim. Both programs had been reduced to club status as a result of budget constraints. Although men's programs were also cut back, the plaintiffs alleged that the cuts discriminated against women at the school. The appellate court approved the district judge's determination that the plaintiffs would most likely prevail on the merits when the case was finally resolved. Further, the court observed that if the volleyball and gymnastics teams continued in their demoted state for any length of time, they would suffer irreparably because they would lose recruitment opportunities and coaches. The court found that these harms outweighed the small financial loss the university would sustain in keeping the teams at a varsity level until final resolution of the suit. (The *Cohen* case is further discussed in Section 4.15.3.)

1.4.5.3. Attorney's fees. Either the plaintiff or the defendant may recover the reasonable costs of attorney's fees in certain situations where they are the prevailing party. For instance, under the Civil Rights Attorney's Fees Awards Act of 1976 (90 Stat. 2641 (1976), 42 U.S.C. § 1988)), the federal courts may grant the prevailing parties in certain federal civil rights suits reasonable attorney's fees as part of the costs of litigation (see this volume, Section 7.5.9). The U.S. Supreme Court has held that this Act applies to state governments and officials who are sued in their official capacities. In *Hutto v. Finney*, 437 U.S. 678 (1978), the Court held that Congress intended to set aside the states' Eleventh Amendment immunity in these cases in order to enforce the protection of individual rights under the Fourteenth Amendment of the Constitution, and that attorney's fees are therefore not barred. Attorney's fees are also sometimes available under the Equal Access to Justice Act, to parties who prevail in litigation involving the federal government (see this volume, Section 7.6.1). More generally, Rule 11 of the Federal Rules of Civil Procedure (28 U.S.C. Appendix) permits federal courts to award attorney's fees in certain situations where a party files with the court a document that is not grounded in fact; is not based on existing law or a nonfrivolous argument for its modification; or is filed for an improper purpose, such as harassment or delay. In such circumstances the court may impose "a variety of sanctions, including attorney's fees and other expenses incurred as a direct result of the violation." Moreover, under Rule 38 of the Federal Rules for Appellate Procedure (28 U.S.C. Appendix), if a party's request for an appeal is frivolous, the court may award costs to the prevailing party, and such an award will typically include attorney's fees.

Weinstein v. University of Illinois, 811 F.2d 1091 (7th Cir. 1987), illustrates how a higher education institution may recover attorney's fees if forced to defend itself against a frivolous lawsuit. The appellate court relied on its authority under Rule 38 of the Federal Rules for Appellate Procedure to order the plaintiff professor to pay attorney's fees even though the university had not requested such an award. The professor, who was nontenured, challenged the refusal to renew his contract, claiming a violation of procedural due process. The court held that the claim was frivolous and may not have been brought in good faith, because it ignored the established rule that a nontenured faculty member has no property interest in continued employment (see Section 3.6.2.1). In fact, as the court emphasized, a prior case before the same court (*McElearney v. University of Illinois,* 612 F.2d 285, 289–91 (7th Cir. 1979)) "holds that a nontenured professor at the same university, employed under the same contract, lacked a property interest." Thus, according to the court, the plaintiff was "litigating a defunct claim. He hasn't a chance; he never did; but he has put the University to some expense. This is frivolous litigation."

Even when the court has authority to award attorney's fees and does so, the parties may challenge the reasonableness of the amount awarded. The case of *Craik v. Minnesota State University Board,* 738 F.2d 348 (8th Cir. 1984), illustrates several of the issues that may arise and suggests the various grounds on which a higher education institution may seek to diminish an award against it or enhance an award in its favor. The plaintiff in *Craik* prevailed in an employment discrimination suit against Minnesota State University and was awarded $126,127.40 in reasonable attorney's fees under 42 U.S.C. § 1988.

In order to reach this figure, and in reviewing the university's challenge to it, the court considered the nature and quality of the legal services rendered to the plaintiff for the appeal, the reasonableness of the rates charged by the plaintiff's out-of-state counsel, the inclusion of ten hours of travel time charged at the out-of-state counsel's normal office hourly rate, and the extent of the plaintiff's success on the appeal. The court rejected the university's arguments for reduction on the first three grounds but accepted its argument on the fourth ground. Because the plaintiff did not prevail on all issues raised on appeal, and because the relief awarded could be further narrowed on remand to the trial court, the appellate court reduced the attorney's fees award by 20 percent. In turn, however, in response to the plaintiff's argument, the court considered the degree of risk to their law practices that the plaintiff's attorneys assumed by taking the case and, on this ground, enhanced the fees of two of the four attorneys by 25 percent, thus leaving the amount awarded almost the same as it was before being challenged.

1.4.5.4. Contempt of court. When a defendant does not comply with the court's award of relief to the plaintiff, or when either party or their witnesses do not comply with some other court order (for example, a subpoena to testify), the court may enforce its own orders by various means. Primary and most powerful is the imposition of criminal or civil contempt. In *United States v. United Mine Workers*, 330 U.S. 258 (1947), the U.S. Supreme Court distinguished the two sanctions. A civil contempt judgment may be used to coerce the contemnor into compliance with a court order or to award compensation to the complaining party for incurred losses. On the other hand, a criminal contempt judgment is used not simply to coerce but rather to punish the contemnor or vindicate the authority of the court. Commonly, the court may impose a monetary fine or imprisonment for either type of judgment. In a civil contempt case, the amount of the fine or term of the imprisonment may be indefinite, since the purpose is to coerce the contemnor into compliance. Thus, a judge may imprison someone until that person is willing to comply, or fine him a certain sum per day until compliance. Further, once it becomes clear that no amount of coercion will work, the fine or imprisonment must stop. Conversely, in criminal contempt, there must be a definite fine or term of imprisonment set at the outset.

Dinnan v. Regents of the University System of Georgia, 625 F.2d 1146 (5th Cir. 1980), illustrates the reach of the contempt power as well as the potential difficulty in determining whether a judge has imposed criminal or civil contempt. The plaintiff was a University of Georgia professor challenging a contempt order against him. He was a member of a committee that had denied a promotion to a female faculty applicant who subsequently sued the university for sex discrimination (see Section 3.3.4). When he refused to testify at the trial (see this volume, Section 3.7.7.1), the court ordered him to pay $100 for every day (up to thirty days) he refused to testify. If he continued in contempt of the order after that time, he would be sentenced to ninety days' imprisonment subject to being released earlier any time he agreed to testify. Dinnan argued that the court's orders constituted criminal contempt and were unlawful because fines and imprisonment cannot be combined as punishment for criminal contempt. Both the trial court and the appellate court rejected his challenge, holding that these were coercive, not punitive, measures and that both sanctions were appropriate components of a civil order of contempt.

An opposite result obtained in *Martin v. Guillot*, 875 F.2d 839 (11th Cir. 1989). There, a university that had dismissed an administrator without affording him due process protections disobeyed a court order to afford the administrator (the plaintiff) an appropriate hearing and appeal. Although university officials (the defendants) eventually complied, the plaintiff requested that the court hold the university in contempt for its earlier delay in doing so. The trial court granted the request and, as a sanction, ordered the defendants to purge themselves of their contempt by giving the plaintiff back pay for the time from his unlawful dismissal to the eventual provision of full due process rights. The appellate court reversed the trial court's order, however, because the order was in the nature of a criminal contempt, and the trial court had not met the procedural requirements of the Federal Rules of Criminal Procedure (Rule 42) for imposing criminal contempt:

> [T]he sanction was not imposed either to coerce or compensate and therefore is not a civil contempt sanction. The defendants had already complied with the court orders and afforded Martin due process; there remained nothing to coerce them to do. The continued contempt could be construed as being compensatory in character because the sanction, approximately equal to back pay, was to be paid to the appellant rather than to the court. However, in its order specifying the amount of the sanction to be imposed, the district court explicitly

stated its "object was and is to sanction defendants rather than to compensate Martin." Because the sanction levied by the district court was clearly designed predominately to punish defendants for their initial failings to comply with court orders, it is a criminal contempt sanction [875 F.2d at 845].

1.4.6. Managing litigation and the threat of litigation.

1.4.6. Managing litigation and the threat of litigation. Managing, settling, and conducting litigation, like planning its avoidance, requires the in-depth involvement of attorneys at all stages.[7] Institutions should place heavy emphasis on this aspect of institutional operations. Both administrators and counsel should cultivate conditions in which they can work together as a team in a treatment law mode (see Section 1.7.2). The administrator's basic understanding of the tactical and technical matters discussed in Sections 1.4.1 through 1.4.5, and counsel's mastery of these technicalities and the tactical options and difficulties they present, will greatly enhance the institution's capacity to engage in treatment law that successfully protects the institution's mission as well as its reputation and financial resources.

Litigation management is a two-way street. It may be employed either in a defensive posture when the institution or its employees are sued or threatened with suit, or in an offensive posture when the institution seeks access to the courts as the best means of protecting its interests in a conflict situation. Administrators, like counsel, will thus do well to consider treatment law from both perspectives and to view courts and litigation as a potential benefit in some circumstances, rather than only as a hindrance.

Although administrators and counsel must accord great attention and energy to lawsuits when they arise, and thus must emphasize the expert practice of treatment law, their primary and broader objective should be to avoid lawsuits or limit their scope whenever that can be accomplished consistent with the institutional mission. Once a lawsuit has been filed, they sometimes can achieve this objective by using summary judgment motions or (if the institution is a defendant) motions to dismiss (Section 1.4.3.5), or by encouraging pretrial negotiation and settlement. Moreover, by agreement of the parties, the dispute may be diverted from the courts to a mediator or an arbitrator. Even better, they may be able to derail disputes from the litigation track before any suit is filed by providing for a suitable alternative mechanism for resolving the dispute. Mediation and arbitration are common and increasingly important examples of such ADR (alternative dispute-resolution) mechanisms (see Section 1.1), which are usable whether the institution is a defendant or a plaintiff, and whether the dispute is an internal campus dispute or an external dispute with a commercial vendor, construction contractor, or other outside entity. For internal campus disputes, internal grievance processes and hearing panels (see, for example, Section 4.5) are also important ADR mechanisms and may frequently constitute reme-

---

[7]The suggestions in this section apply not only to litigation against the institution but also to suits against officers or *employees* of the institution when the institution is providing, or considering providing, legal representation or related assistance to the employee. In suits where both the institution and one or more named institutional officers or employees are defendants, questions may arise concerning possible conflicts of interest that should preclude the institution's legal staff from representing all or some of the officers or employees (see Section 1.4.3.4).

dies that, under the exhaustion doctrine (Section 1.4.2.5), disputants must utilize before resorting to court.

Even before disputes arise, administrators and counsel should be actively engaging in preventive law (Section 1.7.2) as the most comprehensive and forward-looking means of avoiding and limiting lawsuits. Preventive law also has a useful role to play in the wake of a lawsuit, especially a major one in which the institution is sued and loses. In such a circumstance, administrators may engage in a postlitigation audit of the institutional offices and functions implicated in the lawsuit. The purpose would be to use the litigation constructively, as a kind of lens through which to view institutional shortcomings of the type that led to the lawsuit and the judgment against the institution, and to rectify such shortcomings so that lawsuits need not arise again in that area of concern.

Sec. 1.5. *The Public-Private Dichotomy*

1.5.1 Background. Historically, higher education has roots in both the public and the private sectors, although the strength of each one's influence has varied over time (see generally F. Rudolph, *The American College and University: A History* (University of Georgia Press, 1990)). Sometimes following and sometimes leading this historical development, the law has tended to support and reflect the fundamental dichotomy between public and private education.

A forerunner of the present university was the Christian seminary. Yale was an early example. Dartmouth began as a school to teach Christianity to the Indians. Similar schools sprang up throughout the colonies. Though often established through private charitable trusts, they were also chartered by the colony, received some financial support from the colony, and were subject to its regulation. Thus, colonial colleges were often a mixture of public and private activity. The nineteenth century witnessed a gradual decline in governmental involvement with sectarian schools. As states began to establish their own institutions, the public-private dichotomy emerged. (See D. Tewksbury, *The Founding of American Colleges and Universities Before the Civil War* (Anchor Books, 1965).) In recent years this dichotomy has again faded as state and federal governments have provided larger amounts of financial support to private institutions, many of which are now secular.

Although private institutions have always been more expensive to attend than public institutions, private higher education has been a vital and influential force in American intellectual history. The private school can cater to special interests that a public one often cannot serve because of legal or political constraints. Private education thus draws strength from "the very possibility of doing something different than government can do, of creating an institution free to make choices government cannot—even seemingly arbitrary ones—without having to provide a justification that will be examined in a court of law" (H. Friendly, *The Dartmouth College Case and the Public-Private Penumbra* (Humanities Research Center, University of Texas, 1969), 30).

Though modern-day private institutions are not always free from examination "in a court of law," the law often does treat public and private institutions differently. These differences will underlie much of the discussion in this book. They are critically important in assessing the law's impact on the roles of particular institutions and the duties of their administrators.

Whereas public institutions are usually subject to the plenary authority of the government that creates them, the law protects private institutions from such extensive governmental control. Government can usually alter, enlarge, or completely abolish its public institutions (see Section 6.2); private institutions, however, can obtain their own perpetual charters of incorporation, and, since the famous *Dartmouth College* case (*Trustees of Dartmouth College v. Woodward,* 17 U.S. 518 (1819)), government has been prohibited from impairing such charters. In that case the U.S. Supreme Court turned back New Hampshire's attempt to assume control of Dartmouth by finding that such action would violate the Constitution's Contracts Clause (see B. Campbell, *"Dartmouth College* as a Civil Liberties Case: The Formation of Constitutional Policy," 70 *Ky. L. J.* 643 (1981-82)). Subsequently, in three other landmark cases—*Meyer v. Nebraska,* 262 U.S. 390 (1923); *Pierce v. Society of Sisters,* 268 U.S. 510 (1925); and *Farmington v. Tokushige,* 273 U.S. 284 (1927)—the Supreme Court used the Due Process Clause to strike down unreasonable governmental interference with teaching and learning in private schools.

Nonetheless, government does retain substantial authority to regulate private education. But—whether for legal, political, or policy reasons—state governments usually regulate private institutions less than they regulate public institutions. The federal government, on the other hand, has tended to apply its regulations comparably to both public and private institutions or, bowing to considerations of federalism, has regulated private institutions while leaving public institutions to the states.

In addition to these differences in regulatory patterns, the law makes a second and more pervasive distinction between public and private institutions: public institutions and their officers are fully subject to the constraints of the federal Constitution, whereas private institutions and their officers are not. Because the Constitution was designed to limit only the exercise of government power, it does not prohibit private individuals or corporations from impinging on such freedoms as free speech, equal protection, and due process. Thus, *insofar as the federal Constitution is concerned,* a private university can engage in private acts of discrimination, prohibit student protests, or expel a student without affording the procedural safeguards that a public university is constitutionally required to provide.

Indeed, this distinction can be crucial even within a single university. In *Powe v. Miles,* 407 F.2d 73 (2d Cir. 1968), seven Alfred University students had been suspended for engaging in protest activities that disrupted an ROTC ceremony. Four of the students attended Alfred's liberal arts college, while the remaining three were students at the ceramics college. The state of New York had contracted with Alfred to establish the ceramics college, and a New York statute specifically stated that the university's disciplinary acts with respect to students at the ceramics college were considered to be taken on behalf of the state. The court found that the dean's action in suspending the ceramics students was "state action" but the suspension of the liberal arts students was not. Thus, the court ruled that the dean was required to afford the ceramics students due process but was not required to follow any constitutional dictates in suspending the liberal arts students, even though both groups of students had engaged in the same course of conduct.

1.5.2. The state action doctrine. As *Powe* makes clear, before a court will apply constitutional guarantees of individual rights to a postsecondary institution, it must first determine that the institution's action is "state (governmental) action."[8] Although this determination is essentially a matter of distinguishing public from private institutions, or the public part of an institution from the private part, these distinctions do not necessarily depend on traditional notions of public or private. Because of varying patterns of government assistance and involvement, a continuum exists, ranging from the obvious public school (such as the tax-supported state university) to the obvious private school (such as the religious seminary). The large gray area between these extremes provides a continuing source of debate about how far the government must be involved before a "private" institution may be considered "public" under the Constitution. Since the early 1970s, however, the trend of the U.S. Supreme Court's opinions has been to trim back the state action concept, making it less likely that courts will find state action to exist in particular cases. The leading case in this line involving educational institutions is *Rendell-Baker v. Kohn*, 457 U.S. 830 (1982), discussed below.

Though government funding is a relevant consideration, much more than money is involved in a state action determination. Courts and commentators have dissected the state action concept in many different ways, but at heart essentially three approaches have emerged for attributing state action to an ostensibly private entity. When the private entity (1) acts as an agent of government in performing a particular task delegated to it by government (the delegated power theory), or (2) performs a function that is generally considered the responsibility of government (the public function theory), or (3) obtains substantial resources, prestige, or encouragement from its involvement with government (the government contacts theory), its actions may become state action subject to constitutional constraints.

The first theory, delegated power, was relied on in the *Powe v. Miles* case (discussed in Section 1.5.1), where the court found that New York State had delegated authority to Alfred to operate a state ceramics school at the university. This same court also considered the delegated power theory in *Wahba v. New York University*, 492 F.2d 96 (2d Cir. 1974), in which a research professor had been fired from a government-funded research project. But here the court refused to find that the firing was state action, since the government did not exercise any managerial control over the project. This focus on state involvement *in addition to funding* has assumed increasing importance in state action law. In *Greenya v. George Washington University*), 512 F.2d 556 (D.C. Cir. 1975), for instance, the university had a contract with the Navy to provide instruction at the U.S. Naval School of Hospital Administration. When the university fired a teacher assigned to teach in this program, he argued state action on the basis that he had been teaching government employees at government facilities—essentially a delegated power theory. But the court rejected the argument on grounds similar to those in *Wahba:*

> [Plaintiff] was always under the supervision and control of university officials, and . . . he maintained no contractual relations with the Navy. Nothing

[8]Although this inquiry has arisen mainly with regard to the federal Constitution, it may also arise in applying *state* constitutional guarantees. See, for example, *Stone v. Cornell University*, 510 N.Y.S.2d 313 (N.Y. 1987) (no state action).

in the record indicates that the Navy had any right to say who would be hired to teach the English course. Neither does the record indicate that the Navy had anything whatsoever to do with the failure to renew appellant's contract. Appellant was merely the employee of an independent contractor who was providing educational services to the Navy [512 F.2d at 561–62].

The second theory, the public function theory, has generally not been a basis for finding state action in education cases. Though the issue has often been raised, courts have recognized that education has substantial roots in the private sector and cannot be considered a solely public function. In the *Greenya* case, for instance, the court simply remarked: "We have considered whether higher education constitutes 'state action' because it is a 'public function' as that term has been developed . . . and have concluded that it is not. . . . Education . . . has never been a state monopoly in the United States." In the later case of *State v. Schmid*, 423 A.2d 615 (N.J. 1980) (this volume, Section 5.6.3), however, the court was unwilling to accord the public function theory such a summary rejection. The case concerned the applicability of the First Amendment to Princeton University's removal from campus of a nonstudent who was distributing political leaflets. After refusing to find state action under the government contacts theory, the court set out the most comprehensive analysis to date of the application of the public function theory to private college campuses. But because of the absence of decisional authority and "strong cross-currents of policy" regarding the question, the court deferred any final determination on the public function theory, deciding the case instead under the New Jersey state constitution.

It is the third theory, the government contacts theory, that has had the greatest workout in postsecondary education cases. Although this theory is closely related to the delegated power theory, it focuses on less formal and particularized relationships between government and private entities. As the U.S. Supreme Court noted in the landmark *Burton v. Wilmington Parking Authority* case, 365 U.S. 715, 722 (1961), "Only by sifting facts and weighing circumstances can the nonobvious involvement of the state in private conduct be attributed its true significance." The search focuses initially on state involvement in the particular activity that gives rise to the lawsuit: "[T]he inquiry must be whether there is a sufficiently close nexus between the State and the challenged action of the [private] entity so that the action of the latter may be fairly treated as that of the State itself" (*Jackson v. Metropolitan Edison Co.*, 419 U.S. 345, 351 (1974).[9] Alternately, a state action finding may be based on the state's overall involvement with the private institution, if "the state has so far insinuated itself into a position of interdependence with . . . [the institution] that it must be recognized as a joint participant in the challenged activity" (*Burton*, 345 U.S. at 725, establishing the "joint venturer" or "symbiotic relationship" branch of the government contacts theory). When the state is so substantially involved in the whole of the private entity's activities, courts will not normally require proof that it was specif-

[9]In *Jackson*, the U.S. Supreme Court nailed down this point when it rejected the petitioner's state action argument because "there was no . . . [state] imprimatur placed on the practice of . . . [the private entity] about which petitioner complains," and the state "has not put its own weight on the side of the . . . practice by ordering it" (419 U.S. at 357). Such a showing of state involvement in the precise activity challenged may not be required, however, in race discrimination cases (see *Norwood v. Harrison*, 413 U.S. 455 (1973), and the cases discussed later in this section.

ically involved in (or had a "nexus" with) the particular activity challenged in the lawsuit.

The *Greenya* case also illustrates the government contacts theory. In challenging his termination by George Washington University, the plaintiff sought to base state action not only on the government's contract with the university but also on the government's general support for the university. The court quickly affirmed that neither the grant of a corporate charter nor the grant of tax-exempt status is sufficient to constitute state action. It then reached the same conclusion regarding federal funding of certain university programs and capital expenditures. Government funding, in the court's view, would not amount to state action unless and until the conditions placed on such funding "become so all-pervasive that the government has become, in effect, a joint venturer in the recipient's enterprise" (*Greenya* at 561).[10] In contrast, in *Benner v. Oswald*, 592 F.2d 174 (3d Cir. 1979), the court found state action by applying the government contacts theory. The plaintiffs in the case, students at Pennsylvania State University, challenged the process for selecting members of the university's board of trustees. Relying on numerous contacts between the university and the state, the court used the *Burton* joint venturer test to hold that selection of the trustees constituted state action.

Under each of the three state action theories, courts appear more likely to find state action in race discrimination cases than in any other kind of case. In the *Wahba* and *Greenya* cases above, the courts specifically noted as part of their reasoning processes that race discrimination was not involved. In *Williams v. Howard University*, 528 F.2d 658 (D.C. Cir. 1976), which did involve race discrimination, the plaintiff also raised a second claim, involving deprivation of due process; and the court distinguished between the two claims. It held that the defendant's receipt of substantial federal funding was not a sufficient basis for finding government (state) action as to the due process claim but that "the allegation of substantial federal funding would be enough to demonstrate governmental action as to . . . [the] claim of racial discrimination."

In *Weise v. Syracuse University*, 522 F.2d 397 (2d Cir. 1975), the court recognized this same "double standard" in state action cases and extended it in part to claims of sex discrimination. The plaintiffs were two women, one a rejected faculty applicant and the other a terminated faculty member, who claimed that the university had discriminated against them solely on the basis of sex. In remanding the case to the trial court, the appellate court explained the significance of both race and sex discrimination in state action cases:

> If our concern in this case were with discipline and the First Amendment, the alleged indicia of state action—funding and regulation—would most likely be insufficient. . . . [But as the] conduct complained of becomes more offensive, and as the nature of the dispute becomes more amenable to resolution by a court, the more appropriate it is to subject the issue to judicial scrutiny. . . . Class-based discrimination is perhaps the practice most fundamentally opposed to the stuff of which our national heritage is composed, and by far the most evil form of discrimination has been that based on race. It should hardly be surprising, then, that in race discrimination cases courts have been particularly vigilant in requir-

---

[10]This "joint venturer" (or symbiotic relationship) concept comes from the *Burton* case, cited above. See also *Moose Lodge v. Irvis*, 407 U.S. 163 at 176–77 (1972).

ing the states to avoid support of otherwise private discrimination, and that where the conduct has been less offensive, a greater degree of tolerance has been shown. . . . It is not necessary to put sex discrimination into the same hole as race discrimination. . . . It is enough to note that the conduct here alleged—invidious class-based discrimination on account of sex—would appear . . . to be more offensive than the disciplinary steps taken in prior cases [522 F.2d at 405-06].[11]

Most state action cases, like those above, are concerned with whether government is so involved in the activities of a private institution as to render those activities state action. But state action issues may also arise with respect to public institutions. In that context the basic question is whether the public institution is so involved with the activity of some private entity as to render that entity's activity state action. In *Shapiro v. Columbia Union National Bank and Trust Co.*, 576 S.W.2d 310 (Mo. 1978), for example, the question was whether the University of Missouri at Kansas City (a public institution) was so entwined with the administration of a private scholarship trust fund that the fund's activities became state action. The plaintiff, a female student, sued the school and the bank, which was the fund's trustee. The fund had been established as a trust by a private individual, who had stipulated that all scholarship recipients be male. Shapiro alleged that, although the Columbia Union National Bank was named as trustee, the university in fact administered the scholarship fund; that she was ineligible for the scholarship solely because of her sex; and that the university's conduct in administering the trust therefore was unconstitutional. She further claimed that the trust constituted three-fourths of the scholarship money available at the university and that the school's entire scholarship program was thereby discriminatory.

The trial court twice dismissed the complaint for failure to state a cause of action, reasoning that the trust was private and the plaintiff had not stated facts sufficient to demonstrate state action. On appeal the Supreme Court of Missouri reviewed the university's involvement in the administration of the trust, applying the government contacts theory:

> We cannot conclude that by sifting all the facts and circumstances there was state action involved here. Mr. Victor Wilson established a private trust for the benefit of deserving Kansas City "boys." He was a private individual; he established a trust with his private funds; he appointed a bank as trustee; he established a procedure by which recipients of the trust fund would be selected. The trustee was to approve the selections. Under the terms of the will, no public agency or state action is involved. Discrimination on the basis of sex results from Mr. Wilson's personal predilection. That is clearly not unlawful.
>
> The dissemination of information by the university in a catalogue and by other means, the accepting and processing of applications by the financial aid office, the determining of academic standards and financial needs, the making of a tentative award or nomination and forwarding the names of qualified male

---

[11](Author's footnote.) After the appellate court remanded *Weise* to the trial court, that court did not rule on the state action issue until 1982. By then, the U.S. Supreme Court had decided *Rendell-Baker v. Kohn*, (discussed later in this section). In light of that case, the *Weise* trial court held, "with disappointment," that the plaintiffs could not "establish state action under any view of the instant matter" (*Weise v. Syracuse University*, 553 F. Supp. 675 (N.D.N.Y. 1982)).

students to the private trustee . . . does not in our opinion rise to the level of state action [576 S.W.2d at 320].

Disagreeing with this conclusion, one member of the appellate court wrote in a dissenting opinion:

> The university accepts the applications, makes a tentative award, and in effect "selects" the male applicants who are to receive the benefits of the scholarship fund. The acts of the university are more than ministerial. The trust as it has been administered has shed its purely private character and has become a public one. The involvement of the public university is . . . of such a prevailing nature that there is governmental entwinement constituting state action [576 S.W.2d at 323].

Having declined to find state action, thus denying the plaintiff a basis for applying the Constitution to the trust fund, the appellate court majority affirmed the dismissal of the case. (For a discussion of the treatment of sex-restricted scholarships under Title IX, see this volume, Section 4.3.3.)

Four years after *Shapiro*, a major U.S. Supreme Court case added more firepower to the postsecondary arsenal for thwarting state action challenges. *Rendell-Baker v. Kohn*, 457 U.S. 830 (1982), was a suit brought by teachers at a private school who had been discharged as a result of their opposition to school policies. They sued the school and its director, Kohn, alleging that the discharges violated their federal constitutional rights to free speech and due process. The issue before the Court was whether the private school's discharge of the teachers was "state action," subjecting it to the constraints of the Constitution.

The defendant school specializes in dealing with students who have drug, alcohol, or behavioral problems or other special needs. Nearly all students are referred by local public schools or by the drug rehabilitation division of the state's department of health. The school receives funds for student tuition from the local public school boards and is reimbursed by the state department of health for services provided to students referred by the department. The school also receives funds from other state and federal agencies. Virtually all the school's income, therefore, is derived from government funding. The school is also subject to state regulations on various matters, such as record keeping and student/teacher ratios, and to requirements concerning services provided under its contracts with the local school boards and the state health department. Few of these requirements, however, relate to personnel policy.

Using an analysis based on the government contacts theory, the Supreme Court held that neither the government funding nor the government regulation was sufficient to make the school's discharge decisions state action. As to funding, the Court analogized the school's funding situation to that of a private corporation whose business depends heavily on government contracts to build "roads, bridges, dams, ships, or submarines" for the government. And as to regulation:

> Here the decisions to discharge the petitioners were not compelled or even influenced by any state regulation. Indeed, in contrast to the extensive regulation of the school generally, the various regulators showed relatively little interest in the school's personnel matters. The most intrusive personnel regulation promulgated by the various government agencies was the requirement that the Committee on Criminal Justice had the power to approve persons hired as vocational

counselors. Such a regulation is not sufficient to make a decision to discharge, made by private management, state action [457 U.S. at 841].

The Court also considered and rejected two other arguments of the teachers: that the school was engaged in state action because it performs a "public function" and that the school had a "symbiotic relationship" with—that is, was engaged in a "joint venture" with—government, which constitutes state action under *Burton v. Wilmington Parking Authority*, discussed above. As to the former argument, the Court reasoned:

> [T]he relevant question is not simply whether a private group is serving a "public function." We have held that the question is whether the function performed has been "traditionally the *exclusive* prerogative of the state" (*Jackson v. Metropolitan Edison Co.*, 419 U.S. at 353). There can be no doubt that the education of maladjusted high school students is a public function, but that is only the beginning of the inquiry. [Massachusetts law] demonstrates that the state intends to provide services for such students at public expense. That legislative policy choice in no way makes these services the exclusive province of the state. Indeed, the Court of Appeals noted that until recently the state had not undertaken to provide education for students who could not be served by traditional public schools (641 F.2d at 26). That a private entity performs a function which serves the public does not make its acts state action [457 U.S. at 842].

As to the latter argument, the Court concluded simply that "the school's fiscal relationship with the state is not different from that of many contractors performing services for the government. No symbiotic relationship such as existed in *Burton* exists here."

Having rejected all the teachers' arguments, the Court, by a 7-to-2 vote, concluded that the school's discharge decisions did not constitute state action; and it affirmed the lower court's dismissal of the lawsuit.

As part of the narrowing trend evident in the Court's state action opinions since the early 1970s, *Rendell-Baker* illustrates the trend's application to private education. The case serves to confirm the validity of many earlier cases where the court refused to find state action respecting activities of postsecondary institutions, and to cast doubt on some other cases where state action has been found.[12] *Rendell-Baker* thus insulates postsecondary institutions further from state action findings and the resultant application of federal constitutional constraints to their activities.

Lower court cases subsequent to *Rendell-Baker* illustrate the constricting effect of that case on the state action doctrine. In an opinion relying on a companion case to *Rendell-Baker*, *Blum v. Yaretsky*, 457 U.S. 991 (1982), a federal appellate court, after protracted litigation, refused to extend the state action doctrine to the disciplinary actions of a private college (*Albert v. Carovano*, 824 F.2d 1333, *modified on rehearing*, 838 F.2d 871 (2d Cir. 1987), *panel opin. vacated*, 851 F.2d 561 (2d Cir. 1988) (*en banc*)). The suit was brought against Hamilton College by students whom the college had disciplined under authority of its policy guide on freedom of expression and maintenance of public order. The college had promulgated this guide in com-

---

[12]The cases and authorities are collected in Annot., "Action of Private Institution of Higher Education as Constituting State Action, or Action Under Color of Law, for Purposes of Fourteenth Amendment and 42 U.S.C., Section 1983," 37 A.L.R. Fed. 601 (1978 and periodic supp.).

pliance with New York Education Law, Section 6450 (the Henderson Act), which requires colleges to adopt rules for maintaining public order on campus and file them with the state. The trial court dismissed the students' complaint on the grounds that they could not prove that the college's action was state action. After an appellate court panel reversed, the full court affirmed the pertinent part of the trial court's dismissal. The *en banc* court concluded:

> [A]ppellants' theory of state action suffers from a fatal flaw. That theory assumes that either Section 6450 or the rules Hamilton filed pursuant to that statute constitute "a rule of conduct imposed by the state." 457 U.S. at 937. Yet nothing in either the legislation or those rules required that these appellants be suspended for occupying Buttrick Hall. Moreover, it is undisputed that the state's role under the Henderson Act has been merely to keep on file rules submitted by colleges and universities. The state has never sought to compel schools to enforce these rules and has never even inquired about such enforcement [851 F.2d at 568].

Finding that the state had taken no action regarding the disciplinary policies of private colleges in the state, and that the administrators of Hamilton College did not believe that the Henderson Act required them to take particular disciplinary actions, the court refused to find state action.

In *Smith v. Duquesne University*, 612 F. Supp. 72 (W.D. Pa. 1985), *affirmed without opin.*, 787 F.2d 583 (3d Cir. 1985), a graduate student challenged his expulsion on due process and equal protection grounds, asserting that Duquesne's action constituted state action. The court used both the "joint venturer" and the "nexus" analyses to determine that Duquesne was not a state actor. Regarding the former, the court distinguished Duquesne's relationship with the state of Pennsylvania from that of Temple University and the University of Pittsburgh (which were viewed as state actors in *Krynicky v. University of Pittsburgh*, 742 F.2d 94 (3d Cir. 1984)), and held that the relationship with Duquesne was "so tenuous as to lead to no other conclusion but that Duquesne is a private institution and not a state actor" (612 F. Supp. at 77–78). There was no statutory relationship between the state and the university, the state did not review the university's expenditures, and the university was not required to submit the types of financial reports to the state that state-related institutions, such as Temple and Pitt, were required to submit. Regarding the latter (the nexus test), the court determined that the state could not "be deemed responsible for the specific act" complained of by the plaintiff:

> [T]his case requires no protracted analysis to determine that Duquesne's decision to dismiss Smith cannot fairly be attributable to the Commonwealth. . . . The decision to expel Smith, like the decision to matriculate him, turned on an academic judgment made by a purely private institution according to its official university policy. If indirect involvement is insufficient to establish state action, then certainly the lack of any involvement cannot suffice [612 F. Supp. at 78].

And in *Imperiale v. Hahnemann University*, 966 F.2d 125 (3d Cir. 1992), a federal appellate court rejected the plaintiff's claim that the university had engaged in unconstitutional state action when it revoked his medical degree. Considering both the joint venturer and the nexus tests, the court denied the contention that the state action doctrine should apply because the university was "state-aided."

Rendell-Baker and later cases, however, do not create an impenetrable protective barrier for postsecondary institutions. In particular, there may be situations in which government is directly involved in the challenged activity—in contrast to the absence of government involvement in the personnel actions challenged in *Rendell-Baker*. Such involvement may supply the "nexus" missing in the Supreme Court case (see *Milonas v. Williams*, 691 F.2d 931 (10th Cir. 1982)). Moreover, there may be situations, unlike *Rendell-Baker,* in which government officials by virtue of their offices sit on or nominate others for an institution's board of trustees. Such involvement, perhaps in combination with other "contacts," may create the "symbiotic relationship" that did not exist in the Supreme Court case (see *Krynicky v. University of Pittsburgh* and *Schier v. Temple University,* 742 F.2d 94 (3d Cir. 1984)). Because these and other such circumstances continue to pose complex issues, administrators in private institutions should keep the state action concept in mind in major dealings with government. They should also rely heavily on legal counsel for guidance in this technical area. And, most important, administrators should confront the question that the state action cases leave squarely on their doorsteps: When the law does not impose constitutional constraints on your action, to what extent and in what manner will your institution undertake on its own initiative to protect freedom of speech and press, equality of opportunity, due process, and other such values on your campus?

1.5.3. Other bases for legal rights in private institutions. The inapplicability of the federal Constitution to private schools does not necessarily mean that students, faculty members, and other members of the private school community have no legal rights assertable against the school. There are other sources for individual rights, and these sources may resemble those found in the Constitution.

The federal government and, to a lesser extent, state governments have increasingly created statutory rights enforceable against private institutions, particularly in the discrimination area. The federal Title VII prohibition on employment discrimination (42 U.S.C. § 2000e et seq., discussed in Section 3.3.2.1), applicable generally to public and private employment relationships, is a prominent example. Other major examples are the Title VI race discrimination law (42 U.S.C. § 2000d et seq.) and the Title IX sex discrimination law (20 U.S.C. § 1681 et seq.) (see this volume, Sections 7.5.2 and 7.5.3), applicable to federal aid recipients. Such sources provide a large body of nondiscrimination law, which parallels and in some ways is more protective than the equal protection principles derived from the Fourteenth Amendment.

Beyond such statutory rights, several common law theories for protecting individual rights in private postsecondary institutions have been advanced. Most prominent by far is the contract theory, under which students and faculty members are said to have a contractual relationship with the private school. Express or implied contract terms establish legal rights that can be enforced in court if the contract is breached. Although the theory is a useful one that is often referred to in the cases (see Sections 3.1 and 4.1.3), most courts agree that the contract law of the commercial world cannot be imported wholesale into the academic environment. The theory must thus be applied with sensitivity to academic customs and usages. Moreover, the theory's usefulness is somewhat limited. The "terms" of the "contract" may be difficult to identify, particularly in the case of students. (To what extent, for instance, is the college catalogue a source of contract terms?) Some of the terms, once identified, may be too vague or ambiguous to enforce. Or the contract may be so barren of content or so one-sided in favor of the institution that it is an insignificant source of individual rights.

Despite its shortcomings, the contract theory has gained in importance. As it has become clear that the bulk of private institutions can escape the tentacles of the state action doctrine, alternative theories for establishing individual rights are increasingly used. Since the lowering of the age of majority, postsecondary students have had a capacity to contract under state law—a capacity that many previously did not have. In what has become the age of the consumer, students have been encouraged to import consumer rights into postsecondary education. And, in an age of collective negotiation, faculties have often sought to rely on a contract model for ordering employment relationships on campus (see Section 3.2).

Such developments can affect both public and private institutions, although state law may place additional restrictions on contract authority in the public sphere. While contract concepts can of course limit the authority of the institution, they should not be seen only as a burr in the administrator's side. They can also be used creatively to provide order and fairness in institutional affairs and to create internal grievance procedures that encourage in-house rather than judicial resolution of problems. Administrators thus should be sensitive to both the problems and the potentials of contract concepts in the postsecondary environment.

State constitutions have also assumed critical importance as a source of legal rights for individuals to assert against private institutions. The key case is *PruneYard Shopping Center v. Robins*, 592 P.2d 341 (Cal. 1979), *affirmed*, 447 U.S. 74 (1980). In this case a group of high school students who were distributing political material and soliciting petition signatures had been excluded from a private shopping center. The students sought an injunction in state court to prevent further exclusions. The California Supreme Court sided with the students, holding that they had a state constitutional right of access to the shopping center to engage in expressive activity. In the U.S. Supreme Court, the shopping center argued that the California court's ruling was inconsistent with an earlier U.S. Supreme Court precedent, *Lloyd v. Tanner*, 407 U.S. 551 (1972), which held that the First Amendment of the federal Constitution does not guarantee individuals a right to free expression on the premises of a private shopping center. The Court rejected the argument, emphasizing that the state had a "sovereign right to adopt in its own constitution individual liberties more expansive than those conferred by the federal Constitution."

The shopping center also argued that the California court's decision, in denying it the right to exclude others from its premises, violated its property rights under the Fifth and Fourteenth Amendments of the federal Constitution. The Supreme Court rejected this argument as well:

> It is true that one of the essential sticks in the bundle of property rights is the right to exclude others (*Kaiser Aetna v. United States*, 444 U.S. 164, 179–80 (1979)). And here there has literally been a "taking" of that right to the extent that the California Supreme Court has interpreted the state constitution to entitle its citizens to exercise free expression and petition rights on shopping center property. But it is well established that "not every destruction or injury to property by governmental action has been held to be a 'taking' in the constitutional sense" (*Armstrong v. United States*, 364 U.S. 40, 48 (1960)). . . .
>
> Here the requirement that appellants permit appellees to exercise state-protected rights of free expression and petition on shopping center property

clearly does not amount to an unconstitutional infringement of appellants' property rights under the taking clause. There is nothing to suggest that preventing appellants from prohibiting this sort of activity will unreasonably impair the value or use of their property as a shopping center. The PruneYard is a large commercial complex that covers several city blocks, contains numerous separate business establishments, and is open to the public at large. The decision of the California Supreme Court makes it clear that the PruneYard may restrict expressive activity by adopting time, place, and manner regulations that will minimize any interference with its commercial functions. Appellees were orderly, and they limited their activity to the common areas of the shopping center. In these circumstances, the fact that they may have "physically invaded" appellants' property cannot be viewed as determinative [447 U.S. at 82–84].

PruneYard has gained significance in educational settings with the New Jersey Supreme Court's decision in *State v. Schmid*, 423 A.2d 615 (N.J. 1980) (this volume, Section 5.6.3). The defendant, who was not a student, had been charged with criminal trespass for distributing political material on the Princeton University campus in violation of Princeton regulations. The New Jersey court declined to rely on the federal First Amendment, instead deciding the case on state constitutional grounds. It held that, even without a finding of state action (a prerequisite to applying the federal First Amendment), Princeton had a state constitutional obligation to protect Schmid's expressional rights (N.J. Const. (1947), Art. I, para. 6 and para. 18). In justifying its authority to construe the state constitution in this expansive manner, the court relied on *PruneYard*. A subsequent case involving Muhlenberg College, *Pennsylvania v. Tate*, 432 A.2d 1382 (Pa. 1981), follows the *Schmid* reasoning in holding that the Pennsylvania state constitution protected the defendant's rights.

In contrast, a New York court refused to permit a student to rely on the state constitution in a challenge to her expulsion from a summer program for high school students at Cornell. In *Stone v. Cornell University*, 510 N.Y.S.2d 313 (N.Y. App. Div. 1987), the sixteen-year-old student was expelled after she admitted smoking marijuana and drinking alcohol while enrolled in the program and living on campus. No hearing was held. The student argued that the lack of a hearing violated her rights under New York's constitution (Art. I, §6). Disagreeing, the court invoked a "state action" doctrine similar to that used for the federal Constitution (see Section 1.5.2 above) and concluded that there was insufficient state involvement in Cornell's summer program to warrant constitutional due process protections.

Sec. 1.6. Religion and the Public-Private Dichotomy

Under the Establishment Clause of the First Amendment, public institutions must maintain a neutral stance regarding religious beliefs and activities; they must, in other words, maintain religious neutrality. Public institutions cannot favor or support one religion over another, and they cannot favor or support religion over nonreligion. Thus, for instance, public schools have been prohibited from using an official nondenominational prayer (*Engel v. Vitale*, 370 U.S. 421 (1962)) and from prescribing the reading of verses from the Bible at the opening of each school day (*Abington School District v. Schempp*, 374 U.S. 203 (1963)).

The First Amendment contains two "religion" clauses. The first prohibits government from "establishing" religion; the second protects individuals' "free exercise" of religion from governmental interference. Although the two clauses have a common objective of ensuring governmental "neutrality," they pursue it in different ways. As the U.S. Supreme Court explained in *Abington School District v. Schempp:*

> The wholesome "neutrality" of which this Court's cases speak thus stems from a recognition of the teaching of history that powerful sects or groups might bring about a fusion of governmental and religious functions or a concert or dependency of one upon the other to the end that official support of the state or federal government would be placed behind the tenets of one or of all orthodoxies. This the establishment clause prohibits. And a further reason for neutrality is found in the free exercise clause, which recognizes the value of religious training, teaching, and observance and, more particularly, the right of every person to freely choose his own course with reference thereto, free of any compulsion from the state. This the free exercise clause guarantees. . . . The distinction between the two clauses is apparent—a violation of the free exercise clause is predicated on coercion, whereas the establishment clause violation need not be so attended [374 U.S. at 222-23].

Neutrality, however, does not necessarily require a public institution to prohibit all religious activity on its campus or at off-campus events it sponsors. In some circumstances the institution may have discretion to permit noncoercive religious activities (see *Lee v. Weisman,* 112 S. Ct. 2649 (1992) (finding indirect coercion in context of religious invocation at *high school* graduation)). Moreover, if a rigidly observed policy of neutrality would discriminate against campus organizations with religious purposes or could impinge on an individual's right to "free exercise" of religion or to freedom of speech, the institution may be required to allow some religion on campus. In *Keegan v. University of Delaware,* 349 A.2d 14 (Del. 1975), for example, the university had banned all religious worship services from campus facilities. The plaintiffs contended that this policy was unconstitutional as applied to students' religious services in the commons areas of campus dormitories. After determining that the university could permit religious worship in the commons area without violating the Establishment Clause, the court then held that the university was constitutionally *required* by the Free Exercise Clause to make the commons area available for students' religious worship:

> The only activity proscribed by the regulation is worship. . . . The commons area is already provided for student use and there is no request here that separate religious facilities be established. The area in question is a residence hall where students naturally assemble with their friends for many purposes. Religion, at least in part, is historically a communal exercise. . . .
>
> It can be argued, as it has been, that the question is whether the university must permit the students to worship on university property. But, in terms of religious liberty, the question is better put, in our judgment, from the perspective of the individual student. Can the university prohibit student worship in a commons area of a university dormitory which is provided for student use and in which the university permits every other student activity? It is apparent to us that such a regulation impedes the observance of religion [349 A.2d at 17, 18].

In a later case that has now become a landmark decision, *Widmar v. Vincent,* 454 U.S. 263 (1981) (this volume, Section 4.11.4), the U.S. Supreme Court determined that student religious activities on public campuses are also protected by the First Amendment's Free Speech Clause. The Court indicated a preference for using the Free Speech Clause, rather than the Free Exercise of Religion Clause, whenever the institution has created a "public forum" generally open for student use. The Court also concluded that the First Amendment's Establishment Clause would not be violated by an "open-forum" or "equal-access" policy permitting student use of campus facilities for both nonreligious and religious purposes.[13]

A private institution's position under the Establishment and Free Exercise Clauses differs markedly from that of a public institution. Private institutions have no obligation of neutrality under these clauses. Moreover, these clauses affirmatively protect the religious beliefs and practices of private institutions from government interference. For example, establishment and free exercise considerations may restrict the judiciary's capacity to entertain lawsuits against religiously affiliated institutions.[14] Such litigation may involve the court in the interpretation of religious doctrine or in the process of church governance, thus creating a danger that the court—an arm of government—would entangle itself in religious affairs in violation of the Establishment Clause. Or such litigation may invite the court to enforce discovery requests (such as subpoenas) or award injunctive relief that would interfere with the religious practices of the institution or its sponsoring body, thus creating dangers that the court's orders would violate the institution's rights under the Free Exercise Clause. (For discussion of these issues, see Sections 3.1.6 and 7.2.6.2.) Sometimes such litigation may present both types of federal constitutional problems or, alternatively, may present parallel problems under the state constitution. When the judicial involvement requested by the plaintiff(s) would cause the court to intrude upon establishment or free exercise values, the court must decline to enforce certain discovery requests, or must modify the terms of any remedy or relief it orders, or must decline to exercise any jurisdiction over the dispute, thus protecting the institution against governmental incursions into its religious beliefs and practices.

A private institution's constitutional protection under the Establishment and Free Exercise Clauses is by no means absolute. Its limits are illustrated by *Bob Jones University v. United States,* 461 U.S. 574 (1983) (this volume, Section 7.3.1). Because the university maintained racially restrictive policies on dating and marriage, the Internal Revenue Service had denied it tax-exempt status under federal tax laws. The university argued that its racial practices were religiously based and that the denial abridged its right to free exercise of religion. The U.S. Supreme Court, rejecting this argument, emphasized that the federal government has a "compelling" interest in "eradicating racial discrimination in education" and that that interest "substantially outweighs whatever burden denial of tax benefits places on [the university's] exercise of . . . religious beliefs."

Although the institution did not prevail in *Bob Jones,* the "compelling interest" test that the Court used to evaluate free exercise claims does provide substantial protection for religiously affiliated institutions. A new federal statute, the Religious

[13]For a later case (involving elementary and secondary education) that affirms and extends these principles, see *Lamb's Chapel v. Center Moriches Union Free School District,* 113 S. Ct. 2141 (1993).

[14]The federal constitutional principles are developed in *Serbian Orthodox Diocese v. Milivojevich,* 426 U.S. 696 (1976); *Jones v. Wolf,* 443 U.S. 595 (1979); *Presbyterian Church v. Hull Church,* 393 U.S. 440 (1969); *Kedroff v. Saint Nicholas Cathedral* 344 U.S. 94 (1952); and *Watson v. Jones,* 80 U.S. 679 (1871).

Freedom Restoration Act of 1993 (103 Pub. L. No. 141, 107 Stat. 1488 (1993)), also will provide strong protection for such institutions. This Act reaffirms the compelling interest test as the appropriate standard in religious freedom cases and legislatively overrules a post–*Bob Jones* case (*Employment Division v. Smith*, 494 U.S. 872 (1990)), which severely limited protections available under the Free Exercise Clause. (See D. Laycock, "Free Exercise and the Religious Freedom Restoration Act," 62 *Fordham L. Rev.* 883 (1994).) (The Religious Freedom Restoration Act will also reaffirm and provide strong protections for *individuals* who assert free exercise claims against *public* institutions, as in the cases in the earlier part of this subsection.)

Although the Establishment Clause itself imposes no neutrality obligation on private institutions, this clause does have another kind of importance for private institutions that are church related. When government—federal, state, or local—undertakes to provide financial or other support for private postsecondary education, the question arises whether this support, insofar as it benefits church-related education, constitutes government support for religion. If it does, such support would violate the Establishment Clause because government would have departed from its position of neutrality.

Two 1971 cases decided by the Supreme Court provide the basis for the modern law on government support for church-related schools. *Lemon v. Kurtzman*, 403 U.S. 602 (1971), invalidated two state programs providing aid for church-related elementary and secondary schools. *Tilton v. Richardson*, 403 U.S. 672 (1971), held constitutional a federal aid program providing construction grants to higher education institutions, including those that are church related. In deciding the cases, the Court developed a three-pronged test for determining when a government support program passes muster under the Establishment Clause:

> First, the statute must have a secular legislative purpose; second, its principal or primary effect must be one that neither advances nor inhibits religion . . . ; finally, the statute must not foster "an excessive government entanglement with religion" (*Walz v. Tax Commission*, 397 U.S. 664, 674 (1970)) [403 U.S. at 612–13].

The first prong (purpose) has proved easy to meet and has not been of major significance in subsequent cases. But the other two prongs (effect and entanglement) have been both very important and very difficult to apply in particular cases. The Court's major explanation of "effect" came in *Hunt v. McNair*, 413 U.S. 734 (1973):

> Aid normally may be thought to have a primary effect of advancing religion when it flows to an institution in which religion is so pervasive that a substantial portion of its functions are subsumed in the religious mission or when it funds a specifically religious activity in an otherwise substantially secular setting [413 U.S. at 753].

Its major explanation of "entanglement" appeared in the *Lemon* case:

> In order to determine whether the government entanglement with religion is excessive, we must examine (1) the character and purposes of the institutions which are benefitted, (2) the nature of the aid that the state provides, and (3) the resulting relationship between the government and the religious authority [403 U.S. at 615].

Four Supreme Court cases have applied this complex three-pronged test to church-related postsecondary institutions. In each case the aid program passed the test. In *Tilton* the Court approved the federal construction grant program, and the grants to the particular colleges involved in that case, by a narrow 5-to-4 vote. In *Hunt v. McNair*, the Court, by a 6-to-3 vote, sustained a state program that assisted colleges, including church-related colleges, by issuing revenue bonds for their construction projects. In *Roemer v. Board of Public Works*, 426 U.S. 736 (1976), the Court, by a 5-to-4 vote, upheld Maryland's program of general support grants to private, including church-related, colleges. And in the fourth case, *Witters v. Washington Department of Services for the Blind*, 474 U.S. 481 (1986), the Court rejected an Establishment Clause challenge to a state vocational rehabilitation program for the blind that provided assistance directly to a student enrolled in a religious ministry program at a private Christian college. Distinguishing between institution-based aid and student-based aid, the unanimous Court concluded that the aid plan did not violate the second prong of the *Lemon* test, since any state payments that were ultimately channeled to the educational institution were based solely on the "genuinely independent and private choices of the aid recipients." (For a discussion of *Witters* against the backdrop of the earlier Supreme Court cases, and of the aftermath of *Witters* in the Washington Supreme Court, see Note, "The First Amendment and Public Funding of Religiously Controlled or Affiliated Higher Education," 17 *J. Coll. & Univ. Law* 381, 398–409 (1991).) Taken together, these U.S. Supreme Court cases suggest that a wide range of postsecondary support programs can be devised compatibly with the Establishment Clause and that a wide range of church-related institutions can be eligible to receive government support. The *Roemer* case is perhaps the most revealing. There the Court refused to find that the grants given a group of church-related schools constituted support for religion—even though the funds were granted annually and could be put to a wide range of uses, and even though the schools had church representatives on their governing boards, employed Roman Catholic chaplains, held Roman Catholic religious exercises, required students to take religion or theology classes taught primarily by Roman Catholic clerics, made some hiring decisions for theology departments partly on the basis of religious considerations, and began some classes with prayers.[15]

When issues concerning governmental support for religion arise, as in the cases above, the federal Constitution is not the only source of law that may apply. In some states the state constitution will also play an important role. In *Witters* (above), for example, the U.S. Supreme Court remanded the case to the Supreme Court of Washington (whose decision the U.S. Supreme court had reversed), observing that the state court was free to consider the "far stricter" church-state provision of the state constitution. On remand, the state court concluded that the state constitutional provision—prohibiting use of public moneys to pay for any religious instruction—precluded the grant of state funds to the student enrolled in the religious ministry program (*Witters v. State Commission for the Blind*, 771 P.2d 1119 (Wash. 1989)). First the court held that providing vocational rehabilitation funds to the student would violate the state constitution because the funds would pay for "a

---

[15]For a very important subsequent case, not involving postsecondary education but further developing the concepts used in these cases, see *Bowen v. Kendrick*, 487 U.S. 589 (1988).

religious course of study at a religious school, with a religious career as [the student's] goal" (771 P.2d at 1119).

Distinguishing the Establishment Clause of the U.S. Constitution from the state constitution's provision, the court noted that the latter provision "prohibits not only the *appropriation* of public money for religious instruction, but also the *application* of public funds to religious instruction" (771 P.2d at 1121). Then the court held that the student's federal constitutional right to free exercise of religion was not infringed by denial of the funds, because he is "not being asked to violate any tenet of his religious beliefs nor is he being denied benefits 'because of conduct mandated by religious belief'" (771 P.2d at 1123). Third, the court held that denial of the funds did not violate the student's equal protection rights under the Fourteenth Amendment, because the state has a "compelling interest in maintaining the strict separation of church and state set forth" in its constitution, and the student's "individual interest in receiving a religious education must . . . give way to the state's greater need to uphold its constitution" (771 P.2d at 1123).

Though the federal cases have been quite hospitable to the inclusion of church-related institutions in government support programs for postsecondary education, administrators of church-related institutions should still be most sensitive to Establishment Clause issues. As *Witters* indicates, state constitutions may contain clauses that restrict government support for church-related institutions more vigorously than the federal Establishment Clause does.[16] The statutes creating funding programs may also contain provisions that restrict the program's application to religious institutions or activities. Moreover, even the federal Establishment Clause cases have historically been decided by close votes, with great disagreement among the justices. That trend continues, and a number of the justices have accelerated it by raising doubts concerning *Lemon*. The law has not yet settled. Thus, administrators should exercise great care in using government funds and should keep in mind that, at some point, religious influences within the institution can still jeopardize government funding.

Sec. 1.7. Organizing the Postsecondary Institution's Legal Affairs

1.7.1. Organizational arrangements. There are numerous organizational arrangements by which postsecondary institutions can obtain legal counsel. See generally F. B. Manley & Co., *Provision of Legal Services: A Survey of NACUA Primary Representatives* (National Association of College and University Attorneys, 1992). Debate has been growing in recent years concerning which arrangements are most effective and cost-efficient. The issues, which are especially visible in private institutions, range from escalating legal costs, to the appropriate balance between in-house and outside counsel, to new roles and fee schedules for outside counsel, to the use of legal consultants for staff training and other special projects. See generally G. Blumentstyk, "Shake-Ups in Campus Law Offices," *Chron. Higher Educ.*, June 8, 1994, A27.

[16]Some of the cases are collected in Annot., "Validity, Under State Constitution and Laws, of Insurance by State or State Agency of Revenue Bonds to Finance or Refinance Construction Projects at Private Religiously Affiliated Colleges or Universities," 95 A.L.R.3d 1000 (1991 and periodic supp.).

The arrangements for public postsecondary institutions often differ from those for private institutions. The latter have a relatively free hand in deciding whom to employ or retain as counsel and how to utilize their services, and will frequently have in-house counsel and campus-based services. Public institutions, on the other hand, may be served by the state attorney general's office or, for some community colleges, by a county or city attorney's office. Other public institutions that are part of a statewide system may be served by system attorneys appointed by the system's governing authority. In either case, working relationships may vary with the state and the campus, and legal counsel may be located at an off-campus site and may serve other campuses as well. In general, administrators in such situations should seek to have services centralized in one or a small number of assistant attorney generals or other government counsel who devote a considerable portion of their time to the particular campus and become thoroughly familiar with its operations.

A public postsecondary institution's authority to obtain other counsel to supplement or displace that furnished by the state may be confined by the state constitution and statutes. Occasionally, public institutions have challenged the traditional employment arrangements and hired their own counsel to represent the institution. Some courts have acknowledged public institutions' authority to do so, implying this authority from the express authority to manage and operate the institution.

In *Board of Trustees of the University of Illinois v. Barrett*, 46 N.E.2d 951 (Ill. 1943), for example, the board of trustees and two employees it had hired as legal counsel (Hodges and Johnson) sued the state attorney general and the state auditor of public accounts. The plaintiffs sought a judicial affirmation of the board's authority to employ independent legal counsel, as well as an order precluding the attorney general from interfering with Hodges and Johnson and an order compelling the state to pay the compensation due them. In defense, the attorney general asserted that, by virtue of his office, he was sole legal counsel for the university and its board of trustees, and that the board must obtain the attorney general's approval before hiring additional counsel. Since he did not approve of the decision to hire Hodges or Johnson, he had sought their resignations and directed the auditor of public accounts to refrain from paying their salaries.

The Supreme Court of Illinois decided that the board, a "statutory" institution (see Section 6.2.1), had authority to employ independent legal counsel without the attorney general's approval as long as the arrangement complied with the provisions of the statute creating the university and with the legislature's appropriations for its operation and management. Regarding the attorney general's powers, the court concluded that neither the state constitution nor state statutes granted the attorney general express authority to represent public institutions. Thus, the university had "the undoubted right to employ its own counsel or engage the services of any other employees it may deem necessary or proper. . . . This power is, however, always subject to the restriction that when such faculty members or other employees are to be paid from State funds, they must be within the classifications for which funds have been appropriated and are available." Since the legislature had not appropriated funds for Hodges and Johnson, the court refused to compel the auditor to pay their salaries. Thus, although the court recognized the board's authority to hire legal counsel, the court also recognized that the legislature had not provided them the financial means to do so.

Following the *Barrett* decision, three other state courts determined that other public institutions had authority to hire independent legal counsel. Cases from Oklahoma and New Jersey concerned statutory institutions; a case from South Dakota concerned a "constitutional" governing board (see Section 6.2.2). In the Oklahoma case, a public institution was granted authority to hire independent counsel to secure an injunction to prevent individuals from fishing on a college-owned lake (*Blair v. Board of Regents for the Oklahoma Agricultural and Mechanical Colleges*, 421 P.2d 228 (Okla. 1966)). In the New Jersey case, *Frank Briscoe Co., Inc. v. Rutgers, the State University*, 327 A.2d 687 (N.J. Super Ct. Law Div. 1974), a breach-of-contract case defended by the state attorney general, the court determined (despite the attorney general's suggestions to the contrary) that Rutgers had a right to sue and be sued. For purposes of this issue, the court permitted Rutgers' own counsel to participate in the litigation "because the interests of a public university may be different from those of a state and thus need separate representation from the Attorney General."

In the South Dakota case, concerning a constitutional board, *Board of Regents v. Carter*, 228 N.W.2d 621 (S.D. 1975), the court reached a similar result. It authorized the board to hire independent counsel to represent its interests in a lawsuit challenging its definition of a proper employee bargaining unit. The attorney general had challenged the board of regents' authority to do so. He contended that he was the sole legal counsel for the state and that the state constitution did not grant the regents power to institute its own lawsuits or hire its own counsel. Accordingly, he claimed that any legislative attempt to grant the regents this power violated the provisions of the state constitution creating the board and granting the attorney general executive powers. In disagreeing, the court relied on the language of the state constitution granting the regents authority to control South Dakota's public educational institutions, subject to rules and restrictions promulgated by the legislature. (This right of control and the legislature's power to pass rules and restrictions was reaffirmed and explicated in *South Dakota Board of Regents v. Meierhenry*, 351 N.W.2d 450 (S.D. 1984).) Here the legislature had promulgated a statute granting the regents power "to sue and to be sued." The court held that this statute was constitutional and that, in order for the regents to exercise their right "to sue and to be sued," the regents needed the authority to hire independent counsel free from the control of the attorney general.[17]

Many larger colleges and universities, especially private institutions, now employ their own in-house staff counsel. Such an arrangement has the advantage of providing daily coordinated services of resident counsel acclimated to the particular needs and problems of the institution. Though staff attorneys can become specialists in postsecondary education law, they normally will not have the time or exposure to become expert in all the specialty areas (such as labor law, tax law, patent law, or litigation) with which institutions must deal. Thus, these institutions may sometimes retain private law firms for special problems. Other institutions, large and small, may arrange for all their legal services to be provided by one or more private law firms.

---

[17]For cases on the other side of the coin, regarding termination of attorneys, see Annot., "Attorneys—Wrongful Discharge of In-House Counsel," 16 A.L.R.5th 239 (1993 and periodic supp.) (private entities); and *Goffer v. Marbury*, 956 F.2d 1045 (11th Cir. 1992) (public entities).

This arrangement has the advantage of increasing the number of attorneys with particular expertise available for the variety of problems that confront institutions. A potential disadvantage is that no one attorney will be conversant with the full range of the institution's needs and problems or be on call daily for early participation in administrative decision making. Administrators of institutions depending on private firms may thus want to ensure that at least one lawyer is generally familiar with and involved in the institution's affairs and regularly available for consultation even on routine matters.

Whatever the organizational arrangement, and regardless of whether the institution is public or private, counsel and administrators should have clear understandings of who is the "client" to whom counsel is responsible. Generally the client is the institution's board of trustees or, for some public institutions, the state system's board of trustees or regents—the entity in which operating authority is vested (see Section 2.2.1). Counsel generally advises or represents the president, chancellor, or other officers or administrators only insofar as they are exercising authority that derives from the board of trustees. If in certain circumstances institutional personnel or institutional committees have personal interests or legal needs that may be inconsistent with those of the institution, they may have to obtain their own separate legal assistance. Depending on the situation and on institutional policy, the institution and its counsel may or may not arrange for or help them obtain such separate legal representation.

1.7.2. Treatment law and preventive law. With each of the organizational arrangements above, serious consideration must be given to the particular functions that counsel will perform and to the relationships that will be fostered between counsel and administrators. Broadly stated, counsel's role is to identify and define actual or potential legal problems and provide options for resolving or preventing them. There are two basic, and different, ways to fulfill this role: through treatment law or through preventive law. To analogize to another profession, treatment law is aimed at curing legal diseases, whereas preventive law seeks to maintain legal health. Under either approach, counsel will be guided not only by legal considerations and institutional goals and policies but also by ethical requirements of the legal profession, which shape the responsibilities of individual practitioners to their clients and the public (see this volume, Section 1.4.3.4).

Treatment law is the more traditional of the two practice approaches. It focuses on actual challenges to institutional practices and on affirmative legal steps by the institution to protect its interests when they are threatened. When suit is filed against the institution, or litigation is threatened; when a government agency cites the institution for noncompliance with its regulations; when the institution needs formal permission of a government agency to undertake a proposed course of action; when the institution wishes to sue some other party—then treatment law operates. The goal is to resolve the specific legal problem at hand. Treatment law today is indispensable to the functioning of a postsecondary institution, and virtually all institutions have such legal service.

Preventive law, in contrast, focuses on initiatives that the institution can take before actual legal disputes arise. Preventive law involves administrator and counsel in a continual process of setting the legal parameters within which the institution will operate to avoid litigation or other legal disputes. Counsel identifies the legal consequences of proposed actions; pinpoints the range of alternatives for avoiding problems and the legal risks of each alternative; sensitizes administrators to legal issues and the importance of recognizing them early; and determines the impact of new or proposed laws and regulations, and new court decisions, on institutional operations.

Prior to the 1980s, preventive law was not a general practice of postsecondary institutions. But this approach became increasingly valuable as the presence of law on the campus increased, and acceptance of preventive law within postsecondary education grew substantially. Today preventive law is as indispensable as treatment law and provides the more constructive posture from which to conduct institutional legal affairs.

Institutions using or considering the use of preventive law face some difficult questions. To what extent will administrators and counsel give priority to the practice of preventive law? Which institutional administrators will have direct access to counsel? Will counsel advise only administrators, or will he or she also be available to recognized faculty or student organizations or committees, or perhaps to other members of the university community on certain matters? What working arrangements will ensure that administrators are alert to incipient legal problems and that counsel is involved in institutional decision making at an early stage? What degree of autonomy will counsel have to influence institutional decision making, and what authority will counsel have to halt legally unwise institutional action?

The following steps are suggested for administrators and counsel seeking to implement a preventive law system:

1. Review the institution's current organizational arrangement for obtaining legal counsel. Determine whether changes that might facilitate preventive lawyering—for example, from part-time to full-time counsel or from outside firm to house counsel—are appropriate and feasible.

2. Develop a teamwork relationship between administrator and counsel; both should be substantially involved in legal affairs, cooperating with one another on a regular basis, for preventive law to work best. Since the dividing line between the administrator's and the lawyer's functions is not always self-evident, roles should be developed through mutual interchange between the two sets of professionals. While considerable flexibility is possible, institutions should be careful to maintain a distinction between the two roles. The purpose of preventive law is not to make the administrator into a lawyer or the lawyer into an administrator. It is the lawyer's job to resolve doubts about the interpretation of statutes, regulations, and court decisions; to stay informed of legal developments and predict the directions in which law is evolving; and to suggest legal options and advise on their relative effectiveness in achieving the institution's goals. In contrast, it is the administrator's job (and that of the board of trustees) to stay informed of developments in the theory and practice of administration; to devise policy options within the constraints imposed by law and determine their relative effectiveness in achieving institutional goals; and ultimately, at the appropriate level of the institutional hierarchy, to make the policy decisions that give life to the institution.

3. To assist teamwork relationships, arrange for training for administrators that focuses on the legal implications of their administrative responsibilities. Management workshops for new deans and department chairs, or periodic workshops for middle managers, or counseling sessions for the staff of a particular office would be

examples of such training. The institution's legal staff may conduct training sessions, or they may be provided on or off site by third parties. In conjunction with such training, the institution should ensure the availability of relevant and up-to-date legal information for administrators, through distribution of one or more of the newsletters and periodicals available from outside sources, or through legal counsel memos crafted to the particular circumstances of the institution.

4. Have the lawyer-administrator team perform legal audits periodically. A legal audit is a legal "checkup" to determine the legal "health" of the institution. A complete audit would include a survey of every office and function in the institution. For each office and function, the lawyer-administrator team would develop the information and analysis necessary to determine whether that office or function is in compliance with the full range of legal constraints to which it is subject.

5. To supplement legal audits, develop an early-warning system that will apprise counsel and administrators of potential legal problems in their incipiency. The early-warning system should be based on a list of situations that are likely to create significant legal risk for the institution. Such a list might include the following situations: an administrator is revising a standard form contract used by the institution or creating a new standard form contract to cover a type of transaction for which the institution has not previously used such a contract; administrators are reviewing the institution's code of student conduct, student bill of rights, or similar documents; a school or department is seeking to terminate a faculty member's tenure; a committee is drafting or modifying an affirmative action plan; administrators are preparing policies to implement a new set of federal administrative regulations; or administrators are proposing a new security system for the campus or temporary security measures for a particular emergency. Under an early-warning system, all such circumstances, or others that the institution may specify, would trigger a consultative process between administrator and counsel aimed at resolving legal problems before they erupt into disputes.

6. Using the data obtained through legal audits, an early-warning system, and other devices, engage in a continuing course of legal planning. If audits and other means provide detection and diagnosis, legal planning provides measures for legal health maintenance. Legal planning establishes the process and the individual steps by which the institution determines the degree of legal risk exposure it is willing to assume in particular situations, and avoids or resolves legal risks it is unwilling to assume. Successful legal planning depends on a careful sorting out and interrelating of legal and policy issues. Teamwork between administrator and lawyer is therefore a critical ingredient in legal planning. Sensitivity to the authority structure of the institution is also a critical ingredient, so that legal planning decisions are made at the prescribed levels of authority.

7. For the inevitable percentage of potential legal problems that do develop into actual disputes, establish internal grievance mechanisms. These mechanisms may utilize various techniques for dispute resolution, from informal consultation, to mediation or arbitration, to hearings before panels drawn from the academic community. Whatever techniques are adopted should be generally available to students, faculty, and staff members who have complaints concerning actions taken against them by other members of the academic community. Some summary procedure should be devised for dismissing complaints that are frivolous or that contest general academic policy rather than a particular action that has harmed the complainant. Not

every dispute, of course, is amenable to internal solution, since many disputes involve outside parties (such as business firms, government agencies, or professional associations). But for disputes among members of the campus community, grievance mechanisms provide an on-campus forum that can be attuned to the particular characteristics of academic institutions. Grievance mechanisms can encourage collegial resolution of disputes, thus forestalling the complainant's resort to courts or other external bodies.

Selected Annotated Bibliography

General

Bickel, Robert, & Brechner, Jane. *The College Administrator and the Courts* (College Administration Publications, 1977, plus periodic supp.). A basic casebook written for administrators that briefs and discusses leading court cases. Topics include the legal system, sources of law, the role of counsel, distinctions between public and private colleges, and the state action concept. Updated quarterly by Barbara A. Lee and Peter H. Ruger.

Sec. 1.1 (How Far Does the Law Reach and How Loud Does It Speak?)

Dutile, Fernand. "The Law of Higher Education and the Courts: 19XX in Review," *J. Coll. & Univ. Law*. A series of annual articles reviewing cases decided in the prior year in federal and state courts. Each article discusses trends in education law while summarizing the important cases regarding First Amendment problems, tort liability, search and seizure on campus, due process, institutional contracts, sovereign and individual immunities, funding, employment discrimination, and other topics.

Edwards, Harry T. *Higher Education and the Unholy Crusade Against Governmental Regulation* (Institute for Educational Management, Harvard University, 1980). Reviews and evaluates the federal regulatory presence on the campus. Author concludes that much of the criticism directed by postsecondary administrators at federal regulation of higher education is either unwarranted or premature.

Folger, Joseph, & Shubert, J. Janelle. "Resolving Student-Initiated Grievances in Higher Education: Dispute Resolution Procedures in a Non-Adversarial Setting," 3 *NIDR Reports* (National Institute for Dispute Resolution, 1986). A short monograph exploring the various methods employed at twenty different institutions to resolve conflicts. Includes a flow chart entitled "Model of Possible Options for Pursuing Resolutions to Student-Initiated Grievances" and a set of criteria for evaluating the effectiveness of particular grievance procedures.

Gouldner, Helen. "The Social Impact of Campus Litigation," 51 *J. Higher Educ.* 328 (1980). Explores the detrimental effects on the postsecondary community of "the tidal wave of litigation . . . awash in the country"; identifies "increased secrecy on campus," "fragile friendships among colleagues," a "crisis in confidence" in decision making, and "domination by legal norms" as major effects to be dealt with.

Helms, Lelia B. "Litigation Patterns: Higher Education and the Courts in 1988," 57 *West's Educ. Law Rptr.* 1 (1990). Reviews and classifies litigation involving higher education during a one-year period. Uses the geographical area, the court, the parties, and the issue as classifying factors. Includes tables summarizing litigation patterns. Article provides "baseline data for later comparison" and a methodology for collecting later data. See also the Helms entry for Section 1.2.

Hobbs, Walter C. "The Courts," in Philip G. Altbach, Robert O. Berdahl, & Patricia J. Gumport (eds.), *Higher Education in American Society* (3d ed., Prometheus Books, 1994). Reviews the concept of judicial deference to academic expertise and analyzes the impact of courts on postsecondary institutions. Includes illustrative cases. Author concludes that, despite complaints to the contrary from academics, the tradition of judicial deference to academic judgments is still alive and well.

Kaplin, William A. *The Importance of Process in Campus Administrative Decision-Making*, IHELG Monograph 91-10 (Institute for Higher Education Law and Governance, University of Houston, 1992). Distinguishes between the *substance* and the *process* of internal decision making by campus administrators; develops a "process taxonomy" with six generic classifications (rule making, adjudication, mediation, implementation, investigation, and crisis management); examines the "process values" that demonstrate the importance of campus processes; and sets out criteria for identifying "good" processes.

Olivas, Michael A. *The Law and Higher Education: Cases and Materials on Colleges in Court* (Carolina Academic Press, 1989, with 1993 supp.). A casebook presenting both foundational and contemporary case law on major themes in higher education law and governance. Includes supportive commentary by the author, news accounts, and excerpts from and cites to writings of others.

Pavela, Gary (ed.). *Synfax Weekly Report* and *Synfax Bulletin* (Synfax, Inc.). Interrelated newsletter-style publications delivered by FAX technology to maintain optimum currency. Each publication digests and critiques important legal and policy developments as reflected in court opinions, news media accounts, and other sources.

Specialty Law Digest: Education (Bureau of National Affairs). A monthly publication focusing on recent developments in the law of education, both elementary/secondary and postsecondary. Contains an "Education Law Digest" with summaries of cases arranged conceptually; a "Case Survey" with education law cases arranged by jurisdiction; "The Education Law Article," a monograph selected and reprinted by the publishers from among recent commentary; and a selected bibliography of other recent articles.

Weeks, Kent M., & Davis, Derek (eds.). *Legal Deskbook for Administrators of Independent Colleges and Universities* (2d ed., Center for Constitutional Studies, Baylor University/National Association of College and University Attorneys, 1993). A resource containing legal analysis, practical advice, and bibliographical sources on issues of particular import to administrators and counsel at private institutions.

West's Education Law Reporter (West Publishing Co.). A biweekly publication covering education-related case law on both elementary/secondary and postsecondary education. Includes complete texts of opinions, brief summaries written for the layperson, articles and case comments, and a cumulative table of cases and index of legal principles elucidated in the cases.

Sec. 1.2 (Evolution of the Law Relating to Postsecondary Education)

Beach, John A. "The Management and Governance of Academic Institutions," 12 *J. Coll. & Univ. Law* 301 (1985). Reviews the history and development of institutional governance, broadly defined. Discusses the corporate character of postsecondary institutions, the contradictions of "managing" an academic organization, academic freedom, and the interplay among the institution's various constituencies.

Bok, Derek. "Universities: Their Temptations and Tensions," 18 *J. Coll. & Univ. Law* 1 (1991). Author addresses the need for universities to maintain independence with regard to research and public service. Discusses three sources of temptation: politicization, diversion of faculty time and interest from teaching and research to consulting, and the indiscriminate focus on commercial gain when one is seeking funding.

Bureau of National Affairs. *Computer Data Security: A Legal and Practical Guide to Liability, Loss Prevention, and Criminal and Civil Remedies* (Bureau of National Affairs, 1990). Discusses federal and state laws related to fraud, electronic trespass, and other relevant theories. Offers suggestions for storing and protecting confidential data on computer. The book is written for professionals without technical expertise in computer use.

Clark, Burton R. *The Academic Life: Small Worlds, Different Worlds* (Carnegie Foundation for the Advancement of Teaching, 1987). Traces the evolution of postsecondary institutions, the development of academic disciplines, the nature of academic work, the culture of academe, and academic governance. The book emphasizes the rewards and challenges of the faculty role, addressing the significance of the "postmodern" academic role.

El-Khawas, Elaine. *Campus Trends* (American Council on Education). Published annually, this report analyzes survey data from a cross section of colleges and universities. Includes data on enrollments, student and faculty characteristics, financial issues, and other significant information.

Fass, Richard A., Morrill, Richard L., & Mount, C. Eric, Jr. "In Loco Parentis Revisited?" 18 *Change* 34 (Jan./Feb. 1986). Provides two perspectives (one by Fass, the second by Morrill and Mount) on whether "in loco parentis" should be reestablished, in what manner, and what alternatives to that doctrine are appropriate for postsecondary institutions.

Finkin, Matthew. "On 'Institutional' Academic Freedom," 61 *Tex. L. Rev.* 817 (1983). Explores the history and theoretical basis of academic freedom and analyzes the constitutional basis for academic freedom claims. Throughout, author distinguishes between the freedom of private institutions from government interference (institutional autonomy) and the freedom of individual members of the academic community from interference by government or by the institution. Includes analysis of leading U.S. Supreme Court precedents from 1819 (the *Dartmouth College* case) through the 1970s, as well as copious citations to legal and nonlegal sources.

Fishbein, Estelle A. "New Strings on the Ivory Tower: The Growth of Accountability in Colleges and Universities," 12 *J. Coll. & Univ. Law* 381 (1985). Examines the impact of external forces on the management of colleges and universities. Focusing primarily on the effect of federal regulation (including that by federal courts), the author discusses the significance of internal accountability in responding to external regulation.

Helms, Lelia B. "Patterns of Litigation in Postsecondary Education: A Case Law Study," 14 *J. Coll. & Univ. Law* 99 (1987). Analyzes reported cases in one state (Iowa) from 1850 to 1985. Categorizes cases in a variety of ways and develops findings that provide "perspective on patterns of litigation and possible trends."

Kaplin, William A. "Law on the Campus, 1960–1985: Years of Growth and Challenge," 12 *J. Coll. & Univ. Law* 269 (1985). Discusses the legal implications of social and political changes for colleges and universities. Issues addressed in historical context include the concepts of "public" and "private," the distinctions between secular and religious institutions, and preventive legal planning.

Kerr, Clark. *The Great Transformation in Higher Education, 1960–1980* (State University of New York Press, 1991). A collection of essays written over three decades by an eminent participant in and observer of American higher education's era of greatest expansion, development, and change. The essays are collected under four broad rubrics: The American System in Perspective; The Unfolding of the Great Transformation: 1960–1980; Governance and Leadership Under Pressure; and Academic Innovation and Reform: Much Innovation, Little Reform.

Kerr, Clark. *Troubled Times for American Higher Education: The 1990s and Beyond* (State University of New York Press, 1994). Also a collection of essays, this book addresses contemporary issues that face colleges and universities. Part I examines "possible contours of the future and . . . choices to be made by higher education"; Part II concerns the relationship between higher education and the American economy; Part III examines specific issues, such as quality in undergraduate education, teaching about ethics, the "racial crisis" in American higher education, and elitism in higher education.

Lautsch, John C. "Computers and the University Attorney: An Overview of Computer Law on Campus," 5 *J. Coll. & Univ. Law* 217 (1978–79). Explores the developing relationship between computers and the law and the impact of this relationship on the campus. Includes analysis of the role of contract law as it affects computers; the impact of computers on labor questions; the relationship of patent, copyright, and trade-secret laws to computers; and other areas.

Metzger, Walter, et al. *Dimensions of Academic Freedom* (University of Illinois Press, 1969). A series of papers presenting historical, legal, and administrative perspectives on academic freedom. Considers how the concept has evolved in light of changes in the character of faculties and student bodies and in the university's internal and external commitments.

Pavela, Gary (ed.). *Synthesis: Law and Policy in Higher Education* (College Administration Publications). A five-times-yearly periodical primarily for administrators. Each issue focuses on a single topic or perspective of contemporary concern. Includes practical analysis, commentary from and interviews with experts, case studies, samples of documents, and bibliographies and case citations.

Reidhaar, Donald L. "The Assault on the Citadel: Reflections on a Quarter Century of Change in the Relationship Between the Student and the University," 12 *J. Coll. & Univ. Law* 343 (1985). Reviews changes in the legal relationships between students and institutions, with particular emphasis on student protest and equal opportunity challenges.

Stallworth, Stanley B. "Higher Education in America: Where Are Blacks Thirty-Five Years After *Brown?*" 1991 *Wis. Multi-Cultural Law J.* 36 (1991). Reviews the history of historically black colleges, discusses the effect of *Brown v. Board of Education*, analyzes the effect of federal attempts to desegregate public systems of higher education, and reviews the attitudes of alumni of black colleges toward the quality of their educational experience.

Stark, Joan S., et al. *The Many Faces of Education Consumerism* (Lexington Books,

1977). A collection of essays on the history and status of the educational consumerism movement. Discusses the roles of the federal government, state government, accrediting agencies, and the courts in protecting the consumers of education; the place of institutional self-regulation; and suggestions for the future. Provides a broad perspective on the impact of consumerism on postsecondary education.

Tatel, David, & Guthrie, R. Claire. "The Legal Ins and Outs of University-Industry Collaboration," 64 *Educ. Record* 19 (Spring 1983). Examines the complex legal and business issues that arise when universities and businesses seek to join forces to develop new technologies. Reviews various legal arrangements already effectuated, such as the Harvard University–Monsanto Company joint venture; outlines issues, such as conflict of interest, confidentiality, and patent rights, that arise in such arrangements; and discusses the federal government's role in encouraging university-industry relationships.

Terrell, Melvin C. (ed.). *Diversity, Disunity, and Campus Community* (National Association of Student Personnel Administrators, 1992). Describes problems related to an increasingly diverse student body and recommends ways in which the campus climate can be improved. Discusses cultural diversity in residence halls, relationships with campus law enforcement staff, student and faculty perspectives on diversity and racism, and strategies for reducing or preventing hate crimes.

Van Alstyne, William. "The Demise of the Right-Privilege Distinction in Constitutional Law," 81 *Harvard L. Rev.* 1439 (1968). Provides a historical and analytical review of the rise and fall of the right-privilege distinction; includes discussion of several postsecondary education cases to demonstrate that the pursuit of educational opportunities and jobs at public colleges is no longer a "privilege" to which constitutional rights do not attach.

Weiler, William C. "Post-Baccalaureate Educational Choices of Minority Students," 16 *Rev. Higher Educ.* 439 (1993). Analyzes data from the U.S. Department of Education's "High School and Beyond" database to ascertain why minority students are less likely than whites to earn graduate degrees. The author provides suggestions for the development of programs to encourage undergraduates to seek postbaccalaureate education.

Wright, Thomas W. "Faculty and the Law Explosion: Assessing the Impact—A Twenty-Five Year Perspective (1960–85) for College and University Lawyers," 12 *J. Coll. & Univ. Law* 363 (1985). Assesses developments in the law with regard to college faculty. Issues addressed include the impact of the law on teaching (for example, the Buckley Amendment and student challenges to grading decisions), research (federal regulations, academic misconduct), and faculty-administration relationships (for example, in collective bargaining).

Sec. 1.3 (Sources of Postsecondary Education Law)

Bakken, Gordon M. "Campus Common Law," 5 *J. Law & Educ.* 201 (1976). A theoretical overview of custom and usage as a source of postsecondary education law. Emphasizes the impact of custom and usage on faculty rights and responsibilities.

Brennan, William J. "State Constitutions and the Protection of Individual Rights," 90 *Harvard L. Rev.* 489 (1977). Discusses the trend, in some states, toward expansive construction of state constitutional provisions protecting individual rights. The author, then an associate justice of the U.S. Supreme Court, finds that "the very premise of the [U.S. Supreme Court] cases that foreclose federal remedies constitutes a clear call to state courts to step into the breach." For a sequel, see William J. Brennan, "The Bill of Rights and the States: The Revival of State Constitutions as Guardians of Individual Rights," 61 *N.Y.U. L. Rev.* 535 (1986).

Edwards, Harry T., & Nordin, Virginia D. *An Introduction to the American Legal System: A Supplement to Higher Education and the Law* (Institute for Educational Management, Harvard University, 1980). Provides "a brief description of the American legal system for scholars, students, and administrators in the field of higher education who have had little or no legal training." Chapters include summary overviews of "The United States Courts," "The Process of Judicial Review," "Reading and Understanding Judicial Opinions, State Court Systems," "Legislative and Statutory Sources of Law," and "Administrative Rules and Regulations as Sources of Law."

Farnsworth, E. Allan. *An Introduction to the Legal System of the United States* (2d ed., Oceana, 1983). An introductory text emphasizing the fundamentals of the American legal system. Written for the layperson.

Gifis, Steven. *Law Dictionary* (3d ed., Barron's Educational Series, 1991). A paperback study aid for students or laypersons who seek a basic understanding of unfamiliar legal words and phrases. Also includes a table of abbreviations used in legal citations, a map and chart of the federal judicial system, and the texts of the U.S. Constitution and the ABA *Model Rules of Professional Conduct.*

Sec. 1.4 (Litigation in the Courts)

Drinan, Robert F. "Lawyer-Client Confidentiality in the Campus Setting," 19 *J. Coll. & Univ. Law* 305 (1993). Traces traditional and current views of lawyer-client confidentiality and explores inherent conflicts of interest in representation of administration, faculty, students, and alumni. For use primarily by college and university attorneys.

Kane, Mary Kay. *Civil Procedure in a Nutshell* (3d ed., West, 1991). A book-length summary of the entire law of civil procedure, written in clear language; well organized and outlined. Explains the basics of the law and uses case examples for illustration. Includes a discussion of the structure of the court system and a step-by-step guide through a civil case from filing of the complaint to final disposition.

Lieberman, Jethro K. (principal ed.). *The Role of Courts in American Society: The Final Report of the Council on the Role of the Courts* (Council on the Role of the Courts, 1984). A short report discussing sociological, political, and legal issues involving the American legal system. Considers problems with the system, such as overburdened court dockets and the expense of litigation, as well as possible solutions, such as mediation and arbitration.

O'Connell, John B. *Remedies in a Nutshell* (2d ed., West, 1985). A clearly written summary of the entire law of remedies. Explains the basics of the law without the use of case examples. Topics include contempt of court, basic contract remedies, injunctions, and methods of assessing damages.

Reynolds, William L. *Judicial Process in a Nutshell* (2d ed., West 1991). Summarizes the operation of the American court system. Written clearly, the book uses case examples to illustrate such matters as the role of the Constitution, judicial precedent, and general court structure. Topics include the nature of common law, the use of precedent, the use of statutes, and the methods of constitutional interpretation.

Sec. 1.5 (The Public-Private Dichotomy)

Faccenda, Philip, & Ross, Kathleen. "Constitutional and Statutory Regulations of Private Colleges and Universities," 9 *Valparaiso U. L. Rev.* 539 (1975). An overview of the ways in which private institutions are subjected to federal constitutional and regulatory requirements; draws distinctions between public and private institutions. Written primarily for administrators, with footnotes designed for counsel.

Howard, A. E. Dick. *State Aid to Private Higher Education* (Michie, 1977). A comprehensive treatment of state aid programs in each of the fifty states, as well as a general national overview. Provides legal analysis of state and federal constitutional law, historical developments, and descriptive information on aid programs; emphasizes church-state issues, such as those discussed in Section 1.6 of this chapter.

Phillips, Michael J. "The Inevitable Incoherence of Modern State Action Doctrine," 28 *St. Louis U. L.J.* 683 (1984). Traces the historical development of the state action doctrine through the U.S. Supreme Court's 1982 decision in *Rendell-Baker v. Kohn* and analyzes the political and social forces that have contributed to the doctrine's current condition.

Sedler, Robert A. "The State Constitutions and the Supplemental Protection of Individual Rights," 16 *U. Toledo L. Rev.* 465 (1985). Analyzes the use of the "individual rights" clauses of state constitutions to protect individual rights.

Thigpen, Richard. "The Application of Fourteenth Amendment Norms to Private Colleges and Universities," 11 *J. Law & Educ.* 171 (1982). Reviews the development of various theories of state action, particularly the public function and government contacts theories, and their applications to private postsecondary institutions. Also examines theories other than traditional state action for subjecting private institutions to requirements comparable to those that the Constitution places on public institutions. Author concludes: "It seems desirable to have a public policy of protecting basic norms of fair and equal treatment in nonpublic institutions of higher learning."

See Finkin entry for Section 1.2.

Sec. 1.6 (Religion and the Public-Private Dichotomy)

Greenawalt, Kent. "Constitutional Limits on Aid to Sectarian Universities," 4 *J. Coll. & Univ. Law* 177 (1977). Examines the Establishment Clause ramifications of public subsidies for church-related postsecondary institutions. Analyzes the *Tilton*, *Hunt*, and *Roemer* decisions and extracts a composite of operative legal principles from them. Also includes historical perspective and comparison of federal Establishment Clause interpretations with interpretations reached under parallel clauses of state constitutions.

Moots, Philip R., & Gaffney, Edward M. *Church and Campus: Legal Issues in Religiously Affiliated Higher Education* (University of Notre Dame Press, 1979). Directed primarily to administrators and other leaders of religiously affiliated colleges and universities. Chapters deal with the legal relationship between colleges and affiliated religious bodies, conditions under which liability might be imposed on an affiliated religious group, the effect that the relationship between a college and a religious group may have on the college's eligibility for governmental financial assistance, the "exercise of religious preference in employment policies," questions of academic freedom, the influence of religion on student admissions and discipline, the use of federally funded buildings by religiously affiliated colleges, and the determination of property relationships when a college and a religious body alter their affiliation. Ends with a set of conclusions and recommendations and three appendices discussing the relationships between three religious denominations and their affiliated colleges.

Note, "The First Amendment and Public Funding of Religiously Controlled or Affiliated Higher Education," 17 *J. Coll. & Univ. Law* 381 (1991). Distinguishes between "institution-directed" aid and "student-directed" aid, and reviews the federal Establishment Clause law applicable to each. Covers the leading U.S. Supreme Court cases with a special emphasis on the *Witters* case and its aftermath in the Washington Supreme Court. Also analyzes the viability, under the Free Exercise Clause, of various state restrictions on the funding of religiously affiliated higher education.

See Howard entry for Section 1.5.

Sec. 1.7 (Organizing the Postsecondary Institution's Legal Affairs)

Bickel, Robert. "A Revisitation of the Role of College and University Legal Counsel," 85 *West's Educ. Law Rptr.* 989 (1993), updating the author's earlier article published at 3 *J. Law & Educ.* 73 (1974). Explores the various roles of an institution's legal counsel. Roles include representing the university in formal legal proceedings, giving administrators advice in order to prevent legal problems, and preventing unnecessary extensions of technical legal factors into institutional administration. Includes commentary on the viewpoints of others since the author's original publication in 1974 and concludes that the earlier observations are still valid.

Block, Dennis J., & Epstein, Michael A. *The Corporate Counsellor's Deskbook* (4th ed., Prentice-Hall Law & Business, 1992). A sourcebook in loose-leaf binder format. Provides practical information and analysis, checklists, and sample documents on selecting outside counsel, controlling costs of services, managing litigation and other work assignments, and protecting the attorney-client privilege. Designed for counsel of nonprofit institutions, including colleges and universities. Periodic supplements.

Brown, Louis M., & Dauer, Edward A. *Planning by Lawyers: Materials on a Non-adversarial Legal Process* (Foundation Press, 1978). A comprehensive set of materials presenting various perspectives on legal planning. Includes chapters on "Thinking About Planning" and "Techniques and Devices," with a particularly helpful section on "Legal Audit and Periodic Checkup."

Daane, Roderick K. "The Role of University Counsel," 12 *J. Coll. & Univ. Law* 399 (1985). Addresses the ways in which social changes and differences among institutions have affected the role of attorneys that serve colleges and universities. Examines "the way law is now practiced on campuses," focusing especially on counsel's roles as "Advisor-Counsellor," "Educator-Mediator," "Manager-Administrator," "Draftsman," "Litigator," and "Spokesman."

McCarthy, Jane (ed.). *Resolving Conflict in Higher Education,* New Directions for Higher Education, no. 32 (Jossey-Bass, 1980). Describes and discusses mechanisms (such as mediation) that can be used by postsecondary institutions to resolve internal disputes without the necessity of lawsuits. Includes both legal and policy perspectives on alternative dispute-resolution techniques.

Frank B. Manley & Co. *Provision of Legal Services: A Survey of NACUA Primary Representatives* (National Association of College and University Attorneys, 1992). The report of NACUA's latest survey of legal services. Presents and analyzes data on current practices, collected from both public and private institutions. Includes information on in-house staffing and organization, salaries and compensation, budgets, major issue areas and responsibilities of college attorneys, and outside counsel caseloads and billing rates.

National Association of College and University Attorneys. *The Formbook* (2d ed., NACUA, 1994). Includes nearly one hundred legal forms and checklists covering a wide range of institutional functions and transactions. A practical resource for counsel and administrators at both public and private institutions.

Symposium, "Focus on Ethics and the University Attorney," 19 *J. Coll. & Univ. Law* 305 (1993). A collection of three articles examining the role and the ethical duties of the university attorney, especially with respect to other members of the campus community: Robert F. Drinan, "Lawyer-Client Confidentiality in the Campus Setting"; Stephen S. Dunham, "Case Studies on Wrongdoing on Campus: Ethics and the Lawyer's Role"; and Robert M. O'Neil, "The Lawyer and the Client in the Campus Setting: Who Is the Client, What Does the Client Expect and How May the Attorney Respond?"

Symposium, 2 *J. Coll. & Univ. Law* 1 (1974–75). A series of three papers discussing the role and functions of legal counsel: John Corbally, Jr., "University Counsel—Scope and Mission"; J. Rufus Beale, "Delivery of Legal Service to Institutions of Higher Education"; and Richard Sensenbrenner, "University Counselor: Lore, Logic and Logistics." The first paper is written from the perspective of a university president; the other two are from the perspective of practicing university attorneys.

Weeks, Kent M. (ed.). *A Legal Inventory for Independent Colleges and Universities* (Center for Constitutional Studies, Mercer University (now at Baylor University), 1981). A short monograph presenting a checklist of questions to use in conducting a legal audit of a private institution.

II

The College and Trustees, Administrators, and Staff

◆   ◆   ◆

Sec. 2.1. The Question of Authority

Trustees, officers, and administrators of postsecondary institutions—public or private—can take only those actions and make only those decisions that they have authority to take or make. Acting or deciding without authority to do so can have legal consequences, both for the responsible individual and for the institution. It is thus critical, from a legal standpoint, for administrators to understand and adhere to the scope and limits of their authority and that of other institutional functionaries with whom they deal. Such sensitivity to authority questions will also normally be good administrative practice, since it can contribute order and structure to institutional governance and make the governance system more understandable, accessible, and accountable to those who deal with it.

Authority generally originates from some fundamental legal source that establishes the institution as a legal entity. For public institutions the source is usually the constitution or statutes of the state (see Section 6.2); for private institutions it is usually articles of incorporation, sometimes in combination with some form of state license (see Section 6.3). This source, though fundamental, is only the starting point for legal analysis of authority questions. To be fully understood and utilized, an institution's fundamental authority must be construed and implemented in light of all the sources of law described in Section 1.3. For public institutions state administrative law (administrative procedure acts or similar statutes, as well as court decisions) and agency law (court decisions) provide the backdrop against which authority is construed and implemented; for private institutions state corporation or trust law (statutes and court decisions) and agency law (court decisions) are the bases. Authority

76

is particularized and dispersed (delegated) to institutional officers, employees, and organizations by institutional rules and regulations and the institution's employment contracts and, for public institutions, by administrative regulations of the state education boards or agencies. Gaps and ambiguities in authority may be filled in by resort to custom and usage at the institution. And authority may be limited by individual rights guarantees of federal and state constitutions (see especially Sections 3.6 and 3.7 and Sections 4.5 through 4.13) and by federal and state statutes and administrative regulations or adjudications (see especially Sections 6.3 and 6.5 and Sections 7.2 and 7.5).

There are several generic types of authority. As explained in *Brown v. Wichita State University* (Section 2.3.2), authority may be either express, implied, or apparent. Express authority is that which is found within the plain meaning of a written grant of authority. Implied authority is that which is necessary or appropriate for exercising express authority and can therefore be inferred from the express authority. Apparent authority is not actual authority at all; the term is used to describe the situation where someone acting for the institution induces a belief in other persons that authority exists when in fact it does not. Administrators should avoid this appearance of authority and should not rely on apparent authority as a basis for acting, because the institution may be held liable, under the doctrine of "estoppel," for resultant harm to persons who rely to their detriment on an appearance of authority (see Section 2.2.2). When an institutional officer or employee does mistakenly act without authority, the action can sometimes be corrected through "ratification" by the board of trustees or other officer or employee who does have authority to undertake the act in question (see Section 2.2.2).

One other type of authority is occasionally referred to in the postsecondary context: inherent authority. In *Morris v. Nowotny*, 323 S.W.2d 301 (Tex. 1959), for instance, the court remarked that the statutes establishing the University of Texas "imply the power, and, if they do not so imply, then the power is inherent in university officials to maintain proper order and decorum on the premises of the university." In *Esteban v. Central Missouri State College*, 415 F.2d 1077 (8th Cir. 1969), the court held that the college had "inherent authority to maintain order and to discipline students." And in *Waliga v. Board of Trustees of Kent State University*, 488 N.E.2d 850 (Ohio 1986), it found inherent authority in the university's trustees to revoke an academic degree that had been obtained by fraud. (For the facts and reasoning of this case, see Section 4.6.2.) The inherent authority concept is often loosely used in judicial opinions and has no clear definition. Sometimes courts appear to apply the phrase to what is really a very broad construction of the institution's implied powers. In *Goldberg v. Regents of the University of California*, 57 Cal. Rptr. 463 (Cal. Ct. App. 1967), the court held that broad disciplinary authority over students was implicit in the state constitution's grant of power to the university, but then it called that authority "inherent." At other times the inherent authority concept is more clearly distinguished from implied authority; inherent authority then is said to exist not because of any written words but because it would not be sensible, as measured by the norms of postsecondary education, for an institution to be without authority over the particular matter at issue. In all, inherent authority is an elusive concept of uncertain stature and questionable value, and it is a slender reed to rely on to justify actions and decisions. If administrators need broader authority, they should, with counsel's help, seek to expand their express authority or to justify a broader construction of their implied authority.

The law is not clear on how broadly or narrowly authority should be construed in the postsecondary context. To some extent, the answer will vary from state to state and, within a state, may depend on whether the institution is established by the state constitution, by state statutes, or by articles of incorporation. Although authority issues have been addressed in judicial opinions, such as those discussed in Section 2.2, analysis is sometimes cursory, and authority problems are sometimes overlooked. There is debate among courts and commentators about whether postsecondary institutions should be subject to traditional legal principles for construing authority or whether such principles should be applied in a more flexible, less demanding way that takes into account the unique characteristics of postsecondary education. Given the uncertainty, administrators should rely when possible on express rather than implied or inherent authority and should seek clarity in statements of express authority, in order to avoid leaving authority questions to the vagaries of judicial interpretation. If institutional needs require greater flexibility and generality in statements of authority, administrators should consult legal counsel to determine how much breadth and flexibility the courts of the state would permit in construing the various types of authority.

Miscalculations of the institution's authority, or the authority of particular officers or employees, can have various adverse legal consequences. For public institutions unauthorized acts may be invalidated in courts or administrative agencies under the ultra vires doctrine of administrative law (a doctrine applied to acts that are beyond the delegated authority of a public body or official). For private institutions a similar result occasionally can be reached under corporation law.

When the unauthorized act is a failure to follow institutional regulations and the institution is public (see Section 1.5.2), courts will sometimes hold that the act violated procedural due process. In *Escobar v. State University of New York/College at Old Westbury*, 427 F. Supp. 850 (E.D.N.Y. 1977), a student sought to enjoin the college from suspending him or taking any further disciplinary action against him. The student had been disciplined by the judicial review committee, acting under the college's "Code of Community Conduct." After the college president learned of the disciplinary action, he rejected it and imposed more severe penalties on the student. The president purported to act under the "Rules of Public Order" adopted by the board of trustees of the State University of New York rather than under the college code. The court found that the president had violated the rules, and it enjoined enforcement of his decision:

> Even if we assume the president had power to belatedly invoke the Rules, it is clear that he did not properly exercise that power, since he did not follow the requirements of the Rules themselves. The charges he made against the plaintiff were included in the same document which set forth the plaintiff's suspension and the terms for his possible readmission. Contrary to the Rules, the president did not convene the hearing committee, did not give notice of any hearing, and received no report from the hearing committee. There is no authority in either the Rules or the Code for substituting the hearing before the Code's judicial review committee for the one required to be held before the Rule's hearing committee. . . .

Of course, not every deviation from a university's regulations constitutes a deprivation of due process. . . . But where, as here, an offending student has been formally charged under the college's disciplinary code, has been subjected to a hearing, has been officially sentenced, and has commenced compliance with that sentence, it is a denial of due process of law for the chief administrative officer to step in, conduct his own in camera review of the student's record, and impose a different punishment without complying with any of the procedures which have been formally established for the college. Here the president simply brushed aside the college's formal regulations and procedures and, without specific authority, imposed a punishment of greater severity than determined by the hearing panel, a result directly contrary to the Code's appeal provisions [427 F. Supp. at 858].

For both public and private institutions, an unauthorized act violating institutional regulations may also be invalidated as a breach of an express or implied contract with students or the faculty. *Lyons v. Salve Regina College*, 422 F. Supp. 1354 (D.R.I. 1976), *reversed*, 565 F.2d 200 (1st Cir. 1977), involved a student who had received an F grade in a required nursing course because she had been absent from several classes and clinical sessions. After the student appealed the grade under the college's published "Grade Appeal Process," the grade appeal committee voted that the student receive an Incomplete rather than an F. Characterizing the committee's action as a recommendation rather than a final decision, the associate dean overruled the committee, and the student was dismissed from the nursing program.

The parties agreed that the "Grade Appeal Process" was part of the terms of a contract between them. Though the grade appeal committee's determination was termed a "recommendation" in the college's publications, the lower court found that, as the parties understood the process, the recommendation was to be binding on the associate dean. The associate dean's overruling of the committee was therefore unauthorized and constituted a breach of contract. The lower court ordered the college to change the student's grade to an Incomplete and reinstate her in the nursing program. The appellate court reversed but did not disavow the contract theory of authority. Instead, it found that the committee's determination was not intended to be binding on the associate dean and that the dean therefore had not exceeded his authority in overruling the committee.

Authority questions are also central to a determination of various questions concerning liability for harm to third parties. The institution's tort liability may depend on whether the officer or employee committing the tort was acting within the scope of his authority (see Section 2.3.1). The institution's contract liability may depend on whether the officer or employee entering the contract was authorized to do so (Section 2.3.2). And, under the estoppel doctrine, both the institution and the individual may be liable where the institution or individual had apparent authority to act (Section 2.2.2).

Because of these various legal ramifications, a postsecondary institution should carefully organize and document its authority and the delegation of this authority among institutional officers, employees, and organizations. Counsel should be involved in this process. Organizational statements or charts should be generally available to the campus community, so that persons with questions or grievances can know where to turn for assistance. Delegations should be reviewed periodically, to determine whether they accurately reflect actual practice within the institution and maintain an appropriate balance of specificity and flexibility. Where a gap in authority is found, or an unnecessary overlap or ambiguity, it should be corrected. Where questions concerning the permissible scope of authority are uncovered, they should be resolved.

Similarly, administrators should understand the scope of their own authority and that of the officers, employees, and organizations with whom they deal. They should understand where their authority comes from and which higher-level administrators may review or modify their acts and decisions. They should attempt to resolve unnecessary gaps or ambiguities in their authority. They should consider what part of their authority may and should be subdelegated to lower-level administrators or faculty and what checks or limitations should be placed on those delegations. And they should attempt to ensure that their authority is adequately understood by the members of the campus community with whom they deal.

Sec. 2.2. Sources and Scope of Authority

The following discussion illustrates particular kinds of legal challenges that may be made to the authority of various functionaries in postsecondary institutions. Although the discussion reflects general concepts and issues critical to an understanding of authority in the postsecondary context, the specific legal principles that courts apply to particular challenges to authority may vary from state to state.

2.2.1. Trustees. In public institutions the authority of trustees is defined and limited by the state statutes, and sometimes by constitutional provisions, which create trustee boards for individual institutions. Such laws generally confer power on the board itself as an entity separate from its individual members. Individual trustees generally have authority to act only on behalf of the board, pursuant to some board bylaw, resolution, or other delegation of authority from the board. Other state laws, such as conflict-of-interest laws or ethics codes, may place obligations on individual board members as well as on the board itself.

In *First Equity Corp. of Florida v. Utah State University*, 544 P.2d 887 (Utah 1975), the plaintiff, a stock brokerage company, sued the university over its failure to pay for common stocks ordered by the university's assistant president of finance. The university defended itself by asserting that its board of trustees lacked the power to authorize the assistant president to invest in common stocks. The board had general control and supervision "of all appropriations made by the territory [state] for the support" of the school (Comp. Laws of Utah § 1855 (1888)), and the university had authority to handle its own financial affairs under the supervision of the board (Higher Education Act of 1969, Utah Code Ann. § 53-48-10(5)). The court held, however, that these provisions did not give the university unlimited authority to encumber public funds:

> Whether or not the grant of a "general control" of "all appropriations" and the right to "handle its own financial affairs" grant unrestricted power to invest is answered by the *University of Utah v. Board of Examiners of the State*

of Utah [295 P.2d 348 (Utah 1956)] case. After quoting Sections 1 and 2 of Article X of the [state] constitution, which mandates the legislature to provide for the maintenance of the University of Utah and USU, the court states:

> Would it be contended by the university that under Article X, Section 1, it might compel the legislature to appropriate money the university considers essential? Is it contended that the demands of the university are not subject to constitutional debt limits? If so, respondent would have the power to destroy the solvency of the state and all other institutions by demands beyond the power of the state to meet [544 P.2d at 890].

The court then quotes in full Sections 5 and 7 of Article X of the state constitution, which provide, respectively, that the proceeds of the sale of land reserved by Congress for the University of Utah shall constitute permanent funds of the state, and that all public school funds shall be guaranteed by the state against loss or diversion. Then the court concludes:

> It is inconceivable that the framers of the constitution, in light of the provisions of Sections 1, 5, and 7 of Article X and the provisions as to debt limitations, intended to place the university above the only controls available for the people of this state as to the property, management, and government of the university. We are unable to reconcile respondent's position that the university has a blank check as to all its funds with no preaudit and no restraint under the provisions of the constitution requiring the state to safely invest and hold the dedicated funds and making the state guarantor of the public school funds against loss or diversion. To hold that respondent has free and uncontrolled custody and use of its property and funds while making the state guarantee said funds against loss or diversion is inconceivable. We believe the framers of the constitution intended no such result [544 P.2d at 890].

Because of this state constitutional limitation regarding finances, and the absence of any "specific authorizing grant" of investment power under the state statutes, the court held that the board did not have authority to purchase the particular type of stock involved. The board therefore could not authorize the assistant vice president or any other agent to make the purchases.

In *Feldman v. Regents of the University of New Mexico,* 540 P.2d 872 (N.M. 1975), the head football coach at the university sued the regents for discharging him during the term of his contract. According to New Mexico law, the regents have "power to remove any officer connected with the university when in their judgment the interests require it" (N.M. Stat. Ann. § 73-25-9). The regents relied on the statute as sufficient authority for dismissing the coach. In ruling on the regents' motion for summary judgment, the state courts refused to approve the dismissal under this statute. The courts reasoned that additional information was needed to determine whether the coach was an "officer" or an "employee" of the institution, since the statute would not authorize his discharge if he were an employee.

In *Baker v. Southern University,* 604 So. 2d 699 (La. Ct. App. 1992), a custodian who had Civil Service protections charged that the chancellor did not have the authority to dismiss him. The court was required to determine whether the board of supervisors of Southern University was legally authorized to delegate appointing and discharge authority to the university's chancellor. The court had to reconcile the provisions of the state's civil service statute as well as the statute that controls the organization of the state's colleges and universities. These statutes, said the court, give broad powers to the board of supervisors to "supervise and manage the university system . . . to exercise all power to direct, control, supervise and manage the university" (604 So. 2d at 701). This power, said the court, included the power to delegate appointing authority to the chancellor.

The outcome is different, however, if statutes provide that the board itself must act. In *Blanchard v. Lansing Community College*, 370 N.W.2d 23 (Mich. Ct. App. 1985), a faculty member challenged his discharge because the board of trustees had not voted on the matter. The board argued that it had delegated the power to hire and discharge to certain administrators. Turning to the relevant Michigan statute, the court noted that the statute specifies that the faculty employment contract is between the faculty member and the board, and ruled that the power to discharge was expressly committed to the discretion of the board and thus was not delegable.

Authority not delegated to a board by the state legislature, however, may not be assumed by that board. For example, in *Board of Regents v. Board of Trustees for State Colleges and Universities*, 491 So. 2d 399 (La. Ct. App. 1986), the court ruled that the board of trustees for the state's public colleges and universities did not have the authority to change the name of the state university; that was the prerogative of the legislature. Since neither the state constitution nor any statute gave the board of trustees the authority to change the university's name, the court ruled that the legislature had retained that authority.

In private institutions the authority of institutional trustees is defined and limited by the institution's corporate charter (articles of incorporation) and the state corporation laws under which charters are issued. As in public institutions, the power generally lodges in the board of trustees as an entity separate from its individual members. But charter provisions, corporate bylaws, or board resolutions may delegate authority to individual trustees or trustee committees to act for the board in certain situations. Moreover, general state corporate law or trust law may place affirmative obligations on individual board members to act fairly and responsibly in protecting the institution's resources and interests. (For an argument favoring an increased obligation to the public on the part of private colleges and universities, see P. Haskell, "The University as Trustee," 17 *Ga. L. Rev.* 1 (1982).)

The Missouri case of *Burnett v. Barnes*, 546 S.W.2d 744 (Mo. 1977), illustrates how the authority of a private institution's board of trustees may be limited by the institution's articles of incorporation. The institution in this case, the Kansas City College of Osteopathic Medicine, was a "membership" corporation; graduates of the college had the status of members of the corporation. When the college's board of trustees sought to amend the corporate bylaws to eliminate this membership status, the Missouri state courts determined that the trustees had no authority to make such a change. The Missouri General Not-for-Profit Corporation Law gave the trustees power "to make and alter bylaws not inconsistent with its articles of incorporation or with the laws of this state" (Mo. Rev. Stat. § 355.090). The institution's original articles of agreement and its subsequent articles of acceptance each referred to the admission of new members to the corporation. On the basis of these two references, the courts concluded that the board's power to amend the bylaws was limited by the institution's articles of incorporation to matters that did not eliminate membership.

Stern v. Lucy Webb Hayes National Training School for Deaconnesses and Missionaries, 381 F. Supp. 1003 (D.D.C. 1974) (the *Sibley Hospital* case), is the first reported opinion to comprehensively review the obligations of the trustees of private charitable corporations and to set out guidelines for trustee involvement in financial dealings. Although the case concerns a hospital, the court's analysis is clearly transferable to private educational institutions. The court's decision to analyze the trustees' standard of duty in terms of corporate law, rather than trust law, apparently reflects the evolving trend in the law.

The plaintiffs represented patients of Sibley Hospital, a nonprofit charitable corporation in the District of Columbia and the principal concern of the Lucy Webb Hayes National Training School. Nine members of the hospital's board of trustees were among the named defendants. The plaintiffs charged that the defendant trustees had "conspired to enrich themselves and certain financial institutions with which they were affiliated [and which were also named as defendants] by favoring those institutions in financial dealings with the hospital" and that "they breached their fiduciary duties of care and loyalty in the management of Sibley's funds." The court examined evidence of the relationships between the defendant trustees and the defendant institutions. Although most of the hospital's funds were deposited in the defendant institutions, the funds were controlled and managed almost exclusively from the early 1950s until 1972 by a deceased trustee, without the active involvement of any of the defendant trustees.

The court concluded that the plaintiffs had not established a conspiracy but had established serious breaches of duty by the trustees. According to the court, the trustees owed a duty to the institution comparable to, and in some cases greater than, that owed by the directors of a business corporation.

1. Mismanagement

Both trustees and corporate directors are liable for losses occasioned by their negligent mismanagement of investments. However, the degree of care required appears to differ in many jurisdictions. A trustee is uniformly held to a high standard of care and will be held liable for simple negligence, while a director must often have committed "gross negligence" or otherwise be guilty of more than mere mistakes of judgment.

This distinction may amount to little more than a recognition of the fact that corporate directors have many areas of responsibility, while the traditional trustee is often charged only with the management of the trust funds and can therefore be expected to devote more time and expertise to that task. Since the board members of most large charitable corporations fall within the corporate rather than the trust model, being charged with the operation of ongoing businesses, it has been said that they should only be held to the less stringent corporate standard of care. More specifically, directors of charitable corporations are required to exercise ordinary and reasonable care in the performance of their duties, exhibiting honesty and good faith.

2. Nonmanagement

Plaintiffs allege that the individual defendants failed to supervise the management of hospital investments or even to attend meetings of the committees charged with such supervision. Trustees are particularly vulnerable to such a charge, because they not only have an affirmative duty to "maximize the trust income by prudent investment," but they may not delegate that duty, even to a committee of their fellow trustees. A corporate director, on the other hand, may delegate his investment responsibility to fellow directors, corporate officers, or even outsiders, but he must continue to exercise general supervision over the activities of his delegates. Once again, the rule for charitable corporations is closer to the traditional corporate rule: directors should at least be permitted to delegate investment decisions to a committee of board members, so long as all directors assume the responsibility for supervising such committees by periodically scrutinizing their work.

Total abdication of the supervisory role, however, is improper even under traditional corporate principles. A director who fails to acquire the information necessary to supervise investment policy or consistently fails even to attend the meetings at which such policies are considered has violated his fiduciary duty to the corporation. . . .

3. Self-Dealing

Under District of Columbia law, neither trustees nor corporate directors are absolutely barred from placing funds under their control into a bank having an interlocking directorship with their own institution. In both cases, however, such transactions will be subjected to the closest scrutiny to determine whether or not the duty of loyalty has been violated. A deliberate conspiracy among trustees or board members to enrich the interlocking bank at the expense of the trust or corporation would, for example, constitute such a breach and render the conspirators liable for any losses. In the absence of clear evidence of wrongdoing, however, the courts appear to have used different standards to determine whether or not relief is appropriate, depending again on the legal relationship involved. Trustees may be found guilty of a breach of trust even for mere negligence in the maintenance of accounts in banks with which they are associated, while corporate directors are generally only required to show "entire fairness" to the corporation and "full disclosure" of the potential conflict of interest to the board.

Most courts apply the less stringent corporate rule to charitable corporations in this area as well [381 F. Supp. at 1013-15; footnotes omitted].

On the basis of these principles, the court created explicit guidelines for the future conduct of trustees in financial matters:

The court holds that a director or so-called trustee of a charitable hospital organized under the Non-Profit Corporation Act of the District of Columbia (D.C. Code § 29-1001 et seq.) is in default of his fiduciary duty to manage the fiscal and investment affairs of the hospital if it has been shown by a preponderance of the evidence that:

(1) While assigned to a particular committee of the board having general financial or investment responsibility under the bylaws of the corporation, he has failed to use due diligence in supervising the actions of those officers, employees, or outside experts to whom the responsibility for making day-to-day financial or investment decisions has been delegated; or

(2) he knowingly permitted the hospital to enter into a business transaction with himself or with any corporation, partnership, or association in which he then had a substantial interest or held a position as trustee, director, general manager, or principal officer without having previously informed the persons charged with approving that transaction of his interest or position and of any significant reasons, unknown to or not fully appreciated by such persons, why the transaction might not be in the best interests of the hospital; or

(3) except as required by the preceding paragraph, he actively participated in or voted in favor of a decision by the board or any committee or sub-
committee thereof to transact business with himself or with any corporation,
partnership, or association in which he then had a substantial interest or held
a position as trustee, director, general manager, or principal officer; or
(4) he otherwise failed to perform his duties honestly, in good faith, and
with a reasonable amount of diligence and care [381 F. Supp. at 1015].

In *Corporation of Mercer University v. Smith*, 371 S.E.2d 858 (Ga. 1988), the
Georgia Supreme Court echoed the D.C. court in the *Sibley Hospital* case when it
considered whether trust law or corporate law would apply to trustees' merger and
closure decisions; it also considered the scope of private institutional autonomy under
state law. At issue was a challenge to a decision made by Mercer University's trustees
to close Tift College in Atlanta, with which the university had recently merged. The
merger agreement provided that Mercer would make a good-faith effort to continue
operating Tift College at its original location. Plaintiffs—who included a district
attorney, several alumni, and three former trustees—sued to set aside the merger and
to keep the college open. The parties differed as to whether trust law or corporate law
would apply to Mercer's actions. The plaintiffs wanted the court to apply the stricter
fiduciary duty requirements of trust law; the college argued that trustees were bound
only by the dictates of corporate law. Siding with the college, the court applied
corporate law, rather than trust law, and concluded that under corporate law the
trustees had the power to merge the college and then close it:

> [F]ormalities of trust law are inappropriate to the administration of col-
> leges and universities which, in this era, operate as businesses. . . . [T]hose per-
> sons responsible for the operation of the universities need the administrative
> flexibility to make the many day-to-day decisions affecting the operation of the
> institution, including those decisions involving the acquisition of and sale of
> assets [371 S.E.2d at 860–61].

In re Antioch University, 418 A.2d 105 (D.C. 1980), illustrates the delineation
of authority between the board of trustees and the institution's constituent units. The
case arose as a dispute between the university, located in Ohio, and a law school that
it operated in Washington, D.C. The dispute concerned the extent to which the law
school could operate autonomously from the university. According to the court:

> Because of asserted university financial problems, the law school author-
> ities fear that its existence as an accredited institution is threatened if funds paid
> by its students and grants for education and clinic programs are not administered
> by the law school officers. The university urges that its accountability as a trustee
> of all university funds and its ability to administer such funds for the welfare of
> the entire institution will be severely impaired unless its proper officers have full
> and unilateral control over all funds coming into the university. This dispute
> mushroomed into a claim by the . . . co-deans of the law school that the university
> had contractually relinquished its control over the fiscal and administrative af-
> fairs of the law school and that the university was in breach of its fiduciary duties
> to the students of the law school and clients of its clinic. The university counters
> that the co-deans of the law school breached their fiduciary obligations to the

university by refusing to follow its direction in the handling of the funds [418 A.2d at 106].

The law school officials sought a preliminary injunction that would enable the law school to administer its funds independently. When the trial court denied this relief, the officials appealed. The appellate court considered the officials' contract claim in the context of the law governing private boards of trustees:

[The law school officials] argue that "commitments," which are asserted to be actual contractual agreements between the university and the law school, provide for an independent administration of the law school. They argue that a resolution passed by the board of trustees of Antioch University on December 5 and 6, 1975, established the basis for this conclusion. This resolution reaffirmed the board of trustees' commitment to a law school "built around a teaching law firm" and established an "*interim governing structure* pending a determination by the board of trustees of *ultimate governance* relationship between the school of law and the college" [emphasis added by court]. The resolution goes on to name a board of governors of the law school and to delineate its authority. The resolution specifies those matters over which the board of trustees of the university specifically reserves authority unto itself. And finally, the resolution "expressly charges the law school board of governors to develop recommendations respecting the *ultimate structure* of relationship between the law school and the college" [emphasis added by court]. . . .

Upon the basis of this record, we conclude that the trial court was amply justified in impliedly rejecting appellants' contractual argument based upon this resolution. The university is a not-for-profit corporation organized under the law of the state of Ohio. The university, [like] any corporation, is governed by the statutes of the state of its incorporation, its articles of incorporation, and its bylaws. The law school "is not organized as a corporation or other judicial entity." Concededly, it "was established pursuant to a resolution of the board of trustees of Antioch College (the predecessor in name to Antioch University) dated December 3 and 4, 1971." Resolutions adopted by the university in accordance with its articles of incorporation and bylaws effectuate the will of the corporation (see generally *Brown v. National Loan & Investment Co.*, 139 S.W.2d 364 (Tex. Civ. App. 1940)). However, the plain meaning of this resolution bespeaks a delegation of power for the establishment of an "interim governing structure" of the law school as it relates to the university. It cannot be concluded that such a delegation deprived the board of trustees of the power given to them in Article III of the university's Articles of Incorporation, to wit: "All of the rights and powers of the corporation and the entire control and management of its college, property, and affairs shall be vested in and exercised by a board of trustees composed of twenty-five (25) persons." In fact, a contract conveying such plenary power vested by corporation charter in the trustees would be void [418 A.2d at 111–12].

In thus affirming the denial of preliminary relief, the court determined that the board of trustees had acted in accordance with its fiduciary obligations under Ohio law and its charter and bylaws.[1] The court further cautioned that, had the board

---

[1]A later case between the same parties, *Cahn v. Antioch University*, 482 A.2d 120 (D.C. 1984), dealt with the law school officials' fiduciary obligations to the university. See also *In re Antioch University*, 482 A.2d 133 (D.C. 1984), which rejected the law school officials' request that the university pay their attorney's fees for the litigation.

granted to the law school the administrative power it sought, the board's action would have been void. This conclusion is supported by the university's charter, which apparently precludes the trustees from delegating their management powers. It may also find support in the legal principle, recognized in varying degrees by the corporation laws of the states, that excessive delegation of management powers by a corporate board violates state law even if it is not precluded by the charter.

With a little muscle, a framework for analyzing the power relationship between private universities and their constituent units can be squeezed from the opinion in *In re Antioch University*. First, the university is the legal entity that derives power from the state; the constituent unit usually has no separate corporate status and thus derives its authority exclusively from the university. Second, the extent to which the board of trustees may delegate authority to a constituent unit is determined initially by the relevant provisions of the corporate charter; the trustees may delegate management powers only to the extent, and in the manner, authorized by the charter. Third, charter provisions, in turn, may authorize delegation of management powers only to the extent, and in the manner, that the state's corporation statutes and case law permit; charter provisions that conflict with state law on excessive delegation are invalid. Fourth, the extent to which the university has actually delegated authority to a constituent unit is determined by construing the trustees' resolutions, the university's bylaws, and other official acts of the university. Any claimed authority that is not found in these sources, construed consistently with the charter and state law, does not exist.

Another issue related to the authority of trustees involves their role in monitoring the management of assets over which they have no legal control, but which may benefit the institution in the future. In *Shriners Hospitals for Crippled Children v. First Security Bank of Utah*, 835 P.2d 350 (Wyo. 1992), the Wyoming Supreme Court addressed the concerns of two beneficiaries of a trust: the hospital and the University of Utah. A donor had established a "charitable remainder trust" in her will that provided income for her sister during the sister's lifetime and then reverted to the hospital and the university upon the sister's death. The trustee, a bank, had sold some land that was part of the trust's assets, without notifying the contingent beneficiaries (the hospital and the university), and at a price allegedly below its market value. The Wyoming court rejected the challenge to the sale of the land, ruling that the trustee had no duty to notify the contingent beneficiaries of the sale of trust assets. The U.S. Supreme Court declined to review the case. The outcome of this case is troubling for colleges, because donors often use charitable remainder trusts to make gifts to colleges and universities. Although colleges may ask the trustee of the trust to notify them before selling assets, there may not be a legal obligation for the trustee to do so.

2.2.2. Other officers and administrators. The authority of the highest-ranking officers and administrators of postsecondary institutions may occasionally be set out in statutes or state board regulations (for public institutions) or in corporate charters (for private institutions). But more often even the highest-ranking officers and employees, and almost always the lower-ranking ones, derive their authority not directly from statute, state board regulation, or charter but rather from subdelegation by the institution's board of trustees. The lower the administrator in the administrative hierarchy, the greater the likelihood of subsubdelegation—that is, subdelegation of

authority from the board of trustees to an officer or administrator who in turn sub-
delegates part of this authority to some other administrator or employee.

Silverman v. University of Colorado, 555 P.2d 1155 (Colo. 1976), illustrates the
subdelegation of authority. A terminated assistant professor claimed that her termination constituted a breach of contract. In December 1972 the associate dean of the
professor's school wrote the professor that she would be reappointed for 1973–74 if
certain federal funding was renewed and if the professor's peers recommended reappointment. The professor claimed that, although both conditions were fulfilled, the
school did not renew her contract, thus violating the terms of the December 1972
letter. The trial court held for the university, reasoning that the associate dean's letter
could not create a contract because, by statute, only the board of regents had authority
to appoint faculty members. The intermediate appellate court reversed, reasoning that
the associate dean could have created a contract because he could have been acting
under authority subdelegated to him by the board. The Supreme Court of Colorado
then reversed the intermediate court and reinstated the trial court's decision, holding
that hiring authority is not delegable unless "expressly authorized by the legislature."

In *People v. Ware,* 368 N.Y.S.2d 797 (N.Y. App. Div. 1975), however, an appellate court upheld a delegation of power from a systemwide board of trustees to the
president of an individual institution and thence to campus police officers employed
by that institution. The trial court had dismissed a prosecution against an illegal
trespasser at the State University of New York (SUNY) at Buffalo because the officer
making the arrest did not have authority to do so. According to this court, the New
York Education Law (§ 355(2)(m)) designated the SUNY board of trustees to appoint
peace officers, whereas the arresting officer had been appointed by the president of
the university. In reversing, the appellate court reasoned that the board had authority
under the Education Law to promulgate rules and regulations, and the rules and
regulations promulgated by the board provided for the delegation of power to
SUNY's executive and administrative officers. By resolution passed under these rules
and regulations, the board had authorized administrative officers of each state institution to appoint peace officers for their campuses. Since the SUNY president had
properly appointed the arresting officer pursuant to this resolution, the officer had
authority to make the arrest.

In some cases, however, a board is not permitted to delegate its authority to
a president. In *Faculty of City University of New York Law School at Queens College
v. Murphy,* 539 N.Y.S.2d 367 (N.Y. App. Div. 1989), the university chancellor had
declined to forward to the board of trustees the applications of two candidates for
tenure who had not received unanimous approval from a joint law school/college
review committee. The court held that the chancellor did not have authority to withhold the applications and that the board of trustees had the exclusive, nondelegable
power to award tenure.

Even when an institutional officer or administrator acts beyond the scope of
his delegated power, so that the act is unauthorized, the board of trustees may subsequently "ratify" the act if that act was within the scope of the board's own authority.
"Ratification" converts the initially unauthorized act into an authorized act. In *Silverman v. University of Colorado* (above), for instance, the intermediate appellate
court held that, even if the associate dean did not have authority to reappoint the
professor, the professor was entitled to prove that the offer of reappointment had been
ratified by the board of regents (541 P.2d 93, 96 (1975)). Similarly, in *Tuskegee In-*

stitute v. May Refrigeration Co., 344 So. 2d 156 (Ala. 1977), two employees of a special program operated by Tuskegee had ordered an air conditioning unit from the May Company. May delivered and installed the unit but was not paid the agreed-upon price. An intermediate appellate court reversed a damages award for May on the theory that the Tuskegee employees who ordered the unit had no authority to do so. The highest state court then reversed the intermediate court. It reasoned that, even though the employees had no actual or apparent authority, Tuskegee had kept and used the unit that the employees ordered and therefore could have ratified their unauthorized acts.

Even when an officer or administrator acts without authority and a higher officer or administrator or the board of trustees has not ratified the act, a court will occasionally estop the institution from denying the validity of the act. Under this doctrine of estoppel, courts may—in order to prevent injustice to persons who had justifiably relied on an unauthorized act—treat the unauthorized act as if it had been authorized. In the *Silverman* case, the plaintiff professor argued that various officials of the school had "advised her that her position was secure for the coming academic year" and that she had "reasonably relied on these representations to her detriment in that she did not seek other employment." The intermediate appellate court ruled that, if the plaintiff's allegations regarding the assurances, the reasonableness of her reliance, and the detriment were true, then "the doctrine of estoppel may be invoked if necessary to prevent manifest injustice." The Colorado Supreme Court reversed, recognizing the estoppel doctrine but holding that the facts did not justify its application in this case. The court reasoned that, since the professor had received adequate notice of nonrenewal, there was no "manifest injustice" necessitating estoppel and that, since the faculty handbook clearly stated that the board of regents makes all faculty appointments, the professor's "reliance on statements made by university officials was misplaced."

Another illustration of estoppel is provided by *Blank v. Board of Higher Education of the City of New York*, 273 N.Y.S.2d 796 (N.Y. Sup. Ct. 1966). The plaintiff student sought to compel the defendant board to award him a Bachelor of Arts degree. The question about the student's degree developed after he was advised that he could take advantage of a Professional Option Plan allowing him to complete a certain minimum amount of coursework without attending any classes. This arrangement enabled him to begin law school in Syracuse before he had finished all his coursework at Brooklyn College. The student had been advised by faculty members, the head of the department of psychology, and a member of the counseling and guidance staff, and the arrangement had been approved by the professors of the psychology courses involved, each of whom gave him the necessary assignments. At the time of his expected graduation, however, the student was denied his degree because he had not completed the courses "in attendance."

In defending its refusal to grant the degree, the college argued that only the dean of the faculty had the authority to determine a student's eligibility for the Professional Option Plan and that the dean had not exercised such authority regarding the plaintiff. The college further argued that the dean had devised regulations concerning the Professional Option Plan and that these regulations contained residence requirements which the student had not met. While the court did not dispute these facts, it emphasized, as a contrary consideration, that the plaintiff had "acted in obvious reliance upon the counsel and advice of members of the staff of the college administration to whom he was referred and who were authorized to give him such counsel and advice." Moreover:

> "The authority of an agent is not only that conferred upon him by his commission, but also as to third persons that which he is held out as possessing. The principal is often bound by the act of his agent in excess or abuse of his authority, but this is only true between the principal and third persons who, believing and having a right to believe that the agent was acting within and not exceeding his authority, would sustain loss if the act was not considered that of the principal" (*Walsh v. Hartford Fire Insurance Co.*, 73 N.Y. 5, 10).
>
> The dean of faculty may not escape the binding effect of the acts of his agents performed within the scope of their apparent authority, and the consequences that must equitably follow therefrom. Having given permission to take the subject courses in the manner prescribed, through his agents . . . , he cannot, in the circumstances, later assert that the courses should have been taken in another manner [273 N.Y.S.2d at 802-03].

Thus, "all of the elements of an estoppel exist" and the "doctrine should be invoked" against the college. The court ordered the college to award the plaintiff the A.B. degree.

In cases involving apparent authority, plaintiffs must convince a court that reliance on that apparent authority was reasonable. In *Sipfle v. Board of Governors of the University of North Carolina*, 318 S.E.2d 256 (N.C. Ct. App. 1984), the plaintiff had signed up for a trip to China organized by a university faculty member and had paid him $52,000 for the cost of the trip. When the travel agency arranging the tour went bankrupt and did not provide the trip or return the plaintiff's money, she sued the university, claiming that the faculty member was its agent and thus the university was responsible for refunding her money. Although the faculty member had used university stationery to advertise the trip, the university escaped liability for his actions because the court ruled that the plaintiff's belief that the university was the sponsor was unreasonable.

Another institution also escaped contract liability on the theory that the defendant could not properly rely on the representations of a college employee. In *Student House, Inc. v. Board of Regents of Regency Universities*, 254 N.E.2d 496 (Ill. 1969), a corporation that owned and operated a private student housing facility at Northern Illinois University sued the university for building additional residence halls. The plaintiffs stated that several years earlier, the university's director of housing had told them that the university would not build additional residence halls; and in reliance on that representation, the plaintiffs formed the corporation and built a private residence hall. The court found that the board of regents had the authority to decide to build residence halls and that the board had not delegated such authority to the housing director. The plaintiffs had relied on the representations of the director without discussing the matter with the president or any board member, said the court; and such reliance on the statements of "lower echelon members of the University staff" (254 N.E.2d at 499) was not reasonable.

2.2.3. The college's staff. Authority questions occasionally concern college staff—most notably, whether a particular staff member is an agent of the institution or has actual or apparent authority to bind the institution (Section 2.1). But other questions, primarily those related to the staff member's employment, are arising with greater frequency as staff join the various groups that are making increasing demands on colleges.

The legal disputes between a college and its nonfaculty staff do not differ significantly, in most respects, from those between a college and its faculty. With the important exceptions of academic freedom and tenure, which would typically not provide a nonacademic staff member (and one without a faculty appointment) the protections enjoyed by faculty, most of the legal doctrines that apply to faculty also apply to staff.

For example, the question of whether a faculty handbook is a binding contract (discussed in Section 3.1.1) has also arisen with regard to a staff handbook (see, for example, *Wall v. Tulane University*, 499 So. 2d 375 (La. Ct. App. 1986), and *Gilbert v. Tulane University*, 909 F.2d 124 (5th Cir. 1990)). Wrongful-discharge claims, under both common law and nondiscrimination statutes (Section 3.3), have also involved nonacademic staff, particularly when the person who was discharged had complained of sexual harassment (see, for example, *Townsend v. Indiana University*, 995 F.2d 691 (7th Cir. 1993), and *Giordano v. William Paterson College*, 804 F. Supp. 637 (D.N.J. 1992)).

Staff at many public and private institutions are represented by unions for the purpose of collective bargaining. Issues of bargaining unit composition (Section 3.2.3), organization and recognition of the bargaining agent (Section 3.2.2), and appropriate subjects of bargaining (Section 3.2.4) arise under either state or federal law (depending on whether the college is public or private), although they may be resolved differently for staff than for faculty. For example, in some public colleges and universities, staff (but not faculty) are covered by a state's civil service provisions. These provisions are derived from state law and regulation, and thus differ by state and between state systems of higher education. Issues typically involve the classification or reclassification of positions (see *Sindlinger v. State Board of Regents*, 503 N.W.2d 387 (Iowa 1993)), or the amount of due process protections that a college must afford a staff member who is disciplined, discharged, or laid off (see, for example, *Fields v. Durham*, 90 F.2d 94 (4th Cir. 1991), and *Page v. DeLaune*, 837 F.2d 233 (5th Cir. 1988)).

College staff may also assert constitutional claims involving free speech or association (Section 3.7.1) (see *Wilson v. University of Texas Health Center*, 973 F.2d 1263 (5th Cir. 1992)); defamation claims (Sections 2.3.1.2 and 2.4.1) (for instance, in *Wilson v. University of Texas Health Center*); employment discrimination claims (see Section 7.2.6.1); and common law contract and tort claims under state law, particularly in light of the increasing number of limitations to the employment-at-will doctrine (see Sections 3.1.1 and 6.1).

Evaluation and documentation of administrative and staff performance are increasingly significant as legal challenges to negative employment decisions persist. For assistance, see P. Seldin, *Evaluating and Developing Administrative Performance* (Jossey-Bass, 1988).

2.2.4. Campus organizations. Authority in postsecondary institutions may be delegated not only to individual officers or administrators but also to various campus organizations that are accorded some role in governance. Common examples include academic senates, faculty assemblies, department faculties, and student or university judicial systems. (See Section 4.5.3 for a discussion of judicial systems.)

Searle v. Regents of the University of California, 100 Cal. Rptr. 194 (Cal. Ct. App. 1972), is a leading case. By a standing order of the regents, the academic senate was given authority to "authorize and supervise all courses and curricula." Pursuant to this authority, the senate approved a course in which 50 percent of the lectures would be taught by a nonfaculty member (Eldridge Cleaver). Subsequent to the senate's approval of the course, the regents adopted two pertinent resolutions. One resolution provided that a person without an appropriate faculty appointment could not lecture more than once during a university quarter in a course offering university credit; the other provided that the course to be taught by Cleaver could not be offered for credit if it could not be restructured.

The course was taught as originally planned. When the regents resolved that the course not be given academic credit, sixteen students who took the course and six faculty members sued to compel the regents to grant the credit and to rescind the two resolutions. The plaintiffs argued that the standing order granting the academic senate authority over courses and curricula deprived the regents of power to act. The court, however, found that the regents had specifically retained the power to appoint faculty members and concluded that this case involved an appointment to the faculty rather than just the supervisory power over courses provided by the standing order: "To designate a lecturer for a university course is to name the person to conduct the course, at least to the extent of the lectures to be given by him. When the designation is of one to conduct a full half of the course, it appears to be a matter of appointment to the faculty, which is clearly reserved to the regents." Moreover, the court indicated that the authority of the academic senate was subject to further diminishment by the regents:

> In any event, the power granted to the senate is neither exclusive nor irrevocable. The bylaws specifically provide that neither they nor the standing orders "shall be construed, operate as, or have the effect of an abridgment or limitation of any rights, powers, or privileges of the regents." This limitation not only is authorized but seems required by the overriding constitutional mandate which vests the regents with "full powers of organization and government" of the university, and grants to them as a corporation "all the powers necessary or convenient for the effective administration of its trust" (Cal. Const. Art. IX, § 9). To accept appellants' argument would be to hold that a delegation of authority, even though specifically limited, amounts to a surrender of authority [100 Cal. Rptr. at 195–96].

The court therefore determined that the regents, and not the senate, had authority over the structuring of the course in question.

Another case illustrating delegation of authority to a campus organization— this time a student rather than a faculty group—is *Student Association of the University of Wisconsin-Milwaukee v. Baum,* 246 N.W.2d 622 (Wis. 1976). The Wisconsin legislature had passed a statute that accorded specific organizational and governance rights to students in the University of Wisconsin system:

> The students of each institution or campus subject to the responsibilities and powers of the board [of regents], the president, the chancellor, and the faculty

shall be active participants in the immediate governance of and policy development for such institutions. As such, students shall have primary responsibility for the formulation and review of policies concerning student life, services, and interests. Students, in consultation with the chancellor and subject to the final confirmation of the board, shall have the responsibility for the disposition of those student fees which constitute substantial support for campus student activities. The students of each institution or campus shall have the right to organize themselves in a manner they determine and to select their representatives to participate in institutional governance [Wis. Stat. § 36.09(5)].

The chancellor of the Milwaukee campus asserted that, despite the statute's passage, he retained the right to make student appointments to the Physical Environment Committee and the Segregated Fee Advisory Committee. The Student Association, the campuswide student government, argued that the chancellor no longer had this authority because the statute had delegated it to the association. Applying traditional techniques of statutory interpretation, the court agreed with the students. Concerning the student appointments to the Physical Environment Committee, the court held:

> When § 36.09(5), Stats., became effective in July 1974, the chancellor lost his authority to make these appointments. The statute gave this authority to the students as of that time. It is well settled that if a rule or directive of an administrative body or officer is in conflict with a newly enacted statute, the statute must take precedence. The students had the right to select their representatives on the Physical Environment Committee [246 N.W.2d at 626].

Using a similar analysis, the court reached the same result with respect to the Segregated Fee Advisory Committee.

2.2.5. *Captive and affiliated organizations.* The activities of higher education institutions are no longer conducted under the umbrella of a single corporate entity. In addition to the degree-granting entity itself, there may be numerous spin-off or related organizations, such as alumni and booster clubs, hospitals and clinics, organizations to support research or market products, TV or radio stations, museums, and foundations of various kinds (see generally Sections 9.3 and 9.4). Although often created by action of the institution itself, these organizations may have a corporate existence of their own and may be at least partially independent from the institution. In other situations the related organization may have originated and developed completely apart from the institution but later enters an affiliation agreement with the institution, maintaining its separate corporate existence and autonomy but cooperating with the institution in some area of mutual interest. The creation and dissolution of these captive and affiliated organizations, and their authority in relation to that of the institution itself, have been the subject of recent debate as well as litigation. The potential liabilities of these organizations, and the potential liabilities the institution might sustain as a result of its relationship with such an organization, have also raised concerns (see, for example, the *Brown* case in Section 2.3.2 below (contract liability), and *Jaar v. University of Miami*, 474 So. 2d 239 (Fla. Dist. Ct. App. 1985) (tort liability)).

The problem may arise in different contexts. In one scenario an institution may wish to sever part or all of a particular function or department, creating a separately incorporated entity. The separate entity then may operate apart from certain legal requirements that would attach if it were still subsumed within the institution's corporate structure. The question then may become whether the institution has sufficiently relinquished its control over the separate entity so that it may operate independently from the institution and free of restrictions that would apply to the institution itself. In *Colorado Association of Public Employees v. Board of Regents of the University of Colorado*, 804 P.2d 138 (Colo. 1990), for example, the court explored the status of a university hospital. The state had promulgated legislation that purported to reorganize the hospital into a private, nonprofit corporation. The legislation provided that the board of regents of the University of Colorado would still control the hospital through regulations and that, "[s]hould the corporation dissolve, the assets of the corporation less amounts owed to creditors will revert to the Regents." The hospital was also required to secure the approval of the state legislature if it wished to transfer the corporation to anyone other than the regents, or if it were to exceed a sixty-million-dollar debt level within two years of its creation.

Under this reorganization scheme, over two thousand state civil servants employed at the hospital had a choice of either continuing as regular members of the hospital staff, in which case they would lose their civil service status, or being assigned by the university to the hospital for a period of two years, at which point they would have to relinquish their employment. The employees filed a complaint alleging that this action would violate the Colorado constitution. The complaint included alternative theories of unconstitutionality. If the legislation were construed to create an entity having the status of a *private* corporation, the plaintiffs claimed that it would violate Articles V and XI of the state constitution, which prohibit private corporations from receiving public funds or assets. If the legislation were construed to create an entity having the status of a *public* corporation, the plaintiffs claimed that it would violate Article XII, Section 13 (the State Civil Service Amendment) and Article XI, Section 3, which forbids state indebtedness except in limited circumstances.

The Supreme Court of Colorado, with two dissents, held that the legislation reorganized the hospital into a public corporation subject to all laws that governed the University of Colorado itself. The court reasoned that "whether University Hospital may be considered private depends upon whether 1) it is founded and maintained by private individuals or a private corporation and 2) the state is involved in the management or control of its property or internal operations" (804 P.2d at 143). Analyzing the first of these factors, the court determined that "[u]nder the facts before us, the reorganized hospital clearly cannot be characterized as a private hospital [because] the Regents, who are elected officials, established the hospital pursuant to authority granted in Article VIII, Section 5 of the Colorado Constitution and in Colo. Rev. Stat. Section 23-21-403(1)(a)." Regarding the second factor, the court determined that the state maintained control of the hospital by granting the regents power to appoint and remove the hospital directors and to control certain aspects of the hospital's budgeting, spending, and indebtedness. Thus, despite language in the legislation that expressly precluded the hospital from being considered an agency of state government, "it is evident that the Regents have not sufficiently divested themselves of power over the hospital to enable the new corporation to operate independently as a private corporation. Thus, we find that the reorganized hospital is still a public entity."

Since the hospital remained a state entity, and since the legislation would require over two thousand of the hospital's employees to relinquish their civil service status, the court held that the legislation violated the State Civil Service Amendment (Article XII, Section 13 of the state constitution), "which protects state personnel from legislative measures designed to circumvent the constitutional amendment." The court also held that the financing provisions of the reorganizing legislation, allowing the hospital to become indebted, violated Article XI, which prohibits the state from incurring debts.

A different type of structural issue arose in *Gulf Regional Education Television Affiliates v. University of Houston*, 746 S.W.2d 803 (Tex. 1988). The university, because it disapproved of the way in which certain finances were handled by Gulf Regional Education Television (GRETA), had summarily stopped issuing checks to GRETA and had basically dismantled its operations, which the university claimed to be under its control. GRETA hired its own attorney and sued the university. The university challenged GRETA's authority to bring suit, claiming that, as an auxiliary enterprise of the university, it was an arm of the state, and that the attorney general of Texas was the only person authorized to bring suit on the state's behalf. The court had to decide whether GRETA was an agency of the state, which could be represented only by the attorney general, or an independent organization that was merely affiliated with the university and could sue on its own behalf. Relying largely on a letter from the university to GRETA outlining the relationship between the two, the court sided with the university:

> The letter states that auxiliary enterprises are considered part of the University "family" and speaks of the necessity of following University policy on some matters to facilitate the meshing of their operations into the overall institution. Also, auxiliary enterprise employees are employees of the University. Even the language allowing auxiliary enterprises a *major* role in the selection of personnel suggests that the University reserves the option to participate. Finally, and most importantly, while auxiliary enterprises can enter directly into contracts, the University recognizes that, particularly in the case of major contracts, the contracting parties ultimately hold the University legally responsible [746 S.W.2d at 808].

Thus, as in the *University of Colorado* case, the institution's retention of considerable control over the affiliated organization demonstrated that the organization was part of the institution rather than an independent entity. GRETA was thus "subject to governance by the Board of Regents and . . . a suit brought by or on its behalf must be authorized by the Board of Regents."

The creation or reorganization of separate entities may also give rise to taxation issues. Resolution of these issues may also depend on the legal status of the organization in relation to the degree-granting entity and the degree of control the latter asserts over the former (as in cases like the *Colorado* case). In addition, the resolution of taxation problems may depend on the functions that the organization performs and their relation to the functions of the institution itself. In *Yale Club of Chicago v. Department of Revenue*, 574 N.E.2d 31 (Ill. 1991), for example, the court considered whether an alumni association that recruited for Yale University qualified for a purchaser's exemption from the state sales tax. The Yale Club of Chicago (YCC) is a nonprofit corporation that dedicates its efforts to promoting Yale University. One of its central purposes is to use its members to interview potential Yale students in the Chicago area. Although the club follows admissions guidelines prepared by Yale, it is not controlled in any way by the university and does not receive any funding from the university. The club sponsors social events for its members: Yale alumni, parents of alumni, and current Yale students.

The appellate court held that the YCC did not qualify for an educational or a charitable tax exemption under Illinois law. Regarding the educational exemption, the club had argued that "because Yale University is a school to which the exemption would apply, and the YCC is performing the same functions that Yale could, the exemption should apply to those activities performed [to further] Yale's educational objectives." In rejecting this argument, the court, under the statute and case law, reasoned that the club could claim exemption based on its relationship with Yale only if the club's activities were "reasonably necessary" to Yale's pursuit of its educational mission, and that:

> [R]egardless of how important a school's admissions goals may be to the school, we do not believe that a Chicago-based alumni association's recruitment activities on behalf of Yale in Connecticut are reasonably necessary to the administration of that school under the pertinent Illinois case law. We do not mean to minimize the value to Yale of the YCC's recruiting and fund raising. We conclude, however, that the YCC's activities are not so clearly related to the educational goals or administrative needs of Yale as to require this court to reverse the Department's denial of the purchaser's sales tax exemption [574 N.E.2d at 36].

Thus, the *Yale Club* case demonstrates that an affiliated organization performing beneficial functions for the institution does not necessarily qualify for a tax exemption even though the institution itself could receive an exemption on the basis of the same activities.

Creation of or affiliation with another entity may also raise questions about the application of state regulatory statutes. Various state statutes apply to state agencies or public bodies, for instance, but not to private entities. If a public institution creates or affiliates with another entity, the question would be whether the entity is sufficiently controlled by or related to the public institution that the former would be considered an agency or body subject to these state laws.

In *Weston v. Carolina Research and Development Foundation*, 401 S.E.2d 161 (S.C. 1991), for example, the issue was whether South Carolina's Freedom of Information Act (S.C. Code Ann. §§ 30-4-10 to 30-4-110) applied to the Carolina Research and Development Foundation, a nonprofit corporation operating "exclusively for the benefit of the University of South Carolina" (401 S.E.2d at 162), thus allowing the plaintiff media organizations to inspect the foundation's records. The Act applies to all "public bodies," defined in part as "any organization, corporation, or agency supported in whole or in part by public funds or expending public funds" (S.C. Code Ann. § 30-4-20(a)). The court determined that the foundation had received public funds on at least four separate occasions. The foundation had accepted almost 40 percent of the consideration the University of South Carolina received for selling one of the university's buildings; it had accepted over sixteen million dollars in federal grant money on behalf of the university and managed the expenditure of these funds for construction of an engineering center for the university; it had accepted grants of money from the city of Columbia and from Richland County, and a conveyance of real estate from the city, as part of the process of developing a real estate project for the university; and it had retained 15 to 25 percent of the total payments from private third parties under research and development contracts that the university had entered and channeled through the foundation. The court held that any one of these transactions qualified the foundation as a public body under the language of the Act. The foundation was thus required to permit the plaintiffs to inspect its records.

Similarly, in *State v. Nicholls College Foundation*, 564 So. 2d 682 (La. 1990), the inspector general of the state of Louisiana sought to view the records of the foundation pursuant to the state Public Records Act (La. Rev. Stat. Ann. §§ 44:1 et seq.). The foundation, a nonprofit corporation organized to promote the welfare of Nicholls College, had received funds from the Nicholls State University Alumni Federation, another nonprofit organization promoting the college's interests. The federation received its funding through a mandatory fee charged to all Nicholls students registered for more than seven credit hours; it then transferred 10 percent of these funds to the foundation. Under the Public Records Act, the foundation's records would be "public records" subject to public inspection if either (a) the Foundation were a "public body" or (b) the records concerned "the receipt or payment" of public funds. Using the second rationale, the Louisiana Supreme Court determined that the federation's close affiliation with Nicholls College (including its occupying a building on campus at only nominal rent, its use of state employees in its operations, and its inclusion in the college's yearly budget) made the federation a public body and that the student fees provided to the federation were public funds. The foundation's records of its receipt and use of these funds were thus public records subject to the Act (as, presumably, were the federation's records). The state's inspector general thus had a right to view the records. (For further clarifications in later proceedings, see *State v. Nicholls College Foundation*, 592 So. 2d 419 (La. 1991); see also Section 6.5.2.)

A quite different set of problems arises when an organization that is not already part of the institution's structure attempts to connect itself to the institution in some way. The general question then is whether an institution has any obligation to allow particular outside entities to become affiliated with it, and whether and how an institution may restrict the rights of such an organization to claim or publicly assert an affiliation with the school. In *Ad Hoc Committee of Baruch Black and Hispanic Alumni Association v. Bernard M. Baruch College*, 835 F.2d 980 (2d Cir. 1987), the plaintiff committee alleged that the college had improperly refused to recognize its proposed alumni association dedicated to the needs of minority students. This refusal, the committee argued, was a violation of the First Amendment and the Equal Protection Clause of the Fourteenth Amendment. The college countered that an officially recognized alumni organization, which included minority alumni, already existed and that the creation of another alumni association could overburden alumni with fund solicitations and thus dilute the current association's power to raise funds.

After a district court dismissed the committee's complaint, the U.S. Court of Appeals reversed and remanded, holding:

> [I]t is possible that plaintiffs could demonstrate that the College's selective
> denial of official recognition to their alumni association was improperly moti-

vated by discrimination based on political viewpoint or race. . . . In this case, the College has not yet offered any justification for its denial of recognition to the Black and Hispanic Alumni Association, and thus it is impossible to determine at this stage whether this action was motivated by a desire to "discourage one viewpoint and advance another" in violation of the First Amendment [835 F.2d at 982].

On remand, the district court held that universities generally have no responsibilities to their graduates, other than to supply transcripts. In particular:

> The First Amendment does not require colleges to fund or recognize alumni groups. Moreover, a college does not unlawfully impede the associational rights of its alumni when it declines to recognize an alumni group. . . . However, if a college does involve itself in establishing an alumni relationship structure, it must act non-discriminatorily [726 F. Supp. at 523].

The court then held that the committee could show no discrimination or other improper motive by the college in not recognizing the proposed alumni association, and that the college was thus not required to acknowledge and support the new association.[2]

In light of these case illustrations, it is clear that an institution must carefully structure and document its relationships with each organization it creates or with which it affiliates. In so doing, it should focus on the purposes it seeks to fulfill, the degree of control it needs to attain or retain, and the consequences of particular structural relationships on the respective rights of the parties to act autonomously of one another. In addition, the institution should consider how the structural arrangements would affect the applicability of particular regulatory and tax laws to the institution's activities, as well as ascertain whether the institution may be liable for actions of the other entity (see generally Section 2.3) and, if so, how the institution would control that risk (see generally Section 2.5).

Sec. 2.3. Institutional Liability for Acts of Others

2.3.1. Institutional tort liability. A tort is broadly defined as a civil wrong, other than a breach of contract, for which the courts will allow a damage remedy. While there is a broad range of actions that may expose an institution to tort liability, and any act fitting this definition may be considered a tort, there are certain classic torts for which the essential elements of the plaintiff's prima facie case and the defendant's acceptable defenses are already established. The two classic torts that most frequently arise in the setting of postsecondary education are negligence[3] and defamation, both

---

[2]Eventually, the parties resolved their dispute. By agreement, the Black and Hispanic Alumni Association is allowed to use the college's name and some office space, and the committee expressed willingness to discuss a possible relationship with the Baruch Alumni Association ("College Settles Lawsuit Filed by Minority Alumini," *Chron. Higher Educ.*, May 2, 1990, A2).

[3]The relevant cases and authorities are collected in an extensive series of annotations on the tort liability of elementary/secondary schools and postsecondary institutions in particular circumstances: 33 A.L.R.4th 632 (1984) (libel and slander by governing board members); 34 A.L.R.3d 1166 (1970) accidents due to condition of buildings or equipment); 34 A.L.R.3d

of which are discussed in this section; but other tort theories, such as common law fraud, are also appearing in lawsuits against colleges and universities. Various techniques are available to postsecondary institutions for managing the risks of tort liability, as discussed in Section 2.5.

A postsecondary institution is not subject to liability for every tortious act of its trustees, administrators, or other agents. But the institution will generally be liable, lacking immunity or some other recognized defense, for tortious acts committed within the scope of the actor's employment or otherwise authorized by the institution or subject to its control. In the *Lombard* case discussed in Section 2.3.1.1, for instance, the institution was liable for the acts of its janitors committed in the course of their building maintenance duties. And in *Butler v. Louisiana State Board of Education*, 331 So. 2d 192 (La. 1976), after finding that a professor had been negligent in allowing a biology experiment to be conducted without appropriate safeguards, the court asserted that the professor's "negligence must be attributed to the defendant university and to the state board of education."

Unless they are employees of the institution, torts caused by students generally will not result in liability for the institution. Medical students, moreover, will not always be considered agents of the institution. In *Gehling v. St. George's University School of Medicine*, 705 F. Supp. 761 (E.D.N.Y. 1989), *affirmed without opin.*, 891 F.2d 277 (2d Cir. 1989), for example, students who treated a colleague after he collapsed in a road race did not expose the medical school to malpractice liability, because they had not acted as agents of the school.

Even if an individual is not an employee of the institution, however, the college may be found liable under the concept of "gratuitous employee." In *Foster v. Board of Trustees of Butler County Community College*, 771 F. Supp. 1122 (D. Kan. 1991), a basketball coach had asked a student to pick up a potential recruit at the airport and drive him to a nearby motel. On his return from the airport, the student ran a red light and hit a truck, resulting in his death and the injuries of the recruit and the truck driver. Both injured parties sued the college.

A jury awarded the injured recruit $2.26 million against the college and the estate of the driver. On appeal, the college argued that it was not responsible for the actions of the student driver. The court, noting that the student's car was uninsured and unregistered and that the student had no valid driver's license, ruled that "the Butler Community College defendants could have discovered [the driver's] unfitness

---

1210 (1970) (accidents associated with the transportation of students); 35 A.L.R.3d 725 (1970) (accidents occurring during school athletic events); 35 A.L.R.3d 758 (1970) (accidents associated with chemistry experiments, shopwork, and manual or vocational training); 35 A.L.R.3d 975 (1970) (accidents due to condition of buildings, equipment, or outside premises); 36 A.L.R.3d 330 (1970) (injuries caused by acts of fellow students); 36 A.L.R.3d 361 (1970) (accidents occurring in physical education classes); 37 A.L.R.3d 712 (1971) (accidents occurring during use of premises and equipment for other than school purposes); 37 A.L.R.3d 738 (1971) (injuries due to condition of grounds, walks, and playgrounds); 38 A.L.R.3d 830 (1971) (injuries resulting from lack or insufficiency of supervision); 38 A.L.R.3d 908 (1971) (negligence of, or lack of supervision by, teachers and other employees or agents); 60 A.L.R.4th 260 (1988) (hiring or retaining incompetent or otherwise unsuitable teacher); 86 A.L.R.2d 489 (1962) (general tort liability); 1 A.L.R.4th 1139 (1980) (educational malpractice). All annotations are supplemented periodically with recent cases.

for the task had any investigation been conducted" (771 F. Supp. at 1128). The college had policies requiring students driving on the college's behalf to be licensed; the college's failure to follow its policies and its failure to ascertain whether the student was qualified to undertake the responsiblity it assigned him resulted in the court's determination that, for purposes of *respondeat superior* liability, the student was a "gratuitous employee" of the college. (Under the doctrine of *respondeat superior*, an employer is legally responsible for an employee's torts.)

In some circumstances a postsecondary institution may also be liable for the acts of its student organizations. In *Wallace v. Weiss*, 372 N.Y.S.2d 416 (N.Y. Sup. Ct. 1975), a libel action based on material printed in a student publication, the University of Rochester moved for judgment in its favor on the ground that it was not responsible for the acts of a student organization. The court denied the motion because "the question of the university's responsibility should not be determined until all the facts are presented at the trial." According to this court:

> [A university] may be in a position to take precautions against the publication of libelous matter in its student publications. . . .
> The university, by furnishing and providing to the organization money, space, and in lending its name, may well be responsible for the acts of the organization at least insofar as the university has the power to exercise control. By assisting the organization in its activities, it cannot avoid responsibility by refusing to exercise control or by delegating that control to another student organization [372 N.Y.S.2d at 422].

A 1981 New York State Court of Claims case, *Mazart v. State*, 441 N.Y.S.2d 600 (N.Y. Ct. Cl. 1981) (this volume, Section 4.13.4), contains a valuable analysis of an institution's liability for the tortious acts of its student organizations. The case concerned a libelous letter to the editor, published by the student newspaper at SUNY-Binghamton. The court's opinion addressed the liability theories proposed in *Wallace v. Weiss*. The court noted two possible theories for holding postsecondary institutions liable: (1) that the student organization was acting as an agent of the institution, and the institution, as principal, is vicariously liable for its agents' torts (the *respondeat superior* doctrine); and (2) that the institution had a legal duty to supervise the student organization, even if it was not acting as the institution's agent, because the institution supported or provided the environment for the organization's operation. In a lengthy analysis, the court refused to apply either theory against the institution, holding that (1) the institution did not exercise sufficient control over the newspaper to establish an agency relationship; and (2) given the relative maturity of college students and the rudimentary need and generally understood procedure for verifying information, the institution had no legal duty to supervise the newspaper's editorial process.

The second theory articulated in *Mazart*, the institution's purported "duty to control," became an issue in a case that, although it did not involve a tort claim, addressed issues similar to those addressed in tort actions against colleges. An attempt to hold a university responsible for acts of individual students and a faculty member was rejected by the Supreme Court of Vermont. In *Doria v. University of Vermont*, 589 A.2d 317 (Vt. 1991), an unsuccessful political candidate sued the University of Vermont under several sections of the state constitution, arguing that the university had a duty to supervise and control its students and faculty members in order to preserve his constitutional right to a fair election. The students had worked as telephone pollers for a faculty member and two newspapers; and, the plaintiff alleged, the questions and the ensuing poll results had given other candidates an unfair advantage.

The court rejected the plaintiff's "duty to control" theory, stating that "requiring defendant to strictly regulate and control the activity involved here, or any other student and faculty activity that might have an impact on the electoral process, would be basically inconsistent with the academic environment" (589 A.2d at 321). The result in *Doria* is deferential to the activities of faculty members and their students, particularly in matters related to curriculum or faculty research.

Even if the individual causing the injury is acting in a volunteer capacity rather than within the scope of employment, a college may be liable for injury caused by that person. In *Smith v. University of Texas*, 664 S.W.2d 180 (Tex. Ct. App. 1984), the court refused to award summary judgment to the university on its theory that the tortfeasor (the individual whose actions resulted in injury) was acting as a volunteer referee at a sporting event. Questions about the university's duty to supervise the event, the fact that these "volunteers" were also employees of the university, and unresolved questions of fact dictated that the matter go to trial.

An additional source of potential liability for colleges and universities is found in their status as landowners or landlords. The institution may be held liable for the acts of strangers on the campus under certain circumstances. In *Peterson v. San Francisco Community College District*, 685 P.2d 1193 (Cal. 1984), a student was assaulted in a campus parking lot by an unidentified man who had been hiding behind bushes and trees next to the parking lot. The court found that the college had breached its duty to invitees (individuals lawfully on the campus, whether they were students, staff, or members of the general public) because of the foreseeability of this incident, given the history of violent crime in the area in which the assault occurred. (For a discussion of campus security issues, see Section 4.17.)

Public institutions can sometimes escape tort liability by asserting sovereign or governmental immunity. Sovereign immunity is a common law doctrine that protects the state as an entity, and its agencies, from litigation concerning common law or certain statutory claims. (Immunity of a state and its agencies from suit in federal courts is also guaranteed by the Eleventh Amendment to the U.S. Constitution, and is discussed in Section 2.3.3.)

The availability of this defense varies greatly from state to state. While the sovereign immunity doctrine was generally recognized in early American common law, the doctrine has been abrogated or modified in many states by judicial decisions, state legislation, or a combination of the two.[4] When a public institution raises a defense of sovereign immunity, the court must first determine whether the institution is an arm of the state. Because the doctrine does not protect the state's political subdivisions, entities that are separate and distinct from the state are not protected by sovereign immunity. If the court finds that the institution is a state entity, then the court must determine whether the state has taken some action that would divest

---

[4]The cases and authorities are collected in Annot., "Modern Status of Doctrine of Sovereign Immunity as Applied to Public Schools and Institutions of Higher Learning," 33 A.L.R.3d 703 (1970 and periodic supp.).

the institution of sovereign immunity, at least for purposes of the lawsuit. Some states, for example, have passed tort claims acts, which define the types of lawsuits that may be brought against the state and the procedures that must be followed (see, for example, Florida's Tort Claims Act, Fla. Stat. § 768.28 (1985)). Other exceptions have been created by decisions of state supreme courts, such as in *Morash v. Commonwealth*, 363 Mass. 612 (1973), in which the Massachusetts Supreme Court ruled that the state could be sued for intentional torts or for a limited category of negligence claims.

In *Brown v. Wichita State University*, 540 P.2d 66 (Kan. 1975), *vacated in part*, 547 P.2d 1015 (Kan. 1976), the university faced both tort and contract claims for damages arising from the crash of an airplane carrying the university's football team. In Kansas, the university's home state, the common law doctrine of immunity had been partly abrogated by judicial decision in 1969, the court holding that the state and its agencies could be liable for negligence in the conduct of "proprietary" (as opposed to "governmental") activities. But in 1970 the Kansas legislature had passed a statute reinstituting the immunity abrogated by the court. The university in *Brown* relied on this statute to assert immunity to the tort claim. The court, after reconsidering the issue, vacated its prior judgment to the contrary and rejected plaintiffs' arguments that the statute was unconstitutional, thus allowing the university's immunity defense.

A public institution does not necessarily lose its immunity defense even if it subsumes—and then must answer for the actions of—an entity that, when independent, did not enjoy such immunity. In *Kroll v. Board of Trustees of the University of Illinois*, 934 F.2d 904 (7th Cir. 1991), a former employee of an athletic association sued the trustees for wrongful discharge. Although the athletic association had been a nonprofit corporation independent of the university, the state legislature had merged the association into the university through special legislation. The court ruled that the board had not waived its immunity when it absorbed the association, nor had the legislature so provided. Therefore, the university's immunity extended to acts of the former association, and the case was dismissed.

Sovereign immunity may be unavailable as a defense if the institution does not assert this defense in its response to a lawsuit. In *University of Kentucky Board of Trustees v. Hayse*, 782 S.W.2d 609 (Ky. 1989), the Kentucky Supreme Court rejected the university's claim of sovereign immunity in litigation over a tenure denial because it had not been asserted at the beginning of the proceedings. Sovereign immunity is also unavailable in situations where the state entity is not performing a governmental function, but one that a private entity could perform. For example, in *Brown v. Florida State Board of Regents*, 513 So. 2d 184 (Fla. Dist. Ct. App. 1987), a student at the University of Florida drowned in a lake owned and maintained by the university. In response to the university's defense of sovereign immunity in the ensuing wrongful death claim, the appellate court ruled that since the type of activity was not a governmental one, the university could not assert the immunity defense; once the university decided to operate a lake, it then assumed the common law duty of care to those who used it.

Although private institutions can make no claim to sovereign immunity, non-profit schools may sometimes be able to assert a limited "charitable" immunity defense to certain tort actions.[5] The availability of this defense also varies considerably from state to state. Overall, the charitable immunity defense appears to be more limited and less recognized than sovereign immunity. In a leading precedent, *President and Directors of Georgetown College v. Hughes*, 130 F.2d 810 (D.C. Cir. 1942), the court struck a common note by heavily criticizing charitable immunity and refusing to apply it to a tort suit brought by a special nurse injured on the premises of the college's hospital. And in *Mullins v. Pine Manor College*, 449 N.E.2d 331 (Mass. 1983) (discussed in Section 4.17.2), the Supreme Court of Massachusetts, noting that the state legislature had abrogated charitable immunity for torts committed in the course of activity that was primarily commercial (Mass. Gen. Laws ch. 231, § 85K), rejected the college's charitable immunity defense. The court also refused the college president's request to apply a good-faith standard, rather than a negligence standard, to his actions. (A good-faith standard would absolve the president of liability even if he were found negligent, as long as he had acted in good faith.) For a discussion of the continuing viability of charitable immunity, see Note, "The Quality of Mercy: Charitable Torts and Their Continuing Immunity," 100 *Harvard L. Rev.* 1382 (1987).

   2.3.1.1. Negligence. Higher education institutions are facing a growing array of negligence lawsuits, often related to students or others injured on campus or at off-campus functions. Although most college students have reached the age of majority and, theoretically, are responsible for their own behavior, injured students and their parents are increasingly asserting that the institution has a duty of supervision or a duty based on its "special relationship" with the student that goes beyond the institution's ordinary duty to invitees, tenants, or trespassers. For examples of recent negligence lawsuits against colleges and universities, see A. Stevens, "Personal-Injury Lawsuits by Students Are Endangering University Budgets," *Wall Street Journal*, Nov. 18, 1992, B1, B13.

   When the postsecondary institution is not immune from negligence suits under either sovereign or charitable immunity, liability depends, first, on whether the institution's actions fit the legal definition of the tort with which it is charged; and, second, on whether the institution's actions are covered by one of the recognized defenses that protect against liability for the tort with which it is charged. For the tort of negligence, the legal definition will be met if the institution owed a duty to the injured party but failed to exercise due care to avoid the injury. Whether or not a duty exists is a matter of state common law. In *Lombard v. Fireman's Fund Insurance Co.*, 302 So. 2d 394 (La. Ct. App. 1974), the duty was found to depend on the plaintiff's status while on the institution's property. The plaintiff was a student going to a class held on the second floor of a Southern University building. When the student reached the second floor, she noticed that it was slippery but continued to walk the fifteen feet to her classroom. The student slipped and fell, injuring her back. The slipperiness was caused by an excess amount of oil that janitors had placed on

[5]The cases and authorities are collected in Annot., "Immunity of Private Schools and Institutions of Higher Learning from Liability in Tort," 38 A.L.R.3d 480 (1971 and periodic supp.), and Annot., "Tort Immunity of Nongovernmental Charities—Modern Status," 25 A.L.R.4th 517 (1983 and periodic supp.). See also Annot., "Liability of Charitable Organization Under Respondeat Superior Doctrine for Tort of Unpaid Volunteer, " 82 A.L.R.3rd 1213 (1978 and periodic supp.).

the floors. In holding the university liable, the court determined that the plaintiff was an "invitee" on the university's property, as opposed to a trespasser, and applied the general tort law principle "that the owner of property owes to invitees . . . the duty of exercising reasonable care to keep the premises in a safe condition, or of warning invitees of hidden or concealed perils of which he knows or should have known in the exercise of reasonable care."

In addition to the general duty owed to invitees on its campus, there may be a "special relationship" between the institution and its students that gives rise to a duty beyond that owed to invitees or to the general public. For example, when the institution sponsors an activity such as intercollegiate sports, a court may find that the institution owes a duty to student athletes on the basis of a special relationship. In *Kleinknecht v. Gettysburg College*, 989 F.2d 1360 (3d Cir. 1993) (discussed in Section 4.15.6), a federal appellate court applying Pennsylvania law held that a special relationship existed between the college and a student who collapsed as a result of cardiac arrest and died during lacrosse practice, and that because of this special relationship the college had a duty to provide treatment to the student in the event of such a medical emergency. On the other hand, if the student is pursuing private social activities that the institution has not undertaken to supervise or control, a court may find that no duty exists. In *University of Denver v. Whitlock*, 744 P.2d 54 (Colo. 1987), for example, the Supreme Court of Colorado reversed a $5.26 million judgment against the University of Denver for a student rendered a quadriplegic in a trampoline accident.

The accident in *Whitlock* occurred in the front yard of a fraternity house on the university campus. The university had leased the land to the fraternity. Whitlock asserted that the university had a duty, based on a "special relationship," to make sure that the fraternity's trampoline was used only under supervised conditions. The special relationship, Whitlock asserted, arose either from his status as a student or the university's status as landowner and lessor to the fraternity. But the court held that the university's power to regulate student conduct on campus did not give rise to a duty to regulate student conduct or to monitor the conduct of every student on campus. Nothing the university had done justified Whitlock's reliance on the university for aid or protection, the court noted. Citing earlier cases in which no duty to supervise social activity was found (*Bradshaw v. Rawlings* and *Baldwin v. Zoradi*, discussed below), the court concluded that the university did not have a special relationship based merely on the fact that Whitlock was a student. Inspection of the lease between the university and the fraternity disclosed no right to direct or control the activities of the fraternity members, and the fire inspections and drills conducted by the university did not create a special relationship.

In determining whether a duty exists, the court may consider whether the harm that befell the individual was foreseeable. For example, in *Kleinknecht v. Gettysburg College*, discussed above, the court noted that the specific event need not be foreseeable, but that the risk of harm must be both foreseeable and unreasonable. In analyzing the standard of care required, the court noted that the potential for life-threatening injuries occurring during practice or an athletic event was clearly foreseeable, and thus the college's failure to provide facilities for emergency medical attention was unreasonable. In another case, *Nero v. Kansas State University*, 861 P.2d 768 (Kan. 1993) (discussed in Section 4.17.2), the Kansas Supreme Court ruled that the rape of a student by a fellow student in a residence hall was reasonably foreseeable because the alleged rapist had been found guilty of an earlier sexual assault on campus.

If the injury is unforeseeable, however, the court will refuse to create a duty. For example, in *Relyea v. State of Florida*, 385 So. 2d 1378 (Fla. Dist. Ct. App. 1980), the court rejected the claim that the institution had a duty to protect two students who had been abducted on the campus and murdered, since the action was unforeseeable. Similarly, the Supreme Court of Vermont refused to hold Norwich University liable for injuries to two railroad engineers shot by university students, because the injuries were not foreseeable and the students were legally adults (*Smith v. Day*, 538 A.2d 157 (Vt. 1987)).

Lack of foreseeability also undergirded a ruling by New York's highest court that the State University of New York at Buffalo had no legal duty to screen applicants who were ex-convicts for violent tendencies before admitting them. In *Eiseman v. State*, 518 N.Y.S.2d 608, 511 N.E.2d 1128 (N.Y. 1987), the court overturned rulings by two lower courts that the university and the state's prison system were jointly liable for an ex-convict's rape and murder of a fellow student:

> [I]mposing liability on the College for failing to screen out or detect potential danger signals in [the ex-convict] would hold the College to a higher duty than society's experts in making such predictions—the correction and parole officers, who in the present case have been found to have acted without negligence [518 N.Y.S.2d at 616].

On the other hand, when the institution attempts to prohibit, or to control, inherently dangerous activities in which its students participate, a court may find that it has a duty to those students. In *Furek v. University of Delaware*, 594 A.2d 506 (Del. 1991), the Supreme Court of Delaware ruled that the university's pervasive regulation of hazing during fraternity rush created a duty to protect students from injuries suffered as a result of that hazing. Furek, who had pledged the local chapter of Sigma Phi Epsilon, was seriously burned and permanently scarred when a fraternity member poured a lye-based liquid oven cleaner over his back and neck as part of a hazing ritual. After he withdrew from the university and lost his football scholarship, he sued the university and was awarded $30,000 by a jury, 93 percent of which was to be paid by the university and the remainder by the student who poured the liquid on Furek.

The university asserted on appeal that it had no duty to Furek. While agreeing that "the university's duty is a limited one," the court was "not persuaded that none exists" (594 A.2d at 517). Rejecting the rationales of *Bradshaw* (discussed below) and its progeny, the court used a public policy argument to find that the University did have a duty:

> It seems . . . reasonable to conclude that university supervision of potentially dangerous student activities is not fundamentally at odds with the nature of the parties' relationship, particularly if such supervision advances the health and safety of at least some students [594 A.2d at 518].

Although it refused to find a special duty based on the dangerous activities of fraternities and their members, the court held that:

> Certain established principles of tort law provide a sufficient basis for the imposition of a duty on the [u]niversity to use reasonable care to protect resident students against the dangerous acts of third parties. . . . [W]here there is direct university involvement in, and knowledge of, certain dangerous practices of its students, the university cannot abandon its residual duty of control [594 A.2d at 519–20].

The court determined that the university's own policy against hazing, and its repeated warnings to students against the hazards of hazing, "constituted an assumed duty" (594 A.2d at 520). Relying on Section 314A of the *Restatement (Second) of Torts*, the court determined that the "pervasive" regulation of hazing by the university amounted to an undertaking by the university to protect students from the dangers related to hazing, and created a duty to do so.

Once a legal duty is found to exist, the boundaries of that duty must be delineated. That is, a court must determine what standard of care the defendant will be held to under the circumstances. This issue was considered in *Mortiboys v. St. Michael's College*, 478 F.2d 196 (2d Cir. 1973). A student sued the institution for injuries sustained while he was skating on an outdoor ice rink maintained by the college for student pleasure skating. The student had fallen when his skate hit a one-inch-high lump of ice. The court refused to hold the college liable and articulated the standard of care owed by the college as "reasonable care under all the circumstances." For the college to be held liable, the dangerous condition would either have to be "known . . . or [to] have existed for such a time that it was [the college's] duty to know it." The court concluded that it was "a matter of speculation what caused the lump to be formed and whether it had been there for any substantial length of time." Expensive maintenance equipment, which would be used for indoor intercollegiate hockey rinks, "cannot reasonably be required of a college providing an outdoor rink for the kind of use contemplated and to which this rink was actually being put at the time of the accident."

But if the institution undertakes to provide a service, particularly to individuals who depend on the institution for their safety, the court may determine that a higher standard of care exists than that owed to a mere invitee. In *Nova University v. Wagner*, 491 So. 2d 1116 (Fla. 1986), the Supreme Court of Florida ruled that the university, which operated a residential rehabilitation center for children with behavioral problems, could be liable for actions of those children. Two residents at the center had escaped and, while at large, had killed one younger child and severely injured a second. The resident supervisors were university employees, and the court ruled that in operating the facility they had failed to meet the standard of reasonable care to avoid harm to the general public.

Even if a duty and the requisite standard of care have been established, the postsecondary institution still will not be found negligent unless the plaintiff is able to prove that the institution's breach of duty was the proximate cause of the injury. In *Mintz v. State*, 362 N.Y.S.2d 619 (N.Y. App. Div. 1975), the State University at New Paltz was found not liable for the deaths of two students who drowned on a canoe trip sponsored by an outing club. The court held that "it was the terrible, severe, and unforeseen weather conditions on the lake, and not any negligence on the part of the university, which were the proximate cause of the deaths herein."

Even when the plaintiff establishes all the elements for a prima facie case of negligence, as discussed above, the postsecondary institution may avoid liability by asserting and proving the defense of "contributory negligence" or "assumption of risk" of injury by the plaintiff.

While failing to find the plaintiff contributorily negligent, the court in the *Lombard* case (discussed above) acknowledged the acceptability of such a defense: "The invitee in a slip and fall case is under a duty to see dangers which are obvious and can be detected and avoided by the degree of care exercised by a reasonably prudent person"; under the facts presented, however, "it was not unreasonable for plaintiff to traverse the slippery floor [for only a few feet] after she discovered its slippery condition."

Liability also will not be imposed where the plaintiff is found to have assumed the risk of the injury that occurred. This "assumption-of-risk" doctrine was applied in *Rubtchinsky v. State University of New York at Albany*, 260 N.Y.S.2d 256 (N.Y. Ct. Cl. 1965), where a student was injured in a pushball game between freshmen and sophomores conducted by the student association as part of an orientation program. The court found that the student voluntarily assumed the risks of the game, since the student, who was offered various orientation activities, chose to play pushball.

Contemporary problems concerning the consumption of alcohol by college students provide a particularly useful illustration of negligence law's operation on campus. For postsecondary administrators and legal counsel, student drinking is a persistent and troubling issue. Vandalism of campus property is one consequence of alcohol-related student activity. Of more serious concern, however, are the injuries and deaths that result from accidents caused by student drinking, and the potential tort liability of postsecondary institutions for such occurrences.[6]

Surveys have found that alcohol is a factor in most incidents leading to injury or death of students or campus visitors. For example, a survey of claims by an insurer of a national fraternity between 1987 and 1991 showed that 86 percent of all fatalities, 86 percent of injuries resulting in paralysis, 72 percent of the serious injuries reported, 88 percent of psychological injuries, and 97 percent of reported cases of sexual abuse involved alcohol use (Harris & Harris 1992 Fraternity Claims Analysis). Although many institutions have attempted to curb drinking, especially by underage students, their success has been limited (C. Shea, "Party Schools Find the Image Is Difficult to Shed as Efforts to Curb Alcohol Abuse Have Limited Success," *Chron. Higher Educ.*, Apr. 7, 1993, A31–32).

Two cases from Pennsylvania and California consider the responsibility of postsecondary institutions to control student drinking on campus and at college-sponsored activities off campus. The cases also add generally to an understanding of negligence liability by analyzing the relationship between the institution and its students, and the ensuing legal duty of care arising from this relationship. Both of these cases have been relied on in subsequent cases where students claimed that the institution had a duty to protect them from the consequences of their own actions.

In *Bradshaw v. Rawlings*, 612 F.2d 135 (3d Cir. 1979), a sophomore at Delaware Valley College in Doylestown, Pennsylvania, was seriously injured in an automobile accident following the annual sophomore class picnic, which had been held

---

[6]Cases are collected in Annot., "Tort Liability of College or University for Injury Suffered by Student as a Result of Own or Fellow Student's Intoxication," 62 A.L.R.4th 81 (1988 and periodic supp.).

off campus. The injured student was a passenger in a car driven by another student, who had become intoxicated at the picnic. Flyers announcing the picnic were mimeographed by the college duplicating facility. They featured drawings of beer mugs and were prominently displayed across the campus. The sophomore class's faculty adviser, who did not attend the picnic, cosigned the check that was used to purchase beer. The injured student brought his action against the college, as well as the beer distributor and the municipality, alleging that the college owed him a duty of care to protect him from harm resulting from the beer drinking at the picnic. The jury in the trial court awarded the student, who was rendered quadriplegic, damages in the amount of $1,108,067 against all defendants, and each appealed on separate grounds.

The college argued on appeal that the plaintiff had failed to establish that the college owed him a legal duty of care. The appellate court agreed with this argument. Its opinion began with a discussion of the custodial character of postsecondary institutions. Changes that have taken place on college campuses in recent decades lessen the duty of protection that institutions once owed to their students:

> There was a time when college administrators and faculties assumed a role *in loco parentis*. . . . A special relationship was created between college and student that imposed a duty on the college to exercise control over students' conduct and, reciprocally, gave the students certain rights of protection by the college. . . . A dramatic reapportionment of responsibilities and social interests [has taken] place. . . . College administrators no longer control the broad arena of general morals. At one time exercising their rights and duties *in loco parentis*, colleges were able to impose strict regulations. But today students vigorously claim the right to define and regulate their own lives [612 F.2d at 139].

The concept of legal duty is neither rigid nor static. A court can create a new duty if, after evaluating the interests of the parties, it decides that a plaintiff should be entitled to legal protection against a defendant's conduct. According to the *Bradshaw* court, "The plaintiff in this case possessed an important interest in remaining free from bodily injury, and thus the law protects his right to recover compensation from those who negligently cause his injury. The college, on the other hand, has an interest in the nature of its relationship with its adult students, as well as an interest in avoiding responsibilities that it is incapable of performing."

The student had the burden of proving the existence of a legal duty by identifying specific interests that arose from his relationship with the college. Concentrating on the college's regulation prohibiting the possession or consumption of alcoholic beverages on campus or at off-campus college-sponsored functions, he argued that this regulation created a custodial relationship between the college and its students. A basic principle of law holds that one who voluntarily takes custody of another is under a duty to protect that person. The plaintiff reasoned that he was entitled to the protection voluntarily assumed by the college when it promulgated the regulation. The court dismissed this argument on the ground that the college regulation merely tracks state law, which prohibits persons under the age of twenty-one from drinking intoxicants.[7] By promulgating the regulation, then, the college did not

---

[7]In actuality the regulation went beyond the statute because it applied to every student regardless of age—a point that could have favored the plaintiff had the court been sensitive to it. Lawyers will thus want to exercise caution in relying on the court's analysis of this particular issue.

voluntarily assume a custodial relationship but only reaffirmed the necessity of student compliance with Pennsylvania law.

Besides creating new legal duties, courts may rely on existing case or statutory law that recognizes a legal duty arising from the particular relationship at issue. Some states impose a legal duty on a provider of intoxicants to an intoxicated person, making the provider responsible to third parties for the negligent acts of the intoxicated person (known as "social host" liability theories).[8] The plaintiff in *Bradshaw* argued that this duty, already existing in some states, also existed in Pennsylvania. By analogy, the college would then have a duty to protect third persons from the negligent acts of intoxicated student drivers, because it had furnished, or condoned the furnishing of, the alcoholic beverages. Pennsylvania does establish by statute a duty of care to third persons if the provider has a liquor license, but the Pennsylvania Supreme Court had held that a private host who supplies intoxicants to a visibly intoxicated guest may not be held civilly liable for injuries to third persons caused by the intoxicated guest's negligence. The *Bradshaw* court predicted that, since the Pennsylvania courts had refused to impose a legal duty on the private host, "it would be even less willing to find a relationship between a college and its student under the circumstances of this case." (The Pennsylvania Supreme Court has since ruled that individuals who knowingly serve intoxicants to minors are negligent per se and liable for any ensuing damages (*Congino v. Portersville*, 470 A.2d 515 (Pa. 1983).)

Consequently, unable to find a legal duty based on a special relationship existing as a matter of law, and unwilling to obligate the college by creating a new duty, the appellate court reversed the trial court's judgment of liability.

The *Bradshaw* case was quoted with approval in a California case, *Baldwin v. Zoradi*, 176 Cal. Rptr. 809 (Cal. Ct. App. 1981). In *Baldwin* the drinking occurred on campus in a dormitory room, and the plaintiff student was injured by an intoxicated student driver involved in a drag-racing contest. The plaintiff alleged that her dormitory room agreement, which prohibited alcoholic beverages in the residence halls, created a special relationship between her and the dormitory advisers and that the advisers therefore owed her a duty to enforce the provisions of the agreement. Although California courts are particularly willing to find a duty of protection where the defendant stands in a special relationship to both the victim and the person causing the harm, as was argued here, the *Baldwin* court determined that practicality prevented the imposition of a legal duty on the college to control student drinking. The prevalence of alcohol consumption on the modern college campus would make compliance with such a duty almost impossible, and the use of alcohol by college students is not so harshly judged by contemporary standards as to require special efforts to eradicate it.

Bradshaw and *Baldwin* have influenced many courts in subsequent litigation regarding whether the institution owed its students a duty to protect them from drinking, either their own or that of fellow students. In *Beach v. University of Utah*, 726 P.2d 413 (Utah 1986), an underage student who consumed alcohol on a university-sponsored field trip, in full view of the faculty adviser, fell off a cliff, sustaining serious injuries. The court refused to find a duty, based on special relationship, on

---

[8]For a survey and analysis of state law on social host liability, see Special Project, "Social Host Liability for the Negligent Acts of Intoxicated Guests," 70 *Cornell L. Rev.* 1058 (1985).

the university's part, despite the fact that the university had promulgated regulations against drinking and the fact that the faculty adviser had failed to enforce those regulations.

Similarly, in *Crow v. State of California*, 271 Cal. Rptr. 349 (Cal. Ct. App. 1990), a California appellate court rejected a student's claim that the university owed him a duty to protect him from assault by an intoxicated fellow student. The assailant, of legal drinking age, had become intoxicated at a party held in a university residence hall. On a previous occasion he had also assaulted a residence hall adviser. Despite the plaintiff's assertion that the fellow student was "inherently dangerous" and that the prior assault made this one foreseeable, the court found no duty to supervise either the beer party or the assailant.

And in *Van Mastrigt v. Delta Tau Delta*, 573 A.2d 1128 (Pa. Super. Ct. 1990), another university escaped liability when a student, incarcerated for murder, claimed that the alcohol and drugs he consumed at a campus fraternity party induced him to commit the crime, and that both the university and the fraternity were liable for his actions. The appellate court dismissed the claim, finding no duty and thus no breach.

With regard to liability for injuries related to alcohol consumption by students, college administrators, in all probability, may safely rely on *Bradshaw* and *Baldwin* insofar as they reject the notion of a general custodial relationship between the postsecondary institution and its students. Colleges with drinking regulations that do not merely track state law, however, could still be held liable, despite *Bradshaw*, if the regulations can be interpreted as a voluntary assumption of a specific custodial duty regarding alcoholic beverages (such as was found with regard to the University of Delaware's hazing regulations in *Furek*, discussed above). Although many college communities are responding to alcohol abuse by establishing task forces for responsible student drinking and by operating alcohol education clinics, there is also a trend toward initiating or strengthening institutional regulations on alcohol use. Since courts could construe such regulations to constitute voluntary assumption of custodial duty, institutions should have counsel review all drinking regulations.

Moreover, student alcohol abuse is increasingly recognized as a serious campus problem, and special efforts are being made to eradicate it (see D. Magner, "Alcohol-Related Problems Have Not Decreased on Most College Campuses, Survey Indicates," *Chron. Higher Educ.*, Nov. 9, 1988, A35, A37; see also T. Goodale (ed.), *Alcohol and the College Student*, New Directions for Student Services, no. 35 (Jossey-Bass, 1986)). Despite the apparent vitality of the *Baldwin* doctrine, the intractability of the problem and increasingly vigorous institutional efforts to control underage drinking and its associated violence may encourage students to continue to attempt to hold colleges responsible for injuries resulting from student alcohol abuse on campus or at college-sponsored activities off campus.

Additional sources of liability may arise in states where case or statutory law establishes civil liability for private hosts who furnish intoxicating beverages (see *Kelly v. Gwinnell*, 476 A.2d 1219 (N.J. 1984), and *Bauer v. Dann*, 428 N.W.2d 658 (Iowa 1988)) or for retail establishments that sell alcohol to minors. Sponsors of parties at which intoxicants are served, particularly to minors, could be found negligent under the social host doctrine. (See also G. Rinden, "Judicial Prohibition? Erosion of the Common Law Rule of Non-Liability for Those Who Dispense Alcohol," 34 *Drake L. Rev.* 937 (1985–86).) A court in such a jurisdiction could rely on this law to impose a legal duty on the institution when alcohol is served at college-sponsored activities. Many states also have Dram Shop Acts, which strictly regulate licensed establishments engaged in the sale of intoxicants and impose civil liability for dispensing intoxicants to an intoxicated patron. A college or university that holds a liquor license, or contracts with a concessionaire who holds one, may wish to enlist the aid of legal counsel to assess its legal obligations as a license holder.

Colleges and universities may also face liability for negligence with regard to employment decisions. The doctrine of negligent hiring, in which a plaintiff seeks to hold the employer responsible for injuries sustained as a result of violence by an employee, is recognized in approximately thirty states. Liability is found if the plaintiff can demonstrate that the employer knew or should have known that the employee was unfit for the job, often because of a history of violence or criminal activity. For a discussion of this issue, see C. Shattuck, "The Tort of Negligent Hiring and the Use of Selection Devices: The Employee's Right of Privacy and the Employer's Need to Know," 11 *Indust. Rel. Law J.* 2 (1989).

2.3.1.2. Defamation. The second typical tort asserted against a postsecondary institution, defamation, is committed by the oral or written publication of matter that tends to injure a person's reputation. The matter must have been published to some third person and must have been capable of defamatory meaning and understood as referring to the plaintiff in a defamatory sense. (See Sections 4.13.4 and 4.13.5 for a further discussion of defamation.) Defamation claims are also asserted against officials of the institution, such as deans or department chairs. These claims are discussed in Section 2.4.1.

One of the most important defenses against a defamation action is the conditional or qualified privilege of fair comment and criticism. An application of this privilege occurred in *Olsson v. Indiana University Board of Trustees*, 571 N.E.2d 585 (Ind. Ct. App. 1991). A prospective teacher, who had graduated from the university and had performed her student teaching under the supervision of one of its faculty, sued the university, claiming that a letter of reference written by a faculty member was libelous. The faculty member had described both the plaintiff's strengths and weaknesses with apparent candor.

The court ruled that the faculty member and the university were protected by a qualified privilege that may be asserted "if a need exists for full and unrestricted communication regarding matters on which the parties have a common interest or duty" (571 N.E.2d at 587). Such a privilege would cover any communication "if made in good faith on any subject matter in which the party making the communication has an interest or in reference to which he has a duty, either public or private, whether legal or moral, or social, if made to a person having a corresponding interest or duty" (571 N.E.2d at 587). Noting that the university had a responsibility to prepare teachers, the court ruled that this letter of recommendation was an appropriate occasion for the use of the qualified privilege.

Another conditional privilege that is important for administrators in state institutions is the privilege afforded to executive and administrative officers of government. In *Shearer v. Lambert*, 547 P.2d 98 (Or. 1976), an assistant professor at Oregon State University brought a libel action against the head of her department. While admitting that the statement was defamatory, the defendant argued that the privilege of government officers should be extended to lesser executive or adminis-trative officers, such as the head of a department. The court agreed, reasoning that, since "the privilege is designed to free public officials from intimidation in the dis-charge of their duties, we are unable to explain why this policy would not apply equally to inferior as well as to high-ranking officers." This qualified privilege is available, however, only where the defendant "publishes the defamatory matter in the performance of his official duties."

A constitutional "opinion" privilege based on the First Amendment is also sometimes assertable as a defense in a defamation action. Under this privilege, def-amation may be considered protected speech under the First Amendment if the speech meets certain requirements. In *Gertz v. Robert Welch*, 418 U.S. 323, 339–40 (1974), the U.S. Supreme Court stated that "there is no such thing as a false idea." *Gertz* has been interpreted to mean that an allegedly defamatory statement of opinion is actionable only if it implies that "undisclosed defamatory facts" have formed the basis for the opinion (*Restatement (Second) of Torts* § 566 at 170). An example of the application of this doctrine is found in *Belliveau v. Rerick*, 504 A.2d 1360 (R.I. 1986), in which a professor denied tenure by Providence College sued his department chair for def-amation, arguing that the chair had undercounted his "publications" and thus given false information. The court characterized the chair's statement as opinion and said that the chair and the plaintiff had a difference of opinion about what "counted" as a publication. Since the chair and the plaintiff had referred to the same list of "pub-lications," there were no undisclosed facts, and the court applied the constitutional privilege. Furthermore, noted the court, even if the chair's statements could be char-acterized as fact, rather than opinion, he was protected by a qualified privilege of commenting on the qualifications of tenure candidates, as required by his position.

If a defamation lawsuit is brought against a prominent administrator, trustee, or faculty member who would be considered a "public figure," the standard of proof changes to one of "actual malice," and the privilege to defame is thus broader than for defamation of private figures. In *Avins v. White*, 627 F.2d 637 (3d Cir. 1980) (discussed more fully in Section 8.3.2.5), for example, the question was whether the dean of the Delaware Law School was a public figure. After examining his role "as creator, chief architect, and the first dean" of the school, and his active involvement in the school's efforts to achieve accreditation, the court answered the question affirmatively.

If a person is a public figure, another person will not be held liable for de-faming him unless that other person's comment "was made with knowledge of its falsity or in reckless disregard of whether it was false or true" (*Garrison v. Louisiana*, 379 U.S. 64, 74 (1964)). Thus, to the extent that members of the academic community are placeable in the public-figure category, the institution's potential liability for defamation is reduced. Under factors such as those considered by the court in *Avins v. White*, however, it is unlikely on any given campus at any particular time that a substantial proportion of the community would be considered public figures.

2.3.1.3. Other sources of tort liability. One area of potential liability that combines several theories of liability revolves around the issue of acquired immune deficiency syndrome (AIDS, or HIV). Although the potential consequences of con-tracting AIDS are very serious, since the disease itself is usually fatal, the limited avenues of transmission of the disease mean that the liability of most institutions is limited. However, those with medical or dental schools face potential liability for infection of patients, staff, and the general public.

Students and staff who have AIDS or who are HIV-positive are protected by the Rehabilitation Act and the Americans with Disabilities Act (see Sections 3.3.2.5 and 7.5.4 in this volume) against discrimination on the basis of that status. Potential tort issues involving individuals who are HIV-positive could include invasion of privacy for breaches of confidentiality, negligent treatment by student health service personnel, assault and/or battery, fraud, and intentional or negligent infliction of emotional distress.

When an HIV-positive employee or student is involved in clinical programs, such as medicine or dentistry, in which that employee or student comes in contact with members of the general public in university-sponsored clinics, potential negligence liability exists if that employee or student infects a patient. Concern over this liability persuaded Washington University to deny further enrollment in the dental program to an HIV-positive dental student. The student sued the university under Section 504 of the Rehabilitation Act. (For discussion of this and related cases, see Section 7.5.4. in this volume.)

For analyses of an institution's potential liability related to AIDS, see S. Steinbach, "AIDS on Campus: Emerging Issues for College and University Administrators," 16 *Coll. Law Dig.* 113 (Jan. 9, 1986), and J. T. Ranney, "Background Paper on AIDS: Scientific and Legal Issues," 18 *Coll. Law Dig.* 211 (Mar. 31, 1988). For an examination of the legal issues surrounding health care professionals who are HIV-positive, see G. G. Keyes, "Health-Care Professionals with AIDS: The Risk of Transmission Balanced Against the Interests of Professionals and Institutions," 16 *J. Coll. & Univ. Law* 589 (1990).

Another potential source of tort liability, albeit a generally unsuccessful one for plaintiffs, is the doctrine of "educational malpractice." The claim (which may also be based on contract law, as discussed in Sections 2.3.2 and 4.1.3) arises from the duty assumed by a professional not to harm the individuals relying on the professional's expertise. An individual who performs "one of the professions, or a trade, calling or business, . . . [is] required to exercise that degree of skill (a special form of competence) and knowledge usually had by members of such profession or such trade in good standing" (S. Speiser, *The American Law of Torts* (Clark Boardman Callaghan, 1985), 319).

Although they often sympathize with students who claim that they have not learned what they should have learned, or that their professors were negligent in teaching or supervising them, courts have been reluctant to create a cause of action for educational malpractice. In *Ross v. Creighton University,* 740 F. Supp. 1319 (N.D. Ill. 1990), discussed in Section 4.15.2, a trial judge dismissed the claim by a former athlete that the university had failed to educate him. Asserting that the university's curriculum was too difficult for him, the former basketball player argued that Creighton had a duty to educate him and not simply allow him to attend while maintaining his athletic eligibility. The judge disagreed, ruling that the student was ultimately responsible for his academic success. The appellate court affirmed (957 F.2d 410 (7th Cir. 1992)).

A similar result was reached in *Moore v. Vanderloo,* 386 N.W.2d 108 (Iowa 1986), although the plaintiff in this case was a patient injured by a chiropractor trained at Palmer College of Chiropractic. The patient sued the college, claiming that the injuries were a cause of the chiropractor's inadequate training. After reviewing cases from other jurisdictions, the Iowa Supreme Court decided against permitting a cause of action for educational malpractice.

The court gave four reasons for its decision:

1. There is no satisfactory standard of care by which to measure an educator's conduct.
2. The cause of the student's failure to learn is inherently uncertain, as is the nature of damages.
3. Permitting such claims would flood the courts with litigation and would thus place a substantial burden on educational institutions.
4. The courts are not equipped to oversee the day-to-day operation of educational institutions.

The Supreme Court of Kansas reached a similar conclusion in *Finstand v. Washburn University of Topeka*, 845 P.2d 685 (Kan. 1993). Several students in the university's court-reporting program sued the university for consumer fraud (since, they alleged, it had falsely claimed that its program was accredited) and for malpractice (since, they alleged, the performance of students in the program on the state's certification test was worse than that of other students). Although the court found that the students' latter allegation was true, there was no evidence that the students' failure rate was caused by poor instruction. Citing *Ross* and a case in which New York's highest court rejected a malpractice claim against a school system (*Donohue v. Copiague Unified Free School District*, 391 N.E.2d 1352 (N.Y. 1979)), the Kansas Supreme Court refused to recognize such a claim for essentially the same reasons cited in *Moore*.

2.3.2. Institutional contract liability. The institution may be characterized as a "principal" and its trustees, administrators, and other employees as "agents" for purposes of discussing the potential liability of each on contracts transacted by an agent for, or on behalf of, the institution. The fact that an agent acts with the principal in mind does not necessarily excuse the agent from personal liability (see Section 2.4.2), nor does it automatically make the principal liable. The key to the institution's liability is authorization; that is, the institution may be held liable if it authorized the agent's action before it occurred or if it subsequently ratified the action. However, even when an agent's acts were properly authorized, an institution may be able to escape liability by raising a legally recognized defense, such as sovereign immunity. As mentioned in Section 2.3.1, this defense is available in some states to public institutions but not to private institutions.

The existence and scope of sovereign immunity from contract liability vary from state to state. In *Charles E. Brohawn & Bros., Inc. v. Board of Trustees of Chesapeake College*, 304 A.2d 819 (Md. 1973), the court recognized a very broad immunity defense. The plaintiffs had sued the trustees to compel them to pay the agreed-upon price for work and materials provided under the contract, including the construction of buildings for the college. In considering the college's defense, the court reasoned:

The doctrine of sovereign immunity exists under the common law of Maryland. By this doctrine, a litigant is precluded from asserting an otherwise meritorious cause of action against this sovereign state or one of its agencies which has inherited its sovereign attributes, unless [sovereign immunity has been] expressly waived by statute or by a necessary inference from such a legislative enactment. . . . The doctrine of sovereign immunity or, as it is often alternatively referred to, governmental immunity was before this court in *University of Maryland v. Maas,* 173 Md. 554, 197 A. 123 (1938), where our predecessors reversed a judgment recovered against the university for breach of contract in connection with the construction of a dormitory at College Park. That opinion, after extensively reviewing the prior decisions of this court, succinctly summed up [our predecessors'] holdings: "So it is established that neither in contract nor tort can a suit be maintained against a governmental agency, first, where specific legislative authority has not been given, second, even though such authority is given, if there are no funds available for the satisfaction of the judgment, or no power reposed in the agency for the raising of funds necessary to satisfy a recovery against it" (173 Md. at 559, 197 A. at 125) [304 A.2d at 820; notes and citations omitted].

Finding that the cloak of the sovereign's immunity was inherited by the community college and had not been waived, the court rejected the plaintiff's contract claim.

Regarding contract liability, there is little distinction to be made among trustees, administrators, employees, and other agents of the institution. Whether the actor is a member of the board of trustees or its equivalent—the president, the athletic director, the dean of arts and sciences, or some other functionary—the critical question is whether the action was authorized by the institution.

The issue of authorization can become very complex. In *Brown v. Wichita State University,* 540 P.2d 66 (Kan. 1975),[9] the court discussed the issue at length:

To determine whether the record establishes an agency by agreement, it must be examined to ascertain if the party sought to be charged as principal had delegated authority to the alleged agent by words which expressly authorize the agent to do the delegated act. If there is evidence of that character, the authority of the agent is express. If no express authorization is found, then the evidence must be considered to determine whether the alleged agent possesses implied powers. The test utilized by this court to determine if the alleged agent possesses implied powers is whether, from the facts and circumstances of the particular case, it appears there was an implied intention to create an agency, in which event the relation may be held to exist, notwithstanding either a denial by the alleged principal, or whether the parties understood it to be an agency.

"On the question of implied agency, it is the manifestation of the alleged principal and agent as between themselves that is decisive, and not the appearance to a third party or what the third party should have known. An agency will not be inferred because a third person assumed that it existed, or because the alleged agent assumed to act as such, or because the conditions and circumstances were such as to make such an agency seem natural and probable and to the advantage of the supposed principal, or from facts which show that the alleged agent was a mere instrumentality" [quoting *Corpus Juris Secundum,* a leading

_____

[9]This decision reverses and remands a summary judgment in favor of the university by the trial court. In a second opinion in this case, 547 P.2d 1015 (1976), the court reaffirmed (without discussion) the portion of its first opinion dealing with authorization. The tort liability aspects of these two opinions are discussed in Section 2.3.1.

legal encyclopedia]. . . . The doctrine of apparent or ostensible authority is predicated upon the theory of estoppel. An ostensible or apparent agent is one whom the principal has intentionally or by want of ordinary care induced and permitted third persons to believe to be his agent even though no authority, either express or implied, has been conferred upon him.

Ratification is the adoption or confirmation by a principal of an act performed on his behalf by an agent, which act was performed without authority. The doctrine of ratification is based upon the assumption there has been no prior authority, and ratification by the principal of the agent's unauthorized act is equivalent to an original grant of authority. Upon acquiring knowledge of his agent's unauthorized act, the principal should promptly repudiate the act; otherwise it will be presumed he has ratified and affirmed the act [540 P.2d at 74–75].

As mentioned in Section 2.3.1, the *Brown* case arose after the crash of a plane carrying the Wichita State football team. The survivors and personal representatives of the deceased passengers sued Wichita State University (WSU) and the Physical Education Corporation (PEC) at the school for breaching their Aviation Service Agreement by failing to provide passenger liability insurance for the football team and other passengers. The plaintiffs claimed that they were third-party beneficiaries of the service agreement entered into by WSU, the PEC, and the aviation company. The service agreement was signed by the athletic director of WSU and by an agent of the aviation company. The university asserted that it did not have the authority to enter the agreement without the board of regents' approval, which it did not have; that it did not grant the athletic director the authority to enter the agreement on its behalf; that the athletic director only had authority to act as the agent of the PEC; that WSU could not ratify the agreement because it lacked authority to enter it initially; and that, as a state agency, it could not be estopped from denying the validity of the agreement.

The court held that the PEC was the agent of the university and that the athletic director, "as an officer of the corporate agent [PEC], had the implied power and authority to bind the principal—Wichita State University." The court further held that failure to obtain the board of regents' approval did not invalidate the contract:

> The legislature has delegated to the board of regents the authority to control, operate, manage, and supervise the universities and colleges of this state. "For such control, operation, management, or supervision, the board of regents may make contracts and adopt orders, policies, or rules and regulations and do or perform such other acts as are authorized by law or are appropriate for such purposes" (K.S.A. 1974 Supp. 76–712). . . . However, no policy, rule, or regulation of the board of regents has been cited or furnished to this court regarding contract matters, and none can be found in the Kansas Administrative Regulations. . . . Absent any such rules or regulations, Wichita State cannot use the statute to deny the validity of the Aviation Service Agreement following execution and partial performance. Common honesty forbids repudiation now [540 P.2d at 76–77].[10]

[10]Not all courts will be so willing to find institutional authority in cases concerning public institutions. Other courts in other circumstances may assert that a person who deals with

The fact that the agreement had been partly performed was particularly persuasive to the court:

> Today, the use of separate corporate entities in collegiate athletics appears to be common, perhaps widespread, but indeed shadowy as to involvement and responsibility. Whether such arrangements should continue is not a question for this court. But when the involvement is such as presented in the instant case, then it begs logic to hold [that] no agency relations exist and that the principles thereof do not apply. Performance under the contract had begun and payments [were] made; this constituted tacit, effective approval of the Aviation Agreement Contract [540 P.2d at 77].

An institution sued on a contract can raise defenses arising from the contract itself or from some circumstance unique to the institution. Defenses that arise from the contract include the other party's fraud, the other party's breach of the contract, and the absence of one of the requisite elements (offer, acceptance, consideration) in the formation of a contract (see generally Section 9.1). Defenses unique to the institution may include a counterclaim against the other party, the other party's previous collection of damages from the agent, or, for public institutions, the sovereign immunity defense discussed earlier. Even if one of these defenses—for instance, that the agent or institution lacked authority or that a contract element was absent—is successfully asserted, a private institution may be held liable for any benefit it received as a result of the other party's performance. But public institutions may sometimes not even be required to pay for benefits received under such circumstances.

Institutions also face potential contract liability from policy documents or student catalogues (see Section 4.1.3) and from student athletes who argue that the college made contractually binding representations during the recruitment process (see, for example, *Ross v. Creighton University,* discussed in Section 4.15.2).

The variety of contract and agency law principles that may bear on contract liability makes the area a complex one, calling for frequent involvement of legal counsel. The postsecondary institution's main concern in managing liability should be the delineation of the contracting authority of each of its agents. By carefully defining such authority, and by repudiating any unauthorized contracts of which they become aware, postsecondary administrators can protect the institution from unwanted liability. While protection may also be found in other defenses to contract actions, such as sovereign immunity, advance planning of authority is the surest way to limit contract liability and the fairest to the parties with whom the institution's agents may deal.

2.3.3. Institutional liabilities for violations of federal constitutional rights. The tort and contract liabilities of postsecondary institutions (discussed in Sections 2.3.1 and 2.3.2) are based in state law and, for the most part, are relatively well settled. The institution's potential constitutional rights liability, in contrast, is primarily a matter

---

a public institution "does so at his peril," as in *First Equity Corp. of Florida v. Utah State University,* 544 P.2d 887 (Utah 1975), where the court upheld the university's refusal to pay for stocks ordered by one of its employees. (This case is discussed in Section 2.2.1.).

of federal law, which has undergone a complex evolutionary development.[11] The key statute governing the enforcement of constitutional rights,[12] commonly known as "Section 1983," reads:

> Every person who, under color of any statute, ordinance, regulation, custom, or usage, of any state or territory or the District of Columbia, subjects, or causes to be subjected, any citizen of the United States or other person within the jurisdiction thereof to the deprivation of any rights, privileges, or immunities secured by the Constitution and laws, shall be liable to the party injured in an action at law, suit in equity, or other proper proceeding for redress [42 U.S.C. § 1983].

Section 1983's coverage is limited in two major ways. First, it imposes liability only for actions carried out "under color of" state law, custom, or usage. Under this language the statute applies only to actions attributable to the state, in much the same way that, under the state action doctrine (see Section 1.5.2), the U.S. Constitution applies only to actions attributable to the state. While public institutions clearly meet this statutory test, private postsecondary institutions cannot be subjected to Section 1983 liability unless the action complained of was so connected with the state that it can be said to have been done under color of state law, custom, or usage.

Second, Section 1983 imposes liability only on a "person"—a term not defined in the statute. Thus, Section 1983's application to postsecondary education also depends on whether the particular institution or system being sued is considered to be a person, as the courts construe that term.[13] Although private institutions would usually meet this test because they are corporations, which are considered to be legal persons under state law, most private institutions would be excluded from Section 1983 anyway under the color-of-law test. Thus, the crucial coverage issue under Section 1983 is one that primarily concerns administrators of public institutions: whether a public postsecondary institution is a person for purposes of Section 1983 and thus subject to civil rights liability under that statute.

A related issue, which also helps shape a public institution's liability for violations of constitutional rights, is whether the institution is immune from suit in federal courts under Article III and the Eleventh Amendment of the U.S. Constitution.[14] If the suit is against the state itself, or if the suit is against a state official acting in his or her "official capacity" and seeks money damages that would come from the state treasury, the immunity from federal court suit will apply unless the state has consented to suit, expressly or by clear implication, thus waiving its immunity. (Com-

---

[11]In addition to federal *constitutional* rights, there are numerous federal statutes that create *statutory* civil rights, violation of which will also subject institutions to liability. See, for example, Sections 3.3 and 7.5 of this volume.

[12]Legal analyses of the various federal civil rights laws and extensive citations to important cases can be found in C. Antieau, *Federal Civil Rights Acts* (2d ed., Lawyers' Cooperative, 1980 and periodic supp.), and M. Schwartz & J. Kirklin, *Section 1983 Litigation: Claims, Defenses, and Fees* (Wiley Law Publications, 1986 and periodic supp.).

[13]Cases are collected in Annot., "Public Institutions of Higher Learning as 'Persons' Subject to Suit Under 42 USCS § 1983," 65 A.L.R. Fed. 490 (1991 and periodic supp.).

[14]The U.S. Supreme Court cases are collected in Annot., "Supreme Court's Construction of Eleventh Amendment, Restricting Federal Judicial Power over Suits Against States," 106 L. Ed. 2d 660 (1991 and periodic supp.).

pare *Soni v. Board of Trustees of the University of Tennessee,* 513 F.2d 347 (6th Cir. 1975) (waiver) with *Cowan v. University of Louisville School of Medicine,* 900 F.2d 936 (6th Cir. 1990) (no waiver).) As discussed below, the courts have used Eleventh Amendment immunity law as a backdrop against which to fashion a definition of "person" under Section 1983.

In a series of cases beginning in 1978, the U.S. Supreme Court dramatically expanded the potential liability of government entities under Section 1983. As a result of these cases, it is now clear that any political subdivision of a state may be sued under this statute; that such governmental defendants may not assert a qualified immunity from liability based on the reasonableness or good faith of their actions; that they may be liable not only for violations of an individual's federal constitutional rights but also for violations of other rights secured by federal law (*State of Maine v. Thiboutot,* 448 U.S. 1 (1980)); and that they may not require claimants to resort to state administrative forums before seeking redress in court.

The first, and key, case in this series is the U.S. Supreme Court's decision in *Monell v. Department of Social Services of the City of New York,* 436 U.S. 658 (1978). Overruling prior precedents that had held the contrary, the Court decided that local government units, such as school boards and municipal corporations, are "persons" under Section 1983 and thus subject to liability for violating civil rights protected by that statute. Since the definition of "person" is central to Section 1983's applicability, the question is whether the Court's definition in *Monell* is broad enough to encompass postsecondary institutions: Are all or some public postsecondary institutions sufficiently like local government units that they will be considered "persons" subject to Section 1983 liability?

The answer depends not only on a close analysis of *Monell* but also on an analysis of the particular institution's organization and structure under state law (see Section 6.2). Locally based institutions, such as community colleges established as an arm of a county or a community college district, are the most likely candidates for "person" status. At the other end of the spectrum, institutions established as state agencies under the direct control of the state are apparently the least likely candidates. This distinction between local agencies and state agencies is appropriate because the Eleventh Amendment immunizes states, but not local governments, from certain suits in federal courts. Consequently, the *Monell* Court limited its "person" definition "to local government units which are not considered part of the state for Eleventh Amendment purposes." And in a subsequent case, *Quern v. Jordan,* 440 U.S. 332 (1979), the Court emphasized this limitation in *Monell* and asserted that neither the language nor the history of Section 1983 evidences any congressional intention to abrogate the states' Eleventh Amendment immunity.

The clear implication, reading *Monell* and *Quern* together, is that local governments—such as school boards, cities, and counties—are persons suable under Section 1983 and are not immune from suit under the Eleventh Amendment, whereas state governments and state agencies controlled by the state are not persons under Section 1983 and are immune under the Eleventh Amendment. The issue in any particular case, then, as phrased by the Court in another case decided the same day as *Quern,* is whether the entity in question "is to be regarded as a political subdivision" of the state (and thus not immune) or as "an arm of the state subject to its control" (and thus immune) (*Lake County Estates v. Tahoe Regional Planning Agency,* 440 U.S. 391, 401–02 (1979)).

This case law added clarity to what once had been the confusing and uncertain status of postsecondary institutions under Section 1983 and the Eleventh Amendment. But courts continued to have difficulty determining whether to place particular institutions on the immune or nonimmune side of the liability line. A 1982 U.S. Court of Appeals case, *United Carolina Bank v. Board of Regents of Stephen F. Austin State University*, 665 F.2d 553 (5th Cir. 1982), provides an instructive illustration of the problem. The plaintiff in this case was a professor who had been dismissed from his position. He brought a Section 1983 suit against the board of regents, the president of the university, and four university administrators, alleging violations of his First Amendment free speech and Fourteenth Amendment due process rights. When the professor died during the course of the action, the bank, as administrator of his estate, became the plaintiff. The threshold question was whether the Eleventh Amendment barred the federal court from taking jurisdiction over the Section 1983 claims against the university, as opposed to the claims against the four administrators sued in their individual capacities (see this volume, Section 2.4.3). To answer this question, the court had to "decide whether the Board of Regents of SFA is to be treated as an arm of the State, partaking of the State's eleventh amendment immunity, or is instead to be treated as a municipal corporation or other political subdivision to which the eleventh amendment does not extend."

The district court determined that the Eleventh Amendment did not bar suit against SFA. The appellate court disagreed and dismissed the claim, characterizing the university as an arm of the state not subject to Section 1983 suits in federal courts:

> Our analysis will first examine the status of the Board of Regents of SFA under Texas law. . . . The district court omitted this particularly illuminating inquiry. Texas law provides: "'state agency' means a university system or an institution of higher education as defined in section 61.003 Texas Education Code, other than a public junior college." Tex. Rev. Civ. Stat. Ann. art. 6252-9b(8)(B) (Vernon). By contrast, Texas statutory definitions of "political subdivision" typically exclude universities in the category of SFA. . . .
>
> [W]e next examine the state's degree of control over SFA, and SFA's fiscal autonomy. SFA was created by the legislature in 1921, and in 1969 was placed under the control of its own Board of Regents. Texas' statutes authorizing the operation of SFA and providing for its governance are codified at Tex. Educ. Code Ann. § 95.01 *et seq.* and § 101.01 *et seq.* These statutes provide that members of the Board of Regents are to be appointed by the Governor with the advice and consent of the Senate. Tex. Educ. Code Ann. § 101.11. Texas also subjects SFA to some control by the Coordinating Board, Texas College and University System, which exercises broad managerial powers over all of the public institutions of higher learning in Texas. This Board consists of eighteen members appointed by the Governor with the advice and consent of the Senate. Tex. Educ. Code Ann. § 61.001 *et seq.*
>
> SFA's Board has the power of eminent domain, but "the taking of the land is for the use of the state." Tex. Educ. Code Ann. § 95.30. The University's real property is state property, Tex. Rev. Civ. Stat. Ann. art. 601b § 1.02; . . . and the funds used to purchase it were appropriated by the legislature from the general revenues of the state. . . . State law is the source of the University's authority to purchase, sell, or lease real and personal property. *See* Tex. Rev. Civ. Stat. Ann. art. 601b. The University's operating expenses come largely through legislative appropriation. 1981 Tex. Sess. Law Serv. ch. 875 at 3695. Even those public funds

which do not originate with the state are reappropriated to the University, *id.* ch. 875 at 3720, and become subject to rigid control by the state when received. *Id.* ch. 875 at 3719–21. The source and use of the University's monies is governed comprehensively, *id.* ch. 875 at 3716–28, and all funds are subject to extensive reporting requirements and state audits. *E.g., id.* ch. 875 at 3721.

In addition to the functions cited above, because SFA is a state agency it is subject to state regulation in every other substantial aspect of its existence such as employee conduct standards, promotions, disclosure of information, liability for tort claims, [workers'] compensation, inventory reports, meetings, posting of state job opportunities, private consultants, travel rules and legal proceedings. *See generally,* 1981 Tex. Sess. Law Serv. ch. 875 at 3790–3824. Also Texas courts have held repeatedly that suits against Universities within SFA's classification are suits against the state for sovereign immunity purposes. *Martine v. Board of Regents, State Senior Colleges of Texas,* 578 S.W.2d 465, 469–70 (Tex. Civ. App. 1979); *Lowe v. Texas Tech University,* 540 S.W.2d 297, 298 (Tex. 1976). In short, under Texas law SFA is more an arm of the state than a political subdivision [665 F.2d at 557–58].

The court carefully noted that its conclusion concerning Stephen F. Austin University would not necessarily apply to state universities in other states, or to all other postsecondary institutions in Texas: "Each situation must be addressed individually because the states have adopted different schemes, both intra and interstate, in constituting their institutions of higher learning." As an example, the court noted the distinction between Texas institutions such as SFA, on the one hand, and Texas junior colleges, on the other. Relying on Texas statutes, the court reaffirmed its earlier decisions in *Hander v. San Jacinto Junior College,* 519 F.2d 273 (5th Cir. 1975), and *Goss v. San Jacinto Junior College,* 588 F.2d 96 (5th Cir. 1979), that Texas junior colleges are not arms of the state and are thus suable under Section 1983:

Junior colleges, rather than being established by the legislature, are created by local initiative. Tex. Educ. Code Ann. § 130.031. Their governing bodies are elected by local voters rather than being appointed by the Governor with the advice and consent of the Senate. *Id.* § 130.083(e). Most telling is the power of junior colleges to levy *ad valorem* taxes, *id.* § 130.122, a power which the Board of SFA lacks. Under Texas law, political subdivisions are sometimes defined as entities authorized to levy taxes. Tex. Rev. Civ. Stat. Ann. art. 2351b-3. *See generally, Hander,* 519 F.2d at 279 [665 F.2d at 558].

Eleventh Amendment and Section 1983 case law since *United Carolina Bank* has developed along similar lines, with courts frequently equating the Eleventh Amendment immunity analysis with the "person" analysis under Section 1983 (see, for example, *Thompson v. City of Los Angeles,* 885 F.2d 1439 (9th Cir. 1989), upholding dismissal of a claim against the board of regents of the University of California). In the process, the law has become clearer and more refined. In *Kashani v. Purdue University,* 813 F.2d 843 (7th Cir. 1987), for example, the court reaffirmed the proposition that the Eleventh Amendment shields most state universities from damages liability in Section 1983 actions. The plaintiff, an Iranian graduate student, asserted that his termination from a doctoral program during the Iranian hostage crisis was based on his national origin. In dismissing his claim for monetary relief, the court suggested that, although the states have structured their educational systems in many ways and courts review each case on its facts, "it would be an unusual state university that would not receive immunity" (813 F.2d at 845). The court also reaffirmed, however, that under the doctrine of *Ex parte Young*, 209 U.S. 123 (1908), the Eleventh Amendment does not bar claims against university officers in their official capacities for the injunctive relief of reinstatement. In determining whether the defendant, Purdue University, was entitled to Eleventh Amendment immunity, the court placed primary importance on the "extent of the entity's financial autonomy from the state," the relevant considerations being "the extent of state funding, the state's oversight and control of the university's fiscal affairs, the university's ability independently to raise funds, whether the state taxes the university, and whether a judgment against the university would result in the state increasing its appropriations to the university." Applying these considerations, the court concluded that Purdue was entitled to immunity because it "is dependent upon and functionally integrated with the state treasury."

Other courts, particularly in the Third and Sixth Circuits, have applied a more expansive set of nine factors to resolve Eleventh Amendment immunity questions. These factors, known variously as the *"Urbano* factors" or *"Blake* factors" to credit the cases from which they derived, have gained increasing popularity in recent higher education cases. In the case that first articulated these factors, *Urbano v. Board of Managers of New Jersey State Prison*, 415 F.2d 247 (3d Cir. 1969), the court explained:

> (1) [L]ocal law and decisions defining the status and nature of the agency involved in its relation to the sovereign are factors to be considered, but only one of a number that are of significance. Among the other factors, no one of which is conclusive, perhaps that most important is (2) whether, in the event plaintiff prevails, the payment of the judgment will have to be made out of the state treasury; significant here also is (3) whether the agency has the funds or the power to satisfy the judgment. Other relevant factors are (4) whether the agency is performing a governmental or proprietary function; (5) whether it has been separately incorporated; (6) the degree of autonomy over its operations; (7) whether it has the power to sue and be sued and to enter into contracts; (8) whether its property is immune from state taxation; and (9) whether the sovereign has immunized itself from responsibility for the agency's operations [415 F.2d at 250–51; numbering added].

This nine-factor test was applied to higher education in *Hall v. Medical College of Ohio at Toledo*, 742 F.2d 299 (6th Cir. 1984), a case in which a student who had been dismissed from medical school alleged racial discrimination in violation of Section 1983. The district court, looking generally to the extent of the school's functional autonomy and fiscal independence, had held that the school was an "arm of the state" entitled to Eleventh Amendment immunity. Although the appellate court affirmed the district court, it emphasized that the nine-part *Urbano/Blake* test "is the better approach for examining the 'peculiar circumstances' of the different colleges and universities."

Similarly, the court in *Skehan v. State System of Higher Education*, 815 F.2d 244 (3d Cir. 1987), used the *Urbano/Blake* test to determine that the defendant State System "is, effectively, a state agency and therefore entitled to the protection of the eleventh amendment." In contrast, however, the court in *Kovats v. Rutgers, The State*

University, 822 F.2d 1303 (3d Cir. 1987), determined that Rutgers is not an arm of the state of New Jersey and thus is not entitled to Eleventh Amendment immunity. The case involved Section 1983 claims of faculty members who had been dismissed. Focusing on *Urbano/Blake* factors 2 and 3, the court considered whether a judgment against Rutgers would be paid by Rutgers or the state and determined that Rutgers in its discretion could pay the judgment either with segregated nonstate funds or with nonstate funds that were commingled with state funds. Rutgers argued that, if it paid the judgment, the state would have to increase its appropriations to the university, thus affecting the state treasury. The court held that such an appropriations increase following a judgment would be in the legislature's discretion, and that "(i)f the state structures an entity in such a way that the other relevant criteria indicate it to be an arm of the state, then immunity may be retained even where damage awards are funded by the state at the state's discretion." Then, considering the other *Urbano/Blake* factors, the court determined that, although Rutgers "is now, at least in part, a state-created entity which serves a state purpose with a large degree of state financing, it remains under state law an independent entity able to direct its own actions and responsible on its own for judgments resulting from those actions."

Since the Eleventh Amendment provides states with immunity only from federal court suits, it does not apply to Section 1983 suits in state courts. The definition of "person" under Section 1983 is thus the sole focus of the analysis. In *Will v. Michigan Department of State Police*, 491 U.S. 58 (1989), the U.S. Supreme Court ruled that neither the state nor state officials sued in their official capacities are "persons" for the purposes of Section 1983 suits in state courts. But in *Howlett v. Rose*, 496 U.S. 356 (1990), the Court reaffirmed that Section 1983 suits may be brought in state courts against other government entities that are considered "persons" under Section 1983. In such cases *state* law protections of sovereign immunity and other state procedural limitations on suits against the sovereign (see *Felder v. Casey*, 487 U.S. 131 (1988)) will not generally be available to the government defendants.

Fuchilla v. Layman, 537 A.2d 652 (N.J. 1988), provides an example of a higher education case brought in state court under Section 1983. The case also illustrates how courts may continue to rely on Eleventh Amendment analysis in such suits, even though the amendment's immunity applies only in federal courts. A former employee of the University of Medicine and Dentistry of New Jersey sued the university, alleging sexual harassment. The Supreme Court of New Jersey reasoned that if "a governmental entity enjoys immunity as the state or its alter ego under the eleventh amendment, it cannot be liable as a 'person' under Section 1983." The court then looked at Eleventh Amendment law—specifically, the nine-factor *Urbano/Blake* test—to determine whether UMDNJ is a "person" under Section 1983. The court concluded that the "factors tip in favor of finding [that] the UMDNJ is not the alter ego of the State for eleventh amendment purposes and, therefore, is liable as a person under Section 1983."

Even if the institution is characterized as a Section 1983 "person" with no Eleventh Amendment immunity, it may still be able in particular cases to avoid liability. According to *Monell:*

> Local governing bodies . . . can be sued directly under [Section] 1983 . . . [where] the action that is alleged to be unconstitutional implements or executes a policy statement, ordinance, regulation, or decision officially adopted and pro-

mulgated by the body's officers. Moreover, although the touchstone of the Section 1983 action against a government body is an allegation that official policy is responsible for a deprivation of rights protected by the Constitution, local governments, like every other Section 1983 "person," by the very terms of the statute, may be sued for constitutional deprivations visited pursuant to governmental "custom" even though such a custom has not received formal approval through the body's official decision-making channels. . . .

On the other hand, the language of Section 1983 . . . compels the conclusion that Congress did not intend municipalities to be held liable unless action pursuant to official municipal policy of some nature caused a constitutional tort. In particular, we conclude that a municipality cannot be held liable solely because it employs a tortfeasor—or, in other words, a municipality cannot be held liable under Section 1983 on a *respondeat superior* theory [436 U.S. at 690–91].

Thus, along with its expansion of the "persons" suable under Section 1983, *Monell* also clarifies and limits the types of government actions for which newly suable entities can be held liable.

The liability of political subdivisions under the *Monell* decision is not limited by the "qualified immunity" that officers and employees would have if sued personally (see this volume, Section 2.4.3). This type of immunity claim was rejected by the U.S. Supreme Court in *Owen v. City of Independence*, 445 U.S. 622 (1980):

[N]either history nor policy supports a construction of Section 1983 that would justify the qualified immunity. . . . We hold, therefore, that the municipality may not assert the good faith of its officers or agents as a defense to liability under Section 1983.

. . . [O]wing to the qualified immunity enjoyed by most government officials, see *Scheuer v. Rhodes*, 416 U.S. 232 (1974), many victims of municipal malfeasance would be left remediless if the city were also allowed to assert a good-faith defense.

. . . We believe that today's decision, together with prior precedents in this area, properly allocates [the costs of official misconduct] among the three principals in the scenario of the Section 1983 cause of action: the victim of the constitutional deprivation; the officer whose conduct caused the injury; and the public, as represented by the municipal entity. The innocent individual who is harmed by an abuse of governmental authority is assured that he will be compensated for his injury. The offending official . . . may go about his business secure in the knowledge that a qualified immunity will protect him from personal liability for damages that are more appropriately chargeable to the populace as a whole. And the public will be forced to bear only the costs of injury inflicted by the "execution of a government's policy or custom, whether made by its lawmakers or by those whose edicts or acts may fairly be said to represent official policy" [445 U.S. at 638, 651, 657; quoting *Monell v. New York City Dept. of Social Services*, 436 U.S. at 694].

Although *Monell* and *Owen* made clear that political subdivisions could be held liable under Section 1983 for compensatory monetary damages, the cases did not determine whether political subdivisions could also be liable for punitive damages. In an earlier case, *Carey v. Piphus*, 435 U.S. 247 (1978), the Supreme Court had held that punitive damages could be assessed in an appropriate case against a government employee "with the specific purpose of deterring or punishing violations of constitutional rights." But in *City of Newport v. Fact Concerts, Inc.,* 453 U.S. 247 (1981), the Court refused to extend this ruling to political subdivisions. The Court found that the goal of deterrence would not be served by awards of punitive damages against political subdivisions, since it was far from clear that policy-making officials would be deterred from wrongdoing by the knowledge that awards could be assessed against their governments.

In another case, *Memphis Community School District v. Stachura,* 477 U.S. 299 (1986), the Court also determined that compensatory damages awards in Section 1983 cases may not be based on the "value" or "importance" of the constitutional right that has been violated. Citing *Carey v. Piphus,* the Court underscored that actual injuries are the only permissible bases for an award of compensatory damages caused by the denial of a constitutional right.

Various procedural issues of importance to colleges and universities have also arisen in the wake of *Monell.* For instance, in *Patsy v. Board of Regents of the State of Florida,* 457 U.S. 496 (1982), a suit by a staff employee of Florida International University alleging race and sex discrimination, the U.S. Supreme Court had to decide whether a Section 1983 plaintiff must "exhaust" available state administrative remedies before a court may consider her claim (see Section 1.4.2.5). Invoking such an exhaustion requirement would be yet another way for governmental defendants to ameliorate the impact of decisions expanding Section 1983 liability. For many years preceding *Patsy,* however, the Court had refused to impose an exhaustion requirement on Section 1983 suits. The Court in *Patsy* declined the Florida board of regents' invitation to overrule this line of decisions, because "Congress is vested with the power to prescribe the basic procedural scheme under which claims may be heard in federal courts" and "a court should not defer the exercise of jurisdiction under a federal statute unless it is consistent with . . . [Congress's] intent" (which it was not here).[15] And in *Burnett v. Grattan,* 468 U.S. 42 (1984), the Court rejected yet another procedural device for limiting the impact of Section 1983. The defendant, a state university, argued that the federal court should "borrow" and apply a six-month state statute of limitations to the case (see Section 1.4.2.4)—the same time period as applied to the filing of discrimination complaints with the state human rights commission—and that the plaintiffs' complaint should be dismissed because it was not filed within six months of the harm (employment discrimination) that the plaintiffs alleged. The Court concluded that, in order to accomplish the goals of Section 1983, it was necessary to apply a longer, three-year, time period for bringing this particular suit—the same period generally allowed for civil actions under the law of the state whose statutes of limitations were being borrowed.

Given these substantial and complex legal developments, at least some public postsecondary institutions are now subject to Section 1983 liability, both in federal courts and state courts, for violations of federal constitutional rights. Those that are subject may be exposed to extensive judicial remedies, which they are unlikely to

[15]Even though exhaustion is not required under *Patsy,* the unreviewed findings of fact of a state administrative agency may nevertheless have a "preclusive" effect on subsequent federal litigation under Section 1983, as long as the parties in the administrative proceeding had an adequate opportunity to litigate disputed issues (*University of Tennessee v. Elliott,* 478 U.S. 788 (1986); see this volume, Section 1.4.4)).

escape by using procedural technicalities. Moreover, institutions and systems that can escape Section 1983 liability because they are not "persons" or are otherwise protected by the Eleventh Amendment will likely find that they are subject in other ways to liability for violations of constitutional rights. They will be suable under other federal civil rights laws establishing statutory rights that parallel those protected by the Constitution (see, for example, Section 3.3.2, this volume). They may also be suable under similar state civil rights laws or under state statutes similar to Section 1983 that authorize access to state courts for the vindication of federal or state constitutional rights. Moreover, trustees and administrators of public institutions are sometimes suable in their individual capacities under Section 1983 even where the institution could not be sued (see Section 2.4.3).

In such a legal environment, administrators should foster full and fair enjoyment of federal civil rights on their campuses. Even when a particular institution's Section 1983 status is unclear, administrators should seek to comply with the spirit of Section 1983, which compels that where officials "may harbor doubt about the lawfulness of their intended actions . . . [they should] err on the side of protecting citizens' . . . rights" (*Owen*, 445 U.S. at 652).

Sec. 2.4. Personal Liability of Trustees, Administrators, and Staff

2.4.1. Personal tort liability. A trustee, administrator, or other agent of a postsecondary institution who commits a tort may be liable even if the tort was committed while he or she was conducting the institution's affairs.[16] The individual must actually have committed the tortious act, directed it, or otherwise participated in its commission, however, before personal liability will attach. The individual will not be personally liable for torts of other institutional agents merely because he or she represents the institution for whom the other agents were acting. The elements of a tort and the defenses against a tort claim (see Section 2.3.1) in suits against the individual personally are generally the same as those in suits against the institution. An individual sued in his or her personal capacity, however, is usually not shielded by the sovereign immunity and charitable immunity defenses that sometimes protect the institution.

If a trustee, administrator, or other institutional agent commits a tort while acting on behalf of the institution and within the scope of the authority delegated to him or her, both the individual and the institution may be liable for the harm caused by the tort. But the institution's potential liability does not relieve the individual of any measure of liability; the injured party could choose to collect a judgment solely from the individual, and the individual would have no claim against the institution for any part of the judgment he or she was required to pay. However, where individual and institution are both potentially liable, the individual may receive practical relief from liability if the injured party squeezes the entire judgment from the institution or the institution chooses to pay the entire amount.

[16]Cases and authorities are collected in Annot., "Personal Liability of Public School Teacher in Negligence Action for Personal Injury or Death of Student," 34 A.L.R.4th 228 (1984 and periodic supp.); Annot., "Personal Liability of Public School Executive or Administrative Officer in Negligence Action for Personal Injury or Death of Student," 35 A.L.R.4th 272 (1985 and periodic supp.); Annot., "Personal Liability in Negligence Action of Public School Employee, Other Than Teacher or Executive or Administrative Officer, for Personal Injury or Death of Student," 35 A.L.R.4th 328 (1985 and periodic supp.).

If a trustee, administrator, or other institutional agent commits a tort while acting outside the scope of delegated authority, he or she may be personally liable but the institution would not be liable (Section 2.3.1). Thus, the injured party could obtain a judgment only against the individual, and only the individual would be responsible for satisfying the judgment. The institution, however, may affirm the individual's unauthorized action ("affirmance" is similar to the "ratification" discussed in connection with contract liability in Section 2.3.2), in which case the individual will be deemed to have acted within his or her authority, and both institution and individual will be potentially liable. (For a discussion of potential personal liability of trustees and administrators for decisions with environmental consequences, see Comment, "Whistling Past the Waste Site: Directors' and Officers' Personal Liability for Environmental Decisions and the Role of Liability Insurance Coverage," 140 *U. Pa. L. Rev.* 241 (1991); see also Section 7.2.15.)

Officers and employees of public institutions can sometimes escape tort liability by proving the defense of "official immunity." For this defense to apply, the individual's act must have been within the scope of his or her authority and must have been a discretionary act involving policy judgment, as opposed to a "ministerial duty" (the person performing such a duty has little or no discretion with regard to the choices to be made). Because it involves this element of discretion and policy judgment, official immunity is more likely to apply to a particular individual the higher in the authority hierarchy he is.

For example, in *Staheli v. Smith*, 548 So. 2d 1299 (Miss. 1989), the Supreme Court of Mississippi was asked to determine whether the dean of the School of Engineering at the University of Mississippi was a public official for purposes of governmental immunity against a defamation lawsuit. A faculty member sued the dean, stating that a letter from the dean recommending against tenure for the plaintiff was libelous. The court found that the dean was, indeed, a public figure and thus protected by qualified government immunity. Since the faculty handbook authorized administrators to make "appropriate" comments, and since making a subjective evaluation of a faculty member's performance is a discretionary, rather than a ministerial, duty, the court found that the dean had acted within the scope of his authority and had not lost the privilege by exceeding his authority.

Malpractice claims against doctors employed by hospitals affilitated with public institutions provide a potential opportunity for an immunity defense. The breadth of coverage is dependent upon state law. For example, in *Rivera v. Hospital Universitario*, 762 F. Supp. 15 (D.P.R. 1991), the court applied Puerto Rico law to determine that medical school professors who worked part-time as attending physicians at the university hospital were employees, not independent contractors, and thus shared the university's governmental immunity.

On the other hand, the Supreme Court of Virginia in *James v. Jane*, 267 S.E.2d 108 (Va. 1980), rejected a defense of sovereign immunity asserted by physicians who were full-time faculty members at the state university medical center and members of the hospital staff. The defendants had argued that, as state employees, they were immune from a suit charging them with negligence in their treatment of certain patients at the university's hospital. The trial court accepted the physicians' defense. Although agreeing that under Virginia law certain state employees and agents could share the state's own sovereign immunity, the Virginia Supreme Court reversed the trial court and refused to extend this immunity to these particular employees.

In reaching its decision, the appellate court analyzed the current status of the immunity defense and the circumstances in which its assertion is appropriate:

> The Commonwealth of Virginia functions only through its elected and appointed officials and its employees. If, because of the threat of litigation, or for any other reason, they cannot act, or refuse to act, the state also ceases to act. Although a valid reason exists for state employee immunity, the argument for such immunity does not have the same strength it had in past years. This is because of the intrusion of government into areas formerly private, and because of the thousandfold increase in the number of government employees. We find no justification for treating a present-day government employee as absolutely immune from tort liability, just as if he were an employee of an eighteenth-century sovereign. It is proper that a distinction be made between the state, whose immunity is absolute unless waived, and the employees and officials of the state, whose immunity is qualified, depending upon the function they perform and the manner of performance. Certain state officials and state employees must of necessity enjoy immunity in the performance of their duties. These officers are inclusive of, but not limited to, the governor, state officials, and judges. They are required by the Constitution and by general law to exercise broad discretionary powers, often involving both the determination and implementation of state policy.
>
> Admittedly, no single all-inclusive rule can be enunciated or applied in determining entitlements to sovereign immunity. . . . A state employee who acts wantonly, or in a culpable or grossly negligent manner, is not protected. And neither is the employee who acts beyond the scope of his employment, who exceeds his authority and discretion, and who acts individually.
>
> The difficulty in application comes when a state employee is charged with simple negligence, a failure to use ordinary or reasonable care in the performance of some duty, and then claims the immunity of the state. Under such circumstances we examine the function this employee was performing and the extent of the state's interest and involvement in that function. Whether the act performed involves the use of judgment and discretion is a consideration, but it is not always determinative. Virtually every act performed by a person involves the exercise of some discretion. Of equal importance is the degree of control and direction exercised by the state over the employee whose negligence is involved. . . .
>
> In the case under review, the paramount interest of the Commonwealth of Virginia is that the University of Virginia operate a good medical school and that it be staffed with efficient and competent administrators and professors. The state is of course interested and concerned that patients who are treated at the university hospital receive proper medical care. However, the state has this same concern for every patient who is treated in any private hospital or by any doctor throughout the commonwealth. This is evidenced by the numerous statutes enacted by the General Assembly of Virginia designed to assure adequate medical care and medical facilities for the people of the state. The state's interest and the state's involvement, in its sovereign capacity, in the treatment of a specific patient by an attending physician in the university hospital are slight: equally slight is the control exercised by the state over the physician in the treatment accorded that patient. This interest and involvement is not of such moment and value to the commonwealth as to entitle [the defendants] to the immunity enjoyed by the state [267 S.E.2d at 113-14].

The "sovereign" or "state employee" immunity thus created by the Virginia court is potentially broader than the "official immunity" recognized in some other jurisdictions. In states recognizing "official immunity," the likelihood of successfully invoking the defense is, as mentioned, proportional to the officer's or employee's level in the authority hierarchy. This official immunity doctrine seeks to protect the discretionary and policy-making functions of higher-level decision makers, a goal that the *James v. Jane* opinion also recognized. The sovereign immunity defense articulated in *James*, however, encompasses an additional consideration: the degree of state control over the employee's job functions. In weighing this additional factor, the Virginia sovereign immunity doctrine also seeks to protect state employees who are so closely directed by the state that they should not bear individual responsibility for negligent acts committed within the scope of this controlled employment. Sovereign immunity Virginia-style may thus extend to lower-echelon employees not reached by official immunity. Although *James* held that this theory does not apply to physicians treating patients in a state university medical center, the theory could perhaps be applied to other postsecondary employees—such as middle- or low-level administrative personnel (*Messina v. Burden*, 321 S.E.2d 657 (Va. 1984), concerning the superintendent of buildings at a community college); support staff; or even medical interns at a state university hospital (*Lawhorne v. Harlan*, 200 S.E.2d 569 (Va. 1973)).

Although *James* is binding law only in Virginia, it illustrates nuances in the doctrine of personal tort immunity that may also exist, or may now develop, in other states. When contrasted with the cases relying on the official immunity doctrine, *James* also illustrates the state-by-state variations that can exist in this area of the law.

In *Tarasoff v. Regents of the University of California*, 551 P.2d 334 (Cal. 1976), the parents of a girl murdered by a psychiatric patient at the university hospital sued the university regents, four psychotherapists employed by the hospital, and the campus police. The patient had confided his intention to kill the daughter to a staff psychotherapist. Though the patient was briefly detained by the campus police at the psychotherapist's request, no further action was taken to protect the daughter. The parents alleged that the defendants should be held liable for a tortious failure to confine a dangerous patient and a tortious failure to warn them or their daughter of a dangerous patient. The psychotherapists and campus police claimed official immunity under a California statute freeing "public employee(s)" from liability for acts or omissions resulting from "the exercise of discretion vested in [them]" (Cal. Govt. Code § 820.2). The court accepted the official immunity defense in relation to the failure to confine, because that failure involved a "basic policy decision" sufficient to constitute discretion under the statute. But regarding the failure to warn, the court refused to accept the psychotherapists' official immunity claim, because the decision whether to warn was not a basic policy decision. The campus police needed no official immunity from their failure to warn, because, the court held, they had no legal duty to warn in light of the facts in the complaint.

A federal appellate court found several members of the athletic staff protected by a qualified immunity against liability for negligence in the death of a student. In *Sorey v. Kellett*, 849 F.2d 960 (5th Cir. 1988), a football player at the University of Southern Mississippi collapsed during practice and died shortly thereafter. The court applied Mississippi's qualified immunity for public officials performing discretionary, rather than ministerial, acts to the trainer, the team physician, and the football coach, finding that the first two were performing a discretionary act in administering medical treatment to the student. The coach was entitled to qualified immunity because of his general authority over the football program. Noting that "a public official charged only with general authority over a program or institution naturally is exercising discretionary functions" [849 F.2d at 964], the court denied recovery to the plaintiff.

Defamation claims against faculty and administrators have proliferated over the past few years, but few have been successful. For example, a female associate professor denied promotion sued her department chair, claiming that a memo he wrote to her and distributed to higher-level administrators was defamatory. The court rejected the claim on several grounds. First, the plaintiff had requested the promotion and thus "opened herself" to evaluation. Second, the memo had a limited audience and thus did not meet the "publication" requirement for defamation (see Section 2.3.1.2). And third, the memo expressed the chair's opinion, and thus was consitutionally protected (*Gernander v. Winona State University*, 428 N.W.2d 473 (Minn. Ct. App. 1988)).

But a recent ruling by the U.S. Supreme Court in *Milkovich v. Lorain Journal Co.*, 497 U.S. 1 (1990), suggests that this third reason may not be legally sound when applied to a "public figure" (see Section 2.3.1.2). The plaintiff claimed that an article in which he was portrayed as a perjurer was defamatory. The defendant, a newspaper, asserted an "opinion privilege" as its entire defense to the defamation claim. In an opinion by Chief Justice Rehnquist, the Supreme Court denied that an "opinion privilege" existed, although it said that "statements on matters of public concern must be provable as false before liability attaches," at least in situations where "a media defendant is involved" (497 U.S. at 19). Although future nonmedia defendants may attempt to limit *Milkovich* to its narrow facts, the opinion's wholesale rejection of the "opinion privilege" appears to apply to all defendants, not just the media.

The official immunity and state employee immunity defenses are not available to officers and employees of private institutions. But it appears that at least the trustees of private nonprofit institutions will be leniently treated by some courts out of deference to the trustees' special discretionary functions (see W. C. Porth, "Personal Liability of Trustees of Higher Educational Institutions," 2 *J. Coll. & Univ. Law* 143 (1974–75)). As a result, the personal liability of such trustees may be limited in a way somewhat akin to the official immunity limitation available to officers and employees of public institutions.

Administrators acting within the scope of their authority may be protected by a common law qualified privilege for communications between persons sharing a common duty or interest, such as communications between individuals within a business or an academic organization. "The conditional nature of this privilege, or its 'qualification,' depends on whether or not the communication was made on a proper occasion, in good faith and without excessive publication" (F. Bazluke, *Defamation Issues in Higher Education* (National Association of College and University Attorneys, 1990), 8). In *Kraft v. William Alanson White Psychiatric Foundation*, 498 A.2d 1145 (D.C. 1985), the court applied an "absolute privilege" to communications among faculty members about the plaintiff's inadequate academic performance in a postgraduate certificate program. The court stated:

> A person who seeks an academic credential and who is on notice that satisfactory performance is a prerequisite to his receipt of that credential consents

to frank evaluation by those charged with the responsibility to supervise him [498 A.2d at 1149].

In addition, certain university administrators or trustees may be viewed as "public figures" by a court; in such instances the plaintiff would have to demonstrate that the defendants acted with "actual malice" in publishing the defamatory information. The constitutional standard that a public figure must meet was established by the U.S. Supreme Court in *New York Times v. Sullivan*, 376 U.S. 254 (1964), in which the court defined actual malice to include knowledge of the falsity of the statement or reckless disregard for its truth or falsity. Athletic coaches, university trustees and administrators, and even prominent faculty have been determined to be public figures; thus, public comment on their activities or decisions must meet a high standard in order to be actionable.

Defendants in certain defamation cases may be protected by the concept of "invited libel" and thus found not to have been responsible for the "publication" element of a defamation claim. In *Sophianopoulous v. McCormick*, 385 S.E.2d 682 (Ga. Ct. App. 1989), a state appellate court rejected a faculty member's defamation claim against his department chair. The professor had complained to the American Association of University Professors (AAUP) that his chair had mistreated him. When the AAUP contacted the chair to inquire about the professor's performance, the chair sent the AAUP copies of memoranda critical of the professor's performance. The judges ruled that, by involving the AAUP in the dispute with his chair, the plaintiff consented to having the offending information published to the AAUP.

Although personnel decisions and letters of reference for students or faculty provide the impetus for most defamation claims, statements by researchers may also be actionable. For analysis of a case in which a jury found several university researchers liable for defamation (*Neary v. Regents of the University of California* (Cal. Super. Ct. Alameda County, No. 525-839-0, 1988)), see M. Traynor, "Defamation Law: Shock Absorbers for Its Ride into the Groves of Academe," 16 *J. Coll.& Univ. Law* 373 (1990).

Institutions should consider whether or not they wish to protect their personnel from the financial consequences of personal tort liability. Insurance coverage and indemnification agreements, discussed in Section 2.5.2, may be utilized for this purpose. For an overview of liability insurance and related issues, see B. Higgins and E. Zulkey, "Liability Insurance Coverage: How to Avoid Unpleasant Surprises," 17 *J. Coll. & Univ. Law* 123 (1990).

2.4.2. Personal contract liability. A trustee, administrator, or other agent who signs a contract on behalf of an institution may be personally liable for its performance if the institution breaches the contract. The extent of personal liability depends on whether the agent's participation on behalf of the institution was authorized—either by a grant of express authority or by an implied authority, an apparent authority, or a subsequent ratification by the institution. (See the discussion of authority in Section 2.3.2.) If the individual's participation was properly authorized, and if that individual signed the contract only in the capacity of an institutional agent, he or she will not be personally liable for performance of the contract. If, however, the participation was not properly authorized, or if the individual signed in an individual capacity rather than as an institutional agent, he or she may be personally liable.

In some cases the other contracting party may be able to sue both the institution and the agent or to choose between them. This option is presented when the contracting party did not know at the time of contracting that the individual participated in an agency capacity, but later learned that was the case. The option is also presented when the contracting party knew that the individual was acting as an institutional agent, but the individual also gave a personal promise that the contract would be performed. In such situations, if the contracting party obtains a judgment against both the institution and the agent, the judgment may be satisfied against either or against both, but the contracting party may receive no more than the total amount of the judgment. Where the contracting party receives payment from only one of the two liable parties, the paying party may have a claim against the nonpayor for part of the judgment amount.

An agent who is a party to the contract in a personal capacity, and thus potentially liable on it, can assert the same defenses that are available to any contracting party. These defenses may arise from the contract (for instance, the absence of some formality necessary to complete the contract, or fraud, or inadequate performance by the other party), or they may be personal to the agent (for instance, a particular counterclaim against the other party).

Quasi-contractual theories, such as detrimental reliance, may be used to assert personal liability against trustees or administrators. In *Student House, Inc. v. Board of Regents of Regency Universities*, 254 N.E.2d 496 (Ill. 1969), a private housing developer sought to enjoin the trustees of Northern Illinois University from building additional student housing. The developer claimed that several admininistrators, such as the director of student housing and the director of research, had promised that the university would not build housing if private housing met the university's needs. The Illinois Supreme Court ruled that, as a matter of law, the developer's reliance on these oral representations of lower-level administrators was unreasonable, and refused to apply the plaintiff's agency law and estoppel theories.

2.4.3. Personal liability for violations of federal constitutional rights.

The liability of trustees, administrators, and other employees of postsecondary institutions for constitutional rights violations is determined under the same body of law that determines the liability of the institutions themselves, and presents many of the same legal issues (see Section 2.3.3). As with institutional liability, an individual's action must usually be done "under color of" state law, or must be characterizable as "state action," before liability will attach. But, as with tort and contract liability, the liability of individual trustees, administrators, and other employees is not coterminous with that of the institution itself. Defenses that may be available to the institution (such as the constitutional immunity defense) may not be available to individuals sued in their individual (or personal) capacities; conversely, defenses that may be available to individuals (such as the qualified immunity discussed later in this section) may not be available to the institution.

The federal statute referred to as Section 1983, quoted in Section 2.3.3 of this chapter, is again the key statute. Individual state and local government officials and employees sued in their personal capacities are clearly "persons" under Section 1983 and thus subject to its provisions whenever they are acting under color of state law (*Hafer v. Melo*, 112 S. Ct. 358 (1991)). But courts have long recognized a qualified immunity for certain public officials and employees from liability for monetary damages under Section 1983. See K. Blum, "Qualified Immunity: A User's Manual," 26 *Ind. L. Rev.* 187 (1993). In 1974 and again in 1975, the U.S. Supreme Court attempted to explain the scope of this immunity as it applies to school officials.

In *Scheuer v. Rhodes*, 416 U.S. 232 (1974), the Court considered a suit for damages brought on behalf of three students killed in the May 1970 disturbances at Kent State University. The Court rejected the contention that the president of Kent State and other state officials had an absolute "official immunity" protecting them from personal liability. The Court instead accorded the president and officials a "qualified immunity" under Section 1983: "In varying scope, a qualified immunity is available to officers of the executive branch of government, the variation being dependent upon the scope of discretion and responsibilities of the office and all the circumstances as they reasonably appeared at the time of the action on which liability is sought to be based." Because the availability of this immunity depended on facts not yet in the record, the Supreme Court remanded the case to the trial court for further proceedings.[17]

In *Wood v. Strickland*, 420 U.S. 308 (1975), the Supreme Court extended, and added enigma to, its discussion of Section 1983 immunity in the institutional context. After the school board in this case had expelled some students from high school for violating a school disciplinary regulation, several of them sued the members of the school board for damages and injunctive and declaratory relief. In a controversial decision with strong dissents, the Court held that school board members, as public school officials, are entitled to a qualified immunity from such suits:

> We think there must be a degree of immunity if the work of the schools is to go forward; and, however worded, the immunity must be such that public school officials understand that action taken in the good-faith fulfillment of their responsibilities and within the bounds of reason under all the circumstances will not be punished and that they need not exercise their discretion with undue timidity. . . .
>
> The official must himself be acting sincerely and with a belief that he is doing right, but an act violating a student's constitutional rights can be no more justified by *ignorance or disregard of settled, indisputable law* on the part of one entrusted with supervision of students' daily lives than by the presence of actual malice. To be entitled to a special exemption from the categorical remedial language of Section 1983 in a case in which his action violated a student's constitutional rights, a school board member, who has voluntarily undertaken the task of supervising the operation of the school and the activities of the students, must be held to a standard of conduct based not only on permissible intentions, but also on *knowledge of the basic, unquestioned constitutional rights of his charges.* Such a standard neither imposes an unfair burden upon a person assuming a responsible public office requiring a high degree of intelligence and judgment for the proper fulfillment of its duties, nor an unwarranted burden in light of the value which civil rights have in our legal system. Any lesser standard would

---

[17]On remand the case proceeded to trial against all defendants. No defendant was held immune from suit. The president of Kent State was eventually dismissed as a defendant, however, because the facts indicated that he had not personally violated any of the plaintiffs' rights (see *Krause v. Rhodes*, 570 F.2d 563 (6th Cir. 1977)). Eventually the case was settled and an award of $600,000 plus attorney's fees made to the plaintiffs (see *Krause v. Rhodes*, 640 F.2d 214 (6th Cir. 1981)).

deny much of the promise of Section 1983. Therefore, in the specific context of school discipline, we hold that a school board member is not immune from liability for damages under Section 1983 (1) if he knew or reasonably should have known that the action he took within his sphere of official responsibility would violate the constitutional rights of the student affected, or (2) if he took the action with the malicious intention to cause a deprivation of constitutional rights or other injury to the student [420 U.S. at 321-22; emphasis and numbering added].

The Court's reliance on the *Scheuer* case at several points in its *Wood* opinion indicates that the *Wood* liability standard applies to public officials in postsecondary education as well. Clearly, this qualified immunity would be available to trustees and executive heads of public postsecondary institutions. The immunity of lower-level administrators and faculty members is less clear; for, as the Court noted in *Scheuer* and reaffirmed in *Wood*, the immunity's existence and application would depend in each case on the "scope of discretion and responsibilities of the office."

In 1982 the Court modified its *Wood* analysis in ruling on a suit brought against two senior aides in the Nixon administration. The immunity test developed in *Wood* had two parts. One part was subjective; it focused on the defendant's "permissible intentions," asking whether he had acted "with the malicious intention to cause a deprivation of constitutional rights or other injury" to the plaintiff (420 U.S. at 322). The other part was objective; it focused on the defendant's "knowledge of . . . basic, unquestioned constitutional rights," asking whether he "knew or reasonably should have known that the action he took . . . would violate the constitutional rights" of the plaintiff (420 U.S. at 322). The 1982 case, *Harlow v. Fitzgerald*, 457 U.S. 800, deleted the subjective part of the test because it had inhibited courts from dismissing insubstantial lawsuits prior to trial:

> We conclude today that bare allegations of malice should not suffice to subject government officials either to the costs of trial or to the burdens of broad-reaching discovery. We therefore hold that government officials performing discretionary functions generally are shielded from liability for civil damages insofar as their conduct does not violate clearly established statutory or constitutional rights of which a reasonable person would have known (see *Procunier v. Navarette*, 434 U.S. 555, 565 (1978); *Wood v. Strickland*, 420 U.S. at 321).
>
> Reliance on the objective reasonableness of an official's conduct, as measured by reference to clearly established law, should avoid excessive disruption of government and permit the resolution of many insubstantial claims on summary judgment. On summary judgment, the judge appropriately may determine not only the currently applicable law but whether that law was clearly established at the time an action occurred. If the law at that time was not clearly established, an official could not reasonably be expected to anticipate subsequent legal developments, nor could he fairly be said to "know" that the law forbade conduct not previously identified as unlawful. Until this threshold immunity question is resolved, discovery should not be allowed. If the law was clearly established, the immunity defense ordinarily should fail, since a reasonably competent public official should know the law governing his conduct. Nevertheless, if the official pleading the defense claims extraordinary circumstances and can prove that he neither knew nor should have known of the relevant legal standard, the defense should be sustained. But again, the defense would turn primarily on objective factors [457 U.S. at 817-18].

In litigation, qualified immunity is an affirmative defense to be pleaded by the individual seeking to assert the immunity claim (*Gomez v. Toledo,* 446 U.S. 635 (1980)). Once the defendant has asserted the claim, the court must determine (1) whether the plaintiff's complaint alleges the violation of a right protected by Section 1983; and (2), if so, whether this right "was clearly established at the time of [the defendant's] actions" (*Siegert v. Gilley,* 111 S. Ct. 1789, 1793–94 (1991)). If the court answers both of these inquiries affirmatively, it will reject the immunity claim unless the defendant can prove that, because of "extraordinary circumstances," he "neither knew nor should have known" the clearly established law applicable to the case (*Harlow,* above). The burden of proof here is clearly on the defendant, and it would be a rare case in which the defendant would sustain this burden.

Since *Wood* and *Harlow,* courts have often considered the applicability of Section 1983 qualified immunity to officers and administrators of postsecondary institutions, sometimes accepting the defense (for example, *Garvie v. Jackson,* 845 F.2d 647 (6th Cir. 1988)) and sometimes rejecting it (for example, *Dube v. State University of New York,* 900 F.2d 587 (2d Cir. 1990)). The case of *United Carolina Bank v. Board of Regents of Stephen F. Austin State University,* 665 F.2d 553 (5th Cir. 1982) (this volume, Section 2.3.3), is illustrative. Having been denied tenure, a professor sued several administrators at his institution. He argued that the tenure denial had been precipitated by allegations he had made concerning the misuse of funds and that these allegations were an exercise of free speech for which he should not be punished (see this volume, Section 3.7.4). The defendants claimed immunity. Basing their argument on an analysis of the events leading to the tenure denial, they claimed that they neither knew nor should have known that their actions would violate the professor's First Amendment rights. After a detailed review of the facts in the record, the court rejected the defendants' argument and held them liable. The opinion illustrates that, even under the objective immunity test approved by *Harlow,* a court may have to sort out a tangled web of facts in disposing of immunity claims.

Other complexities are illustrated by *Mangaroo v. Nelson,* 864 F.2d 1202 (5th Cir. 1989). The plaintiff had been demoted from a deanship to a tenured faculty position. She sued both Nelson, the acting president who demoted her, and Pierre, Nelson's successor, alleging that their actions violated her procedural due process rights. She sued the former in his *individual* (or personal) capacity, seeking monetary damages, and the latter in his *official* capacity, seeking injunctive relief. The court held that Nelson was entitled to claim the qualified immunity, since the plaintiff sought money damages from him in his individual capacity for the harm he had caused. In contrast, the court held that Pierre was not entitled to qualified immunity, because the plaintiff sued him only in his official capacity, seeking an injunctive order compelling him, as president, to take action to remedy the violation of her due process rights.

As a result of this line of cases, personnel of public colleges and universities are charged with responsibility for knowing "clearly established law" (*Harlow,* above). Unless "extraordinary circumstances" prevent an individual from gaining such knowledge, the disregard of clearly established law is considered unreasonable and thus unprotected by the cloak of immunity. It will often be debatable whether particular principles of law are sufficiently "clear" to fall within the Court's characterization. Moreover, the applicability of even the clearest principles may depend on the particular facts of each case, as the *United Carolina Bank* case well illustrates.

Since it is therefore extremely difficult to predict what unlawful actions would fall within the qualified immunity, administrative efforts will be far better spent taking preventive measures to ensure that Section 1983 violations do not occur, rather than making weak predictions about whether immunity would exist if violations did occur.

Officers and administrators found personally liable under Section 1983 are subject to both court injunctions and money damage awards in favor of the prevailing plaintiff(s). Unlike governmental defendants (see *City of Newport v. Fact Concerts, Inc.*, Section 2.3.3 of this volume), individual defendants may be held liable for punitive as well as compensatory damages. To collect compensatory damages, a plaintiff must prove "actual injury," tangible or intangible; courts usually will not presume that damage occurred from a violation of civil rights and will award compensatory damages only to the extent of proven injury (*Carey v. Piphus*, 435 U.S. 247 (1978)). To collect punitive damages, a plaintiff must show that the defendant's actions either manifested "reckless or callous disregard for the plaintiff's rights" or constituted "intentional violations of federal law" (*Smith v. Wade*, 461 U.S. 30, 51 (1983)).

Besides having a potentially broad scope of liability and a limited, unpredictable immunity from damages under Section 1983, institutional personnel are also generally unprotected by the Eleventh Amendment immunity that sometimes protects their institutions from federal court suits (see Section 2.3.3). In the *Scheuer* case (discussed earlier in this section), for example, the Court held that the president of Kent State had no such immunity:

> The Eleventh Amendment provides no shield for a state official confronted by a claim that he had deprived another of a federal right under the color of state law. . . . When a state officer acts under a state law in a manner violative of the federal Constitution, he "comes into conflict with the superior authority of that Constitution, and he is in that case stripped of his official or representative character and is subjected *in his person* to the consequences of his individual conduct" [416 U.S. at 237; quoting *Ex parte Young*, 209 U.S. 123, 159 (1908)].

If a state university president has no immunity under the Constitution, it follows that lower-level administrators and faculty members (and probably trustees) would also usually have no such immunity. The *Scheuer* case notes one important circumstance, however, under which such persons would enjoy the constitutional immunity: when they are sued only as titular parties in a suit that is actually seeking money damages from the state treasury. In this type of suit, the individual is sued for damages in his or her official (or representational)—rather than personal (or individual)—capacity (see *Papasan v. Allain*, 478 U.S. 265, 276–79 (1986)). In such circumstances the suit will be considered to be against the state itself and thus barred by the Eleventh Amendment.

The state of the law under Section 1983 and the Eleventh Amendment, taken together, gives administrators of public postsecondary institutions no cause to feel confident that either they or other institutional officers or employees are insulated from personal civil rights liability. To minimize the liability risk in this critical area of law and social responsibility, administrators should make legal counsel available to institutional personnel for consultation, encourage review by counsel of institutional policies that may affect civil rights, and provide personnel with information on or training in basic civil rights law and other legal principles. To absolve personnel of the financial drain of any liability that does occur, administrators may wish to consider the purchase of special insurance coverage or the development of indemnity plans. As discussed in Section 2.5.2, however, public policy in some states may limit the use of these techniques in the civil rights area.

Sec. 2.5. Institutional Management of Liability Risk

The risk of financial liability for injury to another party remains a major concern for postsecondary institutions as well as their governing board members and personnel. This section examines some methods for controlling such risk exposure and thus minimizing the detrimental effect of liability on the institution and its personnel. Risk management may be advisable not only because it helps stabilize the institution's financial condition over time but also because it can improve the morale and performance of institutional personnel by alleviating their concerns about potential personal liability. In addition, risk management can implement the institution's humanistic concern for minimizing and compensating any potential injuries that its operations may cause to innocent third parties.

The major methods of risk management may be called risk avoidance, risk control, risk transfer, and risk retention. See generally J. Adams & J. Hall, "Legal Liabilities in Higher Education: Their Scope and Management" (Part II), 3 *J. Coll. & Univ. Law* 335, 360-69 (1976).

2.5.1. Risk avoidance and risk control. The most certain method for managing a known exposure to liability is risk avoidance—the elimination of the behavior, condition, or program that is the source of the risk. This method is often not realistic, however, since it could require institutions to forgo activities important to their educational missions. It might also require greater knowledge of the details of myriad campus activities than administrators typically can acquire and greater certainty about the legal principles of liability (see Sections 2.3 and 2.4) than the law typically affords.

Risk control is less drastic than risk avoidance. The goal is to reduce, rather than eliminate entirely, the frequency or severity of potential exposures to liability—mainly by improving the physical environment or modifying hazardous behavior or activities in ways that reduce the recognized risks. Although this method may have less impact on an institution's educational mission than risk avoidance, it may similarly require considerable detailed knowledge of campus facilities and functions and of legal liability principles.

2.5.2. Risk transfer. By purchasing commercial insurance, entering "hold-harmless" or "indemnification" agreements, or employing releases and waivers, institutions can transfer their own liability risks to others or transfer to themselves the liability risks of their officers and employees or of third parties.

2.5.2.1. Insurance. A commercial insurance policy shifts potential future financial losses (up to a maximum amount) to the insurance company in exchange for payment of a specified premium. (See B. Higgins & E. Zulkey, "Liability Insurance Coverage: How to Avoid Unpleasant Surprises," 17 *J. Coll. & Univ. Law* 123 (1990).) The institution can insure against liability for its own acts, as well as liability transferred to it by a "hold-harmless" agreement with its personnel. With the advice of insurance experts, the institution can determine the kinds and amounts of liability protection it needs and provide for the necessary premium expenditures in its budgeting process.

There are two basic types of insurance policies important to higher education institutions. The first and primary type is general liability insurance; it provides broad coverage of bodily injury and property damage claims such as would arise in the case of a negligently caused injury to a student or staff member. The second type is directors and officers insurance ("D & O" coverage, or sometimes "errors and omissions" coverage). It covers property and nonbodily injury claims such as employment claims, defamation, and violations of due process.

General liability insurance policies usually exclude from their coverage both intentionally or maliciously caused damage and damage caused by acts that violate penal laws. In *Brooklyn Law School v. Aetna Casualty and Surety Co.*, 849 F.2d 788 (2d Cir. 1988), for example, the school had incurred numerous costs in defending itself against a lawsuit in which a former professor alleged that the school, its trustees, and faculty members had intentionally conspired to violate his constitutional rights. The school sued its insurer—which insured the school under an umbrella policy—to recover its costs in defending against the professor's suit. The appellate court held that, under New York Law, the insurer was not required to defend the insured against such a suit, which alleged intentional harm, when the policy terms expressly excluded from coverage injuries caused by the insured's intentional acts.

Liability arising from the violation of an individual's constitutional or civil rights is also commonly excluded from general liability insurance coverage—an exclusion that can pose considerable problems for administrators and institutions, whose exposure to such liability has escalated greatly since the 1960s. In specific cases, questions about this exclusion may become entwined with questions concerning intent or malice. In *Andover Newton Theological School, Inc. v. Continental Casualty Company*, 930 F.2d 89 (1st Cir. 1991), the defendant insurance company had refused to pay on the school's claim after a court had found that the school violated the Age Discrimination in Employment Act (ADEA) (this volume, Section 3.3.6) when it dismissed a tenured, sixty-two-year-old professor. The jury in the professor's case found that the school had impermissibly considered the professor's age in deciding to dismiss him, but the evidence did not clearly establish that the school's administrators had acted deliberately. Under the ADEA, behavior by the school that showed "reckless disregard" for the law was enough to sustain the verdict against it. When the school sought to have its insurance carrier pay the judgment, the insurer objected on grounds that it is against Massachusetts public policy (and that of most other states) to insure against intentional or deliberate conduct of the insured. The district court agreed and held the school's loss to be uninsurable.

On appeal, the appellate court reasoned that the school's suit against the insurer revolved around the following question:

> Does a finding of willfulness under the Age Discrimination in Employment Act (ADEA), if based on a finding of "reckless disregard as to whether [defendant's] conduct is prohibited by federal law," constitute "deliberate or intentional . . . wrongdoing" such as to preclude indemnification by an insurer under the public policy of Massachusetts as codified at Mass. Gen. L. ch. 175, section 47 Sixth (b) [930 F.2d at 91]?

The appellate court certified this question to the Massachusetts Supreme Judicial Court, which answered in the negative. The federal appellate court then reversed the federal district court's decision and remanded the case to that court for further proceedings. The appellate court reasoned that, since the jury verdict did not necessitate a conclusion that the school had acted intentionally or deliberately, the losses incurred by the school were insurable and payment would not contravene public policy.[18]

Exclusions from coverage, as in the examples above, may exist either because state law requires the exclusion (see Section 2.5.4) or because the insurer has made its own business decision to exclude certain actions from its standard coverages. When the exclusion is of the latter type, institutions may nevertheless be able to cover such risks by combining a standard policy with one or more specialty endorsements or companion policies, such as a directors and officers policy. If this arrangement still does not provide all the coverage the institution desires, and if the institution can afford the substantial expense, it may request a "manuscript" policy tailored to its specific needs.

2.5.2.2. Hold-harmless and indemnification agreements. A second method of risk transfer is a "hold-harmless" or indemnification agreement. In a broad sense, the term "indemnification" refers to any compensation for loss or damage. Insurance is thus one method of indemnifying someone. But in the narrower sense used here, indemnification refers to an arrangement whereby one party (for example, the institution) agrees to hold another party (for example, an individual officer or employee) harmless from financial liability for certain acts or omissions of that party which cause damage to another:

> In brief synopsis, the mechanism of a typical indemnification will shift to the institution the responsibility for defense and discharge of claims asserted against institutional personnel individually by reason of their acts or omissions on behalf of the institution, if the individual believed in good faith that his actions were lawful and within his institutional authority and responsibility. That standard of conduct is, of course, very broadly stated; and the question of whether or not it is satisfied must be determined on a case-by-case basis [R. Aiken, "Legal Liabilities in Higher Education: Their Scope and Management" (Part I), 3 *J. Coll. & Univ. Law* 121, 313 (1976)].

Although, with respect to its own personnel, the institution would typically be the "indemnitor"—that is, the party with ultimate financial liability—the institution can sometimes also be an "indemnitee," the party protected from liability loss. The institution could negotiate for "hold-harmless" protection for itself, for instance, in contracts it enters with outside contractors or lessees. In an illustrative case, *Bridston v. Dover Corp. and University of North Dakota v. Young Men's Christian As-*

---

[18]On remand, the district court decided for the school, and the insurance company appealed (*Andover Newton Theological School, Inc. v. Continental Casualty Co.*, 964 F.2d 1237 (1st Cir. 1992)). The company challenged a number of the district court's actions: holding a hearing to determine whether the school had deliberately violated federal law in dismissing the professor; placing the burden of proving deliberateness on the insurance company; and finding that the officers of the school did not act with knowledge that their conduct was illegal. The appellate court rejected all these challenges and upheld the district court.

sociation, 352 N.W.2d 194 (N.D. 1984), the university had leased a campus auditorium to a dance group. One of the group's members was injured during practice, allegedly because of the negligence of a university employee, and sued the university for damages. The university invoked an indemnity clause in the lease agreement and successfully avoided liability by arguing that the clause required the lessee to hold the university harmless even for negligent acts of the university's own employees.

Like insurance policies, indemnification agreements often do not cover liability resulting from intentional or malicious action or from action violating the state's penal laws. Just as public policy may limit the types of acts or omissions that may be insured against, it may also limit those for which indemnification may be received.

Both public and private institutions may enter indemnification agreements. A public institution, however, may need specific authorizing legislation (see, for example, Mich. Comp. Laws § 691.1408 (1992)), while private institutions usually can rely on the general laws of their states for sufficient authority. Some states also provide for indemnification of all state employees for injuries caused by their acts or omissions on behalf of the state (see Cal. Govt. Code § 825 et seq.).

2.5.2.3. Releases and waivers. A third method of risk transfer is the release or waiver agreement. This type of arrangement releases one of two related parties from liability to the other for injuries arising from the relationship. In postsecondary education, this mechanism is most likely to be used in situations such as intercollegiate athletics, provision of medical services, student field trips, and tours of construction sites, where the participant or recipient is required to execute a release or waiver as a precondition to participation or receipt. The *Porubiansky, Tunkl,* and *Wagenblast* cases, discussed in Section 2.5.4, illustrate both the uses of releases and the substantial legal limitations on their use.

2.5.3. Risk retention. The most practical option for the institution in some circumstances may be to retain the risk of financial liability. Risk retention may be appropriate, for instance, in situations where commercial insurance is unavailable or too costly, the expected losses are so small that they can be considered normal operating expenses, or the probability of loss is so remote that it does not justify any insurance expense (see Adams & Hall, "Legal Liabilities in Higher Education" (cited in Section 2.5), at 361–63). Both insurance policy deductibles and methods of self-insurance are examples of risk retention. The deductible amounts in an insurance policy allocate the first dollar coverage of liability, up to the amount of the deductible, to the institution. The institution becomes a self-insurer by maintaining a separate bank account to pay appropriate claims. The institution's risk managers must determine the amount to be available in the account and the frequency and amount of regular payments to the account. This approach is distinguished from simple noninsurance by the planning and actuarial calculations that it involves.

2.5.4. Legal limits on authority to transfer risk. An institution's ability to transfer risk is limited by the law to situations that do not contravene "public policy." When financial liability is incurred as a result of willful wrongdoing, it is generally considered contrary to public policy to protect the institution or individual from responsibility for such behavior through insurance or indemnity. Wrongdoing that is malicious, fraudulent, immoral, or criminal will often fall within this category; thus, insurance companies may decline to cover such action, or provisions in insurance policies or indemnification agreements that do cover it may be void and unenforceable under state law. Common actions to which this public policy may apply include assault and battery, abuse of process, defamation, and invasion of privacy. This public policy may also apply to intentional deprivations of constitutional or civil rights; when the deprivation is unintentional, however, public policy may not operate to prohibit risk transfer (see, for example, *Solo Cup Co. v. Federal Insurance Co.*, 619 F.2d 1178 (7th Cir. 1980)).

Public policy may also prohibit agreements insuring against financial loss from punitive damage awards. Jurisdictions differ on whether such insurance coverage is proscribed. Some courts have prohibited coverage because it would defeat the two purposes served by punitive damages: punishment for egregious wrongdoing and deterrence of future misconduct (see, for example, *Hartford Accident and Indemnity Co. v. Village of Hempstead*, 397 N.E.2d 737 (N.Y. 1979)). Other courts have permitted coverage at least when punitive damages are awarded as the result of gross negligence or wanton and reckless conduct rather than intentional wrongdoing (see, for example, *Hensley v. Erie Insurance Co.*, 283 S.E.2d 227 (W. Va. 1981)).[19]

Depending on their state's public policy, institutions may also be prohibited in some circumstances from using releases, waivers, or other contractual agreements to transfer the risk of negligence to the potential victims of negligence. In *Emory University v. Porubiansky*, 282 S.E.2d 903 (Ga. 1981), for example, the Emory University School of Dentistry Clinic sought to insulate itself from negligence suits by inserting into its consent form a clause indicating that the patient waived all claims against the university or its agents. The Georgia Supreme Court voided the agreement as offensive to public policy because it purported to relieve state-licensed professional practitioners of a duty to exercise reasonable care in dealing with patients. Sometimes it may be difficult to determine what the state's public policy is and in what circumstances it will be deemed to be contravened by a risk transfer arrangement. The case of *Wagenblast v. Odessa School District*, 758 P.2d 968 (Wash. 1988), provides useful guidelines for making these determinations. In this case the Supreme Court of Washington invalidated school district policies requiring that, as a condition of participating in interscholastic athletics, students and their parents sign standardized forms releasing the school district from liability for negligence. The court based its decision on the earlier case of *Tunkl v. Regents of University of California*, 383 P.2d 441 (Cal. 1963), thus suggesting that the legal principles from *Wagenblast* apply to higher education as well. *Tunkl* involved an action by a hospital patient against a charitable hospital operated by the defendant. Upon acceptance into the program and entry into the hospital, Tunkl signed a document releasing the regents and the hospital from any and all liability for negligent or wrongful acts or omissions of its employees. The California Supreme Court invalidated this release agreement, relying on a state statute that prohibited certain agreements exempting a person from his own fraud, willful injury to another, or violation of law. Such agreements were invalid if they were contrary to the public interest, which the *Tunkl* court determined by considering six factors that it had consolidated from previous cases: (1) whether the agreement con-

[19]The cases are collected in Annot., "Liability Insurance Coverage as Extending to Liability for Punitive or Exemplary Damages," 16 A.L.R.4th 11 (1982 and periodic supp.).

cerned an endeavor suitable for public regulation; (2) whether the party seeking exculpation offered a service of public importance or necessity; (3) whether that party held itself out as willing to perform the service for any member of the public, or anyone who met predetermined standards; (4) whether that party possessed a bargaining advantage over members of the public desiring the service; (5) whether the release provision was in the nature of an adhesion contract (see this volume, Section 4.1.3) that did not contain any option for the other party to obtain protection against negligence by paying an extra fee; and (6) whether the party seeking exculpation would be able to exert control over persons seeking its services, thus subjecting these persons to risk. The more these factors are implicated in a release agreement, the more likely it is that a court will declare the agreement invalid on public policy grounds.

Even though the Washington court in *Wagenblast* had no statute similar to California's to rely on, it nevertheless used a public policy approach similar to that of the California court and adopted the six *Tunkl* factors. Noting that all six factors applied to the releases being challenged, the court invalidated the releases. This common law/public policy approach, encapsulated in the six factors borrowed from *Tunkl*, provides an analytical framework for determining whether and when higher education institutions may use releases or waivers of liability to transfer risk to potential victims of the institution's negligence. The specific results reached when an institution applies this *Wagenblast* approach, of course, may vary with the circumstances, including the specific activity for which the release is to be used; the persons for whom the release is sought (students, institutional employees, or outside third parties); and perhaps the type of institution using the release (whether it is a public or a private institution).

A different kind of legal problem may exist for postsecondary institutions that enjoy some degree of sovereign or charitable immunity from financial liability (see Section 2.3.1). Public institutions may not have authority to purchase liability insurance covering acts within the scope of their immunity. Where such authority does exist, however, and the institution does purchase insurance, its sovereign or charitable immunity may thereby be affected. Sometimes a statute authorizing insurance coverage may itself waive sovereign immunity to the extent of coverage. When such a waiver is lacking, in most states the purchase of insurance appears not to affect immunity, and the insurance protection is operable only for acts found to be outside the scope of immunity. In some states, however, courts appear to treat the authorized purchase of insurance as a waiver or narrowing of the institution's immunity, to the extent of the insurance coverage.[20]

Selected Annotated Bibliography

Sec. 2.1 (The Question of Authority)

Bess, James L. *Collegiality and Bureaucracy in the Modern University* (Teachers College Press, 1988). Examines governance in the contemporary university. Dis-

---

[20]Relevant cases are collected in Annot., "Liability or Indemnity Insurance Carried by Governmental Unit as Affecting Immunity from Tort Liability," 68 A.L.R.2d 1438 (1959 and periodic supp.); and Annot., "Immunity of Private Schools and Institutions of Higher Learning from Liability in Tort," 38 A.L.R.3d 480, 501–02 (1971 and periodic supp.).

cusses the relationship between authority structures, power, and collegiality; and between organizational characteristics and faculty perceptions of administrators. A framework for analysis of university governance is provided.

Hornby, D. Brock. "Delegating Authority to the Community of Scholars," 1975 *Duke L.J.* 279 (1975). Provides excellent legal and policy analysis regarding delegations of authority in public systems of postsecondary education. Considers constitutional and statutory delegations to statewide governing boards and individual boards of trustees, and subdelegations of that authority to officials, employees, and other bodies in individual institutions. Contains many useful citations to legal and policy materials.

Reuschlein, Harold G., & Gregory, William A. *Handbook on the Law of Agency and Partnership* (West, 1979). Provides a thorough explanation of the principles of agency law, with copious citations to cases; includes discussion of kinds of authority, estoppel, ratification, and tort and contract liabilities among principals, agents, and third parties.

Sec. 2.2 (Sources and Scope of Authority)

American Association for Higher Education. "Special Issue: Divestment," 38 *AAHE Bulletin* no. 9 (May 1986). Examines issues that arise when an institution decides to divest itself of the stock it holds in corporations doing business in countries whose human rights policies are contrary to democratic principles. Various divestment options are described, and suggestions are made for dealing with the campus community when the institution is considering divestment.

Bakaly, Charles G., Jr., & Grossman, Joel M. *Modern Law of Employment Contracts: Formation, Operation and Remedies for Breach* (Prentice-Hall Law & Business, 1983 and periodic supp.). Analyzes judicial precedents, state and federal employment laws, and recent developments in the employment-at-will doctrine. Also included is information about drug testing, medical screening and HIV, alternative dispute resolution, the drafting of employment policies and manuals, and tort theories that are often appended to contract claims.

Berry, Charles R., & Buchwald, Gerald J. "Enforcement of College Trustees' Fiduciary Duties: Students and the Problem of Standing," 9 *U. San Francisco L. Rev.* 1 (1974). Discusses the history, status, effectiveness, and future direction of the law regarding trustee responsibilities and potential liability, particularly with respect to university finances; emphasis on the question of who, besides the state attorney general, can sue to enforce fiduciary responsibilities.

Christie, George C. "Legal Aspects of Changing University Investment Strategies," 58 *N.C. L. Rev.* 189 (1980). Examines legal aspects of the effort, currently undertaken by most postsecondary institutions, to increase the rate of return from existing endowments. Although it focuses on North Carolina law, the article is also valuable for institutions in other states because of its discussions of the Uniform Management of Institutional Funds Act, Treasury regulations issued under the Internal Revenue Code, and various other sources of federal guidance.

Daugherty, Mary Schmid. "Uniform Management of Institutional Funds Act: The Implications for Private College Board of Regents," 57 *West's Educ. Law Rptr.*, 319 (1990). Examines state laws based on the Uniform Act, which establishes guidelines for the management and use of the investments of nonprofit educational and charitable organizations. Discusses the standards to which regents are held, the issue of restitution, the types of investments that can be made under these laws, and issues that remain for the courts to clarify. Suggestions for monitoring the institution's investment plan are provided.

Fishman, James J. "Standards of Conduct for Directors of Nonprofit Corporations," 7 *Pace L. Rev.* 389 (1987). Surveys the evolution in the law regarding nonprofit directors' duty of care, with emphasis on the *Sibley Hospital* case. Distinguishes between and critiques the "corporate" and the "trust" standards of care, and proposes a new "shifting standard of care," whose application would depend on "the type of nonprofit corporation and the nature of a director's conduct and interest in a particular transaction."

Gross, Allen J. *Employee Dismissal Law: Forms and Procedures* (2d ed., Wiley, 1992). Discusses suits alleging wrongful dismissal. Follows the litigation path from the time a decision to litigate is made through interrogatories, depositions, the trial, and its closing arguments. Useful for attorneys representing either party, the book focuses on the litigation process rather than the substance of the legal claims. Model forms and policies are included, as are suggestions for presenting wrongful-discharge cases before a jury.

Ingram, Richard T., & Associates. *Governing Public Colleges and Universities: A Handbook for Trustees, Chief Executives, and Other Campus Leaders* (Jossey-Bass, 1993). A resource book for college trustees. Divided into three parts: "Understanding the Environment of Public Higher Education," "Fulfilling Board Functions," and "Developing the Public Board." Each part is subdivided into chapters and topics, many of which address legal considerations. Appendices contain resources, including sample statements of board members' responsibilities and desirable qualifications for trustees; a survey of public governing boards' characteristics, policies, and practices; and self-study criteria for public multicampus and system boards. Also included is an extensive annotated list of recommended readings.

King, Harriet M. "The Voluntary Closing of a Private College: A Decision for the Board of Trustees?" 32 *S.C. L. Rev.* 547 (1981). Reviews the legal problems inherent in any decision of a board of trustees to close a private postsecondary institution. The article focuses on questions of trust law, especially the application of the doctrine of cy pres, an equitable doctrine permitting the assets of a charity to be used for a purpose other than that specified in the trust instrument when the original purpose can no longer be carried out.

Langbein, John H., & Posner, Richard. "Social Investing and the Law of Trusts," 79 *Mich. L. Rev.* 72 (1980). Defines "social investing" as the exclusion of "securities of certain otherwise attractive companies from an investor's portfolio because the companies are judged to be socially irresponsible" and the inclusion of "securities of certain otherwise unattractive companies because they are judged to be behaving in a socially laudable way. " Authors demonstrate that social investing invites a number of legal risks under the law of trusts. Despite such risks, authors are unwilling "to say that the law does, or should, absolutely forbid social investing by charitable trustees." Contains a section dealing with risks unique to investment of university endowments.

Larson, Lex K. *Employment Screening* (Matthew Bender, 1988 and annual updates). Discusses employment testing and reference checking, drug and alcohol screening, HIV testing, polygraph and honesty testing, genetic testing, and background checks. Additional chapters address judicial precedent on negligent hiring claims and examine state, federal, and constitutional laws relevant to employee screening. Appendices include model policies, forms, and other practice aids.

Larson, Lex K., & Borowsky, Philip. *Unjust Dismissal* (Matthew Bender, 1985). Provides a comprehensive review and analysis of a variety of claims under the umbrella of "unjust dismissal," including whistleblowing, free speech, workplace privacy, lie detector tests, and personnel manuals. Also discusses the covenant of good faith and fair dealing and other tort claims related to dismissal. Each step of the litigation process is described, and litigation-prevention recommendations for employers are included.

Leonard, Arthur S. "A New Common Law of Employment Termination," 66 *N.C. L. Rev.* 631 (1988). Discusses the assortment of contract and tort theories that state courts have recognized as limiting the employment-at-will doctrine.

Marsh, Gordon H. "Governance of Non-Profit Organizations: An Appropriate Standard of Conduct for Trustees and Directors of Museums and Other Cultural Institutions," 85 *Dickinson L. Rev.* 607 (1981). Compares the different standards of care applied by courts to the common law trustee and the corporate director, respectively, and considers the applicability of these standards to trustees of nonprofit organizations. Although the article will be of particular interest to institutions responsible for the management of museums or other cultural exhibits, its discussion of standards of care and the state of the case law defining a good-faith standard for trustees is of general interest for postsecondary institutions.

Perritt, Henry H., Jr. *Employee Dismissal Law and Practice* (3d ed., Wiley, 1992 and periodic supp.). A guide to litigation for plaintiffs and defendants. Includes information on state statutory and common law of wrongful discharge, discusses common law actions in tort, implied contract, and the implied covenant of good faith. Also discusses the access to these theories by employees covered by collective bargaining agreements.

Porth, William C. "Personal Liability of Trustees of Educational Institutions," 1 *J. Coll. & Univ. Law* 84 (1973) and 2 *J. Coll. & Univ. Law* 143 (1974–75). Collects and discusses the small number of cases on trustee liability and suggests approaches that future courts may take to the problem; emphasis is on the *Sibley Hospital* case.

Seldin, Peter. *Evaluating and Developing Administrative Performance* (Jossey-Bass, 1988). Presents a comprehensive system for assessing administrative performance and helping administrators improve their performance. Chapters discuss the demand for accountability and its effect on evaluation, the use of evaluative information in personnel decisions, characteristics of a successful evaluation system, the process of creating an evaluation system, and legal pitfalls of evaluation.

Waldo, Charles N. *A Working Guide for Directors of Not-for-Profit Organizations* (Greenwood Press, 1986). Provides an overview of the mission of an organization's board of directors in nontechnical terms. Also provided is a discussion of the responsibilities of directors and brief summaries of financial issues, planning, legal issues, and tax problems.

Sec. 2.3 (Institutional Liability for Acts of Others)

Aiken, Ray, Adams, John F., & Hall, John W. *Legal Liabilities in Higher Education: Their Scope and Management* (Association of American Colleges, 1976), printed simultaneously in 3 *J. Coll. & Univ. Law* 127 (1976). Provides an in-depth examination of legal and policy issues of institutional liability and the problems of protecting institutions and their personnel against liability by insurance and risk management.

Bazluke, Francine T. *Defamation Issues in Higher Education* (National Association of College and University Attorneys, 1990). A layperson's guide to defamation law. Author reviews the legal framework for a defamation claim and the possible defenses, and then discusses specific employment issues and student disciplinary actions that may give rise to defamation claims. Also discussed is the institution's potential liability for defamatory student publications. Guidelines are provided to minimize the institution's exposure to defamation claims.

Bickel, Robert D., & Lake, Peter F. "Reconceptualizing the University's Duty to Provide a Safe Learning Environment: A Criticism of the Doctrine of *In Loco Parentis* and the Restatement (Second) of Torts," 20 *J. Coll. & Univ. Law* 261 (1994). Criticizes the majority rule regarding institutional liability from *Rabel* (discussed in Section 4.17.2) and *Bradshaw* and argues that courts have improperly interpreted the *Restatement (Second) of Torts* and its "special relationship" requirement. The authors assert that colleges have a duty to protect, warn, and control their students, and that they should be found liable if they fail to act reasonably to protect students from foreseeable harm.

Bookman, Mark. *Contracting Collegiate Auxiliary Services* (Education and Nonprofit Consulting, 1989). Discusses legal and policy issues related to contracting for auxiliary services on campus. An overview chapter reviews legal terminology, the advantages and disadvantages of contracting, and the ways in which contracting decisions are made. Another chapter explains what should be negotiated when the contract is developed and how contracted services should be managed. Sample documents are included.

Burling, Philip. *Crime on Campus: Analyzing and Managing the Increasing Risk of Institutional Liability* (National Association of College and University Attorneys, 1990). Reviews the legal analyses that courts undertake in responding to claims that liability for injuries suffered on campus should be shifted from the victim to the institution. Includes a review of literature about reducing crime on campus and managing the risk of liability to victims whom the institution may have a duty to protect.

Evans, Richard B. Note, "'A Stranger in a Strange Land': Responsibility and Liability for Students Enrolled in Foreign-Study Programs," 18 *J. Coll. & Univ. Law* 299 (1991). Examines the doctrine of "special relationship" that has been applied to the student-institution relationship and discusses its significance to claims of students injured while participating in a study-abroad program. Suggestions for limiting institutional liability are provided.

Gaffney, Edward M., & Sorensen, Philip M. *Ascending Liability in Religious and Other Non Profit Organizations* (Center for Constitutional Studies, Mercer University (now at Baylor University), 1984). Provides an overview of liability case law related to nonprofit and religiously affiliated organizations, discusses constitutional issues, and provides suggestions for structuring the operations of such organizations to limit liability.

Gehring, Donald D., & Geraci, Christy P. *Alcohol on Campus: A Compendium of the Law and a Guide to Campus Policy* (College Administration Publications, 1989). Examines legal and policy issues related to alcohol on college campuses. Included are chapters reviewing research on student consumption of alcohol, including differences by students' race and gender; sources of legal liability for colleges if intoxicated students injure themselves or others; and procedural and substantive considerations in developing alcohol policies and risk management procedures. A state-by-state analysis of laws relevant to alcohol consumption, sale, and social host liability is included. The book is updated annually.

Green, Ronald M., & Reibstein, Richard J. *Employer's Guide to Workplace Torts* (Bureau of National Affairs, 1992). Reviews each of the areas of employment-related torts, explaining the general principles of law involved, summarizing case law precedent, and providing suggestions for avoiding liability.

Miyamoto, Tia. "Liability of Colleges and Universities for Injuries During Extracurricular Activities," 15 *J. Coll. & Univ. Law* 149 (1988). Examines four theories under which students have attempted to hold institutions liable for injuries incurred while participating in extracurricular activities: (1) in loco parentis, (2) the duty to supervise students, (3) the duty to control the acts of third persons who have injured the student, and (4) the duty to protect students as invitees. Cases in which one or more of these theories were used are analyzed. Author concludes that the fourth theory is the one under which the student is most likely to prevail.

Moots, Philip R. *Ascending Liability: Planning Memorandum* (Center for Constitutional Studies, Mercer University (now at Baylor University), 1987). Discusses planning issues such as risk management, contract drafting, and restructuring of certain activities of the organization. Also discusses the role of the governing board and the institution's role vis-à-vis related organizations.

Nahmod, Sheldon H. *Civil Rights and Civil Liberties Litigation: The Law of Section 1983* (3d ed., Shepard's/McGraw-Hill, 1991, with annual supp.). A guide to litigation brought under Section 1983. Primarily for legal counsel. Focuses on the positions the courts have taken on the procedural and technical questions common to all Section 1983 litigation.

National Association of College and University Attorneys. *Am I Liable? Faculty, Staff, and Institutional Liability in the College and University Setting* (NACUA, 1989). A collection of articles on selected liability issues. Included are analyses of general tort liability theories, liability for the acts of criminal intruders, student groups and alcohol-related liability, academic advising and defamation, and workers' compensation. Also discusses liability releases. A final chapter addresses risk management and insurance issues. Written by university counsel, these articles provide clear, useful information to counsel, administrators, and faculty.

Prosser, William L., & Keeton, W. Page. *Handbook on the Law of Torts* (5th ed., West, 1984). A comprehensive survey of tort doctrines and concepts, with discussion of leading cases and relevant statutes. Includes discussion of sovereign and charitable immunity, defamation, negligence, and the contributory negligence and assumption-of-risk defenses.

Richmond, Douglas. "Institutional Liability for Student Activities and Organizations," 19 *J. Law & Educ.* 309 (1990). Provides an overview of a variety of tort theories, and judicial precedents related to these theories, in which the institution's liability for the allegedly wrongful acts of student organizations was at issue.

Stevens, George E. "Evaluation of Faculty Competence as a 'Privileged Occasion,'" 4 *J. Coll. & Univ. Law* 281 (1979). Discusses the law of defamation as it applies to institutional evaluations of professional competence.

Strohm, Leslie Chambers (ed.). *AIDS on Campus: A Legal Compendium* (National Association of College and University Attorneys, 1991). A collection of materials related to a range of legal, medical, and policy issues concerning AIDS. Included are Centers for Disease Control recommendations, guidelines, and updates regarding precautions to take if employees, patients, or students have AIDS; journal articles; occupational safety and health guidelines; institutional policy statements; and an extensive list of resources.

See Reuschlein & Gregory entry for Section 2.1.

Sec. 2.4 (Personal Liability of Trustees, Administrators, and Staff)

Crandall, Deborah. *The Personal Liability of Community College Officials*, Topical Paper no. 61 (ERIC Clearinghouse for Junior Colleges, 1977). A guide for administrators that "illustrates the kinds of actions taking place in the courts and provides useful background information on personal liability." Though written for community college administrators, can be useful for other postsecondary administrators as well.

Hopkins, Bruce R., & Anderson, Barbara S. *The Counselor and the Law* (3d ed., American Association for Counseling and Development, 1990). Discusses confidentiality, privilege, and civil and criminal liability for counselors in educational, institutional, and community settings.

See Reuschlein & Gregory entry for Section 2.1.

See Langbein & Posner entry for Section 2.2.

See Moots, Nahmod, and NACUA entries for Section 2.3.

Sec. 2.5 (Institutional Management of Liability Risk)

Ad Hoc Committee on Trustee Liability Insurance. *Trustee Liability Insurance* (Association of Governing Boards, 1982). A booklet providing guidance on the selection of liability insurance coverage for trustees of postsecondary institutions.

Burling, Philip, & United Educators Risk Retention Group. "Managing Athletic Liability: An Assessment Guide," 72 *West's Educ. Law Rptr.* 503 (1993). A practical guide for developing and implementing risk management programs for athletics. Covers institutional duties to supervise; to provide safe facilities, adequate equipment, safe transportation, and medical treatment; and to protect spectators. Includes basic requirements and suggestions for risk management programs, "risk management action steps" for effectuating the institution's various duties, suggestions for selection and training of athletic staff, and a list of case citations.

Hollander, Patricia. *Computers in Education: Legal Liabilities and Ethical Issues Concerning Their Use and Misuse* (College Administration Publications, 1986). A monograph cataloguing negligence, contract, criminal, and other problems in one of the newest areas of potential liability. Provides practical guidance for identifying potential liabilities and avoiding or resolving the problems.

Stone, Byron, & North, Carol. *Risk Management and Insurance for Nonprofit Managers* (Society for Nonprofit Organizations, 1988). Provides practical guidance to nonprofit entities in devising risk management programs, including selection and maintenance of insurance coverage.
See Aiken and NACUA entries for Section 2.3.

III

The College and
the Faculty

◆ ◆ ◆

The legal relationship between a college and its faculty is defined by an increasingly complex web of principles and authorities. The core of the relationship is contract law (see especially Section 3.1), but that core is encircled by expanding layers of labor relations law (Section 3.2), employment discrimination law (Sections 3.3 and 3.4), and, in public institutions, constitutional law (see especially Sections 3.6 and 3.7) and public employment statutes and regulations. Federal regulations also affect the employment relationship (Section 7.2).

Most of the legal principles and laws discussed in this chapter also apply generally to the institution's employment relationship with its nonfaculty employees. Administrators will thus be constrained by these legal sources with respect to administration and staff as well as faculty. The particular applications of these sources to faculty will often differ from their applications to other employees, however, because courts and administrative agencies often take account of the unique characteristics of institutional customs and practices regarding faculty (such as tenure) and of academic freedom principles that protect faculty but not all other employees.

Sec. 3.1. The Contract of Employment

3.1.1. Scope and terms of the contract. There is considerable variety among institutions in the contracts they make with their faculties. The written contract may range from a brief notice of appointment on a standard form, with blanks to be filled in for each faculty member, to a lengthy collective bargaining agreement negotiated under state or federal labor laws. Or it may not be called a contract at all, but a faculty handbook or an institutional policy manual. As the discussion below explains, the formal writing does not necessarily include all the terms of the contract.

A contract's meaning is ascertained primarily by reference to its express terms. Where the contract language is unambiguous, it will govern any factual situation to which it clearly applies. *Billmyre v. Sacred Heart Hospital of Sisters of Charity*, 331 A.2d 313 (Md. 1975), illustrates this principle of contract interpretation. A nurse was employed as a coordinator-instructor at the hospital's nursing school under a contract specifying that either the employer or the employee could terminate the contract "at the end of the school year by giving notice in writing to the other not later than May 1 of such school year." On May 18 the nurse received a letter terminating her employment as a teacher. The court held that the hospital had breached the contract, since the contract language unambiguously provided for teacher notification before May 1 to effectuate a termination of the contract.

In the absence of contravening statutes, the clear language of the contract will prevail. But if a public college or university is subject to laws or regulations regarding contract periods or notice provisions, those laws or regulations may supersede the terms of a contract. In *Subryan v. Regents of the University of Colorado*, 698 P.2d 1383 (Colo. Ct. App. 1984), the court determined that the university did not have the authority to offer the plaintiff a one-year contract, because the regents had enacted a "law" governing the university that required appointments of all untenured faculty to be for three years. Although the regents argued that the one-year contract was justified because of a lack of funding for the plaintiff's position, the court declared that the regents could not ignore their own "laws," which they had the power to amend if financial problems so required.

Contracts are governed by common law, which may vary considerably by state. Employee handbooks and oral promises have been ruled to create binding contracts in some states, while other state courts have rejected this theory. For example, in *Sola v. Lafayette College*, 804 F.2d 40 (3d Cir. 1986), a faculty member sought to maintain a cause of action for tenure denial on the faculty handbook's language concerning affirmative action. The court ruled that such language had contractual status and provided the faculty member with a cause of action. Similarly, in *Arneson v. Board of Trustees, McKendree College*, 569 N.E.2d 252 (Ill. App. Ct. 1991), the court ruled that the faculty manual was a contract; however, a state appellate court in Lousiana reached the opposite result in *Marson v. Northwestern State University*, 607 So. 2d 1093 (La. Ct. App. 1992). In *Yates v. Board of Regents of Lamar University System*, 654 F. Supp. 979 (E.D. Tex. 1987), an untenured faculty member who had no written contract challenged a midyear discharge, asserting that oral representations made by the institution's officials constituted a contract not to be dismissed prior to the end of the academic year. The court, in denying summary judgment for the university, agreed that oral promises and policies could create an implied contract, citing *Perry v. Sindermann* (see Section 3.6.2.1).

Some contracts clearly state that another document has been incorporated into the terms of employment. For a postsecondary institution, such typical documents as the faculty handbook, institutional bylaws, or guidelines of the American Association of University Professors (AAUP) may be referred to in the contract. The extent to which the terms of such outside writings become part of the faculty employment contract is discussed in *Brady v. Board of Trustees of Nebraska State Colleges*, 242 N.W.2d 616 (Neb. 1976), where the contract of a tenured professor at Wayne State College incorporated "the college bylaws, policies, and practices relating to academic tenure and faculty dismissal procedures." When the institution dismissed the professor, using procedures that violated a section of the bylaws, the court held that the termination was ineffective: "There can be no serious question but that the bylaws of the governing body with respect to termination and conditions of the employment became a part of the employment contract between the college and [the professor]. At the time of the offer and acceptance of initial appointment . . . [the professor] was advised in writing that the offer and acceptance . . . constituted a contract honoring the policies and practices set forth in the faculty handbook, which was furnished to him at that time."

A case litigated under New York law demonstrates the significance of an institution's decision to adopt certain AAUP policy statements and not to adopt others. Fordham University had adopted the AAUP's 1940 "Statement of Principles on Academic Freedom and Tenure" but not its 1973 statement "On the Imposition of Tenure Quotas," in which the AAUP opposed tenure quotas. (Both statements are included in *AAUP Policy Documents and Reports* (AAUP, 1990), 3–10 and 37–39.) Fordham denied tenure to faculty whose departments would exceed 60 percent tenured faculty if they were awarded tenure. A professor of social service denied tenure because of the quota policy sued the university, claiming that the tenure quota policy violated both of the AAUP statements. In *Waring v. Fordham University*, 640 F. Supp. 42 (S.D.N.Y. 1986), the court, noting that the university had not adopted the 1973 statement, ruled that the university's action was appropriate and not a breach of contract.

But not all institutional policies are contractually binding. For example, in *Goodkind v. University of Minnesota*, 417 N.W.2d 636 (Minn. 1988), a dental school professor sued for breach of contract, stating that the policy for searching for a department chair was part of his employment contract and that the university's failure to follow the dental school's written search policy violated his contractual rights. The Minnesota Supreme Court disagreed, asserting that the search policy was a general statement of policy and not sufficiently related to the faculty member's own terms and conditions of employment to be considered contractually binding on the university.

On occasion a court is asked to fill in the "gaps" in a written or unwritten contract by determining what the intent of the parties was, even if that intent was not directly or indirectly expressed. The parties' intent may sometimes be ascertained from oral statements made at the time a hiring decision is made. In *Lewis v. Loyola University of Chicago*, 500 N.E.2d 47 (Ill. App. Ct. 1986), the plaintiff, a professor of medicine and chair of the pathology department at the university's medical school, argued that two letters from the dean of the medical school, in which the dean promised to recommend Dr. Lewis for early tenure consideration as soon as he obtained a license to practice medicine in Illinois, constituted a contract and that the institution's failure to grant him tenure breached that contract.

In 1980 the dean, as part of the process of recruiting Dr. Lewis as chair of the pathology department, wrote two letters in which he explicitly promised to recommend Lewis for tenure. Lewis accepted the university's offer, and his official appointment letter incorporated by reference the provisions of the faculty handbook. Lewis served as chair for three years on one-year contracts; just before the expiration of the third one-year contract, he received notice relieving him of his duties as department chair and advising him that his next one-year contract would be a terminal contract.

The dean did not submit Dr. Lewis's tenure candidacy at the time he had promised to, and several months later he resigned as dean and became a full-time faculty member. Before his resignation, the dean told Lewis orally that he had forgotten to submit his name for tenure and that he would do it the following year. The dean assured Lewis that the oversight would not be harmful.

Although the university argued that the letters and the dean's oral promises should not be considered part of Lewis's employment contract, the court disagreed. Noting that "the record discloses conversations, meetings and correspondence over a period of a year," the court asserted that "[it] cannot seriously be argued that a form contract for a teaching position . . . embodied the complete agreement and understanding of the parties" (500 N.E.2d at 50). Furthermore, said the court, objective—rather than subjective—criteria were used to make the tenure decision at the medical school, and Lewis was able to demonstrate that deans' tenure recommendations were rarely reversed. The court agreed with the trial judge's finding of "ample evidence" to indicate that Lewis would have been tenured absent the dean's oversight.

The opinion contains a useful discussion of remedies in academic breach-of-contract cases. The trial court had awarded Dr. Lewis the balance of his salary from the terminal contract (about $36,500) but had also awarded him $100,000 annually until he became disabled, died, or reached age sixty-five. The appellate court reversed this latter award, stating that it was based on speculation about the probable length of Dr. Lewis's employment had his contract not been breached. Thus, despite the finding of a contractual breach and the finding that Lewis should have been tenured, his damage award was relatively low. Furthermore, contractual remedies generally do not include reinstatement.

In other cases a court may look beyond the policies of the institution to the manner in which faculty employment terms are shaped in higher education generally. In these cases the court may use "academic custom and usage" to determine what the parties would have agreed to had they addressed a particular issue. For example, in *Greene v. Howard University*, 412 F.2d 1128 (D.C. Cir. 1969), the court looked to outside writings to determine the customs and usual practices of the institution and interpret the contract in light of such custom and usage (see Section 1.3.2.3). The plaintiffs in *Greene* were five nontenured professors who had been fired after a university investigation purported to find that they had been involved in disorders on campus. When the university terminated the professors as of the close of the academic year, the professors asserted that the university had breached a contractual obligation to give appropriate advance notice of nonrenewal or to provide a hearing prior to nonrenewal. The court concluded: "The contractual relationship existing here, when viewed against the regulations provided for, and the practices customarily followed in, their administration, required the university in the special circumstances here involved to afford the teachers an opportunity to be heard."

The court derived the institution's customary practices from the faculty handbook, buttressed by testimony in court, even though the handbook was not specifically incorporated by reference and even though it stated that the university did not have a contractual obligation to follow the notice-of-nonreappointment procedures. The professors were found to be relying "not only on personal assurances from university officials and on their recognition of the common practice of the university, but also on the written statements of university policy contained in the faculty handbook under whose terms they were employed." The court reasoned:

Contracts are written, and are to be read, by reference to the norms of conduct and expectations founded upon them. This is especially true of contracts in and among a community of scholars, which is what a university is. The readings of the marketplace are not invariably apt in this noncommercial context. . . .

The employment contracts of [the professors] here comprehend as essential parts of themselves the hiring policies and practices of the university as embodied in its employment regulations and customs [412 F.2d at 1135].

Another possible source of contractual protection for faculty could be the code of student conduct. In *McConnell v. Howard University*, 818 F.2d 58 (D.C. Cir. 1987), a professor refused to meet his class because the administration would not remove a disruptive student from the class. When the professor was discharged for failure to perform his professional duties, he sued for breach of contract, claiming that both the faculty handbook and the code of student conduct created a duty on the part of the university to protect his professional authority. The court ruled that he should have the opportunity to demonstrate that the university owed him this duty.

Although academic custom and usage can fill in gaps in the employment contract, it cannot be used to contradict the contract's express terms. In *Lewis v. Salem Academy and College*, 208 S.E.2d 404 (N.C. 1974), a professor had been employed from 1950 to 1973 under a series of successive one-year contracts. The college had renewed the contract the last two years, even though the professor had reached age sixty-five, but did not renew the contract for the 1973–74 academic year. The professor argued that he had a right to continue teaching until seventy because that was a usual and customary practice of the college and an implied benefit used to attract and retain faculty. The college's faculty guide, however, which was incorporated into all faculty contracts, had an explicit retirement policy providing for continued service beyond sixty-five to age seventy on a year-to-year basis at the discretion of the board of trustees.[1] The court held that custom and usage could not modify this clear contract provision:

Here . . . plaintiff had his own individual written contracts of employment, and the faculty guide, which was expressly incorporated into each of these contracts, specifically covered in clear and unambiguous language the conditions under which his employment after age 65 might be continued. "A custom or usage may be proved in explanation and qualification of the terms of a contract which otherwise would be ambiguous, or to show that the words in which the contract is expressed are used in a particular sense different from that which they usually impart, and, in some cases, to annex incidents to the contract in matters upon which it is silent; but evidence of a usage or custom is never admitted to make a new contract or to add a new element to one previously made" (55 Am. Jur., Usages and Customs § 31, 292) [208 S.E.2d at 408].

Even if a contractual provision would ordinarily bind the college or university, fraud on the part of the faculty member may result in a contractual *recission*, which

[1] Such a policy is now contrary to the dictates of the Age Discrimination in Employment Act (Section 3.3.6), which prohibits employment decisions made on the basis of an employee's age.

means that the contract no longer exists. For example, when American University learned that a tenure-track professor who had taught at the university for two years held a full-time job concurrently at another institution, it terminated his employment. In *Morgan v. American University*, 534 A.2d 323 (D.C. 1987), the professor challenged the termination because no hearing had been held, as the faculty handbook required. The university argued that its action was not a termination but a contract recission, because the professor had withheld a material fact—that he held a second full-time position. The court agreed with the university's theory. In *Nash v. Trustees of Boston University*, 946 F.2d 960 (1st Cir. 1991), a professor induced the university to give him an early-retirement incentive without informing the university that he had secured a full-time position at another institution. The court said that because the early-retirement agreement was induced by the professor's fraud, the university's refusal to honor that agreement was not a breach but a recission of the contract. The court rejected the plaintiff's claim that the Employee Retirement Income Security Act (ERISA—see Section 7.2.5) preempted the common law doctrine of fraud in the inducement, ruling that ERISA's purpose of protecting the legitimately acquired benefits of employees would be furthered by permitting the university to defend its recission by raising the fraud argument. The distinction between terminating and rescinding a contract is a standard and important one in contract law.

Contracts may not only specify faculty's duties and rights but also may have additional requirements, such as acceptance of the tenets of a particular religion (if the institution is affiliated with a religious organization) or a code of conduct. For example, several colleges and universities have promulgated policies that forbid faculty from entering sexual relationships with students who are in their classes or under their supervision.

A particularly controversial issue with contractual significance for academic and nonacademic organizations alike is whether the institution wishes to prohibit the use of controlled substances and whether it will test its employees to ascertain whether they use such substances. This issue is complicated by federal law requiring federal fund recipients to maintain "drug-free workplaces" (Sections 7.4.3.1 and 7.4.3.2); by the Fourth Amendment (for employees of public institutions); and by provisions of state constitutions, some of which have been interpreted to provide employees in the private sector with privacy rights similar to those guaranteed by the Fourth Amendment (Section 6.1). For an overview of the potential legal claims related to drug testing, see Note, "Drug Testing of College and University Employees," 15 *J. Coll. & Univ. Law* 321 (1989). See also "College and University Policies on Substance Abuse and Drug Testing," 78 *Academe* 17 (May–June 1992).

Whether or not a state or an institution may lawfully require its faculty and staff to submit to drug testing depends on many factors, including the nature of the individual's job, the type of institution (whether it is public or private), and the scope of the testing (whether it is done "for cause" or on a random basis). The legality of drug testing for employees of public institutions has been upheld by the U.S. Supreme Court for individuals holding certain types of jobs. In *National Treasury Employees Union v. Von Raabe*, 489 U.S. 656 (1989), the Court sustained the drug-testing policy of the U.S. Customs Service, which required a urine test for employees seeking a promotion to a position where they would be carrying firearms or confiscating drugs. The employees' union had charged that the policy was an unreasonable search (of the person's urine) and an unreasonable seizure (of evidence in the urine of possible illegal conduct), thus violating the Fourth Amendment of the U.S. Constitution. In a 5-to-4 decision, Justice Kennedy stated that the policy, which was applied to all such employees whether or not they were suspected drug users, was "reasonable" (a necessary finding to defeat a Fourth Amendment claim) because of the nature of the job. The strong government interest in the interdiction of illegal drugs outweighed the employees' interest in avoiding a potentially unreasonable search of their body fluids.

On the same day, the Court also upheld the drug-testing regulations of the Federal Railroad Administration, which required blood and urine testing for alcohol and drugs after accidents and when employees violated certain safety rules (*Skinner v. Railway Labor Executives Association*, 489 U.S. 602 (1989)). In a 7-to-2 opinion written by Justice Kennedy, the Court found this testing policy to be reasonable. The compelling government interest in the safety of both the public and fellow employees justified the policy. Individualized suspicion was not necessary under these circumstances to satisfy the dictates of the Fourth Amendment.

In both cases the Court evaluated the policy under attack by examining the strength of the government interest at stake and the importance of the employees' interest in freedom from unreasonable searches and seizures; and in both cases the Court found it significant that the employees were part of a "pervasively regulated industry." Although the cases may be applied by analogy to employees whose jobs involve public safety, such as police officers, it may be harder to argue that faculty are engaged in a profession where the use of controlled substances poses a safety hazard to society or to their colleagues.

A Georgia law, enacted in 1990, that required all applicants for state jobs (including faculty) to submit to drug tests was challenged under the *Von Raabe* doctrine. The law provided that any applicant who failed the test or refused to take it would be barred from public employment for two years. While the law did not require faculty already employed at public institutions to be tested, it would have permitted testing of employees with "hazardous" jobs, such as campus police.

The Georgia Association of Educators asserted that the law violated the Equal Protection and Due Process Clauses of the Fourteenth Amendment, as well as the Fourth Amendment. In *Georgia Association of Educators v. Harris*, 749 F. Supp. 1110 (N.D. Ga. 1990), a federal district judge agreed, saying that Georgia's general interest in maintaining a drug-free workplace was not sufficiently compelling to outweigh the applicants' Fourth Amendment protections against unreasonable searches and seizures. The judge noted that he could not approve the law under *Von Raabe's* balancing test and criticized the legislature for failing to identify a government interest compelling enough to justify testing all applicants for state jobs.[2]

In addition to drug testing, some states have enacted laws requiring that, as a condition of employment, faculty and graduate teaching assistants be competent in spoken English. In other states a statewide regulatory body or governing body has promulgated a similar requirement. Many of these laws or policies require that the institution certify the English proficiency only of nonnative speakers of English, a requirement that might be interpreted as discrimination on the basis of national

---

[2]Relevant cases and authorities related to drug testing are collected in Annot., "Use of Illegal Drugs as Ground for Dismissal of Teacher, or Denial or Cancellation of Teacher's Certificate," 47 A.L.R.3d 754 (1973 and periodic supp.).

origin (see Section 3.3.3). For a discussion of these laws and policies, see P. Monoson & C. Thomas, "Oral English Proficiency Policies for Faculty in U.S. Higher Education," 16 *Rev. Higher Educ.* 127 (1993).

Given the rapid changes in state common law of contract and the interest of state legislators in the conditions of faculty employment, administrators and faculty should continually be sensitive to the question of what institutional documents or practices are, or should be, part of the faculty contract. Where ambiguity exists, they should decide whether there is some good policy reason for maintaining the ambiguity. If not, the contracts should be clarified. And both faculty and administrators need to understand how the law of their state interprets handbooks, policy manuals, and oral promises. Careful drafting and the use, if desirable, of disclaimers in documents that are not intended to afford contractual rights may protect the institution against liability for claims that arise from oral promises or policy documents in some states, although substantial differences exist among states in judicial attitudes toward disclaimers.

3.1.2. Amendment of the contract. The terms of the original employment contract need not remain static through the entire life of the contract. Courts have accepted the proposition that employment contracts may be amended. In *Rehor v. Case Western Reserve University,* 331 N.E.2d 416 (Ohio 1975), the court found amendments to be valid either where the right to amend was reserved in the original contract or where there was mutual consent of the parties to amend and adequate consideration was given in return for the changed terms. The plaintiff in *Rehor* was a tenured professor employed under contract at Western Reserve University from 1942 to 1967. Throughout this period the retirement age was always seventy. After Case Institute of Technology joined with Western Reserve to form Case Western Reserve University, Case Western, which took over the faculty contracts, adopted a resolution requiring faculty members over sixty-eight to petition to be reappointed. The university bylaws provided that "the board of trustees shall from time to time adopt such rules and regulations governing the appointment and tenure of the members of the faculty as the board of trustees deems necessary." The court held that this bylaw language "includes a reservation of the right to change the retirement age of the faculty" and thus defeats the plaintiff's claim that the university was in breach of contract. Since the retirement policy is part of tenure, "the reserved right to change rules of tenure includes the right to change the retirement policy." The court also approved of the university's assertion that "an employment contract between a university and a tenured faculty member may be amended by the parties in writing when supported by adequate consideration." These considerations were satisfied in *Rehor* by the professor's execution of reappointment forms and acceptance of an increased salary after the new retirement policy was put into effect. (For a criticism of the case, see M. Finkin, "Contract, Tenure, and Retirement: A Comment on *Rehor v. Case Western Reserve University,*" 4 *Human Rights* 343 (1975).)

The outcome in *Rehor* is based in large part upon the apparent renegotiation of the faculty member's terms and conditions of employment. In *Karr v. Board of Trustees of Michigan State University,* 325 N.W.2d 605 (Mich. Ct. App. 1982), the trustees of Michigan State University decided to respond to a budget crisis by placing university employees on a two-and-a-half-day layoff, for which they would receive no pay. Although employees were permitted to specify whether they wanted the reduction in pay deducted in a lump sum or in six equal installments, there was no negotiation with the employees. Although the trial court had granted summary judgment for the university, the appellate court reversed, saying that, if the employees had contracts with the university for a fixed sum, then the university's unilateral decision to withhold two and a half days of the employees' pay was a breach of their employment contract. The existence of such a contract was a question of fact, said the court, and was not amenable to a summary judgment determination.

On the other hand, not all understandings between faculty and a college or university constitute a binding contract. In *Faur v. Jewish Theological Seminary of America*, 536 N.Y.S.2d 516 (N.Y. App. Div. 1989), a male professor of rabbinics resigned when the seminary faculty voted to admit female rabbinical students, claiming that the change in admissions policy was incompatible with his personal religious beliefs. The professor argued that the new admissions policy breached his employment contract and also constituted religious discrimination. The court, citing the impropriety of examining whether the seminary's policy change constituted religious discrimination on First Amendment grounds (see Section 7.2.6.2), dismissed the professor's claim.

Under the common law of many states, a letter may be contractually binding on both parties. In *Levy v. University of Cincinnati*, 616 N.E.2d 1132 (Ohio Ct. App. 1992), a letter outlining the terms of a professor's employment was ruled a contract; a subsequent letter changing those contractual terms was also found to bind both parties. The court ruled that the professor had accepted the terms of the second letter, which established new employment rights and obligations, by continuing to teach at the university.

Occasionally contracts may also be amended unilaterally by subsequent state legislation. But the state's power to modify its own contracts legislatively or to regulate contracts between private parties is circumscribed by Article I, Section 10(1), of the United States Constitution, known as the Contracts Clause: "No state shall . . . pass any . . . law impairing the obligation of contracts." In *Indiana ex rel. Anderson v. Brand*, 303 U.S. 95 (1938) (discussed in Section 3.1.4), for instance, the U.S. Supreme Court held that an Indiana law which had the effect of canceling the tenure rights of certain public school teachers was an unconstitutional impairment of their employment contracts. Under this and subsequent Contracts Clause precedents, a state may not impair either its own or private contracts unless such impairment is both "reasonable and necessary to serve an important public purpose," with "necessary" meaning that the impairment is essential and no viable alternative for serving the state's purpose exists (*United States Trust Company of New York v. New Jersey*, 431 U.S. 1 (1977)).

3.1.3. Waiver of contract rights. Once a contract has been formed, the parties may sometimes waive their contract rights, either intentionally by a written agreement or unintentionally by their actions. *Chung v. Park*, 514 F.2d 382 (3d Cir. 1975), concerned a professor who after teaching at Mansfield State College for five years was notified that his contract would not be renewed. Through his counsel, the professor negotiated with the state attorney general and agreed to submit the issue of the termination's validity to an arbitration panel. When the panel upheld the termination, the professor brought suit, alleging that the college did not follow the termination procedures set out in the tenure regulations and was therefore in breach of contract. The court, after pointing out that under the state law contract rights may be waived by subsequent agreement between the parties, upheld the district court's finding "that the parties had reached such a subsequent agreement when, after extensive negotiations, they specifically stipulated to the hearing procedures actually employed."

Public policy considerations may, however, preclude the waiver of certain contract terms. In *McLachlan v. Tacoma Community College District No. 22*, 541 P.2d 1010 (Wash. 1975), the court addressed this issue but found the rights in question to be properly waivable. The two plaintiffs were employed by the college district under contracts that specifically stated, "The employee waives all rights normally provided by the tenure laws of the state of Washington." The plaintiffs, who were aware that they were employed to replace people on one-year sabbaticals, contended that, for reasons of public policy, the contracts should not be enforced. While avoiding the broad issue of whether a blanket waiver of tenure rights contravenes public policy, the court said, "We envision no serious public policy considerations which would prohibit a teacher from waiving the statutory nonrenewal notice provisions in advance of the notice date, provided he knows the purpose of his employment is to replace the regular occupant of that position who is on a one-year sabbatical leave."

3.1.4. Statutory rights versus contract rights in public institutions. A public institution's legal relationship with faculty members may be defined by statute and administrative regulation as well as by written employment contract.[3] Tenure rights, for instance, may be created by a state tenure statute rather than by the terms of the employment contract; or pay scales may be established by board of regents or state personnel rules rather than by the employment contract. The distinction between statutory rights and contract rights can be critical. A right created by statute or by administrative rule can be revoked or modified by a subsequent statute or rule, with the result that the public institution has no further obligation to recognize that right. A contract right, however, usually cannot be revoked or modified by subsequent statute or rule unless the parties have made provision for such changes in the contract itself, or unless the modification satisfies the requirements of the Constitution's Contracts Clause.

The Supreme Court's test for compliance with the Contracts Clause was created in *United States Trust Co. v. New Jersey*, 431 U.S. 1 (1977). In *Gardiner v. Tschechtelin*, 765 F. Supp. 279 (D. Md. 1991), a federal trial judge applied the *United States Trust* criteria to determine whether the state could abrogate tenure contracts with college faculty. In 1989, by act of the state legislature, the state of Maryland had assumed ownership of a municipal college, the Community College of Baltimore, because of the college's serious financial problems and a strong concern about the quality of the curriculum and the faculty. That legislation abolished faculty tenure and provided that faculty employed at the college would be employed only through

---

[3]Cases related to faculty rights under tenure statutes are collected in Annot., "Construction and Effect of Tenure Provisions of Contract or Statute Governing Employment of College or University Faculty Member," 66 A.L.R.3d 1018 (1975 and periodic supp.); Annot., "Sufficiency of Notice of Intention to Discharge or Not to Rehire Teacher Under Statutes Requiring Such Notice," 52 A.L.R.4th 301 (1987 and periodic supp.); Annot., "Who Is 'Teacher' for Purposes of Tenure Statute," 94 A.L.R.3d 141 (1979 and periodic supp.).

the end of 1990. All faculty were sent termination notices. The faculty sued under Section 1983 of the Civil Rights Act (see this volume, Section 2.3.3), claiming that the legislation violated the Constitution's Contracts Clause (see Section 3.1.2) because their tenure was guaranteed by contract.

Under *United States Trust Co.*, the court was required to determine whether the legislation served a "legitimate public purpose" and whether the faculty contracts were private or public contracts. If the contracts were public, the court's standard of review would be higher, since the state's "self-interest" was at stake (765 F. Supp. at 288, citing 431 U.S. at 26). Because the faculty contracts were public, the court also was required to determine whether the legislation was "reasonable and necessary."

The judge determined that the legislature's concerns about the financial viability and quality of education at the college were legitimate, and that the state had chosen a less drastic means to try to improve the college than it could have by retaining all the faculty for one year and providing that those evaluated as above-average or excellent teachers would receive additional annual contracts. Given the legislature's decision to continue supporting the college for only three years, pending an evaluation of the appropriateness of continuing its existence, the court ruled that the abrogation of tenure and the dismissal of some of the faculty was "reasonable and necessary to serve an important public purpose" (765 F. Supp. at 290) and therefore did not violate the Contracts Clause. For analysis of Contracts Clause litigation, see Note, "Rediscovering the Contracts Clause," 97 *Harvard L. Rev.* 1414 (1984).

Even if particular rights emanate from statutes or regulations, they may become embodied in contracts and thus be enforceable as contract rights. The contract may provide that certain statutory rights become part of the contract. Or the statute or regulation may itself be so written or interpreted that the rights it creates become enforceable as contract rights. This latter approach has twice been dealt with by the U.S. Supreme Court in cases concerning statutory tenure laws. *Phelps v. Board of Education of West New York*, 300 U.S. 319 (1937), concerned a New Jersey Act of 1909, which provided that teachers employed by local school boards could only be dismissed or subject to reduced salary for cause. By an Act of 1933, the state enabled the school boards to fix and determine salaries. When one board invoked this authority to reduce salaries without cause, teachers claimed that this action impaired their contracts in violation of the Constitution's Contracts Clause. The Court held that there was no constitutional impairment, since the Act of 1909 did not create a contract between the state and the teachers. The Court agreed with the New Jersey court that the statute established "a legislative status for teachers" but failed to establish "a contractual one that the legislature may not modify." Thus, "although the Act of 1909 prohibited the board, a creature of the state, from reducing the teacher's salary or discharging him without cause, . . . this was but a regulation of the conduct of the board and not a continuing contract of indefinite duration with the individual teacher."

A year after *Phelps*, the Supreme Court came to a contrary conclusion in a similar impairment case. *Indiana ex rel. Anderson v. Brand*, 303 U.S. 95 (1938), dealt with Indiana's Teachers Tenure Act, adopted in 1927. The Act provided that, once a teacher had tenure, his or her contract "shall be deemed to be in effect for an indefinite period." Sometime after the Act was amended in 1933 to omit township school corporations, the job of the plaintiff, a tenured teacher, was terminated. The Court found that the Act of 1927 created a contract with the teacher because the title of the Act was "couched in terms of contract," the "tenor of the Act indicates that the word 'contract' was not used inadvertently or in other than its usual legal meaning,'' and the state courts had previously viewed the Act of 1927 as creating a contract. The Court then held that the 1933 amendment unconstitutionally impaired the contracts created by the Act of 1927.

Given the fundamental distinction between contract and statutory rights, and the sometimes subtle relationships between them, administrators of public institutions should pay particular attention to the source of faculty members' legal rights and should consult counsel whenever they are attempting to define or change a faculty member's legal status.

3.1.5. Status of part-time faculty members. Facing ever-increasing financial constraints, many colleges and universities have increasingly turned to part-time faculty to provide instruction at considerably lower cost than hiring a full-time faculty member. Part-time faculty often are paid on a per-course basis, and generally are not entitled to employee benefits such as medical insurance or pensions.

The status of part-time faculty members in postsecondary institutions has received attention within and outside the postsecondary community (see, for example, J. Gappa & D. Leslie, *The Invisible Faculty: Improving the Status of Part-Timers in Higher Education* (Jossey-Bass, 1993); H. Bowen & J. Schuster, *American Professors: A National Resource Imperiled* (Oxford University Press, 1986); D. Leslie, S. Kellams, & G. M. Gunne, *Part-Time Faculty in American Higher Education* (Praeger, 1982)). The number and percentage of part-time faculty members in the academic work force has increased substantially over the past decades. According to the AAUP ("Report on the Status of Non-Tenure-Track Faculty," 78 *Academe* 39 (1992), at 40–41), the percentage of part-timers increased from approximately 32 percent of total teaching faculty in 1980 to approximately 38 percent in 1988. Differences by institutional type are striking; 17 percent of the faculty in research universities are part-time, while approximately 52 percent of the total faculty at community colleges were part-timers in 1988. Compared with their representation in full-time positions (27 percent), women tend to be overrepresented among part-time faculty (42 percent), and African-Americans are twice as likely to teach part-time as whites. Legal issues concerning this large and important faculty group are likely to demand special attention.

The questions being raised about part-time faculty involve such matters as pay scales, eligibility for fringe benefits (life insurance, health insurance, sick leave, sabbaticals, retirement contributions), access to tenure, rights upon dismissal or nonrenewal, and status for collective bargaining purposes. Each of these questions may be affected by two more general questions: (1) How is the distinction between a part-time and a full-time faculty member defined? (2) Are distinctions made between (or among) categories of part-time faculty members? The initial and primary source for answering these questions is the faculty contract (see Section 3.1.1). Also important are state and federal statutes and administrative rulings on such matters as defining bargaining units for collective bargaining (see *University of San Francisco and University of San Francisco Faculty Association*, 265 NLRB 1221 (1982), approving part-time faculty unit, and see also Section 3.2.3), retirement plans, civil service classifications, faculty tenure, wage-and-hour requirements, and unemployment compensation. These statutes and rulings may substantially affect what can and cannot be provided for in faculty contracts.

A significant area of controversy has concerned the application of state statutes to part-time faculty in public institutions. Most of the reported court decisions are from California, which has a complex statutory scheme with special provisions applicable to community colleges. This statutory scheme provides the framework for part-time faculty contracts with public institutions. The California experience merits study not only to understand that state's law but also to develop insights on approaches to take and problems to avoid in other states, where the law is less developed.

Generally, California has three classes of community college faculty members: permanent (also known as regular or tenured), probationary (also known as contract), and temporary. In *Balen v. Peralta Junior College District*, 523 P.2d 629 (Cal. 1974), the California Supreme Court explained the statutory classifications of community college teachers:

> The essence of the statutory classification system is that continuity of service restricts the power to terminate employment which the institution's governing body would normally possess. Thus, the legislature has prevented the arbitrary dismissal of employees with positions of a settled and continuing nature—that is, permanent and probationary teachers—by requiring notice and hearing before termination. . . . Substitute and temporary teachers, on the other hand, fill the short-range needs of a school district, and may be summarily released absent an infringement of constitutional or contractual rights. . . . Because the substitute and temporary classifications are not guaranteed procedural due process by statute, they are narrowly defined by the legislature and should be strictly interpreted [523 P.2d at 631–32; citations and footnotes omitted].

The most extensively litigated section of California's statutes, Cal. Educ. Code § 13337.5, has been recodified as Cal. Educ. Code §§ 87482 and 87482.5 (West, 1990). The first subpart of Section 87482 defines as "temporary" those appointees who replace permanent teachers on leave or are employed in response to increased student enrollment. The second subpart limits the duration of temporary employment to no more than two semesters or three quarters within a consecutive three-year period. Faculty members with a work load less than 60 percent of the full-time assignment for permanent faculty are designated as temporary by Section 87482.5; temporary employees as defined by this section can never achieve permanent status. The relationship of this section to the other subsections is the key issue confronted in the court decisions.

The *Balen* case, above, concerned a part-time hourly instructor whose employment was terminated without notice or hearing after four and a half years of service. Since Balen taught less than 40 percent of the hours of a full-time load, the college argued he was a temporary employee under Section 87482.5. But that paragraph had not been enacted when Balen was initially hired, and the court refused to apply it retroactively. Since the plaintiff had attained probationary status under other provisions of the California Education Code, and Section 87482.5 could not be used to divest him of that status, he could be dismissed only for cause after notice and opportunity for a hearing.

In *California Teachers Association v. Santa Monica Community College District*, 144 Cal. Rptr. 620 (Cal. Ct. App. 1978), the association sought reclassification and back pay for teachers whom the district had classified as temporary. The association argued that the language of Section 87482 limited the effect of Section 87482.5

(the prohibition on hiring temporary faculty as regular, or "contract," employees), so that temporary faculty should be reclassified as "contract" faculty, with all the rights of full-time faculty. The court disagreed, concluding that Section 87482.5 stands as independent authority for long-term classification of employees as temporary. Thus, under this case, community colleges could continue hiring their faculty members as temporary employees paid at lower rates of pay and without procedural rights upon dismissal.

The *California Teachers Association* analysis was adopted and expanded by the Supreme Court of California in *Peralta Federation of Teachers (AFL-CIO) v. Peralta Community College*, 595 P.2d 113 (Cal. 1979). The plaintiffs, all employed for less than 60 percent of a full-time load, were separated into two categories: those hired before and those hired after November 8, 1967, the effective date of Section 13337.5 (which was later recodified as Section 87482.5). Both groups sought tenure, higher compensation, and back pay. Those hired after November 8 asserted that their status was unaffected by Section 87482.5 because their employment did not meet the conditions of Section 87482. The court disagreed, thus confirming the independent status of Section 87482.5 as construed in *California Teachers*. These plaintiffs therefore obtained no relief because they were within that section's definition of temporary. Those hired before November 8, 1967, however, were not subject to Section 87482.5 because, under *Balen* (above), Section 87482.5 did not apply retroactively. Construing other statutory provisions defining permanent status, the court held that faculty members in this group were permanent (tenured) employees and awarded them that status along with back pay.

The *Peralta* decision was applied and explained by a lower court in *Warner v. North Orange County Community College District*, 161 Cal. Rptr. 1 (Cal. Ct. App. 1979). A subsequent California Supreme Court opinion in *California Teachers Association v. San Diego Community College District*, 621 P.2d 856 (Cal. 1981), reaffirmed *Peralta* and analyzed the issue of computing pro rata pay for part-time faculty under the California statutes.

Another question regarding the application of state law to part-time faculty is whether full-time faculty at a community college engaged in a reduction in force can "bump" part-time faculty from the courses that faculty to be laid off are qualified to teach. In *Biggiam v. Board of Trustees of Community College District No. 516*, 506 N.E.2d 1011 (Ill. App. Ct. 1987), the court was required to determine whether the Illinois Community College Tenure Act and/or the collective bargaining agreement between the faculty and the board afforded tenured faculty the right to bump any instructor or just full-time faculty members. The court agreed with the board's argument that full-time faculty could bump nontenured or less senior faculty from "positions," but that part-time instructors were not "faculty" and did not have "positions," but only taught courses. Thus, faculty could not bump instructors from courses. Although this case rested on interpretation of a state law, it may have relevance to institutions in other states that will be reducing the number of full-time faculty.

To respond effectively to issues like those in California, and the many other legal and policy issues that are arising, administrators should understand the differences in legal status of part-time and full-time faculty members at their institutions. In consultation with counsel, they should make sure that the existing differences in status and any future changes are adequately expressed in faculty contracts and institutional rules and regulations. Administrators should also consider the extent and clarity of their institution's legal authority to maintain the existing differences if they are challenged or to change the legal status of part-timers if changes are advisable to effectuate new educational policy.

3.1.6. Contracts in religious institutions. In religious institutions employment issues involving the interplay between religious doctrine and civil law have been litigated primarily in cases construing state and federal employment discrimination laws (see Section 7.2.6); however, when the faculty member is a member of a religious order or when the institution makes employment decisions on religious grounds, complex questions of contract law may also arise.

The contract made between a faculty member and a religiously affiliated institution would normally be governed by state contract law unless the parties explictly or implicitly intended that additional sources of law be used to interpret the contract. Some religiously affiliated institutions require their faculty to observe the code of conduct dictated by the doctrine of the religious sponsor; others incorporate church law or canon law into their contracts. Judicial interpretation of contracts is limited by the religion clauses of the First Amendment (see Section 1.6).

Three cases have addressed the nature of the contract between a religious institution and a faculty member who belongs to a religious order. In two of these cases, the courts have determined that the issues involved religious matters and that judicial intervention would be unconstitutional; in the third, the court determined that only secular issues were involved and no constitutional violation was present.

In *Curran v. Catholic University of America*, Civ. No. 1562-87 (D.C. Super. Ct., Feb. 28, 1989), a tenured professor of Catholic theology filed a breach-of-contract claim when the university prohibited him from teaching courses involving Catholic theology. Curran had taken a public stand against several of the Catholic Church's teachings, and the Holy See had ruled him ineligible to teach Catholic theology. The university's board of trustees then withdrew Curran's ecclesiastical license, which is required of all faculty who teach in departments that confer ecclesiastical degrees. Although the university attempted to place Curran in another, nontheological teaching assignment, Curran argued that the university had constructively discharged him without a finding that he was not competent to teach Catholic theology. He also argued that the university had incorporated protections for academic freedom into his contract and that the treatment afforded him because of his scholarly beliefs constituted a violation of those protections.

The court was faced with three potential sources of contract law: District of Columbia common law, canon law, and explicit or implied contractual promises of academic freedom that were judicially enforceable (see Section 3.1.1). The court saw its duty not to interpret canon law, which it was forbidden to do by Establishment Clause principles, but to determine whether the parties had intended to be bound by canon law, a question of fact. The court found that, even though his contract did not explicitly mention canon law or its requirements, Curran knew that ecclesiastical faculties were different from nonecclesiastical faculties, that the Holy See could change the requirements for ecclesiastical faculties, and that the university was obligated to accede to those changes. In fact, the Apostolic Constitution of 1979 required ecclesiastical faculties to have a "canonical mission," meaning that such faculty were required to teach in the name of the Catholic Church and not to oppose its doctrine. The court noted:

> [I]f the court had come to the opposite conclusion on this issue [that Curran was contractually required to maintain a canonical mission], it would have been squarely presented with a substantial constitutional question [the Establishment Clause problem]. . . . In light of the court's conclusion that Professor Curran's contract required him to have a canonical mission as a condition of teaching in the Department of Theology, it is unnecessary to reach the University's "canon law defense" [the argument that the Constitution prohibited the court from interpreting canon law] [Civ. No. 1562-87 at 19].

The court ruled that the university had the right to require faculty who taught theology to meet the requirements of the Holy See, since that body could withdraw the university's authority to award ecclesiastical degrees if the university failed to comply with its requirements. Because the university had a special relationship with the Holy See, the court found implied in Curran's contract with the university an obligation to abide by the Holy See's requirements. The court also found that, whatever academic freedom Curran was due, his academic freedom could not limit the Holy See's authority to determine which ecclesiastical faculty were qualified to teach theology. (For a brief discussion of academic freedom in religiously affiliated institutions, see Section 3.7.5.)

The New Jersey Supreme Court was faced with two cases involving the interplay between religious doctrine and civil contract law. In *Alicea v. New Brunswick Theological Seminary*, 128 N.J. 303 (1992), an ordained minister and untenured assistant professor of theology claimed that the seminary's president offered him a nontenure-track position with the promise of an eventual tenured position. When that promise was not acted upon, Alicea resigned, claiming constructive discharge and breach of contract. The ecclesiastical body that governed the seminary, the Reform Church's Board of Theological Education (BTE), had reserved to itself all final decision power regarding the hiring and retention of faculty. Alicea claimed that the BTE had impliedly ratified the promise made to him by the president, and that the president had the apparent authority to make such promises. The court ruled that it could not determine whether the seminary had breached an implied contract with an untenured professor because such an inquiry would constitute an inquiry into ecclesiastical polity or doctrine. Although the court refused to adopt a per se rule that courts may not hear employees' lawsuits against religious institutions, the court noted that "governmental interference with the polity, *i.e.*, church governance, of a religious institution could also violate the First Amendment by impermissibly limiting the institution's options in choosing those employees whose role is instrumental in charting the course for the faithful" (128 N.J. at 311). Explaining further, the court said:

> When State action would impose restrictions on a religious institution's decisions regarding employees who perform ministerial functions under the employment relationship at issue, courts may not interfere in the employment relationship unless the agreement between the parties indicates that they have waived their free-exercise rights and unless the incidents of litigation—deposi-

tions, subpoenas, document discovery and the like—would not unconstitutionally disrupt the administration of the religious institution [128 N.J. at 312–13].

The court noted that because Alicea taught theology and counseled prospective ministers, he performed a ministerial function. Therefore, although the case involved issues of church governance (rather than doctrine, as in the *Curran* case), the court was similarly required to abstain from exercising jurisdiction.

Although the faculty handbook contained a grievance provision, which the seminary had not honored, the court refused to order the parties to use the procedure, because it was "optional" in light of the BTE's reservation of full authority. The court stated: "Enforcement of the ministerial-employment agreement would have violated the Free Exercise Clause whether based on actual or apparent authority" (128 N.J. at 316). In other words, the court could suggest that the parties abide by the manual but could not enforce the manual because its provisions were "vague and clearly optional" (128 N.J. at 317).

The court outlined the analysis to be applied to such cases:

> [A] court should first ascertain whether, because of the ministerial role played by the employee, the doctrinal nature of the controversy, or the practical effect of applying neutral principles of law, the court should abstain from entertaining jurisdiction. . . . In assessing the extent to which the dispute implicates issues of doctrine or polity, factors such as the function of the employee under the relationship sought to be enforced, the clarity of contractual provisions relating to the employee's function, and the defendant's plausible justifications for its actions should influence the resolution of that threshhold question. . . . If neither the threat of regulatory entanglement, the employee's ministerial function, nor the primarily-doctrinal nature of the underlying dispute mandates abstention, courts should effectuate the intent of the parties to the contract.
>
> Specifically, courts should enforce express agreements or implied promises to comply with religious doctrine when they can determine compliance or non-compliance with such agreements by application of neutral principles of law. Similarly, courts should honor contractual waivers of any rights to act in accordance with or under the compulsion of religious beliefs to the extent that enforcement through litigation would not unconstitutionally entangle church and State. In discerning the reasonable intent of the parties, courts should focus on factors such as the text of the contract or employment manual, on whether the employee's duties included supervision of impressionable adherents, and on the function to have been performed by the employee. Either party's position as a church official is also a relevant, but not dispositive, factor. Conversely, if the employee performs a function that would otherwise require abstention, the court must determine whether the parties nevertheless intended to submit their dispute to the civil courts and, if such intent be found, whether such submission would nonetheless entail impermissible entanglement [128 N.J. at 313–14].

The same court decided a case with similar issues on the same day as *Alicea*. In *Welter v. Seton Hall University*, 128 N.J. 279 (1992), two Ursuline nuns who had taught for three years at Seton Hall, a Catholic university, filed breach-of-contract claims when their contracts were not renewed. The university claimed that the sisters' order, the Ursuline Convent of the Sacred Heart, had refused permission for the sisters to continue teaching at the university, and that the court lacked jurisdiction to entertain the breach-of-contract claims.

The New Jersey Supreme Court ruled against the university on several grounds. First, the sisters did not perform a ministerial (pastoral) function—they taught computer science. Second, the dispute did not implicate either doctrinal issues or matters of church polity; the university simply refused to honor its contractual obligation to give the untenured sisters twelve months' notice (a one-year terminal contract) before discharging them. The contract included no mention of canon law, nor did it require the sisters to obtain the permission of their religious superiors before accepting employment. It was the same contract that the university used for lay faculty. Furthermore, when the Ursuline convent requested that the university forward the sisters' paychecks directly to it, the university refused and advised the sisters to open a checking account and deposit their paychecks.

There was substantial evidence that the university desired to terminate the sisters' employment because of dissatisfaction with their performance. Instead of issuing the terminal contracts, university administrators contacted the sisters' religious superiors and asked that they be recalled. The university then terminated the sisters' employment without the required notice. The university admitted that the issue would be a completely secular one if the sisters were not members of a religious order. In deciding this case, the court applied a two-part test. First, the court analyzed whether the sisters performed any ministerial functions for the university, and found that they did not. Second, the court assessed whether the sisters could have contemplated that canon law would have superseded the procedural safeguards of the contract, and found no such evidence. "The purely secular nature of plaintiffs' employment obligations; the absence of a contractual provision imposing religious obligations on plaintiffs; Seton Hall's rejection of the Ursulines' prior request regarding plaintiffs' paychecks; and the absence of any religious connotations behind the hiring of, tenure of, or decision to terminate plaintiffs all plainly indicate the contrary" (128 N.J. at 299).

In a fourth case involving the question of contract interpretation when the employer is a religious organization, a faculty member who was *not* a member of a religious order was discharged by a Baptist seminary for failing to adhere to the "lifestyle and behavior" expected of a faculty member at the seminary. In *Patterson v. Southwestern Baptist Theological Seminary*, 858 S.W.2d 602 (Tex. Ct. App. 1993), the faculty member filed a wrongful-discharge claim, alleging that his contractual rights had been violated. The faculty handbook required each faculty member to be an "active and faithful member of a Baptist church" and to "subscribe in writing to the Articles of Faith" of the Southern Baptist Convention. The court ruled that the explicit inclusion of these requirements in the faculty handbook made it evident that the seminary "makes employment decisions regarding faculty members largely upon religious criteria" (858 S.W.2d at 1199), rendering judicial review of the discharge decision a violation of the Constitution's First and Fourteenth Amendments.

The cases are consistent in deferring to religious institutions on matters that involve the interpretation of church doctrine (*Curran*) or matters of church governance. The decisions have clear implications for academic freedom disputes at religious institutions (Section 3.7.5.2), especially where issues of adherence to religious doctrine are intertwined with free speech issues. Counsel acting for religiously affiliated institutions whose leaders wish their faculty employment contracts to be interpreted under church law as well as civil contract law should specify in written contracts and other institutional documents that church law or religious doctrine will be binding on the parties to the contract, and that church law will prevail in any conflict between church and civil law.

3.1.7. Legal planning with contracts. Given the wealth of legal theories that faculty, as well as other employees, use to challenge employment decisions, the need for careful drafting of faculty handbooks, institutional policies, and employment contracts is essential. State court opinions regarding the binding nature of a handbook or an employment contract, while often favoring the employee, also suggest that in these documents the faculty member's rights vis-à-vis the institution should be carefully spelled out, in order to reduce potential litigation.

Although careful drafting of contracts and policy documents is important, no amount of careful drafting can prevent litigation. Administrators and counsel might wish to consider the use of individual employment contracts, particularly with faculty, containing a clause that limits the parties to arbitration for resolution of disputes arising under the contract. Arbitration and other alternate dispute-resolution mechanisms (see Section 3.2.5) often provide quicker, less expensive, and less formal resolution of disputes than litigation, and federal courts are beginning to dismiss lawsuits brought by employees who have signed contracts with arbitration clauses.

Beginning with a decision by the U.S. Supreme Court in *Gilmer v. Interstate-Johnson Lane*, 500 U.S. 20 (1991), courts are enforcing arbitration clauses in individual employment contracts, although the law is different for collectively bargained contracts (see Section 3.2.7). Gilmer, a registered securities representative, had signed a contract that required him to submit all employment disputes to compulsory arbitration. When he challenged his discharge by filing an age discrimination claim, his employer filed a motion to compel arbitration, which the trial court upheld. The appellate court reversed, but the U.S. Supreme Court sided with the trial court, ruling that the language of the contract must be enforced.

In several cases decided after *Gilmer*, trial courts have enforced arbitration clauses in situations where plaintiffs have filed employment discrimination claims with an administrative agency or in court. Although the Federal Arbitration Act (9 U.S.C. § 1 et seq.) requires courts, in general, to enforce private arbitration agreements, language in the Act has been interpreted to preclude arbitration of employment contracts. Section 1 of the Act exempts "contracts of employment of seamen, railroad employees, or any other class of workers engaged in foreign or interstate commerce." The U.S. Supreme Court has not interpreted the meaning of "class of workers engaged in foreign or interstate commerce," and the conclusions of federal appellate courts regarding the reach of this language have been inconsistent. Some courts have interpreted the exclusion narrowly and applied it only to those workers actually engaged in the movement of goods in interstate commerce (see, for example, *Miller Brewing Co. v. Brewery Workers Local Union No. 9*, 739 F.2d 1159 (7th Cir. 1984), *cert. denied*, 469 U.S. 1160 (1985)); others have defined the exemption to include all employment contracts (see, for example, *Willis v. Dean Witter Reynolds, Inc.*, 948 F.2d 305 (6th Cir. 1991).[4] While the Supreme Court in *Gilmer* did not expressly

---

[4]Cases related to the enforcement of arbitration clauses are collected in Annot., "Preemption by Federal Arbitration Act (9 U.S.C.S. § 1 et seq.) of State Laws Prohibiting or Restricting Formation or Enforcement of Arbitration Agreements," 108 A.L.R. Fed. 179 (1992 and periodic supp.).

address this language, it did state that the Federal Arbitration Act favors arbitration agreements and that they should be upheld whenever appropriate.

The use of alternative dispute resolution in higher education is discussed in R. Goodman & M. Gooding, *Resolving Faculty and Staff Employment Disputes Through Arbitration* (United Educators Insurance Risk Retention Group, Inc., 1993).

Sec. 3.2. Collective Bargaining

Collective bargaining has existed on some college campuses since the late 1960s, yet some institutions have recently faced the prospect of bargaining with their faculty for the first time. Whether the faculty union is a fixture or a recent arrival, it presents administrators with a complex mixture of the familiar and the foreign. Many faculty demands, such as for lighter teaching loads, smaller class sizes, and larger salaries, may be familiar on many campuses; but other demands sometimes voiced, such as for standardized pay scales rather than individualized "merit" salary determinations, may present unfamiliar situations. Legal, policy, and political issues may arise concerning the extent to which collective bargaining and the bargained agreement ("the contract"; see Section 3.1 above) preempt or circumscribe not merely traditional administrative elbow room but also the customary forms of faculty and student self-government. And potential tension for academia clearly exists when "outsiders" participate in campus affairs through their involvement in all the aspects of collective bargaining: certification of bargaining agents, negotiation of agreements, fact finding, mediation, conciliation, arbitration, and ultimate resolution of internal disputes through state or federal administrative agencies and courts.

An estimated 229,000 faculty, both full-time and adjunct, are represented by collective bargaining agents (J. Douglas (ed.), *Directory of Faculty Contracts and Bargaining Agents in Institutions of Higher Education* (National Center for the Study of Collective Bargaining in Higher Education and the Professions, 1992), at viii). In some states, virtually all college faculty in public institutions and many in private institutions are unionized. The mix of factors involved, the importance of the policy questions, and the complexity of the law make collective bargaining a potentially troublesome area for administrators. Heavy involvement of legal counsel is clearly called for. Use of professional negotiators, or of administrators experienced in the art of negotiation, is also usually appropriate, particularly when the faculty have such professional expertise on their side of the bargaining table.[5]

3.2.1. The public-private dichotomy in collective bargaining. Theoretically, the legal aspects of collective bargaining divide into two distinct categories: public and private. However, these categories are not necessarily defined in the same way as they are for constitutional state action purposes (see Section 1.5.2). In relation to collective bargaining, "public" and "private" are defined by the collective bargaining legislation and interpretive precedents. Private institutions are subject to the federal law control-

[5]The major issues concerning bargaining in postsecondary education have been frequently discussed in articles, books, and speeches. This section will cite the literature extensively, in order to provide a broad range of sources for pursuing the many complexities in this area. Other sources are included in the Selected Annotated Bibliography at the end of this chapter.

ling collective bargaining, whereas collective bargaining in public institutions is regulated by state law. Privately chartered institutions (see Section 6.3) are likely to be considered private for collective bargaining purposes even if they receive substantial government support. Factors that may determine an institution's status under federal or state collective bargaining laws include actions by a state legislature to transform the institution to a public entity, and proportions of public versus private funds, among others. This issue was addressed in a lengthy case regarding the University of Vermont. In *University of Vermont and State Agricultural College*, 223 NLRB 423 (1976), the National Labor Relations Board (NLRB), the agency that enforces the federal labor relations law, asserted jurisdiction over the university because it received only 25 percent of its support directly from the state and because it was chartered as private and nonprofit and was not a political subdivision of the state. However, in 1988 the state legislature passed a law bringing the university under the purview of state labor law. The state sought an advisory opinion from the NLRB on whether the university was still subject to federal law for collective bargaining purposes. In *University of Vermont and State Agricultural College*, 297 NLRB 42 (1989), the Board determined that the university was a political subdivision of the state, reversing its earlier opinion.

Private-sector bargaining is governed by the National Labor Relations Act of 1935 (the Wagner Act) as amended by the Labor-Management Relations Act of 1947 (the Taft-Hartley Act), 29 U.S.C. § 141 et seq. (see Section 7.2.3). The NLRB first asserted jurisdiction over private nonprofit postsecondary institutions in *Cornell University*, 183 NLRB 329 (1970); and in *C. W. Post Center of Long Island University*, 189 NLRB 904 (1971), it specified that its jurisdiction extended to faculty members.[6] The Board's jurisdiction over higher education institutions was judicially confirmed in *NLRB v. Wentworth Institute*, 515 F.2d 550 (1st Cir. 1975), where the court enforced an NLRB order finding that Wentworth had engaged in an unfair labor practice in refusing to bargain with the certified faculty bargaining representative. Today all private postsecondary institutions, at least all those large enough to have a significant effect on interstate commerce, are included within the federal sphere. Disputes about collective bargaining in private institutions are thus subject to the limited body of statutory authority and the vast body of administrative and judicial precedent regarding the National Labor Relations Act.

Legal authority and precedent have provided few easy answers, however, for collective bargaining issues in postsecondary education. The uniqueness of academic

---

[6]The NLRA specifically includes "professional employees," defined as "any employee engaged in work (i) predominantly intellectual and varied in character as opposed to routine mental, manual, mechanical, or physical work; (ii) involving the consistent exercise of discretion and judgment in its performance; (iii) of such a character that the output produced or the result accomplished cannot be standardized in relation to a given period of time; (iv) requiring knowledge of an advanced type in a field of science or learning customarily acquired by a prolonged course of specialized intellectual instruction and study in an institution of higher learning or a hospital, as distinguished from a general academic education or from an apprenticeship or from training in the performance of routine mental, manual, or physical processes." Also included is anyone who has completed the specialized courses described above and is working under the supervision of the professional employee (29 U.S.C. § 152(12)). Cases regarding which types of employees fit this definition are collected in Annot., "Who Are Professional Employees Within Meaning of National Labor Relations Act (29 U.S.C.S. § 152(12))?" 40 A.L.R. Fed. 25 (1978 and periodic supp.).

institutions, procedures, and customs poses problems not previously encountered in the NLRB's administration of the national labor law in other employment contexts. There are, moreover, many ambiguities and unsettled areas in the national labor law even in nonacademic contexts. They derive in part from the intentionally broad language of the federal legislation and in part from the NLRB's historic insistence on proceeding case by case rather than under a policy of systematic rule making (see K. Kahn, "The NLRB and Higher Education: The Failure of Policy Making Through Adjudication," 21 *UCLA L. Rev.* 63 (1973), and A. P. Menard & N. DiGiovanni, Jr., "NLRB Jurisdiction over Colleges and Universities: A Plea for Rulemaking," 16 *William and Mary L. Rev.* 599 (1975)).[7] Administrators will find working with the NLRB's body of piecemeal precedential authority to be a very different experience from working with the detailed regulations of other agencies, such as the U.S. Department of Education.

Public postsecondary education, on the other hand, is exempt from NLRB jurisdiction (see 29 U.S.C. § 152(2)) and subject only to state authority. Thirty-five states either have some type of legislation permitting some form of collective bargaining in public postsecondary education or the governing board has enacted a policy that permits faculty in public institutions to bargain collectively. In 1983 the legislatures of Illinois and Ohio authorized collective bargaining for faculty members (Ohio Rev. Code Ann. § 4117.01 et seq.; Ill. Ann. Stat. ch. 48, § 1701 et seq.), and in 1992 the New Mexico legislature passed the Public Employee Bargaining Act (10-7D-1 et seq. NMSA 1978), which became effective on April 1, 1993. Indiana faculty gained the right to bargain by executive order in 1990 (see Douglas, *Directory of Faculty Contracts* (cited in Section 3.2), at 123).

Legislation that enables public employees to bargain collectively is often limited in coverage or in the extent to which it authorizes or mandates the full panoply of collective bargaining rights and services. A statute may grant employees rights as narrow as the right to "meet and confer" with administration representatives. In *Lipow v. Regents of the University of California,* 126 Cal. Rptr. 515 (Cal. Ct. App. 1976), for instance, the defendant had only the obligation to "meet and confer" with the organization representing the University of California faculty regarding revisions in the defendant's administrative manual—an obligation which the court held was met. The permissibility of strikes is also a major variable among state statutes.

Frequently, state legislation is designed to cover public employees generally and makes little, if any, special provision for the unique circumstances of postsecondary education. (For analyses of what a state statute should contain, see Comment, "The Legislation Necessary to Effectively Govern Collective Bargaining in Public Higher Education," 1971 *Wis L. Rev.* 275 (1971), and R. Sensenbrenner, "Collective Bargaining Legislation for Public Higher Education from the Management Side of the Table," 4 *J. Coll. & Univ. Law* 27 (1977).) State labor law may be as unsettled as the federal labor law, providing few easy answers for postsecondary education, and may also have a smaller body of administrative and judicial precedents. State agencies and courts often fill in the gaps by relying on precedents in federal labor law. State legislatures may also conceivably become directly involved (see J. Henkel & N. Wood,

---

[7]The NLRB, in 1985, issued rules regarding bargaining unit composition in acute care hospitals (see Section 7.2.3). It was the first instance of substantive rule making since the enactment of the NLRA in 1935.

"Legislative Power to Veto Collective Bargaining Agreements by Faculty Unions: An Overlooked Reality?" 11 *J. Law & Educ.* 79 (1982)).

Even where state collective bargaining legislation does not cover public post-secondary institutions, some "extralegal" bargaining may still take place. A public institution's faculty members, like other public employees, have a constitutional right, under First Amendment freedom of speech and association, "to organize collectively and select representatives to engage in collective bargaining" (*University of New Hampshire Chapter AAUP v. Haselton,* 397 F. Supp. 107 (D.N.H. 1975)). But faculty members do not have a constitutional right to require the public institution "to respond to . . . [faculty] demands or to enter into a contract with them." The right to require the employer to bargain in good faith must be created by statute. Even if the public institution desires to bargain with faculty representatives, it may not have the authority to do so under state law. Or state law may remove from the institution the right to set terms and conditions of employment and vest it instead in a state governing or regulatory board (see *Knight v. Minnesota Community College Faculty Association,* discussed in Section 3.2.2).

The employment powers of public institutions may be vested by law in the sole discretion of institutional governing boards; sharing such powers with collective bargaining representatives or arbitrators appointed under collective bargaining agreements may therefore be construed as an improper delegation of authority. In *Board of Trustees of Junior College District No. 508 v. Cook County College Teachers Union,* 343 N.E.2d 473 (Ill. 1976), the court held that the board's powers to decide which faculty members to employ and promote were "nondelegable" and thus not subject to binding arbitration under the collective bargaining agreement. (See generally G. M. Alley & V. J. Facciolo, "Concerted Public Employee Activity in the Absence of State Authorization," 2 *J. Law & Educ.* 401 (1973), and E. Green, "Concerted Public Employer Collective Bargaining in the Absence of Explicit Legislative Authorization," 2 *J. Law & Educ.* 419 (1973).)

An additional distinction has been built into the public-private dichotomy by the U.S. Supreme Court's decision in *NLRB v. Catholic Bishop of Chicago,* 440 U.S. 490 (1979). Given the willingness of both the NLRB and federal appellate courts to apply *Catholic Bishop* to religiously controlled institutions of higher education, the private side of the dichotomy must be subdivided into "private nonreligious" and "private religious" institutions.

The *Catholic Bishop* case arose after teachers at two groups of Catholic high schools voted for union representation in NLRB-sponsored elections. Although the NLRB certified the unions as the teachers' collective bargaining representatives, the schools refused to negotiate and the unions filed unfair labor practice charges against them. In response, the schools claimed that the First Amendment precluded the NLRB from exercising jurisdiction over them. After the Board upheld its authority to order the elections and ordered the schools to bargain with the unions, the U.S. Court of Appeals for the Seventh Circuit denied enforcement of the NLRB's order. By exercising jurisdiction over "church-operated" schools, the court said, the Board was interfering with the freedom of church officials to operate their schools in accord with their religious tenets, thus violating both the Free Exercise Clause and the Establishment Clause of the First Amendment (see Section 1.6).

The U.S. Supreme Court affirmed the appellate court's decision, by a 5-to-4 vote, but it did so on somewhat different grounds. Rather than addressing the First

Amendment issue directly, as had the appeals court, the Supreme Court focused on a question of statutory interpretation: whether Congress intended that the National Labor Relations Act would give the Board jurisdiction over church-operated schools. In deciding that issue, the Court considered the constitutional problem indirectly by positing that an Act of Congress should be construed, whenever possible, in such a way that serious constitutional problems are avoided. Emphasizing the key role played by teachers in religious primary and secondary schools, the Court found that grave First Amendment questions would result if the Act were construed to allow the Board jurisdiction over such teachers:

> It is already clear that the Board's action will go beyond resolving factual issues. The Court of Appeals opinion refers to charges of unfair labor practices filed against religious schools. The court observed that in those cases the schools had responded that their challenged actions were mandated by their religious creeds. The resolution of such charges by the Board, in many instances, will necessarily involve inquiry into the good faith of the position asserted by the clergy-administrators and its relationship to the school's religious mission. It is not only the conclusions that may be reached by the Board which may impinge on rights guaranteed by the religion clauses, but the very process of inquiry leading to findings and conclusions.
>
> The Board's exercise of jurisdiction will have at least one other impact on church-operated schools. The Board will be called upon to decide what are "terms and conditions of employment" and therefore mandatory subjects of bargaining. . . .
>
> Inevitably the Board's inquiry will implicate sensitive issues that open the door to conflicts between clergy-administrators and the Board, or conflicts with negotiators for unions. . . .
>
> The church-teacher relationship in a church-operated school differs from the employment relationship in a public or other nonreligious school. We see no escape from conflicts flowing from the Board's exercise of jurisdiction over teachers in church-operated schools and the consequent serious First Amendment questions that would follow. We therefore turn to an examination of the National Labor Relations Act to decide whether it must be read to confer [such] jurisdiction [440 U.S. at 502–04].

A survey of the Act's legislative history convinced the Court that Congress had not manifested any "affirmative intention" that teachers in church-operated primary and secondary schools be covered by the Act. Since "Congress did not contemplate that the Board would require church-operated schools to grant recognition to unions," and since such a construction of the Act would require the Court "to resolve difficult and sensitive questions" under the First Amendment, the Court held that the Board's jurisdiction does not extend to teachers in church-operated schools.

The result in *Catholic Bishop* raised questions as to whether its reasoning would apply to church-operated institutions of higher education. The Supreme Court's opinion had given short shrift to the possible distinction between elementary/secondary and higher education. It asserted generally that, whenever extension of NLRB jurisdiction over teachers in "church-operated schools" would raise "serious constitutional questions," a court can uphold the NLRB only if it finds a "clear expression of Congress's intent" to authorize jurisdiction. Thus, the extension of

Catholic Bishop to higher education hinged on two questions: (1) whether NLRB jurisdiction would raise "serious constitutional questions" in light of the First Amendment case law distinguishing between elementary/secondary and higher education; and (2) whether the legislative history of the NLRA and its amendments could be construed differently for higher education, so as to reveal a clearly expressed congressional intent to include higher education teachers within the Board's jurisdiction.

Before the courts had an opportunity to consider these questions, the NLRB asserted jurisdiction over three colleges and universities that had claimed to be exempt under *Catholic Bishop*. In these rulings the Board held that *Catholic Bishop* did not apply because the college "is not church operated as contemplated by *Catholic Bishop*." In *Lewis University*, 265 NLRB 1239 (1982), for example, the Board asserted jurisdiction over a historically church-related institution because operating authority had been transferred to a private board of trustees, and the local diocese "does not exercise administrative or other secular control" over, and does not perform any services for, the institution. This approach was contrary to an earlier ruling of a federal appellate court. In *NLRB v. Bishop Ford Central Catholic High School*, 623 F.2d 818 (2d Cir. 1980), the court had denied enforcement of an NLRB order asserting jurisdiction over lay teachers in a Catholic school severed from ownership and control of the local diocese and operated instead by a predominantly lay board of trustees. According to the court, the critical question in determining whether a school is "church operated" under *Catholic Bishop* is not whether a church holds legal title or controls management; it is whether the school has a "religious mission" that could give rise to "entanglement" problems under the Establishment Clause. Since the school's history and "present religious characteristics" indicated that its religious mission continued after separation from the diocese, the court held the school to be exempt from NLRB jurisdiction.

This "religious mission" test was used in the first application of *Catholic Bishop* to an institution of higher education when a federal appellate court, in an *en banc* opinion, split evenly on whether the NLRB could assert jurisdiction over a religiously affiliated university. In *Universidad Central de Bayamon v. NLRB*, 793 F.2d 383 (1st Cir. 1986), the divided court did not enforce the NLRB's bargaining order; it thereby overturned the ruling of a three-judge panel that had ordered the university to bargain with its faculty. The question addressed by both groups of judges was whether a religiously affiliated university is sufficiently different from a parochial elementary or secondary school to justify a departure from *Catholic Bishop*.

The group holding that *Catholic Bishop* should apply cited the substantial religious mission of the university. It also noted that in *Catholic Bishop* the Court had not distinguished postsecondary education from elementary or secondary education and had rejected the NLRB's distinction between "completely religious schools" and "merely religiously associated schools" because of the potential for entanglement when the Board attempted to determine which of those categories an institution belonged in. The group believed that making such distinctions at the postsecondary level would be equally troublesome. The group favoring the application of the NLRA to the university held that the religious mission of the university was far less central than that of the high schools in *Catholic Bishop*. It further believed that most unfair labor practice charges would involve secular matters, and that the university still had the right to assert a First Amendment claim should entanglement be a potential problem in any particular Board action.

The *Bayamon* case dramatizes the difficult law and policy issues involved, and suggests that no resolution to this problem is imminent. In future cases on this same general subject, courts will probably focus on the institution's mission and will try to determine whether employment policies derive from the religious sponsor's doctrines or whether they have been secularized (see Sections 3.1.6 and 7.2.6.2). For a discussion of the interplay between religious doctrine and labor law, see D. L. Gregory & C. J. Russo, "Overcoming *NLRB v. Yeshiva University* by the Implementation of Catholic Labor Theory," 41 *Labor Law J.* 55 (1990). (The *Yeshiva* case is discussed in Section 3.2.3.)

3.2.2. Organization, recognition, and certification. Once a faculty or a substantial portion of it decides that it wants to bargain collectively with the institution, its representatives can ask the administration to recognize them for collective bargaining purposes. A private institution has two choices at this point. It can voluntarily recognize the faculty representatives and commence negotiations, or it can withhold recognition and insist that the faculty representatives seeking recognition petition the NLRB for a certification election (see *Linden Lumber Division v. NLRB*, 419 U.S. 817 (1974)). Public institutions that have authority to bargain under state law usually have the same two choices, although elections and certification would be handled by the state labor board.

Administrators should consider two related legal implications of choosing the first alternative. First, it is a violation of the National Labor Relations Act (NLRA) (and most state acts) for an employer voluntarily to recognize a minority union—that is, a union supported by less than 50 percent of the faculty in the bargaining unit (see 29 U.S.C. § 158(a)(1) and (2), and *International Ladies Garment Workers Union v. NLRB*, 366 U.S. 731 (1961)). Second, it is also a violation of the NLRA (and most state acts) for an employer to recognize any union (even one with apparent majority support) when a rival union makes a "substantial claim of support," which the NLRB interprets to mean a claim "not . . . clearly unsupportable and lacking in substance" (*American Can Co.*, 218 NLRB 102, 103 (1975)). Thus, unless a union seeking recognition can prove the clear support of the majority of the members of the proposed bargaining unit (usually through "authorization cards" or a secret ballot poll), and the administration has no reason to believe that a rival union with a "substantial claim of support" is also seeking recognition, it is usually not wise to recognize any union without a certification election.

In the interim between the beginning of organizational activity and the actual certification of a union, administrators must be circumspect in their actions. In the private sector, the NLRA prohibits the employer from doing anything that would appear to favor any of the contenders for recognition (29 U.S.C. § 158(a)(2)) or that would "interfere with, restrain, or coerce employees in the exercise of their rights" to self-organize, form or join a union, or bargain collectively (29 U.S.C. § 158(a)(1)). This prohibition would apply to promises of benefits, threats of reprisals, coercive interrogation, or surveillance. Furthermore, the institution may not take any action that could be construed as a discrimination against union organizers or supporters because of their exercise of rights under the Act (29 U.S.C. § 158(a)(3)). In the public sector, state laws generally contain comparable prohibitions on certain kinds of employer activities.

Another crucial aspect of the organizational phase is the definition of the "bargaining unit"—that is, the portion of the institution's employees that will be represented by the particular bargaining agent seeking certification. Again, most state laws parallel the federal law. Generally, the NLRB or its state equivalent has considerable discretion to determine the appropriate unit (see 29 U.S.C. § 159(b)). The traditional rule has been that there must be a basic "community of interest" among the individuals included in the unit, so that the union will represent the interests of everyone in the unit when it negotiates with the employer.[8] The question of appropriate bargaining unit arises when a union represents both full-time and adjunct faculty and a board must determine whether they should be in the same unit or in different ones. In *Vermont State Colleges Faculty Federation v. Vermont State Colleges*, 566 A.2d 955 (Vt. 1989), the state college system challenged the state labor board's ruling that both full-time and adjunct faculty should be combined in a single bargaining unit. The Vermont Supreme Court reversed the board's ruling, holding that the adjunct faculty did not share a community of interest with the full-time faculty because they were hired and paid differently, were ineligible for tenure, and had no advising responsibilities.

Under the NLRA (see 29 U.S.C. § 152(3) and (11)) and most state laws, supervisory personnel are excluded from any bargaining unit. Individual determinations must be made, in light of the applicable statutory definition, of whether particular personnel are excluded from the unit as supervisors. Professionals, however, are explicitly included by the NLRA, and its definition clearly applies to college faculty (see note 6 in Section 3.2.1 of this volume).

Generally, several factors have traditionally been used to determine a "community of interest," including the history of past bargaining (if any), the extent of organization, the skills and duties of the employees, and common supervision. But these factors are difficult to apply in postsecondary education's complex world of collegially shared decision making. To define the proposed unit as "all faculty members" does not resolve the issue. For example, does the unit include all faculty of the institution, or only the faculty of a particular school, such as the law school? Part-time as well as full-time faculty members? Researchers and librarians as well as teachers? Graduate teaching assistants? Chairs of small departments whose administrative duties are incidental to their primary teaching and research functions? The problems are compounded in multicampus institutions, especially if the programs offered by the individual campuses vary significantly from one another. (See, for example, R. Head & D. Leslie, "Bargaining Unit Status of Part-Time Faculty," 8 *J. Law & Educ.* 361 (1979); E. Moore, "The Determination of Bargaining Units for College Faculties," 37 *U. Pittsburgh L. Rev.* 43 (1975); M. W. Finkin, "The NLRB in Higher Education," 5 *U. Toledo L. Rev.* 608, 612–45 (1974).)

The question of whether department chairs or coordinators are "employees" (who are protected by the NLRA) or "supervisors" (who are not) was addressed by the Board in *Detroit College of Business and Detroit College of Business Faculty Association*, 296 NLRB 318 (1989). Prior to this case, the Board had used the "fifty

---

[8]Cases are collected in Annot., " 'Community of Interest' Test in NLRB Determination of Appropriateness of Employee Bargaining Unit," 90 A.L.R. Fed. 16 (1988 and periodic supp.), and Annot., "Who May Be Included in 'Unit Appropriate' for Collective Bargaining at School or College, Under Sec. 9(b) of National Labor Relations Act (29 U.S.C.S. § 159(b))," 46 A.L.R. Fed. 580 (1980 and periodic supp.).

percent" rule developed in *Adelphi University*, 195 NLRB 639 (1972), which stated that, unless an individual spent at least half of his or her time in supervisory functions, the supervisory exclusion did not apply. In *Detroit College of Business*, the Board rejected the "fifty percent" rule, stating that even though the department coordinators spent the majority of their time teaching, their responsibilities to evaluate and hire part-time faculty brought them within the definition of "supervisor" and thus excluded them from the NLRA's protection.[9] Given the breadth of this definition of supervisor, it is possible that faculty members who supervise graduate student research or teaching assistants (who are employees also) could theoretically be excluded from the protections of the NLRA.

Once the bargaining unit is defined and the union recognized or certified, the union becomes the exclusive bargaining agent of all employees in the unit, whether or not they become union members and whether or not they are willing to be represented (see *J. I. Case Co. v. NLRB*, 321 U.S. 332 (1944)). Courts have generally upheld the constitutionality of such exclusive representation systems. The leading case for higher education, *Minnesota State Board for Community Colleges v. Knight*, 465 U.S. 271 (1984), examines (but is not particularly sensitive to) the special concerns that exclusive systems may create for higher education governance.

In *Knight* the Court upheld a Minnesota law that requires public employers to "meet and negotiate" with exclusive bargaining representatives of public employees over mandatory subjects of bargaining and, when the employees are professional, to "meet and confer" with their exclusive representatives regarding nonmandatory subjects. (Subjects of bargaining are discussed in Section 3.2.4.) Pursuant to this law, the Minnesota Community College Faculty Association was designated the exclusive bargaining agent for state community college faculty members. The association and the state board established statewide meet-and-confer committees as well as local committees on each campus. These committees discussed various policy matters, such as curriculum, fiscal planning, and student affairs. Only members of the association served on the committees.

This arrangement was challenged by a group of faculty members who were not members of the association and thus could not participate in the meet-and-negotiate or meet-and-confer processes. The faculty members argued that their exclusion deprived them of their First Amendment rights to express their views and also discriminated against them in violation of the Fourteenth Amendment's Equal Protection Clause. The lower court (1) rejected these arguments as applied to the negotiation of mandatory bargaining subjects but (2) agreed with the faculty members that exclusion from the meet-and-confer committees violated the First Amendment (571 F. Supp. 1 (D. Minn. 1982)). On the faculty members' appeal from the first ruling, the U.S. Supreme Court summarily affirmed the lower court (*Knight v. Minnesota Community College Faculty Assn.*, 466 U.S. 284 (1984)). On the state board and the association's appeal from the second ruling, in an opinion joined by only five members, the U.S. Supreme Court overruled the lower court. According to the Court majority, the faculty members' free speech challenge to their exclusion from meet-and-confer committees was unavailing:

[9]Cases are collected in Annot., "Who Are 'Supervisors' Within Meaning of NLRA (29 U.S.C.S. §§ 151 et seq.) in Education and Health Services," 52 A.L.R. Fed. 28 (1981 and periodic supps.).

Appellees have no constitutional right to force the government to listen to their views. They have no such right as members of the public, as government employees, or as instructors in an institution of higher education. . . . The academic setting of the policy making at issue in this case does not alter this conclusion. To be sure, there is a strong, if not universal or uniform, tradition of faculty participation in school governance, and there are numerous policy arguments to support such participation. But this Court has never recognized a constitutional right of faculty to participate in policy making in academic institutions. . . . Even assuming that speech rights guaranteed by the First Amendment take on a special meaning in an academic setting, they do not require government to allow teachers employed by it to participate in institutional policy making. Faculty involvement in academic governance has much to recommend it as a matter of academic policy, but it finds no basis in the Constitution [465 U.S. at 287–88].

The equal protection claim similarly failed:

The interest of appellees that is affected—the interest in a government audience for their policy views—finds no special protection in the Constitution. . . . The state has a legitimate interest in insuring that its public employers hear one, and only one, voice presenting the majority view of its professional employees on employment-related policy questions, whatever other advice they may receive on those questions. Permitting selection of the "meet-and-confer" representatives to be made by the exclusive representative, which has its unique status by virtue of majority support within the bargaining unit, is a rational means of serving that interest. . . . Similarly, the goal of basing policy decisions on consideration of the majority view of its employees makes it reasonable for an employer to give only the exclusive representative a particular formal setting in which to offer advice on policy [465 U.S. at 291–92].

In addition to limiting the independent actions of nonunion faculty members in matters of governance or institutional policy, the exclusivity doctrine has raised other legal issues. Supreme Court precedent interpreting federal labor law (*International Association of Machinists v. Street*, 367 U.S. 740 (1961)) and state labor law (*Abood v. Detroit Board of Education*, 431 U.S. 209 (1977)) permits unions to charge nonmembers an "agency fee" to underwrite the cost of services provided by the union. But if a union represents faculty at public institutions and uses nonmembers' fees to support political activity with which nonmembers do not agree, their First Amendment rights may have been violated by the forced payment (*Chicago Teachers' Union v. Hudson*, 475 U.S. 292 (1986)).

This doctrine has also been imputed to the National Labor Relations Act, which governs labor relations in private organizations. In *Communication Workers v. Beck*, 487 U.S. 735 (1988), the Supreme Court ruled that objecting bargaining unit members must pay for services provided to their bargaining unit by the union, such as the costs of negotiating contracts or processing grievances. But forced payment of agency fees to support other union activities to which the nonmember objected, and which were not chargeable to the bargaining unit, violated Section 7 of the National Labor Relations Act.

Questions concerning the degree to which objecting faculty must pay agency fees; whether and how the union must account for its use of nonmembers' fees; and the interplay between the NLRA, the First Amendment, and civil rights laws have been examined in litigation between unions representing college faculty and dissenting nonmember faculty. In those states that permit collective bargaining contracts to specify nonpayment of union dues or agency fees as a permissible reason for discharging faculty, the issue has been particularly complex.[10] For a discussion of the implications of *Hudson* for faculty tenure, see S. Olswang, "Union Security Provisions, Academic Freedom and Tenure: The Implications of *Chicago Teachers Union v. Hudson*," 15 *J. Coll. & Univ. Law* 539 (1988); the implications of *Beck* are discussed by R. Hartley, "Constitutional Values and the Adjudication of Taft-Hartley Act Dues Objector Cases," 41 *Hastings L.J.* 1 (1989).

In a case decided by the U.S. Supreme Court, *Lehnert v. Ferris Faculty Association*, 111 S. Ct. 1950 (1991), nonmember faculty at Ferris State University sued the union representing them, an affiliate of the National Education Association, over the matter of agency fees. Michigan's Public Employment Relations Act permits a union and a public employer to negotiate an agency shop agreement, and such an agreement was negotiated between the faculty union and the administration of Ferris State College. In their suit the plaintiffs claimed that being forced to support the state and national union's legislative lobbying activities, expenses for travel to conventions by union officers, preparation for a strike, and other activities violated their constitutional rights. The agency fee had been set at an amount equal to union members' dues. In a 5-to-4 decision, the Court ruled that agency fees were permissible for the purpose of supporting union activities directly related to services to bargaining unit members, and that activities by state or national affiliates that were related to collective bargaining, even if not of direct benefit to local union members, could be included in the calculation of the agency fee.

Several justices wrote separate concurring opinions, and the majority joined only portions of the opinion written by Justice Blackmun. In analyzing the issues before the Court, Justice Blackmun, writing for himself and four other justices, used a three-part test drawn from prior precedent. First, the chargeable activities must be "germane" to collective bargaining activity. Second, they must be justified by the "government's vital policy interest in labor peace and avoiding 'free riders.'" And third, the activities must "not significantly add to the burdening of free speech that is inherent in the allowance of an agency or union shop" (111 S. Ct. at 1959).

Activities at the state and national level that were related to collective bargaining, as opposed to political activity, were permissible charges, Blackmun wrote. Lobbying on behalf of the profession or public employees generally was not a permissible charge because it was more "likely to concern topics about which individuals hold strong personal views" and was outside the scope of the collective bargaining context. Therefore, "the State constitutionally may not compel its employees to subsidize legislative lobbying or other political union activities outside the limited context of contract ratification or implementation" (at 1960–61).

The majority was willing, however, to permit the portion of the agency fee paid to the national union to be a chargeable expense because it "is assessed for the bargaining unit's protection, even if it is not actually expended on that unit in any

---

[10]Cases related to this issue are collected in Annot., "Union Security Arrangements in State Public Employment," 95 A.L.R.3d 1102 (1979 and periodic supp.).

particular membership year" (at 1961). But "[t]here must be some indication that the payment is for services that may ultimately enure to the benefit of the members of the local union," rather than a charitable contribution or other payment unrelated to collective bargaining or grievance handling services (at 1961–62).

Public relations expenditures on behalf of the teaching profession, union social activities, and expenses for the national union's magazine were not permissible charges, but the costs of preparing for a strike were allowable, the majority ruled. Although strikes by public-sector employees are illegal in Michigan, strike preparations are not, and the majority believed that these preparations are "substantively indistinguishable from those appurtenant to collective-bargaining negotiations" (at 1965). The case was remanded to the federal appellate court for disposition in light of the Court's determinations.

The remaining four justices, although agreeing with Justice Blackmun's disposition of the chargeable activities, took a much narrower view of the activities appropriate for charging to nonmembers, and argued that the criteria embraced by the majority inappropriately expanded the category of expenses for which dissenting members could be charged. Justice Scalia, joined by Justices O'Connor, Souter, and Kennedy, held that chargeable expenses should be only those costs of performing the union's "statutory duty as exclusive bargaining agent." Scalia asserted, "[A] union cannot constitutionally charge nonmembers for any expenses except those incurred for the conduct of activities in which the union owes a duty of fair representation to the nonmembers being charged" (111 S. Ct. at 1979). Applying this test, Scalia concurred with Blackmun's determination that lobbying, public relations activities, and the union's magazine were not chargeable, but he held that travel to national conferences or general support for the national union's collective bargaining services also should not be chargeable, except for those services actually provided to the local union (at 1981).

Another question concerning the use of nonmembers' agency fees is the potential for such use to violate an individual's First Amendment religious exercise rights by compelling a nonmember to pay for union activities that conflict with the nonmember's religious beliefs (see *EEOC v. University of Detroit,* discussed in Section 3.2.7).

Other issues concerning the relationship between the college or university as employer and the union may raise legal problems. For example, some colleges and universities have sought to insulate themselves against joint liability with the union if nonmembers challenge the amount and use of agency fee payments. In *Weaver v. University of Cincinnati,* 970 F.2d 1523 (6th Cir. 1992), nonmember staff challenged the amount of the agency fee (90 percent of dues) and its use by the union, suing both the union and the university because the university collected the fee through a "dues checkoff" system. The university had negotiated an indemnification clause in the contract that disclaimed liability for any unconstitutional acts or practices by the union. The court refused to enforce the clause, stating that

> both parties to a fair share agreement must be held accountable for their responsibility to see that *Hudson's* commands are followed. A clause that relieves the employer of all consequences for its failure to assume and conscientiously carry out its duties, including even the cost of defending legal actions, is against public policy [970 F.2d at 1538].

The use of a college's internal mail system by the faculty or staff union is a common practice on many campuses. The U.S. Supreme Court dealt a blow to unions in ruling that the University of California's refusal to permit a union to use the university's internal mail system was lawful. The California Public Employment Relations Board had ordered the university to permit the union to use its mail system under a provision of the California Higher Education Employer-Employee Relations Act that requires employers to grant unions access to their "means of communication" (Cal. Govt. Code Ann. §§ 3560–3599). In *Regents of the University of California v. Public Employment Relations Board*, 485 U.S. 589 (1988), the Court ruled that under the Private Express Statutes (18 U.S.C. §§ 1693–1699, 39 U.S.C. §§ 601–606) that protect the monopoly of the U.S. Postal Service, the university could not be compelled, over its objection, to carry the union's mail without postage.

In addition to the numerous and complex issues related to the union's status as exclusive agent of the faculty, the question of when and whether the collective bargaining agreement supersedes or may be supplemented by other institutional policies and procedures can lead to thorny problems. These problems often arise when a faculty member's breach-of-contract claim concerns a matter that is covered by the collective bargaining agreement. In *White v. Winona State University*, 474 N.W.2d 410 (Minn. Ct. App. 1991), the court was asked to determine whether a dean's decision to remove a department chair from office in the middle of a three-year term violated the faculty member's individual (rather than collective) contract rights. The faculty member cited a letter from the dean appointing him to a three-year term as the source of his contractual protection. The collective bargaining agreement that governed the faculty member's terms and conditions of employment contained a "zipper clause," stating that it was the complete agreement between the parties. Furthermore, that agreement stated that removal of department chairs was not subject to the agreement's grievance procedure. Professor White argued that the contractual language excluded this issue from coverage by the agreement, and the letter thus became his contract. The court disagreed. Interpreting Minnesota law, the court ruled that if the collective agreement makes it clear that the grievance procedure is intended to be the exclusive remedy for employment disputes, then Professor White could not bring action for common law breach of contract. A similar result was reached under the NLRA in *McGough v. University of San Francisco*, 263 Cal. Rptr. 404 (Cal. 1989), in which the court ruled that the NLRA preempted a faculty member's claim that his tenure denial breached an implied contract with the university. The NLRA did not, however, preempt the faculty member's common law tort claim of intentional infliction of emotional distress.

Although faculty members covered by a collective agreement have been unsuccessful in filing common law contract claims, they have won the right to file common law tort claims. This is a relatively recent development, for unionized employees had previously been limited to the grievance and arbitration procedures of their collective agreements under the doctrine of *Teamsters v. Lucas Flour Co.*, 369 U.S. 95 (1962), and *Allis-Chalmers Corp. v. Lueck*, 471 U.S. 202 (1985). But in *Lingle v. Norge Division of Magic Chef*, 486 U.S. 399 (1988), the U.S. Supreme Court ruled that an employee who asserts a state law tort claim of wrongful discharge may pursue this claim in court if its resolution does not depend on an interpretation of the collective agreement and even if the employee has already used the contractual grievance system. This ruling gives unionized employees two opportunities to challenge negative employment actions and diminishes some of the benefits afforded by binding arbitration: finality, speed, informality, and low cost. For an analysis of this issue, see Note, "Steering Away from the Arbitration Process: Recognizing State Law Tort Actions for Unionized Employees," 24 *U. Richmond L. Rev.* 233 (1990).

Although higher education is no longer a newcomer to collective bargaining and its complexities, the process and the many related issues continue to raise new and unexamined problems for the academic community. The advice of experienced labor counsel is critical in enabling institutions to comply with the law and, at the same time, to respond to the practical concerns of dealing with an organized faculty.

3.2.3. Bargaining unit eligibility of full-time faculty. The NLRB asserted jurisdiction over higher education in 1970 and determined in 1971 that college faculty in private institutions could organize under the protections of the National Labor Relations Act (see Section 3.2.1). Between 1971 and 1980, the NLRB routinely ruled that faculty were "employees" and thus eligible to form unions under the NLRA, even if they participated in hiring, promotion, and tenure decisions, and controlled the curriculum and their course content. The routine inclusion of faculty under the NLRA came to an abrupt halt, however, in 1980.

In *NLRB v. Yeshiva University*, 444 U.S. 672 (1980), the U.S. Supreme Court considered, for the first time, how federal collective bargaining principles developed to deal with industrial labor-management relations apply to private academic institutions. Adopting a view of academic employment relationships very different from that of the dissenting justices, a bare majority of the Court denied enforcement of an NLRB order requiring Yeshiva University to bargain collectively with a union certified as the representative of its faculty. The Court held that Yeshiva's full-time faculty members were "managerial" personnel and thus excluded from the coverage of the NLRA.

In 1975 a three-member panel of the NLRB had reviewed the Yeshiva University Faculty Association's petition seeking certification as bargaining agent for the full-time faculty members of certain of Yeshiva's schools. The university opposed the petition on the grounds that its faculty members were managerial or supervisory personnel and hence not covered by the Act. After accepting the petition and sponsoring an election, the Board certified the Faculty Association as exclusive bargaining representative. The university refused to bargain, maintaining that its faculty members' extensive involvement in university governance excluded them from the Act. When the Faculty Association charged that the refusal was an unfair labor practice, the NLRB ordered the university to bargain and sought enforcement of its order in federal court. The U.S. Court of Appeals for the Second Circuit denied enforcement, holding that Yeshiva's faculty were endowed with "managerial status" sufficient to remove them from the coverage of the Act (*NLRB v. Yeshiva University*, 582 F.2d 686 (2d Cir. 1978)).

In affirming the appellate court's decision, Justice Powell's majority opinion recognized two distinct exemptions that could support the university's position but focused its analysis on only one:

> Professionals, like other employees, may be exempted from coverage under the Act's exclusion for "supervisors" who use independent judgment in overseeing other employees in the interest of the employer, or under the judicially

implied exclusion for "managerial employees" who are involved in developing and enforcing employer policy. Both exemptions grow out of the same concern: that an employer is entitled to the undivided loyalty of its representatives (*Beasley v. Food Fair of North Carolina*, 416 U.S. 653, 661–62 (1974); see *NLRB v. Bell Aerospace Co.*, 416 U.S. 267, 281–82 (1974)). Because the Court of Appeals found the faculty to be managerial employees, it did not decide the question of their supervisory status. In view of our agreement with that court's application of the managerial exclusion, we also need not resolve that issue of statutory interpretation [444 U.S. at 681–82].

The Court looked to previous NLRB decisions and Supreme Court opinions to formulate a definition of managerial employee:

> Managerial employees are defined as those who "formulate and effectuate management policies by expressing and making operative the decisions of their employer. . . ." Managerial employees must exercise discretion within or even independently of established employer policy and must be aligned with management. Although the Board has established no firm criteria for determining when an employee is so aligned, normally an employee may be excluded [from NLRA coverage] as managerial only if he represents management interests by taking or recommending discretionary actions that effectively control or implement employer policy [444 U.S. at 682–83].

Applying this standard to the Yeshiva faculty, the Court concluded:

> The controlling consideration in this case is that the faculty of Yeshiva University exercise authority which in any other context unquestionably would be managerial. Their authority in academic matters is absolute. They decide what courses will be offered, when they will be scheduled, and to whom they will be taught. They debate and determine teaching methods, grading policies, and matriculation standards. They effectively decide which students will be admitted, retained, and graduated. On occasion their views have determined the size of the student body, the tuition to be charged, and the location of a school. When one considers the function of a university, it is difficult to imagine decisions more managerial than these. To the extent the industrial analogy applies, the faculty determines within each school the product to be produced, the terms upon which it will be offered, and the customers who will be served [444 U.S. at 686].

The NLRB had acknowledged this decision-making function of the Yeshiva faculty but argued that "alignment with management" was the proper criterion for assessing management status:

> The Board argues that the Yeshiva faculty are not aligned with management because they are expected to exercise "independent professional judgment" while participating in academic governance, and because they are neither "expected to conform to management policies [nor] judged according to their effectiveness in carrying out those policies." Because of this independence, the Board contends there is no danger of divided loyalty and no need for the managerial exclusion. In its view, union pressure cannot divert the faculty from adhering to the interests of the university, because the university itself expects its faculty to

pursue professional values rather than institutional interests. The Board concludes that application of the managerial exclusion to such employees would frustrate the national labor policy in favor of collective bargaining [444 U.S. at 684].

In reaching its conclusion, the Court explicitly rejected the Board's approach:

> We are not persuaded by this argument. There may be some tension between the Act's exclusion of managerial employees and its inclusion of professionals, since most professionals in managerial positions continue to draw on their special skills and training. But we have been directed to no authority suggesting that that tension can be resolved by reference to the "independent professional judgment" criterion proposed in this case. Outside the university context, the Board routinely has applied the managerial and supervisory exclusions to professionals in executive positions without inquiring whether their decisions were based on management policy rather than professional expertise. . . .
>
> Moreover, the Board's approach would undermine the goal it purports to serve: to ensure that employees who exercise discretionary authority on behalf of the employer will not divide their loyalty between employer and union. In arguing that a faculty member exercising independent judgment acts primarily in his own interest and therefore does not represent the interest of his employer, the Board assumes that the professional interests of the faculty and the interests of the institution are distinct, separable entities with which a faculty member could not simultaneously be aligned. The Court of Appeals found no justification for this distinction, and we perceive none. In fact, the faculty's professional interests—as applied to governance at a university like Yeshiva—cannot be separated from those of the institution [444 U.S. at 686–88].

Four members of the Court dissented. In a perceptive opinion on behalf of these dissenters, Justice Brennan argued that the NLRB's decision should be upheld:

> Unlike the purely hierarchical decision-making structure that prevails in the typical industrial organization, the bureaucratic foundation of most "mature" universities is characterized by dual authority systems. The primary decisional network is hierarchical in nature: Authority is lodged in the administration, and a formal chain of command runs from a lay governing board down through university officers to individual faculty members and students. At the same time, there exists a parallel professional network, in which formal mechanisms have been created to bring the expertise of the faculty into the decision-making process. (See J. Baldridge, *Power and Conflict in the University* 114 (1971); M. Finkin, "The NLRB in Higher Education," 5 *U. of Toledo L. Rev.* 608, 614–18 (1974).)
>
> What the Board realized—and what the Court fails to apprehend—is that whatever influence the faculty wields in university decision making is attributable solely to its collective expertise as professional educators, and not to any managerial or supervisory prerogatives. Although the administration may look to the faculty for advice on matters of professional and academic concern, the faculty offers its recommendations in order to serve its own independent interest in creating the most effective environment for learning, teaching, and scholarship. And while the administration may attempt to defer to the faculty's competence whenever possible, it must and does apply its own distinct perspective to

those recommendations, a perspective that is based on fiscal and other managerial policies which the faculty has no part in developing. The university always retains the ultimate decision-making authority, and the administration gives what weight and import to the faculty's collective judgment as it chooses and deems consistent with its own perception of the institution's needs and objectives.

The premise of a finding of managerial status is a determination that the excluded employee is acting on behalf of management and is answerable to a higher authority in the exercise of his responsibilities. The Board has consistently implemented this requirement—both for professional and nonprofessional employees—by conferring managerial status only upon those employees "whose interests are closely aligned with management as *true representatives of management*" (emphasis added). (See, for example, *Sutter Community Hospitals of Sacramento*, 227 NLRB 181, 193 (1976); *Bell Aerospace*, 219 NLRB 384, 385 (1975); *General Dynamics Corp.*, 213 NLRB 851, 857 (1974).) Only if the employee is expected to conform to management policies and is judged by his effectiveness in executing those policies does the danger of divided loyalties exist.

Yeshiva's faculty, however, is not accountable to the administration in its governance function, nor is any individual faculty member subject to personal sanction or control based on the administration's assessment of the worth of his recommendations. When the faculty, through the schools' advisory committees, participates in university decision making on subjects of academic policy, it does not serve as the "representative of management." Unlike industrial supervisors and managers, university professors are not hired to "make operative" the policies and decisions of their employer. Nor are they retained on the condition that their interests will correspond to those of the university administration. Indeed, the notion that a faculty member's professional competence could depend on his undivided loyalty to management is antithetical to the whole concept of academic freedom. Faculty members are judged by their employer on the quality of their teaching and scholarship, not on the compatibility of their advice with administration policy. . . .

It is no answer to say, as does the Court, that Yeshiva's faculty and administration are one and the same because their interests tend to coincide. In the first place, the National Labor Relations Act does not condition its coverage on an antagonism of interests between the employer and the employees. The mere coincidence of interests on many issues has never been thought to abrogate the right to collective bargaining on those topics as to which that coincidence is absent. Ultimately, the performance of an employee's duties will always further the interests of the employer, for in no institution do the interests of labor and management totally diverge. Both desire to maintain stable and profitable operations, and both are committed to creating the best possible product within existing financial constraints. Differences of opinion and emphasis may develop, however, on exactly how to devote the institution's resources to achieve those goals. When these disagreements surface, the national labor laws contemplate their resolution through the peaceful process of collective bargaining. And in this regard, Yeshiva University stands on the same footing as any other employer. . . .

Finally, the Court's perception of the Yeshiva faculty's status is distorted by the rose-colored lens through which it views the governance structure of the modern-day university. The Court's conclusion that the faculty's professional interests are indistinguishable from those of the administration is bottomed on an idealized model of collegial decision making that is a vestige of the great medieval university. But the university of today bears little resemblance to the "community of scholars" of yesteryear. Education has become "big business," and the task of operating the university enterprise has been transferred from the faculty to an autonomous administration, which faces the same pressures to cut costs and increase efficiencies that confront any large industrial organization. The past decade of budgetary cutbacks, declining enrollments, reductions in faculty appointments, curtailment of academic programs, and increasing calls for accountability to alumni and other special interest groups has only added to the erosion of the faculty's role in the institution's decision-making process [444 U.S. at 696–703].

Just as the *Yeshiva* case sparked sharp debate within the Court, it generated much dialogue and disagreement among commentators. (See, for example, D. Rabban, "Distinguishing Excluded Managers from Covered Professionals Under the NLRA," 89 *Columbia L. Rev.* 1775 (1989); see also G. Bodner, "The Implications of the *Yeshiva University* Decision for Collective Bargaining Rights of Faculty at Private and Public Institutions of Higher Education," 7 *J. Coll. & Univ. Law* 78 (1980–81), and the response in M. Finkin, "The *Yeshiva* Decision: A Somewhat Different View," 7 *J. Coll. & Univ. Law* 321 (1980–81).) The debate has developed on two levels. The first is whether the Court majority's view of academic governance and its adaptation of labor law principles to that context are justifiable—an issue well framed by Justice Brennan's dissenting opinion. The second level concerns the extent to which the "management exclusion" fashioned by the Court should be applied to university settings and faculty governance systems different from Yeshiva's.

On the latter issue, it is important to take account of the Court's close attention to the specific circumstances of Yeshiva University. The majority opinion described the institution and the faculty's governance role at length:

> The individual schools within the university are substantially autonomous. Each is headed by a dean or director, and faculty members at each school meet formally and informally to discuss and decide matters of institutional and professional concern. At four schools, formal meetings are convened regularly pursuant to written bylaws. The remaining faculties meet when convened by the dean or director. Most of the schools also have faculty committees concerned with special areas of educational policy. Faculty welfare committees negotiate with administrators concerning salary and conditions of employment. Through these meetings and committees, the faculty at each school effectively determine its curriculum, grading system, admission and matriculation standards, academic calendars, and course schedules.
>
> Faculty power at Yeshiva's schools extends beyond strictly academic concerns. The faculty at each school make recommendations to the dean or director in every case of faculty hiring, tenure, sabbaticals, termination, and promotion. Although the final decision is reached by the central administration on the advice of the dean or director, the overwhelming majority of faculty recommendations are implemented. Even when financial problems in the early 1970s restricted Yeshiva's budget, faculty recommendations still largely controlled personnel decisions made within the constraints imposed by the administration. Indeed, the faculty of one school recently drew up new and binding policies expanding their own role in these matters. In addition, some faculties make final decisions regarding the admission, expulsion, and graduation of individual students. Others have decided questions involving teaching loads, student absence policies, tuition and enrollment levels, and in one case the location of a school [444 U.S. at 676–77].

The Court relied on these facts throughout its opinion, focusing on the faculty role at Yeshiva or "a university like Yeshiva." In a final footnote, the majority emphasized the narrowness of its holding that faculty are managers:

> Other factors not present here may enter into the analysis in other contexts. It is plain, for example, that professors may not be excluded merely because they determine the content of their own courses, evaluate their own students, and supervise their own research. There thus may be institutions of higher learning unlike Yeshiva where the faculty are entirely or predominantly nonmanagerial. There also may be faculty members at Yeshiva and like universities who properly could be included in a bargaining unit. It may be that a rational line could be drawn between tenured and untenured faculty members, depending upon how a faculty is structured and operates. But we express no opinion on these questions, for it is clear that the unit approved by the board was far too broad [444 U.S. at 690, n.31].

Thus, the *Yeshiva* decision appears to create a managerial exclusion only for faculty at "Yeshiva-like," or what the Court called "mature," private universities. Even at such institutions, it is unlikely that all faculty would be excluded from bargaining under federal law. Most part-time faculty, for instance, would not be considered managers and would thus remain eligible to bargain. Legitimate questions also exist concerning faculty with "soft-money" research appointments, instructors and lecturers not on a tenure track, visiting professors, and even nontenured faculty generally, at mature universities.

At private institutions that are not "Yeshiva-like," the NLRB and reviewing appellate courts have refused to apply the managerial exclusion to faculty. For example, *NLRB v. Stephens Institute*, 620 F.2d 720 (9th Cir. 1980), concerned the faculty of an art academy on the opposite end of the spectrum from Yeshiva. The academy was a corporation whose principal shareholder was also chief executive officer. Faculty members, except department heads, were paid according to the number of courses they taught each semester. According to the court, "The instructors at the academy . . . have no input into policy decisions and do not engage in management-level decision making. They are simply employees. Also, the academy bears little resemblance to the nonprofit 'mature' university discussed in *Yeshiva*."

Another case, in which the court reached a similar conclusion, concerned the faculty of a liberal arts college that was closer to Yeshiva on the spectrum than was the art academy. In *Loretto Heights College v. NLRB*, 742 F.2d 1245 (10th Cir. 1984), the court determined that "faculty participation in college governance occurs largely through committees and other such groups" and that, outside such committees, faculty members' governance roles were limited to participation in decision making "within or concerning particular program areas" in matters such as hiring and curriculum development. After carefully examining all these facts, the court concluded:

> It is evident from these facts that faculty members at Loretto Heights play a substantial role in college governance, participating in decision making and implementation in a wide range of areas. It is equally clear, however, that the faculty's authority in most aspects of college governance is severely circumscribed. . . . Thus, while [the faculty] committees may in fact perform important functions, the extent of faculty involvement in the committees' work is so limited

as to be only incidental to, or in addition to, their primary function of teaching, research, and writing, rather than truly managerial in nature. . . . In light of the infrequent or insignificant nature of some committee work, the mixed membership of many committees, the faculty's limited decision-making authority, and the layers of administrative approval required for many decisions, the impact of faculty participation in college governance falls far short of the "effective recommendation or control" contemplated by *Yeshiva*. Outside the committee structure, as in the hiring and budget processes for example, faculty participation is similarly limited in authority and ultimately subject to one or more levels of administrative approval [742 F.2d at 1252–54; cites to *Yeshiva* omitted].

Moreover, said the court, since the governance structure of the college limited the administration's need to rely on faculty members' professional judgment, it was unnecessary for faculty to be aligned with management as they had been in *Yeshiva*.

Other cases in which the Board and courts refused to exclude faculty as managerial employees include *Bradford College and Milk Wagon Drivers and Creamery Workers Union, Local 380*, 261 NLRB 565 (1982); *Montefiore Hospital and Medical Center and New York State Federation of Physicians and Dentists*, 261 NLRB 569 (1982); *NLRB v. Cooper Union for Advancement of Science*, 783 F.2d 29 (2d Cir. 1986); *NLRB v. Florida Memorial College*, 820 F.2d 1182 (11th Cir. 1987); and *Kendall Memorial School v. NLRB*, 866 F.2d 157 (6th Cir. 1989).

But the Board and federal courts have applied the *Yeshiva* criteria to exclude faculty from coverage in several other cases. Faculty were found to be "managerial employees" excluded from bargaining in *Ithaca College and Ithaca College Faculty Ass.*, 261 NLRB 577 (1982); *Thiel College and Thiel College Chapter, AAUP*, 261 NLRB 580 (1982); *Duquesne University of the Holy Ghost and Duquesne University Law School Faculty Ass.*, 261 NLRB 587 (1982); *Fairleigh Dickinson University and Fairleigh Dickinson University Council of American Association of University Professors Chapters*, Case no. 22-RC-7198 (1986); *NLRB v. Lewis University*, 765 F.2d 616 (7th Cir. 1985); and *Boston University Chapter, AAUP v. NLRB*, 835 F.2d 399 (1st Cir. 1987).

As of 1992, faculty at twenty-four colleges had been found to be "managerial" and thus unprotected by federal labor law; faculty at another twenty institutions were found to be nonmanagerial (Douglas, *Directory of Faculty Contracts* (cited in Section 3.2), at 120–21). For analysis and criticism of the Board's application of the *Yeshiva* criteria, see B. Lee & J. Begin, "Criteria for Evaluating the Managerial Status of College Faculty: Applications of *Yeshiva University* by the NLRB," 10 *J. Coll. & Univ. Law* 515 (1983–84).

Attempts have been made to apply *Yeshiva* by analogy to public-sector institutions, but without success. The most notable example involved the University of Pittsburgh. Although a hearing examiner for the Pennsylvania Labor Relations Board ruled that the faculty were managerial, the full board reversed that finding and allowed an election to proceed (*University of Pittsburgh*, 21 Pa. Publ. Employee Rpts. 203 (1990)). The faculty elected "no agent," rejecting union representation (D. Blum, "After 7-Year Fight, Pitt Professors Vote Against Union," *Chron. Higher Educ.*, Mar. 20, 1991, A2; see also J. Douglas, "The Impact of *NLRB v. Yeshiva University* on Faculty Unionism at Public Colleges," 19 *J. of Collective Negotiations in the Public Sector* 1 (1990)).

At institutions that are not "Yeshiva-like," the managerial exclusion could apply to individual faculty members who have special governing responsibilities. Department heads, members of academic senates, or members of grievance committees or other institutional bodies with governance functions could be excluded as managerial employees. But the numbers involved are not likely to be so large as to preclude formation and recognition of a substantial bargaining unit.

Given the many possible variations from the circumstances in *Yeshiva*, faculty, administrators, and counsel can estimate the case's application to their campus only by comprehensively analyzing the institution's governance structure, the faculty's governance role in this structure, and the resulting decision-making experience.

On campuses with faculty members who would be considered "managers," bargaining does not become unlawful as a result of *Yeshiva*. The remaining faculty members not subject to exclusion may still form bargaining units under the protection of federal law. And even faculty members subject to the managerial exclusion may still agree among themselves to organize, and the institution may still voluntarily choose to bargain with them. But the administration may block the protection of federal law. Thus, for instance, faculty managers would have no federally enforceable right to be included in a certified bargaining unit or to demand good-faith bargaining over mandatory bargaining subjects (see Section 3.2.4). Conversely, the institution would have no federally enforceable right to file an unfair labor practice charge against a union representing only faculty managers for engaging in recognitional picketing, secondary boycotts, or other activity that would violate Section 8(b) of the NLRA (29 U.S.C. § 158(b)) if the federal law applied. A collective bargaining agreement entered through such a voluntary process could, however, be enforced in state court under the common law of contract.

In addition to raising questions about the legal status of faculties under *Yeshiva*, the decision has had a more subtle impact on relationships between faculty and administration (see generally J. V. Baldridge, F. Kemerer, & Associates, *Assessing the Impact of Faculty Collective Bargaining*, ERIC/Higher Education Research Report no. 8 (American Association for Higher Education, 1982)). It has given rise to numerous policy issues and sociological questions about faculty power on campus, and such matters merit reconsideration. Faculty at "mature" institutions have pressed for new mechanisms for exercising authority that the Supreme Court characterized as "managerial." At "nonmature" institutions administrators have accorded greater authority to faculty in order to forestall their resort to the bargaining process highlighted by *Yeshiva*. And at all types of institutions—mature or not, public or private—all affected constituencies may wish to better define and implement faculty's role in academic governance, not as a legal matter but as an exercise of sound policy judgment.

3.2.4. Bargainable subjects. Once the unit has been defined and the agent certified, the parties must proceed to negotiations. In the private sector, under the NLRA, the parties may negotiate on any subject they wish, although other laws (such as federal employment discrimination laws) may make some subjects illegal. In the public sector, the parties may negotiate on any subject that is not specifically excluded from the state's collective bargaining statute or preempted by other state law, such as a tenure statute. Those terms that may be raised by either party and that are negotiable with the consent of the other are referred to as "permissive" subjects for negotiation. Academic collective bargaining can range, and has ranged, over a wide variety of such permissive subjects (see M. Moskow, "The Scope of Collective Bargaining in Higher Education," 1971 *Wis. L. Rev.* 33 (1971)). A refusal to negotiate on a permissive subject of bargaining is not an unfair labor practice; on the contrary, it may be an unfair labor practice to insist that a permissive subject be covered by the bargaining agreement.

The heart of the collective bargaining process, however, is found in those terms over which the parties must negotiate. These "mandatory" subjects of bargaining are defined in the NLRA as "wages, hours, and other terms and conditions of employment" (29 U.S.C. § 158(d)). Most state laws use similar or identical language but often exclude particular subjects from the scope of that language or add particular subjects to it.[11] The parties must bargain in good faith over mandatory subjects of bargaining; failure to do so is an unfair labor practice under the NLRA (see 29 U.S.C. §§ 158(a)(5) and 158(b)(3)) and most state statutes.

The statutory language regarding the mandatory subjects is often vague (for example, "terms and conditions of employment") and subject to broad construction by labor boards and courts. Thus, the distinction between mandatory and permissive subjects is difficult to draw, particularly in postsecondary education, where faculties have traditionally participated in shaping their jobs to a much greater degree than have employees in industry. Internal governance and policy issues that may never arise in industrial bargaining may thus be critical in postsecondary education. There are few court or labor board precedents in either federal or state law to help the parties determine whether educational governance and educational policy issues are mandatorily or permissibly bargainable. For a thoughtful discussion of the scope of bargaining under federal law for professional employees, see D. Rabban, "Can American Labor Law Accommodate Collective Bargaining by Professional Employees?" 99 *Yale L.J.* 689 (1990).

Under state law, where some subjects may be impermissible, there are few precedents to help administrators determine when particular subjects fall into that category. One court case, *Assn. of New Jersey State College Faculties v. Dungan*, 316 A.2d 425 (N.J. 1974), concerned a state statute that gave public employees the right to bargain over the "terms and conditions of employment" and "working conditions." The court held that rules for granting tenure are not "mandatorily negotiable" under the statute because such rules "represent major educational policy pronouncements entrusted by the legislature [under the state's Education Law] to the board [of higher education's] educational expertise and objective judgment." Under such reasoning, tenure rules could also be beyond the scope of permissible bargaining, as "inherent managerial policy" (*University Education Association v. Regents of the University of Minnesota*, 353 N.W.2d 534 (Minn. 1984)) or as a nondelegable function of the board (see the *Cook County College Teachers Union* case in Section 3.2.1) or as a function preempted by other state laws or administrative agency regulations (see *New Jersey State College Locals v. State Board of Higher Education*, 449 A.2d 1244 (N.J. 1982)).

Other courts or agencies, however, particularly when dealing with private institutions under the NLRA, may reason that tenure is a mandatory, or at least

---

[11]Cases on this issue are collected in Annot., "Bargainable or Negotiable Issues in State Public Employment Labor Relations," 84 A.L.R.3d 242 (1978 and periodic supp.).

permissive, bargaining subject because it concerns job security (see A. Menard, "May Tenure Rights of Faculty Be Bargained Away?" 2 *J. Coll. & Univ. Law* 256 (1975)). In *Hackel v. Vermont State Colleges*, 438 A.2d 1119 (Vt. 1981), for example, the court determined that faculty promotion and tenure are "properly bargainable" under that state's Employee Labor Relations Act and upheld a provision on tenure and promotion in a collective bargaining agreement. Given this variation in judicial results, it is impossible to generalize about whether tenure or promotion standards or procedures are negotiable in general.

When the parties are unable to reach agreement on an item subject to mandatory bargaining (called impasse), a number of resolution techniques may be available to them. In the private sector, the NLRA specifically recognizes that employees have the right to strike under certain circumstances (see 29 U.S.C. § 163). The basic premise of the Act is that, given the free play of economic forces, employer and union can and will bargain collectively and reach agreement, and the ultimate economic force available to a union is the strike. (For an analysis of faculty strikes, see J. Douglas, "Professors on Strike: An Analysis of Two Decades of Faculty Work Stoppages—1966-85," 4 *Labor Lawyer* 87 (1988).) In the public sector, however, it is almost unanimously regarded as unlawful, either by state statute or state judicial decision, for an employee to strike. The rationale is that states have a vital interest in ensuring that government services remain available to the public without the interruption that would be created by a strike.[12]

Consequently, almost all state statutes prescribe impasse-resolution techniques to take the place of strikes. Depending on the statute, these techniques include mediation, fact-finding, and interest arbitration. The most commonly prescribed impasse procedure is mediation, the appointment of a third party who may make recommendations to the disputing parties but who does not dictate any terms of settlement. Fact-finding usually involves the appointment of an independent individual or panel to review the dispute and make findings regarding the critical facts underlying it. This process is sometimes mandatory if the parties fail to reach agreement within a specified time period; at other times a fact finder is appointed by order of a labor board or agreement of the parties (see J. Stern, "The Wisconsin Public Employee Fact-Finding Procedure," 20 *Indust. & Labor Rel. Rev.* 3 (1966)). Interest arbitration (as distinguished from grievance arbitration, discussed below) utilizes a third party to settle the contract terms on which the negotiating parties cannot agree. Interest arbitration can be either compulsory (in which case the statute requires the submission of unresolved issues to an arbitrator, who makes a final decision) or voluntary (in which case the parties decide for themselves whether to resort to binding arbitration).[13]

The same techniques used to resolve an impasse in bargaining may also be available in the public sector to resolve disputes concerning the application or interpretation of the bargaining agreement after it has gone into force. The most common

---

[12]The statutes and cases are collected in Annot., "Labor Law: Right of Public Employees to Strike or Engage in Work Stoppage," 37 A.L.R.3d 1147 (1971 and periodic supp.).

[13]Statutes and cases are collected in Annot., "Validity and Construction of Statutes or Ordinances Providing for Arbitration of Labor Disputes Involving Public Employees," 68 A.L.R.3d 885 (1976 and periodic supp.).

technique for resolving such disputes is grievance arbitration[14] (see M. Finkin, "The Arbitration of Faculty Status Disputes in Higher Education," 30 *Southwestern L.J.* 389 (1976), and J. Douglas, "An Analysis of the Arbitration Clause in Collective Bargaining Agreements in Higher Education," 39 *Arbitration J.* 38 (1984)).

In the private sector, there are only two techniques for resolving an impasse in negotiating an agreement—mediation and interest arbitration—and the latter is rarely used. Mediation is available through the Federal Mediation and Conciliation Service, which may "proffer its services in any labor dispute . . . either upon its own motion or upon the request of one or more of the parties" (29 U.S.C. § 173(b)), state mediation agencies, or the American Arbitration Association. Interest arbitration may be used when the parties have a collective bargaining agreement that is about to expire, and they are willing to have the arbitrator decide any terms they cannot agree upon when negotiating their new agreement. Interest arbitration in the private sector has no statutory basis and is entirely the creature of an existing agreement between the parties.

Negotiated agreements in the private sector usually provide for grievance arbitration to resolve disputes concerning the application or interpretation of the agreement. The arbitrator's power to entertain a grievance and to order a remedy comes from the language of the contract. In an illustrative case, *Trustees of Boston University v. Boston University Chapter, AAUP*, 746 F.2d 924 (1st Cir. 1984), the court upheld an arbitrator's interpretation of his powers under an arbitration clause of a bargaining agreement and affirmed the arbitrator's award of equity and merit raises to three professors who had filed grievances.

The parties specify the degree of authority given to the arbitrator to hear a grievance and the remedy the arbitrator may award. Although most contracts provide that an arbitrator may hear grievances related to any alleged violation of the collective agreement, most contracts limit the arbitrator's authority when the grievance is related to a faculty employment decision, such as reappointment, promotion, or tenure. Although most contracts allow the arbitrator to determine whether a procedural violation has occurred in the decision-making process, the usual remedy is to order the decision to be made a second time, following the appropriate procedures. In the few cases where collective bargaining agreements between institutions of higher education and faculty unions have provided for binding arbitration of employment disputes, arbitrators have overturned a negative employment decision and awarded reappointment, promotion, or tenure in about half of the cases. (For analysis of the outcomes of binding arbitration of faculty employment disputes in the California State College System, see E. Purcell, "Binding Arbitration and Peer Review in Higher Education," 45 *Arbitration J.* 10 (Dec. 1990).)

Another method of dispute resolution is the filing of an unfair labor practice claim with the NLRB (for private colleges and universities) or the state public employment relations agency (for public institutions). Allegations of refusing to bargain over an issue that the union believes is a proper subject of bargaining and the administration does not, or allegations that one of the parties is in some way violating federal or state labor law, are often the subject of unfair labor practices. Remedies available to the federal or state agency include orders to bargain or to desist in the

---

[14]Statutes and cases are collected in Annot., "Rights of State and Municipal Public Employees in Grievance Proceedings," 46 A.L.R.4th 912 (1986 and periodic supp.).

unlawful activity, reinstatement of individuals discharged in violation of the labor laws, and compensatory or equitable remedies.[15]

3.2.5. Coexistence of collective bargaining and traditional academic practices. Collective bargaining contracts traditionally come in two kinds, those with a "zipper" clause and those with a "past practices" clause. A zipper clause usually states that the union agrees to forgo its rights to bargain about any employment term or condition not contained in the contract; prior relationships between the parties thus become irrelevant. A past practices clause incorporates previous customary relationships between the parties in the agreement, at least insofar as they are not already inconsistent with its specific terms. Administrators faced with collective bargaining should carefully weigh the relative merit of each clause. A contract without either clause will likely be interpreted consistently with past practice when there are gaps or ambiguities in the contract terms. (See Sections 1.3.2.3 and 3.1.1.)

The availability of the past practices clause, however, by no means ensures that such traditional academic practices will endure under collective bargaining. In the early days of faculty bargaining, several commentators argued that such academic practices would steadily and inevitably disappear (for example, see D. Feller, "General Theory of the Collective Bargaining Agreement," 61 *Cal. L. Rev.* 663, 718–856 (1973)). One view was that collective bargaining brings with it the economic warfare of the industrial bargaining model, forcing the two parties into much more clearly defined employee and management roles and diminishing the collegial characteristics of higher education. The opposing view was that collective bargaining can be domesticated in the postsecondary environment with minimal disruption of academic practices (see M. Finkin, "Collective Bargaining and University Government," 1971 *Wis. L. Rev.* 125 (1971), and M. Finkin, "Faculty Collective Bargaining in Higher Education: An Independent Perspective," 3 *J. Law & Educ.* 439 (1974)).

As with most opposing theories, the outcome seems to be somewhere between the predictions of those who believed faculty would negotiate away tenure for higher salaries and those who believed that faculty unions would have no effect on traditional governance mechanisms. Although faculty senates have either been abolished or atrophied at a few colleges and universities, relationships between faculty unions and senates have, for the most part, been cooperative and mutually supportive, and there is no evidence that faculty have been willing to weaken or abrogate their tenure protection for greater economic benefits (see J. Begin, "Faculty Bargaining and Faculty Reward Systems: Current Research Findings," in D. Lewis & W. Becker (eds.), *Academic Rewards in Higher Education* (Ballinger, 1979), 245–96).

Thus, the issue for administrators is not whether traditional governance systems will be destroyed, but the extent to which faculty involvement in institutional governance should and can be maintained by incorporating such arrangements in the bargaining agreement, through either a past practices clause or a more detailed description of forms and functions (see F. R. Kemerer & J. V. Baldridge, *Unions on Campus: A National Study of the Consequences of Faculty Bargaining* (Jossey-Bass, 1975), and B. Lee, "Contractually Protected Governance Systems at Unionized Colleges," 5 *Rev. Higher Educ.* 69 (1982)). Given the result in *College of Osteopathic*

---

[15]Statutes and cases are collected in Annot., "What Constitutes Unfair Labor Practice Under State Public Employee Relations Acts," 9 A.L.R.4th 20 (1991 and periodic supp.).

Medicine, 265 NLRB 37 (1982), in which college faculty who attained a role in governance through their collective agreement were found to be managerial employees by the NLRB, faculty union leaders at private institutions may resist the incorporation of governance structures into the collective agreement.

3.2.6. Students and collective bargaining. During the 1970s students became increasingly concerned with the potential impact of collective bargaining between faculty and the administration on their interests. The questions are basically whether faculty and student interests are potentially, or necessarily, inconsistent and whether collective bargaining will reduce student power by reducing the policy issues in which students participate or the internal remedies they can utilize. If either of these effects flows from collective bargaining, another question then arises: Should students have a formal role in bargaining—and, if so, what kind? Several state legislatures have provided such a role for students in public institutions. In 1975 Oregon passed a law providing an independent observer-participant role for students (Or. Rev. Stat. ch. 679(1), §§ 243.650–243.782), and Montana passed a law allowing students to be part of the administration bargaining team (Rev. Code Mont. § 59-1602(1)). In 1976 Maine passed a law giving students the formal opportunity to consult with both administrators and faculty members before bargaining begins and with administrators at reasonable intervals during negotiations (Me. Rev. Stat. Ann. vol. 26, § 1024-A.6). In states without such statutes, some formal student participation has been provided by institutional or state governing board regulations or by agreement of the bargaining parties. Such action, however, may raise legal questions concerning institutional authority, particularly if students are empowered to postpone or veto the resolution of issues by the faculty and administration bargaining teams.

Some students may be more than spectators in collective bargaining in that they may be employees of the institution. Graduate students, for instance, may also be lecturers or laboratory or teaching assistants. If those duties would legally be characterized as employment, these students (as employees) would be eligible to participate in organizational efforts or collective negotiations covering positions of the type that they hold. It is sometimes difficult, however, to determine whether instructional, research, or clinical duties create an employment relationship or, instead, are part of an educational program that the student undertakes as student rather than employee. In *Physicians National House Staff Assn. v. Fanning,* 642 F.2d 492 (D.C. Cir. 1980), for example, the court held that interns, residents, and clinical fellows on staffs belonging to the association were "primarily students" and thus not covered by federal collective bargaining law. But in *Regents of the University of California v. Public Employment Relations Board,* 224 Cal. Rptr. 631 (Cal. 1986), the Supreme Court of California ruled that medical residents at University of California hospitals were employees and thus permitted to bargain. After considering how much time the residents spent in direct patient care, how much supervision they received, and whether they had the "indicia" of employment, the court concluded that their educational goals were subordinate to the services they performed for the hospitals. A similar result was reached in *University Hospital, University of Cincinnati College of Medicine v. State Employment Relations Board,* 587 N.E.2d 835 (Ohio 1992).

Graduate teaching assistants at many public universities are unionized; at some institutions they are in the same bargaining unit as full-time faculty. Administrators on campuses with large numbers of graduate teaching and research assistants can expect vigorous organizing activity from these groups over the next few years (see D. Blum, "Graduate Students on a Growing Number of Campuses Are Stepping Up Efforts to Organize Bargaining Units," *Chron. Higher Educ.*, Aug. 8, 1990, A9, A10).

3.2.7. Collective bargaining and antidiscrimination laws. A body of case law is developing on the applicability of federal and state laws prohibiting discrimination in employment (see Section 3.3) to the collective bargaining process. Courts have interpreted federal labor relations law (Section 3.2.1) to impose on unions a duty to represent each employee fairly—without arbitrariness, discrimination, or bad faith (see *Vaca v. Sipes*, 386 U.S. 171 (1967)).[16] In addition, some antidiscrimination statutes, such as Title VII and the Age Discrimination in Employment Act, apply directly to unions as well as employers. But these laws have left open several questions concerning the relationships between collective bargaining and antidiscrimination statutes. For instance, when employment discrimination problems are covered in the bargaining contract, can such coverage be construed to preclude faculty members from seeking other remedies under antidiscrimination statutes? If a faculty member resorts to a negotiated grievance procedure to resolve a discrimination dispute, can that faculty member then be precluded from using remedies provided under antidiscrimination statutes?

Most cases presenting such issues have arisen under Title VII of the Civil Rights Act of 1964 (see Section 3.3.2.1). The leading case is *Alexander v. Gardner-Denver Co.*, 415 U.S. 36 (1974). A discharged black employee claimed that the discharge was motivated by racial discrimination, and he contested his discharge in a grievance proceeding provided under a collective bargaining contract. Having lost before an arbitrator in the grievance proceeding, and having had a complaint to the federal Equal Employment Opportunity Commission dismissed, the employee filed a Title VII action in federal district court. The district court, citing earlier Supreme Court precedent regarding the finality of arbitration awards, had held that the employee was bound by the arbitration decision and thus had no right to sue under Title VII. The U.S. Supreme Court reversed. The Court held that the employee could still sue under Title VII, which creates statutory rights "distinctly separate" from the contractual right to arbitration under the collective bargaining agreement. Such independent rights "are not waived either by inclusion of discrimination disputes within the collective bargaining agreement or by submitting the nondiscrimination claim to arbitration."

In *McDonald v. City of West Branch*, 466 U.S. 284 (1984), the Court relied on *Gardner-Denver* in holding that a dismissed employee's resort to a union arbitration proceeding did not preclude him from seeking judicial relief under the Section 1983 civil rights statute (see Section 2.3.3). In an opinion that would cover employees who file Section 1983 claims alleging discrimination or other violations of constitutional and statutory rights, the Court concluded that arbitration "cannot provide an adequate substitute for a judicial proceeding in protecting the federal statutory and constitutional rights that Section 1983 is designed to safeguard." The fact that the grievance system is part of a collectively negotiated agreement, and not an individual

---

[16]Cases discussing the union's duty of fair representation are collected in Annot., "Union's Liability in Damages for Refusal or Failure to Process Employee Grievance," 34 A.L.R.3d 884 (1970 and periodic supp.).

employment contract, is important to the reasoning of *Gardner-Denver* and *McDonald*. The Court noted in *Gardner-Denver* that it may be possible to waive a Title VII cause of action (and presumably actions under other statutes) "as part of a voluntary settlement" of a discrimination claim. The employee's consent to such a settlement would have to be "voluntary and knowing," however, and "mere resort to the arbitral forum to enforce contractual rights" could not constitute such a waiver (see 415 U.S. at 52). Furthermore, the U.S. Supreme Court enforced an arbitration clause in an individual employment contract in *Gilmer v. Interstate-Johnson Lane,* 111 S. Ct. 1647 (1991). A registered securities representative had agreed to submit all disputes to compulsory arbitration, and the Court refused to permit him to file an age discrimination claim because he had entered the agreement to arbitrate. Distinguishing *Gardner-Denver,* the Court noted three differences between *Gardner-Denver* and *Gilmer.* First, Gilmer had agreed to arbitrate statutory claims, whereas the arbitration clause at issue in *Gardner-Denver* related to contract-based claims. Second, in *Gardner-Denver* the problem was that the Court did not believe the union should be permitted unilaterally to waive an individual employee's right to seek redress under nondiscrimination laws; in *Gilmer* no such problem existed because the individual employee had voluntarily entered the contract. And third, the Court noted that the Federal Arbitration Act favors arbitration agreements and that such agreements should be upheld whenever appropriate.

Given the holding of *Gardner-Denver,* some institutions have negotiated collective bargaining agreements with their faculty that contain a choice-of-forum provision. For example, the board of governors of the Illinois state colleges and universities negotiated with its faculty union a grievance procedure that gave the board the right to terminate grievance proceedings if a faculty member filed a discrimination claim with an administrative agency or in court. Raymond Lewis, a professor denied tenure, filed a grievance challenging the denial and, in order to preserve his rights under the federal Age Discrimination in Employment Act's (see Section 3.3.2.6) statute of limitations, filed a charge with the EEOC. The board terminated the grievance proceedings, citing the contractual provision. The EEOC filed an age discrimination lawsuit against the board, asserting that this provision constituted retaliation for exercising rights under the ADEA, which is forbidden by Section 4(d) of the Act (29 U.S.C. § 628(d)). After a series of lower court opinions resulting in victory for the board, the U.S. Court of Appeals for the Seventh Circuit reversed, agreeing with the EEOC's position. In *EEOC v. Board of Governors of State Colleges and Universities,* 957 F.2d 424 (7th Cir. 1992), the court, citing *Gardner-Denver,* reaffirmed the right of employees to overlapping contractual and statutory remedies and called the contractual provision "discriminatory on its face" (957 F.2d at 431).

Another situation where Title VII protections may conflict with the rights of the union as exclusive bargaining agent arises in the clash between Title VII's prohibition against religious discrimination and the union's right to collect an agency fee from nonmembers. Robert Roesser, an associate professor of electrical engineering at the University of Detroit, refused to pay his agency fee to the local union because, as a Catholic, he objected to the pro-choice position on abortion taken by the state union and the national union (the National Education Association). According to the university's contract with the union, nonpayment of the agency fee was grounds for termination, and Roesser was discharged.

Roesser filed a complaint with the EEOC, which sued both the union and the university on his behalf. The EEOC claimed that, under Title VII, the union was required to make a reasonable accommodation to Roesser's religious objections unless the accommodation posed an undue hardship (see Section 3.3.7). Roesser had offered to donate to a charity either the entire agency fee or the portion of the fee that was sent to the state and national unions. The union refused, but countered with the suggestion that the amount of the agency fee used for all social and political issues generally, including pro-choice and other issues, be deducted. Roesser refused because he did not want to be associated in any way with the state or national union (adding a First Amendment issue to the Title VII litigation).

The federal district court granted summary judgment to the union and the university, ruling that the union's accommodation was reasonable and that Roesser's proposal imposed undue hardship on the union. That ruling was overturned by the U.S. Court of Appeals for the Sixth Circuit (*EEOC v. University of Detroit*, 701 F. Supp. 1326 (E.D. Mich. 1988), *reversed and remanded*, 904 F.2d 331 (6th Cir. 1990)). The appellate court stated that Roesser's objection to the agency fee had two prongs, only one of which the district court had recognized. Roesser had objected to both the contribution to and the association with the state and national unions because of their position on abortion; the district court had ruled only on the contribution issue. According to the appellate court, the lower court had

> excuse[d] the union from making any effort to accommodate that portion of Roesser's religious belief which prevents him from associating in any way with the MEA and NEA. . . . The union was required to make some effort to accommodate the conflict between Roesser's religious belief against associating with the MEA and NEA and his employment obligation of paying the service fee [904 F.2d at 334–35].

In remanding the case, the appeals court asked the lower court to determine whether the associational prong of Roesser's objection could be reasonably accommodated without undue hardship to the union. In dicta, the appeals court suggested that Roesser might be required to pay the entire fee but that no portion of his fee would be sent to either the state or the national union, since he had stated no objection to the activities of the local union.

Thus, collective bargaining does not provide an occasion for postsecondary administrators to lessen their attention to the institution's Title VII responsibilities or its responsibilities under other antidiscrimination and civil rights laws. In many instances, faculty members can avail themselves of rights and remedies both under the bargaining agreement and under civil rights statutes.

Sec. 3.3. Nondiscrimination in Employment

3.3.1. The statutory, regulatory, and constitutional thicket. The problem of employment discrimination is probably more heavily blanketed with overlapping statutory and regulatory requirements than any other area of postsecondary education law. The federal government has no less than nine major employment discrimination statutes and one major executive order applicable to postsecondary education, each with its own comprehensive set of administrative regulations or guidelines (see Section 3.3.2). All states also have fair employment practices statutes. Some of these statutes (for instance, Md. Ann. Code Art. 49B, § 18) may exclude educational institutions; others may apply to educational institutions and overlap federal statutes.

Because of their national scope and comprehensive coverage of problems and remedies, and because they provide greater protection than the laws of many states, the federal antidiscrimination statutes have assumed greater importance than the state statutes. The federal statutes, moreover, supplemented by those of the states, have outstripped the importance of the federal Constitution as a remedy for employment discrimination. The statutes cover almost all major categories of discrimination and tend to impose more affirmative and stringent requirements on employers than does the Constitution.

Race discrimination in employment is prohibited by Title VII of the Civil Rights Act of 1964 as amended, by 42 U.S.C. § 1981, and by Executive Order 11246 as amended. Sex discrimination is prohibited by Title VII, by Title IX of the Education Amendments of 1972, by the Equal Pay Act, and by Executive Order 11246. Age discrimination is outlawed by the Age Discrimination in Employment Act. Discrimination against employees with disabilities is prohibited by both the Americans with Disabilities Act and the Rehabilitation Act of 1973. Discrimination on the basis of religion is outlawed by Title VII and Executive Order 11246. Discrimination on the basis of national origin is prohibited by Title VII and by Executive Order 11246. Discrimination against aliens is prohibited indirectly under Title VII (see Section 3.3.3). Discrimination against veterans is covered in part by 38 U.S.C. § 4212.

The nondiscrimination aspects of the statutes and Executive Order 11246 are discussed in this section, and they are contrasted with the requirements of the federal Constitution, as interpreted by the courts in the context of discrimination claims. The affirmative action aspects of the statutes and Executive Order 11246 are discussed in Section 3.4.

3.3.2. The legal concept of discrimination. The rationale for laws prohibiting discrimination in employment decisions is that characteristics such as race, sex, religion, or age (among others) are irrelevant for employment decisions. In debates prior to the passage of the Civil Rights Act of 1964, the first comprehensive federal law prohibiting employment discrimination, congressional leaders stressed the financial cost to both business and members of minority groups of employment decisions based not on individual qualifications or merit, but on "immutable" characteristics such as sex or race.

In cases where discrimination is alleged, the parties must follow a prescribed order of proof, which is described later in this subsection. The plaintiff must present sufficient evidence to raise an inference of discrimination; the defense then is allowed to rebut that inference by presenting evidence of a legitimate, nondiscriminatory reason for the action the plaintiff alleges was discriminatory. The plaintiff then has an opportunity to demonstrate that the defendant's "legitimate nondiscriminatory reason" is a pretext, that it is unworthy of belief. Thus, in order to prevail, the plaintiff need not prove that the defendant discriminated but that the defendant's explanation is untrue.

Discrimination claims are particularly complex for college faculty to prove and for colleges to defend against because of the subjective nature of employment decisions in academe. A successful discrimination claim generally depends on a plaintiff's ability to demonstrate unequal treatment of otherwise similar individuals. But identifying "similar" faculty members or demonstrating unequal treatment can be difficult. Particularly at institutions where faculty peers play a significant role in recommending candidates for hiring, promotion, or tenure, the locus of decision-making responsibility and the effect on upper levels of administration of potentially tainted recommendations at lower levels can be difficult to trace and to prove. Furthermore, opinions about what is "excellent" research or teaching may differ, even within the same academic department; and a plaintiff who attempts to compare herself or himself to colleagues in order to demonstrate unequal treatment may have difficulty doing so, especially in a small department.

Other issues facing academic institutions involve shifting performance standards, which may result in greater demands on recently hired faculty than those conducting the evaluation were required to meet—an outcome that can appear discriminatory whether or not there was a discriminatory intent. Comparisons of faculty productivity or quality across disciplines pose difficulties as well. And the practice at many colleges and universities of shielding the deliberations of committees or individuals from the scrutiny of the candidate or, in some cases, the courts (see Section 3.7.6) adds to the complexity of academic discrimination cases.

Because of the many employment discrimination laws and the complexity of their substantive and procedural requirements, each of the relevant laws will be examined in this section. The nature of the remedies available to plaintiffs will also be addressed. Then each type of discrimination (race, sex, etc.) will be examined in subsequent sections, with examples of how these claims typically arise, the types of issues that colleges defending these claims must generally address, and the implications of these cases for administrators and institutional counsel.

3.3.2.1. Title VII of the Civil Rights Act of 1964. Title VII of the Civil Rights Act of 1964, 42 U.S.C. § 2000e et seq., is the most comprehensive and most frequently utilized of the federal employment discrimination laws. It was extended in 1972 to cover educational institutions both public and private. According to the statute's basic prohibition, 42 U.S.C. § 2000e-2(a):

> It shall be an unlawful employment practice for an employer—
> (1) to fail or refuse to hire or to discharge any individual, or otherwise to discriminate against any individual with respect to his compensation, terms, conditions, or privileges of employment, because of such individual's race, color, religion, sex, or national origin; or
> (2) to limit, segregate, or classify his employees or applicants for employment in any way which would deprive or tend to deprive any individual of employment opportunities or otherwise adversely affect his status as an employee, because of such individual's race, color, religion, sex, or national origin.

The law covers not only employers but labor unions and employment agencies as well. Liability under Title VII is corporate; supervisors cannot be held individually liable under Title VII, although they may under other legal theories (*Miller v. Maxwell's International*, 991 F.2d 583 (9th Cir. 1993)).

The major exception to the general prohibition against discrimination is the "BFOQ" exception, which permits hiring and employing based on "religion, sex, or national origin" when such a characteristic is a "bona fide occupational qualification necessary to the normal operation of that particular business or enterprise" (42 U.S.C.

§ 2000e-2(e)(1)). Religion as a BFOQ is examined in Section 7.2.6.2 in the context of employment decisions at religiously affiliated institutions of higher education. Sex could be a permissible BFOQ for a locker room attendant or, perhaps, for certain staff of a single-sex residence hall. Race and national origin would not be permissible BFOQs for positions at colleges and universities.

Title VII is enforced by the Equal Employment Opportunity Commission (EEOC), which has issued a series of regulations and guidelines published at 29 C.F.R. Parts 1600 through 1610. The EEOC may receive, investigate, and conciliate complaints of unlawful employment discrimination and initiate lawsuits against violators in court or issue right-to-sue letters to complainants (29 C.F.R. Part 1601).

Title VII was amended by the Civil Rights Act of 1991 (Pub. L. No. 102-166, 105 Stat. 1071, 1072 (1991)), in large part as a reaction by Congress to seven decisions of the U.S. Supreme Court in 1989 that sharply limited the procedural and substantive rights of civil rights litigants under Title VII and several other nondiscrimination laws. These decisions will be discussed briefly in this section and in Section 3.4. In addition, the Civil Rights Act of 1991 provides for compensatory and punitive damages,[17] as well as jury trials, in cases of intentional discrimination.

Although Title VII broadly prohibits employment discrimination, it does not limit the right of postsecondary institutions to hire faculty members on the basis of job-related qualifications or to distinguish among faculty members on the basis of seniority or merit in pay, promotion, and tenure policies. Institutions retain the discretion to hire, promote, reward, and terminate faculty, as long as they do not make distinctions based on race, color, religion, sex, or national origin. If, however, an institution does distinguish among faculty on one of these bases, courts have broad powers to remedy the Title VII violation by "making persons whole for injuries suffered through past discrimination" (*Albemarle Paper Co. v. Moody*, 422 U.S. 405 (1975)). Remedies may include back-pay awards (*Albemarle*), awards of retroactive seniority (*Franks v. Bowman Transportation Co.*, 424 U.S. 747 (1976)), and various affirmative action measures to benefit the group whose members were the subject of the discrimination (see this chapter, Section 3.4), as well as the newly won right, in disparate treatment cases, to compensatory and punitive damages.

There are two basic types of Title VII claims: the "disparate treatment" claim and the "disparate impact" or "adverse impact" claim. In the former type of suit, an individual denied a job, promotion, or tenure, or subjected to a detrimental employment condition, claims to have been treated less favorably than other applicants or employees because of his or her race, sex, national origin, or religion (see, for example, *Lynn v. Regents of the University of California*, 656 F.2d 1337 (9th Cir. 1981) (alleged sex discrimination in denial of tenure)). In the "disparate impact" or "adverse impact" type of suit, the claim is that some ostensibly neutral policy of the employer has a discriminatory impact on the claimants or the class of persons they represent (see, for example, *Scott v. University of Delaware*, 455 F. Supp. 1102, 1123–

---

[17]At present, compensatory and punitive damages are capped on the basis of the size of the employer: organizations with 15–100 employees may be assessed up to $50,000; 101–201 employees, $100,000; 201–500 employees, $200,000; and over 500 employees, $300,000. A bill, the "Equal Remedies Act," is pending that would remove these caps (S-17, H-224). These damages may be assessed in addition to the "make-whole" remedies of back pay and attorney's fees. Other statutes, most notably Section 1981, do not have these caps.

32 (D. Del. 1978), *affirmed on other grounds*, 601 F.2d 76 (3d Cir. 1979) (alleged race discrimination in hiring, promotions, and tenure); and *Zahorik v. Cornell University*, 729 F.2d 85, 95–96 (2d Cir. 1984) (alleged sex discrimination in denial of tenure)). Of the two types of suits, disparate treatment is the more common for postsecondary education. The disparate treatment and disparate impact theories are also used when claims are litigated under other nondiscrimination laws, such as the Age Discrimination in Employment Act and Title IX of the Education Amendments of 1972.

The paradigm for disparate treatment suits is *McDonnell Douglas Corp. v. Green*, 411 U.S. 792 (1973). Under that decision:

> The complainant in a Title VII trial must carry the initial burden under the statute of establishing a prima facie case of racial discrimination. This may be done by showing (i) that he belongs to a racial minority; (ii) that he applied and was qualified for a job for which the employer was seeking applicants; (iii) that, despite his qualifications, he was rejected; and (iv) that, after his rejection, the position remained open and the employer continued to seek applicants from persons of complainant's qualifications. . . .
>
> The burden then must shift to the employer to articulate some legitimate, nondiscriminatory reason for the employee's rejection [411 U.S. at 802].

Although *McDonnell Douglas* concerned only racial discrimination, its methodology has been applied to other types of discriminatory treatment prohibited by Title VII; likewise, though the case concerned only job applications, courts have adapted its methodology to faculty hiring, promotion, and tenure situations.

This paradigm is used for the litigation of discrimination under other federal nondiscrimination laws as well. A subsequent Supreme Court case adds important gloss to *McDonnell Douglas* by noting that, in a disparate treatment (as opposed to disparate impact) case, "proof of discriminatory motive is critical [to complainant's case], although it can in some situations be inferred from the mere fact of difference in treatment" (*International Brotherhood of Teamsters v. United States*, 431 U.S. 324, 355 n.12 (1977)).

Courts had difficulty interpreting *McDonnell Douglas's* requirements concerning the evidentiary burden of both the plaintiff and the defendant in Title VII cases. The Supreme Court clarified its "burden-of-proof" ruling in *Texas Department of Community Affairs v. Burdine*, 450 U.S. 248 (1981). The case was brought by a state agency employee whose position had been abolished in a staff reorganization. Speaking for a unanimous court, Justice Powell gave this explanation of burdens of proof in Title VII disparate treatment cases:

> The burden of establishing a prima facie case of disparate treatment is not onerous. The plaintiff must prove by a preponderance of the evidence that she applied for an available position, for which she was qualified, but was rejected under circumstances which give rise to an inference of unlawful discrimination. The prima facie case serves an important function in the litigation; it eliminates the most common nondiscriminatory reasons for the plaintiff's rejection (see *Teamsters v. United States*, 431 U.S. 324, 358, and n.44 (1977)). As the Court explained in *Furnco Construction Co. v. Waters*, 438 U.S. 567, 577 (1978), the prima facie case "raises an inference of discrimination only because we presume these acts, if otherwise unexplained, are more likely than not based on the con-

sideration of impermissible factors." Establishment of the prima facie case in effect creates a presumption that the employer unlawfully discriminated against the employee. . . .

The burden that shifts to the defendant, therefore, is to rebut the presumption of discrimination by producing evidence that the plaintiff was rejected, or someone else was preferred, for a legitimate, nondiscriminatory reason. The defendant need not persuade the court that it was actually motivated by the proffered reasons. . . . It is sufficient if the defendant's evidence raises a genuine issue of fact as to whether it discriminated against the plaintiff. To accomplish this, the defendant must clearly set forth, through the introduction of admissible evidence, the reasons for the plaintiff's rejection. The explanation provided must be legally sufficient to justify a judgment for the defendant. If the defendant carries this burden of production, the presumption raised by the prima facie case is rebutted, and the factual inquiry proceeds to a new level of specificity. . . .

The plaintiff retains the burden of persuasion. She now must have the opportunity to demonstrate that the proffered reason was not the true reason for the employment decision. This burden now merges with the ultimate burden of persuading the court that she has been the victim of intentional discrimination. She may succeed in this either directly by persuading the court that a discriminatory reason more likely motivated the employer or indirectly by showing that the employer's proffered explanation is unworthy of credence (see *McDonnell Douglas*, 411 U. S. at 804-05). . . .

The court [of appeals] placed the burden of persuasion on the defendant apparently because it feared that "if an employer need only articulate not prove a legitimate, nondiscriminatory reason for his action, he may compose fictitious, but legitimate, reasons for his actions" (*Turner v. Texas Instruments, Inc.*, 555 F.2d 1251, 1255 (5th Cir. 1977)). We do not believe, however, that limiting the defendant's evidentiary obligation to a burden of production will unduly hinder the plaintiff. First, as noted above, the defendant's explanation of its legitimate reasons must be clear and reasonably specific. . . . Second, although the defendant does not bear a formal burden of persuasion, the defendant nevertheless retains an incentive to persuade the trier of fact that the employment decision was lawful. Thus, the defendant normally will attempt to prove the factual basis for its explanation. Third, the liberal discovery rules applicable to any civil suit in federal court are supplemented in a Title VII suit by the plaintiff's access to the Equal Employment Opportunity Commission's investigatory files concerning her complaint (see *EEOC v. Associated Dry Goods Corp.*, 449 U.S. 590 (1981)) [450 U.S. at 253-56; footnotes omitted].

Burdine clarifies the distinction between the burden of *production* (of producing evidence about a particular fact) and the burden of *persuasion* (of convincing the trier of fact that illegal discrimination occurred). The plaintiff always carries the ultimate burden of persuasion; it is only the burden of production that shifts from plaintiff to defendant and back to plaintiff again. The requirement that the defendant "articulate" rather than "prove" a nondiscriminatory reason does not relieve the defendant of the need to introduce probative evidence; it merely frees the defendant from any obligation to carry the ultimate burden of persuasion on that issue.

In *St. Mary's Honor Center v. Hicks*, 113 S. Ct. 2742 (1993), the Supreme Court reemphasized that the plaintiff carries the ultimate burden of proving intentional discrimination (instead of merely demonstrating that the defendant's reasons for its action were false). In *Hicks* the employer had offered two reasons for the plaintiff's discharge: a series of disciplinary violations and an incident of gross insubordination. In the "pretext" stage of the case, the plaintiff convinced the trial court that these were not the reasons for the discharge, because other employees with similar disciplinary problems had not been discharged. The trial court ruled against the plaintiff because the plaintiff was unable to show racial animus in the decision, but the U.S. Court of Appeals for the Eleventh Circuit reversed, saying that, under the *Burdine* language, if the plaintiff could demonstrate that the employer's reasons were "unworthy of belief," the plaintiff should prevail.

The Supreme Court, in a 5-to-4 opinion written by Justice Scalia, disagreed, saying that Title VII did not afford a plaintiff a remedy simply because an employer gave untruthful reasons, but only if the employer's decision was based on the plaintiff's race. Justice Scalia wrote:

> We have no authority to impose liability upon an employer for alleged discriminatory employment practices unless an appropriate factfinder determines, according to proper procedures, *that the employer has unlawfully discriminated.* . . . [N]othing in law would permit us to substitute for the required finding that the employer's action was the product of unlawful discrimination, the much different (and much lesser) finding that the employer's explanation of its action was not believable [113 S. Ct. at 2751; emphasis in original].

In other words, in order to prevail under Title VII, the plaintiff must show two things: that the employer's stated reasons for the challenged decision are untrue, and that the true reason is discrimination. Few plaintiffs have direct evidence of discrimination, and many plaintiffs who have prevailed in discrimination claims have done so by indirect proof of discrimination of the type that the majority rejected in *Hicks*.

The dissent, written by Justice Souter, criticized the majority's "depart[ure] from settled precedent" and creation of an interpretation of Title VII "that promises to be unfair and unworkable" (113 S. Ct. at 2757). Relying on the *Burdine* language, which appeared to permit plaintiffs to prevail if they prevailed at the pretext stage, the dissent argued that the majority opinion would frustrate the purpose of Title VII by discouraging plaintiffs without direct evidence of discrimination from seeking redress under that law. A bill, H.R. 2787, has been introduced into Congress that would overturn the result in *Hicks*.

Occasionally, however, a plaintiff will have direct evidence of discrimination and alleges the problem of "mixed motives" in an employment decision. In such cases the plaintiff demonstrates that one or more of the prohibited factors (sex, race, etc.) was a motivating factor in a negative employment decision. In *Price Waterhouse v. Hopkins*, 490 U.S. 228 (1989), the plaintiff had proved that a committee evaluating her for partnership in an accounting firm used gender stereotypes to reach its decision not to award her a partnership. Both the plaintiff's and the defendant's burden of proof were at issue in *Hopkins:* the plaintiff argued that, in order to hold the defendant liable for discrimination, she need only demonstrate that gender played a part in the decision; the defendant insisted that, before liability could be found, the plaintiff must prove that gender was the "decisive consideration" in the decision.

A plurality of the Court, in an opinion authored by Justice Brennan, ruled that the plaintiff need only show that gender was one of the considerations in the employment decision. With regard to the defendant's burden of proof, Justice Brennan wrote:

[O]nce a plaintiff in a Title VII case shows that gender played a
motivating part in an employment decision, the defendant may avoid a finding
of liability only by proving that it would have made the same decision even if
it had not allowed gender to play such a role [490 U.S. at 244].

In other words, in "mixed-motive" cases, simply "articulating a legitimate nondiscriminatory reason" in the face of demonstrated bias would be insufficient for a
defendant to rebut the plaintiff's evidence; instead, to be found not liable, an employer
would have to demonstrate that it would have reached the same decision even if the
impermissible factors were absent.

In the Civil Rights Act of 1991, Congress agreed with the plurality's determination regarding the plaintiff's burden, but it overturned its determination that a
defendant could still prevail even if an impermissible factor contributed to an employment decision. The Act amended Title VII's Section 703 by adding subsection (m),
which states that if the plaintiff shows that a prohibited factor motivated an employment decision, an unlawful employment practice is established. But if the plaintiff
establishes a violation under subsection (m) and the employer successfully demonstrates that the same action would have been taken in absence of the prohibited factor,
then a court may not award damages or make-whole remedies (such as reinstatement
or promotion). This amendment permits plaintiffs who do not prevail on the merits
to be awarded attorney's fees and declaratory relief.

Disparate treatment cases may also be brought by a class of plaintiffs. In these
cases, called "pattern and practice" cases, the plaintiffs must prove intentional discrimination by the employer in one or more employment conditions. For example,
in *Penk v. Oregon State Board of Higher Education*, 816 F.2d 458 (9th Cir. 1987),
female faculty alleged systemwide discrimination against women in salary, promotion, and tenure practices, because statistical analysis revealed that women, on the
whole, were paid less than male faculty and tended to be at lower ranks. The appellate
court affirmed the trial court's conclusion that the postsecondary system had provided
legitimate nondiscriminatory reasons for the statistical differentials, such as the fact
that most women faculty were less senior and that external economic factors had
depressed the salaries of junior faculty compared with those of senior faculty, most
of whom were male. The court's careful articulation of the burdens of proof in pattern
and practice cases is instructive.

Although most Title VII litigation in academe involves allegations of disparate treatment, several class action complaints have been brought against colleges and
universities using the disparate impact theory. For example, in *Scott v. University of
Delaware*, 455 F. Supp. 1102 (D. Del. 1987), *affirmed on other grounds*, 601 F.2d 76
(3d Cir. 1979), a black professor alleged, on behalf of himself and other black faculty,
that requiring applicants for faculty positions to hold a Ph.D. had a disparate impact
on blacks because blacks are underrepresented among holders of Ph.D. degrees. The
court agreed with the university's argument that training in research, symbolized by
the doctoral degree, was necessary for universities because of their research mission.

The paradigm for disparate impact suits is *Griggs v. Duke Power Co.*, 401 U.S.
424 (1971). As the U.S. Supreme Court explained in that case:

Under [Title VII] practices, procedures, or tests neutral on their face, and
even neutral in terms of intent, cannot be maintained if they operate to "freeze"
the status quo of prior discriminatory employment practices. . . .

Congress has now provided that tests or criteria for employment or promotion may not provide equality of opportunity merely in the sense of the fabled offer of milk to the stork and the fox. On the contrary, Congress has now required that the posture and condition of the job seeker be taken into account. It has—to resort again to the fable—provided that the vessel in which the milk is proffered be one all seekers can use. The Act proscribes not only overt discrimination but also practices that are fair in form but discriminatory in operation. The touchstone is business necessity. If an employment practice which operates to exclude Negroes cannot be shown to be related to job performance, the practice is prohibited [401 U.S. at 429-31].

In its unanimous opinion in *Griggs,* the Court interpreted Title VII to prohibit employment practices that (1) operate to exclude or otherwise discriminate against employees or prospective employees on grounds of race, color, religion, sex, or national origin, and (2) are unrelated to job performance or not justified by business necessity. Both requirements must be met before Title VII is violated. Under the first requirement, it need not be shown that the employer intended to discriminate; the effect of the employment practice, not the intent behind it, controls. Under the second requirement, the employer, not the employee, has the burden of showing the job relatedness or business necessity of the employment practice in question.

The disparate impact test developed in *Griggs* was applied by the Supreme Court in *Watson v. Fort Worth Bank & Trust,* 487 U.S. 977 (1988). The Court added an element to the *Griggs* tests: where a practice with a disparate impact is justified by business necessity, the plaintiffs may still prevail if they can demonstrate that "other selection processes that have a lesser discriminatory effect could also suitably serve the employer's business needs" (487 U.S. at 1006, Blackmun concurrence). In addition, the Court ruled that plaintiffs could attack subjective decision-making practices under the disparate impact theory—a ruling that is important to faculty plaintiffs, who have frequently alleged that subjective performance standards are susceptible to bias. For an analysis of legal challenges to subjective hiring practices, see P. Swan, "Subjective Hiring and Promotion Decisions in the Wake of *Ft. Worth, Atonio,* and *Price-Waterhouse,*" 16 *J. Coll. & Univ. Law* 1 (1990).

The burdens of proof addressed in *Griggs* were revisited by the U.S. Supreme Court in 1989 in *Wards Cove Packing Co. v. Atonio,* 490 U.S. 642 (1989). In a 5-to-4 opinion, to which Justices Stevens and Blackmun wrote blistering dissents, the Supreme Court changed the requirement that employers demonstrate the "business necessity" of those practices and made the plaintiffs' burden of production much more difficult.

The case involved a challenge to the hiring, promotion, and work assignment practices of two Alaskan salmon canneries by Filipino and Native American unskilled cannery workers. Noncannery workers, who held such positions as truck drivers, cooks, and fishing boat captains, were predominantly white. The plaintiffs charged that the canneries used nepotism, separate hiring channels, and rehire preferences for the better-paying, more highly skilled noncannery jobs, and refused to permit cannery workers to compete for the better jobs. These practices resulted in a segregated work force, which was perpetuated by the canneries' practice of segregating cannery and noncannery workers' eating halls and dormitories.

The Court addressed three issues: the sufficiency of the plaintiffs' statistical evidence in establishing a disparate impact, the evidence necessary to prove that the challenged practices caused the alleged disparity, and the employer's rebuttal burden. Rejecting the plaintiffs' statistical evidence as insufficient, the Court then determined that the plaintiffs could not assert that the cumulative effect of the hiring practices caused the disparate impact; instead, they must specify each practice that caused the disparity and show how each practice operated to exclude the plaintiffs—an extremely difficult, if not impossible, task.

The Court then examined the defendant's burden. In his opinion for the majority, Justice White wrote:

> [T]he dispositive issue is whether a challenged practice serves, in a significant way, the legitimate employment goals of the employer. . . . The touchstone of this inquiry is a reasoned review of the employer's justification for his use of the challenged practice. . . . [T]here is no requirement that the challenged practice be "essential" or "indispensable" to the employer's business for it to pass muster: this degree of scrutiny would be almost impossible for most employers to meet, and would result in a host of evils. . . . [T]he employer carries the burden of producing evidence of a business justification for his employment practice [490 U.S. at 659].

The "business justification" standard articulated by Justice White was much easier for employers to meet than the "business necessity" standard created by *Griggs*. This diminution of the *Griggs* standard (without explicitly overruling *Griggs*) and the resulting heightened burden of producing evidence faced by plaintiffs in these cases created substantial pressure on Congress to amend Title VII to counteract the effect of *Wards Cove*.

Congress responded in the Civil Rights Act of 1991 by codifying the *Griggs* standard, thus nullifying that portion of *Wards Cove*. The Act adds subsection (k) to Section 703. The subsection requires the employer to rebut a showing of disparate impact by demonstrating that "the challenged practice is job related for the position in question and consistent with business necessity" (42 U.S.C. § 2000e-2(k)(1)(a)(i)). The subsection also permits the plaintiff to challenge the combined effects of several employment practices if the plaintiff "can demonstrate to the court that the elements of a respondent's decisionmaking process are not capable of separation for analysis." The new law also codifies the Court's *Watson* holding by adding that unlawful disparate impact may also be established if the plaintiff can demonstrate that a less discriminatory and equally effective alternative practice is available to the employer but the employer refuses to use it.

Two additional issues litigated under Title VII bear on claims under other nondiscrimination laws. The first concerns the time limits within which a Title VII claim must be brought, and the second deals with the nature of the remedies available to plaintiffs denied promotion or tenure as a result of the discriminatory subjective evaluation of the quality of their research or teaching.

Under Title VII an individual claiming discrimination must file a complaint with the EEOC within 180 days "after the alleged unlawful employment practice occurred" (42 U.S.C. § 2000e-5(e)), or within 300 days if a claim has first been filed with a state or local civil rights agency. The claim lapses if the individual does not comply with this time limit. Although this provision may appear straightforward, most colleges and universities use multiple decision levels on faculty status matters. In addition, many individuals and groups are involved in an employment decision. These practices make it difficult to determine exactly when an employment practice "occurred." Did it occur with the first negative recommendation, perhaps made by a department chair, or is the action by an institution's board of trustees the "occurrence"? And since many colleges give a faculty member a "terminal year" contract after denial of tenure, at what point has the alleged discrimination "occurred"?

In *Delaware State College v. Ricks*, 449 U.S. 250 (1980), the U.S. Supreme Court interpreted this time requirement as it applies to faculty members making claims against postsecondary institutions. Overruling the appellate court, the Supreme Court held that the time period commences when an institution officially announces its employment decision and not when the faculty member's employment relationship terminates.

In a 5-to-4 decision, the Court dismissed the claim of Ricks, a black Liberian professor who had been denied tenure, because he had not filed his claim of national origin discrimination within 180 days of the date the college notified him of its decision. Ricks had claimed that his terminal year of employment, after the tenure denial, constituted a "continuing violation" of Title VII, which allowed him to file his EEOC charge within 180 days of his last day of employment. The Court rejected this view:

> Mere continuity of employment, without more, is insufficient to prolong the life of a cause of action for employment discrimination. If Ricks intended to complain of a discriminatory discharge, he should have identified the alleged discriminatory acts that continued until, or occurred at the time of, the actual termination of his employment. . . .
>
> In sum, the only alleged discrimination occurred—and the filing limitations period therefore commenced—at the time the tenure decision was made and communicated to Ricks. That is so even though one of the effects of the denial of tenure—the eventual loss of a teaching position—did not occur until later [449 U.S. at 257–58].

The Court also rejected an intermediate position, adopted by three of the dissenters, that the limitations period should not have begun until after the final decision of the college grievance committee, which had held hearings on Ricks's complaint.

In *Chardon v. Fernandez*, 102 S. Ct. 28 (1981), a per curiam opinion from which three justices dissented, the Court extended the reasoning of *Ricks* to cover nonrenewal or termination of term appointments (as opposed to tenure denials). Unless there are allegations that discriminatory acts continued to occur after official notice of the decision, the 180-day time period for nonrenewal or termination claims also begins to run from the date the complainant is notified.

The U.S. Court of Appeals for the Seventh Circuit was asked to determine at what point the "official notice" of the decision occurs: when an administrator makes a decision to which higher-level administrators routinely defer, or when the chief academic officer confirms that decision? In *Lever v. Northwestern University*, 979 F.2d 552 (7th Cir. 1992), the appellate court ruled that the point at which the discriminatory act occurs is a question of fact, which must be determined by reference to the institution's policies and practices. In this case, language in the faculty handbook indicated that a dean's decision to deny tenure was final unless reversed by the provost on appeal, and that the provost did not review negative recommendations by deans unless asked to do so by the candidate. Citing *Ricks,* the court stated that appeal of a negative decision made by the dean does not toll the limitations period.

The Civil Rights Act of 1991 addresses the issue of timely filing, although it does not overturn *Ricks.* In a case decided in 1989, the U.S. Supreme Court ruled that the limitations period begins to run when a practice that later has a discriminatory effect on an individual or group is first enacted, rather than when the individual or group is harmed. In *Lorance v. AT&T Technologies,* 490 U.S. 900 (1989), a group of women were not permitted to challenge an allegedly discriminatory seniority provision that had been adopted several years earlier, because they waited until they were harmed by the provision's application rather than filing a claim within 180 days of the date the provision took effect. Congress reversed this ruling by adding a new paragraph (2) to Section 112 of Title VII. The law now provides that a seniority system that intentionally discriminates may be challenged when the system is adopted, when an individual becomes subject to it, or when an individual is actually harmed by it.

Remedies available to prevailing parties in Title VII litigation include reinstatement, back pay, compensatory and punitive damages (for disparate treatment discrimination), and attorney's fees. An issue that has troubled courts analyzing academic Title VII cases is the appropriate remedy for a denial of tenure or promotion that is found to have been discriminatory. In nonacademic settings, reinstatement to the position along with retroactive promotion is a routine remedy. But the courts, citing their lack of expertise in evaluating the scholarly or teaching ability of college faculty, sometimes have been reluctant to award "make whole" remedies to college faculty.

Early cases in which courts were asked to review denials of tenure or promotion made clear the judges' discomfort with the request. In situations where peer review committees had determined that a plaintiff's scholarship and/or teaching did not meet the proper standards, judges were reluctant to impose either their own judgments or their own performance standards on peer review committees, external evaluators, or college administrators. In an early case, *Faro v. New York University,* 502 F.2d 1229 (2d Cir. 1974), the U.S. Court of Appeals for the Second Circuit stated:

> [O]f all fields which the federal courts should hesitate to invade and take over, education and faculty appointments at a university level are probably the least suited for federal court supervision. Dr. Faro would remove any subjective judgments by her faculty colleagues in the decisionmaking process [502 F.2d at 1231–32].

The Fourth Circuit, echoing *Faro,* stated that "[c]ourts are not qualified to review and substitute their judgment for the subjective, discretionary judgments of professional experts on faculty promotions" (*Clark v. Whiting,* 607 F.2d 634, 640 (1979)).

Federal appellate courts in subsequent academic discrimination cases were more willing to review academic judgments, although the question of the appropriate remedy was still troublesome. In *Powell v. Syracuse University,* 580 F.2d 1150 (2d Cir. 1978), the court rejected its earlier deference, stating that the courts' "anti-interventionist policy has rendered colleges and universities virtually immune to charges of employment bias," and that the court would not "rely on any such policy of self-abnegation where colleges are concerned" (580 F.2d at 1153). The question of remedy rarely arose, however, because, between 1972 and 1986, plaintiffs won on the merits only about 20 percent of the time (G. LaNoue & B. Lee, *Academics in Court: The Consequences of Faculty Discrimination Litigation* (University of Michigan Press, 1987)).

The issue of a remedy for a discriminatory denial of tenure was addressed squarely in *Kunda v. Muhlenberg College,* 621 F.2d 532 (3d Cir. 1980). The decision, written by Judge Dolores Sloviter, a former law professor, takes into account the need for academic freedom and the significance of peer evaluation while also recognizing that individuals who make academic judgments are still subject to Title VII's prohibitions on discrimination.

Connie Kunda, a physical education instructor, brought suit after the college had denied her applications for promotion and tenure. The trial court (463 F. Supp. 294 (E.D. Pa. 1978)), holding that the college had intentionally discriminated against Kunda because of her sex, awarded her (1) reinstatement to her position; (2) back pay from the date her employment terminated, less amounts earned in the interim; (3) promotion to the rank of assistant professor, back-dated to the time her application was denied; and (4) the opportunity to complete the requirements for a master's degree within two full school years from the date of the court's decree, in which case she would be granted tenure.

In affirming the trial court's award of relief, the appellate court carefully analyzed the particular facts of the case. These facts, as set out below, played a vital role in supporting and limiting the precedent set by this opinion.

When Kunda was appointed an instructor in the Muhlenberg College physical education department in September 1966, she held a Bachelor of Arts degree in physical education. Although the department's terminal degree requirement, for tenure purposes, was the master's, Kunda was never informed that a master's was needed for advancement. Kunda was first recommended for promotion in the academic year 1971–72. The department forwarded its recommendation to the Faculty Personnel and Policies Committee (FPPC) of the college, which rejected the recommendation. The dean of the college, Dean Secor, who seldom attended FPPC deliberations on promotions, spoke against the recommendation. Subsequently, to determine the reasons for the denial, Kunda met individually with her department chairman; Dean Secor; and the college's president, President Morey. The court found that none of these persons told her that she had been denied promotion "because she lacked a master's degree" or stated that "a master's would be mandatory" in any future consideration for promotion or for tenure.

In the two subsequent years, Kunda's department colleagues and all relevant faculty committees recommended that she be promoted and, in the last year, granted tenure. Both times, the dean recommended against promotion and tenure, citing various institutional concerns rather than Kunda's lack of a master's degree, and affirming Kunda's worth to the college by recommending to the president that she be retained in a non-tenure-track status. Both years, President Morey recommended against promotion and tenure, and Kunda was given a terminal contract.

Kunda appealed the tenure denial to the Faculty Board of Appeals (FBA). The FBA recommended that Kunda be promoted and awarded tenure because (1) Kunda displayed the "scholarly equivalent" of a master's degree, (2) the policy of granting promotions only to faculty possessing the terminal degree had been bypassed frequently for the physical education department, and (3) no significant financial considerations mandated a denial of tenure. Despite the FBA recommendation, the board of trustees voted to deny tenure.

After reviewing these facts, the court of appeals examined other facts comparing Kunda's situation with that of similarly situated males at Muhlenberg. With respect to promotion, three male members of the physical education department had been promoted during the period of Kunda's employment, notwithstanding their lack of master's degrees. In another department of the college, a male instructor had been promoted without a terminal degree. There was also a difference between the counseling offered Kunda and that offered similarly situated males; while Kunda was not told that the master's would be a prerequisite for a grant of tenure, male members had been so advised.

Basing its conclusions on its analysis of these facts found by the trial court, and its approval of the trial court's allocation of burdens of proof, the appellate court agreed that Kunda had been discriminated against in both the denial of promotion and the denial of tenure. Concerning promotion, the appellate court affirmed the finding that the defendant's reason for denial articulated at trial, lack of the terminal degree, was a pretext for discrimination. Concerning tenure, the appellate court affirmed the trial court's determination that the articulated reason (lack of terminal degree) was not pretextual but that Kunda had been subjected to intentional disparate treatment with respect to counseling on the need for the degree.

Having held the college in violation of Title VII, the court turned to what it considered the most provocative issue raised on appeal: the propriety of the remedy fashioned by the trial court. Awards of back pay and reinstatement are not unusual in academic employment discrimination litigation; awards of promotion or conditional tenure are. The appellate court therefore treated the latter remedies extensively, emphasizing the special academic freedom context in which they arose:

> Academic freedom, the wellspring of education, is entitled to maximum protection.
>
> It does not follow that because academic freedom is inextricably related to the educational process it is implicated in every employment decision of an educational institution. Colleges may fail to promote or to grant tenure for a variety of reasons, such as anticipated decline in enrollment, retrenchment for budgetary reasons, termination of some departments, or determination that there are higher priorities elsewhere. These are decisions which may affect the quality of education but do not necessarily intrude upon the nature of the educational process itself.
>
> On the other hand, it is beyond cavil that generally faculty employment decisions comprehend discretionary academic determinations which do entail review of the intellectual work product of the candidate. That decision is most effectively made within the university and although there may be tension between the faculty and the administration on their relative roles and responsibilities, it is generally acknowledged that the faculty has at least the initial, if not the primary, responsibility for judging candidates. "The peer review system has evolved as the most reliable method for assuring promotion of the candidates best qualified to serve the needs of the institution" (*Johnson v. University of Pittsburgh*, 435 F. Supp. 1328, 1346 (W.D. Pa. 1977)).
>
> Wherever the responsibility lies within the institution, it is clear that

courts must be vigilant not to intrude into that determination, and should not substitute their judgment for that of the college with respect to the qualifications of faculty members for promotion and tenure. Determinations about such matters as teaching ability, research scholarship, and professional stature are subjective, and unless they can be shown to have been used as the mechanism to obscure discrimination, they must be left for evaluation by the professionals, particularly since they often involve inquiry into aspects of arcane scholarship beyond the competence of individual judges. In the cases cited by appellant in support of the independence of the institution, an adverse judgment about the qualifications of the individual involved for the position in question had been made by the professionals—faculty, administration, or both. It was those adverse judgments that the courts refused to reexamine. (See, for example, *Johnson v. University of Pittsburgh,* above; *Huang v. College of the Holy Cross,* 436 F. Supp. 639 (D. Mass. 1977); *EEOC v. Tufts Institution of Learning,* 421 F. Supp. 152 (D. Mass. 1975). But see *Sweeney v. Board of Trustees of Keene State College,* 604 F.2d 106 (1st Cir. 1979), *on remand from* 439 U.S. 24 . . . (1978).)

The distinguishing feature in this case is that Kunda's achievements, qualifications, and prospects were not in dispute. She was considered qualified by the unanimous vote of both faculty committees which evaluated her teaching, research and creative work, and college and public service. Her department chairman consistently evaluated her as qualified. Even Dean Secor, who did not affirmatively recommend Kunda, commented favorably on her performance, which he rated as "justify[ing] a permanent appointment." . . . The district court made a specific finding of fact (No. 30) that President Morey did not recommend tenure for Kunda "because of her lack of an advanced degree." The record is manifest that if President Morey had recommended Kunda for tenure, the board of trustees would have ratified that decision. The college had ample opportunity during the trial to present testimony as to any other factor on which the decision to deny tenure was based and failed to do so. Thus, the trial judge's finding that plaintiff "had satisfied both alternatives to the terminal degree requirement for promotion and tenure" was based not on his independent judgment, but on the judgment of the university community itself. In the line of cases challenging university decisions not to promote or grant tenure, this case may therefore be *sui generis* or, at least, substantially distinguishable.

Nor can the court's order be construed as appellant does—as a judicial grant of tenure. Underlying the court's order was its finding of fact that "had Mrs. Kunda been counseled in the same manner as male members of the physical education department, we find that she would have done everything possible to obtain a master's degree in order to further enhance her chances of obtaining tenure." The court did not award Kunda tenure. The court instead attempted to place plaintiff in the position she should have been "but for" the unlawful discrimination. Having found she was denied tenure because she did not have a terminal degree, the court gave her the opportunity to secure one within two full school years, the period between the time she should have been counseled in 1972 and the tenure decision in 1974. The direction by the court to the college to grant her tenure after she secured the one missing link upon which her rejection by the college had been based is consistent with the line of Title VII cases awarding seniority and other employment perquisites to those found to have been victims of discrimination (*International Brotherhood of Teamsters v. United States,* 431 U.S. 324 . . . (1977); *Franks v. Bowman Transportation Co.,* 424 U.S. 747 . . . (1976)). The court could have reasonably decided that there would be no purpose to be served to require that the board of trustees reconsider plaintiff's tenure after

she achieved a master's degree because of the impossibility of asking the board
to ignore changes such as the financial situation, student enrollment, and faculty
hiring which may have occurred in the intervening five-year period, as well as
the intangible effect upon that decision because the candidate being considered
was the successful party to a Title VII suit.

The touchstone of Title VII remedies is "to make persons whole for injuries suffered on account of unlawful employment discrimination" (*Albemarle
Paper Co. v. Moody*, 422 U.S. 405, 418 . . . (1975)). In directing the award of
competitive-type seniority, the Court noted the broad scope of the courts' equitable discretion in Title VII cases:

> To effectuate this "make-whole" objective, Congress in Section
> 706(g) vested broad equitable discretion in the federal courts to "order such
> affirmative action as may be appropriate, which may include, but is not
> limited to, reinstatement or hiring of employees, with or without back pay,
> . . . or any other equitable relief as the court deems appropriate" (*Franks v.
> Bowman Transportation Co.*, 424 U.S. 747, 763–64 . . . (1976). . . .

The fact that the discrimination in this case took place in an academic
rather than commercial setting does not permit the court to abdicate its responsibility to insure the award of a meaningful remedy. Congress did not intend that
those institutions which employ persons who work primarily with their mental
faculties should enjoy a different status under Title VII than those which employ
persons who work primarily with their hands.

The legislative history of Title VII is unmistakable as to the legislative
intent to subject academic institutions to its requirements. When originally
enacted, Title VII exempted from the equal employment requirements educational institution employees connected with educational activities. This exemption was removed in 1972. The need for coverage is amply set forth in the Report
of the House Committee on Education and Labor:

> There is nothing in the legislative background of Title VII, nor does
> any national policy suggest itself, to support the exemption of the educa-
> tional institution employees—primarily teachers—from Title VII coverage.
> Discrimination against minorities and women in the field of education is as
> pervasive as discrimination in any other area of employment. In the field of
> higher education, the fact that black scholars have been generally relegated
> to all-black institutions, or have been restricted to lesser academic positions
> when they have been permitted entry into white institutions, is common
> knowledge. Similarly, in the area of sex discrimination, women have long
> been invited to participate as students in the academic process, but without
> the prospect of gaining employment as serious scholars.
> When they have been hired into educational institutions, particu-
> larly in institutions of higher education, women have been relegated to
> positions of lesser standing than their male counterparts. In a study con-
> ducted by Theodore Caplow and Reece J. McGee, it was found that the
> primary factors determining the hiring of male faculty members were pres-
> tige and compatibility, but that women were generally considered to be
> outside of the prestige system altogether.
> The committee feels that discrimination in educational institutions
> is especially critical. The committee cannot imagine a more sensitive area
> than educational institutions, where the nation's youth are exposed to a
> multitude of ideas that will strongly influence their future development. To
> permit discrimination here would, more than in any other area, tend to
> promote misconceptions leading to future patterns of discrimination. . . .
> (Equal Employment Opportunity Act of 1972 . . .). . . .

The lack of success of women and minorities in Title VII suits alleging discrimination against academic institutions can, in large part, be attributed to the subjective factors upon which employment decisions are made, previously discussed. The danger that judicial abnegation may nullify the congressional policy to rectify employment bias in an academic setting has been noted:

> This anti-interventionist policy has rendered colleges and universities virtually immune to charges of employment bias, at least when that bias is not expressed overtly. We fear, however, that the common-sense position we took in [*Faro v. New York University*, 502 F.2d 1229 (2d Cir. 1974)], namely that courts must be ever mindful of relative institutional competence, has been pressed beyond all reasonable limits and may be employed to undercut the explicit legislative intent of the Civil Rights Act of 1964 (*Powell v. Syracuse University*, 580 F.2d 1150, 1153 (2d Cir.), *certiorari denied*, 439 U.S. 984 . . . (1978)).

When a case is presented such as this, in which the discrimination has been proven and the required remedy is clear, we cannot shirk the responsibility placed on us by Congress [621 F.2d at 547–51; footnotes omitted].

Kunda was a ground-breaking case because the court in effect awarded a promotion and conditional tenure as the remedy for the discrimination against the plaintiff. The case was also controversial because the remedy is subject to the charge that it interferes with institutional autonomy in areas (promotion and tenure) where autonomy is most important to postsecondary education. Yet, as a careful reading of the opinion indicates, the court's holding is actually narrow and its reasoning sensitive to the academic community's needs and the relative competencies of college and court. The court emphasizes that "in the line of cases challenging university decisions not to promote or grant tenure, this case may . . . be sui generis [the only one of its kind] or, at least, substantially distinguishable." Thus, the case's significance is tied tightly to its facts. According to those facts, the plaintiff had, by the consensus of her peers, met all requirements for promotion and tenure but one—the terminal degree. And since that requirement had been tainted by the discrimination, the defendant could not rely on it. The court thus made an independent judgment about the existence of discrimination, not about the plaintiff's qualifications. The court's remedy put the plaintiff in the position she would have been in, by the institution's own determination, had the discrimination not occurred. Since she would have been promoted had the administration not discriminatorily imposed the degree requirement, the court ordered the promotion; since she would have had two more years to obtain the degree had she not been the subject of discriminatory counseling, the court ordered that she receive tenure if she earned the degree within two years.

Another federal court of appeals addressed the thorny issue of remedies for academic discrimination in two cases, refusing in both to award tenure to plaintiffs who had prevailed on the merits. In *Gutzwiller v. University of Cincinnati*, 860 F.2d 1317 (6th Cir. 1988), the court, affirming the trial court's finding of discrimination, remanded the case to the trial court on the issue of a remedy, cautioning that court-awarded tenure should be "provided in only the most exceptional cases, [and] [o]nly when the court is convinced that a plaintiff reinstated to her former faculty position could not receive fair reconsideration . . . of her tenure application" (860 F.2d at 1333). The district court awarded Professor Gutzwiller back pay, reinstated her without tenure for the 1989–90 academic year, and ordered that a new tenure review be conducted under the court's supervision within the following year. The university conducted a tenure review during the 1989–90 academic year and awarded Professor Gutzwiller tenure.

In a second case before the same federal circuit court, *Ford v. Nicks,* 866 F.2d 865 (6th Cir. 1989), the appellate court reversed a trial court's award of reinstatement as a tenured full professor to Lanni Ford, who had been denied reappointment as an instructor in 1977 at Middle Tennessee State University. Although Ford had prevailed on the merits in 1984 (741 F.2d 858 (6th Cir. 1984)), the issue of the appropriate remedy had occupied the court for another five years. The plaintiff had argued that only reinstatement as a full professor would provide a "make-whole" remedy; the court disagreed, noting that Ford had taught for only two years and had never been evaluated for promotion or tenure. The court remanded the case to the trial court with instructions to fashion some remedy short of tenure that would compensate Ford for her losses.

The first time a federal appellate court examined and approved the outright award of tenure occurred in *Brown v. Trustees of Boston University,* 891 F.2d 337 (1st Cir. 1989).[18] Julia Brown, an assistant professor of English, had received the unanimous recommendation of her department and positive recommendations from outside evaluators, but was denied tenure by the university's president. After a jury trial, the university was found to have discriminated in its denial of tenure to Brown. The court, in reinstating Brown with tenure, noted that her peers had judged her to be qualified (a factor absent in *Gutzwiller* and *Ford,* but present in *Kunda*), and that the president's sexist remarks about the English department showed evidence of gender bias. The university had raised an academic freedom challenge to a court award of tenure, stating that it infringed upon its First Amendment right to determine "who may teach" (see *Sweezy v. New Hampshire,* discussed in Section 3.7.1). The appellate court rejected that argument, noting that the First Amendment could not insulate the university against civil rights violations.

The court also rejected the university's argument that the appropriate remedy be another three-year probationary period or a nondiscriminatory tenure review, such as was the remedy in *Gutzwiller.* The court said these remedies would not make the plaintiff whole. And in what may be the death knell to the "academic abstention" doctrine, the court engaged in an extensive review of Brown's publications and teaching record. Thus, the appellate court reviewed the substance of the decision as well as its procedural fairness, the approach used by courts in previous cases. This willingness to review the substance of academic judgments is also evident in *Bennun v. Rutgers, The State University of New Jersey,* 737 F. Supp. 1393 (D.N.J. 1990), *affirmed,* 941 F.2d 154 (3d Cir. 1991), and in *Jew v. University of Iowa,* 749 F. Supp. 946 (S.D. Iowa 1990).[19]

Recent court opinions in academic discrimination cases make it clear that

---

[18]Two federal trial courts had awarded tenure to plaintiffs, but in neither case was the remedy examined on appeal. See *Gladney v. Thomas,* 573 F. Supp. 1232 (D. Ala. 1983), and *Younus v. Shabat,* 336 F. Supp. 1137 (N.D. Ill. 1971), *affirmed mem.,* 6 Fair Empl. Prac. Cases 314 (7th Cir. 1973).

[19]Cases related to the issue of discrimination and the award of tenure are collected in Annot., "Application to Tenured Positions in Educational Institutions of Provisions of Civil Rights Act of 1964, as Amended (42 U.S.C.S. §2000e et seq.), Prohibiting Discrimination on Basis of Sex," 55 A.L.R. Fed. 842 (1981 and periodic supp.).

postsecondary institutions have no special dispensation from the requirements of federal antidiscrimination legislation. Courts will defer to institutions' expert judgments concerning scholarship, teaching, and other educational qualifications if they believe that those judgments are fairly reached, but courts will not subject institutions to a more deferential standard of review or a lesser obligation to repair the adverse effects of discrimination. And despite the fact that tenure is an unusual remedy in that it has the potential to give lifetime job security to a faculty member, the federal courts appear to have lost their reluctance to order tenure as a remedy when they believe that discrimination has occurred.

In addition to equitable remedies such as reinstatement or tenure, and damages, prevailing plaintiffs are entitled to attorney's fees under Title VII (42 U.S.C. § 2000e-5(k)). The Wisconsin Supreme Court recently was asked to determine whether a faculty member who prevailed in a sex discrimination claim in an internal university grievance procedure was entitled to attorney's fees under the rationale of Title VII. In *Duello v. Board of Regents, University of Wisconsin*, 501 N.W.2d 38 (Wis. 1993), the Wisconsin Supreme Court ruled that an internal university appeals committee's decision that the plaintiff had suffered sex discrimination was not a "proceeding" under the meaning of Title VII and thus the university was not liable to the plaintiff for her attorney's fees.

3.3.2.2. Salary discrimination and the Equal Pay Act. Both the Equal Pay Act (part of the Fair Labor Standards Act, 29 U.S.C. § 206(d)) and Title VII prohibit sex discrimination in compensation. Because of the similarity of the issues, pay discrimination claims under both laws will be discussed in this subsection.

The Equal Pay Act provides that:

> [N]o employer [subject to the Fair Labor Standards Act] shall discriminate . . . between employees on the basis of sex . . . on jobs the performance of which requires equal skill, effort, and responsibility, and which are performed under similar working conditions, except where such payment is made pursuant to (i) a seniority system; (ii) a merit system; (iii) a system which measures earnings by quantity or quality of production; or (iv) a differential based on any other factor other than sex.

Thus, the determination of whether jobs are equal, and the judgment as to whether one of the four exceptions applies to a particular claim, is the essence of an equal pay claim under this law.

Congress's purpose in enacting this provision was to combat the "ancient but outmoded belief that a man, because of his role in society, should be paid more than a woman" and to establish, in its place, the principle that " 'equal work will be rewarded by equal wages' " (quoting *Corning Glass Workers v. Brennan*, 417 U.S. 188 (1974)).

Some institutions or state systems of higher education have been required to make classwide salary adjustments for women faculty. For example, in *Denny v. Westfield State College*, 669 F. Supp. 1146 (D. Mass. 1987), a trial court ruled for several women faculty who had alleged salary discrimination and had provided anecdotal evidence of intentional salary discrimination. For example, the president had allegedly said that men needed higher salaries because they were supporting families. Furthermore, the college was unable to explain the salary differentials on the basis of rational criteria, such as the faculty member's discipline, market factors, or performance. Similarly, the community college system of Massachusetts settled a sixteen-year equal pay case by agreeing to provide back pay for approximately 1,200 women faculty ("Massachusetts' 15 Community Colleges . . . ," *Chron. Higher Educ.*, Oct. 21, 1992, A20).

The Equal Pay Act has been applied to discrimination against men as well as against women. In *Board of Regents of the University of Nebraska v. Dawes*, 522 F.2d 380 (8th Cir. 1975), the university had, under pressure of a threatened federal fund cutoff, developed a complicated numerical formula for computing the average salary of male faculty members. The university used this average as the minimum salary for female faculty members. In a declaratory judgment action by the university, the court held that the practice violated the Equal Pay Act because ninety-two male faculty members received less than the female minimum even though they had substantially equal qualifications.

The Equal Pay Act is enforced by the Equal Employment Opportunity Commission. The EEOC's procedural regulations for the Act are codified in 29 C.F.R. Parts 1620–1621. For an overview of Equal Pay Act issues in higher education, see D. Green, "Application of the Equal Pay Act to Higher Education," 8 *J. Coll. & Univ. Law* 203 (1981–82).

Salary discrimination claims under Title VII are not subject to the "equal work" requirement of the Equal Pay Act, and thus challenges can be brought to pay discrimination between jobs that are comparable rather than strictly equal. Several "comparable worth" claims have been brought by women faculty who have asserted that Title VII prohibits colleges and universities from setting the compensation of faculty in female-dominated disciplines at a level different from that of faculty in male-dominated disciplines. In each of these cases, plaintiffs have asserted that the Supreme Court's decision in *Gunther* permits a comparable worth claim under Title VII.

In *County of Washington v. Gunther*, 452 U.S. 161 (1981), the U.S. Supreme Court sorted out the relationships between the Equal Pay Act and Title VII as they apply to claims of sex discrimination in pay. Although the *Gunther* decision broadened the avenues that aggrieved employees have for challenging sex-based pay discrimination, the Court's opinion did not adopt the "comparable worth" theory that some forecasters had hoped the case would establish. According to the majority:

> We emphasize at the outset the narrowness of the question before us in this case. Respondents' claim is not based on the controversial concept of "comparable worth," under which plaintiffs might claim increased compensation on the basis of a comparison of the intrinsic worth or difficulty of their job with that of other jobs in the same organization or community. Rather, respondents seek to prove, by direct evidence, that their wages were depressed because of intentional sex discrimination, consisting of setting the wage scale for female guards, but not for male guards, at a level lower than its own survey of outside markets and the worth of the jobs warranted. The narrow question in this case is whether such a claim is precluded by [Title VII] [452 U.S. at 166].

Although the *Gunther* opinion neither rejects nor accepts the comparable worth theory, the Court's application of Title VII to pay disparity claims did provide impetus for further attempts to establish the theory. A number of lawsuits were filed in the wake of the Court's decision. In the first faculty case to reach the appellate courts, *Spaulding v. University of Washington*, 740 F.2d 686 (9th Cir. 1984), members of the university's nursing faculty raised both discriminatory treatment and disparate impact claims to challenge disparities in salary levels between their department and others on campus. The court rejected both claims. As to the former claim, the plaintiffs had not shown that the university acted with discriminatory intent in establishing the salary levels. According to the court, the direct evidence did not indicate such intent, and "we will not infer intent merely from the existence of wage differences between jobs that are only similar." As to the latter claim (which does not require a showing of intent), the court held that the law does not permit use of the disparate impact approach in cases, such as this one, that "involve wide-ranging allegations challenging general wage policies" for jobs that are "only comparable" rather than equal. In particular, said the court, an employer's mere reliance on market forces in setting wages cannot itself constitute a disparate impact violation.

The court emphasized, however, that:

> A plaintiff may show that the jobs are substantially equal, not necessarily that they are identical. Actual job performance and content, rather than job descriptions, titles, or classifications, is determinative. Thus, each claim that jobs are substantially equal necessarily must be determined on a case-by-case basis. . . . We disagree[,] therefore, with the university's contention that jobs from different academic disciplines can never be substantially equal [740 F.2d at 697].

Subsequent comparable worth litigation against nonacademic organizations has also been unsuccessful for plaintiffs. In *American Federation of State, County, and Municipal Employees v. State of Washington*, 770 F.2d 1401 (9th Cir. 1985), the federal appeals court overruled the finding of a trial judge that Washington's failure to implement a statutorily required comparable worth salary system was either intentional discrimination or satisfied the disparate impact theory under Title VII (see Section 3.3.2.1). The Supreme Court has not ruled on the comparable worth theory, either directly or indirectly, since its *Gunther* ruling. Several states have passed laws requiring comparable worth in the public sector, but there has been little activity related to college faculty, although women staff at some unionized colleges and universities have benefited from comparable worth adjustments in collective bargaining agreements.

A particularly troubling issue in salary discrimination claims is the determination of whether pay differentials are, in fact, caused by sex or race discrimination, or by legitimate factors such as performance differences, market factors, or the number of years that have elapsed since a faculty member received the doctorate. These issues have been debated fiercely in the courts and in the literature. While some experts believe that rank and number of years since the doctorate are the strongest predictors of salary differences, others argue that rank may be a "tainted variable" if women or racial minorities are promoted more slowly than their male counterparts. And apart from these arguments, there is evidence that salaries are lower for faculty in predominantly female disciplines, such as English or nursing (a comparable worth issue), as well as for female faculty in predominantly male disciplines (a potential equal pay issue). For a critical discussion of the concept of comparable worth, see P. Weiler,

"The Wages of Sex: The Uses and Limits of Comparable Worth," 99 *Harvard L. Rev.* 1728 (1986).

An extreme example of the debate over the appropriate criteria occurred in *Sobel v. Yeshiva University*, 566 F. Supp. 1166 (S.D.N.Y. 1983), *reversed and remanded*, 797 F.2d 1478 (2d Cir. 1986), *on remand*, 656 F. Supp. 587 (S.D.N.Y. 1987), *reversed and remanded*, 839 F.2d 18 (2d Cir. 1988). In this case a female medical school professor alleged that salaries of women faculty were significantly lower than salaries of male faculty, using multiple regression analysis to isolate the effect of certain variables on salary levels. Although a trial judge twice found the plaintiff's statistical evidence to be inadequate, the appellate court remanded and ordered that the court apply the standard developed by the U.S. Supreme Court in *Bazemore v. Friday*, 478 U.S. 385 (1986). In *Bazemore* the Court had ruled that plaintiffs could rely in their statistical analyses on pre–Title VII enactment salary data if they could show that such data influenced post–Title VII actions (or inaction) by the employer. For analysis of the problems involved in demonstrating salary discrimination through the use of statistics, see J. McKeown, "Statistics for Wage Discrimination Cases: Why the Statistical Models Used Cannot Prove or Disprove Sex Discrimination," 67 *Ind. L.J.* 633 (1992), and T. Campbell, "Regression Analysis in Title VII Cases: Minimum Standards, Comparable Worth, and Other Issues Where Law and Statistics Meet," 36 *Stanford L. Rev.* 1299 (1984). For an analysis of the comparable worth doctrine in general, see "Symposium: Comparable Worth," 20 *J. Law Reform* 1 (1986).

3.3.2.3. Title IX. Title IX of the Education Amendments of 1972, 20 U.S.C. § 1681 et seq., prohibits sex discrimination by public and private educational institutions receiving federal funds (see Section 7.5.3). The statute is administered by the Office for Civil Rights (OCR) of the Department of Education. The department's regulations contain provisions on employment (34 C.F.R. §§ 106.51 through 106.61) that are similar in many respects to the EEOC's sex discrimination guidelines under Title VII. Like Title VII, the Title IX regulations contain a provision permitting sex-based distinctions in employment where sex is a "bona fide occupational qualification" (34 C.F.R. § 106.61). Also like Title VII, Title IX contains an exemption applicable to some religious institutions. Title IX's is differently worded, however, to exempt "an educational institution which is controlled by a religious organization" if Title IX's requirements "would not be consistent with the religious tenets of such organization" (20 U.S.C. § 1681(a)(3); 34 C.F.R. § 106.12).

The applicability of Title IX to employment discrimination was hotly contested in a series of cases beginning in the mid-1970s. The U.S. Supreme Court has resolved the dispute, holding that Title IX does apply to and prohibit sex discrimination in employment (see *North Haven Board of Education v. Bell*, 456 U.S. 512 (1982) (discussed in Section 7.5.7.1)).

The decision of the U.S. Supreme Court in *Franklin v. Gwinnett County Public Schools*, 112 S. Ct. 1028 (1992) (discussed in Sections 7.5.3 and 7.5.9), that plaintiffs alleging discrimination under Title IX may be awarded compensatory and punitive damages will very likely stimulate discrimination claims under Title IX that might otherwise have been brought under Title VII, given Title VII's cap on damages (see Section 3.3.2.1). Title IX does not require the exhaustion of administrative remedies, and it borrows its statute of limitations from state law, which may be more generous than the relatively short period under Title VII. Plaintiffs with dual status as employees and students (for example, graduate teaching assistants, work-study students, and residence hall counselors) may find Title IX appealing because they need not prove they are "employees" rather than students in order to seek relief.

A federal district court has interpreted *Franklin* as permitting plaintiffs alleging sex discrimination in employment to seek compensatory damages. In *Paddio v. Board of Trustees for State Colleges and Universities,* 61 Fair Empl. Prac. Cases 86 (E.D. La. 1993), the court refused to dismiss a claim of sex discrimination by a female volleyball and softball coach at Southeastern University brought under Title IX, stating that *Franklin* did not distinguish between discrimination against students and discrimination against employees.

The order of proof and burdens of production under Title IX follow those of Title VII (see Section 3.3.2.1), which means that a plaintiff must prove intentional discrimination in a claim of disparate treatment. In *Lipsett v. University of Puerto Rico,* 864 F.2d 881 (1st Cir. 1988), the court ruled that a student claiming sexual harassment by supervisors and fellow students must follow the disparate treatment model of *McDonnell Douglas* (discussed in Section 3.3.2.1) and its progeny.[20]

3.3.2.4. Section 1981 (Race). A post–Civil War civil rights statute, 42 U.S.C. § 1981, commonly known as "Section 1981," states:

> All persons within the jurisdiction of the United States shall have the same right in every state and territory to make and enforce contracts, to sue, be parties, give evidence, and to the full and equal benefit of all laws and proceedings for the security of persons and property as is enjoyed by white citizens, and shall be subject to like punishment, pains, penalties, taxes, licenses, and exactions of every kind, and to no other.

Section 1981 is enforced through court litigation by persons denied the equality that the statute guarantees.[21] It prohibits discrimination in both public and private employment, as the U.S. Supreme Court affirmed in *Johnson v. Railway Express Agency,* 421 U.S. 454 (1975).

Section 1981 covers racially based employment discrimination against white persons as well as racial minorities (*McDonald v. Sante Fe Trail Transportation Co.,* 427 U.S. 273 (1976)). Although in earlier cases Section 1981 had been held to apply to employment discrimination against aliens (*Guerra v. Manchester Terminal Corp.,* 498 F.2d 641 (5th Cir. 1974)), more recent federal appellate court rulings suggest that this broad reading of the law is inappropriate. In *Bhandari v. First National Bank of Commerce,* 829 F.2d 1343 (5th Cir. 1987), a federal appellate court overturned *Guerra* and, after a lengthy review of the 1866 Civil Rights Act, determined that Congress had not intended Section 1981 to cover private discrimination against aliens, although the court did not address the issue of such discrimination by a public entity. The U.S. Supreme Court vacated the *Bhandari* opinion because the appellate court had speculated that the Supreme Court would overturn *Runyon v. McCrary* (which

---

[20]Cases related to Title IX's prohibition of sex discrimination in employment are collected in Annot., "Application of Title IX of the Education Amendments of 1972 (20 U.S.C.S. §§ 1681 et seq.) to Sex Discrimination in Educational Employment," 54 A.L.R. Fed. 522 (1981 and periodic supp.).

[21]Cases interpreting Section 1981 are collected in Annot., "Supreme Court's Views as to Constitutionality, Construction, and Application of 42 U.S.C.S. § 1981, Providing for Equal Rights as to Such Matters as Contracts and Legal Proceedings," 105 L. Ed. 2d 737 (1991 and periodic supp.).

had applied Section 1981 to private discrimination) in its opinion in *Patterson v. McLean Credit Union.* (Both cases are discussed below.) On the contrary, the Supreme Court reaffirmed *Runyon* and vacated *Bhandari,* instructing the Fifth Circuit to analyze its case in light of *Patterson.* On remand, the U.S. Court of Appeals, sitting *en banc,* reinstated its holding in *Bhandari* at 887 F.2d 609 (1989), asserting that *Patterson* did not alter the rationale for its earlier ruling. The Supreme Court denied review (494 U.S. 1061 (1990)).[22]

Although Section 1981 does not specifically prohibit discrimination on the basis of national origin (*Ohemeng v. Delaware State College,* 676 F. Supp. 65 (D. Del. 1988), *aff'd,* 862 F.2d 309 (3d Cir. 1988)), some courts have permitted plaintiffs to pursue national origin discrimination claims under Section 1981 in cases where race and national origin were intertwined.[23] In two special cases, moreover, the U.S. Supreme Court has interpreted Section 1981 to apply to certain types of national origin and ethnicity discrimination. In *Al-Khazraji v. St. Francis College,* 481 U.S. 604 (1987), the Court permitted a professor of Arabian descent to challenge his tenure denial under Section 1981. And in *Shaare Tefila Congregation v. Cobb,* 481 U.S. 615 (1987), the Court extended similar protections to Jews. In both cases the Court looked to the dictionary definition of "race" in the 1860s, when Section 1981 was enacted by Congress; the definition included both Arabs and Jews as examples of races.

While Section 1981 overlaps Title VII (see Section 3.3.2.1) in its coverage of racial discrimination in employment, a back-pay award is not restricted to two years of back pay under Section 1981, as it is under Title VII (see *Johnson v. Railway Express Agency,* 421 U.S. 454 (1975)). Section 1981 does not have the short statute of limitations that Title VII imposes, and does not limit the amount of compensatory or punitive damages that can be awarded, as does Title VII. Therefore, individuals alleging race discrimination in employment are more likely to file claims under Section 1981 than under Title VII.

In *General Building Contractors Assn. v. Pennsylvania,* 458 U.S. 375 (1982), the U.S. Supreme Court engrafted an intent requirement onto the Section 1981 statute. To prevail in a Section 1981 claim, therefore, a plaintiff must prove that the defendant intentionally or purposefully engaged in discriminatory acts. This requirement is the same as the Court previously applied to discrimination claims brought under the Equal Protection Clause (see this volume, Section 3.3.2.7).

Section 1981 applies to the employment decisions of private as well as public organizations, according to a U.S. Supreme Court decision in *Runyon v. McCrary,* 427 U.S. 160 (1976). The Court reaffirmed this principle in a 1989 decision, but sharply narrowed the scope of Section 1981 at the same time.

For a brief time, actions brought under Section 1981 were confined to claims of bias in hiring or the "making" of a contract. The U.S. Supreme Court ruled in *Patterson v. McLean Credit Union,* 491 U.S. 164 (1989), that plaintiffs could not use Section 1981 to challenge any employer conduct—such as racial harassment or dis-

---

[22]Cases addressing whether aliens are protected by Section 1981 are collected in Annot., "Application of 42 U.S.C.S. Section 1981 to Private Discrimination Against Aliens," 99 A.L.R. Fed. 835 (1990 and periodic supp.).

[23]Cases related to national origin claims under Section 1981 are collected in Annot., "Applicability of 42 U.S.C.S. § 1981 to National Origin Employment Discrimination Cases," 43 A.L.R. Fed. 103 (1979 and periodic supp.).

criminatory discharge—if that conduct occurred after the formation of a contract. In response, Congress amended Section 1981 in the Civil Rights Act of 1991 by adding subsections (b) and (c), which read:

> (b) For purposes of this section, the term "make and enforce contracts" includes the making, performance, modification, and termination of contracts, and the enjoyment of all benefits, privileges, terms, and conditions of the contractual relationship.
> (c) The rights protected by this section are protected against impairment by nongovernmental discrimination and impairment under color of State law.

Thus, Congress codified the result in *Runyon* and rejected the Court's interpretation in *Patterson*. The amendment restores Section 1981 jurisprudence to its pre-*Patterson* status. For a thoughtful analysis of race discrimination and its legal remedies, see L. Alexander, "What Makes Wrongful Discrimination Wrong? Biases, Preferences, Stereotypes, and Proxies," 141 *U. Pa. L. Rev.* 149 (1992).

3.3.2.5. The Americans with Disabilities Act and the Rehabilitation Act of 1973. Two federal laws forbid employment discrimination against individuals with disabilities. The Americans with Disabilities Act (ADA), 42 U.S.C. § 12101 et seq., prohibits employment discrimination by employers with fifteen or more employees, labor unions, and employment agencies. Section 504 of the Rehabilitation Act, 29 U.S.C. § 794 (also discussed in Section 7.5.4), also prohibits discrimination against individuals with disabilities. It is patterned after the Title VI and Title IX provisions (see Sections 7.5.2 and 7.5.3), which prohibit, respectively, race and sex discrimination in federally funded programs and activities. Each federal funding agency enforces the Rehabilitation Act with respect to its own funding programs.

Title I of the Americans with Disabilities Act of 1990 prohibits employment discrimination against "qualified" individuals who are disabled. (The other titles of the ADA are discussed in Section 7.2.16.) The prohibition of discrimination in the ADA uses language very similar to that of Title VII:

> (a) No covered entity shall discriminate against a qualified individual with a disability because of the disability of such individual in regard to job application procedures, the hiring, advancement, or discharge of employees, employee compensation, job training, and other terms, conditions, and privileges of employment [42 U.S.C. § 12102(a)].

The law defines "discrimination" very broadly, and prohibits the following practices: segregating or limiting the job opportunities of the individual with a disability; participating in a relationship with another entity, such as a labor union or employment agency, that engages in discrimination against an individual with a disability; using hiring or promotion standards that have a discriminatory effect or perpetuate the discrimination of others; denying employment or benefits to an individual who has a relationship with someone who is disabled; not making reasonable accommodation (unless an undue hardship exists); denying employment opportunities in order to avoid having to accommodate an individual; using selection tests or standards that screen out individuals with disabilities unless the tests or standards are job related and a business necessity; failing to use tests that identify an individual's skills rather than his or her impairments.

The law defines a "qualified individual with a disability" as "an individual with a disability who, with or without reasonable accommodation, can perform the essential functions of the employment position that such individual holds or desires" (42 U.S.C. § 12111(8)). This definition, which would apply to an individual with a disability who could perform the job only if accommodated, rejects the U.S. Supreme Court's interpretation of the Rehabilitation Act's definition of "otherwise qualified" in *Southeastern Community College v. Davis*, 442 U.S. 397 (1979). Because the ADA's language is broader than that of the Rehabilitation Act, it is more likely that individuals claiming disability discrimination will seek redress under the ADA rather than the Rehabilitation Act.

The law requires that, if an applicant or a current employee meets the definition of "qualified individual with a disability," the employer must provide a reasonable accommodation unless the accommodation presents an "undue hardship" for the employer. The terms are defined thusly in the statute:

The term "reasonable accommodation" may include—

(A) making existing facilities used by employees readily accessible to and usable by individuals with disabilities; and

(B) job restructuring, part-time or modified work schedules, reassignment to a vacant position, acquisition or modification of equipment or devices, appropriate adjustment or modifications of examinations, training materials or policies, the provision of qualified readers or interpreters, and other similar accommodations for individuals with disabilities [42 U.S.C. § 12111(9)].

(10) (A) The term "undue hardship" means an action requiring significant difficulty or expense, when considered in light of the factors set forth in subparagraph (B).

(B) In determining whether an accommodation would impose an undue hardship on a covered entity, factors to be considered include—

(i) the nature and cost of the accommodation needed under this chapter;

(ii) the overall financial resources of the facility or facilities involved in the provision of the reasonable accommodation; the number of persons employed at such facility; the effect on expenses and resources, or the impact otherwise of such accommodation upon the operation of the facility;

(iii) the overall financial resources of the covered entity; the overall size of the business of a covered entity with respect to the number of its employees, the number, type, and location of its facilities; and

(iv) the type of operation or operations of the covered entity, including the composition, structure, and functions of the workforce of such entity; the geographic separateness, administrative, or fiscal relationship of the facility or facilities in question to the covered entity [42 U.S.C. § 12111(10)].

The ADA also contains provisions regarding the use of preemployment medical examinations, the confidentiality of an individual's medical records, and the individuals who may have access to information about the individual's disability.

The law specifically excludes current abusers of controlled substances from coverage, but it does protect recovering abusers or individuals who are incorrectly perceived to be abusers of controlled substances. Individuals who have completed or are participating in a supervised rehabilitation program, and are no longer using controlled substances, are protected by the ADA. Since the law does not exclude persons with alcoholism, they are protected by the ADA, even if their abuse is current. However, the law permits employers to prohibit the use of alcohol or drugs at the workplace, to outlaw intoxication on the job, and to conform with the Drug-Free Workplace Act of 1988 (41 U.S.C. § 701 et seq.). Employers may also hold users of drugs or alcohol to the same performance standards as other employees, and the law neither requires nor prohibits drug testing.

The ADA's employment discrimination remedies are identical to those of Title VII, and it is enforced by the EEOC, as is Title VII. The same limitation on damages found in Title VII applies to actions brought under the ADA, except that language applicable to the ADA provides that if an employer makes a good-faith attempt at reasonable accommodation, but is still found to have violated the ADA, neither compensatory nor punitive damages will be available to the plaintiff (42 U.S.C. § 1981A). This provision also applies to the Rehabilitation Act. Regulations interpreting the ADA are published at 29 C.F.R. § 1630. In addition to expanding on the concepts of "qualified," "reasonable accommodation," and "undue hardship," they include guidelines for determining whether hiring or retaining an employee with a disability would pose a safety hazard to co-workers or to the employee (29 C.F.R. § 1630.2(r)).

Title II of the ADA prohibits discrimination on the basis of disability by "public entities," which includes public colleges and universities. The language of Title II mirrors the language of Title VI and Section 503 of the Rehabilitation Act:

> [N]o qualified individual with a disability shall, by reason of such disability, be excluded from participation in or be denied the benefits of the services, programs, or activities of a public entity, or be subjected to discrimination by any such entity [42 U.S.C. § 12132].

The regulations interpreting Title II prohibit employment discrimination by a public entity (28 C.F.R. § 35.140). Title II adopts the remedies, rights, and procedures of Section 505 of the Rehabilitation Act, which has been interpreted to provide a private right of action for individuals alleging discrimination under the Rehabilitation Act (see this volume, Section 7.5.4). No exhaustion of administrative remedies is required by either Title II or Section 505.

In 1993 a federal district court examined the relationship between Titles I and II of the ADA—the first time such an examination has been made. An employee of the University of Wisconsin whose one-year contract was not renewed filed a lawsuit in federal court under Title II of the ADA. In *Peterson v. University of Wisconsin Board of Regents*, 818 F. Supp. 1276 (W.D. Wis. 1993), the university argued that the court lacked jurisdiction because Peterson did not exhaust his administrative remedies by first filing a charge with the EEOC, as required by Title I of the ADA. The court, noting the language of the statute, the regulations, and the legislative history, concluded that Title II includes employment discrimination as prohibited conduct and explicitly does not require exhaustion of administrative remedies. This ruling, certain to be appealed, appears to create an exception for employees of public colleges and universities to the requirement that claims of employment discrimination under the ADA be first filed with the EEOC.

Colleges and universities have been subject to the Rehabilitation Act since 1972, and a body of judicial precedent has developed interpreting that Act's requirements. The law was recently amended by the Rehabilitation Act Amendments of 1992 (Pub. L. 102-569, 106 Stat. 4344) to replace the word "handicap" with the word "disability" and to conform the language of the Rehabilitation Act in other ways with that of the ADA (see Section 7.5.4). Regulations interpreting the Rehabilitation Act's prohibitions against disability discrimination by federal contractors have been revised to conform to ADA provisions, and are found at 34 C.F.R. § 104.11 and 29 C.F.R. § 1641.

Regarding employment, the regulations from the Department of Education implementing Section 504 provide:

(a) *General.* (1) No qualified individual with a disability shall, on the basis of disability, be subjected to discrimination in employment under any program or activity. . . .

(2) A recipient that receives assistance under the Education of the Handicapped Act shall take positive steps to employ and advance in employment qualified individuals with disabilities in programs assisted under that Act.

(3) A recipient shall make all decisions concerning employment under any program or activity to which this part applies in a manner which ensures that discrimination on the basis of disability does not occur and may not limit, segregate, or classify applicants or employees in any way that adversely affects their opportunities or status because of disability.

(4) A recipient may not participate in a contractual or other relationship that has the effect of subjecting qualified applicants or employees with disabilities to discrimination prohibited by this subpart. The relationships referred to in this subparagraph include relationships with employment and referral agencies, with labor unions, with organizations providing or administering fringe benefits to employees of the recipient, and with organizations providing training and apprenticeship programs.[24]

The regulations also prohibit discrimination against qualified disabled persons with regard to any term or condition of employment, including selection for training or conference attendance and employers' social or recreational programs. Furthermore, the regulations state that the employer's obligations under the statute are not affected by any inconsistent term of any collective bargaining agreement to which the employer is a party (34 C.F.R. § 104.11).

In language similar to that of the ADA statute, the regulations inplementing

---

[24]Cases related to who is qualified under the Rehabilitation Act are collected in Annot., "Who Is 'Qualified' Handicapped Person Protected from Employment Discrimination Under Rehabilitation Act of 1973 (29 U.S.C.S. §§ 701 et seq.) and Regulations Promulgated Thereunder," 80 A.L.R. Fed. 830 (1986 and periodic supp.). See also Annot., "Construction and Effect of Sec. 504 of the Rehabilitation Act of 1973 (29 U.S.C.S. § 794) Prohibiting Discrimination Against Otherwise Qualified Handicapped Individuals in Specified Programs or Activities," 44 A.L.R. Fed. 148 (1979 and periodic supp.), and Annot., "Who Is 'Individual with Handicaps' Under Rehabilitation Act of 1973 (29 U.S.C.S. § 701 et seq.)," 97 A.L.R. Fed. 40 (1990 and periodic supp.).

Section 504 define a qualified person with a disability as one who "with reasonable accommodation can perform the essential functions" of the job in question (34 C.F.R. § 104.3(k)(1)). The regulations impose an affirmative obligation on the recipient to make "reasonable accommodation to the known physical or mental limitations of an otherwise qualified handicapped applicant or employee unless the recipient can demonstrate that the accommodation would impose an undue hardship on the operation of its program" (34 C.F.R. § 104.12(a)). Reasonable accommodations can take the form of modification of the job site, of equipment, or of a position itself. What hardship would relieve a recipient of the obligation to make reasonable accommodation depends on the facts of each case. As a related affirmative requirement, the recipient must adapt its employment tests to accommodate an applicant's sensory, manual, or speaking disability unless the tests are intended to measure those types of skills (34 C.F.R. § 104.13(b)).

The regulations include explicit prohibitions regarding employee selection procedures and preemployment questioning. As a general rule, the fund recipient cannot make any preemployment inquiry or require a preemployment medical examination to determine whether an applicant is disabled or to determine the nature or severity of a disability (34 C.F.R. § 104.14(a)). Nor can a recipient use any employment criterion, such as a test, that has the effect of eliminating qualified applicants with disabilities, unless the criterion is job related and there is no alternative job-related criterion that does not have the same effect (34 C.F.R. § 104.13(a)). These prohibitions are also found in the ADA and its regulations.

In *Southeastern Community College v. Davis*, 442 U.S. 397 (1979), discussed in Sections 4.2.4.3 and 7.5.4, the U.S. Supreme Court addressed for the first time the extent of the obligation that Section 504 imposes on colleges and universities. The case involved the admission of a disabled applicant to a clinical nursing program, but the Court's opinion also sheds light on the Rehabilitation Act's application to employment of disabled persons.

In *Davis* the Court determined that an "otherwise qualified handicapped individual" protected by Section 504 is one who is qualified *in spite of* his or her disability, and thus ruled that the institution need not make major program modifications to accommodate the individual. Because the definition of "otherwise qualified" appears only in the Department of Education's regulations implementing Section 504, not in the statute, the Court did not consider itself bound by the language of the regulations, which defined a "qualified handicapped individual" for employment purposes as one who, "with reasonable accommodation," can perform the job's essential functions. However, statutory language in the ADA virtually repeats the language of Section 504's regulations; thus, the Court's opinion in *Davis* has limited relevance under the ADA.

The Court apparently equated accommodation of an individual with a disability with affirmative action rather than viewing the accommodation as the removal of barriers for an individual with a disability. The framers of the ADA have rejected the former interpretation; since the accommodation requirement is stated clearly in the ADA, and the term "affirmative action" appears nowhere in the statute, the continued vitality of *Southeastern Community College* in the context of employment is questionable.

The U.S. Supreme Court again interpreted the Rehabilitation Act in *School Board of Nassau County v. Arline*, 480 U.S. 273 (1987), in which the Court determined that persons suffering from a contagious disease (in this case, tuberculosis) were protected by the Act. The Court listed four factors that employers must take into consideration when determining whether an employee with a potentially contagious disease poses a danger to other employees or to clients, customers, or students:

1) the nature of the risk (how the disease is transmitted);
2) the duration of the risk (how long is the carrier infectious);
3) the severity of the risk (what is the potential harm to third parties); and
4) the probabilities the disease will be transmitted and will cause varying degrees of harm [480 U.S. at 288].

Although the Supreme Court did not specifically indicate whether individuals suffering from acquired immune deficiency syndrome (AIDS) are protected by the Act, the Court's reasoning appears to apply with equal force to all contagious diseases. Congress adopted the Court's position in this case in an amendment to the Rehabilitation Act tacked onto the Civil Rights Restoration Act of 1987 (Pub. L. No. 100-259, 102 Stat. 28, § 9).

For many postsecondary institutions, however, even a narrow reading of the "reasonable accommodation" requirement will have little effect on their obligations regarding employment of individuals with disabilities. Section 503 of the Rehabilitation Act requires all institutions holding contracts with the federal government in excess of $10,000 to "take affirmative action to employ and advance in employment qualified handicapped individuals." While the Court in *Davis* emphatically rejected an affirmative action obligation under Section 504, its decision in no way affects the express obligation imposed on federal contractors by Section 503 (see this chapter, Section 3.4).

Administrators and counsel should watch for future litigation interpreting the employment provisions of the ADA and for changes in the interpretation of the Rehabilitation Act by the Education Department and other funding agencies.

3.3.2.6. Age Discrimination in Employment Act (ADEA). The ADEA, 29 U.S.C. § 621 et seq., prohibits age discrimination only with respect to persons who are at least forty years of age. It is contained within the Fair Labor Standards Act (29 U.S.C. §§ 201–219) and is subject to the requirements of that Act (see Section 7.2.4).

Prior to the Act's amendment in 1978, the upper age limit was sixty-five (29 U.S.C. § 631). The 1978 amendments raised that limit to seventy, effective January 1, 1979; and amendments added in 1986 removed the limit completely, except for persons in certain professions. Individuals in public-safety positions (police officers, firefighters), "high-level policy makers," and tenured college faculty could be required to retire at certain ages (seventy for tenured faculty). The amendment provided that the exemption for individuals in public-safety positions and tenured faculty would expire on December 31, 1993.[25] Thus, as of January 1, 1994, mandatory retirement for faculty, whether tenured or not, is unlawful.

The Act, which is applicable to both public and private institutions, makes it unlawful for an employer:

[25]Although a bill that would have retained mandatory retirement for firefighters and police officers was introduced in the House of Representatives in 1993 (H.R. Rep. No. 2554, introduced June 29, 1993), no action had been taken on the bill at press time.)

(1) to fail or refuse to hire or to discharge any individual with respect to his compensation, terms, conditions, or privileges of employment, because of such individual's age;

(2) to limit, segregate, or classify his employees in any way which would deprive or tend to deprive any individual of employment opportunities or otherwise adversely affect his status as an employee, because of such individual's age; or

(3) to reduce the wage rate of any employee in order to comply with this chapter [29 U.S.C. § 623].[26]

The ADEA is enforced by the Equal Employment Opportunity Commission (EEOC), and implementing regulations appear at 29 C.F.R. Parts 1625–1627. Among other matters, the interpretations specify the criteria an employer must meet to establish age as a bona fide job qualification.[27]

As under other statutes, the burden of proof has been an issue in litigation. Generally, the plaintiff must make a prima facie showing of age discrimination, at which point the burden shifts to the employer to show that "age is a bona fide occupational qualification reasonably necessary to the normal operation of the particular business" at issue (29 U.S.C. § 623(f)(1)); or that distinctions among employees or applicants were "based on reasonable factors other than age" (29 U.S.C. § 623(f)(1)); or that, in the case of discipline or discharge, the action was taken "for good cause" (29 U.S.C. § 623(f)(3)). (See *Laugeson v. Anaconda Co.*, 510 F.2d 307 (6th Cir. 1975), and *Hodgson v. First Federal Savings and Loan*, 455 F.2d 818 (5th Cir. 1972).) For analysis of the "reasonable factors other than age" defense, see H. Eglit, "The Age Discrimination in Employment Act's Forgotten Affirmative Defense: The Reasonable Factors Other Than Age Exception," 66 *Boston U. L. Rev.* 155 (1986).

The case of *Leftwich v. Harris-Stowe College*, 702 F.2d 686 (8th Cir. 1983), illustrates the application of these principles to postsecondary education. The plaintiff in *Leftwich* had lost his position as a tenured biology professor when the state legislature transferred control of the college from a local board of education to the state college system. After the governor appointed a board of regents for the "new" college, the board decided to hire a "new" faculty of substantially smaller size. Under the regents' plan, a certain number of tenured and a certain number of nontenured positions from the "old" college were retained. Faculty members were invited to apply for these positions in the "new" college, and those not hired were sent termination letters and offered the opportunity to have their applications reviewed in a hearing with the regents. Of the two biology positions at the "new" college, one was to be filled by a nontenured and the other by a tenured faculty member. Even though Leftwich had scored higher than either of his two competitors on the regents' evaluation measure, these other two men were retained and Leftwich was terminated.

---

[26]Relevant authorities construing the Act are collected in Annot., "Construction and Application of Age Discrimination in Employment Act of 1967," 24 A.L.R. Fed. 808 (1975 and periodic supp.).

[27]Cases regarding age as a BFOQ are collected in Annot., "Age as Bona Fide Occupational Qualification 'Reasonably Necessary' for Normal Conduct of Business under § 4 (f)(1) of Age Discrimination in Employment Act (29 U.S.C.S. § 623 (f)(1)," 63 A.L.R. Fed. 610 (1983 and periodic supp.).

Leftwich filed suit, contending (among other things) that the regents' specification of the numbers of new college positions to be filled by tenured and by
nontenured faculty members had the effect of discriminating by age. The plaintiff's
expert witness testified that tenured faculty at the "old" college were older and higher
paid as a group than nontenured faculty and that the regents' reservation of a specified number of positions for nontenured faculty (and their use of salary as a selection
factor) therefore had an adverse impact on the employment of older faculty members.
The regents did not refute this expert testimony. Instead, they argued that "business
necessity" justified this adverse impact of their selection plan—in other words, that
they could consider nontenured status to be a bona fide occupational qualification
under Section 623(f)(1) of the ADEA statute. The regents asserted that their needs to
cut costs and to promote innovation and quality created the "business necessity" to
hire the specified number of nontenured faculty.

After the district court rejected the regents' contentions and determined that
they had discriminated against Leftwich in violation of the ADEA, the U.S. Court
of Appeals for the Eighth Circuit affirmed:

> To establish a prima facie case of age discrimination under a disparate
> impact theory, a plaintiff need not show that the employer was motivated by a
> discriminatory intent; he or she need only demonstrate that a facially neutral
> employment practice actually operates to exclude from a job a disproportionate
> number of persons protected by the ADEA. . . .
>
> Statistical evidence such as that presented by [the plaintiff's expert] is
> clearly an appropriate method to establish disparate impact (see, for example,
> *Hazelwood School District v. United States*, 433 U.S. 299, 306–09 (1977); *Inter-
> national Brotherhood of Teamsters v. United States*, 431 U.S. 324 (1977)).
>
> Once the plaintiff established his prima facie case, the burden of persua-
> sion shifted to the defendants to prove that their selection plan was justified by
> business necessity (see, for example, *Albemarle Paper Co. v. Moody*, 422 U.S. 405,
> 425 (1975); *Geller v. Markham*, 635 F.2d 1027, 1032 (2d Cir. 1980)).
>
> The defendants' primary justification is that they adopted their selection
> plan as a cost-saving measure. Quite simply, the plan was intended to reduce costs
> by eliminating some positions at the college for tenured faculty, who were gener-
> ally higher paid than the nontenured faculty. The district court held that this cost
> justification did not establish a business necessity defense. We agree. . . .
>
> Here, the defendants' selection plan was based on tenure status rather than
> explicitly on age. Nonetheless, because of the close relationship between tenure
> status and age, the plain intent and effect of the defendants' practice was to
> eliminate older workers who had built up, through years of satisfactory service,
> higher salaries than their younger counterparts. If the existence of such higher
> salaries can be used to justify discharging older employees, then the purpose of
> the ADEA will be defeated. . . .
>
> The other justification offered by the defendants for their selection plan
> is that it promotes innovation and quality among the faculty by giving the
> college flexibility to hire nontenured faculty. The district court also rejected this
> justification. We again affirm that finding.
>
> First, the record makes it clear that the defendants' principal, if not only,
> purpose in adopting their selection plan was to eliminate some tenure positions
> in order to effectuate cost savings. Second, to the extent that the defendants in
> fact utilized their selection plan in an attempt to increase the quality of the

college's faculty, they have failed to establish that the plan was necessary to achieve their goal. . . .

The defendants failed to demonstrate that reserving nontenured slots was necessary to bring new ideas to the college. Instead, their assertion that younger nontenured faculty would have new ideas apparently assumes that older tenured faculty members would cause the college to "stagnate." Such assumptions are precisely the kind of stereotypical thinking about older workers that the ADEA was designed to eliminate [702 F.2d at 690–92].

Having affirmed the lower court's decision for the professor, the appellate court reviewed the relief the lower court had awarded to him. After making several modifications in the lower court's order, the appellate court awarded the professor a position on the "new" college faculty, retroactive seniority for the years missed as a result of his discriminatory termination, back pay, attorney's fees, and court costs.

Individuals claiming age discrimination under the ADEA must first file a claim either with the federal EEOC (within 180 days) or with the appropriate state civil rights agency. Sixty days after such a claim is filed, the individual may bring a civil action in federal court (29 U.S.C. §626(d)). A jury trial is provided for in the statute, and remedies include two years of back pay, liquidated damages (double back pay), front pay, and other make-whole remedies.

In *Oscar Mayer & Co. v. Evans*, 441 U.S. 750 (1979), the U.S. Supreme Court considered whether an employee or a former employee claiming age discrimination must seek relief from appropriate state agencies before bringing an ADEA suit in the federal courts. The Court held that such resort to state agencies is mandatory under Section 14(b) of the ADEA (29 U.S.C. §633(b)) whenever there is a state agency authorized to grant relief against age discrimination in employment, but that the employee need not commence state proceedings within the time limit specified by state law. If the state agency rejects the employee's complaint as untimely or does not resolve the complaint within sixty days, the employee can then turn to the federal courts.

The ADEA was amended in 1990 by the Older Workers Benefit Protection Act (OWBPA), 104 Stat. 981, in part as a reaction to a decision by the U.S. Supreme Court in *Public Employees Retirement System of Ohio v. Betts*, 492 U.S. 158 (1989). In that opinion, the Court had ruled that only employee benefit plans that could be shown to be a subterfuge for discrimination violated the Act, even if their terms had the effect of discriminating against older workers. OWBPA prohibited discriminatory employee benefit plans (29 U.S.C. §623(k)) and codified the "equal benefits or equal cost" principle articulated in *Karlen v. City Colleges of Chicago*, 837 F.2d 314 (7th Cir. 1988). In *Karlen* the appellate court had found discriminatory two provisions of a retirement plan that gave more generous benefits to faculty who are sixty-five years old and under. The court ruled that employers could provide benefits of equal *cost* to the employer, even if older workers received benefits of less *value* because of the higher cost of benefits to older workers. An employer, however, could not vary benefits (such as sick leave or severance pay) in ways that favored younger employees. The new law requires employers to give older workers benefits that are equal to or better than those given younger workers, unless the employer can demonstrate that benefits (such as term life insurance) carry a higher cost for older workers. The legislation also defines requirements for early-retirement plans, and regulates the conditions under which severance benefits may be offset by other benefits included in early-retirement plans (29 U.S.C. sec. 623(*l*)). Furthermore, the law specifies how releases or waivers of an employee's right to sue under the ADEA must be formulated, and requires a twenty-one-day waiting period and a seven-day revocation period for releases (29 U.S.C. § 626(f)(1)). Institutions planning to offer early-retirement incentives should confer with experienced counsel in order to comply with the numerous requirements of OWBPA.[28]

3.3.2.7. ***Constitutional prohibitions against employment discrimination.*** While the Fourteenth Amendment's Equal Protection Clause applies to employment discrimination by public institutions (see Section 1.5.2), the constitutional standards for justifying discrimination are generally more lenient than the various federal statutory standards. (See the discussions of constitutional equal protection standards in Sections 4.2.4 and 4.2.5.) Even where constitutional standards are very strong, as for race discrimination, the courts usually strike down only discrimination found to be intentional; the federal statutes, on the other hand, often do not require a showing of discriminatory intent. In *Washington v. Davis*, 426 U.S. 229 (1976), for instance, the U.S. Supreme Court distinguished between disparate impact cases brought under Title VII (see Section 3.3.2.1) and those brought under the Equal Protection Clause, noting that the equal protection cases "have not embraced the proposition that a law or other official act, without regard to whether it reflects a racially discriminatory purpose, is unconstitutional solely because it has a racially disproportionate impact." Under Title VII, in contrast, "discriminatory purpose need not be proved." Title VII thus "involves a more probing judicial review of, and less deference to, the seemingly reasonable acts of administrators and executives than is appropriate under the Constitution where special racial impact, without discriminatory purpose, is claimed."

In *Personnel Administrator of Massachusetts v. Feeney*, 442 U.S. 256 (1979), the Court elaborated on the requirement of discriminatory intent, which must be met to establish a violation of the Equal Protection Clause. *Feeney* concerned a female civil servant who challenged the constitutionality of a state law providing that all veterans who qualify for civil service positions must be considered ahead of any qualified nonveteran. The statute's language was gender neutral—its benefits extended to "any person" who had served in official United States military units or unofficial auxiliary units during wartime. The veterans' preference law had a disproportionate impact on women, however, because 98 percent of the veterans in Massachusetts were men. Consequently, nonveteran women who received high scores on competitive examinations were repeatedly displaced by lower-scoring male veterans. Feeney claimed that the preference law discriminated against women in violation of the Fourteenth Amendment. The Court summarized the general approach it would take in ruling on such constitutional challenges of state statutes:

> The equal protection guarantee of the Fourteenth Amendment does not take from the states all the power of classification. Most laws classify, and many affect certain groups unevenly, even though the law itself treats them no differently from all other members of the class described by the law. When the basic

---

[28]For analysis of this issue, see Annot., "Pension Plan Designed to Induce Early Retirement of Employees of Certain Age as Violation of Age Discrimination in Employment Act (29 U.S.C.S. §§ 621 et seq.) or ERISA (29 U.S.C.S. §§ 1001 et seq.)," 91 A.L.R. Fed. 296 (1989 and periodic supp.).

classification is rationally based, uneven effects upon particular groups within a class are ordinarily of no constitutional concern. The calculus of effects, the manner in which a particular law reverberates in society, is a legislative and not a judicial responsibility. In assessing an equal protection challenge, a court is called upon only to measure the basic validity of the . . . classification. When some other independent right is not at stake . . . and when there is no "reason to infer antipathy," it is presumed that "even improvident decisions will eventually be rectified by the democratic process" (*Vance v. Bradley*, 440 U.S. 93) [442 U.S. at 271–72; citations omitted].

The Supreme Court agreed with the district court's finding that the law was enacted not for the purpose of preferring males but, rather, to give a competitive advantage to veterans. Since the classification "nonveterans" includes both men and women, both sexes could be disadvantaged by the laws. The Court concluded that too many men were disadvantaged to permit the inference that the classification was a pretext for discrimination against women.

Feeney argued that, although the legislation assisted only veterans, the curtailing of job opportunities for women was an inevitable, foreseeable concomitant of the veterans' preference policy and that where "a law's consequences are that inevitable they cannot meaningfully be described as unintended." The Court disagreed:

> Discriminatory purpose . . . implies more than intent as volition or intent as awareness of consequences. . . . It implies that the decision maker, in this case the state legislature, selected or reaffirmed a particular course of action at least in part "because of," not merely "in spite of," its adverse effects upon an identifiable group [442 U.S. at 279].

Since neither the statute's language nor the facts concerning its passage demonstrated that the preference was designed to deny women opportunity for employment or advancement in the Massachusetts civil service, the Supreme Court, with two justices dissenting, upheld the statute.

Feeney extends the reasoning in *Washington v. Davis* by stating unequivocally that a statute which has a disproportionate impact on a particular group will withstand an equal protection challenge unless the plaintiff can show that it was enacted in order to affect that group adversely. Thus, a statute neutral on its face will be upheld unless the disparate impact of the law "could not plausibly be explained on neutral grounds," in which case "impact itself would signal that the classification made by the law was in fact not neutral." The effect of this reasoning—controversial especially among civil rights advocates—is to increase the difficulty of proving equal protection violations.

The Supreme Court applied its *Feeney* analysis in considering a challenge to an Alabama law that disenfranchised any individual who had been convicted of a crime "involving moral turpitude." Since these crimes included misdemeanors, two individuals who had been found guilty of passing bad checks, a misdemeanor in Alabama, were disenfranchised. The plaintiffs had demonstrated that the framers of the 1901 Alabama constitution, which contained the challenged provision, intended to discriminate against black voters, despite the fact that the law was applied to blacks and whites equally. Justice Rehnquist, writing for a unanimous court in *Hunter v. Underwood*, 471 U.S. 222 (1985), explained that if the intent of the law was discriminatory, then its effects are still discriminatory, and thus the Fourteenth Amendment was violated.

Besides its less vigorous standards, the Equal Protection Clause also lacks the administrative implementation and enforcement mechanisms that exist for most federal statutes. Consequently, postsecondary administrators will have more guidance, via regulations and interpretive bulletins, but will also be subject to more detailed rules and a broader range of remedies for ensuring compliance, under the statutes than under the Constitution.

In employment discrimination the Constitution assumes its greatest importance in areas not covered by any federal statute. Age discrimination against persons less than forty years old is one such area, since the Age Discrimination in Employment Act does not cover individuals under age forty. A second example is discrimination against aliens, which is no longer covered by Section 1981. Another important uncovered area is discrimination on the basis of sexual preference (such as discrimination against homosexuals), which is discussed in Section 3.3.8.[29] Discrimination on the basis of residence is a fourth important example.[30]

Although the Constitution restrains public institutions in areas such as the four mentioned above, the restraints may be more lax than those under federal statutes. In an age discrimination case, *Weiss v. Walsh*, 324 F. Supp. 75 (S.D.N.Y. 1971), for instance, the plaintiff was denied the Schweitzer Chair at Fordham University allegedly because of his age, which at that time was seventy. The court broadly rejected the plaintiff's equal protection argument:

> I am constrained to hold that Professor Weiss is not the victim of an invidious and impermissible discrimination. Notwithstanding great advances in gerontology, the era when advanced age ceases to bear some reasonable statistical relationship to diminished capacity or longevity is still future. It cannot be said, therefore, that age ceilings upon eligibility for employment are inherently suspect, although their application will inevitably fall unjustly in the individual case. If the precision of the law is impugnable by the stricture of general applicability, vindication of the exceptional individual may have to attend the wise discretion of the administrator. On its face, therefore, the denial of a teaching position to a man approaching seventy years of age is not constitutionally infirm [324 F. Supp. at 77, *affirmed*, 461 F.2d 846 (2d Cir. 1972)].

Professor Weiss could not sue under the ADEA because, at the time of the litigation, persons who had reached age seventy were not protected by that law. All faculty forty

---

[29]Such discrimination is often challenged on freedom-of-speech or freedom-of-association grounds rather than equal protection. See *Aumiller v. University of Delaware*, 434 F. Supp. 1273 (D. Del. 1977), where the court ordered reinstatement and $15,000 damages for a lecturer whose freedom of speech was violated when the university refused to renew his contract because of statements he had made on homosexuality.

[30]See, for example, *McCarthy v. Philadelphia Civil Service Commission*, 424 U.S. 645 (1976), upholding a continuing residency requirement for city employees; and *Cook County College Teachers Union v. Taylor*, 432 F. Supp. 270 (N.D. Ill. 1977), upholding a similar requirement for college faculty members. Compare *United Building and Construction Trades Council v. Camden*, 465 U.S. 208 (1984), suggesting that discrimination in employment on the basis of state or local residency may violate the Privileges and Immunities Clause in Article IV, Section 2, of the Constitution. Also compare the student residency cases discussed in Section 4.3.5.

and over are now protected by the ADEA, so it is unlikely that a faculty member would file a constitutional claim to challenge alleged age discrimination.

Similarly, in *Ambach v. Norwick*, 441 U.S. 68 (1979), the U.S. Supreme Court considered the constitutionality of a New York statute that discriminated against aliens by prohibiting their employment as public school teachers. The Court determined that "the Constitution requires only that a citizenship requirement applicable to teaching in the public schools bear a rational relationship to a legitimate state interest." Applying this principle, the Court held that the state's citizenship requirement did not violate equal protection because it was a rational means of furthering the teaching of citizenship in public schools. The Court focused specifically on elementary and secondary education, however, and it is not clear that its reasoning would also permit states to refuse to employ aliens as teachers in postsecondary education, where the interest in citizenship education may be less.

And in *Naragon v. Wharton*, 737 F.2d 1403 (5th Cir. 1984), the court rejected an instructor's claim that Louisiana State University had reassigned her to nonteaching duties because of her homosexual orientation. The instructor had had an intimate relationship with a female undergraduate student who was not in her classes. Over a strong dissent, the court concluded that university officials had transferred the instructor because they considered any intimate relationship between an instructor and a student to be unprofessional, rather than because this particular relationship was homosexual rather than heterosexual. Thus, in the court's view, the university's action did not constitute discrimination based on sexual orientation.

3.3.2.8. Executive orders 11246 and 11375. Executive Order 11246, 30 Fed. Reg. 12319, as amended by Executive Order 11375, 32 Fed. Reg. 14303 (adding sex to the list of prohibited discriminations), prohibits discrimination "because of race, color, religion, sex, or national origin," thus paralleling Title VII (Section 3.3.2.1). Unlike Title VII, the executive orders apply only to contractors and subcontractors under federal government contracts and federally assisted construction contracts. Agreements with each such contractor must include an equal opportunity clause (41 C.F.R. § 60-1.4), and contractors must file compliance reports after receiving the award and annual compliance reports thereafter (41 C.F.R. § 60-1.7(a)) with the federal contracting agency. In addition to their equal opportunity provisions, the executive orders and regulations place heavy emphasis on affirmative action by federal contractors, as discussed in Section 3.4.

The regulations implementing these executive orders exempt various contracts and contractors (41 C.F.R. § 60-1.5), including church-related educational institutions defined in Title VII (41 C.F.R. § 60-1.5(a)(5)). While the regulations contain a partial exemption for state and local government contractors, "educational institutions and medical facilities" are specifically excluded from this exemption (41 C.F.R. § 60-1.5(a)(4)). The enforcing agency may hold compliance reviews (41 C.F.R. § 60-1.20), receive and investigate complaints from employees and applicants (41 C.F.R. §§ 60-1.21 to 60-1.24), and initiate administrative or judicial enforcement proceedings (41 C.F.R. § 60-1.26(a)(1)). It may seek orders enjoining violations and providing other relief, as well as orders terminating, canceling, or suspending contracts (41 C.F.R. § 60-1.26(a)(2)). The enforcing agency may also seek to debar contractors from further contract awards (41 C.F.R. § 60-1.26(a)(2)).

On October 8, 1978, all authority for enforcing compliance with Executive Orders 11246 and 11375 was centralized in the Office of Federal Contract Compliance

Programs, part of the Department of Labor (Executive Order 12086). In 1981 the department issued proposals for modifying (some commentators would say weakening) the regulations implementing these executive orders (see 46 Fed. Reg. 42968 (Aug. 25, 1981)).

The primary remedy for violation of the executive orders is cutoff of federal funds and/or debarment from future contracts. Individuals alleging employment discrimination by federal contractors have sought to file discrimination claims in court, but have been rebuffed. For example, in *Weise v. Syracuse University*, 522 F.2d 397 (2d Cir. 1975), two women faculty members filed sex discrimination claims against the university under authority of the executive orders. Their claims were dismissed; the court found no private right of action in the executive orders. Similar outcomes occurred in *Braden v. University of Pittsburgh*, 343 F. Supp. 836 (W.D. Pa. 1972), *vacated on other grounds*, 477 F.2d 1 (3d Cir. 1973), and *Cap v. Lehigh University*, 433 F. Supp. 1275 (E.D. Pa. 1977).[31]

3.3.3. Race and national origin discrimination.

3.3.3. Race and national origin discrimination. As noted above, race discrimination claims may be brought under Title VII (Section 3.3.2.1), Section 1981 (Section 3.3.2.4), the U.S. Constitution (Section 3.3.2.7), or federal executive orders (Section 3.3.2.8). Claims of national origin discrimination may be brought under Title VII, the U.S. Constitution, or federal executive orders and, sometimes, under Section 1981.[32]

In race discrimination claims, as in other academic discrimination claims, a faculty member alleges that different (usually higher) standards were applied to him or her than were applied to white faculty members, and that the plaintiff's performance was as good as or superior to that of white faculty who were hired, promoted, or tenured when the plaintiff was not.

For example, in *Bennun v. Rutgers, The State University of New Jersey*, 941 F.2d 154 (3d Cir. 1991), an Hispanic professor—stating both Title VII and Section 1981 claims—charged that the university's four refusals to promote him to full professor were based on his race and/or national origin. The trial court compared Professor Bennun's research and publication record with the record of a departmental colleague, a white female who had been promoted to full professor at the same time Bennun's promotion was denied. The trial court found nine instances in which different, and more demanding, standards were applied to Bennun than to the comparator faculty member. In light of these findings, the district court concluded that the university's reason for denying Professor Bennun promotion—inadequate research production—was a pretext for discrimination. Although Bennun apparently had no direct evidence of discrimination, his ability to demonstrate pretext was sufficient to establish liability, the court ruled. (This case predated *St. Mary's Honor Center v. Hicks*, and would very likely have been resolved differently under the *Hicks* standard described in Section 3.3.2.1.)

The comparison of Professor Bennun with his departmental colleague was

---

[31]Cases related to private right of action under the executive orders are collected in Annot., "Right to Maintain Private Employment Discrimination Action Under Executive Order 11246, as Amended, Prohibiting Employment Discrimination by Government Contractors and Subcontractors," 31 A.L.R. Fed. 108 (1977 and periodic supp.).

[32]Cases involving race discrimination are collected in Annot., "Racial Discrimination in Hiring, Retention, or Assignment of Teachers—Federal Cases," 3 A.L.R. Fed. 325 (1970 and periodic supp.).

disputed at the appellate level. The university argued that, because the female professor had been rated "outstanding" in both teaching and service and Bennun had not, they were not "similarly situated" and thus the comparisons were inappropriate. The court rejected the university's argument, stating that the different standards applied to the professors' research quality and productivity were sufficient to establish disparate treatment, and that whether or not the two faculty were similar enough in other respects for comparison purposes was irrelevant.

The university petitioned the Third Circuit for a rehearing by the entire panel of judges, which was denied. Judge Sloviter, who believed that a rehearing should be granted, wrote of her concerns about the activism shown by the trial court in its review of the qualifications of Professor Bennun and the comparator faculty member. Judge Sloviter, a former law school professor, and the author of the *Kunda* decision (discussed in Section 3.3.2.1), wrote:

> I believe that the majority's decision may be read to thrust the federal courts of this circuit into the subjective area of academic tenure and promotion decisions to an unwarranted and unprecedented degree. . . . In the present case, it would appear that this court may have abandoned the doctrine of restraint set forth in *Kunda*. In *Kunda* . . . the plaintiff's qualifications were not in dispute, and the court accordingly did not review the college's assessment of her qualifications. In this case, Professor Bennun's qualifications to be full professor were in dispute among the faculty and administration at Rutgers. Thus . . . it appears that the district court reassessed every decision made by Rutgers regarding Professor Bennun's qualifications and concluded that the court's assessment of the factors under review was superior to the university's. . . . I do not believe that it is proper or desirable for the courts of this circuit to become involved in substantive tenure and promotion decisions in the academic setting unless the evidence of discriminatory action is unmistakable [941 F.2d at 181].

Another race discrimination case decided by the U.S. Court of Appeals for the Third Circuit concerned a claim by a black professor that his department chair and the college president applied stricter standards to his quest for tenure than they did to white candidates. The case has an unusual procedural twist in that it demonstrates the interplay between Title VII and Section 1981, and the effects of a jury decision in the Section 1981 case on the judge's fact-finding in the Title VII case. (This issue has less relevance today because Title VII cases may now be tried before a jury.) In *Roebuck v. Drexel University*, 852 F.2d 715 (3d Cir. 1988), a jury found that the institution had discriminated against Roebuck, a black professor of history, in that both the department chair and the president discounted his service to the local community (which he had, in part, been hired to provide) and made selective use of teaching evaluations in order to rate his teaching as satisfactory rather than outstanding. The trial judge had found the jury verdict to be against the weight of the evidence and had found for the university in the Title VII claim. The appellate court, holding that a reasonable jury could have found for Professor Roebuck, remanded the case for a new trial, and instructed the judge to conform the Title VII fact-finding to the jury verdict in the new trial.

A third race discrimination claim resulted in what appears to be the largest damage award in an academic discrimination lawsuit to date. It also demonstrates the inflammatory effect of racist comments upon a jury's decision concerning the amount of damages to award. Reginald Clark, a black professor of education, asserting that the decision by Claremont Graduate School to deny him tenure was racially motivated, brought suit under California's Fair Employment and Housing Act (Govt. Code § 12900 et seq.), which permitted a jury trial. The jury found for Professor Clark, in part because Clark was able to demonstrate several examples of race-related remarks made by departmental colleagues, both before and during the time that they made the tenure recommendation (a split vote). The jury awarded Professor Clark one million dollars in compensatory damages and $16,327 in punitive damages. The trial judge awarded Clark attorney's fees of over $400,000. The California Court of Appeal affirmed the jury verdict and damage awards (*Clark v. Claremont University Center*, 8 Cal. Rptr. 2d 151 (Cal. Ct. App. 1992)), stating:

> We must add we are not surprised by the jury's verdict. Many employment discrimination cases do not even survive to trial because evidence of the employer's improper motive is so difficult to obtain. This case is unusual, not because of Clark's claims, but because of Clark's strong evidence of improper motive. Our own computer-assisted research of tenure denial cases across the nation revealed none involving university professors who made such blatant remarks as in this case [8 Cal. Rptr. at 170].

White faculty have also used Section 1981 and Title VII to challenge negative employment decisions under a theory of "reverse discrimination."[33] These cases illustrate that Title VII, as well as the Equal Protection Clause (Section 3.3.2.7) and the civil rights statute "Section 1981" (Section 3.3.2.4), can "cut both ways" to protect white as well as black faculty members from discrimination. In *Craig v. Alabama State University*, 451 F. Supp. 1207 (M.D. Ala. 1978), a class action brought on behalf of white faculty and other white employees and former employees at a predominantly black institution, the court concluded on the basis of evidence presented at trial that "in the hiring of its administrative, teaching, and clerical and support staff and the promotion and tenure of its faculty, A.S.U. has . . . engaged in a pattern and practice of discrimination against whites." The U.S. Court of Appeals for the Fifth Circuit affirmed (614 F.2d 1295 (5th Cir. 1980)).

Shortly after *Craig* the Fifth Circuit reached a similar result in a case brought by a single faculty member. In *Whiting v. Jackson State University*, 616 F.2d 116 (5th Cir. 1980), a white psychometry professor working at a predominantly black university claimed that his discharge was motivated by racial discrimination. The court outlined the burdens of proof applicable to the professor's claim, using the same standards applicable to other Title VII "disparate treatment" claims (see the discussion of the *Kunda* case in Section 3.3.2.1). Finding that the university's articulated reason for the discharge was a pretext and that the discharge had been motivated by racial considerations, the court affirmed the trial court's judgment for the professor: "Our traditional reluctance to intervene in university affairs cannot be allowed to undermine our statutory duty to remedy the wrong."

The *Whiting* standards were followed in *Fisher v. Dillard University*, 499 F.

---

[33]Cases and authorities on "reverse discrimination" are collected in Annot., "What Constitutes Reverse or Majority Discrimination on Basis of Sex or Race Violative of Federal Constitution or Statutes," 26 A.L.R. Fed. 13 (1976 and periodic supp.).

Supp. 525 (E.D. La. 1980), in which a predominantly black university had discharged a white Ph.D. psychologist and hired a black psychologist instead at a higher salary. The court entered judgment for the white professor. And in another similar case, *Lincoln v. Board of Regents of the University System of Georgia*, 697 F.2d 928 (11th Cir. 1983), the court affirmed the lower court's ruling that a white professor would have had her contract renewed but for her race.

In several cases that have arisen at traditionally black institutions, the defendants have argued that black faculty are needed to serve as role models for black students. However, in *Wygant v. Jackson Board of Education*, 476 U.S. 267 (1986) (see Section 3.4), the U.S. Supreme Court rejected the role model theory as a defense to race-conscious employment decisions. And in *Arneson v. Southern University*, 911 F.2d 1124 (5th Cir. 1990), a white professor seeking a tenure-track position at Southern University Law School argued that the dean's assertion that no tenure-track position existed was a pretext for race discrimination. The jury hearing Professor Arneson's Section 1981 claim found the school's defense to be pretextual, given the fact that a tenure-track position had been given to a less experienced black woman and the statement made by the chair of the law school's tenure and promotion committee that there were too many white professors on the faculty.

However, the fact that a black institution may attempt to recruit black faculty or emphasizes the role model theory is not necessarily dispositive. In *Dybczak v. Tuskegee Institute*, 737 F.2d 1524 (11th Cir. 1984), the only white academic administrator was returned to the faculty when the institute refused to agree to his demands for additional salary and a sabbatical leave. Although Professor Dybczak alleged that his return to the faculty was racially motivated, a jury found that the plaintiff's replacement, a black professor of aerospace science, was better qualified and that the plaintiff was neither discharged nor discriminated against. The appellate court found the jury's verdict supported by evidence and affirmed the verdict for the Institute.

Title VII also prohibits discrimination "because of [an] individual's . . . national origin" (42 U.S.C. § 2000e-2(a))—that is, discrimination based on the employee's nationality. In *Briseno v. Central Technical Community College Area*, 739 F.2d 344 (8th Cir. 1984), for example, the court held that the defendant had intentionally discriminated against the plaintiff, a Mexican-American, because of his national origin.

The U.S. Supreme Court has ruled that the statutory term "national origin" does not cover discrimination on the basis of alienage—that is, discrimination against employees who are not citizens of the United States (*Espinoza v. Farah Manufacturing Co.*, 414 U.S. 86 (1973)). But the Court cautioned in *Espinoza* that a citizenship requirement may sometimes be part of a scheme of, or a pretext for, national origin discrimination and that "Title VII prohibits discrimination on the basis of citizenship [alienage] whenever it has the purpose or effect of discriminating on the basis of national origin." The Court also made clear that aliens, as individuals, are covered by Title VII if they have been discriminated against on the basis of race, color, religion, or sex, as well as national origin.

To implement the statute and case law, the EEOC has issued guidelines barring discrimination on the basis of national origin (29 C.F.R. Part 1606).

Other claims related to race or national origin discrimination involve accents or English proficiency. State laws requiring colleges and universities to certify that nonnative U.S. residents who are teaching assistants are proficient in English may be challenged as a violation of Title VII or Section 1981, in that no such standards are applied to individuals born in the United States. Testing the language proficiency of all teaching assistants should prevent discrimination claims. A statement in the institution's college catalogue that instruction will be conducted in English would make English proficiency a bona fide occupational qualification, and, as long as that requirement is applied to all instructors, it should not run afoul of the nondiscrimination laws.[34] Similarly, a requirement that unaccented English is required for a certain position would also be vulnerable to a national origin claim if the individual could be understood.[35] For a discussion of bias against accents, see M. Matsuda, "Voices of America: Accent, Antidiscrimination Law, and a Jurisprudence for the Last Reconstruction," 100 *Yale L.J.* 1329 (1991).

In addition to Title VII and Section 1981, another law may pose potential liability for college and universities with regard to race and national origin. The Immigration Reform and Control Act of 1986 (Pub. L. No. 99-603, 100 Stat. 3359, codified in scattered sections of 8 U.S.C.) prohibits employers from hiring workers who cannot document that (1) they are in the United States legally and (2) they are legally entitled to work. Employers must ask applicants for proof of both elements, and civil penalties may be assessed against the employer for each undocumented worker hired.

The law also forbids discrimination against aliens who are lawfully entitled to work, and describes the complaint procedures available through the U.S. Department of Justice (8 U.S.C. § 1324b (West, 1990 supp.)). With the advent of the Immigration Reform and Control Act, discrimination claims by individuals denied employment because the employer believes they may not be in the country lawfully have risen. For discussion of this problem and a comparison of IRCA's antidiscrimination provisions with those of Title VII, see L. S. Johnson, "The Antidiscrimination Provisions of the Immigration Reform and Control Act," 62 *Tulane L. Rev.* 1059 (1988). See also Comment, "IRCA's Antidiscrimination Provisions: Protections Against Hiring Discrimination in Private Employment," 25 *San Diego L. Rev.* 405 (1988).

Race discrimination has also been alleged in the context of standardized hiring tests, which majority applicants pass at a higher rate than minority applicants. For example, the written Civil Service examination has been challenged on several occasions as having a disparate impact on minority applicants who take the test (*Washington v. Davis*, 426 U.S. 229 (1976)), as have the National Teachers Examination and other standardized achievement tests (*Griggs v. Duke Power Co.*, 401 U.S. 424 (1971)). Because of concerns that standardized tests could be culturally biased, and because of a commitment to increase the proportion of minority employees in their work force, some states and other large employers began the practice of "race norming" the passing scores for standardized tests. "Race norming" involves the calcula-

---

[34]Cases related to requiring English proficiency are collected in Annot., "Requirement That Employees Speak English in Workplace as Discrimination in Employment Under Titlte VII of Civil Rights Act of 1964 (42 U.S.C.S. §§ 2000e et seq.)," 90 A.L.R. Fed. 806 (1988 and periodic supp.).

[35]Cases related to employment denials based on an individual's accent are collected in Annot., "When Does Adverse Employment Decision Based on Person's Foreign Accent Constitute National Origin Discrimination in Violation of Title VII of Civil Rights Act of 1964?" 104 A.L.R. Fed. 816 (1988 and periodic supp.).

tion of a passing score for each racial, ethnic, gender, or other protected class that takes the test, and often results in a different passing score for each group. The Civil Rights Act of 1991 outlawed race or gender norming by adding subsection *l* to Section 703 (42 U.S.C. § 2000e-2(*l*)). The subsection reads:

> It shall be an unlawful employment practice for a respondent, in connection with the selection or referral of applicants or candidates for employment or promotion, to adjust the scores of, use different cutoff scores for, or otherwise alter the results of, employment related tests on the basis of race, color, religion, sex, or national origin.

Although faculty generally are not hired on the basis of standardized tests, this new provision would apply to selection tests used for nonfaculty employment decisions.

3.3.4. Sex discrimination and sexual harassment. The largest number of discrimination lawsuits filed by faculty against colleges and universities have involved allegations of sex discrimination. Between 1972 and 1984, women filed more than half of all academic discrimination claims that resulted in decisions on the merits (G. La-Noue & B. Lee, *Academics in Court: The Consequences of Faculty Discrimination Litigation* (University of Michigan Press, 1987), at 35–36). Given the underrepresentation of women among college faculty in general (although not as severe as the underrepresentation of racial and ethnic minority faculty), and particularly at the tenured ranks, the perception that women have not been treated on equal terms with male faculty is not surprising (see "Treading Water: The Annual Report on the Economic Status of the Profession, 1992–93," 79 *Academe* 8, 13 (Mar.–Apr. 1993)).[36] Efforts of women to secure academic positions, and the barriers faced in this quest, are chronicled in N. Aisenberg & M. Harrington, *Women of Academe: Outsiders in the Sacred Grove* (University of Massachusetts Press, 1988).

Sex discrimination claims have ranged from claims by individual women that a department or college applied higher standards to her than to comparable male faculty (*Namenwirth v. Regents of the University of Wisconsin*, 769 F.2d 1235 (7th Cir. 1985)) to class actions alleging that an entire institution's system of recruiting, hiring, and promoting faculty was infected with sex bias (*Lamphere v. Brown University*, 491 F. Supp. 232 (D.R.I. 1980), *affirmed*, 685 F.2d 743 (1st Cir. 1982)). In the *Lamphere* case, Brown University entered a consent decree containing guidelines on how faculty would be recruited and evaluated for hiring, promotion, and tenure. During the fourteen years that the consent decree was in effect, Brown increased the number of tenured women faculty from 12 to 67, and the number of female faculty members overall from 52 to 128 (A. De Palma, "Rare in Ivy League: Women Who Work as Full Professors," *New York Times*, Jan. 24, 1993, at 1, 23). The University of Minnesota entered a similar consent decree after settling a class action sex discrimination case (*Rajender v. University of Minnesota*, 546 F. Supp. 158 (D. Minn. 1982), 563 F. Supp. 401 (D. Minn. 1983).

[36]In academic year 1992–93, 14.4 percent of the full professors in U.S. colleges and universities, 28.9 percent of the associate professors, and 42 percent of the assistant professors were women. Overall, 71 percent of male faculty have tenure, while 46 percent of women faculty have tenure.

Most sex discrimination lawsuits, however, involve a single plaintiff who argues that she was given less favorable treatment than comparable males. For example, in *Namenwirth v. Board of Regents of the University of Wisconsin*, 769 F.2d 1235 (7th Cir. 1985), an assistant professor of zoology, the first woman to be hired in a tenure-track position in the department in thirty-five years, challenged her tenure denial by arguing that her department colleagues had treated her less favorably than a male colleague with a very similar publication record. Despite the plaintiff's demonstration that more stringent standards were applied to her performance than to the comparable male faculty member, the court deferred to the department's judgment that Namenwirth showed "insufficient promise" to be granted tenure.

Women who have challenged the fairness of peer judgments have generally not been successful in court; between 1972 and 1984, only about one-fifth of individual women who claimed sex discrimination prevailed on the merits (see LaNoue & Lee (cited above), at 31). However, women who could demonstrate actual gender bias in employment decisions (such as the sexist language used in *Brown v. Trustees of Boston University*, discussed in Section 3.3.2.1) or a clearly different *objective* standard for men and women (such as in *Kunda v. Muhlenberg College*, also discussed in Section 3.3.2.1) have prevailed in their discrimination claims.

3.3.4.1. Pregnancy discrimination. Regulations issued by the Equal Employment Opportunity Commission (EEOC) pursuant to the Pregnancy Discrimination Act of 1978 make it a violation of Title VII for an employer to discriminate on the basis of pregnancy, childbirth, or related illnesses in either employment opportunities, health or disability insurance programs, or sick leave plans (29 C.F.R. § 1604.10 and Appendix, "Questions and Answers on the Pregnancy Discrimination Act"). Pregnancy-related conditions must be treated the same as any other disabilities, and health insurance for pregnancy-related conditions must extend not only to female employees but also to wives of male employees (*Newport News Shipbuilding and Dry Dock Co. v. EEOC*, 462 U.S. 669 (1983)).

Some states have enacted laws that attempt to "level the playing field" for women, who have the biological responsibility for bearing children, in order to ease their return to work. For example, a California law requires employers to give pregnant employees unpaid maternity leave and to reinstate them to the same or an equivalent position upon their return to work. That law was challenged in *California Federal Savings & Loan v. Guerra*, 479 U.S. 272 (1987), in which the employer claimed that Title VII did not permit more favorable treatment of an individual because of pregnancy, but merely mandated that pregnant women not be discriminated against. The Supreme Court ruled that the Pregnancy Discrimination Act provided a "floor" of protection for pregnant employees, but not a ceiling, and that Title VII did not preempt state laws that recognized the special circumstances of pregnant employees.[37]

However, in a challenge to Missouri's unemployment compensation law, which denies benefits to women who leave work because of the birth of a child, the Supreme Court ruled that Title VII does not prevent a state from categorizing a

---

[37]The federal Family and Medical Leave Act of 1993 (Pub. L. No. 103-3) requires employers with fifty or more employees to grant up to twelve weeks of unpaid leave each year to an employee for the care of a sick, newborn, or recently adopted child, or a seriously ill family member, or for the employee's own serious health condition. This law is discussed in Section 7.2.17.

resignation on account of the birth of a child as a voluntary resignation, resulting in ineligibility for unemployment benefits (*Wimberly v. Labor & Industrial Relations Commission*, 479 U.S. 511 (1987)). For discussion of state unemployment compensation laws, see Section 6.5.4.

Another issue related to pregnancy, or potential pregnancy, is the lawfulness of employer policies that exclude pregnant or potentially pregnant employees from work sites where exposure to substances could cause birth defects. While most faculty do not work with fetotoxins, staff and graduate students may. And some nonacademic employers have excluded from such jobs all women who were capable of becoming pregnant.[38] They have done so in order to avoid liability for litigation by children seeking a remedy for birth defects allegedly traceable to their mothers' workplace exposure to fetotoxins.

These "fetal vulnerability" policies were challenged in *United Auto Workers v. Johnson Controls*, 111 S. Ct. 1196 (1991). The company, which manufactures automobile batteries, argued that exposure to the lead used in the manufacturing process could cause birth defects, and that permitting women to work with the lead was unsafe. The company excluded all women capable of becoming pregnant—unless they could prove that they were unable to conceive a child—from the high-paying jobs involving lead exposure; but the company permitted men, even those who wished to father children, to work in these jobs.

A unanimous Supreme Court ruled that fetal vulnerability policies that excluded only women constituted intentional disparate treatment discrimination, and rejected the company's argument that, on the grounds of safety, inability to become pregnant was a bona fide occupational qualification (BFOQ) for a position involving exposure to fetotoxins. The Court stated that the BFOQ is a narrow concept and is used only in "special situations" (111 St. Ct. at 1204). The opinion clarifies the concept of BFOQ in the following manner:

> Our case law . . . makes it clear that the safety exception is limited to instances in which sex or pregnancy actually interferes with the employee's ability to perform the job. This approach is consistent with the language of the BFOQ provision itself, for it suggests that permissible distinctions based on sex must relate to ability to perform the duties of the job [111 S. Ct. at 1206].

Given the language of *Johnson Controls*, it is unlikely that a college or university could successfully specify gender as a BFOQ for jobs involving exposure to fetotoxins, or for virtually any other job as well.

3.3.4.2. Sex-based retirement plans. In a number of Title VII cases, plaintiffs have challenged the use of sex-based mortality tables to calculate the contributions to be made or the benefits to be received by employees under employer-sponsored retirement plans. In *City of Los Angeles v. Manhart*, 435 U.S. 702 (1978), the U.S. Supreme Court held that employers cannot require women to make larger contributions than males when the benefits to be paid women are the same as those to be paid men. The Court applied its decision only prospectively, to contributions made to the

---

[38]Cases regarding fetal vulnerability policies are collected in Annot., "Exclusion of Women from Employment Involving Risk of Fetal Injury as Violative of Title VII of Civil Rights Act of 1964 (42 U.S.C.S. §§ 2000e et seq.)," 66 A.L.R. Fed. 968 (1984 and periodic supp.).

defendant's plan after the Court's ruling, so that previous contributions and benefits based on them were not affected. Five years later, in *Arizona Governing Committee v. Norris*, 463 U.S. 1073 (1983), the Court applied its *Manhart* ruling to plans under which contributions are equal but women are paid lower monthly retirement benefits than men. Refusing to make fine distinctions based on the type of plan involved, the Court broadly reaffirmed its statement in *Manhart* that "the use of sex-segregated retirement benefits violates Title VII whether or not the tables are an accurate prediction of the longevity of women as a class." Six justices concurred in this ruling. A separate majority of five justices again refused to apply the ruling retroactively, instead holding that the prohibition of sex-based tables would apply only to those retirement benefits under the defendant's plan that were based on contributions made on or after August 1, 1983 (the beginning of the month following the ruling).

On the same day that it decided *Norris*, the Court also vacated the judgments in two U.S. Court of Appeals cases involving the Teachers' Insurance and Annuity Association–College Retirement Equities Fund (TIAA-CREF), the retirement plan widely used at colleges and universities across the country. In the first case, *Spirt v. TIAA & CREF*, 691 F.2d 1054 (2d Cir. 1982), the Second Circuit had held that both TIAA's and CREF's use of sex-based tables to determine retirement benefits violates Title VII. In the second case, *Peters v. Wayne State University*, 691 F.2d 235 (6th Cir. 1982), the Sixth Circuit had held that neither plan's use of sex-based tables violates Title VII. The Supreme Court remanded both cases to the lower courts for further consideration in light of *Norris*. Subsequently, in the second *Spirt v. TIAA & CREF*, 735 F.2d 23 (2d Cir. 1984), the Second Circuit affirmed its earlier ruling as consistent with *Norris*. The court did not agree to apply its ruling only prospectively, however, as the Supreme Court had done in *Norris*. Emphasizing that the TIAA-CREF system for calculating benefits differs fundamentally from that of the Arizona plan in *Norris*, the *Spirt* court determined that retroactive relief would not impose added financial burdens on employers or on the plan. Accordingly, the court ordered TIAA-CREF to use unisex (gender-neutral) tables to calculate benefits for all persons retiring after May 1, 1980 (a date shortly after the trial court's original decision), including benefits based on contributions made prior to that date. The U.S. Supreme Court declined to review the Second Circuit's decision (469 U.S. 881 (1984)).

It is clear, after *Manhart* and *Norris*, that the law now prohibits the use of sex-segregated tables by all types of retirement plans sponsored by postsecondary employers. After *Spirt*, it is also clear that TIAA-CREF, in particular, must use unisex tables for all contributions of all annuitants retiring any time after May 1, 1980.

3.3.4.3. Sexual harassment. Much attention has been given to the issue of sexual harassment in recent years, in contrast to prior years, when the issue was rarely litigated, particularly in academe. However, the number of sexual harassment claims by students and faculty is growing as individuals become aware that such conduct is prohibited by law, whether the target is an employee or a student. Sexual harassment of faculty is addressed in this section; harassment of students is discussed in Section 4.7.3.

Sexual harassment is a violation of Title VII of the Civil Rights Act of 1964 (discussed in this volume, Section 3.3.2.1) because it is workplace conduct directed at an individual on the basis of his or her sex. It is also a violation of Title IX of the Education Amendments of 1972 (discussed in Section 3.3.2.3). Therefore, sexual harassment victims may be male or female, and harassers may be of either gender as well.

Furthermore, homosexual sexual harassment would also be a violation of Title VII and Title IX.

The EEOC's guidelines prohibiting sexual harassment expansively define sexual harassment and establish standards under which an employer can be liable for harassment occasioned by its own acts as well as the acts of its agents and supervisory employees:

(a) Harassment on the basis of sex is a violation of Sec. 703 of title VII. Unwelcome sexual advances, requests for sexual favors, and other verbal or physical conduct of a sexual nature constitute sexual harassment when (1) submission to such conduct is made either explicitly or implicitly a term or condition of an individual's employment, (2) submission to or rejection of such conduct by an individual is used as the basis for employment decisions affecting such individual, or (3) such conduct has the purpose or effect of unreasonably interfering with an individual's work performance or creating an intimidating, hostile, or offensive working environment.

(b) In determining whether alleged conduct constitutes sexual harassment, the Commission will look at the record as a whole and the totality of the circumstances, such as the nature of the sexual advances and the context in which the alleged incidents occurred. The determination of the legality of a particular action will be made from the facts, on a case-by-case basis.

(c) Applying general title VII principles, an employer, employment agency, joint apprenticeship committee, or labor organization (hereinafter collectively referred to as "employer") is responsible for its acts and those of its agents and supervisory employees with respect to sexual harassment regardless of whether the specific acts complained of were authorized or even forbidden by the employer and regardless of whether the employer knew or should have known of their occurrence. The Commission will examine the circumstances of the particular employment relationship and the job functions performed by the individual in determining whether an individual acts in either a supervisory or agency capacity.

(d) With respect to conduct between fellow employees, an employer is responsible for acts of sexual harassment in the work place where the employer (or its agents or supervisory employees) knows or should have known of the conduct, unless it can show that it took immediate and appropriate corrective action.

(e) An employer may also be responsible for the acts of nonemployees, with respect to sexual harassment of employees in the work place, where the employer (or its agents or supervisory employees) knows or should have known of the conduct and fails to take immediate and appropriate corrective action. In reviewing these cases the Commission will consider the extent of the employer's control and any other legal responsibility which the employer may have with respect to the conduct of such nonemployees.

(f) Prevention is the best tool for the elimination of sexual harassment. An employer should take all steps necessary to prevent sexual harassment from occurring, such as affirmatively raising the subject, expressing strong disapproval, developing appropriate sanctions, informing employees of their right to raise and how to raise the issue of harassment under title VII, and developing methods to sensitize all concerned.

(g) Other related practices: Where employment opportunities or benefits are granted because of an individual's submission to the employer's sexual advances or requests for sexual favors, the employer may be held liable for unlawful sex discrimination against other persons who were qualified for but denied that employment opportunity or benefit [29 C.F.R. § 1604.11].

Some thoughtful commentators have cautioned that broad application of Section a(3), on hostile environment, to academic teaching may impair academic freedom. See, for example, W. Van Alstyne, "The University in the Manner of Tiananmen Square," 21 *Hastings Const. Law Q.* 1 (1993).

Two forms of sexual harassment have been considered by the courts, and each has a different consequence with regard to employer liability and potential remedies. Harassment that involves the exchange of sexual favors for employment benefits, or the threat of negative action if sexual favors are not granted, is known as quid pro quo harassment. The U.S. Supreme Court addressed this form of sexual harassment for the first time in *Meritor Savings Bank v. Vinson*, 477 U.S. 57 (1986), ruling that, if quid pro quo harassment were proven, employer liability under Title VII would ensue even if the victim had not reported the harassment. Using principles of agency law, the Court asserted that harassment involving an actual or threatened change in terms and conditions of employment would result in a form of strict liability for the employer.

The Court did not elaborate on the showing that the plaintiff must make to demonstrate that the employer "knew or should have known," but it did mention two tests to assist courts in determining whether a plaintiff's decision not to report alleged sexual harassment was reasonable:

1) the employer should have a clearly-worded policy prohibiting sexual harass-ment in the workplace that is communicated to all employees;
2) the employer should have a system for reporting sexual harassment that pro-vides an alternate channel so that the victim, if harassed by a supervisor, can avoid the traditional complaint procedure of discussing the problem with that supervisor [477 U.S. at 71-73].

The other form of harassment, the creation of a hostile or offensive environ-ment, may involve virtually anyone that the target employee encounters because of the employment relationship. Supervisors, co-workers, clients, customers, and vendors have been accused of sexual harassment. If the allegations are proven, and if the plaintiff establishes that the employer knew or should have known that the harassment had occurred, liability attaches as well.

The U.S. Supreme Court addressed this form of harassment in *Harris v. Fork-lift Systems*, 114 S. Ct. 367 (1993). In *Harris* the plaintiff had demonstrated that her supervisor had repeatedly engaged in verbal sexual harassment. The major issue in the case was not whether the behavior was harassment (the defense had conceded that it was), but whether the plaintiff must demonstrate serious psychological harm in order to convince a court that the harassment was sufficiently severe and pervasive to constitute a "hostile or offensive environment."

In a unanimous opinion, the U.S. Supreme Court rejected the argument that serious harm must be demonstrated. Justice O'Connor, writing for the Court, asserted:

Title VII comes into play before the harassing conduct leads to a nervous breakdown. A discriminatorily abusive work environment, even one that does not seriously affect employees' psychological well-being, can and often will detract from employees' job performance, discourage employees from remaining on the job, or keep them from advancing in their careers. Moreover, even without regard to these tangible effects, *the very fact that the discriminatory conduct was so severe or pervasive that it created a work environment abusive to employees because of their race, gender, religion, or national origin offends Title VII's broad rule of workplace equality.* . . . Certainly Title VII bars conduct that would seriously affect a reasonable person's psychological well-being, but the statute is not limited to such conduct. So long as the environment would reasonably be perceived, and is perceived, as hostile or abusive, there is no need for it also to be psychologically injurious [114 S. Ct. at 370–71; emphasis added].

The Court thus determined that the harassing conduct itself is unlawful, and whether it has a psychological, or even a financial, impact on the plaintiff is irrelevant. Justice O'Connor also took pains to extend the harassment issue beyond gender to any of the categories protected by Title VII.

Although the standard for quid pro quo harassment is clear in that the accused harasser must have the power to affect the target's terms and conditions of employment, the standard for establishing hostile or offensive environment is less clear, for the Supreme Court did not explicitly address this issue. Name calling, sexual jokes, sexual touching, sexually explicit cartoons, and other sexual behavior by supervisors or co-workers have been found to constitute sexual harassment (see, for example, *Bennett v. Corroon and Black Corp.*, 845 F.2d 104 (5th Cir. 1988)). Furthermore, vandalism or harassing conduct of a nonsexual nature directed at a target because of his or her gender has also been found to violate Title VII, sometimes as sexual harassment and sometimes as sex discrimination (see, for example, *Hall v. Gus Construction Co.*, 842 F.2d 1010 (8th Cir. 1988)).

Words alone may be sufficient to constitute sexual harassment. In a case involving a female faculty member, *Jew v. University of Iowa*, 749 F. Supp. 946 (S.D. Iowa 1990), false rumors that the plaintiff had engaged in a sexual relationship with her department chair in order to obtain favorable treatment were found to constitute actionable sexual harassment, and the institution was ordered to promote the plaintiff and to give her back pay and attorney's fees.

The U.S. Court of Appeals for the Ninth Circuit, in *Jordan v. Clark*, 847 F.2d 1368 (9th Cir. 1988), described the showing that the plaintiff must make in order to demonstrate a hostile environment. The plaintiff must prove:

1) that he or she was subjected to demands for sexual favors, or other verbal or physical conduct of a sexual nature;
2) that this conduct was unwelcome;
3) that the conduct was sufficiently severe or pervasive to alter the conditions of the victim's employment and create an abusive working environment [847 F.2d at 1373].

But the definition of an "abusive working environment" has not been uniformly interpreted. Establishing whether the conduct is sufficiently severe or pervasive, and whether the plaintiff's claim that the behavior was offensive meets the standard for liability, has been a problem for the courts.

The U.S. Court of Appeals for the Ninth Circuit created a special standard by which to determine whether the complained-of conduct constituted a hostile environment. In *Ellison v. Brady*, 924 F.2d 872 (9th Cir. 1991), the court created the "reasonable woman" standard, in which the court assumes the perspective of a reasonable person of the plaintiff's gender, since "conduct that many men consider unobjectionable may offend many women" (924 F.2d at 878). The court continued:

> [W]e hold that a female plaintiff states a prima facie case of hostile environment sexual harassment when she alleges conduct which a reasonable woman would consider sufficiently severe or pervasive to alter the conditions of employment and create an abusive working environment [924 F.2d at 879].

The EEOC has adopted the "reasonable woman" standard in proposed guidelines related to hostile evironment harassment, as has the New Jersey Supreme Court in interpreting the state's Law Against Discrimination (*Lehman v. Toys 'R' Us*, 132 N.J. 587 (1993). While the U.S. Supreme Court did not discuss the question of standards in *Harris*, Justice O'Connor appeared to use the "reasonable person" rather than the "reasonable woman" standard. For a brief discussion of interpretation problems related to the "reasonable woman" standard, see E. H. Marcus, "Sexual Harassment Claims: Who Is a Reasonable Woman?" 44 *Labor Law J.* 646 (1993).

Subsection (f) of the EEOC guidelines emphasizes the advisability of implementing clear internal guidelines and sensitive grievance procedures for resolving sexual harassment complaints. The EEOC guidelines' emphasis on prevention suggests that the use of such internal activities may alleviate the postsecondary institution's liability under subsections (d) and (e) and diminish the likelihood of occurrences occasioning liability under subsections (c) and (g). Title IX requires grievance procedures.

In light of the social and legal developments, postsecondary institutions should give serious attention and sensitive treatment to sexual harassment issues. Sexual harassment on campus may be not only an employment issue but, for affected faculty and students, an academic freedom issue as well. Advance preventive planning is the key to successful management of these issues, as the EEOC guidelines indicate. Institutions should involve the academic community in developing specific written policies and information on what the community will consider to be sexual harassment.

Prompt response to complaints of sexual harassment is critical to the avoidance or limitation of liability if harassment claims are filed with an administrative agency or in court. For example, in *Giordano v. William Paterson College*, 804 F. Supp. 637 (D.N.J. 1992), the college was able to secure summary judgment on the issue of hostile environment harassment (but not on the quid pro quo claim) because the college had responded promptly to the report of harassment, had conducted a thorough investigation, and, despite its conclusion that harassment had not occurred, had transferred and demoted the alleged harassers. For an analysis of judicial views on the adequacy of employers' responses to claims of sexual harassment, see H. Comisky, " 'Prompt and Effective Remedial Action?' What Must an Employer Do to Avoid Liability for 'Hostile Work Environment' Sexual Harassment?" 8 *Labor Law-*

yer 181 (1992). In light of these judicial attitudes, institutions should establish processes for receiving, investigating, and resolving complaints and for preserving the privacy of the complainants and charged parties to the maximum practical extent.

An important component of the institution's response is consideration of whether a faculty member charged with harassment should be disciplined or discharged. Tenured faculty members have a property interest in continued employment, as do nontenured faculty members whose contract has not yet expired. Institutions may wish to use their regular hearing procedures when determining whether a faculty member should be disciplined or discharged (see Section 3.6). Whether the regular procedure or one tailored specifically for harassment issues is selected, faculty and administrators may wish to consult the AAUP statement on "Sexual Harassment: Suggested Policy and Procedures for Handling Complaints" (in *AAUP Policy Documents and Reports*, 1990 ed.), supplemented with "Due Process in Sexual Harassment Complaints," 77 *Academe* 47 (Sept.–Oct. 1991). Both statements emphasize the role of a faculty review committee before any disciplinary action is taken against a faculty member accused of harassment.

Sexual harassment is not only an important social problem in the employment context, but it may pose substantial financial liability for a college or university. Although compensatory and punitive damages are capped in lawsuits brought under Title VII, plaintiffs may also sue under Title IX and obtain unlimited monetary damages (see *Franklin v. Gwinnett County Public Schools*, discussed in Section 7.5.3). For a summary of the legal and practical issues involving sexual harassment in employment, see B. Lindeman & D. Kadue, *A Primer on Sexual Harassment* (Bureau of National Affairs, 1992). An especially valuable resource for sexual harassment of both faculty and students is E. Cole (ed.), *Sexual Harassment on Campus: A Legal Compendium* (National Association of College and University Attorneys, 1990), which contains sample policies from various institutions as well as suggestions on how to develop a policy and how to handle complaints of harassment. A resource especially useful for those institutions whose faculty are represented by unions is L. Fitzgerald, *Sexual Harassment in Higher Education: Concepts and Issues* (National Education Association, 1992).

3.3.5. Discrimination on the basis of disability. Very few cases alleging discrimination on the basis of disability have been brought by college faculty, although the passage of the Americans with Disabilities Act may stimulate litigation by faculty in this area. Under the Rehabilitation Act, a faculty member denied tenure by Rice University alleged that the decision was based on his disability (deafness). In *Guertin v. Hackerman*, 25 Fair Empl. Prac. Cases 207 (S.D. Tex. 1981), the court found that the tenure denial was based on the narrowness of the plaintiff's scholarly research and its lack of promise in the field of physics, as well as on the plaintiff's failure to collaborate with the departmental research group.

A recent case decided by the U.S. Court of Appeals for the First Circuit, interpreting the Rehabilitation Act, may have significance for colleges and universities. In *Cook v. State of Rhode Island*, 10 F.3d 17 (1st Cir. 1993), the court ruled that a state agency's refusal to rehire a qualified former employee because of its concern that her weight (320 pounds) would interfere with her ability to evacuate patients in the event of an emergency, and its speculation that she had a higher probability of injury or illness than employees were were not obese, violated Section 504. The court did not say whether, in its view, obesity is a disability, but rather ruled that her obesity was perceived as a disability, which brought her under the law's protections. (The ADA has the same protections for nondisabled individuals who are perceived as disabled.) The EEOC has argued that obesity should be characterized as a disability protected under both Section 504 and the ADA.

Although the ADA is similar to the Rehabilitation Act in most respects (see Section 3.3.2.5), several differences suggest that faculty will turn to this law for relief when they believe discrimination has occurred. The ADA includes reassignment to a vacant position as a form of accommodation that the employer must consider (42 U.S.C. § 12111(9)(B)), a requirement absent from the language of the Rehabilitation Act, although it is included in its regulations. The ADA protects individuals with alcoholism, and it is not yet clear whether, or how often, a college or university would be required to offer a faculty member with alcoholism an opportunity for inpatient rehabilitation. The ADA has strict confidentiality requirements for medical information related to employees' disabilities (42 U.S.C. § 12112(d)(3)(B)); the interplay between these requirements and the right of a labor union to receive information related to an employment grievance is as yet unresolved.

Differences between the Rehabilitation Act and the ADA, and the implications of these differences for employment decisions, are addressed in B. Lee, "Reasonable Accommodation Under the Americans with Disabilities Act: Limitations of Rehabilitation Act Precedents," 14 *Berkeley J. Empl. & Labor Law* 201 (1993). Issues of special interest to colleges and universities are discussed in L. Rothstein, "Students, Staff and Faculty with Disabilities: Current Issues for Colleges and Universities," 17 *J. Coll. & Univ. Law* 471 (1991).

3.3.6. Age discrimination. College faculty alleging age discrimination have directed their complaints at two major areas: discrimination with regard to pensions or other retirement benefits, and salary discrimination. An additional issue with both legal and policy ramifications for institutions of higher education is the "uncapping" of the mandatory age-seventy retirement provision in the ADEA.

The elimination of mandatory retirement means that colleges and universities may divest themselves of older faculty in one of two ways: entice them to retire, usually by providing financial incentives, or dismiss them for cause. Legal issues related to dismissing tenured faculty for cause are discussed in Section 3.5.2; such action would require extensive documentation of performance or discipline problems. For an analysis of this issue, see A. Morris, *Dismissal of Tenured Higher Education Faculty: Legal Implications of the Elimination of Mandatory Retirement* (National Organization on Legal Problems of Education, 1992). See also N. Giovanni, Jr., *Age Discrimination: An Administrator's Guide* (College and University Personnel Association, 1989).

Others have questioned whether, in light of the elimination of mandatory retirement, colleges and universities should consider alternatives to tenure. For discussion of potential alternatives to tenure for older faculty, see O. Ruebhausen, "The Age Discrimination in Employment Act Amendments of 1986: Implications for Tenure and Retirement," 14 *J. Coll. & Univ. Law* 561 (1988); and a rejoinder, M. Finkin, "Tenure After an Uncapped ADEA: A Different View," 15 *J. Coll. & Univ. Law* 43 (1988). For an analysis of the impact of uncapping on college staffing policies and practices, see a report by the National Research Council, *Ending Mandatory Retire-*

ment for Tenured Faculty: The Consequences for Higher Education (National Academy Press, 1991). See also "AAUP Working Paper on the Status of Tenure Without Mandatory Retirement," 73 *Academe* 45 (July–Aug. 1987).

Individual faculty have challenged salary decisions under the ADEA, asserting that their institution favored younger faculty by paying newly hired faculty a higher salary than that of older faculty hired years earlier. In *MacPherson v. University of Montevallo*, 922 F.2d 766 (11th Cir. 1991), two business school professors who were the oldest and the lowest-paid faculty in the college alleged both disparate impact and disparate treatment discrimination in the university's salary practices. Their disparate impact claim was based on the business school's practice of basing the salary of incoming faculty on market factors and research productivity, since the school was seeking accreditation of its business school. The trial judge ordered a directed verdict for the university on the ground that, although the market-rate salary practice did exclude older faculty, the university made market-based salary adjustments for older faculty and each plaintiff had received one. The appellate court affirmed that portion of the ruling, holding that market-linked pay for new hires is a legitimate business reason for paying younger faculty more than older faculty.

With regard to the plaintiffs' claim of disparate treatment, the trial judge found that comparator faculty who were younger and more highly paid had more skills and different disciplines; furthermore, the plaintiffs had done little significant research and had few publications. There was some question, however, about the way in which salary decisions were made, so the appellate court affirmed the trial judge's order for a new trial.

The U.S. Court of Appeals for the Seventh Circuit was presented with a similar claim in *Davidson v. Board of Governors of State Colleges and Universities*, 920 F.2d 441 (7th Cir. 1990). A professor of business hired at age fifty-eight challenged a provision in the collective bargaining agreement that permitted the institution to give a salary adjustment to any faculty member who could present a bona fide offer of employment from another institution. Although Judge Posner, writing for a unanimous panel, agreed that salary practices that relied on market forces had a disparate impact on older faculty members, he noted that comparable worth is not required by the civil rights laws, and that the market is a neutral criterion on which to base salary determinations. Posner observed that the market alternatives of faculty who have been at an institution for a long time are "relatively poor and they fare relatively badly under any market-based compensation scheme, regardless of age" (920 F.2d at 446).

MacPherson and *Davidson* illustrate the difficult problem of salary compression faced by many institutions, and the potential for age discrimination allegations if salary decisions are not clearly based on factors unrelated to age. For example, merit pay systems have been challenged as discriminatory, and the criteria for decisions must relate closely to the institution's need for productive faculty. For an example of a merit pay system that survived judicial scrutiny when sex discrimination was alleged, see *Willner v. University of Kansas*, 848 F.2d 1023 (10th Cir. 1988).

Early-retirement incentive programs are regulated by the ADEA, as amended by the Older Workers Benefit Protection Act, discussed in Section 3.3.2.6. The amendments to the ADEA that took effect January 1, 1988, require, among other things, that institutions continue pension contributions without regard to the individual's age. Prior to 1988, however, some institutions terminated pension contributions when a faculty member reached "normal retirement" age, whether or not that individual remained employed. In a case brought against Purdue University, a class of faculty sued the university for its practice, between 1982 and 1988, of discontinuing pension contributions when a faculty member reached age sixty-five. The university asserted that this practice was lawful prior to the 1988 amendments outlawing the cessation of pension contributions because of age. As evidence, it cited Section 4(f)(2) of the Act, which permits bona fide benefit plans that are not a subterfuge for age discrimination. Although a trial judge ruled in *Bell v. Trustees of Purdue University*, 761 F. Supp. 1360 (N.D. Ind. 1991), that a jury could find the practice "a subterfuge for age-based discrimination in wages" and denied summary judgment for the university, that ruling was reversed by the U.S. Court of Appeals for the Seventh Circuit (975 F.2d 422 (7th Cir. 1992)) in light of the decision of the U.S. Supreme Court in *Public Employee Retirement System of Ohio v. Betts*, 492 U.S. 158 (1989).

In *Betts* the U.S. Supreme Court had upheld a benefit plan that made age-based distinctions, finding that it was not a "subterfuge" under Section 4(f)(2). The Older Workers Benefit Protection Act overruled *Betts*, but the appellate court did not apply OWPBA retroactively.

Given the complexity of the legal and policy issues related to retirement and other benefit plans, consultation with specialized counsel is essential. For a thoughtful analysis of the implications of the Older Workers Benefit Protection Act for early-retirement incentive programs offered by colleges and universities, see P. Swan, "Early Retirement Incentives with Upper Age Limits Under the Older Workers Benefit Protection Act," 19 *J. Coll. & Univ. Law* 53 (1992). Additional information is provided in R. Stith & W. Kohlburn, "Early Retirement Incentive Plans After the Passage of the Older Workers Benefit Protection Act," 11 *St. Louis U. Pub. Law Rev.* 263 (1992).

3.3.7. Religious discrimination. Discrimination "because of [an] individual's . . . religion" is one of the prohibited forms of discrimination under Title VII (42 U.S.C. § 2000e-2(a)), subject to an exception for situations where a particular religious characteristic is a "bona fide occupational qualification" for the job (42 U.S.C. § 2000e-2(e)(1)). A related exception, applicable specifically to educational institutions, permits the employment of persons "of a particular religion" if the institution is "owned, supported, controlled, or managed" by that religion or if the institution's curriculum "is directed toward the propagation of a particular religion" (42 U.S.C. § 2000e-2(e)(2)).

Title VII defines religion to include "all aspects of religious observance and practice, as well as belief" (42 U.S.C. § 2000e(j)). The same section of the statute requires that an employer "reasonably accommodate to" an employee's religion unless the employer can demonstrate an inability to do so "without undue hardship." In *Trans World Airlines v. Hardison*, 432 U.S. 63 (1977), the U.S. Supreme Court narrowly construed this provision, holding that it would be an undue hardship to require an employer to bear more than minimal costs in accommodating an employee's religious beliefs. To further explicate the statute and case law, the EEOC has issued revised guidelines on the employer's duty under Title VII to reasonably accommodate the religious practices of employees and applicants (29 C.F.R. Part 1605).

The Supreme Court addressed religious discrimination a second time in *Ansonia Board of Education v. Philbrook*, 479 U.S. 60 (1986). In *Ansonia* a schoolteacher had asked to use the paid "personal days" provided by the collective bargaining agreement for the observance of religious holidays. The collective bargaining agreement provided that religious holidays taken beyond those that were official school holidays would be taken as unpaid leave. Philbrook sued, alleging religious discrimination under Title VII and stating that the school board should have accommodated his religious needs by permitting him to use paid leave. In analyzing the scope of the "reasonable accommodation" requirement, the Court ruled that the employer need not accede to the employee's preferred accommodation, but could offer its own as long as that accommodation also met the "reasonableness" criterion articulated in *Hardison*. The employer did not have to prove that the employee's preferred accommodation would pose an undue hardship; it only had to prove that the accommodation it offered was a reasonable one.

Under very narrow circumstances, an individual of the Jewish faith may attack religious discrimination under Section 1981 of the 1866 Civil Rights Act (see Section 3.3.2.4).

For related developments on the applicability of Title VII to church-related postsecondary institutions, see Section 7.2.6.2.

3.3.8. Sexual orientation discrimination. Discrimination on the basis of sexual orientation is not prohibited by Title VII, nor is there any other federal law directed at such discrimination. However, eight states prohibit discrimination on the basis of sexual orientation,[39] and numerous municipalities have enacted similar local laws prohibiting such discrimination. And in *Evans v. Romer*, 854 P.2d 1270 (Colo. 1993), an attempt by voters in Colorado to make unconstitutional any state or local laws extending nondiscrimination protection on the basis of sexual orientation was found to violate the Equal Protection Clause.

Employment issues related to sexual orientation go beyond the issues—such as tenure denial or salary discrimination—faced by other protected classes. Access to benefits for unmarried homosexual partners, access to campus housing reserved for heterosexual couples, and the effect of the military's refusal to recruit homosexuals add to the complexity of dealing with this issue. The law is developing rapidly; a few illustrations will demonstrate the changes that have occurred in judicial and legislative attitudes over the last decades.

Challenges to discrimination on the basis of sexual orientation have been brought against federal employers, under the Fourteenth Amendment, and against the U.S. military. In *Padula v. Webster*, 822 F.2d 97 (D.C. Cir. 1987), a female applicant charged that the Federal Bureau of Investigation refused to hire her because of her homosexuality. Padula urged the court to adopt the "strict scrutiny" test for determining whether FBI policy against hiring homosexuals violated the equal protection guarantees implicit in the Fifth Amendment, a test that would require the FBI to demonstrate that the regulation was "suitably tailored to serve a compelling state interest" (822 F.2d at 102). The FBI, however,

---

[39]As of late 1993, the following states prohibited discrimination in employment (and in some states, in public accommodations and/or housing as well) on the basis of sexual orientation: California, Connecticut, Hawaii, Massachusetts, Minnesota, New Jersey, Vermont, and Washington. In nine states sexual orientation discrimination is prohibited in state employment by executive order (Colorado, Louisiana, Minnesota, New Mexico, New York, Ohio, Oregon, Pennsylvania, and Rhode Island).

argued that the U.S. Supreme Court had refused to add homosexuals to the group of "suspect classes" (race, alienage, and national origin) that were entitled to the strict scrutiny test. In *Bowers v. Hardwick*, 478 U.S. 186 (1986), the Court refused to declare a Georgia law criminalizing sodomy unconstitutional, asserting that private sexual behavior outside the "family relationship" was neither a fundamental right nor protected by the Constitution's privacy guarantees. The appellate court in *Padula* followed *Hardwick* and applied the "rational basis" test to the FBI policy, finding that the law enforcement needs of the agency provided a rational basis for the exclusion of homosexuals.

More recently, however, the U.S. Court of Appeals for the Tenth Circuit accepted without comment a lower court's declaration that homosexuals and those regarded as homosexuals were a suspect class for equal protection purposes. In *Jantz v. Muci*, 976 F.2d 623 (10th Cir. 1992), the court analyzed the refusal of a school principal to hire a prospective teacher because he reminded the principal's secretary of her ex-husband, a suspected homosexual. Although the court declared that current legal doctrine prohibited as unconstitutional those employment decisions made on the basis of homosexual status without specific evidence of misconduct, the law in this regard was not clear in 1988, when the challenged decision was made. Therefore, the court granted qualified immunity (see Section 2.4.3) to the principal because the state of the law was not clear at that time.

Two federal courts have held that the military's ban on homosexuals violates the Constitution's Equal Protection Clause. In *Steffan v. Secretary of the Navy*, 8 F.3d 57 (D.C. Cir. 1993), a federal appellate court ruled that the U.S. Naval Academy's action in expelling a high-performing student just prior to graduation on the grounds of homosexuality violated equal protection norms implicit in the Fifth Amendment. The court used the lowest level of equal protection review—the "rational basis" test (the level of review most deferential to the government in equal protection cases)—and determined that the Navy's expulsion of the plaintiff based on his *status* as a homosexual, rather than on any homosexual *conduct* (for which there was no evidence), was irrational in impermissibly burdening the plaintiff because of his thoughts, rather than his actions. The court said:

> Homosexual conduct is more than a practice discouraged by the military: it is grounds for discipline and sometimes (in the case of sodomy) a criminal act. Therefore, the Secretary's justification for the gay ban presumes that a certain class of persons will break the law or the rules solely because of their thoughts and desires. This is inherently unreasonable. . . . A person's status alone, whether determined by his thoughts or by his membership in a certain group, is an inadequate basis upon which to impute misconduct [8 F.3d at 65].

The court concluded that the directives prohibiting homosexuals from serving in the military on the basis of their status, rather than conduct, were not rationally related to any legitimate government goal. The court concluded, "it is apparent that the Directives exclude a particular class of individuals, identifiable only by their thoughts and desires, for no other reason than the military's fear and dislike of that group" (8 F.3d at 70), a finding that, under any standard of review, violates the Constitution.

The full Court of Appeals for the District of Columbia Circuit vacated this opinion and will rehear and redecide this case (E. Schmitt, "Appeals Court to Reconsider a Right to Bar Gay Troops," *New York Times*, Jan. 8, 1994, A7); thus, the opinion of the panel may not stand. Whatever the result of the rehearing, the opinion will very likely be appealed to the U.S. Supreme Court, but it provides a powerful argument for future courts that may be asked to address employment discrimination, particularly by public employers, against individuals on the basis of their sexual orientation.

In *Dahl v. Secretary of the Navy*, 830 F. Supp. 1319 (E.D. Cal. 1993), a federal trial judge also ruled that the Navy's policy of barring homosexuals from service violated the equal protection guarantees of the Fifth Amendment because the policy was based on prejudice against homosexuals.

In none of the cases involving the military have the courts declared homosexuals a suspect class deserving of "strict scrutiny" protection under the Constitution. The opinions that invalidated military prohibitions against homosexual status used the "rational basis" test, the lowest standard. Until, and unless, the U.S. Supreme Court reverses what appears to be a trend, employment discrimination on the basis of sexual orientation may be prohibited by federal precedent as well as in those states that have outlawed such discrimination.

These rulings, if upheld on appeal, have several implications for colleges and universities. They could prohibit Reserve Officer Training Corps programs on college campuses from excluding individuals on the basis of their status as homosexuals. Furthermore, they could settle the dispute over whether colleges and universities that have promulgated nondiscrimination policies on the basis of sexual orientation should, nevertheless, permit the military to recruit on campus.

Access to employment benefits for the partners of homosexual employees is a matter generally governed by state or local law. Laws in California and New York, permitting the registration of "domestic partnerships," are being used to assert that employers must afford benefits to unmarried domestic partners on the same basis that they do to married heterosexual spouses. Law and policy are developing rapidly on this matter; administrators should consult experienced labor and employment counsel when developing or modifying employment benefits policies.

For analyses of the legal issues related to sexual orientation and employment, see "Developments in the Law: Sexual Orientation and the Law," 102 *Harvard L. Rev.* 1508 (1989), and I. B. Capers, "Sex(ual Orientation) and Title VII," 91 *Columbia L. Rev.* 1158 (1991). For an examination of employment issues, see A. Leonard, "Sexual Orientation and the Workplace: A Rapidly Developing Field," 44 *Labor Law J.* 574 (1993).

3.3.9. Coping with the equal employment thicket. There is no magic machete that postsecondary administrators can use to cut through the equal employment thicket. Though they embody critical social goals, the complex statutes, executive orders, regulations, and court cases create a formidable administrative challenge under the best of circumstances. The challenge is not one for amateurs. Postsecondary institutions need equal employment officers and other administrators who are qualified specialists on the subject. Postsecondary institutions also need legal counsel in the formation of equal employment policies and should encourage a smooth working relationship between equal opportunity officers and legal advisers.

The various laws provide many channels for challenging alleged discrimination in an institution's employment decisions. Administrators should be attentive to the increased possibilities for such challenges from faculty members, applicants, or government agencies. In order to avoid or overcome charges of employment discrimination, administrators should be prepared to do more than provide nondiscriminatory reasons, after the fact, for the institution's employment decisions. Instead, administrators should endeavor to ensure that legitimate, nondiscriminatory reasons are the actual basis for each employment decision at the time it is made. As the court noted in an age discrimination case, *Laugeson v. Anaconda Co.,* 510 F.2d 307, 317 (6th Cir. 1975): "There could be more than one factor in the decision to discharge . . . [the employee] and . . . he was nevertheless entitled to recover if one such factor was his age and if in fact it made a difference in determining whether he was to be retained or discharged." (See also the discussion of the *Mt. Healthy* case in Section 3.7.6.)

Sec. 3.4. Affirmative Action in Employment

Affirmative action has been an intensely controversial concept in many areas of American life. While the ongoing debate on affirmative action in student admissions (Section 4.2.5) parallels the affirmative action debate on faculty employment in its intensity, the latter has been even more controversial because it is more crowded with federal regulations and requirements. In addition, beneficiaries of affirmative action in employment may be more visible because they compete for often-scarce faculty openings. While issues relating to affirmative action in student admissions have not been discussed frequently by the courts in recent years, questions about affirmative action in employment continue to engender debate. The future character and mission of postsecondary education continue to depend, in part, on the outcome of the debates.

Affirmative action became a major issue because the federal government's initiatives regarding discrimination have a dual aim: to "bar like discrimination in the future" and to "eliminate the discriminatory effects of the past" (*Albemarle Paper Co. v. Moody,* 422 U.S. 405 (1975)). Addressing this latter objective under Title VII, courts may " 'order such affirmative action as may be appropriate' " (*Franks v. Bowman Transportation Co.,* 424 U.S. 747 (1976), quoting *Albemarle*). Affirmative action can be appropriate under *Franks* even though it may adversely affect other employees, since "a sharing of the burden of the past discrimination is presumptively necessary." Under statutes other than Title VII, and under Executive Orders 11246 and 11375, courts or administrative agencies may similarly require employers, including public and private postsecondary institutions, to engage in affirmative action to eliminate the effects of past discrimination.

Executive Orders 11246 and 11375 (see Section 3.3.2.8) have been the major focus of federal affirmative action initiatives. Aside from their basic prohibition of race, color, religion, sex, and national origin discrimination, these executive orders require federal nonconstruction contractors and subcontractors with specified amounts of contracts and numbers of employees to develop affirmative action plans. Section 60-2.10 of the Department of Labor's implementing order, known as "Revised Order No. 4" (41 C.F.R. Part 60-2, as amended in 1977 by 42 Fed. Reg. 3454), requires that a contractor's affirmative action program include affirmative action goals. There have been considerable confusion and controversy over the concept of goals. While the order states that "goals should be specific for planned results" (§ 60-2.12(d)), it also states that "goals may not be rigid and inflexible quotas which must be met, but must be targets reasonably attainable by means of applying every good faith effort to make all aspects of the entire affirmative action program work" (§ 60-2.12(e)).

An institution's compliance with affirmative action requirements is monitored and enforced by the Office of Federal Contract Compliance Programs (OFCCP), located in the U.S. Department of Labor. The OFCCP may also conduct an investigation of an institution's employment practices before a federal contract is awarded.

Postsecondary institutions contracting with the federal government are also subject to federal affirmative action requirements regarding persons with disabilities, disabled veterans, and Vietnam veterans. Persons with disabilities are covered by Section 503 of the Rehabilitation Act of 1973 (29 U.S.C. § 793):

> Any contract in excess of $10,000 entered into by any federal department or agency for the procurement of personal property and nonpersonal services (including construction) for the United States shall contain a provision requiring that, in employing persons to carry out such contract, the party contracting with the United States shall take affirmative action to employ and advance in employment qualified individuals with disabilities.

The Vietnam Era Veterans' Readjustment Assistance Act of 1974 (38 U.S.C. § 4212) contains similar language covering disabled veterans as well as Vietnam veterans whether or not disabled. That law, however, deletes the language in Section 503 that requires affirmative action only "in employing persons to carry out such contract," thus suggesting that the veterans' law has a broader scope than Section 503.[40]

The Department of Labor has issued regulations to implement both Section 503 (41 C.F.R. Part 60-741) and the veterans' law (41 C.F.R. Part 60-250). Both sets of regulations provide that any job qualification which tends to screen out members of the covered groups must be job related and consistent with business necessity (41 C.F.R. § 60-741.6(c)(1); 41 C.F.R. § 60-250.6(c)(1)). The regulations also require contractors to accommodate the physical and mental limitations of employees and disabled veterans "unless the contractor can demonstrate that such an accommodation would impose an undue hardship on the conduct of the contractor's business" (41 C.F.R. § 60-741.6(d); 41 C.F.R. § 60-250.6(d)).

Under the various affirmative action provisions in federal law, the most sensitive nerves are hit when affirmative action creates "reverse discrimination"; that is, when the employer responds to a statistical "underrepresentation" of women or minorities by granting employment preferences to members of the underrepresented or previously victimized group, thus discriminating "in reverse" against other em-

---

[40]This language distinction between veterans' law and Section 503 (disabled) does not appear to be reflected in the Department of Labor regulations implementing the two statutes. Both sets of regulations, as well as the regulations under Executive Orders 11246 and 11375, contemplate affirmative action for a wider group of employees than those working directly on the contract. All three sets of regulations, however, permit contractors to request waivers of affirmative action requirements for facilities not connected with the contract. Under 41 C.F.R. §§ 60-1.5(b)(2), 60-250.3(a)(5), and 60-741.3(a)(5), the Department of Labor may grant waivers "with respect to any of a prime contractor's or subcontractor's facilities which [it] finds to be in all respects separate and distinct from activities of the prime contractor or subcontractor related to the performance of the contract or subcontract, provided that . . . [it] also finds that such a waiver will not interfere with or impede the effectuation of the Act."

ployees or applicants.[41] Besides creating policy issues of the highest order, such affirmative action measures create two sets of complex legal questions: (1) To what extent does the applicable statute, executive order, or implementing regulation require or permit the employer to utilize such employment preferences? (2) What limitations does the Constitution place on the federal government's authority to require or permit, or the employer's authority to utilize, such employment preferences, particularly in the absence of direct evidence of discrimination by the employer?

The response to the first question depends on a close analysis of the particular legal authority involved. The answer is not necessarily the same under each authority. In general, however, federal law is more likely to require or permit hiring preferences when necessary to overcome the effects of the employer's own past discrimination than it is when no such past discrimination is shown or when preferences are not necessary to eliminate its effects. Section 703 (j) of Title VII, for instance, relieves employers of any obligation to give "preferential treatment" to an individual or group merely because of an "imbalance" in the number or percentage of employed persons from that group compared with the number or percentage of persons from that group in the "community, state, section, or other area" (42 U.S.C. § 2000e-2(j)). But where an imbalance does not arise innocently but, rather, arises because of the employer's discriminatory practices, courts in Title VII suits have sometimes required the use of hiring preferences or goals to remedy the effects of such discrimination (see, for example, *Local 28 of the Sheet Metal Workers' International Assn. v. EEOC*, 478 U.S. 421 (1986).

Constitutional limitations on the use of employment preferences by public employers stem from the Fourteenth Amendment's Equal Protection Clause. (See the discussion of that clause's application to admissions preferences in Section 4.2.5.) Even if the applicable statute, executive order, or regulation is construed to require or permit employment preferences, such preferences may still be invalid under the federal Constitution unless a court or an agency has found that the employer has discriminated in the past. Courts have usually held hiring preferences to be constitutional where necessary to eradicate the effects of the employer's past discrimination, as in *Carter v. Gallagher*, 452 F.2d 315 (8th Cir. 1971). Where there is no such showing of past discrimination, the constitutionality of employment preferences is more in doubt.

The U.S. Supreme Court has analyzed the legality of voluntary affirmative action plans and race- or gender-conscious employment decisions made under the authority of these plans. The cases have involved sharp divisions among the justices and are inconsistent in several ways. Moreover, changes in the composition of the Court during the 1980s and 1990s suggest that future affirmative action cases may have different outcomes from those described below. Therefore, the analysis of Supreme Court jurisprudence in the area of affirmative action is difficult, and predictions about future directions of the Court in this volatile area are nearly impossible.

In its first examination of a voluntary affirmative action plan involving a private employer, the Court strongly endorsed the concept, analyzing the claim under Title VII of the Civil Rights Act of 1964. In *Weber v. Kaiser Aluminum Co.*, 443 U.S.

---

[41]The relevant authorities are collected in Annot., "What Constitutes Reverse or Majority Discrimination on Basis of Sex or Race Violative of Federal Constitution or Statutes," 26 A.L.R. Fed. 13 (1976 and periodic supp.).

193 (1979), the Court considered a white steelworker's challenge to an affirmative action plan negotiated by his union and employer. The plan provided for a new craft-training program, with admission to be on the basis of one black worker for every white worker selected. The race-conscious admission practice was to cease when the proportion of black skilled craft workers at the plant reflected the proportion of blacks in the local labor force. During the first year the plan was in effect, the most junior black selected for the training program was less senior than several white workers whose requests to enter the training program were denied. One of those denied admission to the program filed a class action claim, alleging "reverse discrimination."

The federal district court ruled that the plan unlawfully discriminated against white employees and therefore violated Title VII of the Civil Rights Act (415 F. Supp. 761 (E.D. La. 1976)), and the appellate court affirmed (563 F.2d 216 (5th Cir. 1978)). In a 5-to-2 decision written by Justice Brennan, the Supreme Court reversed, ruling that employers and unions in the private sector may take race-conscious steps to eliminate "manifest racial imbalance" in "traditionally segregated job categories." Such action, the Court said, does not run afoul of Title VII's prohibition on racial discrimination (see Section 3.3.2.1).

The Court considered Weber's claim that, by giving preference to junior black employees over more senior whites, the training program discriminated against white employees in violation of the 1964 Civil Rights Act:

> We emphasize at the outset the narrowness of our inquiry. Since the Kaiser-USWA plan does not involve state action, this case does not present an alleged violation of the equal protection clause of the Constitution. Further, since the Kaiser-USWA plan was adopted voluntarily, we are not concerned with what Title VII requires or with what a court might order to remedy a past proven violation of the Act. The only question before us is the narrow statutory issue of whether Title VII *forbids* private employers and unions from voluntarily agreeing upon bona fide affirmative action plans that accord racial preferences in the manner and for the purpose provided in the Kaiser-USWA plan. . . .
>
> Respondent argues that Congress intended in Title VII to prohibit all race-conscious affirmative action plans. Respondent's argument rests upon a literal interpretation of Sections 703(a) and (d) of the Act. Those sections make it unlawful to "discriminate . . . because of . . . race" in hiring and in the selection of apprentices for training programs. . . .
>
> The prohibition against racial discrimination in Sections 703(a) and (d) of Title VII must . . . be read against the background of the legislative history of Title VII and the historical context from which the Act arose. . . . Examination of those sources makes clear that an interpretation of the sections that forbade all race-conscious affirmative action would "bring about an end completely at variance with the purpose of the statute" and must be rejected (*United States v. Public Utilities Commission*, 345 U.S. 295, 315 (1953)) [443 U.S. at 200–02; footnotes and some citations omitted].

After reviewing the legislative history describing the concerns that led Congress to pass Title VII, the Court concluded that, given Title VII's intent, voluntary efforts to achieve greater racial balance in the work force did not violate the law:

> It would be ironic indeed if a law triggered by a nation's concern over centuries of racial injustice and intended to improve the lot of those who had

"been excluded from the American dream for so long" (110 Cong. Rec. at 6552 (remarks of Sen. Humphrey)) constituted the first legislative prohibition of all voluntary, private, race-conscious efforts to abolish traditional patterns of racial segregation and hierarchy.

Our conclusion is further reinforced by examination of the language and legislative history of [Section] 703(j) of Title VII. . . . The section provides that nothing contained in Title VII "shall be interpreted to *require* any employer . . . to grant preferential treatment . . . to any group because of the race . . . of such . . . group on account of" a de facto racial imbalance in the employer's work force. The section does not state that "nothing in Title VII shall be interpreted to *permit*" voluntary affirmative efforts to correct racial imbalances. The natural inference is that Congress chose not to forbid all voluntary, race-conscious affirmative action. [443 U.S. at 200–07].

Thus concluding that the use of racial preferences in hiring is sometimes permissible, the Court went on to uphold the Kaiser plan in particular. In doing so, the Court found it unnecessary to set forth detailed guidelines for employers and unions. Instead, it noted three criteria for evaluating voluntary affirmative action plans:

[T]he plan does not unnecessarily trammel the interests of the white employees. The plan does not require the discharge of white workers and their replacement with new black hires. Nor does the plan create an absolute bar to the advancement of white employees; half of those trained in the program will be white. Moreover, the plan is a temporary measure; it is not intended to maintain racial balance, but simply to eliminate a manifest racial imbalance. Preferential selection of craft trainees at the Gramercy plant will end as soon as the percentage of black skilled craft workers in the Gramercy plant approximates the percentage of blacks in the local labor force.

We conclude, therefore, that the adoption of the Kaiser-USWA plan for the Gramercy plant falls within the area of discretion left by Title VII to the private sector voluntarily to adopt affirmative action plans designed to eliminate conspicuous racial imbalance in traditionally segregated job categories [443 U.S. at 208–09].

Several factors were critical to the Court's holding in *Weber*. First, there was a "manifest racial imbalance" in the job categories for which Kaiser had established the special training program. While the percentage of blacks in the area work force was approximately 39 percent, less than 2 percent of the craft jobs at Kaiser were filled by blacks. Second, as the Court noted in a footnote to its opinion, these crafts had been "traditionally segregated"; rampant discrimination in the past had contributed to the present imbalance at Kaiser. Third, the Court emphasized that the plan in *Weber* did not "unnecessarily trammel" the interests of white employees; it did not operate as a total bar to whites, and it was temporary, designed to bring minority representation up to that of the area's work force rather than to maintain racial balance permanently.

These factors cited by the Court left several questions open: How great a racial imbalance must there be before it will be considered "manifest"? What kind of showing must be made before a job category will be considered "traditionally segregated"? At what point will the effects of a plan on white workers be so great as to be considered "unnecessary trammeling"? These questions were raised in a subsequent challenge to a gender-conscious employment decision made under the authority of an affirmative action plan, this time by a public employer. To date, it is the only Supreme Court analysis of gender preferences in employment.

In *Johnson v. Transportation Agency, Santa Clara County*, 480 U.S. 616 (1987), Paul Johnson, who had applied for a promotion, alleged that the agency had promoted a less qualified woman, Diane Joyce, because of her gender, in violation of Title VII. In a 6-to-3 opinion, the Supreme Court, relying on its *Weber* precedent, held that neither the affirmative action plan nor Joyce's promotion violated Title VII.

As is the practice in many public agencies, the agency's promotion policies permitted the decision maker to select one of several individuals who were certified to be minimally qualified for the position in question—in this case, a road maintenance dispatcher. Both Joyce and Johnson, as well as several other men, had been rated "qualified," although Johnson's total score (based on experience, an interview, and other factors) was slightly higher than Joyce's.

The agency had developed an affirmative action plan that attempted to increase the number of women and racial minorities in jobs in which they were traditionally underrepresented. The agency had not submitted evidence of any prior discrimination on its part, but noted the statistical disparities between the proportion of potentially qualified women and their low representation in certain occupations.

The majority opinion, written by Justice Brennan, first addressed the burden-of-proof issue. It is up to the plaintiff, wrote Brennan, to establish that the affirmative action plan is invalid. In assessing the plan's validity, the Court applied the three tests from *Weber*. First, the plan had to address a "manifest imbalance" that reflected underrepresentation of women in traditionally segregated job categories. Statistical comparisons between the proportion of qualified women in the labor market and those in segregated job categories would demonstrate the imbalance. Regarding the employer's responsibility for that imbalance, the majority rejected the notion that the employer must demonstrate prior discrimination, a requirement that would be imposed if the case had been brought under the Equal Protection Clause of the Fourteenth Amendment:

> A manifest imbalance need not be such that it would support a prima facie case against the employer . . . since we do not regard as identical the constraints of Title VII and the Federal Constitution on voluntarily adopted affirmative action plans [480 U.S. at 632].

The majority's refusal to apply constitutional standards to voluntary affirmative action plans in *public* employment elicited a sharp response from Justice O'Connor, who had otherwise concurred in the judgment. O'Connor wrote:

> [T]he Court has chosen to follow an expansive and ill-defined approach to voluntary affirmative action by public employers despite the limitations imposed by the Constitution and by the provisions of Title VII. . . .
> In my view, the proper initial inquiry in evaluating the legality of an affirmative action plan by a public employer under Title VII is no different from that required by the Equal Protection Clause. In either case, consistent with the congressional intent to provide some measure of protection to the interests of the

employer's nonminority employees, the employer must have had a firm basis for believing that remedial action was required. An employer would have such a firm basis if it can point to a statistical disparity sufficient to support a prima facie claim under Title VII by the employee beneficiaries of the affirmative action plan of a pattern or practice claim of discrimination. . . . As I read *Weber*, . . . the Court also determined that Congress had balanced these two competing concerns [rooting out discrimination against all persons and eliminating the lasting effects of discrimination] by permitting affirmative action only as a remedial device to eliminate actual or apparent discrimination or the lingering effects of this discrimination [480 U.S. at 615–16].

Having determined that the affirmative action plan satisfied the first part of the *Weber* test, the majority then examined whether the plan "unnecessarily trammeled" the rights of male employees or created an absolute bar to their advancement. Finding that Johnson had no absolute entitlement to the promotion, and that he retained his position, salary, and seniority, the majority found that the plan met the second *Weber* test.

The majority then assessed whether the plan was a temporary measure, the third requirement of *Weber*. Although the plan was silent with regard to its duration, the Court found that the plan was intended to attain, rather than to maintain, a balanced work force, thus satisfying the third *Weber* test. Justice Brennan wrote that "substantial evidence shows that the Agency has sought to take a moderate, gradual approach to eliminating the imbalance in its work force, one which establishes realistic guidance for employment decisions, and which visits minimal intrusion on the legitimate expectations of other employees" (480 U.S. at 640).

Justice Scalia, joined by Justices Rehnquist and White, wrote a stinging dissent, arguing that Title VII outlawed all sex- or race-conscious employment decisions and that *Weber* should be overruled. He was particularly critical of the majority's refusal to apply equal protection requirements to voluntary affirmative action by a public employer. This refusal to impose constitutional requirements under Title VII to a public employer had this effect, according to Justice Scalia:

> The most significant proposition of law established by today's decision is that racial or sexual discrimination is permitted under Title VII when it is intended to overcome the effect not of the employer's own discrimination, but of societal attitudes that have limited the entry of certain races, or of a particular sex, into certain jobs [480 U.S. at 664].

He also criticized the *Weber* opinion for creating "a judicially crafted code of conduct, the contours of which are determined by no discernible standard" [480 U.S. at 670–71]. He warned that the outcome of *Johnson* would require employers to make race- or sex-conscious decisions whenever an imbalance in the work force existed.

Both the *Weber* and the *Johnson* cases involved voluntary affirmative action plans that were challenged under Title VII. A year before *Johnson*, the Supreme Court had addressed the legality, under Title VII, of race-conscious hiring and promotion as part of court-ordered (as opposed to voluntary) remedies after intentional discrimination had been proved. One issue in both cases centered on whether individuals who had not been actual victims of discrimination could benefit from race-conscious remedies applied to hiring and promotion. In both cases the Supreme

Court upheld those remedies in situations where lower courts had found the discrimination to be egregious. In *Local 93, International Association of Firefighters v. City of Cleveland,* 478 U.S. 501 (1986), a majority of six justices approved a consent decree that required race-conscious promotions for Cleveland firefighters as a means of remedying prior discrimination against blacks and Hispanics. In response to the assertion by the city that Title VII prohibited race-conscious remedies for individuals who had not themselves suffered discrimination, Justice Brennan, writing for the majority, said:

> It is equally clear that the voluntary action available to employers and unions seeking to eradicate race discrimination may include reasonable race-conscious relief that benefits individuals who were not actual victims of discrimination [478 U.S. at 516].

A majority of six justices also approved race-conscious selection and promotion requirements in *Local 28 of the Sheet Metal Workers' International Assn. v. EEOC,* 478 U.S. 421 (1986), as a remedy for longstanding and egregious race discrimination in access to union apprenticeship programs and admission to the union. For a review and analysis of the affirmative action cases decided in 1986, see M. Clague, "The Affirmative Action Showdown of 1986: Implications for Higher Education," 14 *J. Coll. & Univ. Law* 171 (1987).

The following year, the Supreme Court again addressed the issue of involuntary remedies for persistent race discrimination, but this time under the equal protection standard rather than Title VII. In *United States v. Paradise,* 480 U.S. 149 (1987), federal courts had ordered that 50 percent of the promotions to corporal within the Alabama State Troopers be awarded to qualified black candidates. Because the lower courts had found systematic exclusion of blacks for over four decades by the state police department, and another decade of resistance to following court orders to increase the proportion of black troopers, the Supreme Court, in a 5-to-4 decision, found ample justification to uphold the one-black-for-one-white promotion requirement imposed by the lower federal courts.

The United States, acting as plaintiff in this case, argued that the remedy imposed by the court violated the Equal Protection Clause. Justice Brennan, writing for the majority, noted that the Court had yet to agree on the appropriate standard of review for affirmative action cases brought under the Equal Protection Clause. He refused to do so in *Paradise* because "we conclude that the relief ordered survives even strict scrutiny analysis: it is 'narrowly tailored' to serve a 'compelling [governmental] purpose' " [480 U.S. at 167]. In reaching this conclusion, the majority determined that "the pervasive, systematic, and obstinate discriminatory conduct of the Department created a profound need and firm justification for the race-conscious relief ordered by the District Court" [480 U.S. at 167]. Unfortunately, the court left for another day the delineation of equal protection guidelines for remedial affirmative action plans.

The Supreme Court's opinions in *Weber, Sheet Metal Workers, Cleveland Firefighters, Johnson,* and *Paradise* involved promotions or other advancement opportunities, and did not result in job loss for majority individuals. When, however, an affirmative action plan was used to justify racial preferences in layoffs, the response of the Supreme Court was very different. In *Firefighters v. Stotts,* 467 U.S. 561 (1984), the Court invalidated a remedial consent decree that approved race-conscious layoff decisions in order to preserve the jobs of more recently hired minorities under the city's affirmative action plan.

The Court addressed the issue of voluntary racial preferences in reductions-in-force in a case brought under the Equal Protection Clause. In *Wygant v. Jackson Board of Education*, 476 U.S. 267 (1986), the school board and the teachers' union responded to a pending race discrimination claim by black teachers and applicants for teaching positions by specifying race-conscious layoff practices in a collective bargaining agreement. The agreement specified that, if a layoff occurred, those teachers with the most seniority would be retained, except that at no time would there be a greater percentage of minority personnel laid off than the percentage of minority personnel employed at the time of the layoff. A layoff occurred, and the board, following the contractual provision, laid off some white teachers with more seniority than minority teachers who were retained in order to meet the proportionality requirement. The more senior white teachers challenged the constitutionality of the contractual provision. Both the federal district court and the U.S. Court of Appeals for the Sixth Circuit upheld the provision as permissible action taken to remedy prior societal discrimination and to provide role models for minority children. In a 5-to-4 decision whose plurality opinion was written by Justice Powell, the Court reversed the lower courts, concluding that the race-conscious layoff provision violated the Equal Protection Clause. Four justices agreed that the contractual provision should be subjected to the "strict scrutiny" test for racial classifications used in other equal protection challenges: a compelling governmental interest, and means chosen by the state that are " 'narrowly tailored to the achievement of that goal' " (476 U.S. at 274, quoting *Fullilove v. Klutznick*, 448 U.S. 448, 480). The fifth, Justice White, who concurred in the judgment, did not address the strict scrutiny issue (476 U.S. at 294–95).

Rejecting the school board's argument that remedying societal discrimination provided a sufficient justification for the race-conscious layoffs, the plurality opinion stated:

> This Court never has held that societal discrimination alone is sufficient to justify a racial classification. Rather, the Court has insisted upon some showing of prior discrimination by the governmental unit involved before allowing limited use of racial classifications in order to remedy such discrimination [476 U.S. at 274].

The plurality then discussed the Court's ruling in *Hazelwood School District v. United States*, 433 U.S. 299 (1977), which established the method to be used to demonstrate prior discrimination by comparing qualified minorities in the labor market with their representation in the employer's work force. The correct comparison was of teachers to qualified blacks in the labor market, not of minority teachers to minority children. The plurality continued:

> Unlike the analysis in *Hazelwood*, the role model theory employed by the District Court has no logical stopping point. The role model theory allows the Board to engage in discriminatory hiring and layoff practices long past the point required by any legitimate remedial purpose. . . .
>
> Moreover, because the role model theory does not necessarily bear a rela-

tionship to the harm caused by prior discriminatory hiring practices, it actually could be used to escape the obligation to remedy such practices by justifying the small percentage of black teachers by reference to the small percentage of black students [476 U.S. at 275–76].

Furthermore, said the plurality, there had been no finding of prior discrimination by the school board. Having rejected the "societal discrimination" and "role model" arguments and finding no history of discrimination, the plurality concluded that the school board had not made the showing of a compelling interest required by the strict scrutiny test.

Justice O'Connor's concurring opinion considered whether specific findings of prior discrimination by a public employer were necessary at the time an affirmative action plan was implemented. She concluded that requiring such a finding would be a powerful disincentive for a public employer to initiate a voluntary affirmative action plan, and stated that "a contemporaneous or antecedent finding of past discrimination by a court or other competent body is not a constitutional prerequisite to a public employer's voluntary agreement to an affirmative action plan" [476 U.S. at 289]. But the employer should "act on the basis of information which gives [the public employer] a sufficient basis for concluding that remedial action is necessary" [476 U.S. at 291], so that findings by a court or an enforcement agency would be unnecessary. As long as the public employer had a "firm basis for believing that remedial action is required" [476 U.S. at 286], presumably through evidence demonstrating statistical disparity between the proportion of minorities in the qualified labor market and those in the work force, a state's interest in affirmative action could be found to be "compelling." In a comment with potential significance for proponents of affirmative action as a tool to promote racial diversity, O'Connor noted, "Although its precise contours are uncertain, a state interest in the promotion of racial diversity has been found sufficiently 'compelling,' at least in the context of higher education, to support the use of racial considerations in furthering that interest" [476 U.S. at 286; citing *Bakke,* discussed in Section 4.2.5].

Justice Marshall, in a dissent joined by Justices Brennan and Blackmun, characterized the case quite differently from the plurality:

> The sole question posed by this case is whether the Constitution prohibits a union and a local school board from developing a collective-bargaining agreement that apportions layoffs between two racially determined groups as a means of preserving the effects of an affirmative hiring policy, the constitutionality of which is unchallenged [476 U.S. at 300].

Justice Marshall found the school board's purpose in preserving minority representation of teachers compelling under the factual record presented to the court. He concluded that the contractual provision was narrowly tailored because it neither burdened nor benefited one race but, instead, substituted a criterion other than absolute seniority for layoff decisions.

The collective implication of these complex decisions and the fragmentation of the justices regarding the lawfulness of race- or gender-conscious employment decisions, along with their disagreement about the standard for reviewing such decisions by public employers, leave college administrators with little certainty regarding voluntary affirmative action plans. It appears that institutions that can document "manifest" underrepresentation of women or minority faculty or staff in certain positions, and that can show a substantial gap between the proportion of qualified women and minorities in the relevant labor market and their representation in the institution's faculty work force, may be able to act in conformance with a carefully developed affirmative action plan. Given the very small numbers of minorities with doctoral degrees,[42] however, establishing this "gap" may be extremely difficult, if not impossible. Making this showing for women in some disciplines will be more successful as the proportion of women earning doctorates in traditionally male fields increases.

Public colleges and universities located in states subject to *Adams* agreements (see Sections 7.5.2 and 7.5.8) will very likely have an easier time meeting the standards of the Equal Protection Clause for voluntary affirmative action plans as articulated by Justice O'Connor in *Wygant* and *Johnson*. Furthermore, for public institutions operating under the dictates of a judicially supervised consent decree regarding remedies for prior discrimination, the Civil Rights Act of 1991 has removed the threat of challenges to remedial employment decisions made under the aegis of the consent decree. In *Martin v. Wilks*, 490 U.S. 755 (1989), the Supreme Court had ruled that any nonparty to the litigation culminating in a consent decree could later challenge both the decree and employment decisions made in conformance with that decree. Congress overturned the result in *Martin v. Wilks* by adding a new subsection to Section 703 of Title VII of the Civil Rights Act of 1964 (42 U.S.C. § 2000e-2). The law now provides that a litigated or consent judgment may not be challenged by a person who had actual notice of the proposed judgment or order prior to its entry and an opportunity to object, or by a person whose interests were adequately represented by another person who had challenged the judgment or order.

For public institutions in states where a history of de jure segregation of public higher education has not been documented or addressed, however, establishing prior discrimination in the employment of faculty may be more difficult. Given the outcome in *Wygant* and related cases, the effect of an affirmative action plan on existing and prospective majority faculty members at both public and private colleges should be carefully analyzed to ensure that racial or gender preferences are not implemented in a way that would "unnecessarily trammel" their interests (under Title VII) or fail the strict scrutiny test (under the Constitution). Two of the factors relied on in *Weber*—that the plan did not require the discharge of any white workers and that the plan was temporary—appear to be easily transferable to and easily met in the postsecondary hiring context. But the third factor—that the plan did not "create an absolute bar to the advancement of white employees"—bears careful watching in postsecondary education. The special training programs at issue in *Weber* benefited

---

[42]Nationally, excluding those teaching at historically black colleges, approximately 2 percent of the faculty are black (P. Applebome, "Goal Unmet, Duke Reveals Perils in Effort to Increase Black Faculty," *New York Times*, Sept. 19, 1993, at 34). According to the National Research Council, of all doctoral degrees awarded in 1992, 6.2 percent were awarded to blacks, 3.2 to Hispanics, 0.5 to Native Americans, 6.2 to Asians, and 84.5 to whites. Patterns differ, however, by discipline. Of the doctorates in education, 8.3 percent were awarded to blacks in 1992, while 1 percent of the doctorates in physical sciences were awarded to blacks that year. Asians were awarded 17.8 percent of the doctorates in engineering in 1992, but 2.4 percent of the doctorates in education (*Summary Report 1992* (National Research Council, 1993)).

both black and white employees. Thirteen workers were selected, seven black and six white. At postsecondary institutions, however, faculty vacancies or special opportunities such as department chairmanships generally occur one at a time and on an irregular basis. A decision that a particular opening will be filled by a minority may, in effect, serve as a complete bar to whites, especially in a small department where there is little turnover and where the date of the next opening cannot be predicted. Institutions that use race or gender as a "plus" factor, rather than targeting specific positions for a particular race or gender, may be able to satisfy the *Weber* test more successfully, although public colleges may have a more difficult time satisfying the requirements of the Equal Protection Clause.

For public institutions, being able to demonstrate a history of race or sex discrimination in employment, rather than simply a statistical disparity between minority representation in the work force and the labor market, is even more significant in light of another decision of the U.S. Supreme Court regarding affirmative action, although not in employment. In *City of Richmond v. J. A. Croson Co.*, 488 U.S. 469 (1989), an again sharply divided court ruled 6-to-3 that a set-aside program of public construction contract funds for minority subcontractors violated the Constitution's Equal Protection Clause. Applying the strict scrutiny test, a plurality of justices (plus Justice Scalia, using different reasoning) ruled that the city's requirement that prime contractors awarded city construction contracts must subcontract at least 30 percent of the amount of each contract to minority-owned businesses was not justified by a compelling governmental interest, and that the 30 percent set-aside program was not narrowly tailored to accomplish a remedial purpose.

Croson, a plumbing and heating contractor, had submitted the only bid on a public construction project. The city initially accepted his bid, but when Croson was unable to secure an acceptable bid from minority subcontractors on supplies for the project, the city denied him a waiver of the minority subcontracting requirement and withdrew its acceptance of the bid. Croson challenged the constitutionality of the city's set-aside plan in federal court.

The district and appellate courts upheld the plan in all respects, citing an earlier Supreme Court decision in *Fullilove v. Klutznick*, 448 U.S. 448 (1980),[43] and *University of California Regents v. Bakke*, 438 U.S. 265 (1978) (see Section 4.2.5). The Supreme Court, however, vacated the appellate court opinion and remanded the case for reconsideration in light of its *Wygant* opinion (*City of Richmond v. J. A. Croson Co.*, 478 U.S. 1016 (1986)). On remand, the U.S. Court of Appeals for the Fourth Circuit struck down the set-aside program, stating that it violated both prongs of the strict scrutiny test (822 F.2d 1355 (4th Cir. 1987)).

The city had cited several factors in support of its determination that the set-

[43]*Fullilove v. Klutznick* upheld a remedial program Congress had fashioned to eliminate traditional barriers to minority participation in public contracting opportunities. The program was implemented in the Minority Business Enterprise (MBE) provision of the Public Works Employment Act of 1977, which allocates federal funds to state and local governments for public works projects. This provision requires that state and local grantees use at least 10 percent of the funds they receive under the Act to procure services from minority-owned business. Although six opinions were written, and six justices voted to uphold the MBE provision, no opinion gathered a majority vote. For this reason, and because the opinions emphasize the unique power and competence of Congress to combat discrimination, the case's significance for postsecondary education is limited.

aside program was necessary. It noted the small number of minority businesses in the local contracting industry, these businesses' lack of working capital, their inability to meet bonding requirements, their unfamiliarity with bidding procedures, and the disadvantage of an inadequate record of successful bidding on public projects. The Court recognized the historical fact of race discrimination, but it characterized as "sheer speculation" the city's claim that some amount of prior discrimination justified the imposition of "a rigid racial quota" (488 U.S. at 499).

Justice O'Connor, writing for the Court, asserted that the city's generalized findings of prior race discrimination in the award of public construction contracts, unsupported by statistical or other evidence of actual discrimination, was as inadequate as the "role model" theory offered by the defendant in *Wygant*. She wrote:

> [A] generalized assertion that there has been past discrimination in an entire industry provides no guidance for a legislative body to determine the precise scope of the injury it seeks to remedy. . . .
> While there is no doubt that the sorry history of both private and public discrimination in this country has contributed to a lack of opportunities for black entrepreneurs, this observation, standing alone, cannot justify a rigid racial quota in the awarding of public contracts in Richmond, Virginia [488 U.S. at 498–99].

Criticizing the city for relying on statistical disparities between the number of city contracts awarded to minority firms and the city's minority population, O'Connor again noted that the proper standard for determining underrepresentation was contained in *Hazelwood School District v. United States*, 433 U.S. 299 (1977). Distinguishing *Fullilove*, O'Connor stated that Richmond could not simply cite congressional findings of nationwide discrimination in the construction industry and apply them to its own situation:

> While the States and their subdivisions may take remedial action when they possess evidence that their own spending practices are exacerbating a pattern of prior discrimination, they must identify that discrimination, public or private, with some specificity before they may use race-conscious relief [488 U.S. at 504].

Finding only generalizations about prior discrimination against blacks, and no evidence at all of discrimination against the other minority groups included in the set-aside program ("Spanish-speaking, Orientals, Indians, Eskimos, or Aleuts"), O'Connor concluded that the city's interest was not compelling.

O'Connor also concluded that the set-aside plan was not narrowly tailored to remedy prior discrimination, the second element of the strict scrutiny test. First, she noted that no consideration had been given to race-neutral means of increasing minority participation in city construction projects. Second, there was no justification for selection of 30 percent as the appropriate quota, beyond its correspondence to the proportion of minorities in Richmond's population.

Three justices joined another portion of O'Connor's opinion, which discussed race-neutral mechanisms for increasing the proportion of minority subcontractors. One portion of her opinion, however, which discusses circumstances in which state and local governments might lawfully use race-conscious remedies, was joined by only two justices and was attacked by Justice Scalia. Justice Stevens, although he concurred in the opinion and agreed with Justice O'Connor, argued that the limitations placed on the actions of legislative bodies should not necessarily be applied to courts when they are asked to fashion a remedy for prior discrimination. Justices Marshall, Brennan, and Blackmun dissented, asserting that Richmond's plan was indistinguishable from the plan upheld in *Fullilove* and thus should have been permitted.

Although *Croson* does not address employment, public institutions will clearly be required to comply with the standards the opinion establishes for review under the Equal Protection Clause. Specific evidence of prior discrimination, either by the institution or by others, whose effects have persisted, and additional evidence of attempts to remedy the prior discrimination by neutral practices will apparently be required before an institution's race- or gender-conscious employment actions will survive the strict scrutiny test.

Principles from the Supreme Court's affirmative action cases have been applied to postsecondary education, and in particular to public postsecondary institutions. In *Valentine v. Smith*, 654 F.2d 503 (8th Cir. 1981), Valentine, a disappointed white job applicant, challenged an affirmative action plan in place at Arkansas State University (ASU). The plaintiff had taught on ASU's business education faculty from 1967 until she resigned in 1974. In 1976 Valentine's replacement, the only black member of the department, resigned. Valentine then applied for her former position and was rated first on a list of applicants that the head of the division submitted to the university's vice president for instruction. Following a meeting of the division head, the vice president, and ASU's affirmative action officer, Valentine's name was deleted from the list, and a new list, containing only the names of two black applicants, was submitted. ASU hired one of these applicants.

At the time Valentine sought to be rehired, ASU had an affirmative action program for faculty hiring that was implemented as part of an effort to desegregate the Arkansas state college and university system. In 1973 a federal court, in *Adams v. Richardson*, 356 F. Supp. 92 (D.D.C. 1973) (discussed in Section 7.5.8), had ordered the Department of Health, Education and Welfare (HEW) to bring Arkansas and other southern states into compliance with Title VI of the Civil Rights Act of 1964. ASU submitted an affirmative action hiring program to HEW in 1975; it was this program, implemented to remedy the past effects of racial discrimination, that ASU relied on when it deleted Valentine from the applicant list.

Valentine charged that the ASU program was unconstitutional as applied to her because it constituted reverse discrimination, violating the Constitution's Equal Protection Clause. In rejecting Valentine's challenge, the appellate court first determined that findings of past discrimination had been made by an appropriate decision-making body:

> The Supreme Court has determined that the Congress, federal courts, and, in some instances, the states have the competency to make such findings of past discrimination as are sufficient to justify a race-conscious remedy. The record reflects that HEW and the District Court for the District of Columbia [in *Adams v. Richardson*, above] found that Arkansas's colleges and universities did not comply with Title VI. Because of these findings and the action taken by OCR [HEW's Office for Civil Rights], ASU developed its affirmative action program. HEW and the district court are competent to make findings of past discrimina-

tion sufficient to justify the remedial purpose of an affirmative action program.
. . . Findings of previous statutory violations of Title VI by a district court and
OCR justify the use of some type of race-conscious remedy by a state to serve its
constitutionally permissible objective of remedying past discrimination [654 F.2d
at 507–09].

The court next determined that racial preferences may be used to remedy the
effects of past employment discrimination, and it specified the criteria that the institution's plan must meet:

> The test for determining whether Arkansas has adopted constitutionally
> permissible means is whether the affirmative action plan is "substantially re-
> lated" to the objective of remedying prior discrimination. A race-conscious affir-
> mative action program is substantially related to remedying past discrimination
> if (1) its implementation results or is designed to result in the hiring of a sufficient
> number of minority applicants so that the racial balance of the employer's work
> force approximates roughly, but does not unreasonably exceed, the balance that
> would have been achieved absent the past discrimination; (2) the plan endures
> only so long as is reasonably necessary to achieve its legitimate goals; (3) the plan
> does not result in hiring unqualified applicants; and (4) the plan does not com-
> pletely bar whites from all vacancies or otherwise unnecessarily or invidiously
> trammel their interests [654 F.2d at 509–10].

Finally, the court determined that the ASU affirmative action program was itself
a constitutionally permissible use of racial preferences to remedy past discrimination:

> ASU's affirmative action plan set a goal of raising the percentage of blacks
> on the faculty to a total of 5 percent by 1979. To reach this goal, ASU planned
> that 25 percent of the faculty hired between 1976 and 1979 would be black. These
> goals do not exceed reasonable efforts to remedy ASU's past discrimination. In
> 1976, when Valentine was not hired for the position, ASU had 10 black faculty
> members among a total faculty of 296 (3.4 percent of faculty was black). Upon
> [the] retirement [of Valentine's replacement], the business college had no black
> faculty members. If Valentine had been rehired, the business college would have
> continued to have no black faculty members at least until the next vacancy oc-
> curred. ASU attracts students from an area which has a population which is
> approximately 23.6 percent black.[44] We find that the plaintiff has failed to show
> that ASU's goals exceed those which would be substantially related to ASU's
> legitimate purpose.
> ASU's 25 percent hiring goal is neither permanent nor even long lasting.
> Instead, ASU's plan extends over a four-year period and contemplates the achieve-
> ment of a modest increase in black faculty members. Nothing about the duration
> of the plan suggests any purpose other than a remedial one, and Valentine has
> not shown that the period of the plan exceeds the time substantially necessary for
> achieving the plan's remedial purpose. . . .
> ASU's affirmative action plan does not require firing any employees to
> make room for minority applicants. Nor does the plan deprive innocent persons
> of employment rights or benefits they already enjoyed. The plan contemplates

---

[44](Author's note.) Under *Hazelwood,* discussed earlier in this section, this comparison
is not the appropriate one.

that only 25 percent of new faculty over a four-year period will be black; we cannot say that this plan completely bars whites from faculty positions.

    In summary, because we find ASU's affirmative action goals substantially related to the legitimate goal of ending and remedying previous racial discrimination, because the plan does not require the hiring of unqualified persons, because it is temporary, and because it does not completely bar whites or otherwise invidiously trammel their interests, we conclude that ASU's plan, on its face, is a constitutionally permissible solution to a difficult problem (*United States v. City of Miami*, 614 F.2d at 1338-40; *Detroit Police Officers Ass'n v. Young*, 608 F.2d at 696) [654 F.2d at 510-11].

    Although *Valentine*, unlike *Weber*, is an equal protection case, the court's equal protection analysis of affirmative action plans is similar to the *Weber* and *Johnson* Title VII analyses, but does not apply the strict scrutiny test suggested in *Croson*. The court's opinion focuses, for example, on the existence of racial imbalance in the relevant job categories, on the temporary character of the affirmative action plan, and on the absence of "unnecessary trammeling" on white employees' interests—the same factors emphasized in *Weber*. *Valentine* states that specific findings of discrimination must be made by a "competent" or "qualified" governmental authority before the affirmative action plan is implemented. In *Valentine* the findings substantiated that the Arkansas state college system had itself discriminated in the past. But the court's reliance on *Fullilove* proved to have been misplaced, since the findings in that case were superseded by the Supreme Court's subsequent rulings in *Wygant* and *Croson*—namely, that findings of general societal discrimination in the relevant employment category are insufficient and that the strict scrutiny standard will be applied.

    Once findings of historical discrimination by the institution are made, a public college or university apparently has much the same authority as a private institution to implement an affirmative action plan. There is still some question whether the public institution can use explicit racial or sexual quotas. *Weber* allows private employers to use explicit quotas. But of the cases involving public employers, *Johnson* and *Valentine* concerned goals rather than quotas, and the majority of justices in *Bakke* and *Croson* prohibited the use of explicit quotas. Subsequent cases in which the affirmative action plans of public institutions were challenged affirmed the right of such institutions to use goals (but not quotas).

    In *Palmer v. District Board of Trustees of St. Petersburg Junior College*, 748 F.2d 595 (11th Cir. 1984), a federal appellate court upheld a race-conscious hiring based on goals set in the college's affirmative action plan. Both the U.S. Department of Health, Education and Welfare and a federal district court had found that the state of Florida had maintained a racially segregated system of higher education (in *Adams v. Richardson*, see above). The state of Florida then developed a statewide desegregation plan for its higher education system, and the defendant college was subject to the plan.

    Clarence Palmer, a white male, applied for a teaching position at the college. When no qualified black applicants could be found, Palmer was appointed for a one-year temporary position. A new search was conducted the following year, and a black applicant was selected. Palmer's one-year position ended, and he sued for age and race discrimination.

Because Palmer stipulated that the affirmative action plan was valid, the court did not need to address its lawfulness. Applying the *Weber* test, it held that Palmer was not discharged (as he had claimed), but was simply not reappointed, and thus his interests were not trammeled. Citing *Sester v. Novack Investment Co.*, 657 F.2d 962 (8th Cir. 1981), the court noted that because the college had demonstrated that its treatment of Palmer was a direct consequence of following its affirmative action plan, the only way Palmer could prevail was either to show that the plan's purpose was not remedial or that the plan as adopted exceeded its remedial purpose. Since Palmer, in agreeing that the plan was lawful, could not make either of these showings, the appellate court affirmed the trial court's grant of summary judgment to the college.

A later challenge to a gender-conscious hiring decision used a somewhat different analysis but reached the same conclusion. In *Enright v. California State University*, 57 Fair Empl. Prac. Cases 56 (E.D. Cal. 1989), brought under Title VII, a trial judge, using the *Weber* test and relying on the Supreme Court's *Johnson* case, granted summary judgment to the university. The judge noted that the statistical disparity between women with Ph.D. degrees in sociology and the proportion of women in the department constituted the required "manifest imbalance," and ruled that the difference between the proportion of women in the population (50 percent) and the proportion of women with Ph.D.s in sociology (34 percent) rendered the sociology profession a traditionally segregated field. Furthermore, the judge ruled, the university's affirmative action plan employed goals, not quotas; the plaintiff, a male who was not hired, was not displaced and had no entitlement to the job; and the plan was a temporary one.

An unusual lawsuit against the City University of New York demonstrates that administrators should consider carefully the implications of including certain ethnic groups (beyond the traditional categories of black, Asian, Hispanic, and Native American) in affirmative action plans. In *Scelsa v. City University of New York*, 806 F. Supp. 1126 (S.D.N.Y. 1992), an Italian-American professor challenged a decision by CUNY to transfer the Calendra Italian American Institute from Manhattan to Staten Island and to reassign its director of nearly twenty years to other administrative responsibilities. Scelsa, the director, sued the university under Title VI of the Civil Rights Act (see Section 7.5.2 of this volume), as well as under Title VII (Section 3.3.2.1, this volume) and equal protection theories. He asserted that the university's affirmative action plan, developed nearly two decades earlier, had designated Italian-Americans an underrepresented group among its faculty and staff, but the university had done little to correct that underrepresentation. The plaintiffs sought a preliminary injunction to halt the transfer of the institute and its director, which the judge granted, citing evidence of underrepresentation of Italian-Americans among CUNY's faculty and staff and the evident failure of the university to follow its voluntarily adopted affirmative action plan.

Because of the split among the justices regarding whether Title VII and the Fourteenth Amendment permit affirmative action, and the lack of clarity in the post-*Weber* affirmative action opinions, designing a "safe harbor" for affirmative action employment decisions is virtually impossible. *Wygant* and *Croson* sharply limit the ability of public institutions to use race- or gender-conscious hiring or promotion policies to redress historical imbalance unless clear evidence of discrimination, either by the institution itself or from some other related source (such as a state agency), is documented. Private institutions have more leeway under *Weber* and *Johnson*, as long as they follow the tests of *Weber* and as long as they do not use quotas. For a critique of Supreme Court affirmative action doctrine, see M. Daly, "Some Runs, Some Hits, Some Errors—Keeping Score in the Affirmative Action Ballpark from *Weber* to *Johnson*," 30 *Boston Coll. L. Rev.* 1 (1988). See also T. A. Aleinikoff, "A Case for Race-Consciousness," 1991 *Columbia L. Rev.* 1060 (1991), and M. Rosenfeld, "Decoding *Richmond:* Affirmative Action and the Elusive Meaning of Constitutional Equality," 87 *Mich L. Rev.* 1729 (1989).

Furthermore, affirmative action in higher education employment, as in non-academic organizations, has been under attack by both black and white scholars. *See,* for example, S. Carter, *Reflections of an Affirmative Action Baby* (Basic Books, 1991), and S. Steele, *The Content of Our Character* (HarperCollins, 1990). In addition, the change in composition of the U.S. Supreme Court, and its shift during the 1980s and early 1990s to a conservative majority, call into question the future of affirmative action. Administrators and counsel will need to continue their careful attention to identifying underrepresentation and its underlying reasons, to crafting affirmative action plans that meet the requirements of *Weber* and *Johnson*, and to following the (albeit limited) guidance of *Wygant* and *Croson*.

Sec. 3.5. Standards and Criteria for Faculty Personnel Decisions

3.5.1. General principles. Postsecondary institutions commonly have written and published standards or criteria to guide decisions regarding faculty appointments, contract renewals, promotions, and the granting and termination of tenure. Since they will often constitute part of the contract between the institution and the faculty member (see Section 3.1) and thus bind the institution, such evaluative standards and criteria should receive the careful attention of administrators and faculty members alike. If particular standards are not intended to be legally binding or are not intended to apply to certain kinds of personnel decisions, those limitations should be made clear in the standards themselves.

While courts will enforce standards or criteria found to be part of the faculty contract, the law accords postsecondary institutions wide discretion in determining the content and specificity of those standards and criteria. Courts are less likely to become involved in disputes concerning the substance of standards and criteria than in disputes over procedures for applying standards and criteria. (Courts draw the same distinction in cases concerning students; see the discussion in Sections 4.6 through 4.8.) In rejecting the claims of a community college faculty member, for example, the court in *Brouillette v. Board of Directors of Merged Area IX*, 519 F.2d 126 (8th Cir. 1975), quoted an earlier case to note that "such matters as the competence of teachers and the standards of its measurement are not, without more, matters of constitutional dimensions. They are peculiarly appropriate to state and local administration." And in *Riggin v. Board of Trustees of Ball State University*, 489 N.E.2d 616 (Ind. Ct. App. 1986), the court indicated that it "must give deference to [the board of trustees'] expertise and that it "may not reweigh the evidence or determine the credibility of witnesses," since "peer groups make the judgment on the performance of a faculty member." And in *Dorsett v. Board of Trustees for State Colleges and Universities*, 940 F.2d 121, 123 (5th Cir. 1991) (quoting earlier cases), the court warned that "Of all fields that the federal courts 'should hesitate to invade and take over, education and faculty appointments at the university level are probably the least suited for federal court supervision.' "

Despite this generally deferential judicial attitude, there are several bases on which an institution's standards and criteria may be legally scrutinized. For both public and private institutions, question regarding consistency with AAUP policies may be raised in AAUP investigations (this volume, Section 8.5) or in court (Section 3.1.1). When standards or criteria are part of the faculty contract, both public and private institutions' disputes over interpretation may wind up in court or in the institution's internal grievance process. Cases on attaining tenure and on dismissal from tenured positions for "just cause" are prominent examples. For public institutions standards or criteria may also be embodied in state statutes or administrative regulations that are subject to interpretation by courts, state administrative agencies (such as boards of regents or civil service commissions), or decision makers within the institution's internal grievance process. The tenure denial and termination cases are again excellent examples.[45] And under the various federal nondiscrimination statutes discussed in Section 3.3, courts or federal administrative agencies may scrutinize the standards and criteria of public and private institutions for their potential discriminatory applications (see, for example, *Bennun v. Rutgers, The State University of New Jersey*, 941 F.2d 154 (3d Cir. 1991)); these standards and criteria also may be examined in the course of an internal grievance process when one is required by federal regulations or otherwise provided by the institution.

In public institutions standards and criteria may also be subjected to constitutional scrutiny under the First and Fourteenth Amendments. Under the First Amendment, a standard or criterion can be challenged as "overbroad" if it is so broadly worded that it can be used to penalize faculty members for having exercised constitutionally protected rights of free expression. Under the Fourteenth Amendment, a standard or criterion can be challenged as "vague" if it is so unclear that institutional personnel cannot understand its meaning in concrete circumstances. (The overbreadth and vagueness doctrines are discussed further in Sections 4.5.2, 4.6.1, and 4.9.2.) The leading U.S. Supreme Court case on overbreadth and vagueness in public employment standards is *Arnett v. Kennedy*, 416 U.S. 134 (1974). A federal civil servant had been dismissed under a statute authorizing dismissal "for such cause as will promote the efficiency of the service." A majority of the Court held that this standard, as applied in the federal service, was neither overboard nor vague.

While the result in *Arnett* suggests that the overbreadth and vagueness doctrines do not substantially restrict the standard-setting process, it does not necessarily mean that public postsecondary institutions can use the same "cause" standard approved in *Arnett*. Employment standards should be adapted to the characteristics and functions of the group to which the standards apply. A standard acceptable for a large heterogeneous group such as the federal civil service may not be acceptable for a smaller, more homogeneous group such as a college faculty. (See, for example, *Bence v. Breier*, 501 F.2d 1185 (7th Cir. 1974), which held that the discharge standard of a local police force must be more stringently scrutinized for overbreadth and vagueness than was the federal discharge standard in *Arnett*.) Courts may thus be somewhat

---

[45]The cases and authorities for both statutes and contract clauses are collected in Annot., "Construction and Effect of Tenure Provisions of Contract or Statute Governing Employment of College or University Faculty Member," 66 A.L.R.3d 1018 (1975 and periodic supp.).

stricter with a postsecondary institution's standards than with the federal government's—particularly when the standards are applied to what is arguably expressive activity, in which case the overbreadth and vagueness doctrines would combine with academic freedom principles (see Section 3.7) to create important limits on institutional discretion in devising employment standards.

3.5.2. Terminations of tenure for cause. Perhaps the most sensitive issues concerning standards arise in situations where institutions attempt to dismiss a tenured faculty member "for cause" (see T. Lovain, "Grounds for Dismissing Tenured Postsecondary Faculty for Cause," 10 *J. Coll. & Univ. Law* 419 (1983-84)). Such dismissals should be distinguished from dismissals due to financial exigency or program discontinuance, discussed in Section 3.8. For-cause dismissals—being more personal, potentially more subjective, and more debilitating to the individual concerned—may be even more troublesome and agonizing for administrators than dismissals for reasons of financial exigency or program discontinuance. Similarly, they may give rise to even more complex legal issues concerning adequate procedures for effecting dismissal (see Section 3.6); the adequacy of standards for defining and determining "cause"; and the types and amount of evidence needed to sustain a termination decision under a particular standard of cause.

The American Association of University Professors' 1976 "Recommended Institutional Regulations on Academic Freedom and Tenure" (in *AAUP Policy Documents and Reports* (AAUP, 1990), 21-30) acknowledges "adequate cause" as an appropriate standard for dismissal of tenured faculty. These guidelines caution, however, that "adequate cause for a dismissal will be related, directly and substantially, to the fitness of faculty members in their professional capacities as teachers or researchers." Since the guidelines do not further define the concept, institutions are left to devise cause standards on their own or, occasionally for public institutions, to find standards in state statutes or agency regulations.

For-cause dismissals may raise numerous questions about contract interpretation. In *McConnell v. Howard University*, 818 F.2d 58 (D.C. Cir. 1987), for example, a mathematics professor had been verbally abused during class by a student and refused to resume teaching his course until "the proper teaching atmosphere was restored" (818 F.2d at 61). The university did not take any disciplinary action against the student, did not take other initiatives to resolve the situation, and rejected a grievance committee's recommendation in favor of the professor. It then dismissed the professor for "neglect of professional responsibilities"—an enumerated "cause" stated in the faculty handbook. The professor sued the institution for breach of contract. Construing the pertinent contract provisions in light of custom and usage (see Section 1.3.2.3), the court held that the institution, in a for-cause dismissal, must consider not only the literal meaning of the term "cause" but also all surrounding and mitigating circumstances; in addition, the institution must evaluate the professor's actions "according to the standards of the profession." Since the institution had not done so, the court remanded the case to the district court for further proceedings.

Courts also might question the clarity or specificity of an institution's dismissal standards. In *Garrett v. Matthews*, 625 F.2d 658 (5th Cir. 1980), the University of Alabama had dismissed the plaintiff, a tenured professor, for "insubordination and dereliction of duty." The charges had been brought pursuant to a faculty handbook provision permitting dismissal for "adequate cause" as found after a hearing. The plaintiff argued that the handbook's adequate-cause standard was so vague that it violated constitutional due process. Although due process precedents suggest that this argument is one to be taken seriously,[46] the court rejected it in one terse sentence that contains no analysis and relies on a prior opinion in *Bowling v. Scott*, 587 F.2d 229 (5th Cir. 1979) (this volume, Section 3.6.2.3), which does not even address the argument. Thus, although *Garrett* is authority for the constitutionality of a bare adequate-cause standard, it is anemic authority indeed.

In a more instructive case, *Korf v. Ball State University*, 726 F.2d 1222 (7th Cir. 1984), the university had adopted the AAUP's 1987 "Statement on Professional Ethics" (in *AAUP Policy Documents and Reports* (AAUP, 1990), 75–76) and published it in the faculty handbook. Subsequently, the university applied the statement's ethical standards to a tenured professor who, according to the findings of a university hearing committee, had made sexual advances toward and exploited male students. Specifically, the university relied on the portions of the AAUP statement that prohibit "exploitation of students . . . for private advantage" and require that a professor "demonstrates respect for the student as an individual and adheres to his proper role as intellectual guide and counsellor." When the university dismissed the professor for violating these standards, the professor sued, claiming that the dismissal violated due process because the statement did not specifically mention sexual conduct and therefore did not provide him adequate notice of the standard to which he was held. The court rejected this claim (which was essentially a claim of unconstitutional vagueness):

> It is unreasonable to assume that the drafters of the "Statement on Professional Ethics" could and must specifically delineate each and every type of conduct (including deviant conduct) constituting a violation. . . . We agree with [the professor's] academic peers on the hearing committee and the board of trustees in their application of [the statement]. . . . They were well qualified to interpret the AAUP "Statement on Professional Ethics" as well as to determine what is and is not acceptable faculty conduct within an academic setting. . . . The facts and circumstances clearly demonstrate that [the professor] should have understood both the standards to which he was being held and the consequences of his conduct [726 F.2d at 1227–28].

In a later case, *San Filippo v. Bongiovanni*, 961 F.2d 1125 (3d Cir. 1992), Rutgers University had adopted the AAUP's "Statement on Professional Ethics" (University Regulation 3.91). In separate regulations, however, it had also adopted an adequate-cause standard to govern dismissals of tenured faculty (University Regulation 3.93) and had defined "adequate cause" as "failure to maintain standards of sound scholarship and competent teaching, or gross neglect of established University obligations appropriate to the appointment, or incompetence, or incapacitation, or conviction of a crime of moral turpitude" (University Regulation 3.94). Relying on both the AAUP statement and the adequate-cause regulations, the university dis-

---

[46]See, for example, *H & V Engineering, Inc. v. Board of Professional Engineers and Land Surveyors*, 747 P.2d 55 (Idaho 1987) (invalidating disciplinary action taken under "misconduct" and "gross negligence" standard); *Tuma v. Board of Nursing*, 593 P.2d 711 (Idaho 1979) (invalidating suspension under standard of "unprofessional conduct"); and *Davis v. Williams*, 598 F.2d 916 (5th Cir. 1979) (invalidating regulation prohibiting "conduct prejudicial to good order").

missed the plaintiff, a tenured chemistry professor. The charges stemmed from the professor's "conduct towards visiting Chinese scholars brought to the University to work with him on research projects." A university hearing panel found that the professor had "'exploited, threatened and been abusive'" to these student scholars and had "'demonstrated a serious lack of integrity in his professional dealings'" (961 F.2d at 1132; quoting the panel report).

The professor challenged his dismissal in federal court, arguing (among other things) that the university's dismissal regulations were unconstitutionally vague because they did not give him fair notice that he could be dismissed for the conduct charged against him. The university argued that the adequate-cause regulations (3.93 and 3.94) "incorporated" the AAUP "Statement on Professional Ethics" (3.91), which applied to the professor's conduct and gave him sufficient notice. The appellate court (like the district court) rejected the university's "incorporation" argument and determined that the grounds for dismissal must be found in the adequate-cause regulations themselves, apart from the AAUP statement. But the appellate court (unlike the district court) nevertheless rejected the professor's vagueness argument because the portion of the adequate-cause regulation on "failure to maintain standards of sound scholarship and competent teaching" (3.94) was itself sufficient to provide fair notice:

> A reasonable, ordinary person using his common sense and general knowledge of employer-employee relationships would have fair notice that the conduct the University charged Dr. San Filippo with put him at risk of dismissal under a regulation stating he could be dismissed for "failure to maintain standards of sound scholarship and competent teaching." Regulation 3.94. He would know that the standard did not encompass only actual teaching or research skills. . . . It is not unfair or foreseeable for a tenured professor to be expected to behave decently towards students and coworkers, to comply with a superior's directive, and to be truthful and forthcoming in dealing with payroll, federal research funds or applications for academic positions. Such behavior is required for the purpose of maintaining sound scholarship and competent teaching [961 F.2d at 1137].

But an Ohio court overturned the termination of a tenured professor in *Ohio Dominican College v. Krone*, 560 N.E.2d 1340 (Ohio Ct. App. 1990). The court interpreted the faculty handbook's specification of "grave cause" for tenure termination as limiting the college's ability to discharge a faculty member with whom it had a contractual dispute. Joan Krone was a tenured assistant professor and chair of the mathematics department at Ohio Dominican (ODC). After the college received federal funds to initiate a computer science department, Krone was granted a one-year paid leave for academic year 1982–83 to obtain a master's degree in computer science, in return for her agreement to return and to teach for at least two years. Leaving ODC prior to her two-year teaching obligation would require her to reimburse ODC for the costs of her education.

Krone completed her master's degree in 1983 but continued her graduate work in computer science under a series of agreements with ODC, including a one-semester unpaid leave during which she had agreed to perform several tasks for the college. Her obligation was now to teach for three years upon returning to the college. In contemplating Krone's return to work in the fall of 1984, the academic vice president offered her a half-time contract for the fall semester for $5,500 in salary. Krone signed the contract after changing the salary to $10,000.

ODC rejected the change made by Krone and offered her a full-time teaching contract at an annual salary of $22,000. The letter making this offer stated that failure to sign and return it within ten days would be interpreted as a resignation and forfeiture of tenure. The day before the contract was due, Krone requested a meeting with the ODC president. The meeting was held, and ODC officials refused to change the most recent offer. At the same time, the college was negotiating with a male professor, who accepted the college's offer eleven days after Krone's signed contract was due. A week after that, ODC sent a letter to Krone, informing her that she had forfeited her tenured faculty position and must begin reimbursing the college for her educational expenses within a month.

When Krone refused to reimburse the college, stating that the terms of its offer were unacceptable, the college sued her for reimbursement; Krone countersued for wrongful termination. A trial judge granted judgment for the college based on the written contracts.

Krone appealed, asserting that the college had breached its contract (contained in the faculty handbook), and also arguing that under the Ohio constitution and the U.S. Constitution's Fourteenth Amendment she was entitled to a pretermination hearing. The ODC faculty handbook contained the following provision: "An appointment with continuous tenure is terminable by the institution only for grave cause or on account of extraordinary financial emergencies. Grave cause shall include demonstrated incompetence, crime, or similar matters" (560 N.E.2d at 1343). Krone also noted that the faculty handbook defined a full-time teaching load as three courses per semester; the college's last offer to Krone was to teach five courses and to serve as department chair. This portion of the contract was the basis for Krone's refusal to sign it.

The court concluded that the contract negotiations between ODC and Krone were separate from her status as a tenured professor. It noted:

> [Krone's] conduct, in not signing and returning a proposed contract that included terms of employment which were unacceptable to her, cannot serve as the basis for ODC terminating appellant for grave cause as set forth . . . in the Faculty Handbook. Furthermore, upon review of the record, there is no contractual provision in the Faculty Handbook which ODC can invoke that grants authority to ODC to unilaterally demand the signing and returning of a contract from a tenured professor by a specified date, and interpret the failure of that action to be a forfeiture of tenure. . . . Thus, [Krone] had a contractual right to continued employment . . . unless there was a finding of grave cause which would terminate her employment before that time period. . . . Accordingly, ODC breached appellant's contract for tenure by unilaterally setting forth a condition for continued employment [560 N.E.2d at 1344–45].

The court refused to address Krone's constitutional claims but upheld Krone's claim of wrongful discharge and concluded that she was entitled to reinstatement in order to meet her three-year teaching obligation to ODC.

Freedom-of-expression issues may also become implicated in the institution's application of its dismissal standards. In *Adamian v. Jacobson*, 523 F.2d 929 (9th Cir.

1975), a professor from the University of Nevada at Reno had allegedly led a disruptive demonstration on campus. Charges were brought against him under a university code provision requiring faculty members "to exercise appropriate restraint [and] to show respect for the opinions of others," and the board of regents determined that violation of this provision was adequate cause for dismissal. In court the professor argued that this standard was not only unconstitutionally vague but also unconstitutionally "overbroad" in violation of the First Amendment (see Sections 4.5.2, 4.6.1, 4.6.2, and 4.9.2 regarding overbreadth). The appellate court held that the standard would violate the First Amendment if interpreted broadly but could be constitutional if interpreted narrowly, as prescribed by AAUP academic freedom guidelines, so as not to refer to the content of the professor's remarks. The court therefore remanded the case to the trial court for further findings on how the university interpreted its code provision. On a second appeal, the court confined itself to the narrow issue of the construction of the code provision. Determining that the university's construction was consistent with the AAUP guidelines and reflected a limitation on the manner, rather than the content, of expression, the court held that the code provision was sufficiently narrow to avoid an overbreadth (as well as a vagueness) challenge (608 F.2d 1224 (9th Cir. 1979).

Despite the summary approval in *Garrett*, institutions should not comfortably settle for a bald adequate-cause standard. Good policy and (especially for public institutions) good law should demand more. Since incompetency, insubordination, immorality, unethical conduct, and medical disability are the most commonly asserted grounds for dismissals for cause, institutions may wish to specifically include them in their dismissal policies.[47] If unethical conduct is a stated ground for dismissal, the institution should consider adopting the AAUP "Statement on Professional Ethics," as did the institution in the *Korf* case. If it adopts the AAUP statement or its own version of ethical standards, the institution should make clear how and when violations of the statement or standards may be considered grounds for dismissal— thus avoiding the problem in *San Filippo*. If medical disability (either physical or mental) is a stated ground for dismissal, the institution should consider the ramifications of Section 504 and the Americans with Disabilities Act (this volume, Section 3.3.2.5). The AAUP's recommended regulation on termination for medical reasons (regulation 4(e), in *AAUP Policy Documents and Reports* (AAUP, 1990), 25) may also be helpful.

For each ground (or "cause") included in its dismissal policy, the institution should also include a definition of that ground, along with the criteria or standards for applying the definition to particular cases. (The AAUP statement may serve this purpose for the "unethical conduct" ground.) Since such definitions and criteria may become part of the institution's contract with faculty members, they should be drafted clearly and specifically enough, and applied sensitively enough, to avoid contract interpretation problems such as those faced by the institution in the *McConnell* case.

---

[47]Another ground for dismissal or other discipline that gained currency in the 1980s is the ground of "scientific misconduct." The ground refers to particular types of ethical problems that arise in the context of scientific research. See generally *Framework for Institutional Policies and Procedures for Dealing with Fraud in Research* (final draft) (Association of American Universities, 1989). See also this volume, Section 7.4.2, regarding federal regulations on scientific misconduct.

Such definitions and criteria should also be sufficiently clear to guide the decision makers who will apply them and to forewarn the faculty members who will be subject to them, thus avoiding vagueness problems; and (as in *Adamian*) they should be sufficiently specific to preclude dismissal of faculty members because of the content of their expression. In addition, they should conform to the AAUP's caution that cause standards must have a direct and substantial relationship to the faculty member's professional fitness. Hand in hand with such standards, if it chooses to adopt them, the institution will want to develop record-keeping policies, and perhaps periodic faculty review policies (see S. Olswang & J. Fantel, "Tenure and Periodic Performance Review: Compatible Legal and Administrative Principles," 7 *J. Coll. & Univ. Law* 1 (1980–81)), that will provide the facts necessary to make reliable termination decisions. The case of *King v. University of Minnesota*, 774 F.2d 224 (8th Cir. 1985), provides an instructive example of a university's success in this regard.

Administrators will also want to keep in mind that involuntary terminations of tenured faculty, because of their coercive and stigmatizing effect on the individuals involved, usually create a far greater number of legal problems than voluntary means for dissolving a tenured faculty member's employment relationship with the institution. Thus, another way to minimize legal vulnerability is to rely on voluntary alternatives to dismissals for cause. For example, the institution might provide increased incentives for retirement, or opportunities for phased or partial retirement, or retraining for mid-career shifts to underpopulated teaching or research fields (see J. Chronister & T. Kepple, *Incentive Early Retirement Programs for Faculty: Innovative Responses to a Changing Environment*, ERIC Clearinghouse Rpt. no. 1 (Association for the Study of Higher Education, 1987)). Or it might maintain flexibility in faculty development by increased use of fixed-term contracts, visiting professorships, part-time appointments, and other non-tenure-track appointments. All these alternatives have one thing in common with involuntary termination: their success depends on thorough review of personnel policies, coordinated planning for future contingencies, and careful articulation into written institutional policies.

Sec. 3.6. Procedures for Faculty Personnel Decisions

3.6.1. General principles. Postsecondary educational institutions have established varying procedural requirements for making and internally reviewing faculty personnel decisions. Administrators should look first at these requirements when they are attempting to resolve procedural issues concerning appointment, retention, promotion, and tenure. Whenever such requirements can reasonably be construed as part of the faculty member's contract with the institution (see Section 3.1), the law will usually expect both public and private institutions to comply with them. In *Skehan v. Board of Trustees of Bloomsburg State College*, 501 F.2d 31 (3d Cir. 1976), for instance, a nonrenewed professor alleged that the institution had not complied with a college policy statement providing for hearings in academic freedom cases. The appellate court held that the college would have to follow the policy statement if, on remand, the lower court found that the statement granted a contractual right under state law and that the professor's case involved academic freedom within the meaning of the statement. Upon remand and a second appeal, the court held that the professor did have a contractual right to the procedures specified in the statement and that the college had violated this right (590 F.2d 470 (3d Cir. 1978)). Similarly, in *Zuelsdorf* *v. University of Alaska, Fairbanks,* 794 P.2d 932 (Alaska 1990), the court held that a notice requirement in the university's personnel regulations was part of the faculty contract, and that the university had breached the contract by not giving the plaintiffs timely notice of nonrenewal.

Public institutions will also often be subject to state statutes or administrative regulations that establish procedures applicable to faculty personnel decisions. In *Brouillette v. Board of Directors of Merged Area IX,* 519 F.2d 126 (8th Cir. 1975), for example, the court determined that a state statute requiring a public pretermination hearing for public school teachers applied to the termination of a community college faculty member as well. The institution had, however, complied with the statutory requirements. In a "turnabout" case, *Rutcosky v. Board of Trustees of Community College District No. 18,* 545 P.2d 567 (1976), the court found that the plaintiff faculty member had not complied with a state procedural requirement applicable to termination-of-employment hearings and therefore refused to grant him any relief.

Institutional procedures and/or state laws also control the conditions under which a faculty member acquires tenured status. Many institutions have adopted policies that state that only the trustees can grant tenure, and courts have denied an award of de facto tenure in those cases. For example, in *Hill v. Talladega College,* 502 So. 2d 735 (Ala. 1987), the court refused to award de facto tenure to a faculty member employed at the college for ten years because the faculty handbook specifically stated that only the trustees could grant tenure and that tenure could not be acquired automatically at the college.

In other cases, however, faculty members have claimed that, by virtue of longevity, they had acquired tenure de facto, even though no official action was taken to grant tenure. For example, in *Dugan v. Stockton State College,* 586 A.2d 322 (N.J. Super. Ct. App. Div. 1991), a faculty member who had been employed at a state college for thirteen years, during several of which she was in a nonfaculty status, claimed that her years of service entitled her to tenure. The court examined the state law in effect at the time of her hiring, which stated that any individual consecutively employed for five years in a state college was tenured. Although the state board of higher education had issued regulations providing that only the board could confer tenure, the court noted that the regulations were contrary to the clear language of the statute, and thus beyond the power of the board to promulgate.

The procedures used by a state institution or other institution whose personnel decision is considered state action (see Section 1.5.2) are also subject to constitutional requirements of procedural due process. These requirements are discussed in Section 3.6.2.

Since private institutions are not subject to these constitutional requirements, or to state procedural statutes and regulations, contract law may be the primary or sole basis for establishing and testing the scope of their procedural obligation to faculty members. In *Johnson v. Christian Brothers College,* 565 S.W.2d 872 (Tenn. 1978), for example, an associate professor instituted suit for breach of his employment contract when the college did not grant him tenure. The college, a religiously affiliated institution in Memphis, had a formal tenure program detailed in its faculty handbook. The program included a seven-year probationary period, during which the faculty member worked under a series of one-year contracts. After seven years, on the prior recommendation of the tenure committee and approval of the president, the faculty member either received tenure along with the award of the eighth contract or was dismissed. The plaintiff claimed that, once he had reached the final probationary year and was being considered for tenure, he was entitled to the formal notice and hearing procedures utilized by the college in terminating tenured faculty. The Supreme Court of Tennessee held that nothing in the terms of the one-year contracts, the published tenure program, or the commonly used procedure of the college evidenced an agreement or practice of treating teachers in their final probationary year as equivalent to tenured faculty. The college therefore had no express or implied contractual obligation to afford the professor notice and an opportunity to be heard.

3.6.2. The public faculty member's right to constitutional due process. In two landmark cases, *Board of Regents v. Roth*, 408 U.S. 564 (1972), and *Perry v. Sindermann*, 408 U.S. 593 (1972), the U.S. Supreme Court established that faculty members have a right to a fair hearing whenever a personnel decision deprives them of a "property interest" or a "liberty interest" under the Fourteenth Amendment's Due Process Clause. The "property" and "liberty" terminology is derived from the wording of the Fourteenth Amendment itself, which provides that states shall not "deprive any person of life, liberty, or property, without due process of law." (The identification of property and liberty interests is also important to many procedural due process questions concerning students; see Sections 4.3.1, 4.3.7.2, 4.8.2, and 4.17.1.)

In identifying these property and liberty interests, one must make the critical distinction between faculty members who are under continuing contracts and those whose contracts have expired. It is clear, as *Roth* notes, that "a public college professor dismissed from an office held under tenure provisions . . . and college professors and staff members dismissed during the terms of their contracts . . . have interests in continued employment that are safeguarded by due process." But the situation is not clear with respect to faculty members whose contracts are expiring and are up for renewal or a tenure review. Moreover, when a personnel decision would infringe a property or liberty interest, as in tenure termination, other questions then arise concerning the particular procedures that the institution must follow.

3.6.2.1. Nonrenewal of contracts. *Roth* and *Perry* (above) are the leading cases on the nonrenewal of faculty contracts. The respondent in *Roth* had been hired as an assistant professor at Wisconsin State University for a fixed term of one year. A state statute provided that all state university teachers would be employed for one-year terms and would be eligible for tenure only after four years of continuous service. The professor was notified before February 1 that he would not be rehired. No reason for the decision was given, nor was there an opportunity for a hearing or an appeal.

The question considered by the Supreme Court was "whether the [professor] had a constitutional right to a statement of reasons and a hearing on the university's decision not to rehire him for another year." The Court ruled that he had no such right because neither a "liberty" nor a "property" interest had been violated by the nonrenewal. Concerning liberty interests, the Court reasoned:

> The state, in declining to rehire the respondent, did not make any charge against him that might seriously damage his standing and associations in his community. It did not base the nonrenewal of his contract on a charge, for example, that he had been guilty of dishonesty or immorality. Had it done so, this would be a different case. For "where a person's good name, reputation,

honor, or integrity is at stake because of what the government is doing to him, notice and an opportunity to be heard is essential" (*Wisconsin v. Constantineau*, 400 U.S. 433, 437 (1971)) [other citations omitted]. In such a case, due process would accord an opportunity to refute the charge before university officials. In the present case, however, there is no suggestion whatever that the respondent's "good name, reputation, honor, or integrity" is at stake.

Similarly, there is no suggestion that the state, in declining to reemploy the respondent, imposed on him a stigma or other disability that foreclosed his freedom to take advantage of other employment opportunities. The state, for example, did not invoke any regulations to bar the respondent from all other public employment in state universities. Had it done so, this, again, would be a different case. . . .

Hence, on the record before us, all that clearly appears is that the respondent was not rehired for one year at one university. It stretches the concept too far to suggest that a person is deprived of "liberty" when he simply is not rehired in one job but remains as free as before to seek another [408 U.S. at 573–74, 575].

The Court also held that the respondent had not been deprived of any property interest in future employment:

The Fourteenth Amendment's procedural protection of property is a safeguard of the security of interests that a person has already acquired in specific benefits. . . . To have a property interest in a benefit, a person clearly must have more than an abstract need or desire for it. He must have more than a unilateral expectation of it. He must, instead, have a legitimate claim of entitlement to it. . . .

Property interests, of course, are not created by the Constitution. Rather, they are created and their dimensions are defined by existing rules or understandings that stem from an independent source such as state law—rules or understandings that secure certain benefits and that support claims of entitlement to those benefits. . . . Respondent's "property" interest in employment at Wisconsin State University-Oshkosh was created and defined by the terms of his appointment, [which] specifically provided that the respondent's employment was to terminate on June 30. They did not provide for contract renewal absent "sufficient cause." Indeed, they made no provision for renewal whatsoever. . . .

In these circumstances, the respondent surely had an abstract concern in being rehired, but he did not have a property interest sufficient to require the university authorities to give him a hearing when they declined to renew his contract of employment [408 U.S. at 578].

Since the professor had no protected liberty or property interest, his Fourteenth Amendment rights had not been violated, and the university was not required to provide a reason for its nonrenewal of the contract or to afford the professor a hearing on the nonrenewal.

In the *Perry* case, the respondent had been employed as a professor by the Texas state college system for ten consecutive years. While employed, he was actively involved in public disagreements with the board of regents. He was employed on a series of one-year contracts, and at the end of his tenth year the board elected not to rehire him. The professor was given neither an official reason nor the opportunity for a hearing. Like Roth, Perry argued that the board's action violated his Fourteenth Amendment right to procedural due process.

But in the *Perry* case, unlike the *Roth* case, the Supreme Court ruled that the professor had raised a genuine claim to de facto tenure, which would create a constitutionally protected property interest in continued employment. The professor relied on tenure guidelines promulgated by the coordinating board of the Texas College and University System and on an official faculty guide's statement that "Odessa College has no tenure system. The administration of the college wishes the faculty member to feel that he has permanent tenure as long as his teaching services are satisfactory and as long as he displays a cooperative attitude toward his coworkers and his superiors, and as long as he is happy in his work."

According to the Court:

> The respondent [professor] offered to prove that a teacher with his long period of service at this particular state college had no less a "property" interest in continued employment than a formally tenured teacher at other colleges, and had no less a procedural due process right to a statement of reasons and a hearing before college officials upon their decision not to retain him.
>
> We have made clear in *Roth* . . . that "property" interests subject to procedural due process protection are not limited by a few rigid technical forms. Rather, "property" denotes a broad range of interests that are secured by "existing rules or understandings." A person's interest in a benefit is a "property" interest for due process purposes if there are such rules or mutually explicit understandings that support his claim of entitlement to the benefit and that he may invoke at a hearing.
>
> A written contract with an explicit tenure provision clearly is evidence of a formal understanding that supports a teacher's claim of entitlement to continued employment unless sufficient "cause" is shown. Yet absence of such an explicit contractual provision may not always foreclose the possibility that a teacher has a "property" interest in reemployment. . . . In this case, the respondent has alleged the existence of rules and understandings, promulgated and fostered by state officials, that may justify his legitimate claim of entitlement to continued employment absent "sufficient cause." We disagree with the court of appeals insofar as it held that a mere subjective "expectancy" is protected by procedural due process, but we agree that the respondent must be given an opportunity to prove the legitimacy of his claim of such entitlement in light of "the policies and practices of the institution" [citation omitted]. Proof of such a property interest would not, of course, entitle him to reinstatement. But such proof would obligate officials to grant a hearing at his request, where he could be informed of the grounds for his nonretention and challenge their sufficiency [408 U.S. at 603].

One other Supreme Court case should be read together with *Roth* and *Perry* for a fuller understanding of the Court's due process analysis. *Bishop v. Wood*, 426 U.S. 341 (1976), concerned a policeman who had been discharged, allegedly on the basis of incorrect information, and orally informed of the reasons in a private conference. With four judges strongly dissenting, the Court held that the discharge infringed neither property nor liberty interests of the policeman. Regarding property, the Court, adopting a stilted lower court interpretation of the ordinance governing employment of policemen, held that the ordinance created no expectation of continued employment but only required the employer to provide certain procedural protections, all of which had been provided in this case. Regarding liberty, the Court held that the charges against an employee cannot form the basis for a deprivation-of-liberty claim if they are privately communicated to the employee and not made public. The Court also held that the truth or falsity of the charges is irrelevant to the question of whether a liberty interest has been infringed.

Under *Roth, Perry,* and *Bishop,* there are three basic situations in which courts will require that a nonrenewal decision be accompanied by appropriate procedural safeguards:

1. The existing rules, policies, or practices of the institution, or "mutually explicit understandings" between the faculty member and the institution, support the faculty member's claim of entitlement to continued employment. Such circumstances would create a property interest. In *Soni v. Board of Trustees of University of Tennessee,* 513 F.2d 347 (6th Cir. 1975), for example, the court held that a nonrenewed, nontenured mathematics professor had such a property interest because voting and retirement plan privileges had been extended to him and he had been told that he could expect his contract to be renewed.

2. The institution, in the course of nonrenewal, makes charges against the faculty member that could seriously damage his or her reputation, standing, or associations in the community. Such circumstances would create a liberty interest.[48] *Roth,* for instance, suggests that charges of dishonesty or immorality accompanying nonrenewal could infringe a faculty member's liberty interest. And in *Wellner v. Minnesota State Junior College Board,* 487 F.2d 153 (8th Cir. 1973), the court held that charges of racism deprived the faculty member of a liberty interest.

The *Bishop* case makes clear that charges or accusations against a faculty member must in some way be made public before they can form the basis of a liberty claim. Although *Bishop* did not involve faculty members, a pre-*Bishop* case, *Ortwein v. Mackey,* 511 F.2d 696 (5th Cir. 1975), applies essentially the same principle in the university setting. Under *Ortwein* the institution must have made, or be likely to make, the stigmatizing charges "public 'in any official or intentional manner, other than in connection with the defense of [related legal] action'" (511 F.2d at 699; quoting *Kaprelian v. Texas Woman's University,* 509 F.2d 133, 139 (5th Cir. 1975)). Thus, there are still questions to be resolved concerning when a charge has become sufficiently "public" to fall within *Ortwein* and *Bishop.*

3. The nonrenewal imposes a "stigma or other disability" on the faculty member that "foreclose[s] his freedom to take advantage of other employment opportunities." Such circumstances would create a liberty interest. *Roth,* for instance, suggests that a nonrenewal that bars the faculty member from other employment in the state higher education system would infringe a liberty interest. Presumably, charges impugning the faculty member's professional competence or integrity could also infringe a liberty interest if the institution keeps records of the charges and if the

---

[48]In *Paul v. Davis,* 424 U.S. 693 (1976), the U.S. Supreme Court held that "defamation, standing alone," does not infringe a liberty interest. But defamation can still create a liberty infringement when combined with some "alteration of legal status" under state law, and termination or nonrenewal of public employment is such a change in status. Defamation "in the course of declining to rehire" would therefore infringe a faculty member's liberty interest even under *Paul v. Davis.*

contents of these records could be divulged to potential future employers of the faculty member. But if the faculty member's contract is merely not renewed, the fact that it may be difficult for an individual to locate another teaching position does not mean that the nonrenewal creates a liberty interest.

A liberty or property interest might also be infringed when the nonrenewal is based on, and thus would penalize, the faculty member's exercise of freedom of expression. The Supreme Court dealt with this issue briefly in a footnote in the *Roth* case (408 U.S. at 575 n.14), appearing to suggest that a hearing may be required in some circumstances where the nonrenewal "would directly impinge upon interests in free speech or free press."

Whenever a nonrenewed faculty member has a basis for making a liberty or property interest claim (see Sections 3.7.1 through 3.7.4), administrators should consider providing a hearing. Properly conducted, a hearing may not only vitiate any subsequent procedural due process litigation by the faculty member but may also resolve or defuse First Amendment claims that otherwise might be taken to court.

In 1971 the American Association of University Professors adopted a "Statement on Procedural Standards in the Renewal or Nonrenewal of Faculty Appointments" (in *AAUP Policy Documents and Reports* (AAUP, 1990), 11–14). The procedures include notice of criteria for reappointment, periodic review of the performance of probationary faculty, notice of reasons for nonreappointment, and an appeal process for decisions that allegedly involved academic freedom violations or gave inadequate consideration to the department's recommendation.

3.6.2.2. Denial of tenure. Denials of tenure, like contract nonrenewals, must be distinguished analytically from terminations of tenure. Whereas a tenure termination always infringes the faculty member's property interests, a tenure denial may or may not infringe a property or liberty interest, triggering due process protections. The answer in any particular case will depend on application of the teachings from *Roth* and *Perry* (Section 3.6.2.1) and their progeny. Denials of promotions, for due process purposes, are generally analogous to denials of tenure and thus are subject to the general principles developed in the tenure denial cases below. For a leading illustration, see *Clark v. Whiting*, 607 F.2d 634 (4th Cir. 1979), where the court held that an associate professor had no right to an evidentiary hearing upon denial of promotion to full professor.

In 1978 a West Virginia court determined that a faculty member denied tenure had been deprived of a property interest (*McLendon v. Morton*, 249 S.E.2d 919 (W. Va. 1978)). Parkersburg Community College published eligibility criteria for tenure, which included six years as a teaching member of the full-time faculty and attainment of the rank of assistant professor. Having fulfilled both requirements, McLendon applied for tenure. After her tenure application was rejected on grounds of incompetence, McLendon filed suit, claiming that the institution's failure to provide her a hearing abridged her due process rights. The court held that (1) satisfying "objective eligibility standards gave McLendon a sufficient entitlement, so that she could not be denied tenure on the basis of her competence without some procedural due process"; and (2) minimal due process necessitates notice of the reasons for denial and a hearing before an unbiased tribunal, at which the professor can refute the issues raised in the notice. This decision thus extends the *Roth* doctrine to include, among persons who have a property interest in continued employment, faculty members who teach at public institutions and have met specified objective criteria for tenure eligibility (assuming that the institution uses objective criteria). In West Virginia and any other jurisdiction that may accept the *McLendon* reasoning, institutions must give such faculty members notice and an opportunity for a hearing before any final decision to deny tenure. Most institutions, however, use subjective criteria, or a combination of objective and subjective criteria, for making tenure decisions, and thus would not be bound by *McLendon*.

In contrast to *McLendon*, the court in *Beitzel v. Jeffrey*, 643 F.2d 870 (1st Cir. 1981), held that a professor hired as a "probationary employee" did not have a sufficient property interest at stake under *Roth* to challenge his denial of tenure on due process grounds. The standards for the granting or denial of tenure were outlined in the university handbook; but, unlike those in *McLendon*, these standards were subjective. The court determined that the professor had no basis for the expectation that he would be granted tenure automatically. Similarly, in *Goodisman v. Lytle*, 724 F.2d 818 (9th Cir. 1984), the court rejected a professor's claim that he had a property interest in the university's procedures and guidelines for making tenure decisions. The court concluded that the procedures and guidelines "do not significantly limit university officials' discretion in making tenure decisions. They provide only an outline of relevant considerations. They do not enhance a candidate's expectation of obtaining tenure enough to establish a constitutionally protected interest."

In *Davis v. Oregon State University*, 591 F.2d 493 (9th Cir. 1978), the same court that later decided *Goodisman* rejected a different type of professorial claim to a hearing prior to tenure denial. The plaintiff had been an associate professor in the university's department of physics. He alleged that the department chairman had assured him at the time of his appointment that he would be granted tenure "as a matter of course." In 1972 and again in 1973, under the university's published tenure policy, the university tenure committee reviewed Davis's case and on both occasions obtained insufficient votes to either grant or deny tenure. Davis was thereafter terminated at the end of the 1973–74 academic year and brought suit, contending that he had de facto tenure arising from an oral contract with the department chairman. The court ruled that the university's written tenure policy defeated any claim to a contractual tenure agreement, since the policy vested no authority to grant tenure in department chairmen, and Davis was fully aware of this fact. The court thus held that Davis had no property interest that would support his claim to a hearing.

Institutional procedures for making a tenure decision do not themselves create a property interest, according to *Siu v. Johnson*, 748 F.2d 238 (4th Cir. 1984). Siu was denied tenure by George Mason University, a public institution, despite the positive recommendation of her departmental colleagues. Citing language in the faculty handbook that "the faculty is primarily responsible for recommendations involving appointments, reappointments, promotions, [and] the granting of tenure" (748 F.2d at 241) (although the final decision was explicitly afforded to the board or president), Siu asserted that the university's written procedures for making tenure decisions created a constitutionally protected property interest, and that the institution's failure to defer to the peer evaluation violated that property interest. The court stated that most untenured faculty were at-will employees and thus had no legitimate expectation of reemployment, adding:

> We doubt that [*Roth* and its progeny] directly support Siu's position and question whether, in any event, under *Roth* the property interest claimed by Siu

would exist unless the University's procedures and their application over time had given rise to an institutional "common law of re-employment" by which the interest created by her probationary appointment had been elevated to something firmer than a mere "unilateral expectation" [748 F.2d at 243–44].

The court then turned to Siu's contention that detailed procedures for making tenure decisions created a property interest in having those procedures followed. The court responded:

> Put this way the claim is a circular one: the state's detailed procedures provide the due process guarantees which create the very property interest protected by those guarantees. This is conceptually unacceptable. Its logical effect would be to "constitutionalize" all state contractual provisions respecting the continuation of public employment [748 F.2d at 244].

The court then provided guidance regarding the analysis of whether a property interest exists.

> Where a property interest—including one involving academic employment—is claimed to be derived from state law sources, see *Roth*, 408 U.S. at 577, it is obviously necessary to look to those sources to determine the general nature of the interest, for the process constitutionally due is dependent upon that [citations omitted]. And in making that inquiry the procedures provided in those sources for creating and terminating the interest are obviously relevant to the extent that they help define the general nature of the interest. But that is the limit of their relevance to the constitutional inquiry. They do not define in detail the process constitutionally due for protection of the interest, except to the extent that they may coincide with elements of that process as independently defined by federal [constitutional] law.
>
> The special relevance of the procedures to this limited inquiry is their indication of the general nature of the decisional process by which it is contemplated that the "interest" may be terminated. In particular, the procedures will likely indicate whether the decisional process is intended to be essentially an objective one designed to find facts establishing fault, or cause, or justification or the like, or instead to be essentially a subjective, evaluative one committed by the sources to the professional judgment of persons presumed to possess special competence in making the evaluation [748 F.2d at 244].

Concluding that the process in tenure decisions was subjective rather than objective, the court held that "the process due one subject to this highly subjective evaluative decision can only be the exercise of professional judgment by those empowered to make the final decision in a way not so manifestly arbitrary and capricious that a reviewing court could confidently say of it that it did not in the end involve the exercise of professional judgment" (748 F.2d at 245).

The court then turned to Siu's claim that the institution's refusal to defer to the faculty's judgment violated its tenure procedures, an alleged violation of substantive, rather than procedural, due process:

> Peer faculty primacy in this respect may obviously be a matter of rightful and great concern to faculties. Both in the governance of particular institutions

and in the general protection of essential academic freedom in our society at large, such a safeguard may rightly be thought by responsible members of the professoriat to be vital. Required deference to "working" faculty judgments in evaluating the professional qualifications of their peers may therefore be a proper subject for vigorous faculty associational efforts, for negotiated contractual ordering, or for voluntary conferral by sufficiently enlightened and secure academic institutions. But we are not prepared to hold that it is an essential element of constitutionally guaranteed due process, whether or not it is contractually ordered or otherwise observed as a matter of custom in a particular institution [748 F.2d at 245].

In another case a federal district court concluded that the tenure decision-making criteria and policies at Rutgers University created neither a property nor a liberty interest. The faculty union and a class of individuals denied tenure by Rutgers had asserted that probationary faculty had a legitimate expectation of being evaluated under the same standards that were in effect when currently tenured faculty were evaluated (in other words, that raising the standards for achieving tenure infringed the probationary faculty members' property interests). In an unpublished opinion, *Varma v. Bloustein,* Civ. No. 84-2332 (D.N.J. 1988), the trial judge granted summary judgment for the university, ruling that the tenure criteria and procedures did not "provide the significant substantive restrictions on University discretion in tenure appointments required to create a protected property interest." Furthermore, she wrote, previous patterns of tenure decisions did not bind the university to similar outcomes in the future, particularly in light of the very general nature of the tenure criteria and their reliance on subjective assessments of faculty performance.

As evidence of the existence of a liberty interest, the plaintiffs cited prisoners' rights cases in which the U.S. Supreme Court analyzed the factors that establish a liberty interest in state regulations or procedures. In *Olin v. Wakinekona,* 461 U.S. 238 (1983), the Court noted that "a state creates a protected liberty interest by placing substantive limitations on official discretion." When a state's regulations contain such substantive limitations, the plaintiff may have a protected liberty interest (*Hewitt v. Helms,* 459 U.S. 460 (1983)). The judge rejected the application of *Olin* and *Hewitt* to tenure decisions at Rutgers, stating that a liberty interest arises only when there are "particularized standards or criteria." The university's tenure standards did not restrict its discretion to award or deny tenure, and thus no liberty interest was created.

The court in *Kilcoyne v. Morgan,* 664 F.2d 940 (4th Cir. 1981), rejected yet another argument for procedural protections prior to denial of tenure. The plaintiff, a nontenured faculty member at East Carolina University, argued that his employment contract incorporated a provision of the faculty manual requiring department chairmen to apprise nontenured faculty—both by personal conference and written evaluation—of their progress toward tenure. Although Kilcoyne received a letter from the department chairman and had a follow-up conference toward the end of each of his first two years at the university, he argued that these procedures did not conform to the faculty manual. University guidelines also mandated a tenure decision following a three-year probationary period. At the beginning of his third year, Kilcoyne was notified that he would be rehired for a fourth year; later in the third year, however, he was informed that he would not be granted tenure or employed beyond the fourth year. After his claim of "de facto tenure" was summarily dismissed by the courts (405 F. Supp. 828 (E.D.N.C. 1975), *affirmed*, 530 F.2d 968 (4th Cir. 1975)), Kilcoyne argued that the alleged failure of the university to conform precisely to the faculty manual procedures incorporated into his contract deprived him of procedural due process. The court held that Kilcoyne lacked any *Roth* property interest in further employment at the university; denial of tenure would thus have been constitutionally permissible even if accompanied by no procedural safeguards. According to the court, if a state university gratuitously provides procedural safeguards that are not constitutionally mandated, deviations from such procedures will not violate due process even if the procedures are enumerated in the faculty contract. Although the contract may provide a basis for a breach-of-contract action, the mere fact that the state is a contracting party does not raise the contract problem to the status of a constitutional issue.

Other potential sources of property interests relevant to tenure denials (as well as to terminations of tenured faculty, discussed in Section 3.6.2.3) are the fair employment laws enacted by the states. In *Logan v. Zimmerman Brush Co.*, 455 U.S. 422 (1982), the U.S. Supreme Court ruled that a former employee challenging his dismissal had a property interest in the adjudicatory processes of the Illinois Fair Employment Practices Commission. The commission had failed to schedule a hearing on Logan's timely complaint of discriminatory dismissal, and the Illinois courts had ruled that the commission's procedural error deprived the commission of jurisdiction and thus extinguished Logan's cause of action. The court, in an opinion written by Justice Blackmun, disagreed. Justice Blackmun wrote:

> [Logan's] right to use the [state law] adjudicatory procedures is a species of property protected by the Due Process Clause. . . . The hallmark of property is an individual entitlement grounded in state law, which cannot be removed except for cause [455 U.S. at 431].

The statute created a property interest because it gave Logan an entitlement to use the state's enforcement process; the state's own error deprived Logan of this protected property interest, and no due process protections had been afforded him.

With the exception of *McLendon*, which addressed issues not usually present in challenges to tenure denials, the courts have clearly stated that denial of tenure is not a "termination" per se, and affords no constitutional due process guarantees (although state statutes or regulations may provide procedural guarantees, which, if violated, could form the basis for a claim under state law). As is the case with nonreappointment, however, if the faculty member alleges that the tenure denial was grounded in unconstitutional reasons (retaliation for constitutionally protected speech, for example), then liberty interests would arguably have been infringed and procedural due process protections would therefore apply.

3.6.2.3. Termination of tenure. Whenever an institution's personnel decision would infringe a property or liberty interest, constitutional due process requires that the institution offer the faculty member procedural safeguards before the decision becomes final. The crux of these safeguards is notice and opportunity for a hearing. In other words, the institution must notify the faculty member of the reasons for the decision and provide a fair opportunity for him or her to challenge these reasons in a hearing before an impartial body.

Decisions to terminate tenured faculty members must always be accompanied by notice and opportunity for a hearing, since such decisions always infringe property interests. The cases in this section provide specific illustrations of the procedural due process requirements applicable to tenure termination cases. Decisions to terminate a nontenured faculty member during the contract term are generally analogous to tenure terminations and thus are subject to principles similar to those in the cases below; the same is true for nonrenewal and denial-of-tenure decisions when they would infringe property or liberty interests.

Because of the significance of the property interest, a pretermination hearing is required. The standards for the pretermination hearing that must be provided to a discharged faculty member were developed by the U.S. Supreme Court in *Cleveland Board of Education v. Loudermill,* 470 U.S. 532 (1985). Prior to making the final termination decision, the institution should hold a pretermination hearing, according to the *Loudermill* opinion. "The tenured public employee is entitled to oral or written notice of the charges against him, an explanation of the employer's evidence, and an opportunity to present his side of the story" (470 U.S. at 546). If the pretermination hearing is as informal as the *Loudermill* criteria suggest is permissible, then a post-termination hearing is necessary to permit the individual to challenge the decision in a manner designed to protect his or her rights to due process. The nature of the hearing and the degree of formality of the procedures have been the subjects of much litigation by tenured faculty who were discharged.

Although there is no requirement that the termination hearing have all the elements of a judicial hearing (*Toney v. Reagan,* 467 F.2d 953 (9th Cir. 1972), such hearings must meet minimal constitutional standards. A federal appeals court set forth such standards in *Levitt v. University of Texas,* 759 F.2d 1224 (5th Cir. 1985):

1. The employee must be given notice of the cause for dismissal.
2. The employee must be given notice of the names of witnesses and told what each will testify to.
3. The employee must be given a meaningful opportunity to be heard.
4. The hearing must be held within a reasonable time.
5. The hearing must be conducted before an impartial panel with appropriate academic expertise.

Many institutions, however, have adopted the procedures recommended by the American Association of University Professors. Formal adoption of the AAUP's 1958 "Statement on Procedural Standards in Faculty Dismissal Proceedings" (in *AAUP Policy Documents and Reports* (AAUP, 1990), 11–14) will require the institution to follow them.

A federal trial court developed a set of carefully reasoned and articulated due process standards in *Potemra v. Ping,* 462 F. Supp. 328 (E.D. Ohio 1978). In that case a tenured member of the economics department at Ohio University claimed that he was denied due process when the university dismissed him for failure to perform his faculty duties and inability to communicate with students. The court ruled that the teacher's minimum due process safeguards included (1) a written statement of the reasons for the proposed termination prior to final action, (2) adequate notice of a hearing, (3) a hearing at which the teacher has an opportunity to submit evidence to controvert the grounds for dismissal, (4) a final statement of the grounds for dismissal

if it does occur. The court held that the university had complied with these requirements and had not infringed the faculty member's due process rights.

In a similar case, *Bowling v. Scott*, 587 F.2d 229 (5th Cir. 1979), a tenured
English professor at the University of Alabama filed suit after the university terminated his tenure. The court enunciated a minimum due process standard similar to
that used in *Potemra* and ruled that no deprivation of procedural due process had
occurred, since the university had served Bowling with a list of charges; informed him
that formal proceedings would commence; given advance notice of each of fourteen
hearing sessions, all of which the faculty member had attended with his lawyer; and
subsequently issued a twelve-page report stating the grounds for dismissal.

In another case, *King v. University of Minnesota*, 774 F.2d 224 (8th Cir. 1985),
the court upheld the university's dismissal of a tenured faculty member for neglect
of his teaching responsibilities and lack of scholarship. The university had provided
the following due process protections:

1. Frequent communications with King concerning his poor teaching, his unex-
    cused absences, and his refusal to cooperate with the department.
2. A departmental vote, with King present, to remove him from the department
    because of his history of poor performance.
3. Notice to King of the charges against him and the university's intent to initiate
    removal proceedings.
4. A hearing panel of tenured faculty and the right to object to any of the individ-
    ual members (which King did for one member, who was replaced).
5. Representation by counsel and substantial documentary discovery, including
    depositions of administrators.
6. A prehearing conference in which the parties exchanged issue lists, witness
    lists, and exhibit lists.
7. A hearing occurring over a two-week period, during which King was repre-
    sented by counsel, who cross-examined witnesses, presented witnesses and
    documentary evidence, and made oral and written arguments.
8. Review of the entire record by the university president.
9. Review by the regents of the panel's findings, the president's recommendation,
    and briefs from each of the parties.
10. An opportunity for King to appear before the regents before they made the
    termination decision.

The appellate court characterized the procedural protections that King received as
"exhaustive" and determined that they satisfied constitutional requirements (774 F.2d
at 228).

In *Frumkin v. Board of Trustees, Kent State*, 626 F.2d 19 (6th Cir. 1980), the
court focused particularly on the type of hearing an institution must provide prior
to a decision to terminate tenure. The university had slated the professor for dismissal
after federal funding for his position was cut. In support of the recommendation for
dismissal, the university charged the professor with "unsatisfactory performance as
grant director, recurring unproven charges against faculty members, unprofessional
conduct, false charges against the department, and violation of university policy."
When the professor chose to contest his dismissal, the university scheduled a hearing.
The professor was permitted to have a lawyer present at the hearing, but the lawyer's

role was limited. He was permitted to consult and advise his client and to make closing arguments in his client's behalf. But he was prohibited from conducting any cross-examination or direct examination of witnesses or from raising objections.

Reasoning that this limited hearing was well suited to the type of decision to be made, the court held that the university had not violated the professor's due process rights:

> The criteria which determine the parameters of procedural due process are set out in *Mathews v. Eldridge,* 424 U.S. 319, 334 . . . (1976):
>
>> Identification of the specific dictates of due process generally requires consideration of three distinct factors: first, the private interest that will be affected by the official action; second, the risk of an erroneous deprivation of such interest through the procedures used, and the probable value, if any, of additional or substitute procedural safeguards; and finally, the government's interest, including the function involved and the fiscal and administrative burdens that the additional or substitute procedural requirement would entail.
>
> The Supreme Court has consistently rejected a concept of due process which would afford all complaining parties, whatever the context of the dispute, an inflexible "checklist" of legal rights. On the contrary, procedural due process issues, originating as they may in diverse situations, demand a more sensitive judicial approach. Thus, we find in *Mathews, supra,* an analysis designed to balance competing interests in lieu of imposing rigid legal formulae. . . .
>
> The narrow issue is . . . whether procedural due process required the university to permit Dr. Frumkin's retained counsel to conduct direct and cross-examination of witnesses at the pretermination hearing. The second *Mathews* criterion requires us to assess the "risk of erroneous deprivation" and the "value of the additional procedural safeguards" at issue. Under certain circumstances, the active participation of a legal representative is likely to mitigate an otherwise considerable risk of "erroneous deprivation." The Supreme Court has, for example, recognized the potential importance of counsel's role in welfare benefits pretermination hearings (see *Goldberg v. Kelly,* 397 U.S. 254 . . . (1970)). . . .
>
> We cannot, however, accept appellant's contention that we should rule in his favor on the basis of an analogy between the problems which beset an unrepresented welfare recipient confronted with an administrative court and the position of a professional academic who, under the direction of his attorney, presents his case to a panel of fellow faculty members. As the *Mathews* court noted:
>
>> The judicial model of an evidentiary hearing is neither a required nor even the most effective method of decision making in all circumstances. . . . All that is necessary is that the procedures be tailored, in light of the decision to be made, to the "capacities and circumstances of those who are to be heard" to insure that they are given a meaningful opportunity to present their case (424 U.S. at 348 . . . ; see also *Toney v. Reagan,* 467 F.2d 953, 958 (9th Cir. 1972)).
>
> We believe that Dr. Frumkin had ample opportunity to present his case to the hearing committee in a manner calculated to achieve a fair result. . . .
>
> The third guideline set out in *Mathews* requires an analysis of "the government's interest, *including the function involved,* and the fiscal and administrative burden that the additional . . . procedure would entail" (emphasis added).

The administrative burden, in this instance, of permitting appellant's counsel to examine witnesses would have been comparatively slight. However, we are persuaded that the university has a legitimate argument in its expressed reluctance to transform the type of inquiry involved here into a full-fledged adversary trial. Because universities have traditionally been afforded broad discretion in their administration of internal affairs (see *Downing v. Le Britton*, 550 F.2d 689, 692 (1st Cir. 1977)), we do not deem it necessary to interfere where, as here, there is no showing that the overall procedure was prejudicial to the rights [of the] terminated employee [626 F.2d at 21–22].

Another case, *Clarke v. West Virginia Board of Regents*, 279 S.E.2d 169 (W. Va. 1981), also focuses on one specific part of the termination process but is not as deferential to institutions as *Frumkin* is. It provides particularly useful guidance to administrators and counsel in developing a written decision based on the record upon which a reviewing court may rely. In this case the court considered the reasons and evidence an institution must provide to support a decision terminating tenure. Clarke, a tenured professor at Fairmont State College, had been dismissed following a hearing before a hearing examiner. The hearing examiner made a written report, which merely cited the testimony of witnesses who supported dismissal and did not state any specific reasons or factual basis for affirming the dismissal. The professor argued in court that this report did not comply with due process requirements. Although the court's analysis is based on the state constitution, the opinion relied on federal constitutional precedents and is indicative of federal constitutional analysis as well.

As a starting point for determining what a hearing examiner's report must contain, the court consulted a policy bulletin of the West Virginia board of regents:

> The hearing examiner is not required by statute to make written findings of fact and conclusions of law, nor does the bulletin specifically require him to state on the record the reasons for his decision or to specify the evidence which supports those reasons. The bulletin does, however, require the hearing examiner to "enter such recommendations *as the facts justify and the circumstances may require*" (emphasis added). Clearly, the bulletin contemplates that the hearing examiner will make a reasoned determination which is supported by the evidence adduced at the hearing. At the very least, the hearing examiner should make some sort of findings on the record and indicate the evidence supporting those findings in order to demonstrate that he has fulfilled his obligations as a fact finder and has not acted arbitrarily and capriciously in reaching his conclusions. "The decision maker should state the reasons for his determination and indicate the evidence he relied on, though his statements need not amount to a full opinion or even formal findings of fact and conclusions of law" (*Goldberg v. Kelly*, 397 U.S. 254, 271 . . . (1970)) [279 S.E.2d at 177].

The court then stressed the importance of an adequate report to give a reviewing court a basis for review and to give the affected individual a basis for identifying grounds for review:

> The need for an adequate statement of the hearing examiner's reasons for his determination and the evidence supporting them is obvious. Our function as a reviewing court is to review the record to determine if the evidence adduced at

the hearing supports the findings of the hearing examiner and whether his conclusions follow from those findings. We must rely on the facts and logic upon which the hearing examiner ruled . . . and determine whether he erroneously applied them in reaching his final determination. If the record of the administrative proceeding does not reveal those facts which were determinative of the ruling or the logic behind the ruling, we are powerless to review the administrative action. We are thrust into the position of a trier of fact and are asked to substitute our judgment for that of the hearing examiner. That we cannot do.

Equally important is the burden placed on the individual seeking review of the administrative action. Where the hearing examiner fails to make adequate findings on the record to support his conclusions, the appellant cannot assert his grounds for review. He cannot allege error with particularity because he is unable to determine where the error was committed. Where, as here, the proceeding involves more than one ground for dismissal, the party seeking review is unable to discuss which of those charges the hearing examiner found to be supported by the evidence. The failure of the hearing examiner to state on the record adequate reasons for his determination and the evidence he relied upon infringes upon the right of the party to have an effective and meaningful review of the administrative action taken against him in violation of due process (see *Specht v. Patterson*, 386 U.S. 605 . . . (1967); *Gardner v. Louisiana*, 368 U.S. 157 . . . (1961)) [279 S.E.2d at 178].

On the basis of its review of the regents' bulletin and applicable constitutional principles, the court held that the hearing examiner's report did not meet due process standards:

The only statement made by the hearing examiner here was his conclusion that, in view of the "particularly impressive" testimony of other faculty members, Dr. Clarke's dismissal was for cause and pursuant to the procedures of the board of regents. This comment is nothing more than a conclusory pronouncement of the hearing examiner's decision on the ultimate question before him. Neither this court nor Dr. Clarke is informed of the reasons for the conclusion nor the specific evidence relied on. A proper statement of the hearing examiner's reasons and a clear indication of the evidence on which he relied is especially important where there are myriad charges and hundreds of pages of testimony. In the report of findings and recommendations, a hearing examiner should list the specific charges found to be supported by the evidence adduced at the hearing and provide some reference to the evidence supporting those findings. In view of our discussion above, we conclude that the failure of the hearing examiner to state on the record the charges against Dr. Clarke which were found to be supported by the evidence constitutes reversible error [279 S.E.2d at 178].

In termination proceedings, questions may arise as to whether defects in one segment of the proceeding constitute a sufficient violation of due process to invalidate the entire proceeding. In *Fong v. Purdue University*, 692 F. Supp. 930 (N.D. Ind. 1988), for example, Professor Fong had asked for several delays in the scheduling of the hearing on his dismissal. The faculty hearing committee granted one delay, but decided to proceed on the rescheduled date. Although Fong was available on that date, he refused to attend the hearing because his attorney was not present. The hearing panel recorded and had transcribed the proceedings; and Fong later appeared with his attorney and presented his own witnesses and cross-examined the university's witnesses. In appealing the university's decision to dismiss him, Fong asserted that his absence from part of the hearing was a denial of due process. The court found that Professor Fong had been given, and had taken advantage of, ample opportunity to present his side of the case and that no due process denial had occurred.

> The university's procedural due process, to suffice, does not require . . . the full-blown application of either the Federal Rules of Civil Procedure or Evidence. . . . Any problems that might have arisen in this regard from the fact that the university panel proceeded without Dr. Fong and without his counsel at the early stages, were adequately obviated by permitting him to call witnesses at a time when counsel was present. He was afforded an opportunity to cross-examine witnesses and to present his own witnesses. He was provided full and complete notice of the charges against him, and had an opportunity to confront and challenge those charges. Considering the record in its totality, and not in isolated segments, it is difficult to imagine what other procedural due process the officials at Purdue University could have provided to Dr. Fong [692 F. Supp. at 957].

Even if hearing procedures are lengthy, however, a substantive due process claim may ensue. In *Dismissal Proceedings Against Huang*, 431 S.E.2d 541 (N.C. Ct. App. 1993), a tenured faculty member was dismissed as a result of several assaults. Because the assaults had occurred as long as fifteen years earlier, the professor claimed that the use of "old" misconduct violated his substantive due process rights. Although the appellate court agreed, characterizing the university's actions as arbitrary and capricious, the state's supreme court reversed (441 S.E.2d 696 (1994)), finding ample evidence that the professor had engaged in conduct that constituted just cause for dismissal. Although the university ultimately prevailed, the case underscores the importance of prompt administrative response to faculty misconduct.

Procedural due process may also be required for a faculty member whose employment contract has been rescinded (see Section 3.1). In *Garner v. Michigan State University*, 462 N.W.2d 832 (Mich. Ct. App. 1990), the university, without holding a hearing, rescinded the contract of a tenured professor who allegedly lied to the dean about allegations of unprofessional conduct in his prior faculty position. When the dean discovered that serious charges had been made against the professor at his former place of employment, the university rescinded the professor's tenured contract of employment. The professor denied that he had lied about the charges. Although the university asserted its right to rescind an employment contract because of the employee's misrepresentations, citing *Morgan v. American University*, 534 A.2d 323 (D.C. 1987) (see Section 3.1.1), the court disagreed, distinguishing *Morgan* on two grounds. First, the plaintiff in *Morgan* had admitted the misrepresentation, meaning that there was no factual dispute. Second, *Morgan* involved a private institution. The court noted that the plaintiff, as a tenured professor, had a property interest in continued employment and must be afforded the same due process protections that he would be entitled to if the university had terminated him.

Due process protections are not necessary, however, if a tenured professor abandons his position and permits several years to elapse before reclaiming it. In *Osborne v. Stone*, 536 So. 2d 473 (La. Ct. App. 1988), a state court applied the doctrine of laches in determining that a tenured law professor at Southern University who failed to report for class for an entire academic year had abandoned his position and thus was deemed to have resigned. Since Southern University did not discharge Professor Osborne, the university owed him no hearing or other due process protections.

Taken together, these cases provide a helpful picture of how courts will craft procedural requirements for tenure termination decisions. When reviewing such decisions, courts will generally look for compliance with basic elements of due process, as set out in *Potemra*. When an institution fails to accord the faculty member one or more of these basic elements, *Clarke, Garner,* and *Huang* indicate that courts will invalidate the institution's decision. But *Bowling* and *Frumkin* illustrate judicial reluctance to provide more specific checklists of procedures mandated by due process. Beyond the minimum requirements, such as those in *Potemra*, courts will usually defer to institutional procedures that appear suited to the needs and expectations of the faculty member and the institution.

3.6.2.4. *Other personnel decisions.* Courts interpreting *Roth* and *Sindermann* have made it clear that in only a narrow range of employment decisions will the claim that the faculty member has a property interest in the decision apply. For example, in *Swartz v. Scruton*, 964 F.2d 607 (7th Cir. 1992), a professor sued Ball State University, alleging a constitutionally defective failure to follow the proper procedures in determining the recipients of merit salary raises. The court ruled that there was no constitutionally protected property interest in the process of determining merit raises that would support a substantive due process claim, and that the faculty member's procedural interests were not themselves property rights (in other words, the purpose of due process was to protect a property interest, had one existed, but the process itself was not a property interest). Furthermore, the professor had no property interest in a specific pay increase, and even if the professor could have demonstrated a contractual right to the use of proper procedures, this right would not equal a property interest.

Courts have similarly refused to find a protected property interest in other decisions related to faculty employment—for instance, decisions to transfer faculty members to other departments or to less desirable office space within a department. In *Maples v. Martin*, 858 F.2d 1546 (11th Cir. 1988), the plaintiffs, all of whom were tenured professors, were transferred from the mechanical engineering department to other engineering departments at Auburn University. (The professors also asserted academic freedom claims, discussed in Section 3.7.3.) The plaintiffs claimed that they were denied due process in the transfer decision, but the court concluded that their claim was unfounded.

Considering first whether the property interests that they asserted were sufficient to satisfy the Fourteenth Amendment's Due Process Clause, the court determined that "[t]ransfers and reassignments have generally not been held to implicate a property interest" (858 F.2d at 1550). It indicated that, in this case, neither the faculty handbook nor state law contained any provision protecting a profesor from transfer to another department without his or her consent, and such decisions apparently were left to the discretion of university administrators. Thus rejecting the professors' property interest claim, the court also summarily rejected their liberty interest claim, because they had not suffered any loss of rank or salary, could still teach in their areas of specialization, and could not show any stigma resulting from the transfers that would damage their professional reputations or foreclose them from other employment opportunities (858 F.2d at 1550–51, n.5 and accompanying text).

The court held further that, even if the transfer had infringed a property or liberty interest, the professors still would not have been denied procedural due process. The professors had been given notice of the transfers, and the grievance procedures in the faculty handbook were available to them to challenge the transfers (an opportunity that the professors did not pursue).

Another federal court, asked to determine whether a tenured professor had a property interest in a particular position, ruled that no property interest existed in the position itself and that the faculty member's only property interest was in receiving his full compensation (*Huang v. Board of Governors of the University of North Carolina*, 902 F.2d 1134 (4th Cir. 1990). Furthermore, the court ruled that the university had afforded the plaintiff ample due process because he had had an opportunity to present his grievances to a faculty committee during a nine-day hearing. The procedures used were sufficient, the court ruled, to ensure that the transfer decision was not arbitrary and that it was reached impartially.

Unless an administrative position is explicitly identified as a tenured position, incumbents have no property interest in retaining their administrative positions. In *Garvie v. Jackson*, 845 F.2d 647 (6th Cir. 1988), the former head of the speech and theater department at the University of Tennessee argued that his removal from that position (to a position as a tenured faculty member) without a hearing violated his rights to due process. The court disagreed. The faculty handbook stated clearly that positions as department heads were not tenured; furthermore, a letter appointing the plaintiff as head stated that he would serve at the pleasure of the chancellor. To the plaintiff's claim that removal as department head violated his liberty interests because "rumors" accompanied the removal, the court determined that, since the plaintiff returned to a tenured faculty position, he could not demonstrate the kind of interference with career opportunities that would normally give rise to a liberty interest.

3.6.3. The private faculty member's procedural rights.

The rights of faculty employed by private colleges and universities are governed primarily by state contract law and, where applicable, by state constitutions. Although the lack of constitutional protections for faculty at private institutions gives the institution more flexibility in fashioning its decision-making procedures and in determining what procedural protections it will afford faculty, written policies, faculty handbooks, and other policy documents are interpreted as binding contracts in many states (see Section 3.1), and "academic custom and usage" (see Section 1.3.2.3) may also be used by judges to evaluate whether a private institution afforded a faculty member the appropriate protections. Because challenges to negative employment decisions brought by faculty against private institutions are interpreted under state law, the outcomes and reasoning of any particular case must be applied with care to institutions in states other than the state in which the litigation occurred.

Many private institutions have adopted, either in whole or in part, policy statements promulgated by the American Association of University Professors with regard to reappointment and dismissal of tenured faculty. Formal adoption of these policy statements, or consistent adherence to their terms (which could create an implied contract, as discussed in Section 3.1.1), will require the private institution to follow them. Failure to follow these policies can result in breach-of-contract claims.

The term of the contract, the conditions under which it may be renewed, and the individual's right to certain procedures in the renewal decision are all matters of contract law. If the contract states a specific term (one year, three years), then language to the contrary in other documents may not afford the faculty member greater protection. For example, in *Upadhya v. Langenburg*, 834 F.2d 661 (7th Cir. 1987), a faculty member was employed under several one-year contracts, which stated that the tenure evaluation would take place during the fifth year of employment. The faculty member was notified that he would not be given a fourth one-year contract. Asserting that language in the contracts guaranteed him five years of employment, the faculty member sued for breach of contract. The court disagreed with the plaintiff's interpretation, stating that the language regarding a fifth-year tenure review was not contractually binding on the college and that the contract was clearly intended to be issued for only a one-year period. Furthermore, the faculty handbook stated that there was no guaranteed right to renewal for probationary faculty members.

The written terms of the contract will generally prevail, even if the faculty member can demonstrate that oral representations were made that modified the written contract. In *Baker v. Lafayette College*, 504 A.2d 247 (Pa. Super. Ct. 1986), the plaintiff argued that the head of his department had promised him a full four-year probationary period. When Baker's two-year contract was not renewed, he sued for breach of contract. Pointing to language in the faculty handbook that gave the faculty member a right to *consideration* for reappointment, rather than an absolute right to reappointment, the court denied the claim.

Even handbook language that appears to afford probationary faculty members rights to reappointment may not bind the institution. In *Brumbach v. Rensselaer Polytechnic Institute*, 510 N.Y.S.2d 762 (N.Y. App. Div. 1987), the plaintiff, an assistant professor of public archaeology, was given a three-year contract. Her work was evaluated formally each year and was found to be satisfactory. Just before the contract's expiration, the department faculty decided to change the plaintiff's position to one in computer archaeology, a position for which the plaintiff was not qualified. The department offered the plaintiff a one-year terminal contract. At its expiration, she instituted an action for breach of contract, asserting that the faculty handbook's statement "If the result of the evaluation is satisfactory, it is normal for an assistant professor to be re-employed for a second three-year period" obligated the institution to reappoint her.

The court disagreed, stating that, upon expiration of the contract, the plaintiff became an employee at will. The handbook's language regarding evaluation did not amount to a promise to dismiss a probationary faculty member only for just cause, and there was no showing that the decision to modify the plaintiff's position was arbitrary or capricious. For those reasons, the trial court's grant of summary judgment to the institution was affirmed.

An often-litigated issue in nonreappointment decisions is the timeliness of notice. Depending on the wording of the contract, faculty handbook, or policy document, failure to notify a faculty member of a nonrenewal decision in a timely manner may give rise to contractual damages and, in some cases, to tenure. In *Howard University v. Best*, 547 A.2d 144 (D.C. 1988), a trial court and an appellate court considered the issue of timeliness of notice—specifically, whether a faculty member was entitled to "indefinite tenure" if timely notice of nonreappointment was not given—and the meaning of the term "prior appointment."

Marie Best had initially held a three-month nonfaculty appointment at Howard University. She was then given a three-year faculty appointment but was not given the one-year notice of nonrenewal of that appointment in a timely manner. Best sued for breach of contract, arguing that the university's failure to notify her of the nonrenewal entitled her to tenure. Alternatively, she argued that the three-year faculty appointment was really a reappointment, since she had previously held a position at Howard, and that the faculty handbook's provision that faculty received tenure upon reappointment after a previous appointment entitled her to tenure.

The court attempted to determine whether it was Howard University's "custom and practice" to grant tenure to a faculty member who had served in a part-time, nonfaculty position. Finding no evidence of a pattern of such tenure awards, the court ruled against Best's theory of tenure on reappointment. With regard to Best's theory that late notice of nonreappointment entitled her to tenure, or at least to an additional three-year appointment without tenure, the court found evidence that the university had given other faculty additional appointments in situations where reappointment notices were late. For that reason, the appellate court affirmed the jury verdict for a second three-year appointment without tenure, and $155,000 in damages.

3.6.4. Implementing procedural requirements. An institution's procedures for making and internally reviewing faculty personnel decisions should be put in writing and made generally available. Public institutions must, at a minimum, comply with the constitutional due process requirements in Section 3.6.2 and may choose to provide additional procedures beyond those required by the Constitution. Private institutions are not required to comply with constitutional requirements but may wish to use these requirements as a guide in establishing their own procedures.

Though personnel procedures can be administratively burdensome, that is not the whole story. They can also help the institution avoid or rectify mistaken assessments, protect the academic freedom of the faculty, foster faculty confidence in the institution, and encourage the resolution of nonrenewal and termination disputes in-house rather than in the courts. When effective personnel procedures do exist, courts may require, under the "exhaustion-of-remedies" doctrine (see Section 1.4.2.5), that the faculty member "exhaust" those procedures before filing suit. In *Rieder v. State University of New York*, 366 N.Y.S.2d 37 (N.Y. App. Div. 1975), *affirmed*, 351 N.E.2d 747 (N.Y 1976), for instance, employees at a state institution were covered by a collective bargaining agreement containing a four-step grievance procedure. When some employees filed suit while awaiting a determination at step 2, the appellate courts ordered the suit dismissed for failure to exhaust administrative remedies.[49]

In cases such as *Rieder* (and see also *Beck v. Board of Trustees of State Colleges*, Section 1.4.2.5), where public institutions are involved, the administrative law of the state provides the source of the exhaustion doctrine. Such administrative law principles do not apply to private institutions, since they are not agencies of the state. Private institutions may be subject to a comparable exhaustion doctrine, however, stemming from the common law of "private associations" (see Section 4.8.4). For an overview of this common law exhaustion doctrine, see "Developments in the Law—

[49]Plaintiffs filing civil rights claims under "Section 1983," the federal civil rights statute, need not exhaust state administrative remedies (see *Patsy v. Board of Regents of the State of Florida*, 457 U.S. 496 (1982), discussed in Section 2.3.3).

Judicial Control of Actions of Private Associations," 76 *Harvard L. Rev.* 983, 1069–80 (1963).

In devising or reviewing procedures, administrators should carefully consider what procedural safeguards they should provide before making a personnel decision or before suspending or terminating job benefits, as opposed to after. In public institutions, for example, a full-scale hearing need not be provided before the personnel decision is tentatively made. Some courts, however, require a hearing before an institution actually implements the decision by terminating the faculty member's pay or other substantial employment benefits. In *Skehan v. Board of Trustees of Bloomsburg State College*, 501 F.2d 31 (3d Cir. 1974), for instance, the plaintiff had been relieved of his duties, dismissed, and removed from the payroll for almost three months before he was afforded a hearing. The court held that the hearing, because of its timing, did not meet due process requirements. In *Peacock v. Board of Regents of University and State Colleges of Arizona*, 510 F.2d 1324 (9th Cir. 1975), however, the court upheld a post-termination hearing where the faculty member had been removed only from a nonpaying position as department head; and in *Chung v. Park*, 514 F.2d 382 (3d Cir. 1975), the court upheld a hearing that had been provided after the decision to terminate was made but before job benefits were actually terminated.

The question of when and in what detail statements of reasons for personnel decisions are to be given must also be carefully considered. The question of who shall preside over hearings is likewise important, with impartiality being the key consideration. Other critical issues are the confidentiality of the statements of reasons—and of any proceedings in which the faculty member challenges these reasons—and the question of what permanent records should be kept of adverse personnel decisions and who should have access to them. While the legal principles in Sections 3.6.1 and 3.6.2 create some limits on administrative discretion in these areas, considerable flexibility remains for administrators to make wise policy choices.

Sec. 3.7. Faculty Academic Freedom

3.7.1. General concepts and principles. The concept of academic freedom eludes precise definition. It draws meaning from both the world of education and the world of law. Educators usually use the term "academic freedom" in reference to the custom and practice, and the ideal, by which faculties may best flourish in their work as teachers and researchers (see, for example, the AAUP's 1940 "Statement of Principles on Academic Freedom and Tenure," in *AAUP Policy Documents and Reports* (AAUP, 1990), 3–10). Lawyers and judges, in comparison, often use "academic freedom" as a catch-all term to describe the legal rights and responsibilities of the teaching profession, and courts hearing such cases attempt to reconcile basic constitutional principles with prevailing views of academic freedom's social and intellectual role in American life. Moreover, academic freedom refers not only to the prerogatives of faculty members and students but also to the prerogatives of institutions ("institutional academic freedom" or "institutional autonomy"). As the court stated in *Piarowski v. Illinois Community College*, 759 F.2d 625 (7th Cir. 1985), "though many decisions describe 'academic freedom' as an aspect of the freedom of speech that is protected against governmental abridgment by the First Amendment, . . . the term is equivocal. It is used to denote both the freedom of the academy to pursue its ends without interference from the government . . . and the freedom of the individual teacher (or in some versions—indeed in most cases—the student) to pursue his ends without interference from the academy; and these two freedoms are in conflict." And in *Regents of the University of Michigan v. Ewing*, 474 U.S. 214, 226 n.12 (1985), the U.S. Supreme Court itself confirmed that "[a]cademic freedom thrives not only on the independent and uninhibited exchange of ideas among teachers and students . . . but also, and somewhat inconsistently, on autonomous decision making by the academy itself."

In the realm of law and courts (the primary focus of this section), yet another distinction regarding academic freedom must be made: the distinction between constitutional law and contract law. Though courts usually discuss academic freedom in cases concerning the constitutional rights of faculty members, the legal boundaries of academic freedom are initially defined by contract law. Faculty members possess whatever academic freedom is guaranteed them under the faculty contract (see Section 3.1). The AAUP's 1940 "Statement of Principles on Academic Freedom and Tenure," its 1970 "Interpretive Comments," and its 1982 "Recommended Institutional Regulations on Academic Freedom and Tenure" (all included in *AAUP Policy Documents and Reports* (AAUP, 1990), 3–10, 21–30) are often considered the preeminent policy statements on academic freedom, and it is crucial for administrators to determine whether either document has been—or should be—incorporated into the faculty contract. For any document that has been incorporated, courts will interpret and enforce its terms by reference to contract law principles. Even when these documents have not been incorporated into the contract, they may be an important source of academic "custom and usage" that courts will consider in interpreting unclear contract terms (see Sections 1.3.2.3 and 3.1).

In public institutions administrators are limited by both contract law and constitutional concepts of academic freedom,[50] and perhaps also by state statutes or administrative regulations on academic freedom. But in private institutions (see Sections 1.5.1 and 1.5.3), the faculty contract may be the only legal restriction on the administrator's authority to limit academic freedom. In religiously affiliated institutions, concern for the institution's special mission may add additional complexities to contract law's application to academic freedom problems (see, for example, the *Curran* case discussed in Section 3.1.6 and the *Quilichini* case discussed in Section 3.7.5.2). In addition, concerns regarding the establishment and free exercise of religion may limit the capacity of the courts to entertain lawsuits against religiously affiliated institutions by faculty members alleging breach of contract (see, for example, the *Welter* and *Alicea* cases discussed in Section 3.1.6).

While contractual and statutory provisions may distinguish between tenured and nontenured faculty, tenure and job status are immaterial to most constitutionally based academic freedom claims. In *Perry v. Sindermann*, 408 U.S. 593 (1972), dis-

---

[50]The same constitutional concepts would limit legislatures and government officials whose regulatory actions affected academic freedom, whether in public or in private institutions. One contemporary manifestation of this problem is the debate on whether government regulation of sexual harassment in the workplace would implicate First Amendment concerns and thus, as applied to faculty members and higher education institutions, may impinge upon academic freedom. See, for example, E. Volokh, "Freedom of Speech and Workplace Harassment," 39 *UCLA L. Rev.* 1809 (1992). For another manifestation, see the problem of keeping academic information confidential in the face of government requests for disclosure, discussed in this volume, Section 3.7.7.

cussed in Section 3.6.2.1, the U.S. Supreme Court held that a nonrenewed faculty member's "lack of a contractual or tenure right to reemployment . . . is immaterial to his free speech claim" and that, "regardless of the . . . [teacher's] contractual or other claim to a job," government cannot "deny a benefit to a person because of his constitutionally protected speech or associations."[51]

Constitutional principles of academic freedom have developed in two stages, each occupying a distinct time period and including distinct types of cases. The earlier cases of the 1950s and 1960s focused on faculty and institutional freedom from external (political) intrusion. These cases pitted the faculty and the institution against the state. Since the early 1970s, however, academic freedom cases have focused primarily on faculty freedom from institutional intrusion. In these later cases, faculty academic freedom has collided with institutional academic freedom.

In the 1950s and 1960s cases, the U.S. Supreme Court gave academic freedom constitutional status under the First Amendment freedoms of speech and association, and to a lesser extent under the Fifth Amendment protection against self-incrimination and the Fourteenth Amendment guarantee of procedural due process. The opinions in these cases include a number of ringing declarations on the importance of academic freedom. In *Sweezy v. New Hampshire*, 354 U.S. 234 (1957), for example, both the plurality opinion and Justice Frankfurter's concurring opinion lauded academic freedom in the course of reversing a contempt judgment against a professor who had refused to answer questions concerning a lecture delivered at the state university. In *Shelton v. Tucker*, 364 U.S. 479 (1960), where it invalidated a state statute that compelled public school and college teachers to reveal all organizational affiliations or contributions for the previous five years, the Court remarked:

> The vigilant protection of constitutional freedoms is nowhere more vital than in the community of American schools. "By limiting the power of the states to interfere with freedom of speech and freedom of inquiry and freedom of association, the Fourteenth Amendment protects all persons, no matter what their calling. But, in view of the nature of the teacher's relation to the effective exercise of the rights which are safeguarded by the Bill of Rights and by the Fourteenth Amendment, inhibition of freedom of thought, and of action upon thought, in the case of teachers brings the safeguards of those amendments vividly into operation. Such unwarranted inhibition upon the free spirit of teachers . . . has an unmistakable tendency to chill that free play of the spirit which all teachers ought especially to cultivate and practice; it makes for caution and timidity in their associations by potential teachers" (*Wieman v. Updegraff*, 344 U.S. 183, 195 . . . (concurring opinion)) [364 U.S. at 487].

And in *Keyishian v. Board of Regents*, 385 U.S. 589 (1967), discussed below, the Court quoted both *Sweezy* and *Shelton*, and added:

> Our nation is deeply committed to safeguarding academic freedom, which is of transcendent value to all of us and not merely to the teachers concerned. That

---

[51]The *Perry* Court also held, in contrast, that the professor's job status, "though irrelevant to his free speech claim, is highly relevant to his procedural due process claim." The Fourteenth Amendment due process clause is the one constitutional basis for an academic freedom claim that distinguishes among faculty members on the basis of job status.

freedom is therefore a special concern of the First Amendment, which does not tolerate laws that cast a pall of orthodoxy over the classroom. . . . The classroom is peculiarly the "marketplace of ideas." The nation's future depends upon leaders trained through wide exposure to that robust exchange of ideas which discovers truth "out of a multitude of tongues, [rather] than through any kind of authoritative selection" (*United States v. Associated Press,* 52 F. Supp. 362, 372) [385 U.S. at 603].

The legal principles that emerge from the 1950s and 1960s cases, however, are not as broad as the Court's academic freedom declarations might suggest. The faculty's constitutional rights evolving from these cases are succinctly summarized by William Van Alstyne in "The Constitutional Rights of Teachers and Professors," 1970 *Duke L.J.* 841, 847–48:

1. Membership per se in political organizations, not excluding the Communist Party, or economic organizations such as labor unions is not a permissible ground for terminating teachers or disqualifying applicants to the profession. Arguably, moreover, not even active and knowing membership including some degree of personal sympathy for the illegal objectives of the group may be sufficient, short of some concrete act in furtherance of an illegal objective inconsistent with one's lawful obligations as a teacher.

2. Correspondingly, disclaimer oaths requiring that one forswear activities or associations he is otherwise constitutionally privileged to pursue as a private citizen are beyond the constitutional pale. In all likelihood, the state may go no further than to require that one be willing to affirm a general commitment to uphold the Constitution and faithfully to perform the duties of the position he holds.[52]

3. While neither the First Amendment nor the Fifth Amendment entitles a teacher to withhold information when his employer has questioned his competence or professional integrity on the basis of reasonably specific and creditable allegations "of impropriety related to his job," information elicited under such circumstances by a public employer may not be utilized for purposes of criminal prosecution, and vague or general fishing expeditions on mere suspicion are not permissible.

The centerpiece of these constitutional developments is the Supreme Court's 1967 decision in the *Keyishian* case, quoted above. The appellants were State University of New York faculty members who refused to sign a certificate (the "Feinberg Certificate") stating that they were not and never had been Communists. This certificate was required under a set of laws and regulations designed to prevent "subversives" from obtaining employment in the state's educational system. The faculty members lost their jobs and sued the state on the grounds that the dismissal violated

---

[52](Author's footnote.) In *Cole v. Richardson,* 405 U.S. 676 (1972), the U.S. Supreme Court later upheld an oath that included not only a general commitment to "uphold and defend" the Constitution but also a commitment to "oppose the overthrow of the government . . . by force, violence, or by any illegal or unconstitutional method." To maintain the second commitment's constitutionality, the Court read it very narrowly as merely "a commitment not to use illegal and constitutionally unprotected force to change the constitutional system." So interpreted, the second commitment "does not expand the obligation of the first [commitment]."

their First Amendment rights. They challenged the certificate requirements and the underlying law barring employment to members of subversive organizations, as well as other provisions authorizing dismissal for the "utterance of any treasonable or seditious word or words or the doing of any treasonable or seditious act" and for "by word of mouth or writing wilfully and deliberately advocating, advising, or teaching the doctrine of forceful overthrow of the government."

The Court held that the faculty members' First Amendment freedom of association had been violated by the existence and application of a series of laws and rules that were both vague and overbroad (see Section 3.5.1 regarding the vagueness and overbreadth doctrines). The word "seditious" was held to be unconstitutionally vague, even when defined as advocacy of criminal anarchy:

> The possible scope of "seditious utterances or acts" has virtually no limit. For under Penal Law § 161, one commits the felony of advocating criminal anarchy if he "publicly displays any book . . . containing or advocating, advising or teaching the doctrine that organized government should be overthrown by force, violence, or other unlawful means." Does the teacher who carries a copy of the Communist Manifesto on a public street thereby advocate criminal anarchy? . . . The teacher cannot know the extent, if any, to which a "seditious" utterance must transcend mere statement about abstract doctrine, the extent to which it must be intended to and tend to indoctrinate or incite to action in furtherance of the defined doctrine. The crucial consideration is that no teacher can know just where the line is drawn between "seditious" and nonseditious utterances and acts [385 U.S. at 598-99].

The Court also found that the state's entire system of "intricate administrative machinery" was "a highly efficient *in terrorem* mechanism. . . . It would be a bold teacher who would not stay as far as possible from utterances or acts which might jeopardize his living by enmeshing him in this intricate machinery. . . . The result may be to stifle 'that free play of the spirit which all teachers ought especially to cultivate and practice' " (385 U.S. at 601; quoting *Wieman v. Updegraff*, 344 U.S. 183, 195 (Frankfurter, concurring)).

The Court rejected the older case of *Adler v. Board of Education*, 342 U.S. 485 (1951), which permitted New York to bar employment to teachers who were members of listed subversive organizations. Noting that "the stifling effect on the academic mind from curtailing freedom of association in such a manner is manifest," the Court applied a new rule:

> Mere knowing membership without a specific intent to further the unlawful aims of an organization is not a constitutionally adequate basis for exclusion from such positions as those held by appellants. . . . Legislation which sanctions membership unaccompanied by specific intent to further the unlawful goals of the organization or which is not active membership violates constitutional limitations [385 U.S. at 606, 608].

One year after *Keyishian*, the Supreme Court stepped gingerly into a new type of academic freedom controversy that became the primary focus for the second stage of academic freedom's development in the courts. *Pickering v. Board of Education*,

391 U.S. 563 (1968), concerned a public high school teacher who had been dismissed for writing the local newspaper a letter in which he criticized the board of education's financial plans for the high schools. Pickering brought suit alleging that the dismissal violated his First Amendment freedom of speech. The school board argued that the dismissal was justified because the letter "damaged the professional reputations of . . . [the school board] members and of the school administrators, would be disruptive of faculty discipline, and would tend to foment 'controversy, conflict, and dissention' among teachers, administrators, the board of education, and the residents of the district."

The Court balanced the teacher's free speech interests against the state's interest in maintaining an efficient educational system, using the following considerations in the balance: (1) Was there a close working relationship between the teacher and those he criticized? (2) Is the substance of the letter a matter of legitimate public concern? (3) Did the letter have a detrimental impact on the administration of the educational system? (4) Was the teacher's performance of his daily duties impeded? (5) Was the teacher writing in his professional capacity or as a private citizen? The Court found that Pickering had no working relationship with the board, that the letter dealt with a matter of public concern, that Pickering's letter was greeted with public apathy and therefore had no detrimental effect on the schools, that Pickering's performance as a teacher was not hindered by the letter, and that he wrote as a citizen, not as a teacher. The Court concluded that under all these facts the school administration's interest in limiting teachers' opportunities to contribute to public debate was not significantly greater than its interest in limiting a similar contribution by any member of the general public and that "in a case such as this, absent proof of false statements knowingly or recklessly made by him, a teacher's exercise of his right to speak on issues of public importance may not furnish the basis for his dismissal from public employment."

The *Pickering* balancing test was further explicated in two later Supreme Court cases: *Givhan v. Western Line Consolidated School District*, 439 U.S. 410 (1979), and *Connick v. Myers*, 461 U.S. 138 (1983).

In *Givhan* the issue was whether *Pickering* protects public school teachers who communicate their views in private rather than in public. In a series of private meetings with her school principal, the plaintiff teacher in *Givhan* had made complaints and expressed opinions about school employment practices that she considered racially discriminatory. When the school district did not renew her contract, the teacher filed suit, claiming an infringement of her First Amendment rights. The trial court found that the school district had not renewed the teacher's contract primarily because of her criticisms of school employment practices, and it held that such action violated the First Amendment. The U.S. Court of Appeals reversed, reasoning that the teacher's expression was not protected by the First Amendment because she had expressed her views privately. The U.S. Supreme Court, in a unanimous opinion, disagreed with the appeals court and remanded the case to the trial court for further consideration. According to the Court, "neither the [First] Amendment itself nor our decisions indicate that . . . freedom [of speech] is lost to the public employee who arranges to communicate privately with his employer rather than to spread his views before the public." Rather, private expression, like public expression, is subject to the same balancing of factors that the Court utilized in *Pickering*. The Court did suggest in a footnote, however, that private expression may involve some different considerations:

   Although the First Amendment's protection of government employees extends to private as well as public expression, striking the *Pickering* balance in each context may involve different considerations. When a teacher speaks publicly, it is generally the content of his statements that must be assessed to determine whether they "in any way either impeded the teacher's proper performance of his daily duties in the classroom or . . . interfered with the regular operation of the schools generally" (*Pickering v. Board of Education*, 391 U.S. at 572–73). Private expression, however, may in some situations bring additional factors to the *Pickering* calculus. When a government employee personally confronts his immediate superior, the employing agency's institutional efficiency may be threatened not only by the content of the employee's message but also by the manner, time, and place in which it is delivered [439 U.S. at 415 n.4].

   In *Connick v. Myers*, the issue was whether *Pickering* protects public employees who communicate views to office staff about office personnel matters. The plaintiff, Myers, was an assistant district attorney who had been scheduled for transfer to another division of the office. In opposing the transfer, she circulated a questionnaire on office operations to other assistant district attorneys. Later on the same day, she was discharged. In a 5-to-4 decision, the Court declined to apply *Givhan*, arguing that Givhan's statements about employment practices "involved a matter of public concern." Then, applying the *Pickering* factors, the Court majority determined that the questions posed by Myers (with one exception) "do not fall under the rubric of matters of 'public concern'"; that Myers spoke "not as a citizen upon matters of public concern, but instead as an employee upon matters only of personal interest"; and that circulation of the questionnaire interfered with "close working relationships" within the office. The balance of factors therefore indicated that the discharge did not violate the plaintiff's freedom of speech.
   Givhan and *Connick* emphasize the need to distinguish between communications on matters of public concern and communications on matters of private or personal concern—a distinction that does not depend on whether the communication is itself made in public or in private. The dispute between the majority and dissenters in *Connick* reveals how slippery this distinction can be. Although *Connick* may appear to limit the protections originally provided by *Pickering*, the Court emphasized that its opinion was limited to the case's specific facts and that courts must remain attentive to the "enormous variety of fact situations" that other cases may present.
   Besides its reliance on free speech and press, self-incrimination, and procedural due process, the U.S. Supreme Court has tapped two other constitutional guarantees to develop additional protections for academic freedom. In *Epperson v. Arkansas*, 393 U.S. 97 (1968), and *Edwards v. Aguillard*, 482 U.S. 578 (1987), the Court used the First Amendment's Establishment Clause (see this volume, Section 1.6) to strike down state statutes that interfered with public school teachers' teaching of evolution. (See A. Morris, "Fundamentalism, Creation, and the First Amendment," 41 *West's Educ. Law Rptr.* 1 (1987).) In *O'Connor v. Ortega*, 480 U.S. 709 (1987), the Court used the Fourth Amendment Search and Seizure Clause. The plaintiff, who was in charge of training physicians in the psychiatric residency program at a state hospital, had his office searched by hospital officials. The Court concluded that public employees may have reasonable expectations of privacy in their offices, desks, and files; these expec-

tations may, in certain circumstances, be protected by the Fourth Amendment. A plurality of the justices, however, agreed that an employer's warrantless search of such property will nevertheless be permissible if it is done for "noninvestigatory, work-related purposes" or for "investigations of work-related misconduct," and if it meets "the standard of reasonableness under all the circumstances."[53]

In recent years lower courts have had occasion to apply U.S. Supreme Court precedents to a variety of academic freedom disputes pitting faculty members against their institutions. The source of law most frequently invoked in these cases is the First Amendment's Free Speech Clause, as interpreted in the *Pickering/Connick* line of cases. Some cases have also relied on *Keyishian* and its forerunners, either in lieu of or as a supplement to the *Pickering/Connick* line. As could be expected, courts have reached varying conclusions that depend on the specific facts of the case, the particular court's disposition on liberal construction of First Amendment protections, and its sensitivities to the nuances of academic freedom. Sections 3.7.2 through 3.7.5 below provide examples in four primary areas of concern, and Sections 3.7.6 and 3.7.7 address some additional special problems.

3.7.2. Academic freedom in the classroom. Courts are generally reticent to become involved in academic freedom disputes concerning course content, teaching methods, grading, or classroom behavior, viewing these matters as best left to the competence of the administrators and educators who have primary responsibility over academic affairs. Two classical cases from the early 1970s illustrate this judicial attitude.

Hetrick v. Martin, 480 F.2d 705 (6th Cir. 1973), concerned a state university's refusal to renew a nontenured faculty member's contract. Her troubles with the school administration apparently began when unnamed students and the parents of one student complained about certain of her in-class activities. To illustrate the "irony" and "connotative qualities" of the English language, for example, the faculty member once told her freshman students, "I am an unwed mother." At that time she was a divorced mother of two, but she did not reveal that fact to her class. On occasion she also apparently discussed the war in Vietnam and the military draft with one of her freshman classes.

The faculty member sued the university, alleging an infringement of her First Amendment rights. The court ruled that the university had not based the nonrenewal on any statements the faculty member had made but rather on her "pedagogical attitude." The faculty member believed that her students should be free to organize assignments in accordance with their own interests, while the university expected her to "go by the book." Thus, viewing the case as a dispute over teaching methods, the court refused to equate the teaching methods of professors with constitutionally protected speech:

> We do not accept plaintiff's assertion that the school administration abridged her First Amendment rights when it refused to rehire her because it considered her teaching philosophy to be incompatible with the pedagogical aims of the university. Whatever may be the ultimate scope of the amorphous

[53]Related cases are collected in Annot., "Warrantless Search by Government Employer of Employee's Workplace, Locker, Desk, or the Like as Violation of Fourth Amendment Privacy Rights—Federal Cases," 91 A.L.R. Fed. 13 (1989 and periodic supp.).

"academic freedom" guaranteed to our nation's teachers and students . . . , it does not encompass the right of a nontenured teacher to have her teaching style insulated from review by her superiors . . . just because her methods and philosophy are considered acceptable somewhere in the teaching profession [480 F.2d at 709].

Clark v. Holmes, 474 F.2d 928 (7th Cir. 1972), also involved a teacher's methods and behavior. Clark was a nontenured, temporary substitute teacher at Northern Illinois University, a state institution. He had been told that he could be rehired if he was willing to remedy certain deficiencies—namely, that he "counseled an excessive number of students instead of referring them to NIU's professional counselors; he overemphasized sex in his health survey course; he counseled students with his office door closed; and he belittled other staff members in discussions with students." After discussions with his superiors, in which he defended his conduct, Clark was rehired; but in the middle of the year he was told that he would not teach in the spring semester because of these same problems.

Clark brought suit, claiming that, under *Pickering*, the university had violated his First Amendment rights by not rehiring him because of his speech activities. The court, disagreeing, refused to apply *Pickering* to this situation: (1) Clark's disputes with his colleagues about course content were not matters of public concern, as were the matters raised in Pickering's letter; and (2) Clark's disputes involved him as a teacher, not as a private citizen, whereas Pickering's situation was just the opposite. The court then held that the institution's interest as employer overcame any free speech interest the teacher may have had:

> But we do not conceive academic freedom to be a license for uncontrolled expression at variance with established curricular contents and internally destructive of the proper functioning of the institution. First Amendment rights must be applied in light of the special characteristics of the environment in the particular case (*Tinker v. Des Moines Indep. Community School Dist.*, 393 U.S. 503, 506 . . . (1969); *Healy v. James*, 408 U.S. 169 (1972)). The plaintiff here irresponsibly made captious remarks to a captive audience, one, moreover, that was composed of students who were dependent upon him for grades and recommendations. . . .
>
> Furthermore, *Pickering* suggests that certain legitimate interests of the state may limit a teacher's right to say what he pleases: for example, (1) the need to maintain discipline or harmony among coworkers; (2) the need for confidentiality; (3) the need to curtail conduct which impedes the teacher's proper and competent performance of his daily duties; and (4) the need to encourage a close and personal relationship between the employer and his superiors, where that relationship calls for loyalty and confidence [474 F.2d at 931].

Most of the more recent cases are consistent with *Hetrick* and *Clark*. In *Lovelace v. Southeastern Massachusetts University*, 793 F.2d 419 (1st Cir. 1986), for instance, the court rejected the free speech claim of a faculty member whose contract was not renewed after he rejected administration requests to lower the academic standards he applied to his students. Citing *Hetrick* and *Clark*, the court concluded that universities must themselves have the freedom to set their own standards on "matters such as course content, homework load, and grading policy" and that "the first amendment does not require that each nontenured professor be made a sovereign unto himself."

Similarly, in *Wirsing v. Board of Regents of the University of Colorado,* 739 F. Supp. 551 (D. Colo. 1990), *affirmed without opin.,* 945 F.2d 412 (10th Cir. 1991), a tenured professor of education taught her students "that teaching and learning cannot be evaluated by any standardized test." Consistent with these beliefs, the professor refused to administer the university's standardized course evaluation forms for her classes. The dean denied her a pay increase because of her refusal. The professor sought a court injunction ordering the regents to award her the pay increase and to desist from requiring her to use the form. She argued that the forms were "contrary to her theory of education. Hence, by being forced to give her students the standardized form, the university is interfering arbitrarily with her classroom method, compelling her speech, and violating her right to academic freedom." The court rejected her argument:

> Here, the record is clear that Dr. Wirsing was not denied her merit salary increase because of her teaching methods, presentation of opinions contrary to those of the university, or otherwise presenting controversial ideas to her students. Rather, she was denied her merit increase for her refusal to comply with the University's teacher evaluation requirements. . . . [A]lthough Dr. Wirsing may have a constitutionally protected right under the First Amendment to disagree with the University's policies, she has no right to evidence her disagreement by failing to perform the duty imposed upon her as a condition of employment. *Shaw v. Board of Trustees,* 396 F. Supp. 872, 886 (D.C. Md. 1975), aff'd, 549 F.2d 929 (4th Cir. 1976) [739 F. Supp. at 553].

Since the professor remained free to "use the form as an example of what not to do . . . [and to] criticize openly both the [standardized] form and the University's evaluation form policy," the university's requirement was "unrelated to course content [and] in no way interferes with . . . academic freedom." Moreover, according to the court, adoption of a method of teacher evaluation "is part of the University's own right to academic freedom."

Similarly, in *Martin v. Parrish,* 805 F.2d 583 (5th Cir. 1986), the court upheld the dismissal of an economics instructor at Midland College in Texas, ruling that the instructor's use of vulgar and profane language in a college classroom did not fall within the scope of First Amendment protection. Applying *Connick v. Myers,* the court held that the instructor's language did not constitute speech on "matters of public concern." In the process, the court noted the professor's claim that, apart from *Connick,* he had "a first amendment right to 'academic freedom' that permits use of the language in question," but refused to address this claim because "such language was not germane to the subject matter in his class and had no educational function" (805 F.2d at 584 n.2). The court also approved an alternative for upholding the dismissal. Applying elementary/secondary education precedents (see *Bethel School District v. Fraser,* 478 U.S. 675 (1986)), it held that the instructor's use of the language was unprotected because "it was a deliberate, superfluous attack on a 'captive audience' with no academic purpose or justification." In a separate opinion, a concurring judge accepted the court's reasoning based on *Connick* but rejected its alternative analysis, on the grounds that the precedents the court had invoked should not apply to higher education. The concurring judge also agreed with the court in refusing to address the professor's argument based on an independent "first amendment right to 'academic freedom'"': "While some of [his] comments arguably bear on economics and could be viewed as relevant to Martin's role as a teacher in motivating the interest of his students, his remarks *as a whole* are unrelated to economics and devoid of any educational function."[54]

A leading 1990s case, *Bishop v. Aronov,* 926 F.2d 1066 (11th Cir. 1991), strikes a similar note while treading into new areas that involve religion as well as speech. An exercise physiology professor, as the court explained, "occasionally referred to his religious beliefs during instructional time. . . . Some of his references concerned his understanding of the creative force behind human physiology. Other statements involved brief explanations of a philosophical approach to problems and advice to students on coping with academic stresses." He also organized an optional after-class meeting, held shortly before the final examination, to discuss "Evidences of God in Human Physiology." But "[h]e never engaged in prayer, read passages from the Bible, handed out religious tracts, or arranged for guest speakers to lecture on a religious topic during instructional time." Some students nevertheless complained about the in-class comments and the optional meeting. The university responded by sending the professor a memo requiring that he discontinue "(1) the interjection of religious beliefs and/or preferences during instructional time periods and (2) the optional classes where a 'Christian Perspective' of an academic topic is delivered." The professor challenged the university's action as violating both his freedom of speech and his freedom of religion (see Section 1.6) under the First Amendment. The district court emphasized that "the university has created a forum for students and their professors to engage in a free interchange of ideas" and granted summary judgment for the professor (732 F. Supp. 1562 (N.D. Ala. 1990)). The U.S. Court of Appeals disagreed and upheld the university's actions.

With respect to the professor's free speech claims, the appellate court, like the majority in *Martin* (above), applied recent elementary/secondary education precedents that display considerable deference to educators (see *Hazelwood School District v. Kuhlmeier,* 484 U.S. 260 (1988)). Using *Kuhlmeier* especially, and without satisfactorily justifying its extension either to higher education in general or to faculty members (since *Kuhlmeier* concerned the free speech of *students*), the court asserted that administrators "do not offend the First Amendment by exercising editorial control over style and content of student [or professor] speech in school-sponsored expressive activities so long as their actions are reasonably related to legitimate pedagogical concerns." Addressing the academic freedom implication of its position, the court concluded:

[54]This modest elaboration of the court's brief statement apparently sows the seeds of an alternative analysis that could yield academic freedom protections for professors when their classroom speech is "germane" and has an "educational function," even if the speech is not on a "matter of public concern." For other seeds of such an alternative analysis, see *State Board for Community Colleges v. Olson,* 687 P.2d 429, 437 (Colo. 1984), and for classic elementary/secondary cases with parallel reasoning, see *Pred v. Board of Instruction of Dade County, Florida,* 415 F.2d 851, 857 n.17 (5th Cir. 1969); and *Mailloux v. Kiley,* 323 F. Supp. 1387 (D. Mass. 1971). For other analysis, focusing on the problem of hate speech in the classroom, and also distinguishing between germane and nongermane comments, see J. Weinstein, "A Constitutional Roadmap to the Regulation of Campus Hate Speech," 38 *Wayne L. Rev.* 163, 192–214 (1991).

Though we are mindful of the invaluable role academic freedom plays in our public schools, particularly at the post-secondary level, we do not find support to conclude that academic freedom is an independent First Amendment right. And, in any event, we cannot supplant our discretion for that of the University. Federal judges should not be ersatz deans or educators. In this regard, we trust that the University will serve its own interests as well as those of its professors in pursuit of academic freedom [926 F.2d at 1075].

In upholding the university's authority in matters of course content as superior to that of the professor, the court accepted the validity and applicability of two particular institutional concerns underlying the university's decision to limit the professor's instructional activities. First was the university's "concern . . . that its courses be taught without personal religious bias unnecessarily infecting the teacher or the students." Second was the concern that optional classes not be conducted under circumstances that give "the impression of official sanction, which might [unduly pressure] students into attending and, at least for purposes of examination, into adopting the beliefs expressed" by the professor. Relying on these two concerns, against the backdrop of its general deference to the institution in curricular matters, the court concluded:

In short, Dr. Bishop and the University disagree about a matter of content in the course he teaches. The University must have the final say in such a dispute. Though Dr. Bishop's sincerity cannot be doubted, his educational judgment can be questioned and redirected by the University when he is acting under its auspices as a course instructor, but not when he acts as an independent educator or researcher. The University's conclusions about course content must be allowed to hold sway over an individual professor's judgments. By its memo to Dr. Bishop, the University seeks to prevent him from presenting his religious viewpoint during instructional time, even to the extent that it represents his professional opinion about his subject matter. We have simply concluded that the University as an employer and educator can direct Dr. Bishop to refrain from expression of religious viewpoints in the classroom and like settings [926 F.2d at 1076–77].

Though the appellate court's opinion may seem overly deferential to the institution's prerogatives as employer, and insufficiently sensitive to the particular role of faculty academic freedom in higher education (see R. O'Neil, "*Bishop v. Aronov*: A Comment," 18 *J. Coll. & Univ. Law* 381 (1992)), at least the court was careful to demarcate limits on its holding. These limits are very important. Regarding the professor's classroom activities, the court clearly stated that the university's authority applies only "to the classroom speech of the professor, . . . wherever he purports to conduct a class for the university." "[T]he university has not suggested that [the professor] cannot hold his particular views; express them, on his own time, far and wide and to whomever will listen; or write and publish, no doubt authoritatively, on them; nor could it so prohibit him." The court also conceded that "[o]f course, if a student asks about [the professor's] religious views, he may fairly answer the question." Moreover, regarding the optional meetings, the court noted that "[t]he University has not suggested that [the professor] cannot organize such meetings, make notice of them on campus, or request University space to conduct them; nor could it so prohibit him." As long as the professor "makes it plain to his students that such meetings are not mandatory, not considered part of the coursework, and not related to grading, the university cannot prevent him from conducting such meetings."

The court rejected the professor's free exercise of religion claim in a single paragraph, noting that the professor "has made no true suggestion, much less demonstration, that any proscribed conduct of his impedes the practice of religion. . . . [T]he university's restrictions of him are not directed at his efforts to practice religion, per se, but rather are directed at his practice of teaching." The court likewise gave scant attention to the potential Establishment Clause ramifications of the case: "we do not reach the establishment clause questions raised by [the professor's] conduct. The university can restrict speech that falls short of an establishment violation, and we have already disposed of the university's restrictions of [the professor] under the free speech clause."[55] (For a suggested framework for analyzing the religion and free speech claims in *Bishop* and related cases, see O'Neil, above.)

Although the above cases strongly support institutional authority over professors' instructional activities, it does not follow that institutions invariably prevail. The courts in *Wirsing, Martin,* and *Bishop,* in limiting their holdings, all suggest situations in which faculty members could prevail. In the following three cases, faculty members—and thus faculty academic freedom—actually did prevail over institutional authority.

In *Parate v. Isibor,* 868 F.2d 821 (6th Cir. 1989), the court used the First Amendment to limit the deference traditionally accorded administrative decisions about grading of students. The defendant, dean of the school in which the plaintiff was a nontenured professor, ordered the plaintiff, over his objections, to execute a grade-change form raising the final grade of one of his students. The plaintiff argued that this incident, and several later incidents alleged to be in retaliation for his lack of cooperation regarding the grade change, violated his First Amendment academic freedom. Relying on the Free Speech Clause, the court agreed that "[b]ecause the assignment of a letter grade is symbolic communication intended to send a specific message to the student, the individual professor's communicative act is entitled to some measure of First Amendment protection." The court reasoned (without reliance on the *Pickering/Connick* methodology) that:

> [T]he professor's evaluation of her students and assignment of their grades is central to the professor's teaching method. . . . Although the individual professor does not escape the reasonable review of university officials in the assignment of grades, she should remain free to decide, according to her own professional judgment, what grades to assign and what grades not to assign. . . . Thus, the individual professor may not be compelled, by university officials, to change a grade that the professor previously assigned to her student. Because the individual professor's assignment of a letter grade is protected speech, the university officials' action to compel the professor to alter that grade would severely burden a protected activity [868 F.2d at 828].

Thus, the defendant's act of ordering the plaintiff to change the grade, contrary to the plaintiff's professional judgment, violated the First Amendment. The

---

[55]For an example of a classroom case in which the court did find an Establishment Clause violation, see *Lynch v. Indiana State University Board of Trustees,* 378 N.E.2d 900 (Ind. 1978).

court indicated, however, that had university administrators changed the student's grade themselves, this action would not have violated the plaintiff's First Amendment rights. The protection that *Parate* accords to faculty grading and teaching methods is therefore quite narrow—more symbolic than real, perhaps, but nonetheless an important step away from the deference normally paid institutions in these matters. (For a more extended critique and criticism of *Parate*, see D. Sacken, "Making No Sense of Academic Freedom: *Parate v. Isibor*," 56 *West's Educ. Law Rptr.* 1107 (Jan. 4, 1990).)

Another case, *DiBona v. Matthews*, 269 Cal. Rptr. 882 (Cal. Ct. App. 1990), illustrates that the First Amendment can provide a measure of protection for a professor's artistic and literary expression as it relates to the choice of class content and materials. In this case the California Court of Appeal held that San Diego Community College District administrators violated a teacher's free speech rights when they canceled a play production and a drama class in which the controversial play was to have been performed. The teacher had selected a play entitled *Split Second* for performance by students enrolled in the drama class. The play was about a black police officer who, in the course of an arrest, shot a white suspect after the suspect had subjected him to racial slurs and epithets. The play's theme closely paralleled the facts of a criminal case that was then being tried in San Diego. The court determined that the college administrators had canceled the class because of the content of the play. While the First Amendment Free Speech Clause did not completely prevent the college from considering the play's content in deciding to cancel the drama class, the court held that the college's particular reasons—that the religious community opposed the play and that the subject was controversial and sensitive—were not valid reasons under the First Amendment. Moreover, distinguishing the present case from those involving minors in elementary and secondary schools, the court held that the college could not cancel the drama class solely because of the vulgar language included in the play.

Yet another case, *McConnell v. Howard University*, 818 F.2d 58 (D.C. Cir. 1987), discussed further in Sections 1.4.3.6 and 3.5.2, provides some academic freedom protection in the private institution context and signals another type of step away from the traditional deference that courts give to administrators' decisions regarding classroom behavior. The *McConnell* court raised questions about the university's handling of a conflict between professor and student and ordered the case remanded for a de novo trial. The case was a breach-of-contract action, and the court's reasoning suggests that, at least in circumstances like those being addressed, the contract claim may be a more promising vehicle for faculty members than the constitutional claims in cases such as *Hetrick* and *Clark*. (Contrast *McConnell*, however, with another contract case raising academic freedom issues—the unusual case of *Curran v. Catholic University of America*, discussed in Section 3.1.6.)

3.7.3. Academic freedom in research and publication.

Academic freedom protections clearly extend to the research and publication activities of faculty members. Such activities are apparently the most ardently protected of all faculty activities. The highly publicized case of *Levin v. Harleston*, 770 F. Supp. 895, *affirmed*, 966 F.2d 85 (2d Cir. 1992), is illustrative.

In *Levin* a philosophy professor at City College of the City University of New York had advocated in certain writings and publications that blacks are less intelligent on average than whites. In addition, he had opposed all use of affirmative action quotas. As a result of these writings, he became controversial on campus. Student groups staged demonstrations; documents affixed to his door were burned; and students distributed pamphlets outside his classroom. On several occasions groups of students made so much noise outside his classrooms that he could not continue the class. The college's written regulations prohibited student demonstrations that have the effect of disrupting or obstructing teaching and research activities. Despite this regulation and the professor's repeated reports about the disruptions, the university took no action against the student demonstrators. The college did, however, take two affirmative steps to deal with the controversy regarding the professor. First, the college dean (one defendant) created "shadow sections" (alternative sections) for the professor's required introductory philosophy course. Second, the college president (another defendant) appointed an ad hoc faculty committee "to review the question of when speech both in and outside the classroom may go beyond the protection of academic freedom or become conduct unbecoming a member of the faculty."

To implement the shadow sections, the college dean sent letters to the professor's students, informing them of the option to enroll in these sections. The dean stated in the letter, however, that he was "aware of no evidence suggesting that Professor Levin's views on controversial matters have compromised his performance as an able teacher of Philosophy who is fair in his treatment of students." After implementation of the shadow sections, enrollment in the professor's classes decreased by one-half. The college had never before used such sections to allow students to avoid a particular professor because of his views.

To implement the ad hoc committee, the president charged the members "to specifically review information concerning Professor Michael Levin . . . and to include in its report its recommendations concerning what the response of the College should be." The language of the charge tracked certain language in college bylaws and professional contracts concerning the discipline of faculty members and the revocation of tenure. Three of the seven committee members had previously signed a faculty petition condemning the professor. Moreover, although the committee met more than ten times, it never extended the professor an opportunity to address it. The committee's report, as summarized by the district court, stated "that Professor Levin's writings constitute unprofessional and inappropriate conduct that harms the educational process at the college, and that the college has properly intervened to protect his students from his views by creating the shadow sections."

The professor sought declaratory and injunctive relief, claiming that the defendants' failure to enforce the student demonstration regulations, the creation of the shadow sections, and the operation of the ad hoc committee violated his rights under the federal Constitution's Free Speech and Due Process Clauses. After trial the district court issued a lengthy opinion agreeing with the professor.

Relying on *Keyishian* (Section 3.7.1), the court noted the chilling and stigmatizing effect of the ad hoc committee's activities, as demonstrated by the fact that the professor declined over twenty invitations to speak or write about his controversial views. The court thus held that the professor had an objective and reasonable basis to fear losing his position, and that the effects on him were "exactly that predicted in *Keyishian*. . . . Professor Levin was forced to 'stay as far away as possible from utterances or acts which might jeopardize his living.'" To determine whether this infringement on the professor's speech was nonetheless legitimate, the court then undertook a *Pickering/Connick* analysis. It held that there was "no question" that the professor's speech was "protected expression," since his writings and statements addressed matters that were "quintessentially 'issues of public importance.'" The only justification advanced by the defendants for the ad hoc committee and shadow sections was the need to protect the professor's students from harm that could accrue "if they thought, because of the expression of his views, that he might expect less of them or grade them unfairly." The court, however, rejected this justification because City College had presented no evidence at trial to support it. Consequently, the trial court granted injunctive relief, compelling the defendants to investigate the alleged violations of the college's student demonstration regulations and prohibiting the defendants from any further use of the shadow sections or the ad hoc committee.

The federal appeals court disagreed with the district court's conclusion regarding the failure to enforce the student demonstration regulations, since the college generally had not enforced these regulations and there was no evidence that "the college treated student demonstrations directed at Professor Levin any differently than other student demonstrations." The defendants' inaction could thus not be considered a violation of any of the professor's constitutional rights.

The appellate court generally agreed, however, with the district court's conclusion regarding the shadow sections and the ad hoc committee. The court noted that the "formation of the alternative sections would not be unlawful if done to further a legitimate educational purpose that outweighed the infringement on Professor Levin's First Amendment rights." But the defendants had presented no evidence to support their contention that the professor's expression of his ideas outside the classroom harmed the educational process within the classroom. In fact, "none of Professor Levin's students had ever complained of unfair treatment on the basis of race." The court concluded that the defendants' "encouragement of the continued erosion in the size of Professor Levin's class if he does not mend his extracurricular ways is the antithesis of freedom of expression." The appellate court also agreed that the operation of the ad hoc committee had a "chilling effect" on the professor's speech and thus violated his First Amendment rights. Affirming that "governmental action which falls short of direct prohibition on speech may violate the First Amendment by chilling the free exercise of speech," the court determined that, when the president "deliberately formed the committee's inquiry into Levin's conduct to mirror the contractual standard for disciplinary action, he conveyed the threat that Levin would be dismissed if he continued voicing his racial theories."

To implement its conclusions, the appellate court vacated the portion of the trial court's injunction ordering the defendants to investigate the alleged violations of the demonstration regulations. It affirmed the portion of the injunction prohibiting the defendants from using the shadow sections. Regarding the ad hoc committee, the appellate court modified the relief ordered by the trial court. Since the ad hoc committee had recommended no disciplinary action and had no further investigations or disciplinary proceedings pending, the injunction was unnecessary. It was sufficient to issue an order that merely declared the unconstitutionality of the defendants' use of the committee, since such declaratory relief would make clear that "disciplinary proceedings, or the threat thereof, predicated solely upon Levin's continued expression of his views outside of the classroom" would violate his free speech rights.

Levin is an important case for several reasons. It painstakingly chronicles a major academic freedom dispute centering on faculty publication activities; it demonstrates a relationship between academic freedom and the phenomenon of "political correctness";[56] and it strongly supports faculty academic freedom in research by using the federal Constitution as a basic source of protection. The courts' opinions do not break new legal ground, however, since they use established principles and precedents applicable to public employees generally and do not emphasize the unique circumstances of academic freedom on the college campus. Nor is the decision, once limited by its special and unique facts, as broadly applicable as may at first appear. The case dealt with traditionally protected speech—writing and outside publication expressing opinions on matters of public concern—and not with classroom lectures, teaching methods, or course materials, or with intramural speech on institutional affairs. Not only is such speech given the highest protection, but the defendants produced no evidence that the professor's writings and views had any adverse impact on his classroom performance or his treatment of students. Nor did the defendants claim that the professor's statements were false. The college had never before created such shadow sections and had advanced no "legitimate educational interest" in using them in this circumstance. Finally, the numerous procedural flaws in the establishment and operation of the ad hoc committee greatly supported, if only circumstantially, the professor's claims that his constitutional rights were being chilled.[57]

3.7.4. Academic freedom in institutional affairs. Just as a faculty member's duties extend beyond instruction and research, so do the possibilities for academic freedom disputes. Faculty members may claim academic freedom protections for opinions and behavior involving other official or unofficial job responsibilities or campus activities. In these situations the interests that both the institution and the faculty member seek to protect are different from those relating to the classroom. The institution may be less concerned with the effect that faculty speech or behavior has on students and more concerned with promoting harmonious working relationships among faculty and administration and maintaining the public's confidence in the institution. The faculty member's interest is not in maintaining an atmosphere of free debate in the classroom and other instructional areas but rather in protecting the right to express views or personality on campus without fear of reprisal.

In the cases involving institutional affairs, as seen below, the First Amendment Free Speech Clause has been the primary focus of analysis, and courts have increasingly resorted to the *Pickering/Connick* line of cases as the governing authority. From those cases the lower courts have extracted a three-stage decision-making methodology. At the first stage, as required by *Connick*, the question is whether the faculty member's speech is on a matter of public concern. If it is not, the inquiry ends and the faculty member is afforded no First Amendment protection. If the speech *is* on a matter of public concern, the court moves to the second stage and applies the

---

[56]According to the trial court, "[t]his case raises serious constitutional questions that go to the heart of the current national debate on what has come to be denominated as 'political correctness' in speech and thought on the campuses of the nation's colleges and universities" (footnote omitted). See generally P. Berman (ed.), *Debating P. C.: The Controversy over Political Correctness on College Campuses* (Dell, 1992).

[57]Special academic freedom problems concerning research and publication may arise in religiously affiliated institutions, especially for theologians. See, for example, *Curran v. Catholic University* in Section 3.1.6 of this volume; and see generally M. Collison, "Church's Proposed Rules Raise Fears at Some Catholic Colleges," *Chron. Higher Educ.*, Sept. 15, 1993, A20.

Pickering/Connick balancing test. If the balance of interests weighs in favor of the institution, the inquiry ends and the faculty member again obtains no First Amendment protection. If the balance of interests weighs in favor of the faculty member, however, the court will either protect the faculty member or proceed to a third stage of analysis, where questions of causation are considered. At this stage, if the institution would have taken adverse action against the faculty member anyway for reasons apart from the faculty member's speech activities, the court will afford no First Amendment protection to the faculty member even if the speech was on a matter of public concern and the balance of interests weighed in the faculty member's favor. (This potential third stage of the analysis is discussed in Section 3.7.6 below.)

With some exceptions, the trend in the cases concerning institutional affairs has been to deny First Amendment protection to faculty speech. In many cases courts accomplish this result by finding that the speech activities at issue were not "matters of public concern" (stage 1); in other cases courts acknowledge that the speech addressed matters of public concern, but they deny protection by applying the balancing analysis in a manner inhospitable to the faculty member (stage 2); and in an occasional case the court will find no causation (stage 3). In contrast, an occasional court that is sensitive to the uniqueness of higher education will employ the balancing analysis hospitably to extend First Amendment protections to faculty speech. The following cases are illustrative. (See also *San Filippo v. Bongiovanni*, 30 F.3d 424 (3d Cir. 1994), where the court extended First Amendment *freedom of petition* protections to faculty members.)

Ayoub v. Texas A&M University, 927 F.2d 834 (5th Cir. 1991), involved an Egyptian-born professor, originally hired in 1968, who made repeated complaints that his starting salary was low and that, as a result, his salary in each succeeding year remained too low. In 1985 the professor's interim department head reviewed the salary and recommended no raise for the professor (as well as four other professors who were white U.S. citizens), and the college dean also determined that the salary was appropriate. Later in 1985, the new department head attempted to move the professor's office to a different building, allegedly because of complaints other department members had made about his disruptiveness. The professor then initiated legal action, "alleging that his civil rights had been violated when his office was relocated in retaliation against his complaints about the University's past discriminatory pay scale."

The court recognized the difficulty in distinguishing between public and private concerns, as required by *Connick* (Section 3.7.1), "because almost anything that occurs within a public agency could be of concern to the public." The court's role was "not [to] focus on the inherent interest or importance of the matters discussed by the employee [but instead] to decide whether the speech at issue in a particular case was made *primarily* in the plaintiff's role as a citizen or *primarily* in his role as employee. In making this distinction, the mere fact that the topic of the employee's speech was one in which the public might or would have had a great interest is of little moment" (emphasis added). Applying this test, the court determined that the professor had spoken primarily as an employee, because his speech "involved only his personal situation." Only after the professor filed suit did he "characterize his complaint in terms of a 'two-tier' system perpetuated by the University, whereby foreign-born professors were paid less than white, native-born professors." Nor was there any evidence that the professor "ever uttered such a protest at any time before the alleged retaliatory acts by the defendants." Thus, even if his comments were viewed "in terms of a disparate, 'two-tier' pay system, the record is absolutely clear that he only complained about its application to him." Consequently, the court concluded that the professor "consistently spoke not as a citizen upon matters of public concern, but rather as an employee upon matters of only personal interest. . . . [T]here is no evidence that [he] expressed concern about anything other than his own salary. Although pay discrimination based on national origin can be a matter of public concern, in the context in which it was presented in this case by [the professor] it was a purely personal and private matter."

Colburn v. Trustees of Indiana University, 973 F.2d 581 (7th Cir. 1992), involved two nontenured sociology professors employed under one-year renewable contracts. Their department had for several years been split into two contending factions. The majority faction controlled the department's primary committee, which constituted the first level of review for all promotion and tenure decisions. The two professors, members of the minority faction, each wrote a letter to university officials asserting that the "department was so divided that individual careers, and the effective functioning of the department, were being threatened," and requesting an external review of the sociology department's internal peer review system for professional advancement. University officials responded to the letters by urging the department to resolve its conflict internally. The primary committee continued to be controlled by the majority faction, however, and the two professors, along with the other members of the minority faction, wrote to the department chair describing "the deplorable and intolerable [situation], especially for junior members of the department who face discrimination by the now unchallenged dominant group." Each professor subsequently nominated himself for promotion, but the primary committee recommended against promotion. The committee also recommended that one of the plaintiffs not be reappointed, noting that his "written and verbal comments to people outside the department have hurt the image of the Sociology faculty and undermined the integrity of the peer review process." The second professor was also considered for tenure; although he received a favorable recommendation from the committee, the recommendation of the department chair was negative and he was ultimately denied not only tenure but reappointment as well.

The two professors challenged these actions in court, charging that the university had retaliated against them for engaging in expression protected by the First Amendment. The trial court granted summary judgment for the university, finding that the professors' speech was not on matters of public concern. On appeal, the professors advanced four arguments for classifying their speech as a matter of public concern. The appellate court rejected each argument and affirmed the trial court's judgment.

First, the professors argued that "their letters were not simply an internal matter, but revealed that the integrity of the university was being threatened." The court recognized that "[e]xposing wrongdoing within a public entity may be a matter of public concern," and that there is "[n]o doubt [that] the public would be displeased to learn that faculty members at a public university were evaluating their colleagues on personal biases." The court asserted, however, that "the fact the issue could be 'interesting' to the community does not make it an issue of public concern." The court viewed the plaintiffs' letters as "principally an attempt to seek intervention in a clash of hostile personalities rather than an "attempt to expose some malfeasance that would directly affect the community at large."

Second, the professors argued that the "division in the department fell along the lines of membership and non-membership in the faculty union, and that pressures to join a union make the faculty clashes of deep public concern." Again, the court recognized that "[s]peech which is related to collective activity may be a matter of public concern." In this case, however, "[a]lthough union affiliation may have been a factor in determining membership in one of the two competing groups, pressure to join the union was not the central reason for the request for review of the department, nor were [the plaintiffs] attempting to inform the public that faculty members were being pushed into union membership. . . . [T]he point of their speech . . . was to highlight how the department's in-fighting had affected them and would affect their futures at the university."

Third, the professors argued that "simply because they had some personal interest in calming the tensions in the department does not prevent their requests for review from being matters of public concern." The court recognized that "[s]peech is not unprotected simply because it raises complaints or other issues personal to the speaker. . . . However, where the overriding reason for the speech is the concern of a few individuals whose careers may be on the line, the speech looks much more like an internal personal dispute than an effort to make the public aware of wrongdoing." Although the plaintiffs "emphasize[d] that they did not speak simply to further their own career interests but everyone in the department's interest," the court believed that the department's "deterioration was principally of importance to the few faculty members who had to tolerate the bickering."

Fourth, the professors argued that "the forum in which [they] raised their concerns is relevant to whether their statements should be characterized as a matter of public concern." The court recognized that "[e]mployee speech does not go unprotected simply because the chosen forum is private and addressed solely to others in the workplace. . . . But statements made privately in the workplace themselves must be of some public concern in order to be protected." The fact that the plaintiffs had communicated their concerns to only a few university officials "underscores the internal nature of the dispute."

Thus, the court concluded, consistent with the trial court, that the professors' letters and statements "are most reasonably characterized as relating to matters of personal interest. Plaintiffs were not speaking primarily as citizens, but as faculty members concerned about the private matter of the processes by which they were evaluated."

In *Dorsett v. Board of Trustees for State Colleges and Universities*, 940 F.2d 121 (5th Cir. 1991), a tenured mathematics professor at a state university claimed that he had been retaliated against because he had "challenged several departmental decisions and [had] publicly supported another professor who had been attacked by the administration for refusing to lower academic standards." The departmental decisions he challenged concerned teaching assignments, pay increases, and other administrative and procedural matters. The appellate court held that "the alleged harms suffered by Dorsett [did] not rise to the level of a constitutional deprivation" and that, even if they did, nothing in the content, form, or context of the speech indicated an intent to address an issue of public concern, as required by *Connick*. The court specifically noted that the professor's complaints had been directed to persons within the university and had not arisen in the context of a public debate about academic standards or about the administration of the university or the mathematics department. The court did not reach the *Pickering* balance test because the speech in question was a matter of personal rather than public concern.

In contrast to *Ayoub, Colburn,* and *Dorsett,* the court in *Maples v. Martin,* 858 F.2d 1546 (11th Cir. 1988), declared professors' intramural speech to be a matter of public concern but then used a *Pickering* balancing analysis to determine that the institution's interests in efficiency and harmony outweighed the professors' interests. The case involved five disgruntled tenured professors in the mechanical engineering department at Auburn University who continually opposed the personnel and administrative decisions of their department head. In anticipation of an accreditation review by the American Board of Education Technology, the professors distributed a survey to departmental faculty and students, to some alumni and administrators, and to the accreditation board. The professors compiled the data from these surveys into a report that discussed departmental problems, especially a morale problem, and was highly critical of the department head. Largely as a result of this report and related events that preceded and followed it, the university reassigned the five professors to other engineering departments, without loss of pay or rank.

The professors argued that reassigning them for having published the report violated their rights to freedom of speech. The district and appellate courts disagreed, upholding the reassignment. Applying *Connick,* the appellate court concluded that a portion of the professors' report was speech on matters of public concern because it would influence the public's perception of the quality of education at the university. The court then used the *Pickering* balancing test to weigh the professors' free speech interests in publishing the report against the report's "disruptive impact on the workplace." The report had "distracted both students and faculty from the primary academic tasks of education and research"; it was "produced in an atmosphere of tension created by the authors' longstanding grievance" against the department's administration; and the report's publication "contributed to a lack of harmony among the faculty and . . . severely hampered communication between the members of the faculty and the Department Head." The court therefore concluded that the report's "interference with the efficient operation of the [Mechanical Engineering] Department at Auburn was sufficient to justify the transfer[s]" and outweighed the professors' need to speak on matters of public concern.

Taken together, these cases illustrate how lower courts have adapted the U.S. Supreme Court's directives in *Pickering* and *Connick* to the particular circumstances of higher education. Most important, these cases establish a framework for determining whether the speech at issue was a matter of public concern. As discussed below, this framework, and much of the courts' reasoning under *Pickering* and *Connick,* is insensitive to the shared-governance context of higher education and may be criticized on numerous grounds.

These cases accord relatively little weight to the particular "context" of the speech. According to *Connick,* "[w]hether an employee's speech addresses a matter of public concern must be determined by the content, form, *and context* of a given statement, as revealed by the whole record" (emphasis added). The courts have generally used the same analysis in faculty cases that they use in cases involving other types of public employees, thereby attaching no significance to the special context of higher education. While there are many similarities between college and university employees and other public employees, there are also important differences. Primary among them are the special governance structure of higher education and the special status of academic freedom. When courts are inattentive to such matters, the strictness of the "public concern" test and the fact sensitivity and malleability of the balancing test may combine to chill the faculty member's willingness to participate forthrightly in departmental and institutional debate.

Similarly, these cases employ a cramped version of the *Connick* distinction between speaking out as a "private citizen" and as a "public employee." This distinction is useful in the general employment context, as in *Connick,* but in the higher education context it ignores the fact that shared governance requires professors to speak out as professionals on matters of institutional concern. Those who do so may enhance rather than threaten the operation of the institution. When a court ends its inquiry because the speech is not a matter of public concern, as strictly conceived in *Ayoub, Colburn,* and *Dorsett,* it never considers the vital participatory role professors may play in shared-governance systems or the constructive impact that speech about "institutional concerns" may have on institutional operations over the long haul.

Perhaps most problematic, these cases assign excessive weight to whether or not the speech was communicated to the general public. The *Ayoub* opinion relied on a previous case (*Terrell v. University of Texas System Police,* 792 F.2d 1360, 1362 (5th Cir. 1982)), in which the court, holding that First Amendment protections did not apply to a diary, "emphasized that [the claimant] made no effort to communicate its contents to the public." Applying this reasoning to the professor's claims, the *Ayoub* court noted that "[c]ertainly, [he] never attempted to air his complaints in a manner that would call the public's attention to the alleged wrong." Similarly, the *Colburn* court considered the fact that the professors had brought their concerns only to the attention of university officials and viewed this fact as underscoring the private, internal character of the speech. This heavy emphasis on the audience of the speech, along with precious little emphasis on the subject matter, appears to conflict with the U.S. Supreme Court's holding in *Givhan* (Section 3.7.1). There the Court made clear that the determination of whether speech is a matter of public concern does not depend on whether the communication itself was made in public or private. As the appeals court explained in *Kurtz v. Vickrey,* 855 F.2d 723 (11th Cir. 1988): "Although an employee's efforts to communicate his or her concerns to the public are relevant to a determination of whether or not the employee's speech relates to a matter of public concern, focusing solely on such behavior, or on the employee's motivation, does not fully reflect the Supreme Court's directive that the content, form, and context of the speech must all be considered. The content of the speech is notably overlooked in such an analysis. . . . Moreover, such a focus overlooks the Court's holding in *Givhan.*"

When courts ignore the nature of the higher education context while focusing on the "private citizen"/"public employee" distinction and the public/private context of the speech, they undercut the concepts of shared governance and collegiality. In the cases described above, the professors who followed administrative channels and did not communicate their criticisms to persons outside the institution did not receive First Amendment protection. Those professors who did communicate outside the institution, specifically to accrediting agencies, were afforded at least threshold First Amendment protections. These results seem to suggest that, to guarantee themselves protection under the First Amendment, faculty members should bypass internal administrative procedures and go directly to persons or agencies outside the institution. A First Amendment rule that would encourage, if not require, such behavior would conflict with the best interests and the customs of institutions that protect shared governance and collegiality.

One case that avoids these problems, and could serve as a model for later judicial developments, is *Johnson v. Lincoln University*, 776 F.2d 443 (3d Cir. 1985). The court's language and methodology are much more amenable to the protection of faculty speech in institutional affairs. In declining to side with the university, the court found that the speech in question was a matter of public concern, and although it remanded the case to the trial court to apply the balancing test, it clearly signaled its inclination to give great weight to the faculty member's free speech interests.

The *Johnson* plaintiff was a chemistry professor challenging the termination of his tenure. The lawsuit grew out of a dispute within the university that began in 1977. At that time the university decided to make substantial reductions in its faculty. Led in part by the professor, the faculty responded with sharp criticism of both the university and its president. An initial lawsuit ensued, in which the faculty asserted that "various disciplinary actions had been taken in order to suppress faculty criticism of university policy." That case eventually was settled out of court. Four months later, the chemistry department chair initiated dismissal proceedings against the professor. The charges were based primarily on events related to the "rancorous, longstanding dispute within the chemistry department." After a hearing, the presiding committee recommended the termination of the professor's tenure. The university president accepted the committee's recommendation, and the board of trustees upheld his decision. The professor thereupon sued in federal court, challenging the termination of his tenure on several grounds, including the ground that the termination was in retaliation for his statements about university policies and academic standards. The trial court focused both on the professor's speech regarding disputes within the chemistry department and on letters he had written to the Middle States Association of Colleges and Schools regarding the university's academic standards in general. Reasoning that disputes within the chemistry department were of interest only to those within the department and that the professor's letters were "merely an outgrowth of his personal dispute with the university," the trial court held that each of these speech activities concerned matters of "purely private concern" and therefore were not protected.

The appellate court vacated the trial court's judgment, holding that it had erred as a matter of law in determining that the professor's speech activities did not involve matters of public concern. First the court emphasized "that the mere fact that an employee's statement is an 'outgrowth of his personal dispute' does not prevent some aspect of it from touching upon matters of public concern." While the controversies within the department may have some personal aspects, other aspects are "concerned [with] questions of educational standards and academic policy of a scope broader than their application within the department." As an example, the court quoted from a memorandum written by the professor regarding departmental standards: "I believe such grade inflation is a kind of crime against students, Lincoln University, and Black people. Standards of Black Colleges are always suspect and it took 50–60 years for Lincoln to earn a high reputation for quality education and high standards. . . . What [the department chair] has done is to encourage non-quality education and non-quality character. . . . A good reputation for academic quality was the only thing of value Lincoln ever had or ever will have." Commenting on this passage, the court asserted that "[i]t is difficult to imagine a theme that touches more upon matters of public concern." The court then noted that the same theme was present in the professor's letters to the Middle States Association, in which he criticized the standards of a master's degree program at Lincoln because it did not require a bachelor's degree. In these letters the professor "proceeded to connect the decline of academic standards at Lincoln with the demoralization caused by the suppression of academic freedom during the [prior] controversy, and encouraged the Middle States Association to investigate Lincoln." The professor specifically emphasized "the vital importance of high educational standards to the future of mankind—and the special circumstances that make it a kind of crime to allow lower standards at Black institutions."

Tracking the language of *Connick,* the court declared that "questions of academic standards are of 'apparent . . . interest to the community upon which it is essential that public employees be able to speak out freely without fear of retaliatory dismissal.'" As to the letters, the court stated that "it is difficult to see any distinguishing features between these letters and the one which the *Pickering* court held to be protected activity."

The appellate court also found that the trial court erred in limiting its inquiry to the two types of speech activities identified above. The professor's claims also included "his role in [the prior] litigation [against the university], his role in the underlying activities leading up to that litigation, his longstanding criticisms of [the current] administration's academic policy, his newspaper articles proposing that Lincoln eliminate the F grade, his attempts to have other faculty members censured for allowing students to take advanced courses without passing the prerequisites, and his criticisms of his department chairman over academic standards." The court observed that whether these items "touch[ed] upon matters of public concern seems hardly open to question."

In remanding the case to the trial court so that it could undertake the *Pickering* balancing analysis, the appellate court provided considerable guidance. First, quoting one of its own prior decisions, it noted that "'even if there were some evidence of disruption caused by plaintiff's speech, such a finding is not controlling. . . . *Pickering* is truly a balancing test, with office disruption or breached confidences being only weights on the scales.'" The appellate court further cautioned that "a stronger showing [of the employer's justification] may be necessary if the employee's speech more substantially involved matters of public concern."

Of special interest, and in marked contrast to *Ayoub, Colburn,* and *Dorsett,* the *Johnson* court placed significant importance on the circumstances of the academic environment. It began by declaring that "[d]espite the inappropriateness of this forum for resolving issues of academic policy and academic freedom, we find ourselves reviewing charges [of wrongful] termination of tenure." Then, after asserting the importance of context, the court, tracking the language of *Tinker v. Des Moines School District* (this volume, Sections 4.9.1 and 4.9.2), stated:

> It is particularly important that in cases dealing with academia, the standard applied in evaluating the employer's justification should be the one applicable to the rights of teachers and students "in light of the special characteristics of the school environment. . . . In an academic environment, suppression of speech or opinion cannot be justified by an "undifferentiated fear or apprehension of disturbance," . . . nor by "a mere desire to avoid the discomfort and un-

pleasantness that always accompany an unpopular viewpoint" [776 F.2d at 453–54; citations omitted].

Whereas all the cases above concerned "intramural" speech, *Starsky v. Williams*, 353 F. Supp. 900 (D. Ariz. 1972), *affirmed in pertinent part*, 512 F.2d 109 (9th Cir. 1975), presents a different type of academic freedom problem. The case involved institutional affairs not in the sense that the speech concerned campus issues but rather in the sense that the professor's on-campus speech activities allegedly conflicted with his institutional responsibilities. Although the speech at issue did take place on campus, it concerned external public affairs rather than internal institutional operations. The case illustrates that, when speech regarding external affairs is at issue, the "public concern" test is easily met and the analysis will focus either on the *Pickering* balancing test or on the concept of "chilling effect" created by institutional imposition of an orthodoxy (see the *Keyishian* case in Section 3.7.1).

The plaintiff in *Starsky* was a tenured philosophy professor who had taught at Arizona State for six years before the university dismissed him on a series of eight charges, some involving on-campus activity and others involving off-campus activity. (The charges in the latter category are discussed in Section 3.7.5.1.) After several incidents, generally involving the professor's dissemination on campus of information about socialism, the board of regents directed the president to institute proceedings against him. After carefully considering the evidence, the disciplinary committee found that the charges did not support a recommendation for dismissal. The board nevertheless terminated the professor's employment, and the professor sought redress in the courts.

The federal district court held that the termination violated the professor's constitutional right to free speech. Discussing the eight charges at length, the court dismissed some as unsupported by the evidence. One charge it found to be substantiated was that the professor had deliberately cut a class in order to participate in a campus rally. The court ruled that he had broken no specific regulation by canceling the class and that the incident was a minor one, usually handled informally within the department. The court chastised the board for selectively enforcing its general attendance policy and dismissed the charge. Another more serious charge concerned the peaceful distribution of a leaflet to other faculty members. The leaflet was a philosophical and political discussion of activity taking place at Columbia University and quoted a Columbia student who advocated socialism. The university charged that the professor had "failed to exercise appropriate restraint or to exercise critical self-discipline and judgment in using, extending, and transmitting knowledge" and that his activity was not in keeping with "the austere surroundings of a faculty meeting" and exhibited "complete disrespect for authority." The court, quoting the academic freedom declaration from the *Keyishian* case, stated:

> There is a serious constitutional question as to whether speech can be stifled because the ideas or wording expressed upset the "austere" faculty atmosphere; certainly the board has no legitimate interest in keeping a university in some kind of intellectual austerity by an absence of shocking ideas. Insofar as the plaintiff's words upset the legislature or faculty because of the contents of his views, and particularly the depth of his social criticism, this is not the kind of

detriment for which plaintiff can constitutionally be penalized [353 F. Supp. at 920].

3.7.5. Academic freedom in private life. Faculty members' activities would seem most insulated from state or institutional interference when they are engaging in private activities. Indeed, the faculty member can be seen as an ordinary citizen who happens to teach in a postsecondary institution. But the faculty member's private activities are not completely immune from interference by the state or the institution, because such activities may have an impact on teaching responsibilities or other legitimate interests of the institution.

3.7.5.1. Public institutions. A professor's private life may involve activities not traditionally thought of as academic freedom concerns or as First Amendment rights. *Hander v. San Jacinto Junior College*, 519 F.2d 273 (5th Cir. 1975), for instance, concerned a state college's authority to enforce faculty grooming regulations. The college dismissed the professor when he refused to shave his beard. In holding for the professor on due process and equal protection grounds, the court first distinguished faculty members from other government employees: "Teachers even at public institutions such as San Jacinto Junior College simply do not have the exposure or community-wide impact of policemen and other employees who deal directly with the public. Nor is the need for discipline as acute in the educational environment as in other types of public service." The court then enunciated this role for teachers:

> School authorities may regulate teachers' appearance and activities only when the regulation has some relevance to legitimate administrative or educational functions. . . .
> The mere subjective belief in a particular idea by public employers is, however, an undeniably insufficient justification for the infringement of a constitutionally guaranteed right. . . . It is illogical to conclude that a teacher's bearded appearance would jeopardize his reputation or pedagogical effectiveness with college students [519 F.2d at 277].

Another aspect of faculty freedom in private life is illustrated by *Trister v. University of Mississippi*, 420 F.2d 499 (5th Cir. 1969), where the court ruled that it was unconstitutional for a state law school to prohibit some part-time faculty members from working part-time at outside legal jobs while allowing other faculty members to do so. Certain part-time faculty members had continued working at a legal services office of the Office of Economic Opportunity (OEO) despite a warning from the administration that they would lose their jobs at the university if they did so. There was no evidence that the OEO jobs consumed any more time than the part-time jobs of other faculty members. In upholding the plaintiffs' right to work at the OEO office, the court based its decision not on the First Amendment but on the Fourteenth Amendment's Equal Protection Clause:

> We are not willing to take the position that plaintiffs have a constitutional right to participate in the legal services program of the OEO, or in any other program. Nor do they have a constitutional right to engage in part-time employment while teaching part time at the law school. No such right exists in isolation. Plaintiffs, however, do have the constitutional right to be treated by a state agency in no significantly different manner from others who are members

of the same class; that is, members of the faculty of the University of Mississippi school of law [420 F.2d at 502].

While this narrow reasoning was sufficient to uphold the plaintiffs' claim, other courts may be more willing to find a limited constitutional right to outside employment, as an aspect of First Amendment freedom of association or Fourteenth Amendment due process privacy rights, where such employment does not interfere with any substantial interest of the institution.

Yet another aspect of faculty freedom in private life is illustrated by *Starsky v. Williams* (cited and discussed further in Section 3.7.4). The plaintiff filed suit seeking reinstatement as a member of the faculty at Arizona State University. He had made a television speech criticizing the board of regents and calling them hypocrites. He had also issued a press release in which he criticized the board. The court, finding for the professor, stated:

> In each of these communications, plaintiff spoke or wrote as a private citizen on a public issue, and in a place and context apart from his role as faculty member. In none of these public utterances did he appear as a spokesman for the university, or claim any kind of expertise related to his profession. He spoke as any citizen might speak, and the board was, therefore, subject to its own avowed standard that when a faculty member "speaks or writes as a citizen, he should be free from institutional censorship or discipline" [353 F. Supp. at 920].

More recently, in *Jeffries v. Harleston*, 820 F. Supp. 741 (S.D.N.Y. 1993), *motion to set aside jury verdict granted in part and denied in part, and permanent injunction granted*, 828 F. Supp. 1066 (S.D.N.Y. 1993), a tenured professor and chair of the Black Studies Department at the City College of New York had made a controversial off-campus speech in the capacity of "an appointed consultant of the State Education Commissioner." While addressing the topic of reforming the educational system to promote diversity, the professor "made strident attacks against particular individuals, and made derogatory comments about specific ethnic groups." When CCNY subsequently removed the professor from his position as department chair, he claimed a violation of the First Amendment. The trial judge upheld a jury verdict in the professor's favor. The court first held (relying on *Pickering* and *Connick* (this volume, Section 3.7.1)) that the speech was on a matter of public concern and that "Professor Jeffries's statements, when spoken outside the classroom, remain under the umbrella of constitutional protection, as long as those statements do not impede the efficient and effective operation of the College or University." In the course of a lengthy analysis based on the *Mt. Healthy* case (this volume, Section 3.7.6)—an analysis that is highly critical of CCNY—the court concluded: "While there may have been compelling and legitimate grounds upon which to discipline Professor Jeffries, the University chose to act upon illegitimate and unconstitutional grounds, specifically upon [the off-campus speech] and the publicity surrounding it." The appellate court affirmed the trial court in all pertinent respects (remanding the case, however, for further proceedings regarding punitive damages); 21 F.3d 1238 (2d Cir. 1994).

3.7.5.2. Religious institutions. In religiously affiliated institutions, special problems concerning academic or personal freedom may arise, because such institutions may claim additional authority over certain aspects of faculty members' private lives that implicate religious doctrine or morality. Although the faculty member would have no constitutional rights to assert in this context (see Section 1.5.2), contract rights would continue to apply (see Section 3.1.6). The religious institution's own constitutional rights to religious freedom, however, may limit the faculty member's ability to maintain contract or other actions in court (see Section 1.6). In lieu of or in addition to resort to the courts, the faculty member may seek the protection of the American Association of University Professors. An AAUP report on the case of Jeannette Quilichini Paz, a professor from the Catholic University of Puerto Rico, is illustrative.

The university had dismissed the professor when it learned that she had remarried, even though her previous Catholic marriage had ended in civil divorce rather than ecclesiastical annulment. According to the report of the AAUP investigating committee ("Academic Freedom and Tenure: The Catholic University of Puerto Rico," 73 *Academe* 33 (May–June 1987)), the Catholic University of Puerto Rico was canonically established by the Holy See in 1972 and has a policy, printed in its faculty manual, that "The faculty member should conduct himself in accordance with the values and ethical principles of the Catholic Church (both within and without the University) and be loyal to the Institution. Such loyalty presumes, among other things, the preservation of the good name of the Catholic University." Each year, the faculty also recited the following oath: "I also swear to embrace and preserve each and every matter of faith and morals propounded by the Church, and in the same form which the Church proposes, whether they have been defined by a solemn judgment, or asserted and declared by the ordinary magisterium, especially those which refer to the mysteries of the Holy Church of Christ and its Sacraments, the Sacrifice of the Mass, and the Primacy of the Roman Pontiff."

When the university hired the professor as a full-time faculty member in 1975, she was informed of "what will happen" if she remarried. (Her earlier marriage had ended in 1973.) She claimed to have informed the university vice president at that time of her objection to any authority the university might assert over her private behavior. In 1982 the university granted the professor tenure. In 1986 she remarried. Having learned of her remarriage, considered sinful under Catholic doctrine, the university suspended her with pay, reasoning that faculty must adhere to the laws of the Church in their academic and private lives. After the completion of internal hearing and appeal processes, the university dismissed the professor solely because of her remarriage.

In disapproving the university's actions, the AAUP investigating committee report emphasized that "The issue of direct concern in Professor Quilichini's case, however, is not academic freedom but personal freedom. It was her private conduct rather than her conduct as a teacher and researcher or any intramural or extramural statements she may have made that was the administration's ground for dismissal." Regarding the effect of the university's action on this "personal freedom"—that is, the professor's "private life unconnected to her professional duties"—the report concluded: "The administration of CUPR, in dismissing Professor Quilichini from her tenured position for reasons unrelated to her fitness as a teacher or researcher, acted in disregard of the applicable provisions of the Association's *Recommended Institutional Regulations on Academic Freedom and Tenure.*" Regarding the broader effects of the university's action, the report concluded:

3.7.6. Administrators' Authority over Faculty Academic Freedom

> The administration of CUPR, in basing the dismissal of Profes
> chini from her tenured position on vaguely stated religious standards ׀
> strably related to professional performance, has placed in question the acau
> freedom of all faculty members at CUPR. The statement in the faculty manual
> that a faculty member is expected to "conduct himself in accordance with the
> values and ethical principles of the Catholic Church (both within and without
> the University) . . ." is subject to such broad interpretation that it would allow
> the administration to dimiss almost any faculty member at will [73 *Academe* at
> 38].

The AAUP's Committee A accepted the investigating committee's report and recommended that the university be placed on the AAUP's list of censured administrations (73 *Academe* 45, at 48 (Sept.–Oct. 1987)). At the AAUP's 73rd annual meeting, the membership approved Committee A's recommendation (73 *Academe* 39 (Sept.–Oct. 1987). For a discussion of the censuring process, see Section 8.5.

Quilichini subsequently filed suit against the university in the Superior Court of Puerto Rico (*Quilichini v. Universidad Católica*, Civ. Case No. CS87-235), where the trial judge refused to intervene in the dispute because to do so would infringe on separation of church and state (see Section 1.6). The case has since been pending on appeal in the Puerto Rico Supreme Court (docket No. R-90-578).

3.7.6. Administrators' authority over faculty academic freedom. The foregoing discussions make clear that academic freedom is an area in which the law provides few firm guidelines for administrators—particularly those in private institutions, since the decided cases are mostly constitutional decisions applicable only to public schools. Even the constitutional cases are sometimes incompletely reasoned or difficult to reconcile with one another. Because the decisions often depend heavily on a vague balancing of faculty and institutional interests in light of the peculiar facts of the case, it is difficult to generalize from one case to another. Thus, institutions need to develop their own guidelines on academic freedom and to have internal systems for protecting academic freedom in accordance with institutional policy. The AAUP guidelines (see this volume, Sections 3.7.1 and 8.5) often can be of considerable assistance in this endeavor.

When drafting or reviewing internal institutional regulations on academic freedom, administrators should ensure that these regulations avoid the constitutional dangers of "overbreadth" and "vagueness" (see Section 3.5.1). In addition, such regulations should not interfere with the content (or substance) of faculty members' speech, at least outside the classroom; courts permit narrow regulation of the time, place, or manner of speech but seldom of its content as such (see Sections 4.9.2 and 4.10). Finally, the regulations must follow procedural due process requirements in situations where their application would deprive a faculty member of a "liberty" or "property" interest (see Section 3.6.2). Although these requirements bind only public institutions, they may provide useful guidance for private institutions as well.

For both public and private institutions, faculty handbooks and other documents may provide some guidance for administrators, and contract law does create limitations on administrators' authority to regulate academic freedom. Whether those limits are meaningful, however, depends on the content of the particular faculty-institution contract (see Section 3.1.1). Express academic freedom clauses, or clauses incorporating AAUP guidelines, may create substantial limits. So may clauses establishing procedural safeguards that must precede adverse personnel actions (see Section 3.6.1) and clauses establishing "for-cause" standards that limit administrative discretion to terminate the contract (see Section 3.5.2).

For public institutions the constitutional cases, despite their difficulties, do provide other guidance and do also restrict administrators' authority to limit faculty academic freedom. The classroom (Section 3.7.2) is the arena where institutional authority is greatest and courts are most hesitant to enter. Research and publication (Section 3.7.3) is the arena where the institution is likely to have the least authority. Beyond these two arenas, faculty members have considerable freedom to express themselves on public issues and, as private citizens, to associate with whom they please and engage in outside activities of their choice. In general, whether in the classroom or out, administrative authority over teacher behavior or activities increases as the job-relatedness of the behavior or activities increases and as the adverseness of their impact on academic performance or other institutional functions increases.

Using all these contractual and constitutional, internal and external, sources, administrators should carefully avoid decisions based on activities protected by academic freedom whenever they are deciding whether to hire, renew, promote, grant tenure to, or dismiss a particular faculty member. Sticky problems can arise when the faculty member has engaged in possibly protected action but has also engaged in unprotected action that might justify an adverse personnel decision. Suppose, for instance, that a faculty member up for renewal has made public statements critical of state policy on higher education (probably protected) and has also often failed to meet his classes (unprotected). What must an administrator do to avoid later judicial reversal of a decision not to renew?

The U.S. Supreme Court addressed this problem in *Mt. Healthy City School District Board of Education v. Doyle,* 429 U.S. 274 (1977). The plaintiff schoolteacher had made statements regarding school policy to a radio broadcaster, who promptly broadcast the information as a news item. A month later the school board informed the teacher that he would not be rehired and gave the radio broadcast as one reason. It also gave several other reasons, however, including an incident in which the teacher made an obscene gesture to two students in the school cafeteria. The Supreme Court determined that the radio communication was protected by the First Amendment and had played a substantial part in the nonrenewal decision, but that the nonrenewal was nevertheless valid if the school board could prove that it would not have rehired the teacher even if the radio incident had never occurred:

> Initially, in this case, the burden was properly placed upon . . . [the teacher] to show that his conduct was constitutionally protected, and that this conduct was a "substantial factor"—or, to put it in other words, that it was a "motivating factor" in the board's decision not to rehire him. [The teacher] having carried that burden, however, the district court should have gone on to determine whether the board had shown by preponderance of the evidence that it would have reached the same decision as to . . . [the teacher's] reemployment even in the absence of the protected conduct [429 U.S. at 287].

Numerous court decisions have applied the *Mt. Healthy* test to postsecondary education in situations where both proper and improper considerations are alleged

to have contributed to a particular decision. In *Goss v. San Jacinto Junior College,*
588 F.2d 96 (5th Cir. 1979), the plaintiff, a junior college instructor, claimed that her
contract had not been renewed because of her political and union activities, which
were protected activities under the First Amendment. The college responded that the
instructor had not been rehired because of declining enrollment and poor evaluation
of her work. After a jury trial, the jury agreed with the instructor and awarded her
$23,400 in back pay. In affirming the jury verdict, the federal appeals court issued an
opinion illustrating what administrators should *not* do if they wish to avoid judicial
invalidation of their personnel decisions:[58]

> There was ample evidence to support the jury finding that Mrs. Goss had
> not been rehired "because of her political and/or professional activities." Dr.
> Spencer [the president of the college] testified that, when Mrs. Goss sought to
> organize a local chapter of the National Faculty Association, he distributed by
> campus mail a faculty newsletter expressing his concern about the organization,
> while denying proponents of the National Faculty Association the privilege of
> distributing literature by campus mail. Mrs. Goss testified that, after her husband
> had filed a petition to run for a seat on the board of regents, Dr. Carl Burney,
> chairman of the Division of Social and Behavioral Sciences, advised her to have
> her husband withdraw from the election. In deposition testimony, Dr. O. W.
> Marcom, academic dean, stated that, when Mrs. Goss presided at an organiza-
> tional meeting of a local chapter of the Texas Junior College Teachers Associ-
> ation in the spring of 1971, he attended and voiced his objection to the group.
> Dr. Spencer himself testified by deposition that he had recommended the non-
> renewal of Mrs. Goss's contract to discipline her for "creating or trying to create
> ill will or lack of cooperation . . . with the administration."
>
> There was sufficient evidence to support the jury finding that "matters
> other than Mrs. Goss's political and/or professional activities" were not respon-
> sible for the board of regents' action. Appellants justified the nonrenewal of Mrs.
> Goss's contract on the grounds that declining enrollment necessitated a staff
> reduction and that Mrs. Goss received a poor evaluation from Dr. Edwin Lehr,
> chairman of the history department, and Dr. Burney. Although Dr. Spencer had
> recommended a reduction of three faculty members in the history department,
> Mrs. Goss was one of four faculty members in the history department in 1971–
> 72 who did not teach at San Jacinto Junior College in 1972–73.
>
> Furthermore, Dr. Lehr's evaluation of Mrs. Goss, upon which Dr. Spencer
> allegedly relied in making his recommendation to the board of regents, was
> inconsistent with the objective criteria established for the rating. The criteria by
> which the teachers were rated include the number of years of teaching at San
> Jacinto Junior College, enrollment in a doctoral program, the number of
> doctoral-level courses completed, the percentage of the teacher's students earning
> credits, and other factors. Mrs. Goss was not awarded five points to which she
> was entitled on the objective scale for academic courses she had taken while
> employed as an instructor. Thus, she was assigned eighty points, rather than
> eighty-five. If she had been awarded the points to which she was entitled, she
> would have ranked in the middle of the seventeen history instructors rather than
> in the bottom three [588 F.2d at 99–100].

---

[58]For other classic "what-not-to-do" examples, see *Jeffries v. Harleston* (Section 3.7.5.1
above) and *Levin v. Harleston* (Section 3.7.3 above).

Evidence of an intrusion into academic freedom is not always as clear as it was to the court in *Goss*, however, and postsecondary institutions have often emerged victorious in court. In *Allaire v. Rogers*, 658 F.2d 1055 (5th Cir. 1981), the court considered whether a university president had denied merit raises to a group of tenured professors because they had lobbied for increased salary appropriations at the state legislature (protected) or because of their lack of merit (unprotected). Only one of the eight original plaintiffs ultimately prevailed on appeal. In *Hillis v. Stephen F. Austin State University*, 665 F.2d 547 (5th Cir. 1982), the court considered whether the contract of a nontenured faculty member had not been renewed because of his private criticism of his superiors (apparently protected) or his insubordination and uncooperativeness (unprotected). After losing at trial, the university prevailed on appeal. In *Hildebrand v. Board of Trustees of Michigan State University*, 607 F.2d 705 (6th Cir. 1979), *appeal after remand*, 662 F.2d 439 (6th Cir. 1981) (further discussed in Section 1.4.1), the court considered whether a faculty member had been denied tenure because of his criticism of the department's curriculum (protected), his election to the departmental advisory committee (protected), or his unsuitability for the multidisciplinary emphasis of the department (unprotected). After extended litigation, the university eventually emerged victorious. In *Ollman v. Toll*, 518 F. Supp. 1196 (D. Md. 1981), *affirmed*, 704 F.2d 139 (4th Cir. 1983), the court considered whether the University of Maryland refused to appoint the plaintiff as department chair, after his selection by a search committee, because he held Marxist political views (protected) or because he lacked the necessary qualifications to develop the department according to the university's plans (unprotected). The university prevailed at trial and on appeal. And in *Harden v. Adams*, 841 F.2d 1091 (11th Cir. 1988), the court considered whether a professor's tenure had been terminated because he helped maintain discrimination charges against the university and helped organize a chapter of a state education association (protected) or because he quarreled with supervising faculty members and sought to draw students into the disputes, caused dissension within the faculty, neglected faculty duties, and violated minor institutional rules (unprotected). The court concluded that the latter reasons had been the basis for the termination.

By placing burdens on faculty members who assert violations of academic freedom, *Mt. Healthy* and its progeny give administrators breathing space to make personnel decisions where faculty members may have engaged in protected activity. The goal for administrators still should be a decision untainted by any consideration of protected conduct. But in the real world, that goal is not always attainable, either because under current legal standards it is difficult to determine whether particular conduct is protected or because events that involve conduct protected by academic freedom are so widely known that administrators cannot claim to be unaware of their existence. In situations where both protected and unprotected conduct have occurred, administrators can still avoid judicial invalidation if they make sure that strong and dispositive grounds, independent of any grounds impinging academic freedom, exist for every adverse decision, and that such independent grounds are considered in the decision-making process and are documented in the institution's records.

Administrators should also consider what procedures they will use in investigating situations that could give rise or have given rise to a claim of an academic freedom violation. The need to investigate in order to resolve factual disputes, and to clarify the nuances of what may be subtle and complex circumstances, may be especially great when the institution is contemplating disciplinary action against a faculty member because of activities that he or she may claim are protected by academic freedom. The recent U.S. Supreme Court case of *Waters v. Churchill*, 114 S.Ct. 1878 (1994), underscores the need for caution in such situations and provides some (although murky) guidance to public employers regarding investigations in cases with First Amendment overtones. The case concerned a nurse whom a public hospital had dismissed based on a third-party report that she had made disruptive statements concerning the hospital to a co-worker. There was a fact dispute about the content of these statements; in the nurse's version, the statements were on matters of public concern protected under *Connick* (this volume, Section 3.7.1). Although the justices filed four opinions with differing perspectives on the constitutional issues, a majority apparently did agree that, in these circumstances, the employer had a duty to conduct a "reasonable" investigation of the facts and could not dismiss the employee unless it had a "reasonable" belief that the third party's or the employer's version of the facts was accurate (see 114 S.Ct. at 1891–93 (concurring opinion of Justice Souter)).

While the *Mt. Healthy* case and the *Waters* case, as First Amendment precedents, bind only public institutions, they can guide private institutions in establishing review standards for their own internal hearings on personnel disputes, and they may, by analogy, assist courts in reviewing academic freedom claims based on a contract theory (see Section 3.7.1).

3.7.7. Protection of confidential academic information: "Academic freedom privilege." A decade of litigation has centered on a difficult and divisive academic freedom problem for postsecondary faculty members and administrators: whether courts or administrative agencies may compel faculty members or their institutions to disclose confidential academic information if such information is relevant to issues in litigation. Faculty members may confront this problem if they are asked to provide a deposition, to answer interrogatories, or to be a witness in ongoing litigation, or if they are served with a subpoena or a contempt citation or are otherwise ordered by a court or administrative agency to surrender information within their control.

Administrators may become entwined in the problem if the institution seeks to assist a faculty member with such matters or, more generally, if the institution seeks to monitor institutional affairs so as to avoid litigation. Although faculty members and administrators may disagree on how best to respond to demands for confidential information, the primary clash is not between members of the academic community—as in the cases in Sections 3.7.2 through 3.7.5—but between the academic community, on the one hand, and the courts, administrative agencies, and opposing litigants on the other.

Issues related to the protection of confidential information tend to arise in two contexts: (1) requests to disclose the views of individual evaluators of faculty performance at the time that reappointment, promotion, or tenure decisions are made; and (2) the demand that unpublished data or research findings be released against the will of the researcher. These issues are examined in Sections 3.7.7.1 and 3.7.7.2.

3.7.7.1. Personnel issues. Many colleges and universities rely on the judgments of a faculty member's peers—either colleagues within the institution or experts in the faculty member's discipline from other institutions—to assess the quality of that individual's scholarship, teaching, and service and to recommend whether reappointment, promotion, or tenure should be conferred. Historically, candidates have not been given access to peer evaluations at many institutions; in fact, many external reviewers have been willing to provide candid judgments about a faculty colleague only if the institution provided assurances that the candidate would not have access to the evaluation. Institutions, their faculty, and external evaluators have argued that confidentiality is essential to encourage candor. On the other hand, candidates denied reappointment, promotion, or tenure have argued that refusing to give them access to the confidential evaluations upon which a negative decision may have been based is unfair and restricts their ability to challenge what may be an unlawful decision in court. Although this latter view prevailed in a decision of the U.S. Supreme Court, which required a university to disclose "confidential" evaluations to the EEOC (*University of Pennsylvania v. EEOC*, 493 U.S. 182 (1990)), it took ten years of litigation and a sharp division among the federal appellate courts to obtain an answer to this dilemma.[59]

The official beginning of judicial attention to this issue, and the most celebrated of the cases, occurred when a trial court had ordered a University of Georgia professor serving on a faculty review committee to reveal and explain his vote on a promotion and tenure application that the committee had rejected. The professor refused, citing an "academic freedom privilege."

The appellate court (in *In re Dinnan*, 661 F.2d 426 (11th Cir. 1981)) rejected the professor's claim to an academic freedom privilege:

> The appellant argues that the instant case is one of "academic freedom." We, however, are unable to accept this characterization and, indeed, believe that any such view of the present case requires a gross distortion of its facts.
>
> This case simply involves the law of evidence: there are no issues of constitutional dimension raised. The appellant is claiming a privilege, that is, a right to refrain from testifying, that heretofore has not been considered or recognized by any court. The issue before this court then is whether the privilege claimed by the appellant should be endorsed by this circuit.
>
> We hold that no privilege exists that would enable Professor Dinnan to withhold information regarding his vote on the promotion of the appellee. This result is required on the basis of fundamental principles of law and sound public policy [661 F.2d at 427].

While recognizing the significance of academic freedom, the court characterized Dinnan's claim as seeking to suppress information, and stressed the potential for frustrating the plaintiff's attempt to ascertain the reasons for her tenure denial. "This possibility is a much greater threat to our liberty and academic freedom than the compulsion of discovery in the instant case" (661 F.2d at 431).

The opinion demonstrates apparent irritation with Professor Dinnan's claim that forcing disclosure of votes and evaluations will harm colleges and universities:

> We fail to see how if a tenure committee is acting in good faith, our decision today will adversely affect its decision-making process. Indeed, this opinion should work to reinforce responsible decision-making in tenure questions as it sends out a clear signal to would-be wrongdoers that they may not hide behind

---

[59]Cases are collected in Annot., "Academic Peer Review Privilege in Federal Court," 85 A.L.R. Fed. 691 (1987 and periodic supp.).

"academic freedom" to avoid responsibility for their actions. . . . Society has no strong interest in encouraging timid faculty members to serve on tenure committees [661 F.2d at 431–32].

The court therefore affirmed the trial court's orders that Dinnan answer deposition questions about his committee vote and that he be fined and jailed for contempt if he continued to refuse. Dinnan again refused, and the court ordered him jailed. He arrived at the jail dressed in full academic regalia.

Although the point of view expressed in *Dinnan* foreshadows the unanimous opinion of the U.S. Supreme Court in the *Pennsylvania* decision, nine years would elapse and several more appellate decisions would consider this issue before the high court resolved it.

The following year, another court, in *Gray v. Board of Higher Education*, 692 F.2d 901 (2d Cir. 1982), reached the same result as *Dinnan*, but on much narrower grounds, and left the door open for the creation of such a privilege under appropriate circumstances. Gray had not been given reasons why he was denied tenure, and believed that the decision had been infected with racial discrimination. He therefore demanded to see the letters and memos used by the college to make its decision. The court used a balancing test that weighed the plaintiff's need for the materials against the institution's interest in maintaining their confidentiality. Had Gray received a full statement of the reasons for his tenure denial, the court suggested, the university's legitimate interests in the confidentiality of evaluators' comments may have prevailed. There was no protected interest on the university's part, however, in not giving Gray a full explanation of the reasons for the decision. By leaving room for recognition of an academic freedom privilege in other cases, the court in effect adopted a middle-ground position earlier espoused by the AAUP (see "A Preliminary Statement on Judicially Compelled Disclosure in the Nonrenewal of Faculty Appointments," 67 *Academe* 27 (Feb.–Mar. 1981)).

The U.S. Court of Appeals for the Seventh Circuit created and applied an academic freedom privilege in *EEOC v. University of Notre Dame*, 715 F.2d 331 (7th Cir. 1983). When a faculty member charged the university with discrimination under Title VII (see this volume, Section 3.3.2.1), Notre Dame had agreed to provide the Equal Employment Opportunity Commission (EEOC) with the files of the unsuccessful candidate for tenure and other faculty, but had insisted that the names of evaluators be redacted (removed) to protect their identity. The EEOC had refused to accept redacted files, arguing that the writer's identity was necessary and relevant to the plaintiff's claim of discrimination. The court ordered the EEOC to accept the redacted files, asserting that the identity of the evaluators was protected by an "academic freedom privilege." The court also accepted the university's argument that the EEOC should be required to sign a nondisclosure agreement before it obtained the files of faculty who were not parties to the lawsuit.

But the U.S. Court of Appeals for the Third Circuit rejected the attempt of Franklin and Marshall College to assert an academic freedom privilege when the EEOC requested "confidential" evaluative information in order to investigate a professor's claim that his denial of tenure was a result of national origin discrimination. In *EEOC v. Franklin and Marshall College*, 775 F.2d 110 (3d Cir. 1985), the court, while recognizing the importance of confidentiality in obtaining candid evaluations, nevertheless ruled that the plaintiff's need for information relevant to his discrimination claim outweighed the college's interests in confidentiality.

Given the sharp differences among the four federal appellate courts that had addressed this issue, the U.S. Supreme Court granted review of a case in which Rosalie Tung, a professor in the University of Pennsylvania's business school, sued the university for race, sex, and national origin discrimination in denying her tenure. The EEOC had subpoenaed the confidential peer evaluations on which the university had relied to make its negative decision. Although the university complied with much of the EEOC's request, it refused to submit confidential letters written by Tung's evaluators, letters from the department chair, and accounts of a faculty committee's deliberations. It also refused to submit similar materials for five male faculty in the business school who were granted tenure during that year, which the EEOC wanted to review for comparison purposes. The EEOC filed an action to enforce the subpoena; both the district court and the U.S. Court of Appeals for the Third Circuit ordered the university to produce the documents, relying on *Franklin and Marshall*. Still refusing to produce the materials, the university appealed the ruling to the U.S. Supreme Court. The university argued that quality tenure decisions require candid peer evaluations, which in turn require confidentiality. It asserted that requiring such disclosure would "destroy collegiality" and that either a common law privilege or a constitutionally based privilege should be created. The Court agreed to determine whether a qualified "academic freedom privilege" should be created or whether a balancing test should be used that would require the EEOC to show "particularized need" for the information before it was disclosed.

Writing for a unanimous court, Justice Harry Blackmun upheld the EEOC's need for peer evaluations and refused either to create a privilege or to require the EEOC to show "particularized need" (*University of Pennsylvania v. EEOC*, 493 U.S. 182 (1990)). Justice Blackmun first noted that Title VII contains no language excluding peer evaluations from discovery and that the EEOC's need for relevant information was not diminished simply because the defendant in this case was a university.

The Court gave the following reasons for its refusal to create a common law privilege:

1. Congress, in amending Title VII in 1972 to extend its protections to employees of colleges and universities, had not included such a privilege.
2. Title VII confers upon the EEOC a broad right of access to relevant evidence, and peer evaluations were clearly relevant.
3. Title VII includes sanctions for the disclosure of confidential information by EEOC staff.
4. Evidence of discrimination is particularly likely to be "tucked away in peer review files" (493 U.S. at 193).
5. Requiring the EEOC to show particularized need for the information could frustrate the purpose of Title VII by making the EEOC's investigatory responsibilities more difficult.

The Court also rejected the university's request that a constitutionally based academic freedom privilege be created. While acknowledging academe's strong interest in protecting academic freedom, the Court viewed the EEOC's request as an "extremely attenuated" infringement on academic freedom, characterizing it as a "content-neutral" government action to enforce a federal law rather than a government attempt to supress free speech (493 U.S. at 198–99).

It was clear that the Court regarded the potential injury to academic freedom as speculative, and the argument that academe deserved special treatment as inappropriate:

> We are not so ready as petitioner seems to be to assume the worst about those in the academic community. Although it is possible that some evaluators may become less candid as the possibility of disclosure increases, others may simply ground their evaluations in specific examples and illustrations in order to deflect potential claims of bias or unfairness. Not all academics will hesitate to stand up and be counted when they evaluate their peers [493 U.S. at 200].

The result in this case appears to require an institution, when confronted with an EEOC subpoena, to produce relevant information, whether or not the institution has promised to keep it confidential. Although the Supreme Court did not address the issue of whether an institution could provide peer review materials with identifying information redacted, the Court's very broad language upholding the need of the EEOC for relevant information suggests that, should the EEOC assert that identifying information is relevant to a particular claim, the information would have to be provided. And although this case involves access to information by the EEOC, rather than by a private plaintiff, it is likely that the case will be interpreted to permit faculty plaintiffs in discrimination cases to see letters from outside evaluators, written recommendations of department or other committees, and other information relevant to a negative employment decision. For analysis of the *Pennsylvania* case's implications for faculty personnel decisions, see B. Lee, *Peer Review Confidentiality: Is It Still Possible?* (National Association of College and University Attorneys, 1990). See also Note, "Shifting Meanings of Academic Freedom: An Analysis of *University of Pennsylvania v. EEOC*," 17 *J. Coll. & Univ. Law* 329 (1991).

For public institutions (and some private ones as well) in states with open-records laws, the result in *Pennsylvania* may have little significance, because several of these laws have been interpreted to apply to faculty personnel decisions. For example, in *Pennsylvania State University v. Commissioner, Department of Labor and Industry*, 536 A.2d 852 (Pa. Commw. Ct. 1988), a state court interpreted the open-records law as permitting faculty to see peer evaluations solicited for promotion or tenure decisions, calling them "performance evaluations" (for which the state law requires disclosure) rather than "letters of reference" (which are exempted from the law's disclosure requirements). The state law was applied in the same manner when a faculty member at a private college sought access to peer evaluations after he was denied tenure (*Lafayette College v. Commissioner, Department of Labor and Industry*, 546 A.2d 126 (Pa. Commw. Ct. 1988)). Similarly, the Supreme Court of Alaska ruled that promotion and tenure decisions are subject to the state's "sunshine law" (*University of Alaska v. Geistauts*, 666 P.2d 424 (Alaska 1983)).

But a Michigan court exempted some peer evaluations from disclosure in *Muskovitz v. Lubbers*, 452 N.W.2d 854 (Mich. Ct. App. 1990), ruling that a letter from a dean to the provost regarding a faculty member's performance was exempt from the Michigan Employee Right-to-Know Act (Mich. Comp. Laws § 423.501 et seq.). The court characterized the letter as a "staff planning document" (one of the law's exemptions). It also ruled that the names of persons who prepared the evaluations, and specific words used in them (if those words would reveal the identity of the writer), were exempt under the law as "employee references supplied to an employer" and could be removed from documents submitted to a plaintiff. The court noted the Supreme Court's ruling in *Pennsylvania* but stated that it did not control interpretation of the Michigan law. Similarly, a state appellate court in Florida, in interpreting that state's open-records law, ruled that tenure committee votes are exempt from disclosure (*Cantanese v. Ceros-Livingston*, 599 So. 2d 1021 (Fla. Dist. Ct. App. 1992)).

Faculty in California attempted to use that state's education laws to seek access to their confidential peer evaluations, but without success. Section 92612 of the state's Education Code guarantees a faculty member access to material in his or her personnel files (although the name and affiliation of the writer may be redacted). In *Scharf v. Regents of the University of California*, 286 Cal. Rptr. 227 (Cal. Ct. App. 1991), six faculty members denied tenure and the American Federation of Teachers asserted that the state's Education Code gave them the right to review letters from outside reviewers and other confidential material in their personnel files. The university had given the faculty members summaries of the material but refused to provide the actual letters. The appellate court, citing Article IX, Section 9 of the California constitution, noted that the University of California has constitutional autonomy and that the provision in the state Education Code giving faculty access to confidential evaluations was, in its application to the university, unconstitutional. Distinguishing the *Pennsylvania* decision, the court noted that the faculty were not involved in litigation regarding their promotion or tenure decisions and that the reasoning of that case did not bind the California court in this case.

In light of the *Pennsylvania* decision and the proliferation of open-records laws at the state level, the American Association of University Professors developed a policy on access to faculty personnel files. The report provides a thoughtful discussion of the two conflicting interests—preserving confidentiality in order to ensure complete candor, and ensuring access to evaluative material in order to encourage responsible and careful evaluation and to ascertain whether inappropriate grounds for a negative employment decision exist.

The report, "Access to Faculty Personnel Files," 78 *Academe* 24 (July-Aug. 1992), which is a joint report of Committee A on Academic Freedom and Tenure and Committee W on the Status of Women in the Academic Profession, reaches the following conclusions:

1. Faculty members should, at all times, have access to their own files, including unredacted letters, both internal and external.

2. A faculty member should be afforded access upon request to general information about other faculty members such as is normally contained in a *curriculum vitae*.

3. Files of a faculty complainant and of other faculty members, for purposes of comparison, should be available in unredacted form to faculty appeals committees to the extent such committees deem the information relevant and necessary to the fair disposition of the case before them.

4. A faculty appeals committee should make available to the aggrieved faculty member, in unredacted form and without prejudging the merits of the case, all materials it deems relevant to the complaint, including personnel files

of other faculty members, having due regard for the privacy of those who are not parties to the complaint.

The report acknowledges that these recommendations "go beyond the practices regarding access to personnel files that are common in many colleges and universities" (at 28).

Given the broadened access of candidates for reappointment, promotion, and tenure to formerly confidential evaluative information, college and university administrators and faculty should assess their policies and practices regarding peer evaluation and access of candidates to such information. Particularly in those states where access is afforded by state law, faculty evaluators should be well informed about the institution's criteria for such decisions and should be trained to provide appropriate documentation to support their recommendations. Given the heightened judicial scrutiny of institutions' denials of tenure to faculty (see Sections 3.3.2, 3.6.2.2, and 3.6.3.2), time spent ensuring that peer evaluations and the ensuing employment decisions are amply supported by evidence is an excellent investment.

3.7.7.2. Research findings. Researchers are asked from time to time to provide their findings for a variety of lawsuits, the most common of which is product liability. In some of these cases, the data have not been fully analyzed and the researcher is unwilling to make them public at that time. In other cases the type of disclosure required would violate the confidentiality of research subjects. The legal question presented in these cases is whether, under evidence law or under the First Amendment, the information can be said to be privileged—protected from disclosure by a "researcher's privilege."

In *Dow Chemical Co. v. Allen,* 672 F.2d 1262 (7th Cir. 1982), the court recognized a claim to a researcher's privilege. It therefore refused to enforce subpoenas issued by an administrative law judge presiding over a hearing convened by the Environmental Protection Agency to consider canceling the registration of certain herbicides manufactured by Dow:

> Relevant portions of the affidavits of Dr. Allen and Mr. Van Miller [the university researchers served with the subpoenas] stated, without contradiction by Dow [the company seeking the information], that public access to the research data would make the studies an unacceptable basis for scientific papers or other research; that peer review and publication of the studies was crucial to the researchers' credibility and careers and would be precluded by whole or partial public disclosure of the information; that loss of the opportunity to publish would severely decrease the researchers' professional opportunities in the future; and that even inadvertent disclosure of the information would risk total destruction of months or years of research.
>
> The precise contours of the concept of academic freedom are difficult to define. . . . One First Amendment scholar has written: "The heart of the system consists in the right of the individual faculty member to teach, carry on research, and publish without interference from the government, the community, the university administration, or his fellow faculty members" (T. Emerson, *The System of Freedom of Expression* 594 (1970)). We think it clear that whatever constitutional protection is afforded by the First Amendment extends as readily to the scholar in the laboratory as to the teacher in the classroom (see generally Emerson at 619). Of course, academic freedom, like other constitutional rights, is not

absolute and must on occasion be balanced against important competing interests. . . . Case law considering the standard to be applied where the issue is academic freedom of the university to be free of governmental interference, as opposed to academic freedom of the individual teacher to be free of restraints from the university administration, is surprisingly sparse. But what precedent there is at the Supreme Court level suggests that to prevail over academic freedom the interests of government must be strong and the extent of intrusion carefully limited. . . .

In the present case, the . . . subpoenas by their terms would compel the researchers to turn over to Dow virtually every scrap of paper and every mechanical or electronic recording made during the extended period that those studies have been in progress at the university. The ALJ's [administrative law judge's] decision would have further obliged the researchers to continually update Dow on "additional useful data" which became available during the course of the proceedings. These requirements threaten substantial intrusion into the enterprise of university research, and there are several reasons to think they are capable of chilling the exercise of academic freedom. To begin with, the burden of compliance certainly would not be insubstantial. More important, enforcement of the subpoenas would leave the researchers with the knowledge throughout continuation of their studies that the fruits of their labors had been appropriated by and were being scrutinized by a not-unbiased third party whose interests were arguably antithetical to theirs. It is not difficult to imagine that that realization might well be both unnerving and discouraging. Indeed, it is probably fair to say that the character and extent of intervention would be such that, regardless of its purpose, it would "inevitably tend to check the ardor and fearlessness of scholars, qualities at once so fragile and so indispensable for fruitful academic labor" (*Sweezy* [*v. New Hampshire*, 354 U.S. 234, 262 (1957)] (Frankfurter, J., concurring in result)). In addition, the researchers could reasonably fear that additional demands for disclosure would be made in the future. If a private corporation can subpoena the entire work product of months of study, what is to say further down the line the company will not seek other subpoenas to determine how the research is coming along? To these factors must be added the knowledge of the researchers that even inadvertent disclosure of the subpoenaed data could jeopardize both the studies and their careers. Clearly, enforcement of the subpoenas carries the potential for chilling the exercise of First Amendment rights.

We do not suggest that facts could not arise sufficient to overcome respondents' academic freedom interests in the . . . studies. Nor do we say that a waiver of the protection afforded by the First Amendment is impossible. If, for example, Dr. Allen, Mr. Van Miller, or other researchers were likely to testify about the . . . studies at the [Environmental Protection Agency] hearing, there might well be justification for granting at least partial or conditional enforcement of the subpoenas. Of course, we need not decide that question now [672 F.2d at 1273–76; footnotes omitted].

In an earlier case, *Richards of Rockford, Inc. v. Pacific Gas and Electric Co.*, 71 F.R.D. 388 (N.D. Cal. 1976), a federal district court judge reached a similar conclusion in an opinion that identified and balanced the various competing interests at stake. But in *Wright v. Jeep Corp.*, 547 F. Supp. 871 (E.D. Mich. 1982), decided seven months after *Allen*, a federal district court rejected a privilege claim and enforced a subpoena requiring a University of Michigan professor to produce research data from a study that was apparently completed (unlike the study in Allen).[60]

Allen was again cited by a scholar attempting to protect the confidentiality of his data, but without success this time. In *Deitchman v. E. R. Squibb & Sons, Inc.*, 740 F.2d 556 (9th Cir. 1984), the drug company was a defendant in a products liability lawsuit by women whose mothers had taken diethylstilbestrol (DES) and who had contracted cancer, allegedly as a result of their prenatal exposure to DES. Dr. Arthur Herbst, a professor at the University of Chicago medical school, maintained a registry of individuals suffering from certain forms of cancer. Herbst had promised confidentiality to all patients whose records had been submitted to the registry. Herbst also conducted research using information from the registry.

Squibb asked Herbst to produce the entire registry, and Herbst, citing both the confidentiality issue and his "academic freedom" not to release research results before they had undergone peer review, refused. Although a trial judge quashed the subpoena, the appellate court required the parties to negotiate about the scope of discovery and the methods to be used to protect the patients' confidentiality. The court stated that, although Squibb's discovery demand was far too broad, the company had a legitimate need for some of the information contained in the registry. The court suggested that the parties consider redaction, a protective order, and other measures calculated to minimize the burden on Herbst and to protect the confidentiality of the patients.

Another federal appellate court enforced a subpoena for unpublished data in *In re Mt. Sinai School of Medicine v. American Tobacco Co.*, 880 F.2d 1520 (2d Cir. 1989). The tobacco company was a defendant in a products liability lawsuit. The company had asked a researcher at the medical school to produce research data on the effects of smoking on asbestos workers. The researcher was not a party to the lawsuit and refused to produce the data, saying that he had promised the subjects confidentiality and that redacting the data would be very expensive and would take thousands of hours of his time. A motion to compel production of the evidence, filed in state court, was quashed.

The tobacco company filed a second motion in federal court, this time seeking only the data from already published scientific papers, covering two years of the study, and offering to pay the costs of deleting the confidential information. The court agreed to enforce the subpoena and issued a protective order to guard the identities of the research subjects.

The Second Circuit denied that there was an "absolute privilege for scholars," noting that the researcher's interest in avoiding disruption of his ongoing research is only one factor that the court considers in applying a balancing test; another factor would be the public's interest in accurate information. The court concluded that it was not unreasonable for the tobacco company to wish to examine the data that formed the basis for the articles, upon which expert witnesses (but not the researcher) were expected to testify on the plaintiffs' behalf. No qualified privilege was used in

[60]In a second case involving the same University of Michigan professor and the same research data, *Buchanan v. American Motors Corp.*, 697 F.2d 151 (6th Cir. 1983), the appellate court refused to decide the privilege issue, instead holding that to compel an "expert who has no direct connection with the litigation" to testify was "unreasonably burdensome." The court therefore quashed a subpoena seeking the professor's appearance.

this case; instead, the court used the usual criteria for determining whether a discovery request is appropriate: relevance, burdensomeness, and the party's need for the information.

This case differs from *Allen* in that the data sought had already been published, so the researcher could not make the premature disclosure argument that the court considered so important in *Allen*. Also, the tobacco company was not seeking to compel the researcher to testify, so the privilege against compelled testimony was not an issue in this case. The interest in *Mt. Sinai* was primarily the researcher's time, the effect on his ongoing research program, and the potential for disclosure of the names of research subjects. The court applied a balancing test, weighing the tobacco company's need for the information against the adverse effect on the researcher and the research subjects. The court apparently concluded that these interests did not outweigh the tobacco company's need for the information, primarily because redaction would preserve the subjects' confidentiality.

Federal courts have been particularly unsympathetic to researchers when their data are required for criminal, rather than civil, proceedings. In *In re Grand Jury Subpoena*, 583 F. Supp. 991 (E.D.N.Y. 1984), *reversed*, 750 F.2d 223 (2d Cir. 1984), a doctoral student was conducting "participant observation" research for his dissertation at a restaurant on Long Island. When a suspicious fire and explosion destroyed the restaurant, the student's observations and notes on his conversations at the restaurant were subpoenaed by a grand jury. The student moved to quash the subpoena, claiming a "scholar's privilege" because he had promised confidentiality to his research subjects. The federal trial judge quashed the subpoena, comparing the student's interest in confidentiality to that of a news reporter's, as recognized in *Branzburg v. Hayes*, 408 U.S. 665 (1972). A federal appellate court reversed the trial judge's ruling and sent the case back to the trial judge for further analysis in light of the criteria specified by the appellate court.

The appellate court was not convinced that a "scholar's privilege" exists or that one should be applied under these circumstances. First the court discussed the showing that an individual claiming a scholar's privilege would need to make:

> Surely the application of a scholar's privilege, if it exists, requires a threshold showing consisting of a detailed description of the nature and seriousness of the scholarly study in question, of the methodology employed, of the need for assurances of confidentiality to various sources to conduct the study, and of the fact that the disclosure requested by the subpoena will seriously impinge upon that confidentiality [750 F.2d at 225].

The court explained further that no evidence had been presented about

> the nature of the work or of its role in the scholarly literature of sociology. One need not quip that "You can't tell a dissertation by its title" to conclude that the words "The Sociology of the American Restaurant" afford precious little information about the subject matter of [the student's] thesis [750 F.2d at 225].

The opinion suggests that the student would have been required to present testimony from recognized scholars justifying the seriousness of the subject and the appropriateness of the methodology. This requirement appears to be based upon the individual's status as a student rather than a holder of a Ph.D. The opinion describes the showing that must be made before a scholar's privilege could be considered:

> What exactly [the student's] role is, what kinds of material he hopes to collect, and how that role and that material relate to a need for confidentiality . . . , evidence of a considered research plan, conceived in light of scholarly requirements or standards, contemplating assurances of confidentiality for certain parts of the inquiry [750 F.2d at 225].

The court then discussed the limited nature of the scholar's privilege (if it exists), which would cover only those portions of the research material that required confidentiality. The court also noted that the scholar would be required to permit inspection of the material by a judge and redaction under the judge's supervision. The broad privilege claimed by the student, that all his research notes and journals were included, was roundly rejected by the court.

Another federal appeals court extended the trend against a "scholar's privilege." In *Scarce v. United States*, 5 F.3d 397 (9th Cir. 1993), the court ruled that there is no constitutional right or federal common law privilege that shelters a scholar's refusal to answer questions before a grand jury. Scarce, a doctoral student in sociology at Washington State University, had been asked to testify about conversations with some of his friends, animal rights activists who were accused of breaking into and damaging animal research facilities at the university.

Scarce, who was conducting research on the animal rights movement and had written a book on the radical environmental movement, refused to testify and was jailed for six months. (For an account of this matter, see P. Monaghan, "Free After 6 Months: Sociologist Who Refused to Testify Is Released," *Chron. Higher Educ.*, Nov. 3, 1993, A14–15.) The court rejected the concept of a "scholar's privilege," stating that no cases had recognized the right of a scholar to withhold information from a grand jury where the information was relevant to a legitimate grand jury inquiry and was sought in good faith.

It appears that judges are increasingly hostile to claims of a researcher's or scholar's privilege, especially when the information is sought for a criminal, rather than a civil, proceeding. Clearly, absolute privileges appear to be unavailable to scholars, because judges have several strategies for protecting confidentiality and reducing the burden on the researcher. In light of these developments, faculty and administrators need to understand that promises of absolute confidentiality to research subjects may not be enforceable.

Close attention should be paid to the particular context in which potential issues arise. Especially important are (1) the procedural and evidentiary rules of the court or administrative agency that would entertain the litigation and (2) the impact that disclosure of the requested information would have on academic freedom. Suggestions for ways in which administrators and researchers can limit access to or interest in their research findings are found in N. Miller, "Subpoenas in Academe: Controlling Disclosure," 17 *J. Coll. & Univ. Law* 1 (1990).

A second major issue involving confidentiality of research results is the requirement of some funding sources, both governmental and private, that research results be kept secret. Although this requirement presents the opposite dilemma of compelled disclosure, it is no less troubling from an academic freedom perspective.

When it is the government imposing the secrecy restrictions, the Constitution is asserted as the source of protection for the researcher's academic freedom right to publish research results. The regulations of several federal agencies authorize officials to prohibit release of certain findings without the funding agency's permission (see, for example, 48 C.F.R. §§ 324.70, 352.224-70 (1991), which authorize contract officers from the Department of Health and Human Services to place restrictions on disclosure of preliminary findings).

In *Board of Trustees of Stanford University v. Sullivan,* 773 F. Supp. 472 (D.D.C. 1991), the National Institutes of Health conditioned the university's receipt of research funds for medical research on its agreement to include a clause regarding disclosure in the funding contract. The clause would have prohibited the university from disclosing "preliminary unvalidated findings" that "could create erroneous conclusions which might threaten public health or safety if acted upon" (773 F. Supp. at 474, n.5) as well as findings that could have "adverse effects" on the agency. Upon Stanford's refusal, the NIH withdraw the contract and Stanford sued in federal district court, asserting that the agency's confidentiality requirement was unconstitutional.

In defending against Stanford's claim, the NIH cited *Rust v. Sullivan,* 111 S. Ct. 1759 (1991) (discussed in Section 7.4.5., this volume), and its distinction between decisions not to subsidize protected activity and attempts to prohibit protected activity. Relying on *Rust,* the NIH argued that it was simply engaging in a "nonsubsidy" activity, not prohibiting protected activity, when it stipulated that all release of information be subject to prior government approval.

The federal trial judge disagreed, stating that the NIH confidentiality requirement was broad and would prohibit the researchers from speaking about their research without prior permission whether they were acting for themselves or on behalf of the university. Furthermore, the judge cited the language from *Rust* in which the Court recognized the university's role as a "traditional sphere of free expression" and appeared to limit the reach of the "nonsubsidy doctrine" when it was applied to institutions of higher education and their faculty (Section 7.4.5., this volume). Applying strict scrutiny to the federal regulation, the trial judge rejected as noncompelling the NIH's argument that secrecy was required in order to protect prospective patients from "unwarranted hope" that could be raised by the release of preliminary findings (773 F. Supp. at 477, n.16).

Should the result in *Stanford University* be upheld on appeal or followed in similar cases, there may be a "university exception" to the nonsubsidy doctrine, as suggested by the *Rust* dicta. Such a development would be a welcome event for researchers and administrators when the funding source is public. But constitutional protections would typically not apply to funding restrictions imposed by private funding sources, such as corporations or foundations. Such restrictions, if incorporated into the contract, could be removed only if the funding source agreed. And unless certain state constitutions or cases decided under their authority included free speech guarantees that applied to private entities as well as the government (see, for example, *State v. Schmid,* discussed in Sections 1.5.2 and 5.6.3), it is not clear that a faculty member or an institution would have a cause of action against a private funding source that withdrew funding after the faculty member refused to agree to secrecy requirements.

For an extended discussion of secrecy and university research in the context of government restrictions on disclosure, see "Focus on Secrecy and University Research," 19 *J. Coll. & Univ. Law* 199 (1993). This special issue of the journal includes four articles devoted to this subject.

Sec. 3.8. Staff Reduction Due to Financial Exigency and Program Discontinuance

The financial difficulties that began for postsecondary education in the late 1960s created a new and particularly sensitive faculty personnel issue, an issue with equal salience in the 1990s.[61] In an era of inflation and shrinking resources, what are the legal responsibilities of an institution that must terminate an academic program or otherwise initiate a reduction in force? What are its obligations to faculty and students? And is there a difference between the institution's legal obligations during financial exigency and its obligations when it decides to close or reduce an academic program? On these questions, which should continue to stalk postsecondary education for the foreseeable future, the law is still developing. But enough judicial ink has been spilled to give administrators a fair idea of how to prepare for the unwelcome necessity of terminating faculty jobs in a financial crunch.

3.8.1. Contractual considerations. The faculty contract (Section 3.1) is the starting point for determining both a public and a private institution's responsibilities regarding staff reductions. Administrators should consider several questions concerning the faculty contract. Does it, and should it, provide for termination due to financial exigency or program discontinuance? Does it, and should it, specify the conditions that will constitute a financial exigency or justify discontinuance of a program and stipulate how the institution will determine when such conditions exist? Does it, and should it, set forth criteria for determining which faculty members will be released? Does it, and should it, require that alternatives be explored (such as transfer to another department) before termination becomes permissible? Does it, and should it, provide a hearing or other recourse for a faculty member chosen for dismissal? Does it, and should it, provide the released faculty member with any priority right to be rehired when other openings arise or the financial situation eases?

Whenever the faculty contract has any provision on financial exigency or program discontinuance, the institution should follow it; failure to do so will likely be a breach of contract. Whether such contractual provisions exist may depend on whether the AAUP guidelines[62] have been incorporated into the faculty contract. In

---

[61]This section is limited to financial exigency and program discontinuance problems concerning faculty. But such problems also affect students, and an institution's response may occasionally give students a basis on which to sue. See *Eden v. Board of Trustees of State University, Beukas v. Board of Trustees of Fairleigh Dickinson University*, and *Unger v. National Residents Matching Program*, discussed in Section 4.2.3.; see also *Aase v. South Dakota Board of Regents*, 400 N.W.2d 269 (S.D. 1987). See generally Section 4.1.3, concerning an institution's contractual obligation to students.

[62]See "Recommended Institutional Regulations on Academic Freedom and Tenure," Regulation 4 (in *AAUP Policy Documents and Reports* (AAUP, 1990), at 21), and "On Institutional Problems Resulting from Financial Exigency: Some Operating Guidelines" (in *AAUP Policy Documents and Reports*, at 128). An earlier (1968) version of the "Recommended Institutional Regulations"—specifically the 1968 version of Regulation 4(c)—was interpreted in the *Browzin* case, discussed in the text in this section. The court concluded that the defendant university had not violated the requirement that it "make every effort" to place terminated faculty members "in other suitable positions."

Browzin v. Catholic University of America, 527 F.2d 843 (D.C. Cir. 1975), for instance, the parties stipulated that the AAUP guidelines had been adopted as part of the faculty contract, and the court noted that such adoption was "entirely consistent with the statutes of the university and the university's previous responses to AAUP actions." As in *Browzin,* it is important for administrators to understand the legal status of AAUP guidelines within their institutions; any doubt should be resolved by consulting counsel.

The contract provisions for tenured and nontenured faculty members may differ, and administrators should note any differences. Nontenured faculty members generally pose far fewer legal problems, since administrators may simply not renew their contracts at the end of the contract term (see Section 3.6.2.1). If the faculty contract is silent regarding financial exigency or program discontinuance, in relation to either tenured or nontenured faculty members, the institution still may have the power to terminate. Under the common law doctrine of "impossibility," the institution may be able to extricate itself from contractual obligations if unforeseen events have made it impossible to perform those obligations. The doctrine of impossibility has been stated as follows:

> When an unforeseen event which makes impossible the performance of a contractual duty occurs subsequent to the formation of the contract, it is often held that the promisor is excused from performing. Such holdings are exceptions to the general rule that when a contractual promise is made, the promisor must perform or pay damages for his failure to perform no matter how burdensome performance has become as a result of unforeseen circumstances [J. D. Calamari and J. M. Perillo, *Contracts* (2d ed., West, 1977), § 13-1 at 456-77; and see generally ch. 13].

The first major contract case on financial exigency was *AAUP v. Bloomfield College,* 322 A.2d 846 (N.J. Super. Ct. Ch. Div. 1974), *affirmed,* 346 A.2d 615 (App. Div. 1975). On June 29, 1973, Bloomfield College, a private school, notified thirteen tenured faculty members that their services would not be needed as of June 30, 1973. The college gave financial exigency as the reason for this action. The college also notified the remaining faculty members, tenured and nontenured, that they would be put on one-year terminal contracts for 1973-74, after which they would have to negotiate new contracts with the school.

The thirteen fired faculty members brought suit based on their contracts of employment. Paragraph C(3) of the "policies" enumerated in the contract provided that "a teacher will have tenure and his services may be terminated only for adequate cause, except in case of retirement for age, or under extraordinary circumstances because of financial exigency of the institution." Paragraph C(6) provided that "termination of continuous appointment because of financial exigency of the institution must be demonstrably bona fide. A situation which makes drastic retrenchment of this sort necessary precludes expansion of the staff at other points at the same time, except in extraordinary circumstances."

The faculty members alleged that no bona fide financial exigency existed and that the hiring of twelve new staff members three months after the plaintiffs were dismissed violated the requirement that during a financial exigency new staff persons would be hired only "in extraordinary circumstances." Thus, the court had to determine whether there was a "demonstrably bona fide" financial exigency and whether there were such extraordinary circumstances as would justify the hiring of new faculty members.

The trial court analyzed the college's finances and determined that no bona fide financial exigency existed because the college owned a large piece of valuable property that it could have sold to meet its needs. The appellate court, however, disagreed:

> In our opinion, the mere fact that this financial strain existed for some period of time does not negate the reality that a "financial exigency" was a fact of life for the college administration within the meaning of the underlying contract. The interpretation of "exigency" as attributed by the trial court is too narrow a concept of the term in relation to the subject matter involved. A more reasonable construction might be encompassed within the phrase "state of urgency." In this context the evidence was plentiful as to the proof of the existence of the criterion of the financial exigency required by the contract.
>
> In this vein it was improper for the judge to rest his conclusion in whole or in part upon the failure of the college to sell the knoll property which had been acquired several years before in anticipation of the creation of a new campus at a different locale. . . . Whether such a plan of action to secure financial stability on a short-term basis is preferable to the long-term planning of the college administration is a policy decision for the institution. Its choice of alternative is beyond the scope of judicial oversight in the context of this litigation [346 A.2d at 617].

Though the appellate court thus held that the college was in a state of financial exigency, it was unwilling to find that the faculty members were fired because of the college's financial condition. The trial court had determined that the reason for the terminations was the college's desire to abolish tenure, and the appellate court found ample evidence to support this finding.

On the question of whether extraordinary circumstances existed sufficient to justify the hiring of twelve new faculty members, the trial court also held in favor of the plaintiffs. The college had argued that its actions were justified because it was developing a new type of curriculum, but the court noted that the evidence put forth by the college was vague and did not suggest that any financial benefit would result from the new curriculum. The appellate court did not disturb this part of the trial court's decision, nor did it even discuss the issue.

A major overarching issue of the case concerned the burden of proof. Did the college have the burden of proving that it had fulfilled the contract conditions justifying termination? Or did the faculty members have the burden of proving that the contractual conditions had not been met? The issue has critical practical importance; because the evidentiary problems can be so difficult, the outcome of financial exigency litigation may often depend on who has the burden of proof. The trial court assigned the burden to the college, and the appellate court agreed:

> It is manifest that under the controlling agreement among the parties the affected members of the faculty had attained the protection of tenure after completing a seven-year probationary service. This was their vested right which could be legally divested only if the defined conditions occurred. The proof of existence

of those conditions as a justifiable reason for terminating the status of the plaintiffs plainly was the burden of the defendants [346 A.2d at 616].

Since the college had not proved that it had met the contract conditions justifying termination, the courts ordered the reinstatement of the terminated faculty members.

A similar result occurred in *Pace v. Hymas*, 726 P.2d 693 (Idaho 1986). The University of Idaho's faculty handbook stated that a tenured faculty member's service could be terminated for cause or for financial exigency. The handbook defined financial exigency as

> a demonstrably bona fide, imminent financial crisis which threatens the viability of an agency, institution, office or department as a whole or one or more of its programs . . . and which cannot be adequately alleviated by means other than a reduction in the employment force [726 P.2d at 695].

Pace, a professor of home economics, was laid off after the State Board of Education issued a declaration of financial exigency. Relying on *Bloomfield College*, as well as on more recent cases, the Idaho Supreme Court ruled that the university had the burden of proof regarding the existence of financial exigency, and that it had not carried that burden.

Although the university had sustained a budget shortfall in the Agricultural Extension Service, the unit to which Pace was appointed, the university had received an increased appropriation from the state, it had received funds for a 7 percent salary increase for faculty, and it had a surplus of uncommitted funds at the end of its fiscal year. No alternatives to laying off faculty—including salary freezes, reduction in travel and other expenses, or other cost-saving practices—had been considered prior to Pace's layoff. Because the university had not determined if the financial crisis could be alleviated by less drastic means than firing tenured faculty, the court ruled that the university had not met the faculty handbook's definition of a bona fide financial exigency.

In *Pace* the faculty handbook explicitly mentioned financial exigency as a permissible reason for termination of a tenured faculty member. Two U.S. Court of Appeals cases upheld institutional authority to terminate tenured faculty members even in the absence of any express contractual provision granting such authority. The first case, *Krotkoff v. Goucher College*, 585 F.2d 675 (4th Cir. 1978), concerned a termination due to bona fide financial exigency; the second case, *Jimenez v. Almodovar*, 650 F.2d 363 (1st Cir. 1981), concerned a termination due to discontinuance of an academic program. Both cases resort to academic custom and usage (Sections 1.3.2.3 and 3.1.1) to imply terms into the faculty contract. Both cases also identify implicit rights of tenured faculty members that limit the institution's termination authority. The opinion in *Krotkoff* is discussed at some length as an illustration of the type of showing that, in this court's opinion, attested to the good faith of the college's actions.

Krotkoff was a tenured professor of German at Goucher College, a private liberal arts college for women. After having taught at the college for thirteen years, she was notified in June of 1975 that she would be terminated on the grounds of financial exigency. Her performance had been at all times acceptable. Since her contract was silent on the question of financial exigency, the professor argued that the termination was a breach of contract. The college argued that it had implied authority to terminate in order to combat bona fide financial exigency.

The college had sustained budget deficits each year from 1968 through 1975, and the trustees decided not to renew the contracts of eleven untenured faculty members and to terminate four tenured faculty members. A faculty committee had made recommendations concerning curricular changes, one of which was to eliminate all but introductory courses in German. Krotkoff had taught advanced German literature courses, while another tenured faculty member had taught introductory German. The department chair and dean recommended that the other faculty member be retained because she was experienced in teaching introductory German and because she could also teach French. The president concurred and notified Krotkoff that she would be laid off.

Although a faculty committee reviewing Krotkoff's ensuing grievance recommended her retention, it did not recommend that the other faculty member be discharged, nor did it consider how the college could retain both professors. The president rejected the committee's recommendation and the trustees concurred. The committee had made an alternate recommendation that Krotkoff teach German courses and the other professor replace an assistant dean, who would be dismissed. This suggestion was also rejected by the president.

The college provided Krotkoff with a list of all positions available for the next year, and Krotkoff suggested that she assume a position in the economics department at her present faculty rank and salary and with tenure. The college refused her suggestion because she had no academic training in economics, and terminated her appointment.

In a four-part opinion, the appellate court analyzed the facts regarding the college's overall retrenchment program and the particular termination at issue. It concluded that the faculty contract, read in light of "the national academic community's understanding of the concept of tenure," permitted termination due to financial exigency; that a bona fide financial exigency existed; and that the college had used reasonable standards in selecting which faculty to terminate and had taken reasonable measures to afford the plaintiff alternative employment. The well-reasoned and organized opinion not only discusses the difficult legal issues but also touches on practical considerations, such as the complexities of relying on faculty committees to recommend candidates for termination.

Since the college's policy statements and bylaws did not specify financial exigency as a reason for the discharge of a tenured professor, the court first turned to "academic custom and usage" to determine whether such a reason for discharge was subsumed within the concept of tenure:

> The national academic community's understanding of the concept of tenure incorporates the notion that a college may refuse to renew a tenured teacher's contract because of financial exigency so long as its action is demonstrably bona fide. Dr. Todd Furniss, director of the Office of Academic Affairs of the American Council on Education, testified on behalf of Goucher:
>
> > The [common] understanding was that the person who held tenure would be employed for an indeterminate or indefinite period up to retirement, unless two conditions held. The first condition would be some inade-

quacy on that person's part, either incompetency or neglect of duty or moral turpitude. . . .

The second instance under which the tenure contract might be terminated is a group that includes, of course, death, includes disability, includes resignation, obviously, but chiefly includes what has been called financial exigency [585 F.2d at 678].

The court noted that Furniss had based his opinion in part on the AAUP's 1940 "Statement of Principles on Academic Freedom and Tenure.[63] The court then continued:

Probably because it was formulated by both administrators and professors, all of the secondary authorities seem to agree that [the 1940 statement] is the "most widely accepted academic definition of tenure" (R. Brown, "Tenure Rights in Contractual and Constitutional Context," 6 *J. of Law and Education* 279, 280 (1977); see also M. Mix, *Tenure and Termination in Financial Exigency* 4 (1978); C. Byse, "Academic Freedom, Tenure, and the Law," 73 *Harvard L. Rev.* 304, 305 (1959)).

The reported cases support the conclusion that tenure is not generally understood to preclude demonstrably bona fide dismissal for financial reasons. In most of the cases, the courts have interpreted contracts which contained an explicit reference to financial exigency (see *Browzin v. Catholic University*, 527 F.2d 843 (1975); *Bellak v. Franconia College*, 386 A.2d 1266 (N.H. 1978); *American Association of University Professors v. Bloomfield College*, . . . 322 A.2d 846 ([N.J. Super. Ct.] Ch. Div. 1974), *affirmed*, 346 A.2d 615 (App. Div. 1975); *Scheuer v. Creighton University*, . . . 260 N.W.2d 595 [Neb.] (1977)). In others, where the contracts did not mention this term, the courts construed tenure as implicitly granting colleges the right to make bona fide dismissals for financial reasons (see *Johnson v. Board of Regents*, 377 F. Supp. 227, 234–35 (W.D. Wis. 1974), *affirmed*, 510 F.2d 975 (7th Cir. 1975) (table); *Levitt v. Board of Trustees*, 376 F. Supp. 945 (D. Neb. 1974); cf. *Rehor v. Case Western Reserve University*, . . . 331 N.E.2d 416 ([Ohio] 1975)). No case indicates that tenure creates a right to exemption from dismissal for financial reasons. . . .

A concept of tenure that permits dismissal based on financial exigency is consistent with the primary purpose of tenure. Tenure's "real concern is with arbitrary or retaliatory dismissals based on an administrator's or a trustee's distaste for the content of a professor's teaching or research, or even for positions taken completely outside the campus setting. . . . It is designed to foster our society's interest in the unfettered progress of research and learning by protecting the profession's freedom of inquiry and instruction" (*Browzin* . . . [at] 846; see also *Rehor* . . . [at] 421; Note, "Dismissal of Tenured Faculty for Reasons of

[63]The statement (in *AAUP Policy Documents and Reports* (AAUP, 1990), at 3, 4) reads, in pertinent part, "After the expiration of a probationary period, teachers or investigators should have permanent or continuous tenure, and their services should be terminated only for adequate cause, except in the case of retirement for age, or under extraordinary circumstances because of financial exigencies.

"In the interpretation of this principle, it is understood that the following represents acceptable academic practice:

. . .

(5) Termination of a continuous appointment because of financial exigency should be demonstrably bona fide."

Financial Exigency," 51 *Indiana L.J.* 417 n.2 (1976)). Dismissals based on financial exigency, unlike those for cause or disability, are impersonal; they are unrelated to the views of the dismissed teachers. A professor whose appointment is terminated because of financial exigency will not be replaced by another with more conventional views or better connections. Hence, bona fide dismissals based on financial exigency do not threaten the values protected by tenure. . . .

In sum, there was no evidence of a general understanding in the Goucher community that the tenured faculty had greater protection from dismissal for financial reasons than the faculty at other colleges. The Krotkoff-Goucher contract must be interpreted consistently with the understanding of the national academic community about tenure and financial exigency. . . . By defining Krotkoff's relationship with the college in terms of tenure, the contract did not exempt her from demonstrably bona fide dismissal if the college confronted financial exigency (see Note, "Financial Exigency as Cause for Termination of Tenured Faculty Members in Private Post Secondary Educational Institutions," 62 *Iowa L. Rev.* 481, 508–09 (1976)) [585 F.2d at 678–80].

After the court determined that the contract between Krotkoff and Goucher permitted termination on the basis of financial exigency, it then considered Krotkoff's claim that a jury should have determined whether the college had breached its contract. In particular, Krotkoff argued that the court should submit for the jury's determination the question of whether the trustees' belief that financial exigency existed was reasonable. The court disagreed:

Courts have properly emphasized that dismissals of tenured professors for financial reasons must be demonstrably bona fide. Otherwise, college administrators could use financial exigency to subvert academic freedom. The leading case on this aspect of tenure is *American Association of College* [sic] *Professors v. Bloomfield College* . . . [discussed above in this section]. . . .

Bloomfield, however, establishes that the trustees' decision to sell or retain a parcel of land was not a proper subject for judicial review. . . . The same principle, we believe, should apply to the dissipation of an endowment. The reasonableness of the trustees' decision concerning the disposition of capital did not raise an issue for the jury. Stated otherwise, the existence of financial exigency should be determined by the adequacy of a college's operating funds rather than its capital assets (see Note, "Dismissal of Tenured Faculty for Reasons of Financial Exigency," . . . [at] 420–23; cf. *Scheuer v. Creighton University*, . . . [at] 599–601.

Krotkoff has acknowledged that the trustees and other college officials did not act in bad faith. The evidence overwhelmingly demonstrates that the college was confronted by pressing financial need. As a result of the large annual deficits aggregating more than $1,500,000 over an extended period and the steady decline in enrollment, the college's financial position was precarious. Action undoubtedly was required to secure the institution's future. Because of Krotkoff's disavowal of bad faith on the part of the college and because of the unrefuted evidence concerning the college's finances and enrollment, we believe that this aspect of the case raised no question for the jury. The facts and all the inferences that properly can be drawn from them conclusively establish that the trustees reasonably believed that the college was faced with financial exigency [585 F.2d at 681].

Finally, the court considered whether Goucher had used reasonable standards to determine that Krotkoff's appointment should be terminated, and whether the college had made reasonable efforts to find her another position. Although Goucher had argued that neither of these subjects was appropriate for judicial review, the court disagreed:

> Krotkoff's claims must be resolved by reference to her contract. This involves ascertaining, first, what contractual rights she had and, second, whether the college breached them. Viewing the evidence in the light most favorable to Krotkoff, as we must for purposes of this appeal, we believe that the district court correctly held that she was contractually entitled to insist (a) that the college use reasonable standards in selecting which faculty appointments to terminate and (b) that it take reasonable measures to afford her alternative employment.
>
> Neither the letter granting Krotkoff tenure nor the documents setting forth Goucher's policy concerning tenure mention the procedural rights to which a faculty member is entitled when the college proposes to terminate her appointment for financial reasons. Therefore, we must examine again the academic community's understanding concerning tenure to determine the nature of this unique contractual relationship.
>
> . . . [T]he 1940 Statement on Academic Freedom and Tenure sanctions terminations of faculty appointments because of financial exigency. But it also stipulates: "Termination of a continuous appointment because of financial exigency should be demonstrably bona fide." The evidence discloses that the academic community commonly understands that inherent in the concept of a "demonstrably bona fide" termination is the requirement that the college use fair and reasonable standards to determine which tenured faculty members will not be reappointed. The college's obligation to deal fairly with its faculty when selecting those whose appointments will be terminated is an attribute of tenure. Consequently, it is an implicit element of the contract of appointment.
>
> Nevertheless, the evidence questioning the reasonableness of Goucher's procedures was insufficient to submit this issue to the jury. The necessity for revising Goucher's curriculum was undisputed. A faculty committee accepted elimination of the classics department and reduction of the German section of the modern language department as reasonable responses to this need. The only substantial controversy was whether the college should have retained Krotkoff or Ehrlich, both tenured professors. Nothing in Krotkoff's contract gave her precedence, and the college did not breach it by retaining Ehrlich instead of Krotkoff. Nor was the college under any contractual obligation to retain Krotkoff by demoting Ehrlich to part-time teaching and part-time administrative work. Therefore, the district court did not err in ultimately ruling for the college on this issue.
>
> Whether the college was contractually obliged to make reasonable efforts to find Krotkoff alternate employment at Goucher was the subject of conflicting evidence. It is reasonable, however, to infer from the evidence that a demonstrably bona fide termination includes this requirement (see Note, "Financial Exigency as Cause for Termination of Tenured Faculty Members in Private Post Secondary Educational Institutions," . . . [at] 504–05; cf. *Browzin v. Catholic University*, . . . [at] 847. On the other hand, in the absence of an explicit contractual undertaking, the evidence discloses that tenure does not entitle a professor to training for appointment in another discipline (cf. *Browzin v. Catholic University* . . . [at] 850–51.
>
> The evidence conclusively establishes that the college did not breach any contractual obligation concerning alternative employment. The constraints of tenure, rank, and pay that Krotkoff placed on alternative employment severely

restricted the college's efforts to accommodate her. Apart from Ehrlich's position, the only vacancy in which she expressed interest was in the economics department. No evidence suggested that the head of that department or the president acted unreasonably in assessing the time and expense of retraining Krotkoff for this position or in deciding that her transfer would not be feasible. Again, we conclude that the district court did not err in holding that the college was entitled to judgment on these issues.

The judgment is affirmed [585 F.2d at 682–83].

Krotkoff provides an instructive analysis of postsecondary institutions' authority and obligations when terminating tenured faculty because of financial exigency. The case also provides an outstanding example of judicial reliance on academic custom and usage to resolve postsecondary education contractual disputes.

Somewhat different issues arise when the reduction is caused by a program closure, which may be done either on "educational" grounds or because of financial exigency. The plaintiffs in *Jimenez v. Almodovar* were two professors who had been appointed to a pilot program in physical education and recreation at a regional college of the University of Puerto Rico. Their teaching positions were eliminated as a result of low enrollment and poor evaluation of the program. The court had to resolve some contractual questions in ruling on the plaintiffs' claim of deprivation of property without procedural due process (see Section 3.6.2). The parties stipulated that the plaintiffs had property interests established by their letters of appointment, but the letters did not detail the extent of these interests. Therefore, in order to determine the scope of procedures required by due process, the court had to determine the extent of the plaintiffs' contractual rights.

According to the court:

> American courts and secondary authorities uniformly recognize that, unless otherwise provided in the agreement of the parties, or in the regulations of the institution, or in a statute, an institution of higher education has an implied contractual right to make in good faith an unavoidable termination of right to the employment of a tenured member of the faculty when his position is being eliminated as part of a change in academic program. The American court decisions are consistent with the 1940 Statement of Principles on Academic Freedom and Tenure widely adopted by institutions of higher education and professional organizations of faculty members (60 *AAUP Bulletin* 269-72 (1974); see *Bignall v. North Idaho College*, 538 F.2d 243 (9th Cir. 1976); *Browzin v. Catholic University of America*, 527 F.2d 843 (D.C. Cir. 1975); and *Scheuer v. Creighton University*, . . . 260 N.W.2d 595 ([Neb.] 1977)). That the [institution's] implied right of bona fide unavoidable termination due to changes in academic program is wholly different from its right to termination for cause or on other personal grounds is plainly recognized in the following definition of tenure of the [AAUP/AAC] Commission on Academic Tenure in Higher Education [in] *Faculty Tenure: A Report and Recommendations* [Jossey-Bass, 1973]:
>
> > An arrangement under which faculty appointments in an institution of higher education are continued until retirement for age or disability, subject to dismissal for adequate cause or unavoidable termination on account of financial exigency or change of institutional program (emphasis in original omitted).

The foregoing authorities lead to the conclusion that, unless a Puerto Rican statute or a university regulation otherwise provides, the instant contracts should be interpreted as giving the University of Puerto Rico an implied right of bona fide unavoidable termination on the ground of change of academic program [650 F.2d at 368; footnotes omitted].

Finding no Puerto Rican statute or university regulation to the contrary, the court confirmed the university's implied contractual right to terminate tenured faculty. The court then analyzed the procedures available to the plaintiffs to challenge their terminations and concluded that they met procedural due process requirements.

The *Jimenez* decision is consistent with earlier precedents and AAUP policy in recognizing, first, a distinction between dismissals for causes personal to the individual and dismissals for impersonal institutional reasons and, second, a distinction between institutional reasons of financial exigency and reasons of program discontinuance. AAUP policy on the latter distinction, however, is found not in the 1940 statement cited by the court but in the 1976 "Recommended Institutional Regulations on Academic Freedom and Tenure" (*AAUP Policy Documents and Reports* (AAUP, 1990), at 21), which authorize program discontinuances "not mandated by financial exigency" when "based essentially upon educational considerations" and implemented according to AAUP specifications. Under this policy, if the institution adheres to it, or under the precedent now established by *Jimenez*, postsecondary institutions may, if they follow prescribed standards and procedures for doing so, terminate tenured faculty because of a bona fide academic program change. (See generally M. Clague, "*Jimenez v. Almodovar:* Program Discontinuance as a Cause for Termination of Tenured Faculty in Public Institutions," 9 *West's Educ. Law Rptr.* 805 (1983).)

If faculty handbooks, collective bargaining agreements, or other institutional policy documents specify a faculty role in determining how program reductions or closures, or the criteria for selecting faculty, will be accomplished, then excluding faculty from this process will invite breach-of-contract claims. But in some instances, despite the fact that handbooks and policy documents did not specify a faculty role in the process, breach-of-contract claims have been brought. For example, when Mercer University closed its Atlanta College of Arts and Sciences, the faculty asserted that excluding them from participating in the closure decision breached their contract because in the academic community the term "bona fide discontinuance of a program," used in the faculty handbook, meant that faculty must be involved in the decision (C. Houpt, "The Age of Austerity: Downsizing for the 90s," in *Academic Program Closures: A Legal Compendium* (National Association of College and University Attorneys, 1991)).

Students have also asserted contract claims against a college or university for reducing or eliminating an academic program. These cases are discussed in Section 4.1.3.

3.8.2. Constitutional considerations. Public institutions (see Section 1.5.2) must be concerned not only with contract considerations relating to financial exigency and program termination but also with constitutional considerations under the First and Fourteenth Amendments. Even if a termination (or other personnel decision) does not violate the faculty contract or any applicable state statutes or administrative regulations, it will be subject to invalidation by the courts if it infringes the faculty member's constitutional rights.

Under the First Amendment, a faculty member may argue that financial exigency was only a pretext for termination and that termination was actually a retaliation for the faculty member's exercise of First Amendment rights (see Note, "Economically Necessitated Faculty Dismissal as a Limit on Academic Freedom," 52 *Denver L.J.* 911 (1975); and see generally Section 3.7). The burden of proof on this issue is primarily on the faculty member (see the *Mt. Healthy* case discussed in Section 3.7.6). *Mabey v. Reagan*, 537 F.2d 1036 (9th Cir. 1976), is illustrative. The defendant college had not renewed the appointment of a nontenured philosophy instructor. The instructor argued that the nonrenewal was due to an argument he had had with other faculty members in an academic senate meeting and that his argument was a protected First Amendment activity. The college argued that this activity was not protected under the First Amendment and that, at any rate, the nonrenewal was also due to overstaffing in the philosophy department. In remanding the case to the trial court for further fact findings, the appellate court noted:

> We emphasize that the trier [of fact] must be alert to retaliatory terminations. . . . Whenever the state terminates employment to quell legitimate dissent or punishes protected expressive behavior, the termination is unlawful. . . .
>
> We stress that this holding does not shield those who are legitimately not reappointed. Where the complainant . . . does not meet his burden of proof that the state acted to suppress free expression, . . . the termination will stand [537 F.2d at 1045].

Under the Fourteenth Amendment, a faculty member whose job is terminated by a public institution may argue that the termination violated the Due Process Clause. To proceed with this argument, the faculty member must show that the termination infringed a "property" or "liberty" interest, as discussed in Section 3.6.2.1. If such a showing can be made, the questions then are (1) what procedural protections is the faculty member entitled to, and (2) what kinds of arguments can the faculty member raise in his or her "defense"? A case that addresses both issues is *Johnson v. Board of Regents of University of Wisconsin System*, 377 F. Supp. 227 (W.D. Wis. 1974), *affirmed without opin.*, 510 F.2d 975 (7th Cir. 1975).

In this case the Wisconsin legislature had mandated budget reductions for the university system. To accommodate this reduction, as well as a further reduction caused by lower enrollments on several campuses, the university officials devised a program for "laying off" tenured faculty. The chancellor of each campus determined who would be laid off, after which each affected faculty member could petition a faculty committee for "reconsideration" of the proposed layoff. The faculty committee could consider only two questions: whether the layoff decision was supported by sufficient evidence, and whether the chancellor had followed the procedures established for identifying the campus's fiscal and programmatic needs and determining who should be laid off. Thirty-eight tenured professors selected for layoff sued the university system.

The court determined that the Due Process Clause required the following minimum procedures in a financial exigency layoff: "furnishing each plaintiff with a reasonably adequate written statement of the basis for the initial decision to lay off;

furnishing each plaintiff with a reasonably adequate description of the manner in which the initial decision had been arrived at; making a reasonably adequate disclosure to each plaintiff of the information and data on which the decision makers had relied; and providing each plaintiff the opportunity to respond" (377 F. Supp. at 240). Measuring the procedures actually used against these requirements, the court held that the university system had not violated procedural due process. The most difficult issue was the adequacy of information disclosure (the third requirement above), about which the court said:

> Plaintiffs have shown in this court that the information disclosed to them was bulky and some of it amorphous. They have shown that it was not presented to the reconsideration committees in a manner resembling the presentation of evidence in court. They have shown that in some situations . . . they encountered difficulty in obtaining a coherent explanation of the basis for the initial layoff decisions, and that, as explained in some situations, the basis included judgments about personalities. But as I have observed, the Fourteenth Amendment does not forbid judgments about personalities in this situation, nor does it require adversary proceedings. The information disclosed was reasonably adequate to provide each plaintiff the opportunity to make a showing that reduced student enrollments and fiscal exigency were not in fact the precipitating causes for the decisions to lay off tenured teachers in this department and that; and it was also reasonably adequate to provide each plaintiff the opportunity to make a showing that the ultimate decision to lay off each of them, as compared with another tenured member of their respective departments, was arbitrary and unreasonable. I emphasize the latter point. On this record, plaintiffs' allegations about the inadequacy and imprecision of the disclosure related principally to those stages of the decision making which preceded the ultimate stage at which the specific teachers, department by department, were selected.
>
> Had the disclosure as it was made not been "reasonably adequate," it is possible that it could have been made adequate by permitting plaintiffs some opportunity to confront and even to cross-examine some of the decision makers. But I hold that the opportunity to confront or to cross-examine these decision makers is not constitutionally required when the disclosure is reasonably adequate, as it was here [377 F. Supp. at 242].

The court also determined that the university system could limit the issues which the faculty members could address in challenging a termination under the above procedures:

> I am not persuaded that, after the initial decisions had been made, the Fourteenth Amendment required that plaintiffs be provided an opportunity to persuade the decision makers that departments within their respective colleges, other than theirs, should have borne a heavier fiscal sacrifice; that non-credit-producing, nonacademic areas within their respective campus structures should have borne a heavier fiscal sacrifice; that campuses, other than their respective campuses, should have borne a heavier fiscal sacrifice; or that more funds should have been appropriated to the university system. However, I believe that *each plaintiff was constitutionally entitled to a fair opportunity to show: (1) that the true reason for his or her layoff was a constitutionally impermissible reason; or (2) that, given the chain of decisions which preceded the ultimate decision desig-*

nating him or her by name for layoff, that ultimate decision was nevertheless wholly arbitrary and unreasonable. I believe that each plaintiff was constitutionally entitled to a fair opportunity to make such a showing in a proceeding within the institution, in order to permit prompt reconsideration and correction in a proper case. Also, if necessary, each plaintiff was and is constitutionally entitled to a fair opportunity to make such a showing thereafter in a court [377 F. Supp. at 239–40; emphasis added].

Although the Constitution requires that institutions avoid terminations for a "constitutionally impermissible reason" and "wholly arbitrary" terminations, the court made clear that the Constitution does not prescribe any particular bases for selection of the faculty members to be terminated:

[The Constitution does not require] that the selection be made on one specific basis or another: in inverse order of seniority within the department, for example; or in order of seniority; or in terms of record of performance or potential for performance; or in inverse order of seniority, but with exceptions for the necessity to retain teachers in the department with specific skills or funds of knowledge. I believe that the federal Constitution is silent on these questions, and that the identity of the decision maker and the choice of a basis for selection lie within the discretion of the state government [377 F. Supp. at 238].

A federal appellate court found constitutional violations in the treatment of two professors who were laid off without being granted a hearing on the criteria for selecting faculty for layoff. In *Johnson-Taylor v. Gannon*, 907 F.2d 1577 (6th Cir. 1990), the trustees of Lansing Community College determined that financial exigency required the layoff of several faculty members. Under the collective bargaining agreement with the faculty, the trustees had the right to make the ultimate decision about how many faculty were to be laid off, but the union had the right to recommend criteria for selecting faculty and the procedure to be used.

Two faculty who were laid off argued that they were denied due process because no hearing had been held regarding their selection for layoff. Both asserted that they had been chosen to be laid off because of their criticisms of the institution and their union activity. Although both had filed grievances under the collective bargaining agreement, an arbitrator had concluded that they had been afforded all the protections which the contract required.

The court first examined whether the professors had a property or liberty interest at stake. Finding that the collective bargaining agreement provided for continued employment, the court concluded that the professors, indeed, had a property interest, which required the college to afford them due process. Furthermore, one of the professors was tenured, and thus had a second basis for a protected property interest.

The court concluded that the professors' due process rights had been violated because neither had been afforded a hearing at which they were informed why they were selected for layoff, nor had they had an opportunity to challenge the existence of financial exigency. The court remanded the matter to the trial court for an evidentiary hearing on both of these issues.

In *Milbouer v. Keppler*, 644 F. Supp. 201 (D. Idaho 1986), the plaintiff, a tenured professor of German, was laid off because of financial exigency and charged

Boise State University with constitutional violations of her substantive and due process rights under the Fourteenth Amendment. A federal district court sketched out the basic due process rights to which a tenured faculty member is entitled when financial exigency requires termination.

First, said the court, the institution must demonstrate that a genuine financial exigency exists. It can do so by submitting evidence of budget shortfalls, legislative or executive branch reductions in funding, or other financial data indicating that funds are limited or may not be used to retain the faculty member.

With regard to the substantive due process claim, the court stated, the institution must demonstrate that uniform procedures were used to determine how the reduction would be effected and which faculty members would be terminated. In this case the institution had used enrollment trends, faculty/student ratios, and historical data on the number of majors in the foreign language department. The elimination of the department was justified, the judge ruled, by the small number of majors and low enrollments.

The plaintiff had been offered a part-time position teaching in the English department, which she had refused. She had also been offered retraining as a linguistic specialist in the business education department, but did not avail herself of that opportunity either. Although the plaintiff argued that a one-month notice prior to her termination was insufficient, the court ruled that that period of time was long enough to permit the plaintiff to write a detailed letter of appeal and to have her appeal heard by a hearing committee, which had been done.

Despite the fact that the university hired fifteen new faculty members for other "viable" programs at the same time that it closed its foreign language department, the judge ruled that the institution had demonstrated that a genuine financial exigency existed, and that its procedures afforded the plaintiff both substantive and procedural due process.

If faculty members have property interests in their jobs, the cases make it clear that the institution must provide a hearing for those selected for layoff, so that they can be told the reasons for their selection and given an opportunity to challenge the sufficiency of those reasons. But must faculty members be given a hearing when the institution decides to reduce or eliminate an academic program?

This question was considered in *Texas Faculty Association v. University of Texas at Dallas*, 946 F.2d 379 (5th Cir. 1991). The deans of the education school and the school of natural sciences and mathematics decided to eliminate two academic programs because of low enrollment and the desire to reallocate the resources devoted to those programs. The university was not facing a situation of financial exigency. The faculty teaching in those programs were told that their employment would be terminated.

The tenured faculty asserted that they had a right to a hearing on the merits of the decision to eliminate the two programs. They also asserted a right to a hearing to determine whether their employment should be terminated. No hearings were held, although the university counsel sent the faculty a letter stating that they could meet with the deans informally to discuss the reasons for the program elimination. The faculty responded by filing a lawsuit claiming denial of procedural due process with respect to both the closure decision and their terminations.

The court refused to require the university to hold adversarial hearings on the decision to eliminate academic programs. The court stated that such a requirement would "seriously impair the university's significant interest in administering its educational programs in the manner it deems best" (946 F.2d at 385). Noting that courts are typically deferential to decisions based on academic judgments (citing *Board of Curators v. Horowitz*, 435 U.S. 78 (1978), discussed in Section 4.8.3), the court concluded that the judicial system was poorly equipped to review the substance of academic decisions, stating that "only the barest procedural protections of notice and an opportunity to be heard need be afforded the individual faculty member" (946 F.2d at 387). Because the faculty had been given nearly two years' notice and had been invited on several occasions to discuss the matter with their dean, the institution had met this portion of its due process obligation.

With regard to the propriety of decisions to terminate individual faculty, however, the court's attitude differed:

> [W]e perceive the risk that a particular faculty member will be terminated erroneously to be somewhat greater [than the risk of incorrectly deciding to eliminate a program] under the rather unusual facts of this case. Unlike many, if not most, institutions of higher learning, faculty in the University of Texas system are tenured to their particular component *institution* rather than to a particular school or program within that institution [citing regulations of the board of regents]. . . . Consequently, UTD faculty had a right of continuing appointment to the University of Texas at Dallas as a *whole*, and not merely to their particular schools or academic programs [946 F.2d at 386; emphasis in original].

The court noted that many of the faculty were qualified to teach in other programs within the university. "Unless the procedures afforded appellants meaningfully considered whether each appellant should be retained at UTD in *some* teaching capacity, then the risk that a given faculty member could be terminated erroneously seems to us patent" (946 F.2d at 386; emphasis in original).

The court concluded that the university had failed to provide due process with regard to the termination decisions:

> Because UTD faculty are tenured to the *institution,* each appellant was entitled to a meaningful opportunity to demonstrate that, even if his or her program was to be discontinued and the number of faculty positions associated with that program eliminated, he or she should nevertheless be retained to teach in a field in which he or she is qualified.
>
> We do not believe affording faculty such an opportunity would unduly interfere with the university's interest in academic freedom. A procedure ensuring that (1) an instructor was not terminated for constitutionally impermissible reasons, (2) the administration's actions were taken in good faith, and (3) objective criteria were employed and fairly applied in determining whom, from *among the faculty at large,* to terminate, is all that the Fourteenth Amendment requires [946 F.2d at 387; emphasis in original].

The court elaborated on the practical consequences of its ruling, saying that not all faculty would need to be afforded adversarial hearings:

> Initially, the administration probably need only consider, in good faith, a written submission from each affected faculty member setting out why he or

she deserves to be retained. Only if a particular faculty member makes a colorable showing that, under the objective criteria the university employs, he or she deserves to be retained in another academic program, must any sort of "hearing" be offered. Otherwise, a brief written statement from the decision maker of the reasons why the faculty member does not deserve to be retained would suffice. The "hearing" offered need only be an opportunity for the aggrieved faculty member to meet with the ultimate decision maker, to present his or her case orally, and to explore with the decision maker the possible alternatives to termination. If the decision maker nevertheless decides not to retain the faculty member, a written statement of reasons is required. Of course, if the retention of one faculty member results in the displacement of another, the displaced faculty member is equally entitled to due process [946 F.2d at 388].

The court discussed the faculty members' contention that they were entitled to a full-blown adversarial hearing, with counsel, before an official other than the one who made the initial termination decision; the right to cross-examination; and a written record. Absent clear evidence of bias on the part of the decision maker, said the court, the official responsible for the termination decision may conduct the hearing. Because the termination was not for performance reasons, the presence of counsel, the right to cross-examine, and a written record were not necessary. But the court agreed that the plaintiffs did have a right to present documentary evidence and to receive a written statement of the hearing officer's conclusions. Because the faculty had not been afforded the type of due process outlined by the court, the court remanded the case for further proceedings.

The UTD case is very helpful to administrators at public institutions seeking guidance about program reduction or closure. Unless the institution has adopted procedures that require additional due process protections, or unless state statutes or regulations require more, the due process protections described in the UTD case should satisfy the institution's constitutional obligations to tenured faculty.

3.8.3. Statutory considerations. A public institution's legal responsibilities during financial exigency or program discontinuance may be defined not only by contract and by constitutional considerations but also by state statutes or their implementing administrative regulations. The case of *Hartman v. Merged Area VI Community College*, 270 N.W.2d 822 (Iowa 1978), illustrates how important statutory analysis can be.

In *Hartman* a community college had dismissed a faculty member as part of a staff reduction occasioned by declining enrollment and a worsening financial condition. For authority for its action, the institution relied on a state statute authorizing it to discharge faculty "for incompetency, inattention to duty, partiality, or any good cause" (Iowa Code of 1973 § 279.24). The institution's position was that the phrase "good cause" supported its action because it is a broad grant of authority encompassing any rational reason for dismissal asserted by the board of directors in good faith. The appellate court disagreed and invalidated the dismissal. It reasoned that "good cause," interpreted in light of the statute's legislative history and in conjunction with other related Iowa statutes, "refer[s] only to factors personal to the teacher"; that is, factors that can be considered the teacher's own "personal fault" (see Section 3.5.2 for a consideration of such personal factors).

While *Hartman* deals only with substantive standards for staff reduction, state statutes or administrative regulations may also establish procedures with which institutions must comply. In *Mabey v. Reagan*, 537 F.2d 1036 (9th Cir. 1976), for instance, a college did not renew an instructor's contract, in part because his department was overstaffed. The instructor challenged the nonrenewal, arguing that the college had followed the wrong procedures in reaching its decision. The court rejected the challenge, agreeing with the college that the applicable procedures were found in the statutes dealing with tenure and nonreappointment, rather than in the statutes dealing with separation for "lack of work or lack of funds."

Public institutions considering staff reductions must therefore identify not only the applicable substantive standards but also the applicable procedures specified by state law. The procedures may be contained in a legal source different from that setting out the standards (see, for example, *Council of New Jersey State College Locals v. State Board of Higher Education*, 449 A.2d 1244 (N.J. 1982) (substantive criteria from state board policy on financial exigency applicable despite collective bargaining agreement, but some procedures derived from board policy bargainable); *Board of Trustees of Ohio State University v. Department of Administrative Services*, 429 N.E.2d 428 (Ohio 1981) (state administrative procedure act applicable to termination of nonfaculty personnel)).

3.8.4. Preparing for staff reductions. Everyone agrees that institutions, both public and private, should plan ahead to avoid the legal difficulties that can arise if financial or programmatic pressures necessitate staff reductions. Much can be done to plan ahead. Faculty contracts should be reviewed in light of the questions raised in Section 3.8.1. Where the contract does not clearly reflect the institution's desired position concerning staff reductions, its provisions should be revised to the extent possible without breaching existing contracts.

For institutional planning purposes, administrators should carefully distinguish between the two alternative approaches to faculty termination—financial exigency and program discontinuance:

1. When drafting or amending contracts for nontenured, tenure-track faculty, the institution should consider specific provisions on both alternatives. Public institutions should consult state law (Section 3.8.3 above) to determine whether it permits use of both alternatives. If the institution chooses, the AAUP's recommended regulations on either alternative (see Section 3.8.1, note 62) may be incorporated by reference into its faculty contracts. The institution may also draft provisions altogether different from the AAUP'S, although it will want to give close attention to the competing policy considerations.

2. When interpreting existing tenure contracts, the institution should determine whether it has already, either expressly or by institutional custom, adopted AAUP policy for either alternative; or whether, in the face of institutional silence, courts would likely fill the gap with AAUP policy (see Section 3.8.1 above). In such circumstances the institution should consider itself bound to follow AAUP requirements and thus not free under existing contracts to strike out unilaterally on a different course.

3. When faced with circumstances mandating consideration of tenured faculty terminations, and when authorized to follow either alternative approach, the institution should carefully consider its choice. Which alternative—institution-wide fi-

nancial exigency or discontinuance of specific programs—can better be substantiated by existing circumstances? Which would better serve the institution's overall mission? If the institution decides to pursue one of the alternatives, it should be careful to identify and follow the particular decision-making requirements and protections for faculty specified for that alternative.

When the institution does have authority for staff reductions necessitated by financial exigency, it should have a policy and standards for determining when a financial exigency exists and which faculty members' positions will be terminated. It should also specify the procedures by which the faculty member can challenge the propriety of his or her selection for termination. Before administrators make a termination decision, they should be certain (1) that a financial exigency does actually exist under the institution's policy, (2) that the terminations will alleviate the exigency, and (3) that no other motivation for a particular termination may exist. After dismissing faculty members, administrators should be extremely careful in hiring new ones, to avoid the impression, as in the *Bloomfield* case (see Section 3.8.1), that the financial exigency was a pretext for abolishing tenure or otherwise replacing old faculty members with new. Similar considerations would apply in implementing program discontinuations.

Finally, administrators should remember that, in this sensitive area, some of their decisions may wind up in court despite careful planning. Administrators should thus keep complete records and documentation of their staff reduction policies, decisions, and internal review processes for possible use in court and should work closely with counsel both in planning ahead and in making the actual termination decisions.

Selected Annotated Bibliography

General

American Association of University Professors. *AAUP Policy Documents and Reports* (the "Redbook") (AAUP, 1990). A collection of the AAUP's major policy statements on academic freedom, tenure, collective bargaining, professional ethics, institutional governance, sexual harassment, part-time faculty, and other topics. Includes a discussion of the role and usefulness of AAUP policy statements and an appendix with selected judicial decisions and articles referring to AAUP statements.

American Association of University Professors/Association of American Colleges, Commission on Academic Tenure in Higher Education. *Faculty Tenure: A Report and Recommendations* (Jossey-Bass, 1973). An evaluation of the status and limitations of tenure. Includes special essays on "Legal Dimensions of Tenure" by Victor Rosenblum and "Faculty Unionism and Tenure" by W. McHugh.

Brown, Ralph S., & Kurland, Jordan E. "Academic Tenure and Academic Freedom," 53 *Law & Contemporary Problems* 325 (1990). Discusses the role of tenure in reinforcing academic freedom; the costs of tenure; benefits of tenure, in addition to its role in protecting academic freedom; and various alternatives to tenure. Also discusses various perceived weaknesses in tenure and several methods of protecting the academic freedom of faculty who are not tenured.

Chait, Richard P., & Ford, Andrew T. *Beyond Traditional Tenure: A Guide to Sound*

Policies and Practices (Jossey-Bass, 1982). Includes chapters on "Tenure in Context," "Institutions Without Tenure," "Life Without Tenure," "Tenure and Nontenure Tracks," "Extended Probationary Periods and Suspension of 'Up-or-Out' Rule," "Tenure Quotas," "Sound Tenure Policy," "Evaluating Tenured Faculty," "Distributing Rewards and Applying Sanctions," and "Auditing and Improving Faculty Personnel Systems." Based on authors' survey and analysis of tenure options in existence at various institutions around the country. Provides case studies of leading examples. For extended reviews of the book, see 10 *J. Coll. & Univ. Law* 93–112 (1983–84).

Finkin, Matthew W. "Regulation by Agreement: The Case for Private Higher Education," 65 *Iowa L. Rev.* 1119 (1980), reprinted in 67 *AAUP Bulletin* no. 1 (Parts I and II of the article), no. 2 (Part III), and no. 3 (Part IV) (1981). Provides a multifaceted review of various problems unique to employment relations in higher education. Part I of the article serves as a general introduction; Part II discusses the nature of the contract of academic employment and various questions that arise in contract litigation; Part III discusses the continued relevance of academic organization by collective agreement, notwithstanding *NLRB v. Yeshiva University;* Part IV sets out a proposal for an alternative system of self-regulation of employment matters.

Furniss, W. Todd. "The Status of 'AAUP Policy,' " 59 *Educ. Record* 7 (1978). Reviews the role that AAUP policy statements play in the university employment scheme. Notes the increasing use of such statements in employment litigation and urges institutions of higher education to clarify the extent to which they accept AAUP policy statements as their own institutional policy. The arguments raised in this article are challenged in a companion article: Ralph S. Brown, Jr., and Matthew W. Finkin, "The Usefulness of AAUP Policy Statements," 59 *Educ. Record* 30 (1978).

McCarthy, Jane, Ladimer, Irving, & Sirefman, Josef. *Managing Faculty Disputes: A Guide to Issues, Procedures, and Practices* (Jossey-Bass, 1984). Addresses the problem of faculty disputes on campus and proposes processes for resolving them. Covers both disputes that occur regularly and can be subjected to a standard dispute-resolution process, and special disputes that occur irregularly and may require a resolution process tailored to the circumstances. Includes model grievance procedures, case studies of actual disputes, and worksheets and checklists to assist administrators in implementing dispute-resolution processes.

Sec. 3.1 (The Contract of Employment)

Biles, George E., & Tuckman, Howard P. *Part-Time Faculty Personnel Management Policies* (ACE/Macmillan, 1986). Chapters include discussions on how to define a part-time faculty member, equal employment opportunity and affirmative action issues, appointment and reappointment practices, salaries and benefits for part-timers, tenure eligibility, the professional obligations of part-time faculty, evaluation of part-time faculty, and due process and collective bargaining issues. Also included are suggestions for a handbook for part-time faculty.

McKee, Patrick W. "Tenure by Default: The Non-Formal Acquisition of Academic Tenure," 7 *J. Coll. & Univ. Law* 31 (1980–81). Analyzes the impact of *Board of Regents v. Roth* and *Perry v. Sindermann* on the concept of nonformal tenure.

Distinguishes between "automatic tenure," "tenure by grant," "nonformal or de facto tenure," and "tenure by default." To resolve confusion in lower court opinions applying *Roth* and *Perry* to nonformal tenure claims, the article develops a common law analysis covering employment relationships in both private and public institutions.

Sec. 3.2 (Collective Bargaining)

Angell, George W., Kelly, Edward P., Jr., & Associates. *Handbook of Faculty Bargaining* (Jossey-Bass, 1977). A comprehensive guide to collective bargaining for administrators. Provides information and recommendations on preparing for collective bargaining, negotiating contracts, administering contracts, and exerting institutional leadership in the bargaining context. Includes a special chapter on statewide bargaining in state postsecondary systems.

Bartosic, Florian, & Hartley, Roger. *Labor Relations Law in the Private Sector* (2d ed., American Law Institute, 1986). A restatement and analysis of the federal law of union organization and collective bargaining. Primarily for legal counsel who are not labor law specialists; also usable by specialists as a ready-reference manual and by administrators as a readable explanatory text. Can also help in dealing with public-sector labor law in states with law patterned after the federal law.

Chandler, Margaret, & Julius, Daniel. "By Whose Right? Management Rights and Governance in the Unionized Institution," in Joel M. Douglas (ed.), *Unionization and Academic Excellence* (National Center for the Study of Collective Bargaining in Higher Education and the Professions, 1985), at 91. A paper in the Proceedings of the Center's 13th Annual Conference. Discusses management rights in institutions where faculty participate in governance and where faculty are represented by a union.

Finkin, Matthew. "The NLRB in Higher Education," 5 *U. Toledo L. Rev.* 608 (1974). Probes the whole gamut of NLRB authority and activity in postsecondary education. Discusses and criticizes NLRB decisions dealing with jurisdiction over private institutions; faculty status as managers, supervisors, or employees; appropriate bargaining units; and employers' unfair labor practices.

Head, Ronald B., & Leslie, David. "Bargaining Unit Status of Part-Time Faculty," 8 *J. Law & Educ.* 361 (1979). Discusses court cases, labor board decisions, and other problems related to unionized part-time faculty.

Lee, Barbara A. "Faculty Role in Academic Governance and the Managerial Exclusion: Impact of the *Yeshiva University* Decision," 7 *J. Coll. & Univ. Law* 222 (1980–81). An in-depth analysis of the *Yeshiva* case. Discusses origins and definitions of the terms "supervisory," "managerial," and "professional" employees; the faculty's role in academic governance; and "the implications of the *Yeshiva* decision for both unionized and nonunionized colleges and universities."

Rabban, David. "Is Unionization Compatible with Professionalism?" 45 *Indust. & Labor Rel. Rev.* 97 (1991). Analyzes the compatibility of unionization with professionalism by examining the provisions of over one hundred collective bargaining agreements involving a variety of professions. Author discusses the effect of contractual provisions on professional standards, participation by professionals in organizational decision making, and other issues of professional concern, and concludes that unionization and professionalism are not "inherently incompatible."

Shark, Alan R., et al. *Final Reports of the Research Project on Students and Collective Bargaining* (National Student Educational Fund, 1976). A study of student participation in faculty collective bargaining. Surveys the law and practice regarding student participation, analyzes bargaining's impact on students, and discusses various bargaining contract provisions.

Williams, Gwen, & Zirkel, Perry. "Academic Penetration in Faculty Collective Bargaining Contracts in Higher Education," 28 *Research in Higher Educ.* 76 (1988). Presents the findings of an analysis of collective bargaining agreements and identifies the degree to which academic governance issues are included in these agreements.

Sec. 3.3 (Nondiscrimination in Employment)

"The Academy in the Courts: A Symposium on Academic Freedom," 16 *U. Cal. Davis L. Rev.* 831 (1983). A two-part article. The second part is titled "Discrimination in the Academy" (for a description of the first part, see "Academy in the Courts" entry for Section 3.7). This part contains three articles: Christine Cooper, "Title VII in the Academy: Barriers to Equality for Faculty Women"; John D. Gregory, "Secrecy in University and College Tenure Deliberations: Placing Appropriate Limits on Academic Freedom"; and Harry F. Tepker, "Title VII, Equal Employment Opportunity, and Academic Autonomy: Toward a Principled Deference."

Achtenberg, Roberta. *Sexual Orientation and the Law* (Clark Boardman Callaghan, 1985 and periodic supp.). A comprehensive treatise on many areas of the law related to homosexuality. Employment-related subjects include civil rights and discrimination, First Amendment issues, employment and AIDS, insurance and AIDS, and tax issues. Written for attorneys who represent gay clients, the book includes sample forms and contracts.

Baldus, David C., & Cole, James L. *Statistical Proof of Discrimination* (Shepards/McGraw-Hill, 1980). A guide to the proper uses of statistics in discrimination litigation, with emphasis on employment discrimination. The book will be helpful to both plaintiffs' and defendants' counsel in such actions. Includes useful glossary and bibliography.

Bompey, Stuart H., & Witten, Richard E. "Settlement of Title VII Disputes: Shifting Patterns in a Changing World," 6 *J. Coll. & Univ. Law* 317 (1980). Reviews the types of settlements available to plaintiffs and defendants and the various means of reaching such settlements. Examines the settlement process from the commencement of an action (when a plaintiff files charges with the EEOC) to the culmination of litigation through the entry of consent decrees.

Cole, Elsa Kircher (ed.). *Sexual Harassment on Campus: A Legal Compendium* (2d ed., National Association of College and University Attorneys, 1990). A collection of resources on sexual harassment: law review articles; EEOC policy guidelines; and sexual harassment policy statements from five universities, the AAUP, and the American Council on Education. Also includes a list of additional resources and suggestions for developing a sexual harassment policy.

DiGiovanni, Nicholas. *Age Discrimination: An Administrator's Guide* (College and University Personnel Association, 1989). Written for campus administrators. Includes an overview of the ADEA, a discussion of how an age discrimination lawsuit is conducted and defended, and suggestions for minimizing the risk of liability. Additional chapters discuss planning for retirement (including the EEOC guidelines for retirement incentives), practical considerations in evaluating and counseling older workers, waivers and releases, and a table of state laws prohibiting age discrimination. (This book predates the passage of the Older Workers Benefit Protection Act, discussed in Section 3.3.6, this volume.)

Fitzgerald, Louise F. *Sexual Harassment in Higher Education: Concepts and Issues* (National Education Association, 1992). A brief, practical guide to the major issues facing faculty and administrators with regard to sexual harassment. Includes definitions of harassment, an estimate of its prevalence, and a brief summary of the legal issues. Also includes suggestions for developing institutional sexual harassment policies and complaint procedures; a discussion of whether institutions should extend their prohibitions to include consensual amorous relationships between faculty and students; a comprehensive bibliography; a typology of sexual harassment; a sexual harassment experiences questionnaire; sample campus policies on sexual harassment; and the NEA's Sexual Harassment Statement.

Gamble, Barbara S. (ed.). *Sex Discrimination Handbook* (Bureau of National Affairs, 1992). A concise guidebook to sex discrimination claims, their defense, and their avoidance. Case summaries and the text of federal nondiscrimination laws and regulations are included, as well as sample forms and policies. A directory of EEOC offices and the states' fair employment agencies is also provided.

Gutek, Barbara. "Understanding Sexual Harassment at Work," 6 *Notre Dame J. Law, Ethics & Public Policy* 335 (1992). A review of social science research related to sexual behavior in the workplace. Discusses the definition of sexual harassment, the frequency of sexual behavior in the workplace, the impacts of such behavior, and the concept of "sex role spillover" and its implications for workplace behavior.

LaNoue, George, & Lee, Barbara A. *Academics in Court: The Consequences of Faculty Discrimination Litigation* (University of Michigan Press, 1987). A comprehensive study of all academic discrimination lawsuits between 1972 and 1986. Chapter 2 describes the sources of protection against employment discrimination and discusses their application in the academic context. Five academic discrimination cases are discussed, and interview data from the parties involved are presented. The final chapter provides a series of recommendations for faculty members considering filing discrimination claims and for administrators who must determine how and whether to defend these claims in court.

Leap, Terry. *Tenure, Discrimination, and the Courts* (Industrial and Labor Relations Press, 1993). An examination of significant issues that arise in academic discrimination lawsuits. Chapters include "The Reappointment, Promotion, and Tenure Process," "Judicial Intervention in Promotion and Tenure Disputes," "Criteria for Making Promotion and Tenure Decisions," and "The Burden of Proof in College and University Discrimination Cases." Suggestions for preventing discrimination lawsuits are also provided.

Lee, Barbara A. "Balancing Confidentiality and Disclosure in Faculty Peer Review: Impact of Title VII Litigation," 9 *J. Coll. & Univ. Law* 279 (1982-83). Analyzes recent Title VII litigation brought by faculty of higher education institutions. Includes a section on "Burdens of Proof and Persuasion," which elucidates the three stages of a Title VII case—the "prima facie case," "the institution's rebuttal," and plaintiff's proof of "pretextual behavior"—using illustrations from higher education cases. Also reviews issues concerning "evidence admitted by courts in challenges to peer review decisions" and "standards applied by courts to the peer review process," and examines the question of whether courts should recognize an "academic freedom privilege."

Lindemann, Barbara, & Kadue, David D. *Primer on Sexual Harassment* (Bureau of National Affairs, 1992). A concise overview of the legal, social, and policy issues related to sexual harassment in the workplace. Written for a nonlegal audience, the primer discusses the definition of sexual harassment; appropriate employer responses to reports of alleged harassment; significant court opinions; discipline and discharge issues; and other issues, such as workers' compensation for harassment claims.

National Association of College and University Business Officers (NACUBO). *Federal Regulations and the Employment Practices of Colleges and Universities* (NACUBO, 1977 and periodic supp.). A loose-leaf service that provides information and guidance on applying federal regulations affecting personnel administration in postsecondary institutions.

Paludi, Michele A. (ed.). *Ivory Power: Sexual Harassment on Campus* (State University of New York Press, 1991). A collection of articles and essays on sexual harassment. Include discussions of the definition of harassment; the impact of sexual harassment on the cognitive, physical, and emotional well-being of victims; the characteristics of harassers; and procedures for dealing with sexual harassment complaints on campus. Sample materials for training faculty, draft forms for receiving harassment complaints, lists of organizations and other resources concerned with sexual harassment, and references to other written materials are also included.

Perritt, Henry H., Jr. *Americans with Disabilities Act Handbook* (2d ed., Wiley, 1991 and periodic supp.). A comprehensive practice guide to Title I of the ADA. Chapters include a description of the statute, the legislative history, the various categories of protection, the employer's legal obligations, procedural and evidentiary issues, and suggestions for modifying employment policies and practices to comply with the ADA. The Rehabilitation Act of 1973 also is described, and an appendix provides a summary of the ADA's public accommodation provisions.

Sandin, Robert T. *Autonomy and Faith: Religious Preference in Employment Decisions in Religiously Affiliated Higher Education* (Omega Publications, 1990). Discusses the circumstances under which religiously affiliated colleges and universities may use religion as a selection criterion. Provides a taxonomy of religiously affiliated colleges and models of their preferential hiring policies, reviews state and federal nondiscrimination statutes, summarizes judicial precedent regarding secular and religious functions in Establishment Clause litigation, and discusses the interplay between religious preference and academic freedom.

Sullivan, Charles A., Zimmer, Michael J., & Richards, Richard F. *Federal Statutory Law of Employment Discrimination* (Michie/Bobbs-Merrill, 1980). A one-volume basic text on the federal law of employment discrimination, supplemented annually. Includes discussions of Title VII, the Equal Pay Act, the Age Discrimination in Employment Act, and 42 U.S.C. § 1981. Examines both the substantive and the procedural law developed under these statutes and integrates this law with other areas of law, such as the National Labor Relations Act. Includes extensive case citations and table of cases.

Symposium, "Age Discrimination," 32 *Hastings L.J.* 1093 (1981). A collection of articles on various issues concerning age discrimination. Topics of articles include age discrimination issues under the Equal Protection Clause; evidentiary standards under the ADEA; EEOC's role in enforcing age discrimination legislation; the use of statistics in age discrimination cases; and the relationships between federal and state pension laws. Ends with a comprehensive bibliography of scholarly publications, government documents, and other resources on age discrimination.

Van Tol, Joan E. "Eros Gone Awry: Liability Under Title VII for Workplace Sexual Favoritism," 13 *Indust. Rel. Law J.* 153 (1991). Examines the difficult issue of workplace romance and its potential legal implications for the employer. Although the article does not focus specifically on academic organizations, the issues addressed are relevant for academic workplaces as well as others.

Sec. 3.4 (*Affirmative Action in Employment*)

Bureau of National Affairs. *Affirmative Action Compliance Manual for Federal Contractors* (BNA, published and updated periodically). A comprehensive loose-leaf guide. Provides detailed and continually updated information on the federal government's affirmative action program and the compliance responsibilities and procedures of the Departments of Labor, Education, Defense, and other federal agencies.

Clague, Monique Weston. "Affirmative Action Employment Discrimination: The Higher Education Fragment," in John B. Smart (ed.), *Higher Education: Handbook of Theory and Research*, vol. 2 (Agathon Press, 1986), 109–62. Discusses significant decisions by the U.S. Supreme Court, including *Weber* and *Wygant*. Although the article predates more recent Supreme Court decisions in this area, it provides a thorough and thoughtful analysis of the legal and historical context for affirmative action in the 1970s and early 1980s.

Foster, Sheila. "Difference and Equality: A Critical Assessment of the Concept of 'Diversity,'" 1993 *Wis. L. Rev.* 105 (1993). Explores and criticizes the concept of diversity as developed through equal protection jurisprudence, with special emphasis on *Bakke* and *Metro Broadcasting*. Examines the concept of "difference" and discusses that concept against the history of exclusion of various groups. Also discussed is the tension between equal treatment and equal outcomes.

Oppenheimer, David B. "Distinguishing Five Models of Affirmative Action," 4 *Berkeley Women's Law J.* 42 (1988). Discusses quotas, preference systems, the use of goals and timetables for selected occupations, expanded recuitment pools, and affirmative commitment not to discriminate as alternate models for increasing the proportion of underrepresented persons in the work force. Selected discrimination lawsuits are also analyzed.

Taylor, Bron Raymond. *Affirmative Action at Work: Law, Politics and Ethics* (University of Pittsburgh Press, 1991). Reports the result of a survey of state agency employees' attitudes toward affirmative action and provides suggestions for organizations that wish to strengthen their affirmative action programs. Includes a brief legal history of affirmative action, as well as philosophical and ethical perspectives on affirmative action.

Sec. 3.5 (*Standards and Criteria for Faculty Personnel Decisions*)

Olswang, Steven G., & Fantel, Jane I. "Tenure and Periodic Performance Review: Compatible Legal and Administrative Principles," 7 *J. Coll. & University Law* 1

(1980–81). Examines the "separate concepts of tenure and academic freedom and their relation to one form of accountability measure: systematic reviews of the performance of tenured faculty." Identifies the "differences between tenure and academic freedom" and the purposes and uses of periodic performance reviews "in an overall system of faculty personnel management." Includes discussion of tenure terminations for cause based on incompetence, immorality, insubordination, and other such factors.

Sec. 3.6 (Procedures for Faculty Personnel Decisions)

Baird, James, & McArthur, Matthew R. "Constitutional Due Process and the Negotiation of Grievance Procedures in Public Employment," 5 *J. Law & Educ.* 209 (1976). Compares and contrasts grievance procedures in the public and private sectors. Analyzes due process aspects of the collective bargaining process and suggests ways that public employers can deal with due process requirements in devising grievance procedures.

Olswang, Steven G., & Lee, Barbara A. "Scientific Misconduct: Institutional Procedures and Due Process Considerations," 11 *J. Coll. & Univ. Law* 51 (1984–85). Identifies the types of misconduct that qualify as "scientific misconduct," reviews appropriate and inappropriate means of investigating charges of scientific misconduct, and examines the due process issues to be considered before any action is taken against an individual charged with scientific misconduct.

See Brown & Kurland entry for "General" section.

See Biles & Tuckman entry for Section 3.1.

Sec. 3.7 (Faculty Academic Freedom)

"The Academy in the Courts: A Symposium on Academic Freedom," 16 *U. Cal. Davis L. Rev.* 831 (1983). A two-part article. (The second part, "The First Amendment in the Academy," is described in the "Academy in the Courts" entry for Section 3.3.) The first part contains three articles: Robert O'Neil, "Scientific Research and the First Amendment: An Academic Privilege"; Katheryn Katz, "The First Amendment's Protection of Expressive Activity in the University Classroom: A Constitutional Myth"; and Martin Malin & Robert Ladenson, "University Faculty Members' Right to Dissent: Toward a Unified Theory of Contractual and Constitutional Protection." Symposium also includes a foreword by John Poulos, which briefly recounts the history of institutional academic autonomy and reviews each article's critique of this concept.

Byrne, J. Peter. "Academic Freedom: A 'Special Concern of the First Amendment,'" 99 *Yale L.J.* 251 (1989). Develops a framework and foundation for the academic freedom that is protected by the First Amendment. Traces the development of academic freedom as construed by both academics and the courts and then espouses a new theory of "academic freedom based on the traditional legal status of academic institutions and on the appropriate role of the judiciary in academic affairs."

DeChiara, Peter. "The Need for Universities to Have Rules on Consensual Sexual Relationships Between Faculty Members and Students," 21 *Columbia J. Law & Social Problems* 137 (1988). Reviews the issue of faculty-student sexual relationships and possible responses by universities. Reports on the author's survey of thirty-eight institutions. Discusses constitutional right-to-privacy implications of regulation. Author asserts that regulation is needed because consensual sexual relationships between faculty and students can create problems of pressured decisions, sexual harassment, and favoritism.

Hoornstra, Charles D., & Liethen, Michael A. "Academic Freedom and Civil Discovery," 10 *J. Coll. & Univ. Law* 113 (1983–84). Focuses on the federal appeals court opinions in *Dow Chemical Co. v. Allen* and *Buchanan v. American Motors Co.* Analyzes the cases, provides a critique of "wide-open" approaches to pretrial discovery of the work product of academic researchers, and suggests limits appropriate to academic pretrial discovery. Primarily for counsel.

Menard, Louis (ed.). *Academic Freedom and the Future of the Academy* (University of Chicago Press, forthcoming). A collection of lectures by noted scholars from various disciplines, who debate the cutting-edge issues of academic freedom. This collection is the product of a lecture series sponsored by the AAUP.

Olivas, Michael. "Reflections on Professional Academic Freedom: Second Thoughts on the Third 'Essential Freedom,'" 45 *Stanford L. Rev.* 1835 (1993). Presents the author's perspective on faculty academic freedom, with particular emphasis on conflicts that arise in the classroom. Considers and interrelates professional norms, First Amendment case law, and recent scholarly commentary.

O'Neil, Robert. "The Private Lives of Public Employees," 51 *Or. L. Rev.* 70 (1971). Discusses the types of problems that can arise in the interaction of life-style and public employment. Symbolic expression, hair length, homosexual and heterosexual association, extracurricular writing, and other questions are examined. Although written primarily for the lawyer, the article is also useful for administrators of public postsecondary institutions.

O'Neil, Robert. *Is Academic Freedom a Constitutional Right?* Monograph 84-7 (Institute for Higher Education Law and Governance, University of Houston, 1984), reprinted (under title "Academic Freedom and the Constitution") in 11 *J. Coll. & Univ. Law* 275 (1984). An argument on behalf of the continued vitality of constitutionally based claims of academic freedom. Examines the current status of and conceptual difficulties regarding such claims and makes suggestions for faculty members and other academics to consider before submitting such claims to the courts for vindication.

"Symposium on Academic Freedom," 66 *Tex. L. Rev.* no. 7 (1988). Contains eighteen commentaries and responses preceded by a lengthy foreword by Julius Getman and Jacqueline Mintz. Commentaries include, among others, (1) Walter P. Metzger, "Profession and Constitution: Two Definitions of Academic Freedom in America"; (2) Matthew W. Finkin, "Intramural Speech, Academic Freedom, and the First Amendment"; (3) Charles E. Curran, "Academic Freedom and Catholic Universities"; (4) Lonnie D. Kliever, "Academic Freedom and Church-Affiliated Universities"; (5) Phoebe A. Haddon, "Academic Freedom and Governance: A Call for Increased Dialogue and Diversity"; (6) Rebecca S. Eisenberg, "Academic Freedom and Academic Values in Sponsored Research"; (7) David M. Rabban, "Does Academic Freedom Limit Faculty Autonomy?"; and (8) Douglas Laycock and Susan E. Waelbroeck, "Academic Freedom and the Free Exercise of Religion."

Van Alstyne, William W. (special ed.). "Freedom and Tenure in the Academy: The Fiftieth Anniversary of the 1940 Statement of Principles," 53 *Law & Contemporary*

Problems no. 3 (1990); also published as a separate book, *Freedom and Tenure in the Academy* (Duke University Press, 1993). A symposium containing nine articles: (1) Walter P. Metzger, "The 1940 Statement of Principles on Academic Freedom and Tenure"; (2) William W. Van Alstyne, "Academic Freedom and the First Amendment in the Supreme Court of the United States: An Unhurried Historical Review"; (3) Judith Jarvis Thomson, "Ideology and Faculty Selection"; (4) Robert M. O'Neil, "Artistic Freedom and Academic Freedom"; (5) Rodney A. Smolla, "Academic Freedom, Hate Speech, and the Idea of a University"; (6) David M. Rabban, "A Functional Analysis of 'Individual' and 'Institutional' Academic Freedom Under the First Amendment"; (7) Michael W. McConnell, "Academic Freedom in Religious Colleges and Universities"; (8) Ralph S. Brown and Jordan E. Kurland, "Academic Tenure and Academic Freedom"; and (9) Matthew W. Finkin, "A Higher Order of Liberty in the Workplace: Academic Freedom and Tenure in the Vortex of Employment Practices and Law." Also includes a helpful bibliography of sources: Janet Sinder, "Academic Freedom: A Bibliography," listing 174 journal articles, books, and reports; and three appendices containing the 1915 AAUP "General Report," the 1940 "Statement of Principles," and the 1967 "Joint Statement on Rights and Freedoms of Students."
See Finkin entry for Section 1.2.

Sec. 3.8 (Staff Reduction Due to Financial Exigency and Program Discontinuance)

Houpt, Corinne A. *Academic Program Closures: A Legal Compendium* (National Association of College and University Attorneys, 1991). A comprehensive resource for administrators, faculty, and legal counsel. Included are six chapters and law review articles discussing legal issues and planning issues, such as the roles of trustees, administrators, faculty, students, and other constituencies in planning for and implementing program closures. Also included are AAUP guidelines, policies from five institutions on faculty reductions and program termination, and documents on related issues, as well as a list of relevant books and articles.

Johnson, Annette B. "The Problems of Contraction: Legal Considerations in University Retrenchment," 10 *J. Law & Educ.* 269 (1981). Examines the financial circumstances that justify retrenchment, how and by whom retrenchment decisions should be made, and the procedures to follow after the decision in order to preserve the legal rights of individuals affected by the retrenchment.

Ludolph, Robert Charles. "Termination of Faculty Tenure Rights Due to Financial Exigency and Program Discontinuance," 63 *U. Detroit L. Rev.* 609 (1986). Reviews faculty property rights (for both tenured and untenured faculty), discusses constitutional requirements for reductions in force and program closures, and analyzes contractual issues related to faculty terminations. Author proposes an analytical model that helps counsel develop an appropriate defense to challenges to program closures, reductions based on financial exigency, and the closing of a campus or an institution.

Martin, James, Samels, James E., & Associates. *Merging Colleges for Mutual Growth* (Johns Hopkins University Press, 1993). Provides practical and theoretical advice, by college administrators and legal counsel experienced in these matters, about merging colleges to avoid bankruptcy. Discusses a typology of models of mergers, the role of trustees and governing boards, the role of administrators and faculty, and financial planning. Attention is also given to planning for the effects of mergers on students and alumni, as well as academic support concerns, such as the merging of libraries.

Mingle, James R., & Associates. *Challenges of Retrenchment: Strategies for Consolidating Programs, Cutting Costs, and Reallocating Resources* (Jossey-Bass, 1981). Describes the actual retrenchment efforts of public and private institutions through an extensive set of case studies. Analyzes the complex organizational, legal, and political issues that arise when colleges and universities lay off faculty and cut back programs and departments because of rising inflation, declining enrollments, or both.

Olswang, Steven G. "Planning the Unthinkable: Issues in Institutional Reorganization and Faculty Reductions," 9 *J. Coll. & Univ. Law* 431 (1982–83). Examines the legal and policy issues inherent in institutional reorganization and faculty reduction. Analyzes the "three primary alternatives"—"financial exigency declarations, program eliminations, and program reductions"—for achieving reorganization and reduction. Also provides policy guidelines for determining which faculty to lay off and discusses faculty members' rights and prerogatives when they are designated for removal.

IV

The College and
the Students

◆　◆　◆

Sec. 4.1. The Legal Status of Students

4.1.1. The evolutionary process. The legal status of students in postsecondary institutions changed dramatically in the 1960s, changed further in the 1970s and 1980s, and is still evolving. For most purposes students are no longer second-class citizens under the law. They are recognized under the federal Constitution as "persons" with their own enforceable constitutional rights. They are recognized as adults, with the rights and responsibilities of adults, under many state laws. And they are accorded their own legal rights under various federal statutes. The background of this evolution is traced in Section 1.2; the legal status that emerges from these developments, and its impact on postsecondary administration, is explored throughout this chapter.

Perhaps the key case in forging the new student status was *Dixon v. Alabama State Board of Education* (1961), discussed in Section 4.8.2. The court in this case rejected the notion that education in state schools is a "privilege" to be dispensed on whatever conditions the state in its sole discretion deems advisable; it also implicitly rejected the "in loco parentis" concept, under which the law had bestowed on schools all the powers over students that parents had over minor children. The *Dixon* approach became a part of U.S. Supreme Court jurisprudence in cases such as *Tinker v. Des Moines School District* (see Section 4.9.1), *Healy v. James* (Sections 4.9.1 and 4.11.1), and *Goss v. Lopez* (Section 4.8.2). The impact of these public institution cases spilled over onto private institutions, as courts increasingly viewed students as contracting parties having rights under express and implied contractual relationships with the institution. Congress gave students at both public and private schools new rights under various civil rights acts and, in the Buckley Amendment (Section 4.16.1),

371

gave postsecondary students certain rights that were expressly independent of and in lieu of parental rights. State statutes lowering the age of majority also enhanced the independence of students from their parents and brought the bulk of postsecondary students, even undergraduates, into the category of adults.

The latest stage in the evolution of the legal status of students is the stage of institutional self-regulation. Increasingly, higher education associations and commentators have urged, and assisted, individual institutions to redefine and extend their own internal regulations as an alternative or supplement to government regulation. (See generally E. El-Khawas, "Solving Problems Through Self-Regulation, " 59 *Educ. Record* 323 (1978); C. Saunders, "How to Keep the Government from Playing the Featured Role," 59 *Educ. Record* 61 (1978).) But self-regulation has not displaced the continuing flow of federal regulation regarding student rights and responsibilities (see Sections 4.17.3 and 7.4.3).

4.1.2. The age of majority. The age of majority is established by state law in all states. There may be a general statute prescribing an age of majority for all or most business and personal dealings in the state, or there may be specific statutes or regulations establishing varying ages of majority for specific purposes. Until the 1970s twenty-one was typically the age of majority in most states. But since the 1971 ratification of the Twenty-Sixth Amendment, lowering the voting age to eighteen, most states have lowered the age of majority to eighteen or nineteen for many other purposes as well. The Michigan statute (Mich. Comp. Laws Ann. § 722.52) illustrates the comprehensive approach adopted by some states:

> Notwithstanding any other provision of law to the contrary, a person who is eighteen years of age but less than twenty-one years of age when this Act takes effect, and a person who attains eighteen years of age thereafter, is deemed to be an adult of legal age for all purposes whatsoever and shall have the same duties, liabilities, responsibilities, rights, and legal capacity as persons heretofore acquired at twenty-one years of age.

Other states have adopted more limited or more piecemeal legislation, sometimes using different minimum ages for different purposes. Given the lack of uniformity, administrators and counsel should carefully check state law in their own states.

The age-of-majority laws can affect many postsecondary regulations and policies. For example, students at age eighteen may be permitted to enter binding contracts without the need for a cosigner, give consent to medical treatment, declare financial independence, or establish a legal residence apart from the parents. But although students' legal capacity enables institutions to deal with them as adults at age eighteen, it does not necessarily require that institutions do so. Particularly in private institutions, administrators may still be able as a policy matter to require a cosigner on contracts with students, for instance, or to consider the resources of parents in awarding financial aid, even though the parents have no legal obligations to support the student. An institution's legal capacity to adopt such policy positions depends on the interpretation of the applicable age-of-majority law and the possible existence of special state law provisions for postsecondary institutions. A state loan program, for instance, may have special definitions of dependency or residency, which may not conform to general age-of-majority laws. Administrators will thus confront two questions: What do the age-of-majority laws require that I do in particular areas? And should I, where I am under no legal obligation, establish age requirements higher than the legal age in particular areas, or should I instead pattern institutional policies on the general legal standard?

4.1.3. The contractual rights of students. Both public and private institutions often have express contractual relationships with students. The most common examples are probably the housing contract or lease, the food service contract, and the loan agreement. When problems arise in these areas, the written contract, including institutional regulations incorporated by reference in the contract, is usually the first source of legal guidance.[1]

The contractual relationship between student and institution, however, extends beyond the terms of express contracts. There also exists the more amorphous contractual relationship recognized in *Carr v. St. John's University, New York*, 187 N.E.2d 18 (N.Y. 1962), the modern root of the contract theory of student status. In reviewing the institution's dismissal of students for having participated in a civil marriage ceremony, the court based its reasoning on the principle that "when a student is duly admitted by a private university, secular or religious, there is an implied contract between the student and the university that, if he complies with the terms prescribed by the university, he will obtain the degree which he sought." Construing a harsh and vague regulation in the university's favor, the court upheld the dismissal because the students had failed to comply with the university's prescribed terms.

Although *Carr* dealt only with a private institution, a subsequent New York case, *Healy v. Larsson*, 323 N.Y.S.2d 625, *affirmed*, 318 N.E.2d 608 (N.Y. 1974) (discussed below in this section), indicated that "there is no reason why . . . the *Carr* principle should not apply to a public university or community college."

Other courts have increasingly utilized the contract theory for both public and private institutions, as well as for both academic and disciplinary disputes. The theory, however, does not necessarily apply identically to all such situations. A public institution may have more defenses against a contract action. *Eden v. Board of Trustees of State University*, 374 N.Y.S.2d 686 (N.Y. App. Div. 1975), for instance, recognizes both an ultra vires defense and the state's power to terminate a contract when necessary in the public interest. ("Ultra vires" means "beyond authority," and the defense is essentially "You can't enforce this contract against us because we didn't have authority to make it in the first place.") And courts may accord both public and private institutions more flexibility in drafting and interpreting contract terms involving academics than they do contract terms involving discipline. In holding that

---

[1]The contract theory is by far the primary theory for according legal status to students beyond that derived from the Constitution and state and federal statutes. Other theories have occasionally been suggested by commentators, but they are seldom reflected in court opinions (see, for example, A. L. Goldman, "The University and the Liberty of Its Students—A Fiduciary Theory," 54 *Ky. L.J.* 643 (1966); Note, "Judicial Review of the University-Student Relationship: Expulsion and Governance," 26 *Stanford L. Rev.* 95 (1973) (common law of private associations)). For a comparison of the various theories and cites to illustrative cases, see *Tedeschi v. Wagner College*, 404 N.E.2d 1302, 1304–06 (N.Y. 1980).

Georgia State University had not breached its contract with a student by withholding a master's degree, for example, the court in *Mahavongsanan v. Hall,* 529 F.2d 448 (5th Cir. 1976), recognized the "wide latitude and discretion afforded by the courts to educational institutions in framing their academic requirements."

In general, courts have applied the contract theory to postsecondary institutions in a deferential manner. Courts have accorded institutions considerable latitude to select and interpret their own contract terms and to change the terms to which students are subjected as they progress through the institution. In *Mahavongsanan,* for instance, the court rejected the plaintiff student's contract claim in part because an institution "clearly is entitled to modify [its regulations] so as to properly exercise its educational responsibility." Nor have institutions been subjected to the rigors of contract law as it applies in the commercial world. The plaintiff student in *Slaughter v. Brigham Young University* (Sections 4.6.2 and 4.8.4) had been awarded $88,283 in damages in the trial court in a suit alleging erroneous dismissal from school. The appellate court reversed:

> The trial court's rigid application of commercial contract doctrine advanced by plaintiff was in error, and the submission on that theory alone was error. . . .
>
> It is apparent that some elements of the law of contracts are used and should be used in the analysis of the relationship between plaintiff and the university to provide some framework into which to put the problem of expulsion for disciplinary reasons. This does not mean that "contract law" must be rigidly applied in all its aspects, nor is it so applied even when the contract analogy is extensively adopted. . . . The student-university relationship is unique, and it should not be and cannot be stuffed into one doctrinal category [514 F.2d at 676].

Despite the generally deferential judicial attitude, the contract theory creates a two-way street; it has become a source of meaningful rights for students as well as for institutions. In *Healy v. Larsson,* for instance, the plaintiff student had transferred to the Schenectady County Community College and had taken all the courses his guidance counselors specified, but he was denied a degree. The court held that he was contractually entitled to the degree because he had "satisfactorily completed a course of study at . . . [the] community college as prescribed to him by authorized representatives of the college." Similarly, in the *Steinberg* and *Eden* cases, discussed in Section 4.2.3, students won victories in admissions cases. Other examples include *Paynter v. New York University,* 319 N.Y.S.2d 893 (N.Y. App. Div. 1971), and *Zumbrun v. University of Southern California,* 101 Cal. Rptr. 499 (Cal. Ct. App. 1972), both suits seeking tuition refunds after classes had been canceled for part of a semester during antiwar protests. Although in *Paynter* the court held in favor of the university and in *Zumbrun* it remanded the case to the trial court for further proceedings, both opinions recognized that the courses to be taken by a student and the services to be rendered in the courses are part of the student-institution contract. Moreover, the opinions indicate that the institution may make only "minor" changes in the schedule of classes and in the course of study that a student has undertaken for a particular semester; more substantial deviations could constitute a breach of contract.

But in *Doherty v. Southern College of Optometry,* 862 F.2d 570 (6th Cir. 1988), the court rejected a student's claim that deviations from the stated curriculum breached his contractual rights. The college's handbook had specifically reserved the right to change degree requirements, and the college had uniformly applied curricular changes to current students in the past. Therefore, the court ruled that the changes were neither arbitrary nor capricious, and dismissed the student's contract claim.

An express disclaimer in a state university's catalogue defeated a student's contract claim in *Eiland v. Wolf*, 764 S.W.2d 827 (Tex. Ct. App. 1989). Although the catalogue stated that the student would be entitled to a diploma if he successfully completed required courses and met other requirements, the express disclaimer that the catalogue was not an enforceable contract and was subject to change without notice convinced the court to dismiss the student's challenge to his academic dismissal.

A reservation-of-rights clause was also present, but less important, in *Beukas v. Fairleigh Dickinson University*, 605 A.2d 776 (N.J. Super. Ct. Law Div. 1991), *affirmed*, 605 A.2d 708 (N.J. Super. Ct. App. Div. 1992). The court ruled that no express contract existed between the dental students and the university and that, under principles of "quasi-contract," the university could close the dental school as long as it acted in good faith (see Section 4.2.3).

The contract theory is still developing. Debate continues on issues such as the means for identifying the terms and conditions of the student-institution contract, the extent to which the school catalogue constitutes part of the contract, and the extent to which the institution retains implied or inherent authority (see Section 2.1) not expressed in any written regulation or policy. For example, in *Prusack v. State*, 498 N.Y.S.2d 455 (N.Y. App. Div. 1986), the court rejected the student's claim that a letter of admission from the university which had quoted a particular tuition rate was an enforceable contract, since other university publications expressly stated that tuition was subject to change. In *Eiland v. Wolf*, 764 S.W.2d 827 (Tex. Ct. App. 1989), reservation-of-rights language in a catalogue for the University of Texas Medical School at Galveston absolved the institution of contractual liability. The catalogue stated: "The provisions of this catalogue are subject to change without notice and do not constitute an irrevocable contract between any student . . . and the University." Furthermore, the catalogue gave the faculty the right to determine whether a student's performance was satisfactory, and stated that "the Faculty of the School of Medicine has the authority to drop any student from the rolls . . . if circumstances of a legal, moral, health, social, or academic nature justify such a request" (764 S.W.2d at 838). The court said: "Given the express disclaimers in the document alleged to be a contract here, it is clear that no enforceable 'contract' existed" (764 S.W.2d at 838).

Also still debatable is the extent to which courts will rely on certain contract law concepts, such as "unconscionable" contracts and "contracts of adhesion." An unconscionable contract is one which is so harsh and unfair to one of the parties that a reasonable person would not freely and knowingly agree to it. Unconscionable contracts are not enforceable in the courts. In *Albert Merrill School v. Godoy*, 357 N.Y.S.2d 378 (Civ. Ct., N.Y. City, 1974), for example, the school sought to recover money due on a contract to provide data-processing training. Finding that the student did not speak English well and that the bargaining power of the parties was uneven, the court held the contract unconscionable and refused to enforce it. A contract of adhesion is one offered by one party (usually the party in the stronger bargaining position) to the other party on a "take-it-or-leave-it" basis, with no opportunity to negotiate the terms. Although courts will often construe adhesion contracts in favor of the weaker party where there is ambiguity, such contracts are enforceable unless a court holds that they are unconscionable. In *K. D. v. Educational Testing Service*, 386 N.Y.S.2d 747 (N.Y. Sup. Ct. 1976), the court viewed the plaintiff's agreement with ETS to take the Law School Admissions Test (LSAT) as a contract of adhesion, explaining:

> Where the court finds that an agreement is a contract of adhesion, effort will frequently be made to protect the weaker party from the agreement's harsher terms by a variety of pretexts, while still keeping the elementary rules of the law of contracts intact (Kessler, "Contracts of Adhesion—Some Thoughts About Freedom of Contract," 43 *Columbia L. Rev.* 629, 633 (1943)). The court may, for example, find the obnoxious clause "ambiguous," even where no ambiguity exists, and then construe it against its author; or it may find the clause to be against public policy and declare it unenforceable [386 N.Y.S.2d at 752].

Nevertheless, the court held the agreement valid because it was not "so unfair and unreasonable" that it should be disregarded by use of the available "pretexts."

Since these contract principles depend on the weak position of one of the parties, and on overall determinations of "fairness," courts are unlikely to apply them against institutions that deal openly with their students—for instance, by following a good-practice code, operating grievance mechanisms for student complaints (see Sections 4.5.1 through 4.5.3), and affording students significant opportunity to participate in institutional governance.

Other contractual issues may arise as a result of the action of institutional or state-level actors. For example, in *Arriaga v. Members of Board of Regents*, 825 F. Supp. 1 (D. Mass. 1992), students challenged the constitutionality of retroactive tuition increases ordered by the state board of regents after the state legislature, responding to a fiscal crisis, passed a law increasing tuition for nonresident students. Claiming that the institution's statements about the amount of tuition for nonresident students was a contract, the students argued that the regents' action impaired their contractual rights in violation of the U.S. Constitution's Contracts Clause, Article I, Section 10 (see this volume, Section 3.1.4).

The regents filed a motion to dismiss the lawsuit, arguing that they had the unilateral power to impose tuition increases, and thus it was not the legislature's action that was dispositive of the constitutional claim. The court was required to determine whether it was the action of the legislature or the regents that resulted in the tuition increase, for the Contracts Clause would apply only to the acts of the legislature unless it had delegated its power to the executive branch (here, the regents). The court concluded that, although the regents determined that tuition increases were necessary before the legislature formally passed the law, their action was in anticipation of the law and thus was controlled by the provisions of the Contracts Clause.

As further developments unfold, postsecondary administrators should be sensitive to the language used in all institutional rules and policies affecting students. Language suggestive of a commitment (or promise) to students should be used only when the institution is prepared to live up to the commitment. Limitations on the institution's commitments should be clearly noted where possible. Administrators should consider the adoption of an official policy, perhaps even a "code of good practice," on fair dealing with students. (See E. H. El-Khawas, *New Expectations for Fair Practice: Suggestions for Institutional Review* (American Council on Education, 1976).)

Sec. 4.2. Admissions

4.2.1. Basic legal requirements. Postsecondary institutions have traditionally been accorded wide discretion in formulating admissions standards. The law's deference to administrators' autonomy stems from the notion that tampering with admissions criteria is tampering with the expertise of educators. In recent years, however, some doorways have been opened in the wall of deference, as dissatisfied applicants have successfully pressed the courts for relief, and legislatures and administrative agencies have sought to regulate certain aspects of the admissions process.

Administrators are subject to three general constraints in formulating admissions policies: (1) the selection process must not be arbitrary or capricious; (2) the institution may be bound, under a contract theory, to adhere to its published admissions standards and to honor its admissions decisions; and (3) the institution may not have admissions policies that unjustifiably discriminate on the basis of race, sex, age, disability, or citizenship.

Although administrators are also constrained in the admissions process by the "Buckley" regulations on school records (Section 4.16.1), the regulations have only limited applicability to admissions records. The regulations do not apply to the records of persons who are not or have not been students at the institution; thus, admissions records are not covered until the applicant has been accepted and is in attendance at the institution (34 C.F.R. §§ 99.1(d), 99.3 ("student")). The institution may also maintain the confidentiality of letters of recommendation if the student has waived the right of access; such a waiver may be sought during the application process (34 C.F.R. § 99.12). Moreover, when a student from one component unit of an institution applies for admission to another unit of the same institution, the student is treated as an applicant rather than a student with respect to the second unit's admissions records; those records are therefore not subject to Buckley until the student is in attendance in the second unit (34 C.F.R. § 99.5).

Falsification of information on an application may be grounds for discipline or expulsion. In *North v. West Virginia Board of Regents*, 332 S.E.2d 141 (W. Va. 1985), a medical student provided false information on his application concerning his grade point average, courses taken, degrees, birth date, and marital status. The court upheld the expulsion on two theories: that the student had breached the university's disciplinary code (even though he was not a student at the time) and that the student had committed fraud.

Students may also make constitutional claims, based on the due process and equal protection provisions of the Fourteenth Amendment. For example, in *Martin v. Helstad*, 578 F. Supp. 1473 (W.D. Wis. 1983), a law school revoked its acceptance of an applicant when the school learned he had neglected to include on his application that he had been convicted of a felony and incarcerated. The court held that, although the applicant was entitled to minimal procedural due process to respond to the school's charge that he had falsified information on his application, the school had provided him sufficient due process in allowing him to explain his nondisclosure.

In *Phelps v. Washburn University of Topeka*, 634 F. Supp. 556 (D. Kan. 1986), rejected applicants attempted to state due process claims, asserting that the university denied them admission because they were active in racial justice issues and because of similar activities of their father. The court found no racial discrimination, and also ruled that the plaintiffs had no property interest in being admitted to the university, thus defeating their procedural due process claims.

4.2.2. Arbitrariness. The "arbitrariness" standard of review is the one most protective of the institution's prerogatives. The cases reflect a judicial hands-off attitude toward any admissions decision arguably based on academic qualifications. Under the arbitrariness standard, the court will overturn an institution's decision only if there is no reasonable explanation for its actions. *Lesser v. Board of Education of New York*, 239 N.Y.S.2d 776 (N.Y. App. Div. 1963), provides a classic example. Lesser sued Brooklyn College after being rejected because his grade average was below the cutoff. He argued that the college acted arbitrarily and unreasonably in not considering that he had been enrolled in a demanding high school honors program. The court declined to overturn the judgment of the college:

> Courts may not interfere with the administrative discretion exercised by agencies which are vested with the administration and control of educational institutions, unless the circumstances disclosed by the record leave no scope for the use of that discretion in the matter under scrutiny. . . .
> More particularly, a court should refrain from interjecting its views within those delicate areas of school administration which relate to the eligibility of applicants and the determination of marking standards, unless a clear abuse of statutory authority or gross error has been shown [239 N.Y.S.2d at 779].

The court in *Arizona Board of Regents v. Wilson*, 539 P.2d 943 (Ariz. Ct. App. 1975), expressed similar sentiment. In that case a woman was refused admission to the graduate school of art at the University of Arizona because the faculty did not consider her art work to be of sufficiently high quality. She challenged the admissions process on the basis that it was a rolling admissions system with no written guidelines. The court entered judgment in favor of the university:

> This case represents a prime example of when a court should not interfere in the academic program of a university. It was incumbent upon appellee to show that her rejection was in bad faith, or arbitrary, capricious, or unreasonable. The court may not substitute its own opinions as to the merits of appellee's work for that of the members of the faculty committee who were selected to make a determination as to the quality of her work [539 P.2d at 946].

Another court, in considering whether a public university's refusal to admit a student to veterinary school involved constitutional protections, rejected arbitrariness claims based on the due process and equal protection clauses. In *Grove v. Ohio State University*, 424 F. Supp. 377 (S.D. Ohio 1976), the plaintiff, denied admission to veterinary school three times, argued that the use of a score from a personal interview introduced subjective factors into the admissions decision process that were arbitrary and capricious, thus depriving him of due process. Second, he claimed that the admission of students less well qualified than he deprived him of equal protection. And third, he claimed that a professor had told him he would be admitted if he took additional courses.

Citing *Roth* (Section 3.6.2), the court determined that the plaintiff had a liberty interest in pursuing veterinary medicine. The court then examined the admissions procedure and concluded that, despite its subjective element, it provided sufficient due process protections. The court deferred to the academic judgment of the admissions committee with regard to the weight that should be given to the interview score. The court also found no property interest, since the plaintiff had no legitimate entitlement to a space in a class of 130 when over 900 individuals had applied.

The court rejected the plaintiff's second and third claims as well. The plaintiff had not raised discrimination claims, but had asserted that the admission of students with lower grades was a denial of equal protection. The court stated, "This Court is reluctant to find that failure to adhere exactly to an admissions formula constitutes a denial of equal protection" (424 F. Supp. at 387), citing *Bakke* (see Section 4.2.5). Nor did the professor's statement that the plaintiff would be reconsidered for admission if he took additional courses constitute a promise to admit him once he completed the courses.

The review standards in these cases establish a formidable barrier for disappointed applicants to cross. But occasionally someone succeeds. *State ex rel. Bartlett v. Pantzer*, 489 P.2d 375 (Mont. 1971), arose after the admissions committee of the University of Montana Law School had advised an applicant that he would be accepted if he completed a course in financial accounting. He took such a course and received a D. The law school refused to admit him, claiming that a D was an "acceptable" but not a "satisfactory" grade. The student argued that it was unreasonable for the law school to inject a requirement of receiving a "satisfactory grade" after he had completed the course. The court agreed:

> Thus, we look to the matter of judgment or "discretion" in the legal sense. To cause a young man, who is otherwise qualified and whose entry into law school would not interfere with the educational process in any discernible fashion, to lose a year and an opportunity for education on the technical, unpublished distinction between the words "satisfactory" and "acceptable" as applied to a credit-earning grade from a recognized institution is, in our view, an abuse of discretion [489 P.2d at 379].

All these cases involve public institutions, and whether their principles would apply to private institutions is unclear. The "arbitrary and capricious" standard apparently arises from concepts of due process and administrative law that are applicable only to public institutions. Courts may be even less receptive to arbitrariness arguments lodged against private schools, although common law may provide some relief even here. In *In re Press*, 45 U.S.L.W. 2238 (N.Y. Sup. Ct., Oct. 27, 1976), for instance, the court held that an arbitrariness claim was a valid basis on which New York University, a private institution, could be sued. And in *Levine v. George Washington University* and *Paulsen v. Golden Gate University* (Section 4.2.6), common law principles protected students at private institutions against arbitrary interpretation of institutional policy.

The cases discussed in this section demonstrate that, if the individuals and groups who make admissions decisions adhere carefully to their published (or unwritten) criteria, give individual consideration to every applicant, and provide reasonable explanations for the criteria they use, judicial review will be deferential.

4.2.3. The contract theory. The plaintiffs in *Eden v. Board of Trustees of the State University,* 374 N.Y.S.2d 686 (N.Y. App. Div. 1975), had been accepted for admission to a new school of podiatry being established at the State University of New York at Stony Brook. Shortly before the scheduled opening, the state suspended its plans for the school, citing fiscal pressures in state government. The students argued that they had a contract with SUNY entitling them to instruction in the podiatry school. The court agreed that SUNY's "acceptance of the petitioners' applications satisfies the classic requirements of a contract." Though the state could legally abrogate its contracts when necessary in the public interest to alleviate a fiscal crisis, and though "the judicial branch . . . must exercise restraint in questioning executive prerogative," the court nevertheless ordered the state to enroll the students for the ensuing academic year. The court found that a large federal grant as well as tuition money would be lost if the school did not open, that the school's personnel were already under contract and would have to be paid anyway, and that postponement of the opening therefore would not save money. Since the fiscal crisis would not be alleviated, the state's decision was deemed "arbitrary and capricious" and a breach of contract.

The *Eden* case establishes that a prospective student has a contract with the school once the school accepts his or her admission application. A subsequent case takes the contract analysis one step further, applying it to applicants not yet accepted. In *Steinberg v. University of Health Sciences/Chicago Medical School,* 354 N.E.2d 586 (Ill. App. Ct. 1976), the court held that a rejected applicant could sue for breach of contract on the theory that the medical school had deviated from the admissions criteria in its catalogue. The applicant alleged that the school had used unstated criteria, such as the existence of alumni in the applicant's family and the ability to pledge large sums of money to the school. Although conceding that it had no authority to interfere with the substance of a private school's admissions requirements, the court asserted that the school had a contractual duty to its applicants to judge their qualifications only by its published standards unless it had specifically reserved the right to reject any applicant.

The court reasoned that the school's catalogue was an invitation to make an offer; the plaintiff's application in response to that invitation was an offer; and the medical school's retention of the application fee was the acceptance of the offer.

> We believe that he [Steinberg] and the school entered into an enforceable contract; that the school's obligation under the contract was stated in the school's bulletin in a definitive manner; and that by accepting his application fee—a valuable consideration—the school bound itself to fulfill its promises. Steinberg accepted the school's promises in good faith, and he was entitled to have his application judged according to the school's stated criteria [354 N.E.2d at 591].

The court thus ordered a trial on the applicant's allegations that the school had breached a contract. The Illinois Supreme Court affirmed the order and also held that the applicant had a cause of action for fraud (371 N.E.2d 634 (Ill. 1977)).

Thus, the contract theory clearly applies to both public and private schools, although, as *Eden* suggests, public institutions may have defenses not available to private schools. While the contract theory does not require administrators to adopt or to forgo any particular admissions standard, it does require that administrators honor their acceptance decisions once made and honor their published policies in deciding whom to accept and to reject. Administrators should thus carefully review their published admissions policies and any new policies to be published. The institution may wish to omit standards and criteria from its policies in order to avoid being pinned down under the contract theory. Conversely, the institution may decide that full disclosure is the best policy. In either case administrators should make sure that published admissions policies state only what the institution is willing to abide by. If the institution needs to reserve the right to depart from or supplement its published policies, such reservation should be clearly inserted, with counsel's assistance, into all such policies.

Even if a catalogue is not viewed as a contract, a court may hold an institution to a good-faith standard. In *Beukas v. Fairleigh Dickinson University*, 605 A.2d 776 (N.J. Super. Ct. Law Div. 1991), *affirmed*, 605 A.2d 708 (N.J. Super. Ct. App. Div. 1992), former dental students sued the university for closing its dental school when the state withdrew its subsidy. The university pointed to language in the catalogue reserving the right to eliminate programs and schools, arguing that the language was binding on the students. But instead of applying a contract theory, the trial court preferred to analyze the issue using quasi-contract theory, and applied an arbitrariness standard:

> [T]his court rejects classic contract doctrine to resolve this dispute. . . . [T]he "true" university-student "contract" is one of mutual obligations implied, not in fact, but by law; it is a quasi-contract which is "created by law, for reasons of justice without regard to expressions of assent by either words or acts" [citing *West Caldwell v. Caldwell*, 26 N.J. 9 (1958)]. . . . This theory is the most efficient and legally-consistent theory to resolve a university-student conflict resulting from an administrative decision to terminate an academic or professional program. The inquiry should be: did the university act in good faith and, if so, did it deal fairly with its students?" [605 A.2d at 783, 784].

Citing *AAUP v. Bloomfield College* (this volume, Section 3.8.1), the court explained its reasoning for using a good-faith standard rather than contract law:

> This approach will give courts broader authority for examining university decisionmaking in the administrative area than would a modified standard of judicial deference and will produce a more legally cohesive body of law than will application of classic contract doctrine with its many judicially created exceptions, varying as they must from jurisdiction to jurisdiction [605 A.2d at 784–85].

The state's appellate court upheld the result and the reasoning, but stated that if the catalogue was a contract (a question that this court did not attempt to answer), the reservation-of-rights language would have permitted the university to close the dental school.

The existence of a contractual relationship between student and institution is significant if the student wishes to assert constitutional claims based on a property interest. In *Unger v. National Residents Matching Program*, 928 F.2d 1392 (3d Cir. 1991), the plaintiff, admitted to Temple University's residency program in dermatology, challenged the university's decision to terminate the program five months before she was to enroll. Unger claimed constitutional violations of both liberty and property interests. The court rejected the liberty interest claim, stating that Unger was inconvenienced by Temple's actions but was not precluded from seeking other training.

To Unger's claim that Temple's decision deprived her of a property interest, based on her contract with the university, the court replied that the claim failed for two reasons. First, Unger had no legitimate expectation that she would continue her graduate medical training; second, she had no entitlement to the training provided by the program. The court did find that Temple's offer of admission was a contract; but it was not the type of contract that created a property interest enforceable under federal civil rights law (see Section 2.3.3).

Common law developments in employment contract interpretation (see Section 3.1) have implications for student admissions as well. Oral promises, the effect of disclaimers, and other issues related to whether a contract exists and how it should be interpreted may affect student challenges to admission decisions. For an examination of some of these issues, see E. Bunting, "The Admissions Process: New Legal Questions Creep Up the Ivory Tower," 60 *West's Educ. Law Rptr.* 691 (1990).

4.2.4. The principle of nondiscrimination.

Postsecondary institutions are prohibited in varying degrees and by varying legal authorities from discriminating in their admissions process on the basis of race, sex, disability, age, residence, and alien status. The first four are discussed in this section. The other two types—discrimination against nonresidents (residents of other states) and discrimination against aliens (citizens of other countries who are residing in the United States)—are discussed in Sections 4.3.5 and 4.3.6 because the leading cases concern financial aid rather than admissions. The legal principles in these sections also apply generally to admissions. Under these principles, generally speaking, admissions preferences for state residents (see, for example, Cal. Educ. Code § 22522) may be permissible (see *Rosenstock v. Board of Governors of the University of North Carolina*, 423 F. Supp. 1321, 1326-27 (M.D.N.C. 1976)), but among state residents a preference for those who are United States citizens or a bar to those who are nationals of particular foreign countries is probably impermissible (see *Tayyari v. New Mexico State University*, 495 F. Supp. 1365 (D.N.M. 1980)). For an analysis of residency requirements, see M. Olivas, "*Plyler v. Doe, Toll v. Moreno* and Postsecondary Admissions: Undocumented Adults and Enduring Disability," 15 *J. Law & Educ.* 19 (1986).

4.2.4.1. Race.

It is clear under the Fourteenth Amendment's Equal Protection Clause that, in the absence of a "compelling state interest" (see Section 4.2.5), no public institution may discriminate in admissions on the basis of race. The leading case is *Brown v. Board of Education*, 347 U.S. 483 (1954), which, although it concerned elementary and secondary schools, clearly applies to postsecondary education as well. The Supreme Court affirmed its relevance to higher education in *Florida ex rel. Hawkins v. Board of Control*, 350 U.S. 413 (1956). Cases involving postsecondary education have generally considered racial segregation within a state postsecondary system rather than within a single institution, and suits have been brought under

Title VI of the Civil Rights Act of 1964 as well as the Constitution. These cases are discussed in Section 7.5.2.

Although most of the racial segregation cases focus on a broad array of issues, a recent decision by the U.S. Supreme Court addressed admissions issues, among others. In *United States v. Fordice*, 112 S. Ct. 2727 (1992), private plaintiffs and the U.S. Department of Justice asserted that the Mississippi public higher education system was segregated, in violation of both the U.S. Constitution and Title VI of the Civil Rights Act of 1964. Although a federal trial judge had found the state system to be in compliance with both Title VI and the Constitution, a federal appellate court and the U.S. Supreme Court disagreed. (This case is discussed at length in Section 7.5.2.)

Justice White, writing for a unanimous Court, found that the state's higher education system retained vestiges of its prior de jure segregation. With regard to admissions, Justice White cited the state's practice (initiated in 1963, just prior to Title VI's taking effect) of requiring all applicants for admission to the three flagship universities (which were predominantly white) to have a minimum composite score of 15 on the American College Testing (ACT) Program. Testimony had demonstrated that the average ACT score for white students was 18, and the average ACT score for black students was 7. Justice White wrote, "Without doubt, these requirements restrict the range of choices of entering students as to which institution they may attend in a way that perpetuates segregation" (112 S. Ct. at 2739).

These admissions standards were particularly revealing of continued segregation, according to Justice White, when one considered that institutions given the same mission within the state (regional universities) had different admissions standards, depending on the race of the predominant student group. For example, predominantly white regional universities had ACT requirements of 18 or 15, compared to minimum requirements of 13 at the black universities. Because the differential admissions standards were "remnants of the dual system with a continuing discriminatory effect" (112 S. Ct. at 2739), the state was required to articulate an educational reason for those disparities, and it had not done so.

Furthermore, the institutions looked only at ACT scores and did not consider high school grades as a mitigating factor for applicants who could not meet the minimum ACT score. The gap between the grades of black and white applicants was narrower than the gap between their ACT scores, "suggesting that an admissions formula which included grades would increase the number of black students eligible for automatic admission to all of Mississippi's public universities" (112 S. Ct. at 2740). Although the state had argued that grade inflation and the lack of comparability among high schools' course offerings and grading practices made grades an unreliable indicator, the Court dismissed that argument:

> In our view, such justification is inadequate because the ACT was originally adopted for discriminatory purposes, the current requirement is traceable to that decision and seemingly continues to have segregative effects, and the State has so far failed to show that the "ACT-only" admission standard is not susceptible to elimination without eroding sound educational policy [112 S. Ct. at 2740].

The use of high school grades as well as scores on standardized tests is common in higher education admissions decisions, and the state's attempt to rely solely on ACT scores was an important element of the Court's finding of continued segregation.

Although most challenges to allegedly discriminatory admissions requirements have come from black students, Asian and Latino students have filed challenges
as well. In *United States v. League of United Latin American Citizens*, 793 F.2d 636
(5th Cir. 1986), black and Latino college students raised Title VI and constitutional
challenges to the state's requirement that college students pass a reading and mathematics skills test before enrolling in more than six hours of professional education
courses at Texas public institutions. Passing rates on these tests were substantially
lower for minority students than for white, non-Latino students.

Although the trial court had enjoined the practice, the appellate court vacated
the injunction, noting that the state had validated the tests and that they were
appropriate:

> The State's duty . . . to eliminate the vestiges of past discrimination would
> indeed be violated were it to thrust upon minority students, both as role models
> and as pedagogues, teachers whose basic knowledge and skills were inferior to
> those required of majority race teachers [793 F.2d at 643].

In response to the students' equal protection claim, the court found that the state had
demonstrated a compelling interest in teacher competency and that the test was a valid
predictor of success in the courses. Because the students could retake the test until they
passed it, their admission was only delayed, not denied. In response to the students'
liberty interest claim, the court found a valid liberty interest in pursuing a chosen
profession, but also found that the state could require a reasonable examination for
entry into that profession.

Latino students and civil rights groups also challenged the state's funding for
public colleges and universities located near the Mexican border, arguing that they
were more poorly funded because of their high proportion of Latino students. A jury,
applying the state constitution's requirement of equal access to education, found that
the state higher education system did not provide equal access to citizens in southern
Texas, although it also found that state officials had not discriminated against these
persons (K. Mangan, "Texas Jury Faults State on Equal Access to Top Universities,"
Chron. Higher Educ., Nov. 27, 1991, A25). A state court judge later ordered the state
to eliminate the funding inequities among state institutions (K. Mangan, "9 State
Colleges in South Texas to Get Massive Budget Increase," *Chron. Higher Educ.*, June
23, 1993, A23). But in *Richards v. League of United Latin American Citizens*, 868
S.W.2d 306 (Tex. 1993), the Texas Supreme Court ruled later that year that allegedly
inequitable resource allocation to predominantly Hispanic public colleges did not
violate students' equal protection rights.

Asian students have challenged the admissions practices of several institutions,
alleging that they either have "quotas" limiting the number of Asians who may be
admitted or that the institutions exclude Asians from minority admissions programs.
Complaints filed with the Education Department's Office for Civil Rights, which
enforces Title VI (see this volume, Section 7.5.2), have resulted in changes in admissions practices at both public and private colleges and universities. For a discussion
of this issue, see Note, "Assuring Equal Access of Asian Americans to Highly Selective
Universities," 90 *Yale L.J.* 659 (1989).

In addition to the Constitution's Equal Protection Clause and the desegregation criteria developed under Title VI, there are two other major legal bases for

attacking racial discrimination in higher education. The first is the civil rights statute called "Section 1981" (42 U.S.C. § 1981) (this volume, Section 3.3.2.4). A post–Civil War statute guaranteeing the freedom to contract, Section 1981 has particular significance because (like Title VI) it applies to private as well as public institutions. In the leading case of *Runyon v. McCrary*, 427 U.S. 160 (1976), the U.S. Supreme Court used Section 1981 to prohibit two private, white elementary schools from discriminating against blacks in their admissions policies. Since the Court has applied Section 1981 to discrimination against white persons as well as blacks (*McDonald v. Santa Fe Trail Transportation Co.*, 427 U.S. 273 (1976)), this statute would also apparently prohibit predominantly minority private institutions from discriminating in admissions against white students.

The other legal source is federal income tax law. In Revenue Ruling 71-447, 1971-2 C.B. 230 (*Cumulative Bulletin,* an annual multivolume compilation of various tax documents published by the IRS), the Internal Revenue Service revised its former policy and ruled that schools practicing racial discrimination were violating public policy and should be denied tax-exempt status. Other IRS rulings enlarged on this basic rule. Revenue Procedure 72-54, 1972-2 C.B. 834, requires schools to publicize their nondiscrimination policies. Revenue Procedure 75-50, 1975-2 C.B. 587, requires that a school carry the burden of "show[ing] affirmatively . . . that it has adopted a racially nondiscriminatory policy as to students" and also establishes record-keeping and other guidelines through which a school can demonstrate its compliance. And Revenue Ruling 75-231, 1975-1 C.B. 158, furnishes a series of hypothetical cases to illustrate when a church-affiliated school would be considered to be discriminating and in danger of losing tax-exempt status. The U.S. Supreme Court upheld the basic policy of Revenue Ruling 71-447 in *Bob Jones University v. United States*, 461 U.S. 574 (1983), discussed in Section 7.3.1 of this volume.[2]

The combined impact of these various legal sources—the Equal Protection Clause, Title VI, Section 1981, and IRS tax rulings—is clear: neither public nor private postsecondary institutions may maintain admissions policies (with a possible exception for affirmative action policies, as discussed in Section 4.2.5) that discriminate against students on the basis of race, nor may states maintain plans or practices that perpetuate racial segregation in a statewide system of postsecondary education.

4.2.4.2. Sex. Title IX of the Education Amendments of 1972 (20 U.S.C. § 1681 et seq.) (see this volume, Section 7.5.3) is the primary legal source governing sex discrimination in admissions policies. While Title IX and its implementing regulations, 34 C.F.R. Part 106, apply nondiscrimination principles to both public and private institutions receiving federal funds, there are special exemptions concerning admissions. For the purposes of applying these admissions exemptions, each "administratively separate unit" of an institution is considered a separate institution (34 C.F.R. § 106.15(b)). An "administratively separate unit" is "a school, department, or college . . . admission to which is independent of admission to any other component of such institution" (34 C.F.R. § 106.2(o)). Private undergraduate institutions are not prohibited from discriminating in admissions on the basis of sex (20 U.S.C. § 1681(a)(1), 34 C.F.R. § 106.15(d)). Nor are public undergraduate institutions that have always been single-sex institutions (20 U.S.C. § 1681(a)(5), 34 C.F.R. § 106.15(e);

[2]Cases and materials are collected in Annot., "Allowability of Federal Tax Benefits to a Private, Racially Segregated School or College," 7 A.L.R. Fed. 548 (1971 and periodic supp.).

but compare the *Hogan* case, discussed later in this section). In addition, religious institutions, including all or any of their administratively separate units, may be exempted from nondiscrimination. The remaining institutions, which are prohibited from discriminating in admissions, are (1) graduate schools; (2) professional schools, unless they are part of an undergraduate institution exempted from Title IX's admissions requirements (see 34 C.F.R. § 106.2(m)); (3) vocational schools, unless they are part of an undergraduate institution exempted from Title IX's admissions requirements (see 34 C.F.R. § 106.2(n)); and (4) public undergraduate institutions that are not, or have not always been, single-sex schools.[3]

Institutions subject to Title IX admissions requirements are prohibited from treating persons differently on the basis of sex in any phase of admissions and recruitment (34 C.F.R. §§ 106.21-106.23). Specifically, Section 106.21(b) of the regulations provides that a covered institution, in its admissions process, shall not

   (i) Give preference to one person over another on the basis of sex, by ranking applicants separately on such basis, or otherwise;
  (ii) Apply numerical limitations upon the number or proportion of persons of either sex who may be admitted; or
 (iii) Otherwise treat one individual differently from another on the basis of sex.

Section 106.21(c) prohibits covered institutions from treating the sexes differently in regard to "actual or potential parental, family, or marital status"; from discriminating against applicants because of pregnancy or conditions relating to childbirth; and from making preadmission inquiries concerning marital status. Sections 106.22 and 106.23(b) prohibit institutions from favoring single-sex or predominantly single-sex schools in their admissions or recruitment practices if such practices have "the effect of discriminating on the basis of sex."

Institutions that are exempt from Title IX admissions requirements are not necessarily free to discriminate at will on the basis of sex. Some will be caught in the net of other statutes or of constitutional equal protection principles. A state statute such as the Massachusetts statute prohibiting sex discrimination in vocational training institutions may catch other exempted undergraduate programs (Mass. Gen. Laws Ann. ch. 151C, § 2A(a)). More important, the Fourteenth Amendment's Equal Protection Clause places restrictions on public undergraduate schools even if they are single-sex schools exempt from Title IX.

After a period of uncertainty concerning the extent to which equal protection principles would restrict a public institution's admissions policies, the U.S. Supreme Court considered the question in *Mississippi University for Women v. Hogan*, 458 U.S. 718 (1982). In this case the plaintiff challenged an admissions policy that excluded males from a professional nursing school. Ignoring the dissenting justices'

---

[3]The admissions exemption for private undergraduate institutions in the regulations may be broader than that authorized by the Title IX statute. For an argument that "administratively separate" professional and vocational components of private undergraduate institutions should not be exempt and that private undergraduate schools which are primarily professional and vocational in character should not be exempt, see W. Kaplin & M. McGillicuddy, "Scope of Exemption for Private Undergraduate Institutions from Admissions Requirements of Title IX," memorandum printed in 121 *Congressional Record* 1091 (94th Cong., 1st Sess., 1975).

protestations that Mississippi provided baccalaureate nursing programs at other state coeducational institutions, the majority of five struck down the institution's policy as unconstitutional sex discrimination. In the process, the Court developed an important synthesis of constitutional principles applicable to sex discrimination claims. These principles would apply not only to admissions but also to all other aspects of a public institution's operations:

> Because the challenged policy expressly discriminates among applicants on the basis of gender, it is subject to scrutiny under the equal protection clause of the Fourteenth Amendment (*Reed v. Reed*, 404 U.S. 71, 75 (1971)). That this statute discriminates against males rather than against females does not exempt it from scrutiny or reduce the standard of review (*Caban v. Mohammed*, 441 U.S. 380, 394 (1979); *Orr v. Orr*, 440 U.S. 268, 279 (1979)). Our decisions also establish that the party seeking to uphold a statute that classifies individuals on the basis of their gender must carry the burden of showing an "exceedingly persuasive justification" for the classification (*Kirchberg v. Feenstra*, 450 U.S. 455, 561 (1981); *Personnel Administrator of Massachusetts v. Feeney*, 442 U.S. 256, 273 (1979)). The burden is met only by showing at least that the classification serves "important governmental objectives and that the discriminatory means employed" are "substantially related to the achievement of those objectives" (*Wangler v. Druggists Mutual Insurance Co.*, 446 U.S. 142, 150 (1980)).
>
> Although the test for determining the validity of a gender-based classification is straightforward, it must be applied free of fixed notions concerning the roles and abilities of males and females. Care must be taken in ascertaining whether the statutory objective itself reflects archaic and stereotypic notions. Thus, if the statutory objective is to exclude or "protect" members of one gender because they are presumed to suffer from an inherent handicap or to be innately inferior, the objective itself is illegitimate (see *Frontiero v. Richardson*, 411 U.S. 677, 684–85 (1973) (plurality opinion)).
>
> If the state's objective is legitimate and important, we next determine whether the requisite direct, substantial relationship between objective and means is present. The purpose of requiring that close relationship is to assure that the validity of a classification is determined through reasoned analysis rather than through the mechanical application of traditional, often inaccurate, assumptions about the proper roles of men and women [458 U.S. at 723–24].

Applying the principles regarding the legitimacy and importance of the state's objective, the Court noted that the state's justification for prohibiting men from enrolling in the nursing program was to compensate for discrimination against women. On the contrary, the Court pointed out, women had never been denied entry to the nursing profession, and limiting admission to women actually perpetuated the stereotype that nursing is "women's work." The state had made no showing that women needed preferential treatment in being admitted to nursing programs, and the Court did not believe that that was the state's purpose in discriminating against men.

Even if the state had a valid compensatory objective, its policy would still be unconstitutional, according to the Court, because it also violated other equal protection principles:

> The state has made no showing that the gender-based classification is substantially and directly related to its proposed compensatory objective. To the

contrary, MUW's policy of permitting men to attend classes as auditors fatally undermines its claim that women, at least those in the school of nursing, are adversely affected by the presence of men.

MUW permits men who audit to participate fully in classes. Additionally, both men and women take part in continuing education courses offered by the school of nursing, in which regular nursing students also can enroll. . . . The uncontroverted record reveals that admitting men to nursing classes does not affect teaching style, . . . and that men in coeducational nursing schools do not dominate the classroom. . . . In sum, the record in this case is flatly inconsistent with the claim that excluding men from the school of nursing is necessary to reach any of MUW's educational goals [458 U.S. at 730–31].

The Court's opinion on its face invalidated single-sex admissions policies only at MUW's school of nursing and, by extension, other public postsecondary nursing schools. The majority noted: "We decline to address the question of whether MUW's admissions policy, as applied to males seeking admission to schools other than the school of nursing, violates the Fourteenth Amendment," and "We are not faced with the question of whether states can provide 'separate but equal' undergraduate institutions for males and females." But the majority's reasoning cannot so easily be confined, as two of the three dissenting opinions pointed out. It is likely that this reasoning would also invalidate single-sex policies in programs other than nursing and in entire institutions. The most arguable exception to this broad reading would be a single-sex policy that redresses the effects of past discrimination on a professional program in which one sex is substantially underrepresented. But even such a compensatory policy would be a form of explicit sexual quota, which could be questioned by analogy to the racial affirmative action cases (this volume, Section 4.2.5).

Whatever the remaining ambiguity about the scope of the *Hogan* decision, it will not be resolved by further litigation at the Mississippi University for Women. After the Supreme Court decision, MUW's board of trustees—perhaps anticipating a broad application of the Court's reasoning—voted to admit men to all divisions of the university.

The *Hogan* opinion provided important guidance in a challenge to the lawfulness of male-only public military colleges. In *United States v. Commonwealth of Virginia*, 766 F. Supp. 1407, *vacated*, 976 F.2d 890 (4th Cir. 1992), the U.S. Department of Justice challenged the admissions policies of the Virginia Military Institute (VMI), which admits only men. The government claimed that those policies violated the Equal Protection Clause (it did not include a Title IX claim, since military academies and historically single-sex institutions are exempt from Title IX). Equal protection challenges to sex discrimination require the state to demonstrate "an exceedingly persuasive justification" for the classification (*Hogan*, 458 U.S. at 739). In this case the state argued that enhancing diversity by offering a distinctive single-sex military education to men was an important state interest. The district court found that the single-sex policy was justified because of the benefits of a single-sex education, and that requiring VMI to admit women would "fundamentally alter" the "distinctive ends" of the educational system (766 F. Supp. at 1411).

The appellate court vacated the district court's opinion, stating that Virginia had not articulated an important objective sufficient to overcome the burden on equal protection. While the appellate court agreed with the trial court's finding that the admission of women would materially affect several key elements of VMI's program—physical training, lack of privacy, and the adversative approach to character development—it was homogeneity of gender, not maleness, that justified the program (976 F.2d at 897). The appellate court also accepted the trial court's findings that single-sex education has important benefits. But these findings did not support the trial court's conclusion that VMI's male-only policy passed constitutional muster. Although VMI's single-gender education and "citizen-soldier" philosophy were permissible, the state's exclusion of women from such a program was not, and no other public postsecondary education institution in Virginia was devoted to educating only one gender.

The court did not order VMI to admit women, but remanded the case to the district court to give Virginia the option to (1) admit women to VMI, (2) establish parallel institutions or programs for women, or (3) terminate state support for VMI. On appeal, the U.S. Supreme Court refused to hear the case (113 S. Ct. 2431 (1993)). Following that action, the trustees of VMI voted to underwrite a military program at a neighboring private women's college, Mary Baldwin College ("Virginia Military Institute to Establish Courses at Women's College," *New York Times*, Sept. 26, 1993, A26). The U.S. Department of Justice has challenged the plan, saying that it is "based on gender stereotypes," and has asked the court to order VMI to admit women and to integrate them into its full program ("Ways and Means," *Chron. Higher Educ.*, Nov. 24, 1993, A21). A trial judge approved the parallel program at Mary Baldwin College (S. Jaschik, "Judge Says Va. Military Institute Can Maintain All-Male Admissions," *Chron. Higher Educ.*, May 11, 1994, A30).

The only other all-male public college, The Citadel, was ordered by a panel of the U.S. Court of Appeals for the Fourth Circuit to admit a female applicant whom that college had admitted on the mistaken belief that she was male (*Faulkner v. Jones*, 1993 U.S. App. LEXIS 29885 (4th Cir. 1993); see also "Military College Is Ordered to Admit Woman," *New York Times*, Nov. 18, 1993, B16). The court ordered that she be admitted as a day student, and remanded to the district court the issue of whether she can become a full member of the college's corps of cadets. On remand the trial judge ordered that she become a member of the corps of cadets. The college appealed this ruling (see S. Jaschik, "Citadel Vows to Fight U.S. Judge's Order That It Admit a Woman," *Chron. Higher Educ.*, Aug. 3, 1994, A27), and an appeals court panel ordered her status as a cadet to be delayed until the court could hear the college's arguments.

Important as *Hogan* may be to the law regarding sex discrimination in admissions, it is only part of the bigger picture, which already includes Title IX. Thus, to view the law in its current state, one must look both to *Hogan* and to Title IX. *Hogan* and its progeny have at least limited, and apparently undermined, the Title IX exemption for public undergraduate institutions that have always had single-sex admissions policies (20 U.S.C. § 1681(a)(5), 34 C.F.R. § 106.15(e)). Thus, until the disputes over public single-sex military colleges are resolved, the only programs and institutions that are still legally free to have single-sex admissions policies are (1) private undergraduate institutions and their constituent programs and (2) religious institutions, including their graduate, professional, and vocational programs, if they have obtained a waiver of Title IX admission requirements on religious grounds (20 U.S.C. § 1681(a)(3); 34 C.F.R. § 106.12).

Another potential area for sex discrimination in admissions is in the use of standardized tests for making admission decisions. Some of the standardized tests used to make admission decisions—the Scholastic Aptitude Test, for example—have been challenged because of the systematic gender differences in scores. When these test scores are used to make decisions about awarding scholarships, they may be especially vulnerable to legal challenge. In *Sharif v. New York State Education Department* (discussed in Section 4.3.3), a federal district court ruled that this practice violated Title IX and the Fourteenth Amendment's Equal Protection Clause. The American Civil Liberties Union has filed a sex discrimination complaint with the Office for Civil Rights, alleging that the use of scores on the Scholastic Aptitude Test to determine the winners of National Merit Scholarships disproportionately favors boys (M. Winerip, "Merit Scholarship Program Faces Sex Bias Complaint," *New York Times*, Feb. 16, 1994, A18). For analysis of the potential discriminatory effects of standardized testing, see K. Connor & E. Vargyas, "The Legal Implications of Gender Bias in Standardized Testing," *Berkeley Women's Law J.* 13 (1992). See also L. Silverman, "Unnatural Selection: A Legal Analysis of the Impact of Standardized Test Use on Higher Education Resource Allocation," 23 *Loyola of Los Angeles L. Rev.* 1433 (1990).

In addition to Title IX, other laws include prohibitions on sex discrimination in admissions. For example, one section of the Public Health Service Act's provisions on nurse education (42 U.S.C. § 298(b)(2)) prohibits the secretary of health and human services from making grants, loan guarantees, or interest subsidy payments to schools of nursing unless the schools provide "assurances satisfactory to the Secretary that the school will not discriminate on the basis of sex in the admission of individuals to its training programs."

4.2.4.3. Disability. The country's conscience has awakened to the problem of discrimination against people with disabilities. Accommodating students with disabilities is a particularly significant issue for colleges and universities because of the sheer numbers of these students. According to a study by the American Council on Education, in 1992 nearly one in eleven freshmen reported that they had a disability, compared with one in thirty-eight in 1978 (*College Freshmen with Disabilities: A Statistical Profile* (American Council on Education, 1992)). And disability discrimination complaints by students are increasing in proportion to their growth in numbers. In 1992, for example, the Education Department found that forty-six colleges had violated the rights of either students or employees with disabilities (S. Jaschik, "46 Colleges Found to Have Violated Rights of Disabled, U.S. Documents Show," *Chron. Higher Educ.*, Apr. 21, 1993, A18).

Two pieces of landmark federal legislation—Section 504 of the Rehabilitation Act of 1973 (29 U.S.C. § 794) and the Americans with Disabilities Act (ADA) (42 U.S.C. § 12101 et seq.)—prohibit discrimination against individuals with disabilities. Before those laws were passed, these individuals had been the subject of a few scattered federal provisions (such as 20 U.S.C. § 1684, which prohibits discrimination against blind persons by institutions receiving federal funds) and a few constitutional equal protection cases (such as *PARC v. Pennsylvania*, 334 F. Supp. 1257 (E.D. Pa. 1971), which challenged discrimination against disabled students by public elementary and secondary schools). But none of these developments have had nearly the impact on postsecondary admissions that Section 504 and the ADA have.

As applied to postsecondary education, Section 504 generally prohibits discrimination on the basis of disability in federally funded programs and activities (see this volume, Section 7.5.4). Section 104.42 of the implementing regulations, 34 C.F.R. Part 104, prohibits discrimination on the basis of disability in admissions and recruitment. This section contains several specific provisions similar to those prohibiting sex discrimination in admissions under Title IX (see this volume, Section 4.2.4.2). These provisions prohibit (1) the imposition of limitations on "the number or proportion of individuals with disabilities who may be admitted" (§ 104.42(b)(1)); (2) the use of any admissions criterion or test "that has a disproportionate, adverse effect" on individuals with disabilities, unless the criterion or test, as used, is shown to predict success validly and no alternative, nondiscriminatory criterion or test is available (§ 104.42(b)(2)); and (3) any preadmission inquiry about whether the applicant has a disability, unless the recipient needs the information in order to correct the effects of past discrimination or to overcome past conditions that resulted in limited participation by people with disabilities (§§ 104.42(b)(4) and 104.42(c)).

These prohibitions apply to discrimination directed against "qualified" individuals with disabilities. A disabled person is qualified, with respect to postsecondary and vocational services, if he or she "meets the academic and technical standards requisite to admission or participation in the recipient's education program or activity" (§ 104.3(k)(3)). Thus, while the regulations do not prohibit an institution from denying admission to a person with a disability who does not meet the institution's "academic and technical" admissions standards, they do prohibit an institution from denying admission on the basis of the disability as such. (After a student is admitted, however, the institution can make confidential inquiry concerning the disability (34 C.F.R. § 104.42(b)(4)); in this way the institution can obtain advance information about disabilities that may require accommodation.)

In addition to these prohibitions, the institution has an affirmative duty to ascertain that its admissions tests are structured to accommodate applicants with disabilities that impair sensory, manual, or speaking skills, unless the test is intended to measure these skills. Such adapted tests must be offered as often and in as timely a way as other admissions tests and must be "administered in facilities that, on the whole, are accessible" to people with disabilities (§ 104.42(b)(3)).

In *Southeastern Community College v. Davis*, 442 U.S. 397 (1979), the U.S. Supreme Court issued its first interpretation of Section 504. The case concerned a nursing school applicant who had been denied admission because she is deaf. The Supreme Court ruled that an "otherwise qualified handicapped individual" is one who is qualified *in spite of* (rather than except for) his disability. Since an applicant's disability is therefore relevant to his or her qualification for a specific program, Section 504 does not preclude a college or university from imposing "reasonable physical qualifications" on applicants for admission, where such qualifications are necessary for participation in the school's program. The Department of Education's regulations implementing Section 504 provide that a disabled applicant is "qualified" if he or she meets "the academic and technical standards" for admission; the Supreme Court has made it clear, however, that "technical standards" may sometimes encompass reasonable physical requirements. Under *Davis* an applicant's failure to meet such requirements can be a legitimate ground for rejection.

The Court's 9-to-0 ruling was a disappointment to many advocates on behalf of people with disabilities, who feared the decision's effects on their entry into academic and professional pursuits and, more generally, on an institution's willingness to accommodate the needs of people with disabilities. The impact of *Davis* may be substantially limited, however, by the rather narrow and specific factual context in which the case arose. The plaintiff, who was severely hearing-impaired, sought admission to a nursing program. The college denied her admission, believing that she would not be able to perform nursing duties in a safe manner and could not participate fully in the clinical portion of the program.

The U.S. District Court had decided the case in favor of the college, concluding that the plaintiff's disability "prevents her from safely performing in both her training program and her proposed profession" and that she therefore was not "otherwise qualified" under Section 504 (424 F. Supp. 1341 (E.D.N.C. 1976)). The U.S. Court of Appeals had reversed, concluding that the district court had erred in taking the plaintiff's handicap into account in determining whether she was "otherwise qualified" (574 F.2d 1158 (4th Cir. 1978)). Determining that the district court had the better of the argument, the Supreme Court reversed the appellate court:

> Section 504 by its terms does not compel educational institutions to disregard the disabilities of handicapped individuals or to make substantial modifications in their programs to allow disabled persons to participate. Instead, it requires only that an "otherwise qualified handicapped individual" not be excluded from participation in a federally funded program "solely by reason of his handicap," indicating only that mere possession of a handicap is not a permissible ground for assuming an inability to function in a particular context.
>
> The court [of appeals], however, believed that the "otherwise qualified" persons protected by Section 504 include those who would be able to meet the requirements of a particular program in every respect except as to limitations imposed by their handicap. Taken literally, this holding would prevent an institution from taking into account any limitation resulting from the handicap, however disabling. It assumes, in effect, that a person need not meet legitimate physical requirements in order to be "otherwise qualified." We think the understanding of the district court is closer to the plain meaning of the statutory language. An otherwise qualified person is one who is able to meet all of a program's requirements in spite of his handicap [442 U.S. at 405–07].

The Court cited the regulations interpreting Section 504, noting that the individual must be able to meet both academic and "technical" standards in order to be deemed a "qualified" individual with a disability (34 C.F.R. § 104.3(k)(3)). Furthermore, the Court noted, the regulations emphasize that legitimate physical qualifications could be essential to participation in particular programs.

The plaintiff had argued that Section 504 requires affirmative action and that the court should order the college to modify the program by giving her individualized instruction, exempting her from required courses, and adapting the program in other ways to enable her to participate. The Court rejected this argument:

> [I]t . . . is reasonably clear that Section 84.44(a) [of the regulations, now 34 C.F.R. § 104.44(a)] does not encompass the kind of curricular changes that would be necessary to accommodate respondent in the nursing program. In light of respondent's inability to function in clinical courses without close supervision, Southeastern with prudence could allow her to take only academic classes. Whatever benefits respondent might realize from such a course of study, she would not receive even a rough equivalent of the training a nursing program normally

gives. Such a fundamental alteration in the nature of a program is far more than the "modification" the regulation requires.

Moreover, an interpretation of the regulations that required the extensive modifications necessary to include respondent in the nursing program would raise grave doubts about their validity. If these regulations were to require substantial adjustments in existing programs beyond those necessary to eliminate discrimination against otherwise qualified individuals, they would do more than clarify the meaning of Section 504. Instead, they would constitute an unauthorized extension of the obligations imposed by that statute.

The language and structure of the Rehabilitation Act of 1973 reflect a recognition by Congress of the distinction between the evenhanded treatment of qualified handicapped persons and affirmative efforts to overcome the disabilities caused by handicaps. . . . Congress understood [that] accommodation of the needs of handicapped individuals may require affirmative action and knew how to provide for it in those instances where it wished to do so. . . .

Here neither the language, purpose, nor history of Section 504 reveals an intent to impose an affirmative action obligation on all recipients of federal funds. Accordingly, we hold that, even if HEW has attempted to create such an obligation itself, it lacks the authority to do so [442 U.S. at 409–12].

The Court carefully limited its holding to the circumstances of this case, noting that technological advances might one day enable certain persons with disabilities to qualify for certain programs that they were not presently qualified for.

It is important to emphasize that *Davis* involved admission to a professional, clinical training program. The demands of such a program, designed to train students in the practice of a profession, raise far different considerations from those involved in admission to an undergraduate or a graduate academic program, or even a nonclinically oriented professional school. While the Court approved the imposition of "reasonable physical qualifications," it did so only for requirements that the institution can justify as necessary to the applicant's successful participation in the particular program involved. In *Davis* the college had shown that an applicant's ability to understand speech without reliance on lipreading was necessary to ensure patient safety and to enable the student to realize the full benefit of its nursing program. For programs without clinical components, or without professional training goals, it would be much more difficult for the institution to justify such physical requirements. Even for other professional programs, the justification might be much more difficult than in *Davis*. In a law school program, for example, the safety factor would be lacking. Moreover, in most law schools, clinical training is offered as an elective rather than a required course. By enrolling only in the nonclinical courses, a deaf student would be able to complete the required program with the help of an interpreter.

Furthermore, the Court did not say that affirmative action is never required to accommodate the needs of disabled applicants. Although the Court asserted that Section 504 does not require institutions "to lower or to effect substantial modifications of standards" or to make "fundamental alteration[s] in the nature of a program," the Court did suggest that less substantial and burdensome program adjustments may sometimes be required. The Court also discussed, and did not question, the regulation requiring institutions to provide certain "auxiliary aids," such as interpreters for students with hearing impairments, to qualified students with disabilities (see Sections 4.4 and 7.5.4). This issue was addressed in *United States v.*

Board of Trustees for the University of Alabama, 908 F.2d 740 (11th Cir. 1990), in which the court ordered the university to provide additional transportation for students with disabilities. Moreover, the Court said nothing that in any way precludes institutions from voluntarily making major program modifications for applicants who are disabled.

Several appellate court cases have applied the teachings of *Davis* to other admissions problems. The courts in these cases have refined the *Davis* analysis, especially in clarifying the burdens of proof in a discrimination suit under Section 504. In *Pushkin v. Regents of the University of Colorado,* 658 F.2d 1372 (10th Cir. 1981), the court affirmed the district court's decision that the plaintiff, a medical doctor suffering from multiple sclerosis, had been wrongfully denied admission to the university's psychiatric residency program. Agreeing that *Davis* permitted consideration of handicaps in determining whether an applicant is "otherwise qualified" for admission, the court outlined what the plaintiff had to prove in order to establish his case of discrimination:

> 1. The plaintiff must establish a prima facie case by showing that he was an otherwise qualified handicapped person *apart from* his handicap, and was rejected under circumstances which gave rise to the inference that his rejection was based solely on his handicap.
>
> 2. Once plaintiff establishes his prima facie case, defendants have the burden of going forward and proving that plaintiff was not an otherwise qualified handicapped person—that is, one who is able to meet all of the program's requirements *in spite of* his handicap—or that his rejection from the program was for reasons other than his handicap.
>
> 3. The plaintiff then has the burden of going forward with rebuttal evidence showing that the defendants' reasons for rejecting the plaintiff are based on misconceptions or unfounded factual conclusions, and that reasons articulated for the rejection other than the handicap encompass unjustified consideration of the handicap itself [658 F.2d at 1387].

In another post-*Davis* case, *Doe v. New York University,* 666 F.2d 761 (2d Cir. 1981), the court held that the university had not violated Section 504 when it denied readmission to a woman with a long history of "borderline personality" disorders. This court also set out the elements of the case a plaintiff must make to comply with the *Davis* reading of Section 504:

> Accordingly, we hold that in a suit under Section 504 the plaintiff may make out a prima facie case by showing that he is a handicapped person under the Act and that, although he is qualified apart from his handicap, he was denied admission or employment because of his handicap. The burden then shifts to the institution or employer to rebut the inference that the handicap was improperly taken into account by going forward with evidence that the handicap is relevant to qualifications for the position sought (cf. *Dothard v. Rawlinson,* 433 U.S. 321 . . . (1977)). The plaintiff must then bear the ultimate burden of showing by a preponderance of the evidence that in spite of the handicap he is qualified and, where the defendant claims and comes forward with some evidence that the plaintiff's handicap renders him less qualified than other successful applicants, that he is at least as well qualified as other applicants who were accepted [666 F.2d at 776–77].

The *Doe* summary of burdens of proof is articulated differently from the *Pushkin* summary, and the *Doe* court disavowed any reliance on *Pushkin*. In contrast to the *Pushkin* court, the *Doe* court determined that a defendant institution in a Section 504 case "does not have the burden, once it shows that the handicap is relevant to reasonable qualifications for readmission (or admission), of proving that . . . [the plaintiff is not an otherwise qualified handicapped person]" (666 F.2d at 777 n.7).

The *Doe* case is also noteworthy because, in deciding whether the plaintiff was "otherwise qualified," the court considered the fact that she had a recurring illness, even though it was not present at the time of the readmission decision. This was an appropriate factor to consider because the illness could reappear and affect her performance after readmission:

> The crucial question to be resolved in determining whether Doe is "otherwise qualified" under the Act is the substantiality of the risk that her mental disturbances will recur, resulting in behavior harmful to herself and others. The district court adopted as its test that she must be deemed qualified if it appeared "more likely than not" that she could complete her medical training and serve as a physician without recurrence of her self-destructive and antisocial conduct. We disagree with this standard. In our view she would not be qualified for readmission if there is a significant risk of such recurrence. It would be unreasonable to infer that Congress intended to force institutions to accept or readmit persons who pose a significant risk of harm to themselves or others, even if the chances of harm were less than 50 percent. Indeed, even if she presents any appreciable risk of such harm, this factor could properly be taken into account in deciding whether, among qualified applicants, it rendered her less qualified than others for the limited number of places available. In view of the seriousness of the harm inflicted in prior episodes, NYU is not required to give preference to her over other qualified applicants who do not pose any such appreciable risk at all [666 F.2d at 777].

Doe is thus the first major case to deal directly with the special problem of disabling conditions that are recurring or degenerative. The question posed by such a case is this: To what extent must the university assume the risk that an applicant capable of meeting program requirements at the time of admission may be incapable of fulfilling these requirements at a later date because of changes in his or her disabling conditions? *Doe* makes clear that universities may weigh such risks in making admission or readmission decisions and may consider an applicant unqualified if there is "significant risk" of recurrence (or degeneration) that would incapacitate the applicant from fulfilling program requirements. This risk factor thus becomes a relevant consideration for both parties in carrying their respective burdens of proof in Section 504 litigation. In appropriate cases, where there is medical evidence for doing so, universities may respond to the plaintiff's prima facie case by substantiating the risk of recurrence or degeneration that would render the applicant unqualified. The plaintiff would then have to demonstrate that his condition is sufficiently stable or, if it is not, that any change during his enrollment as a student would not render him unable to complete program requirements.

Another case interpreting Section 504 in light of *Davis* is *Kling v. County of Los Angeles,* 633 F.2d 876 (9th Cir. 1980), 769 F.2d 532 (9th Cir. 1985), *reversed without opin.,* 474 U.S. 936 (1985). The apppellate court granted a preliminary injunction admitting the plaintiff, who suffered from Crohn's disease, into the defendant's school of nursing pending the completion of litigation. The school did not argue that the plaintiff failed to meet its admissions requirements but rather that, because of her disability, she would miss too many classes. In rejecting the school's argument, the court relied on the opinion of the plaintiff's physician that she would be able to complete the program and that hospitalization, if necessary, could be planned to minimize interruptions in her schooling. The appellate court remanded the case to the district court, directing it to grant a preliminary injunction.

The district court, however, determined that the plaintiff had been properly denied admission to the college, and denied damages. In its second opinion, the appellate court said that the plaintiff was otherwise qualified and that damages were appropriate. It again remanded the case for calculation of damages.

The U.S. Supreme Court granted review and reversed the appellate court on the same day, ordering it to reconsider its ruling in light of *Anderson v. Bessemer City*, 470 U.S. 564 (1985), a case that addresses the standard for determining whether a district court's fact-finding is clearly erroneous. Three justices filed dissents to the reversal. Justice Stevens pointed out that the college's doctor had never evaluated the plaintiff on an individual basis but had made generalized assumptions about the nature of her disability, which Section 504 prohibits.

In *Doherty v. Southern College of Optometry*, 862 F.2d 570 (6th Cir. 1988), a federal appellate court considered the relationship between Section 504's "otherwise qualified" requirement and the institution's duty to provide a "reasonable accommodation" for a student with a disability. The plaintiff—a student with retinitis pigmentosa (RP), which restricted his field of vision, and a neurological condition which affected his motor skills—asserted that the college should exempt him from recently introduced proficiency requirements related to the operation of optometric instruments. The student could not meet these requirements and claimed that they were a pretext for discrimination on the basis of disability, since he was "otherwise qualified" and therefore had the right to be accommodated.

In ruling for the school, the district court considered the "reasonable accommodation" inquiry to be separate from the "otherwise qualified" requirement; thus, in its view, the institution was obligated to accommodate only a student with a disability who has already been determined to be "otherwise qualified." The appeals court disagreed, indicating that the "inquiry into reasonable accommodation is one aspect of the 'otherwise qualified' analysis" (862 F.2d at 577). To explain the relationship, the court quoted from *Brennan v. Stewart*, 834 F.2d 1248, 1261–62 (5th Cir. 1988):

> "[I]t is clear that the phrase 'otherwise qualified' has a paradoxical quality; on the one hand, it refers to a person who has the abilities or characteristics sought by the [institution]: but on the other, it cannot refer only to those already capable of meeting all the requirements—or else no reasonable requirement could ever violate Section 504, no matter how easy it would be to accommodate handicapped individuals who cannot fulfill it. This means that we can no longer take literally the assertion of *Davis* that 'an otherwise qualified person is one who is able to meet all of a program's requirements in spite of his handicap.' The question . . . is the rather mushy one of whether some 'reasonable accommodation' is available to satisfy the legitimate interests of both the [institution] and the handicapped person" [862 F.2d at 575].

The appellate court's interpretation did not change the result in the case; since the proficiency requirements were reasonably necessary to the practice of optometry, waiver of these requirements would not have been a "reasonable accommodation." But the court's emphasis on the proper relationship between the "otherwise qualified" and "reasonable accommodation" inquiries does serve to clarify and strengthen the institution's obligation to accommodate the particular needs of students with disabilities.

In another case concerning the qualifications of a student with a disability, the court determined that the plaintiff was not qualified for admission. In *Wood v. President and Trustees of Spring Hill College*, 978 F.2d 1214 (11th Cir. 1992), the plaintiff, who had schizophrenia, attended college for one week, and alleged constructive dismissal from the college on the basis of her disability. Resting her claim on Section 504, the plaintiff said that the college's insistence that she take remedial courses was based on her disability. The college disagreed, arguing that its admission decision had been erroneous and that its request that she defer her admission for one semester while taking remedial courses was reasonable. A jury found for the college, and the plaintiff appealed.

Because the plaintiff was seeking compensatory damages, she was required to demonstrate intentional discrimination, said the appellate court, which she had not done. And although the judge should have instructed the jury to consider whether the college had acted "solely on the basis of handicap" (as articulated in 29 U.S.C. § 794(a)), the lack of objection at trial to this omission prevented its assertion on appeal. Furthermore, the plaintiff had presented no evidence that she had requested an accommodation, so there was no need for the jury to determine whether the college should have provided the plaintiff with a reasonable accommodation.

The Rehabilitation Act and the ADA also prohibit retaliation against students with disabilities who request accommodations or who file complaints alleging discrimination. In *Rothman v. Emory University*, 828 F. Supp. 537 (N.D. Ill. 1993), a former law student who had epilepsy charged that the university had failed to give him appropriate accommodations (including additional time to take examinations) and, when he complained, had retaliated by writing a letter to the Illinois Board of Law Examiners asserting that he was hostile and attributing his behavior to "chronic epilepsy." In considering the university's motion for summary judgment, the court ruled that, if proven, such actions could support a claim of discrimination and retaliation against a person with disabilities.

Students alleging discrimination on the basis of disability may file a complaint with the Education Department's Office for Civil Rights (OCR), or they may file a private lawsuit and receive compensatory damages (*Tanberg v. Weld County Sheriff*, 787 F. Supp. 970 (D. Colo. 1992)). Section 504 does not, however, provide a private right of action against the secretary of education, who enforces Section 504 (*Salvador v. Bennett*, 800 F.2d 97 (7th Cir. 1986)).

The provisions of the ADA are similar in many respects to those of Section 504, upon which, in large part, it was based. In addition to employment (see this volume, Section 3.3.2.5), Title II of the ADA prohibits discrimination in access to services or programs of a public entity (such as a public college or university), and Title III prohibits discrimination in access to places of public accommodation (such as private colleges and universities).

The ADA specifies ten areas in which colleges and universities may not discriminate against a qualified individual with a disability: eligibility criteria; modifications of policies, practices, and procedures; auxiliary aids and services; examinations and courses; removal of barriers in existing facilities; alternatives to barriers in existing facilities; personal devices and services; assistive technology; seating in assembly areas; and transportation services (28 C.F.R. § 36.301–310). The law also addresses accessibility issues for new construction or renovation of existing facilities (28 C.F.R. § 36.401–406). The law is discussed more fully in Section 7.5.4.

The law's language regarding "eligibility criteria" means that in their admissions or placement tests or other admission-related activities, colleges and universities must accommodate the needs of applicants or students with disabilities. For example, one court held that, under Section 504, the defendant medical school must provide a dyslexic student with alternate exams unless it could demonstrate that its rejection of all other testing methods was based on rational reasons (*Wynne v. Tufts University School of Medicine*, 932 F.2d 19 (1st Cir. 1991)).

Students with learning disabilities are protected by both Section 504 and the ADA, and legal challenges by such students are on the rise. For example, in *Fruth v. New York University*, 2 A.D. Cases 1197 (S.D.N.Y. 1993), a student with learning disabilities challenged the university's decision to rescind his acceptance because he had failed to attend a required summer orientation session for students with learning disabilities. Relying heavily on *Doe v. New York University* (discussed above), the court ruled that, since the student's grades were lower than the university's required grade point average, the university's insistence that the student attend the summer program was reasonable and not in violation of the ADA. It is likely that courts will continue to rely on precedent developed under Section 504 until a body of ADA law has developed.

In sum, postsecondary administrators should still proceed very sensitively in making admission decisions concerning disabled persons. *Davis* can be expected to have the greatest impact on professional and paraprofessional health care programs; beyond that, the circumstances in which physical requirements for admission may be used are unclear. Furthermore, while *Davis* relieves colleges and universities of any obligation to make substantial modifications in their program requirements, a refusal to make lesser modifications may in some instances constitute discrimination. Furthermore, interpretation of Section 504's requirements has evolved since *Davis*, as evidenced by the *Doherty* case; and in some cases the ADA provides additional protections for students. Administrators and counsel should watch for further litigation involving different factual settings, as well as for possible new policy interpretations by the Department of Education.

4.2.4.4. Age. In *Massachusetts Board of Retirement v. Murgia*, 427 U.S. 307 (1976), the U.S. Supreme Court held that age discrimination is not subject to the high standard of justification that the Equal Protection Clause of the Constitution requires, for instance, for race discrimination. Rather, age classifications are permissible if they "rationally further" some legitimate governmental objective. The Court confirmed the use of the "rational basis" standard for age discrimination cases in *City of Dallas v. Stanglin*, 490 U.S. 19 (1989), saying that this standard is "the most relaxed and tolerant form of judicial scrutiny under the Equal Protection Clause" (490 U.S. at 26).

In *Miller v. Sonoma County Junior College District*, No. C-74-0222 (N.D. Cal. 1974) (unpublished opinion decided before *Murgia*), two sixteen-year-old students won the right to attend a California junior college. The court held that the college's minimum-age requirement of eighteen was an arbitrary and irrational basis for exclusion because it was not related to the state's interest in providing education to qualified students.

In *Purdie v. University of Utah,* 584 P.2d 831 (Utah 1978), a case that can usefully be compared with *Miller,* the court considered the constitutional claim of a fifty-one-year-old woman who had been denied admission to the university's department of educational psychology. Whereas the Miller plaintiffs were allegedly too young for admission, Purdie was allegedly too old. But in both cases the courts used the Equal Protection Clause to limit the institution's discretion to base admission decisions on age. In *Purdie* the plaintiff alleged, and the university did not deny, that she exceeded the normal admissions requirements and was rejected solely because of her age. The trial court held that her complaint did not state a viable legal claim and dismissed the suit. On appeal the Utah Supreme Court reversed, holding that rejection of a qualified fifty-one-year-old would violate equal protection unless the university could show that its action bore a "rational relationship to legitimate state purposes." Since the abbreviated trial record contained no evidence of the department's admissions standards or its policy regarding age, the court remanded the case to the trial court for further proceedings.

Both public and private institutions that receive federal funds are subject to the federal Age Discrimination Act of 1975 (42 U.S.C. § 6101 et seq). Section 6101 of the Act, with certain exceptions listed in Sections 6103(b) and 6103(c), originally prohibited "unreasonable discrimination on the basis of age in programs or activities receiving federal financial assistance." In 1978 Congress deleted the word "unreasonable" from the Act (see this volume, Section 7.5.5), thus lowering the statute's tolerance for discrimination and presumably making its standards more stringent than the Constitution's "rationality" standard used in *Purdie.* As amended and interpreted in the implementing regulations (45 C.F.R. Part 90), the Age Discrimination Act clearly applies to the admissions policies of postsecondary institutions.

The age discrimination regulations, however, do not prohibit all age distinctions. Section 90.14 of the regulations permits age distinctions that are necessary to the "normal operation" of, or to the achievement of a "statutory objective" of, a program or activity receiving federal financial assistance (see this volume, Section 7.5.5). Moreover, Section 90.15 of the regulations permits recipients to take an action based on a factor other than age—"even though that action may have a disproportionate effect on persons of different ages"—if the factor has a "direct and substantial relationship" to the program's operation or goals. The practical impact of these provisions on admissions policies is illustrated by two examples in the explanatory commentary accompanying the regulations:

1. A medical school receiving federal financial assistance generally does not admit anyone over 35 years of age, even though this results in turning away highly qualified applicants over 35. The school claims it has an objective, the teaching of qualified medical students who, upon graduation, will practice as long as possible. The school believes that this objective requires it to select younger applicants over older ones. The use of such an age distinction is *not necessary* to normal operation of the recipient's program because it does not meet the requirement of Section 90.14(b). Age of the applicant may be a reasonable

measure of a nonage characteristic (longevity of practice). This characteristic may be impractical to measure directly on an individual basis. Nevertheless, achieving a high average of longevity of practice cannot be considered a program objective for a medical school within the meaning of the Act. The "normal operation" exception is not intended to permit a recipient to use broad notions of efficiency or cost-benefit analysis to justify exclusion from a program on the basis of age. The basic objectives of the medical school involve training competent and qualified medical school graduates. These objectives are not impaired if the average length its graduates practice medicine is lowered by a fraction of a year (or even more) by the admission of qualified applicants over 35 years of age.

2. A federally assisted training program uses a physical fitness test as a factor for selecting participants to train for a certain job. The job involves frequent heavy lifting and other demands for physical strength and stamina. Even though older persons might fail the test more frequently than younger persons, the physical fitness test measures a characteristic that is *directly and substantially related* to the job for which persons are being trained and is, therefore, permissible under the Act [44 Fed. Reg. 33773-74 (June 12, 1979)].

State law also occasionally prohibits age discrimination against students. In its Fair Educational Practices statute, for example, Massachusetts prohibits age discrimination in admissions to graduate programs and vocational training institutions (Mass. Gen. Laws Ann. ch. 151C, §§ 2(d), 2A(a)).

Taken together, the Constitution, the federal law and regulations, and occasional state laws now appear to create a substantial legal barrier to the use of either maximum- or minimum-age policies in admissions. The federal Age Discrimination Act, applicable to both public and private institutions regardless of whether they receive federal funds, is the most important of these developments; administrators should watch for further implementation of this statute.

4.2.5. Affirmative action programs. Designed to increase the number of minority persons admitted to educational programs, affirmative action policies pose delicate social and legal questions. Educators have agonized over the extent to which the social goal of greater minority representation justifies the admission of less or differently qualified applicants into educational programs, particularly in the professions, while courts have grappled with the complaints of qualified but rejected nonminority applicants who claim to be victims of "reverse discrimination" because minority applicants were admitted in preference to them. Though two cases have reached the U.S. Supreme Court, *DeFunis* and *Bakke* (both discussed later), neither case established comprehensive requirements regarding affirmative action. But the varied opinions of the justices in the *Bakke* decision, 438 U.S. 265 (1978), contain valuable insight and guidance concerning the legal and social issues of affirmative action. Read together with two lower court cases (discussed below) that followed it, *Bakke* forms a baseline against which all affirmative action programs should be measured.

The legal issues can be cast in both constitutional and statutory terms and apply to both public and private institutions. The constitutional issues, pertaining only to public institutions, arise under the Fourteenth Amendment's Equal Protection Clause. The statutory issues arise under Title VI of the Civil Rights Act of 1964 and Title IX of the Education Amendments of 1972, which prohibit race and sex discrimination by public and private institutions receiving federal funds (see Sections

4.2.4.1 and 4.2.4.2) and under 42 U.S.C. § 1981, which has been construed to prohibit race discrimination in admissions by private schools whether or not they receive federal money (see Section 4.2.4.1). In the *Bakke* case, a majority of the justices agreed that Title VI uses constitutional standards for determining the validity of affirmative action programs (see 438 U.S. at 284–87, 328–41, 414–18). Standards comparable to the Constitution's would presumably also be used for any affirmative action question arising under 42 U.S.C. § 1981 or under Title IX. Thus, *Bakke* establishes the foundation for a core of uniform legal parameters for affirmative action, applicable to public and private institutions alike.[4]

Both the Title VI and the Title IX regulations address the subject of affirmative action. These regulations preceded *Bakke* and are brief and somewhat ambiguous. After *Bakke* HEW issued a "policy interpretation" of Title VI, indicating that the department had reviewed its regulations in light of *Bakke* and "concluded that no changes in the regulation are required or desirable" (44 Fed. Reg. 58509, at 58510 (Oct. 10, 1979)). In this policy interpretation, however, HEW did set forth guidelines for applying its affirmative action regulation consistent with *Bakke*.

When an institution has discriminated in the past, the Title VI and Title IX regulations require it to implement affirmative action programs to overcome the effects of that discrimination (34 C.F.R. §§ 100.3(b)(6)(i) and 100.5(i); 34 C.F.R. § 106.3(a)).[5] When the institution has not discriminated, the regulations nevertheless permit affirmative action to overcome the effects of societal discrimination (34 C.F.R. §§ 100.3(b)(6)(ii) and 100.5(i); 34 C.F.R. § 106.3(b)). The HEW policy interpretation contains guidelines for such voluntary uses of affirmative action to increase minority student enrollments.

The first case to confront the constitutionality of affirmative action admissions programs in postsecondary education was *DeFunis v. Odegaard*, 507 P.2d 1169 (Wash. 1973), *dismissed as moot*, 416 U.S. 312 (1973), *on remand*, 529 P.2d 438 (Wash. 1974). After DeFunis, a white male, was denied admission to the University of Washington law school, he filed suit alleging that less qualified minority applicants had been accepted and that, but for the affirmative action program, he would have been admitted. He claimed that the university discriminated against him on the basis of his race, in violation of the Equal Protection Clause.

The law school admissions committee had calculated each applicant's predicted first-year average (PFYA) through a formula that considered the applicant's Law School Admissions Test (LSAT) scores and junior-senior undergraduate average. The committee had attached less importance to a minority applicant's PFYA and had considered minority applications separately from other applications. Although the

---

[4]Cases and authorities are collected in Annot., "Standing to Challenge College or Professional School Admissions Program Which Gives Preference to Minority or Disadvantaged Applicants," 60 A.L.R. Fed. 612 (1982 and periodic supp.).

[5]The department, however, cannot require the institution to use admissions quotas as part of an affirmative action plan. Section 408 of the Education Amendments of 1976 (20 U.S.C. § 1232i(c)) provides that:

> It shall be unlawful for the secretary [of education] to defer or limit any federal assistance on the basis of any failure to comply with the imposition of quotas (or any other numerical requirements which have the effect of imposing quotas) on the student admission practices of an institution of higher education or community college receiving federal financial assistance.

committee accepted minority applicants whose PFYAs were lower than those of other applicants, in no case did it accept any person whose record indicated that he or she would not be able to complete the program successfully. The committee established no quotas; rather, its goal was the inclusion of a reasonable representation of minority groups. DeFunis's PFYA was higher than those of all but one of the minority applicants admitted in the year he was rejected.

The state trial court ordered that DeFunis be admitted, and he entered the law school. The Washington State Supreme Court reversed the lower court and upheld the law school's affirmative action program as a constitutionally acceptable admissions tool justified by several "compelling" state interests. Among them were the "interest in promoting integration in public education," the "educational interest . . . in producing a racially balanced student body at the law school," and the interest in alleviating "the shortage of minority attorneys—and, consequently, minority prosecutors, judges, and public officials."

When DeFunis sought review in the U.S. Supreme Court, he was permitted to remain in school pending the Court's final disposition of the case. Subsequently, in a per curiam opinion with four justices dissenting, the Court declared the case moot because, by then, DeFunis was in his final quarter of law school and the university had asserted that his registration would remain effective regardless of the case's final outcome. The Court vacated the Washington State Supreme Court's judgment and remanded the case to that court for appropriate disposition. Though the per curiam opinion does not discuss the merits of the case, Justice Douglas's dissent presents a thought-provoking analysis of affirmative action in admissions:

> The equal protection clause did not enact a requirement that law schools employ as the sole criterion for admissions a formula based upon the LSAT and undergraduate grades, nor does it prohibit law schools from evaluating an applicant's prior achievements in light of the barriers that he had to overcome. A black applicant who pulled himself out of the ghetto into a junior college may thereby demonstrate a level of motivation, perseverance, and ability that would lead a fair-minded admissions committee to conclude that he shows more promise for law study than the son of a rich alumnus who achieved better grades at Harvard. That applicant would be offered admission not because he is black but because as an individual he has shown he has the potential, while the Harvard man may have taken less advantage of the vastly superior opportunities offered him. Because of the weight of the prior handicaps, that black applicant may not realize his full potential in the first year of law school, or even in the full three years, but in the long pull of a legal career his achievements may far outstrip those of his classmates whose earlier records appeared superior by conventional criteria. There is currently no test available to the admissions committee that can predict such possibilities with assurance, but the committee may nevertheless seek to gauge it as best it can and weigh this factor in its decisions. Such a policy would not be limited to blacks, or Chicanos, or Filipinos, or American Indians, although undoubtedly groups such as these may in practice be the principal beneficiaries of it. But a poor Appalachian white, or a second-generation Chinese in San Francisco, or some other American whose lineage is so diverse as to defy ethnic labels, may demonstrate similar potential and thus be accorded favorable consideration by the committee.
>
> The difference between such a policy and the one presented by this case is that the committee would be making decisions on the basis of individual

attributes, rather than according a preference solely on the basis of race. To be sure, the racial preference here was not absolute—the committee did not admit all applicants from the four favored groups. But it did accord all such applicants a preference by applying, to an extent not precisely ascertainable from the record, different standards by which to judge their applications, with the result that the committee admitted minority applicants who, in the school's own judgment, were less promising than other applicants who were rejected. Furthermore, it is apparent that because the admissions committee compared minority applicants only with one another, it was necessary to reserve some proportion of the class for them, even if at the outset a precise number of places were not set aside. That proportion, apparently 15 to 20 percent, was chosen because the school determined it to be "reasonable," although no explanation is provided as to how that number rather than some other was found appropriate. Without becoming embroiled in a semantic debate over whether this practice constitutes a "quota," it is clear that given the limitation on the total number of applicants who could be accepted, this policy did reduce the total number of places for which DeFunis could compete—solely on account of his race [416 U.S. at 331-33].

Justice Douglas did not conclude that the university's policy was therefore unconstitutional but, rather, that it would be unconstitutional unless, after a new trial, the court found that it took account of "cultural standards of a diverse rather than a homogeneous society" in a "racially neutral" way.

Five years after it had avoided the issue in *DeFunis,* the Supreme Court considered the legality of affirmative action in *Regents of the University of California v. Bakke,* 438 U.S. 265 (1978). The plaintiff, a white male twice rejected from the medical school of the University of California at Davis, had challenged the affirmative action program that the school used to select a portion of its entering class each year that he was rejected. The particular facts concerning this program's operation were critical to its legality and were subject to dispute in the court proceedings. They are best taken from Justice Powell's opinion in the U.S. Supreme Court, in a passage with which a majority of the justices agreed:

The faculty devised a special admissions program to increase the representation of "disadvantaged" students in each medical school class. The special program consisted of a separate admissions system operating in coordination with the regular admissions process. . . .

The special admissions program operated with a separate committee, a majority of whom were members of minority groups. On the 1973 application form, candidates were asked to indicate whether they wished to be considered as economically and/or educationally disadvantaged" applicants; on the 1974 form, the question was whether they wished to be considered as members of a "minority group," which the medical school apparently viewed as "blacks," "Chicanos," "Asians," and "American Indians." If these questions were answered affirmatively, the application was forwarded to the special admissions committee. No formal definition of "disadvantaged" was ever produced, but the chairman of the special committee screened each application to see whether it reflected economic or educational deprivation. Having passed this initial hurdle, the applications then were rated by the special committee in a fashion similar to that used by the general admissions committee, except that special candidates did not have to meet the 2.5 grade point average cutoff applied to regular applicants. About one fifth of the total number of special applicants were invited for interviews in 1973 and 1974. Following each interview, the special committee assigned each special applicant a benchmark score. The special committee then presented its top choices to the general admissions committee. The latter did not rate or compare the special candidates against the general applicants but could reject recommended special candidates for failure to meet course requirements or other specific deficiencies. The special committee continued to recommend special applicants until a number prescribed by faculty vote were admitted. While the overall class size was still fifty, the prescribed number was eight; in 1973 and 1974, when the class size had doubled to 100, the prescribed number of special admissions also doubled, to sixteen.

From the year of the increase in class size—1971—through 1974, the special program resulted in the admission of twenty-one black students, thirty Mexican-Americans, and twelve Asians, for a total of sixty-three minority students. Over the same period, the regular admissions program produced one black, six Mexican-Americans, and thirty-seven Asians, for a total of forty-four minority students. Although disadvantaged whites applied to the special program in large numbers, none received an offer of admission through that process. Indeed, in 1974 at least, the special committee explicitly considered only "disadvantaged" special applicants who were members of one of the designated minority groups [438 U.S. at 272–76].

The university sought to justify its program by citing the great need for doctors to work in underserved minority communities, the need to compensate for the effects of societal discrimination against minorities, the need to reduce the historical deficit of minorities in the medical profession, and the need to diversify the student body. In analyzing these justifications, the California Supreme Court had applied a "compelling state interest" test, such as that used in *DeFunis*, along with a "less objectionable alternative test" (*Bakke v. Regents of the University of California*, 553 P.2d 1152 (Cal. 1976)). Although it assumed that the university's interests were compelling, this court held the affirmative action program unconstitutional because the university had not demonstrated that the program was the least burdensome alternative available for achieving its goals. The court suggested these alternatives:

The university is entitled to consider, as it does with respect to applicants in the special program, that low grades and test scores may not accurately reflect the abilities of some disadvantaged students, and it may reasonably conclude that although their academic scores are lower, their potential for success in the school and the profession is equal to or greater than that of an applicant with higher grades who has not been similarly handicapped.

In addition, the university may properly, as it in fact does, consider other factors in evaluating an applicant, such as the personal interview, recommendations, character, and matters relating to the needs of the profession and society, such as an applicant's professional goals. . . .

In addition to flexible admission standards, the university might increase minority enrollment by instituting aggressive programs to identify, recruit, and provide remedial schooling for disadvantaged students of all races who are interested in pursuing a medical career and have an evident talent for doing so.

Another ameliorative measure which may be considered is to increase the number of places available in the medical schools, either by allowing additional students to enroll in existing schools or by expanding the schools. . . .

None of the foregoing measures can be related to race, but they will provide for consideration and assistance to individual applicants who have suffered previous disabilities, regardless of their surname or color [553 P.2d at 1166-67].

Thus concluding that the university's program did not satisfy applicable constitutional tests, the California court held that the program operated to exclude Bakke on account of his race and ordered that Bakke be admitted to medical school. It further held that the Constitution prohibited the university from giving any consideration to race in its admissions process and enjoined the university from doing so.

The U.S. Supreme Court affirmed this decision in part and reversed it in part (438 U.S. 265 (1978)). The justices wrote six opinions (totaling 157 pages), none of which commanded a majority of the Court. Three of these opinions deserve particular consideration: (1) Justice Powell's opinion—in some parts of which various of the other justices joined; (2) Justice Brennan's opinion—in which Justices White, Marshall, and Blackmun joined (referred to below as the "Brennan group"); and (3) Justice Stevens's opinion—in which Justices Stewart, Rehnquist, and Chief Justice Burger joined (referred to below as the "Stevens group").

A bare majority of the justices, four (the "Stevens group") relying on Title VI and one (Justice Powell) relying on the Equal Protection Clause of the Fourteenth Amendment, agreed that the University of California at Davis program unlawfully discriminated against Bakke, thus affirming the first part of the California court's judgment (ordering Bakke's admission). A different majority of five justices—Justice Powell and the "Brennan group"—agreed that "the state has a substantial interest that legitimately may be served by a properly devised admissions program involving the competitive consideration of race and ethnic origin" (438 U.S. at 320), thus reversing the second part of the California court's judgment (prohibiting the consideration of race in admissions). The various opinions debated the issues of what equal protection tests should apply, how Title VI should be interpreted in this context, what the appropriate justifications for affirmative action programs are, and to what extent such programs can be race conscious. No majority agreed on any of these issues, however, except that Title VI embodies constitutional principles of equal protection.

Since the Supreme Court's decision in *Bakke,* two critically important state court decisions have applied the teachings of the *Bakke* opinions to uphold affirmative action programs of state professional schools in Washington and California. The first of these two cases was *McDonald v. Hogness,* 598 P.2d 707 (Wash. 1979). The particular facts, like the facts in *Bakke,* were singularly important to the outcome. McDonald, a white male, sought admission to the University of Washington's medical school. After being rejected, he challenged the school's admissions policy as racially discriminatory against whites.

According to its published admissions policy then in effect, the medical school considered candidates "comparatively on the basis of academic performance, medical aptitude, motivation, maturity, and demonstrated humanitarian qualities." Unlike the admissions policy at issue in *Bakke,* the University of Washington's policy did not provide for any separate treatment or consideration of minority applicants. Nor did the policy explicitly recognize race as an admission criterion. It did, however, provide that "extenuating background circumstances are considered as they relate to [the five listed] selection factors." Similarly, the guidelines given members of the school's interviewing committee listed "special considerations, including extenuating circumstances" as one of the criteria for rating applicants. According to the Washington Supreme Court's analysis of the school's admissions practices, the race of applicants could be and was considered under this criterion.

In its opinion the Washington court further described the school's admissions policy and its application to McDonald:

> Medical school personnel believe grade point average (GPA) is the best measure of academic performance, while the Medical College Admissions Test (MCAT) score is the best measure of medical aptitude. Noncognitive criteria— motivation, maturity, and demonstrated humanitarian qualities—are assessed from the applicant's file and the interview. . . .
>
> The medical school's selection process was aptly summarized by the trial court:
>
>> The committee on admissions functions simultaneously at three levels.
>>
>> Generally, the paper credentials of each applicant are reviewed independently by two members of the admissions committee. . . . Candidates considered potentially competitive . . . are invited to meet with an interview-conference committee. . . . Interview-conference committees evaluate the candidates' paper credentials and the candidates . . . and forward their evaluations to the executive committee [EXCOM] of the committee on admissions as a part of each . . . application. . . . [The EXCOM], which reviews applicants in the context of the total applicant pool, makes final determinations.
>
> The "first screen" score calculated upon receipt of an application is based on GPA and MCAT. It is the "bright-line" test for referral to the admissions committee and is considered later by admissions committee application readers and interview-conference committee members. Of the 1,703 applicants, 816 were referred to the reading committee. Interviews were granted to 546 applicants considered potentially competitive by reading committee analyses. . . .
>
> After the twenty- to thirty-minute interview, the candidate is excused and each member [of the interview-conference committee] independently places the applicant in one of four categories: (1) Unacceptable (specific deficiencies); (2) Possible (with comparative deficiencies academically and/or with regard to noncognitive features); (3) Acceptable (no deficiencies that are not balanced by other abilities, would be an average medical student); and (4) Outstanding (no apparent deficiencies, high probability of making an excellent physician and scholar). Following each interview-conference, committee staff calculate an average of the individual committee members' ratings based on a scale of 4 for "outstanding" downward through 1 for "unacceptable." The average is entered on the interview-conference summary.
>
> The Skeletal Consideration List (SCL) serves as a rough agenda for EXCOM selection meetings. Placement is determined by one's total score—first screen score plus interview-conference score—grouped again in categories 4, 3, 2, and 1. Placement in category 2 or 1 nearly always leads to application denial. McDonald averaged 2.17 on the interview and was placed in category 2. His SCL position was at the number 237 level. When corrected for "ties" of 546 candidates interviewed for 175 slots, more than 300 placed higher than McDonald. However, every black, Chicano, and American Indian placing higher than McDonald on the SCL had a lower "first screen" score than he did. On April 30, 1976, EXCOM

voted that all candidates not otherwise acted upon, which included McDonald, be considered noncompetitive for the [1976 entering] class and his application was denied [598 P.2d at 709-10].

Noting at the outset that McDonald would not have been admitted even if the race of applicants had not been considered, the court held that this fact alone[6] justified denying relief. But because of the public importance of the case and the likelihood of its recurrence, the court proceeded to address the merits of McDonald's discrimination claim. It based its analysis on the Equal Protection Clause and noted, as a majority of the justices in *Bakke* had held, that an admissions program which was consistent with the Fourteenth Amendment would also be consistent with Title VI of the Civil Rights Act of 1964.

In holding that the medical school's admissions program was constitutional, the court relied heavily on Justice Powell's opinion in *Bakke*. That opinion, according to the Washington court, discouraged the separate consideration of minority applicants but permitted race to be considered as a factor in an admissions policy when its consideration "(1) is designed to promote a compelling state interest and (2) does not insulate an applicant from competition with remaining applicants." Like Justice Powell, the Washington court acknowledged that the attainment of a diverse student body is a compelling interest because it is central to the university's academic freedom:

> The University of Washington argues that the denial of McDonald's application was an exercise of its constitutionally protected freedom to decide who shall be admitted to study. It quotes Mr. Justice Frankfurter's concurring opinion in *Sweezy v. New Hampshire*, 354 U.S. 234, 263 . . . (1957), also quoted by Mr. Justice Powell in *Bakke*, 438 U.S. at 312 . . .
>
>> It is the business of a university to provide that atmosphere which is most conducive to speculation, experiment, and creation. It is an atmosphere in which there prevail "the four essential freedoms" of a university— to determine for itself on academic grounds who may teach, what may be taught, how it shall be taught, and who may be admitted to study.
>
> Like Mr. Justice Powell, we believe that the atmosphere of "speculation, experimentation, and creation" is promoted by a diverse student body. We agree that, in seeking diversity, the U.W. medical school must be viewed "as seeking to achieve a goal that is of paramount importance in the fulfillment of its mission" (438 U.S. at 313 . . .). But though a university must have wide discretion in making admission judgments, "constitutional limitations protecting individual rights may not be disregarded" (438 U.S. at 314 . . .) [598 P.2d at 712-13 n.7].

[6]Plaintiffs in other affirmative action cases have encountered similar problems. In *Henson v. University of Arkansas*, 519 F.2d 576 (8th Cir. 1975), for example, the court affirmed the dismissal of the complaint because the petitioner had failed to show that she would have been admitted if no minority admissions program had been in effect. In the *Bakke* case, the California Supreme Court presumed that the plaintiff would have been admitted unless the defendant school could affirmatively show otherwise (553 P.2d at 1172). The U.S. Supreme Court did not address the issue (438 U.S. at 280 nn.13, 14).

The Washington court then compared the medical school's admissions program with another program—the Harvard plan—that had been cited approvingly in *Bakke,* finding the two plans similar:

> In *dicta* Mr. Justice Powell indicates that the Harvard admission plan— which, like the plan here, employs race as an admission factor—furthers a compelling state interest in diversity of the student body (438 U.S. at 316-18 . . .). Justices Brennan, White, Marshall, and Blackmun also found the Harvard plan constitutional under their approach (438 U.S. at 326 n.1 . . .). Thus, a majority of the Court find constitutional a plan without a quota or separate consideration for minority groups but where race may be a beneficial factor. The University of Washington school of medicine's admission policies and procedures have the same redeeming characteristics [598 P.2d at 713].

For further support, the Washington court also relied on the opinion of Justice Brennan's group of four justices in *Bakke* and its own earlier opinion in *DeFunis:*

> In the second *Bakke* opinion which supports the UW medical school on this issue, Justices Brennan, White, Marshall, and Blackmun pronounce the [University of California at] Davis program constitutionally valid. In their opinion, the state need only show [that the racial criterion] (1) serves an important, articulated purpose, (2) does not stigmatize any discrete group, and (3) is reasonably used in light of the program's objectives (438 U.S. at 361 . . .). The Brennan group believes Davis's goal of admitting students disadvantaged by effects of past discrimination is sufficiently important. They reasonably read Mr. Justice Powell's opinion as agreeing [that] this can constitute a compelling purpose (438 U.S. at 366 n.42 . . .).
>
> In *DeFunis v. Odegaard,* . . . 507 P.2d 1169 ([Wash.] 1973), this court rejected the argument that a state law school violated equal protection rights by denying plaintiff admission, yet accepting minority applicants with lower objective indicators than plaintiff. We stressed gross underrepresentation in law schools and the legal profession in finding an overriding interest in promoting integration in public education. We held [that] the interest in eliminating racial imbalance within public legal education is compelling (. . . 507 P.2d 1169).
>
> In the instant case, the trial court determined the school had decided that, in order to serve the educational needs of the school and the medical needs of the region, the school should seek greater representation of minorities "where there has been serious underrepresentation in the school and in the medical profession." Thus, the program furthers a compelling purpose of eliminating racial imbalance within public medical education.
>
> Furthermore, the program here meets the additional elements of the Brennan group's test. The racial classification does not stigmatize any discrete group and is reasonably used in light of its objectives [598 P.2d at 713-14].

The court in *McDonald* thus accepted the authority of both the Powell opinion and the Brennan group's opinion in *Bakke,* holding that the University of Washington plan met the tests established by each of these opinions. In so doing, the court also accepted two separate interests—attainment of a diverse student body and elimination of racial imbalance by admitting minority students disadvantaged by past societal discrimination—as compelling interests that can justify the use of affirmative action plans.

The second affirmative action case, to be read in tandem with *McDonald*, is *DeRonde v. Regents of the University of California*, 625 P.2d 220 (Cal. 1981). The plaintiff was an unsuccessful applicant for admission to King Hall, the University of California at Davis law school. Following his rejection, the plaintiff was accepted at and graduated from a different law school and was admitted to the state bar. The California court chose not to dismiss the case as moot, however, citing the need for "appellate resolution of important issues of substantial and continuing public interest."

The court first examined the operation of the law school's admissions policy:

> The record discloses that, in selecting candidates for admission to King Hall in 1975, the university relied principally on a formula which combined an applicant's previous academic grade point average (GPA) with his or her score on the standardized Law School Admissions Test (LSAT). This formula yielded a predicted first-year average (PFYA) which, it was hoped, measured, at least roughly, the applicant's potential for law study.

> Believing, however, that the foregoing formula tended to ignore other significant and relevant selection factors, the university considered several additional background elements to supplement or mitigate a lower PFYA. These factors included (1) growth, maturity, and commitment to law study (as shown by prior employment, extracurricular and community activities, advanced degrees or studies, and personal statements and recommendations); (2) factors which, while no longer present, had affected previous academic grades (such as temporary physical handicaps or disruptive changes in school or environment); (3) wide discrepancies between grades and test scores where there was indicated evidence of substantial ability and motivation; (4) rigor of undergraduate studies; (5) economic disadvantage; and (6) "ethnic minority status" contributing to diversity.

> It is the consideration by the university of the final factor, "ethnic minority status," which is the principal target of DeRonde's attack. Trial testimony established that "ethnic minority status" was defined by the university as including Asians, blacks, Chicanos, Native Americans, and Filipinos. This grouping generally corresponds to the ethnic categories defined by the federal Equal Employment Opportunity Commission in its public reports. The record reflects that the university's reasons for considering minority status were primarily twofold: First, an appreciable minority representation in the student body will contribute a valuable cultural diversity for both faculty and students; and, second, a minority representation in the legal pool from which future professional and community leaders, public and private, are drawn will strengthen and preserve minority participation in the democratic process at all levels. In short, it was believed that the individual and group learning experience is enriched with broadly beneficial consequences both to the profession and to the public at large. We carefully emphasize that, although minority status was included as one of several pertinent selection factors, the university did not employ any quota system or reserve a fixed number of positions for any minority applicants in its entering class.

> Just as a relatively low PFYA might be increased by utilization of any of the foregoing factors, alternatively, a relatively high PFYA could be reduced by considering (1) the applicant's prior schools attended, (2) the difficulty of his or her prior course of study, (3) variations in an applicant's multiple LSAT scores,

(4) the absence of any factors indicating maturity or motivation, and (5) the applicant's advanced age.

As a consequence of this formulation, in 1975 the 406 students to whom the university offered admission included 135 minority applicants, and more than 1,800 applicants, including DeRonde, were rejected. DeRonde's 3.47 GPA and 575 LSAT score produced a 2.70 PFYA. The PFYAs of successful applicants ranged from 2.24 to 3.43. Sixty-nine minority applicants were accepted with PFYAs lower than DeRonde's. On the other hand, the more than 800 unsuccessful applicants who had higher PFYAs than DeRonde included 35 minority applicants [625 P.2d at 222–23].

Noting that the *McDonald* court had employed similar analysis, the *DeRonde* court focused on the Equal Protection Clause and began its analysis by referring to Justice Powell's *Bakke* opinion. The court then compared the Davis program to the Harvard plan discussed by Justice Powell and similarly found it acceptable:

In our view the admissions procedures used by the university to select its 1975 entering class at King Hall does not vary in any significant way from the Harvard program. Minority racial or ethnic origin was one of several competing factors used by the university to reach its ultimate decision whether or not to admit a particular applicant. Each application, as contemplated by the program, was individually examined and evaluated in the light of the various positive and negative admission factors. As Justice Powell pointedly observed, the primary and obvious defect in the quota system in *Bakke* was that it *precluded* individualized consideration of every applicant without regard to race (438 U.S. at 317–18 and n.52 . . .). That fatal flaw does not appear in the admissions procedure before us. This is not a quota case. Thus, we conclude that the race-attentive admissions procedure used by the university in 1975 would have passed federal constitutional muster under the standards prescribed by Justice Powell in *Bakke* [625 P.2d at 225].

The *DeRonde* court then turned, as had the *McDonald* court, to Justice Brennan's opinion:

The Brennan opinion, representing the views of four justices, would have upheld the Davis quota system invalidated by the majority in *Bakke*. It may fairly be concluded that a race-conscious law school admissions program that did not involve a quota, *a fortiori*, would be sustained by those holding the Brennan view [625 P.2d at 225].

The court noted that the Brennan group had also explicitly approved the Harvard plan but had focused on different interests than those relied on by Powell:

Justice Brennan "agree[d] with Mr. Justice Powell that a plan like the 'Harvard' plan . . . is constitutional under our approach, at least so long as the use of race to achieve an integrated student body is necessitated by the lingering effects of past discrimination" (438 U.S. at 326, n.1 . . . ; see also 438 U.S. at 378–79 . . . (expressing the view that the Harvard plan is "no more or less constitutionally acceptable" than the Davis quota system ruled invalid by the majority)). Justice Brennan expands the foregoing requirement of a past discriminatory effect and would hold that even a racial quota system such as involved in *Bakke* was constitutional if its purpose "is to remove the disparate racial impact [the university's] actions might otherwise have and if there is reason to believe that the disparate impact is itself the product of past discrimination, whether its own or that of society at large" [625 P.2d at 225; quoting 438 U.S. at 369].

Since the *DeRonde* trial had preceded the U.S. Supreme Court's *Bakke* opinions, the question of whether the university's admissions program was "necessitated by the lingering effects of past discrimination" was neither framed nor litigated by the parties. The court nevertheless studied the record and found evidence that a race-conscious admissions program was needed to prevent a disproportionate underrepresentation of minorities at King Hall. The primary evidence was the testimony of a former dean of the law school, who "stressed that if admission selection was based solely upon numbers (i.e., GPA and LSAT scores), 'the greatest bulk of the minority applicants' would be excluded." The court then looked to the Brennan opinion to develop a nexus between past societal discrimination and present underrepresentation of minorities:

> Finally, the existence of a nexus between past discrimination and present disproportionate academic and professional underrepresentation was fully acknowledged in the Brennan opinion itself, wherein it was readily assumed that societal discrimination against minorities has impaired their access to equal educational opportunity. As the opinion states, "Davis clearly could conclude that the serious and persistent underrepresentation of minorities in medicine . . . *is the result of handicaps under which minority applicants labor as a consequence of a background of deliberate, purposeful discrimination against minorities in education and in society generally,* as well as in the medical profession (438 U.S. at 370-71 . . .). . . . Judicial decrees recognizing discrimination in public education in California testify to the fact of widespread discrimination suffered by California-born minority applicants. . . . The conclusion is inescapable that applicants to medical school must be few indeed who endured the effects of *de jure* segregation, the resistance to *Brown I* [*Brown v. Board of Education,* 347 U.S. 483 (1954)], or the equally debilitating pervasive private discrimination fostered by our long history of official discrimination, and yet come to the starting line with an education equal to whites" (438 U.S. at 372 . . . , italics added, footnotes omitted) [625 P.2d at 226].

Combining its reliance on the Brennan opinion with its reliance on the Powell opinion, the court concluded:

> Accordingly, we conclude that, whether based on the Powell reasoning of assuring an academically beneficial diversity among the student body, or on the Brennan rationale of mitigating the effects of historical discrimination, it is abundantly clear that the university's 1975 admissions program would, on its face, meet federal constitutional standards as declared by a majority of the justices of the high Court [625 P.2d at 226].

Having upheld the facial validity of the Davis law school's admissions policy, the court next considered DeRonde's argument that the policy had been unconstitutionally applied to his particular circumstances. In rejecting this argument, the court again relied heavily on the Powell opinion in *Bakke:*

> We readily acknowledge, of course, that a facially valid procedure may in its actual application produce a constitutionally discriminatory result. Indeed, Justice Powell in *Bakke* fully and fairly both raised the possibility and anticipated the answer, noting:
>
>> It has been suggested that an admissions program which considers race only as one factor is simply a subtle and more sophisticated—but no less effective—means of according racial preference than the Davis program. A facial intent to discriminate, however, is evident in petitioner's preference program and not denied in this case. *No such facial infirmity exists in an admissions program where race or ethnic background is simply one element—to be weighed fairly against other elements—in the selection process.* . . . And a court would not assume that a university, professing to employ a facially nondiscriminatory admissions policy, would operate it as a cover for the functional equivalent of a quota system. In short, *good faith would be presumed in the absence of a showing to the contrary* in the manner permitted by our cases (438 U.S. at 318–19 . . . , italics added; but see 438 U.S. at 378–79 . . . (opn. of Brennan, J.)).
>
> Again, we emphasize Justice Powell's analysis on the point because the Brennan group presumably would permit even a deliberate and systematic exclusion of white applicants if supported by the requisite showing of past discrimination.
>
> Justice Powell further observed that "So long as the university proceeds on an individualized, case-by-case basis, there is no warrant for judicial interference in the academic process. If an applicant can establish that the institution does not adhere to a policy of individual comparisons, or can show that a systematic exclusion of certain groups results, the presumption of legality might be overcome, creating the necessity of proving legitimate educational purpose" (438 U.S. at 319, n.53 . . .).
>
> The record before us is barren of any evidence showing that the university was deliberately using the challenged admissions procedure either as a "cover" for a quota system or as a means of systematic exclusion of, or discrimination against, white male applicants such as DeRonde. The trial court made no such finding. Without proof of such an intent, the university's procedures must be upheld against a claim of unlawful racial discrimination even if accompanied by some evidence of a disproportionate impact (see *Bakke*, 438 U.S. at 289, n.27 (opn. of Powell, J.); *Arlington Heights v. Metropolitan Housing Corp.* (1977), 429 U.S. 252, 264–66 . . .).
>
> Moreover, the evidence fails to support a finding of such disproportionate impact. The record does reflect that, between 1971 and 1977, the percentage of minorities in the entering classes at King Hall has been substantial, fluctuating from a low of 22.78 percent in 1971 to a high of 41.6 percent in 1976. From this arithmetic, DeRonde argues that "for six straight years, from 1971 to 1976, the percentage of minority students entering classes at Davis law school averaged 33 percent of those classes. This was at a time when more *highly qualified* male Caucasians were applying for admission than in the history of the school. . . . How can there be said to exist no 'disproportionate' impact when *extremely well-qualified* male Caucasian applicants outnumber *poorly qualified* minority applicants by over three to one and are admitted to the school in a lesser percentage?" (Italics added.)

As the italicized portion of the argument reveals, the principal difficulty with DeRonde's statistical analysis is that it is based upon the faulty premise that it is only a high PFYA or GPA which truly "qualifies" an applicant for admission to law school. Yet as Justice Powell carefully explained in *Bakke,* racial or ethnic origin, as well as other "nonobjective" factors, such as personal talents, work experience, or leadership potential, properly may be considered in weighing each applicant's qualifications (438 U.S. at 317–20 . . . ; for a probing analysis of the concept of "merit" within the academic context, see Fallon, "To Each According to His Ability, from None According to His Race: The Concept of Merit in the Law of Anti-discrimination," 60 *Boston University L. Rev.* 815, 871–76 (1980)).

DeRonde's statistics may indicate that the university has placed considerable weight upon racial or ethnic factors in determining the composition of its entering law classes. Yet nothing in *Bakke* prohibits such a practice, so long as individualized personal consideration is given to the varied qualifications of each applicant. Furthermore, the fact remains that male Caucasian applicants to King Hall continue to gain admission in respectable numbers. For example, according to DeRonde's own figures, in 1975, the year of DeRonde's application, 157 white males were offered admission as opposed to 133 minority applicants. We do not know the number of white females who were admitted. These statistics alone, however, would appear to contradict any assertion that the university has adopted or implemented a systematic plan or scheme to exclude male Caucasians [625 P.2d at 226–28].

Taken together, *McDonald* and *DeRonde* add considerably to the law on affirmative action. The courts adopted the same analytical approach to determining the validity of particular admissions policies. In developing this analysis, both courts affirmed the authority of the Powell opinion and the Brennan group's opinion in *Bakke,* illustrating how these two opinions may be read together to provide a guide to the validity of affirmative action admissions plans. By accepting both opinions, the *McDonald* and *DeRonde* courts also accepted two separate justifications for implementing affirmative action: the "diverse student body" justification espoused by Powell and the "alleviation of past discrimination" justification espoused by the Brennan group.

A federal district court applied the teachings of *Bakke* and its progeny to evaluate the claim of a white male applicant to New York Law School that his rejection violated Titles VI and IX and the Equal Protection Clause. The plaintiff had applied to, and been rejected by, the law school eight times. In *Davis v. Halperin,* 768 F. Supp. 968 (E.D.N.Y. 1991), the plaintiff challenged the school's use of "diversity" as one of the criteria on which admissions decisions were made. Although the court rejected the plaintiff's sex discrimination claim, it applied strict scrutiny to his race discrimination claim, saying that the provisions of Title VI have been interpreted to proscribe discrimination that also violates the Equal Protection Clause. The court found that the plaintiff had made out a prima facie case of race discrimination because the law school had admitted minority applicants with lower LSAT scores and lower undergraduate grades than the plaintiff's.

In response to the law school's motion for summary judgment, the judge ruled that, although the law school had rebutted the plaintiff's prima facie case of race discrimination by demonstrating that it had followed an affirmative action plan, the court could not determine whether the plan's purpose was to remedy past discrimination by the law school itself (which was permissible) or to remedy past societal discrimination (which was impermissible). The court remarked:

> *Bakke* makes it clear that in the absence of prior discrimination by the university the consideration of race as one factor among many by a university admissions process is constitutional only so far as it seeks to procure for the university the educational benefits which flow from having a diverse student body [768 F. Supp. at 981].

The judge ordered the matter to be tried to a jury.

As interpreted and applied in *McDonald, DeRonde,* and *Davis,* the *Bakke* case has brought some clarity to the law of affirmative action in admissions. The legal and social issues remain sensitive, however, and administrators should involve legal counsel fully when considering any adoption or change of an affirmative action admissions policy. The following five guidelines can assist institutions in any such consideration:

1. As a threshold matter, the institution should consider whether it or the educational system of which it is a part has ever discriminated against minorities or women in its admissions policies. If any illegal discrimination has occurred, the law will require that the institution use affirmative action to the extent necessary to overcome the present effects of the past discrimination. (See the discussion in the *Bakke* opinions, 438 U.S. at 284, 328, and 414.) The limits that the *Bakke* decision places on the use of racial preferences do not apply to situations where "an institution has been found, by a court, legislature, or administrative agency, to have discriminated on the basis of race, color, or national origin. Race-conscious procedures that are impermissible in voluntary affirmative action programs may be required [in order] to correct specific acts of past discrimination committed by an institution or other entity to which the institution is directly related" (U.S. Dept. HEW, Policy Interpretation of Title VI, 44 Fed. Reg. 58509 at 58510 (Oct. 10, 1979)).

For example, in *Geier v. Alexander,* 801 F.2d 799 (6th Cir. 1986), a federal appellate court upheld a consent decree that required race-conscious recruitment and admissions practices at the formerly de jure–segregated Tennessee system of public higher education. (For a discussion of this case and its history, see Section 7.5.2.) The Department of Justice had attacked the consent decree, asserting that it denied equal protection to nonminority students because it was not victim-specific. The court applied strict scrutiny to the challenged practices, finding that the elimination of persistent racial segregation in public higher education was a "compelling state interest," that the five-year life of the consent decree was reasonable, that its goals regarding the admission of minority students were "modest," and that the plan was "narrowly tailored" to achieve the purpose of remedying prior discrimination.

2. In considering whether to employ an affirmative action program, the institution should carefully determine its purposes and objectives and make its decisions in the context of these purposes and objectives. The institution may choose one or a combination of three basic approaches to affirmative action: the uniform system, the differential system, and the preferential system. While all three systems can be implemented lawfully, the potential for legal challenge increases as the institution proceeds down the list. The potential for substantially increasing minority enroll-

ments also increases, however, so that an institution which is deterred by the possibility of legal action may also be forsaking part of the means to achieve its educational and societal goals.

3. A uniform system of affirmative action consists of changing the institution's general admissions standards or procedures so that they are more sensitively attuned to the qualifications and potential contributions of disadvantaged and minority individuals. These changes are then applied uniformly to all applicants. For example, all applicants might be given credit for work experience, demonstrated commitment to working in a particular geographical area, or overcoming handicaps or disadvantages. Such a system would thus allow all candidates—regardless of race, ethnicity, or sex—to demonstrate particular qualities that may not be reflected in grades or test scores. It would not preclude the use of numerical cutoffs where administrators believe that applicants with grades or test scores above or below a certain number should be automatically accepted or rejected. In *DeFunis* Justice Douglas discussed aspects of such a system (416 U.S. at 331–32), as did the California Supreme Court in *Bakke* (553 P.2d at 1165–66).

4. A differential system of affirmative action is based on the concept that equal treatment of differently situated individuals may itself create inequality; different standards for such individuals become appropriate when use of uniform standards would in effect discriminate against them. If, for instance, the institution determined, using appropriate psychometric procedures, that a standardized admissions test that it used was culturally biased as applied to its disadvantaged or minority applicants, it might use a different standard for assessing their performance on the test or employ some other criterion in lieu of the test.

In *Bakke* Justice Powell referred to a differential system by noting: "Racial classifications in admissions conceivably could serve a . . . purpose . . . which petitioner does not articulate: fair appraisal of each individual's academic promise in light of some bias in grading or testing procedures. To the extent that race and ethnic background were considered only to the extent of curing established inaccuracies in predicting academic performance, it might be argued that there is no 'preference' at all" (438 U.S. at 306 n.43). Justice Douglas's *DeFunis* opinion also referred extensively to differential standards and procedures:

> Professional persons, particularly lawyers, are not selected for life in a computerized society. The Indian who walks to the beat of Chief Seattle of the Muckleshoot tribe in Washington has a different culture than examiners at law schools. . . .
>
> The admissions committee acted properly in my view in setting minority applications apart for separate processing. These minorities have cultural backgrounds that are vastly different from the dominant Caucasian. Many Eskimos, American Indians, Filipinos, Chicanos, Asian Indians, Burmese, and Africans come from such disparate backgrounds that a test sensitively tuned for most applicants would be wide of the mark for many minorities. . . .
>
> I think a separate classification of these applicants is warranted, lest race be a subtle force in eliminating minority members because of cultural differences. . . .
>
> The reason for the separate treatment of minorities as a class is to make more certain that racial factors do not militate *against an applicant or on his behalf.* . . .

The key to the problem is consideration of such applications *in a racially neutral way* [416 U.S. at 334–36, 340].

To remain true to the theory of a differential system, an institution can modify standards or procedures only to the extent necessary to counteract the discriminatory effect of applying uniform standards; and the substituted standards or procedures must be designed to select only candidates whose qualifications and potential contributions are comparable to those of candidates selected under the general standards.

5. A preferential system of affirmative action is explicitly "race conscious" and allows some form of preference for minority applicants. The admissions programs at issue in the cases discussed above can be viewed, for the most part, as preferential systems. It is the preference available only to minorities that creates the reverse discrimination claim. Depending on the institution's objectives, some form of racial preference may indeed be necessary. In *Bakke* the Brennan group of justices agreed that:

> There are no practical means by which . . . [the university] could achieve its ends in the foreseeable future without the use of race-conscious measures. With respect to any factor (such as poverty or family educational background) that may be used as a substitute for race as an indicator of past discrimination, whites greatly outnumber racial minorities simply because whites make up a far larger percentage of the total population and therefore far outnumber minorities in absolute terms at every socioeconomic level. . . . Moreover, while race is positively correlated with differences in . . . [grades and standardized test] scores, economic disadvantage is not. Thus, it appears that economically disadvantaged whites do not score less well than economically advantaged whites while economically advantaged blacks score less well than do disadvantaged whites. These statistics graphically illustrate that the university's purpose to integrate its classes by compensating for past discrimination could not be achieved by a general preference for the economically disadvantaged or the children of parents of limited education unless such groups were to make up the entire class [438 U.S. at 376–77].

Preferential systems may fulfill objectives broader than those of differential systems. As *McDonald* and *DeRonde* demonstrate, the leading examples are the objectives of diversifying the student body and alleviating the effects of past institutional or societal discrimination. In a preferential system, the institution must exercise special care in determining its objectives and relating its system to them. Administrators should rely demonstrably on the institution's educational expertise and involve policy makers at the highest levels of authority over the institution. As emphasized by the court in an important pre-*Bakke* case, *Hupart v. Board of Higher Education of the City of New York*, 420 F. Supp. 1087 (S.D.N.Y. 1976):

> Every distinction made on a racial basis . . . must be justified. . . . It cannot be accomplished thoughtlessly or covertly, then justified after the fact. The defendants cannot sustain their burden of justification by coming to court with an array of hypothetical and *post facto* justifications for discrimination that has occurred either without their approval or without their conscious and formal choice to discriminate as a matter of official policy. It is not for the court to supply a rational or compelling basis (or something in between) to sustain the

questioned state action. That task must be done by appropriate state officials
before they take any action [420 F. Supp. at 1106].

The permissible types and scope of preference are also subject to continuing
debate. Under *Bakke* a preferential system that employs explicit racial or ethnic quotas is, by a 5-to-4 vote, reverse discrimination and thus prohibited. But other forms
of preference are permissible. Until the U.S. Supreme Court speaks again, the best
guideline is Justice Powell's opinion in *Bakke*. The Brennan group of justices approved of explicit, specific preferences; a fifth vote was needed to form a majority; and
of the remaining justices, only Powell acknowledged support for any form of preferential admissions system.[7] Justice Powell's opinion thus sets a boundary that administrators should stay within to reasonably ensure legality.

Although the Supreme Court has not addressed affirmative action preferences
in college admissions since *Bakke,* it has considered such preferences in the employment context and in the allocation of public funding. For example, the Supreme
Court, in *Johnson v. Transportation Agency,* 480 U.S. 616 (1987), cited with approval
Justice Powell's opinion in *Bakke* in a case upholding affirmative action plans that
allowed employers to consider "ethnicity or sex" as "a factor" in making hiring
decisions. This case is discussed in Section 3.4. And the Court, in analyzing another
voluntary affirmative action plan under the Equal Protection Clause, determined that
the "strict scrutiny" test would be applied. This case, *City of Richmond v. J. A.
Croson Co.,* is discussed in Section 3.4. Although the Court's rulings in the employment context must be interpreted with care when applied to college admissions, the
cases analyzed in Section 3.4 are clearly relevant for the determination of how affirmative action programs may lawfully be developed and implemented.

For Powell, and thus currently for administrators, the key to a lawful preference system is "a policy of individual comparisons" that "assures a measure of competition among all applicants" and does not result in any "systematic exclusion of
certain groups" on grounds of race or ethnicity from competition for a portion of the
places in a class (see 438 U.S. at 319 n.53). In such a system, "race or ethnic background may be deemed a 'plus' in a particular applicant's file" as long as it is only
"one element—to be weighed fairly against other elements—in the selection process.
. . . A court would not assume that a university, professing to employ [such] a racially
nondiscriminatory admissions policy, would operate it as a cover for the functional
equivalent of a quota system" (438 U.S. at 317–18). (As discussed above, Powell's
model of a constitutional preference policy is the Harvard plan, a copy of which is
set out in an appendix to his opinion.)

But affirmative action programs that reserve a certain number of slots for
minority applicants, or that evaluate minority applicants only against each other and
not against the entire group of applicants, may run afoul of the Constitution and/

---

[7]The position of the other four justices is not entirely clear. Justice Stevens's opinion
expressing their views can be read both broadly and narrowly. He stated that, under Title VI,
"race cannot be the basis of excluding anyone from participation in a federally funded program," suggesting that all racial preferences may be unlawful. But he also stated that "the
question whether race can ever be used as a factor in an admissions decision is not an issue in
this case, and . . . discussion of that issue is inappropriate." If this issue is indeed left open,
possibly one or more of these four justices or their successors will in the future accept some
form of racial consideration in admissions.

or Title VI. In 1992 the U.S. Department of Education and the University of California at Berkeley entered an agreement whereby the law school at Berkeley agreed to halt its practice of separating applicants by race into separate pools for admissions purposes. The law school had admission goals for each minority or ethnic group, and had separate waiting lists by ethnic/minority group as well. Berkeley, and other law schools as well, now require admissions committee members to read and evaluate a random group of applicants, rather than having particular individuals evaluate and make admissions decisions only for minority applicants (S. Jaschik, "2 Law Schools Scale Back Affirmative-Action Programs as Education Dept. Continues Scrutiny of Such Plans," *Chron. Higher Educ.*, Dec. 16, 1992, A19–A20).

Institutions should also take care that they do not exclude certain underrepresented groups from their affirmative action programs. The Office for Civil Rights ruled that a decision by the state of Connecticut to exclude Asians and Native Americans from programs to recruit and retain minority students violated Title VI. The ruling was based on an examination of representation of students from these groups at each institution, rather than the statewide figures that had been used to justify the exclusion. Asian groups had argued that their exclusion was based on stereotypes (S. Jaschik, "Affirmative-Action Ruling on Connecticut Called a 'Big Step' for Asian Americans," *Chron. Higher Educ.*, May 19, 1993, A19).

By following the five guidelines presented in this section, and by tailoring its affirmative action program to recent concerns articulated by the Office for Civil Rights, an institution—with the active involvement of legal counsel—can maximize the elbow room it has to make policy choices about affirmative action. By carefully considering and justifying its choice under these guidelines, the institution can reasonably ensure that even an express preferential system will meet constitutional and statutory requirements.

For a thoughtful discussion of affirmative action in admissions, see R. O'Neil, "Preferential Admissions Revisited: Some Reflections on *DeFunis* and *Bakke,* 14 *J. Coll. & Univ. Law* 423 (1987).

4.2.6. Readmission. The readmission of previously excluded students can pose additional legal problems for postsecondary institutions. Although the legal principles in Section 4.2 apply generally to readmissions, the contract theory (Section 4.2.3) may assume added prominence, because the student-institution contract (see Section 4.1.3) may include provisions concerning exclusion and readmission. The principles in Sections 4.6 through 4.8 may also apply generally to readmissions where the student challenges the validity of the original exclusion.

Institutions should have an explicit policy on readmission, even if that policy is simply "Excluded students will never be considered for readmission." An explicit readmission policy can give students advance notice of their rights, or lack of rights, concerning readmission and, where readmission is permitted, can provide standards and procedures to promote fair and evenhanded decision making. If the institution has an explicit admissions policy, administrators should take pains to follow it, especially since its violation could be considered a breach of contract. Similarly, if administrators make an agreement with a student concerning readmission, they should firmly adhere to it. *Levine v. George Washington University,* C.A. (Civil Action) 8230-76 (D.C. Super. Ct. 1976), for instance, concerned a medical student who had done poorly in his first year but was allowed to repeat the year, with the stipulation that he would be excluded for a "repeated performance of marginal quality." On the second try, he passed all his courses but ranked low in each. The school excluded him. The court used contract principles to overturn the exclusion, finding that the school's subjective and arbitrary interpretation of "marginal quality," without prior notice to the student, breached the agreement between student and school. In contrast, the court in *Giles v. Howard University*, 428 F. Supp. 603 (D.D.C. 1977), held that the university's refusal to readmit a former medical student was not a breach of contract, because the refusal was consistent with the "reasonable expectations" of the parties.

The California case of *Paulsen v. Golden Gate University* illustrates the flexibility that courts may accord institutions in devising and applying readmission standards; at the same time, the case illustrates the legal and practical difficulties an institution may encounter if it has no written readmission policy or does not administer its policy evenhandedly. The plaintiff in *Paulsen* had been excluded from law school at the end of his third year and petitioned the school to be allowed to attend for another year to make up his deficiencies. The school ultimately permitted him to continue on the condition that he could not receive a degree, but only a "certificate of attendance," no matter how high his grades were. After attending for a fourth year and removing his deficiencies, the student sued for a degree. The trial court ordered the institution to award the degree, and the intermediate appellate court affirmed (156 Cal. Rptr. 190 (Cal. Ct. App. 1979)). This court found that the school "apparently maintained an unwritten policy" of permitting deficient students to continue for an extra year but that no other students who had done so had been subjected to the "no-degree" condition. On this basis, the intermediate appellate court held for the student because the no-degree condition was "arbitrary, a manifest abuse of discretion, and an unreasonable discrimination between students."

On further appeal in *Paulsen*, the California Supreme Court reversed the intermediate appellate court (159 Cal. Rptr. 858 (Cal. 1979)). Although the school had allowed other students to return for an additional year without imposing the "no-degree" condition, the Court noted, none of the other students had "flunked out," as Paulsen had.

> The imposition of reasonable conditions on the readmission of academically disqualified students was apparently a regular practice of Golden Gate. Although the no-degree condition may have been novel at the time, this fact in itself does not demonstrate its impermissibility. The only unacceptable conditions are those imposed for reasons extraneous to a student's qualifications for a degree (*Shuffer v. Board of Trustees*, 67 Cal. App. 3d 208, 220, 136 Cal. Rptr. 527). Here, there was an obvious relationship between Paulsen's special fourth-year program, even if unique, and his remarkably unsatisfactory academic record [159 Cal. Rptr. at 862].

Even though the institution ultimately prevailed, a written and consistently adhered-to readmission policy might have saved it from the uncertainties of having others guess about the bases for its decisions.

Another case, decided in 1980, illustrates the importance of carefully considering the procedures to be used in making readmission decisions. In *Evans v. West Virginia Board of Regents*, 271 S.E.2d 778 (W. Va. 1980), a student in good standing at a state school of osteopathic medicine had been granted a one-year leave of absence because of illness. When he sought reinstatement two months after termination of the leave, he was informed that because of his lateness he would have to reapply for admission. He did so but was rejected without explanation. The West Virginia Supreme Court of Appeals found that the student was "not in the same class as an original applicant to a professional school." Nor was he in the same position as a student who had been excluded for academic reasons, since "nothing appears of record even remotely suggesting his unfitness or inability to complete the remainder of his education." Rather, since he had voluntarily withdrawn after successfully completing two and a half years of his medical education, the student had a "reasonable expectation that he would be permitted to complete his education." He thus had "a sufficient property interest in the continuation and completion of his medical education to warrant the imposition of minimal due process protections." The court prescribed that the following procedures be accorded the student if the school again sought to deny him readmission: "(1) a formal written notice of the reasons should he not be permitted to continue his medical education; (2) a sufficient opportunity to prepare a defense to the charges; (3) an opportunity to have retained counsel at any hearings on the charges; (4) a right to confront his accusers and present evidence on his own behalf; (5) an unbiased hearing tribunal; and (6) an adequate record of the proceedings" (271 S.E.2d at 781).

The appellate court in *Evans* did not indicate the full terms of the school's policies regarding leave of absence and readmission or the extent to which these policies were put in writing. Perhaps, as in *Paulsen*, other schools in the defendant's position may avoid legal hot water by having a clear statement of their policies, including any procedural protections that apply and the consequences of allowing a leave of absence to expire.

Although private institutions would not be subject to the Fourteenth Amendment due process reasoning in *Evans*, they should nevertheless note the court's assertion that readmission decisions encompass different considerations and consequences than original admission decisions. Even private institutions may therefore choose to clothe readmission decisions with greater procedural safeguards than they apply to admission decisions. Moreover, private institutions, like public institutions, should clearly state their readmission policies in writing and coordinate them with their policies on exclusion and leaves of absence.

Once such policies are stated in writing, or if the institution has a relatively consistent practice of readmitting former students, contract claims may ensue if the institution does not follow its policies. For discussion of an unsuccessful contract claim by a student seeking readmission to medical school, see *North v. State of Iowa*, discussed in Section 4.2.1.

Students may also allege that denials of readmission are grounded in disability or race discrimination. In *Anderson v. University of Wisconsin*, 841 F.2d 737 (7th Cir. 1988), a black former law student sued the university when it refused to readmit him for a third time because of his low grade point average. To the student's race discrimination claim, the court replied that the law school had consistently readmitted black students with lower grades than those of whites it had readmitted; thus, no systemic race discrimination could be shown against black students. With regard to the plaintiff's claim that the law school had refused to readmit him, in part, because of his alcoholism, the court determined that Section 504 requires a plaintiff to demonstrate that he is "otherwise qualified" before relief can be granted. Given the plaintiff's inability to maintain the minimum grade point average required for retention, the court determined that the plaintiff was not "otherwise qualified," and ruled that "[l]aw schools may consider academic prospects and sobriety when deciding whether an applicant is entitled to a scarce opportunity for education" (841 F.2d at 742). For analysis of this case, see Comment, "*Anderson v. University of Wisconsin:* Handicap and Race Discrimination in Readmission Procedures," 15 *J. Coll. & Univ. Law* 431 (1989).

Sec. 4.3. Financial Aid

4.3.1. General principles. The legal principles affecting financial aid have a wide variety of sources. Some principles apply generally to all financial aid, whether awarded as scholarships, assistantships, loans, fellowships, preferential tuition rates, or in some other form. Other principles depend on the particular source of funds being used and thus may vary with the aid program or the type of award. Sections 4.3.2 through 4.3.7 discuss the principles, and specific legal requirements resulting from them, that present the most difficult problems for financial aid administrators. This section discusses more general principles affecting financial aid.

The principles of contract law may apply to financial aid awards, since an award once made may create a contract between the institution and the aid recipient. Typically, the institution's obligation is to provide a particular type of aid at certain times and in certain amounts. The student recipient's obligation depends on the type of aid. With loans the typical obligation is to repay the principal and a prescribed rate of interest at certain times and in certain amounts. With other aid the obligation may be only to spend the funds for specified academic expenses or to achieve a specified level of academic performance in order to maintain aid eligibility. Sometimes, however, the student recipient may have more extensive obligations—for instance, to perform instructional or laboratory duties, play on a varsity athletic team, or provide particular services after graduation. The defendant student in *State of New York v. Coury,* 359 N.Y.S.2d 486 (N.Y. Sup. Ct. 1974), for instance, had accepted a scholarship and agreed, as a condition of the award, to perform internship duties in a welfare agency for one year after graduation. When the student did not perform the duties, the state sought a refund of the scholarship money. The court held for the state because the student had "agreed to accept the terms of the contract" and had not performed as the contract required.[8]

The law regarding gifts, grants, wills, and trusts may also apply to financial

---

[8]Illustrative cases are collected in Annot., "Construction and Application of Agreement by Medical or Social Work Student to Work in Particular Position or at Particular Location in Exchange for Financial Aid in Meeting Costs of Education," 83 A.L.R.3d 1273 (1978 plus periodic supp.). State age-of-majority laws (regarding a parent's obligation to support a child) are an important supplement to general contract law principles. These laws help the institution determine whether it should contract with the parent or the child in awarding aid and whether it should take parental resources into account in computing the amount of aid. Administrative and policy problems in determining dependency and possible constitutional challenges to the dependency determinations of public institutions are discussed in D. J. Hanson, *The Lowered Age of Majority: Its Impact on Higher Education* (Association of American Colleges, 1975), 11–17, 36–37.

aid awards. These legal principles would generally require aid administrators to adhere to any conditions that the donor, grantor, testator, or settlor placed on use of the funds. But the conditions must be explicit at the time of the gift. For example, in *Hawes v. Emory University*, 374 S.E.2d 328 (Ga. Ct. App. 1988), a scholarship donor demanded that the university return the gift, asserting that the funds had not been dispersed as agreed upon. The court found the contribution to be a valid gift without any indication that its use was restricted in the way the donor later alleged.

Funds provided by government agencies or private foundations must be used in accordance with conditions in the program regulations, grant instrument, or other legal document formalizing the transaction. Section 4.3.2 illustrates such conditions in the context of federal aid programs.[9]

Similarly, funds made available to the institution under wills or trusts must be used in accordance with conditions in the will or trust instrument, unless those conditions are themselves illegal. Conditions that discriminate by race, sex, or religion have posed the greatest problems in this respect. If a public agency or entity has compelled or affirmatively supported the imposition of such conditions, they will usually be considered to violate the federal Constitution's Equal Protection Clause (see *In re Wilson*, 465 N.Y.S.2d 900 (N.Y. 1983)).[10] But if such conditions appear in a privately established and administered trust, they will usually be considered constitutional because no state action is present. In *Shapiro v. Columbia Union National Bank and Trust Co.* (this volume, Section 1.4.2), for instance, the Supreme Court of Missouri refused to find state action to support a claim of sex discrimination lodged against a university's involvement in a private trust established to provide scholarships exclusively for male students. Even in the absence of state action, however, a discriminatory condition in a private trust may still be declared invalid if it violates one of the federal nondiscrimination requirements applicable to federal fund recipients (see Sections 4.3.3 and 4.3.4).[11]

Conditions in testamentary or inter vivos trusts can sometimes be modified by a court under the cy pres doctrine. In *Howard Savings Institution v. Peep*, 170 A.2d 39 (N.J. 1961), Amherst College was unable to accept a trust establishing a scholarship loan fund, because one of its provisions violated the college's charter. The provision, stipulating that recipients of the funds had to be "Protestant" and "Gentile," was deleted by the court. Similarly, in *Wilbur v. University of Vermont*, 270 A.2d 889 (Vt. 1970), the court deleted a provision in a financial aid trust that had placed numerical restrictions on the size of the student body at the university's college of arts and sciences. In each case the court found that the dominant purpose of the person establishing the trust could still be achieved with the restriction removed. As the court in the *Peep* case explained:

---

[9]For trusts generally, see G. T. Bogert, *Trusts* (6th ed., West, 1987). For wills, see T. E. Atkinson, *Wills* (2d ed., West, 1985). For grants, see R. B. Cappalli, *Rights and Remedies Under Federal Grants* (Bureau of National Affairs, 1979).

[10]Cases analyzing gender restrictions in charitable gifts or trusts are collected in Annot., "Validity of Charitable Gift or Trust Containing Gender Restrictions on Beneficiaries," 90 A.L.R.4th 836 (1991 and periodic supp.).

[11]The relevant cases are collected in Annot., "Validity and Effect of Gift for Charitable Purposes Which Excludes Otherwise Qualified Beneficiaries Because of Their Race or Religion," 25 A.L.R.3d 736 (1969 plus periodic supp.).

> The doctrine of *cy pres* is a judicial mechanism for the preservation of a charitable trust when accomplishment of the particular purpose of the trust becomes impossible, impracticable, or illegal. In such a situation, if the settlor manifested an intent to devote the trust to a charitable purpose more general than the frustrated purpose, a court, instead of allowing the trust to fail, will apply the trust funds to a charitable purpose as nearly as possible to the particular purpose of the settlor [170 A.2d at 42].

Given the numerous legal and public relations issues involved in institutional fund-raising and gift acceptance, administrators should develop a clear policy on the acceptance of gifts. For assistance with the development of such a policy, see F. S. Smith, *Looking the Gift Horse in the Mouth* (National Association of College and University Attorneys, 1993).

A third relevant body of legal principles is that of constitutional due process. These principles apply generally to public institutions; they also apply to private institutions when those institutions make awards from public funds (see Section 1.5.2). Since termination of aid may affect both "property" and "liberty" interests (see Section 3.6.2.1) of the student recipients, courts may sometimes require that termination be accompanied by some form of procedural safeguard. *Corr v. Mattheis*, 407 F. Supp. 847 (D.R.I. 1976), for instance, involved students who had had their federal aid terminated in midyear, under a federal "student unrest" statute, after they had participated in a campus protest against the Vietnam War. The court found that the students had been denied a property interest in continued receipt of funds awarded to them, as well as a liberty interest in being free from stigmas foreclosing further educational or employment opportunities. Termination thus had to be preceded by notice and a meaningful opportunity to contest the decision. In other cases, if the harm or stigma to students is less, the required procedural safeguards may be less stringent. Moreover, if aid is terminated for academic rather than disciplinary reasons, procedural safeguards may be almost nonexistent, as courts follow the distinction between academic deficiency problems and misconduct problems drawn in Section 4.8.3.

In *Conrad v. University of Washington*, 834 P.2d 17 (Wash. 1992), the Washington Supreme Court ruled that student athletes do not have a constitutionally protected property interest in the renewal of their athletic scholarships. The court reversed a lower court's finding that the students, who had been dropped from the football team after several instances of misconduct, had a property interest in renewal of their scholarships. The financial aid agreements that the students had signed were for one academic year only, and did not contain promises of renewal. The supreme court interpreted the financial aid agreements as contracts that afforded the students the right to *consideration* for scholarship renewal and—citing *Board of Regents v. Roth* (see this volume, Sections 3.6.2 and 3.6.2.1)—refused to find a "common understanding" that athletic scholarships were given for a four-year period. Furthermore, the court said, the fact that both the university and the NCAA provided minimal due process guarantees did not create a property interest. See generally Section 4.15.2.

Federal and state laws regulating lending and extensions of credit provide a fourth body of applicable legal constraints. At the federal level, for example, the Truth-in-Lending Act (15 U.S.C. § 1601 et seq.) establishes various disclosure requirements for loans and credit sales (see R. Rohner and J. L. Greenfield, *The Law of*

Truth in Lending (Warren, Gorham, and Lamont, 1984 and supp.)). Such provisions are of concern not only to institutions with typical loan programs but also to institutions with credit plans allowing students or parents to defer payment of tuition for extended periods of time. The federal Truth-in-Lending Act, however, exempts National Direct Student Loans (now Perkins Loans), and Guaranteed Student Loans (now Federal Family Education Loans) (see Section 4.3.2) from its coverage (15 U.S.C. § 1603(6)).

As tuition increases have outpaced the rate of inflation and tax law changes have depressed the incentives for savings, state policy makers have looked for other ways to help parents finance their children's college education. One strategy that has received substantial attention in recent years is the creation of prepaid tuition plans by individual colleges and also by some states. For example, a few institutions adopted a program whereby parents of a baby could pay a specified amount to the institution at the time the child was born; later, if the child was admitted, no tuition would be due. If the child was not admitted or did not wish to attend, the payment would be returned with little or no interest. Several states have adopted such plans as well. For example, in 1987 Michigan adopted a prepaid tuition plan that promised to pay four years of tuition at a state institution (or the equivalent amount if the child attended college elsewhere) for a one-time payment by the parents. The funds were put into a trust fund, which invested the money. The assumption underlying the plan was that the investment would produce the anticipated returns and that tuition increases would be stable. That assumption later proved to be incorrect. (For a description of state prepaid tuition plans, see A. Gunn, "Economic and Tax Aspects of Prepaid-Tuition Plans, 17 *J. Coll. & Univ. Law* 243 (1990).) Michigan suspended its program in 1991 ("Michigan Halts Sale of Prepaid-Tuition Contracts While It Re-Examines the Pioneering Program," *Chron. Higher Educ.*, Oct. 2, 1991, A29). Ohio did the same in the spring of 1994 (J. Carmona, "Ohio Agency Suspends Marketing of Prepaid-Tuition Program," *Chron. Higher Educ.*, Apr. 27, 1994, A24). For a critical analysis of the Michigan program, see J. S. Lehman, "Social Irresponsibility, Actuarial Assumptions, and Wealth Redistribution: Lessons About Public Policy from a Prepaid Tuition Program," 88 *Mich. L. Rev.* 1035 (1990). For further discussion of these plans, see J. T. Philipps, "Federal Taxation of Prepaid College Tuition Plans," 47 *Washington and Lee L. Rev.* 291 (1990).

Because of the potential problems with prepaid tuition plans, other states have adopted savings plans rather than prepayment plans. In many states parents are encouraged to buy general-obligation bonds issued by the state for the construction and renovation of campus buildings, with the interest tax free. In other states parents who buy U.S. Savings Bonds pay no state income tax on interest from the bonds if the funds are used to pay college tuition. (Interest on the bonds is also free of federal tax.) Critics of the savings plans say that they will not produce enough income to meet tuition costs; but others believe that plans that encourage saving for college costs will reduce pressure on federal student loan funds and will benefit students who need financial assistance the most.

Given the multitude of tax (see Section 7.3.1), contract, and other legal complications of prepaid tuition plans, institutions should consult with counsel knowledgeable in these areas of the law before implementing such plans.

The gap between the cost of inflation and tuition increases, combined with growing pressure to reduce expenditures for federal student assistance, may lead to changes in student financial assistance policies, both by colleges and by the federal and state governments. Some colleges, when making admission decisions, are considering the prospective student's ability to pay; others are targeting students from affluent communities for heavy recruitment. (See S. Lubman, "A 'Student of Value' Means a Student Who Can Pay the Rising Cost of College," *Wall Street Journal,* Jan. 5, 1994, B1.) Although these are policy rather than legal issues for the moment, they may have legal consequences (such as the antitrust case against the Ivy League, discussed in Section 7.2.13).[12]

4.3.2. Federal programs. The federal government provides or guarantees many millions of dollars per year in student aid for postsecondary education through a multitude of programs.[13] To protect its investment and ensure the fulfillment of national priorities and goals, the federal government imposes many requirements on the way institutions manage and spend funds under federal programs. Some are general requirements applicable to student aid and all other federal assistance programs. Others are specific programmatic requirements applicable to one student aid program or to a related group of such programs. These requirements constitute the most prominent—and, critics would add, most prolific and burdensome—source of specific restrictions on an institution's administration of financial aid.

The most prominent general requirements are the nondiscrimination requirements discussed in Section 4.3.3, which apply to all financial aid, whether or not it is provided under federal programs. In addition, the federal Buckley Amendment (FERPA) (discussed in Section 4.16.1) imposes various requirements on the institution's record-keeping practices for all the financial aid that it disburses. The FERPA regulations, however, do partially exempt financial aid records from nondisclosure requirements. They provide that an institution may disclose personally identifiable information from a student's records, without the student's consent, to the extent "necessary for such purposes as" determining the student's eligibility for financial aid, determining the amount of aid and the conditions that will be imposed regarding it, or enforcing the terms or conditions of the aid (34 C.F.R. §99.31(a)(4)).

Also important are the Student Assistance General Provisions, 34 C.F.R. Part 668, which impose numerous requirements on institutions participating in programs under the Higher Education Act (see below). In determining a student's eligibility for federal assistance, for instance, an institution must ascertain whether the student is in default on any federally subsidized or guaranteed loan or owes a refund on a federal

---

[12]Changing interpretations of parental support obligations may also affect the way colleges calculate a candidate's eligibility for financial aid. See, for example, Annot., "Responsibility of Noncustodial Divorced Parent to Pay for, or Contribute to, Costs of Child's College Education," 99 A.L.R.3d 322 (1980 and periodic supp.). See also Annot., "Postsecondary Education as Within Nondivorced Parent's Child-Support Obligation," 42 A.L.R.4th 819 (1985 and periodic supp.).

[13]The number, complexity, and volatility of federal student assistance programs pose legal issues far too lengthy and specialized for treatment in this volume. The discussion in this section relies heavily on D. Rigney & B. Butler, *Federal Student Financial Aid Programs: A Legal and Policy Overview* (National Association of College and University Attorneys, 1993). The annotated bibliography provides additional sources for individuals wishing more detailed information about these programs.

grant, and must obtain the student's "financial aid transcript(s)" from other institutions to assist in this task (34 C.F.R. § 668.19).

Most of the federal student aid programs were created by the Higher Education Act of 1965 (20 U.S.C. §§ 1070–1099), which has been reauthorized and amended regularly since that year. The most recent changes are contained in the Higher Education Amendments of 1992 (106 Stat. 448, 479–652). Financial aid programs for students in health-related studies are in the Public Health Service Act (42 U.S.C. § 294 et seq. and § 297 et seq.), and programs for veterans and military personnel are in various acts (see Section 7.4.2). The names and requirements of most of the federal student assistance programs have changed in recent years, and Congress has imposed new accountability requirements on colleges and universities participating in these programs.

The specific programmatic restrictions on federal student aid depend on the particular program. There are various types of programs, with different structures, by which the government makes funds available:

1. Programs in which the federal government provides funds to institutions to establish revolving loan funds—as in the Perkins Loan program (20 U.S.C. §§ 1087aa–1087hh, 34 C.F.R. Part 674) and the Health Professions Student Loan program (42 U.S.C. § 294m et seq., 42 C.F.R. Part 57, subpart C).

2. Programs in which the government grants funds to institutions, which in turn grant them to students—as in the Supplemental Educational Opportunity Grant (SEOG) program (20 U.S.C. §§ 1070b–1070b-3, 34 C.F.R. Part 676) and the Federal Work-Study (FWS) program (42 U.S.C. §§ 2751–2756(a), 34 C.F.R. Part 675).

3. Programs in which students receive funds from the federal government—as in the GI Bill program (38 U.S.C. §§ 3451–4393, 38 C.F.R. 21.1020) and the Pell Grant program (20 U.S.C. §§ 1070a–1070a-6, 34 C.F.R. Part 690).

4. Programs in which students receive funds from the federal government through the states—as in the State Student Incentive Grant (SSIG) program (20 U.S.C. § 1070c et seq., 34 C.F.R. Part 692).

5. Programs in which students receive funds from third-party lenders—as in the Federal Family Educational Loan program (20 U.S.C. §§ 1071–1087-2, 34 C.F.R. Part 682).

The Federal Family Educational Loan program includes three types of loans: Stafford Loans, Supplemental Loans for Students (SLS), and Parent Loans for Undergraduate Students (PLUS). Each of these programs has its own regulations placing various requirements on the institution. The new Federal Direct Student Loan Program (FDSLP) allows institutions, authorized by the Department of Education, to lend money directly to students through loan capital provided by the federal government (20 U.S.C. § 1087a et seq., 34 C.F.R. Part 685). Since the Direct Loan Program eliminates third-party lenders, the Department of Education hopes eventually to replace the FFEL program with this program in order to streamline the student loan system.

A further complication was interjected into the student aid arena in 1982, when Congress amended the Military Selective Service Act to require that students subject to the draft registration law must register as a condition to receiving federal student financial aid (Defense Department Authorization Act of 1983, 50 U.S.C. § 462(f)). In order to receive aid, students required to register with Selective Service must file statements with the institutions they attend, certifying that they have complied with the Selective Service law and regulations. The validity of this requirement was upheld by the U.S. Supreme Court in *Selective Service System v. Minnesota Public Interest Research Group*, 468 U.S. 841 (1984). Regulations implementing the certification requirement are published in 34 C.F.R. Part 668 (the Student Assistance General Provisions), §§ 668.31–668.36.

A section of the Higher Education Act of 1965 requires institutions that participate in any federal financial aid program to make certain information "readily available, through appropriate publications and mailings," to prospective or enrolled students upon request and to the secretary of education on an annual basis (20 U.S.C. § 1092(a)). This information must accurately describe (1) the financial aid programs available to students and the methods by which such aid is distributed; (2) the forms, applications, and other requirements that students must complete to be eligible for such assistance; (3) the responsibilities of students receiving such assistance; and (4) the personnel who can assist students with questions regarding financial assistance (20 U.S.C. § 1092(a)(1)(A–D, H)). The institution also must provide other information, such as the cost of attendance (tuition, fees, books and supplies, room and board, and related items); its refund policy; the services available to students with disabilities; the institution's standards for "satisfactory progress" toward completion of the degree; and the terms and conditions under which students receiving guaranteed student loans or direct loans may receive deferral of repayment or partial cancellation under the Peace Corps Act or the Domestic Volunteer Service Act, or for comparable full-time community service (20 U.S.C. § 1092(a)(1)(E–G, I–L). Regulations implementing these requirements are found at 34 C.F.R. §§ 668.41–668.45 (the Student Assistance General Provisions). In 1990 the Student Right-to-Know and Campus Security Act (Pub. L. No. 101-542, 104 Stat. 2381, 20 U.S.C. § 1001 et seq. (also discussed in Section 4.15.1 of this volume)) added more consumer information requirements to the Higher Education Act, particularly with regard to graduation rates of the student body and of athletes, and crime statistics. Regulations interpreting these new disclosure requirements will also be published in 34 C.F.R. Part 668.

The Immigration Reform and Control Act of 1986 (IRCA) amended Section 484 of the Higher Education Act of 1965 (20 U.S.C. § 1091) by conditioning the receipt of Title IV funds upon compliance with a number of verification measures affecting both educational institutions and alien students. In order to participate in grants, loans, or work assistance under Title IV programs, all students must declare in writing that they are U.S. citizens or in an immigrant status that does not preclude their eligibility (§ 121(a)(3) of IRCA). The IRCA also requires alien students to provide the institution with documentation that clearly establishes their immigration status, and further requires the institution to verify the status of such students with the Immigration and Naturalization Service (INS). Institutions are prohibited from denying, delaying, reducing, or terminating Title IV funds without providing students with a reasonable opportunity to establish eligibility. If, after complying with these requirements, an institution determines that a student is ineligible, it is required to deny or terminate Title IV aid and provide the student with an opportunity for a hearing concerning his or her eligibility (34 C.F.R. § 668.136(c)).

Another provision of the Higher Education Act requires an institution participating in the federal student aid program to certify "that it has in operation a drug abuse prevention program that is determined by the institution to be accessible to any officer, employee, or student at the institution" (20 U.S.C. § 1094(a)(10)). Similar provisions in other laws that place obligations on institutions receiving federal funds are discussed in Section 7.4.3.

Much of the controversy surrounding the federal student aid programs has concerned the sizable default rates on student loans, particularly at institutions that enroll large proportions of low-income students. Several reports issued by the General Accounting Office have been sharply critical of the practices of colleges, loan guaranty agencies, and the Department of Education in implementing the federally guaranteed student loan programs. As a result, substantial changes have been made in the laws and regulations related to eligibility, repayment, and collection practices. Collection requirements of federal student loan programs are discussed in Section 4.3.7.3. For an extensive analysis of many troubling issues facing federal student aid policy makers, see R. P. Guerre, Note, "Financial Aid in Higher Education: What's Wrong, Who's Being Hurt, What's Being Done," 17 *J. Coll. & Univ. Law* 483 (1991).

Institutions that participate in federal student aid programs must have their program records audited annually by an independent auditor. Regulations regarding the conduct of the audit and reporting requirements appear at 34 C.F.R. § 668.24.

Finally, the program integrity provisions of the Higher Education Act Amendments of 1992 (Pub. L. No. 102-325) will enable the federal government, with the help of state entities, to keep a watchful eye over institutions participating in federal financial aid programs. These provisions allow State Postsecondary Review Entities (SPREs) to perform an extensive review of institutions identified by the Department of Education, through statutory criteria, as troublesome. One trigger for this extensive review is an institution's high default rate on federal student loans (20 U.S.C. § 1099a et seq.).

Federal courts have refused to authorize a private right of action under the Higher Education Act for students to enforce the financial assistance laws and regulations (see, for example, *L'ggrke v. Benkula,* 966 F.2d 1346 (10th Cir. 1992)). But a few courts have permitted students to use state common law fraud or statutory consumer protection theories against the Education Department, colleges, or lenders when the college either ceased operations or provided a poor-quality education (see, for example, *Tipton v. Alexander,* 768 F. Supp. 540 (S.D. W. Va. 1991)). (See Section 7.4.4 for a discussion of private rights of action under federal funding laws.) One court has permitted students to file a RICO (Racketeer Influenced Corrupt Organization) claim against a trade school, alleging mail fraud. In *Gonzalez v. North American College of Louisiana,* 700 F. Supp. 362 (S.D. Tex. 1988), the students charged that the school induced them to enroll and to obtain federal student loans, which they were required to repay. The school was unaccredited; and, after it had obtained the federal funds in the students' name, it closed and did not refund the loan proceeds.

Federal student aid programs bring substantial benefits to students and the colleges they attend. Their administrative and legal requirements, however, are complex and change constantly. It is imperative that administrators and counsel become conversant with these requirements and monitor legislative and judicial developments closely.

4.3.3. Nondiscrimination. The legal principles of nondiscrimination apply to the financial aid process in much the same way they apply to the admissions process (see Sections 4.2.4 and 4.2.5). The same constitutional principles of equal protection apply to financial aid. The relevant statutes and regulations on nondiscrimination—Title

VI, Title IX, Section 504, the Americans with Disabilities Act, and the Age Discrimination Act—all apply to financial aid, although Title IX's and Section 504's coverage and specific requirements for financial aid are different from those for admissions. And affirmative action poses difficulties for financial aid programs similar to those it poses for admissions programs.

Of the federal statutes, Title IX has the most substantial impact on the financial aid programs and policies of postsecondary institutions. The regulations (34 C.F.R. § 106.37), with four important exceptions, prohibit the use of sex-restricted scholarships and virtually every other sex-based distinction in the financial aid program. Section 106.37(a)(1) prohibits the institution from providing "different amount[s] or types" of aid, "limit[ing] eligibility" for "any particular type or source" of aid, "apply[ing] different criteria," or otherwise discriminating "on the basis of sex" in awarding financial aid. Section 106.37(a)(2) prohibits the institution from giving any assistance, "through solicitation, listing, approval, provision of facilities, or other services," to any "foundation, trust, agency, organization, or person" that discriminates on the basis of sex in providing financial aid to the institution's students. Section 106.37(a)(3) also prohibits aid eligibility rules that treat the sexes differently "with regard to marital or parental status."

The four exceptions to this broad nondiscrimination policy permit sex-restricted financial aid under certain circumstances. Section 106.37(b) permits an institution to "administer or assist in the administration of" sex-restricted financial assistance that is "established pursuant to domestic or foreign wills, trusts, bequests, or similar legal instruments or by acts of a foreign government." Institutions must administer such awards, however, in such a way that their "overall effect" is "nondiscriminatory" according to standards set out in Section 106.37(b)(2). Section 106.31(c) creates the same kind of exception for sex-restricted foreign-study scholarships awarded to the institution's students or graduates. Such awards must be established through the same legal channels specified for the first exception, and the institution must make available "reasonable opportunities for similar [foreign] studies for members of the other sex." The third exception, for athletic scholarships, is discussed in Section 4.15.2. A fourth exception was added by an amendment to Title IX included in the Education Amendments of 1976. Section 412(a)(4) of the amendments (20 U.S.C. § 1681(a)(9)) permits institutions to award financial assistance to winners of pageants based on "personal appearance, poise, and talent," even though the pageant is restricted to members of one sex.

Section 504 of the Rehabilitation Act of 1973 (see this volume, Section 7.5.4), as implemented by the Department of Education's regulations, restricts postsecondary institutions' financial aid processes as they relate to disabled persons. Section 104.46(a) of the regulations (34 C.F.R. Part 104) prohibits the institution from providing "less assistance" to qualified disabled students, from placing a "limit [on] eligibility for assistance," and from otherwise discriminating or assisting any other entity to discriminate on the basis of disability in providing financial aid. The major exception to this nondiscrimination requirement is that the institution may still administer financial assistance provided under a particular discriminatory will or trust, as long as "the overall effect of the award of scholarships, fellowships, and other forms of financial assistance is not discriminatory on the basis of handicap" (34 C.F.R. § 104.46(a)(2)).

The Americans with Disabilities Act also prohibits discrimination on the basis of disability in allocating financial aid. Title II, which covers state and local government agencies, applies to public colleges and universities that meet the definition of a state or local government agency. The regulations prohibit institutions from providing a benefit (here, financial aid) "that is not as effective in affording equal opportunity . . . to reach the same level of achievement as that provided to others" (34 C.F.R. § 35.130(b)(1)(iii)). Both public and private colleges and universities are covered by Title III as "places of public accommodation" (34 C.F.R. § 36.104), and are prohibited from limiting the access of individuals with disabilities to the benefits enjoyed by other individuals (34 C.F.R. § 36.202(b)).

Regulations interpreting the Age Discrimination Act of 1975 (42 U.S.C. § 6101 et seq.) (see Section 7.5.5 of this volume) include the general regulations applicable to all government agencies dispensing federal aid as well as regulations governing the federal financial assistance programs for education. These regulations are found at 34 C.F.R. Part 110, and were published at 58 Fed. Reg. 40194 (July 27, 1993).

The regulations set forth a general prohibition against age discrimination in "any program or activity receiving Federal financial assistance" (34 C.F.R. § 110.10(a), but permit funding recipients to use age as a criterion if the recipient "reasonably takes into account age as a factor necessary to the normal operation or the achievement of any statutory objective of a program or activity" (34 C.F.R. § 110.12) or if the action is based on "reasonable factors other than age," even though the action may have a disproportionate effect on a particular age group (34 C.F.R. § 110.13). With respect to the administration of federal financial aid, the regulations would generally prohibit age criteria for the receipt of student financial assistance.

The affirmative action/reverse discrimination dilemma first hit the financial aid area in *Flanagan v. President and Directors of Georgetown College,* 417 F. Supp. 377 (D.D.C. 1976). The law school at Georgetown had allocated 60 percent of its financial aid for the first-year class to minority students, who constituted 11 percent of the class. The remaining 40 percent of the aid was reserved for nonminorities, the other 89 percent of the class. Within each category, funds were allocated on the basis of need; but, because of Georgetown's allocation policy, the plaintiff, a white law student, received less financial aid than some minority students, even though his financial need was greater. The school's threshold argument was that this program did not discriminate by race because disadvantaged white students were also included within the definition of minority. The court quickly rejected this argument:

> Certain ethnic and racial groups are automatically accorded "minority" status, while whites or Caucasians must make a particular showing in order to qualify. . . . Access to the "favored" category is made more difficult for one racial group than another. This in itself is discrimination as prohibited by Title VI as well as the Constitution [417 F. Supp. at 382].

The school then defended its policy as part of an affirmative action program to increase minority enrollment. The student argued that the policy discriminated against nonminorities in violation of Title VI of the Civil Rights Act (see this volume, Section 7.5.2). The court sided with the student:

> Where an administrative procedure is permeated with social and cultural factors (as in a law school's admission process), separate treatment for "minor-

ities" may be justified in order to insure that all persons are judged in a racially neutral fashion.

But in the instant case, we are concerned with the question of financial need, which, in the final analysis, cuts across racial, cultural, and social lines. There is no justification for saying that a "minority" student with a demonstrated financial need of $2,000 requires more scholarship aid than a "nonminority" student with a demonstrated financial need of $3,000. To take such a position, which the defendants have, is reverse discrimination on the basis of race, which cannot be justified by a claim of affirmative action [417 F. Supp. at 384].

Although *Flanagan* broadly concludes that allotment of financial aid on an explicit racial basis is impermissible, the subsequent decision in *Bakke* (see Section 4.2.5) and its progeny may appear to provide some room for racial considerations in financial aid programs. Exactly how much room remains, however, is presently uncertain, given the *Podberesky* litigation (discussed in Section 4.3.4).

Criteria used to make scholarship awards may have discriminatory effects even if they appear facially neutral. For example, research demonstrates that women students tend to score approximately sixty points lower on the Scholastic Aptitude Test than male students do, although women's high school and college grades tend to be higher than men's. In *Sharif by Salahuddin v. New York State Education Department*, 709 F. Supp. 345 (S.D.N.Y. 1989), a class of female high school students filed an equal protection claim, seeking to halt New York's practice of awarding Regents and Empire State Scholarships exclusively on the basis of SAT scores. The plaintiffs alleged that the practice discriminated against female students. The judge issued a preliminary injunction, ruling that the state should not use SAT scores as the sole criterion for awarding scholarships. For a thorough analysis of legal and policy issues related to this issue, see K. Connor & E. J. Vargyas, "The Legal Implications of Gender Bias in Standardized Testing," 7 *Berkeley Women's Law J.* 13 (1992).

4.3.4. Minority scholarships. Many U.S. colleges and universities reserve a portion of their financial aid funds for scholarships given only to members of certain racial or ethnic groups. A 1993 study conducted by the General Accounting Office, an independent federal agency, found that 5 percent of the financial aid awards for undergraduates, and 4 percent of the financial aid funds, were given to minority students through exclusive scholarships. Although the percentages are relatively low, the study found that two-thirds of undergraduate institutions, one-third of graduate schools, and three-fourths of professional schools awarded at least one minority scholarship during the 1991–92 academic year (S. Jaschik, "Government Finds Few Scholarships Reserved for Ethnic or Racial Minorities," *Chron. Higher Educ.*, Jan. 26, 1994, A36).

The legal status of race-exclusive minority scholarships was challenged in several federal court actions. One case is particularly instructive, showing the complexity of the interplay between forbidden racial discrimination and the recognition that prior discrimination, whether by an institution or by society, has resulted in unequal educational opportunities for some individuals. In *Podberesky v. Kirwan*, 764 F. Supp. 364 (D. Md. 1991), a Hispanic student brought Title VI and equal protection challenges against the University of Maryland–College Park's Banneker

Scholarship program, which was restricted to black students. Defending the progam against strict scrutiny analysis, the university argued that the program served the compelling state interest of remedying prior de jure discrimination (see Section 7.5.2), given the fact that the state was still under order by the Office for Civil Rights to remedy its formerly segregated system of public higher education. The university also argued that its goal of diversity was served by the Banneker Scholarship program.

The district court ruled that the university had provided "overwhelming" evidence of present effects of prior discrimination, and found the program lawful without considering the university's diversity argument. The federal appeals court, however, reversed the district court in *Podberesky v. Kirwan*, 956 F.2d 52 (4th Cir. 1992). Although the appellate court agreed that the university had provided sufficient evidence of prior discrimination, it found the Office for Civil Rights' observations about the present effects of discrimination unconvincing because they had been made too long ago (between 1969 and 1985); and it ordered the district court to make new findings regarding the present effects of prior discrimination. The appellate court also noted that race-exclusive programs violate the *Bakke* precedent if their purpose is to increase diversity and not to remedy prior discrimination.

On remand the university presented voluminous evidence of the present effects of prior discrimination, including surveys of black high school students and their parents, information on the racial climate at the university, research on the economic status of black citizens in Maryland and the effect of unequal educational opportunity, and other studies. In *Podberesky v. Kirwan*, 838 F. Supp. 1075 (D. Md. 1993), the trial court found that the university had demonstrated a "strong basis in evidence" for four present effects of past discrimination: the university's poor reputation in the black community, underrepresentation of blacks in the student body, the low retention and graduation rates of black students at the university, and a racially hostile campus climate. Furthermore, the court found that the Banneker program was narrowly tailored to remedy the present effects of past discrimination because it demonstrated the university's commitment to black students, it increased the number of peer mentors and role models available to black students, it increased the enrollment of high-achieving black students, and it improved the recipients' academic performance and persistence. Less restrictive alternatives did not produce these results.

With regard to the university's evidence of the present effects of past discrimination, the court made this comment:

> It is worthy of note that the University is (to put it mildly) in a somewhat unusual situation. It is not often that a litigant is required to engage in extended self-criticism in order to justify its pursuit of a goal that it deems worthy [838 F. Supp. at 1082 n.47].

The court did not address the university's diversity argument. (As this book went to press, the appellate court again reversed the district court and held the Banneker program invalid (1994 West Law 587092 (4th Cir. 1994)).)

In December 1991, as the *Podberesky* litigation was proceeding, the U.S. secretary of education in the Bush administration, Lamar Alexander, issued a proposed Title VI policy guidance that would have required race neutrality in scholarships awarded by colleges and universities unless a court, administrative agency, or local legislative body had found present effects of past discrimination (*Nondiscrimination in Federally Assisted Programs: Title VI of the Civil Rights Act of 1964; Proposed Policy Guidance*, 56 Fed. Reg. 64548). The proposed policy guidance would have permitted colleges to use privately funded race-exclusive scholarship funds for scholarships awarded to minority students on a race-neutral basis, but would have prohibited colleges from using race as a criterion for awarding scholarships.

Shortly after the proposed policy guidance was issued, several members of Congress asked the General Accounting Office to ascertain how many students received race-exclusive scholarships and how much funding these scholarships represented. Secretary Alexander agreed to postpone the effective date of the policy guidance until the GAO report was completed. By the time the study was completed, President Clinton had replaced President Bush; and the new education secretary, Richard Riley, issued a statement on February 17, 1994, which said that college scholarships could be awarded on the basis of race to remedy past discrimination *and* to promote diversity on college campuses. The proposed guidelines permit colleges to determine on their own—without the need for court, administrative, or legislative findings—that present effects of prior discrimination exist. The policy guidelines are published at 59 Fed. Reg. 8756–8764 (Feb. 23, 1994).

After Secretary Alexander deferred the issuance of the department's policy guidance, but before the results of the GAO study were available, several white undergraduate and law students sued the department, asking the federal court to intervene into the controversy regarding the policy. In *Washington Legal Foundation v. Alexander*, 984 F.2d 483 (D.C. Cir. 1993), the students asserted that they had been discriminated against on the basis of their race because the colleges they attended offered minority-exclusive scholarships. The plaintiffs sought a declaratory judgment that Title VI prohibits federally funded colleges from giving minority-exclusive scholarships, as well as an injunction that would require the department to issue regulations prohibiting all minority scholarships.

The trial court dismissed all claims, holding that the Administrative Procedure Act did not provide a private cause of action against the department because the plaintiffs had a private right of action against their college under Title VI (see generally Section 7.5.9). Furthermore, ruled the court, the department's delay, given the requests of several congressional representatives to await the findings of the GAO report, was reasonable. The appellate court affirmed the trial court's conclusions in their entirety.

Much has been written about the legality, social need for, and effect of minority scholarships. For an account of the *Podberesky* ligitation by one of the university's attorneys, see A. H. Baida, "Not All Minority Scholarships Are Created Equal: Why Some May Be More Constitutional Than Others," 18 *J. Coll. & Univ. Law* 333 (1992). For a criticism of the Bush Administration's policy on minority scholarships, see M. A. Olivas, "Federal Law and Scholarship Policy: An Essay on the Office for Civil Rights, Title VI, and Racial Restrictions," 18 *J. Coll. & Univ. Law* 21 (1991). For an analysis that concludes that minority scholarships are not permissible to address societal discrimination but may be used to redress prior institutional discrimination, see J. A. Ward, "Comment: Race-Exclusive Scholarships: Do They Violate the Constitution and Title VI of the Civil Rights Act of 1964?" 18 *J. Coll. & Univ. Law* 73 (1991). See also J.W.D. Stokes & M. B. Pachman, "Are Race-Based Scholarships Illegal?" 69 *West's Educ. Law Rptr.* 663 (1991).

4.3.5. Discrimination against nonresidents. State institutions have often imposed significantly higher tuition fees on out-of-state students, and courts have generally permitted such discrimination in favor of the state's own residents. The U.S. Supreme Court, in the context of a related issue, said, "We fully recognize that a state has a legitimate interest in protecting and preserving the quality of its colleges and universities and the right of its own bona fide residents to attend such institutions on a preferential tuition basis" (*Vlandis v. Kline*, 412 U.S. 441, 452-53 (1973)). Not all preferential tuition systems, however, are beyond constitutional challenge.

In a variety of cases, students have questioned the constitutionality of the particular criteria used by states to determine who is a resident for purposes of the lower tuition rate.[14] In *Starns v. Malkerson*, 326 F. Supp. 234 (D. Minn. 1970), students challenged a regulation that stipulated: "No student is eligible for resident classification in the university, in any college thereof, unless he has been a bona fide domiciliary of the state for at least a year immediately prior thereto." The students argued, as have the plaintiffs in similar cases, that discrimination against nonresidents affects "fundamental" rights to travel interstate and to obtain an education and that such discrimination is impermissible under the Equal Protection Clause unless necessary to the accomplishment of some "compelling state interest." The court dismissed the students' arguments, concluding that "the one-year waiting period does not deter any appreciable number of persons from moving into the state. There is no basis in the record to conclude, therefore, that the one-year waiting period has an unconstitutional 'chilling effect' on the assertion of the constitutional right to travel." The U.S. Supreme Court affirmed the decision without opinion (401 U.S. 985 (1971)).

Other cases are consistent with *Starns* in upholding durational residency requirements of up to one year for public institutions. Courts have agreed that equal protection law requires a high standard of justification when discrimination infringes fundamental rights. But, as in *Starns*, courts have not agreed that the fundamental right to travel is infringed by durational residency requirements. Since they have also rejected the notion that access to education is a fundamental right (see *San Antonio Independent School District v. Rodriguez*, 411 U.S. 1 (1973)), courts have not applied the "compelling interest" test to durational residency requirements of a year or less. In *Sturgis v. Washington*, 414 U.S. 1057 (1973), *affirming* 368 F. Supp. 38 (W.D. Wash. 1973), the Supreme Court again recognized these precedents by affirming, without opinion, the lower court's approval of Washington's one-year durational residency statute.

However, in *Vlandis v. Kline* (cited earlier in this section), the Supreme Court held another kind of residency requirement to be unconstitutional. A Connecticut statute provided that a student's residency at the time of application for admission would remain her residency for the entire time she was a student. The Supreme Court noted that, under such a statute, a person who had been a lifelong state resident, except for a brief period in another state just prior to admission, could not reestablish Connecticut residency as long as she remained a student. But a lifelong out-of-state

---

[14]Citations to state statutes and regulations on residency determinations, and an analysis of the governance structure by which each state implements its requirements, are contained in M. A. Olivas et al., "State Residency Requirements: Postsecondary Authorization and Regulations," 13 *Coll. Law Dig.* 157, printed in *West's Educ. Law. Rptr.* (NACUA Special Pamphlet, Feb. 1983).

resident who moved to Connecticut before applying could receive in-state tuition benefits even if she had lived in the state for only one day. Because such unreasonable results could flow from Connecticut's "permanent irrebuttable presumption" of residency, the Court held that the statute violated due process. At the same time, the Court reaffirmed the state's broad discretion to use more flexible and individualized criteria for determining residency, such as "year-round residence, voter registration, place of filing tax returns, property ownership, driver's license, car registration, marital status, vacation employment," and so on. In subsequent cases the Court has explained that *Vlandis* applies only to "those situations in which a state 'purports to be concerned with [domicile but] at the same time den[ies] to one seeking to meet its test of [domicile] the opportunity to show factors clearly bearing on that issue'" (*Elkins v. Moreno*, 435 U.S. 647 (1978), quoting *Weinberger v. Salfi*, 422 U.S. 749, 771 (1975)).

Lower courts have considered other types of residency criteria, sometimes (like the Supreme Court in *Vlandis*) finding them invalid. In *Kelm v. Carlson*, 473 F.2d 1267 (6th Cir. 1973), for instance, a U.S. Court of Appeals invalidated a University of Toledo requirement that a law student show proof of employment in Ohio before being granted resident status. And in *Samuel v. University of Pittsburgh*, 375 F. Supp. 1119 (W.D. Pa. 1974), a class action brought by female married students, a federal district court invalidated a residency determination rule that made a wife's residency status dependent on her husband's residency. While the state defended the rule by arguing the factual validity of the common law presumption that a woman has the domicile of her husband, the court held that the rule discriminated on the basis of sex and thus violated equal protection principles.

Other courts (like the Supreme Court in *Starns* and in *Sturgis*) have upheld particular residency criteria against constitutional as well as state administrative law objections. In the most recent case, *Peck v. University Residence Committee of Kansas State University*, 807 P.2d 652 (Kan. 1991), the student plaintiff had applied to the defendant Residence Committee for approval to pay the lower tuition charge for Kansas resident students. The committee denied his request despite the fact that he "(1) registered to vote and voted in Kansas; (2) registered an automobile in Kansas and paid personal property tax in Kansas; (3) insured his automobile in Kansas; (4) acquired a Kansas driver's license; (5) had a checking and savings account in Kansas; and (6) registered with the selective service in Kansas" (807 P.2d at 656). The state district court overruled the committee's decision, stating that its "action in denying Peck resident status is not supported by substantial evidence." Reversing the district court, the Supreme Court of Kansas held that, although the student had established physical residence in Kansas, he had not established the requisite intent to remain permanently in Kansas after graduation. Reviewing the committee's application of eight primary and nine secondary factors set out in state regulations for use in determining intent, the court concluded that most of the student's evidence related to secondary factors, which, standing alone, were "not probative for an intent determination because many are capable of being fulfilled within a few days of arriving in Kansas." The court also rejected the student's arguments that the residency regulations were inconsistent with the authorizing state statute (Kan. Stat. Ann. §76-729(c)(4)) and that the regulations violated equal protection and procedural due process. The court therefore reinstated the findings and decision of the Residence Committee.

In addition to establishing acceptable criteria, institutions must ensure that the procedures they follow in making residency determinations will not be vulnerable to challenges. For instance, they will be expected to follow any procedures established by state statutes or administrative regulations. Their procedures also must not violate the notice requirements of the federal Due Process Clause. In *Lister v. Hoover,* 706 F.2d 796 (7th Cir. 1983), however, the court held that the Due Process Clause did not obligate the University of Wisconsin to provide students denied resident status with a written statement of reasons for the denial; see also *Michaelson v. Cox,* 476 F. Supp. 1315 (S.D. Iowa, 1979).

4.3.6. Discrimination against aliens. In *Nyquist v. Jean-Marie Mauclet,* 432 U.S. 1 (1977), the U.S. Supreme Court set forth constitutional principles applicable to discrimination against resident aliens in student financial aid programs. The case involved a New York state statute that barred resident aliens from eligibility for regents' college scholarships, tuition assistance awards, and state-guaranteed student loans. Resident aliens denied financial aid argued that the New York law unconstitutionally discriminated against them in violation of the Equal Protection Clause of the Fourteenth Amendment. The Supreme Court agreed.

The Court's opinion makes clear that alienage, somewhat like race, is a "suspect classification." Discrimination against resident aliens in awarding financial aid can thus be justified only if the discrimination is necessary in order to achieve some compelling governmental interest. The *Nyquist* opinion indicates that offering an incentive for aliens to become naturalized, or enhancing the educational level of the electorate, is not a state governmental interest sufficient to justify discrimination against resident aliens with regard to financial aid. (For a different analysis of alienage classifications, which may apply when government uses citizenship as an employment criterion, see Section 3.3.3.)

Since the case was brought against the state rather than against individual postsecondary institutions, *Nyquist's* most direct effect is to prohibit states from discriminating against resident aliens in state financial aid programs. It does not matter whether the state programs are for students in public institutions, in private institutions, or both, since in any case the state has created the discrimination. In addition, the case clearly would prohibit public institutions from discriminating against resident aliens in operating their own separate financial aid programs. Private institutions are affected by these constitutional principles only to the extent that they are participating in government-sponsored financial aid programs or are otherwise engaging in "state action" (see Section 1.5.2) in their aid programs.

It does not necessarily follow from *Nyquist* that all aliens must be considered eligible for financial aid. *Nyquist* concerned legal resident aliens and determined that such aliens as a class do not differ sufficiently from United States citizens to permit different treatment. Courts might not reach the same conclusion about temporary nonresident aliens. In *Ahmed v. University of Toledo,* 664 F. Supp. 282 (N.D. Ohio 1986), for example, the court considered a challenge to the University of Toledo's requirement that all international students purchase health insurance. Students not able to show proof of coverage were deregistered, and their financial aid was discontinued. The trial court ruled that the affected international students were not a suspect class for equal protection purposes, because only nonresident aliens were required to purchase the insurance; resident aliens were not. Since the situation was thus unlike

Nyquist, where the challenged policy had affected resident rather than nonresident aliens, the court used the more relaxed "rational relationship" standard of review for equal protection claims rather than the strict scrutiny standard (see Section 3.4) and held that the university's policy was rational and therefore constitutional. The U.S. Court of Appeals dismissed the students' appeal as moot (822 F.2d 26 (6th Cir. 1987)). In an earlier case, however, the court in *Tayyari v. New Mexico State University,* 495 F. Supp. 1365 (D.N.M. 1980), did invalidate a university policy denying reenrollment (during the Iranian hostage crisis) to Iranian students who were nonimmigrant aliens in this country on student visas. The court considered the students to be a suspect class and determined that the university's reasons for treating them differently could not pass strict scrutiny.

Despite the *Tayyari* reasoning, administrators whose institutions are subject to the *Nyquist* principles can probably comply by making sure that they do not require students to be U.S. citizens or to show evidence of intent to become citizens in order to be eligible for financial aid administered by the institution. (The U.S. Department of Education has a similar eligibility standard for the federal Stafford Loan program (34 C.F.R. § 668.7).) Institutions thus may deem temporary nonresident aliens ineligible, at least if they have no demonstrable present intention to become permanent residents. The distinction between resident and temporary nonresident aliens may be justifiable on grounds that institutions (and states) need not spend their financial aid resources on individuals who have no intention to remain in and contribute to the state or the United States. Whether institutions may also make undocumented resident aliens ineligible for financial assistance is a separate question not controlled by *Nyquist* and is discussed below.

Moreover, since *Nyquist* does not affect state residency requirements, aliens who are not state residents may still be deemed ineligible when the principles discussed in Section 4.3.5 permit it—not because they are aliens but because they are nonresidents of the state. Although state residency for aliens may be determined in part by their particular status under federal immigration law (see especially 8 U.S.C. § 1101(a)(15)), it is well to be cautious in relying on federal law. In *Elkins v. Moreno,* 435 U.S. 647 (1978), the University of Maryland had denied "in-state" status, for purposes of tuition and fees, to aliens holding G-4 nonimmigrant visas (for employees of international treaty organizations and their immediate families) under federal law. The university argued that their federal status precluded such aliens from demonstrating an intent to become permanent Maryland residents. The U.S. Supreme Court rejected this argument, holding that G-4 aliens (unlike some other categories of nonimmigrant aliens) are not incapable under federal law of becoming permanent residents and thus are not precluded from forming an intent to reside permanently in Maryland. The Court then certified to the Maryland Court of Appeals the question whether G-4 aliens or their dependents are incapable of establishing Maryland residency under the state's common law.

In "act 2" of this litigation drama, *Toll v. Moreno,* 397 A.2d 1009 (Md. 1979), *judgment vacated,* 441 U.S. 458 (1979), the Maryland court answered no to the Supreme Court's question. In the interim, however, the university had adopted a new in-state policy, which no longer used state residency as the paramount factor in determining in-state status for tuition and fees. Because the changed policy raised new constitutional issues, the Supreme Court ended act 2 by vacating the Maryland court's judgment and remanding the case to the federal district court where the *Elkins* case had begun.

After the district court invalidated Maryland's new policy and the U.S. Court of Appeals affirmed, the case returned to the U.S. Supreme Court (*Toll v. Moreno,* 458 U.S. 1 (1982)) for act 3. The Court held that the university's new policy, insofar as it barred G-4 aliens and their dependents from acquiring in-state status, violated the Supremacy Clause (Art. VI, para. 2) of the United States Constitution. The Supremacy Clause recognizes the primacy of federal regulatory authority over subjects within the scope of federal constitutional power and prevents state law from interfering with federal law regarding such subjects. Since the federal government's broad constitutional authority over immigration has long been recognized, federal law on immigration is supreme, and states may not interfere with it. Applying these principles in *Toll,* the Court reasoned:

> [Our cases] stand for the broad principle that "state regulation not congressionally sanctioned that discriminates against aliens lawfully admitted to the country is impermissible if it imposes additional burdens not contemplated by Congress." *De Canas v. Bica,* 424 U.S. 351, 358 n.6 (1976). . . .
>
> The Immigration and Nationality Act of 1952, 66 Stat. 163, as amended, 8 U.S.C. § 1101 et seq., . . . recognizes two basic classes of aliens, immigrant and nonimmigrant. With respect to the nonimmigrant class, the Act establishes various categories, the G-4 category among them. For many of these nonimmigrant categories, Congress has precluded the covered alien from establishing domicile in the United States. . . . But significantly, Congress has allowed G-4 aliens—employees of various international organizations, and their immediate families—to enter the country on terms permitting the establishment of domicile in the United States. . . . In light of Congress' explicit decision not to bar G-4 aliens from acquiring domicile, the State's decision to deny "in-state" status to G-4 aliens, *solely* on account of the G-4 alien's federal immigration status, surely amounts to an ancillary "burden not contemplated by Congress" in admitting these aliens to the United States [458 U.S. at 12–14; citations and footnotes omitted].[15]

As a result of the *Elkins/Toll* litigation, it is now clear that postsecondary institutions may not use G-4 aliens' immigration status as a basis for denying them in-state status for tuition and fees purposes. It does not follow, however, that institutions are similarly limited with respect to other categories of nonimmigrant aliens. Most nonimmigrant categories, other than G-4, are comprised of aliens who enter the United States temporarily for a specific purpose and must maintain domicile in a foreign country (see, for example, 8 U.S.C. § 1101(a)(15)(B) (temporary visitors for pleasure or business); § 1101(a)(15)(C) (aliens in transit); § 1101(a)(15)(F) (temporary foreign students); § 1101(a)(15)(H) (temporary workers); see generally this volume, Section 7.2.7). Such restrictions, not applicable to G-4s, preclude these other classes of nonimmigrant aliens from forming an intent to establish permanent residency (or

---

[15]The Court's opinion also includes alternative grounds for invalidating the university's policy—namely, that it interferes with federal tax policies under which G-4 visa holders are relieved of federal and some state and local taxes on their incomes. See 458 U.S. at 14–16.

domicile), which is required under the residency laws of most states. Thus, federal and state law would apparently still allow public institutions to deny in-state status to nonimmigrant aliens other than G-4s or to other narrow categories that are not required to maintain domicile in their home countries.

It also remains important, after *Elkins/Toll*, to distinguish between nonimmigrant (nonresident) and immigrant (resident) aliens. Because immigrant aliens, like G-4 aliens, are permitted under federal law to establish United States and state residency, denial of in-state status because of their alienage would apparently violate the federal supremacy principles relied on in *Toll* (act 3). Such discrimination against immigrant aliens is also prohibited by the Equal Protection Clause of the Fourteenth Amendment, as established in *Nyquist v. Jean-Marie Mauclet*, discussed earlier in this section.

Since the *Elkins/Toll* litigation, yet another critical distinction has emerged: the distinction between legal (immigrant or nonimmigrant) aliens and illegal (undocumented) aliens. In some circumstances the Equal Protection Clause will also protect undocumented aliens from state discrimination in the delivery of educational services. In *Plyler v. Doe*, 457 U.S. 202 (1982), for instance, the U.S. Supreme Court used equal protection principles to invalidate a Texas statute that "den[ied] to undocumented school age children the free public education that [the state] provides to children who are citizens of the United States or legally admitted aliens." Reasoning that the Texas law was "directed against children [who] can have little control" over their undocumented status, and that the law "den[ied] these children a basic education," thereby saddling them with the "enduring disability" of illiteracy, the Court held that the state's interests in protecting its education system and resources could not justify this discriminatory burden on the affected children. *Plyler* dealt with elementary education; the key question, then, is whether the case's reasoning and the equal protection principles that support it would apply to higher education as well— in particular to state policies that deny to undocumented aliens financial aid or in-state tuition status that is available to U.S. citizens and documented aliens.

This question has attracted a great deal of attention in California, where courts have wrestled with it in a complex chain of litigation. In 1983 the California legislature passed a statute providing that "[a]n alien, including an unmarried minor alien, may establish his or her residence, unless precluded by the Immigration and Nationality Act (8 U.S.C. § 1101 et seq.) from establishing domicile in the United States" (Cal. Educ. Code § 68062(h)). It was not clear how this statute would apply to undocumented aliens who had been living in California and sought to establish residency for in-state tuition purposes. At the request of the chancellor of the California State University, the attorney general of California issued an interpretation of the statute, indicating that an illegal alien's incapacity to establish residence in the United States under federal immigration law precluded that same alien from establishing residency in California for in-state tuition purposes (67 *Opinions of the Attorney General* 241 (Cal.) (1984), Opinion No. 84-101). Subsequently, the University of California and the California State University and College System formulated identical policies charging all undocumented aliens out-of-state tuition.

In *Leticia A. v. Regents of the University of California*, No. 588-982-5 (Cal. Super. Ct., Alameda County, Apr. 3, 1985), *judgment vacated*, June 10, 1985, *judgment amended and reinstated*, June 19, 1985, four undocumented alien students challenged the constitutionality of these policies on equal protection grounds. The plaintiffs had been brought into this country during their minority and had graduated from California high schools. Relying on the Supreme Court's reasoning in *Plyler*, and on the Equal Protection Clause of the *state* constitution, the *Leticia A.* court determined that "higher education is an 'important' interest in California" and that the defendants' policies can survive equal protection scrutiny only if "there is a 'substantial' state interest served by the [blanket] classification" of undocumented aliens as nonresidents. The court then compared the rationales supporting this classification and those supporting the federal immigration laws:

> The policies underlying the immigration laws and regulations are vastly different from those relating to residency for student fee purposes. The two systems are totally unrelated for purposes of administration, enforcement and legal analysis. The use of unrelated policies, statutes, regulations or case law from one system to govern portions of the other is irrational. The incorporation of policies governing adjustment of status for undocumented aliens into regulations and administration of a system for determining residence for student fee purposes is neither logical nor rational [*Leticia A.* at 9–10].

The court therefore declared the defendants' policies unconstitutional (without rendering any judgment on the validity of Section 68062(h), on which the policies were based) and ordered the defendants to determine the state residence status of undocumented students and applicants for purposes of in-state tuition in the same way as it would make that determination for U.S. citizens.

Neither defendant appealed the *Leticia A.* decision. In 1990, however, a former employee of the University of California sued that institution to require it to reinstate its pre-*Leticia* policy. The employee, Bradford, had been terminated by the University of California for his "unwillingness to comply with the ruling of the [*Leticia A.*] court." The trial court granted summary judgment in favor of the employee. On appeal, in *Regents of the University of California v. Superior Court*, 276 Cal. Rptr. 197 (Cal. Ct. App. 1990) (known as the *Bradford* case), the court reviewed the purpose and constitutionality of the defendant's pre-*Leticia A.* residency policy, as well as of Section 68062(h) itself. The court held that, as originally argued by the defendants in the *Leticia A.* litigation, Section 68062(h) "precludes undocumented alien students from qualifying as residents of California for tuition purposes." Then the court examined whether such an interpretation denied undocumented alien students the equal protection of the laws. Reasoning that undocumented aliens are commonly and legitimately denied basic rights and privileges under both state and federal law, that the university also denies the lower tuition rate to residents of other states and to aliens holding student visas, and that the state had "manifest and important" interests in extending this denial to undocumented aliens, the appellate court upheld the trial court's ruling.

Unlike the *Leticia A.* court, the appellate court in the *Bradford* case did not rely on the Supreme Court's *Plyler* decision but distinguished it on the basis of the "significant difference between an elementary education and a university education." Thus, the *Bradford* court's decision is in direct conflict with *Leticia A.* and serves to uphold the constitutionality of Section 68062(h) as well as the University of California's pre-*Leticia A.* policy. Since *Bradford*, litigation has continued in the California superior courts to work out the implementation of that decision and its application to the California State University and College System, which was not a defendant in *Bradford*. See, for example, L. Gordon, "Immigrants Face Cal. State Fee Hike," *Los Angeles Times*, Sept. 9, 1992, A3.

4.3.7. Collection of student debts. When a postsecondary institution extends financial aid to its students in the form of loans, it has the additional problem of making sure that students repay their loans according to the schedule and conditions in the loan agreement.[16] Enforcing payment of loans can involve the institution in a legal quagmire, several aspects of which are discussed in this section.

    4.3.7.1. Federal bankruptcy law. Student borrowers have often sought to extinguish their loan obligations to their institutions by filing for bankruptcy under the federal Bankruptcy Code contained in Title 11 of the *United States Code*.[17] The Bankruptcy Code supersedes all state law inconsistent with its provisions or with its purpose of allowing the honest bankrupt a "fresh start," free from the burden of indebtedness. A debtor may institute bankruptcy proceedings by petitioning the appropriate federal court for discharge of all his provable debts. Following receipt of the bankruptcy petition, the court issues an order fixing times for the filing and hearing of objections to the petition before a bankruptcy judge. Notice of this order is given to all potential creditors, usually by mail.

    Debtors may petition for bankruptcy under either Chapter 7 or Chapter 13 of the Bankruptcy Code. Under a Chapter 7 "straight" bankruptcy, debts are routinely and completely discharged unless the creditors can show reasons why no discharge should be ordered (11 U.S.C. § 727) or unless a creditor can demonstrate why its particular claim should be "excepted" from the discharge order as a "nondischargeable debt" (11 U.S.C. § 523). Chapter 13, on the other hand, provides for the adjustment of debts for debtors with regular income. After filing a Chapter 13 petition, the debtor must submit a plan providing for full or partial repayment of debts (11 U.S.C. §§ 1321–1323), and the bankruptcy court must hold a hearing and decide whether to confirm the plan (11 U.S.C. §§ 1324–1325, 1327). Prior to the hearing, the bankruptcy court must notify all creditors whom the debtor has included in the plan; these creditors may then object to the plan's confirmation (11 U.S.C. § 1324). If the plan is confirmed and the debtor makes the payments according to the plan's terms, the bankruptcy court will issue a discharge of those debts included in the plan (11 U.S.C. § 1328(a)).

    In 1976, responding to an escalation in defaults on student loans and in the number of students seeking discharge of their loans in bankruptcy, Congress amended the Higher Education Act to prohibit the discharge, under certain circumstances, of loans guaranteed or insured under the federal Guaranteed Student Loan program (20 U.S.C. § 1087-3). Subsequently, Congress replaced this provision with a broader provision, included in the Bankruptcy Reform Act of 1978. In 1979 Congress amended this new provision in order to clarify its language and correct some inequities that

---

    [16]See generally, Annot., "Rights and Obligations of Federal Government, Under 20 U.S.C.S. § 1080, When Student Borrower Defaults on Federally Insured Loan," 73 A.L.R. Fed. 303 (1985 and periodic supp.).

    [17]Because of the complexity of the law of bankruptcy, and its particular implications for the collection of student loans, a summary of the major issues is provided in this section. The discussion relies on D. Dunham & R. A. Buch, "Educational Debts Under the Bankruptcy Code," 22 *Memphis State U. L. Rev.* 679 (1992).

it had inadvertently created. As amended, the new student bankruptcy provision took effect, along with the rest of the revised Bankruptcy Code, on October 1, 1979. Further amendments were made in 1990 to extend the statutory period from five to seven years. The provision is contained in 11 U.S.C. § 523(a)(8):

> *Section 523. Exceptions to discharge:*
> (a) A discharge under Section 727, 1141, 1228(a), 1228(b), or 1328(b) of this title does not discharge an individual debtor from any debt—
>   . . .
> (8) for an educational benefit overpayment or loan made, insured, or guaranteed by a governmental unit, or made under any program funded in whole or in part by a governmental unit or nonprofit institution of higher education, or for an obligation to repay funds received as an educational benefit, scholarship or stipend, unless—
> (A) such loan, benefit, scholarship or stipend overpayment first became due more than seven years (exclusive of any applicable suspension of the repayment period) before the date of the filing of the petition; or
> (B) excepting such debt from discharge under this paragraph will impose an undue hardship on the debtor and the debtor's dependents.

The 1990 amendments also made student loans nondischargeable under Chapter 13 (11 U.S.C. § 1328(a)). For analysis of the prior version of the bankruptcy law and the problems it posed for student loan collection, see Note, "Forging a Middle Ground: Revision of Student Loan Debts in Bankruptcy as an Impetus to Amend 11 U.S.C. § 523(a)(8)," 75 *Iowa L. Rev.* 733 (1990).

Section 523(a)(8) covers loans made under any Department of Education student loan program as well as student loans made, insured, guaranteed, or funded by other "governmental units," such as state and local governments, and by nonprofit higher education institutions. Loans made by profit-making postsecondary institutions or privately owned banks (and not guaranteed or insured under a government program) are not covered by the provision and thus continue to be dischargeable. Moreover, Section 523(a)(8) applies to bankruptcies under both Chapter 7 and Chapter 13.

In re Shore, 707 F.2d 1337 (11th Cir. 1983), illustrates the broad scope of the "governmental unit" language of Section 523(a)(8). A student at Columbus College, part of the University of Georgia System, had borrowed money from the Greentree-Sevier Trust, a trust to benefit Columbus College and its students. The student sought to discharge the loan in bankruptcy, arguing that the loan was made by a trust fund rather than a governmental unit and therefore did not fall within the reach of Section 523. The court disagreed:

> Columbus College is the beneficiary of the Greentree-Sevier Trust. Columbus College made the educational loan to Shore using funds from this trust. Appellant agreed "to pay to Columbus College" the sum of the amount signed for in the space provided on the Loan Agreement. An educational loan "made by" a governmental unit within the meaning of Section 523(a)(8) is one in which a governmental unit is the lender and the holder of the loan obligation. The particular fund on which the governmental unit draws to fund the loan does not alter the definition [707 F.2d at 1339].

The student loan bankruptcy provision defuses what previously had been a major issue in Chapter 7 student bankruptcies: the issue of "provability." In *State v. Wilkes,* 41 N.Y.2d 655 (N.Y. 1977), for example (decided when the old code was in effect), a college had initiated collection procedures against a student who claimed that his prior bankruptcy had discharged his student loans (a point not made clear in the bankruptcy proceeding). The New York Court of Appeals rejected the student's claim. It held that contingencies such as a repayment plan extending over ten years, provision for termination of the debt if the student died or became disabled, and provision for reduction of the debt if the student taught in certain schools made the "ultimate amount of liability impossible to ascertain or even approximate." The debt was therefore not "provable," and because not provable it was nondischargeable.

Section 523(a)(8) obviates the need for an institution to claim lack of provability in order to prevent the discharge of student loans that have been due for less than seven years. During that period the student loan is ordinarily nondischargeable, regardless of provability. Thus, the institution no longer has the burden of filing a proof of claim and asserting lack of provability as a bar to discharge unless the debt has been due for seven years or more. Instead, Section 523(a)(8) "is intended to be self-executing and the lender or institution is not required to file a complaint to determine the nondischargeability of any student loan" (S. Rep. No. 95-989, 95th Cong., 2d Sess., reprinted in 1978 *U.S. Code Cong. & Admin. News,* 5865).[18]

Even if a student loan is nondischargeable under Chapter 7, the filing of a bankruptcy petition may nevertheless affect the institution's efforts to collect the debt. Under the Bankruptcy Code, creditors are automatically prohibited during the pendency of the bankruptcy proceedings from continuing with collection efforts (11 U.S.C. § 362). The bankruptcy judge may modify or cancel this prohibition during the proceedings, however, if the institution can show cause why such action should be taken (11 U.S.C. § 362(d)(1)).

There has been considerable litigation on the scope of the "undue hardship" exception to nondischargeability in Section 523(a)(8)(B).[19] In general, bankruptcy courts have interpreted this exception narrowly, looking to the particular facts of each case (see J. Kasel, "Running the Gauntlet of 'Undue Hardship'—The Discharge of Student Loans in Bankruptcy," 11 *Golden Gate U. L. Rev.* 457 (1981)). Primary importance has been attached to whether the student debtor's economic straits were foreseeable and within his control. Although several courts have established tests for undue hardship, the test created in *Brunner v. New York State Higher Education Services Corp.,* 831 F.2d 395 (2d Cir. 1987), has been adopted by several federal appellate courts. The three-part test requires the court to determine

1. that the debtor cannot maintain, based on current income and expenses, a "minimal" standard of living for [himself or] herself and [his or] her dependents if forced to repay the loans; and

---

[18]There may nevertheless be practical difficulties for college counsel in determining how and when to respond to a notice of the student's filing of a bankruptcy petition (see T. Ayres & D. Sagner, "The Bankruptcy Reform Act and Student Loans: Unraveling New Knots," 9 *J. Coll. & Univ. Law* 361, 385–88 (1982–83)).

[19]Cases and authorities are collected in Annot., "Bankruptcy Discharge of Student Loan on Ground of Undue Hardship Under sec. 523(a)(8) of Bankruptcy Code of 1978 (11 U.S.C.S. § 523(a)(8)(B)," 63 A.L.R. Fed. 570 (1983 and periodic supp.).

2. that additional circumstances exist indicating that this state of affairs is likely
   to persist for a significant portion of the repayment period of the student
   loans; and
3. that the debtor has made good faith efforts to repay the loans [831 F.2d at
   396].

In *In re Perkins*, 11 Bankr. Rptr. (*Bankruptcy Reporter*) 160 (D. Vt. 1980), the
court held that the undue hardship exception "is not intended to shelter the debtor
from self-imposed hardship resulting from a reluctance to live within his means." *In
re Price*, 1 Bankr. Rptr. 768 (D. Haw. 1980), held that the bankrupt's sending three
children to private schools constituted a failure to live within means; and *In re Brock*,
4 Bankr. Rptr. 491 (S.D.N.Y. 1980), held that "the necessity of careful budgeting is
not evidence of undue hardship." Even unemployment or underemployment will not
suffice for a hardship discharge when future prospects are bright (see, for example,
In re Hemmen, 7 Bankr. Rptr. 63 (N.D. Ala. 1980); *In re Tobin*, 18 Bank. Rptr. 560
(W.D. Wis. 1982)). In *Matter of Robinson*, 999 F.2d 1132 (7th Cir. 1993), the court
ruled that, because the debtor's hardship was temporary, he had not met the test for
undue hardship. On the other hand, courts will consider such factors as insufficient
income to maintain a minimum standard of living, excessive unavoidable debts and
expenses, and the failure of education to increase the debtor's earning power. In *In
re Diaz*, 5 Bankr. Rptr. 253 (W.D.N.Y. 1980), for instance, the bankruptcy judge
discharged the student loans of a debtor with personal and family medical problems
and poor employment prospects; and in *In re Birden*, 17 Bankr. Rptr. 891 (E.D. Pa.
1982), the bankruptcy judge, in deciding to discharge the student loans, considered
the presence of large nondischargeable obligations for taxes and child support payments. A debtor's longstanding and serious mental and emotional problems convinced a judge that her situation met the "undue hardship" test in *Kline v. United
States*, 155 Bankr. Rptr. 762 (W.D. Mo. 1993).

Cosigners and nonstudents (such as parents) who take out federally guaranteed
student loans also appear to be covered by the nondischargeability provisions of the
bankruptcy law. In *Webb v. Student Loan Funding Corp.*, 151 Bankr. Rptr. 804 (N.D.
Ohio 1992), the parent, the obligor on a federal PLUS loan (Parent Loans for Undergraduate Students) taken out for her daughter's college education, argued that she
had not received a direct benefit from the loan (her daughter, not she, had received
the education). The court disagreed, stating that the parent did receive at least an
indirect benefit, and that this reason was insufficient to exempt PLUS loans from the
clear intent of the bankruptcy law's statutory language. Similarly, in *In re Hammar-
strom*, 95 Bankr. Rptr. 160 (N.D. Cal. 1989), the court held that the exception to
dischargeability in Section 523(a)(8) unambiguously applied to the debtor, whether
or not the debtor received a direct benefit from the loan. And in *In re Pelkowski*, 990
F.2d 737 (3d Cir. 1993), the court overturned a lower court ruling that the loan was
not an "educational" loan if the debtor was a cosigner or guarantor of the loan for
the student borrower. After analyzing the legislative history of the amendments to the
Bankruptcy Code related to federal student loans, the court concluded that Congress
had acted for the purpose of reducing debtor abuse of the federal student loan program; extending the nondischargeability provisions to nonstudent debtors would
further the intent of Congress in this regard. For analysis of this issue, see Note, "Non-

Student Co-Signers and Sec. 523(a)(8) of the Bankruptcy Code," 1991 *U. Chicago Legal Forum* 357 (1991).

Students may be precluded from further borrowing under the federal student loan program if they have had earlier loans discharged in bankruptcy. In *Elter v. Great Lakes Higher Education Corp.*, 95 Bankr. Rptr. 618 (E.D. Wis. 1989), a bankruptcy court allowed a state guaranty agency to deny a new educational loan to such students. For analysis of this issue, see Comment, "*Elter v. Great Lakes Higher Education Corporation:* State Agencies That Grant Educational Loans May Discriminate Against Student Bankrupts Who Default on Prior Educational Loans," 17 *J. Coll. & Univ. Law* 261 (1990).

For suggestions regarding appropriate institutional actions in collecting student loans from debtors in bankruptcy (written prior to the amendments to Chapter 13), see R. W. Rieder, "Student Loans and Bankruptcies: What Can a University-Creditor Do?" 56 *West's Educ. Law Rptr.* 691 (1989).

4.3.7.2. Withholding certified transcripts. Like its predecessor, the revised (1978) Bankruptcy Code generally forbids creditors from resorting to the courts or other legal process to collect debts discharged in bankruptcy (11 U.S.C. § 524(a)(2)). Under the old Bankruptcy Act, however, there was considerable debate on whether informal means of collection, such as withholding certified grade transcripts from a student bankrupt, were permissible. In *Girardier v. Webster College*, 563 F.2d 1267 (8th Cir. 1977), decided under the old Act, the court held that the Act did not prohibit private institutions from withholding certified transcripts. Besides reducing the scope of this problem by limiting the dischargeability of student loans, the 1978 Bankruptcy Act appears to have legislatively overruled the result in the *Girardier* case.

The provision of the old Act that was applied in *Girardier* prohibited formal attempts, by "action" or "process," to collect discharged debts. In the 1978 Act, this provision was amended to read (with further amendments in 1984):

> A discharge in a case under this title . . . operates as an injunction against the commencement or continuation of an action, the employment of process, or an act, to collect, recover or offset any such debt as a personal liability of the debtor, whether or not discharge of such debt is waived [11 U.S.C. § 524(a)(2)].

The language, especially the phrase "or an act," serves to extend the provision's coverage to informal, nonjudicial means of collection, thus "insur[ing] that once a debt is discharged, the debtor will not be pressured in any way to repay it" (S. Rep. No. 95-989, 95th Cong., 2d Sess., reprinted in 1978 *U.S. Code Cong. Admin. News* 5866).

The 1978 Act also added the words "any act" to a related provision, Section 362(a)(6), which prohibits creditors from attempting to collect debts during the pendency of a bankruptcy proceeding. Bankruptcy courts have construed this new language to apply to attempts to withhold certified transcripts (see *In re Lanford*, 10 Bank. Rptr. 132 (D. Minn. 1981)). This legislative change, together with the change in Section 524(a)(2), apparently prevents postsecondary institutions from withholding transcripts both during the pendency of a bankruptcy proceeding and after the discharge of debts, under either Chapter 7 or Chapter 13.[20]

---

[20]Public institutions may also be restrained by Section 525 of the Bankruptcy Code, which forbids "governmental units" from discriminating against bankrupts in various ways—

The charge typically made when a college refuses to provide a transcript for a student who has filed a bankruptcy petition is that the college has violated the "automatic stay" provisions of the Bankruptcy Code (11 U.S.C. § 362) (*In re Parham,* 56 Bankr. Rptr. 531 (E.D. Va. 1986); *Parraway v. Andrews University,* 50 Bankr. Rptr. 316 (W.D. Mich. 1986)). Even though the debt is nondischargeable, the college may not withhold the transcript during the automatic stay period (*California State University, Fresno v. Gustafson,* 934 F.2d 216 (9th Cir. 1990); *In re Weiner Merchant, Debtor,* 958 F.2d 738 (6th Cir. 1992)). For analysis of the limitations that the bankruptcy law places on colleges with regard to withholding transcripts, see P. Tanaka, *The Permissibility of Withholding Transcripts Under the Bankruptcy Law* (National Association of College and University Attorneys, 1986).

The situation is different if, as in the majority of situations, the student has not filed a bankruptcy petition. Nothing in the Bankruptcy Code would prohibit postsecondary institutions from withholding transcripts from such student debtors. Moreover, the code does not prevent institutions from withholding transcripts if the bankruptcy court has refused to discharge the student loan debts. In *Johnson v. Edinboro State College,* 728 F.2d 163 (3d Cir. 1984), for example, the bankruptcy court had declared a former student to be bankrupt but did not discharge his student loans because he had failed to prove that a hardship existed. Nevertheless, the bankruptcy court had held that the college was obligated to issue the student a transcript because of the Bankruptcy Code's policy to guarantee debtors "fresh starts." When the college appealed, the Court of Appeals overruled the bankruptcy court, holding that when a bankrupt's student loans are nondischargeable under Section 523(a)(8), the policy of that section overrides the code's general fresh-start policy. The college therefore remained free to withhold transcripts from the student.

Similarly, nothing in the federal Family Educational Rights and Privacy Act (FERPA) concerning student records (see this volume, Section 4.16.1) prohibits institutions from withholding certified transcripts from student debtors. If an institution enters grades in a student's records, FERPA would give the student a right to see and copy the grade records. But FERPA would not give the student any right to a *certified* transcript of grades, nor would it obligate the institution to issue a certified transcript or other record of grades to third parties (see *Girardier v. Webster College,* 421 F. Supp. 45, 48 (D. Mo. 1976)).

The most likely legal difficulty would arise under the federal Constitution's Due Process Clause, whose requirements limit only public institutions (see Section 1.5.2). The basic question is whether withholding a certified transcript deprives the student of a "liberty" or "property" interest protected by the Due Process Clause (see generally Section 3.6.2). If so, the student would have the right to be notified of the withholding and the reason for it, and to be afforded some kind of hearing on the sufficiency of the grounds for withholding. Courts have not yet defined liberty or property interests in this context. But under precedents in other areas, if the institution has regulations or policies entitling students to certified transcripts, these reg-

---

apparently including denial of transcripts (see *In re Howren,* 10 Bankr. Rptr. 303 (D. Kan. 1980)).

ulations or policies could create a property interest that would be infringed if the institution withholds a transcript without notice or hearing. And withholding certified transcripts from a student applying to professional or graduate school, or for professional employment, may so foreclose the student's freedom to pursue educational or employment opportunities as to be a deprivation of liberty. Thus, despite the lack of cases on point, administrators at public institutions should consult counsel before implementing a policy of withholding transcripts for failure to pay loans, or for any other reason.[21]

4.3.7.3. Debt collection requirements in federal student loan programs. The Perkins Loan (formerly NDSL) program's statute and regulations contain several provisions affecting the institution's debt collection practices.[22] The statute provides (in 20 U.S.C. § 1087cc(4)), that where a note or written agreement evidencing such a loan has been in default for at least six months despite the institution's due diligence in attempting to collect the debt, the institution, under certain circumstances, may assign its rights under the note or agreement to the United States. If the debt is thereafter collected by the United States, the amount, less 30 percent, is returned to the institution as an additional capital contribution. The Perkins Loan regulations (34 C.F.R. § 674.41 et seq.) provide that each institution maintaining a Perkins Loan fund must accept responsibility for, and use due diligence in effecting, collection of all amounts due and payable to the fund. Due diligence includes the following elements: (1) providing borrowers with information about changes in the program that affect their rights and responsibilities (34 C.F.R. § 674.41(a)); (2) conducting exit interviews with borrowers when they leave the institution and providing them with copies of repayment schedules that indicate the total amount of the loans and the dates and amounts of installments as they come due (34 C.F.R. § 674.42(a)); (3) keeping a written record of interviews and retaining signed copies of borrowers' repayment schedules (34 C.F.R. § 674.42(a)(3)); and (4) staying in contact with borrowers both before and during the repayment period, in order to facilitate billing and keep the borrowers informed of changes in the program that may affect rights and obligations (34 C.F.R. § 674.42(b)). The institution must also use specified "billing procedures" (set forth at 34 C.F.R. § 674.43), including statements of notice and account and demands for payment on accounts that are more than fifteen days overdue. If an institution is unable to locate a borrower, it must conduct an address search (34 C.F.R. § 674). If the billing procedures are unsuccessful, the institution must either obtain the services of a collection agency or utilize its own resources to compel repayment

---

[21]Cases and authorities are collected in Annot., "Validity, Construction, and Application of Statutes, Regulations, or Policies Allowing Denial of Student Loans, Student Loan Guarantees, or Educational Services to Debtors Who Have Had Student Loans Scheduled in Bankruptcy," 107 A.L.R. Fed. 192 (1992 and periodic supp.).

[22]Besides the student loan requirements discussed in this section, there is a growing body of state and federal statutes and court decisions on debt collection practices. See generally *Uniform Consumer Credit Code*, § 5.108(5) (Commissioners on Uniform State Laws, 1974); R. Geltzer & L. Woocher, "Debt Collection Regulation: Its Development and Direction for the 1980's," 37 *Business Lawyer* 1401 (1982); S. Rester, "Regulating Debt Collection Practices: The Social and Economic Needs and a Congressional Response," 11 *Clearing-House Rev.* 547 (1977); M. Greenfield, "Coercive Collection Tactics—An Analysis of the Interests and the Remedies," 1972 *Washington U. L.Q.* 117 (1972).

(34 C.F.R. § 675(a)). (See J. Hunter, "Collecting Defaulted Student Loans: How Much Diligence Is Due?" 9 *J. Coll. & Univ. Law* 149 (1982–83).)

The Federal Family Education Loan (FFEL, formerly GSL) program includes fewer provisions related to debt collection, since postsecondary institutions are not usually the lenders under the program (see T. Naegele, "The Guaranteed Student Loan Program: Do Lenders' Risks Exceed Their Rewards?" 34 *Hastings L.J.* 599 (1983)). The regulations require (at 34 C.F.R. § 682.610(a)), that participating institutions establish and maintain such administrative and fiscal procedures and records as may be necessary to protect the United States from unreasonable risk of loss due to defaults. Another approach to debt collection, with more specifics than FFEL but fewer than Perkins, is illustrated by the Health Professions Student Loan program (42 C.F.R. Part 57, subpart C). Participating institutions must exercise "due diligence" in collecting loan payments (42 C.F.R. § 57.210(b)) and must maintain complete repayment records for each student borrower, including the "date, nature, and result of each contact with the borrower or proper endorser in the collection of an overdue loan" (42 C.F.R. § 57.215(c)). The regulations also establish a quantitative performance standard, requiring institutions to maintain a "defaulted principal amount outstanding" rate of not more than 5 percent (42 C.F.R. § 57.216(a)).

In order to step up collection activities under the Health Education Assistance Loan (HEAL) program (42 U.S.C. § 294 et seq., 42 C.F.R. Part 60), the Public Health Service of the Department of Health and Human Services issued regulations authorizing institutions to withhold transcripts of HEAL defaulters. The regulations also require schools to note student loan defaults on *academic* transcripts. (For a discussion of the lawfulness of withholding student transcripts, see Section 4.3.7.2.)

Prior to 1991 the statute of limitations for defaulted student loans was six years. However, the Higher Education Technical Amendments of 1991 (Pub. L. No. 102-26, 105 Stat. 123, codified as amended at 20 U.S.C. § 1091(a)) deleted the six-year statute of limitations temporarily. The Higher Education Amendments of 1992 made the deletion permanent. Following passage of the amendments, the question before the courts was whether student loans in default for more than six years prior to the amendments' enactment were now subject to collection. The courts have ruled that they are (see, for example, *United States v. Glockson,* 998 F.2d 896 (11th Cir. 1993); see also *United States v. Mastronito,* 830 F. Supp. 1281 (D. Ariz. 1993)).

In 1986 the Department of Education, in order to stimulate repayment of Title IV obligations, amended the regulations governing the Perkins Loan program to revise the definition of "default" status. Under the former default provisions, a borrower in default could remain eligible to receive federal loans if he or she submitted to the institution a written statement of intent to repay. The new provision (codified at 34 C.F.R. § 668.7) directs that borrowers who default on their student loans forfeit eligibility for continued Title IV assistance.

A law passed by Congress in October 1990, the Student Loan Default Prevention Initiative Act of 1990 (Pub. L. No. 101–508, 104 Stat. 1388, codified at various sections of 20 U.S.C.), is aimed at reducing the number of defaulted loans by rendering institutions with high default rates ineligible to participate in certain student loan programs. Section 1085 provides that any institution whose "cohort default rate" exceeds a certain threshold percentage for three consecutive years loses its eligibility for participation in the FFEL program for the fiscal year in which the determination is made and for the two succeeding years. The regulations specifying how default rates are calculated appear at 34 C.F.R. §668.15. The process for calculating the cohort default rate was described in *Canterbury Career School, Inc. v. Riley,* 833 Supp. 1097 (D.N.J. 1993). In this case the threshhold beyond which termination would occur was 30 percent. The court also discussed the due process protections (particularly the opportunity for a hearing) available to schools threatened with termination of their eligibility to participate in federal student aid programs.

In another case a chain of cosmetology schools challenged the secretary of education's decision to terminate the schools' eligibility to participate in the FFEL program. The plaintiffs charged that a "paper" appeal process, rather than a full-blown adversary hearing on the record, violated their rights of due process on both procedural and substantive grounds. The schools also charged that the secretary had miscalculated the default rate. In *Pro Schools, Inc. v. Riley,* 824 F. Supp. 1314 (E.D. Wis. 1993), the trial court disagreed, noting that the secretary was permitted to use default data from years prior to the enactment of the Student Loan Default Prevention Initiative Act, and that the use of these data did not make the Act itself retroactive because the issue was the schools' present eligibility, not their past eligibility (citing *Association of Accredited Cosmetology Schools v. Alexander,* 979 F.2d 859 (D.C. Cir. 1992)). Although the court accepted the plaintiffs' argument that continued eligibility for participation in the federal programs was both a property and a liberty interest (citing *Continental Training Services, Inc. v. Cavazos,* 893 F.2d 877 (7th Cir. 1990)), it viewed the written appeal process as sufficient to protect the schools' due process rights.

Institutions have several weapons in their fight to collect Perkins Loans from defaulting student borrowers. The Student Loan Default Prevention Initiative Act permits colleges to use collection agencies to recover defaulted loans, and also permits judges to award attorney's fees to institutions that must litigate to recover the unpaid loans. In *Trustees of Tufts College v. Ramsdell,* 554 N.E.2d 34 (Mass. 1990), the court noted these provisions, but limited the attorney's fees to the state law standard, rather than the more generous ceiling that the university argued was permitted by federal regulations. The regulations interpreting the Act are found at 34 C.F.R. §§675 and 676.

For those loans that have been assigned to the federal government for collection, federal agency heads may seek a tax offset against the debtor's tax refunds by request to the Internal Revenue Service (as provided in 26 U.S.C. §6402(d)). According to *Thomas v. Bennett,* 856 F.2d 1165 (8th Cir. 1988), the six-year statute of limitations on actions for money damages brought by the United States (28 U.S.C. §2415(a)) does not bar the tax offset, because the statute of limitations does not negate the debt but only bars a court suit as a means of collection; the debt is still collectible by other means. By regulation, however, the Internal Revenue Service has provided that it will not use the offset procedure for any debt that has been delinquent for more than ten years at the time offset is requested (26 C.F.R. §301.6402-6(c)(1)). This regulation was upheld in *Grider v. Cavazos,* 911 F.2d 1158 (5th Cir. 1990). The appellate court refused to permit the secretary of education to intercept the tax refunds of two individuals who had defaulted on their loans fifteen and eleven years earlier. Although the secretary had argued that the loans became delinquent when the banks assigned the loans to the secretary for collection, the court sided with the debtors' argument that the loans went into default when the required payments to the bank (the lender) were not made. The court commented:

> [We] take no pleasure in giving aid and comfort to those former students
> who shirk their loan repayment obligations by hiding behind statutes of limita-
> tion. We can only ask in rhetorical wonderment why the Secretary continues
> quixotically to pursue judicial construction of the Regulation instead of simply
> asking his counterpart in the Department of the Treasury to close the loophole
> in the Regulation with a proverbial stroke of his pen [911 F.2d at 1164].

Students challenging their obligation to repay federal student loans are finding some creative solutions in situations where the college involved either has closed
or did not provide the promised educational services. In some cases students have
argued that the lending banks or the state agency guarantors of their federal student
loans must be subject to state law regarding secured transactions. For example, in
Tipton v. Alexander, 768 F. Supp. 540 (S.D. W. Va. 1991), former students of a defunct
business college sued the secretary of education, the banks, and the state guaranty
agency, asserting that the school had fraudulently misrepresented the training it
would provide the students. The students claimed that the defendants could not
enforce the repayment obligation because the students had rights under state consumer protection laws. Although the defendants argued that the Higher Education
Act of 1965 preempted state law defenses to collection attempts under the federal
student loan program, the trial court disagreed, stating that the defendants were
subject to the students' state law defenses regarding secured transactions. The law in
West Virginia provides that, in making a consumer loan, the lender is subject to the
borrower's defenses against the seller if the lender participated in or was connected
with the sales transaction. The students argued that the lender (the bank) and the
school worked together to induce the students to take out the federally guaranteed
loans. And in *Keans v. Tempe Technical Institute, Inc.,* 807 F. Supp. 569 (D. Ariz.
1992), the court ruled that the Higher Education Act did not preempt state law
regarding the circumstances under which a loan obligation is enforceable. Although
the court dismissed the students' claims under the Higher Education Act (finding no
private right of action), it allowed the state law claims to proceed. Because of their
concern that students might successfully avoid their student loan obligations under
state law, some banks may become hesitant to participate in the federal student loan
programs; and their reluctance to participate could, in turn, limit the access of some
students to these loans. See S. Jaschik, "U.S. Court Ruling on Bank Liability Worries
Aid Experts," *Chron. Higher Educ.,* Aug. 7, 1991, A17 (discussing *Tipton*).

Students arguing under other state law theories, however, have been less successful. In *Bogart v. Nebraska Student Loan Program,* 858 S.W.2d 78 (Ark. 1993), the
Supreme Court of Arkansas rejected a group of students' claim that the guaranty
agency and the banks who actually loaned the money to the students were agents of
the stenographic school, against which the students had obtained a judgment for
fraud, which they were then unable to collect. The court ruled that the Higher Education Act preempted the students' claims under agency law. A similar result occurred in *Veal v. First American Savings Bank,* 914 F.2d 909 (7th Cir. 1990). And in
Jackson v. Culinary School of Washington, 811 F. Supp. 714 (D.D.C. 1993), the court
rejected the claims of students seeking to have their loan obligations declared null and
void because of the secretary of education's negligent supervision of the school's
default rate and the quality of its curriculum. The court said that the student loan
program

is not a warranty or guarantee of the quality of the educational program. As a matter of policy, the plaintiffs would require the current defendants [the banks and the Department of Education] to police the curriculum and activities of all schools throughout the nation, and the practicalities of this would effectively bring about the end of the student loan program as we have known it in this country over the last several years [811 F. Supp. at 719].

Collection of student loans is a critical issue for colleges and universities, for legal reasons and because of the implications of student default rates for continued eligibility. College and university officials should use experienced counsel and student aid professionals to develop and enforce student financial aid policies that fully comply with state and federal requirements.

Sec. 4.4. Support Services

In addition to financial aid services (Section 4.3), institutions provide numerous support services to students. Health services, counseling services, auxiliary services for students with disabilities, child-care services, and legal services are prominent examples that are discussed in this section. Other examples include housing services (see Section 4.14), placement services, resident life programming, campus security (see Section 4.17), parking, food services, and various other student convenience services (see generally Section 9.3). An institution may provide some of these services directly through its own staff members; other services may be performed by outside third parties under a contract with the institution (see Section 9.3.2) or by student groups subsidized by the institution. Funding may come from the institution's regular budget, from mandatory student fees, from revenues generated by charging for the service, or from grants or other governmental assistance. In all of these contexts, the provision of support services may give rise to a variety of legal issues and liability concerns (see generally Sections 2.3 and 2.4), some of which are illustrated below.

When students need support services in order to remove practical impediments to their full participation in the institution's educational program, provocative questions arise concerning the extent of the institution's obligation to provide such services. Courts have considered these questions in two contexts: auxiliary aids for disabled students—in particular, interpreter services for hearing-impaired students; and child-care facilities for students with young children.

University of Texas v. Camenisch, 451 U.S. 390 (1981), was an early, and highly publicized, case on interpreter services. A deaf graduate student at the University of Texas alleged that the university had violated Section 504 of the Rehabilitation Act of 1973 by refusing to provide him with sign-language interpreter services, which he claimed were necessary to the completion of his master's degree. The university had denied the plaintiff's request for such services on the grounds that he did not meet the university's established criteria for financial assistance to graduate students and should therefore pay for his own interpreter. The district court had issued a preliminary injunction ordering the university to provide the interpreter services, irrespective of the student's ability to pay for them. The U.S. Court of Appeals affirmed the district court (616 F.2d 127 (5th Cir. 1980)). The U.S. Supreme Court, however, held that the issue concerning the propriety of the preliminary injunction had become moot because the plaintiff had graduated. Thus, the *Camenisch* case did not furnish answers to questions concerning institutional responsibilities to provide interpreter services and other auxiliary aids to disabled students. A regulation promulgated under Section 504 (34 C.F.R. § 104.44(d)) does obligate institutions to provide such services, and this obligation apparently is not negated by the student's ability to pay. But the courts have not ruled definitively on whether this regulation, so interpreted, is consistent with the Section 504 statute. That is the issue raised but not answered in *Camenisch*.

A related issue concerns the obligations of federally funded state vocational rehabilitation (VR) agencies to provide auxiliary services for eligible college students. The plaintiff in *Camenisch* argued that the Section 504 regulation (now § 104.44(d)) does not place undue financial burdens on the universities because "a variety of outside funding sources," including the VR agencies, "are available to aid universities" in fulfilling their obligation. This line of argument suggests two further questions: whether the state VR agencies are legally obligated to provide auxiliary services to disabled college students and, if so, whether their obligation diminishes the obligation of universities to pay the costs (see J. Orleans and M. A. Smith, "Who Should Provide Interpreters Under Section 504 of the Rehabilitation Act?" 9 *J. Coll. & Univ. Law* 177 (1982–83)).

Two cases decided since *Camenisch* provide answers to these questions. In *Schornstein v. New Jersey Division of Vocational Rehabilitation Services*, 519 F. Supp. 773 (D.N.J. 1981), *affirmed*, 688 F.2d 824 (3d Cir. 1982), the court held that Title I of the Rehabilitation Act of 1973 (29 U.S.C. § 100 et seq.) requires state VR agencies to provide eligible college students with interpreter services they require to meet their vocational goals. In *Jones v. Illinois Department of Rehabilitation Services*, 504 F. Supp. 1244 (N.D. Ill. 1981), *affirmed*, 689 F.2d 724 (7th Cir. 1982), the court agreed that state VR agencies have this legal obligation. But it also held that colleges have a similar obligation under Section 104.44(d) and asked whose responsibility is primary. The court concluded that the state VR agencies have primary financial responsibility, thus diminishing universities' responsibility in situations where the student is eligible for state VR services. There is a catch, however, in the application of these cases to the *Camenisch* problem. As the district court in *Schornstein* noted, state VR agencies may consider the financial need of disabled individuals in determining the extent to which the agency will pay the costs of rehabilitation services (see 34 C.F.R. § 361.47). Thus, if a VR agency employs a financial-need test and finds that a particular disabled student does not meet it, the primary obligation would again fall on the university, and the issue raised in *Camenisch* would again predominate.

Child care, the second context in which a court has addressed a claim for support services needed to overcome some practical impediment to education, was the focus of *De La Cruz v. Tormey*, 582 F.2d 45 (9th Cir. 1978). Several low-income women brought suit in a federal district court, challenging the lack of child-care facilities on the campuses of the San Mateo Community College District. The plaintiffs alleged that the impact of the district's decision not to provide child-care facilities fell overwhelmingly on women, effectively barring them from the benefits of higher education and thus denying them equal educational opportunity. The women claimed that the policy constituted sex discrimination in violation of the Equal Protection Clause and Title IX of the Education Amendments of 1972. The district court dismissed the case for failure to state any claim on which relief could be granted, and the plaintiffs appealed.

The appellate court, reversing the district court, ruled that the complaint could not be summarily dismissed on the pleadings and remanded the case for a trial on the plaintiffs' allegations. Although the district's policy did not rest on an explicit gender classification, the appellate court acknowledged that a facially neutral policy could still violate equal protection if it affected women disproportionately and was adopted or enforced with discriminatory intent. And while Title IX would similarly require proof of disproportionate impact, "a standard less stringent than intentional discrimination" may be appropriate when a court is considering a claim under that statute. (For more recent developments regarding discriminatory intent, see Sections 3.3.3 and 7.5.7.2.)

Regarding disproportionate impact, the court explained:

> There can be little doubt that a discriminatory effect, as that term is properly understood and has been used by the Supreme Court, has been adequately alleged. The concrete human consequences flowing from the lack of sufficient child care facilities, very practical impediments to beneficial participation in the District's educational programs, are asserted to fall overwhelmingly upon women students and would-be students. . . .
>
> [T]he essence of the plaintiffs' grievance is that the absence of child care facilities renders the *included* benefits less valuable and less available to women; in other words, that the effect of the District's child care policy is to render the entire "package" of its programs of lesser worth to women than to men. . . . Were the object of their challenge simply a refusal to initiate or support a program or course of particular interest and value to women—women's studies, for instance—the case might be a much easier one [582 F.2d at 53, 56–57].

After remand the parties in *De La Cruz* agreed to an out-of-court settlement that provided for the establishment of child-care centers on the defendant's campuses. A trial was never held. It is therefore still not known whether the novel claim raised in *De La Cruz,* or similar claims regarding other support services or other forms of discrimination, will be recognized by the courts.

Other types of legal issues may arise when members of the campus community object on grounds of conscience to the institution's provision of a particular service. Health services involving birth control—abortion, sterilization, and distribution of contraceptive devices—are a primary example. The problem may be compounded when the contested service is funded by a student activities fee or other mandatory fee. Students who oppose abortion on grounds of conscience, for instance, may also object to the mandatory fees and the use of their own money to fund such services. The sparse law on this point suggests that such challenges will not often succeed. In *Erzinger v. Regents of the University of California,* 187 Cal. Rptr. 164 (Cal. Ct. App. 1982), for instance, students objected to the defendants' use of mandatory fees to provide abortion and pregnancy counseling as a part of campus student health services. The court rejected the students' claim that such use infringed their free exercise of religion. (See generally Note, "First Amendment Challenges to the Use of Mandatory Student Fees to Help Fund Student Abortions," 15 *J. Coll. & Univ. Law* 61 (1988); and see also the cases in Section 4.11.2, this volume.)

Other questions concerning abortion services arose during Congress's consideration of the Civil Rights Restoration Act of 1987 (see this volume, Section 7.5.7.4). The basic issue was whether an institution's decision to exclude abortion services from its campus health care or its student health insurance coverage could be considered sex discrimination under the Title IX regulations (see 34 CFR §§ 106.39 and 106.40). Congress responded by including two "abortion neutrality" provisions in the 1987 Act: Section 3(a), which adds a new Section 909 (20 U.S.C. § 1688) to Title IX, and Section 8 (20 U.S.C. § 1688 note). Under these provisions neither Title IX nor the Civil Rights Restoration Act may be construed (1) to require an institution to provide abortion services, (2) to prohibit an institution from providing abortion services, or (3) to permit an institution to penalize a person for seeking or receiving abortion services related to legal abortion.

Another development that affected abortion services was the 1988 amendments to the regulations for Title X of the Public Health Service Act (42 U.S.C. §§ 300 to 300a-6), which provides federal funds for family-planning clinics. These amendments (codified at 42 C.F.R. §§ 59.2, 59.5, and 59.7–59.10) prohibited fund recipients (some of whom are campus health clinics or university-affiliated hospitals) from providing counseling or referrals regarding abortion. The U.S. Supreme Court upheld these regulations against a challenge that they violated the free speech rights of physicians and the privacy rights of pregnant women (*Rust v. Sullivan*, 500 U.S. 173 (1991)). However, soon after he was inaugurated, President Clinton issued a memorandum directing the secretary of HHS to suspend the so-called Gag Rule (58 Fed. Reg. 7455 (1993)). Consequently, the secretary suspended the rules, reinstated the previous rules during the pendency of the rule-making process, and proposed to return the family-planning program to the regulatory provisions that were in effect prior to the promulgation of the Gag Rule (58 Fed. Reg. 7462 and 7464 (1994)). (The comment period ended in August 1993, but no final rules had yet been published as this book went to press.)

In yet another context—student legal services—the case of *Student Government Assn. v. Board of Trustees of the University of Massachusetts*, 868 F.2d 473 (1st Cir. 1989), illustrates complex questions concerning the First Amendment. The court held that the First Amendment did not bar the university from terminating its existing campus legal services office (LSO), which represented students in criminal matters and in suits against the university. In order for students' access to legal services to be protected under the First Amendment, the legal services office must be considered a "public forum" (see Section 4.9.2) that provides a "channel of communication" between students and other persons (868 F.2d at 476). Here the students sought to communicate with two groups through the LSO: persons with whom they have disagreements, and the attorneys staffing the LSO. Since the court system, rather than the LSO itself, was the actual channel of communication with the first group, the only channel of communication the LSO provided was with the LSO attorneys in their official capacities. The court did not extend First Amendment public forum protection to this channel because the university was not *regulating* communication in the marketplace of ideas, but only determining whether to *subsidize* communication. Having only extended a subsidy to the LSO, the university could terminate this subsidy unless the plaintiffs could prove that the university was doing so for a reason that itself violated the First Amendment—for instance, to penalize students who had brought suits against the university, or to suppress the assertion (in legal proceedings) of ideas the university considered dangerous or offensive. The court determined that the termination was "nonselective," applying to all litigation rather than only to litigation that reflected a "particular viewpoint," and thus did not serve to penalize individual students or suppress particular ideas. The termination therefore did not violate the Free Speech Clause of the First Amendment. (See Comment, *"Student Government Association v. Board of Trustees of the University of Massachusetts:* Forum and Subsidy Analysis Applied to University Funding Decisions," 17 *J. Coll. & Univ. Law* 65 (1990).)

Sec. 4.5. Disciplinary and Grievance Systems

Colleges and universities develop codes of student conduct (discussed in Section 4.6) and standards of academic performance (discussed in Section 4.7), and expect students to conform to those codes and standards. Sections 4.5 through 4.8 discuss student challenges to institutional attempts to discipline students for violations of these codes and standards. First, Section 4.5 presents the guidelines for disciplinary and grievance systems that afford students appropriate statutory and constitutional protections. Section 4.6 analyzes the courts' response to student challenges to colleges' disciplinary rules and regulations, emphasizing the different standards that public and private institutions must meet. Section 4.7 addresses "academic" matters, such as student challenges to grades, degree revocation, allegations of sexual harassment by faculty, and the special issues raised by students with disabilities who request accommodations of an academic nature. Section 4.8 reviews the guidelines developed by courts reviewing challenges to the *procedures* used by colleges when they seek to discipline or expel a student for either social or academic misconduct.

4.5.1. Establishment of systems. Postsecondary institutions have extensive authority to regulate both the academic and the nonacademic activities and behavior of students. This power is summarized in an often-cited judicial statement:

> In the field of discipline, scholastic and behavioral, an institution may establish any standards reasonably relevant to the lawful missions, processes, and functions of the institution. It is not a lawful mission, process, or function of . . . [a public] institution to prohibit the exercise of a right guaranteed by the Constitution or a law of the United States to a member of the academic community in the circumstances. Therefore, such prohibitions are not reasonably relevant to any lawful mission, process, or function of . . . [a public] institution.
>
> Standards so established may apply to student behavior on and off the campus when relevant to any lawful mission, process, or function of the institution. By such standards of student conduct the institution may prohibit any action or omission which impairs, interferes with, or obstructs the missions, processes, and functions of the institution.
>
> Standards so established may require scholastic attainments higher than the average of the population and may require superior ethical and moral behavior. In establishing standards of behavior, the institution is not limited to the standards or the forms of criminal laws ["General Order on Judicial Standards of Procedure and Substance in Review of Student Discipline in Tax-Supported Institutions of Higher Education," 45 F.R.D. 133, 145 (W.D. Mo. 1968)].

It is not enough, however, for an administrator to understand the extent and limits of institutional authority. The administrator must also skillfully implement this authority through various systems for the resolution of disputes concerning students. Such systems should include procedures for processing and resolving disputes; substantive standards or rules to guide the judgment of the persons responsible for dispute resolution; and mechanisms and penalties with which decisions are enforced. The procedures, standards, and enforcement provisions should be written and made available to all students. Dispute-resolution systems, in their totality, should create a two-way street; that is, they should provide for complaints by students against other members of the academic community as well as complaints against students by other members of the academic community.

The choice of structures for resolving disputes depends on policy decisions made by administrators, preferably in consultation with representatives of various interests within the institution. Should a single system cover both academic and nonacademic disputes, or should there be separate systems for separate kinds of disputes? Should there be a separate disciplinary system for students, or should there be a broader system covering other members of the academic community as well? Will the systems use specific and detailed standards of student conduct, or will they operate on the basis of more general rules and policies? To what extent will students participate in establishing the rules governing their conduct? To what extent will students, rather than administrators or faculty members, be expected to assume responsibility for reporting or investigating violations of student conduct codes or honor codes? To what extent will students take part in adjudicating complaints by or against students? What kinds of sanctions can be levied against students found to have been engaged in misconduct? Can they be fined, made to do volunteer work on campus, expelled from the institution, given a failing grade in a course or denied a degree, or required to make restitution? To what extent will the president, provost, or board of trustees retain final authority to review decisions concerning student misconduct?

Devices for creating dispute-resolution systems may include honor codes or codes of academic ethics; codes of student conduct; bills of rights, or rights and responsibilities, for students or for the entire academic community; the use of various legislative bodies, such as a student or university senate; a formal judiciary system for resolving disputes concerning students; the establishment of grievance mechanisms for students, such as an ombudsman system or a grievance committee; and mediation processes that provide an alternative or supplement to judiciary and grievance mechanisms. On most campuses security guards or some other campus law enforcement system will also be involved in the resolution of disputes and regulation of student behavior.

Occasionally, specific procedures or mechanisms will be required by law. Constitutional due process, for instance, requires the use of certain procedures before a student is suspended or dismissed from a public institution (see this volume, Section 4.8). The Title IX regulations (Section 7.5.3) and the Family Educational Rights and Privacy Act (FERPA) regulations (Section 4.16.1) require both public and private institutions to establish certain procedures for resolving disputes under those particular statutes. Even when specific mechanisms or procedures are not required by law, the procedures or standards adopted by an institution will sometimes be affected by existing law. A public institution's rules regarding student protest, for instance, must comply with First Amendment strictures protecting freedom of speech (Section 4.10).

And its rules regarding administrative access to or search of student rooms, and the investigatory techniques of its campus police, must comply with Fourth Amendment strictures regarding search and seizure (Section 4.14.2). Though an understanding of the law is thus crucial to the establishment of disciplinary and grievance systems, the law by no means rigidly controls their form and operation. To a large extent, the kind of system adopted will depend on the institution's notions of good administrative practice.

Fair and accessible dispute-resolution systems, besides being useful administrative tools in their own right, can also insulate institutions from lawsuits. Students who feel that their arguments or grievances will be fairly considered within the institution may forgo resort to the courts. If students ignore internal mechanisms in favor of immediate judicial action, the courts may refer the students to the institution. Under the "exhaustion-of-remedies" doctrine (see Section 1.4.2.5), courts may require plaintiffs to exhaust available remedies within the institution before bringing the complaint to court. In *Pfaff v. Columbia-Greene Community College,* 472 N.Y.S.2d 480 (N.Y. App. Div. 1984), for example, the New York courts dismissed the complaint of a student who had sued her college, contesting a C grade entered in a course, because the college had an internal appeal process and the student "failed to show that pursuit of the available administrative appeal would have been fruitless."

For a report on the use of campus grievance mechanisms for students, including examples from twenty institutions and advice on planning and implementation, see J. Folger & J. J. Shubert, *Resolving Student-Initiated Grievances in Higher Education: Dispute Resolution Procedures in a Non-Adversarial Setting* (National Institute for Dispute Resolution, 1986).

4.5.2. Codes of student conduct. Three major issues are involved in the drafting or revision of codes of student conduct: the type of conduct the code will encompass, the procedures to be used when infractions of the code are alleged, and the sanctions for code violations.

Codes of student conduct typically proscribe both academic and social misconduct, whether or not the misconduct violates civil or criminal laws, and whether or not the misconduct occurs on campus. Academic misconduct may include plagiarism, cheating, forgery, or alteration of institutional records. In their review of sanctions for academic misconduct, and of the degree of procedural protection required for students accused of such misconduct, courts have been relatively deferential (see Section 4.8.3). For a comprehensive discussion of academic dishonesty, including preventive strategies, disciplinary systems, and a model code of academic integrity, see W. Kibler, E. Nuss, B. Peterson, & G. Pavela, *Academic Integrity and Student Development* (College Administration Publications, 1988).

Social misconduct may include disruption of an institutional function (including teaching and research) and abusive or hazing behavior (but limitations on speech may run afoul of free speech protections, as discussed in Section 4.10). It may also encompass conduct that occurs off-campus,[23] particularly if the misconduct also violates criminal law and the institution can demonstrate that the restrictions are

---

[23]Cases and authorities are collected in Annot., "Misconduct of College or University Students Off Campus as Grounds for Expulsion, Suspension, or Other Disciplinary Action," 28 A.L.R.4th 463 (1984 and periodic supp.).

directly related to its educational mission or the campus community's welfare (*Krasnow v. Virginia Polytechnic Institute*, 551 F.2d 591 (4th Cir. 1977); *Wallace v. Florida A&M University*, 433 So. 2d 600 (Fla. Dist. Ct. App. 1983)).

Sanctions for code violations may range from a warning to expulsion, with various intermediate penalties, such as suspension or public service requirements. Students who are expelled may seek injunctive relief under the theory that they will be irreparably harmed; some courts have ruled that sanctions short of expulsion would not be appropriate for injunctive relief (*Boehm v. University of Pennsylvania School of Veterinary Medicine*, 573 A.2d 575 (Pa. Super. Ct. 1990), but see *Jones v. Board of Governors*, 557 F. Supp. 263 (W.D.N.C.), *affirmed*, 704 F.2d 713 (4th Cir. 1983)). Students at public institutions may assert constitutional claims related to deprivation of a property and/or liberty interest (see Section 3.6.2), while students at private institutions may file actions based on contract law.

If a code of conduct defines the offenses for which a student may be penalized by a public institution, that code must comply with constitutional due process requirements concerning vagueness. The requirement is a minimal one: the code must be clear enough for students to understand the standards with which their conduct must comply, and it must not be susceptible to arbitrary enforcement. A public institution's code of conduct must also comply with the constitutional doctrine of overbreadth in any area where the code could affect First Amendment rights. Basically, this doctrine requires that the code not be drawn so broadly and vaguely as to include protected First Amendment activity along with behavior subject to legitimate regulation (see Sections 4.9.2 and 4.10). Finally, a public institution's student conduct code must comply with a general requirement of evenhandedness; that is, the code cannot arbitrarily discriminate in the range and types of penalties, or in the procedural safeguards, afforded various classes of offenders. *Paine v. Board of Regents of the University of Texas System*, 355 F. Supp. 199 (W.D. Tex. 1972), *affirmed per curiam*, 474 F.2d 1397 (5th Cir. 1973), concerned such discriminatory practices. The institution had given students convicted of drug offenses a harsher penalty and fewer safeguards than it gave to all other code offenders, including those charged with equally serious offenses. The court held that this differential treatment violated the Equal Protection and Due Process Clauses.

As noted in Section 4.5.1, codes of conduct can apply to the off-campus actions as well as the on-campus activity of students. But the extension of a code to off-campus activity can pose significant legal and policy questions. In the *Paine* case above, the institution automatically suspended students who had been put on probation by the criminal courts for possession of marijuana. The court invalidated the suspensions partly because they were based on an off-campus occurrence (court probation) that did not automatically establish a threat to the institution. And in *Thomas v. Granville Board of Education*, 607 F.2d 1043 (2d Cir. 1979), a high school case with pertinent ramifications for postsecondary education, several students had been suspended for their off-campus activities in publishing a newspaper of sexual satire. The court also invalidated these suspensions, according the students the same First Amendment rights as citizens generally and emphasizing that "our willingness to grant school officials substantial autonomy within their academic domain rests in part on the confinement of that power within the metes and bounds of the school itself." (For a contrary view, in which the court upheld the authority of a public college to discipline its students for off-campus violations of laws dealing with controlled substances, see *Hart v. Ferris State College,* 557 F. Supp. 1379 (W.D. Mich. 1983).)

To avoid problems in this area, administrators should ascertain that an off-campus act has a direct detrimental impact on the institution's educational functions before using that act as a basis for disciplining students. See, for example, the opinion of the attorney general of Maryland upholding the right of the state university to discipline "for off-campus conduct detrimental to the interests of the institution, subject to the fundamental constitutional safeguards that apply to all disciplinary actions by educational officials" (74 *Opinions of the Attorney General* 1 (Md.) (1989), Opinion No. 89-002).

Private institutions not subject to the state action doctrine (see Section 1.5.2) are not constitutionally required to follow these principles regarding student codes. Yet the principles reflect basic notions of fairness, which can be critical components of good administrative practice; thus, administrators of private institutions may wish to use them as policy guides in formulating their codes.

A question that colleges and universities, irrespective of control, may wish to consider is whether the disciplinary code should apply to student organizations as well as to individual students. Should students be required to assume collective responsibility for the actions of an organization, and should the university impose sanctions, such as withdrawal of institutional recognition, on organizations that violate the disciplinary code? For a model student disciplinary code that includes student organizations within its ambit, see E. Stoner & K. Cerminara, "Harnessing the 'Spirit of Insubordination': A Model Student Disciplinary Code," 17 *J. Coll. & Univ. Law* 89 (1990).

4.5.3. Judicial systems. Judicial systems that adjudicate complaints of student misconduct must be very sensitive to procedural safeguards. The membership of judicial bodies, the procedures they use,[24] the extent to which their proceedings are open to the academic community, the sanctions they may impose, the methods by which they may initiate proceedings against students, and provisions for appealing their decisions should be set out in writing and made generally available within the institution.

Whenever the charge could result in a punishment as serious as suspension, a public institution's judicial system must provide the procedures required by the Due Process Clause (see Section 4.8.2). The focal point of these procedures is the hearing at which the accused student may present evidence and argument concerning the charge. The institution, however, may wish to include preliminary stages in its judicial process for more informal disposition of complaints against students. The system may provide for negotiations between the student and the complaining party, for instance, or for preliminary conferences before designated representatives of the judicial system. Full due process safeguards need not be provided at every such preliminary stage. *Andrews v. Knowlton,* 509 F.2d 898 (2d Cir. 1975), dealt with the procedures required at a stage preceding an honor code hearing. The court held that due process procedures were not required at that time because it was not a "critical stage" that could have a "prejudicial impact" on the final determination of whether

---

[24]Cases and authorities related to student judicial procedures are collected in Annot., "Admissibility of Hearsay Evidence in Student Disciplinary Proceedings," 30 A.L.R.4th 935 (1984 and periodic supp.).

the student violated the honor code. Thus, administrators have broad authority to construct informal preliminary proceedings—as long as a student's participation in such stages does not adversely affect his or her ability to defend the case in the final stage.

A question receiving increased attention is whether the judicial system will permit the accused student to have an attorney present. Several models are possible: (1) Neither the college nor the student will have attorneys. (2) Attorneys may be present to advise the student but may not participate by asking questions or making statements. (3) Attorneys may be present and participate fully in questioning and making opening and closing statements. A federal appellate court was asked to rule on whether a judicial system at Northern Illinois University that followed the second model—attorney present but a nonparticipant—violated a student's due process rights. In *Osteen v. Henley*, 13 F.3d 221 (7th Cir. 1993), the court wrote:

> Even if a student has a constitutional right to *consult* counsel . . . we don't think he is entitled to be represented in the sense of having a lawyer who is permitted to examine or cross-examine witnesses, to submit and object to documents, to address the tribunal, and otherwise to perform the traditional function of a trial lawyer. To recognize such a right would force student disciplinary proceedings into the mold of adversary litigation. The university would have to hire its own lawyer to prosecute these cases and no doubt lawyers would also be dragged in—from the law faculty or elsewhere—to serve as judges. The cost and complexity of such proceedings would be increased, to the detriment of discipline as well as of the university's fisc [13 F.3d at 225].

The court then, citing *Mathews v. Eldridge* (see Section 3.6.2.3, this volume), balanced the cost of permitting lawyers to participate against the risk of harm to students if lawyers were excluded. Concluding that the risk of harm to students was "trivial," the court refused to rule that attorneys were a student's constitutional right.

Occasionally, a campus judicial proceeding may involve an incident that is also the subject of criminal court proceedings. The same student may thus be charged in both forums at the same time. In such circumstances the postsecondary institution is not legally required to defer to the criminal courts by canceling or postponing its proceedings. As held in *Paine* (Section 4.5.2) and other cases, even if the institution is public, such dual prosecution is not double jeopardy because the two proceedings impose different kinds of punishment to protect different kinds of state interests. The Constitution's double jeopardy clause applies only to successive criminal prosecutions for the same offense. Nor will the existence of two separate proceedings necessarily violate the student's privilege against self-incrimination. In several cases—for instance, *Grossner v. Trustees of Columbia University*, 287 F. Supp. 535 (S.D.N.Y. 1968)—courts have rejected student requests to stay campus proceedings on this ground pending the outcome of criminal trials. One court emphasized, however, that if students in campus proceedings "are forced to incriminate themselves . . . and if that testimony is offered against them in subsequent criminal proceedings, they can then invoke . . . [Supreme Court precedents] in opposition to the offer" (*Furutani v. Ewigleben*, 297 F. Supp. 1163 (N.D. Cal. 1969)). In another case the court rejected as speculative a student's claim that his being identified in campus disciplinary proceedings would jeopardize the fairness of his criminal trial (*Nzuve v. Castleton State College*, 335 A.2d 321 (Vt. 1975)).

While neither double jeopardy nor self-incrimination need tie the administrator's hands, administrators may nevertheless choose, for policy reasons, to delay or dismiss particular campus proceedings when the same incident is in the criminal courts. It is possible that the criminal proceedings will adequately protect the institution's interests. Or, as *Furutani* and *Nzuve* suggest, student testimony at a campus proceeding could create evidentiary problems for the criminal court.

If a public institution proceeds with its campus action while the student is subject to charges still pending in criminal court, the institution may have to permit the student to have a lawyer with him during the campus proceedings. In *Gabrilowitz v. Newman*, 582 F.2d 100 (1st Cir. 1978), a student challenged a University of Rhode Island rule that prohibited the presence of legal counsel at campus disciplinary hearings. The student obtained an injunction prohibiting the university from conducting the hearing without permitting the student the advice of counsel. The appellate court, affirming the lower court's injunction order, held that when a criminal case based on the same conduct giving rise to the disciplinary proceeding is pending in the courts, "the denial to [the student] of the right to have a lawyer of his own choice to consult with and advise him during the disciplinary proceeding would deprive [him] of due process of law."

The court emphasized that the student was requesting the assistance of counsel to consult with and advise him during the hearing, not to conduct the hearing on the student's behalf. Such assistance was critical to the student because of the delicacy of the legal situation he faced:

> Were the appellee to testify in the disciplinary proceeding, his statement could be used as evidence in the criminal case, either to impeach or as an admission if he did not choose to testify. Appellee contends that he is, therefore, impaled on the horns of a legal dilemma: if he mounts a full defense at the disciplinary hearing without the assistance of counsel and testifies on his own behalf, he might jeopardize his defense in the criminal case; if he fails to fully defend himself or chooses not to testify at all, he risks loss of the college degree he is within weeks of receiving, and his reputation will be seriously blemished [582 F.2d at 103].

If a public institution delays campus proceedings, and then uses a conviction in the criminal proceedings as the basis for its campus action, the institution must take care to protect the student's due process rights. In the *Paine* case, a university rule required the automatic two-year suspension of any student convicted of a narcotics offense. The court held that the students must be given an opportunity to show that, despite their conviction and probation, they posed "no substantial threat of influencing other students to use, possess, or sell drugs or narcotics." Thus, a criminal conviction does not automatically provide the basis for suspension; administrators should still ascertain that the conviction has a detrimental impact on the campus, and the affected student should have the opportunity to make a contrary showing.

For analysis of this issue in the context of acquaintance rape cases, see P. Burling, *Acquaintance Rape on Campus: A Model for Institutional Response* (National Association of College and University Attorneys, 1993). See also *Statement*

Concerning Campus Disciplinary Procedures and the Criminal Law in Sexual Assault Cases (National Association of Student Personnel Administrators, Mar. 1993).

Sec. 4.6. Disciplinary Rules and Regulations

Postsecondary institutions customarily have rules of conduct or behavior, which students are expected to follow. It has become increasingly common to commit these rules to writing and embody them in codes of conduct binding on all students (see Section 4.5.2). Although the trend toward written codes is a sound one, legally speaking, because it gives students fairer notice of what is expected from them and often results in a better-conceived and administered system, written rules also provide a specific target to aim at in a lawsuit.

Students have challenged institutional attempts to discipline them by attacking the validity of the rule they allegedly violated or by attacking the nature of the disciplinary proceeding which determined that the alleged violation occurred. This section discusses student challenges to the validity of institutional rules and regulations; Section 4.8 discusses challenges to the procedures used by colleges to determine whether, in fact, violations have occurred.

4.6.1. Public institutions. In public institutions students frequently contend that the rules of conduct violate some specific guarantee of the Bill of Rights, as made applicable to state institutions by the Fourteenth Amendment (see Section 1.5.2). These situations, the most numerous of which implicate the Free Speech and Press Clauses of the First Amendment, are discussed in Section 4.5 and various other sections of this chapter. In other situations the contention is a more general one—that the rule is so vague that its enforcement violates due process; that is (as was noted in Section 4.5.2), the rule is unconstitutionally "vague" or "void for vagueness."

Soglin v. Kauffman, 418 F.2d 163 (7th Cir. 1969), is illustrative. The University of Wisconsin had expelled students for attempting to block access to an off-campus recruiter as a protest against the Vietnam War. The university had charged the students under a rule prohibiting "misconduct" and argued in court that it had inherent power to discipline, which need not be exercised through specific rules. Both the U.S. District Court and the U.S. Court of Appeals held that the misconduct policy was unconstitutionally vague. The appellate court reasoned:

> No one disputes the power of the university to protect itself by means of disciplinary action against disruptive students. Power to punish and the rules defining the exercise of that power are not, however, identical. Power alone does not supply the standards needed to determine its application to types of behavior or specific instances of "misconduct." As Professor Fuller has observed: "The first desideratum of a system for subjecting human conduct to the governance of rules is an obvious one: there must be rules" (L. Fuller, *The Morality of Law*, p. 46 (rev. ed., [Yale University Press,] 1969)). The proposition that government officers, including school administrators, must act in accord with rules in meting out discipline is so fundamental that its validity tends to be assumed by courts engaged in assessing the propriety of specific regulations. . . . The [doctrine] of vagueness . . . , already applied in academic contexts, [presupposes] the existence of rules whose coherence and boundaries may be questioned. . . . These same considerations also dictate that the rules embodying standards of discipline be

contained in properly promulgated regulations. University administrators are not immune from these requirements of due process in imposing sanctions. Consequently, in the present case, the disciplinary proceedings must fail to the extent that the defendant officials of the University of Wisconsin did not base those proceedings on the students' disregard of university standards of conduct expressed in reasonably clear and narrow rules.

. . . The use of "misconduct" as a standard in imposing the penalties threatened here must therefore fall for vagueness. The inadequacy of the rule is apparent on its face. It contains no clues which could assist a student, an administrator, or a reviewing judge in determining whether conduct not transgressing statutes is susceptible to punishment by the university as "misconduct."

Pursuant to appropriate rule or regulation, the university has the power to maintain order by suspension or expulsion of disruptive students. Requiring that such sanctions be administered in accord with preexisting rules does not place an unwarranted burden upon university administration. We do not require university codes of conduct to satisfy the same rigorous standards as criminal statutes. We only hold that expulsion and prolonged suspension may not be imposed on students by a university simply on the basis of allegations of "misconduct" without reference to any preexisting rule which supplies an adequate guide [418 F.2d at 167–68].

While similar language about vagueness is often found in other court opinions, the actual result in *Soglin* (the invalidation of the rule) is unusual. Most university rules subjected to judicial tests of vagueness have survived, sometimes because the rule at issue is less egregious than the "misconduct" rule in *Soglin*, sometimes because a court accepts the "inherent power to discipline" argument raised by the *Soglin* defendants and declines to undertake any real vagueness analysis, and sometimes because the student conduct at issue was so contrary to the judges' own standards of decency that they tended to ignore the defects in the rules in light of the obvious "defect" in behavior. *Esteban v. Central Missouri State College*, 415 F.2d 1077 (8th Cir. 1969), the case most often cited in opposition to *Soglin*, reveals all three of these distinctions. In this case students contested their suspension under a regulation prohibiting "participation in mass gatherings which might be considered as unruly or unlawful." In upholding the suspension, the court emphasized the need for "flexibility and reasonable breadth, rather than meticulous specificity, in college regulations relating to conduct" and recognized the institution's "latitude and discretion in its formulation of rules and regulations." The approach has often been followed in later cases—for instance, in *Jenkins v. Louisiana State Board of Education*, 506 F.2d 992 (5th Cir. 1975), where the court upheld a series of regulations dealing with disorderly assembly and disturbing the peace on campus.

Although the judicial trend suggests that most rules and regulations will be upheld, administrators should not thus assume that they have a free hand in promulgating codes of conduct. *Soglin* signals the institution's vulnerability where it has no written rules at all or where the rule provides no standard to guide conduct. And even the *Esteban* court warned: "We do not hold that any college regulation, however loosely framed, is necessarily valid." To avoid such pitfalls, disciplinary rules should provide standards sufficient to guide both the students in their conduct and the disciplinarians in their decision making. A rule will likely pass judicial scrutiny if the standard "conveys sufficiently definite warning as to the proscribed conduct when measured by common understanding and practices" (*Sword v. Fox*, 446 F.2d 1091 (4th Cir. 1971), upholding a regulation that "demonstrations are forbidden in any areas of the health center, inside any buildings, and congregating in the locations of fire hydrants"). Regulations need not be drafted by a lawyer—in fact, heavy student involvement in drafting may be valuable to ensure an expression of their "common understanding"—but it would usually be wise to have a lawyer play a general advisory role in the process.

Once the rules are promulgated, institutional officials have some latitude in interpreting and applying them, as long as the interpretation is reasonable. In *Board of Education of Rogers, Ark. v. McCluskey*, 458 U.S. 966 (1982), a public school board's interpretation of one of its rules was challenged as unreasonable. The board had held that its rule against students being under the influence of "controlled substances" included alcoholic beverages. The U.S. Supreme Court, quoting *Wood v. Strickland* (see Section 2.4.3, this volume), asserted that "federal courts [are] not authorized to construe school regulations" unless the board's interpretation "is so extreme as to be a violation of due process" (458 U.S. at 969–70).

4.6.2. Private institutions. Private institutions, not being subject to federal constitutional constraints (see Section 1.5.2), have even more latitude than public institutions do in promulgating disciplinary rules. Courts are likely to recognize a broad right to make and enforce rules that is inherent in the private student-institution relationship or to find such a right implied in some contractual relationship between student and school. Under this broad construction, private institutional rules will not be held to specificity standards such as those in *Soglin* (discussed in Section 4.6.1). Thus, in *Dehaan v. Brandeis University*, 150 F. Supp. 626 (D. Mass. 1957), the court upheld the plaintiff's suspension for misconduct under a policy where the school "reserves the right to sever the connection of any student with the university for appropriate reason"; and in *Carr v. St. John's University, New York*, 231 N.Y.S.2d 410 (N.Y. App. Div. 1962), *affirmed*, 187 N.E.2d 18 (N.Y. 1962), the courts upheld the dismissal of four students for off-campus conduct under a regulation providing that "in conformity with the ideals of Christian education and conduct, the university reserves the right to dismiss a student at any time on whatever grounds the university judges advisable."

Despite the breadth of such cases, the private school administrator, like his or her public counterpart, should not assume a legally free hand in promulgating disciplinary rules. Under one developing theory or another (see Section 1.5.3), courts can now be expected to protect private school students from clearly arbitrary disciplinary actions. When a school has disciplinary rules, courts may overturn administrators' actions taken in derogation of the rules. And when there is no rule or the applicable rule provides no standard of behavior, courts may overturn suspensions for conduct that the student could not reasonably have known was wrong. Thus, in *Slaughter v. Brigham Young University*, 514 F.2d 622 (10th Cir. 1975), though the court upheld the expulsion of a graduate student for dishonesty under the student code of conduct, it first asked "whether the . . . [expulsion] was arbitrary" and indicated that the university's findings would be accorded a presumption of correctness only "if the regulations concerned are reasonable [and] if they are known to the student or should have been." To avoid such situations, private institutions may want to adhere to much the same guidelines for promulgating rules as are suggested above for public institutions, despite the fact that they are not required by law to do so.

4.6.3. Disciplining students with psychiatric illnesses.

4.6.3. Disciplining students with psychiatric illnesses. Students with mental or psychological disabilities are protected against discrimination by the Rehabilitation Act and the Americans with Disabilities Act (see Sections 4.2.4.3. and 7.5.4). Yet a student's mental illness may disrupt campus activities, or the student may be dangerous to herself or to other students, faculty, or administrators. Opinion is divided among educators and mental health professionals as to whether students suffering from mental disorders who violate the institution's code of student conduct should be subject to the regular disciplinary procedure or should be given a "medical withdrawal" if their presence on campus becomes disruptive or dangerous.[25]

Several issues arise in connection with mentally ill students who are disruptive or dangerous. If campus counseling personnel have gained information from a student indicating that he or she is potentially dangerous, the teachings of *Tarasoff v. Regents of the University of California* (Section 2.4.1) and its progeny (as well as many state statutes codifying *Tarasoff*) regarding a duty to warn the potential target(s) of the violence would apply (see D. Gehring, "More Than a Duty to Warn," *Synthesis: Law and Policy in Higher Education,* Nov. 1989, at 47–48). If administrators or faculty know that the student is potentially dangerous and that student subsequently injures someone, negligence claims based on the foreseeability of harm may arise (Section 2.3.1.1). On the other hand, potential violations of the federal Family Educational Rights and Privacy Act (discussed in this volume, Section 4.16.1) could also be implicated if institutional officials warned a student's family or others of suicide threats or other serious medical or psychological conditions.

Given the potential for constitutional claims at public institutions and discrimination claims at all institutions, administrators who are considering disciplinary action against a student with a mental or emotional disorder should provide due process protections (see Section 4.8.2). If the student has violated the institution's code of conduct and is competent to participate in the hearing, some experts recommend subjecting the student to the same disciplinary proceedings that a student without a mental or emotional impairment would receive (see, for example, G. Pavela, *The Dismissal of Students with Mental Disorders* (College Administration Publications, 1985)). For an analysis of the issues facing public colleges and universities in these circumstances, and recommended actions, see J. DiScala, S. G. Olswang, & C. S. Niccolls, "College and University Responses to the Emotionally or Mentally Impaired Student," 19 *J. Coll. & Univ. Law* 17 (1992).

Sec. 4.7. Grades, Credits, and Degrees

Fewer legal restrictions pertain to an institution's application of academic standards to students than to its application of behavioral standards. Courts are more deferential to academia when evaluation of academic work is the issue, believing that such evaluation resides in the expertise of the faculty rather than the court.

---

[25]Cases and authorities are collected in Annot., "Physical or Mental Illness as Basis of Dismissal of Student from School, College or University," 17 A.L.R. Fed. 519 (1973 and periodic supp.).

4.7.1. Awarding of grades and degrees. When a student alleges that a grade has been awarded improperly or a degree has been denied unfairly, the courts must determine whether the defendant's action reflected the application of academic judgment or an arbitrary or unfair application of institutional policy. In one leading case, *Connelly v. University of Vermont,* 244 F. Supp. 156 (D. Vt. 1965), a medical student challenged his dismissal from medical school. He had failed the pediatrics-obstetrics course and was excluded, under a College of Medicine rule, for having failed 25 percent or more of his major third-year courses. The court described its role, and the institution's legal obligation, in such cases as follows:

> Where a medical student has been dismissed for a failure to attain a proper standard of scholarship, two questions may be involved; the first is, was the student in fact delinquent in his studies or unfit for the practice of medicine? The second question is, were the school authorities motivated by malice or bad faith in dismissing the student, or did they act arbitrarily or capriciously? In general, the first question is not a matter for judicial review. However, a student dismissal motivated by bad faith, arbitrariness, or capriciousness may be actionable. . . .
>
> This rule has been stated in a variety of ways by a number of courts. It has been said that courts do not interfere with the management of a school's internal affairs unless "there has been a manifest abuse of discretion or where [the school officials'] action has been arbitrary or unlawful" (*State ex rel. Sherman v. Hyman,* 180 Tenn. 99, 171 S.W.2d 822, *certiorari denied,* 319 U.S. 748 . . . (1942)), or unless the school authorities have acted "arbitrarily or capriciously" (*Frank v. Marquette University,* 209 Wis. 372, 245 N.W. 125 (1932)), or unless they have abused their discretion (*Coffelt v. Nicholson,* 224 Ark. 176, 272 S.W.2d 309 (1954); *People ex rel. Bluett v. Board of Trustees of University of Illinois,* 10 Ill. App. 2d 207, 134 N.E.2d 635, 58 A.L.R.2d 899 (1956)), or acted in "bad faith" (*Barnard v. Inhabitants of Shelburne* . . . [102 N.E. 1095 (Mass. 1913)] and see . . . 109 N.E. 818 (same case)).
>
> The effect of these decisions is to give the school authorities absolute discretion in determining whether a student has been delinquent in his studies, and to place the burden on the student of showing that his dismissal was motivated by arbitrariness, capriciousness, or bad faith. The reason for this rule is that, in matters of scholarship, the school authorities are uniquely qualified by training and experience to judge the qualifications of a student, and efficiency of instruction depends in no small degree upon the school's faculty's freedom from interference from other noneducational tribunals. It is only when the school authorities abuse this discretion that a court may interfere with their decision to dismiss a student [244 F. Supp. at 159–60].

The plaintiff had alleged that his instructor decided before completion of the course to fail him regardless of the quality of his work. The court held that these allegations met its requirements for suits. They therefore stated a cause of action, which if proven at trial would justify the entry of judgment against the college.

In 1975 a federal appeals court issued an important reaffirmation of the principles underlying the *Connelly* case. *Gaspar v. Bruton,* 513 F.2d 843 (10th Cir. 1975), concerned a practical nurse student who had been dismissed for deficient performance in clinical training. In rejecting the student's suit against the school, the court held that:

Courts have historically refrained from interfering with the authority vested in school officials to drop a student from the rolls for failure to attain or maintain prescribed scholastic rating (whether judged by objective and/or subjective standards), absent a clear showing that the officials have acted arbitrarily or have abused the discretionary authority vested in them. . . .

The courts are not equipped to review academic records based upon academic standards within the particular knowledge, experience, and expertise of academicians. Thus, when presented with a challenge that the school authorities suspended or dismissed a student for failure re academic standards, the court may grant relief, as a practical matter, only in those cases where the student presents positive evidence of ill will or bad motive [513 F.2d at 850–51].

The U.S. Supreme Court has twice addressed the subject of the standard of review of academic judgments. It first considered this subject briefly in *Board of Curators of the University of Missouri v. Horowitz*, 435 U.S. 78 (1978) (discussed in Section 4.8.3). A dismissed medical student claimed that the school applied stricter standards to her because of her sex, religion, and physical appearance. Referring particularly to *Gaspar v. Bruton*, the Court rejected the claim in language inhospitable to substantive judicial review of academic decisions:

A number of lower courts have implied in dictum that academic dismissals from state institutions can be enjoined if "shown to be clearly arbitrary or capricious." . . . Even assuming that the courts can review under such a standard an academic decision of a public educational institution, we agree with the district court that no showing of arbitrariness or capriciousness has been made in this case. Courts are particularly ill equipped to evaluate academic performance. The factors discussed . . . with respect to procedural due process [see Section 4.8.3] speak *a fortiori* here and warn against any such judicial intrusion into academic decision making [435 U.S. at 91–92].

In a case in which the Court relied heavily on *Horowitz*, a student filed a substantive due process challenge to his academic dismissal from medical school. The student, whose entire record of academic performance in medical school was mediocre, asserted that the school's refusal to allow him to retake the National Board of Medical Examiners examination violated his constitutional rights because other students had been allowed to retake the exam. In *Regents of the University of Michigan v. Ewing*, 474 U.S. 214 (1985), the Court assumed without deciding the issue that Ewing had a property interest in continued enrollment in medical school. The Court noted that it was not the school's procedures that were under review—the question was "whether the record compels the conclusion that the University acted arbitrarily in dropping Ewing from the Inteflex program without permitting a reexamination" (474 U.S. at 225). The court then stated:

Ewing's claim, therefore, must be that the University misjudged his fitness to remain a student in the Inteflex program. The record unmistakably demonstrates, however, that the faculty's decision was made conscientiously and with careful deliberation, based on an evaluation of the entirety of Ewing's academic career [474 U.S. at 225].

Citing *Horowitz,* the Court emphasized:

> When judges are asked to review the substance of a genuinely academic
> decision, such as this one, they should show great respect for the faculty's pro-
> fessional judgment. Plainly, they may not override it unless it is such a substan-
> tial departure from accepted academic norms as to demonstrate that the person
> or committee responsible did not actually exercise professional judgment [474
> U.S. at 225].

Citing *Keyishian* (discussed in Section 3.7.1), the Court reminded the parties that
concerns about institutional academic freedom also limited the nature of judicial
review of substantive academic judgments.

Although the result in *Ewing* represents the standard to be used by lower
courts, the Court's willingness to assume the existence of a property or liberty interest
is questionable in light of a subsequent Supreme Court ruling. In *Siegert v.
Gilley,* 111 S. Ct. 1789 (1991), the Court ruled that when defendants who are state officials
or state agencies raise a defense of qualified immunity (see Section 2.3.3), federal
courts must determine whether a property or liberty interest was "clearly established"
at the time the defendant acted. Applying *Siegert,* the Supreme Court of Hawaii in
Soong v. University of Hawaii, 825 P.2d 1060 (Haw. 1992), ruled that a student had
no clearly established substantive constitutional right to continued enrollment in an
academic program.

Courts may resolve legal questions concerning the award of grades, credits, or
degrees not only by applying standards of arbitrariness or bad faith but also by
applying the terms of the student-institution contract (Section 4.1.3). A 1979 Kentucky
case, *Lexington Theological Seminary v. Vance,* 596 S.W.2d 11 (Ky. Ct. App. 1979),
illustrates the deference that may be accorded postsecondary institutions—especially
church-related institutions—in identifying and construing the contract. The case also
illustrates the problems that may arise when institutions attempt to withhold academic recognition from students because of their homosexuality.

The Lexington Theological Seminary, a seminary training ministers for the
Disciples of Christ and other denominations, had denied Vance, a student who had
successfully completed all his academic requirements, a Master of Divinity degree
because of his admitted homosexuality. The student had enrolled in the seminary in
1972. In September 1975 he advised the dean of the school and the president of the
seminary of his homosexuality. In January 1976 the student was informed that his
degree candidacy would be deferred until he completed one additional course. In May
1976, after he had successfully completed the course, the faculty voted to grant the
Master of Divinity degree. The seminary's executive committee, however, voted not
to approve the faculty recommendation, and the board of trustees subsequently ratified the committee's decision. The student brought suit, seeking conferral of the
degree.[26]

The trial court dealt with the suit as a contract case and held that the seminary
had breached its contract with the plaintiff student. The Kentucky Court of Appeals,

---

[26]See generally Annot., "Certificates and Certification: Student's Right to Compel
School Officials to Issue Degree, Diploma, or the Like," 11 A.L.R.4th 1182 (1982 and periodic
supp.).

although it overruled the trial court, also agreed to apply contract principles to the case: "The terms and conditions for graduation from a private college or university are those offered by the publications of the college at the time of enrollment and, as such, have some of the characteristics of a contract."

The appellate court relied on various phrases from the seminary's catalogue—such as "Christian ministry," "gospel transmitted through the Bible," "servants of the Gospel," "fundamental character," and "display traits of character and personality which indicate probable effectiveness in the Christian ministry"—which it determined to be contract terms. It held that these terms created "reasonably clear standards" and interpreted them to permit the seminary to bar a homosexual student from receiving a degree. The court found that the seminary, being a religious institution preparing ministers to preach the gospel, had "a most compelling interest" in allowing only "persons possessing character of the highest Christian ideals" to graduate and that it had exercised sound discretion in denying the degree.

The court's reasoning sparked a strong dissenting opinion, which examined not only the language in the seminary catalogue but also the conduct of the seminary's dean, president, and faculty. To the dissenting judge, "Since neither the dean, the president, nor the faculty understood the catalogue to clearly exclude homosexuals, their view certainly cloud[ed] any contrary meaning." The dissent also argued that the language used in the catalogue was not sufficiently clear: "In the future, the board should consider revising the catalogue to be more explicit on what is meant by 'fundamental character.' The board might also make it clear that applications for degree candidacy will not only be 'evaluated by the faculty' but will also be reviewed by the board."

The *Lexington Theological Seminary* case illustrates that courts may resolve questions of academic credits or degrees by viewing the school catalogue as a contract binding on both student and institution. The majority opinion also illustrates the flexibility that courts may accord postsecondary institutions in drafting and interpreting this contract, and the special deference that may be accorded church-related institutions in enforcing terms dealing with morality. The dissent in this case, however, deserves as much attention as the majority opinion. It cautions administrators against construing ambiguous catalogue or policy language in a way that is inconsistent with their prior actions (see Section 1.3.2.3) and illustrates the potential for ambiguity that resides in general terms such as "fundamental character." Postsecondary administrators should heed these warnings. Other courts may not be as deferential to the institution as the Kentucky Court of Appeals was, especially in cases that involve life-style or off-campus behavior rather than the quality of academic works as such. Even if administrators could confidently expect broad deference from the courts, the dissent's cautions are still valuable as suggestions for how institutions can do better, of their own accord rather than through judicial compulsion, in ordering their own internal affairs.

An example of a court's refusal to defer to a college's interpretation of its catalogue and policy documents is *Russell v. Salve Regina College*, 890 F.2d 484 (1st Cir. 1989). Sharon Russell had been asked to withdraw from the nursing program at the college because the administrators believed her obesity was unsatisfactory for a nursing student. Although Russell's academic performance in all but one course was satisfactory or better, the instructor in one clinical course gave her a failing grade, which the jury found was related to her weight, not to her performance. Although the nursing program's rules specified that failing a clinical course would result in expulsion, the college promised Russell that she could remain in the program if she would sign a contract promising to lose weight on a regular basis. She did so, and attended Weight Watchers during that year, but did not lose weight. At the end of her junior year, Russell was asked to withdraw from Salve Regina, and she transferred to another nursing program, where she was required to repeat her junior year because of a two-year residency requirement. She completed her nursing degree, but in five years rather than four.

Although the trial judge dismissed her tort claims of intentional infliction of emotional distress and invasion of privacy (stemming from administrators' conduct regarding her obesity), the contract claim had been submitted to the jury, which had found for Russell and had awarded her approximately $44,000. On appeal, the court discussed the terms of the contract:

> From the various catalogs, manuals, handbooks, etc., that form the contract between student and institution, the district court, in its jury charge, boiled the agreement between the parties down to one in which Russell on the one hand was required to abide by disciplinary rules, pay tuition, and maintain good academic standing, and the College on the other hand was required to provide her with an education until graduation. The court informed the jury that the agreement was modified by the "contract" the parties signed during Russell's junior year. The jury was told that, if Russell "substantially performed" her side of the bargain, the College's actions constituted a breach [890 F.2d at 488].

The college had objected to the trial court's use of commercial contract principles of substantial performance rather than using a more deferential approach, such as was used in *Slaughter v. Brigham Young University* (Sections 4.6.2 and 4.8.4, this volume). But the appellate court disagreed, noting that the college's actions were based not on academic judgments but on a belief that the student's weight was inappropriate, despite the fact that the college knew of the student's obesity when it admitted her to both the college and the nursing program:

> Under the circumstances, the "unique" position of the College as educator becomes less compelling. As a result, the reasons against applying the substantial performance standard to this aspect of the student-college relationship also become less compelling. Thus, Salve Regina's contention that a court cannot use the substantial performance standard to compel an institution to graduate a student merely because the student has completed 124 out of 128 credits, while correct, is inapposite. The court may step in where, as here, full performance by the student has been hindered by some form of impermissible action [890 F.2d at 489].

Unlike the student in the *Lexington Theological Seminary* case, Russell was not asking the court to award her a degree; she was asking for contract damages, which included one year of forgone income (while she attended the other college for the extra year). The appellate court found that this portion of the award, $25,000, was appropriate. (The U.S. Supreme Court subsequently reversed and remanded the appellate court's decision (499 U.S. 255 (1991)); on remand the appellate court reinstated its prior judgment and opinion (938 F.2d 315 (1st Cir. 1991)).)

Although infrequent, challenges to grades or examination results have been brought by students. For example, in *Olsson v. Board of Higher Education of the City of New York*, 402 N.E.2d 1150 (N.Y. 1980), a student had not passed a comprehensive examination and therefore had not been awarded the M.A. degree for which he had been working. He claimed that his professor had misled him about the required passing grade on the examination. The professor had meant to say that a student must score three out of a possible five points on four of the five questions; instead, the professor said that a student must pass three of five questions. The student invoked the estoppel doctrine—the doctrine that justifiable reliance on a statement or promise estops the other from contradicting it if the reliance led directly to a detriment or injustice to the promisee. He argued that (1) he had justifiably relied on the professor's statement in budgeting both his study and test time, (2) he had achieved the grade the professor had stated was necessary, and (3) injustice would result if the university was not estopped from denying the degree.

The trial court and the intermediate appellate court both accepted the student's argument. The state's highest appellate court, however, did not. Deferring to the academic judgment of the institution, and emphasizing that the institution had offered the student an opportunity to retake the exam, the court refused to grant a "degree by estoppel":

> In reversing the determinations below, we are mindful that this case involves more than a simple balancing of equities among various competing commercial interests. While it is true that in the ordinary case, a principal must answer for the misstatements of his agent when the latter is clothed with a mantle of apparent authority (see, for example, *Phillips v. West Rockaway Land Co.*, 226 N.Y. 507, 124 N.E. 87), such hornbook rules cannot be applied mechanically where the "principal" is an educational institution and the result would be to override a determination concerning a student's academic qualifications. Because such determinations rest in most cases upon the subjective professional judgment of trained educators, the courts have quite properly exercised the utmost restraint in applying traditional legal rules to disputes within the academic community (see, for example, *Board of Curators, University of Missouri v. Horowitz*, 435 U.S. 78 . . .).
>
> This judicial reluctance to intervene in controversies involving academic standards is founded upon sound considerations of public policy. When an educational institution issues a diploma to one of its students, it is, in effect, certifying to society that the student possesses all of the knowledge and skills that are required by his chosen discipline. In order for society to be able to have complete confidence in the credentials dispensed by academic institutions, however, it is essential that the decisions surrounding the issuance of these credentials be left to the sound judgment of the professional educators who monitor the progress of their students on a regular basis. Indeed, the value of these credentials from the point of view of society would be seriously undermined if the courts were to abandon their longstanding practice of restraint in this area and instead began to utilize traditional equitable estoppel principles as a basis for requiring institutions to confer diplomas upon those who have been deemed to be unqualified.
>
> Certainly [in this case John Jay College] was not obliged to confer a diploma upon Olsson before he demonstrated his competence in accordance with the institution's academic standards. The mere circumstance that Olsson may have been misled by Professor Kim's unfortunate remark cannot serve to enhance the student's position in this regard. Despite Olsson's speculative contention that

he might have passed the examination had he not been misinformed about the grading criteria, the fact remains that neither the courts nor the college authorities have any way of knowing whether the outcome of the testing would have been different if Olsson had not "relied" upon Professor Kim's misstatement. Indeed, the fact that 23 of the 35 students enrolled in Professor Kim's review course managed to pass the examination despite the faculty member's "slip-of-the-tongue" serves to demonstrate that there was no necessary connection between Olsson's exposure to the "three out of five" comment and his failure to achieve a passing score. Under these circumstances, requiring the college to award Olsson a diploma on equitable estoppel grounds would be a disservice to society, since the credential would not represent the college's considered judgment that Olsson possessed the requisite qualifications [402 N.E.2d at 1152–53].

Although the court refused to apply the estoppel doctrine to the particular facts of this case, it indicated that in other, more extreme, circumstances estoppel could apply to problems concerning grading and other academic judgments. The court compared Olsson's situation to that of the plaintiff in *Blank v. Board of Higher Education of the City of New York*, 273 N.Y.S.2d 796 (see this volume, Section 2.2.2), in which the student had completed all academic requirements for his bachelor's degree but had not spent his final term "in residence." The student demonstrated reliance on the incorrect advice of several advisers and faculty members, and had only failed to satisfy a technical requirement rather than an academic one. The court explained:

> The outstanding feature which differentiates *Blank* from the instant case is the unavoidable fact that in *Blank* the student unquestionably had fulfilled the academic requirements for the credential he sought. Unlike the student here, the student in *Blank* had demonstrated his competence in the subject matter to the satisfaction of his professors. Thus, there could be no public policy objection to [the court's] decision to award a "diploma by estoppel" (accord *Matter of Healy v. Larsson*, . . . [323 N.Y.S.2d 625, *affirmed*, 348 N.Y.S.2d 971 (App. Div.), *affirmed*, 318 N.E.2d 608 (N.Y. 1971)]. Moreover, although the distinction is not dispositive, it cannot be overlooked that the student in *Blank* had relied upon a continuous series of deliberate and considered assurances from several faculty members, while Olsson, the student in this case, premised his estoppel claim upon a single inadvertent "slip-of-the-tongue" made by one professor during the course of a single presentation [402 N.E.2d at 1154].[27]

The *Olsson* case thus provides both an extensive justification of "academic deference"—that is, judicial deference to an educational institution's academic judgments—and an extensive analysis of the circumstances in which courts, rather than

[27]Another case in which the court ordered the award of a degree is *Kantor v. Schmidt*, 423 N.Y.S.2d 208 (N.Y. App. Div. 1979), a mandamus proceeding under New York law. The State University of New York at Stony Brook had withheld the degree because the student had not made sufficient progress, within established time limits, toward completion of the degree. A New York trial court ordered the defendant to award a B.A. degree to the student because the university had not complied with the state commissioner of education's regulations on student progress and informing students of progress. The appellate court affirmed but, on reargument, vacated its decision and dismissed the appeal as moot (432 N.Y.S.2d 156 (1980)).

4.7.1. Awarding of Grades and Degrees

deferring, should invoke estoppel principles to protect students challenging academic decisions. Synthesizing its analysis, the court concluded:

> It must be stressed that the judicial awarding of an academic diploma is an extreme remedy which should be reserved for the most egregious of circumstances. In light of the serious policy considerations which militate against judicial intervention in academic disputes, the courts should shun the "diploma by estoppel" doctrine whenever there is some question as to whether the student seeking relief has actually demonstrated his competence in accordance with the standards devised by the appropriate school authorities. Additionally, the courts should be particularly cautious in applying the doctrine in cases such as this, where a less drastic remedy, such as retesting, may be employed without seriously disrupting the student's academic or professional career [402 N.E.2d at 1154].

A challenge to grades in two law school courses provided the New York courts with an opportunity to address another issue similar to that in *Olsson*—the standard of review to be used when students challenge particular grades. In *Susan M v. New York Law School*, 544 N.Y.S.2d 829 (N.Y. App. Div. 1989), *reversed*, 556 N.E.2d 1104 (N.Y. 1990), a law student dismissed for inadequate academic performance sought judicial review of her grades in her constitutional law and corporations courses. The student claimed that she had received poor grades because of errors made by the professors in both courses. In the constitutional law course, she alleged, the professor gave incorrect instructions on whether the exam was open-book; in the corporations course, the professor evaluated a correct answer as incorrect. The law school asserted that these allegations were beyond judicial review because they were a matter of professional discretion.

Although Susan M's claims were dismissed by the trial court, the intermediate appellate court disagreed with the law school's characterization of both grade disputes as beyond judicial review. It agreed that the dispute over the constitutional law examination was "precisely the type of professional, educational judgment the courts will not review" (544 N.Y.S.2d at 830); but the student's claim regarding her answer in the corporations exam, for which she received no credit, was a different matter. The court said:

> At least when a student's very right to remain in school depends on it, we think the school owes the student some manner of safeguard against the possibility of arbitrary or capricious error in grading, and that, in the absence of any such safeguards, concrete allegations of flagrant misapprehension on the part of the grader entitle the student to a measure of relief [544 N.Y.S.2d at 831-32].

The court then described the type of review it believed appropriate, an approach that, had it been upheld on appeal, would have subjected the professor's reasoning process in grading the examination to judicial scrutiny:

> At issue is not what grade petitioner should have received but whether the grade received was arbitrary and capricious; not whether petitioner deserved a C+ instead of a D in Corporations but whether she deserved a zero on this particular essay; not the quality of petitioner's answer but the rationality of the professor's grading [544 N.Y.S.2d at 832].

The court remanded this issue to the law school "for further consideration of petitioner's grade in Corporations." It asked the school to provide "reasonable assurances that the zero given her on the essay in question was a rational exercise of discretion by the grader" (544 N.Y.S.2d at 832). The law school appealed, and the state's highest court unanimously reversed the appellate division's holding, reinstating the outcome in the trial court.

The court strongly endorsed the academic deference argument made by the law school, stating in the opinion's first paragraph:

> Because [the plaintiff's] allegations are directed at the pedagogical evaluation of her test grades, a determination best left to educators rather than the courts, we conclude that her petition does not state a judicially cognizable claim [556 N.E.2d at 1105].

After reviewing the outcomes in earlier challenges to the academic determinations of colleges and universities, the state's highest court stated:

> As a general rule, judicial review of grading disputes would inappropriately involve the courts in the very core of academic and educational decision making. Moreover, to so involve the courts in assessing the propriety of particular grades would promote litigation by countless unsuccessful students and thus undermine the credibility of the academic determinations of educational institutions. We conclude, therefore, that, in the absence of demonstrated bad faith, arbitrariness, capriciousness, irrationality or a constitutional or statutory violation, a student's challenge to a particular grade or other academic determination relating to a genuine substantive evaluation of the student's academic capabilities, is beyond the scope of judicial review [556 N.E.2d at 1107].

Concluding that the plaintiff's claims concerned substantive evaluation of her academic performance, the court refused to review them.

For a summary of legal challenges to academic judgments and a review of the *Susan M* case, see Note, "Student Challenges to Grades and Academic Dismissals: Are They Losing Battles?" 18 *J. Coll. & Univ. Law* 577 (1992). See also F. Faulkner, "Judicial Deference to University Decisions Not to Grant Degrees, Certificates, and Credit—The Fiduciary Alternative," 40 *Syracuse L. Rev.* 837 (1990), and T. A. Schweitzer, " 'Academic Challenge' Cases: Should Judicial Review Extend to Academic Evaluations of Students?" 41 *American U. L. Rev.* 267 (1992). *Susan M* is also humorously reviewed in verse by R. E. Rains in 40 *J. Legal Educ.* 485 (1990) and 43 *J. Legal Educ.* 149 (1993).

Although students apparently may not obtain academic credentials through litigation, they occasionally obtain them fraudulently, either by claiming degrees from "diploma mills" or by altering transcripts to make it appear that they completed a degree. For analysis of this issue, see J. Van Tol, "Detecting, Deterring and Punishing the Use of Fradulent Academic Credentials: A Play in Two Acts," 29 *Santa Clara L. Rev.* 1 (1990).

4.7.2 Degree revocation. Generally, both public and private colleges and universities ᴊthority to revoke improperly awarded degrees when good cause for doing so, such as discovery of fraud or misrepresentation, is shown.[28] Public institutions must afford the degree recipient notice and an opportunity for a hearing before making a decision on whether to revoke a degree, following due process guidelines (see Section 4.8.2). Private institutions, although generally not subject to constitutional requirements, are subject to contract law, and generally must use procedures that will protect the degree recipient from potentially arbitrary or capricious conduct by the institution (see Section 4.8.4).

Degree revocations by both public and private institutions have been challenged in lawsuits. In *Waliga v. Board of Trustees of Kent State University*, 488 N.E.2d 850 (Ohio 1986), the Ohio Supreme Court upheld the university's right to rescind a degree. Two individuals had been awarded baccalaureate degrees, one in 1966 and one in 1967, from Kent State University. University officials discovered, over ten years later, discrepancies such as credits granted for courses the students never took, and grades on official records different from those reported by course professors. The university rescinded the degrees on the grounds that the students had not completed the appropriate number of credits for graduation.

The students sought a declaratory judgment on the university's power to rescind a degree. The Ohio Supreme Court found such power under two theories. First, the Court interpreted Ohio law as permitting any action necessary for operating the state university unless such action was expressly prohibited by statute. As long as a fair hearing had been held, the university had the power to rescind a degree procured by fraud. Second, the court addressed the significance of the public's confidence in the integrity of degrees awarded by colleges and universities:

> Academic degrees are a university's certification to the world at large of the recipient's educational achievement and the fulfillment of the institution's standards. To hold that a university may never withdraw a degree, effectively requires the university to continue making a false certification to the public at large of the accomplishment of persons who in fact lack the very qualifications that are certified [488 N.E.2d at 852].

Just as a university has the power to refuse to confer a degree if a student does not complete the requirements for graduation, it also has the power, the court ruled, to rescind a degree awarded to a student who did not complete those requirements.

Given an institution's power to rescind a degree, what procedural protections must the institution give the student? If the institution is public, the Fourteenth Amendment's Due Process Clause may require certain protections, particularly if the court finds a property interest in the student's possession of the degree. In *Crook v. Baker*, 813 F.2d 88 (6th Cir. 1987), a federal appeals court addressed this issue.

After awarding Crook an M.A. in geology, the University of Michigan determined that the data he had used in his master's thesis were fabricated, and notified him that a hearing would be held to determine whether the degree should be revoked. Crook filed a complaint in federal court, asserting that the university lacked the power to rescind a degree and, if such power were present, that the procedures used by the

[28]Cases and authorities are collected in Annot., "College's Power to Revoke Degree," 57 A.L.R.4th 1243 (1987 and periodic supp.).

university violated his due process rights because they did not permit him to cross-examine witnesses.

The court first considered whether the university had the power to rescind the degree. Summarizing the opinion in *Waliga* at some length, the court determined that "there is nothing in Michigan constitutional, statutory or case law that indicates that the Regents do not have the power to rescind the grant of a degree" (813 F.2d at 92), and noted that the state constitution gave the universitiy significant indpendence in educational matters.

Turning to the student's procedural claims, the court applied the teachings of *Goss v. Lopez* (Section 4.8.2) to evaluate the sufficiency of the procedural protections afforded Crook. Although the trial court had ruled that the hearing violated Crook's right to due process, the appellate court found that the university had given Crook sufficient notice of the charges against him and that the hearing—at which he was permitted to have counsel present, to present witnesses in his behalf, and to respond to the charges against him—complied with the requirements of *Goss*. The appellate court characterized the hearing as "informal," in that hearing panel members asked questions and neither the university nor Crook was permitted to ask questions of the witnesses. Citing its earlier opinion in *Frumkin v. Board of Trustees* (see this volume, Section 3.6.2.3), the court found that Crook had no procedural due process right to have his attorney examine and cross-examine witnesses, and that the procedures provided by the university were sufficient for due process purposes.

Crook had also claimed violation of his substantive due process rights, alleging no rational basis for the rescission of his degree. Citing *Ewing* (see Section 4.7.1), the court found that the hearing committee had exercised professional judgment and that the committee's determination that Crook's data were fabricated was neither arbitrary nor capricious.

Waliga and *Crook* establish the power of a public institution to rescind a degree, and *Crook* discusses the type of procedural protection required to meet constitutional due process standards. When private institutions are involved, however, constitutional requirements typically do not apply. Unless the institution can meet the "state action" test (see Section 1.5.2), constitutional protections are not available to the student (*Imperiale v. Hahnemann University*, 966 F.2d 125 (3d Cir. 1992)).

In a lawsuit filed against Claremont University Center by a student whose doctoral degree was revoked on the grounds that his dissertation was plagiarized, a California appellate court analyzed the university's actions under a deferential standard of review—whether or not the university abused its discretion. In *Abalkhail v. Claremont University Center*, 2d Civ. No. B014012 (Cal. Ct. App. 1986), the court detailed the procedures used to determine whether the degree should be revoked. The university had received a report that portions of the dissertation might have been plagiarized, and it appointed a committee of investigation to determine whether plagiarism had occurred and degree revocation was warranted.

After the committee concluded that plagiarism might have occurred, the graduate school dean informed Abalkhail that a hearing would be held and described the procedures that would be followed. Abalkhail did not receive a copy of the letter that instigated the investigation until the day of the hearing, but he was given the opportunity to respond to the charges against him and was asked if there were additional procedures necessary to give him a fair hearing. The hearing committee met again with Abalkhail to inform him of additional evidence against him and to permit him to respond to that evidence by a particular time. After the time for response had elapsed, the committee found that much of Abalkhail's dissertation was plagiarized and recommended that his degree be rescinded. The university did so, and Abalkhail filed a complaint, alleging deprivation of due process and fairness protections.

Applying the California common law doctrine of fair procedures required of nonprofit groups, the court ruled that Abalkhail was entitled to "the minimum requisites of procedural fairness" (2d Civ. No. B014012 at 15). These "minimum requisites" included notice of the charges and the probable consequences of a finding that the charges would be upheld, a fair opportunity to present his position, and a fair hearing. These had been provided to the plaintiff, according to the court.

For analysis of *Waliga, Crook,* and *Abalkhail,* see B. Reams, Jr., "Revocation of Academic Degrees by Colleges and Universities," 14 *J. Coll. & Univ. Law* 283 (1987).

Although institutions of higher education appear to have the authority to revoke degrees, the revocation must be an act of the same entity that has the authority to award the degree. In *Hand v. Matchell,* 957 F.2d 791 (10th Cir. 1992), a federal appellate court affirmed a federal trial court's award of summary judgment to a former student who challenged his degree revocation. The board of regents of New Mexico State University had not acted on the degree revocation, but had delegated that decision to the graduate dean and, when the student appealed the dean's decision, to the executive vice president. Although the university had developed a procedure that involved both faculty and external experts in the determination that the plaintiff's dissertation had been plagiarized, the court, interpreting New Mexico law, said that the board could not delegate its authority to revoke a degree to a subordinate individual or body.

4.7.3 *Sexual harassment by faculty.* Although students typically have not prevailed in challenges to grades or the denial of degrees on academic grounds, they are meeting with somewhat more success when the allegation is that sexual harassment influenced the grading decision. Sexual harassment of faculty, a violation of Title VII and Title IX as well as states' fair employment laws, is discussed in Section 3.3.4.3.

Sexual harassment of students is a violation of Title IX of the Education Amendments of 1972 (discussed in Section 7.5.3) in that it may interfere with a student's ability to benefit from an educational program by subjecting the student to behavioral or grading criteria not applied to other students. If the student works for the college or university and is harassed by a co-worker or supervisor, the harassment may also be a violation of Title VII or the state's fair employment law (see, for example, *Karibian v. Columbia University,* 14 F.3d 773 (2d Cir. 1994), where the university was held strictly liable for the sexual harassment of a student employee by her supervisor).

The existence and extent of sexual harassment against students is well documented (see, for example, B. W. Dziech & L. Weiner, *The Lecherous Professor: Sexual Harassment on Campus* (Beacon Press, 1984)). Colleges and universities that have promulgated policies prohibiting harassment of students have forbidden such behaviors as sexist behavior (using sexual images or sexual language when sex is irrelevant to the subject matter, or sexual joking that embarrasses or humiliates students of one sex); romantic relationships between professors and students; and unwanted demands for sexual favors with overt or implied threats or promises of academic rewards or punishments.

Although Title IX has been in effect for over two decades, only in recent years have students succeeded in litigation charging faculty and their institutions with liability for sexual harassment, and most of these cases have turned on procedural issues. In an early case, *Alexander v. Yale University*, 631 F.2d 178 (2d Cir. 1980), five female students alleged that Yale's practices and procedures for dealing with sexual harassment of students violated Title IX of the Education Amendments of 1972. One of the plaintiffs alleged that a faculty member had "offered to give her a grade of 'A' in the course in exchange for her compliance with his sexual demands" and that, when she refused, he gave her a C, which "was not the result of a fair evaluation of her academic work but the result of her failure to accede to [the professor's] sexual demands." The remaining plaintiffs made other allegations concerning acts of harassment and the inadequacies of campus procedures to deal with them.

The district court entered judgment for Yale, and the U.S. Court of Appeals affirmed. With the exception of the lowered-grade claim of one plaintiff, all the various claims and plaintiffs were dismissed for technical reasons: the plaintiffs had graduated and their claims were therefore "moot"; Yale had already adopted procedures for dealing with sexual harassment and thus, in effect, had already granted the primary remedy requested in the suit; other claims of harm were too "speculative" or "uncertain." The lowered-grade claim was dismissed because the plaintiff, at trial, did not prove the allegations.

Although it rejected all claims, the *Alexander* court by no means shut the door on Title IX actions alleging that the integrity of grading or other academic processes has been compromised by faculty's sexual harassment of students. Both trial and appellate courts made clear that the grade claim was a "justifiable claim for relief under Title IX." A denial or threatened denial of earned academic awards would be a deprivation of an educational benefit protected by Title IX; and when imposed for sexual reasons, that deprivation becomes sex discrimination prohibited by Title IX. As the district court held, and the appellate court quoted with apparent approval, "Academic advancement conditioned upon submission to sexual demands constitutes sex discrimination in education" (459 F. Supp. 1, 4 (D. Conn. 1977), 631 F.2d at 182).

A federal appellate court clarified several significant issues relating to sexual harassment in *Lipsett v. University of Puerto Rico*, 864 F.2d 881 (1st Cir. 1988). Lipsett, a female surgical resident at the university hospital, was dismissed from her residency after complaining on several occasions about sexual harassment from both her fellow residents and some of the faculty members supervising her. The harassment involved statements by her fellow students and faculty supervisors that women should not be surgeons, sexual advances and unwelcome touching by some residents, name-calling, and the posting of centerfolds from *Playboy* magazine in the residents' dining area. Her supervisors ignored her complaints and dismissed her from the program for insubordination and violation of rules, behavior that Lipsett either denied or asserted was general practice among the residents.

Lipsett filed claims under Title IX against the residents and under Section 1983 (on equal protection grounds) against the faculty and program staff. In reviewing the district court's grant of summary judgment to the university and its administrators, the appellate court evaluated whether, using Lipsett's version of the facts, she could have prevailed on her discrimination claims. Because Lipsett was both a student and an employee of the university, the court used Title VII precedent to interpret Title IX's application to the plaintiff's claims that the sexual harassment had created a hostile environment.

Applying the order-of-proof model of *McDonnell Douglas v. Green* (discussed in Section 3.3.2.1), the court found that Lipsett had established a prima facie case of hostile work environment and quid pro quo sexual harassment by the residents,[29] that the complaints about her work performance were "infused with discriminatory bias," that most of her supervisors knew of the harassment, and that the failure of the supervising faculty to investigate her complaints could constitute gross negligence. These findings suggested that the supervising faculty could be held individually liable under Section 1983 (Section 2.3.3).

With regard to the standard for determining liability for quid pro quo harassment, the court found, citing *Meritor Savings Bank v. Vinson* (discussed in Section 3.3.4.3), that an educational institution is "absolutely liable" whether or not it knew, should have known, or approved of a supervisor's actions (864 F.2d at 901). With regard to hostile environment harassment, the court adopted *Meritor's* agency theory of liability, stating:

> [I]n a Title IX case, an educational institution is liable upon a finding of hostile environment sexual harassment perpetrated by its supervisors upon employees *if* an official representing that institution knew, or in the exercise of reasonable care, should have known, of the harassment's occurrence, *unless* that official can show that he or she took appropriate steps to halt it [864 F.2d at 901].

While the analysis in *Lipsett* is useful in those unusual cases where the student is both an employee and a student, it may have limited application in cases in which the student is not an employee.

Two federal courts addressed the issue of whether Title IX permitted claims of hostile environment sexual harassment, with different outcomes. In *Moire v. Temple University School of Medicine*, 613 F. Supp. 1360 (E.D. Pa. 1985), *affirmed without opin.*, 800 F.2d 1136 (3d Cir. 1986), the court rejected for lack of evidence a female medical student's claim that her supervisor's sexually oriented comments had created a hostile environment. The court did, however, express its willingness to apply Title VII theories of hostile environment harassment to claims brought under Title IX:

> [H]arassment from an abusive environment occurs where multiple incidents of offensive conduct lead to an environment violative of a victim's civil rights. Here there is no allegation of *quid pro quo* harassment. . . . The issue is whether plaintiff because of her sex was in a harassing or abusive environment [613 F. Supp. at 1366-67].

Conversely, a federal district court refused to find that Title IX permitted hostile environment claims. In *Bougher v. University of Pittsburgh*, 713 F. Supp. 139 (W.D.

---

[29]"Hostile work environment" sexual harassment is sexually oriented conduct by peers, nonemployees, or supervisors that creates an abusive or hostile work environment on the basis of the individual's gender. Quid pro quo sexual harassment is an exchange of sexual favors in return for a supervisor's promise either to grant employment benefits or to refrain from taking adverse action against an employee.

Pa. 1989), *affirmed*, 882 F.2d 74 (3d Cir. 1989), the court rejected the plaintiff's argument that Title VII theories should be applied to Title IX:

> [T]o suggest, as plaintiff must, that unwelcome sexual advances, from *whatever* source, official or unofficial, constitute Title IX violations is a leap into the unknown which, whatever its wisdom, is the duty of Congress or an administrative agency to take. Title IX simply does not permit a "hostile environment" claim as described for the workplace [713 F. Supp. at 145].

Because the appellate court found that the plaintiff's claim was barred by the state statute of limitations, it did not determine whether Title IX includes hostile environment claims. It made this comment, however: "[W]e decline to adopt [the district court's] reasoning *in toto* and we find it unnecessary to reach the question, important though it may be, whether evidence of a hostile environment is sufficient to sustain a claim of sexual discrimination in education in violation of Title IX" (882 F.2d at 77). For analysis of Title IX's application to both theories of sexual harassment, see R. Schneider, "Sexual Harassment and Higher Education," 65 *Tex. L. Rev.* 525 (1987).

Another federal district court stated unequivocally that Title IX contemplated hostile environment claims. In *Patricia H. v. Berkeley Unified School District*, 830 F. Supp. 1288 (N.D. Cal. 1993), the court relied on the findings in *Meritor* and *Franklin* (see Section 7.5.3.) to decide that the continuing presence of a teacher who had allegedly molested a high school student created a hostile environment, and that the student's claim was actionable under Title IX.

Students have used theories in addition to Title IX to seek remedies for alleged sexual harassment. In *George v. University of Idaho*, 822 P.2d 549 (Idaho Ct. App. 1991), a law student, who had ended a consensual relationship with a law professor, filed a breach-of-contract claim against the university, asserting that the professor's efforts to resume the relationship, and his retaliation in the form of actions disparaging her character within the law school and the legal community, constituted breach of an implied contract. The court denied summary judgment for the university, noting the existence of several questions of fact concerning the nature and scope of the university's responsibility to the student. First of all, the court noted, the university had an implied contract with the student—as evidenced by the university's sexual harassment policy and by its statement in the faculty handbook that it would "fulfill its responsibilities in pursuit of the academic goals and objectives of all members of the community." Furthermore, when the student brought the professor's actions to the attention of the school, a written agreement had been executed, in which the professor promised to stop harassing the plaintiff if she would drop claims against him and the law school. The court found that the university had an obligation under that agreement independent of its implied contract with the plaintiff, an obligation that extended beyond her graduation, to take reasonable measures to enforce the agreement.

An unpublished case brought under Minnesota's nondiscrimination law illustrates the nature of contemporary judicial review of student sexual harassment claims. In *Smith v. Hennepin County Technical Center*, 1988 U.S. Dist. LEXIS 4876 (D. Minn. 1988), two students charged the instructor in a dental laboratory with offensive touching and retaliation when they complained of his conduct. The court, using Title

VII law by analogy, adopted a five-step prima facie test for demonstrating sexual harassment in an educational setting:

[The plaintiff must show that]
1. she was a member of a protected class;
2. she was subject to unwelcome harassment;
3. the harassment was based on sex;
4. the harassment had the purpose or effect of unreasonably interfering with her education or created an intimidating, hostile, or offensive learning environment; and
5. the educational institution knew or should have known of the harassment and failed to take proper remedial action [1988 U.S. Dist. LEXIS 4876 at 39].

Because the instructor was an employee of the institution, the court ruled that the institution was directly liable for torts committed by its employee if the employer could have prevented the tort through the exercise of reasonable care.

The decision by the U.S. Supreme Court in *Franklin v. Gwinnett County* (discussed in Section 7.5.3) that plaintiffs demonstrating intentional discrimination under Title IX may be awarded money damages raises the stakes for both plaintiffs and institutions in these cases. To that end, institutions of higher education have developed policies that both define prohibited sexually harassing conduct and provide a grievance system for students who believe they have been sexually harassed by a faculty member or an administrator.

One particularly difficult decision institutions may face in drafting sexual harassment policies is whether to prohibit all sexual relationships between students and faculty, consensual or not. Proponents of the total ban argue that the unequal power relationships between student and faculty member mean that no relationship is truly consensual. Opponents of total bans, on the other hand, argue that students are beyond the legal age of consent, and that institutions infringe on constitutional rights of free association or risk invasion-of-privacy claims if they attempt to regulate the personal lives of faculty and students. For discussion of this difficult issue, see M. Chamallas, "Consent, Equality and the Legal Control of Sexual Conduct," 61 *Southern Cal. L. Rev.* 777 (1988). See also P. DeChiara, "The Need for Universities to Have Rules on Consensual Sexual Relationships Between Faculty Members and Students," 21 *Columbia J. of Law & Social Problems* 137 (1988). For another point of view, see E. Keller, "Consensual Amorous Relationships Between Faculty and Students: The Constitutional Right to Privacy," 15 *J. Coll. & Univ. Law* 21 (1988).

Before it receives its first sexual harassment complaint from a student against a faculty member, the institution should determine what complaint procedure will be used. If there is a procedure for disciplining faculty, the institution could use such a procedure. The AAUP has released a statement on "Sexual Harassment: Suggested Policy and Procedures for Handling Complaints" (in *AAUP Policy Documents and Reports* (AAUP, 1990), 113-15), which includes due process protections for the accused and a faculty committee as fact finder. If the institution's procedure permits the faculty member to have an attorney present, the institution should determine whether it will provide counsel for the student, particularly if the faculty member sues the student as a result of the harassment complaint. Of course, the institution is exposed to potential litigation by both the accused faculty member and the student (see K. S.

Mangan, "Thorny Legal Issues Face Colleges Hit by Sexual-Harassment Cases," *Chron. Higher Educ.*, Aug. 4, 1993, A13).

Although it now appears to be established that institutions will face liability under Title IX for harassment by faculty, the issue of potential institutional liability for peer sexual harassment remains to be resolved. Although students are not agents of the institution (unless, perhaps, they are also employees), some commentators have argued that Title IX creates a duty upon colleges and universities to provide equal access to academic programs, and that sexual harassment, whether by students or faculty, denies women students that equal access. Recent Supreme Court rulings in free speech cases (see Section 4.10) have complicated the efforts of public institutions to outlaw harassing or threatening speech, but Title IX might provide an avenue for relief in cases of egregious harassment that the institution was aware of. For analysis of the complex legal issues involved, see J. Faber, "Expanding Title IX of the Education Amendments of 1972 to Prohibit Student to Student Sexual Harassment," 2 *UCLA Women's Law J. 85* (1992). For a report on peer sexual harassment, see *Peer Harassment: Hassles for Women on Campus* (Center for Women Policy Studies, 1992).

The Supreme Court's expansion of Title IX to permit compensatory damages might give rise to a plethora of claims for money damages by students who argue that they left college as a result of harassment and therefore suffered the loss of career opportunities as well as emotional distress. Courts have made it very clear in the employment context that prompt and effective remedial action must be taken when the organization is on notice that sexual harassment may have occurred. That standard is now being applied to the responses of colleges and universities, since students—increasingly aware of their rights and the availability of remedies—are losing their reluctance to complain about sexual harassment by faculty.

4.7.4 Students with disabilities. As noted in Section 4.2.4.3, the Rehabilitation Act and the Americans with Disabilities Act of 1990 require colleges and universities to provide reasonable accommodations for students with disabilities. Although the laws do not require institutions to change their academic criteria for disabled students, they may need to change the format of tests; to provide additional time, or readers or aides to help students take examinations; or to change minor aspects of course requirements.

The question of how much change is required arose in *Wynne v. Tufts University School of Medicine*, 976 F.2d 791 (1st Cir. 1992). A medical student dismissed on academic grounds asserted that the medical school had refused to accommodate his learning disability by requiring him to take a multiple-choice test rather than an alternative that would minimize the impact of his learning disability. Initially, the trial court granted summary judgment for Tufts, but the appellate court reversed on the grounds that the record was insufficient to enable the court to determine whether Tufts had attempted to accommodate Wynne and whether Tufts had evaluated the impact of the requested accommodation on its academic program (932 F.2d 19 (1st Cir. 1991, *en banc*)).

On remand, the university provided extensive evidence to the trial court that it had permitted Wynne to repeat his first year of medical school, had paid for the neuropsychological testing of Wynne that had identified his learning disabilities, and had provided him with tutors, note takers, and other assistance. It had permitted him to take make-up examinations for courses he failed, and had determined that there was not an appropriate alternative method of testing his knowledge in the biochemistry course.

On the strength of the school's evidence of serious consideration of alternatives to the multiple-choice test, the district court again awarded summary judgment for Tufts, and the appellate court affirmed. In deferring to the school's judgment on the need for a certain testing format, the court said:

> [T]he point is not whether a medical school is "right" or "wrong" in making program-related decisions. Such absolutes rarely apply in the context of subjective decision-making, particularly in a scholastic setting. The point is that Tufts, after undertaking a diligent assessment of the available options, felt itself obliged to make "a professional, academic judgment that [a] reasonable accommodation [was] simply not available" [976 F.2d at 795].

Given the multiple forms of assistance that Tufts had provided Wynne, and its ability to demonstrate that it had evaluated alternate test forms and determined that none would be an appropriate substitute for the multiple-choice format, the court was satisfied that the school had satisfied the requirements of the Rehabilitation Act.

In *Halasz v. University of New England*, 816 F. Supp. 37 (D. Me. 1993), a federal trial court relied on *Wynne* to review the challenge of a student, dismissed from the University of New England on academic grounds, that the school had failed to provide him with necessary accommodations and had discriminated against him on the basis of his disability. The school had a special program for students with learning disabilities who lacked the academic credentials necessary for regular admission to the university. The program provided a variety of support services for these students, and gave them an opportunity for regular admission to the university after they completed the special one-year program. Despite the special services, such as tutoring, taped texts, untimed testing, and readers for some of his classes, the plaintiff was unable to attain an academic record sufficient for regular admission to the university. His performance in the courses and tests that he took during his year in the special program indicated, the university alleged, that he was not an "otherwise qualified" student with a disability and thus was not protected by the Rehabilitation Act. The university was able to demonstrate the academic rationale for its program requirements and to show that the plaintiff had been given the same amount and quality of assistance that had been given to other students who later were offered admission to the university's regular academic program.

The decisions in *Wynne* and *Halasz* stress the significance of an institution's consideration of potential accommodations for students with disabilities. Given the tendency of courts to defer to academic judgments, but to hold colleges and universities to strict procedural standards, those institutions that can demonstrate, as could Tufts, that they gave careful consideration to the student's request, and reached a decision on *academic* grounds that the accommodation was either unnecessary or unsuitable, should be able to prevail against challenges under either the Rehabilitation Act or the ADA.

Sec. 4.8. Procedures for Suspension, Dismissal, and Other Sanctions

4.8.1. General principles. As Sections 4.6 and 4.7 indicate, both public and private postsecondary institutions have the clear right to dismiss, suspend, or impose lesser sanctions on students for behavioral misconduct or academic deficiency. But just as that right is limited by the principles set out in those sections, so it is also circumscribed by a body of procedural requirements that institutions must follow in effecting disciplinary or academic sanctions. These procedural requirements tend to be more specific and substantial than the requirements set out above, although they do vary depending on whether behavior or academics is involved and whether the institution is public or private (see Section 1.5.2).

At the threshold level, whenever an institution has established procedures that apply to the imposition of sanctions, the law will usually require that they be followed. In *Woody v. Burns*, 188 So. 2d 56 (Fla. 1966), for example, the court invalidated an expulsion from a public institution because a faculty committee had "circumvented . . . [the] duly authorized [disciplinary] committee and arrogated unto itself the authority of imposing its own penalty for appellant's misconduct." And in *Tedeschi v. Wagner College*, 49 N.Y.2d 652 (N.Y. 1980), New York's highest court invalidated a suspension from a private institution, holding that "when a university has adopted a rule or guideline establishing the procedure to be followed in relation to suspension or expulsion, that procedure must be substantially observed."

There are three exceptions, however, to this "follow-the-rules" principle. An institution may be excused from following its own procedures if the student knowingly and freely waives his or her right to them, as in *Yench v. Stockmar*, 483 F.2d 820 (10th Cir. 1973), where the student neither requested that the published procedures be followed nor objected when they were not. Second, deviations from established procedures may be excused when they do not disadvantage the student, as in *Winnick v. Manning*, 460 F.2d 545 (2d Cir. 1972), where the student contested the school's use of a panel other than that required by the rules, but the court held that the "deviations were minor ones and did not affect the fundamental fairness of the hearing." And third, if an institution provides more elaborate protections than constitutionally required, failure to provide nonrequired protections may not imply constitutional violations (see Section 4.8.3).

4.8.2. Public institutions: Disciplinary sanctions. State institutions may be subject to state administrative procedure acts, state board of higher education rules, or other state statutes or administrative regulations specifying particular procedures for suspensions or expulsions. In *Moresco v. Clark*, 473 N.Y.S.2d 843 (N.Y. App. Div. 1984), the court refused to apply New York State's Administrative Procedure Act to a suspension proceeding at SUNY-Cortland; but in *Mull v. Oregon Institute of Technology*, 538 P.2d 87 (Or. 1975), the court applied that state's administrative procedure statutes to a suspension for misconduct and remanded the case to the college with instructions to enter findings of fact and conclusions of law as required by one of the statutory provisions.

The primary external source of procedural requirements for public institutions, however, is the Due Process Clause of the federal Constitution, which prohibits the government from depriving an individual of life, liberty, or property without certain procedural protections.[30] Since the early 1960s, the concept of procedural due

[30]Cases are collected in Annot., "Expulsion, Dismissal, Suspension, or Other Discipline of Student of Public School, College, or University as Violating Due Process Clause of Federal Constitution's Fourteenth Amendment—Supreme Court Cases," 88 L. Ed. 2d 1015 (1985).

process has been one of the primary legal forces shaping the administration of postsecondary education. For purposes of due process analysis, courts typically assume, without deciding, that a student has a property interest in continued enrollment at a public institution (see, for example, *Marin v. University of Puerto Rico*, 377 F. Supp. 613, 622 (D.P.R. 1974)). One court stopped short of finding a property interest, but said that the Fourteenth Amendment "gives rights to a student who faces expulsion for misconduct at a tax-supported college or university" (*Henderson State University v. Spadoni*, 848 S.W.2d 951 (Ark. Ct. App. 1993). As did the court in *Marin*, the U.S. Supreme Court has assumed a property interest in continued enrollment in a public institution (for example, in *Ewing* and *Horowitz*, discussed in Sections 4.7.1 and 4.8.3 respectively), but has not yet directly ruled on this point.

A landmark 1961 case on suspension procedures, *Dixon v. Alabama State Board of Education*, 294 F.2d 150 (5th Cir. 1961), is still very instructive. Several black students at Alabama State College had been expelled during a period of intense civil rights activity in Montgomery, Alabama. The students, supported by the NAACP, sued the state board, and the court faced the question "whether [the] due process [clause of the Fourteenth Amendment] requires notice and some opportunity for hearing before students at a tax-supported college are expelled for misconduct." On appeal this question was answered in the affirmative, with the court establishing standards by which to measure the adequacy of a public institution's expulsion procedures:

> The notice should contain a statement of the specific charges and grounds which, if proven, would justify expulsion under the regulations of the board of education. The nature of the hearing should vary depending upon the circumstances of the particular case. The case before us requires something more than an informal interview with an administrative authority of the college. By its nature, a charge of misconduct, as opposed to a failure to meet the scholastic standards of the college, depends upon a collection of the facts concerning the charged misconduct, easily colored by the point of view of the witnesses. In such circumstances, a hearing which gives the board or the administrative authorities of the college an opportunity to hear both sides in considerable detail is best suited to protect the rights of all involved. This is not to imply that a full-dress judicial hearing, with the right to cross-examine witnesses, is required. Such a hearing, with the attending publicity and disturbance of college activities, might be detrimental to the college's educational atmosphere and impractical to carry out. Nevertheless, the rudiments of an adversary proceeding may be preserved without encroaching upon the interests of the college. In the instant case, the student should be given the names of the witnesses against him and an oral or written report on the facts to which each witness testifies. He should also be given the opportunity to present to the board, or at least to an administrative official of the college, his own defense against the charges and to produce either oral testimony or written affidavits of witnesses in his behalf. If the hearing is not before the board directly, the results and findings of the hearing should be presented in a report open to the student's inspection. If these rudimentary elements of fair play are followed in a case of misconduct of this particular type, we feel that the requirements of due process of law will have been fulfilled [294 F.2d at 158–59].

Since the *Dixon* case, courts at all levels have continued to recognize and extend the due process safeguards available to students charged by college officials with misconduct. Such safeguards must now be provided for all students in publicly supported schools, not only before expulsion, as in *Dixon*, but before suspension and other serious disciplinary action as well. In 1975 the U.S. Supreme Court itself recognized the vitality and clear national applicability of such developments when it held that even a secondary school student faced with a suspension of less than ten days is entitled to *"some* kind of notice and . . . *some* kind of hearing" (*Goss v. Lopez*, 419 U.S. 565, 579 (1975)).

Although the Court in *Goss* was not willing to afford students the right to a full-blown adversary hearing (involving cross-examination, written transcripts, and representation by counsel), it set out minimal requirements for compliance with the Due Process Clause. The Court said:

> We do not believe that school authorities must be totally free from notice and hearing requirements. . . . [T]he student [must] be given oral or written notice of the charges against him and, if he denies them, an explanation of the evidence the authorities have and an opportunity to present his side of the story. The [Due Process] Clause requires at least these rudimentary precautions against unfair or mistaken findings of misconduct and arbitrary exclusion from school [419 U.S. at 581].

In cases subsequent to *Goss*, most courts have applied these "minimal" procedural standards and, for the most part, have ruled in favor of the college.

Probably the case that has set forth due process requirements in greatest detail and, consequently, at the highest level of protection, is *Esteban v. Central Missouri State College*, 277 F. Supp. 649 (W.D. Mo. 1967) (see also later litigation in this case, discussed in Section 4.6.1 above). The plaintiffs had been suspended for two semesters for engaging in protest demonstrations. The lower court held that the students had not been accorded procedural due process and ordered the school to provide the following protections for them: (1) a written statement of the charges, for each student, made available at least ten days before the hearing; (2) a hearing before the person(s) having power to expel or suspend; (3) the opportunity for advance inspection of any affidavits or exhibits the college intends to submit at the hearing; (4) the right to bring counsel to the hearing to advise them (but not to question witnesses); (5) the opportunity to present their own version of the facts, by personal statements as well as affidavits and witnesses; (6) the right to hear evidence against them and question (personally, not through counsel) adverse witnesses; (7) a determination of the facts of each case by the hearing officer, solely on the basis of the evidence presented at the hearing; (8) a written statement of the hearing officer's findings of fact; and (9) the right, at their own expense, to make a record of the hearing.

The judicial imposition of specific due process requirements rankles many administrators. By and large, courts have been sufficiently sensitive to avoid such detail in favor of administrative flexibility (see, for example, *Moresco v. Clark*, 473 N.Y.S.2d 843 (N.Y. App. Div. 1984); *Henson v. Honor Committee of the University of Virginia*, 719 F.2d 69 (4th Cir. 1983), discussed in Section 4.8.2.2). Yet for the internal guidance of an administrator responsible for disciplinary procedures, the *Esteban* requirements provide a useful checklist. The listed items not only suggest the outer limits of what a court might require but also identify those procedures most often considered valuable for ascertaining facts where they are in dispute. Within this framework of concerns, the constitutional focus remains on the notice-and-opportunity-for-hearing concept of *Dixon*.

Although the federal courts have not required the type of protection provided at formal judicial hearings, deprivations of basic procedural rights can result in judicial rejection of an institution's disciplinary decision. In *Weideman v. SUNY College at Cortland*, 592 N.Y.S.2d 99 (N.Y. App. Div. 1992), the court annulled the college's dismissal of a student who had been accused of cheating on an examination, and ordered a new hearing. Specifically, the court found these procedural defects:

1. Evidence was introduced at the hearing of which the student was unaware.
2. The student was not provided the five-day written notice required by the student handbook about evidence supporting the charges against him, and had no opportunity to defend against that evidence.
3. The hearing panel contacted a college witness after the hearing and obtained additional evidence without notifying the student.
4. The student was given insufficient notice of the date of the hearing and the appeal process.
5. The student was given insufficient notice (one day) of his right to appeal.
6. The student's attorney had advised college officials of these violations, but the letter had been ignored.

4.8.2.1. Notice. Notice should be given of both the conduct with which the student is charged and the rule or policy that allegedly proscribes the conduct. The charges need not be drawn with the specificity of a criminal indictment, but they should be "in sufficient detail to fairly enable . . . [the student] to present a defense" at the hearing (*Jenkins v. Louisiana State Board of Education*, 506 F.2d 992 (5th Cir. 1975), holding notice in a suspension case to be adequate, particularly in light of information provided by the defendant subsequent to the original notice). Factual allegations not enumerated in the notice may be developed at the hearing if the student could reasonably have expected them to be included.

There is no clear constitutional requirement concerning how much advance notice the student must have of the charges. As little as two days before the hearing has been held adequate (*Jones v. Tennessee State Board of Education*, 279 F. Supp. 190 (M.D. Tenn. 1968), *affirmed*, 407 F.2d 834 (6th Cir. 1969); see also *Nash v. Auburn University*, 812 F.2d 655 (11th Cir. 1987)). *Esteban* required ten days, however, and in most other cases the time has been longer than two days. In general, courts handle this issue case by case, asking whether the amount of time was fair under all the circumstances.

4.8.2.2. Hearing. The minimum requirement is that the hearing provide students with an opportunity to speak in their own defense and explain their side of the story. Since due process apparently does not require an open or a public hearing, the institution has the discretion to close or partially close the hearing or to leave the choice to the accused student. But courts usually will accord students the right to hear the evidence against them and to present oral testimony or, at minimum, written statements from witnesses. Formal rules of evidence need not be followed. Cross-examination, the right to counsel, the right to a transcript, and an appellate procedure have generally not been constitutional essentials, but where institutions have voluntarily provided these procedures, courts have often cited them approvingly as enhancers of the hearing's fairness. In upholding the validity of the University of Virginia's student-operated honor system, for example, the court in *Henson v. Honor Committee of the University of Virginia*, 719 F.2d 69 (4th Cir. 1983), reasoned that:

> The university's honor system provides the accused student with an impressive array of procedural protections. The student, for example, receives what is essentially an indictment, specifying both the charges and the factual allegations supporting them (Virginia Honor Code, Art. III § C(l)). He has a right to a hearing before a committee of his peers. He is entitled, at no personal cost, to have a student lawyer represent his interests at all critical stages in the proceedings. He may also retain a practicing attorney to assist in his defense, although the attorney can assume no active role in the honor trial itself (Art. III § C(l)). The individuals who brought the charges must face the student at the hearing and state the basis of their allegations (Art. III § D(2)). They, in turn, must submit to cross-examination by the student, or his designated student counsel, and by the members of the hearing committee. The student then has the right to present evidence in opposition to the charges and to offer witnesses for the sole purpose of bolstering his character (Art. III § D(5)(a)). He may, if he chooses, demand that the hearing be conducted in public, where impartial observers can make an independent assessment of the proceeding's fairness (Art. VIII § E). If, after hearing the evidence, four fifths (4/5) of the committee members find the student guilty beyond a reasonable doubt, he has the right to appeal the decision to a five-member board comprised of members of the student government (Art. V). This board is empowered to review the record of the honor trial and to grant new trials when, in its judgment, the correct procedures were not followed or the evidentiary findings of the trial committee were deficient.
>
> In some respects, these procedures concededly fall short of the stringent protections afforded the criminal defendant; that is not, however, a defect of constitutional dimension. . . . The Supreme Court has made it plain that "the judicial model of an evidentiary hearing is neither a required, nor even the most effective, method of decision making in all circumstances" [quoting *Mathews v. Eldridge*, 424 U.S. 319, 348 (1976)]. . . .
>
> It is true that Henson [the student plaintiff] was not permitted to have a practicing attorney conduct his defense, but this is not a right generally available to students facing disciplinary charges (*Gabrilowitz v. Newman*, 582 F.2d 100, 104 (1st Cir. 1978)). Henson was provided with two student lawyers, who consulted extensively with his personally retained attorney at all critical stages of the proceedings. The due process clause would impose no greater obligations on the university than it placed on itself in conducting its disciplinary proceedings [719 F.2d at 73–74].

When the conduct with which the student is charged in the disciplinary proceeding is also the subject of a criminal court proceeding, the due process obligations of the institution will likely increase. Since the student then faces additional risks and strategic problems, some of the procedures usually left to the institution's discretion may become constitutional essentials. In *Gabrilowitz v. Newman*, 582 F.2d 100 (1st Cir. 1978) (discussed in Section 4.5.3), for example, the court required that the institution allow the student to have a professional lawyer present to advise him during the disciplinary hearing.

The person(s) presiding over the disciplinary proceedings and the person(s) with authority to make the final decision must decide the case on the basis of the evidence presented and must, of course, weigh the evidence impartially. Generally the student must show malice, bias, or conflict of interest on the part of the hearing officer or panel member before a court will make a finding of partiality. In *Blanton v. State University of New York*, 489 F.2d 377 (2d Cir. 1973), the court held that—at least where students had a right of appeal—due process was not violated when a dean who had witnessed the incident at issue also sat on the hearing committee. And in *Jones v. Tennessee State Board of Education*, 279 F. Supp. 190 (M.D. Tenn. 1968), *affirmed*, 407 F.2d 834 (6th Cir. 1969), the court even permitted a member of the hearing committee to give evidence against the accused student, in the absence of proof of malice or personal interest. But other courts may be less hospitable to such practices, and it would be wise to avoid them whenever possible.

The hearing must normally take place before the suspension or expulsion goes into effect. The leading case on this point has been *Stricklin v. Regents of the University of Wisconsin*, 297 F. Supp. 416 (W.D. Wis. 1969), where the court limited the use of interim suspensions, pending a final decision, to situations where "the appropriate university authority has reasonable cause to believe that danger will be present if a student is permitted to remain on campus pending a decision following a full hearing." The court also noted that "an interim suspension may not be imposed without a prior preliminary hearing, unless it can be shown that it is impossible or unreasonably difficult to accord it prior to an interim suspension," in which case "procedural due process requires that . . . [the student] be provided such a preliminary hearing at the earliest practical time." These requirements would protect a student from being "suspended in ex parte proceedings . . . without any opportunity, however brief and however limited, to persuade the suspending authority that there is a case of mistaken identity or that there was extreme provocation or that there is some other compelling justification for withholding or terminating the interim suspension." While case law on these points has been sparse, the U.S. Supreme Court's 1975 ruling in *Goss v. Lopez* affirms that at least part of *Stricklin* applies nationwide:

> As a general rule notice and hearing should precede removal of the student from school. We agree . . . , however, that there are recurring situations in which prior notice and hearing cannot be insisted upon. Students whose presence poses a continuing danger to persons or property or an ongoing threat of disrupting the academic process may be immediately removed from school . . . [and notice and hearing] should follow as soon as practicable [419 U.S. at 583 (1975)].

The extent to which the notice and hearing procedures set forth above apply to disciplinary sanctions less severe than suspension or expulsion is unclear. On the one hand, a pre-*Goss* case, *Yench v. Stockmar*, 483 F.2d 820 (10th Cir. 1973), held the Due Process Clause inapplicable to disciplinary probation cases in which students are not required to interrupt their education. On the other hand, any penalty that deprives the student of substantial educational benefits or seriously affects his or her reputation and employment prospects is, under *Goss*, arguably subject to at least the "rudimentary" protections of due process. In general, an institution should provide increasingly more formal and comprehensive due process procedures as the severity of the potential penalty increases and should gear its procedures to the maximum penalty that can be meted out in each type of proceeding it authorizes.

A federal appellate court considered the question of the specific protections necessary to satisfy the Constitution's Due Process Clause. In *Gorman v. University of Rhode Island*, 837 F.2d 7 (1st Cir. 1988), a student suspended for a number of disciplinary infractions charged that the university's disciplinary proceedings were defective in several respects. He asserted that two students on the student-faculty University Board on Student Conduct were biased against him because of earlier encounters; that he had been denied the assistance of counsel at the hearing; that he had been denied a transcript of the hearing; and that the director of student life had served as adviser to the board and also had prepared a record of the hearing, thereby compromising the board's independence.

Finding no evidence that Gorman was denied a fair hearing, the court commented:

> [T]he courts ought not to extol form over substance, and impose on educational institutions all the procedural requirements of a common law criminal trial. The question presented is not whether the hearing was ideal, or whether its procedure could have been better. In all cases the inquiry is whether, under the particular circumstances presented, the hearing was fair, and accorded the individual the essential elements of due process [837 F.2d at 16].

For analyses of student rights in disciplinary hearings, see J. M. Picozzi, "University Disciplinary Process: What's Fair, What's Due and What You Don't Get," 96 *Yale L.J.* 2132 (1987), and D. R. Richmond, "Students' Right to Counsel in University Disciplinary Proceedings, 15 *J. Coll. & Univ. Law* 289 (1989).

When students are accused of academic misconduct, such as plagiarism or cheating, conduct issues become mixed with academic evaluation issues (compare the *Napolitano* case in Section 4.8.4). Courts typically require some due process protections for students suspended or dismissed for academic misconduct, but not elaborate ones. For example, in *Easley v. University of Michigan Board of Regents*, 853 F.2d 1351 (6th Cir. 1988), the court found no constitutional deprivation in a law school's decision to suspend a student for one year after finding that he had plagiarized a course paper. The school had given the student an opportunity to respond to the charges against him, and the court also determined that the student had no property interest in his law degree because he had not completed the degree requirements.

But in *Jaksa v. Regents of the University of Michigan*, 597 F. Supp. 1245 (E.D. Mich. 1984), a trial court noted that a student challenging a one-semester suspension for cheating on a final examination had both a liberty interest and a property interest in continuing his education at the university. Applying the procedural requirements of *Goss v. Lopez*, the court ruled that the student had been given a meaningful opportunity to present his version of the situation to the hearing panel. It rejected the student's claims that due process was violated because he was not allowed to have a representative at the hearing, was not given a transcript, could not confront the student who charged him with cheating, and was not provided with a detailed statement of reasons by the hearing panel.

4.8.3. Public institutions: Academic sanctions. At noted above, the Fourteenth Amendment's Due Process Clause also applies to students facing suspension or dismissal from publicly supported schools for deficient academic performance. But even though academic dismissals may be even more damaging to students than disciplinary dismissals, due process affords substantially less protection to students in the former situation. Courts grant less protection because they recognize that they are less competent to review academic evaluative judgments than factually based determinations of misconduct and that hearings and the attendant formalities of witnesses and evidence are less meaningful in reviewing grading than in determining misconduct.

Gaspar v. Bruton, 513 F.2d 843 (10th Cir. 1975), was apparently the first case to provide any procedural due process rights to a student facing an academic suspension or dismissal. The plaintiff was a forty-four-year-old high school graduate pursuing practical nurse training in a vocational-technical school. After completing more than two-thirds of the program, she was dismissed for deficient performance in clinical training. She had been on probation for two months owing to such deficiencies and had been informed that she would be dismissed if they were not corrected. When they were not, she was notified of dismissal in a conference with the superintendent and some of her instructors and was subsequently offered a second conference and an opportunity to question other staff and faculty members who had participated in the dismissal decision.

The trial and appellate courts upheld the dismissal, rejecting the student's contention that before dismissal she should have been confronted with and allowed to challenge the evidence supporting the dismissal and permitted to present evidence in her defense. Although the appellate court recognized a "property interest" in continued attendance, it held that school officials had only minimal due process obligations in this context:

> Gaspar was provided much more due process than that which we hold must be accorded in cases involving academic termination or suspension. We hold that school authorities, in order to satisfy due process prior to termination or suspension of a student for deficiencies in meeting minimum academic performance, need only advise that student with respect to such deficiencies in any form. All that is required is that the student be made aware prior to termination of his failure or impending failure to meet those standards [513 F.2d at 850–51].

More significant protection was afforded in *Greenhill v. Bailey,* 519 F.2d 5 (8th Cir. 1975), where another U.S. Court of Appeals invalidated a medical student's dismissal because he had not been accorded procedural due process. The school had dismissed the student for "lack of intellectual ability or insufficient preparation" and had conveyed that information to the liaison committee of the Association of American Medical Colleges, where it was available to all other medical schools. The court ruled that "the action by the school in denigrating Greenhill's intellectual ability, as distinguished from his performance, deprived him of a significant interest in liberty, for it admittedly 'imposed on him a stigma or other disability that foreclose[s] his freedom to take advantage of other . . . opportunities' (*Board of Regents v. Roth,* 408 U.S. at 573, 92 S. Ct. at 2707)." In such circumstances, due process required more than the school had provided:

At the very least, Greenhill should have been notified in writing of the alleged deficiency in his intellectual ability, since this reason for his dismissal would potentially stigmatize his future as a medical student elsewhere, and should have been accorded an opportunity to appear personally to contest such allegation.

We stop short, however, of requiring full trial-type procedures. . . . But an "informal give-and-take" between the student and the administrative body dismissing him—and foreclosing his opportunity to gain admission at all comparable institutions—would not unduly burden the educational process and would, at least, give the student "the opportunity to characterize his conduct and put it in what he deems proper context" (*Goss v. Lopez*, 419 U.S. at 584, 95 S. Ct. at 741) [519 F.2d at 9].

The next year the same U.S. Court of Appeals extended its *Greenhill* ruling in another medical school case, *Horowitz v. Board of Curators of the University of Missouri*, 538 F.2d 1317 (8th Cir. 1976). But on appeal the U.S. Supreme Court clipped this court's wings and put an apparent halt to the development of procedural due process in academic disputes (*Board of Curators of the University of Missouri v. Horowitz*, 435 U.S. 78 (1978)). The university had dismissed the student, who had received excellent grades on written exams, for deficiencies in clinical performance, peer and patient relations, and personal hygiene. After several faculty members repeatedly expressed dissatisfaction with her clinical work, the school's council on evaluation recommended that Horowitz not be allowed to graduate on time and that, "absent radical improvement" in the remainder of the year, she be dropped from the program. She was then allowed to take a special set of oral and practical exams, administered by practicing physicians in the area, as a means of appealing the council's determination. After receiving the results of these exams, the council reaffirmed its recommendation. At the end of the year, after receiving further clinical reports on Horowitz, the council recommended that she be dropped from school. The school's coordinating committee, then the dean, and finally the provost for health sciences affirmed the decision.

Though there was no evidence that the reasons for the dismissal were conveyed to the liaison committee, as in *Greenhill*, the appellate court held that "Horowitz's dismissal from medical school will make it difficult or impossible for her to obtain employment in a medically related field or to enter another medical school." The court concluded that dismissal would so stigmatize the student as to deprive her of liberty under the Fourteenth Amendment and that, under the circumstances, the university could not dismiss the student without providing "a hearing before the decision-making body or bodies, at which she shall have an opportunity to rebut the evidence being relied upon for her dismissal and accorded all other procedural due process rights."

The Supreme Court found it unnecessary to decide whether Horowitz had been deprived of a liberty or property interest. Even assuming she had, Horowitz had no right to a hearing:

Respondent has been awarded at least as much due process as the Fourteenth Amendment requires. The school fully informed respondent of the faculty's dissatisfaction with her clinical progress and the danger that this posed to timely graduation and continued enrollment. The ultimate decision to dismiss respondent was careful and deliberate. These procedures were sufficient under the due process clause of the Fourteenth Amendment. We agree with the district court that respondent

> was afforded full procedural due process by the [school]. In fact, the court is of the opinion, and so finds, that the school went beyond [constitutionally required] procedural due process by affording [respondent] the opportunity to be examined by seven independent physicians in order to be absolutely certain that their grading of the [respondent] in her medical skills was correct [435 U.S. at 85].

The Court relied on the distinction between academic and disciplinary cases that lower courts had developed in cases prior to *Horowitz*, finding that distinction to be consistent with its own due process pronouncements, especially in *Goss v. Lopez* (Section 4.8.2):

> The Court of Appeals apparently read *Goss* as requiring some type of formal hearing at which respondent could defend her academic ability and performance. . . . But we have frequently emphasized that "the very nature of due process negates any concept of inflexible procedures universally applicable to every imaginable situation" (*Cafeteria Workers v. McElroy*, 367 U.S. 886, 895 (1961)). The need for flexibility is well illustrated by the significant difference between the failure of a student to meet academic standards and the violation by a student of valid rules of conduct. This difference calls for far less stringent procedural requirements in the case of an academic dismissal. . . .
>
> A school is an academic institution, not a courtroom or administrative hearing room. In *Goss*, this Court felt that suspensions of students for disciplinary reasons have a sufficient resemblance to traditional judicial and administrative fact finding to call for a "hearing" before the relevant school authority. . . .
>
> Academic evaluations of a student, in contrast to disciplinary determinations, bear little resemblance to the judicial and administrative fact-finding proceedings to which we have traditionally attached a full hearing requirement. In *Goss*, the school's decision to suspend the students rested on factual conclusions that the individual students had participated in demonstrations that had disrupted classes, attacked a police officer, or caused physical damage to school property. The requirement of a hearing, where the student could present his side of the factual issue, could under such circumstances "provide a meaningful hedge against erroneous action." The decision to dismiss respondent, by comparison, rested on the academic judgment of school officials that she did not have the necessary clinical ability to perform adequately as a medical doctor and was making insufficient progress toward that goal. Such a judgment is by its nature more subjective and evaluative than the typical factual questions presented in the average disciplinary decision. Like the decision of an individual professor as to the proper grade for a student in his course, the determination whether to dismiss a student for academic reasons requires an expert evaluation of cumulative information and is not readily adapted to the procedural tools of judicial or administrative decision making [435 U.S. at 85–90].

Horowitz signals the Court's lack of receptivity to procedural requirements for academic dismissals. Clearly, an adversary hearing is not required. Nor are all the procedures used by the university in *Horowitz* required, since the Court suggested that Horowitz received more due process than she was entitled to. But the Court's opinion does not say that no due process is required. Institutions apparently must afford some minimal protections, the exact character of which is not yet clear. Due process probably requires the institution to inform the student of the inadequacies in performance and their consequences on academic standing. Apparently, due process also generally requires that the institution's decision making be "careful and deliberate." For the former requirements, courts are likely to be lenient on how much information or explanation the student must be given and also on how far in advance of formal dismissal the student must be notified. For the latter requirement, courts are likely to be very flexible, not demanding any particular procedure but rather accepting any decision-making process that, overall, supports reasoned judgments concerning academic quality. Even these minimal requirements would be imposed on institutions only when their academic judgments infringe on a student's "liberty" or "property" interest, and it is not yet clear what constitutes such infringements in the postsecondary context.

Since courts attach markedly different due process requirements to academic sanctions than to disciplinary sanctions, it is crucial to be able to place particular cases in one category or the other. The characterization required is not always easy. The *Horowitz* case is a good example. The student's dismissal was not a typical case of inadequate scholarship, such as poor grades on written exams; rather, she was dismissed at least partly for inadequate peer and patient relations and personal hygiene. It is arguable that such a decision involves "fact-finding," as in a disciplinary case, more than an "evaluative," "academic judgment." Indeed, the Court split on this issue: five judges applied the "academic" label to the case, two judges applied the "disciplinary" label or argued that no labeling was appropriate, and two judges refused to determine either which label to apply or "whether such a distinction is relevant." For an analysis of *Horowitz*, and a criticism of its deference to the university's academic judgment, see W. G. Buss, "Easy Cases Make Bad Law: Academic Expulsion and the Uncertain Law of Procedural Due Process," 65 *Iowa L. Rev.* 1 (1979).

Another illustration of the categorization difficulty is provided by a pre-*Horowitz* case, *Brookins v. Bonnell,* 362 F. Supp. 379 (E.D. Pa. 1973). A nursing student was dismissed from a community college for (1) failing to submit a state-required physical examination report, (2) failing to inform the college that he had previously attended another nursing school, and (3) failing to attend class regularly. The student disputed these charges and argued that he should have been afforded a hearing before his dismissal. The court indicated that the right to a hearing depended on whether the student had been dismissed "because of disciplinary misconduct" or "solely because of an academic failure." After noting that the situation "does not fit neatly" into either category, the court decided the issue as follows:

> This case is not the traditional disciplinary situation where a student violates the law or a school regulation by actively engaging in prohibited activities. Plaintiff has allegedly failed to act and comply with school regulations for admission and class attendance by passively ignoring these regulations. These alleged failures do not constitute misconduct in the sense that plaintiff is subject to disciplinary procedures. They do constitute misconduct in the sense that plaintiff was required to do something. Plaintiff contends that he did comply with the requirements. Like the traditional disciplinary case, the determination of whether

plaintiff did or did not comply with the school regulations is a question of fact. Most importantly, in determining this factual question, reference is not made to a standard of achievement in an esoteric academic field. Scholastic standards are not involved, but rather disputed facts concerning whether plaintiff did or did not comply with certain school regulations. These issues adapt themselves readily to determination by a fair and impartial "due process" hearing [362 F. Supp. at 383].

The distinction made by the court is sound and is generally supported in the various justices' opinions in *Horowitz*.

But two federal appellate courts weighed in on the "academic" side in cases involving mixed issues of misconduct and poor academic performance. In *Mauriello v. University of Medicine and Dentistry of New Jersey*, 781 F.2d 46 (3d Cir. 1986), the court ruled that the dismissal of a medical student who repeatedly failed to produce thesis data was on academic rather than disciplinary grounds. And in *Harris v. Blake*, 798 F.2d 419 (10th Cir. 1986), in reviewing a student's involuntary withdrawal for inadequate grades, the court held that a professor's letter to a student's file, charging the student with incompetent performance (including absence from class) and unethical behavior in a course, concerned academic rather than disciplinary matters.

When dismissal or other serious sanctions depend more on disputed factual issues concerning conduct than on expert evaluation of academic work, the student should be accorded procedural rights akin to those for disciplinary cases (Section 4.8.2), rather than the lesser rights for academic deficiency cases. Of course, even when the academic label is clearly appropriate, administrators may choose to provide more procedural safeguards than the Constitution requires. Indeed, there may be good reason to provide some form of hearing prior to academic dismissal whenever the student has some basis for claiming that the academic judgment was arbitrary, in bad faith, or discriminatory (see Section 4.7.1). The question for the administrator, therefore, is not merely what procedures are constitutionally required but also what procedures would make the best policy for the particular institution.

There have been several reported opinions applying *Horowitz* to other academic dismissal problems in public institutions. Typical of these is *Schuler v. University of Minnesota*, 788 F.2d 510 (8th Cir. 1986). Schuler was dismissed from the doctoral program in psychology after failing a required oral examination on two occasions. Schuler alleged that she had been misinformed about the subject matter of both examinations, and she used the university's internal process to appeal the dismissal. Her appeal was denied, and she filed constitutional claims, alleging that she had not been notified about the subject matter of the examination or the evaluative criteria. She also alleged that the appeal procedure was defective because department faculty members were on the appeal board. The court noted that she had been given adequate notice of the faculty's dissatisfaction with her performance and, citing *Horowitz*, said that a student need not be made aware of the criteria by which she would be judged:

The full procedural safeguards of the fourteenth amendment are inapplicable where, as here, a student is dismissed from a state educational institution for failure to meet academic standards. . . . Dismissal of a student for academic reasons comports with the requirements of procedural due process if the student had prior notice of faculty dissatisfaction with his or her performance and of the possibility of dismissal, and if the decision to dismiss the student was careful and deliberate [788 F.2d at 514].

The court addressed a second issue—one that clearly illustrates the deferential standard of review that courts have interpreted *Horowitz* to imply. The plaintiff argued that the university did not follow its written procedures in reviewing her appeal, and that this failure to adhere to its own procedures violated her due process rights. On the contrary, said the court,

> the University's noncompliance with its own grievance appeal procedures would not violate Schuler's right to procedural due process, because the hearing she received at the departmental level exceeded the process constitutionally required to protect her interest in continued enrollment at that institution [788 F.2d at 515].

In other words, because academic dismissal does not involve more than minimal due process rights, the university's written policies went beyond constitutional requirements, and failure to follow these policies did not trigger constitutional protections. (See also *Delaney v. Heimstra*, 288 N.W.2d 769 (S.D. 1980); *Gamble v. University of Minnesota*, 639 F.2d 452 (8th Cir. 1981); *Lunde v. Iowa Board of Regents*, 487 N.W.2d 357 (Iowa Ct. App. 1992); *Bleicher v. University of Cincinnati College of Medicine*, 604 N.E.2d 783 (Ohio Ct. App. 1992).)

More frequently, courts have relied on *Horowitz* for guidance in contexts other than student academic dismissals from public institutions—namely, in challenges to academic decisions other than dismissals, to academic dismissals from private institutions, and to judgments concerning faculty rather than students. In *Olsson v. Board of Higher Education of the City of New York*, 402 N.E.2d 1150 (N.Y. 1980) (this volume, Section 4.7.1), for example, the court cited *Horowitz* in rejecting a public college student's challenge to an examination grade. In *Maas v. Corp. of Gonzaga University*, 618 P.2d 106 (Wash. Ct. App. 1980), and *Miller v. Hamline University School of Law*, 601 F.2d 970 (8th Cir. 1979), the courts used *Horowitz* to reject student challenges to academic decisions of private institutions. And in *Clark v. Whiting*, 607 F.2d 634 (4th Cir. 1979), another court relied on *Horowitz* to reject an associate professor's challenge to a denial of promotion to full professor.

Overall, two trends are emerging from the reported decisions in the wake of *Horowitz*. First, extensive appellate litigation challenging academic dismissals is not occurring, and the cases that have been reported have usually been decided in favor of the institutions. Apparently *Horowitz*, with its strong support for institutional discretion in devising academic dismissal procedures, has depressed the market for such litigation. Second, courts have read *Horowitz* as a case whose message has meaning well beyond the context of constitutional due process and academic dismissal. Thus, *Horowitz* also supports the broader concept of "academic deference," or judicial deference to the full range of an academic institution's academic decisions. Both trends help insulate postsecondary institutions from judicial intrusion into their dealings with students and other members of the academic community. But just as surely, these trends emphasize the institution's own responsibilities to deal fairly with students and others and to provide appropriate internal means of accountability regarding institutional academic decision making.

4.8.4. Private institutions. Federal constitutional guarantees of due process do not bind private institutions unless their imposition of sanctions falls under the state action doctrine explained in Section 1.5.2. But the inapplicability of constitutional protections, as Sections 4.6 and 4.7 suggest, does not necessarily mean that the student stands procedurally naked before the authority of the school.

The old view of a private institution's authority is illustrated by *Anthony v. Syracuse University*, 231 N.Y.S. 435 (N.Y. App. Div. 1928), where a student's dismissal was upheld even though "no adequate reason [for it] was assigned by the university authorities." The court held that "no reason for dismissing need be given," though the institution "must . . . have a reason" that falls within its dismissal regulations. "Of course, the university authorities have wide discretion in determining what situation does and what does not fall within . . . [its regulations], and the courts would be slow indeed in disturbing any decision of the university authorities in this respect."

In more recent times, however, many courts have become faster on the draw with private schools. In *Carr v. St. John's University, New York* (see Section 4.6.2), a case limiting the impact of *Anthony* within New York State, the court indicated, although ruling for the university, that a private institution dismissing a student must act "not arbitrarily but in the exercise of an honest discretion based on facts within its knowledge that justify the exercise of discretion." In subsequently applying this standard to a discipline case, another New York court ruled that "the college or university's decision to discipline that student [must] be predicated on procedures which are fair and reasonable and which lend themselves to a reliable determination" (*Kwiatkowski v. Ithaca College*, 368 N.Y.S.2d 973 (N.Y. Sup. Ct. 1975)).

A federal appellate court has taken a similar approach. *Slaughter v. Brigham Young University*, 514 F.2d 622 (10th Cir. 1975), concerned a student who was dismissed for violating the honesty provision of the student code, having made unauthorized use of a professor's name as coauthor of an article. After the lower court had awarded $88,283 in damages to the student, the appellate court set aside the judgment and upheld the dismissal. But in doing so, it tested "whether the action was arbitrary" by investigating both the "adequacy of the procedure" and the substantiality of the evidence supporting the institution's determination. In judging the procedures, the court used *constitutional* due process as a guide, holding that the "proceedings met the requirements of the constitutional procedural due process doctrine as it is presently applied to public universities," and it is therefore unnecessary "to draw any distinction, *if there be any*, between the requirements in this regard for private and for public institutions" (emphasis added).

Another federal appellate court, however, has made it clear that private colleges and universities are not held to the same constitutional standards as are public institutions, even if state law requires them to promulgate disciplinary rules. In *Albert v. Carovano*, 851 F.2d 561 (2d Cir. 1988), students suspended by Hamilton College for occupying the college's administration building brought constitutional claims under a state action theory (see Section 1.5.2). Section 6450 of New York's Education Law required all institutions of higher education to adopt disciplinary rules, and to file them with the state, which the college had done. Although the college's rules and disciplinary procedures provided for a judiciary board that would review the charges and evidence and determine the sanctions to be levied, the procedures also reserved to the president the right to dispense with the written procedures. In dealing with the students, who continued to occupy the building even after the college had secured a court order enjoining the occupation, the president suspended them effective the end of the semester, but invited them to state in writing their views on the situation to either the trustees or himself. The students demanded a hearing before the Judiciary Board, which was not granted. The lawsuit ensued.

The *en banc* court provided a lengthy discussion of the state action doctrine. In this case, it noted, the state law required that the disciplinary rules be placed on file, but the state had made no attempt to evaluate the rules or to ensure that the colleges followed them. Given the lack of state action, the plaintiffs' constitutional claims were dismissed. The court remanded for further consideration the students' claim that the college's selective enforcement of its disciplinary regulations violated Section 1981's prohibitions against race discrimination (see Section 4.2.4.1).

As is true of public institutions, judges are more likely to require procedural protections in the misconduct area than in the academic sphere. For example, in *Melvin v. Union College*, 600 N.Y.S.2d 141 (N.Y. App. Div. 1993), a breach-of-contract claim, a state appellate court enjoined the suspension of a student accused of cheating on an examination; the court took this action because the college had not followed all the elements of its written disciplinary procedure. But in *Ahlum v. Administrators of Tulane Educational Fund*, 617 So. 2d 96 (La. Ct. App. 1993), the appellate court of another state refused to enjoin Tulane University's suspension of a student found guilty of sexual assault. Noting that the proper standard of judicial review of a private college's disciplinary decisions was the "arbitrary and capricious" standard, the court upheld the procedures used and the sufficiency of the factual basis for the suspension. Since the court determined that Tulane's procedures exceeded even the due process protections required in *Goss v. Lopez*, it did not attempt to determine the boundaries of procedural protections appropriate for the disciplinary actions of private colleges and universities.

In *Boehm v. University of Pennsylvania School of Veterinary Medicine*, 573 A.2d 575 (Pa. Super. Ct. 1990), the court, after reviewing case law, legal scholarship, and other sources, concluded that:

> A majority of the courts have characterized the relationship between a private college and its students as contractual in nature. Therefore, students who are being disciplined are entitled only to those procedural safeguards which the school specifically provides. . . . The general rule, therefore, has been that where a private university or college establishes procedures for the suspension or expulsion of its students, substantial compliance with those established procedures must be had before a student can be suspended or expelled [573 A.2d at 579].

Determining that the school had "followed its Code of Rights punctiliously and that the disciplinary proceedings complied with due process and were fundamentally fair" (573 A.2d at 582), the appellate court reversed the trial court's order for a preliminary injunction, viewing that order as "interference with the legitimate authority of the school to sanction students who, after compliance with established procedure, had been found guilty of violating the school's Honor Code" (573 A.2d at 586).

In an opinion extremely deferential to a private institution's disciplinary procedure, and allegedly selective administrative enforcement of the disciplinary code, a federal appellate court refused to rule that Dartmouth College's suspension of several white students violated federal nondiscrimination laws. In *Dartmouth Review v. Dartmouth College,* 889 F.2d 13 (1st Cir. 1989), the students alleged that the college's decision to charge them with disciplinary code violations, and the dean's refusal to help them prepare for the hearing (which was promised in the student handbook), was based on their race. The court disagreed, stating that unfairness or inconsistency of administrative behavior did not equate to racial discrimination, and, since they could not demonstrate a causal link between their race and the administrators' conduct, the students' claims failed.

In reviewing determinations of academic performance, rather than disciplinary misconduct, the courts have crafted lesser procedural requirements. In *Militana v. University of Miami,* 236 So. 2d 162 (Fla. Dist. Ct. App. 1970), for example, the court upheld the dismissal of a medical student, stating flatly that notice and opportunity to be heard, though required in discipline cases, are "not required when the dismissal is for academic failure." Yet even here, the contract theory (see Section 4.1.3) may provide some lesser procedural protections for students in academic jeopardy at private institutions.

As is also true for public institutions, the line between academic and disciplinary cases may be difficult to draw. In *Napolitano v. Trustees of Princeton University,* 453 A.2d 263 (N.J. Super. Ct., App. Div. 1982), the court reviewed the university's withholding of a degree, for one year, from a student whom a campus committee had found guilty of plagiarizing a term paper. In upholding the university's action, the court determined that the problem was one "involving academic standards and not a case of violation of rules of conduct." In so doing, the court distinguished "academic disciplinary actions" from disciplinary actions involving other types of "misconduct," according greater deference to the institution's decisions in the former context and suggesting that lesser "due process" protection was required. The resulting dichotomy differs from the "academic/disciplinary" dichotomy delineated in Section 4.8.3 and suggests the potential relevance of a third, middle category for "academic disciplinary" cases. (Compare the *Easley* and *Jaksa* cases in Section 4.8.2.2.) Because such cases involve academic standards, courts should be sufficiently deferential to avoid interference with the institution's expert judgments on such matters; however, because such cases may also involve disputed factual issues concerning student conduct, courts should afford greater due process rights than they would in academic cases involving only the evaluation of student performance.

While the doctrinal bases for procedural rights in the public and private sectors are different, and while the law accords private institutions greater deference, some courts may nevertheless encourage a rough similarity of treatment by seeking guidance from public-sector precedents when deciding private-sector cases. The *Slaughter* case above provides a good illustration. So does *Miller v. Hamline University School of Law,* 601 F.2d 970 (8th Cir. 1979), in which the court applied the *Horowitz* due process analysis (Section 4.8.3) to a private school's dismissal of a student for academic deficiency. For analysis of such cross-fertilization, see H. L. Silets, "Of Students' Rights and Honor: The Application of the Fourteenth Amendment's Due Process Strictures to Honor Code Proceedings at Private Colleges and Universities, 64 *Denver U. L. Rev.* 47 (1987). Such a similarity of treatment may also make good policy sense for many private institutions. It may thus be prudent for private school administrators to use the constitutional due process principles in Sections 4.8.2 and 4.8.3 of this volume as general guides in implementing their own procedural systems. And if a private school makes a conscious policy choice not to use certain procedures that due process would require for public schools, that choice should be clearly reflected in its rules and regulations, so as to inhibit a court from finding such procedures implicit in the rules or in the student-institution relationship.

Sec. 4.9. Student Protest and Demonstrations

4.9.1. General principles. Freedom of expression for students (see also Sections 4.10 and 4.13) is protected mainly by the free speech and press provisions in the First Amendment of the U.S. Constitution, which applies only to "public" institutions (see Section 1.5.2). In some situations student freedom of expression may also be protected by state constitutional provisions (see Section 1.3.1.1 and the *Schmid* case in Section 5.6.3), by state statutes (see, for example, Cal. Educ. Code § 66301 (public institutions) and § 94367 (private institutions)), or by the institution's own bill of rights or other internal rules (see Section 1.3.2.1). These latter sources of law may apply to private as well as public institutions; they may also consciously adopt First Amendment norms that have been developed in the courts and that bind public institutions, so that these norms may sometimes be operative on private as well as public campuses. The following discussion focuses on these First Amendment norms and the case law in which they have been developed.

In a line of cases arising mainly from the campus unrest of the late 1960s and early 1970s, courts have affirmed that students have a right to protest and demonstrate peacefully—a right that public institutions may not infringe. This right stems from the Free Speech Clause of the First Amendment as reinforced by that amendment's protection of "the right of the people peaceably to assemble, and to petition the Government for a redress of grievances." The keystone case is *Tinker v. Des Moines School District*, 393 U.S. 503 (1969). Several high school students had been suspended for wearing black armbands to school to protest the United States' Vietnam War policy. The U.S. Supreme Court ruled that the protest was a nondisruptive exercise of free speech and could not be punished by suspension from school. The Court made clear that "First Amendment rights, applied in light of the special characteristics of the school environment, are available to teachers and students" and that students "are possessed of fundamental rights which the state must respect, just as they themselves must respect their obligations to the state." The Court also made clear that the First Amendment protects more than just words; it also protects certain "symbolic acts" that are performed "for the purpose of expressing certain views."

Though *Tinker* involved secondary school students, the Supreme Court soon applied its principles to postsecondary education in *Healy v. James*, 408 U.S. 169 (1972), discussed further in Section 4.11.1. The *Healy* opinion carefully notes the First Amendment's important place on campus:

> State colleges and universities are not enclaves immune from the sweep of the First Amendment. . . . [T]he precedents of this Court leave no room for the view that . . . First Amendment protections should apply with less force on college campuses than in the community at large. Quite to the contrary, "The

vigilant protection of constitutional freedoms is nowhere more vital than in the community of American schools" (*Shelton v. Tucker*, 364 U.S. 479, 487 (1960)). The college classroom with its surrounding environs is peculiarly the "marketplace of ideas," and we break no new constitutional ground in reaffirming this nation's dedication to safeguarding academic freedom [408 U.S. at 180].

The free speech protections for students are at their peak when the speech takes place in a "public forum"—that is, an area of the campus that is, traditionally or by official policy, available to students or the entire campus community for expressive activities. See generally G. Sorenson, "The 'Public Forum Doctrine' and Its Application in School and College Cases," 20 *J. Law & Educ.* 445 (1991). This judicially created concept and its attendant "public forum" analysis (see, for example, *Widmar v. Vincent*, discussed in Section 4.11.4) have become increasingly important in student freedom-of-expression cases. Under the currently employed definitions and guidelines, set out by the U.S. Supreme Court in *Perry Education Assn. v. Perry Local Educators' Assn.*, 460 U.S. 37, 45-46 (1983), expressive activities undertaken in a public forum receive far more protection than expressive activities not undertaken in a public forum.

Although *Tinker, Healy,* and *Widmar* apply the First Amendment to the campus just as fully as it applies to the general community, the cases also make clear that academic communities are "special environments," and that "First Amendment rights . . . [must be] applied in light of the special characteristics of the school environment" (*Tinker* at 506). In this regard, "[a] university differs in significant respects from public forums such as streets or parks or even municipal theaters. A university's mission is education, and decisions of this Court have never denied a university's authority to impose reasonable regulations compatible with that mission upon the use of its campus and facilities" (*Widmar v. Vincent*, 454 U.S. 263, 268 n.5 (1981)). The interests that academic institutions may protect and promote, and the nature of threats to these interests, may thus differ from the interests that may exist for other types of entities and in other contexts. Therefore, although First Amendment principles do apply with full force to the campus, their application may be affected by the unique interests of academic communities.

Moreover, colleges and universities may assert and protect their interests in ways that create limits on student freedom of speech. The *Tinker* opinion recognizes "the need for affirming the comprehensive authority of the states and of school officials, consistent with fundamental constitutional safeguards, to prescribe and control conduct in the schools" (at 507). That case also emphasizes that freedom to protest does not constitute freedom to disrupt: "[C]onduct by the student, in class or out of it, which for any reason—whether it stems from time, place, or type of behavior—materially disrupts classwork or involves substantial disorder or invasion of the rights of others is . . . not immunized by the constitutional guarantee of freedom of speech" (at 513). *Healy* makes the same points.

4.9.2. Regulation of student protest. By following the *Tinker/Healy* guidelines above, postsecondary institutions may promulgate rules that prohibit certain types of group or individual demonstrations or protest. Students may be suspended if they violate such rules by actively participating in a disruptive demonstration—for example, entering the stands during a college football game and "by abusive and disorderly acts and conduct" depriving the spectators "of the right to see and enjoy the game in peace and with safety to themselves" (*Barker v. Hardway*, 283 F. Supp. 228 (S.D. W. Va.), *affirmed*, 399 F.2d 638 (4th Cir. 1968)), or physically blocking entrances to campus buildings and preventing personnel or other students from using the buildings (*Buttney v. Smiley*, 281 F. Supp. 280 (D. Colo. 1968)).[31]

The critical problem in prohibiting or punishing disruptive protest activity is determining when the activity has become sufficiently disruptive to lose its protection under *Tinker* and *Healy*. In *Shamloo v. Mississippi State Board of Trustees*, 620 F.2d 516 (5th Cir. 1980), for example, the plaintiffs, Iranian nationals who were students at Jackson State University, had participated in two on-campus demonstrations in support of the regime of Ayatollah Khomeini in Iran. The university disciplined the students for having violated campus regulations that required advance scheduling of demonstrations and other meetings or gatherings. When the students filed suit, claiming that the regulations and the disciplinary action violated their First Amendment rights, the defendant argued that the protests were sufficiently disruptive to lose any protection under the First Amendment. The appellate court asked whether the demonstration had "materially and substantially interfered with the requirements of appropriate discipline in the operation of the school"—the standard developed in an earlier Fifth Circuit case and adopted by the U.S. Supreme Court in *Tinker*. Applying this standard to the facts of the case, the court rejected the defendant's claim:

> There was no testimony by the students or teachers complaining that the demonstration was disrupting and distracting. Shamloo testified that he did not think any of the classes were disrupted. Dr. Johnson testified that the demonstration was quite noisy. Dr. Smith testified that he could hear the chanting from his office and that, in his opinion, classes were being disrupted. The only justification for his conclusion is that there are several buildings within a close proximity of the plaza that students may have been using for purposes of study or for classes. There is no evidence that he received complaints from the occupants of these buildings.
>
> The district court concluded that "the demonstration had a disruptive effect with respect to other students' rights." But this is not enough to conclude that the demonstration was not protected by the First Amendment. The court must also conclude (1) that the disruption was a *material* disruption of classwork or (2) that it involved *substantial* disorder or invasion of the rights of others. It must constitute a *material* and *substantial* interference with discipline. The district court did not make such a conclusion and we certainly cannot, especially in light of the conflicting evidence found in the record. We cannot say that the demonstration did not constitute activity protected under the First Amendment [620 F.2d at 522].

As *Shamloo* suggests, and *Tinker* states expressly, administrators seeking to regulate protest activity on grounds of disruption must base their action on something more substantial than mere suspicion or fear of possible disruption:

[31]Cases are collected in Annot., "Participation of Student in Demonstration on or near Campus as Warranting Expulsion or Suspension from School or College," 32 A.L.R.3d 864 (1991 and periodic supp.).

Undifferentiated fear or apprehension of disturbance is not enough to overcome the right to freedom of expression. Any departure from absolute regimentation may cause trouble. Any variation from the majority's opinion may inspire fear. Any word spoken, in class, in the lunchroom, or on the campus, that deviates from the views of another person may start an argument or cause disturbance. But our Constitution says we must take this risk (*Terminiello v. Chicago,* 337 U.S. 1 (1949)); and our history says that it is this sort of hazardous freedom—this kind of openness—that is the basis of our national strength and of the independence and vigor of Americans who grow up and live in this relatively permissive, often disputatious, society [*Tinker* at 508–09].

Yet substantial disruption need not be a fait accompli before administrators can take action. It is sufficient that administrators have actual evidence on which they can "reasonably . . . forecast" (*Tinker* at 514) that substantial disruption is imminent.

The administrator should also determine whether the disruption is created by the protesters themselves or by the onlookers' reaction to their presence. In striking down a regulation limiting off-campus speakers at Mississippi state colleges, the court in *Stacy v. Williams,* 306 F. Supp. 963 (N.D. Miss. 1969), emphasized that "one simply cannot be restrained from speaking, and his audience cannot be prevented from hearing him, unless the feared result is likely to be engendered by what the speaker himself says or does." Either the protesters must themselves engage in conduct that is physically disruptive, as in *Barker* and *Buttney* above, or their words and acts must be "directed to inciting or producing imminent" disruption by others and "likely to produce" such disruption (*Brandenburg v. Ohio,* 395 U.S. 444 (1969)) before an administrator may stop the protest or discipline the protesters. Where the onlookers rather than the protesters have created the disruption, the administrator's proper recourse is against the onlookers.

Besides adopting regulations prohibiting disruptive protest, public institutions may also promulgate "reasonable regulations with respect to the time, the place, and the manner in which student groups conduct their speech-related activities" (*Healy* at 192–93). Students who violate such regulations may be disciplined even if their violation did not create substantial disruption. As applied to speech in the public forum, however, such regulations may cover only those times, places, or manners of expression that are "basically incompatible with the normal activity of a particular place at a particular time" (*Grayned v. Rockford,* 408 U.S. 104, 116 (1972)). Incompatibility must be determined by the physical impact of the speech-related activity on its surroundings and not by the content or viewpoint of the speech (see Section 4.10).

In the *Shamloo* case (above), for instance, the court invalidated a campus regulation requiring that "all events sponsored by student organizations, groups, or individual students must be registered with the director of student activities, who, in cooperation with the vice-president for student affairs, approves activities of a wholesome nature." The court reasoned that:

[R]egulations must be reasonable as limitations on the time, place, and manner of the protected speech and its dissemination (*Papish v. Board of Curators of the University of Missouri,* 410 U.S. 667 . . . (1973); *Healy v. James,* 408 U.S. 169 . . . (1972)). Disciplinary action may not be based on the disapproved *content* of the protected speech (*Papish,* 410 U.S. at 670 . . .).

The reasonableness of a similar university regulation was previously addressed by this court in *Bayless v. Martine,* 430 F.2d 872, 873 (5th Cir. 1970). In *Bayless* ten students sought injunctive relief from their suspension for violating a university regulation. The regulation in *Bayless* created a Student Expression Area that could be reserved forty-eight hours in advance for any nonviolent purpose. All demonstrations similar to the one held by the Iranian students were regulated to the extent that they could only be held at the Student Expression Area "between the hours of 12:00 noon to 1:00 P.M. and from 5:00 to 7:00 P.M." but there was no limitation on the content of the speech. This court noted that the requirement of forty-eight hours advance notice was a reasonable method to avoid the problem of simultaneous and competing demonstrations and it also provided advance warning of the possible need for police protection. This court upheld the validity of the regulation as a valid exercise of the right to adopt and enforce reasonable nondiscriminatory regulations as to the time, place, and manner of a demonstration.

There is one critical distinction between the regulation examined in *Bayless* and the Jackson State regulation. The former made no reference to the *content* of the speech that would be allowed in the Student Expression Area. As long as there was no interference with the flow of traffic, no interruption of the orderly conduct of university affairs, and no obscene material, the students were not limited in what they could say. Apparently, the same cannot be said with respect to the Jackson State regulations, which provide that only "activities of a *wholesome* nature" will be approved. And if a demonstration is not approved, the students participating may be subjected to disciplinary action, including the possibility of dismissal.

Limiting approval of activities only to those of a "wholesome" nature is a regulation of *content* as opposed to a regulation of time, place, and manner. Dr. Johnson testified that he would disapprove a student activity if, in his opinion, the activity was unwholesome. The presence of this language converts what might have otherwise been a reasonable regulation of time, place, and manner into a restriction on the content of speech. Therefore, the regulation appears to be unreasonable on its face [620 F.2d at 522–23].

Clark v. Community for Creative Non-Violence, 468 U.S. 288 (1984), although not a higher education case, has become a leading precedent on the validity of "time, place, and manner" restrictions on protest demonstrations in the public forum. (The case also speaks importantly to the "symbolic acts" or "symbolic speech" issue developed by the *Tinker* case.) In *Clark* the U.S. Supreme Court upheld National Park Service regulations limiting protests in parks. The Court noted that these regulations were "manner" regulations conforming to this three-part judicial test: "they are justified without reference to the content of the regulated speech, . . . they are narrowly tailored to serve a significant governmental interest, and . . . they leave open ample alternative channels for communication of the information."

Another recent U.S. Supreme Court precedent with important ramifications for "time, place, and manner" regulation of student protests is *Ward v. Rock Against Racism,* 491 U.S. 781 (1989). The Court affirmed that government has a substantial interest in regulating noise levels to prevent annoyance to persons in adjacent areas and refined the first two parts of the *Clark* test: " '[A] regulation of the time, place, or manner of protected speech must be narrowly tailored to serve the government's legitimate content-neutral interests but . . . need not be the least restrictive or least intrusive means of doing so. Rather, the requirement of narrow tailoring is satisfied so long as the . . . regulation promotes a substantial government interest that would be achieved less effectively absent the regulation' " (quoting *United States v. Albertini*, 472 U.S. 675, 689 (1985)). The overall effect of the *Ward* case, combined with the *Clark* case, is to create a more deferential standard, under which it is more likely that courts will uphold the constitutionality of time, place, and manner regulations of speech.

Postsecondary administrators who are drafting or implementing protest regulations must be attentive not only to the various judicial requirements just discussed but also to the doctrines of "overbreadth" and "vagueness" (both discussed in Sections 3.5.1, 4.5.2, and 4.6.1). The overbreadth doctrine provides that regulations of speech must be "narrowly tailored" to avoid sweeping within their coverage speech activities that would be constitutionally protected under the First Amendment. The vagueness doctrine provides that regulations of conduct must be sufficiently clear so that the persons to be regulated can understand what is required or prohibited and conform their conduct accordingly. Vagueness principles apply more stringently when the regulations deal with speech-related activity: " 'Stricter standards of permissible statutory vagueness may be applied to a statute having a potentially inhibiting effect on speech; a man may the less be required to act at his peril here, because the dissemination of ideas may be the loser' " (*Hynes v. Mayor and Council of Oradell*, 425 U.S. 610, 620 (1976), quoting *Smith v. California*, 361 U.S. 147, 151 (1959)). In the *Shamloo* case (above), the court utilized both doctrines in invalidating campus regulations prohibiting demonstrations that are not "of a wholesome nature." Regarding the vagueness doctrine, the court reasoned that:

> The restriction on activities other than those of a "wholesome" nature raises the additional issue that the Jackson State regulation may be void for vagueness. . . . An individual is entitled to fair notice or a warning of what constitutes prohibited activity by specifically enumerating the elements of the offense (*Smith v. Goguen*, 415 U.S. 566 . . . (1974)). The regulation must not be designed so that different officials could attach different meaning to the words in an arbitrary and discriminatory manner (*Smith v. Goguen, supra*). But, of course, we cannot expect "mathematical certainty" from our language (*Grayned v. City of Rockford*, 408 U.S. 104 . . . (1972)). The approach adopted by this court with respect to university regulations is to examine whether the college students would have any "difficulty in understanding what conduct the regulations allow and what conduct they prohibit" [quoting *Jenkins v. Louisiana State Board of Education*, 506 F.2d 992, 1004 (5th Cir. 1975)].
>
> The requirement that an activity be "wholesome" before it is subject to approval is unconstitutionally vague. The testimony revealed that the regulations are enforced or not enforced depending on the purpose of the gathering or demonstration. Dr. Johnson admitted that whether or not something was wholesome was subject to interpretation and that he, as the vice-president of student affairs, and Dr. Jackson, director of student activities, could come to different conclusions as to its meaning. . . . The regulation's reference to wholesome activities is not specific enough to give fair notice and warning. A college student would have great difficulty determining whether or not his activities constitute prohibited unwholesome conduct. The regulation is void for vagueness [620 F.2d at 523–24].

The time, place, and manner tests and the overbreadth and vagueness doctrines, as well as principles concerning "symbolic" speech, all played an important role in another leading case, *Students Against Apartheid Coalition v. O'Neil*, 660 F. Supp. 333 (W.D. Va. 1987), and 671 F. Supp. 1105 (W.D. Va. 1987), *affirmed*, 838 F.2d 735 (4th Cir. 1988). At issue in this case was a University of Virginia regulation prohibiting student demonstrations against university policies on investment in South Africa. In the first phase of the litigation, students challenged the university's policy prohibiting them from constructing shanties—flimsy structures used to protest apartheid conditions in South Africa—on the university's historic central grounds, "the Lawn." The federal district court held that the university's policy created an unconstitutional restriction on symbolic expression in a public forum. Specifically, the court declared that the "current lawn use regulations . . . are vague, are too broad to satisfy the University's legitimate interest in esthetics, and fail to provide the plaintiffs with a meaningful alternative channel for expression."

UVA subsequently revised its policy to tailor it narrowly to the achievement of the university's goals of historic preservation and aesthetic integrity. The students again brought suit to enjoin the enforcement of the new policy on the same constitutional grounds they had asserted in the first suit. The case was heard by the same judge, who this time held in favor of the defendant university and upheld the revised policy. The court determined that the amended policy applied only to "structures," as narrowly defined in the policy; that the policy restricted such structures from only a small section of the Lawn; and that the policy focused solely on concerns of architectural purity. Applying the *Clark* test, the court held that:

> [UVA] may regulate the symbolic speech of its students to preserve and protect the Lawn area as an architectural landmark. To be constitutionally permissible, the regulation must be reasonable in time, place and manner. The revised Lawn Use Policy lies within the constitutional boundaries of the first amendment. The new policy is content-neutral, precisely aimed at protecting the University's esthetics concern in architecture, and permits students a wide array of additional modes of communication. The new policy is also sufficiently detailed to inform students as to the types of expression restricted on the Lawn [671 F. Supp. at 1108].

On appeal by the students, the U.S. Court of Appeals for the Fourth Circuit agreed with the reasoning of the district court and affirmed its decision.

The *O'Neil* case, together with the *Shamloo* case (above), serves to illuminate pitfalls that administrators will wish to avoid in devising and enforcing their own campus's demonstration regulations. The *O'Neil* litigation also provides a good example of how to respond to and resolve problems concerning the validity of campus regulations.

4.9.3. Prior approval of protest activities. Sometimes institutions have attempted to avoid disruption and disorder on campus by requiring that protest activity be approved in advance and by approving only those activities that will not pose problems. Under this strategy a protest would be halted, or its participants disciplined, not because the protest was in fact disruptive or violated reasonable time, place, and manner requirements but merely because it had not been approved in advance. Administrators at public institutions should be extremely leery of such a strategy. A prior approval system constitutes a "prior restraint" on free expression—that is, a temporary or permanent prohibition of expression imposed before the expression has occurred rather than a punishment imposed afterward. Prior restraints "are the most serious and the least tolerable infringement of First Amendment rights" (*Nebraska Press Assn. v. Stuart*, 427 U. S. 539, 559 (1976)).

Hammond v. South Carolina State College, 272 F. Supp. 947 (D.S.C. 1967), provides a classic example of prior restraint. The defendant college had a rule providing that "the student body is not to celebrate, parade, or demonstrate on the campus at any time without the approval of the office of the president." Several students were expelled for violating this rule after they held a demonstration for which they had not obtained prior approval. The court found the rule to be "on its face a prior restraint on the right to freedom of speech and the right to assemble" and held the rule and the expulsions under it to be invalid.

The courts have not asserted, however, that all prior restraints on expression are invalid. *Healy v. James* (Sections 4.9.1 and 4.11.1) summarizes the current judicial attitude: "While a college has a legitimate interest in preventing disruption on campus, which under circumstances requiring the safeguarding of that interest may justify . . . [a prior] restraint, a 'heavy burden' rests on the college to demonstrate the appropriateness of that action." Although it is difficult to ascertain what restraints would be valid under *Healy*, such restraints probably could be imposed for the limited purpose of ensuring that student protest activities will not violate time, place, or manner regulations meeting the guidelines in Section 4.9.2. In *Auburn Alliance for Peace and Justice v. Martin*, 684 F. Supp. 1072 (M.D. Ala. 1988), *affirmed without opin.*, 853 F.2d 931 (11th Cir. 1988), for instance, the trial and appellate courts upheld the facial validity of Auburn's regulations of a campus public forum and also held that the university's denial of a student-faculty group's request for week-long, round-the-clock use of this forum was an appropriate means of implementing time, place, and manner requirements. Probably a prior approval mechanism could also be used for the limited purpose of determining that protest activities will not cause substantial disruption (see Section 4.9.2). In either case, however, it is questionable whether prior approval requirements would be appropriate if applied to small-scale protests that have no reasonable potential for disruption. Also in either case, prior approval regulations would have to contain a clear definition of the protest activity to which they apply, precise standards to limit the administrator's discretion in making approval decisions, and procedures for ensuring an expeditious and fair decision-making process. Administrators must always assume the burden of proving that the protest activity would violate a reasonable time, place, or manner regulation or would cause substantial disruption.[32] Given these complexities, prior approval requirements may invite substantial legal challenges. Administrators should carefully consider whether and when the prior approval strategy is worth the risk. There are always alternatives: disciplining students who violate regulations prohibiting disruptive protest; disciplining students who violate time, place, or manner requirements; or using injunctive or criminal processes, as set out in Section 4.9.4.

[32]These prior restraint requirements have been established in bits and pieces in various court cases. *Healy* is a leading case on burden of proof. *Kunz v. New York*, 340 U.S. 290 (1951), *Shuttlesworth v. Birmingham*, 394 U.S. 147 (1969), and *Forsyth County v. Nationalist Movement*, 112 S. Ct. 2395 (1992), are leading cases on standards to guide administrative discretion. *Southeastern Promotions v. Conrad*, 420 U.S. 546 (1975), is a leading case on procedural requirements.

4.9.4. Court injunctions and criminal prosecutions. When administrators are faced with a mass disruption that they cannot end by discussion, negotiation, or threat of disciplinary action, they may want to seek judicial assistance. A court injunction terminating the demonstration is one option. Arrest and criminal prosecution is the other.[33] Although both options involve critical tactical considerations and risks, commentators favor the injunction for most situations, primarily because it provides a more immediate judicial forum for resolving disputes and because it shifts the responsibility for using law enforcement officials from administrators to the court. Injunctions may also be used in some instances to enjoin future disruptive conduct, whereas criminal prosecutions are limited to punishing past conduct. The use of the injunctive process does not legally foreclose the possibility of later criminal prosecutions; and injunctive orders or criminal prosecutions do not legally prevent the institution from initiating student disciplinary proceedings. Under U.S. Supreme Court precedents, none of these combinations would constitute double jeopardy. (For other problems regarding the relationship between criminal prosecutions and disciplinary proceedings, see Section 4.5.3.)

The legality of injunctions or criminal prosecutions depends on two factors. First, the conduct at issue must be unlawful under state law. To warrant an injunction, the conduct must be an imminent or continuing violation of property rights or personal rights protected by state statutory law or common law; to warrant a criminal arrest and prosecution, the conduct must violate the state criminal code. Second, the conduct at issue must not constitute expression protected by the First Amendment. Both injunctive orders and criminal convictions are restraints on speech-related activity and would be tested by the principles discussed in Section 4.9.2, concerning the regulation of student protest. Since injunctions act to restrain future demonstrations, they may operate as prior restraints on expression and would also be subject to the First Amendment principles described in Section 4.9.3.

When the assistance of the court is requested, public and private institutions are on the same footing. Since the court, rather than the institution, will ultimately impose the restraint, and since the court is clearly a public entity subject to the Constitution, both public and private institutions' use of judicial assistance must comply with First Amendment requirements. Also, for both public and private institutions, judicial assistance depends on the same technical requirements regarding the availability and enforcement of injunctions and the procedural validity of arrests and prosecutions.

Sec. 4.10. The Special Problem of Hate Speech

Since the late 1980s, colleges and universities have increasingly confronted the legal, policy, and political aspects of the "hate speech" problem.[34] Responding to escalating

---

[33]Cases are collected in Annot., "Participation of Student in Demonstration on or near Campus as Warranting Imposition of Criminal Liability for Breach of Peace, Disorderly Conduct, Trespass, Unlawful Assembly, or Similar Offense," 32 A.L.R.3d 551 (1991 and periodic supp.).

[34]Portions of this section are extracted and adapted (without further attribution) from W. Kaplin, "A Proposed Process for Managing the First Amendment Aspects of Campus Hate Speech," 63 *J. Higher Educ.* 517 (1992), copyright © 1992 by the Ohio State University Press; and from W. Kaplin, "Hate Speech on the College Campus: Freedom of Speech and Equality

racial, anti-Semitic, homophobic, and sexist incidents on campus, as well as to developments in the courts, institutions have enacted, revised, and sometimes revoked rules of conduct that regulate certain types of harassing or abusive student behavior directed against members of minority groups (see M. Olivas, "The Political Economy of Immigration, Intellectual Property, and Racial Harassment: Case Studies of the Implementation of Legal Change on Campus," 63 *J. Higher Educ.* 570, 580–84 (1992)). Often the harassment or abuse involved in campus incidents or covered by conduct rules has been conveyed by the spoken or written word or by symbolic conduct—thus raising difficult issues concerning students' free speech and press rights and having important implications for both academic freedom and equal educational opportunity for students.[35]

"Hate speech" is an imprecise catch-all term that generally includes verbal and written words and symbolic acts that convey a grossly negative assessment of particular persons or groups based on their race, gender, ethnicity, religion, sexual orientation, or disability. Hate speech thus is highly derogatory and degrading, and the language is typically coarse. The purpose of the speech is more to humiliate or wound than it is to communicate ideas or information. Common vehicles for such speech include epithets, slurs, insults, taunts, and threats. Because the viewpoints underlying hate speech may be considered "politically incorrect," the debate over hate speech codes has sometimes become intertwined with the political correctness phenomenon on American campuses.

Hate speech is not limited to a face-to-face confrontation or shouts from a crowd. It takes many forms. It may appear on T-shirts, posters, classroom blackboards, bulletin boards, or in flyers and leaflets, phone calls, letters, or electronic mail messages on a computer screen. It may be a cartoon appearing in a student publication or a joke told on a campus radio station or at an after-dinner speech, a skit at a student event, an anonymous note slipped under a dormitory door, or graffiti scribbled on a wall or sidewalk. It may be conveyed through defacement of posters or displays; through symbols such as burning crosses, swastikas, KKK insignia, and Confederate flags; and even through themes for social functions, such as black-face Harlem parties or parties celebrating white history week.

When hate speech is directed at particular individuals, it may cause real psychic harm to those individuals and may also inflict pain on the broader class of persons who belong to the group denigrated by the hate speech. Moreover, the feelings of vulnerability, insecurity, and alienation that repeated incidents of hate speech can engender in the victimized groups may prevent them from taking full advantage of the educational, employment, and social opportunities on the campus and may undermine the conditions necessary for constructive dialogue with other persons or groups. Ultimately, hate speech may degrade the intellectual environment of the campus, thus harming the entire academic community.

Since hate speech regulations may prohibit and punish particular types of

---

at the Crossroads," 27 *Land & Water L. Rev.* 243 (1992), copyright © 1992 by the University of Wyoming.

[35]Similar issues may arise concerning hate speech of faculty members and staff members. See, for example, *Dambrot v. Central Michigan University*, 839 F. Supp. 477 (E. D. Mich. 1993); *Barrett v. University of Colorado Health Sciences Center*, 61 Fair Empl. Prac. Cases 386 (Colo. 1993). Institutions will generally have more constitutional leeway to regulate faculty and staff hate speech than they do for student hate speech; see this volume, Sections 3.7.2 and 3.7.3.

messages, pressing constitutional issues arise under the First Amendment, for public institutions (see Section 1.5.2), as well as for private institutions that are subject to state constitutional provisions or statutes employing First Amendment norms (see Section 4.9.1, this volume) or that voluntarily adhere to First Amendment norms. A number of important cases have reached the courts since 1989, some involving university hate speech codes and others involving city ordinances or state statutes that were construed to cover hate speech activities or that enhanced the penalties for conduct undertaken with racist or other biased motivations.

The U.S. Supreme Court's 1992 decision in *R.A.V. v. City of St. Paul*, 112 S. Ct. 2538 (1992), addresses the validity of a city ordinance directed at hate crimes. This ordinance made it a misdemeanor to place on public or private property any symbol or graffiti that one reasonably knew would "arouse anger, alarm or resentment in others on the basis of race, color, creed, religion or gender." R.A.V., a juvenile who had set up and burned a cross in the yard of a black family, challenged the ordinance as overbroad (see this volume, Section 4.9.2). The lower courts upheld the validity of the statute by narrowly construing it to apply only to expression that would be considered fighting words or incitement. The U.S. Supreme Court disagreed and invalidated the ordinance, but the majority opinion by Justice Scalia did not use overbreadth analysis. Instead, it focused on the viewpoint discrimination evident in the ordinance and invalidated the ordinance because its restriction on speech content was too narrow rather than too broad:

> Although the phrase in the ordinance, "arouses anger, alarm or resent- ment in others," has been limited by the Minnesota Supreme Court's construction to reach only those symbols or displays that amount to "fighting words," the remaining, unmodified terms make clear that the ordinance applies only to "fighting words" that insult, or provoke violence, "on the basis of race, color, creed, religion or gender." Displays containing abusive invective, no matter how vicious or severe, are permissible unless they are addressed to one of the specified disfavored topics. Those who wish to use "fighting words" in connection with other ideas—to express hostility, for example, on the basis of political affiliation, union membership, or homosexuality—are not covered. The First Amendment does not permit St. Paul to impose special prohibitions on those speakers who express views on disfavored subjects [112 S. Ct. at 2547].

The Court did note several narrow exceptions to this requirement of viewpoint neutrality but found that the St. Paul ordinance did not fall into any of these narrow exceptions (112 S. Ct. at 2545-47). The Court also determined that the city could not justify its narrow viewpoint-based ordinance. The city did have a compelling interest in promoting the rights of those who have traditionally been subject to discrimina- tion. But because a broader ordinance without the viewpoint-based restriction would equally serve this interest, the law was not "reasonably necessary" to the advancement of the interest and was thus invalid.

The Supreme Court visited the hate speech problem again in *Wisconsin v. Mitchell*, 113 S. Ct. 2194 (1993). At issue was the constitutionality of a state law that enhanced the punishment for commission of a crime when the victim was intention- ally selected because of his "race, religion, color, disability, sexual orientation, na- tional origin or ancestry" (Wis. Stat. § 939.645(1)(b)). The state had applied the statute to a defendant who, with several other black males, had seen and discussed a movie that featured a racially motivated beating and thereupon had brutally assaulted a white male. Before the attack, the defendant had said, among other things, "There goes a white boy; go get him." A jury convicted the defendant of aggravated battery, and the court enhanced his sentence because his actions were racially motivated.

The Court unanimously upheld the statute because it focused on the defendant's motive, traditionally a major consideration in sentencing. Unlike the *R.A.V.* case, the actual crime was not the speech or thought itself, but the assault—"conduct unprotected by the First Amendment." Moreover, the statute did not permit enhancement of penalties because of "mere disagreement with offenders' beliefs or biases" but rather because "bias-inspired conduct . . . is thought to inflict greater individual and societal harm." The Court did caution, moreover, "that a defendant's abstract beliefs, however obnoxious to most people, may not be taken into consideration by a sentencing judge." Thus, in order for a penalty-enhancing statute to be constitutionally applied, the prosecution must show more than the mere fact that a defendant is, for example, a racist. Such evidence alone would most likely be considered irrelevant and unduly prejudicial by a trial judge. Instead, the prosecution must prove that the defendant's racism motivated him to commit the particular crime; there must be a direct connection between the criminal act and a racial motive. This showing will generally be difficult to make and may necessitate direct evidence such as that in *Mitchell*, where the defendant's own contemporaneous statements indicated a clear and immediate intent to act on racial or other proscribed grounds.

Although no case involving campus hate speech has yet reached the U.S. Supreme Court, there have been several important cases in the lower courts. The first was *Doe v. University of Michigan*, 721 F. Supp. 852 (E.D. Mich. 1989). The plaintiff, a graduate student, challenged the university's hate speech policy, whose central provision prohibited "[a]ny behavior, verbal or physical, that stigmatizes or victimizes an individual on the basis of race, ethnicity, religion, sex, sexual orientation, creed, national origin, ancestry, age, marital status, handicap, or Vietnam-era veteran status." The policy prohibited such behavior if it "[i]nvolves an express or implied threat to" or "[h]as the purpose or reasonably foreseeable effect of interfering with" or "[c]reates an intimidating, hostile, or demeaning environment" for individual pursuits in academics, employment, or extracurricular activities. This prohibition applied to behavior in "educational and academic centers, such as classroom buildings, libraries, research laboratories, recreation and study centers." Focusing on the wording of the policy and the way in which the university interpreted and applied this language, the court held that the policy was unconstitutionally overbroad on its face because its wording swept up and sought to punish substantial amounts of constitutionally protected speech. In addition, the court held the policy to be unconstitutionally vague on its face. This fatal flaw arose primarily from the words "stigmatize" and "victimize" and the phrases "threat to" or "interfering with," as applied to an individual's academic pursuits—language which was so vague that students would not be able to discern what speech would be protected and what would be prohibited.

Similarly, in *UWM Post, Inc. v. Board of Regents of the University of Wisconsin System*, 774 F. Supp. 1163 (E.D. Wis. 1991), the court utilized both overbreadth and vagueness analysis to invalidate a campus hate speech regulation. The regulation applied to "racist or discriminatory comments, epithets, or other expressive behavior directed at an individual" and prohibited any such speech that "intentionally" (1) "demean[s]" the race, sex, or other specified characteristics of the individual, and (2) "create[s] an intimidating, hostile, or demeaning environment for education." The court held this language to be overbroad because it encompassed many types of speech that would not fall within any existing exceptions to the principle that government may not regulate the content of speech. Regarding vagueness, the court rejected the plaintiffs' argument that the phrase "discriminatory comments, epithets, or other expressive behavior" and the word "demean" were vague. But the court nevertheless held the regulation unconstitutionally vague because another of its provisions, juxtaposed against the language quoted above, created confusion as to whether the prohibited speech must actually demean the individual and create a hostile educational environment, or whether the speaker must only *intend* those results and they need not actually occur.

A third case, *Iota Xi Chapter of Sigma Chi Fraternity v. George Mason University*, 993 F.2d 386 (4th Cir. 1993), was decided (unlike the other two) after the U.S. Supreme Court's decision in *R.A.V. v. City of St. Paul.* In this case a fraternity had staged an "ugly woman contest" in which one member wore black face, used padding and women's clothes, and presented an offensive caricature of a black woman. After receiving numerous complaints about the skit from other students, the university imposed heavy sanctions on the fraternity. The fraternity, relying on the First Amendment, sought an injunction that would force the school to lift the sanctions. The trial court granted summary judgment for the fraternity, and the appellate court affirmed the trial court's ruling.

Determining that the skit was "expressive entertainment" or "expressive conduct" protected by the First Amendment and that the sanctions constituted a content-based restriction on speech, the court applied reasoning similar to that in *R.A.V.:*

> The mischief was the University's punishment of those who scoffed at its goals of racial integration and gender neutrality, while permitting, even encouraging, conduct that would further the viewpoint expressed in the University's goals and probably embraced by a majority of society as well. . . .
>
> The University, however, urges us to weigh Sigma Chi's conduct against the substantial interests inherent in educational endeavors. . . . The University certainly has a substantial interest in maintaining an environment free of discrimination and racism, and in providing gender-neutral education. Yet it seems equally apparent that it has available numerous alternatives to imposing punishment on students based on the viewpoints they express. We agree wholeheartedly that it is the University officials' responsibility, even their obligation, to achieve the goals they have set. On the other hand, a public university has many constitutionally permissible means to protect female and minority students. We must emphasize, as have other courts, that "the manner of [its action] cannot consist of selective limitations upon speech." [*R.A.V.*], 112 S. Ct. at 2548. . . . The First Amendment forbids the government from "restrict[ing] expression because of its message [or] its ideas." *Police Department v. Mosley*, 408 U.S. 92, 95 (1972). The University should have accomplished its goals in some fashion other than silencing speech on the basis of its viewpoint [993 F.2d at 393].[36]

[36]In a strong concurring opinion, one judge agreed with the decision only because the university had "tacitly approv[ed]" of the skit without giving any indication that the fraternity would be punished, and then imposed sanctions only after the skit had been performed. More

The three campus cases, combined with *R.A.V.*, make clear the exceeding difficulty public institutions face in attempting to promulgate hate speech regulations that would survive First Amendment scrutiny. Read against the backdrop of earlier Supreme Court cases on freedom of speech, the hate speech cases reflect and confirm five major free speech principles, which, together, severely constrain the authority of government to regulate hate speech. Under the first principle, regulations on the content of speech—that is, the speaker's message—are highly suspect. As the U.S. Supreme Court has frequently stated, "[A]bove all else, the First Amendment means that government has no power to restrict expression because of its message, its ideas, its subject matter, or its content. . . . There is an 'equality of status in the field of ideas,' and government must afford all points of view an equal opportunity to be heard" (*Police Department v. Mosley*, 408 U.S. 92, 95-96 (1972), quoting A. Meiklejohn, *Political Freedom: The Constitutional Powers of the People* (1948), 27 (reprinted by Greenwood Press, 1979)).

Under the second free speech principle, the emotional content as well as the cognitive content of speech is protected from government regulation. As the U.S. Supreme Court explained in *Cohen v. California*, 403 U.S. 15 (1971):

> [M]uch linguistic expression serves a dual communicative function: it conveys not only ideas capable of relatively precise, detached explication, but otherwise inexpressible emotions as well. In fact, words are often chosen as much for their emotive as their cognitive force. We cannot sanction the view that the Constitution, while solicitous of the cognitive content of individual speech, has little or no regard for that emotive function which, practically speaking, may often be the more important element of the overall message [403 U.S. at 26].

Under the third free speech principle, speech may not be prohibited merely because persons who hear or view it are offended by the message. In a flag-burning case, *Texas v. Johnson*, 491 U.S. 397 (1989), the U.S. Supreme Court reaffirmed that "[i]f there is a bedrock principle underlying the First Amendment, it is that the government may not prohibit the expression of an idea simply because society finds the idea itself offensive or disagreeable."

Under the fourth free speech principle, government may not regulate speech activity with provisions whose language is either overbroad or vague and would thereby create a chilling effect on the exercise of free speech rights (see this volume, Section 3.5.1). As the U.S. Supreme Court has stated, "Because First Amendment freedoms need breathing space to survive, government may regulate in the area only with narrow specificity" (*NAACP v. Button*, 371 U.S. 415, 433 (1963)).

And under the fifth free speech principle, when government is regulating what is considered an unprotected type of speech—for example, fighting words or obscenity—it generally may not restrict expression of certain topics or viewpoints in that unprotected area without also restricting expressions of other topics and viewpoints

---

generally, the concurring judge asserted that the university had "greater authority to regulate expressive conduct within its confines as a result of the unique nature of the educational forum" (see this volume, Section 4.9.1) and therefore could regulate certain offensive speech that interferes with its ability to "provide the optimum conditions for learning" and thus "runs directly counter to its mission."

within that same area. For example, if government utilizes the "fighting words" rationale for regulation, it must generally regulate all fighting words or none; it cannot selectively regulate only fighting words that convey disfavored messages. This principle, sometimes called the "underbreadth" principle, is a new addition to First Amendment jurisprudence derived from the *R.A.V.* case (above).

In light of the imposing barriers to regulation erected by these principles, it is critical that institutions (public and private alike) emphasize *nonregulatory* approaches for dealing with hate speech. Such approaches do not rely on the prohibition of certain types of speech or the imposition of involuntary sanctions on transgressors, as do regulatory approaches. Moreover, nonregulatory initiatives may reach or engage a wider range of students than regulatory approaches can. They also may have more influence on student attitudes and values and may be more effective in creating an institutional environment that is inhospitable to hate behavior. Thus, nonregulatory initiatives may have a broader and longer-range impact on the hate speech problem. Nonregulatory initiatives may also be more in harmony with higher education's mission to foster critical examination and dialogue in the search for truth. See generally S. Sherry, "Speaking of Virtue: A Republican Approach to University Regulation of Hate Speech," 75 *Minn. L. Rev.* 933, 934-36, 942-44 (1991). Nonregulatory initiatives, moreover, do not raise substantial First Amendment issues. For these reasons, institutions should move to regulatory options only if they are certain that nonregulatory initiatives cannot suitably alleviate existing or incipient hate speech problems.

In addition to nonregulatory initiatives, institutions may regulate hate *conduct* or *behavior* (as opposed to speech) on their campuses. Hateful impulses that manifest themselves in such behavior or conduct are not within the constitutional protections accorded speech (that is, the use of words or symbols to convey a message). Examples include kicking, shoving, spitting, throwing objects at persons, trashing rooms, and blocking pathways or entryways. Since such behaviors are not speech, they can be aggressively prohibited and punished in order to alleviate hate problems on campus.

If an institution also deems it necessary to regulate speech itself, either in formulating general policies or in responding to particular incidents, it should first consider the applicability or adaptability of regulations that are already in or could readily be inserted into its general code of student conduct. The question in each instance would be whether a particular type of disciplinary regulation can be applied to some particular type of hate speech without substantially intruding on free speech values and without substantial risk that a court would later find the regulation's application to hate speech unconstitutional. Under this selective incremental approach, much hate speech must remain unregulated because no type of regulation could constitutionally reach it. But some provisions in conduct codes might be applied to some hate speech. The following discussion considers six potential types of such regulations.

First, when hate speech is combined with nonspeech actions in the same course of behavior, institutions may regulate the nonspeech elements of behavior without violating the First Amendment. A campus building may be spray-painted with swastikas; homophobic graffiti may be painted on a campus sidewalk; a KKK insignia may be carved into the door of a dormitory room; a student may be shoved or spit on in the course of enduring verbal abuse. All these behaviors convey a hate message and therefore involve speech; but all also have a nonspeech element characterizable as destruction of property or physical attack. While the institution cannot prohibit particular messages, it can prohibit harmful acts; such acts therefore may be covered under neutral regulations governing such nonspeech matters as destruction and defacement of property or physical assaults of persons.

Second, institutions may regulate the time or place at which hate speech is uttered, or the manner in which it is uttered, as long as they use neutral regulations that do not focus on the content or viewpoint of the speech. For example, an institution could punish the shouting of racial epithets in a dormitory quadrangle in the middle of the night, as long as the applicable regulation would also cover (for example) the shouting of cheers for a local sports team at the same location and time.

Third, institutions may regulate the content of hate speech that falls within one of the various exceptions to the principle forbidding content-based restrictions on speech. Thus, institutions may punish hate speech that constitutes fighting words, obscenity, incitement, or private defamation. Any such regulation, however, must comply with the new "underbreadth" principle announced in the *R.A.V.* case. Under this principle, an institution could not have a specific hate speech code based on (for example) a "fighting words" rationale, but it could have a broader regulation that applies to hate speech constituting fighting words as well as to all other types of fighting words.

Fourth, institutions probably may regulate hate speech in the form of threats or intimidation aimed at particular individuals and creating in them a realistic fear for their physical safety or the security of their property. Speech activities with such effects are analogous to assaults, which typically are punishable under both criminal law and tort law. Such activities, even though carried out in part through speech, may be reached under code provisions dealing generally with physical assaults or other threats of physical harm to person or property. (See *United States v. Hayward,* 6 F.3d 1241, 1249–52 (7th Cir. 1993).)

Fifth, institutions probably may regulate hate speech that occurs on or is projected onto private areas, such as dormitory rooms or library study carrels, and thereby infringes on privacy interests of individuals who legitimately occupy these places. For First Amendment purposes, such private areas are not considered "public forums" open to public dialogue; and the persons occupying such places may be "captive audiences" who cannot guard their privacy by avoiding the hate speech (see *Frisby v. Schultz,* 487 U.S. 474 (1988)). For these two reasons, it is likely that hate speech of this type could be constitutionally reached under provisions dealing generally with unjustified invasions of students' personal privacy.

Sixth, institutions probably may regulate hate speech that furthers a scheme of racial or other discrimination. If a fraternity places a sign in front of its house reading "No blacks allowed here," the speech is itself an act of discrimination, making it unlikely that black students would seek to become members of that fraternity. When such speech is an integral element of a pattern of discriminatory behavior, institutions should be able to cover it and related actions under a code provision prohibiting discrimination on the basis of identifiable group characteristics such as race, sex, or ethnicity. The *R.A.V.* majority opinion itself apparently supports such a rationale when it suggests that the nondiscrimination requirements of Title VII (the federal employment discrimination statute) would not violate the "underbreadth" principle and could constitutionally be applied to sexual harassment accomplished in part through speech.

In addition to these six bases for regulating hate speech, institutions may also—as was suggested above—devise enhanced penalties under their conduct codes for hate *behavior* or *conduct* (such as the racially inspired physical attack in *Wisconsin v. Mitchell* above) that does not itself involve speech. An offense that would normally merit a semester of probation, for instance, might be punished by a one-semester suspension upon proof that the act was undertaken for racial reasons. Institutions must proceed most cautiously, however. The delicate inquiry into the perpetrator's motives that penalty enhancement requires is usually the domain of courts, lawyers, and expert witnesses, guided by formal procedures and rules of evidence as well as a body of precedent. An institution should not consider itself equipped to undertake this type of inquiry unless its disciplinary system has well-developed fact-finding processes and substantial assistance from legal counsel or a law-trained judicial officer. Institutions should also assure themselves that the system's "judges" can distinguish between the perpetrator's actual motivation for the offense (which is a permissible basis for the inquiry) and the perpetrator's thoughts or general disposition (which, under *Mitchell,* is an impermissible consideration).

Sec. 4.11. Student Organizations

Student organizations provide college students with the opportunity to learn leadership skills, supplement their formal academic experience, or pursue diverse interests that their academic program may not provide. Although administrators typically view student organizations as an important supplement to classroom learning, colleges may face liability for the actions of student organizations or for decisions to award or deny funding to these organizations. Recognition of a student organization as an "official" college group may lead to claims that the organization is the agent of the college, raising concerns about the institution's potential liability in contract and tort (see Section 2.3).

4.11.1. Right to organize. Students in public postsecondary institutions have a general right to organize; to be officially recognized whenever the school has a policy of recognizing student groups;[37] and to use meeting rooms, bulletin boards, and similar facilities open to campus groups. Occasionally a state statute will accord students specific organizational rights (see *Student Assn. of the University of Wisconsin–Milwaukee v. Baum,* 246 N.W.2d 622 (Wis. 1976), discussed in Section 2.2.4). More generally, organizational rights are protected by the freedom-of-association and freedom-of-expression concepts of the First Amendment. However, public institutions retain authority to withhold or revoke recognition in certain instances and to evenhandedly regulate the organizational use of campus facilities. The balance between the organization's rights and the institution's authority was struck in *Healy v. James,* 408 U.S. 169 (1972), the leading case in the field.[38]

---

[37]See the cases and authorities collected in Annot., "Student Organization Registration Statement, Filed with Public School or State University or College, as Open to Inspection by Public," 37 A.L.R.3d 1311 (1971 and periodic supp.).

[38]The later case of *Widmar v. Vincent,* discussed in Section 4.11.4, affirms many of the principles of *Healy* and adds important new guidance on the particular question of when a

Healy arose after a student organization's request for recognition was denied. The request for recognition as a local Students for a Democratic Society (SDS) organization had been approved by the student affairs committee at Central Connecticut State College, but the college's president denied recognition, asserting that the organization's philosophy was antithetical to the college's commitment to academic freedom and that the organization would be a disruptive influence on campus. The denial of recognition had the effect of prohibiting the student group from using campus meeting rooms and campus bulletin boards and placing announcements in the student newspaper. The U.S. Supreme Court found the president's reasons insufficient under the facts to justify the extreme effects of nonrecognition on the organization's ability to "remain a viable entity" on campus and "participate in the intellectual give and take of campus debate." The Court therefore overruled the president's decision and remanded the case to the lower court, ruling that the college had to recognize the student group if the lower court determined that the group was willing to abide by all reasonable campus rules.

The associational rights recognized in *Healy* are not limited to situations where recognition is the issue. In *Gay Students Organization of the University of New Hampshire v. Bonner*, 509 F.2d 652 (1st Cir. 1974), for instance, the plaintiff (GSO) was an officially recognized campus organization. After it sponsored a dance on campus, the state governor criticized the university's policy regarding GSO; in reaction, the university announced that GSO could no longer hold social functions on campus. GSO filed suit, and the federal appeals court found that the university's new policy violated the students' freedom of association and expression.[39] *Healy* was the controlling precedent, even though GSO had not been denied recognition:

> The Court's analysis in *Healy* focused not on the technical point of recognition or nonrecognition, but on the practicalities of human interaction. While the Court concluded that the SDS members' right to further their personal beliefs had been impermissibly burdened by nonrecognition, this conclusion stemmed from a finding that the "primary impediment to free association flowing from nonrecognition is the denial of use of campus facilities for meetings and other appropriate purposes." The ultimate issue at which inquiry must be directed is the effect which a regulation has on organizational and associational activity, not the isolated and for the most part irrelevant issue of recognition per se [509 F.2d at 658–59].

Healy and related cases reveal three broad bases on which administrators may regulate the recognition of student organizations without violating associational rights. First,

---

student group may have access to meeting rooms and other campus facilities. See also *Gay Student Services v. Texas A&M University*, 737 F.2d 1317, 1331–33 (5th Cir. 1984), in which the court used *Widmar's* "public forum" analysis in invalidating the defendant's refusal to recognize the plaintiff groups.

[39]Cases and authorities are collected in Annot., "Validity, Under First Amendment and 42 U.S.C.S § 1983, of Public College or University's Refusal to Grant Formal Recognition to, or Permit Meetings of, Student Homosexual Organizations on Campus," 50 A.L.R. Fed. 516 (1980 and periodic supp.).

a college administrator may impose a requirement . . . that a group seeking official recognition affirm in advance its willingness to adhere to reasonable campus
law. Such a requirement does not impose an impermissible condition on the
students' associational rights. Their freedom to speak out, to assemble, or to
petition for changes in school rules is in no sense infringed. It merely constitutes
an agreement to conform to reasonable standards respecting conduct. This is a
minimal requirement, in the interest of the entire academic community, of any
group seeking the privilege of official recognition [*Healy* at 193].

Such standards of conduct, of course, must not themselves violate the First Amendment or other constitutional safeguards. Recognition, for instance, could not be conditioned on the organization's willingness to abide by a rule prohibiting all peaceful
protest demonstrations on campus (see Section 4.9.2) or requiring all campus newspaper announcements to be approved in advance by the administration (see Section
4.13.1). But as long as campus rules avoid such pitfalls, student organizations must
comply with them, just as individual students must. If the organization refuses to
agree in advance to obey campus law, recognition may be denied until such time as
the organization does agree. If a recognized organization violates campus law, its
recognition may be suspended or withdrawn for a reasonable period of time.

Second, "associational activities need not be tolerated where they . . . interrupt
classes . . . or substantially interfere with the opportunity of other students to obtain
an education" (*Healy* at 189). Thus, administrators may also deny recognition to a
group that would create substantial disruption on campus, and they may revoke the
recognition of a group that has created such disruption. In either case the institution
has the burden of demonstrating with reasonable certainty that substantial disruption
will or did in fact result from the organization's actions—a burden that the college
failed to meet in *Healy*. This burden is a heavy one because "denial of recognition
. . . [is] a form of prior restraint" of First Amendment rights (*Healy* at 184).

Third, the institution may act to prevent organizational activity that is itself
illegal under local, state, or federal laws, as well as activity "directed to inciting or
producing imminent lawless action and . . . likely to incite or produce such action"
(*Brandenburg v. Ohio*, 395 U.S. 444, 447 (1969), quoted in *Healy* at 188). While the
GSO case specifically supported this basis for regulation, the court found that the
institution had not met its burden of demonstrating that the group's activities were
illegal or inciting. A similar conclusion was reached in *Gay Lib v. University of
Missouri*, 558 F.2d 848 (8th Cir. 1977), *reversing* 416 F. Supp. 1350 (W.D. Mo. 1976).
The trial court found, on the basis of the university's expert evidence, that recognition
of the student group "would predictably lead to increased homosexual activities,
which include sodomy [a felony under state law] as one of the most prevalent forms
of sexual expression in homosexuality." Relying on this finding and on the fact that
sodomy is an illegal activity that can be prohibited, the trial court upheld the university's refusal to recognize the group. Overruling the trial court, the appellate court
held that the university's proof was insufficient to demonstrate that the student organization intended to breach university regulations or advocate or incite imminent
lawless acts. At most, the group intended peaceably to advocate the repeal of certain
criminal laws—expression that constitutionally could not be prohibited. Thus, the
appellate court concluded that the university's denial of recognition impermissibly
penalized the group's members because of their status rather than their conduct. (To

the same effect, see *Gay Activists Alliance v. Board of Regents,* 638 P.2d 1116 (Okla. 1981); and see generally Note, "The Rights of Gay Student Organizations," 10 *J. Coll. & Univ. Law* 397 (1983–84).)

All rules and decisions regarding student organizations should be supportable on one or more of these three regulatory bases. Administrators should apply the rules evenhandedly, carefully avoiding selective applications to particular groups whose philosophy or activities are repugnant to the institution. Decisions under the rules should be based on a sound factual assessment of the impact of the group's activity rather than on speculation or on what the Supreme Court calls "undifferentiated fear or apprehension." Decisions denying organizational privileges should be preceded by "some reasonable opportunity for the organization to meet the university's contentions" or "to eliminate the basis of the denial" (*Wood v. Davison,* 351 F. Supp. 543, 548 (N.D. Ga. 1972)). Keeping these points in mind, administrators can retain substantial yet sensitive authority over the recognition of student groups.

Denial of funding by a public institution to a group because of the views its members espouse is a clear violation of constitutional free speech protections, even if the denial comes from a student government committee rather than from an institutional official. In *Gay and Lesbian Students Assn. v. Gohn,* 850 F.2d 361 (8th Cir. 1988), a committee of the student senate denied funds to an organization that provided education about homosexuality. The court, noting that the administration had upheld the committee's denial of funding, said: "The University need not supply funds to student organizations; but once having done so, it is bound by the First Amendment to act without regard to the content of the ideas being expressed" (850 F.2d at 362). An exception to this principle may be recognized, however, if a public institution refuses to fund certain religiously affiliated organizations because to do so would violate the Establishment Clause (see Section 4.11.4)).

Although most challenges to denials of funding or recognition have been against public institutions, a significant case brought against Georgetown University illustrates some of the issues facing private, religiously affiliated institutions. Two student gay rights groups sought official recognition by the university, which refused, citing Catholic doctrine that condemns homosexuality. Denial of recognition meant that the groups could not use the university's facilities or its mailing and labeling services, could not have a mailbox in the student activities office, and could not request university funds. The student group sued under a District of Columbia law (D.C. Code § 1-2520) that outlaws discrimination (in the form of denying access to facilities and services) on the basis of (among other characteristics) sexual orientation. The university defended its actions on the grounds of free exercise of religion.

In *Gay Rights Coalition of Georgetown University Law Center v. Georgetown University,* 536 A.2d 1 (D.C. 1987), the court issued seven separate opinions, which— although none attracted a majority of the judges—reached a collective result of not requiring the university to recognize the groups but requiring it to give them access to facilities, services, and funding.

By severing the recognition process from the granting of access to university facilities and funding, the court avoided addressing the university's constitutional claim with regard to recognition. In interpreting the D.C. statute, the court found no requirement that "one private actor . . . 'endorse' another" (536 A.2d at 5). For that reason, Georgetown's denial of recognition to the student groups did not violate the statute. But the statute did require equal treatment, according to the court. And, the court concluded, the District of Columbia's compelling interest in eradicating discrimination based on sexual preference outweighed any burden on the university's freedom of religion that providing equal access would imply. For a critical analysis of this case and the conflicts it embodies, see F. N. Dutile, "God and Gays at Georgetown: Observations on *Gay Rights Coalition of Georgetown University Law Center v. Georgetown University*," 15 *J. Coll. & Univ. Law* 1 (1988).

In the wake of the *Gay Rights Coalition* case, the U.S. Congress, which has legislative jurisdiction over the District of Columbia, passed The Nation's Capitol Religious Liberty and Academic Freedom Act, 102 Stat. 2269 (1988). The law provided that the District government would not receive further appropriations unless it adopted legislation authorizing religiously affiliated institutions to deny endorsement or benefits in a situation like that in the *Gay Rights Coalition* case. The constitutionality of the law was challenged by D.C. City Council members in *Clarke v. United States*, 898 F.2d 162 (D.C. Cir. 1990). Although a panel of the appellate court affirmed a trial court's ruling that the law was an unconstitutional burden on the free speech of City Council members, the *en banc* court vacated the panel opinion as moot in *Clarke v. United States*, 898 F.2d 161 (D.C. Cir. 1990) (*en banc*) because the appropriation act had expired. The next year's appropriations act did not contain a funding limitation because Congress used its power under the District of Columbia Self-Government and Governmental Reorganization Act (Pub. L. No. 93-198 (1973)) to amend the District of Columbia law directly to permit religious institutions to discriminate on the basis of sexual orientation.

The regulations that student organizations themselves may promulgate can be subject to constitutional challenges as well. For example, in *Alabama Student Party v. Student Government Assn. of Alabama*, 867 F.2d 1344 (11th Cir. 1989), students challenged the student government's regulations that severely restricted campaigning for student government offices. The students claimed that these regulations violated their free speech rights. Declaring that the elections were an educational function of the university and deserved great deference, the court upheld the regulations.

4.11.2. Right not to organize. The right-to-organize concept has a flip side. Students often are organized into a large campuswide or collegewide association recognized by the institution as a student government or similar representational organization. Mandatory student activities fees sometimes are collected by the institution and channeled to the student association. Where such circumstances pertain at a public institution, may students argue that their constitutional rights are violated—either by a requirement that they be members of the association or by a requirement that their activity fees be used to support the association? Or may a public institution channel funds from a mandatory student activities fee to nonrepresentational, special-purpose organizations (such as minority or foreign student groups, social action groups, and academic or honorary societies) when other students object to supporting those organizations' beliefs or statements?

An early case, *Good v. Associated Students of the University of Washington*, 542 P.2d 762 (Wash. 1975), distinguished between the university's requirement that students be *members* of the ASUW, a nonprofit organization that purported to represent all of the university's students, and the university's ability to impose a mandatory student fee. The court found that the membership requirement was unconstitutional for those students who disagreed with the organization's political viewpoints: "There is no room in the First Amendment for such absolute compulsory support, advocation, and representation" (542 P.2d at 768). With regard to the mandatory fee, however, the court balanced the students' First Amendment rights against the university's interest in providing an environment for diverse ideas. The court concluded that "dissenting students should not have the right to veto every event, speech, or program with which they disagree." Accordingly, student associations like the ASUW may use mandatory fees as long as (1) such use does not "exceed the statutory purposes" for which fees may be spent and (2) the group does not "become the vehicle for the promotion of one particular viewpoint, political, social, economic or religious" (542 P.2d at 769).

A similar approach can be taken toward the validity of mandatory fee allocations to special-purpose organizations. If students have no "right to veto every event, speech, or program" they disagree with, they also should not be able to veto university support for every organization that they disagree with. Thus, unlike broad representational groups such as the ASUW, special-purpose groups can promote a "particular viewpoint." In *Larson v. Board of Regents of the University of Nebraska*, 204 N.W.2d 568 (Neb. 1973), for instance, the court rejected student challenges to mandatory fee allocations for the student newspaper and the visiting-speakers program, whose views the plaintiffs opposed. Because restrictions on the content or purpose of the organization (assuming they are lawful) violate constitutional guarantees, the institution's fee allocations, as a whole, must provide a forum for a broad spectrum of viewpoints rather than selectively supporting particular ones with which the institution feels comfortable.

In a more recent case, the Supreme Court of California considered the question of mandatory student fees. In *Smith v. Regents of California*, 844 P.2d 500 (Cal. 1993), students challenged the regents' authority to impose a mandatory student fee; they also argued that the allocation of these fees to on-campus groups whose political activities these students opposed violated their constitutional rights. The court made short work of the students' first claim, stating that the regents had broad discretion to carry out the university's educational mission. With regard to the constitutional claim, after reviewing *Abood* and its progeny (regarding mandatory union dues—see Section 3.2.2.), the court characterized the issue as a conflict between the regents' authority in educational matters and the students' right to be free of compelled speech and association:

> The solution to this problem is to set a rational limit on the use of mandatory fees. We can do this by recognizing what is obviously true, namely, that a group's dedication to achieving its political or ideological goals, at some point, begins to outweigh any legitimate claim it may have to be educating students on the University's behalf. To fund such a group through mandatory fees will usually constitute more of a burden on dissenting students' speech and associational rights than is necessary to achieve any significant educational goal. The University can teach civics in other ways that involve a lesser burden on those rights, or no burden at all [844 P.2d at 508].

The court gave the regents a choice. They could develop a system of evaluating student organizations to ensure that only those whose primary purpose was educational rather than political would receive student fees; or, if they chose to continue the present system of recognizing any group of at least four students who wished to establish a student organization, they would have to follow the guidelines laid down by the U.S. Supreme Court in *Chicago Teachers' Union v. Hudson* (see Section 3.2.2., this volume). These guidelines require the regents to ascertain which groups are predominantly educational (eligible for funds) and which are predominantly political and/or ideological (ineligible for funds), and to "offer students the option of deducting a corresponding amount from the mandatory fee" (844 P.2d at 513). Furthermore, students "who disagree with the Regents' calculation of the corresponding deduction will be entitled to the procedural safeguards" set forth in *Hudson* and related cases (844 P.2d at 516).

One judge, strongly dissenting from the outcome in *Smith*, argued that the distinction between "educational" and "ideological" speech was "spurious," and warned that the outcome would expose the regents to protracted litigation. Believing that all campus groups engaged in any form of speech have an educational purpose, the judge would have permitted their funding as long as the funds were allocated in a neutral fashion. For analysis of the use of mandatory student fees, see C. E. Wells, "Mandatory Student Fees: First Amendment Concerns and University Discretion," 55 *U. Chicago L. Rev.* 363 (1988).

Several courts have addressed student challenges to the allocation of mandatory student fees to outside groups, loosely linked to the institution, that espouse views that some students oppose. In *Galda v. Rutgers, The State University of New Jersey*, 772 F.2d 1060 (3d Cir. 1985), a federal appellate court enjoined the state university from imposing a compulsory fee on students to fund an outside, nonpartisan public interest organization. The students argued that the levy of the fee violated the First Amendment, since the university compelled them to contribute to an organization that espoused and promoted ideological causes they opposed. Rutgers contended that the educational benefits to the students justified university funding. The court concluded that the educational benefits provided students through university funding were incidental to the group's ideological activities and that the university had neither demonstrated a compelling state interest to override the students' First Amendment rights nor attempted any less drastic means of satisfying its educational interests.

In *Carroll v. Blinken*, 957 F.2d 991 (2d Cir. 1992), the court faced a similar set of issues. Students who opposed the activities of the New York Public Interest Research Group (NYPIRG) sued the State University of New York at Albany, arguing that allocating a portion of their mandatory student fees to NYPIRG constituted compelled speech and association in violation of the First Amendment. Although the court agreed that using mandatory fees to support NYPIRG did constitute compelled speech and association, it held that the infringement on the student's First Amendment rights was justified. It pointed out that the university had a strong interest in supporting NYPIRG because the organization promoted extracurricular activities, its activities provided educational experiences for participating students, and it contributed to the exchange of diverse ideas on campus. The court therefore ruled that the university could allocate mandatory fees to a group whose ideas and activities the students opposed, but it also held that the organization must spend at least the equivalent of the students' contributions on campus. Furthermore, said the court, NYPIRG's practice of defining its membership to include all fee-paying students, whether they wished membership status or not, unjustifiably compelled the students' association and thus violated the First Amendment.

The collective outcomes in the cases discussed above suggest that, in overseeing student organizations, administrators should avoid imposing compulsory membership requirements. In allocating mandatory student fees, they should develop evenhanded processes devoid of artificial limits on the number or type of viewpoints that may be supported. If the process does include limits on the purposes or groups that may be supported, these limits should be demonstrably consistent with the three bases for regulation set out in Section 4.11.1 or some other substantial and evenly applied educational priority of the institution, and with the special rules regarding discrimination (Section 4.11.3) and religious activities (Section 4.11.4). And, given the outcome in *Smith,* they may wish to consider developing a system that permits students to deduct from their fees an amount equivalent to the proportion of funds allocated to "political or ideological" groups.

4.11.3. Principle of nondiscrimination. While the law prohibits administrators from imposing certain restrictions on student organizations (as Sections 4.11.1 and 4.11.2 indicate), there are other restrictions that administrators may be required to impose. The primary example concerns discrimination, particularly on the basis of race or sex. Just as the institution usually cannot discriminate on grounds of race or sex, neither can the student organization discriminate—either as the agent of (see generally Section 2.1) or with the substantial support of the institution. The institution has an obligation either to prohibit discrimination by student organizations or to withhold institutional support from those that do discriminate.

In public institutions student organizations may be subject to constitutional equal protection principles under the state action doctrine (Section 1.5.2) if they act as agents of the institution or make substantial use of institutional facilities, resources, or funds. Thus, in *Joyner v. Whiting,* 477 F.2d 456 (4th Cir. 1973) (also discussed in Section 4.13.2), a black-oriented student newspaper allegedly had a segregationist editorial policy and had discriminated by race in staffing and in accepting advertising. Although the court prohibited the university president from permanently cutting off the paper's funds, because of the restraining effect of such a cutoff on free press, it did hold that the president could and must prohibit the discrimination in staffing and advertising: "The equal protection clause forbids racial discrimination in extracurricular activities of a state-supported institution . . . and freedom of the press furnishes no shield for discrimination."

Uzzell v. Friday, 547 F.2d 801 (4th Cir. 1977), concerned certain rules of student organizations at the University of North Carolina. The Campus Governing Council, legislative branch of the student government, was required under its constitution to have at least two minority students, two males, and two females among its eighteen members. The student Honor Court, under its rules, permitted defendants to demand that a majority of the judges hearing the case be of the same race or the same sex as the defendant. Eschewing the need for any extended analysis, the court invalidated each of the provisions as race discrimination: "Without either reasonable basis or compelling interest, the composition of the council is formulated on the basis of race. This form of constituency blatantly fouls the letter and the spirit of both the Civil Rights Act [42 U.S.C. § 2000d] and the Fourteenth Amendment." (The sex discrimination aspects of the provisions were not challenged by the plaintiff students or addressed by the court.) In *Friday v. Uzzell,* 438 U.S. 912 (1978), the U.S. Supreme Court, seeing possible affirmative action issues underlying this use of racial considerations, vacated the appellate court's judgment and remanded the case for further consideration in light of the *Bakke* decision (see Section 4.2.5).

In 1979 the appeals court reconsidered its earlier decision and, by a vote of 4 to 3, again invalidated the rules (*Uzzell v. Friday*, 591 F.2d 997 (4th Cir. 1979) (*en banc*)). The majority held that the rules were contrary to the teaching of *Bakke*:

> The permeating defect in the organization of . . . the governing council is the imposition of an artificial racial structure upon this elective body that bars nonminority students from eligibility for appointment to the council. This resort to race affronts *Bakke*. Although the regulation seeks to provide "protective representation," its effect is to establish a racial classification, as it relies exclusively on race to preclude nonminority students from enjoying opportunities and benefits available to others [591 F.2d at 998].

The minority, reading *Bakke* more liberally, argued that more facts were necessary before the court could ascertain whether the student government rules were invalid race discrimination, on the one hand, or valid affirmative action, on the other. They therefore asserted that the case should be returned to the district court for a full trial:

> The present record simply does not permit a firm conclusion as to the extent of discrimination at the University of North Carolina and the need for and efficacy of the present regulations. The majority's condemnation of the regulations because they impinge upon the rights of others is simplistic. *Bakke* teaches that as a necessary remedial measure a victimized group may be preferred at the expense of other innocent persons. What cries out for determination in the instant case is whether such preferment is justified under the principles of *Bakke* [591 F.2d at 1001].

In June 1980 the Fourth Circuit recalled its 1979 decision because the *en banc* court that had heard the appeal was improperly constituted: a senior judge sat as a member of the panel—a violation of a federal statute (28 U.S.C. § 46) requiring that an *en banc* panel consist only of active circuit court judges. The new rehearing *en banc* placed the matter before the appeals court for the third time (*Uzzell v. Friday*, 625 F.2d 1117 (4th Cir. 1980) (*en banc*)). On this occasion the court ruled 5 to 3 to remand the case to the district court for a full development of the record and reconsideration in light of *Bakke*. In so ruling, the court expressly adopted the dissenting view of the 1979 decision. The majority indicated that racially conscious actions which impinge on one class of persons in order to ameliorate past discrimination against another class are not unlawful per se, and that "the university should have the opportunity to justify its regulations so that the district court can apply the *Bakke* test: is the classification necessary to the accomplishment of a constitutionally permissible purpose?"

Federal civil rights laws (see Section 7.5) may require private as well as public institutions to ensure, as a condition to receiving federal funds, that student organizations do not discriminate. The Title VI regulations (Section 7.5.2) contain several provisions broad enough to cover student organizations; in particular, 34 C.F.R. § 100.3(b)(1) prohibits institutions from discriminating by race, either "directly or through contractual or other arrangements," and 34 C.F.R. § 100.3(b)(4) prohibits institutions from discriminating in the provision of services or benefits that are offered "in or through a facility" constructed or operated in whole or part with federal funds. And the Title IX regulations (Section 7.5.3) prohibit institutions from "providing significant assistance" to any organization "which discriminates on the basis of sex in providing any aid, benefit, or service to students" (34 C.F.R. § 106.31(b)(7); see also § 106.6(c)). Title IX does not apply, however, to the membership practices of tax-exempt social fraternities and sororities (20 U.S.C. § 1681(a)6(A)). (For a discussion of the civil rights statutes' application to student organizations and other activities that do not receive federal funds, see this volume, Sections 7.5.7.3 and 7.5.7.4.)

State law may also provide protection against discrimination by student organizations at both public and private institutions. In *Frank v. Ivy Club*, 576 A.2d 241 (N.J. 1990), the court was asked to determine whether two private "eating clubs" affiliated with Princeton University, which at the time admitted only men to membership, were subject to the state's nondiscrimination law as places of public accommodation.

In 1979 Sally Frank, then an undergraduate at Princeton, filed a charge with the New Jersey Division on Civil Rights (the state's human rights agency), asserting that she was denied membership in the clubs on the basis of her gender, and that this denial constituted unlawful discrimination by a place of public accommodation. She also filed a charge against the university, asserting that it was responsible for supervising the clubs and therefore was partially responsible for their discriminatory activities. The clubs characterized themselves as private organizations, and the university asserted that the clubs were private organizations not formally affiliated with the university.

After protracted procedural battles, the Division on Civil Rights asserted jurisdiction over Frank's claim and determined that the clubs were places of public accommodation and thus subject to the nondiscrimination requirements of state law. It also ruled that the clubs enjoyed a "symbiotic relationship" with the university, since the university had assisted them in their business affairs, a majority of upper-division Princeton students took their meals at the clubs (relieving the university of the responsibility of providing meals for them), and the clubs would not have come into being without the existence of the university. From these findings, the Division on Civil Rights concluded that probable cause existed to believe that the clubs had unlawfully discriminated against Frank on the basis of her gender.

After several appeals to intermediate courts and other procedural wrangling, the New Jersey Supreme Court finally considered both the procedural and the substantive issues, affirming the jurisdiction of the Division on Civil Rights and its findings and conclusions that the clubs must cease their discriminatory membership policies. The court reasoned that "where a place of public accommodation [the university] and an organization that deems itself private [the clubs] share a symbiotic relationship, particularly where the allegedly 'private' entity supplies an essential service which is not provided by the public accommodation, the servicing entity loses its private character and becomes subject to laws against discrimination" (576 A.2d at 257). The court also upheld the Division on Civil Rights' ruling that the clubs not be permitted to sever their ties with Princeton, but that they be ordered to obey the law.

While the state court proceedings were in progress, one of the clubs filed a claim in federal court, asserting that the state civil rights agency's assertion of jurisdiction over its activities violated its rights to free association under the First Amendment of the U.S. Constitution. A federal appellate court affirmed a trial court's finding that the club's federal claims were not moot (they had not been addressed in the state proceedings), and that the club would be permitted to litigate its federal claims, although it would be bound by the undisputed stipulations of fact that had been reached in the state proceedings (*Ivy Club v. Edwards*, 943 F.2d 270 (3d Cir. 1991)).

In light of such constitutional and regulatory requirements, it is clear that administrators cannot ignore alleged discrimination by student organizations. In some areas of concern, discrimination being the primary example, administrators must deal affirmatively with the rules and practices of campus student organizations in order to fulfill their institution's obligations under the law.

4.11.4. Religious activities. In *Widmar v. Vincent*, 454 U.S. 263 (1981), a case involving the University of Missouri–Kansas City (UMKC), the United States Supreme Court established important rights for student religious groups at public postsecondary institutions who seek to use the institution's facilities. In 1972 the board of curators of UMKC promulgated a regulation prohibiting the use of university buildings or grounds "for purposes of religious worship or religious teaching." In 1977 UMKC applied this regulation to a student religious group called Cornerstone and denied it permission to continue meeting in university facilities. According to the Court:

> Cornerstone is an organization of evangelical Christian students from various denominational backgrounds. . . . Cornerstone held its on-campus meetings in classrooms and in the student center. These meetings were open to the public and attracted up to 125 students. A typical Cornerstone meeting included prayer, hymns, Bible commentary, and discussion of religious views and experiences [454 U.S. at 265 n.2].

Following this denial, eleven members of Cornerstone sued the university, alleging that it had abridged their rights to free exercise of religion and freedom of speech under the First Amendment. The district court rejected the students' arguments, holding that UMKC's regulation was necessary to fulfill the university's obligation, under the Establishment Clause of the First Amendment, to refrain from supporting religion (*Chess v. Widmar*, 480 F. Supp. 907 (W.D. Mo. 1979)). The appellate court reversed the district court (635 F.2d 1310 (8th Cir. 1980)). It determined that the group's activities were protected by the Free Speech Clause of the First Amendment. Applying a classic free speech analysis, the appellate court held that the university had violated the students' rights by placing content-based restrictions on their speech. The Supreme Court agreed with the appellate court.

For the Supreme Court, as for the lower courts, the threshold question was whether the case would be treated as a free speech case. In considering this question, Justice Powell's opinion for the Court (with Justice White dissenting) characterized the students' activities as "religious speech," which, like other speech, is protected by the Free Speech Clause. The university, by making its facilities generally available to student organizations, had created a "forum" open to speech activities, which the Court described both as a "limited public forum" and an "open forum." The Free Speech Clause therefore applied to the situation. This clause did not require UMKC to establish a forum; once UMKC had done so, however, the clause required it to justify any exclusion of a student group from this forum because of the content of its activities:

> In order to justify discriminatory exclusion from a public forum based on the religious content of a group's intended speech, the university must satisfy the standard of review appropriate to content-based exclusions. It must show that its regulation is necessary to serve a compelling state interest and that it is narrowly drawn to achieve that end [454 U.S. at 269–70].

In attempting to justify its regulation under this standard, UMKC relied on the First Amendment's Establishment Clause and on the establishment clause in the Missouri state constitution. Its argument was that maintaining separation of church and state, as mandated by these clauses, was a "compelling state interest," which justified its no-religious-worship regulation under the Free Speech Clause. Resorting to Establishment Clause jurisprudence, the Court rejected this argument. Although the Court agreed that maintaining separation of church and state was a compelling interest, it did not believe that an equal-access policy violated the Establishment Clause. The Court applied the three-part test of *Lemon v. Kurtzman*, 403 U.S. 602 (1971):

> "First, the [governmental policy] must have a secular legislative purpose; second, its principal or primary effect must be one that neither advances nor inhibits religion . . . ; finally, the [policy] must not foster an excessive government entanglement with religion" [403 U.S. at 612–13].

The court then applied the test:

> In this case two prongs of the test are clearly met. Both the district court and the court of appeals held that an open-forum policy, including nondiscrimination against religious speech, would have a secular purpose and would avoid entanglement with religion. But the district court concluded, and the university argues here, that allowing religious groups to share the limited public forum would have the "primary effect" of advancing religion.
>
> The university's argument misconceives the nature of this case. The question is not whether the creation of a religious forum would violate the establishment clause. The university has opened its facilities for use by student groups, and the question is whether it can now exclude groups because of the content of their speech (see *Healy v. James*, 408 U.S. 169 . . . (1972)). In this context we are unpersuaded that the primary effect of the public forum, open to all forms of discourse, would be to advance religion.
>
> We are not oblivious to the range of an open forum's likely effects. It is possible—perhaps even foreseeable—that religious groups will benefit from access to university facilities. But this Court has explained that a religious organization's enjoyment of merely "incidental" benefits does not violate the prohibition against the "primary advancement" of religion [citations omitted].
>
> We are satisfied that any religious benefits of an open forum at UMKC would be "incidental" within the meaning of our cases. Two factors are especially relevant.
>
> First, an open forum in a public university does not confer any imprimatur of state approval on religious sects or practices. As the court of appeals

quite aptly stated, such a policy "would no more commit the university . . . to religious goals" than it is "now committed to the goals of the Students for a Democratic Society, the Young Socialist Alliance," or any other group eligible to use its facilities (*Chess v. Widmar*, 635 F.2d at 1317).

Second, the forum is available to a broad class of nonreligious as well as religious speakers; there are over 100 recognized student groups at UMKC. The provision of benefits to so broad a spectrum of groups is an important index of secular effect [citations omitted]. If the establishment clause barred the extension of general benefits to religious groups, "a church could not be protected by the police and fire departments, or have its public sidewalk kept in repair" (*Roemer v. Maryland Public Works Board*, 426 U.S. 736, 747 . . . (1976) (plurality opinion). . . . At least in the absence of empirical evidence that religious groups will dominate UMKC's open forum, we agree with the court of appeals that the advancement of religion would not be the forum's "primary effect" [454 U.S. at 270-75].

With regard to the university's argument that its interest in enforcing the Missouri constitution's prohibition against public support for religious activities outweighed the students' free speech claim, the Court stated:

> Our cases have required the most exacting scrutiny in cases in which a state undertakes to regulate speech on the basis of its content (see, for example, *Carey v. Brown*, 447 U.S. 455 . . . (1980); *Police Dept. v. Mosley*, 408 U.S. 92 . . . (1972)). On the other hand, the state interest asserted here—in achieving greater separation of church and state than is already ensured under the establishment clause of the federal Constitution—is limited by the free exercise clause and in this case by the free speech clause as well. In this constitutional context, we are unable to recognize the state's interest as sufficiently "compelling" to justify content-based discrimination against respondents' religious speech [454 U.S. at 276].

Since UMKC could not justify its content-based restriction on access to the forum it had created, the Court declared the university's regulation unconstitutional. The plaintiff students thereby obtained the right to have their religious group hold its meetings in campus facilities generally open to student groups. It follows that other student religious groups at other public postsecondary institutions have the same right to use campus facilities; institutions may not exclude them, whether by written policy or otherwise, on the basis of the religious content of their activities. [40]

Widmar has substantial relevance for public institutions, most of which have created forums similar to the forum at UMKC. The opinion falls far short, however, of requiring institutions to relinquish all authority over student religious groups. There are substantial limits to the opinion's reach:

1. *Widmar* does not require (nor does it permit) institutions to create forums especially for religious groups, or to give them any other preferential treatment. As the Court noted, "Because this case involves a forum already made generally available to student groups, it differs from those cases in which this Court has invalidated

---

[40]In 1984 Congress passed and the President signed the Equal Access Act, 98 Stat. 377, giving limited statutory recognition to the principles underlying Widmar. By its terms, however, the Act extends these principles to, and applies only to, "public secondary school[s] . . . receiv[ing] federal financial assistance."

statutes permitting school facilities to be used for instruction by religious groups but not by others" (454 U.S. at 271 n.10; see also 454 U.S. at 273 n.13).

2. Nor does *Widmar* require institutions to create a forum for student groups generally, or to continue to maintain one, if they choose not to do so. The case applies only to situations where the institution has created and voluntarily continues to maintain a forum for student groups.

3. *Widmar* requires access only to facilities that are part of a forum created by the institution, not to any other facilities. Similarly, *Widmar* requires access only for students: "We have not held . . . that a campus must make all of its facilities equally available to students and nonstudents alike, or that a university must grant free access to all of its grounds or buildings" (454 U.S. at 267 n.5).

4. *Widmar* does not prohibit all regulation of student organizations' use of forum facilities; it prohibits only content-based restrictions on access. Thus, the Court noted that "a university's mission is education, and decisions of this Court have never denied its authority to impose reasonable regulations compatible with that mission upon the use of its campus and facilities" (454 U.S. at 267 n.5). In particular, according to the Court, the *Widmar* opinion "in no way undermines the capacity of the university to establish reasonable time, place, and manner regulations" (454 U.S. at 276) for use of the forum. Such regulations must be imposed on all student groups, however, not just student religious organizations, and must be imposed without regard to the content of the group's speech activities (see *Heffron v. International Society for Krishna Consciousness*, 452 U.S. 640 (1981)). If a student religious group or other student group "violate[s] [such] reasonable campus rules or substantially interfere[s] with the opportunity of other students to obtain an education" (454 U.S. at 277), the institution may prohibit the group from using campus facilities for its activities.

5. *Widmar* does not rule out every possible content-based restriction on access to a forum. The Court's analysis quoted above makes clear that a content-based regulation would be constitutional under the First Amendment if it were "necessary to serve a compelling state interest and . . . narrowly drawn to achieve that end." As *Widmar* and other First Amendment cases demonstrate, this standard is exceedingly difficult to meet. But the *Widmar* opinion suggests at least two possibilities, the contours of which are left for further development should the occasion arise. First, the Court hints that, if there is "empirical evidence that religious groups will dominate . . . [the institution's] open forum" (454 U.S. at 275, also quoted above), the institution apparently may regulate access by these groups to the extent necessary to prevent domination. Second, if the student demand for use of forum facilities exceeds the supply, the institution may "make academic judgments as to how best to allocate scarce resources" (454 U.S. at 276). In making such academic judgments, the institution may apparently prefer the educational content of some group activities over others and allocate its facilities in accord with these academic preferences. Justice Stevens's opinion concurring in the Court's judgment contains an example for consideration:

> If two groups of twenty-five students requested the use of a room at a particular time—one to view Mickey Mouse cartoons and the other to rehearse an amateur performance of *Hamlet*—the First Amendment would not require that the room be reserved for the group that submitted its application first. . . .

A university should be allowed to decide for itself whether a program that illuminates the genius of Walt Disney should be given precedence over one that may duplicate material adequately covered in the classroom. . . . A university legitimately may regard some subjects as more relevant to its educational mission than others. But the university, like the police officer, may not allow its agreement or disagreement with the viewpoint of a particular speaker to determine whether access to a forum will be granted [454 U.S. at 278].

For another example of a content-based restriction—approved by a federal appellate court subsequent to *Widmar*—see *Chapman v. Thomas*, 743 F.2d 1056 (4th Cir. 1984). In this case the court ruled that North Carolina State University could prohibit a student from door-to-door canvassing in dormitories to publicize campus Bible study meetings, even though it permitted candidates for top student government offices to campaign door to door.

If a university funds student organizations, may it exclude certain categories of religiously affiliated organizations from eligibility for funding? This question was addressed in *Rosenberger v. Rector and Visitors of the University of Virginia*, 795 F. Supp. 175 (W.D. Va. 1992) *affirmed*, 18 F.3d 269 (4th Cir. 1994). A student group, Wide Awake Productions (WAP), had been recognized by the university and was entitled to use university facilities just as other organizations did. But the university's guidelines for allocating mandatory student fees excluded certain types of organizations, including fraternities and sororities, political and religious organizations, and organizations whose membership policies were exclusionary. The guidelines also prohibited the funding of, among others, religious and political activities. WAP published a journal containing articles written from a religious perspective, and its constitution stated that the organization's purpose included the expression of religious views. The student council, which had been delegated the authority to disburse the funds from student fees, had denied funding to WAP, characterizing its publication of the journal as "religious activity."

The plaintiffs, members of WAP, sued the university, alleging that the denial of funding violated their rights to freedom of speech, press, association, religious exercise, and equal protection under both the federal and state constitutions and state law. The central question, according to the trial court, in determining whether to grant summary judgment, was whether the university's Student Activities Fund (SAF) constituted a limited public forum (as asserted by the plaintiffs) or a nonpublic forum (as argued by the university). The answer to this question was dispositive, according to the court, because if the SAF was a limited public forum, the university would have to demonstrate a compelling interest in denying access to its funds to various categories of organizations (*Perry Education Assn. v. Perry Local Educators' Assn.*, 460 U.S. 37 (1983)), a form of strict scrutiny. However, if the forum were nonpublic, the university's guidelines would be subject to scrutiny under a reasonableness standard, a much more deferential standard of review.

Citing *Widmar* and other Supreme Court cases dealing with access to property, the court determined that the SAF was a nonpublic forum. Relying on *Gay and Lesbian Students Assn. v. Gohn* (see Section 4.11.1, this volume), the court determined that the university had limited eligibility for SAF funds to organizations that, in its view, furthered the educational purposes of the university. The university's actions to exclude those organizations not deemed to further its educational purposes demonstrated the nonpublic nature of the forum.

Having determined that SAF was a nonpublic forum, the court then assessed the reasonableness of the university's exclusion of religious organizations from access to funding. The university had argued that it might violate the Establishment Clause if it provided public funds to a religious organization. The court agreed that the university's concerns over potential constitutional violations were reasonable and justified its policy: "Given the complexity of the law [regarding the Establishment Clause], this court has little trouble in finding that the Guideline restriction is a reasonable limit to access to SAF funds" (795 F. Supp. at 181).

The court quickly rejected WAP's argument that the denial of funds violated the Free Exercise Clause, stating that all organizations denied funds by the university were similarly burdened, and thus WAP was not unconstitutionally deprived of its religious exercise rights. Similarly, the court rejected the plaintiffs' contention that their equal protection rights had been denied, finding no discriminatory intent in the denial of funding. The court granted the university's motion for summary judgment on all claims.

The appellate court, while upholding the trial court in all respects, focused on free speech and Establishment Clause issues. Characterizing the university's prohibition against funding religious organizations as a prior restraint on religious speech, the court analyzed whether the university's funding guidelines constituted a compelling interest (to avoid Establishment Clause violations). The court examined the guidelines in light of the *Lemon v. Kurtzman* test and determined that the funding guidelines were motivated by a secular purpose (the advancement of the university's educational mission). Funding religious activity (in this case, religious speech) would advance religion, however, thus violating the second prong of *Lemon*. And such funding would constitute impermissible entanglement: "for the University to subsidize [the magazine's] publication would, we believe, send an unmistakably clear signal that the University of Virginia supports Christian values and wishes to promote the wide promulgation of such values" (18 F.3d at 286).

Another federal appellate court, using a somewhat different analytical approach, upheld the University of Hawaii's decision to deny funding to any student organization whose purpose is to promote a particular religious point of view. The university did, however, permit funding of student religious groups for secular activities. The student government organization adopted the criteria of *Lemon v. Kurtzman* to determine the eligibility of student organizations for funding. In *Tipton v. University of Hawaii*, 15 F.3d 922 (9th Cir. 1994), representatives of several of the religious groups denied funding alleged violations of their First Amendment rights to free speech, free association, and the free exercise of religion, and an Equal Protection Clause violation as well. The appellate court upheld the summary judgment awarded to the university, relying on the decision of the U.S. Supreme Court in *Rust v. Sullivan*, 111 S. Ct. 1759 (1991), which permitted the government to decide not to subsidize certain forms of constitutionally protected activity (see Section 7.4.2). Since the university had not refused to fund all student religious organizations, the court characterized the policy as a choice "to encourage student 'participation in co-curricular activities' by funding a[n organization] in which a wide range of student groups are eligible for support" (15 F.3d at 926).

The issues addressed in *Widmar*, *Rosenberg*, and *Tipton* demonstrate the continuing tension between free speech and Establishment Clause issues as they relate to the actions of public colleges and universities. Current legal doctrine distinguishes between the responsibility to *recognize* student organizations and the right to *fund* them, although with different results for public colleges (which must recognize but need not fund) than for private ones (which need not recognize but must sometimes provide equal access to facilities—see Section 4.11.1).

Sec. 4.12. Fraternities and Sororities

Fraternal organizations have been part of campus life at many colleges and universities for over a century. Some, such as Phi Beta Kappa, were founded to recognize academic achievement, while others have a predominantly social focus. Because of their strong ties to colleges and universities, whether because the houses occupied by members are on or near the college's property or because their members are students at the college, the consequences of the individual and group behavior of fraternity and sorority members can involve the college in legal problems.

The legal issues that affect nonfraternal student organizations (see Section 4.11) may also arise with respect to fraternities and sororities. But because fraternal organizations have their own unique histories and traditions, are related to national organizations that may influence their activities, and play a significant social role on many campuses, they may pose unique legal problems for the college with which they are affiliated.

Supporters of fraternal, or "Greek," organizations argue that members perform more service to the college and the community and make larger alumni contributions than nonmembers, and that fraternity houses provide room and board to undergraduate students whom the college would otherwise be required to accommodate. Critics of fraternal organizations argue that they foster "elitism, sexism, racism and in worst instances, criminal activity" (V. L. Brown, "College Fraternities and Sororities: Tort Liability and the Regulatory Authority of Public Institutions of Higher Education," 58 *West's Educ. Law Rptr.* (1990)). Institutions have responded to problems such as hazing, alcohol and drug abuse, sexual harassment and assault, and the death or serious injury of fraternity members in various ways—for instance, by regulating social activities, suspending or expelling individual fraternities, or abolishing the entire Greek system on campus.

Fraternities and sororities may be chapters of a national organization or independent organizations. The local chapters, whether or not they are tied to a national organization, may be either incorporated or unincorporated associations. If the fraternity or sorority provides a house for some of its members, it may be located on land owned by the colleges or it may be off campus. In either case, the college may own the fraternity house, or an alumni organization (sometimes called a "house corporation") may own the house and assume responsibility for its upkeep.

4.12.1. Institutional recognition and regulation of fraternal organizations. Recognition by a college is significant to fraternal organizations because many national fraternal organizations require such recognition as a condition of the local organization's continued affiliation with the national. The conditions under which recognition is awarded by the college are important because they may determine, or

enhance, the college's power to regulate the conduct of the organization or its members.

Some colleges and universities require, as a condition of recognition of fraternal organizations, that each local fraternity sign a "relationship statement." These statements outline the college's regulations and elicit the organization's assurance that it will obtain insurance coverage, adhere to fire and building codes, and comply with the institution's policy on the serving of alcohol.[41] Some of these statements also require members to participate in alcohol awareness programs or community service. Some statements include restrictions on parties and noise, and extend the jurisdiction of the college's student conduct code and disciplinary system to acts that take place where students live, even if they live off campus.

On some campuses, institutional regulation of fraternal organizations extends to their membership practices. Traditionally, fraternities and sororities have limited their membership to one gender, and in the past many of these organizations prohibited membership for nonwhite and non-Christian individuals (see Brown, "College Fraternities" (cited in section 4.12), at 2). In recent years, however, several colleges and universities, including Middlebury, Bowdoin, and Trinity (Conn.) Colleges, have required fraternities and sororities to admit to members of both sexes (see N. S. Horton, "Traditional Single-Sex Fraternities on College Campuses: Will They Survive in the 1990s?" 18 *J. Coll. & Univ. Law* 419 (1992)) and, in general, to avoid discriminatory practices.

Other colleges have banned fraternities altogether. For example, Colby College, a private liberal arts college, withdrew recognition of all its fraternities and sororities in 1984 because administrators believed that fraternal activities were incompatible with its goals for student residential life. When a group of students continued some of the activities of a banned fraternity, despite numerous attempts by the college's administration to halt them, the president and college dean imposed discipline on the "fraternity" members, ranging from disciplinary probation to one-semester suspensions.

In *Phelps v. President and Trustees of Colby College*, 595 A.2d 403 (Me. 1991), the students sought to enjoin the discipline and the ban on fraternities under Maine's Civil Rights Act, 5 M.R.S.A. §§ 4681–4683 (Supp. 1990) and the state constitution's guarantees of free speech and the right to associate. Maine's Supreme Judicial Court rejected the students' claims. It held that the state law, directed against harassment and intimidation, did not apply to the actions of the college because it "stopped short of authorizing Maine courts to mediate disputes between private parties exercising their respective rights of free expression and association" (595 A.2d at 407). The court also held that the actions of private entities, such as the college, were not subject to state constitutional restrictions.

But public colleges and universities face constitutional obstacles to banning fraternities, including the First Amendment's guarantee of the right to associate (see sections 4.9.1, 4.9.2, and 4.11). Although the University of Colorado surmounted a First Amendment challenge to its imposition of sanctions on a fraternity for race discrimination in membership (*Sigma Chi Fraternity v. Regents of the University of*

---

[41]Cases and authorities are collected in Annot., "Regulations as to Fraternities and Similar Associations Connected with Educational Institution," 10 A.L.R.3d 389 (1966 and periodic supp.).

Colorado, 258 F. Supp. 515 (D. Colo. 1966), the decision of the U.S. Supreme Court in *Roberts v. United States Jaycees,* 468 U.S. 609 (1983), which established the parameters of constitutionally protected rights of association, could provide the impetus for other constitutional challenges to the banning of one, or all, fraternal organizations at public institutions. For analysis of how *Roberts* may apply to fraternal organizations at public colleges, see J. Harvey, "Fraternities and the Constitution: University-Imposed Relationship Statements May Violate Student Associational Rights," 17 *J. Coll. & Univ. Law* 11 (1990)); and see also G. F. Hauser, "Social Fraternities at Public Institutions of Higher Education: Their Rights Under the First and Fourteenth Amendments," 19 *J. Law & Educ.* 433 (1990).

Although a clear articulation of the college's expectations regarding the behavior of fraternity members may provide a deterrent to misconduct, some courts have viewed institutional attempts to regulate the conduct of fraternity members as an assumption of a duty to control their behavior, with a correlative obligation to exercise appropriate restraint over members' conduct. For example, in *Furek v. University of Delaware,* 594 A.2d 506 (Del. 1991), the state's Supreme Court ruled that the university could be found liable for injuries a student received during fraternity hazing, since the university's strict rules against hazing demonstrated that it had assumed a duty to protect students against hazing injuries. (See Section 4.12.2 below for further discussion of these liability issues.)

Because of the potential for greater liability when regulation is extensive, some institutions have opted for "recognition" statements such as those used to recognize other student organizations. Although this minimal approach may defeat a claim that the institution has assumed a duty to supervise the activities of fraternity members, it may limit the institution's authority to regulate the activities of the organization, although the institution can still discipline individual student members who violate its code of student conduct.

A study that examined tort liability issues related to fraternal organizations (E. D. Gulland & M. B. Powell, *Colleges, Fraternities and Sororities: A White Paper on Tort Liability Issues* (American Council on Education, 1989), at 14–15) recommends that recognition statements include the following provisions:

1. Description of the limited purpose of recognition (no endorsement, but access to institutional facilities).
2. Specification of the lack of principal-agent relationship between college and fraternity.
3. Acknowledgment that the fraternity is an independently chartered corporation existing under state laws.
4. Confirmation that the college assumes no responsibility for supervision, control, safety, security, or other services.
5. Restrictions on use of the college's name, tax identification number, or other representations that the fraternity is affiliated with the college.
6. Requirement that the fraternity furnish evidence that it carries insurance sufficient to cover its risks.

One area where institutional regulation of fraternal organizations is receiving public—and legislative—attention is the "ritual" of hazing, often included as part of pledging activities. Over thirty states have passed laws outlawing hazing. Illinois's antihazing law (Ill. Rev. Stat. ch. 144, para. 221 (1989)) was upheld against a constitutional challenge in *People v. Anderson*, 591 N.E.2d 461 (Ill. 1992). (See also Mass. Ann. Laws ch. 269, §§ 17-19 (Supp. 1987); Cal. Educ. Code § 32050 (West 1990); and Virginia Hazing, Civil and Criminal Liability, Va. Code Ann. § 18.2-56.)

Although an institution may not wish explicitly to assume a duty to supervise the conduct of fraternity members, it does have the power to sanction fraternal organizations and their members if they violate institutional policies against hazing or other dangerous conduct. In *Psi Upsilon v. University of Pennsylvania*, 591 A.2d 755 (Pa. Super. Ct. 1991), a state appellate court refused to enjoin the university's imposition of sanctions against a fraternity whose members kidnapped and terrorized a nonmember as part of a hazing activity. The student filed criminal charges against the twenty students who participated in the prank, and the university held a hearing before imposing sanctions on the fraternity. After the hearing the university withdrew its recognition of the fraternity for three years, took possession of the fraternity house without compensating the fraternity, and prohibited anyone who took part in the kidnapping from participating in a future reapplication for recognition.

In evaluating the university's authority to impose these sanctions, the court first examined whether the disciplinary procedures met legal requirements. Noting that the university was privately controlled, the court ruled that the students were entitled "'only to those procedural safeguards which the school specifically provides'" (591 A.2d at 758, quoting *Boehm v. University of Pennsylvania School of Veterinary Medicine*, 573 A.2d 575 (Pa. Super. Ct. 1990). The court then turned to the relationship statement that the fraternity had entered into with the university.

Characterizing the relationship statement as contractual, the court ruled that it gave ample notice to the members that they must assume collective responsibility for the activities of individual members, and that breaching the statement was sufficient grounds for sanctions. After reviewing several claims of unfairness in the conduct of the disciplinary proceeding, the court upheld the trial judge's denial of injunctive relief.

Although institutions may have the authority to sanction fraternities and their members for criminal conduct or violations of the campus conduct code, conduct that may be construed as antisocial, but is not unlawful, may be difficult to sanction. For example, some public institutions have undertaken to prohibit such fraternity activities as theme parties with ethnic or gender overtones or offensive speech. These proscriptions, however, may run afoul of the First Amendment's free speech guarantees. For example, George Mason University sanctioned Sigma Chi fraternity for holding an "ugly woman contest," a fund-raising activity where fraternity members dressed as caricatures of various types of women, including an offensive caricature of a black woman. (For the facts of this case, see Section 4.10.) The fraternity sued the university under 42 U.S.C. § 1983 (see this volume, Section 2.3.3), alleging a violation of its rights under the First and Fourteenth Amendments.

Although the university argued forcefully that the racial parody violated its goals of promoting cultural and racial diversity, as well as its affirmative action plan, a trial court granted summary judgment for the fraternity, and a federal appellate court affirmed that ruling in *Iota Xi Chapter of Sigma Chi Fraternity v. George Mason University*, 993 F.2d 386 (4th Cir. 1993). The court acknowledged that the skit was "an exercise in teenage campus excess" and noted that determining whether it deserved First Amendment protection was "all the more difficult because of [the skit's] obvious sophomoric nature" (993 F.2d at 389). The court determined that the skit was protected both as expressive entertainment under *Barnes v. Glen Theatre, Inc.*, 111 S. Ct. 2456 (1991) (which decided that nude dancing is expressive conduct and is protected under the First Amendment) and as expressive conduct under *Texas v. Johnson*, 491 U.S. 397 (1989) (which ruled that burning an American flag is protected expressive conduct). It also cited the prohibitions against content-based suppression of speech described by the Supreme Court in *R.A.V. v. City of St. Paul* (discussed in Section 4.10).

Although colleges are limited in their ability to sanction fraternities for offensive speech (or expressive conduct), they can hold individual student members to the same code of conduct expected of all students, particularly with regard to social activities and the use of alcohol.

4.12.2. Institutional liability for the acts of fraternal organizations. Despite the fact that fraternal organizations are separate legal entities, colleges and universities have faced legal liability from injured students, parents of students injured or killed as a result of fraternity activity, or victims of violence related to fraternity activities.[42] Because most claims are brought under state tort law theories, the response of the courts has not been completely consistent. The various decisions suggest, however, that colleges and universities can limit their liability in these situations but that fraternities and their members face increased liability, particularly for actions that courts view as intentional or reckless.

As discussed in Section 2.3.1, liability may attach if a judge or jury finds that the college owed an individual a duty of care, then breached that duty, and that the breach was the proximate cause of the injury. Because colleges are legally separate entities from fraternal organizations, the college owes fraternities, their members, and others only the ordinary duty of care to avoid injuring others. But in some cases courts have found either that a special relationship exists between the college and the injured student or that the college has assumed a duty to protect the student.

In *Furek v. University of Delaware*, 594 A.2d 506 (Del. 1991), the Delaware Supreme Court reversed a directed verdict for the university and ordered a new trial on the issue of liability in a lawsuit by a student injured during a hazing incident. The court noted the following factors in determining that a jury could hold the institution at least partially responsible for the injuries: (1) The university owned the land on which the fraternity house was located, although it did not own the house. The injury occurred in the house. (2) The university prohibited hazing and was aware of earlier hazing incidents by this fraternity. The court stated:

> In view of past hazing incidents involving physical harm to students, the occurrence of the unusual activities preceding fraternity hazing as witnessed by campus security . . . and the common knowledge on campus that hazing occurred, there was sufficient evidence for jury determination on the issue of whether the hazing which caused injury to Furek was foreseeable. . . . The like-

---

[42]Cases and authorities are collected in Annot., "Tort Liability of College, University, or Fraternity or Sorority for Injury or Death of Member or Prospective Member by Hazing or Initiation Activity," 68 A.L.R.4th 228 (1989 and periodic supp.).

lihood of injury during fraternity activities occurring on university campuses is greater than the utility of university inaction [594 A.2d at 522–23].

While *Furek* may be an anomaly among the cases in which colleges are sued for negligence (see Section 2.3.1.1), the opinion suggests some of the dangers of institutional attempts to regulate the conduct of fraternities or their members—for instance, by assuming duties of inspecting kitchens or houses, requiring that fraternities have faculty or staff advisers employed by the college, providing police or security services for off-campus houses, or assisting these organizations in dealing with local municipal authorities. Such actions may suggest to juries deliberating a student's negligence claim that the institution had assumed a duty of supervision (see Gulland & Powell, *Colleges, Fraternities and Sororities,* cited in Section 4.12.1).

Colleges and universities have been codefendants with fraternities in several cases. In most of these cases, the institution has escaped liability. For example, in *Thomas v. Lamar University-Beaumont,* 830 S.W.2d 217 (Tex. Ct. App. 1992), the mother of a student who died as a result of pledge hazing sued both the fraternity and the university, which owned the track that was used during the hazing incident. The plaintiff asserted that the university had waived its sovereign immunity because it had failed to supervise those who used its track. The trial court determined that the university had no duty of supervision and awarded summary judgment for the university. The appellate court affirmed.

In *Estate of Hernandez v. Board of Regents,* 838 P.2d 1283 (Ariz. Ct. App. 1991), the personal representative of a man killed in an automobile accident caused by an intoxicated fraternity member sued the University of Arizona and the fraternity. The plaintiff asserted that the university was negligent in continuing to lease the fraternity house to the house corporation when it knew that the fraternity served alcohol to students who were under the legal drinking age of twenty-one.

The plaintiff cited the "Greek Relationship Statement," which required all fraternities to participate in an alcohol awareness educational program, as evidence of the university's assumption of a duty to supervise. The statement also required an upper-division student to be assigned to each fraternal organization to educate its members about responsible conduct relating to alcohol. Furthermore, the university employed a staff member who was responsible for administering its policies on the activities of fraternities and sororities. Despite these attempts to suggest that the university had assumed a duty to supervise the activities of fraternities, the court applied Arizona's social host law, which absolved both the fraternity and the university of liability, and affirmed the trial court's award of summary judgment.

When the student's own behavior is a cause of the injury, the courts have typically refused to hold colleges or fraternities liable for damages. In *Whitlock v. University of Denver,* 744 P.2d 54 (Colo. 1987), the Colorado Supreme Court rejected a student's contention that the university had undertaken to regulate the use of a trampoline in the yard of a fraternity house, even though the university owned the land and had regulated other potentially dangerous activities in the past. Similarly, students injured in social events sponsored by fraternities have not prevailed when the injury was a result of the student's voluntary and intentional action. For example, in *Foster v. Purdue University,* 567 N.E.2d 865 (Ind. Ct. App. 1991), a student who became a quadriplegic after diving headfirst into a fraternity's "water slide" was unsuccessful in his suit against both the university and the fraternity of which he was a member. Similarly, in *Hughes v. Beta Upsilon Building Assn.*, 619 A.2d 525 (Me. 1993), a student who was paralyzed after diving into a muddy field on the fraternity's property at the University of Maine was unsuccessful because the court ruled that the Building Association, landlord for the local fraternity chapter, was not responsible for the chapter's activities.

When, however, the injury is a result of misconduct by *other* fraternity members, individual and organizational liability will attach. Particularly in cases where pledges have been forced to consume large amounts of alcohol as part of a hazing ritual, fraternities and their members have been held responsible for damages.[43]

Because of the increasing tendency of plaintiffs to look to national fraternities for damages, several national fraternities have developed risk management information and training programs for local chapters. College administrators responsible for oversight of fraternal organizations should work with national fraternities to advance their mutual interest in minimizing dangerous activity, student injuries, and ensuing legal liability. Given the seriousness of injuries related to misconduct by fraternities and their members, administrators should examine their institutional regulations, their relationship or recognition statements, and their institutional code of student conduct to ascertain the extent of the college's potential liability. Educational programs regarding the responsible use of alcohol, swift disciplinary action for breaches of the code of student conduct, and monitoring (rather than regulation) of the activities of fraternal organizations may reduce the likelihood of harm to students or others and of liability for the college.

Sec. 4.13. Student Press

4.13.1. General perspectives. A public institution's relationships with student newspapers, magazines, and other publications should be viewed in the first instance under the same principles that are set out in Section 4.11, on student organizations. Often student publications are under the auspices of some student organization (such as the newspaper staff), which may be recognized by the school or funded from mandatory student activity fees. Such organizations can claim the same freedom of association as the organizations discussed in Section 4.11, and a public institution's regulation of such organizations is limited by the principles set out in that section.

Objecting students have no more right to challenge the allocation of mandatory student fees to student newspapers that express a particular viewpoint than they

---

[43]In *Ballou v. Sigma Nu General Fraternity*, 352 S.E.2d 488 (S.C. Ct. App. 1986), a state appellate court found that the *national* fraternity owes a duty of care to initiates not to injure them; the court therefore held that fraternity responsible for damages related to a pledge's wrongful death from alcohol poisoning. A student who sustained serious neurological damage after forced intoxication was similarly successful in *Quinn v. Sigma Rho Chapter*, 507 N.E.2d 1193 (Ill. App. Ct. 1987), as was the father of a student who died after being forced to drink as part of an initiation ritual for the lacrosse team at Western Illinois University. In that case the students were found liable as individuals (*Haben v. Anderson*, 597 N.E.2d 655 (Ill. App. Ct. 1993)). For a review of the potential liability of national fraternities for hazing injuries, see Note, "Alcohol and Hazing Risks in College Fraternities: Re-evaluating Vicarious and Custodial Liability of National Fraternities," 7 *Review of Litigation* 191 (1988).

have to challenge such allocations to other student organizations expressing particular viewpoints. In *Arrington v. Taylor*, 380 F. Supp. 1348 (M.D.N.C. 1974), *affirmed*,
526 F.2d 587 (4th Cir. 1975), for example, the court rejected a challenge to the University of North Carolina's use of mandatory fees to subsidize its campus newspaper,
the *Daily Tar Heel*. Since the paper did not purport to speak for the entire student
body and its existence did not inhibit students from expressing or supporting opposing viewpoints, the subsidy did not infringe First Amendment rights. Eight years later
the same court reconsidered and reaffirmed *Arrington* in *Kania v. Forham*, 702 F.2d
475 (4th Cir. 1983); and in 1992 another U.S. Court of Appeals (citing *Kania*) reached
the same result (*Hays County Guardian v. Supple*, 969 F.2d 111, 123 (5th Cir. 1992)).

However, student publications must also be viewed from an additional perspective, not directly involved in the section on student organizations: the perspective
of freedom of the press.[44] As perhaps the most staunchly guarded of all First Amendment rights, the right to a free press protects student publications from virtually all
encroachments on their editorial prerogatives by public institutions. In a series of
forceful cases, courts have implemented this student press freedom, using First
Amendment principles akin to those that would apply to a big-city daily published
by a private corporation.[45]

The chief concern of the First Amendment's free press guarantee is censorship.
Thus, whenever a public institution seeks to control or coercively influence the content of a student publication, it will have a legal problem on its hands. The problem
will be exacerbated if the institution imposes a prior restraint on publication; that
is, a prohibition imposed in advance of publication rather than a sanction imposed
subsequently (see Section 4.9.3). Conversely, the institution's legal problems will be
alleviated if the institution's regulations (concerning, for example, the allocation of
office space or limitations on the time, place, or manner of distribution) do not affect
the message, ideas, or subject matter of the publication and do not permit prior
restraints on publication.

4.13.2. Permissible scope of regulation. *Joyner v. Whiting*, 477 F.2d 456 (4th Cir.
1973), arose after the president of North Carolina Central University permanently
terminated university financial support for the campus newspaper. The president
asserted that the newspaper had printed articles urging segregation and had advocated
the maintenance of an all-black university. The court held that the president's action
violated the student staff's First Amendment rights:

> It may well be that a college need not establish a campus newspaper, or,
> if a paper has been established, the college may permanently discontinue pub-
> lication for reasons wholly unrelated to the First Amendment. But if a college has

---

[44]Cases are collected in Annot., "Validity, Under Federal Constitution, of Public School
or State College Regulation of Student Newspapers, Magazines, or Other Publications—Federal
Cases," 16 A.L.R. Fed. 182 (1973 and periodic supp.).

[45]Problems may also arise concerning outside newspapers that are distributed on campus, and the students' rights to obtain such newspapers. In *Hays County Guardian v. Supple*,
969 F.2d 111 (5th Cir. 1992), for example, the court invalidated restrictions on distribution of
a free newspaper distributed throughout the county. See generally *City of Cincinnati v. Discovery Network*, 113 S. Ct. 1505 (1993).

a student newspaper, its publication cannot be suppressed because college officials dislike its editorial comment. . . .

The principles reaffirmed in *Healy* [*v. James,* discussed in Section 4.11.1] have been extensively applied to strike down every form of censorship of student publications at state-supported institutions. Censorship of constitutionally protected expression cannot be imposed by suspending the editors, suppressing circulation, requiring imprimatur of controversial articles, excising repugnant materials, withdrawing financial support, or asserting any other form of censorial oversight based on the institution's power of the purse [477 F.2d at 460].

The president had also asserted, as grounds for terminating the paper's support, that the newspaper would employ only blacks and would not accept advertising from white-owned businesses. While such practices were not protected by the First Amendment and could be enjoined, the court held that the permanent cutoff of funds was an inappropriate remedy for such problems because of its broad effect on all future ability to publish.

Subsequent to *Joyner,* less drastic attempts by a university to reduce the funding of a student newspaper were struck down in *Stanley v. Magrath,* 719 F.2d 279 (8th Cir. 1983). The University of Minnesota changed the funding mechanism of one of its student newspapers by eliminating mandatory student fees and instead allowing students to elect individually whether or not a portion of their fees would go to the *Minnesota Daily.* Institution of this refundable fee system came on the heels of intense criticism from students, faculty, religious groups, and the state legislature over a satirical "Humor Issue" of the paper.

Although the university argued that the change in funding mechanism came in response to student objections about having to fund the paper (which the court assumed *arguendo* was a legitimate motivation), the court pointed to evidence suggesting that, at least in part, the change was impermissibly in retaliation for the content of the "Humor Issue." It then held that the school failed to carry its burden of showing that the permissible motive would have produced the same result even in the absence of the impermissible one and struck down the funding change.

Bazaar v. Fortune, 476 F.2d 570, *rehearing,* 489 F.2d 225 (5th Cir. 1973), is also illustrative. The University of Mississippi had halted publication of an issue of *Images,* a student literary magazine written and edited with the advice of a professor from the English department, because a university committee had found two stories objectionable on grounds of "taste." While the stories concerned interracial marriage and black pride, the university disclaimed objection on this basis and relied solely on the stories' inclusion of "earthy" language. The university argued that the stories would stir an adverse public reaction, and, since the magazine had a faculty adviser, their publication would reflect badly on the university. The court held that the involvement of a faculty adviser did not enlarge the university's authority over the magazine's content. The university's action violated the First Amendment because "speech cannot be stifled by the state merely because it would perhaps draw an adverse reaction from the majority of people, be they politicians or ordinary citizens, and newspapers. To come forth with such a rule would be to virtually read the First Amendment out of the Constitution and, thus, cost this nation one of its strongest tenets."

Schiff v. Williams, 519 F.2d 257 (5th Cir. 1975), concerned the firing of the editors of the *Atlantic Sun,* the student newspaper of Florida Atlantic University. The university's president based his action on the poor quality of the newspaper and on the editors' failure to respect university guidelines regarding the publication of the paper. The court characterized the president's action as a form of direct control over the paper's content and held that such action violated the First Amendment. Poor quality, even though it "could embarrass, and perhaps bring some element of disrepute to the school," was not a permissible basis on which to limit free speech. The university president in *Schiff* attempted to bolster his case by arguing that the student editors were employees of the state. The court did not give the point the attention it deserved. Presumably, if a public institution chose to operate its own publication (such as an alumni magazine) and hired a student editor, the institution could fire that student if the technical quality of his or her work was inadequate. The situation in *Schiff* did not fit this model, however, because the newspaper was not set up as the university's own publication. Rather, it was recognized by the university as a publication primarily by and for the student body, and the student editors were paid from a special student activities fee fund under the general control of the student government association.

While arrangements such as those in *Schiff* may insulate the student newspaper from university control, it might nevertheless be argued that a newspaper's use of mandatory student fees and university facilities constitutes state action (Section 1.5.2), thus subjecting the student editors themselves to First Amendment restraints when dealing with other students and with outsiders. However, the court rejected a state action argument (over a strong dissent) in *Mississippi Gay Alliance v. Goudelock*, 536 F.2d 1073 (5th Cir. 1976), a suit against a student newspaper that had refused to print an ad for a gay counseling service. And in *Sinn v. The Daily Nebraskan*, 829 F.2d 662 (8th Cir. 1987), the court held that the newspaper was not engaged in state action when it refused to print sexual preferences in classified ads. In *Gay and Lesbian Students Assn. v. Gohn*, 850 F.2d 361 (8th Cir. 1988) (further discussed in Section 4.11.1 above), however, the court distinguished *Sinn* and found state action in a situation where the student organization's activity was "not free from university control."

Joyner, *Stanley*, *Bazaar*, and *Schiff* clearly illustrate the very substantial limits on an administrator's authority to control the student press in public institutions. Though each case involves a different regulatory technique and a different rationale for regulation, the administrators lost each time. Yet even these cases suggest grounds on which student publications can be subjected to some regulation. The *Joyner* case indicates that the student press can be prohibited from racial discrimination in its staffing and advertising policies. *Stanley* suggests that institutions may alter the funding mechanisms for student publications as long as it does not do so for reasons associated with a publication's content. *Bazaar* indicates that institutions may dissociate themselves from student publications to the extent of requiring or placing a disclaimer on the cover or format of the publication. (The court specifically approved the following disclaimer after it reheard the case: "This is not an official publication of the university.") *Schiff* suggests enigmatically that there may be "special circumstances" where administrators may regulate the press to prevent "significant disruption on the university campus or within its educational processes."

In these and other student press cases, the clear lesson is not "don't regulate" but rather "don't censor." As long as administrators avoid direct or indirect control of content, they may regulate publications by student organizations or individual students in much the same way that they may regulate other organizations (Section 4.11) or students generally (Section 4.9). Even content need not be totally beyond an administrator's concern. A disclaimer requirement can be imposed to avoid confusion about the publication's status within the institution. Content that is illegal under state law because it is obscene or libelous may also be regulated, as the next two subsections suggest. As the *Rosenberger* case in Section 4.11.4 suggests, religious content may be regulated to an extent necessary to prevent Establishment Clause violations. And advertising content in a publication also can be controlled to some extent. In *Pittsburgh Press Co. v. Pittsburgh Commission on Human Relations*, 413 U.S. 376 (1973), for instance, the U.S. Supreme Court upheld a regulation prohibiting newspapers from publishing "help-wanted" advertisements in sex-designated columns. And in *Virginia State Board of Pharmacy v. Virginia Citizens Consumer Council*, 425 U.S. 748 (1976), while invalidating a statutory ban on advertising prescription drug prices, the Court did affirm the state's authority to regulate false or misleading advertising and advertising that proposes illegal transactions.

Issues regarding advertising in student newspapers are considered at length in *Lueth v. St. Clair County Community College*, 732 F. Supp. 1410 (E.D. Mich. 1990). The plaintiff, a former editor of the student newspaper, sued the college because it had prohibited the publication of ads for an off-campus nude-dancing club. Concluding that the advertising was "commercial speech" (Section 5.6.4.1) and that the student-run newspaper was a public forum (Section 4.9.1), the court applied the First Amendment standards for commercial speech set out in *Central Hudson Gas & Electric Corp. v. Public Service Commission*, 447 U.S. 557 (1980), as modified by *Board of Trustees of the State University of New York v. Fox*, 492 U.S. 469 (1989) (both discussed in Section 5.6.4.1). Although the college had substantial interests in not fostering underage drinking or the degradation of women, the court held the advertising prohibition unconstitutional because the college had no advertising guidelines or other limits on its authority which would ensure that its regulation of advertising was "narrowly tailored" to achieve its interests. (This case should be of particular interest to institutions considering the regulation of alcohol-related ads in student publications; see S. Dodge, "Many Colleges Move to Restrict Alcohol-Related Ads in Student Papers, Vendors' Sponsorship of Events," *Chron. Higher Educ.*, Feb. 21, 1990, A39.)

4.13.3. Obscenity. It is clear that public institutions may discipline students or student organizations for having published obscene material. Public institutions may even halt the publication of such material if they do so under carefully constructed and conscientiously followed procedural safeguards. A leading case is *Antonelli v. Hammond*, 308 F. Supp. 1329 (D. Mass. 1970), which invalidated a system of prior review and approval by a faculty advisory board, because the system did not place the burden of proving obscenity on the board, or provide for a prompt review and internal appeal of the board's decisions, or provide for a prompt final judicial determination. *Baughman v. Freimuth*, 478 F.2d 1345 (4th Cir. 1973), which sets out prior review requirements in the secondary school context, is also illustrative. Clearly, the constitutional requirements for prior review are stringent, and the creation of a constitutionally acceptable system is a very difficult and delicate task. (For U.S. Supreme Court teaching on prior review, see *Southeastern Promotions, Ltd. v. Conrad*, 420 U.S. 546 (1975).)

Moreover, institutional authority extends only to material that is actually obscene, and the definition or identification of obscenity is, at best, an exceedingly difficult proposition. In a leading Supreme Court case, *Papish v. Board of Curators of the University of Missouri*, 410 U.S. 667 (1973), the plaintiff was a graduate student who had been expelled for violating a board of curators bylaw prohibiting distribution of newspapers "containing forms of indecent speech." The newspaper at issue had a political cartoon on its cover which "depicted policemen raping the Statue of Liberty and the Goddess of Justice. The caption under the cartoon read: 'With Liberty and Justice for All.'" The newspaper also "contained an article entitled 'M—— F—— Acquitted,' which discussed the trial and acquittal on an assault charge of a New York City youth who was a member of an organization known as 'Up Against the Wall, M—— F——.'" After being expelled, the student sued the university, alleging a violation of her First Amendment rights. The Court, in a per curiam opinion, ruled in favor of the student:

> We think *Healy* [*v. James*, Section 4.11.1] makes it clear that the mere dissemination of ideas—no matter how offensive to good taste—on a state university campus may not be shut off in the name alone of "conventions of decency." Other recent precedents of this Court make it equally clear that neither the political cartoon nor the headline story involved in this case can be labeled as constitutionally obscene or otherwise unprotected [410 U.S. at 670].

Obscenity, then, is not definable in terms of an institution's or an administrator's own personal conceptions of taste, decency, or propriety. Obscenity can be defined only in terms of the guidelines that courts have constructed to prevent the concept from being used to choke off controversial social or political dialogue:

> We now confine the permissible scope of . . . regulation [of obscenity] to works which depict or describe sexual conduct. That conduct must be specifically defined by the applicable state law, as written or authoritatively construed. A state offense must also be limited to works which, taken as a whole, appeal to the prurient interest in sex, which portray sexual conduct in a patently offensive way, and which, taken as a whole, do not have serious literary, artistic, political, or scientific value [*Miller v. California*, 413 U.S. 15, 24 (1973)].

Although these guidelines were devised for the general community, the Supreme Court made clear in *Papish* that "the First Amendment leaves no room for the operation of a dual standard in the academic community with respect to the content of speech." Administrators devising campus rules for public institutions are thus bound by the same obscenity guidelines that bind the legislators promulgating obscenity laws. Under these guidelines the permissible scope of regulation is very narrow, and the drafting or application of rules is a technical exercise that administrators should undertake with the assistance of counsel, if at all.

4.13.4. Libel. As they may for obscenity, institutions may discipline students or organizations that publish libelous matter. Here again, however, the authority of public institutions extends only to matter that is libelous according to technical legal definitions. It is not sufficient that a particular statement be false or misleading. Common law and constitutional doctrines require that (1) the statement be false; (2) the publication serve to identify the particular person libeled; (3) the publication cause at least nominal injury to the person libeled, usually including but not limited to injury to reputation; and (4) the falsehood be attributable to some fault on the part of the person or organization publishing it. The degree of fault depends on the subject of the alleged libel. If the subject is a public official or what the courts call a "public figure," the statement must have been made with "actual malice"; that is, with knowledge of its falsity or with reckless disregard for its truth or falsity. In all other situations governed by the First Amendment, the statement need only have been made negligently. Courts make this distinction in order to give publishers extra breathing space when reporting on certain matters of high public interest.[46]

Given the complexity of the libel concept, administrators should approach it most cautiously. Because of the need to assess both injury and fault, as well as identify the defamatory falsehood, libel may be even more difficult to combat than obscenity. Suppression in advance of publication is particularly perilous, since injury can only be speculated about at that point, and reliable facts concerning fault may not be attainable. Much of the material in campus publications, moreover, may involve public officials or public figures and thus be protected by the higher fault standard of actual malice.

Though these factors might reasonably lead administrators to forgo any regulation of libel, there is a countervailing consideration: institutions or administrators may occasionally be held liable in court for libelous statements in student publications. (See Sections 2.3.1 and 2.4.1 for a general discussion of tort liability.) Such liability could exist where the institution sponsors a publication (such as a paper operated by the journalism department as a training ground for its students), employs the editors of the publication, establishes a formal committee to review material in advance of publication, or otherwise exercises some control (constitutionally or unconstitutionally) over the publication's content. In any case, liability would exist only for statements deemed libelous under the criteria set out above.

Such potential liability, however, need not necessarily prompt increased surveillance of student publications. Increased surveillance would demand regulations that stay within constitutional limits yet are strong enough to weed out all libel— an unlikely combination. And since institutional control of the publication is the predicate to the institution's liability, increased regulation increases the likelihood of liability should a libel be published. Thus, administrators may choose to handle liability problems by lessening rather than enlarging control. The privately incorporated student newspaper operating independently of the institution would be the clearest example of a no-control/no-liability situation.

A 1981 decision by the New York State Court of Claims provides a leading example of libel law's application to student newspapers at public institutions. The court's opinion in the case, *Mazart v. State*, 441 N.Y.S.2d 600 (N.Y. Ct. Cl. 1981), illustrates the basic steps in establishing libel and affirms that institutional control

---

[46]The U.S. Supreme Court has developed the constitutional boundaries of libel law in a progression of decisions beginning with *New York Times v. Sullivan*, 376 U.S. 254 (1964). See also *Curtis Publishing Co. v. Butts*, 388 U.S. 130 (1967); *Associated Press v. Walker*, 388 U.S. 162 (1967); *Gertz v. Robert Welch, Inc.*, 418 U.S. 323 (1974); and *Time, Inc. v. Firestone*, 424 U.S. 448 (1976).

over the newspaper, or lack thereof, is a key to establishing or avoiding institutional liability. The opinion also discusses the question of whether an institution can ever restrain in advance the planned publication of libelous material.

The plaintiffs (claimants) in *Mazart* were two students at the State University of New York–Binghamton who were the targets of an allegedly libelous letter to the editor published in the student newspaper, the *Pipe Dream*. The letter described a prank that had occurred in a male dormitory and characterized it as an act of prejudice against homosexuals. The plaintiffs' names appeared at the end of the letter, although they had not in fact written it, and the body of the letter identified them as "members of the gay community." Applying accepted principles of libel law to the educational context in which the incident occurred, the court determined that this letter was libelous:

> Did the letter in the *Pipe Dream* expose claimants to hatred, contempt, or aversion, or induce an evil or unsavory opinion of them in the minds of a substantial number of the community? The answer to the question is far from simple. In general, the community we are concerned with here was the university community located on a campus outside of the City of Binghamton, Broome County, New York. According to the chairman of the English Department at the university, . . . sexual orientation had no more bearing in the classroom than religious affiliation. The assistant vice president for finance, management, and control of the university opined that the published letter had a "very low, very little effect" on the campus community.
>
> No doubt the impact of the published letter on the collective mind of the university was considerably less than it might have been had the letter been published in a conservative rural American village. Nonetheless, the court finds that an unsavory opinion of the claimants did settle in the minds of a substantial number of persons in the university community. . . . The question of homosexuality was a significant one on the university campus. . . . Both claimants testified that they were accosted by numerous fellow students after the event and queried about their sexual orientation, and the court finds their testimony, in this respect, credible. Deviant sexual intercourse and sodomy were crimes in the state of New York at the time the letter was published (Penal Law, §§ 130 and 130.38). Certainly those members of the university community who did not personally know the claimants would logically conclude that claimants were homosexual, since the letter identified them as being members of the "gay community." The court finds that a substantial number of the university community would naturally assume that the claimants engaged in homosexual acts from such identification [441 N.Y.S.2d at 603–04].

The court then rejected the state's argument that, even if the letter was libelous, its publication was protected by a qualified privilege because the subject matter was of public concern. Again using commonly accepted libel principles, the court concluded that a privilege did not apply because

> the editors of the *Pipe Dream* acted in a grossly irresponsible manner by failing to give due consideration to the standards of information gathering and dissemination. It is obvious that authorship of a letter wherein the purported author appears to be libeled should be verified. Not only was the authorship of the letter herein not verified but it appears that the *Pipe Dream*, at least in November of

1977, had no procedures or guidelines with regard to the verification of the authorship of any letters to the editor [441 N.Y.S.2d at 604].

Third, the court held that, although the letter was libelous and not privileged, the university (and thus the state) was not liable for the unlawful acts of the student newspaper. In its analysis the court considered and rejected two theories of liability: "(1) [that] the state, through the university, may be vicariously liable for the torts of the *Pipe Dream* and its editors on the theory of *respondeat superior* (that is, the university, as principal, might be liable for the torts of its agents, the student paper and editors); and (2) [that] the state, through the university, may have been negligent in failing to provide guidelines to the *Pipe Dream* staff regarding libel generally and, specifically, regarding the need to review and verify letters to the editor."

In rejecting the first theory, the court relied heavily on First Amendment principles:

> The state could be held vicariously liable if the university and the *Pipe Dream* staff operated in some form of agency relationship. However, it is characteristic of the relationship of principal and agent that the principal has a right to control the conduct of the agent with respect to matters entrusted to him. While this control need not apply to every detail of an agent's conduct and can be found where there is merely a right held by the principal to make management and policy decisions affecting the agent, there can be no agency relationship where the alleged principal has no right of control over the alleged agent.
>
> There are severe constitutional limitations on the exercise of any form of control by a state university over a student newspaper . . . (*Panarella v. Birenbaum*, 37 A.D.2d 987, 327 N.Y.S.2d 755, *affirmed*, 32 N.Y.2d 108, 343 N.Y.S.2d 333, 296 N.E.2d 238). . . . Censorship or prior restraint of constitutionally protected expression in student publications at state-supported institutions has been uniformly proscribed by the courts. Such censorship or prior restraint cannot be imposed by suspending editors (*Scoville v. Board of Education of Joliet Township High School District 204*, 425 F.2d 10), by suppressing circulation (*Channing Club v. Board of Regents of Texas Tech. University*, 317 F. Supp. 688), by requiring prior approval of controversial articles (*Quarterman v. Byrd*, 453 F.2d 54 (4th Cir.); *Trujillo v. Love*, 322 F. Supp. 1266; *Antonelli v. Hammond*, 308 F. Supp. 1329), by excising or suppressing distasteful material (*Trujillo v. Love, supra; Korn v. Elkins*, 317 F. Supp. 138; *Zucker v. Panitz*, 299 F. Supp. 102), or by withdrawing financial support (*Joyner v. Whiting*, 477 F.2d 456 (4th Cir.); *Antonelli v. Hammond, supra*). Claimants' counsel argues that "the issue of prior restraint has never been extended to libel . . . cases." . . . In fact, in the absence of special circumstances, the publication of libelous material will not be restrained by the courts:

>> A court of equity will not, except in special circumstances, issue an injunctive order restraining libel or slander or otherwise restricting free speech.
>> To enjoin any publication, no matter how libelous, would be repugnant to the First Amendment to the Constitution (. . . *Parker v. Columbia Broadcasting System, Inc.*, 320 F.2d 937 (2d Cir. 1963); cf. *Near v. State of Minnesota, ex rel. Olson*, 283 U.S. 697 . . . (1931)), and to historic principles of equity [*Konigsberg v. Time, Inc.*, 288 F. Supp. 989 (S.D.N.Y. 1968)].

Thus, it appears that a policy of prior approval of items to be published in a student newspaper, even if directed only to restraining the publication of potentially libelous material (cf. *Trujillo v. Love, supra*), would run afoul of *Near v. State of Minnesota, supra*, wherein the Court stated that "liberty of the press, historically considered and taken up by the federal Constitution, has meant, principally although not exclusively, immunity from previous restraints or censorship" (283 U.S. at 716 . . .). . . . The court, therefore, finds that the university was powerless to prevent the publication of the letter.

Although claimants' counsel suggests in his argument that the university's involvement with the funding of the *Pipe Dream* might afford it some measure of control, this involvement affords little, if any, actual control over the funding and expenditures of the newspaper . . . and, in any event, it is settled that no form of editorial control over constitutionally protected expression in student publications can be based on the university's power of the purse.

No doubt the university benefits, and did benefit at the time of the publication of the letter, from the existence of the *Pipe Dream*. That the university recognized participation on the newspaper as a form of independent study indicates that it received educational benefits. Furthermore, the *Pipe Dream* served as a means of disseminating information to the university community and as a forum for debate and discussion for members of the university community. However, these factors, which might suggest an agency relationship, are insufficient to overcome the university's lack of control over the newspaper.

The fact that the university created a climate wherein the student newspaper flourished by furnishing office space and janitorial services hardly creates an agency relationship which would permit recovery against the state. Such accoutrements are nothing more than a form of financial aid to the newspaper which cannot be traded off in return for editorial control (see *Joyner v. Whiting, supra; Antonelli v. Hammond, supra*).

The court recognizes that the *Pipe Dream* and its staff may be incapable of compensating claimants for any damages flowing from the libel. But, in light of the university's eschewing control, editorial or otherwise, over the paper and the constitutionally imposed barriers to the exercise by the university of any editorial control over the newspaper, the court must reluctantly conclude that the relationship of the university and the *Pipe Dream* is not such as would warrant the imposition of vicarious liability on the state for defamatory material appearing in the student newspaper (see "Tort Liability of a University for Libelous Material in Student Publications," 71 *Michigan L. Rev.* 1061) [441 N.Y.S.2d at 604–06; some citations omitted].

Focusing on the tort law concept of "duty," the court then rejected the claimant's second liability theory:

The second theory . . . involves the question of whether the state university, and therefore the state, can be cast in damages in simple negligence for failing to provide to the student editors guidelines and procedures designed to avoid the publication of libelous material. As discussed above, there are constitutional limitations on the actual exercise of editorial control by the university, but this does not necessarily preclude the existence of a duty on the part of the university to furnish guidance.

In view of the absolute hands-off policy adopted by the university administration, it is clear that no such guidelines were furnished, and from the evidence adduced at trial, it does not appear that student editors verified the authorship of controversial letters to the editor prior to the subject publication. The issue then is whether there was a duty on the part of the university administration. The court concludes that there was not. It is clear from a reading of the published cases dealing with the rights of college students that the courts uniformly regard them as young adults and not children. . . .

Furthermore, the establishment by statute of the minimum voting age (Election Law, § 5-102), drinking age (Alcoholic Beverage Control Law, § 65), and the age of consent for marriage (Domestic Relations Law, § 7) at 18 years, is indicative of a recognition, at least on the part of the legislature, of a substantial degree of maturity in college-aged persons.

. . . [T]he court in *Greenberg v. CBS, Inc.*, 69 A.D.2d 693, 419 N.Y.S.2d 988, stated: "The elementary standards of basic news reporting are common knowledge. News articles and broadcasts must contain the answers to the essential inquiries of who, what, where, when, why, and how" (419 N.Y.S.2d 988). Certainly the need to verify the authorship of a letter wherein the purported author appears to be libeled is rudimentary. A conclusion that the university had a duty to furnish guidance to the *Pipe Dream* concerning libel would in effect be a finding that the *Pipe Dream* editors lacked that degree of maturity and common sense necessary to comprehend the normal procedures for information gathering and dissemination. But surely such a finding would be anomalous since those editors' contemporaries might well be selected to sit on a jury (Judiciary Law, § 510(2)), assigned the task of determining, without the aid and guidance of expert testimony, whether a newspaper (the *Pipe Dream* or any other) had failed to adhere to generally followed standards, resulting in the publication of libel. . . .

The court must, therefore, find that the university had no duty to supply news gathering and dissemination guidelines to the *Pipe Dream* editors since they were presumed to already know those guidelines. Admittedly, it appears that the student editors of the *Pipe Dream* in 1977 either did not know or simply ignored common-sense verification guidelines with regard to the publication of the instant letter. But that was not the fault of the university. In either event, there was no duty on the part of the university. The editors' lack of knowledge of or failure to adhere to standards which are common knowledge (*Greenberg v. CBS, Inc., supra*) and ordinarily followed by reasonable persons . . . was not reasonably foreseeable [441 N.Y.S.2d at 606-07].

Mazart v. State is an extensively reasoned precedent in an area where there has been a dearth of precedent. The court's opinion provides much useful guidance for administrators of public institutions. The opinion's reasoning depends, however, on particular circumstances concerning the campus setting in which the libel occurred, the irresponsibility of the student editors, the degree of control the institution exercised over the newspaper, and the foreseeability of the student editors' irresponsible acts. Administrators will therefore want to consult with counsel before attempting to apply the principles in *Mazart* to occurrences on their own campuses.

4.13.5. Obscenity and libel in private institutions. Since the First Amendment does not apply to private institutions that are not engaged in state action (Section 1.5.2), such institutions have a freer hand in regulating obscenity and libel. Yet private institutions should devise their regulatory role cautiously. Regulations broadly construing libel and obscenity based on lay concepts of those terms could stifle the flow of dialogue within the institution, while attempts to avoid this problem with narrow regulations may lead the institution into the same definitional complexities that public institutions face when seeking to comply with the First Amendment. More-over, in devising their policies on obscenity and libel, private institutions will want to consider the potential impact of state law. Violation of state obscenity or libel law by student publications could subject the responsible students to injunctions, damage actions, and even criminal prosecutions, causing unwanted publicity for the institu-tion. But if the institution regulates the student publications to prevent such prob-lems, it could be held liable along with the students if it exercises sufficient control over the publication (see Sections 2.1 and 4.13.4.)

Sec. 4.14. Student Housing

4.14.1. Housing regulations. Postsecondary institutions with residential campuses usually have policies specifying which students may, and which students must, live in campus housing. Such regulations sometimes apply only to certain groups of students, using classifications based on the student's age, sex, class, or marital status. Institutions also typically have policies regulating living conditions in campus hous-ing. Students in public institutions have sought to use the federal Constitution to challenge such housing policies.[47]

In *Prostrollo v. University of South Dakota*, 507 F.2d 775 (8th Cir. 1974), students claimed that the university's regulation requiring all single freshmen and sophomores to live in university housing was unconstitutional because it denied them equal protection under the Fourteenth Amendment and infringed their constitutional rights of privacy and freedom of association. The university admitted that one pur-pose of the regulation was to maintain a certain level of dormitory occupancy to secure revenue to repay dormitory construction costs. But the university also offered testimony that the regulation was instituted to ensure that younger students would educationally benefit from the experience in self-government, community living, and group discipline and the opportunities for relationships with staff members that dormitory life provides. In addition, university officials contended that the dormito-ries provided easy access to study facilities and to films and discussion groups.

After evaluating these justifications, the lower court determined that the pri-mary purpose of the housing regulation was financial and that the regulation's dif-ferentiation of freshmen and sophomores from upper-division students had no rational relationship to the purpose of ensuring housing income. The lower court therefore held the regulation unconstitutional under the Equal Protection Clause. The appellate court reversed the lower court's decision. It reasoned that, even if the regulation's primary purpose was financial, there was no denial of equal protection because there was another rational basis for differentiating freshmen and sophomores from upper-division students: the university officials' belief that the regulation con-tributed to the younger students' adjustment to college life. The appellate court also rejected the students' right-to-privacy and freedom-of-association challenges. The court gave deference to school authorities' traditionally broad powers in formulating educational policy.

A similar housing regulation that used an age classification to prohibit certain

[47]The cases are collected in Annot., "Validity, Under Federal Constitution, of Policy or Regulation of College or University Requiring Students to Live in Dormitories or Residence Halls," 31 A.L.R. Fed. 813 (1977 and periodic supp.).

students from living off campus was at issue in *Cooper v. Nix,* 496 F.2d 1285 (5th Cir. 1974). The regulation required all unmarried full-time undergraduate students, regardless of age and whether or not emancipated, to live on campus. The regulation contained an exemption for certain older students, which in practice the school enforced by simply exempting all undergraduates twenty-three years old and over. Neither the lower court nor the appeals court found any justification in the record for a distinction between twenty-one-year-old students and twenty-three-year-old students. Though the lower court had enjoined the school from requiring students twenty-one and older to live on campus, the appeals court narrowed the remedy to require only that the school not automatically exempt all twenty-three-year-olds. Thus, the school could continue to enforce the regulation if it exempted students over twenty-three only on a case-by-case basis.

A regulation that allowed male students but not female students to live off campus was challenged in *Texas Woman's University v. Chayklintaste,* 521 S.W.2d 949 (Tex. Civ. App. 1975), and found unconstitutional. Though the university convinced the court that it did not have the space or the money to provide on-campus male housing, the court held that mere financial reasons could not justify the discrimination. The court concluded that the university was unconstitutionally discriminating against its male students by not providing them with any housing facilities and also was unconstitutionally discriminating against its female students by not permitting them to live off campus.

The university subsequently made housing available to males and changed its regulations to require both male and female undergraduates under twenty-three to live on campus. Although the regulation was now like the one found unconstitutional in *Cooper,* above, the Texas Supreme Court upheld its constitutionality in a later appeal of *Texas Woman's University v. Chayklintaste,* 530 S.W.2d 927 (Tex. 1975). In this case the university justified the age classification with reasons similar to those used in *Prostrollo,* above, which upheld the freshman and sophomore classification. The university argued that on-campus dormitory life added to the intellectual and emotional development of its students and supported this argument with evidence from two professional educational journals and the testimony of a vice president of student affairs, a professor of education, and an instructor of social work.

In *Bynes v. Toll,* 512 F.2d 252 (2d Cir. 1975), another university housing regulation was challenged—in this case a regulation that permitted married students to live on campus but barred their children from living on campus. The court found that there was no denial of equal protection, since the university had several very sound safety reasons for not allowing children to reside in the dormitories. The court also found that the regulation did not interfere with the marital privacy of the students or their natural right to bring up their children.

For analysis of legal challenges to on-campus residency requirements, see F. T. Bazluke, "Validity of On-Campus Residency Requirements," 20 *Coll. Law Dig.* 99 (Dec. 7, 1989).

Housing regulations limiting dormitory visitors have also been constitutionally challenged.[48] In *Futrell v. Ahrens,* 540 P.2d 214 (N.M. 1975), students claimed that

---

[48]Cases and authorities are collected in Annot., "Validity of Regulation of College or University Denying or Restricting Right of Student to Receive Visitors in Dormitory," 78 A.L.R.3d 1109 (1977 and periodic supp.).

a regulation prohibiting visits by members of the opposite sex in dormitory bedrooms violated their rights of privacy and free association. The regulation did not apply to the lounges or lobbies of the dorms. The court held for the institution, reasoning that even if the regulation affected rights of privacy and association, it was a reasonable time-and-place restriction on exercise of those rights, since it served legitimate educational interests and conformed with accepted standards of conduct.

Taken together, these cases indicate that the Constitution affords public universities broad leeway in regulating on-campus student housing. An institution may require some students to live on campus; may regulate living conditions to fulfill legitimate health, safety, or educational goals; and may apply its housing policies differently to different student groups. If students are treated differently, however, the Constitution requires that the basis for classifying them be reasonable. The cases above suggest that classification based solely on financial considerations may not meet that test. Administrators should thus be prepared to offer sound nonfinancial justifications for classifications in their residence rules—such as the promotion of educational goals, the protection of the health and safety of students, or the protection of other students' privacy interests. Differing treatment of students based on sex may require a relatively stronger showing of justification, and differing treatment based on race would require a justification so compelling that perhaps none exists.

Besides these limits on administrators' authority over student housing, the Constitution also limits public administrators' authority to enter student rooms (see Section 4.14.2) and to regulate solicitation, canvassing, and voter registration in student residences (see Sections 5.4.3 and 5.6.4).

For private as well as public institutions, federal civil rights regulations limit administrators' authority to treat students differently on grounds of race, sex, age, or disability. The Title VI regulations (see Section 7.5.2) apparently prohibit any and all different treatment of students by race (34 C.F.R. §§ 100.3(b)(1)–(b)(5) and 100.4(d)). The Title IX regulations (see Section 7.5.3) require that the institution provide amounts of housing for female and male students proportionate to the number of housing applicants of each sex, that such housing be comparable in quality and in cost to the student, and that the institution not have different housing policies for each sex (34 C.F.R. §§ 106.32 and 106.33). Furthermore, a provision of Title IX (20 U.S.C. § 1686) states:

> Notwithstanding anything to the contrary contained in this chapter, nothing contained herein shall be construed to prohibit any educational institution receiving funds under this Act from maintaining separate living facilities for the different sexes.

The Section 504 regulations on discrimination against people with disabilities (see Section 7.5.4) require institutions to provide "comparable, convenient, and accessible" housing for students with disabilities at the same cost as for nondisabled students (34 C.F.R. § 104.45). The regulations also provide that colleges provide a variety of housing and that students with disabilities be given a choice among several types of housing (34 C.F.R. § 104.45(a)).

In *Fleming v. New York University*, 865 F.2d 478 (2d Cir. 1989), a graduate student who used a wheelchair claimed that the university overcharged him for his room, in violation of Section 504 of the Rehabilitation Act. The trial court dismissed his claim, and the appellate court affirmed. The student had requested single occupancy of a double room as an undergraduate; the university charged him twice the rate that a student sharing a double room paid. After intervention by the U.S. Office for Civil Rights, the university modified its room charge to 75 percent of the rate for two students in a room.

When the student decided to enroll in graduate school at the university, he asked to remain in the undergraduate residence hall. The university agreed, and charged him the 75 percent fee. However, because of low occupancy levels in the graduate residence halls, graduate students occupying double rooms there were charged a single room-rate. When the student refused to pay his room bills, the university withheld his master's degree. The court ruled that the student's claim for his undergraduate years was time-barred. The claim for disability discrimination based on the room charges during his graduate program was denied because the student had never applied for graduate housing; he had requested undergraduate housing. There was no discriminatory denial of cheaper graduate housing, the court said, because the student never requested it.

The Age Discrimination Act regulations (see Section 7.5.5) apparently apply to discrimination by age in campus housing. As implemented in the general regulations, the ADA apparently limits administrators' authority to use explicit age distinctions (such as those used in *Cooper v. Nix* and *Texas Woman's University v. Chayklintaste*) in formulating housing policies. Policies that distinguish among students according to their class (such as those used in *Prostrollo v. University of South Dakota*) may also be prohibited by the ADA, since they may have the effect of distinguishing by age. Such age distinctions will be prohibited (under § 90.12 of the general regulations) unless they fit within one of the narrow exceptions specified in the regulations (in §§ 90.13, 90.14, and 90.15) or constitute affirmative action (under § 90.49) (see generally Sections 7.5.5 and 7.5.6 of this volume). The best bet for fitting within an exception may be the regulation that permits age distinctions "necessary to the normal operation . . . of a program or activity" (§ 90.14). But administrators should note that the four-part test set out in the regulation carefully circumscribes this exception. For policies based on the class of students, administrators may also be helped by the regulation that permits the use of a nonage factor with an age-discriminatory effect "if the factor bears a direct and substantial relationship to the normal operation of the program or activity" (§ 90.15).

Moreover, the Fair Housing Act prohibits discrimination in housing on the basis of "familial status" (42 U.S.C. § 3604 (1989)). An advisory letter from the U.S. Department of Housing and Urban Development discussing the application of the law to accommodations for students and their children in college or university residence halls is reproduced at 20 *Coll. Law Dig.* 326–29 (July 19, 1990). This statute may create rights for married students greater than they are afforded under the Constitution in cases such as *Bynes v. Toll* above.

Another group protesting discrimination in housing policies are same-sex couples. These couples have claimed that because they are not allowed to marry, they are unfairly excluded from a benefit extended to married students. Furthermore, since many colleges and universities prohibit discrimination on the basis of sexual orientation, gay couples have argued that denying them housing violates the institution's nondiscrimination regulations. Several universities, including the University of

Pennsylvania and Stanford University, have provided university housing to unmarried couples, including those of the same sex.

4.14.2. Searches and seizures. The Fourth Amendment secures an individual's expectation of privacy against government encroachment by providing that "the right of the people to be secure in their persons, houses, papers, and effects, against unreasonable searches and seizures, shall not be violated, and no warrants shall issue, but upon probable cause, supported by oath or affirmation, and particularly describing the place to be searched, and the persons or things to be seized." Searches or seizures conducted pursuant to a warrant meeting the requirements of this provision are deemed reasonable. Warrantless searches may also be found reasonable if they are conducted with the consent of the individual involved, if they are incidental to a lawful arrest, or if they come within a few narrow judicial exceptions, such as an emergency situation.

The applicability of these Fourth Amendment mandates to postsecondary institutions has not always been clear. In the past, when administrators' efforts to provide a "proper" educational atmosphere resulted in noncompliance with the Fourth Amendment, the deviations were defended by administrators and often upheld by courts under a variety of theories. While the previously common justification of in loco parentis is no longer appropriate (see Section 4.1.1), several remaining theories retain vitality. The leading case of *Piazzola v. Watkins*, 442 F.2d 284 (5th Cir. 1971), provides a good overview of these theories and their validity.

In *Piazzola* the dean of men at a state university, at the request of the police, pledged the cooperation of university officials in searching the rooms of two students suspected of concealing marijuana there. At the time of the search, the university had the following regulation in effect: "The college reserves the right to enter rooms for inspection purposes. If the administration deems it necessary, the room may be searched and the occupant required to open his personal baggage and any other personal material which is sealed." The students' rooms were searched without their consent and without a warrant by police officers and university officials. When police found marijuana in each room, the students were arrested, tried, convicted, and sentenced to five years in prison. The U.S. Court of Appeals for the Fifth Circuit reversed the convictions, holding that "a student who occupies a college dormitory room enjoys the protection of the Fourth Amendment" and that the warrantless searches were unreasonable and therefore unconstitutional under that amendment.

Piazzola and similar cases establish that administrators of public institutions cannot avoid the Fourth Amendment simply by asserting that a student has no reasonable expectation of privacy in institution-sponsored housing. (Compare *State v. Dalton*, 716 P.2d 940 (Wash. Ct. App. 1986).) Similarly, administrators can no longer be confident of avoiding the Fourth Amendment by asserting the in loco parentis concept or by arguing that the institution's landlord status, standing alone, authorizes it to search to protect its property interests. Nor does the landlord status, by itself, permit the institution to consent to a search by police, since it has been held that a landlord has no authority to consent to a police search of a tenant's premises (see, for example, *Chapman v. United States*, 365 U.S. 610 (1961)).

However, two limited bases remain on which administrators of public institutions or their delegates can enter a student's premises uninvited and without the authority of a warrant.[49] Under the first approach, the institution can obtain the student's general consent to entry by including an authorization to enter in a written housing agreement or in housing regulations incorporated in the housing agreement. *Piazzola* explains the limits on this approach. Citing the regulation quoted above, the court explained:

> The university retains broad supervisory powers which permit it to adopt . . . [this regulation], provided that regulation is reasonably construed and is limited in its application to further the university's function as an educational institution. The regulation cannot be construed or applied so as to give consent to a search for evidence for the primary purpose of a criminal prosecution. Otherwise, the regulation itself would constitute an unconstitutional attempt to require a student to waive his protection from unreasonable searches and seizures as a condition to his occupancy of a college dormitory room [442 F.2d at 289].

Thus, housing agreements or regulations must be narrowly construed to permit only such entry and search as is expressly provided, and in any case to permit only entries undertaken in pursuit of an educational purpose rather than a criminal enforcement function. *State v. Hunter*, 831 P.2d 1033 (Utah App. 1992), illustrates the type of search that may come within the *Piazzola* guidelines. The director of housing at Utah State University had instigated and conducted a room-to-room inspection to investigate reports of vandalism on the second floor of a dormitory. Upon challenge by a student in whose room the director discovered stolen university property in plain view, the court upheld the search because the housing regulations expressly authorized the room-to-room inspection and because the inspection served the university's interest in protecting university property and maintaining a sound educational environment.

   Under the second approach to securing entry to a student's premises, the public institution can sometimes conduct searches (often called "administrative searches") whose purpose is to protect health and safety—for instance, to enforce health regulations or fire and safety codes. Although such searches, if conducted without a student's consent, usually require a warrant, it may be obtained under less stringent standards than those for obtaining a criminal search warrant. The leading case is *Camara v. Municipal Court*, 387 U.S. 523 (1967), where the U.S. Supreme Court held that a person cannot be prosecuted for refusing to permit city officials to conduct a warrantless code-enforcement inspection of his residence. The Court held that such a search required a warrant, which could be obtained "if reasonable legislative or administrative standards for conducting an area inspection are satisfied"; such standards need "not necessarily depend upon specific knowledge of the condition of the particular dwelling."

[49]In *New Jersey v. T.L.O.*, 469 U.S. 325 (1985), the U.S. Supreme Court created a judicial exception to the warrant requirement for certain searches of public school students. However, the Court's opinion directly applies only to public elementary and secondary schools. Moreover, the opinion applies (1) only to searches of the person or property (such as a purse) carried on the person, as opposed to searches of dormitory rooms, lockers, desks, or other such locations (469 U.S. at 337 n.5), and (2) only to "searches carried out by school authorities acting alone and on their own authority," as opposed to "searches conducted by school officials in conjunction with or at the behest of law enforcement agencies" (469 U.S. at 341 n.7).

In emergency situations where there is insufficient time to obtain a warrant, health and safety searches may be conducted without one. The U.S. Supreme Court emphasized in the *Camara* case (387 U.S. at 539) that "nothing we say today is intended to foreclose prompt inspections, even without a warrant, that the law has traditionally upheld in emergency situations." In other cases courts have recognized firefighters' authority to enter "a burning structure to put out the blaze" and remain there to investigate its cause (*Michigan v. Tyler*, 436 U.S. 499 (1978)), and police officers' authority to "enter a dwelling without a warrant to render emergency aid and assistance to a person whom they reasonably believe to be in distress and in need of that assistance" (*Root v. Gauper*, 438 F.2d 361 (8th Cir. 1971)).

Before entering a room pursuant to the housing agreement or an administrative (health and safety) search, administrators should usually seek to notify and obtain the specific consent of the affected students when it is feasible to do so. Such a policy not only evidences courtesy and respect for privacy but would also augment the validity of the entry in circumstances where there may be some doubt about the scope of the administrator's authority under the housing agreement or the judicial precedents on administrative searches.

In addition to these two limited approaches (housing agreements and administrative searches) to securing entry, other even narrower exceptions to Fourth Amendment warrant requirements may be available to security officers of public institutions who have arrest powers. Such exceptions involve the intricacies of Fourth Amendment law on arrests and searches (see generally *Welsh v. Wisconsin*, 104 S. Ct. 2091 (1984)). The case of *State of Washington v. Chrisman*, 102 S. Ct. 812 (1982), is illustrative. A campus security guard at Washington State University had arrested a student, Overdahl, for illegally possessing alcoholic beverages. The officer accompanied Overdahl to his dormitory room when Overdahl offered to retrieve his identification. Overdahl's roommate, Chrisman, was in the room. While waiting at the doorway for Overdahl to find his identification, the officer observed marijuana seeds and a pipe lying on a desk in the room. The officer then entered, confirmed the identity of the seeds, and seized them. Chrisman was later convicted of possession of marijuana and LSD, which security officers also found in the room.

By a 6-to-3 vote, the U.S. Supreme Court applied the "plain view" exception to the Fourth Amendment and upheld the conviction. The plain view doctrine allows a law enforcement officer to seize property that is clearly incriminating evidence or contraband when that property is in "plain view" in a place where the officer has a right to be. The Court determined that, since an arresting officer has a right to maintain custody of a subject under arrest, this officer lawfully could have entered the room with Overdahl and remained at Overdahl's side for the entire time Overdahl was in the room. Thus, the officer not only had the right to be where he could observe the drugs; he also had the right to be where he could seize the drugs. According to the Court, "It is of no legal significance whether the officer was in the room, on the threshold, or in the hallway, since he had a right to be in any of these places as an incident of a valid arrest. . . . This is a classic instance of incriminating evidence found in plain view when a police officer, for unrelated but entirely legitimate reasons, obtains lawful access to an individual's area of privacy."

Chrisman thus recognizes that a security officer may enter a student's room "as an incident of a valid arrest" of either that student or his roommate. The case also indicates that an important exception to search warrant requirements—the plain view doctrine—retains its full vitality in the college dormitory setting. The Court accorded no greater or lesser constitutional protection from search and seizure to student dormitory residents than to the population at large. Clearly, under *Chrisman* students do enjoy Fourth Amendment protections on campus; but, just as clearly, the Fourth Amendment does not accord dormitory students special status or subject campus security officials to additional restrictions that are not applicable to the nonacademic world.

The Supreme Court placed an important restriction on the plain view doctrine in *Arizona v. Hicks*, 480 U.S. 321 (1987). A police officer, who had entered an apartment lawfully for Fourth Amendment purposes, noticed some stereo equipment that he believed might be stolen. He moved the equipment slightly to locate the serial numbers and later ascertained that the equipment was, in fact, stolen. The Court ruled that the search and seizure were unlawful because the police officer did not have probable cause to believe the equipment was stolen—only a reasonable suspicion, which is insufficient for Fourth Amendment purposes.

Administrators at private institutions are generally not subject to Fourth Amendment restraints, since their actions are usually not state action (Section 1.5.2). But if local, state, or federal law enforcement officials are in any way involved in a search at a private institution, such involvement may be sufficient to make the search state action and therefore subject to the Fourth Amendment. In *People v. Boettner*, 362 N.Y.S.2d 365 (N.Y. Sup. Ct. 1974), *affirmed*, 376 N.Y.S.2d 59 (N.Y. App. Div. 1975), for instance, the question was whether a dormitory room search by officials at the Rochester Institute of Technology, a private institution, was state action. The court answered in the negative only after establishing that the police had not expressly or implicitly requested the search; that the police were not aware of the search; and that there was no evidence of any implied participation of the police by virtue of a continuing cooperative relationship between university officials and the police. A Virginia appellate court reached a similar conclusion in *Duarte v. Commonwealth*, 407 S.E.2d 41 (Va. Ct. App. 1991), because the dean of students at a private college had told college staff to search the plaintiff's room, and police were not involved in the search. And in a leading case involving a security officer of a private business firm, another court judged the validity of the search by determining whether the officer had "acted at the behest or suggestion, with the aid, advice, or encouragement, or under the direction or influence of" government law enforcement officials (*United States v. Clegg*, 509 F.2d 605 (5th Cir. 1975)). Thus, a private institution's authority to conduct searches unshackled by the Fourth Amendment depends on the absence of direct or indirect involvement of such officials in such searches. In addition, if security officers at a private institution have been given public arrest or search powers, they and their institution will be subject to Fourth Amendment strictures in exercising these state-delegated powers (see *People v. Zelinski*, 594 P.2d 1000 (Cal. 1979), discussed in this volume, Section 4.17.1).

Sec. 4.15. Athletics

4.15.1. General principles. Athletics, as a subsystem of the postsecondary institution, is governed by the general principles set forth elsewhere in this chapter and this book. These principles, however, must be applied in light of the particular characteristics and problems of curricular, extracurricular, and intercollegiate athletic programs. A student athlete's eligibility for financial aid, for instance, would be viewed under the general principles in Section 4.3, but aid conditions related to the student's eligibility for or performance in intercollegiate athletics create a special focus for the problem (see Section 4.15.2 below). The institution's tort liability for injuries to students would be subject to the general principles in Section 2.3.1, but the circumstances and risks of athletic participation provide a special focus for the problem (see Section 4.15.6 below). Similarly, the due process principles in Section 4.8 may apply when a student athlete is disciplined, and the First Amendment principles in Section 4.9 may apply when student athletes engage in protest activities. But in each case the problem may have a special focus.

If a student athlete is being disciplined for some infraction, the penalty may be suspension from the team. In such instances the issue raised is whether the procedural protections accompanying suspension from school are also applicable to suspension from a team. For institutions engaging in state action (see Sections 1.5.2 and 8.4.2), the constitutional issue is whether the student athlete has a "property interest" or "liberty interest" in continued intercollegiate competition sufficient to make suspension of that interest a deprivation of "liberty or property" within the meaning of the Due Process Clause. Several federal court cases have addressed this question. (Parallel "liberty or property" issues also arise in the context of faculty dismissals (Section 3.6.2) as well as student suspensions and dismissals (Section 4.8.2).)

In *Behagen v. Intercollegiate Conference of Faculty Representatives*, 346 F. Supp. 602 (D. Minn. 1972), a suit brought by University of Minnesota basketball players suspended from the team for participating in an altercation during a game, the court reasoned that participation in intercollegiate athletics has "the potential to bring [student athletes] great economic rewards" and is thus as important as continuing in school. The court therefore held that the students' interests in intercollegiate participation were protected by procedural due process and granted the suspended athletes the protections established in the *Dixon* case (Section 4.8.2). In *Regents of the University of Minnesota v. NCAA*, 422 F. Supp. 1158 (D. Minn. 1976), the same district court reaffirmed and further explained its analysis of student athletes' due process rights. The court reasoned that the opportunity to participate in intercollegiate competition is a property interest entitled to due process protection, not only because of the possible remunerative careers that result but also because such participation is an important part of the student athlete's educational experience.[50] The same court later used much the same analysis in *Hall v. University of Minnesota*, 530 F. Supp. 104 (D. Minn. 1982).

In contrast, the court in *Colorado Seminary v. NCAA*, 417 F. Supp. 885 (D. Colo. 1976), relying on an appellate court's opinion in a case involving high school athletes (*Albach v. Odle*, 531 F.2d 983 (10th Cir. 1976)), held that college athletes have no property or liberty interests in participating in intercollegiate sports, participating in postseason competition, or appearing on television. The appellate court affirmed (570 F.2d 320 (10th Cir. 1978)). (The trial court did suggest, however, that revocation of an athletic scholarship would infringe a student's property or liberty interests and

---

[50]Although the appellate court reversed this decision, 560 F.2d 352 (8th Cir. 1977), it did so on other grounds and did not question the district court's due process analysis.

therefore would require due process safeguards (see Section 4.15.2 below).) And in *Hawkins v. NCAA*, 652 F. Supp. 602, 609–11 (C.D. Ill. 1987), the court held that student athletes have no property interest in participating in postseason competition. Given this disagreement among the courts, the extent of student athletes' procedural due process protections remains an open question, and administrators should tread cautiously in this area.

When student athletes are participants in a protest or demonstration, their First Amendment rights must be viewed in light of the institution's particular interest in maintaining order and discipline in its athletic programs. An athlete's protest that disrupts an athletic program would no more be protected by the First Amendment than any other student protest that disrupts institutional functions. While the case law regarding athletes' First Amendment rights is even more sparse than that regarding their due process rights, *Williams v. Eaton*, 468 F.2d 1079 (10th Cir. 1972), does specifically apply the *Tinker* case (Section 4.9.1) to a protest by intercollegiate football players. Black football players had been suspended from the team for insisting on wearing black armbands during a game to protest the alleged racial discrimination of the opposing church-related school. The court held that the athletes' protest was unprotected by the First Amendment because it would interfere with the religious freedom rights of the opposing players and their church-related institution. The *Williams* opinion is unusual in that it mixes considerations of free speech and freedom of religion. The court's analysis would have little relevance to situations where religious freedom is not involved. Since the court did not find that the athletes' protest was disruptive, it relied solely on the seldom-used "interference with the rights of others" branch of the *Tinker* case.

More recently, in *Marcum v. Dahl*, 658 F.2d 731 (10th Cir. 1981), the court considered a First Amendment challenge to an institution's nonrenewal of the scholarships of several student athletes. The plaintiffs, basketball players on the University of Oklahoma's women's team, had been involved during the season in a dispute with other players over who should be the team's head coach. At the end of the season, they had announced to the press that they would not play the next year if the current coach was retained. The plaintiffs argued that the institution had refused to renew their scholarships because of this statement to the press and that the statement was constitutionally protected. The trial court and then the appellate court disagreed. Analogizing the scholarship athletes to public employees for First Amendment purposes (see this volume, Sections 3.7.1 and 3.7.3), the appellate court held that (1) the dispute about the coach was not a matter of "general public concern" and the plaintiffs' press statement on this subject was therefore not protected by the First Amendment and (2) the plaintiffs' participation in the dispute prior to the press statement, and the resultant disharmony, provided an independent basis for the scholarship nonrenewal.

Similarly, state and federal statutory law has some special applications to an institution's athletes or athletic programs. Questions have arisen, for example, about the eligibility of injured intercollegiate athletes for workers' compensation (see this volume, Section 6.5.5). Criminal laws in some states prohibit agents from entering representation agreements with student athletes (see, for example, Mich. Comp. Laws Ann. §750.411e) or from entering into such an agreement without notifying the student's institution (see, for example, Fla. Stat. Ann. §240.537). State antihazing statutes may have applications to the activities of athletic teams and clubs (see, for example, Ill. Rev. Stat. ch. 144, para. 222, as construed and upheld in *People v.*

Anderson, 591 N.E.2d 461 (Ill. 1992), a prosecution brought against members of a university lacrosse club). Regarding federal law, the antitrust statutes may have some application to the institution's relations with its student athletes when those relations are governed by athletic association and conference rules (this volume, Section 8.4.3). And the Student Right-to-Know Act and Campus Security Act, discussed below, contains separate provisions dealing with low graduation rates of student athletes in certain sports.

The Student Right-to-Know Act (Title I of the Student-Right-to-Know and Campus Security Act), 104 Stat. 2381–2384 (1990), ensures that potential student athletes will have access to data that will help them make informed choices when selecting an institution. Under the Act, an institution of higher education that participates in federal student aid programs and that awards "athletically related student aid" must annually provide the Department of Education with certain information about its student athletes. Athletically related student aid is defined as "any scholarship, grant, or other form of financial assistance the terms of which require the recipient to participate in a program of intercollegiate athletics at an institution of higher education in order to be eligible to receive such assistance" (104 Stat. 2384, 20 U.S.C. § 1092(e)(8)).

Institutions must report the following information, broken down by race and gender: (1) the number of students receiving athletically related student aid in basketball, football, baseball, cross country/track, and all other sports combined (20 U.S.C. § 1092(e)(1)(A)); (2) the completion or graduation rates of those students (20 U.S.C. § 1092(e)(1)(C)); and (3) the average completion or graduation rate for the four most recent classes (20 U.S.C. § 1092(e)(1)(E)). The same types of information must be collected on students in general (20 U.S.C. § 1092(e)(1)(B, D, & F)). In addition to reporting to the Department of Education, institutions must provide this information to potential student athletes and their parents, guidance counselors, and coaches (20 U.S.C. § 1092(e)(2)). Other students may receive the information upon request.[51] The secretary of education may waive the annual reporting requirements if, in his opinion, an institution of higher education is a member of an athletic association or conference that publishes data "substantially comparable" to the information specified in the Act (20 U.S.C. § 1092(e)(6)). Regulations implementing the Act are published at 34 C.F.R. Part 668.

Surrounding these special applications of the law to athletics, there are major new legal and policy issues that pertain specifically to the status of "big-time" intercollegiate athletics within the higher education world. In addition to the low graduation rates mentioned above, the debate has focused on academic entrance requirements for student athletes (see L. Greene, "The New NCAA Rules of the Game: Academic Integrity or Racism?" 28 *St. Louis U. L.J.* 101 (1984)); postsecondary institutions' recruiting practices; alleged doctoring or padding of high school and college transcripts to obtain or maintain athletic eligibility; drug use among athletes and mandatory drug testing (Section 4.15.5 below); alleged exploitation of black athletes; improper financial incentives and rewards or improper academic assistance for student athletes; and the authority and practices of the NCAA and athletic conferences

---

[51]This information is in addition to other information institutions must provide to prospective and enrolled students under 20 U.S.C. § 1092. See this volume, Section 4.3.2, and see also Section 7.4.3.3.

(Section 8.4) regarding such matters. The overarching concern prompted by these issues is one of integrity: the integrity of individual institutions' athletic programs, the integrity of academic standards at institutions emphasizing major intercollegiate competition, the integrity of higher education's mission in an era when athletics has assumed such a substantial role in the operation of the system. See J. Thelin & L. Wiseman, *The Old College Try: Balancing Academics and Athletics in Higher Education* (George Washington University, 1989).

4.15.2. Athletic scholarships. An athletic scholarship will usually be treated in the courts as a contract between the institution and the student. Typically the institution offers to pay the student's educational expenses in return for the student's promise to participate in a particular sport and maintain athletic eligibility by complying with university, conference, and NCAA regulations (see generally Section 8.4). Unlike other student-institutional contracts (see Section 4.1.3), the athletic scholarship contract may be a formal written agreement signed by the student and, if the student is underage, by a parent or guardian. Moreover, the terms of the athletic scholarship may be heavily influenced by athletic conference and NCAA rules regarding scholarships and athletic eligibility (see Section 8.4).

In NCAA member institutions, a letter-of-intent document is provided to prospective student athletes. The student athlete's signature on this document functions as a promise that the student will attend the institution and participate in intercollegiate athletics in exchange for the institution's promise to provide a scholarship or other financial assistance. Courts have generally not addressed the issue of whether the letter of intent, standing alone, is an enforceable contract that binds the institution and the student athlete to their respective commitments. Instead, courts have viewed the signing of a letter of intent as one among many factors to consider in determining whether a contractual relationship exists. Thus, although the letter of intent serves as additional evidence of a contractual relationship, it does not yet have independent legal status and, in effect, must be coupled with a financial aid offer in order to bind either party. See generally M. Cozzillio, "The Athletic Scholarship and the College National Letter of Intent: A Contract by Any Other Name," 35 *Wayne L. Rev.* 1275 (1989).

Although it is possible for either the institution or the student to breach the scholarship contract and for either party to sue, as a practical matter the cases generally involve students who file suit after the institution terminates or withdraws the scholarship. Such institutional action may occur if the student becomes ineligible for intercollegiate competition, has fraudulently misrepresented information regarding his or her academic credentials or athletic eligibility, has engaged in serious misconduct warranting substantial disciplinary action, or has declined to participate in the sport for personal reasons. The following three cases illustrate how such issues arise and how courts resolve them.

In *Begley v. Corp. of Mercer University*, 367 F. Supp. 908 (E.D. Tenn. 1973), the university withdrew from its agreement to provide an athletic scholarship for Begley after realizing that a university assistant coach had miscalculated Begley's high school GPA, and that his true GPA did not meet the NCAA's minimum requirements. Begley filed suit, asking the court to award money damages for the university's breach of contract. The court dismissed the suit, holding that the university was justified in not performing its part of the agreement, since the agreement also required Begley to abide by all NCAA rules and regulations. Because Begley, from the outset, did not have the minimum GPA, he was unable to perform his part of the agreement. Thus, the court based its decision on the fundamental principle of contract law that " 'where one party is unable to perform his part of the contract, he cannot be entitled to the performance of the contract by the other party'" (quoting 17 Am. Jur. 2d at 791–92, *Contracts*, § 355).

In *Taylor v. Wake Forest University*, 191 S.E.2d 379 (N.C. Ct. App. 1972), the university terminated the student's scholarship after he refused to participate in the football program. Originally, the student had withdrawn from the team to concentrate on academics when his grades fell below the minimum that the university required for athletic participation. Even after he raised his GPA above the minimum, however, the student continued his refusal to participate. The student alleged that the university's termination of his athletic scholarship was a breach and asked the court to award money damages equal to the costs incurred in completing his degree. He argued that, in case of conflict between his educational achievement and his athletic involvement, the scholarship terms allowed him to curtail his participation in the football program in order to "assure reasonable academic progress." He also argued that he was to be the judge of "reasonable academic progress." The court rejected the student's argument and granted summary judgment for the university. According to the court, permitting the student to be his own judge of his academic progress would be a "strange construction of the contract." Further, by accepting the scholarship, the student was obligated to "maintain his athletic eligibility . . . both physically and scholastically. . . . When he refused to [participate] in the absence of any injury or excuse other than to devote more time to his studies, he was not complying with his contractual agreements."

In *Conard v. University of Washington*, 814 P.2d 1242 (Wash. Ct. App. 1991), after three years of providing financial aid, the university declined to renew the scholarships of two student athletes for a fourth year because of the students' "serious misconduct." Although the scholarship agreement stipulated a one-year award of aid that would be considered for renewal under certain conditions, the students argued that it was their expectation, and the university's practice, that the scholarship would be automatically renewed for at least four years. The appellate court did not accept the students' evidence to this effect because the agreement, by its "clear terms," lasted only one academic year and provided only for the *consideration* of renewal (see generally Section 1.3.2.3). The university's withdrawal of aid, therefore, was not a breach of the contract.

Due process issues may also arise if an institution terminates or withdraws an athletic scholarship. The contract itself may specify certain procedural steps that the institution must take before withdrawal or termination. Conference or NCAA rules may contain other procedural requirements. And for public institutions, the federal Constitution's Fourteenth Amendment (or comparable state constitutional provision) may sometimes superimpose other procedural obligations upon those contained in the contract and rules. In the *Conard* case above, for example, the Washington Court of Appeals held that the students had a "legitimate claim of entitlement" to the renewal of their scholarships because each scholarship was "issued under the representation that it would be renewed subject to certain conditions," and because it was the university's practice to renew athletic scholarships for at least four years. Since this "entitlement" constituted a property interest under the Fourteenth Amendment, the court held that any deprivation of this entitlement "warrants the protection of due process" (see Section 4.15.1).

The Washington Supreme Court reversed the court of appeals on the due process issue (834 P.2d 17 (Wash. 1992)). The students' primary contention was that a "mutually explicit understanding" (see generally Section 3.6.2.1) had been created by "the language of their contracts and the common understanding, based upon the surrounding circumstances and the conduct of the parties." The court rejected this argument, stating that "the language of the offers and the NCAA regulations are not sufficiently certain to support a mutually explicit understanding, [and] the fact that scholarships are, in fact, normally renewed does not create a 'common law' of renewal, absent other consistent and supportive [university] policies or rules." Consequently, the court held that the students had no legitimate claim of entitlement to renewal of the scholarships, and that the university thus had no obligation to extend them due process protections prior to nonrenewal.

Although the appellate court's decision in *Conard* is no longer good law, it is illustrative of the types of due process safeguards a court would require in a misconduct case *if* it found that a particular scholarship agreement created a protected property interest in renewal:

> Clearly, at least notice and an opportunity to be heard are required. In addition, the student athlete who faces nonrenewal of his or her scholarship based on misconduct must be given a written copy of any information on which the nonrenewal recommendation is based in time to prepare to address that information at the hearing. The student should be given the opportunity to present and rebut evidence, and the hearing must be conducted by an objective decisionmaker. The student has a right to be represented by counsel and to have a record made of the hearing for review purposes. Finally, the student has the right to a written decision from the hearing board setting forth its determination of contested facts and the basis for its decision [814 P.2d at 1246].

Apparently a court would also require the same protections in a situation where the institution had terminated a multiyear athletic scholarship.

Occasionally student athletes have sued their institutions even when the institution has not terminated or withdrawn the athlete's scholarship. Such cases are likely to involve alleged exploitation or abuse of the athlete, and may present not only breach-of-contract issues paralleling those in the cases above but also more innovative tort law issues. The leading case, highly publicized in its day, is *Ross v. Creighton University*, 957 F.2d 410 (7th Cir. 1992). The plaintiff in this case had been awarded a basketball scholarship from Creighton even though his academic credentials were substantially below those of the average Creighton student. The plaintiff alleged that the university knew of his academic limitations but nevertheless lured him to Creighton with assurances that it would provide sufficient academic support so that he would "receive a meaningful education." While at Creighton, the plaintiff maintained a D average; and, on the advice of the athletic department, his curriculum consisted largely of courses such as "Theory of Basketball." After four years he "had the overall language skills of a fourth grader and the reading skills of a seventh grader."

The plaintiff based his suit on three tort theories and a breach-of-contract theory. The trial court originally dismissed all four claims. The appellate court agreed with the trial court on the tort claims but reversed the trial court and allowed the plaintiff to proceed to trial on the breach-of-contract claim. The plaintiff's first tort claim was a claim of "educational malpractice" based on Creighton's not providing him with "a meaningful education [or] preparing him for employment after college." The court refused to recognize educational malpractice as a cause of action, listing four policy concerns supporting its decision: (1) the inability of a court to fashion "a satisfactory standard of care by which to evaluate" instruction; (2) its inability to determine the cause and nature of damage to the student; (3) the potential flood of litigation that would divert institutions' attention from their primary mission; and (4) the threat of involving courts in the oversight of daily institutional operations. The plaintiff's second claim was that Creighton had committed "negligent admission" because it owed a duty to "recruit and enroll only those students reasonably qualified to and able to academically perform at CREIGHTON." The court rejected this novel theory because of similar problems in identifying a standard of care by which to judge the institution's admissions decisions. The court also noted that, if institutions were subjected to such claims, they would admit only exceptional students, thus severely limiting the opportunities for marginal students. The plaintiff's last tort claim was negligent infliction of emotional distress. The court quickly rejected this claim because its rejection of the first two claims left no basis for proving that the defendant had been negligent in undertaking the actions that may have distressed the plaintiff.

Although the court rejected all the plaintiff's negligence claims, it did embrace his breach-of-contract claim. In order to discourage "any attempt to repackage an educational malpractice claim as a contract claim," however, the court required the plaintiff to "do more than simply allege that the education was not good enough. Instead, he must point to an identifiable contractual promise that the defendant failed to honor. . . . [T]he essence of the plaintiff's complaint would not be that the institution failed to perform adequately a promised educational service, but rather that it failed to perform that service at all." Judicial consideration of such a claim is therefore not an inquiry "into the nuances of educational processes and theories, but rather an objective assessment of whether the institution made a good faith effort to perform on its promise."

Following this approach, the court reviewed the plaintiff's allegations that the university failed (1) to provide adequate tutoring; (2) to require that the plaintiff attend tutoring sessions; (3) to allow the plaintiff to "red-shirt" for one year to concentrate on his studies; and (4) to afford the plaintiff a reasonable opportunity to take advantage of tutoring services. The court concluded that these allegations were sufficient to warrant further proceedings and therefore remanded the case to the trial court. (Soon thereafter, the parties settled the case.)

The court's disposition of the tort claims in *Ross* does not mean that student athletes can never succeed with such claims. In a similar case, *Jackson v. Drake University*, 778 F. Supp. 1490 (S.D. Iowa 1991), the court did recognize two tort claims—negligent misrepresentation and fraud—brought by a former student athlete. After rejecting an educational malpractice claim for reasons similar to those in *Ross*, the court allowed the plaintiff to proceed with his claims that "Drake did not exercise reasonable care in making representations [about its commitment to academic excellence] and had no intention of providing the support services it had promised." The court reasoned that the policy concerns "do not weigh as heavily in favor of precluding the claims for negligent misrepresentation and fraud as in the claim for [educational malpractice]."

4.15.3. Sex discrimination. Sex discrimination remains a major issue in athletics programs. Before the passage of Title IX (20 U.S.C. § 1681 et seq.) (see this volume, Section 7.5.3), the legal aspects of this controversy centered on the Fourteenth Amendment's Equal Protection Clause. As in earlier admissions cases (Section 4.2.4.2), courts searched for an appropriate analysis by which to ascertain the constitutionality of sex-based classifications in athletics.[52] Since the implementation in 1975 of the Title IX regulations (34 C.F.R. Part 106), the equal protection aspects of sex discrimination in high school and college athletics have played second fiddle to Title IX. Title IX applies to both public and private institutions receiving federal aid and thus has a broader reach than equal protection, which applies only to public institutions (see this volume, Section 1.5.2). Title IX also has several provisions on athletics that establish requirements more extensive than anything devised under the banner of equal protection. And Title IX is supported by enforcement mechanisms beyond those available for the Equal Protection Clause (see Sections 7.5.8 and 7.5.9).

In addition to Title IX, state law (including state equal rights amendments) also has significant applications to college athletics.[53] In *Blair v. Washington State University*, 740 P.2d 1379 (Wash. 1987), for example, women athletes and coaches at Washington State University used the state's equal rights amendment and the state nondiscrimination law to challenge the institution's funding for women's athletic programs. The trial court had ruled against the university, saying that funding for women's athletic programs should be based on the percentage of women enrolled as undergraduates. In calculating the formula, however, the trial court had excluded football revenues. The Washington Supreme Court reversed on that point, declaring that the state's equal rights amendment "contains no exception for football." It remanded the case to the trial court for revision of the funding formula. See "Comment: *Blair v. Washington State University:* Making State ERA's a Potent Remedy for Sex Discrimination in Athletics," 14 *J. Coll. & Univ. Law* 575 (1988).

Although the regulations interpreting Title IX with regard to athletics were effective in 1975, they were not appreciably enforced at the postsecondary level until the late 1980s—partly because the U.S. Supreme Court, in *Grove City College v. Bell* (discussed in Section 7.5.7.3), had held that Title IX's nondiscrimination provisions applied only to those programs that were direct recipients of federal aid. Congress reversed the result in *Grove City* in the Civil Rights Restoration Act of 1987, making it clear that Title IX applies to all activities of colleges and universities that receive federal funds.

Section 106.41 of the Title IX regulations is the primary provision on athletics; it establishes various equal opportunity requirements applicable to "interscholastic, intercollegiate, club, or intramural athletics." Section 106.37(c) establishes equal opportunity requirements regarding the availability of athletic scholarships. Physical

[52]The cases are collected in Annot., "Validity, Under Federal Law, of Sex Discrimination in Athletics," 23 A.L.R. Fed. 664 (1975 and periodic supp.).

[53]The cases are collected in Annot., "Application of State Law to Sex Discrimination in Sports," 66 A.L.R.3d 1262 (1991 and periodic supp.).

education classes are covered by Section 106.34, and extracurricular activities related to athletics, such as cheerleading and booster clubs, are covered generally under Section 106.31. The regulations impose nondiscrimination requirements on these activities whether or not they are directly subsidized by federal funds (see this volume, Section 7.5.7.4), and they do not exempt revenue-generating sports, such as men's football or basketball, from the calculation of funds available for the institution's athletic programs.

One of the greatest controversies stirred by Title IX concerns the choice of sex-segregated versus unitary (integrated) athletic teams. The regulations develop a compromise approach to this issue, which roughly parallels the equal protection principles that emerged from the earlier court cases.[54]

Under Section 106.41(b):

> [An institution] may operate or sponsor separate teams for members of each sex where selection for such teams is based upon competitive skill or the activity involved is a contact sport. However, where a recipient operates or sponsors a team in a particular sport for members of one sex but operates or sponsors no such team for members of the other sex, and athletic opportunities for members of that sex have previously been limited, members of the excluded sex must be allowed to try out for the team offered unless the sport involved is a contact sport. For the purposes of this part, contact sports include boxing, wrestling, rugby, ice hockey, football, basketball, and other sports the purpose or major activity of which involves bodily contact.

This regulation requires institutions to operate unitary teams only for noncontact sports where selection is not competitive. Otherwise, the institution may operate either unitary or separate teams and may even operate a team for one sex without having any team in the sport for the opposite sex, as long as the institution's overall athletic program "effectively accommodate[s] the interests and abilities of members of both sexes" (34 C.F.R. § 106.41(c)(1)). In a noncontact sport, however, if an institution operates only one competitively selected team, it must be open to both sexes whenever the "athletic opportunities" of the traditionally excluded sex "have previously been limited" (34 C.F.R. § 106.41(b)).

Regardless of whether its teams are separate or unitary, the institution must "provide equal athletic opportunity for members of both sexes" (34 C.F.R.

---

[54]It is still somewhat an open question whether Title IX's athletic regulations fully comply with constitutional equal protection and due process requirements. There is some basis for arguing that the Title IX regulations do not fully meet the equal protection requirements that courts have constructed or will construct in this area (see W. Kaplin and S. Marmur, "Validity of the 'Separate but Equal' Policy of the Title IX Regulations on Athletics," a memorandum reprinted in 121 *Congressional Record* 1090, 94th Cong., 1st Sess. (1975)). One court has ruled on the question, holding Section 86.41(b) (now 106.41(b)) of the Title IX regulations unconstitutional as applied to exclude physically qualified girls from competing with boys in contact sports (*Yellow Springs Exempted Village School District v. Ohio High School Athletic Association*, 443 F. Supp. 753 (S.D. Ohio 1978)). On appeal, however, a U.S. Court of Appeals reversed the district court's ruling (647 F.2d 651 (6th Cir. 1981)). The appellate court held that, because of the posture of the case and the absence of evidence in the record, "we believe it inappropriate for this court to make any ruling on the matter at this time." The majority opinion and a concurring/dissenting opinion include extensive constitutional analysis of sex segregation in athletic teams.

§ 106.41(c)). While equality of opportunity does not require either equality of "aggregate expenditures for members of each sex" or equality of "expenditures for male and female teams," an institution's "failure to provide necessary funds for teams for one sex" is a relevant factor in determining compliance (34 C.F.R. § 106.41(c)). Postsecondary administrators grappling with this slippery equal opportunity concept will be helped by Section 106.41(c)'s list of ten nonexclusive factors by which to measure overall equality:

1. Whether the selection of sports and levels of competition effectively accommodate the interests and abilities of members of both sexes.
2. The provision of equipment and supplies.
3. Scheduling of games and practice time.
4. Travel and per diem allowance.
5. Opportunity to receive coaching and academic tutoring.
6. Assignment and compensation of coaches and tutors.
7. Provision of locker rooms, practice and competitive facilities.
8. Provision of medical and training facilities and services.
9. Provision of housing and dining facilities and services.
10. Publicity.

The equal opportunity focus of the regulations also applies to athletic scholarships. Institutions must "provide reasonable opportunities for such awards for members of each sex in proportion to the number of each sex participating in . . . intercollegiate athletics" (34 C.F.R. § 106.37(c)(1)). If the institution operates separate teams for each sex (as permitted in § 106.41), it may allocate athletic scholarships on the basis of sex to implement its separate-team philosophy, as long as the overall allocation achieves equal opportunity.

In 1979, after a period of substantial controversy, the Department of Health, Education and Welfare (now Department of Education) issued a lengthy Policy Interpretation of its Title IX regulations as they apply to intercollegiate athletics (44 Fed. Reg. 71413 (Dec. 11, 1979)). This Policy Interpretation is still considered authoritative and is currently used by federal courts reviewing allegations of Title IX violations. It addresses each of the ten factors listed in Section 106.41(c) of the regulations, providing examples of information the Department of Education will use to determine whether an institution has complied with Title IX. For example, "opportunity to receive coaching and academic tutoring" would include the availability of full-time and part-time coaches for male and female athletes, the relative availability of graduate assistants, and the availability of tutors for male and female athletes. "Compensation of coaches" includes attention to the rates of compensation, conditions relating to contract renewal, nature of coaching duties performed, and working conditions of coaches for male and female teams (44 Fed. Reg. at 71416). Further elucidation of the ten factors is found in the *Investigator's Manual* published in 1990 by the ED's Office for Civil Rights (which enforces Title IX). This manual may be revised in the near future, so administrators and counsel should ascertain which version of the manual is effective when they are assessing their institution's Title IX compliance.

Most Title IX disputes have involved complaints to the Office for Civil Rights. In the past, this office has been criticized for its "lax" enforcement efforts and for permitting institutions to remain out of compliance with Title IX (*Gender Equity in Intercollegiate Athletics: The Inadequacy of Title IX Enforcement by the U.S. Office for Civil Rights* (Lyndon B. Johnson School of Public Affairs, University of Texas, 1993)). Perhaps partly for this reason, women athletes in recent years have often chosen to litigate their claims in the courts.

Although the first major court challenge to an institution's funding for intercollegiate athletics ended with a settlement rather than a court order (*Haffer v. Temple University*, 678 F. Supp. 517 (E.D. Pa. 1987)), this case set the tone for subsequent litigation. In *Haffer* a federal trial judge certified a class of "all current women students at Temple University who participate, or who are or have been deterred from participating because of sex discrimination[,] in Temple's intercollegiate athletic program." Although the case was settled, with the university agreeing to various changes in scholarships and support for women athletes, it encouraged women students at other colleges and universities to challenge the revenues allocated to women's and men's sports. For discussion see "Comment: *Haffer v. Temple University:* A Reawakening of Gender Discrimination in Intercollegiate Athletics," 16 *J. Coll. & Univ. Law* 137 (1989).

The leading case to date on Title IX's application to intercollegiate athletics is *Cohen v. Brown University*, 991 F.2d 888 (1st Cir. 1993). In that case a U.S. Court of Appeals upheld a district court's preliminary injunction ordering Brown University to reinstate its women's gymnastics and women's volleyball programs to full varsity status pending the trial of a Title IX claim. Until 1971 Brown had been an all-male university. At that time it merged with a women's college and, over the next six years, upgraded the women's athletic program to include fourteen varsity teams. It later added one other such team. It thus had fifteen women's varsity teams as compared to sixteen men's varsity teams; the women had 36.7 percent of all the varsity athletic opportunities available at the university, and the men had 63.3 percent. (Brown's student population is approximately 48 percent women.) In 1991, however, the university cut four varsity teams: two men's teams (for a savings of $15,795) and two women's teams (for a savings of $62,028). These cuts disproportionately reduced the budgeted funds for women, but they did not significantly change the ratio of athletic opportunities, since women retained 36.6 percent of the available slots.

In upholding the district court's injunction, the appellate court first noted that an institution would not be found in violation of Title IX merely because there was a statistical disparity between the percentage of women and the percentage of men in its athletic programs. The court then focused on the ten factors listed in Section 106.41(c) of the Title IX regulations (see above) and noted that the district court based its injunction on the first of these factors: "Brown's failure effectively to accommodate the interests and abilities of female students in the selection and level of sports." To be in compliance with this factor, a university must satisfy at least one of three tests set out in the Title IX Policy Interpretation:

> (1) Whether intercollegiate level participation opportunities for male and female students are provided in numbers substantially proportionate to their respective enrollments; or
> (2) Where the members of one sex have been and are underrepresented among intercollegiate athletes, whether the institution can show a history and

continuing practice of program expansion which is demonstrably responsive to the developing interest and abilities of the members of that sex; or

(3) Where the members of one sex have been and are underrepresented among intercollegiate athletes, and the institution cannot show a continuing practice of program expansion such as that cited above, whether it can be demonstrated that the interests and abilities of the members of that sex have been fully and effectively accommodated by the present program [44 Fed. Reg. at 71418].

The appellate court agreed with the district court that Brown clearly did not fall within the first option. Further, the district court did not abuse its discretion in deciding that, although the university had made a large burst of improvements between 1971 and 1977, the lack of continuing expansion efforts precluded the university from satisfying the second option. Thus, since the university could not comply with either of the first two options, "it must comply with the third benchmark. To do so, the school must fully and effectively accommodate the underrepresented gender's interests and abilities, even if that requires it to give the underrepresented gender . . . what amounts to a larger slice of a shrinking athletic-opportunity pie." The appellate court then focused on the word "fully" in the third option, interpreting it literally to the effect that the underrepresented sex must be "fully" accommodated, not merely proportionately accommodated as in the first option. Since Brown's cuts in the women's athletic programs had created a demand for athletic opportunities for women that was not filled, women were not "fully" accommodated. Thus, since Brown could meet none of the three options specified in the Policy Interpretation, the court concluded that the university had likely violated Title IX, and it therefore affirmed the district court's entry of the preliminary injunction.[55]

Holding that the plaintiffs had made their required showing and that Brown had not, the court turned to the issue of remedy. Although the appellate court upheld the preliminary injunction, it noted the need to balance the institution's academic freedom with the need for an effective remedy for the Title IX violation. The appellate court stated that, since the lower court had not yet held a trial on the merits, its order that Brown maintain women's varsity volleyball and gymnastics teams pending trial was within its discretion. The appellate court noted, however, that a more appropriate post-trial remedy, assuming that a Title IX violation was established, would be for Brown to propose a program for compliance. In balancing academic freedom against Title IX's regulatory scheme, the court noted:

> This litigation presents an array of complicated and important issues at a crossroads of the law that few courts have explored. The beacon by which we must steer is Congress's unmistakably clear mandate that educational institutions not use federal monies to perpetuate gender-based discrimination. At the same time, we must remain sensitive to the fact that suits of this genre implicate the discretion of universities to pursue their missions free from governmental interference and, in the bargain, to deploy increasingly scarce resources in the most advantageous way [991 F.2d at 907].

[55]The appellate court's opinion also contained an important discussion of the plaintiff's and defendant's burdens of proof in presenting and rebutting a Title IX athletics claim (991 F.2d at 902). See also *Roberts v. Colorado State Board of Agriculture*, 998 F2d 824, 831–32 (10th Cir. 1993); and compare *Cook v. Colgate University*, 802 F. Supp. 737 (N.D.N.Y. 1992), vacated on other grounds, 992 F.2d 17 (2d Cir. 1993).

See also *Roberts v. Colorado State Board of Agriculture,* 998 F.2d 824, 833–34 (10th Cir. 1993), which includes a contrasting discussion of remedies.

For later cases reaching results similar to the *Cohen* case, see *Favia v. Indiana University of Pennsylvania,* 7 F.3d 332 (3d Cir. 1993); *Roberts v. Colorado State Board of Agriculture,* 998 F.2d 824 (10th Cir. 1993). For a different result, compare *Kelley v. Board of Trustees of the University of Illinois,* 832 F. Supp. 237 (C.D. Ill. 1993), rejecting a Title IX challenge by members of the *men's* swimming team after the university eliminated the team; and see generally B. Kramer, *Title IX in Intercollegiate Athletics: Litigation Risks Facing Colleges and Universities,* Public Policy Series no. 93-2 (Association of Governing Boards, 1993).

Both in *Cohen* and in *Roberts,* the courts appeared to serve warning on institutions that do not provide equivalent funding for men's and women's sports, and that have either a stringently limited athletic budget or one that must be cut. For such institutions compliance with Title IX can occur only if the institution downgrades by reducing opportunities for men's sports to the level available for women's sports. Both appellate opinions deferred to the institution's right to determine for itself how it will structure its athletic programs, but once the institution was out of Title IX compliance, these courts did not hesitate to order specific remedies. Financial problems do not exempt an institution from Title IX compliance.

4.15.4. Discrimination on the basis of disability. Under Section 504 of the Rehabilitation Act of 1973 and its implementing regulations (this volume, Section 7.5.4), institutions must afford disabled students an equal opportunity to participate in physical education, athletic, and recreational programs. Like Title IX, Section 504 applies to athletic activities even if they are not directly subsidized by federal funds (see this volume, Section 7.5.7.4). The Department of Education's regulations set forth the basic requirement:

> (1) In providing physical education courses and athletics and similar programs and activities to any of its students, a recipient to which this subpart applies may not discriminate on the basis of handicap. A recipient that offers physical education courses or that operates or sponsors intercollegiate, club, or intramural athletics shall provide to qualified handicapped students an equal opportunity for participation in these activities.
>
> (2) A recipient may offer to handicapped students physical education and athletic activities that are separate or different from those offered to nonhandicapped students only if separation or differentiation is consistent with the requirements . . . [that the programs and activities be operated in "the most integrated setting appropriate"] and only if no qualified handicapped student is denied the opportunity to compete for teams or to participate in courses that are not separate or different [34 C.F.R. § 104.47(a)].

By these regulations, a student in a wheelchair could be eligible to participate in a regular archery program, for instance, or a deaf student on a regular wrestling team (34 C.F.R. Part 104 Appendix A), because they would retain full capacity to play those sports despite their disabilities. In these and other situations, however, questions may arise concerning whether the student's skill level would qualify him to participate in the program or allow him to succeed in the competition required for selection to intercollegiate teams.

The case law on Section 504's application to disabled athletes is exceedingly sparse. In what is still the leading case, *Wright v. Columbia University*, 520 F. Supp. 789 (E.D. Pa. 1981), the court relied on Section 504 to protect a disabled student's right to participate in intercollegiate football. The student had been blind in one eye since infancy; because of the potential danger to his "good" eye, the institution had denied him permission to participate. In issuing a temporary restraining order against the university, the court accepted (pending trial) the student's argument that the institution's decision was discriminatory within the meaning of Section 504 because the student was qualified to play football despite his disability and was capable of making his own decisions about "his health and well-being."

In addition to Section 504, the Americans with Disabilities Act (see this volume, Section 7.2.16), may also provide protections for student athletes subjected to discrimination on the basis of a disability in institutional athletic programs. Title II of the Act (public services) (42 U.S.C. §§ 12131–12134) would apply to students in public institutions, and Title III (public accommodations) (42 U.S.C. §§ 12181–12189) would apply to students in private institutions. See generally C. Jones, "College Athletes: Illness or Injury and the Decision to Return to Play," 40 *Buffalo L. Rev.* 113, 189–97 (1992).

4.15.5. Drug testing. Drug testing of athletes has become a focus of controversy in both amateur and professional sports. Intercollegiate athletics is no exception. Legal issues may arise under the federal Constitution's Fourth Amendment Search and Seizure Clause and its Fourteenth Amendment Due Process Clause; under search-and-seizure, due process, or right-to-privacy clauses of state constitutions; under various state civil rights statutes; under state tort law (see generally Section 2.3.1); or under the institution's own regulations, including statements of students' rights. Public institutions may be subject to challenges based on any of these sources; private institutions generally are subject only to challenges based on tort law, their own regulations, civil rights statutes applicable to private action, and (in some states) state constitutional provisions limiting private as well as public action (see generally Section 1.5).

For public institutions the primary concern is the Fourth Amendment of the federal Constitution, which protects individuals against unreasonable searches and seizures, and parallel state constitutional provisions that may provide similar (and sometimes greater) protections. In *Skinner v. Railway Labor Executives Assn.*, 489 U.S. 602, 619 (1989) (discussed generally in Section 3.1.1, this volume), the U.S. Supreme Court held that the collection of urine or blood for drug testing constitutes a search within the meaning of the Fourth Amendment and that the validity of such a search is determined by a reasonableness test:

> What is reasonable . . . "depends on all of the circumstances surrounding the search or seizure and the nature of the search or seizure itself." . . . Thus, the permissibility of a particular practice "is judged by balancing its intrusion on the individual's Fourth Amendment interests against its promotion of legitimate governmental interests" [quoting *United States v. Montoya de Hernandez*, 473 U.S. 531, 537 (1985); citations omitted].

Derdeyn v. University of Colorado, 832 P.2d 1031 (Colo. Ct. App. 1991), *affirmed*, 863 P.2d 929 (Colo. 1993), provides an example of a university drug-testing program held to be unreasonable under the *Skinner* standard. The university initiated a program for testing its student athletes when it had a "reasonable suspicion" that they were using drugs. As a condition to participation in intercollegiate athletics, all athletes were asked to sign a form consenting to such tests. The university initiated the program "because of a desire to prepare its athletes for drug testing in NCAA sanctioned sporting events, a concern for athletes' health, an interest in promoting its image, and a desire to ensure fair competition" (832 P.2d at 1032). In a class action suit, student athletes challenged this program on several grounds. The Supreme Court of Colorado held that the program violated both the federal Constitution's Fourth Amendment and a similar provision of the Colorado constitution. Applying the *Skinner* reasonableness test, the court determined, "based on a balancing of the privacy interests of the student athletes and the governmental interests of CU, that CU's drug-testing program is unconstitutional" (863 P.2d at 946). In addition, the court held that the university's consent form was not sufficient to waive the athletes' constitutional rights. The university bore the burden of proof in showing that the waiver was signed voluntarily. Relying on the trial testimony of several athletes, which "revealed that, because of economic or other commitments the students had made to the University, [the students] were not faced with an unfettered choice in regard to signing the consent" (832 P.2d at 1035), the Colorado Supreme Court invalidated the university's program and prohibited its continuation. (To similar effect, see *Acton v. Vernonia School District 47J*, 23 F.3d 1514 (9th Cir. 1994), invalidating a high school's random drug testing under the state constitution.)

While the state constitution was only a secondary consideration in *Derdeyn*, it was the primary focus in *Hill v. NCAA*, 273 Cal. Rptr. 402 (Cal. Ct. App. 1990), *reversed*, 865 P.2d 633 (Cal. 1994), a case in which Stanford University student athletes challenged the university's implementation of the NCAA's required drug-testing program. The constitutional clause at issue was not a search-and-seizure clause as such but rather a right-to-privacy guarantee (Cal. Const. Art. I, § 1). Both the intermediate appellate court and the Supreme Court of California determined that this guarantee covered drug testing, an activity designed to gather and preserve private information about individuals. Further, both courts determined that the privacy clause limited the information-gathering activities of private as well as public entities, since the language revealed that privacy was an "inalienable right" that no one may violate. Although the private entity designated as the defendant in the *Hill* case was an athletic conference (the NCAA) rather than a private university, the courts' reasoning would apply to the latter as well.

In *Hill* the intermediate appellate court's privacy analysis differed from the Fourth Amendment balancing test of *Skinner* because the court required the NCAA "to show a compelling interest before it can invade a fundamental privacy right"— a test that places a heavier burden of justification on the alleged violator than does the Fourth Amendment balancing test. The Supreme Court of California disagreed on this point, holding that the correct approach "requires that privacy interests be specifically identified and carefully compared with competing or countervailing privacy and nonprivacy interests in a 'balancing test'" (865 P.2d at 655). Under this approach, "[i]nvasion of a privacy interest is not a violation of the state constitutional right to privacy if the invasion is justified by a legitimate and important competing interest" (865 P.2d at 655–56), rather than a compelling interest, as the lower court had specified. Using this balancing test, the California Supreme Court concluded that "the NCAA's decision to enforce a ban on the use of drugs by means of a drug testing program is reasonably calculated to further its legitimate interest in maintaining the integrity of intercollegiate athletic competition" and therefore does not violate the California constitution's privacy guarantee.

In addition to its illustration of state privacy concepts, the *Hill* case also demonstrates the precarious position of institutions that are subject to NCAA or conference drug-testing requirements. As the intermediate appellate court indicated, Stanford, the institution that the *Hill* plaintiffs attended, was in a dilemma: "as an NCAA member institution, if it refused to enforce the consent provision, it could be sanctioned, but if it did enforce the program, either by requiring students to sign or withholding them from competition, it could be sued." To help resolve the dilemma, Stanford intervened in the litigation and sought its own declaratory and injunctive relief. These are the same issues and choices that other institutions will continue to face until the various legal issues concerning drug testing have finally been resolved.

In *Bally v. Northeastern University*, 532 N.E.2d 49 (Mass. 1989), a state civil rights law provided the basis for a challenge to a private institution's drug-testing program. The defendant, Northeastern University, required all students participating in intercollegiate athletics to sign an NCAA student athlete statement that includes a drug-testing consent form. The institution's program called for testing of each athlete once a year as well as other random testing throughout the school year. When a member of the cross-country and track teams refused to sign the consent form, the institution declared him ineligible. The student claimed that this action breached his contract with the institution and violated his rights under both the Massachusetts Civil Rights Act and a state right-to-privacy statute. A lower court granted summary judgment for Northeastern on the contract claim and for the student on the civil rights and privacy claims.

The Massachusetts Supreme Court reversed the lower court's judgment for the student. To prevail on the civil rights claim, according to the statute, the student had to prove that the institution had interfered with rights secured by the Constitution or laws of the United States or the Commonwealth and that such interference was by "threats, intimidation, or coercion." Although the court assumed *arguendo* that the drug-testing program interfered with the student's rights to be free from unreasonable searches and seizures and from invasions of reasonable expectations of privacy, it nevertheless denied his claim because he had made no showing of "threats, intimidation, or coercion." Similarly, the court denied the student's claim under the privacy statute because "[t]he majority of our opinions involving a claim of an invasion of privacy concern the public dissemination of information," and the student had made no showing of any public dissemination of the drug-testing results. In addition, because the student was not an employee, state case law precedents regarding employee privacy, on which the student had relied, did not apply.

Since the courts have not spoken definitively, it is not clear what drug-testing programs and procedures will be valid. In the meantime, institutions (and athletic conferences) that wish to engage in drug testing of student athletes may follow these minimum suggestions, which are likely to enhance their program's capacity to survive challenge under the various sources of law listed at the beginning of this section:

1. Articulate *and document* both the strong institutional interests that would be compromised by student athletes' drug use and the institution's basis for believing that such drug use is occurring in one or more of its athletic programs.

2.   Limit drug testing to those athletic programs where drug use is occurring and is interfering with institutional interests.
3.   Develop evenhanded and objective criteria for determining who will be tested and in what circumstances.
4.   Specify the substances whose use is banned and for which athletes will be tested, limiting the named substances to those whose use would compromise important institutional interests.
5.   Develop detailed and specific protocols for testing of individuals and lab analysis of specimens, limiting the monitoring of specimen collection to that which is necessary to ensure the integrity of the collection process, and limiting the lab analyses to those necessary to detect the banned substances (rather than to discover other personal information about the athlete).
6.   Develop procedures for protecting the confidentiality and accuracy of the testing process and the laboratory results.
7.   Embody all the above considerations into a clear written policy that is made available to student athletes before they accept athletic scholarships or join a team.

4.15.6. Tort liability for athletic injuries. Tort law (see Sections 2.3.1 and 2.4.1) poses special problems for athletic programs and departments. Because of the physical nature of athletics and because athletic activities often require travel to other locations, the danger of injury to students and the possibilities for institutional liability are greater than those resulting from other institutional functions. In *Scott v. State,* 158 N.Y.S.2d 617 (N.Y. Ct. Cl. 1956), for instance, a student collided with a flagpole while chasing a fly ball during an intercollegiate baseball game; the student was awarded $12,000 in damages because the school had negligently maintained the playing field in a dangerous condition and the student had not assumed the risk of such danger.

When negligence is alleged against a public institution (as in the case above), the general principles of tort immunity may also apply. In *Lowe v. Texas Tech University,* 530 S.W.2d 337 (Tex. Civ. App. 1975), for instance, a varsity football player with a knee injury had his damages suit dismissed by the intermediate appellate court because the university had sovereign immunity; but on further appeal, the suit was reinstituted because it fell within a specific statutory waiver of immunity (540 S.W.2d 297 (1976)).

Several recent cases have focused on whether a university can be held liable for its failure to prepare adequately for emergency medical situations. In *Kleinknecht v. Gettysburg College,* 989 F.2d 1360 (3d Cir. 1993), parents of a student athlete sued the college for the wrongful death of their son, who had died from a heart attack suffered during a practice session of the intercollegiate lacrosse team. The student had no medical history that would indicate any danger of such an occurrence. No trainers were present when he was stricken, and no plan prescribing steps to take in medical emergencies was in effect. Students and coaches reacted as quickly as they could to reach the nearest phone, over 200 yards away, and call an ambulance. The parents sued the college for negligence (see generally Section 2.3.1.1), alleging that the college owed a duty to its student athletes to have measures in place to provide prompt medical attention in emergencies. They contended that the delay in securing an ambulance, caused by the college's failure to have an emergency plan in effect, resulted in their son's death. The federal district court, applying Pennsylvania law, granted summary judgment for the college, holding that the college owed no duty to the plaintiffs' son in the circumstances of this case and that, even if a duty were owed, the actions of the college's employees were reasonable and did not breach the duty.[56]

The appellate court reversed the district court's judgment and remanded the case for a jury trial, stressing that

> Drew [the athlete] was not engaged in his own private affairs as a student at Gettysburg College. Instead, he was participating in a scheduled athletic practice for an intercollegiate team sponsored by the College under the supervision of College employees. On these facts we believe that [under the law of Pennsylvania] a special relationship existed between the College and Drew that was sufficient to impose a duty of reasonable care on the College [989 F.2d at 1367].

Having determined the existence of a duty of reasonable care, the court then delineated the specific demands that that duty placed on the college in the circumstances of this case. Since it was generally foreseeable that a life-threatening injury could occur during sports activities such as lacrosse, and given the magnitude of such a risk and its consequences, "the College owed a duty to Drew to have measures in place at the lacrosse team's practice . . . to provide prompt treatment in the event that he or any other members of the lacrosse team suffered a life-threatening injury." However, "the determination whether the College has breached this duty at all is a question of fact for the jury."

Even when the institution does or may owe a duty to the student athlete in a particular case, the student athlete will have no cause of action against the institution if its breach of duty was not the cause of the harm suffered. In *Hanson v. Kynast,* 494 N.E.2d 1091 (Ohio 1986), for example, the court avoided the issue of whether the defendant university owed a duty to a student athlete to provide for a proper emergency plan, because the delay in treating the athlete, allegedly caused by the university's negligent failure to have such a plan, caused the athlete no further harm. The athlete had suffered a broken neck in a lacrosse game and was rendered a quadriplegic; the evidence made it clear that, even if medical help had arrived sooner, nothing could have been done to lessen the injuries. In other words, the full extent of these injuries had been determined before any alleged negligence by the university could have come into play.

As the *Kleinknecht* court's reasoning suggests, the scope of the institution's duty to protect student athletes in emergencies and otherwise may depend on a number of factors, including whether the activity is intercollegiate (versus a club team) or an extracurricular activity, whether the particular activity was officially scheduled or sponsored, and perhaps whether the athlete was recruited or not. The institution's duty will also differ if the student athlete is a member of a visiting team rather than the institution's own team. In general, there is no special relationship

---

[56]The district court's opinion also contains an interesting discussion of the application of the state's Good Samaritan law to athletic injuries. See 786 F. Supp. 449, 457 (M.D. Pa. 1992).

such as that in *Kleinknecht* between the institution and a visiting athlete; there is only the relationship arising from the visiting student's status as an invitee of the institution (see generally Section 2.3.1.1). In *Fox v. Board of Supervisors of Louisiana State University and Agricultural and Mechanical College*, 576 So. 2d 978 (La. 1991), for example, a visiting rugby player from St. Olaf's club team was severely injured when he missed a tackle during a tournament held at LSU. The court determined that the injured player had no cause of action against LSU based on the institution's own actions or omissions. The only possible direct liability claim he could have had would have been based on a theory that the playing field onto which he had been invited was unsafe for play, a contention completely unsupported by the evidence.

In addition to the institution's liability for its own negligent acts, there are also issues concerning the institution's possible vicarious liability for the acts of its student athletes or its athletic clubs. In the *Fox* case above, the visiting athlete also claimed that the university was vicariously liable for negligent actions of its rugby club in holding a cocktail party the night before the tournament, in scheduling teams to play more than one game per day (the athlete was injured in his second match of the day), and in failing to ensure that visiting clubs were properly trained and coached. His theory was that these actions had resulted in fatigued athletes playing when they should not have, thus becoming more susceptible to injury. The appellate court held that LSU could not be vicariously liable for the actions of its rugby club. Although LSU provided its rugby team with some offices, finances, and supervision, and a playing field for the tournament, LSU offered such support to its rugby club (and other student clubs) only to enrich students' overall educational experience by providing increased opportunities for personal growth. The university did not recruit students for the club, and it did not control the club's activities. The club therefore was not an agent of the university and could not bind LSU by its actions.

The same conclusion was reached in *Hanson v. Kynast* (cited above), which concerned a university's vicarious liability for a student's actions. During an intercollegiate lacrosse game, Kynast body-checked and taunted a player on the opposing team. When Hanson (another opposing team player) grabbed Kynast, Kynast threw Hanson to the ground, breaking his neck. Hanson sued Kynast and Ashland University, the team for which Kynast was playing when the incident occurred. The court held that Ashland University, which Kynast attended, was not liable for his actions because he received no scholarship, joined the team voluntarily, used his own playing equipment, and was guided but not controlled by the coach. In essence, the court held that Kynast was operating as an individual, voluntarily playing on the team, not as an agent of the university. (See also *Townsend v. State*, 237 Cal. Rptr. 146 (Cal. Ct. App. 1987), in which the court, relying on state statutes, similarly refused to hold a university vicariously liable for a nonscholarship varsity basketball player's assault on another team's player.)

A similar result would also likely pertain when a student is injured in an informal recreational sports activity. In *Swanson v. Wabash College*, 504 N.E. 2d 327 (Ind. Ct. App. 1987), for example, a student injured in a recreational basketball game sued the college for negligence. The court ruled that the college had no legal duty to supervise a recreational activity among adult students, and that the student who had organized the game was neither an agent nor an employee of the college, so *respondeat superior* liability did not attach.

Sec. 4.16. Student Files and Records

4.16.1. The Buckley Amendment. The Family Educational Rights and Privacy Act of 1974 (20 U.S.C. § 1232g), popularly known as the Buckley Amendment or FERPA, has created a substantial role for the federal government with respect to student records. The Act and its implementing regulations, 34 C.F.R. Part 99, apply to all public and private educational agencies or institutions that receive federal funds from the U.S. Department of Education or whose students receive such funds (under the Guaranteed Student Loan program, for example) and pay them to the agency or institution (34 C.F.R. § 99.1).[57] While FERPA does not invalidate common law or state statutory law applicable to student records (see this volume, Section 4.16.2), the regulations are so extensive that they are the predominant legal consideration in dealing with student records.[58]

FERPA and its regulations establish requirements pertaining to (1) students' right of access to their education records (34 C.F.R. §§ 99.10-99.12); (2) students' right to challenge the content of their records (34 C.F.R. §§ 99.20-99.22); (3) disclosure of "personally identifiable" information from these records to personnel of the institution or to outsiders (34 C.F.R. §§ 99.30-99.37); (4) the institution's obligation to notify students of their rights under the Act and regulations (34 C.F.R. §§ 99.6-99.7); and (5) recourse for students and the federal government when an institution may have violated the Act or regulations (34 C.F.R. §§ 99.60-99.67). Recourse includes a formal system for receipt, investigation, and adjudication of complaints by the Family Policy Compliance Office of the Department of Education and by a review board (34 C.F.R. § 99.60).[59] All students enrolled or formerly enrolled in postsecondary institutions have rights under the Act and regulations regardless of whether they are eighteen and regardless of whether they are dependent on their parents (34 C.F.R. § 99.5). (If students are dependents for federal income tax purposes, however, they cannot prevent their parents from seeing their education records (§ 99.3 (1)(a)(8)).)

The records that are protected under FERPA are all "those records that are (1) [d]irectly related to a student; and (2) [m]aintained by an educational agency or institution or by a party acting for the agency or institution" (20 U.S.C. § 1232g(a)(4)(A),

[57]Cases and authorities are collected in Annot., "Validity, Construction, and Application of Family Educational Rights and Privacy Act of 1974 (20 U.S.C.S. § 1232g)." 112 A.L.R. Fed. 1 (1993 and periodic supp.).

[58]The FERPA regulations provide that "[i]f an educational agency or institution determines that it cannot comply with the Act or [regulations] due to a conflict with State or local law, it shall notify the [Family Policy Compliance] Office within 45 days, giving the text and citation of the conflicting law" (34 C.F.R. § 99.61). Where such conflict exists, the federal law will take precedence unless the institution is willing to relinquish federal funding (see generally *Rosado v. Wyman*, 397 U.S. 397, 420-23 (1970)). The federal government would, however, allow a period of negotiation and encourage the institution to seek an official interpretation of the state law compatible with FERPA or an amendment of the state law.

[59]Two federal appellate courts have refused to recognize a private cause of action under the Buckley Amendment that would permit an individual to sue an institution under that law rather than filing a complaint with the U.S. Department of Education (see *Girardier v. Webster College*, 563 F.2d 1267 (8th Cir. 1977), and *Smith v. Duquesne University*, 612 F. Supp. 72 (W.D. Pa. 1985), *affirmed without opin.*, 787 F.2d 583 (3d Cir. 1985); see also K. Cudlipp, "The Buckley Amendment Two Years Later," a memo printed in 122 *Congressional Record* 16447 (94th Cong., 2d Sess., 1976)).

34 C.F.R. §99.3). This section of the regulations contains five exceptions to this definition, which exclude from coverage certain personal and private records of institutional personnel,[60] certain campus law enforcement records, certain student employment records, certain records regarding health care, and "records . . . [such as alumni records] that only contain information about an individual after he or she is no longer a student at [the] . . . institution." There is also a partial exception for "directory information," which is exempt from the regulations' nondisclosure requirements under certain conditions (34 C.F.R. §99.37).

The key to success in dealing with FERPA is a thorough understanding of the implementing regulations. Administrators should keep copies of the regulations at their fingertips and should not rely on secondary sources to resolve particular problems. Counsel should review the institution's record-keeping policies and practices, and every substantial change in them, to ensure compliance with the regulations. Administrators and counsel should work together to maintain appropriate legal forms to use in implementing the regulations, such as forms for a student's waiver of his or her rights under the Act or regulations, forms for securing a student's consent to release personally identifiable information from his or her records (34 C.F.R. §99.30), and forms for notifying parties to whom information is disclosed of the limits on the use of that information (34 C.F.R. §99.34). Questions concerning the interpretation or application of the regulations may be directed to the Family Policy Compliance Office at the U.S. Department of Education.

Since FERPA has been in effect, questions about who has access, and to what types of records, have proliferated. For example, students at Harvard University who wished to examine the comments that admissions staff had made about them on "summary sheets" filed a complaint with the Department of Education when Harvard denied their request. Harvard had told the students that the summary sheets were kept in a file separate from the student's academic record, that they included direct quotes from the confidential letters of recommendation, and that they had no further significance once a student was admitted. Therefore, Harvard believed that these documents were not accessible under FERPA.

In an advisory letter, reprinted in 22 *Coll. Law Dig.* 299 (July 16, 1992), the Department of Education ruled that the students had a right to examine the summary sheets. Applying FERPA's definition of an "education record" (documents containing information related to a student which are maintained by an educational agency—20 U.S.C. §1232g(a)(4)(A)), the Department of Education determined that the summary sheets met that definition. However, the department ruled that the university could redact from the documents any excerpts specifically derived from confidential letters of recommendation if the student had waived his or her right of access to these letters.

Questions also have been raised about the status of campus law enforcement records under FERPA. Originally, the Department of Education had interpreted the law to mean that any record released by the campus law enforcement unit to other campus officials became part of the student's "education record" and could not be

---

[60]In *Klein Independent School District v. Mattox*, 830 F.2d 576 (5th Cir. 1987), a school district had been asked, under the Texas open-records law, to produce the college transcript of one of its teachers. The court ruled that, since the teacher was an employee, not a student, FERPA did not protect her transcript from disclosure, which was required under the Texas law.

shared, even with other law enforcement agencies, without the student's permission. A federal trial judge ruled, however, that the department's interpretation of FERPA regarding arrest records violated certain constitutional provisions. In *Student Law Press Center v. Alexander,* 778 F. Supp. 1227 (D.D.C. 1991), student journalists challenged a FERPA provision authorizing the withdrawal of federal funds from a college or university that discloses to the public personally identifiable information contained in campus police reports. The plaintiffs sought a preliminary injunction against the enforcement of that provision, claiming that the restriction violated their First Amendment right to receive information and their implied Fifth Amendment right to equal protection. The court ruled that the plaintiffs had demonstrated the likelihood of success on their claim. It therefore granted the preliminary injunction, noting that there was no legitimate privacy interest in arrest records and thus no constitutional basis for upholding that provision of FERPA.

Similar cases have also been brought under state open-records laws (see Section 6.5.3), with similar results. In *Bauer v. Kincaid,* 759 F. Supp. 575 (W.D. Mo. 1991), the editor of the student newspaper at Southwest Missouri State University, suing under the state's sunshine law, charged that the university's refusal to provide access to campus law enforcement records was unlawful. A federal trial court ruled that FERPA did not protect these records from disclosure and that, alternatively, if it did protect law enforcement records from disclosure, FERPA violated the Constitution's Equal Protection Clause by creating a classification (student vs. nonstudent) that had no rational basis. But another federal trial court rejected the request of a nonstudent to gain access to campus law enforcement records in *Norwood v. Slammons,* 788 F. Supp. 1020 (W.D. Ark. 1991), ruling that the general public had no First Amendment right to a college's disciplinary or law enforcement records.

For discussion of these challenges to FERPA, see E. J. Ogg, "Student Records Privacy and Campus Crime Reporting: The Buckley Amendment After *Bauer,*" 13 *Communications and the Law* 39 (1991).

Following this flurry of judicial activity, Congress passed the Higher Education Amendments of 1992 (Pub. L. No. 102-325, codified at 20 U.S.C. § 1232g(a)(4)(B)(ii)), which amended FERPA to exclude from the definition of "education records" records that are maintained by a law enforcement unit of an educational agency or institution for the purpose of law enforcement. This change enables institutions to disclose information about campus crime contained in law enforcement unit records to parents, the media, other students, and other law enforcement agencies. The Department of Education has issued proposed revised regulations to implement the amendments to FERPA at 34 C.F.R. § 99.8 (58 Fed. Reg. 65298 (Dec. 14, 1993)).

The Education Department has also revised the FERPA regulations to clarify the definition of a disciplinary record and to specify the conditions for its release. Disciplinary records are considered "education records" and thus subject to FERPA's limitations on disclosure. However, the revised regulations permit the institution to disclose to the alleged victim of a violent crime the results of a disciplinary proceeding involving the student accused of the crime (34 C.F.R. § 99.3). Student press groups have sought access to disciplinary records, in some cases successfully, under state open-records laws (see the discussion of *The Red and the Black* case, Section 6.5.1).

Although federal courts have consistently refused to find a private right of action under FERPA (see this section, note 59), one federal district court permitted students to base a constitutional claim on the deprivation of their rights under FERPA. In *Krebs v. Rutgers, The State University of New Jersey,* 797 F. Supp. 1246

(D.N.J. 1992), students filed claims under Section 1983 (Section 2.3.3, this volume) and the federal Privacy Act (discussed in Section 4.16.3), challenging Rutgers' use of their Social Security numbers as identification numbers on class rosters, identification cards, meal tickets, and other university documents. Although the judge granted summary judgment for Rutgers on the Privacy Act claim (noting that the university was not subject to that law because it is not a state agency), he issued a preliminary injunction requiring the university to halt the practice of some faculty members who took attendance by circulating rosters containing students' names and their Social Security numbers. The university and the students settled the case, with Rutgers agreeing to remove the numbers from meal cards, to stop mailing letters to students with the numbers on the outside of the envelope, to permit students to obtain substitute identification numbers, and to hold public hearings on student privacy twice a year for the next two years.

The judge acknowledged that the students had no private right of action under FERPA. However, he stated that limiting the students to the administrative complaint procedure was unsatisfactory because he did not believe that the Education Department would withhold federal funds from the university for the relatively minor violation of disclosing Social Security numbers. Therefore, he ruled, the students had rights under federal law that were being violated. Since Section 1983 permitted individuals to claim violations of their federally guaranteed rights, he ruled that the students could make out a Section 1983 claim based on the underlying federal law (FERPA).

4.16.2. State law. In a majority of states, courts now recognize a common law tort of invasion of privacy, which, in some circumstances, protects individuals against the public disclosure of damaging private information about them and against intrusions into their private affairs. A few states have similarly protected privacy with a statute or constitutional provision. Although this body of law has seldom been applied to educational record-keeping practices, the basic legal principles appear applicable to record-keeping abuses by postsecondary institutions. This body of right-to-privacy law could protect students against abusive collection and retention practices where clearly intrusive methods are used to collect information concerning private affairs. In *White v. Davis,* 533 P.2d 222 (Cal. 1975) (see Section 5.5), for example, the court held that undercover police surveillance of university classes and meetings violated the right to privacy because "no professor or student can be confident that whatever he may express in class will not find its way into a police file." Similarly, right-to-privacy law could protect students against abusive dissemination practices that result in unwarranted public disclosure of damaging personal information.

In addition to this developing right-to-privacy law, many states also have statutes or administrative regulations dealing specifically with record keeping. These include subject-access laws, open-record or public-record laws, and confidentiality laws. Such laws usually apply only to state agencies, and a state's postsecondary institutions may or may not be considered state agencies subject to record-keeping laws (see Section 6.5.2). Occasionally a state statute deals specifically with postsecondary education records. A Massachusetts statute, for instance, makes it an "unfair educational practice" for any "educational institution," including public and private postsecondary institutions, to request information or make or keep records concerning certain arrests or misdemeanor convictions of students or applicants (Mass. Gen. Laws Ann. ch. 151C, § 2(f)).

Since state laws on privacy and records vary greatly from state to state, administrators should check with counsel to determine the law in their particular state. Since state record requirements may occasionally conflict with FERPA regulations, counsel must determine whether any such conflict exists (see this volume, Section 4.16.1, n.58). Regarding right-to-privacy concepts, an institution in compliance with FERPA regulations is not likely to be violating any state right to privacy. The two exceptions concern information collection practices and the particular types of records kept, which are not treated in the FERPA regulations (except that FERPA (§ 99.32) requires that a "record of disclosures" of information be kept). In these situations, developing state laws may carve out requirements, as in the *White* case and the Massachusetts statute above, independent of and supplementary to FERPA.

4.16.3. The federal Privacy Act. The Privacy Act of 1974 (88 Stat. 1896, partly codified in 5 U.S.C. § 552a) applies directly to federal government agencies and, with two exceptions discussed below, does not restrict postsecondary education institutions. The Act accords all persons—including students, faculty members, and staff members—certain rights enforceable against the federal government regarding information about them in federal agency files, whether collected from a postsecondary institution or from any other source. The Act grants the right to inspect, copy, and correct such information and limits its dissemination by the agency. Regulations implementing the Privacy Act are found at 34 C.F.R. Part 5b.

Section 7 of the Act prohibits federal, state, and local government agencies from requiring persons to disclose their Social Security numbers. This provision applies to public but not to private postsecondary institutions (see the *Krebs* case in Section 4.16.1, which also discusses when an institution is considered a state agency for purposes of this provision) and thus prevents public institutions from requiring either students or employees to disclose their Social Security numbers. The two exceptions to this nondisclosure requirement permit an institution to require disclosure (1) where it is required by some other federal statute and (2) where the institution maintains "a system of records in existence and operating before January 1, 1975, if such disclosure was required under statute or regulation adopted prior to such date to verify the identity of an individual" (88 Stat. 1896 at 1903).

The second provision of the Act potentially relevant to some postsecondary institutions is Section 3(m) (5 U.S.C. § 552a(m)), which applies the Act's requirements to government contractors who operate record-keeping systems on behalf of a federal agency pursuant to the contract.

Sec. 4.17. Campus Security

Crime is an unfortunate fact of life on many college campuses. Consequently, campus security and the role of security officers have become high-visibility issues. Although contemporary jurisprudence rejects the concept that colleges are responsible for the safety of students (see Section 2.3.1), institutions of higher education have, in some cases, been found liable for injury to students when the injury was foreseeable or when there was a history of criminal activity on campus.[61]

---

[61]Cases and authorities are collected in Annot., "Liability of University, College, or Other School for Failure to Protect Student from Crime," 1 A.L.R.4th 1099 (1980 and periodic supp.).

4.17.1. Security officers. The powers and responsibilities of campus security officers should be carefully delineated. Administrators must determine whether such officers should be permitted to carry weapons and under what conditions. They must determine the security officers' authority to investigate crime on campus or to investigate violations of student codes of conduct. Record-keeping practices also must be devised.[62] The relationship that security officers will have with local and state police must be cooperatively worked out with local and state police forces. Because campus security officers may play dual roles, partly enforcing public criminal laws and partly enforcing the institution's codes of conduct, administrators should carefully delineate the officers' relative responsibilities in each role.

Administrators must also determine whether their campus security guards have, or should have, arrest powers under state or local law. For public institutions state law may grant full arrest powers to certain campus security guards. In *People v. Wesley,* 365 N.Y.S.2d 593 (City Ct., Buffalo, 1975), for instance, the court determined that security officers at a particular state campus were "peace officers" under the terms of Section 355(2)(m) of the New York Education Law. For public institutions not subject to such statutes, and for private institutions, deputization under city or county law or the use of "citizen's arrest" powers may be options (see *Hall v. Virginia,* 389 S.E.2d 921 (Va. Ct. App. 1990)).

Although security guards may have authority to make arrests off campus as well as on campus, their off-campus authority may be more limited. In *State v. Lyon,* 584 P.2d 844 (Utah 1978), for instance, the Supreme Court of Utah vacated the conviction of a motorcyclist (Lyon) who had been arrested by a college security officer four blocks from the campus. The state argued that, under Utah law, the officer had "all of the powers possessed by a policeman" and was "required" to make the arrest to protect the interests of the college. The court rejected this argument, noting that the officer's "suspicion" that Lyon had committed vandalism or theft did not justify the off-campus arrest. Rather, the court stated, for the arrest to be valid, a "present danger" to the college, its students, or its employees must have been evident. (See D. Berman, "Law and Order on Campus: An Analysis of the Role and Problems of the Security Police," 49 *J. Urban Law* 513 (1971–72).)

Conversely, in *Commonwealth of Pennsylvania v. Mitchell,* 554 A.2d 542 (Pa. Super. Ct. 1989), a state court defined the territorial jurisdiction within which campus police in that state may exercise their authority. The defendants, suspected of attempted theft, had been arrested by University of Pennsylvania campus police on the sidewalk of a commercial district on the university's property. The defendants argued that Pennsylvania law did not authorize the campus police to arrest them on commercial property owned and held by the university for investment purposes. Under the applicable statute (71 Pa. Stat. § 646), security and campus police may exercise their powers and perform their duties only on the "premises" and "grounds and buildings" of state colleges and universities. Relying on the statute's legislative history and purpose, the court concluded that these statutory terms include not only

---

[62]For a general discussion of the legal restrictions on record keeping, see Sections 4.16.1 and 4.16.2. The Federal Educational Rights and Privacy Act, discussed in Section 4.16.1, has a specific provision on law enforcement records (20 U.S.C. § 1232g(a)(4)(B)(ii)). Regulations implementing this provision are in 34 C.F.R. §§ 99.3 (definitions of "disciplinary action or proceeding" and "education records") and 99.8.

academic and residential areas but also commercial property used for investment purposes. It reasoned that to limit "premises" to academic and residential areas would ignore the layout and everyday operations of colleges and universities, because business establishments owned by institutions are typically frequented by students. Thus, the court upheld the validity of the arrest.

State laws vary considerably regarding the off-campus authority of campus police officers, and the particular facts of each incident may also have an effect on the court's determination. For additional cases addressing this issue, see *People v. Doherty*, 487 N.E.2d 1222 (Ill. App. Ct. 1986); *State v. Harris*, 609 A.2d 945 (R.I. 1992); and *Baris v. State*, 846 S.W.2d 764 (Mo. Ct. App. 1993).

Police work is subject to a variety of constitutional restraints concerning such matters as investigations, arrests, and searches and seizures of persons or private property. Security officers for public institutions are subject to all these restraints. In private institutions security officers who are operating in conjunction with local or state police forces (see Section 4.14.2) or who have arrest powers (see *Zelinski* case below) may also be subject to constitutional restraints under the state action doctrine (see Section 1.5.2). In devising the responsibilities of such officers, therefore, administrators should be sensitive to the constitutional requirements regarding police work.

In *People v. Zelinski*, 594 P.2d 1000 (Cal. 1979), the California Supreme Court issued a major opinion concerning the applicability of constitutional restraints to private security personnel. Although it concerned security guards at a department store rather than a college campus, and applied the state constitution rather than the United States Constitution, the case nevertheless speaks meaningfully to the question of when a private college's security officers would be subject to state or federal constitutional restraints on their activities. In reversing the conviction of a person who had been arrested and searched by private store detectives, the *Zelinski* court reasoned:

> Here the store security forces did not act in a purely private capacity but rather were fulfilling a public function in bringing violators of the law to public justice. For reasons hereinafter expressed, we conclude that under such circumstances—that is, *when private security personnel conduct an illegal search or seizure while engaged in a statutorily authorized citizen's arrest and detention of a person in aid of law enforcement authorities*—the constitutional proscriptions of Article I, Section 13 [whose words parallel the Fourth Amendment to the U.S. Constitution] are applicable. . . .
>
> The store employees arrested defendant pursuant to the authorization contained in Penal Code Section 837 [citizen's arrest], and the search which yielded the narcotics was conducted incident to that arrest. Their acts, engaged in pursuant to the statute, were not those of a private citizen acting in a purely private capacity. Although the search exceeded lawful authority, it was nevertheless an integral part of the exercise of sovereignty allowed by the state to private citizens. In arresting the offender, the store employees were utilizing the coercive power of the state to further a state interest. Had the security guards sought only the vindication of the merchant's private interests, they would have simply exercised self-help and demanded the return of the stolen merchandise. Upon satisfaction of the merchant's interests, the offender would have been released. By holding defendant for criminal process and searching her, they went beyond their employer's private interests.
>
> Persons so acting should be subject to the constitutional proscriptions

that secure an individual's right to privacy, for their actions are taken pursuant to statutory authority to promote a state interest in bringing offenders to public accounting. Unrestrained, such action would subvert state authority in defiance of its established limits. It would destroy the protection those carefully defined limits were intended to afford to everyone, the guilty and innocent alike. It would afford de facto authorizations for searches and seizures incident to arrests or detentions made by private individuals that even peace officers are not authorized to make. Accordingly, we hold that in any case *where private security personnel assert the power of the state to make an arrest or to detain another person for transfer to custody of the state,* the state involvement is sufficient for the court to enforce the proper exercise of that power (cf. *People v. Haydel* [524 P.2d 866 (Cal. 1974)] by excluding the fruits of illegal abuse thereof [594 P.2d at 1006; emphasis added].

Administrators should also be sensitive to the tort law principles applicable to security work (see generally Sections 2.3.1, 2.4.1, and 2.5). Like athletic activities (Section 4.15.6), campus security actions are likely to expose the institution to a substantial risk of tort liability. Using physical force or weapons, detaining or arresting persons, entering or searching private property can all occasion tort liability if they are undertaken without justification or accomplished carelessly. *Jones v. Wittenberg University,* 534 F.2d 1203 (6th Cir. 1976), for example, dealt with a university security guard who had fired a warning shot at a fleeing student. The shot pierced the student's chest and killed him. The guard and the university were held liable for the student's death, even though the guard did not intend to hit the student and may have had justification for firing a shot to frighten a fleeing suspect. The appellate court reasoned that the shooting could nevertheless constitute negligence "if it was done so carelessly as to result in foreseeable injury."

Institutions may also incur liability for malicious prosecution if an arrest or search is made in bad faith. In *Wright v. Schreffler,* 618 A.2d 412 (Pa. Super. Ct. 1992), a former college student's conviction for possession and delivery of marijuana was reversed because the court found that the defendant had been entrapped by campus police at Pennsylvania State University. The former student then sued the arresting officer for malicious prosecution, stating that the officer had no probable cause to arrest him, since the arrest was a result of the entrapment. The court agreed, and denied the officer's motion for dismissal.

Campus police may also be held liable under tort law for their treatment of individuals suspected of criminal activity. In *Hickey v. Zezulka,* 443 N.W.2d 180 (Mich. Ct. App. 1989), a university public-safety officer had placed a Michigan State University student in a holding cell at the university's department of public safety. The officer had stopped the student for erratic driving, and a breathalyzer test had shown that the student had blood alcohol levels of between 0.15 and 0.16 percent. While in the holding cell, the student hanged himself by a noose made from his belt and socks that he connected to a bracket on a heating unit attached to the ceiling of the cell.

The student's estate brought separate negligence actions against the officer and the university, and both were found liable after trial. Although an intermediate appellate court upheld the trial verdict against both the university and the officer, the state's supreme court, in *Hickey v. Zezulka,* 487 N.W.2d 106 (Mich. 1992), reversed the finding of liability against the university, applying Michigan's sovereign immunity law. The court upheld the negligence verdict against the officer, however, noting that the officer had violated university policies about removing harmful objects from persons before placing them in holding cells and about checking on them periodically. The court characterized the officer's actions as "ministerial" rather than discretionary, which, under Michigan law, eliminated her governmental immunity defense.

In light of *Hickey*, universities with local holding cells should make sure that campus police regulations are clear about the proper procedures to be used, particularly in handling individuals who are impaired by alcohol and drugs, and should ensure that the procedures are followed to reduce both the potential for harm to individuals and liability to the institution or its employees.

4.17.2. Protection against violent crime on campus.

The extent of the institution's obligation to protect students from crime on campus—particularly, violent crimes committed by outsiders from the surrounding community—has become a sensitive issue for higher education. The number of such crimes reported, especially sexual attacks on women, has increased steadily over the years. As a result, postsecondary institutions now face substantial tactical and legal problems concerning the planning and operation of their campus security systems, as well as a federal law requiring them to report campus crime statistics.

In an early case, *P. D. v. Catholic University*, Civ. No. 75-2198 (D.D.C. 1976), a jury found the defendant liable for injuries incurred by a student who was raped in the locker room of the campus gym. While the case supports the general proposition that institutions have some legal duty to protect their students against outside criminal assailants, the court did not issue any opinion explaining the source or extent of this duty. Since then, however, a number of other courts have provided answers to these questions.

The court's response may depend, in part, on where the attack took place and whether the assailant was a student or an intruder. When students have encountered violence in residence halls from intruders, the courts have found a duty to protect the students similar to that of a landlord. For example, in *Mullins v. Pine Manor College*, 449 N.E.2d 331 (Mass. 1983), the court approved several legal theories for establishing institutional liability in residence hall security cases. The student in *Mullins* had been abducted from her dormitory room and raped on the campus of Pine Manor College, a women's college located in a suburban area. Although the college was located in a low-crime area and there was relatively little crime on campus, the court nevertheless held the college liable.

Developing its first theory, the court determined that residential colleges have a general legal duty to exercise due care in providing campus security:

> We think it can be said with confidence that colleges of ordinary prudence customarily exercise care to protect the well-being of their resident students, including seeking to protect them against the criminal acts of third parties. An expert witness hired by the defendant testified that he had visited eighteen area colleges, and, not surprisingly, all took steps to provide an adequate level of security on their campus. He testified also that standards had been established for determining what precautions should be taken. Thus, the college community itself has recognized its obligation to protect resident students from the criminal

acts of third parties. This recognition indicates that the imposition of a duty of care is firmly embedded in a community consensus.

This consensus stems from the nature of the situation. The concentration of young people, especially young women, on a college campus, creates favorable opportunities for criminal behavior. The threat of criminal acts of third parties to resident students is self-evident, and the college is the party which is in the position to take those steps which are necessary to ensure the safety of its students. No student has the ability to design and implement a security system, hire and supervise security guards, provide security at the entrance of dormitories, install proper locks, and establish a system of announcement for authorized visitors. Resident students typically live in a particular room for a mere nine months and, as a consequence, lack the incentive and capacity to take corrective measures. College regulations may also bar the installation of additional locks or chains. Some students may not have been exposed previously to living in a residence hall or in a metropolitan area and may not be fully conscious of the dangers that are present. Thus, the college must take the responsibility on itself if anything is to be done at all [449 N.E.2d at 335].

Developing its second theory, the court determined "that a duty voluntarily assumed must be performed with due care." Quoting from Section 323 of the *Restatement (Second) of Torts*, a scholarly work of the American Law Institute, the court held that when a college has taken responsibility for security, it is "subject to liability . . . for physical harm resulting from [the] failure to exercise reasonable care to perform [the] undertaking." An institution may be held liable under this theory, however, only if the plaintiff can establish that its "failure to exercise due care increased the risk of harm, or . . . the harm is suffered because of the student's reliance on the undertaking."

Analyzing the facts of the case under these two broad theories, the appellate court affirmed the trial court's judgment in favor of the student. The facts relevant to establishing the college's liability included the ease of scaling or opening the gates that led to the dormitories, the small number of security guards on night shift, the lack of a system for supervising the guards' performance of their duties, and the lack of dead bolts or chains for dormitory room doors.

Courts have ruled in two cases that universities provided inadequate residence hall security and that lax security was the proximate cause of a rape in one case and a death in a second. In *Miller v. State*, 478 N.Y.S.2d 829 (N.Y. App. Div. 1984), a student was abducted from the laundry room of a residence hall and taken through two unlocked doors to another residence hall where she was raped. The court noted that the university was on notice that nonresidents frequented the residence hall, and it criticized the university for failing to take "the rather minimal security measure of keeping the dormitory doors locked when it had notice of the likelihood of criminal intrusions" (478 N.Y.S.2d at 833). "Notice" consisted of knowledge by university agents that nonresidents had been loitering in the lounge of the residence hall, and the occurrence of numerous robberies, burglaries, criminal trespass, and a rape. The court applied traditional landlord-tenant law and increased the trial court's damage award of $25,000 to $400,000.

In the second case, *Nieswand v. Cornell University*, 692 F. Supp. 1464 (N.D.N.Y. 1988), a federal trial court refused to grant summary judgment for Cornell University when it denied that its residence hall security was inadequate and thus the proximate cause of a student's death. A rejected suitor (not a student) had entered the residence hall without detection and shot the student and her roommate. The roommate's parents filed both tort and contract claims (see Sections 2.3.1 and 2.3.2) against the university. The court, citing *Miller*, ruled that whether or not the attack was foreseeable was a question of material fact, which would have to be determined by a jury. Furthermore, the representations made by Cornell in written documents, such as residence hall security policies and brochures, regarding the locking of doors and the presence of security personnel could have constituted an implied contract to provide appropriate security. Whether a contract existed and, if so, whether it was breached was again a matter for the jury.

In another case involving Cornell, the university was found not liable for an assault in a residence hall by an intruder. The intruder had scaled a two-story exterior metal grate and then kicked open the victim's door, which had been locked and dead-bolted. In *Vangeli v. Schneider*, 598 N.Y.S.2d 837 (N.Y. App. Div. 1993), the court ruled that Cornell had met its duty to provide "minimal security" as a landlord.

Although colleges and universities have a duty to provide security for students living in residence halls, courts have distinguished between their duty as a landlord and the more general duty to provide security on campus. For example, in *Nola M. v. University of Southern California*, 20 Cal. Rptr. 2d 97 (Cal. Ct. App. 1993), the court refused to find the university liable for a sexual assault on campus. Although there was a history of violent crimes on the campus, the court did not believe that additional security measures would have prevented the injury to the plaintiff. The university's duty as a landowner does not extend, said the court, to ensuring absolute safety against random acts of violence. This result is the majority rule, since most cases involving colleges and universities charged with liability when a student is injured by the violent act of a stranger have resulted in findings of no liability for the college (see, for example, *Relyea v. State of Florida*, 385 So. 2d 1378 (Fla. Dist. Ct. App. 1980); for a contrary result, see *Peterson v. San Francisco Community College District*, 205 Cal. Rptr. 842 (Cal. 1984), which was based on the theory that the premises were unsafe and which is discussed below).

Campus security issues also arise when the assailant is a fellow student. Again, in most instances the college is absolved of liability unless the violent act was clearly foreseeable. Although courts have continued to reject the claim that colleges must ensure the safety of their students, a few courts have applied the common law duty imposed on landlords to protect their invitees against foreseeable harm. For example, in *Nero v. Kansas State University*, 861 P.2d 768 (Kan. 1993), the Supreme Court of Kansas ruled that the university might be found negligent for permitting a student who had earlier been found guilty of a sexual assault on campus to live in a coeducational residence hall, where he sexually assaulted the plaintiff, a fellow student. The court reversed a summary judgment for the university, declaring that a jury would have to determine whether the attack was foreseeable and, if so, whether the university had breached a duty to the plaintiff. The court said:

> We hold [that] the university-student relationship does not in and of itself impose a duty upon universities to protect students from the actions of fellow students or third parties. The *in loco parentis* doctrine is outmoded and inconsistent with the reality of contemporary college life.

> There are, however, other theories under which a university might be held

liable. . . . [A] university has a duty of reasonable care to protect a student against certain dangers, including criminal actions against a student by another student or a third party if the criminal act is reasonably foreseeable and within the university's control [861 P.2d at 778, 780].

In most cases where the assailants were students, however, the courts have found for the college. In *Rabel v. Illinois Wesleyan University*, 514 N.E.2d 552 (Ill. App. Ct. 1987), the court ruled that the university had no duty to protect a student against a "prank" by fellow students that involved her abduction from a residence hall, despite the fact that the assailant had violated the college's policy against underage drinking. A similar result was reached in *Tanja H. v. Regents of the University of California*, 278 Cal. Rptr. 918 (Cal. Ct. App. 1991); the court stated that the university had no duty to supervise student parties in residence halls or to prevent underage consumption of alcohol. Even in *Eiseman v. State*, 518 N.Y.S.2d 608 (N.Y. 1987), the highest court of New York State refused to find that the university had a legal duty to screen applicants who were ex-convicts for violent tendencies before admitting them. For analysis of this case, see D. M. Kobasic, E. R. Smith, & L. S. Barmore Zucker, "*Eiseman v. State of New York:* The Duty of a College to Protect Its Students from Harm by Other Students Admitted Under Special Programs," 14 *J. Coll. & Univ. Law* 591 (1988).

Although colleges typically prevail in situations where plaintiffs allege that security was lax and thus directly linked to their injuries, liability may attach if an agent of the college has knowledge of the particular threat of harm to the victim and does not act with appropriate care. In *Jesik v. Maricopa County Community College District*, 611 P.2d 547 (Ariz. 1980), a student, during registration at the college, reported to a security guard employed by the college that, following an argument, another individual had threatened to kill him. The security guard took no steps to protect the student. About an hour after the report, the assailant returned to campus carrying a briefcase. The student pointed out the assailant to the same security guard, and the guard assured him that he would be protected. The guard then questioned the assailant, turned to walk away, and the assailant shot and killed the student.

The plaintiff, the father of the murdered student, sued the president and the individual members of the governing board of the Community College District, the executive dean and dean of students at Phoenix College, the security guard (Hilton), and the Community College District. The trial court summarily dismissed the case against all defendants except the security guard. The plaintiff appealed this dismissal to the Arizona Supreme Court, which first considered the potential liability of the officials and administrators. The plaintiff argued that "[the individual] defendants controlled an inadequate and incompetent security force [and thus should be] liable for any breach of duty by that security force." To establish the "duty" that had been breached, the plaintiff relied on a series of Arizona statutes that required the Community College District's governing board, where necessary, to appoint security officers (Ariz. Rev. Stat. Ann. § 15-679(A)(3) and (9)); "to adopt rules and regulations for the maintenance of public order" (§ 13-1093); and to prevent "trespass upon the property of educational institutions [or] interference with its lawful use" (§ 13-1982). The court rejected this argument, finding that the statutes in question did not establish any specific standard of care but "only set forth a general duty to provide security to members of the public on school property."

Having discovered no specific legal duty chargeable to the individual defendants (excluding the security officer, whose potential liability the trial court had not rejected), the Arizona court next considered the liability of the Community College District itself. Rejecting the plaintiff's request to adopt two liability principles from the *Restatement (Second) of Torts*,[63] the court found this principle controlling in Arizona:

> A public school district in Arizona is liable for negligence when it fails to exercise ordinary care under the circumstances. [Arizona cases have] established that students are invitees and that schools have a duty to make the premises reasonably safe for their use. If a dangerous condition exists, the invitee must show that the employees of the school knew of or created the condition at issue [611 P.2d at 550].

The court then determined that the *respondeat superior* doctrine applies to governmental defendants under Arizona law, so that the Community College District could be held liable for the negligence of its employees. Therefore, if the plaintiff could show at trial that the district's security guard had breached the duty set out above, while acting within the scope of employment, the district would be liable (along with the employee) for the death of the plaintiff's son.

The *Jesik* court also discussed an Arizona statute (Ariz. Rev. Stat. Ann. § 15-442(A)(16)) that imposes a standard of care on public school districts and community college districts (see 611 P.2d at 550 (original opinion) and 551 (supplemental opinion)). The court did not base its decision on this statute, since the statute was not yet in effect at the time the crime was committed. But the court's discussions provide a useful illustration of how state statutes may affect liability questions about campus security. In a later case, *Peterson v. San Francisco Community College District*, 205 Cal. Rptr. 842 (Cal. 1984), the court did rely on a statutory provision to impose liability on the defendant. The plaintiff was a student who had been assaulted while leaving the campus parking lot. Her assailant had concealed himself behind "unreasonably thick and untrimmed foliage and trees." Several other assaults had occurred at the same location and in the same manner. Community college officials had known of these assaults but did not publicize them. The court held that the plaintiff could recover damages under Section 835 of the California Tort Claims Act (Cal. Govt. Code § 810 et seq.), which provides that "a public entity is liable for injury caused by a dangerous condition of its property" if the dangerous condition was caused by a public employee acting in the scope of his employment or if the entity "had actual or constructive notice of the dangerous condition" and failed to correct it. The court concluded that the failure to trim the foliage or to warn students of the earlier assaults constituted the creation of such a dangerous condition.

The cases in this section illustrate a variety of campus security problems and a variety of legal theories for analyzing them. Each court's choice of theories depended on the common and statutory law of the particular jurisdiction and the specific

---

[63]Section 318 of the *Restatement* deals with the duty of a possessor of land to control the conduct of persons permitted to use the land. Section 344 deals with the duty of a possessor of land held open to the public for business purposes to protect members of the public from physical harm caused by third persons.

factual setting of the case. The theories used in *Nero,* where the security problem occurred in campus housing and the institution's role was comparable to a landlord's, differ from the theories used in *Jesik* and *Relyea,* where the security problems occurred elsewhere and the student was considered the institution's "invitee." Similarly, the first theory used in *Mullins,* establishing a standard of care specifically for postsecondary institutions, differs from theories in the other cases, which borrow and apply standards of care for landlords or landowners generally. Despite the differences, however, a common denominator can be extracted from these cases that can serve as a guideline for postsecondary administrators: When an institution has foreseen or ought to have foreseen that criminal activity will likely occur on campus, it must take reasonable, appropriate steps to safeguard its students and other persons whom it has expressly or implicitly invited onto its premises. In determining whether this duty has been met in a specific case, courts will consider the foreseeability of violent criminal activity on the particular campus and the reasonableness and appropriateness of the institution's response to that particular threat.

4.17.3. Federal statutes and campus security. Following what appears to be an increase in violent crime on campus, the legislatures of several states and the U.S. Congress passed laws requiring colleges and universities to provide information on the numbers and types of crimes on and near campus. The federal legislation, known as the "Crime Awareness and Campus Security Act" (Title II of Pub. L. No. 101-542 (1990)), amends the Higher Education Act of 1965 (this volume, Section 4.3.2) at 20 U.S.C. § 1092. The Campus Security Act, in turn, was amended by the Higher Education Amendments of 1992 (Pub. L. No. 102-325) and imposes requirements on colleges and universities for preventing, reporting, and investigating sex offenses that occur on campus.

The Campus Security Act, as amended by the Higher Education Amendments of 1992, requires colleges to report, on an annual basis,

> statistics concerning the occurrence on campus, during the most recent calendar year, and during the 2 preceding calendar years for which data are available, of the following criminal offenses reported to campus security authorities or local police agencies—
>
> (i) murder;
> (ii) sex offenses, forcible or nonforcible;
> (iii) robbery;
> (iv) aggravated assault;
> (v) burglary; and
> (vi) motor vehicle theft.

The law requires that colleges report the number of arrests for liquor law violations, drug abuse violations, and weapons possessions as well. The law also requires colleges to develop and distribute to students, prospective students and their parents, and the secretary of education,

> (1) a statement of policy regarding—
> (i) such institution's campus sexual assault programs, which shall be aimed at prevention of sex offenses; and
> (ii) the procedures followed once a sex offense has occurred.

The law also requires colleges to include in their policy (1) educational programs to promote the awareness of rape and acquaintance rape, (2) sanctions that will follow a disciplinary board's determination that a sexual offense has occurred, (3) procedures students should follow if a sex offense occurs, and (4) procedures for on-campus disciplinary action in cases of alleged sexual assault.

The Campus Security Act also requires colleges to provide information on their policies regarding the reporting of other criminal actions and regarding campus security and campus law enforcement. They must also provide a description of the type and frequency of programs designed to inform students and employees about campus security.

In one of its most controversial provisions, the law defines "campus" as

(i) any building or property owned or controlled by the institution of higher education within the same reasonably contiguous geographic area and used by the institution in direct support of, or related to its educational purposes; or

(ii) any building or property owned or controlled by student organizations recognized by the institution.

The second part of the definition would, arguably, make fraternity and sorority houses part of the "campus," even if they are not owned by the college and are not on land owned by the college.

Regulations to implement the Campus Security Act were proposed by the secretary of education at 57 Fed. Reg. 30826 (July 10, 1992). Before those regulations became final, additional regulations were proposed to include the additions made by the Higher Education Amendments of 1992 (58 Fed. Reg. 54902 (Oct. 22, 1993)). The proposed regulations amend 34 C.F.R. § 668 by adding § 668.48, which sets out the procedures an institution must follow in reporting campus crimes and its obligations in instances of campus sexual assault, summarized above. Final regulations were published at 59 Fed. Reg. 22314 (Apr. 29, 1994). These regulations require that crimes reported to counselors be included in the college's year-end report, but they do not require counselors to report crimes to the campus community at the time that they learn of them if the student victim requests that no report be made. The regulations require other college officials, however, to make timely reports to the campus community about crimes that could pose a threat to other students.

For analysis of this federal legislation and its implications for potential institutional liability for violent crime, see M. C. Griffaton, Note, "Forewarned Is Forearmed: The Crime Awareness and Campus Security Act of 1990 and the Future of Institutional Liability for Student Victimization," 43 *Case Western Reserve L. Rev.* 525 (1993).

Several states have promulgated laws requiring colleges and universities either to report campus crime statistics or to open their law enforcement logs to the public. For example, a Massachusetts law (Mass. Ann. Laws ch. 41, § 98F (1993)) has the following requirement:

Each police department and each college or university to which officers have been appointed pursuant to the provisions of [state law] shall make, keep and maintain a daily log, written in a form that can be easily understood [, of]

. . . all responses to valid complaints received [and] crimes reported. . . . All entries in said daily logs shall, unless otherwise provided by law, be public records available without charge to the public.

Pennsylvania law requires colleges to provide students and employees, as well as prospective students, with information about crime statistics and security measures on campus. It also requires colleges to report to the Pennsylvania State Police all crime statistics for a three-year period (24 Pa. Cons. Stat. Ann. § 2502 (1992)).

These federal and state requirements to give "timely warning" may be interpreted as creating a legal duty for colleges to warn students, staff, and others about persons on campus who have been accused of criminal behavior. If the college does not provide such a warning, its failure to do so could result in successful negligence claims against it in the event that a student or staff member is injured by someone who one or more administrators know has engaged in allegedly criminal behavior in the past. For analysis of institutional liability and potential defenses, see Section 2.3.1.

Selected Annotated Bibliography

General

Carnegie Council on Policy Studies in Higher Education. *Fair Practices in Higher Education: Rights and Responsibilities of Students and Their Colleges in a Period of Intensified Competition for Enrollments* (Jossey-Bass, 1979). Concluding that serious decay has occurred in the ethical conduct of institutions and their students, the council directs numerous recommendations to institutions, students, accrediting associations, the states, and the federal government. It specifically recommends that institutions provide more and better information on institutional practices and develop codes of rights and responsibilities covering such matters as admissions, financial aid, tuition, record keeping, academic requirements, support services, student conduct penalties for infractions, and grievance procedures.

Cole, Elsa Kircher, & Shiels, Barbara L. (eds). *Student Legal Issues* (National Association of College and University Attorneys, 1989). A collection of articles, originally published in the *Journal of College and University Law,* that cover a wide array of legal issues related to students. Articles focus on academic dismissals, student discipline, student fees, breach-of-contract litigation by students, student loan problems, and a variety of other significant matters. Also includes an index to all articles appearing in the *Journal* related to students.

"Joint Statement on Rights and Freedoms for Students," 52 *AAUP Bulletin* 365 (1967). A set of model guidelines for implementing students' rights on campus, drafted by the Association of American Colleges, the American Association of University Professors, the National Student Association, the National Association of Student Personnel Administrators, and the National Association of Women Deans and Counselors, and endorsed by a number of other professional organizations. (See discussion of the Joint Statement by William Van Alstyne in Grace W. Holmes (ed.), *Student Protest and the Law* (Institute of Continuing Legal Education, 1969), 181–86.) In the early 1990s, a larger group of associations affirmed the Joint Statement and updated it with a set of interpretive notes (see

"Report: Joint Statement on Rights and Freedoms of Students," 79 *Academe* 47 (July/Aug. 1993)).

Laudicina, Robert, & Tramutola, Joseph, Jr. *A Legal Overview of the New Student as Educational Consumer, Citizen, and Bargainer* (Thomas, 1976). A survey of legal developments concerning students. Suggests legal and administrative models for dealing with legal and policy developments. Written by an administrator and a lawyer, with commentary by many other contributors.

Young, D. Parker, & Gehring, Donald D. *The College Student and the Courts* (College Administration Publications, 1973 and periodic supp.). Briefs and supporting comments on court cases concerning students, with new cases added in quarterly supplements.

Sec. 4.1 (The Legal Status of Students)

Cherry, Robert L., Jr. "The College Catalog as a Contract," 21 *J. Law & Educ.* 1 (1992). A review of litigation regarding the contractual status of college catalogues. Discusses disclaimers, reservation-of-rights clauses, and other significant drafting issues.

Dodd, Victoria J. "The Non-Contractual Nature of the Student-University Relationship," 33 *U. Kan. Law Rev.* 701 (1985). Reviews breach-of-contract claims by students, and concludes that courts have manipulated traditional contract law principles in order to defer to institutional autonomy. Analyzes the elements of the student-institution "contract" and argues that courts should impose duties on institutions in addition to their "contract" obligations.

Jennings, Eileen K. "Breach of Contract Suits Against Postsecondary Institutions: Can They Succeed?" 7 *J. Coll. & Univ. Law* 191 (1980–81). A detailed study of suits brought by students alleging breach of contract. Cases are divided into the categories of "Tuition and Fees," "Scholarships," "Student Discipline," "Miscellaneous," and "The Academic Relationship." In the last category, cases are subdivided into "Program Termination," "Quality of Academic Program," "Refusal to Grant Degree," "Change of Requirements During Student's Tenure," and "Academic Dismissal Procedures."

LaTourette, Audrey Wolfson, & King, Robert D. "Judicial Intervention in the Student-University Relationship: Due Process and Contract Theories," 65 *U. Detroit L. Rev.* 199 (1988). Reviews constitutional and contract law disputes between students and colleges. Authors conclude that heightened judicial scrutiny of institutional due process has strengthened students' procedural rights, but that courts remain deferential to substantive academic judgments. Includes a comprehensive analysis of due process in academic and disciplinary decisions, as well as an overview of the application of contract law to student-institution relationships.

Nordin, Virginia D. "The Contract to Educate: Toward a More Workable Theory of the Student-University Relationship," 8 *J. Coll. & Univ. Law* 141 (1981–82). A historical and theoretical overview of the development and current interpretation of the "contract to educate." Includes discussion of the academic abstention doctrine, the application of implied contract and quasi-contract theories to education, the reasonable expectations of the parties, and the legal significance of the college bulletin.

Olswang, Steven G., Cole, Elsa Kircher, & Wilson, James B. "Program Elimination,

Financial Emergency, and Student Rights," 9 *J. Coll. & Univ. Law* 163 (1982-83). Analyzes one particular aspect of the contract relationship between institution and student: the obligations the institution may have to the student when the institution has slated an academic program for elimination. A useful supplement to the Jennings and the Nordin entries above.

Sec. 4.2 (Admissions)

Hurley, Brigid. Note, "Accommodating Learning Disabled Students in Higher Education: Schools' Legal Obligations under Section 504 of the Rehabilitation Act," 32 *Boston College L. Rev.* 1051 (1991). Reviews statutory and regulatory provisions of Section 504 of the Rehabilitation Act of 1973, as well as judicial interpretations of Section 504 for higher education. Examines the reasonable accommodation requirement, the feasibility of the "undue financial burden" defense on behalf of the college, and the practice of "flagging" disabled students in institutional records.

Johnson, Alex M., Jr. "Bid Whist, Tonk and *United States v. Fordice:* Why Integrationism Fails African-Americans Again," 81 *Cal. L. Rev.* 1401 (1993). Criticizes the Supreme Court's *Fordice* opinion regarding the present effects of former de jure segregation in public colleges and universities, particularly the potential effect of the opinion on traditionally black colleges.

McCormack, Wayne (ed.). *The Bakke Decision—Implications for Higher Education Admissions* (American Council on Education, 1978). A report of the American Council on Education/Association of American Law Schools committee convened to study *Bakke*. Reviews the various opinions in *Bakke* and discusses their implications for admissions and financial aid. The report also "analyzes the various objectives to be served by race and ethnic group–conscious admission programs and examines several models of admission procedures and criteria that might be used to serve these objectives."

O'Neil, Robert M. *Discriminating Against Discrimination: Preferential Admissions and the DeFunis Case* (Indiana University Press, 1976). A detailed examination of the *DeFunis* case and the continuing issues emerging from it. Author argues in favor of special admissions programs for minorities, considering and rejecting various nonracial alternatives in the process.

Orleans, Jeffrey H. "Memorandum: First Thoughts on *Southeastern Community College v. Davis*," 6 *J. Coll. & Univ. Law* 263 (1979-80). Analyzes the U.S. Supreme Court's *Davis* opinion and explores its impact on the postsecondary institution's obligations to students with disabilities. Also explores the potential impact of *Davis* on issues such as "academic treatment, adjustments, and assistance" and "preadmission inquiries."

Sindler, Allan P. *Bakke, DeFunis, and Minority Admissions: The Quest for Equal Opportunity* (Longman, 1978). A thought-provoking analysis of the various issues raised by affirmative admissions policies. Traces the issues and their implications through the U.S. Supreme Court's pronouncement in *Bakke*.

"Symposium: *Regents of the University of California v. Bakke*," 67 *Cal. L. Rev.* 1 (1979). Contains articles, comments, and a book review on issues relating to *Bakke*. Lead articles, all by noted legal scholars, are Derrick A. Bell, Jr., "*Bakke*, Minority Admissions, and the Usual Price of Racial Remedies"; Vincent Blasi, "*Bakke* as

Precedent: Does Mr. Justice Powell Have a Theory?"; Robert G. Dixon, Jr., "*Bakke:* A Constitutional Analysis"; R. Kent Greenawalt, "The Unresolved Problems of Reverse Discrimination"; Louis Henkin, "What of a Right to Practice a Profession?"; Robert M. O'Neil, "*Bakke* in Balance: Some Preliminary Thoughts"; and Richard A. Posner, "The *Bakke* Case and the Future of Affirmative Action."

Tribe, Lawrence. "Perspectives on *Bakke:* Equal Protection, Procedural Fairness, or Structured Justice, " 92 *Harvard L. Rev.* 864 (1978). A theoretical discussion of *Bakke*'s ramifications. Draws on broad themes of constitutional law of particular interest to lawyers.

Van Tol, Joan E. (ed.). *College and University Student Records: A Legal Compendium* (National Association of College and University Attorneys, 1989). A collection of articles, sample policies and forms, and state and federal statutes concerning student records. Included are discussions of fraudulent academic credentials, degree revocation, maintenance of computerized academic records, and requests for information from student records.

Sec. 4.3 *(Financial Aid)*

Ayres, Ted D., & Sagner, Dianne R. "The Bankruptcy Reform Act and Student Loans: Unraveling New Knots," 9 *J. Coll. & Univ. Law* 361 (1982–83). Reviews legal issues presented by the Bankruptcy Reform Act of 1978 and other efforts to curtail discharge of student loans in bankruptcy. Examines discharge of debts under both Chapter 7 and Chapter 13 of the Bankruptcy Code and reviews the case law explicating bankruptcy law concepts such as the "undue hardship" exception and the "good-faith" and related tests. Includes, in appendices, a listing of the documents composing the legislative history of the Bankruptcy Reform Act of 1978, a standard interrogatory form used by university counsel, selected resources on bankruptcy law, and a discussion of bankruptcy procedures under the 1978 Act.

Butler, Blaine B., & Rigney, David P. *Managing Federal Student Aid Programs* (National Association of College and University Attorneys, 1993). An overview of the federal student aid programs. Discusses institutional eligibility for participation in these programs, federal oversight of institutional participation, and the audit process. A primer for attorneys unfamiliar with federal student aid programs and their complexity.

Cohen, Arnold B. *Bankruptcy, Secured Transactions, and Other Debtor-Creditor Matters* (Michie, 1981). A comprehensive volume providing an overview of this area of the law, including the new Bankruptcy Code; case citations; and an analysis of important issues that arise. A general resource rather than one focusing specifically on problems of student aid.

Dorian, James C., & Ward, Diane M. *Student Loan Programs: Management and Collection* (National Association of College and University Business Officers, 1991). A guidebook to the management of federal student loan programs. In addition to chapters on each of the major federal loan programs, the book includes chapters on administrative and fiscal standards, loan collection, contracting for services, litigation and bankruptcy, audits and program reviews, the regulatory process, and consumer credit protection. Appendices provide forms, sample letters, federal regulations, a glossary of terms, and a list of references and resources.

Lines, Patricia M. "Tuition Discrimination: Valid and Invalid Uses of Tuition Differentials," 9 *J. Coll. & Univ. Law* 241 (1982–83). Addresses the constitutional validity of tuition differentials between state residents, on one hand, and nonresidents, aliens, or new residents, on the other. Reviews issues arising under equal protection clauses of federal and state constitutions, the federal Privileges and Immunities Clause, the "irrebuttable presumption" doctrine of federal due process, and the federal Supremacy Clause.

Olivas, Michael A. "*Plyler v. Doe, Toll v. Moreno,* and Postsecondary Admissions: Undocumented Adults and 'Enduring Disability,'" 15 *J. Coll. & Univ. Law* 19 (1986). Examines the impact of two important U.S. Supreme Court cases on the rights of undocumented aliens to attend and receive resident status at public higher education institutions. Proposes that the Court's treatment of undocumented alien elementary school students in Texas (in *Plyler v. Doe*) may be extended to other jurisdictions as well as to the higher education arena. Includes a table, with accompanying explanatory text, of the regulatory or policy-making entities that formulate higher education residency requirements in each of the states.

Olivas, Michael A. "Administering Intentions: Law, Theory, and Practice of Postsecondary Residency Requirements," 59 *J. Higher Educ.* 263 (1988). Traces the legal basis for resident and nonresident tuition charges through examination of the statutes, regulations, and administrative practices governing the fifty state systems and the District of Columbia. Explores seven types of alternative models for making residency determinations and sets out suggestions for reform. Includes four helpful tables organizing and summarizing data.

Sagner, Dianne. "Consumer Credit and Higher Education," 6 *J. Coll. & Univ. Law* 3 (1979). Discusses the truth-in-lending provisions of the Consumer Credit Protection Act of 1968 (15 U.S.C. § 160 et seq.) and the university's obligations in disclosing the terms of student loans and credit sales.

Tanaka, Paul. *The Permissibility of Withholding Transcripts Under the Bankruptcy Law* (National Association of College and University Attorneys, 1986). Discusses provisions of the bankruptcy law relevant to an institution's right to withhold a transcript.

Verville, Richard E., & Leyton, Peter S. "Department of Education Student Financial Assistance Audit and Regulatory Proceedings: Limitations, Suspensions, and Terminations," 36 *Administrative Law Rev.* 1 (1984). A review of the enforcement proceedings used in several of the federal grant and loan programs. Topics include who may conduct an audit; the objectives to be achieved by an audit; procedures for the suspension, freezing, and termination of federal student assistance funds; the statutory and regulatory authorization for these procedures; and the procedural safeguards afforded institutions facing regulatory proceedings.

Williams, Rosemary E. *Bankruptcy Practice Handbook* (Callaghan and Co., 1983). "Takes you through a sample case from initial contact and interview through conclusion under each chapter of the Code." Written for attorneys on both sides of a bankruptcy case. Includes forms, sample letters, and checklists as well as discussion of the roles of trustees, examiners, and attorneys representing creditors.

Sec. 4.4 (Support Services)

See Hurley entry for Section 4.2.

Sec. 4.5 (Disciplinary and Grievance Systems)

Beaney, William M., & Cox, Jonathan C. S. "Fairness in University Disciplinary
Proceedings," 22 *Case Western L. Rev.* 390 (1971). Legal and policy analyses, and
suggested guidelines, concerning the development of fair disciplinary proceedings
on campus.

Folger, Joseph P., & Shubert, J. Janelle. *Resolving Student-Initiated Grievances in
Higher Education: Dispute Resolution Procedures in a Non-Adversarial Setting*
(National Institute for Dispute Resolution, 1986). See entry in bibliography for
Section 1.1.

Pavela, Gary. "Limiting the Pursuit of Perfect Justice on Campus: A Proposed Code
of Student Conduct," 6 *J. Coll. & Univ. Law* 137 (1980). A well-drafted sample
code, including standards of conduct and hearing procedures, with comprehensive
annotations explaining particular provisions and cites to relevant authorities. The
code represents an alternative to the procedural complexities of the criminal justice
model.

Pavela, Gary. "Therapeutic Paternalism and the Misuse of Mandatory Psychiatric
Withdrawals on Campus," 9 *J. Coll. & Univ. Law* 101 (1982-83). Analyzes the
pitfalls associated with postsecondary institutions' use of "psychiatric withdrawals" of students. Pitfalls include violations of Section 504 (on disability discrimination) and of students' substantive and procedural due process rights. The article
concludes with "Policy Considerations," including the limits of psychiatric diagnosis, the danger of substituting a "therapeutic" approach as a solution for disciplinary problems, and the "appropriate uses for a psychiatric withdrawal
policy." For a later monograph adapted from this article, with model standards
and procedures, hypothetical case studies, and a bibliography, see Gary Pavela,
*The Dismissal of Students with Mental Disorders: Legal Issues, Policy Consider-
ations, and Alternative Responses* (College Administration Publications, 1985);
and see also Pavela entry for Section 4.8.

Picozzi, James M. "University Disciplinary Process: What's Fair, What's Due, and
What You Don't Get," 96 *Yale L.J.* 2132 (1987). Written by a defendant in a student
disciplinary case. Provides a critical review of case law and institutional grievance
procedures, concluding that the minimal due process protections endorsed by the
courts are insufficient to protect students' interests.

U.S. District Court, Western District of Missouri (*en banc*). "General Order on Judicial Standards of Procedure and Substance in Review of Student Discipline in
Tax-Supported Institutions of Higher Education," 45 *Federal Rules Decisions* 133
(1968). A set of guidelines promulgated for the guidance of the district court in
deciding students' rights cases. The guidelines are similarly useful to administrators and counsel seeking to comply with federal legal requirements.

See Brown & Buttolph entry for Section 4.6.

Sec. 4.6 (Disciplinary Rules and Regulations)

Brown, Valerie L., & Buttolph, Katherine (eds.). *Student Disciplinary Issues: A Legal
Compendium* (National Association of College and University Attorneys, 1993). A
collection of law review articles, institutional policies, judicial opinions, and conference outlines related to student disciplinary rules and disciplinary systems.

Issues related to both academic and nonacademic misconduct are included. A list of additional resources is also provided.
See the bibliography for Section 4.5.

Sec. 4.7 (Grades, Credits, and Degrees)

Kibler, William L., Nuss, Elizabeth M., Peterson, Brent G., & Pavela, Gary. *Academic Integrity and Student Development* (College Administration Publications, 1988). Examines student academic dishonesty from several perspectives: student development, methods for preventing academic dishonesty, and the legal issues related to student dishonesty. A model code of academic integrity and case studies are included in the appendix.

LaMorte, Michael W., & Meadows, Robert B. "Educationally Sound Due Process in Academic Affairs," 8 *J. Law & Educ.* 197 (1979). Analyzes cases up to and including *Board of Curators of the University of Missouri v. Horowitz,* (discussed in Section 4.8.3 of this chapter). Provides extended discussion of educationally and legally sound practices in student evaluation, academic dismissals, and awarding of degrees.

Schneider, Ronna G. "Sexual Harassment and Higher Education," 65 *Tex. L. Rev.* 525 (1987). Reviews the federal laws prohibiting sexual harassment and their regulations, including both Title VII and Title IX. Author compares the enforcement of Title IX with that of Title VI, and discusses the U.S. Supreme Court's ruling in *Meritor Savings Bank.* Provides a thorough legal analysis of sexual harassment theory.

Schweitzer, Thomas A. " 'Academic Challenge' Cases: Should Judicial Review Extend to Academic Evaluations of Students?" 41 *American U. L. Rev.* 267 (1992). Compares judicial review of student discipline cases with "academic challenge" cases (in which the student challenges an academic decision made by the institution). Provides a thorough and penetrating analysis of a variety of challenges to academic decisions, including degree revocation.

Zirkel, Perry A., & Hugel, Paul S. "Academic Misguidance in Colleges and Universities," 56 *West's Educ. Law Rptr.* 709 (1989). Discusses the legal and practical implications of erroneous or inadequate academic advice by faculty and administrators. Reviews four legal theories used by students to seek damages when they are harmed, allegedly by "misguidance," and concludes that most outcomes favor the institution, not the student.

See Jennings entry for Section 4.1, especially at 204–15.

Sec. 4.8 (Procedures for Suspension, Dismissal, and Other Sanctions)

Dessem, R. Lawrence. "*Board of Curators of the University of Missouri v. Horowitz:* Academic Versus Judicial Expertise," 39 *Ohio State L.J.* 476 (1978). Thoroughly canvasses the ramifications and limitations of the *Horowitz* decision.

Golden, Edward J. "Procedural Due Process for Students at Public Colleges and Universities, " 11 *J. Law & Educ.* 337 (1982). Reviews postsecondary education's response to *Goss v. Lopez,* the leading Supreme Court case on disciplinary procedures, and the later *Horowitz* case on academic procedures. After reviewing *Goss*'s and *Horowitz*'s application to dismissals and long-term suspensions, the author reports results of his survey of procedural protections extended by public colleges and universities to students faced with disciplinary or academic dismissal. Includes data on notice, hearing, evidentiary standards, and other procedural issues.

Jennings, Eileen K., & Strope, John L., Jr. "Procedural Due Process in Academia: *Board of Curators v. Horowitz* Seven Years Later," 28 *West's Educ. Law Rptr.* 973 (1986). Reviews the outcome of *Horowitz* and discusses the required elements of due process in academic dismissals.

Pavela, Gary. *The Dismissal of Students with Mental Disorders* (National Association of College and University Attorneys, 1990). Reviews the protections provided by the Rehabilitation Act of 1973 (Section 504) for students with mental disabilities. Recommends elements of an appropriate policy for psychiatric withdrawal, and provides a checklist for responding to students with mental disorders. Includes a case study about a disruptive student and suggests an appropriate institutional response. For related work by the same author, see Pavela, "Therapeutic Paternalism," entry for Section 4.5.

Sec. 4.9 (Student Protest and Demonstrations)

Blasi, Vincent. "Prior Restraints on Demonstrations," 68 *Mich. L. Rev.* 1482 (1970). A comprehensive discussion of First Amendment theory and case law and the specific manner in which the law bears on the various components of a student demonstration.

Herman, Joseph. "Injunctive Control of Disruptive Student Demonstrations," 56 *Va. L. Rev.* 215 (1970). Analyzes strategic, constitutional, and procedural issues concerning the use of injunctions to control disruptive student protest.

Sec. 4.10 (The Special Problem of Hate Speech)

Byrne, J. Peter. "Racial Insults and Free Speech Within the University," 79 *Georgetown L.J.* 399 (1991). Author argues that, to protect "the intellectual values of academic discourse," universities may regulate racial (and other similar) insults on campuses even if the state could not constitutionally enact and enforce the same type of regulation against society at large. He asserts, however, that public universities may not use such regulations "to punish speakers for advocating any idea in a reasoned manner." Article analyzes the evolution of relevant constitutional law and examines polices enacted at the University of Wisconsin, the University of Michigan, and Stanford University. Author was a member of a committee to formulate a "student speech and expression policy" at Georgetown University.

Kaplin, William. "A Proposed Process for Managing the Free Speech Aspects of Campus Hate Speech," 63 *J. Higher Educ.* 517 (1992). Describes a process for dealing with "hate speech" while preserving individuals' rights to free speech. Identifies key principles of First Amendment law that circumscribe the institution's discretion to deal with hate speech, suggests regulatory options that may be implemented consistent with these principles, and emphasizes the need to consider nonregulatory options prior to considering regulatory options.

Lawrence, Charles R., III. "If He Hollers Let Him Go: Regulating Racist Speech on Campus," 1990 *Duke L.J.* 431 (1990). Develops an argument for the constitutionality of hate speech regulations based on an interpretation of *Brown v. Board of*

Education, calls for carefully drafted hate speech regulations on the campuses, explores the injurious nature of hate speech, and criticizes the position of free speech libertarians.

Massaro, Toni M. "Equality and Freedom of Expression: The Hate Speech Dilemma," 32 *William and Mary L. Rev.* 211 (1991). Summarizes theoretical and practical aspects of the hate speech debate; critiques the approaches of "civil liberties theorists," "civil rights theorists," and "accommodationists"; and reviews various narrow approaches to regulating campus hate speech.

Strossen, Nadine. "Regulating Racist Speech on Campus: A Modest Proposal?" 1990 *Duke L.J.* 484 (1990). Reviews the First Amendment principles and doctrines applicable to campus hate speech regulations; responds to Charles Lawrence's advocacy of hate speech regulations (see entry above); and argues that "prohibiting racist speech would not effectively counter, and could even aggravate, the underlying problem of racism," and that "means consistent with the first amendment can promote racial equality more effectively than can censorship." Includes substantial discussion of ACLU policies and activities regarding hate speech.

Sunstein, Cass. "Liberalism, Speech Codes, and Related Problems," 79 *Academe* 14 (July–Aug. 1993). Traces the tension between academic freedom and hate speech and relates hate speech regulation to the "low-value speech" versus "high-value speech" dichotomy developed in United States Supreme Court precedents. Author's primary purpose is to "defend the constitutionality of narrowly drawn restrictions on hate speech, arguing in the process against the broader versions that have become popular in some institutions." (This is a condensed version of a lecture that will be included in the Menard entry in bibliography for Section 3.7.)

Sec. 4.11 (Student Organizations)

Comment, "'Fee Speech': First Amendment Limitations on Student Fee Expenditures," 20 *Cal. Western L. Rev.* 279 (1984). Focuses on the particular problem of "using mandatory student fees to finance political or ideological activities." Analyzes the constitutional issues raised by this practice, from the perspectives of both the university and the students who object to such uses of mandatory fees; reviews prior cases on student fees as well as on mandatory labor union dues; and proposes a new analytical scheme for determining the constitutionality of particular mandatory student fees.

Sec. 4.12 (Fraternities and Sororities)

Curry, Susan J. "Hazing and the 'Rush' Toward Reform: Responses from Universities, Fraternities, State Legislatures, and the Courts," 16 *J. Coll. & Univ. Law* 93 (1989). Examines the various legal theories used against local and national fraternities, universities, and individual fraternity members to redress injury or death resulting from hazing. Also reviews the response of one university to the hazing death of a pledge and its revised regulation of fraternities. Two state antihazing laws are also discussed.

Lewis, Darryll M. H. "The Criminalization of Fraternity, Non-Fraternity and Non-Collegiate Hazing," 51 *Miss. L.J.* 111 (1991). Describes state laws that make hazing and associated activities subject to criminal penalties.

Walton, Spring J., Bassler, Stephen E., & Cunningham, Robert Briggs. "The High Cost of Partying: Social Host Liability for Fraternities and Colleges," 14 *Whittier L. Rev.* 659 (1993). Discusses the implications of state social host laws for local and national fraternities and for colleges and universities. Concludes that increased regulation of fraternities by colleges may prompt judicial imposition of a duty on colleges to prevent injuries related to fraternity social activity.

Sec. 4.13 (Student Press)

Comment, "Student Editorial Discretion, the First Amendment, and Public Access to the Campus Press," 16 *U. Cal. Davis L. Rev.* 1089 (1983). Reviews the constitutional status of student newspapers under the First Amendment, analyzes the applicability of the state action doctrine to student newspapers on public campuses, and discusses the question of whether noncampus groups have any right to have material published in campus newspapers on public campuses.

Duscha, Julius, & Fischer, Thomas. *The Campus Press: Freedom and Responsibility* (American Association of State Colleges and Universities, 1973). A handbook that provides historical, philosophical, and legal information on college newspapers. Discusses case law that affects the campus press and illustrates the variety of ways the press may be organized on campus and the responsibilities the institution may have for its student publications.

Ingelhart, Louis E. *Student Publications: Legalities, Governance, and Operation* (Iowa State University Press, 1993). An overview of issues regarding publication of student newspapers, yearbooks, and magazines. Aimed primarily at administrators, the book discusses organizational, management, and funding issues as well as censorship and other potential legal problems associated with such publications.

Nichols, John E. "Vulgarity and Obscenity in the Student Press, 10 *J. Law & Educ.* 207 (1981). Examines the legal definitions of vulgarity and obscenity as they apply to higher education and secondary education and reviews the questions these concepts pose for the student press.

Note, "Tort Liability of a University for Libelous Material in Student Publications," 71 *Mich. L. Rev.* 1061 (1973). Provides the reader with a general understanding of libel law and discusses the various theories under which a university may be held liable for the torts of its student press. Author also recommends preventive measures to minimize university liability.

Sec. 4.14 (Student Housing)

Delgado, Richard. "College Searches and Seizures: Students, Privacy and the Fourth Amendment," 26 *Hastings L.J.* 57 (1975). Discusses the legal issues involved in dormitory searches and analyzes the validity of the various legal theories used to justify such searches.

Gehring, Donald D. (ed.). *Administering College and University Housing: A Legal Perspective* (rev. ed., College Administration Publications, 1992). An overview of legal issues that can arise in the administration of campus housing. Written in layperson's language and directed to all staff involved with campus housing. Contains chapters by Gehring, Pavela, and others, covering the application of constitutional law, statutory and regulatory law, contract law, and tort law to the residence hall setting, and provides suggestions for legal planning. Includes an appendix with a "Checklist of Housing Legal Issues" for use in legal audits of housing programs.

Note, "Admissibility of Evidence Seized by Private University Officials in Violation of Fourth Amendment Standards, " 56 *Cornell L. Rev.* 507 (1971). Discusses the applicability of Fourth Amendment standards to actions by private universities, as well as the degree of involvement by school and police authorities that may render private university actions subject to the state action doctrine.

Sec. 4.15 (Athletics)

Berry, Robert C., & Wong, Glenn M. *Law and Business of the Sports Industries: Common Issues in Amateur and Professional Sports* (2d ed., Greenwood Press, 1993). The second volume of a comprehensive, two-volume overview of the law applicable to athletics. Most of the discussion either focuses on or has direct application to intercollegiate sports. The twelve chapters cover such topics as "The Amateur Athlete," "Sex Discrimination in Athletics," "Application of Tort Law," "Drug Testing," and "Criminal Law and Its Relationship to Sports." Includes numerous descriptions or edited versions of leading cases, set off from and used to illustrate the textual analysis.

Cross, Harry M. "The College Athlete and the Institution," 38 *Law & Contemporary Problems* 151 (1973). A legal analysis of the student athlete's status within the institution. Discusses admissions, recruitment, athletic eligibility, and the athlete's status as a member of the student body. Written by a law professor and former NCAA president.

Davis, Timothy. "An Absence of Good Faith: Defining a University's Educational Obligation to Student Athletes," 28 *Houston L. Rev.* 743 (1991), examines the relationship between the student athlete and the university, the potential exploitation of the student athlete, and the resulting compromise of academic integrity. Author argues that the good-faith doctrine of contract law should be used to define the university's obligation, so that the contract will be breached if the university "obstructs or fails to further the student-athlete's educational opportunity."

Gaal, John, DiLorenzo, Louis P., & Evans, Thomas S. "HEW's Final Policy Interpretation on Title IX and Intercollegiate Athletics," 6 *J. Coll. & Univ. Law* 345 (1980). A critical analysis of the Department of Education's (then HEW's) final guidelines on how Title IX applies to postsecondary athletic programs. The article should be read together with John Gaal and Louis P. DiLorenzo, "The Legality and Requirements of HEW's Proposed Policy Interpretation of Title IX and Intercollegiate Athletics," 6 *J. Coll. & Univ. Law* 161 (1979–80), an earlier article on the proposed guidelines and the underlying Title IX regulations.

Jones, Cathy J. "College Athletes: Illness or Injury and the Decision to Return to Play," 40 *Buffalo L. Rev.* 113 (1992). Discusses the rights and liabilities in situations where a student athlete seeks to play or return to play after being diagnosed with a medical condition that could cause injury or death. Analyzes the rights of the athletes under the U.S. Constitution, Section 504 of the Rehabilitation Act of 1973, and the Americans with Disabilities Act of 1990. Suggests that athletes' autonomy must be respected and that "[l]iability on the part of the institution and its employees should be judged by a reasonableness standard."

Langerman, Samuel, & Fidel, Noel. "Sports Injury—Negligence," 15 *Proof of Facts 2d* 1 (American Jurisprudence, 1978, with periodic supp.). A thorough examination of the issues involved in this increasingly litigated area of the law. Covers "Duty of Administrator of Sports Program," "Unsafe Facilities or Equipment," "Inadequate Coaching or Supervision," "Effect of Age and Experience of Plaintiff," "Contributory Negligence," "Assumption of Risk," and other topics. Includes "Practice Comments" of the authors and model question-and-answer dialogues with expert witnesses. Primarily for lawyers.

Mitten, Matthew. "Amateur Athletes with Handicaps or Physical Abnormalities: Who Makes the Participation Decision?" 71 *Neb. L. Rev.* 987 (1992). Discusses the circumstances under which athletes with disabilities may participate in competitive sports. Outlines the problem from the perspectives of the athletic associations, the athlete, the team physician, and university administrators. Traces the rights and obligations of the parties under state statutory law, federal constitutional law, and Section 504 of the Rehabilitation Act. Does not discuss the ramifications of the Americans with Disabilities Act.

"On Collegiate Athletics," 60 *Educ. Record* no. 4 (Fall 1979). A symposium with articles and other material, including Elaine H. El-Khawas, "Self-Regulation and Collegiate Athletics"; Cym H. Lowell, "The Law and Collegiate Athletics in Public Institutions"; and "Responsibilities in the Conduct of Collegiate Athletic Programs: American Council on Education Policy Statements" (three policy statements, directed respectively to institutional trustees, presidents, and athletic directors, developed by ACE and its Commission on Collegiate Athletics).

Ranney, James T. "The Constitutionality of Drug Testing of College Athletes: A Brandeis Brief for a Narrowly-Intrusive Approach," 16 *J. Coll. & Univ. Law* 397 (1990). Identifies the legal and policy issues that institutions should consider in developing a drug-testing program. Author concludes that the threat of "performance-enhancing drugs" justifies random warrantless searches while the threat of "street drugs" only justifies searches based on reasonable suspicion or probable cause. Article also discusses procedural safeguards to guarantee the reliability of the testing and protect the athletes' due process rights.

"Symposium on Athletics in Higher Education," 8 *J. Coll. & Univ. Law* 291 (1981–82). Contains the following lead articles: Ann V. Thomas & Jan Sheldon Wildgen, "Women in Athletics: Winning the Game but Losing the Support"; Larry R. Thompson & J. Timothy Young, "Taxing the Sale of Broadcast Rights to College Athletics—An Unrelated Trade or Business?"; Robert H. Ruxin, "Unsportsmanlike Conduct: The Student Athlete, the NCAA, and Agents"; and Edward Branchfield & Melinda Grier, "*Aiken v. Lieuallen* and *Peterson v. Oregon State University*—Defining Equity in Athletics" (includes a conciliation agreement settling the *Peterson* case).

"Symposium on Postsecondary Athletics and the Law," 5 *J. Coll. & Univ. Law* nos. 1 and 2 (1978–79). Contains numerous articles, including Anne M. C. Hermann, "Sports and the Handicapped: Section 504 of the Rehabilitation Act of 1973 and Curricular, Intramural, Club, and Intercollegiate Athletic Programs in Postsecondary Educational Institutions"; Philip R. Hochberg, "The Four Horsemen Ride Again: Cable Communications and Collegiate Athletics"; Stephen Horn, "Intercollegiate Athletics: Waning Amateurism and Rising Professionalism"; Cym H. Lowell, "Judicial Review of Rule-Making in Amateur Athletics"; John C. Weistart, "Antitrust Issues in the Regulation of College Sports"; and Harvey L. Zuckman, "Throw 'em to the Lions (or Bengals): The Decline and Fall of Sports Civilization as Seen Through the Eyes of a United States District Court." Also includes a bibliography on postsecondary athletics and the law by Edmund Edmonds.

Weistart, John C., & Lowell, Cym H. *The Law of Sports* (Michie, 1979, with 1985 supp.). A reference work, with comprehensive citations to authorities, treating the legal issues concerning sports. Of particular relevance to postsecondary institutions are the chapters on "Regulation of Amateur Athletics," "Public Regulation of Sports Activities," and "Liability for Injuries in Sports Activities."

Wong, Glenn M. *Essentials of Amateur Sports Law* (2d ed., Praeger, 1994). Provides background information and a quick reference guide on sports law issues. Covers contract and tort law problems, sex discrimination in athletics, broadcasting, trademark law, drug testing, and various matters regarding athletic associations and athletic eligibility. Also includes detailed descriptions of the NCAA; sample forms for athletic contracts, financial aid agreements, and releases of liability; and a glossary of legal and sports terms. Of particular interest to nonlawyers such as athletic directors, coaches, and student athletes.

See Burling entry in bibliography for Section 2.5.

Sec. 4.16 (Student Files and Records)

American Association of Collegiate Registrars and Admissions Officers, Task Force on Buckley Amendment. *A Guide to Postsecondary Institutions for Implementation of the Family Educational Rights and Privacy Act of 1974 as Amended* (AACRAO, 1976). Explains the Act and its regulations, as well as the procedures and strategies for compliance, and provides sample forms for use in complying and a copy of the Act and its regulations.

Michigan Law Review Editorial Board. "Government Information and the Rights of Citizens," 73 *Mich L. Rev.* 971 (1975). An exhaustive review of federal and state constitutional, statutory, and common law protections of the right to privacy. Includes lengthy discussions of the Privacy Act of 1974 and state law applicable to education records, as well as a brief discussion of the Buckley Amendment. Focuses primarily on the limitations applicable to public agencies and institutions.

Schatken, Steven N. "Student Records at Institutions of Postsecondary Education: Selected Issues Under the Family Educational Rights and Privacy Act of 1974," 4 *J. Coll. & Univ. Law* 147 (1977). Identifies the major Buckley issues, explains why they are issues, suggests resolutions, and gives practical advice for administrators and counsel dealing with student records.

See Van Tol entry for Section 4.2.

Sec. 4.17 (Campus Security)

Hauserman, Nancy, & Lansing, Paul. "Rape on Campus: Postsecondary Institutions as Third Party Defendants," 8 *J. Coll & Univ. Law* 182 (1981–82). Traces the evolution of tort actions by rape and assault victims against third-party institutional defendants. Reviews the procedural issues that may be raised by such suits, the availability and scope of sovereign and charitable immunity defenses, the elements a plaintiff must prove in order to establish the case, and the potential availability of Title IX as an additional ground for litigation.

Oshagan, Georgi-Ann. "Obscuring the Issue: The Inappropriate Application of *in loco parentis* to the Campus Crime Victim Duty Question," 39 *Wayne L. Rev.* 1335 (1993). Reviews the propensity for crime victims and/or their parents to attempt to hold the university liable for the acts of third parties or the negligence of the students themselves.

Raddatz, Anita. *Crime on Campus: Institutional Tort Liability for the Criminal Acts of Third Parties* (National Association of College and University Attorneys, 1988). A pamphlet for college administrators that reviews the basic elements of negligence liability and discusses their implications for campus security. Includes a statement from the American Council on Education regarding campus security and a selected list of references on institutional liability for crimes on campus.

Smith, Michael Clay. *Coping with Crime on Campus* (American Council on Education/Macmillan, 1988). Reviews the increase in campus crime since the late 1960s, the effect of alcohol and drugs on campus crime, sexual assaults, and security issues.

Smith, Michael Clay. *Crime and Campus Police: A Handbook for Campus Police Officers and Administrators* (College Administration Publications, 1989). Discusses risk management, the proper procedure for searches and seizures and arrests on campus, campus judicial procedures, frequent problems encountered by campus police and administrators, white-collar crime on campus, and alcohol issues.

V

The College and
the Community

◆　◆　◆

Sec. 5.1. General Principles

Postsecondary institutions are typically subject to the regulatory authority of one or
more local government entities, such as a city, village, town, or county government.
Some local regulations, such as certain fire and safety codes, are relatively noncon-
troversial. Others may be highly controversial. Controversies have arisen, for instance,
over local governments' attempts to regulate or prohibit genetic experimentation,
nuclear weapons research or the production or storage of nuclear weapons components or radioactive materials, and the use of animals in laboratory experiments.
Other examples include ordinances requiring permits for large-group gatherings at
which alcohol will be served, ordinances restricting smoking in the workplace, and
rent-control ordinances. Land use regulations and zoning board rulings are also
frequently controversial, as Section 5.2 below illustrates. In addition to such exertions
of regulatory power, local governments also exert tax powers that may become controversial either when a postsecondary institution is taxed or when it is exempted,
thus raising claims that the institution does not contribute its fair share to the local
government's coffers. In dealing with ordinances and issues such as these, postsecondary administrators must be aware of the extent of, and limits on, each local government's regulatory and taxing authority.

A local government has only the authority delegated to it by state law. When
a local government has been delegated "home rule" powers, its authority will usually
be broadly interpreted; otherwise, its authority will usually be narrowly construed.
Even where a local body has general authority, it cannot exercise that authority in
a way that conflicts with state law, which generally prevails over local law in case

of conflict.[1] Nor can a local government regulate matters that the state otherwise has "preempted" by its own extensive regulation of the field, or matters that are considered protected by the state's sovereign immunity. Nor, of course, can local governments regulate in a way that violates the federal Constitution.

Although these principles apply to regulation and taxation of both public and private institutions, public institutions are more likely than private institutions to escape the local government's net. Since public institutions are more heavily regulated by the states (see Section 6.2), for instance, they are more likely in particular cases to have preemption defenses. Public institutions may also defend against local regulation by asserting sovereign immunity, a defense not available to private institutions.[2]

The preemption doctrine governs situations in which state and local regulatory activities overlap. If a local government ordinance regulates the same kind of activity as a state law, the institution may be bound only by the state law. Courts will resolve any apparent overlapping of state law and local ordinances by determining, on a case-by-case basis, whether state law has preempted the field and precluded local regulation. A rather unusual case concerning colleges and universities illustrates the application of these principles. *Board of Trustees v. City of Los Angeles*, 122 Cal. Rptr. 361 (Cal. Ct. App. 1975), arose after a state university leased one of its facilities to a circus and claimed that the municipal ordinance regulating circus operations was preempted by a state statute authorizing the board of regents to promulgate rules for the governance of state colleges. In upholding the ordinance, the court found as follows:

> The general statutory grant of authority ([Cal. Educ.] Code §§ 23604, 23604.1, 23751) to promulgate regulations for the governing of the state colleges and the general regulations promulgated pursuant to that authority (Cal. Admin. Code Title 5, § 4000 et seq.) contain no comprehensive state scheme for regulating the conduct of circuses or similar exhibitions with specific references to the safety, health, and sanitary problems attendant on such activities. Nor can the board point to any attempt by it to control the activities of its lessees for the purpose of protecting the public, the animals, or the neighboring community.
>
> In the absence of the enforcement of the city's ordinance, there would be a void in regulating circuses and similar exhibitions when those activities were

---

[1]Occasionally, state laws may be held invalid because they regulate matters of "purely local concern" that the state constitution reserves to local "home rule" governments or because they constitute "local" or "special" legislation prohibited by the state constitution. In such a case, there is no conflict, and local law may prevail.

[2]Issues regarding local regulation of public institutions usually involve state colleges and universities, which are considered state entities. Somewhat different issues may arise when regulation is directed instead at a local community college. The college may be considered a local political subdivision (community college district) rather than a state entity, and the question may be whether the community college is subject to the local laws of some other local government whose territory overlaps its own. Or the community college may be established by a county government (pursuant to state law), and the question may be whether the college is an arm of the county government, and whether county law or state law governs the college on some particular matter. *Atlantic Community College v. Civil Service Commission*, 279 A.2d 820 (N.J. 1971) (discussed in Section 6.2.1), illustrates some of these issues. See also *Appeal of Community College of Delaware County*, 254 A.2d 641 (Pa. 1969) (Section 5.2.2), and *People v. Rancho Santiago College*, 277 Cal. Rptr. 69 (Cal. Ct. App. 1990) (Section 5.2.6).

conducted on university property, thereby creating a status for tenants of the university which would be preferential to tenants of other landowners. This preferential status, under the circumstances, serves no governmental purpose. The subject matter of Los Angeles Municipal Code section 53.50 has not been preempted by the state [122 Cal. Rptr. at 365].

The sovereign immunity doctrine holds that state institutions, as arms of state government, cannot be regulated by a lesser governmental authority that has only the powers delegated to it by the state. In order to claim sovereign immunity, the public institution must be performing state "governmental" functions, not acting in a merely "proprietary" capacity. In *Board of Trustees v. City of Los Angeles,* above, the court rejected the board's sovereign immunity defense by using this distinction:

> In the case at bar, the board leases . . . [its facilities] as a revenue-producing activity. The activities which are conducted thereon by private operators have no relation to the governmental function of the university. "The state is acting in a proprietary capacity when it enters into activities . . . to amuse and entertain the public. The activities of [the board] do not differ from those of private enterprise in the entertainment industry" (*Guidi v. California,* 41 Cal. 2d 623, 627, 262 P.2d 3, 6). The doctrine of sovereign immunity cannot shield the university from local regulation in this case. Even less defensible is the university's attempt here to extend its immunity to private entrepreneurs who are involved in the local commercial market where their competitors are subject to local regulation. By the terms of the lease, the university specifically disavowed any governmental status for its lessee [122 Cal. Rptr. at 364].

In contrast, a sovereign immunity defense was successful in *Board of Regents of Universities v. City of Tempe,* 356 P.2d 399 (Ariz. 1960). The board sought an injunction to prohibit the city from applying its local construction codes to the board. In granting the board's request, the court reasoned:

> The essential point is that the powers, duties, and responsibilities assigned and delegated to a state agency performing a governmental function must be exercised free of control and supervision by a municipality within whose corporate limits the state agency must act. The ultimate responsibility for higher education is reposed by our constitution in the state. The legislature has empowered the board of regents to fulfill that responsibility subject only to the supervision of the legislature and the governor. It is inconsistent with this manifest constitutional and legislative purpose to permit a municipality to exercise its own control over the board's performance of these functions. A central, unified agency, responsible to state officials rather than to the officials of each municipality in which a university or college is located, is essential to the efficient and orderly administration of a system of higher education responsive to the needs of all the people of the state [356 P.2d at 406–07].

A similar result was reached in *Inspector of Buildings v. Salem State College,* 546 N.E.2d 388 (Mass. App. Ct. 1989). The inspector of buildings for a city had issued a stop-work order interrupting the construction of six dormitories at the defendant college because they did not adhere to local zoning requirements regarding height and other dimensional criteria. The question for the court was whether the local zoning ordinance could apply to the college, and to the state college building authority, when they were engaged in governmental functions. In answering "no" to this question, the court noted that generally "the State and State instrumentalities are immune from municipal zoning regulations, unless a statute otherwise expressly provides to the contrary." Analyzing the state statute that delegated zoning powers to municipalities, as it applied to state building projects for state educational institutions, the court concluded that the statute's language did not constitute an "express and unmistakable suspension of the usual state supremacy." The court therefore held that the college could continue the project without complying with the local zoning laws. The court noted, however, that the college did not have free rein to construct buildings without regard to air pollution, noise, growth, traffic, and other considerations, since it still must comply with state environmental requirements imposed on state instrumentalities.

The state preemption doctrine (above) also has a counterpart in federal law. Under the federal preemption doctrine, courts may sometimes invalidate local regulations because the federal government has preempted that particular subject of regulation. In *United States v. City of Philadelphia*, 798 F.2d 81 (3d Cir. 1986), for example, the court invalidated an order of the city's human relations commission that required Temple University's law school to bar military recruiters from its placement facilities because the military discriminated against homosexuals. By statute, Congress had prohibited the expenditure of defense funds at colleges or universities that did not permit military personnel to recruit on campus. The court held that the city commission's order conflicted with the congressional policy embodied in this legislation and was therefore preempted.

Careful consideration of all these principles concerning authority is necessary for determining whether particular local government regulations can be construed to apply to a college or university, and whether the college or university will be bound by such regulations.

Sec. 5.2. Zoning and Land Use Regulation

5.2.1. Overview. The zoning and other land use regulations of local governments can influence the operation of postsecondary institutions in many ways.[3] The institution's location, the size of its campus, its ability to expand its facilities, the density and character of its building, the traffic and parking patterns of its campus—all can be affected by zoning laws. Zoning problems are not the typical daily fare of administrators; but when problems do arise, they can be critical to the institution's future development. Local land use laws can limit, and even prevent, an institution's building programs, expansion of the campus area, use of unneeded land for commercial real estate ventures, development of branch campuses or additional facilities in other locations (see especially the *New York Institute of Technology* case in Section 5.2.4), or program changes that would increase the size and change the character of the student body (see especially the *Marjorie Webster Junior College* case in Section 5.2.4). Thus, administrators should be careful not to underestimate the formidable challenge that zoning and other land use laws can present in such circumstances.

---

[3]The relevant cases and authorities are collected in Annot., "Zoning Regulations as Applied to Colleges, Universities, or Similar Institutions for Higher Education," 64 A.L.R.3d 1138 (1975 and periodic supp.).

Since successful maneuvering through such laws necessitates many legal strategy choices and technical considerations, administrators should involve counsel at the beginning of any land use problem.

Local governments that have the authority to zone typically do so by enacting zoning ordinances, which are administered by a local zoning board. Ordinances may altogether exclude educational uses of property from certain zones (called exclusionary zoning). Where educational uses are permitted, the ordinances may impose general regulations, such as architectural and aesthetic standards, setback requirements, and height and bulk controls, which limit the way that educational property may be used (called regulatory zoning). Public postsecondary institutions are more protected from zoning, just as they are from other types of local regulation, than are private institutions, because public institutions often have sovereign immunity.

5.2.2. *Sovereign immunity of public institutions.* The courts have employed three tests to determine whether a unit of government, such as a state university, is subject to another government's local zoning law. As summarized in *City of Temple Terrace v. Hillsborough Assn.*, 322 So. 2d 571 (Fla. Dist. Ct. App. 1975), *affirmed without opin.*, 332 So. 2d 610 (Fla. 1976), these tests are (1) the superior sovereign test, (2) the governmental/proprietary distinction, and (3) the balancing test. The court's opinion summarizes the case law on the first two tests:

> One approach utilized by a number of courts is to rule in favor of the superior sovereign. Thus, where immunity from a local zoning ordinance is claimed by an agency occupying a superior position in the governmental hierarchy, it is presumed that immunity was intended in the absence of express statutory language to the contrary. . . . A second test frequently employed is to determine whether the institutional use proposed for the land is "governmental" or "proprietary" in nature. If the political unit is found to be performing a governmental function, it is immune from the conflicting zoning ordinance. . . . On the other hand, when the use is considered proprietary, the zoning ordinance prevails. . . . Where the power of eminent domain has been granted to the governmental unit seeking immunity from local zoning, some courts have concluded that this conclusively demonstrates the unit's superiority where its proposed use conflicts with zoning regulations. . . . Other cases are controlled by explicit statutory provisions dealing with the question of whether the operation of a particular governmental unit is subject to local zoning. . . .
>
> When the governmental unit which seeks to circumvent a zoning ordinance is an arm of the state, the application of any of the foregoing tests has generally resulted in a judgment permitting the proposed use. This has accounted for statements of horn-book law to the effect that a state agency authorized to carry out a function of the state is not bound by local zoning regulations [322 So. 2d at 576; citations omitted].

In applying these tests to postsecondary education, the court in *City of Newark v. University of Delaware*, 304 A.2d 347 (Del. Ch. 1973), used a traditional sovereign immunity analysis combining tests 1 and 2: "It has generally been held that a state agency is immune from local zoning ordinances. . . . The University of Delaware is an agency of the state of Delaware. . . . Its function is governmental. . . . It has the power of eminent domain. . . . Traditionally these characteristics and/or power have been cited as establishing immunity" (304 A.2d at 348).

Rutgers, The State University v. Piluso, 286 A.2d 697 (N.J. 1972), is the leading case on the third and newest test—the balancing test. A balancing approach weighs the state's interest in providing immunity for the institution against the local interest in land use regulation. In determining the strength of the state's interest, the *Rutgers* court analyzed the implied legislative intent to confer immunity on the university:

> The rationale which runs through our cases and which we are convinced should furnish the true test of immunity in the first instance, albeit a somewhat nebulous one, is the legislative intent in this regard with respect to the particular agency or function involved. That intent, rarely specifically expressed, is to be divined from a consideration of many factors, with a value judgment reached on an overall evaluation. All possible factors cannot be abstractly catalogued. The most obvious and common ones include the nature and scope of the instrumentality seeking immunity, the kind of function or land use involved, the extent of the public interest to be served thereby, the effect local land use regulation would have upon the enterprise concerned, and the impact upon legitimate local interests. . . . In some instances one factor will be more influential than another or may be so significant as to completely overshadow all others. No one, such as the granting or withholding of the power of eminent domain, is to be thought of as ritualistically required or controlling. And there will undoubtedly be cases, as there have been in the past, where the broader public interest is so important that immunity must be granted even though the local interests may be great. The point is that there is no precise formula or set of criteria which will determine every case mechanically and automatically [286 A.2d at 702-03].

On the facts of the *Rutgers* case, the court decided that the legislative intent was to immunize the university from local zoning laws:

> With regard to a state university . . . there can be little doubt that, as an instrumentality of the state performing an essential governmental function for the benefit of all the people of the state, the legislature would not intend that its growth and development should be subject to restriction or control by local land use regulation. Indeed, such will generally be true in the case of all state functions and agencies [286 A.2d at 703].

The court emphasized, however, that immunity is not absolute and may be conditioned by local needs:

> Even where . . . [immunity] is found to exist, it must not . . . be exercised in an unreasonable fashion so as to arbitrarily override all important legitimate local interests. This rule must apply to the state and its instrumentalities as well as to lesser governmental entities entitled to immunity. For example, it would be arbitrary, if the state proposed to erect an office building in the crowded business district of a city where provision for off-street parking was required, for the state not to make some reasonable provision in that respect. And, at the very least, even if the proposed action of the immune governmental instrumentality does not reach the unreasonable stage for any sufficient reason, the instrumentality ought to consult with the local authorities and sympathetically listen and give every

consideration to local objections, problems, and suggestions in order to minimize the conflict as much as possible [286 A.2d at 703].

The court then held that, under the facts of the case, the local interests did not outweigh the university's claim of immunity:

> As far as Rutgers' proposal here, to erect the student family housing on the Kilmer tract, is concerned, we fail to see the slightest vestige of unreasonableness as far as Piscataway's local interests are concerned or in any other respect. (The university did present the proposal to the local authorities by its variance application.) The possible additional local cost of educating children living in the housing is clearly not a legitimate local interest from any proper land use impact point of view [286 A.2d at 703].

State institutions may be in a stronger position to assert sovereign immunity successfully than are community colleges sponsored by local governments. In confrontations with a local zoning board, a state institution is clearly the superior sovereign, whereas an institution of another local government may not be. Moreover, the legislature's intent regarding immunity may be clearer for state institutions than for local ones. (For an example of a case where a community college was subjected to local zoning laws, see *Appeal of Community College of Delaware County*, 254 A.2d 641 (Pa. 1969).) Constitutionally autonomous state universities (see Section 6.2.2) would usually have the strongest claim to immunity. In *Regents of the University of California v. City of Santa Monica*, 143 Cal. Rptr. 276 (Cal. Ct. App. 1978), for example, the city had attempted to apply various requirements in its zoning and building codes to a construction project undertaken within the city by the university. Relying on various provisions of the California constitution and statutes, and applying a variation of the superior sovereign test; the court held the university to be immune from such regulation:

> In view of the virtually plenary power of the regents in the regulation of affairs relating to the university and the use of property owned or leased by it for educational purposes, it is not subject to municipal regulation. . . . Thus, the regents in constructing improvements solely for educational purposes are exempt from local building codes and zoning regulations [case citations omitted] and also specifically exempt from payment of local permit and inspection fees [143 Cal. Rptr. at 279–80; statutory provisions omitted].

5.2.3. Private institutions and zoning regulations. In seeking redress against a local government's zoning regulations, private postsecondary institutions may challenge the zoning board's interpretation and application of the zoning ordinance or may argue that the ordinance conflicts with the federal Constitution or some state law limiting the local government's zoning authority. Where those arguments are unavailing, the institution may seek an exception (Section 5.2.4), a variance (Section 5.2.5), or an amendment to the zoning ordinance (Section 5.2.6).

The Constitution limits a local government's zoning power in several ways. The ordinance may not create classifications that burden certain groups of people, unless there is a rational public purpose for its doing so (see Section 5.2.8). And although a municipality may attempt to regulate the use of land through its zoning ordinances and their application, it may not deprive individuals of the use of their land in such a fashion as to constitute a "taking."

In an early case dealing with constitutional limits, *Nectow v. Cambridge*, 277 U.S. 183 (1928), the Court stated that "the governmental power to interfere . . . with the general rights of the landowner by [establishing zoning regulations that restrict] the character of his use is not unlimited, and, other questions aside, such restriction cannot be imposed if it does not bear a substantial relation to the public health, safety, morals, or general welfare" (277 U.S. at 188). Later, in *Nollan v. California Coastal Commission*, 483 U.S. 825 (1987), the U.S. Supreme Court distinguished between a governmental entity's power to limit the way that land is used and its power to so limit the landowner's rights that the limitation becomes a "taking" without compensation. The Coastal Commission had placed a condition on the permit issued to the owners of beachfront property so that they could rebuild their home: they must give the public access to the beach through their property, which was located between two public beaches. In determining whether the commission's condition on the permit substantially furthered a governmental purpose, the Court considered the commission's purpose, which was to increase public access to the beach. The Court held that the required easement was a "taking" and that the commission must pay the plaintiffs for the easement. Similarly, in *Dolan v. City of Tigard*, 114 S. Ct. 2309 (1994), the U.S. Supreme Court considered the city's requirement that, as a condition to improving its commercial property, the landowner dedicate certain portions to a public greenway and a bicycle pathway. The Court held these requirements to be an unconstitutional taking because the city had not demonstrated "a reasonable relationship" between the requirements and the adverse impact of the proposed development.

Despite these constitutional limitations, however, constitutional challenges to governmental land use restrictions have seldom succeeded. One major success is *Prentiss v. American University*, 214 F.2d 282 (D.C. Cir. 1954), where a U.S. Court of Appeals overturned a rezoning action of the local zoning board because it did not bear a substantial relation to the public welfare and therefore constituted an unconstitutional taking of property without due process, an outcome similar to that of *Nollan*. A second, more recent, success is *Northwestern College v. City of Arden Hills*, 281 N.W.2d 865 (Minn. 1979), in which the court ruled that, in the particular circumstances, the city's denial of a zoning variance to the college was arbitrary and discriminatory, thus violating constitutional equal protection principles. The Court's subsequent decisions in *Nollan* and *Dolan* apparently increase the likelihood that higher education institutions may have other successes in the future, especially with regard to "dedication" requirements that are placed on property development projects.

In several cases educational institutions have challenged zoning ordinances that exclude educational uses of land in residential zones. In *Yanow v. Seven Oaks Park*, 94 A.2d 482 (N.J. 1953), a postsecondary religious training school challenged the reasonableness of an ordinance that excluded schools of higher or special education from residential zones where elementary and secondary schools were permitted. The court, determining that the former schools could be "reasonably placed in a separate classification" from the latter, upheld the exclusion. But in *Long Island University v. Tappan*, 113 N.Y.S.2d 795 (N.Y. App. Div., 1952), *affirmed* 114 N.E.2d 432 (N.Y. 1953), the institution won its battle against an exclusionary ordinance. After the university had obtained a certificate of occupancy from the local township, a nearby village annexed the tract of land where the university was located. The village then passed a zoning ordinance that would have prohibited the operation of the university. The court concluded: "Insofar as the zoning ordinance seeks to prohibit entirely the use of plaintiff's lands in the village for the purposes for which it is chartered, the zoning ordinance is void and ineffectual, as beyond the power of the village board to enact and as bearing no reasonable relation to the promotion of the health, safety, morals, or general welfare of the community" (113 N.Y.S.2d at 799).

Even when the zoning ordinance permits all or particular kinds of educational institutions to operate in a residential or other zone, the zoning board may not consider all the institution's uses of its land and buildings to be educational use.[4] The distinction is much the same as that drawn in local taxation law (see Section 5.3), where the tax status of an educational institution's property depends not only on the character of the institution but also on whether the particular property is being used for educational purposes. When there are no specific definitions or restrictions in the ordinance itself, courts tend to interpret phrases such as "educational use" broadly, to permit a wide range of uses. In *Scheuller v. Board of Adjustment,* 95 N.W.2d 731 (Iowa 1959), the court held that a seminary's dormitory building was an educational use under an ordinance that permitted educational uses but did not permit apartment houses or multiple dwellings. And in *Property Owners Assn. v. Board of Zoning Appeals,* 123 N.Y.S.2d 716 (N.Y. Sup. Ct. 1953), the court held that seating to be constructed adjacent to a college's athletic field was an educational use.

Where a zoning ordinance prohibits or narrowly restricts educational uses in a particular zone, an educational institution may be able to argue that its proposed use is a permissible noneducational use under some other part of the ordinance. In *Application of LaPorte,* 152 N.Y.S.2d 916 (N.Y. App. Div. 1956), *affirmed,* 141 N.E.2d 917 (N.Y. 1957), a college was allowed to construct a residence to accommodate more than sixty students because the residence came within the ordinance's authorization of single-family dwelling units:

> The city's legislative body has the right to define the term "family." It has done so, placing no limitation on the number of persons constituting a family, nor does it require that the members thereof be related by blood or marriage. We may not impose any restrictions not contained in the ordinance. The petition does not allege, nor does the record disclose, facts from which it can be determined that the proposed building does not constitute a single dwelling unit, or that the members of the order will occupy the dwelling unit other than as a "single, nonprofit housekeeping unit," within the purview of the ordinance [152 N.Y.S.2d at 918].

Fraternity houses may be excluded from residential districts or may be a permissible educational or noneducational use, depending on the terms of the ordinance

---

[4]The relevant cases and authorities are collected in Annot., "What Constitutes 'School,' 'Educational Use,' or the Like Within Zoning Ordinance," 64 A.L.R.3d 1087 (1975 and periodic supp.); Annot., "Zoning Regulations as Applied to Colleges, Universities, or Similar Institutions for Higher Education," 64 A.L.R.3d 1138, §§ 9–11 (1975 and periodic supp.); Annot., "What Constitutes Accessory or Incidental Use of Religious or Educational Property Within Zoning Ordinance," 11 A.L.R.4th 1084 (1982 and periodic supp.); and Annot., "Eminent Domain: Right to Condemn Property Owned or Used by Private Educational, Charitable, or Religious Organization," 80 A.L.R.3d 833 (1977 and periodic supp.).

and the facts of the case.[5] In *City of Baltimore v. Poe,* 168 A.2d 193 (Md. 1961), a fraternity was permitted in a zone that excluded any "club, the chief activity of which is a service customarily carried on as a business." The court found that "the chief activities carried on at this fraternity house . . . have clearly been established to be social and educational functions for the benefit of the whole membership." But in *Theta Kappa, Inc. v. City of Terre Haute,* 226 N.E.2d 907 (Ind. Ct. App. 1967), the court found that a fraternity did not come within the term "dwelling" as defined by the zoning ordinance and was therefore not a permissible use in the residential district in which it was located.

Other problems concerning zoning ordinances arise not because the ordinances exclude a particular use of property but because they regulate the way in which the landholder implements the permitted use. The validity of such "regulatory zoning" also often depends on the interpretation and application of the ordinance and its consistency with state law. In *Franklin and Marshall College v. Zoning Hearing Board of the City of Lancaster,* 371 A.2d 557 (Pa. Commw. Ct. 1977), for example, the college sought to convert a single-family home it owned into a fraternity house. The fraternity house was a permissible use under the ordinance. The town opposed the conversion, however, arguing that it would violate other provisions of the zoning ordinance dealing with the adequacy of parking and the width of side yards. Applying these provisions, the court held that the proposed number of parking spaces was adequate but that the width of the side yard would have to be increased before the conversion would be allowed.

In *Sisters of Holy Cross v. Brookline,* 198 N.E.2d 624 (Mass. 1964), a state statute was the focus of the dispute about regulatory zoning. A local zoning authority had attempted to apply construction requirements for single-family homes to the facilities of a private college. A state statute provided that "no ordinance or bylaw which prohibits or limits the use of land for any church or other religious purpose or for any educational purpose . . . shall be valid." The court rejected the town's claim that the statute did not cover ordinances regulating the dimensions of buildings: "We think that this bylaw, as applied to Holy Cross, 'limits the use' of its land and, therefore, we think such application valid." In contrast, the court in *Radcliffe College v. City of Cambridge,* 215 N.E.2d 892 (Mass. 1966), held that the same state statute did not conflict with a Cambridge zoning ordinance requiring the college to provide off-street parking for newly constructed facilities:

> Providing for the parking or housing of the automobiles of students, instructors, and employees of an educational institution is within the broad scope of the educational powers of the institution, just as is providing for the feeding and housing of such personnel. These are secondary functions incidental to the main educational purpose. Hence, a regulation that requires that some of the college land be used for parking does not lessen the availability of all or any of the institution's land for some appropriate educational purpose. We think the statute does not bar such regulation. Plainly the statute does not do so in express terms. At most the Cambridge ordinance requires choices among the proper educational purposes of the institution. In so doing, it does not impede the reasonable use of the college's land for its educational purposes. We rule, there-

[5]The relevant cases and authorities are collected in Annot., "Application of Zoning Regulations to College Fraternities and Sororities," 25 A.L.R.3d 921 (1969 and periodic supp.).

fore, that it does not limit "the use of [its] land for any . . . educational purpose" within the meaning of . . . [the statute] [215 N.E.2d at 895–96].

5.2.4. Special exceptions. Particular educational or noneducational uses may be permitted as "conditional uses" in an otherwise restricted zone. In this situation the institution must apply for a special exception, "a special use which is considered by the local legislative body to be essential or desirable for the welfare of the community and its citizenry and not essentially incompatible with basic uses in the zone involved, but not at every or any location therein or without restrictions or conditions being imposed on such use" (*Piscatelli v. Township of Scotch Plains*, 248 A.2d 274, 277 (N.J. Super. Ct. Law Div. 1968)). An educational institution may seek a special exception by demonstrating that it satisfies the conditions imposed by the zoning board. If it cannot do so, it may challenge the conditions as being unreasonable or beyond the zoning board's authority under the ordinance or state law.

The plaintiff in *Marjorie Webster Junior College v. District of Columbia Board of Zoning Adjustment*, 309 A.2d 314 (D.C. 1973), had operated a girls' finishing school in a residential zone under a special exception granted by the zoning board. The discretion of the zoning board was limited by a regulation specifying that exceptions would be granted only where "in the judgment of the board such special exceptions will be in harmony with the general purpose and intent of the zoning regulations and maps and will not tend to affect adversely the use of neighboring property in accordance with said zoning regulations and maps." Another regulation specifically authorized exceptions for colleges and universities, but only if "such use is so located that it is not likely to become objectionable to neighboring property because of noise, traffic, number of students, or other objectionable conditions." The college was sold to new owners, who instituted new programs (mostly short-term continuing education programs) that altered the curriculum of the school and attracted a new clientele to the campus. After a citizens' group complained that this new use was outside the scope of the college's special exception, the college filed an amendment to the campus plan that the prior owners had filed in order to obtain the special exception. The zoning board rejected the amendment after extensive hearings, concluding that, under the applicable regulations, the new use of the college property would not be in harmony with the general purpose and intent of the zone and would adversely affect neighboring property by attracting large numbers of transient men and women to the campus and increasing vehicular traffic in the neighborhood. On appeal by the college, the court held that the zoning regulations contained adequate standards to control the board's discretion and that the board's decision was supported by sufficient evidence.

New York Institute of Technology v. LeBoutillier, 305 N.E.2d 754 (N.Y. 1973), took up a similar issue. A private college had entered an agreement with the local government regarding the use of the college's existing property. Subsequent to the agreement, the college acquired property not contiguous with the main campus, in a residential zone that permitted educational use by special exception. The college's application for a special exception was denied by the zoning board, and the court upheld the board's decision in an interesting opinion combining fact, policy, and law:

> Several factors persuade us that there should be an affirmance in this case. To begin with, the institute seeks to expand an existing educational use without

a demonstrable need to expand. Need, of course, is not a criterion for granting a special exception permit. But a reading of the cases dealing with the expansion of existing educational or religious uses clearly indicates that need was apparent. . . . The institute already owns in excess of four hundred acres in Old Westbury. To date it has built on only about 1 percent of its land, whereas, pursuant to the 1965 agreement, it is permitted to build on up to 10 percent. Moreover, its master plan contemplates buildings on only about 8 percent of its acreage, again less than the allowable percentage. Then, too, student enrollment is only about three thousand, whereas the permissible enrollment under the agreement is seventy-five hundred. Need to expand, it seems, is highly questionable.

The institute contends, however, that it is more feasible economically to purchase the Holloway estate and to renovate the existing structures for its teacher education program than to undertake new construction at its main campus. It also contends that certain aspects of the planned teacher education program make separation from the main campus desirable. There is force to the argument that these judgments should be made by college administrators, not zoning boards of appeal or courts. But at some point, probably not definable with precision, a college's desire to expand, here by the path of least economic resistance, should yield to the legitimate interests of village residents. The village has, in the past, acceded to the incorporation of after-acquired properties into the site plan for the campus. But the right to expand is not absolute. . . .

Here, the 1965 agreement becomes relevant. That agreement, although not expressly applicable to after-acquired property, governs the relationship between the institute and the village. By its adoption it became part of the village's comprehensive plan. Approval of this application would constitute a substantial departure from that agreement. The property is not contiguous with the existing campus. It is located in the center of the village in a single-family residential district with two-acre minimum building lots, one-half mile straight-line distance from the main campus, and about four miles over interior village roads. Approval of the institute's application would negate village planning objectives of keeping college uses on the perimeter of the village in an area buffered by golf courses, thereby minimizing the impact on area residents. Approval would also negate the planning objective of routing traffic to and from the colleges over perimeter county roads, rather than interior village routes. There is ample evidence that a traffic problem already exists on Wheatley Road, which the planning board found would be aggravated by students commuting between the main campus and the proposed one at the Holloway estate.

Finally, it should be quite evident that Old Westbury, containing parts of four college campuses occupying substantial acreage in the village, is not pursuing a policy of exclusion or insularism. On the contrary, it has attempted to accommodate these uses to the essentially residential character of the community by placing reasonable restrictions upon them. Moreover, it has, in the past, approved incorporations of contiguous properties into the institute's campus. However, having approved expansion of the institute on previous applications does not require the board to grant the institute's present request to expand its existing educational use irrespective of the effect it may have on the overall character of the community [305 N.E.2d at 758–59].

Similarly, in *Lafayette College v. Zoning Hearing Board of the City of Easton*, 588 A.2d 1323 (Pa. Commw. Ct. 1991), the college failed in its attempt to convert a single-family residence to a "mini-dorm" in a residential area restricted to low-density housing. The college argued that its proposed use qualified as a special exception under the zoning ordinance. After the zoning board disagreed and denied the college's application, the trial court overruled the zoning board's decision and granted the exception conditioned on some changes in the parking arrangements. Reversing the trial court, the appellate court asserted that "an applicant for a special exception has the burden of proving that the request complies with the objective requirements of the zoning ordinance" (588 A.2d at 1326), and held that the college had not met this burden because it had not provided parking that met the ordinance's requirements.

5.2.5. Variances. If a proposed use by an educational institution does not conform to the general standards of the zone or to the terms of a special exception, the institution may seek a variance. "A variance is an exercise of the power of the governmental authority to grant relief, in a proper case, from the liberal application of the terms of an ordinance. It is to be used where strict application of the ordinance would cause unnecessary and substantial hardship to the property holder peculiar to the property in question, without serving a warranted and corresponding benefit to the public interest" (*Arcadia Development Corp. v. Bloomington*, 125 N.W.2d 846, 851 (Minn. 1964)).

Zoning boards may grant variances only in these narrow circumstances and only on the basis of standards created by state or local law. Variances that constitute substantial changes in the zoning plan or alter the boundaries of established zones may be considered in excess of the zoning board's authority. The college in *Ranney v. Instituto Pontificio Delle Maestre Filippini*, 119 A.2d 142 (N.J. 1955), had applied for a variance to expand its existing facilities, located in a restrictive residential zone. The zoning board granted the variance. The New Jersey Supreme Court reversed the board's decision, however, relying on a statutory provision that authorized variances only where there would be no "substantial detriment to the public good" and "the intent and purpose of the zone plan and zoning ordinance" would not be "substantially impair[ed]" (N.J. Stat. Ann. § 40:55-39(d)):

> The existing use and structure cannot justify an enlargement in the face of a zoning plan which has prescribed and fostered the overwhelmingly residential character of the area in which Villa Walsh is located. . . . A variance here would be directly antagonistic to the design and purpose of the ordinance and sound zoning. The "disintegrating process would be set in motion" (*Beirn v. Morris* . . . [103 A.2d 365]). "The zoning act does not contemplate variations which would frustrate the general regulations and impair the overall scheme which is set up for the general welfare of the several districts and the entire community" (*Dolan v. DeCapua*, 109 A.2d 615, 621 (N.J. 1954)) [119 A.2d at 147].

In another case, *Salve Regina College v. Zoning Board of Review of City of Newport*, 594 A.2d 878 (R.I. 1991), the college had applied for a variance so that it could convert a carriage house into a small residence hall for twenty students. A neighbor opposed the variance because, he alleged, it would increase noise and traffic in the vicinity; and the zoning board denied the college's request. The Supreme Court of Rhode Island reversed the zoning board's denial of the variance, because the college had provided experts whose testimony supported Salve Regina's right to the variance.

Since that testimony had been unrefuted by other experts, the court ruled that the variance must be granted.

5.2.6. Amendment of zoning ordinances.

If an educational institution's proposed use is prohibited within a zone, and the institution cannot obtain an exception or a variance, it may petition the local government to amend the zoning ordinance. Unlike an exception or a variance, an amendment is designed to correct an intrinsic flaw in the zoning ordinance, rather than to relieve individual hardship imposed by zoning requirements. An institution seeking an amendment should be prepared to demonstrate that the proposed change is in the public interest rather than just for its own private advantage.

Courts vary in the presumptions and standards they apply to zoning amendments. In some jurisdictions courts give amendments a presumption of reasonableness; in others they presume that the original ordinance was reasonable and require that any amendment be justified. Many courts require that an amendment conform to the comprehensive zoning plan. "Spot zoning," which reclassifies a small segment of land, is frequently overturned for nonconformance with a comprehensive plan.

Bidwell v. Zoning Board of Adjustment, 286 A.2d 471 (Pa. Commw. Ct. 1972), illustrates many of the important legal considerations regarding zoning amendments. An amendment reclassified a tract of land from single-family to multifamily residential and granted an exception to a college to allow the construction of a library, a lecture hall, and an off-street parking area. The court upheld the amendment:

> From the very nature of the proposed use as a library and lecture hall, it is not unreasonable to conclude that commercial activity will not intensify. Nor is there evidence that danger to residents will be significantly increased. Excessive congestion is also not a factor since off-street parking is to be provided. The ordinance in question here merely extended a preexisting zone in accordance with the legislative judgment. . . .
>
> Appellants have not borne their burden of proving that the amendments in question were not in accordance with a comprehensive plan. . . . Public hearings regarding the proposed changes were held and the well-contemplated decision of the legislative body was to amend the zoning ordinance. Considering the presumption afforded this judgment, and taking into account the tenor of the general area, we are of the opinion that this legislation reflects and implements the "totality of a municipality's program of land utilization, considering both the land resources available and the needs and desires of the community" (*Donahue v. Zoning Board of Adjustment,* 194 A.2d 610, 612 ([Pa.] 1963)) [286 A.2d at 473, 474].

Some states may have a statute that enables the state courts to invalidate certain provisions of, and thus in effect to amend, local zoning ordinances. *Trustees of Tufts College v. City of Medford,* 602 N.E.2d 1105 (Mass. App. Ct. 1992), illustrates the operation of such a statute. The parties could not agree on how the off-street parking provisions in the city's zoning ordinance would apply to three new buildings Tufts was constructing in the heart of its campus. Tufts brought suit under a Massachusetts law that invalidated local zoning ordinances which prohibited or restricted the use for educational purposes of land or buildings owned by a nonprofit educational institution (Mass. Gen. Laws ch. 40A, § 3). The trial court invalidated portions of the city ordinance's parking provisions. The appellate court determined that invalidation was unnecessary, however, and modified the trial court's judgment. Recognizing the incongruity of zoning requirements that assume that all property occurs in "lots," when a college's property may consist of a "green" surrounded by clusters of buildings, the appellate court accepted the city's concession that parking spaces in Tufts' new parking garage, located several blocks away, could "count" as off-street parking for the new buildings.

In at least one state, community colleges (as school districts) have yet another means for securing an amendment to a local zoning ordinance. California's Government Code, Section 53094, provides that a school district may declare a city zoning ordinance inapplicable to a proposed use of its own property unless the proposed use is for "nonclassroom facilities." In *People v. Rancho Santiago College*, 277 Cal. Rptr. 69 (Cal. Ct. App. 1990), the college had contracted with a community group to use the college's parking lot for a weekly "swap meet." The parking lot was zoned for "open space," and the city sued the college, arguing that the use of the parking lot for a "swap meet" was not permitted. The court rejected the college's assertion that it could exempt this use from the zoning ordinance, noting that both uses—as a parking lot and for a swap meet—were "nonclassroom facilities" under Section 53094 and thus were not exempt from the ordinance.

5.2.7. Rights of other property owners. In considering various approaches to zoning problems, administrators should be aware that other property owners may challenge zoning decisions favorable to the institution or may intervene in disputes between the institution and the zoning board. The procedures of the zoning board may require notice to local property owners and an opportunity for a hearing before certain zoning decisions are made. Thus, zoning problems may require administrators to "do battle" with the local community in a very real and direct way.

Landowners usually can challenge a zoning decision if they have suffered a special loss different from that suffered by the public generally. Adjacent landowners almost always are considered to have suffered such loss and thus to have "standing" (that is, a legal capacity) to challenge zoning decisions regarding the adjacent land. Property owners' associations may or may not have standing based on their special loss or that of their members, depending on the jurisdiction. In *Peirce Junior College v. Schumaker*, 333 A.2d 510 (Pa. Commw. Ct. 1975), neighboring landowners were denied permission to intervene in a local college's appeal of a zoning decision because they were not the owners or tenants of the property directly involved. But in *Citizens Assn. of Georgetown v. District of Columbia Board of Zoning Adjustment*, 365 A.2d 372 (D.C. 1976), a citizens' association from the neighboring area was successful in challenging and overturning, on procedural grounds, a special exception granted to Georgetown University.

In *Sharp v. Zoning Hearing Board of the Township of Radnor*, 628 A.2d 1223 (Pa. Commw. Ct. 1993), Villanova University had had a tract of its land rezoned from residential to institutional use. The tract, which was to be developed for dormitories, was contiguous to existing dormitory and classroom buildings, but had been in a residential zone. The university had negotiated with owners of adjacent property regarding setbacks, lighting, traffic, security measures, and other measures to reduce the impact of the university's building plans on its neighbors. One of the adjacent property owners challenged the rezoning in court, arguing that the ordinance was invalid because of procedural defects in its enactment and that the zoning board's action was unconstitutional "spot zoning." Quickly rejecting the first argument, the court turned to the constitutional claim. Asserting that "a zoning ordinance is presumed to be valid and constitutional, and the challenging party has the heavy burden of proving otherwise" (628 A.2d at 1227), the court upheld the board's decision. Since most of the land surrounding the rezoned tract was already used by the university for educational purposes, and since the university's need for additional on-campus student housing had a "substantial relation[ship] to the public health, safety, morals and general welfare," the zoning board's action could not be considered to be arbitrary and unreasonable spot zoning.

American University encountered similar objections from some of its neighbors when it proposed a new location for its law school and changes in the campus border. In *Glenbrook Road Assn. v. District of Columbia Board of Zoning Adjustment*, 605 A.2d 22 (D.C. 1992), two groups of neighbors challenged the zoning board's decision to grant the university's request. The court found that the zoning board had required the university to comply with several actions that would minimize the effect of the law school on the neighborhood, and had sufficiently taken into consideration the concerns of the neighbors during the hearing process.

5.2.8. Zoning off-campus housing. Zoning ordinances that prevent groups of college students from living together in residential areas may create particular problems for institutions that depend on housing opportunities in the community to help meet student housing needs. Some communities have enacted ordinances that specify the number of unrelated individuals who may live in the same residential dwelling, and many of these ordinances have survived constitutional challenge (see, for example, *Village of Belle Terre v. Boraas*, 416 U.S. 1 (1974), where the Court rejected the argument that such a restriction violated the residents' freedom-of-association rights).

In *Borough of Glassboro v. Vallorosi*, 568 A.2d 888 (N.J. 1990), the borough had sought an injunction against the leasing of a house in a residential district to ten unrelated male college students. The borough had recently amended its zoning ordinance to limit "use and occupancy" in the residential districts to "families" only. The ordinance defined "family" as "one or more persons occupying a dwelling unit as a single nonprofit housekeeping unit, who are living together as a stable and permanent living unit, being a traditional family unit or the functional equivalency [*sic*] thereof."

Tracking the ordinance's language, the court determined that the ten students constituted a "single housekeeping unit" which was a "stable and permanent living unit" (568 A.2d at 894). The court relied particularly on the fact that the students planned to live together for three years, and that they "ate together, shared household chores, and paid expenses from a common fund" (568 A.2d at 894). The court also cautioned that zoning ordinances are not the most appropriate means for dealing with problems of noise, traffic congestion, and disruptive behavior.

Another type of restriction on off-campus housing was invalidated in *Kirsch v. Prince Georges County*, 626 A.2d 372 (Md. 1993). Prince Georges County, Maryland, had enacted a "mini-dorm" ordinance that regulated the rental of residential property to students attending college. Homeowners and the students they wished to rent to brought an equal protection claim against the county. The ordinance defined a "mini-dormitory" as

[a]n off-campus residence, located in a building that is, or was originally constructed as[,] a one-family, two-family, or three-family dwelling which houses at least three (3), but not more than five (5), individuals, *all or part of whom are unrelated to one another by blood, adoption or marriage and who are registered full-time or part-time students at an institution of higher learning* [§ 27-107.1(a) (150.1), cited in 626 A.2d at 373–74; emphasis added].

For each mini-dorm, the ordinance specified a certain square footage per person for bedrooms, one parking space per resident, and various other requirements. The ordinance also prohibited local zoning boards from granting variances for mini-dorms, from approving departures from the required number of parking spaces, and from permitting nonconforming existing uses.

The court determined that Maryland's constitution provides equal protection guarantees similar to those of the U.S. Constitution's Fourteenth Amendment. Relying on *City of Cleburne v. Cleburne Living Center*, 473 U.S. 432 (1985), as the source of a strengthened "rational basis" test to use for Fourteenth Amendment challenges to restrictive zoning laws, the court determined that this test was the appropriate one to evaluate whether the mini-dorm ordinance was "rationally related to a legitimate governmental purpose." The court then examined the purpose of the ordinance:

> The stated purpose of the Prince Georges County "mini-dorm" ordinance is to "prevent or control detrimental effects upon neighboring properties, such as illegal parking and saturation of available parking by residents of mini-dormitories, litter, and noise." . . . At argument, the County Attorney conceded that the ordinance was passed to address complaints regarding noise, litter, and parking problems from residents of the College Park area, the site of the principal campus of the University of Maryland. . . . Notwithstanding the county-wide effect of the ordinance, the County failed to identify any other neighborhoods in the County where similar off-campus student housing created noise, litter, or parking problems [626 A.2d at 380].

The court was careful to distinguish the *Boraas* case (above), on which the county had relied in its defense of the ordinance:

> Unlike the zoning ordinance analyzed in *Boraas*, the Prince Georges County "mini-dorm" ordinance does not differentiate based on the nature of the use of the property, such as a fraternity house or a lodging house, but rather on the occupation of the persons who would dwell therein. Therefore, under the ordinance a landlord of a building . . . is permitted to rent the same for occupancy by three to five unrelated persons so long as they are not pursuing a higher education without incurring the burdens of complying with the arduous requirements of the ordinance [626 A.2d at 381].

Noting that the problems the ordinance sought to avoid would occur irrespective of whether the tenants were students, the court held that the ordinance "creat[ed] more strenuous zoning requirements for some [residential tenant classes] and less for others based solely on the occupation which the tenant pursues away from that residence," thus establishing an irrational classification forbidden by both the federal and the state constitutions.

Sec. 5.3. Local Government Taxation

5.3.1. General tax concepts. Local government taxation is one of the most traditional problems in postsecondary education law. Although the basic concepts are more settled here than they are in many other areas, these concepts often prove difficult to apply in particular cases. Moreover, in an era of tight budgets, where local governments seek new revenue sources and postsecondary institutions attempt to minimize expenditures, the sensitivity of local tax questions has increased. Pressures to tax institutions' auxiliary services (Section 9.3.5) have grown, for instance, as have pressures for institutions to make payments "in lieu of taxes" to local governments. See generally D. Kay, W. Brown, & D. Allee, *University and Local Government Fiscal Relations,* IHELG Monograph 89-2 (University of Houston Law Center, 1989).

The real property tax is the most common tax imposed by local governments on educational institutions. Sales taxes and admission taxes are also imposed in a number of jurisdictions. A local government's authority to tax is usually grounded in state enabling legislation, which delegates various types of taxing power to various types of local governments. Most local tax questions involving postsecondary institutions concern the interpretation of this state legislation, particularly its exemption provisions. A local government must implement its taxing power by local ordinance, and questions may also arise concerning the interpretation of these ordinances.

A public institution's defenses against local taxation may differ from those of a private institution. Public institutions may be shielded from local taxation by tax exemptions for state government contained in state constitutional provisions or statutes. Public institutions may also make sovereign immunity claims (see Section 5.1) against attempts by a local government to impose taxes or tax collection responsibilities on them. Private institutions, on the other hand, depend on state constitutional or statutory exemptions (or, occasionally, special legislation and charter provisions) that limit the local government's authority to tax. Although the provisions vary, most tax codes contain some form of tax exemption for religious, charitable, and educational organizations. These exemptions are usually "strictly construed to the end that such concessions will be neither enlarged nor extended beyond the plain meaning of the language employed" (*Cedars of Lebanon Hospital v. Los Angeles County,* 221 P.2d 31, 34 (Cal. 1950)). The party requesting the exemption has the burden of proving that the particular activity for which it seeks exemption is covered by the exemption provision. The strictness with which exemptions are construed depends on the state and the type of exemption involved.

5.3.2. Property taxes. Public institutions are often exempt from local real property taxation under state law exemptions for state property. One of the threshold issues that may arise when courts apply these exemptions is whether the particular property that the government seeks to tax actually belongs to the institution and, therefore, the state. In *Southern Illinois University v. Booker,* 425 N.E.2d 465 (Ill. App. Ct. 1981), for instance, the county in which Southern Illinois University is located attempted to assess a property tax on low-cost housing that the university maintained for its married students. The housing consisted of apartments financed by the Federal Housing Administration and the Southern Illinois University Foundation. The foundation was the legal owner of the property. It is a nonprofit corporation whose purpose, under its bylaws, is "to buy, sell, lease, own, manage, convey, and mortgage real estate" and "in a manner specified by the board of trustees of Southern Illinois University, to act as the business agent of the said board in respect to . . . acquisition, management, and leasing of real property and buildings."

The university claimed that the married students' apartments were state property and thus exempt from local government taxation. The county argued, however, that legal ownership vested in the foundation, not the university, thus making the exemption for state property inapplicable. In rejecting the county's argument, the court relied on the time-honored distinction between "legal title" and "equitable title":

> With respect to control and enjoyment of the benefits of the property, the stipulated facts show that the university, not the foundation, in fact controls the property and has the right to enjoy the benefits of it in the manner of an owner in fee simple absolute. The foundation acquired title to the property from the university solely as a convenience to the university with regard to long-term financing. The property is used to house students of the university. The facilities are controlled, operated, and maintained by the university. From funds derived from the operation of the property, the university pays annually as rent the amount of the foundation's mortgage payment and, as agent of the foundation, transmits that sum to the Federal National Mortgage Association. Furthermore, when the mortgage is eventually retired, the university will receive title to the improved property with no further payment whatsoever required as consideration for the transfer. The foundation holds but naked legal title to property plainly controlled and enjoyed by the university and, hence, the state. . . .
>
> Although the foundation is a corporate entity legally distinct from that of the university, the function of the one is expressly "to promote the interests and welfare" of the other, and some of the highest officers of the university are required, under the bylaws of the foundation, to serve in some of the highest positions of the foundation. Thus, a further reality of the ownership of this property is the identification to a certain extent between the holder of bare legal title and the state as holder of the entire equitable interest. In this case, then, not only does the foundation hold but naked legal title to property controlled and enjoyed by the state, but a certain identity exists as well between the holder of naked legal title and the state. For these reasons we hold the property exempt from taxation as property belonging to the state [425 N.E.2d at 471].

Private nonprofit institutions are also often exempt from local real property taxation. Generally, the applicable state law provisions will exempt property of institutions organized for an educational purpose if the property at issue is used for that purpose. Sometimes such exemptions will extend to public institutions as well as private.[6] In the *Southern Illinois University* case above, for example, the court held that the housing for married students was exempt not only as state property but also as property of an educational institution devoted to an educational use. (The latter feature of this case is discussed later in this section.)

The states vary in the tests they apply to implement the "educational use" exemption. Some require that the property be used "exclusively" for educational

---

[6]Some of the cases are collected in Annot., "What Are Educational Institutions or Schools Within State Property Tax Exemption Provisions," 34 A.L.R.4th 698 (1991 and periodic supp.).

purposes to qualify for an exemption. Others require only that the property be used "primarily" for educational purposes. The cases below illustrate the variety of decisions reached under different standards of "use" and differing factual circumstances.

Appeal of the University of Pittsburgh, 180 A.2d 760 (Pa. 1962), is a leading case concerning the exemption of houses provided by postsecondary institutions for their presidents or chancellors.[7] The court allowed an exemption under a lenient standard of use:

> The head of such an institution, whether he be called president or chancellor, represents to the public eye the "image" of the institution. Both an educator and an administrator of the tremendous "business" which any university or college now is, he must also be the official representative to host those who, for one reason or the other, find the university or college a place of interest and, if he is to assume the full scope and responsibility of his duties to the university or college, he must be universal in his contacts. Many years ago the Supreme Court of Massachusetts in *Amherst College v. Assessors,* . . . 79 N.E. 248, stated: "At the same time the usage and customs of the college impose upon the president certain social obligations. . . . The scope, observations, and usage of the character mentioned are not matters of express requirement or exaction. They are, however, required of a president in the use of the house, and noncompliance with them unquestionably would subject him to unfavorable comment from the trustees and others, or, at least, be regarded as a failure on his part to discharge the obligations and hospitality associated with his official position." . . . The residence of the head of a university or college necessarily renders a real function, tangibly and intangibly, in the life of the institution. While its utility to the purposes and objectives of the institution is incapable of exact measurement and evaluation, it is nonetheless real and valuable [180 A.2d at 763].

Another court, citing the *Pittsburgh* case and using the same lenient test, denied an exemption for the house of a president emeritus. The court made a finding of fact that the house was not actually used for institutional purposes:

> [The court in the *Pittsburgh* case] held that a president's or chancellor's residence could enjoy tax exemption where the record showed that the majority of the events for which the residence was utilized bore a direct relationship to the proper functioning of the University of Pittsburgh and served its aims and objectives. In this appeal the record does not support the test laid down in [that case]. This record reflects that the president emeritus is retained on a consultative basis in development and public relations. The residence provided the president emeritus by the trustees appears to properly afford him an appropriate dwelling house commensurate with his past worthy service to Albright College. The record does not support, as in the case of the chancellor's residence of the University of Pittsburgh, that the residence in fact was used for the general purposes of Albright College [*In re Albright College,* 249 A.2d 833, 835 (Pa. Super. Ct. 1968)].

[7]Cases on housing for institutional personnel are collected in Annot., "Tax Exemption of Property of Educational Body as Extending to Property Used by Personnel as Living Quarters," 55 A.L.R.3d 485 (1991 and periodic supp.).

In *Cook County Collector v. National College of Education*, 354 N.E.2d 507 (Ill. App. Ct. 1976), the institution introduced extensive evidence of the institutional use of the president's house. The vice president for business affairs testified that the house, "although used as the residence of the president, . . . is used as well for a number of educational, fund-raising, business, alumni, and social activities of the college," citing many examples. The exemption was denied, however, because the evidence did not satisfy the more stringent use test applied in that jurisdiction:

> On cross-examination . . . [the vice president] stated that classes are not held in the home; that access to the home is by invitation only; and that the primary use of the premises is to house the president and his family.
> The trial court found that the property was not exempt, stating that it is used primarily for residential purposes as an accommodation for the president and only incidentally for college-related purposes [354 N.E.2d at 508].

More recently, a Texas court reached the same result in a similar case, denying a tax exemption for a college president's house under a strictly construed "exclusive use" statute (*Bexar Appraisal v. Incarnate Word College*, 824 S.W.2d 295 (Tex. Ct. App. 1992)).

Cases dealing with faculty and staff housing illustrate a similar split of opinions, depending on the facts of the case and the tests applied. In *MacMurray College v. Wright*, 230 N.E.2d 846 (Ill. 1967), for example, the court, applying a "primary use" test, denied tax exemptions for MacMurray College and Rockford College:

> The colleges have failed to demonstrate clearly that the faculty and staff housing was primarily used for purposes which were reasonably necessary for the carrying out of the schools' educational purposes. The record does not show that any of the faculty or staff members of either college were required, because of their educational duties, to live in these residences or that they were required to or did perform any of their professional duties there. Also, though both records before us contain general statements that there were associations between the concerned faculty and students outside the classroom, there was no specific proof presented, aside from one isolated example, to show that student, academic, faculty, administrative, or any other type of college-connected activities were ever actually conducted at home by any member of the faculty or staff of either of the colleges [230 N.E.2d at 850].

The same result was reached by the California Supreme Court in a case involving the taxability of the leasehold interests of faculty and staff members who owned homes situated on land they leased from their employer, a state university that owned the land. In *Connolly v. County of Orange*, 824 P.2d 663 (Cal. 1992), a faculty member, supported by the university and the university housing corporation, sought exemption under a state constitutional provision applicable to "property used exclusively for . . . state colleges and state universities" (Cal. Const. Art. XIII, § 3(d)). The state university's own ownership interest in the property was tax exempt under another constitutional provision (§ 3(a)), which exempted property owned by the state. In an elaborate opinion, the court held that, although the leasehold interest in the land could qualify as property under Section 3(d), land that is the site for a private residence is not "used exclusively" for the state university's purposes, and the lease-hold interest in the land is therefore not exempt from taxation.

Student dormitories present a clearer case. They are usually exempt from property taxation, even if the institution charges students rent. Other types of student housing, however, may present additional complexities. In *Southern Illinois University v. Booker*, 425 N.E.2d 465 (Ill. App. Ct. 1981) (discussed earlier in this section), the court considered whether apartments for married students were exempt from taxation. The question was whether this housing was more like dormitory housing for single students, which is generally considered an exempt educational use in Illinois, or like faculty and staff housing, which is generally not considered an exempt educational use in Illinois. Making ample use of the facts, the court chose the former:

> Without belaboring the point, we think that married students, for purposes of the comparison with faculty members, are first and foremost students. They are, therefore, more nearly analogous to single students, whose dormitory housing, as we have said, has long enjoyed tax-exempt status in Illinois. Married students seeking an education seem analogous to faculty members, for purposes of this comparison, only insofar as faculty members are often married and raising families. Faculty members, however, have usually completed their educations and are obviously employed, whereas students, by their very nature, have not completed their educations and are, if not unemployed, generally living on quite limited incomes. If a student cannot both attend school and afford to support his or her family in private housing, family obligations being what they are, the student cannot attend school, at least in the absence of low-cost family housing of the kind in issue here. Similarly, if a student cannot find available private housing for his or her family in a community crowded by students seeking housing not provided by the educational institution itself, the student cannot attend school. Therefore, we consider married student housing as necessary to the education of a married student as single-student housing is to a single student. Since the use of dormitory housing, serving essentially single students, is deemed primarily educational rather than residential, the use of family housing for married students should likewise be deemed primarily educational, and such property should enjoy tax-exempt status [425 N.E.2d at 474].

Similarly, courts may or may not accord sorority and fraternity houses the same tax treatment as student dormitories. If the institution itself owns the property, it must prove that the property is used for the educational purposes of the institution. In *Alford v. Emory University*, 116 S.E.2d 596 (Ga. 1960), the court held that fraternity houses operated by the university as part of its residential program were entitled to a tax exemption:

> Under the evidence in this case, these fraternity buildings were built by the university; they are regulated and supervised by the university; they are located in the heart of the campus, upon property owned by the university, required to be so located and to be occupied only by students of the university; adopted as a part of the dormitory and feeding system of the college, and an integral part of the operation of the college. In our opinion these fraternity houses are buildings erected for and used as a college, and not used for the purpose of making either private or corporate income or profit for the university, and our law says that they shall be exempt from taxes [116 S.E.2d at 601].

More recently, *Alford* was followed in *Johnson v. Southern Greek Housing Corp.*, 307 S.E.2d 491 (Ga. 1983). Georgia Southern College, part of the University of Georgia System, organized the Southern Greek Housing Corporation in order to provide the college's fraternities and sororities with housing close to campus. The corporation, not the college, held title to the property on which the fraternity houses were to be built. The Georgia Supreme Court concluded that the fraternity and sorority houses would be "'buildings erected for and used as a college' [quoting *Alford*] and that such buildings [would be] used for the operation of an educational institution." The court held that, even though the property was owned by a corporation and not the college, the fact that the corporation "performs an educational function with and under the auspices of" the college sufficed to bring the case within *Alford*.

In contrast, the court in *Cornell University v. Board of Assessors*, 260 N.Y.S.2d 197 (N.Y. App. Div. 1965), focused on the social uses of university-owned fraternity houses to deny an exemption under an "exclusive use" test:

> It is true, of course, that the fraternities perform the essential functions of housing and feeding students, but it is clear that, in each case, the use of the premises is also devoted, in substantial part, to the social and other personal objectives of a privately organized, self-perpetuating club, controlled by graduate as well as student members. The burden of demonstrating these objectives to be educational purposes was not sustained and thus . . . [the lower court] properly found that the premises were not used "exclusively" for educational purposes, within the intendment of the exemption statute [260 N.Y.S.2d at 199].

But in a later case, *University of Rochester v. Wagner*, 408 N.Y.S.2d 157 (N.Y. App. Div. 1978), *affirmed*, 392 N.E.2d 569 (N.Y. 1979), the New York courts qualified the *Cornell University* holding. The University of Rochester owned nine fraternity houses for which it sought tax-exempt status. Unlike the *Cornell* case, where the houses served "social and other personal objectives" (but somewhat like the *Alford* case), the University of Rochester houses had become integrated into the university's housing program: the university controlled the houses' "exterior grounds, walkways, and access points"; the houses' dining programs were part of the university's dining program; the university periodically "review[ed] the health and viability" of the houses; and the university occasionally assigned nonfraternity members to live in the houses. Applying the "exclusive use" test, and analogizing these fraternity houses to dormitories, the courts granted the university's application for tax exemption:

> Like dormitories, the fraternity houses here serve the primary function of housing and feeding students while they attend the university and complete the required curriculum. This use has been held to be in furtherance of the university's educational purposes. Moreover, the social intercourse and recreational activities that take place in the fraternity houses are similar both in quantity and quality to that which occurs in the dormitories. This social activity, although incidental to the primary use of the facilities, is essential to the personal, social, and moral development of the student and should not be found to change the character of the property from one whose use is reasonably incident to and in furtherance of the university's exempt purposes to a use which is not. For the same reason that dormitories have traditionally been held tax exempt, we see no

reason why under the facts of this case the fraternity houses should not be accorded similar treatment [408 N.Y.S.2d at 164–65].

If an independently incorporated fraternity or sorority seeks its own property tax exemption, it must demonstrate an educational, religious, or charitable purpose independent of the university and prove that the property is used for that purpose. Greek letter and other social fraternities usually do not qualify for exemptions. In *Kappa Alpha Educational Foundation v. Holliday*, 226 A.2d 825 (Del. 1967), the court found that a fraternity house was being held as an investment by the corporation that owned it and therefore did not qualify for exemption. Professional fraternities may be somewhat more successful in establishing the educational purpose and use of their property in order to qualify for exemption. In *City of Memphis v. Alpha Beta Welfare Assn.*, 126 S.W.2d 323 (Tenn. 1939), the Supreme Court of Tennessee upheld a district court's finding of fact that a medical fraternity's house was used exclusively for educational purposes:

> It is shown in proof that the student members of the fraternity by reason of being housed together receive medical, ethical, and cultural instruction that they otherwise would not get. The acquisition of the property in order that the students might be housed together was but the means to the end that the purpose of the Phi Chi Medical Fraternity to promote the welfare of medical students morally and scientifically might be more effectively carried out [126 S.W.2d at 326].

Moreover, even if a campus sorority or fraternity does not qualify for an educational exemption, it may qualify in some jurisdictions under a general statutory exemption for social organizations. In *Gamma Phi Chapter of Sigma Chi Building Fund Corp. v. Dade County*, 199 So. 2d 717 (Fla. 1967), the court held that the property of a national college fraternity was eligible for a statutory exemption designed for fraternal lodges. The exemption was denied on a technicality, however, because the fraternity missed the filing date.[8]

Athletic and recreational facilities owned by an educational institution may be exempt if the institution can prove that the facilities are used for educational purposes. Facilities far in excess of the institution's potential use may be subject to judicial scrutiny. In *Trustees of Rutgers University v. Piscataway Township*, 46 A.2d 56 (N.J. 1946), the court held that a stadium with a seating capacity of twenty thousand owned by an institution with a student body of seventeen hundred was not entitled to a property tax exemption.

Dining facilities that are located on the property of an educational institution and whose purpose is to serve the college community rather than to generate a profit have long been recognized as part of the educational program and therefore entitled to a property tax exemption.[9] In *Goodman v. University of Illinois Foundation*, 58

---

[8]The relevant cases on sorority and fraternity houses are collected in Annot., "Exemption from Taxation of College Fraternity or Sorority House," 66 A.L.R.2d 904 (1959 and periodic supp.).

[9]Cases on dining facilities are collected in Annot., "Property Used as Dining Rooms or Restaurants as Within Tax Exemptions Extended to Property of Religious, Educational, Charitable, or Hospital Organizations," 60 A.L.R.2d 521 (1960 and periodic supp.).

N.E.2d 33 (Ill. 1944), the court upheld an exemption for dining halls (as well as dormitory and recreational facilities) even though the university derived incidental income by charging for the services. Dining facilities may be tax exempt even if the institution contracts with a private caterer to provide food services. In *Blair Academy v. Blairstown*, 232 A.2d 178 (N.J. Super Ct. App. Div. 1967), the court held:

> The use of a catering system to feed the students and faculty of this boarding school cannot be regarded as a commercial activity or business venture of the school. Blair pays for this catering service an annual charge of $376 per person. It has been found expedient by the management of the school to have such a private caterer, in lieu of providing its own personnel to furnish this necessary service. The practice has been carried on for at least ten years. Nor do we find material as affecting Blair's nonprofit status that the catering system uses Blair's kitchen equipment and facilities in its performance or that some of the caterer's employees were permitted by the school to occupy quarters at the school, rent-free [232 A.2d at 181–82].

Exemptions of various other kinds of institutional property also depend on the particular use of the property and the particular test applied in the jurisdiction. In *Princeton University Press v. Borough of Princeton*, 172 A.2d 420 (N.J. 1961), a university press was denied exemption under an "exclusive use" test.

> There is no question that the petitioner has been organized exclusively for the mental and moral improvements of men, women, and children. The press's publication of outstanding scholarly works, which the trade houses would not be apt to publish because of insufficient financial returns, carries out not only the purposes for which it was organized but also performs a valuable public service. It cannot be likewise concluded, however, that the property is *exclusively used* for the mental and moral improvement of men, women, and children as required by the statute. A substantial portion of the press's activity consists of printing work taken in for the purpose of offsetting the losses incurred in the publication of scholarly books. Such printing, which includes work done for educational and nonprofit organizations other than Princeton University, is undertaken for the purpose of making a profit. Hence, in this sense the printing takes on the nature of a commercial enterprise and, therefore, it cannot be said that the property is *exclusively used* for the statutory purpose [172 A.2d at 424].

But in *District of Columbia v. Catholic Education Press*, 199 F.2d 176 (D.C. Cir. 1952), a university press was granted an exemption:

> The Catholic Education Press does not stand alone. It is a publishing arm of the [Catholic University of America]. It is an integral part of it. It has no separate life except bare technical corporate existence. It is not a private independent corporation, but to all intents and purposes it is a facility of the university. . . .
>
> If the Catholic University of America, in its own name, should engage in activities identical with those of its subsidiary, the Catholic Education Press, we suppose its right to exemption from taxation on the personal property used in such activities would not be questioned. We see no reason for denying the exemp-

tion to the university merely because it chooses to do the work through a separate nonprofit corporation [199 F.2d at 178–79].

In *City of Ann Arbor v. University Cellar*, 258 N.W.2d 1 (Mich. 1977), the issue was the application of a local personal property tax to the inventory of a campus bookstore at the University of Michigan. The statute provided an exemption for property "belonging to" the state or to an incorporated educational institution. The bookstore, the University Cellar, was a nonprofit corporation whose creation had been authorized by the university's board of regents. The majority of the corporation's board of directors, however, were appointed by the student government. The court determined that the directors did not represent the board of regents or the university administration and that the regents did not control the operation of the bookstore. Distinguishing the *Catholic Education Press* case, where the separately incorporated entity was essentially the alter ego of the university, the court denied the exemption because the property could not be said to "belong to" the university.

As the *University Cellar* case demonstrates, some of the most important tax exemption issues that arise concern the property of separate entities which the institution establishes or with which it affiliates (see generally Sections 2.2.5 and 9.3.5). The cases about fraternities, housing or facilities corporations, and university presses also illustrate this problem. Another interesting illustration comes from a recent case concerning the property of an athletic conference whose members were universities. In *In re Atlantic Coast Conference*, 434 S.E.2d 865 (N.C. Ct. App. 1993), the county in which the ACC maintained its headquarters denied the ACC's request for an exemption from property taxes for the building it used as administrative offices. Reviewing the county's decision, the Court of Appeals of North Carolina examined "the four separate and distinct requirements" of the statute that must be met before an exemption will be granted: (1) the property is owned by an educational institution, (2) the owner is organized and operated as a nonprofit entity, (3) the property must be used for activities incident to the operation of an educational institution, and (4) the property is used by the owner only for educational purposes (N.C. Gen. Stat. § 105-278.4).

The court found that, since the ACC was an unincorporated association whose only members were institutions that were themselves exempt from property taxes, the first element was satisfied. The third element was satisfied because "athletic activities are a natural part of the education process," and "in collegiate athletics, the negotiation of network contracts and management of broadcasts [functions of the ACC for which it used its building] are . . . necessarily incidental to the operation of educational institutions. . . ." The fourth element was also satisfied because the ACC's main activities, negotiating TV contracts and managing tournaments, both "qualify as 'educational.'" The court, however, could not determine whether the second element (a nonprofit entity) was met. Because neither the member institutions nor the ACC had disclosed adequate financial information for the court's review, the court remanded the case to the lower court for a ruling on the second element. The Supreme Court of North Carolina affirmed without opinion (441 S.E.2d 550 (N.C. 1994)).

Similar tax exemption problems may also arise when a postsecondary institution enters a lease arrangement with a separate entity. If the institution leases some of its property to another entity, the property may or may not retain its exempt status. In such cases exemption again depends on the use of the property and the exemption tests applied in the jurisdiction,[10] and particular consideration may be given to the extent to which the institution controls the property in the hands of the separate entity. Parallel tax exemption problems may also be encountered when an institution leases property *from* (rather than *to*) another entity. *Wheaton College v. Department of Revenue*, 508 N.E.2d 1136 (Ill. App. Ct. 1987) (although a case involving the state rather than a local government), is illustrative. The college had entered a thirty-year lease for an apartment building that it used for student housing—concededly a tax-exempt purpose. The question was whether the college had sufficient indicia of ownership to be considered the property's owner for tax purposes. Although recognizing that "ownership of real estate is a broad concept and can apply to one other than the record titleholder" (508 N.E.2d at 1137), the court held that the college was not the actual owner of the property and was not entitled to the tax exemption. The court found that the "leasing arrangement in question was undertaken primarily for the benefit" of the lessor rather than the college, and "the tax and other advantages of the transaction inured" to the lessors' benefit (508 N.E.2d at 1138). Moreover, "although the lease gives [the college] several incidents of ownership, including the right to remove existing structures and the right to sublease the property, it does not give others, such as the right to alienate fully the property" (508 N.E.2d at 1138).

If institutional property (or that of a separate entity) is denied an exemption and subjected to property taxation, the institution's (or the separate entity's) administrators must then deal with the problem of valuation. After a property tax assessor makes the initial assessment, the institution may challenge the assessment through procedures established by the local government. The assessment of institutional property may be difficult because of the absence of comparable market values. In *Dartmouth Corp. of Alpha Delta v. Town of Hanover*, 332 A.2d 390 (N.H. 1975), an independent fraternity challenged the assessment of its property. To arrive at an evaluation, the town had compared the fraternity property to dormitory facilities. The court upheld the assessor's estimate, reasoning that "in view of the functional similarity between fraternities and dormitories and considering that the college regulates the rents of both types of facilities, it was not unlawful for the board to consider the income and costs of the fraternity buildings if used as dormitories in ascertaining their assessed value."

5.3.3. Sales, admission, and amusement taxes. A local government may have authority to impose a sales tax on the sales or purchases of an educational institution. The institution may claim a specific exemption based on a particular provision of the sales tax ordinance or a general exemption provided by a state statute or the state constitution. The language of the provision may limit the exemption only to the sales or to the purchases of an educational institution or may cover both. The institution's eligibility for exemption from these taxes, as from property taxes, depends on the language of the provision creating the exemption, as interpreted by the courts, and the particular factual circumstances."[11]

[10]Cases dealing with leased property are collected in Annot., "Tax Exemption—Leased Property," 55 A.L.R.3d 430 (1974 and periodic supp.).

[11]The relevant cases on sales taxes, as well as "use" taxes sometimes levied in place of sales taxes, are collected in Annot., "Exemption of Charitable or Educational Organization from Sales or Use Tax," 53 A.L.R.3d 748 (1973 and periodic supp.).

New York University v. Taylor, 296 N.Y.S. 848 (N.Y. App. Div. 1937), *affirmed without opin.*, 12 N.E.2d 606 (N.Y. 1938), arose after the comptroller of the city of New York tried to impose a sales tax on both the sales and the purchases of a non-profit educational institution. The law in effect at that time provided that "receipts from sales or services . . . by or to semipublic institutions . . . shall not be subject to tax hereunder." Semipublic institutions were defined as "those charitable and reli-gious institutions which are supported wholly or in part by public subscriptions or endowment and are not organized or operated for profit." The court made a finding of fact that the university was a "semipublic institution" within the meaning of the statute and therefore was not subject to taxation on its sales or purchases.

Sales by an educational institution may be exempt even if some of the insti-tution's activities generate a profit. The exemption will depend on the use of the profits and the language of the exemption. In *YMCA v. City of Philadelphia*, 11 A.2d 529 (Pa. Super. Ct. 1940), the court held that the sale was not subject to taxation under an ordinance that exempted sales by or to semipublic institutions:

> Certainly, the ordinance contemplated a departure by such institutions from the activities of a public charity, which, in its narrowest sense, sells nothing and is supported wholly by public subscriptions and contributions or endow-ment; and may be said to recognize that many institutions organized for chari-table purposes and supported in part by public subscriptions or endowment do engage in certain incidental activities, of a commercial nature, the proceeds of which, and any profits derived therefrom, are devoted to the general charitable work of the institution and applied to no alien or selfish purpose [11 A.2d at 531].

City of Boulder v. Regents of the University of Colorado, 501 P.2d 123 (Colo. 1972), concerned the attempt of the local government to impose an admission tax on various events, including intercollegiate football games, held on the University of Colorado campus. The court held that the city could not impose tax collection re-sponsibilities on the university because the university, as a branch of the state govern-ment, could claim sovereign immunity. The Supreme Court of Colorado quoted the trial court's opinion with approval:

> "In the instant case the city is attempting to impose duties on the board of regents which would necessarily interfere with the regents' control of the university. The constitution establishes a statewide university and vests control in the board of regents. The board of regents has exclusive control and direction of all funds of, and appropriations to, the university. . . . Thus, the city of Boulder cannot force the regents to apply any funds toward the collection of the tax in question. Even if the city claims that sufficient funds would be generated by the tax to compensate the regents for collection expense and, arguably, such funds could be paid to the regents by the city, the regents are still vested with the 'general supervision' of the university. The university would necessarily be re-quired to expend both money and manpower for the collection, identification, and payment of such funds to the city. This interferes with the financial conduct of the university and the allocation of its manpower for its statewide educational duties. . . .
>
> "Thus, since the constitution has established a statewide university at Boulder and vested general supervisory control in a statewide board of regents and

management in control of the state, a city, even though a home rule city, has no power to interfere with the management or supervision of the activities of the University of Colorado. If the city of Boulder was allowed to impose duties on the university, such duties would necessarily interfere with the functions of the state institution. There is no authority to permit the city of Boulder to force a state institution to collect such a local tax. Consequently, the city of Boulder cannot require the board of regents of the University of Colorado to become involuntary collectors of the city of Boulder's admission tax" [501 P.2d at 125].

The court also held, over two dissents, that the admission tax was itself invalid as applied to various university functions:

> When academic departments of the university, or others acting under the auspices of the university, sponsor lectures, dissertations, art exhibitions, concerts, and dramatic performances, whether or not an admission fee is charged, these functions become a part of the educational process. This educational process is not merely for the enrolled students of the university, but it is a part of the educational process for those members of the public attending the events. In our view the home rule authority of a city does not permit it to tax a person's acquisition of education furnished by the state. We hold that the tax is invalid when applied to university lectures, dissertations, art exhibitions, concerts, and dramatic performances [501 P.2d at 126].

With respect to football games, however, the Colorado court affirmed the tax's validity because the university had not made "a showing that football is so related to the educational process that its devotees may not be taxed by a home rule city." This latter ruling is "probably academic," as the court acknowledged, since under sovereign immunity the university could not be required to collect the tax, even if it were valid.[12] Subsequently, another court reached much the same result, but on different reasoning, in *City of Morgantown v. West Virginia Board of Regents*, 354 S.E.2d 616 (W. Va. 1987). At issue was an amusement tax that the city attempted to apply to ticket sales for university entertainment and athletic events. Under the authorizing statute, only amusements conducted "for private gain" could be taxed. Determining that the university's ticket receipts were "public moneys" and that the university did not conduct these events for private profit, the court held the tax to be contrary to the statute and invalid.

Sec. 5.4. *Student Voting in the Community*

The passage of the Twenty-Sixth Amendment to the U.S. Constitution in 1971, lowering the voting age to eighteen, created several new problems for postsecondary administrators. On some voting issues, administrators may at most play an intermediary or advocate role in disputes between students and the community. Other issues require positive action by administrators to establish guidelines for voting activities on campus.

---

[12]Relevant cases on admission taxes are collected in Annot., "Validity of Municipal Admission Tax for College Football Games or Other College Sponsored Events," 60 A.L.R.3d 1027 (1974 and periodic supp.).

5.4.1. Registering to vote. The extension of the franchise did not automatically give every citizen over eighteen the right to vote. All potential voters must register with the board of elections of their legal residence in order to exercise their right. Determining the legal residence of students attending residential institutions has created major controversies. Some small communities near colleges and universities, fearful of the impact of the student vote, have tried to limit student registration, while students eager to participate in local affairs and to avoid the inconveniences of absentee voting have pushed for local registration.

The trend of the cases has been to overturn statutes and election board practices that impede student registration, and sometimes to overturn state statutes that authorize such practices. In *Jolicoeur v. Mihaly*, 488 P.2d 1 (Cal. 1971), the court considered a statute that created an almost conclusive presumption that an unmarried minor's residence was his or her parents' home. The court held that this statute violated the Equal Protection Clause and the Twenty-Sixth Amendment:

> Sophisticated legal arguments regarding a minor's presumed residence cannot blind us to the real burden placed on the right to vote and associated rights of political expression by requiring minor voters residing apart from their parents to vote in their parents' district. . . .
>
> An unmarried minor must be subject to the same requirements in proving the location of his domicile as is any other voter. Fears of the way minors may vote or of their impermanency in the community may not be used to justify special presumptions—conclusive or otherwise—that they are not bona fide residents of the community in which they live.
>
> It is clear that respondents have abridged petitioners' right to vote in precisely one of the ways that Congress sought to avoid—by singling minor voters out for special treatment and effectively making many of them vote by absentee ballot. . . .
>
> Respondents' policy would clearly frustrate youthful willingness to accomplish change at the local level through the political system. Whether a youth lives in Quincy, Berkeley, or Orange County, he will not be brought into the bosom of the political system by being told that he may not have a voice in the community in which he lives, but must instead vote wherever his parents live or may move to. Surely as well, such a system would give any group of voters less incentive "in devising responsible programs" in the town in which they live [488 P.2d at 4, 7].

Another court invalidated a Michigan statute that created a rebuttable presumption that students are not voting residents of the district where their institution is located. The statute was implemented through elaborate procedures applicable only to students. The court held that the statute infringed the right to vote in violation of the Equal Protection Clause (*Wilkins v. Bentley*, 189 N.W.2d 423 (Mich. 1971)). And in *United States v. State of Texas*, 445 F. Supp. 1245 (S.D. Tex. 1978), a three-judge federal court enjoined the voting registrar of Waller County from applying a burdensome presumption of nonresidency to unmarried dormitory students at Prairie View A&M University. The U.S. Supreme Court summarily affirmed the lower court's decision without issuing any written opinion (*Symm v. United States*, 439 U.S. 1105 (1979)).

In contrast, courts have upheld statutory provisions making attendance at a local college or university irrelevant as a factor in determining a student's residence. In *Whittingham v. Board of Elections*, 320 F. Supp. 889 (N.D.N.Y. 1970), a special three-judge court upheld a "gain or loss provision" of the New York constitution. This provision, found in many state constitutions and statutes, requires a student to prove residency by indicia other than student status. The *Whittingham* case was followed by *Gorenberg v. Onondaga County Board of Elections*, 328 N.Y.S.2d 198 (N.Y. App. Div. 1972), *modified*, 286 N.E.2d 247 (N.Y. 1972), upholding the New York State voting statute specifying criteria for determining residence, including dependency, employment, marital status, age, and location of property.

A series of more recent New York cases illustrates and refines the principles developed in these earlier cases. In *Auerbach v. Rettaliata*, 765 F.2d 350 (2d Cir. 1985), students from two State University of New York (SUNY) campuses challenged the constitutionality of the New York voting residency statute, a virtually identical successor to the statute upheld in *Gorenberg*. The students claimed that the statute—by authorizing county voting registrars to consider factors such as students' financial independence and the residence of their parents—imposed unduly heavy burdens on their eligibility to vote. The court upheld the *facial* validity of the statute because it did not establish any "presumption against student residency." As interpreted by the court, the statute merely specified criteria that could demonstrate "physical presence and intention to remain for the time at least." Although these criteria would require "classes of likely transients" to demonstrate more than physical presence in the county, such treatment was permissible under the Equal Protection Clause.

The *Auerbach* court did caution, however, that even though the New York statute was constitutional on its face, courts would nevertheless intervene in residency determinations if election officials administered the law in a manner that discriminated against students. In *Williams v. Salerno*, 792 F.2d 323 (2d Cir. 1986), the same U.S. Court of Appeals had occasion to put that caution into practice. Students from another SUNY campus challenged an election board's ruling that a dormitory could not be considered a voting residence under the New York voter residency statute, thus prohibiting college dormitory residents from registering. Building on *Auerbach*, the court agreed that the state election law would allow election boards to make more searching inquiries about the residence of students and other presumably transient groups, as long as the boards did not apply more rigorous substantive requirements regarding residency to these groups than they did to other voters. But the court nevertheless invalidated the election board's action under the Equal Protection Clause because it did impose a more rigorous requirement on dormitory students that barred them from voting regardless of the presence of other circumstances that could demonstrate an intent to remain.

Similarly, in *Levy v. Scranton*, 780 F. Supp. 897 (N.D.N.Y. 1991), another court in a suit brought by students at Skidmore College used *Auerbach* and *Williams v. Salerno* to invalidate a county board of elections policy under which the board disqualified students from voting if they had an on-campus residence. The court enjoined the board from denying the right to vote solely on this basis. At the same time, however, the court reconsidered and upheld the validity of the New York statute itself.

Some general rules for constitutionally sound determinations of student residency emerge from these cases. The mere fact that the student lives in campus housing is not a sufficient basis to deny residency. On the other hand, mere presence as a student is not itself sufficient to establish voting residency. Rather, election boards can require not only physical presence but also manifestation of an intent to establish residency in the community. Present intent to establish residency is probably sufficient. Students who intend to leave the community after graduation do not have such intent. Students who are uncertain about their postgraduate plans, but consider the community to be their home for the time being, probably do have such intent. A statute that required proof of intent to remain indefinitely in the community after graduation was held a denial of equal protection in *Whatley v. Clark*, 482 F.2d 1230 (5th Cir. 1973).

Uncertainties concerning future plans and the difficulties of proving intent complicate the application of these general rules. To address these complexities, election boards may use a range of criteria for determining whether a student intends to establish residency. Such criteria may include vacation activity, the location of property owned by the student, the choice of banks and other services, membership in community groups, location of employment, and the declaration of residence for other purposes, such as tax payment and automobile registration. Election officials must be careful to apply such criteria evenhandedly to all voter registrants and, if more searching inquiries are made of some registrants, to apply the same level of inquiry to all potential transient groups.

5.4.2. Scheduling elections. The only reported case that deals with the timing of an election in a district with a substantial student population is *Walgren v. Board of Selectmen of the Town of Amherst*, 519 F.2d 1364 (1st Cir. 1975). The appellate court's opinion lays out the special facts of the case:

> The controversy arises from events which took place over a ten-day period in December 1972, during which the town selectmen, at plaintiff Walgren's urging, endeavored to change the scheduled date for the town caucus, the primary election in which nominees for the positions of town officer and town meeting member are selected. On December 10, 1972, Walgren protested the then recently published schedule for the 1973 elections on the ground that the caucus date of January 19 would be during the winter recess of the University of Massachusetts, when some ten thousand dormitory students would be out of town. On December 11, the board voted to reconsider the schedule at its December 18 meeting. After a week of public reaction, both pro and con, a long and animated meeting was held on December 18, at the end of which the board voted to establish a new calendar. But the dates for the caucus and the final election proposed by Walgren, January 29 and March 1, raised the possibility of a conflict with a state requirement that thirty-one days separate the two dates. The board, being of the opinion that statutory notice for the proposed new dates would have to be published by the following day, provisionally adopted them, subject to advice of counsel. When, on December 19, the advice was received that the dates would be illegal, the board, at a special meeting in the evening, turned down its counsel's proposal that the town meeting itself be moved ahead by a week, and reinstated the original calendar [519 F.2d at 1365].

The lower court refused to set aside the election. Although disagreeing with the lower court's finding that the burden on students' and faculty members' right to vote was insignificant, the appellate court relied on the good-faith efforts of the selectmen to schedule an appropriate date:

> In short, we would be disturbed if, given time to explore alternatives and given alternatives which would satisfy all reasonable town objectives, a town continued to insist on elections during vacations or recess, secure in the conviction that returning to town and absentee voting would be considered insignificant burdens.
>
> The critical element which in our view serves to sustain the 1973 election is the foreshortened time frame within which the selectmen were forced to face up to and resolve a problem which was then novel. . . .
>
> We would add that, under the circumstances of this case, even if we had found the burden impermissible, we would have looked upon the novelty and complexity of the issue, the shortness of time, and the good-faith efforts of the defendants as sufficient justification for refusing to order a new election at this late date [519 F.2d at 1368].

The special facts of the case and the narrowness of the court's holding limit *Walgren's* authority as precedent. But *Walgren* does suggest that, under some circumstances, an election deliberately scheduled so as to disenfranchise an identifiable segment of the student electorate can be successfully challenged.

5.4.3. Canvassing and registration on campus. The regulation of voter canvassing and registration on campus is the voting issue most likely to require the direct involvement of college and university administrators. Any regulation must accommodate the First Amendment rights of the canvassers; the First Amendment rights of the students, faculty, and staff who may be potential listeners; the privacy interests of those who may not wish to be canvassed; the requirements of local election law; and the institution's interests in order and safety. Not all of these considerations have been explored in litigation.[13]

James v. Nelson, 349 F. Supp. 1061 (N.D. Ill. 1972), illustrates one type of challenge to a campus canvassing regulation. Northern Illinois University had for some time prohibited all canvassing in student living areas. After receiving requests to modify this prohibition, the university proposed a new regulation, which would have permitted canvassing under specified conditions. Before the new regulation could go into effect, however, it had to be adopted in a referendum by two-thirds of the students in each dormitory, after which individual floors could implement it by a two-thirds vote. The court held that this referendum requirement unconstitutionally infringed the freedom-of-association and freedom-of-speech rights of the students who wished to canvas or be canvassed. The basis for the *James* decision is difficult to discern. The court emphasized that the proposed canvassing regulation was not "in any way unreasonable or beyond the powers of the university administration to impose in the interests of good order and the safety and comfort of the student body." If the proposed regulation was constitutional, a referendum adopting it would not infringe anyone's constitutional rights. The court's implicit ruling must be that the

---

[13]Cases are collected in Annot., "Validity of College or University Regulation of Political or Voter Registration Activity in Student Housing Facilities," 39 A.L.R.4th 1137 (1991 and periodic supp.).

university's blanket prohibition on canvassing was an infringement of First Amendment rights, and a requirement that this prohibition could be removed only by a two-thirds vote of the students in each dormitory and each floor was also an infringement on the rights of those students who would desire a liberalized canvassing policy.

National Movement for the Student Vote v. Regents of the University of California, 123 Cal. Rptr. 141 (Cal. Ct. App. 1975), was decided on statutory grounds. A local statute permitted registrars to register voters at their residence. University policy, uniformly enforced, did not allow canvassing in student living areas. Registrars were permitted to canvass in public areas of the campus and in the lobbies of the dormitories. The court held that the privacy interest of the students limited the registrars' right to canvass to reasonable times and places and that the limitations imposed by the university were reasonable and in compliance with the law. In determining reasonableness, the court emphasized the following facts:

> There was evidence and findings to the effect that dining and other facilities of the dormitories are on the main floor; the private rooms of the students are on the upper floors; the rooms do not contain kitchen, washing, or toilet facilities; each student must walk from his or her room to restroom facilities in the halls of the upper floors in order to bathe or use the toilet facilities; defendants, in order to "recognize and enhance the privacy" of the students and to minimize assaults upon them and thefts of their property, have maintained a policy and regulations prohibiting solicitation, distribution of materials, and recruitment of students in the upper-floor rooms; students in the upper rooms complained to university officials about persons coming to their rooms and canvassing them and seeking their registrations; defendants permitted signs regarding the election to be posted throughout the dormitories and permitted deputy registrars to maintain tables and stands in the main lobby of each dormitory for registration of students; students in each dormitory had to pass through the main lobby thereof in order to go to and from their rooms; a sign encouraging registration to vote was at each table, and students registered to vote at the tables [123 Cal. Rptr. at 146].

Though the *National Movement v. Regents* decision is based on a statute, the court's language suggests that it would use similar principles and factors in considering the constitutionality of a public institution's canvassing regulations under the First Amendment. In a later case, *Harrell v. Southern Illinois University*, 457 N.E.2d 971 (Ill. App. Ct. 1983), the court did use similar reasoning in upholding, against a First Amendment challenge, a university policy that prohibited political candidates from canvassing dormitory rooms except during designated hours in the weeks preceding elections. The court also indicated that the First Amendment (as well as that state's election law) would permit similar restrictions on canvassing by voter registrars. Thus, although public institutions may not completely prohibit voter canvassing on campus, they may impose reasonable restrictions on the "time, place, and manner" of canvassing in dormitories and other such "private" locations on campus. (See also Section 5.6.4.2.)

5.4.4. Reapportionment. A series of U.S. Supreme Court decisions in the early 1960s established that "the fundamental principle of representative government in this country is one of equal representation for equal numbers of people, without regard to race, sex, economic status, or place of residence within a state" (*Reynolds v. Sims*, 377 U.S. 533, 560-61 (1964)). This "one person, one vote" standard was extended to local government elections in *Avery v. Midland County*, 390 U.S. 474 (1968), and *Hadley v. Junior College District*, 397 U.S. 50 (1970):

> Whenever a state or local government decides to select persons by popular election to perform governmental functions, the equal protection clause of the Fourteenth Amendment requires that each qualified voter must be given an equal opportunity to participate in that election, and when members of an elective body are chosen from separate districts, each district must be established on a basis that will insure, as far as is practicable, that equal numbers of voters can vote for proportionately equal numbers of officials [*Hadley*, 397 U.S. at 56].

Consistent with this basic constitutional requirement, local and state governments must periodically "reapportion" the populations of election districts and redraw their boundaries accordingly. If the election districts containing the largest percentages of student voters were to include more voters per elected official than other districts, thus diluting the voting strength of district voters (malapportionment), students or other voters could claim a violation of "one person, one vote" principles. Even if the districts with concentrations of student voters have populations substantially equal to those of other districts, students could still raise an equal protection challenge if the district lines were drawn in a way that minimized their voting strength (gerrymandering). Case law indicates, however, that both types of claims would be difficult to sustain. Beginning with *Abate v. Mundt*, 403 U.S. 182 (1971) (local elections), and *Mahan v. Howell*, 410 U.S. 315 (1973) (state elections), the U.S. Supreme Court has accepted various justifications for departing from strict population equality among districts, thus making it harder for plaintiffs to prevail on malapportionment claims. And in *Gaffney v. Cummings*, 412 U.S. 735 (1973), and later cases, the Court has flagged its reluctance to scrutinize gerrymandering that is undertaken to balance or maintain the voting strengths of political groups within the jurisdiction (but see *Shaw v. Reno*, 113 S. Ct. 2816 (1993) (racial gerrymander)).

In re House Bill 2620, 595 P.2d 334 (Kan. 1979)—apparently the only reported case dealing with student challenges to reapportionment—also illustrates the difficulty of prevailing on such claims.[14] The student senate of the University of Kansas (and others) filed suit objecting to the reapportionment of two state legislative districts covering the city of Lawrence. Prior to reapportionment, the three voting precincts with the most concentrated student vote ("L," "K," and "O") were located in one legislative district. The reapportionment plan placed two of these precincts in one district and the third in a separate district. The students contended that this redistricting was done in order to split the student vote, thus diluting student voting power. The Kansas Supreme Court disagreed, holding that the redistricting did not inviolously discriminate against students:

[14]Although no other reported cases deal with student challenges to reapportionment, dilution of minority voting power as a result of inclusion or exclusion of student populations in redistricting has been challenged by other plaintiffs. See, for example, *Houston v. Lafayette County Democratic Executive Committee*, 841 F. Supp. 751 (N.D. Miss. 1993); *Fauley v. Forrest County, Mississippi*, 814 F. Supp. 1327 (S.D. Miss. 1993).

There are presently 22,228 students enrolled in the University of Kansas. It is stated [that] a large portion of the students hold similar political beliefs, and those living in precincts identified as "L," "K," and "O" form a cohesive homogeneous unit that cannot be separated without discrimination. . . . In 1978 there were 5,138 "census persons" residing in these three precincts, and 3,156 voters were registered on October 27, 1978. Even assuming that all registered voters in these three precincts were students, which is highly questionable, the three precincts involved would represent no more than 14.2 percent of the students in the university.

Other factors militate against a solid cohesive student body. The students come from different family and political backgrounds and from different localities. Many students vote in their home districts. It is extremely doubtful that all would be of one party. Considering modern trends in higher education, each student is trained for independent thinking. Unanimity among a student body seems unlikely. Keeping all these factors in mind, we cannot say that removing precincts K and O from District 44 and placing them in the newly constituted District 46 was done for the purpose of canceling the voting strength of the 22,228 students attending the University of Kansas. We are not convinced that invidious discrimination resulted [595 P.2d at 343–44].

Sec. 5.5. *Relations with Local Police*

Since the academic community is part of the surrounding community, it will generally be within the geographical jurisdiction of one or more local (town, village, city, county) police forces. The circumstances under which local police may and will come onto the campus, and their authority once on campus, are thus of concern to every administrator. Their role on campus depends on a mixture of considerations: the state and local law of the jurisdiction, federal constitutional limitations on police powers, the adequacy of the institution's own security services, and the terms of any explicit or implicit understanding between local police and campus authorities.

If the institution has its own uniformed security officers, administrators must decide what working relationships these officers will have with local police. This decision will depend partly on the extent of the security officers' authority, especially regarding arrests, searches, and seizures—authority that should also be carefully delineated (see generally Section 4.17.1). Similarly, administrators must understand the relationship between arrest and prosecution in local courts, on the one hand, and campus disciplinary proceedings on the other (see Section 4.5.3). Although administrators cannot make crime an internal affair by hiding evidence of crime from local police, they may be able to assist local law enforcement officials in determining prosecution priorities. Campus and local officials may also be able to cooperate in determining whether a campus proceeding should be stayed pending the outcome of a court proceeding, or vice versa.

The powers of local police are circumscribed by various federal constitutional provisions, particularly the Fourth Amendment strictures on arrests, searches, and seizures. These provisions limit local police authority on both public and private campuses. Under the Fourth Amendment, local police usually must obtain a warrant before arresting or searching a member of the academic community or searching or seizing any private property on the campus (see Section 4.14.2). On a private institution's campus, nearly all the property may be private, and local police may need a warrant or the consent of whoever effectively controls the property before entering most areas of the campus. On a public institution's campus, it is more difficult to determine which property would be considered public and which private, and thus more difficult to determine when local police must have a warrant or consent prior to entry. In general, for both public and private institutions, police will need a warrant or consent before entering any area in which members of the academic community have a "reasonable expectation of privacy" (see generally *Katz v. United States,* 389 U.S. 347 (1967)). The constitutional rules and concepts are especially complex in this area, however; and administrators should consult counsel whenever questions arise concerning the authority of local police on campus.

In *People v. Dickson,* 154 Cal. Rptr. 116 (Cal. Ct. App. 1979), the court considered the validity of a warrantless search of a chemistry laboratory conducted by local police and campus security officers at the Bakersfield campus of California State University. The search uncovered samples of an illegal drug and materials used in its manufacture—evidence that led to the arrest and conviction of the defendant, a chemistry professor who used the laboratory. The court upheld the search and the conviction because, under the facts of the case (particularly facts indicating ready access to the laboratory by many persons, including campus police), the professor had no "objectively reasonable expectation of privacy" in his laboratory.

Under a similar rationale, a Pennsylvania appellate court rejected the argument that undercover police were required to obtain a search warrant before they entered a fraternity party. In *Commonwealth. v. Tau Kappa Epsilon,* 560 A.2d 786 (Pa. Super. Ct. 1989), *reversed on other grounds,* 609 A.2d 791 (Pa. 1992), two undercover officers, recent graduates of Pennsylvania State University, entered parties at eleven fraternities and observed the serving of beer to minors. The fraternities were convicted of serving beer to minors, and appealed their convictions, arguing that the police officers' warrantless entry violated the Fourth Amendment. The court disagreed:

> Security was so lax as to be virtually nonexistent; a person could enter and be furnished beverages almost at will. Under these circumstances, the fraternities could be found to have consented to the entry of [the police] and to have surrendered any reasonable expectation of privacy with respect to the events occurring in their houses [560 A.2d at 791].

That these particular searches were upheld even though the officers did not procure a warrant, however, does not mean that the practice of obtaining warrants can be routinely dispensed with. When there is time to do so, procuring a warrant or the consent of the person whose expectation of privacy may be invaded is still the surest policy.

In 1980 Congress enacted legislation that limits police search-and-seizure activities on college campuses. The legislation, the Privacy Protection Act of 1980 (42 U.S.C. § 2000aa et seq.), was passed in part to counter the U.S. Supreme Court's decision in *Zurcher v. Stanford Daily,* 436 U.S. 547 (1978). In *Zurcher* the Palo Alto, California, Police Department had obtained a warrant to search the files of the *Stanford Daily,* a student newspaper, for photographs of participants in a demonstration during which several police officers had been assaulted. The lower court found probable cause to believe that the *Stanford Daily*'s files did contain such photographs, but no probable cause to believe that the newspaper itself was engaged in any wrongdoing. The U.S. Supreme Court held that the *Stanford Daily,* even though an innocent third party and even though engaged in publication activities, had no First or Fourth Amendment rights to assert against the search warrant.

The Privacy Protection Act's coverage is not confined to newspapers, the subject of the *Zurcher* case. As its legislative history makes clear, the Act also protects scholars and other persons engaged in "public communication"—that is, the "flow of information to the public" (see S. Rep. No. 874, 96th Cong., 2d Sess., in 4 *U.S. Code Cong. & Admin. News* 3950, 3956 (1980)).

Section 101(a) of the Act pertains to the "work product materials" of individuals intending "to disseminate to the public a newspaper, book, broadcast, or other similar form of public communication." The section prohibits the searching for or seizure of the work product of such individuals by any "government officer or employee [acting] in connection with the investigation or prosecution of a criminal offense." There are several exceptions, however, to the general prohibition in Section 101(a). Search and seizure of work-product material is permitted (1) where "there is probable cause to believe that the person possessing such materials has committed or is committing the criminal offense to which the materials relate" and this offense does not consist of "the receipt, possession, communication, or withholding of such materials"; (2) where there is probable cause to believe that the possessor has committed or is committing an offense consisting "of the receipt, possession, or communication of information relating to the national defense, classified information, or restricted data" prohibited under specified provisions of national security laws; and (3) where "there is reason to believe that the immediate seizure of such materials is necessary to prevent the death of, or serious bodily injury to, a human being."

Section 101(b) of the Act covers "documentary materials, other than work product materials." The section prohibits search and seizure of such materials in the same way that Section 101(a) prohibits search and seizure of work product. The same exceptions to the general prohibition also apply. There are also two additional exceptions unique to Section 101(b), under which search and seizure of documentary materials is permitted if:

> (3) there is reason to believe that the giving of notice pursuant to a subpoena duces tecum would result in the destruction, alteration, or concealment of such materials; or
>
> (4) such materials have not been produced in response to a court order directing compliance with a subpoena duces tecum, and—
>   (A) all appellate remedies have been exhausted; or
>   (B) there is reason to believe that the delay in an investigation or trial occasioned by further proceedings relating to the subpoena would threaten the interests of justice.

Section 106 of the Act authorizes a civil suit for damages for any person subjected to a search or seizure that is illegal under Section 101(a) or 101(b).

The Act's language and legislative history clearly indicate that the Act applies to local and state, as well as federal, government officers and employees. It thus limits the authority of city, town, and county police officers both on campus and in off-campus investigations of campus scholars or journalists. The Act limits police officers and other government officials, however, only when they are investigating criminal, as opposed to civil, offenses. Scholars and journalists thus are not protected, for example, from the seizure of property to satisfy outstanding tax debts or from the regulatory inspections or compliance reviews conducted by government agencies administering civil laws. Moreover, the Act's legislative history makes clear that traditional subpoena powers and limitations are untouched by the Act (see S. Rep. No. 874, 96th Cong., 2d Sess., in 4 *U.S. Code Cong. & Admin. News* 3950, 3956–60 (1980)). (Subpoenas of scholarly information are discussed in this volume, Section 3.7.7.2.)

Different problems arise when local police enter a campus not to make an arrest or conduct a search but to engage in surveillance of members of the institutional community. In *White v. Davis*, 533 P.2d 222 (Cal. 1975), a history professor at UCLA sued the Los Angeles police chief to enjoin the use of undercover police agents for generalized surveillance in the university. Unidentified police agents had registered at the university and compiled dossiers on students and professors based on information obtained during classes and public meetings. The California Supreme Court held that such action was a prima facie violation of students' and faculty members' First Amendment freedoms of speech, assembly, and association, as well as the "right-to-privacy" provision of the California constitution. The case was returned to the trial court to determine whether the police were acting on any compelling state interest that would justify the infringement of constitutional rights.

The court's opinion differentiates the First Amendment surveillance problem from the more traditional Fourth Amendment search-and-seizure problem:

> The most familiar limitations on police investigatory and surveillance activities, of course, find embodiment in the Fourth Amendment of the federal Constitution and article I, section 13 (formerly art. I, § 19) of the California constitution. On numerous occasions in the past, these provisions have been applied to preclude specific ongoing police investigatory practices. Thus, for example, the court in *Wirin v. Parker,* 48 Cal. 2d 890, 313 P.2d 844, prohibited the police practice of conducting warrantless surveillance of private residences by means of concealed microphones. . . .
>
> Unlike these past cases involving the limits on police surveillance prescribed by the constitutional "search-and-seizure" provisions, the instant case presents the more unusual question of the limits placed upon police investigatory activities by the guarantees of freedom of speech (U.S. Const. 1st and 14th Amends.; Cal. Const., art. I, § 2). As discussed below, this issue is not entirely novel; to our knowledge, however, the present case represents the first instance in which a court has confronted the issue in relation to ongoing police surveillance of a university community.
>
> Our analysis of the limits imposed by the First Amendment upon police surveillance activities must begin with the recognition that with respect to First Amendment freedoms "the Constitution's protection is not limited to direct interference with fundamental rights" (*Healy v. James* (1972) 408 U.S. 169, 183 . . .). Thus, although police surveillance of university classrooms and organizations' meetings may not constitute a direct prohibition of speech or association, such surveillance may still run afoul of the constitutional guarantee if the effect of such activity is to chill constitutionally protected activity. . . .
>
> As a practical matter, the presence in a university classroom of undercover officers taking notes to be preserved in police dossiers must inevitably inhibit the exercise of free speech both by professors and students [533 P.2d at 228–29].

The court also emphasized the special danger that police surveillance poses for academic freedom:

> The threat to First Amendment freedoms posed by any covert intelligence gathering network is considerably exacerbated when, as in the instant case, the police surveillance activities focus upon university classrooms and their environs. As the United States Supreme Court has recognized time and again: "The vigilant protection of constitutional freedoms is nowhere more vital than in the community of American schools" (*Shelton v. Tucker*, 364 U.S. 479, 487 . . . (1960)).
>
> The police investigatory conduct at issue unquestionably poses . . . [a] debilitating . . . threat to academic freedom. . . . According to the allegations of the complaint, which for purposes of this appeal must be accepted as true, the Los Angeles Police Department has established a network of undercover agents which keeps regular check on discussions occurring in various university classes. Because the identity of such police officers is unknown, no professor or student can be confident that whatever opinion he may express in class will not find its way into a police file. . . . The crucible of new thought is the university classroom; the campus is the sacred ground of free discussion. Once we expose the teacher or the student to possible future prosecution for the ideas he may express, we forfeit the security that nourishes change and advancement. The censorship of totalitarian regimes that so often condemns developments in art, science, and politics is but a step removed from the inchoate surveillance of free discussion in the university; such intrusion stifles creativity and to a large degree shackles democracy [533 P.2d at 229–31].

The principles of *White v. Davis* would apply equally to local police surveillance at a private institution. As an agency of government, the police are prohibited from violating any person's freedom of expression or right to privacy, whether on a public campus or a private one.[15]

Sec. 5.6. Community Access to Institutional Property

5.6.1. Public versus private institutions. Postsecondary institutions have often been the location for many types of events that attract people from the surrounding community and sometimes from other parts of the state, country, or world. Because of their capacity for large audiences and the sheer numbers of students and faculty and staff members on campus every day, postsecondary institutions provide an excellent forum for speakers, conferences, exhibits, pamphleteering, and other kinds of information exchanges. In addition, cultural, entertainment, and sporting events attract large numbers of outside persons. The potential commercial market presented by concentrations of student consumers may also attract entrepreneurs to the campus,

---

[15]The right-to-privacy reasoning used in *White v. Davis* would apply only to states that recognize an individual right to privacy similar to that created under the California constitution. The applicability of the case's First Amendment reasoning may be limited to states whose courts would grant professors or students standing to raise claims of illegal surveillance. The *White* plaintiffs obtained standing under a California "taxpayer standing" statute. They apparently would not have succeeded in the federal court, since the U.S. Supreme Court has held, in *Laird v. Tatum*, 408 U.S. 1 (1972), that government surveillance does not cause the type of specific harm necessary to establish federal court standing.

and the potential labor pool that these students represent may also attract employ-ment recruiters. Whether public or private, postsecondary institutions have consider-able authority to determine how and when their property will be used for such events and activities and to regulate access by outside persons. Although a public institu-tion's authority is more limited than that of a private institution, the case of *State v. Schmid*, 423 A.2d 615 (N.J. 1980) (discussed in Section 5.6.3 below), diminishes the distinction between public and private institutions' authority to deny access to out-siders who want to engage in expressional activities.

Both private and public institutions customarily have ownership or leasehold interests in their campuses and buildings—interests protected by the property law of the state. Subject to this statutory and common law, both types of institution have authority to regulate how and by whom their property is used. Typically, an insti-tution's authority to regulate use by its students and faculty members is limited by the contractual commitments it has made to these groups (see Sections 3.1 and 4.1.3). Thus, for instance, students may have contractual rights to the reasonable use of dormitory rooms and the public areas of residence halls or of campus libraries and study rooms; and faculty members may have contractual rights to the reasonable use of office space or classrooms. For the outside community, however, such contractual rights usually do not exist.

A public institution's authority to regulate the use of its property is further limited by the federal Constitution, in particular the First Amendment (see, for ex-ample, *Lamb's Chapel v. Center Moriches Union Free School District*, 113 S. Ct. 2141 (1993)), and may also be affected by state statutes or regulations applicable to state property in general or specifically to the property of state educational institutions. Unlike contract law limitations, these limitations on institutional authority may provide rights of access and use not only to faculty members and students (see, for example, Sections 4.9.1, 4.9.2, and 4.11.1 on the First Amendment usage rights of students) but also to the outside community.

Sections 5.6.2 to 5.6.4 explore various statutes, regulations, and constitutional considerations that affect outsiders' access to the property of postsecondary institutions.

5.6.2. Speaker bans. Administrators may seek to exclude particular speakers or events from campus in order to avoid campus disruption, hate mongering (see R. O'Neil, "Hateful Messages That Force Free Speech to the Limit," *Chron. Higher Educ.*, Feb. 16, 1994, A52), or other perceived harms. Such attempts inevitably precipitate clashes, not only with the participants but also with those on campus who demand the right to hear the speaker or attend the event. These clashes have sometimes resulted in litigation. Most of the cases on access to campus facilities have involved regulations on off-campus speakers, commonly referred to as "speaker bans."[16]

Since rules regulating off-campus speakers provide a convenient target for a First Amendment attack, such rules should be drafted with extreme care. Much of the law that has developed concerning faculty members' and students' free speech rights on campus also applies to the issue of off-campus speakers (see Sections 3.7, 4.9, and 4.10).

[16]Cases are collected in Annot., "Validity, Under Federal Constitution, of Regulation for Off-Campus Speakers at State Colleges and Universities—Federal Cases," 5 A.L.R. Fed. 841 (1991 and periodic supp.).

Under the First Amendment, administrators of public institutions may reasonably regulate the time, place, and manner of speeches and other communicative activities engaged in by on- or off-campus persons. Problems arise when these basic rules of order are expanded to include regulations under which speakers can be banned because of the content of their speech or their political affiliation or persuasion. Such regulations are particularly susceptible to judicial invalidation because they are prior restraints on speech (see Section 4.9.3). *Stacy v. Williams*, 306 F. Supp. 963 (N.D. Miss. 1969), is a leading example. The board of trustees of the Institutions of Higher Learning of the State of Mississippi promulgated rules providing, in part, that "all speakers invited to the campus of any of the state institutions of higher learning must first be investigated and approved by the head of the institution involved and when invited the names of such speakers must be filed with the executive secretary of the board of trustees." The regulations were amended several times to prohibit "speakers who will do violence to the academic atmosphere," "persons in disrepute from whence they come," persons "charged with crime or other moral wrongs," any person "who advocates a philosophy of the overthrow of the United States," and any person "who has been announced as a political candidate or any person who wishes to speak on behalf of a political candidate." In addition, political or sectarian meetings sponsored by any outside organization were prohibited.

Under the authority of these regulations, the board prevented political activists Aaron Henry and Charles Evers from speaking on any Mississippi state campus. Students at several schools joined faculty members and other persons as plaintiffs in an action to invalidate the regulations. The court struck down the regulations because they created a prior restraint on the students' and faculties' First Amendment right to hear speakers. Not all speaker bans, however, are unconstitutional under the court's opinion. When the speech "presents a 'clear and present danger' of resulting in serious substantive evil," a ban would not violate the First Amendment:

> For purpose of illustration, we have no doubt that the college or university authority may deny an invitation to a guest speaker requested by a campus group if it reasonably appears that such person would, in the course of his speech, advocate (1) violent overthrow of the government of the United States, the state of Mississippi, or any political subdivision thereof; (2) willful destruction or seizure of the institution's buildings or other property; (3) disruption or impairment, by force, of the institution's regularly scheduled classes or other educational functions; (4) physical harm, coercion, or intimidation or other invasion of lawful rights of the institution's officials, faculty members, or students; or (5) other campus disorder of violent nature. In drafting a regulation so providing, it must be made clear that the "advocacy" prohibited must be of the kind which prepares the group addressed for imminent action and steels it to such action, as opposed to the abstract espousal of the moral propriety of a course of action by resort to force; and there must be not only advocacy to action but also a reasonable apprehension of imminent danger to the essential functions and purposes of the institution, including the safety of its property and the protection of its officials, faculty members, and students [306 F. Supp. at 973–74].

The court also promulgated a set of "Uniform Regulations for Off-Campus Speakers," which, in its view, complied with the First Amendment (306 F. Supp. at 979–80). These regulations provide that all speaker requests come from a recognized student or faculty group, thus precluding any outsider's insistence on using the campus as a forum. This approach accords with the court's basis for invalidating the regulations: the rights of students or faculty members to hear a speaker.

Besides meeting a "clear and present danger" or incitement test, speaker ban regulations must use language that is sufficiently clear and precise to be understood by the average reader. Ambiguous or vague regulations run the risk of being struck down, under the First and Fourteenth Amendments, as "void for vagueness" (see Sections 4.5.2, 4.6.1, and 4.9.2). In *Dickson v. Sitterson*, 280 F. Supp. 486 (M.D.N.C. 1968), the court relied on this ground to invalidate a state statute and regulations prohibiting a person from speaking at state colleges or universities if he was a "known member of the Communist party," was "known to advocate the overthrow of the Constitution of the United States or the state of North Carolina," or had "pleaded the Fifth Amendment" in response to questions relating to the Communist party or other subversive organizations.

The absence of rules can be just as risky as poorly drafted ones, since either situation leaves administrators and affected persons with insufficient guidance. *Brooks v. Auburn University*, 412 F.2d 1171 (5th Cir. 1969), is illustrative. A student organization, the Human Rights Forum, had requested that the Reverend William Sloan Coffin speak on campus. After the request was approved by the Public Affairs Seminar Board, the president of Auburn overruled the decision because the Reverend Coffin was "a convicted felon and because he might advocate breaking the law." Students and faculty members filed suit contesting the president's action, and the U.S. Court of Appeals upheld their First Amendment claim:

> Attributing the highest good faith to Dr. Philpott in his action, it nevertheless is clear under the prior restraint doctrine that the right of the faculty and students to hear a speaker, selected as was the speaker here, cannot be left to the discretion of the university president on a pick and choose basis. As stated, Auburn had no rules or regulations as to who might or might not speak and thus no question of a compliance with or a departure from such rules or regulations is presented. This left the matter as a pure First Amendment question; hence the basis for prior restraint. Such a situation of no rules or regulations may be equated with a licensing system to speak or hear and this has been long prohibited.
>
> It is strenuously urged on behalf of Auburn that the president was authorized in any event to bar a convicted felon or one advocating lawlessness from the campus. This again depends upon the right of the faculty and students to hear. We do not hold that Dr. Philpott could not bar a speaker under any circumstances. Here there was no claim that the Reverend Coffin's appearance would lead to violence or disorder or that the university would be otherwise disrupted. There is no claim that Dr. Philpott could not regulate the time or place of the speech or the manner in which it was to be delivered. The most recent statement of the applicable rule by the Supreme Court, perhaps its outer limits, is contained in the case of *Brandenburg v. Ohio*, [395 U.S. 444]: . . . "[T]he constitutional guarantees of free speech and free press do not permit a state to forbid or proscribe advocacy of the use of force or of law violation except where such advocacy is directed to inciting or producing imminent lawless action and is likely to incite or produce such action." . . . There was no claim that the Coffin speech would fall into the category of this exception [412 F.2d at 1172-73].

Under these cases regulations concerning off-campus speakers present sensitive legal and policy issues for public institutions. If such regulations are determined to be necessary, they should be drafted with the aid of counsel. The cases clearly permit reasonable regulation of "the time or place of the speech or the manner in which it . . . [is] delivered," as the *Brooks* opinion notes. But regulating a speech because of its content is permissible only in the narrowest of circumstances, such as those set out in *Stacy* and in *Brooks*. The regulations promulgated by the court in *Stacy* provide useful guidance in drafting legally sound regulations. The five First Amendment principles set out in Section 4.10 of this volume will also be helpful.

5.6.3. Trespass statutes and ordinances.

States and local governments often have trespass or unlawful-entry laws that limit the use of a postsecondary institution's facilities by outsiders. Such statutes or ordinances typically provide that offenders are subject to ejection from the campus and that violation of an order to leave, made by an authorized person, is punishable as a misdemeanor. Counsel for institutions should carefully examine these laws, and the court decisions interpreting them, to determine each law's particular coverage. Some laws may cover all types of property; others may cover only educational institutions. Some laws may cover all postsecondary institutions, public or private; others may apply only to public or only to private institutions. Some laws may be broad enough to restrict members of the campus community under some circumstances; others may be applicable only to outsiders. There may also be technical differences in the standards for determining what acts will be considered a trespass or when an institution's actions will constitute implied consent to entry. (For an illustrative case, see *People v. Leonard*, 405 N.E.2d 831 (N.Y. 1984), in which the court reviewed the applicability of state trespass law to the exclusion of a sometime student from the SUNY-Binghamton campus.)

A number of reported cases have dealt with the federal and state constitutional limitations on a state or local government's authority to apply trespass laws to the campus setting.[17] *Braxton v. Municipal Court*, 514 P.2d 697 (Cal. 1973), is a leading example. Several individuals had demonstrated on the San Francisco State campus against the publication of campus newspaper articles that they considered "racist and chauvinistic." A college employee notified the protestors that they were temporarily barred from campus. When they disobeyed this order, they were arrested and charged under Section 626.4 of the California Penal Code. This statute authorized "the chief administrative officer of a campus or other facility of a community college, state college, or state university or his designate" to temporarily bar a person from the campus if there was "reasonable cause to believe that such person has wilfully disrupted the orderly operation of such campus or facility." The protestors argued that the state trespass statute was unconstitutional for reasons of overbreadth and vagueness (see Sections 4.6.1, 4.9.2, and 4.10).

The California Supreme Court rejected the protestors' argument. Regarding overbreadth, the court concluded:

---

[17]Cases are collected in Annot., "Validity and Construction of Statute or Ordinance Forbidding Unauthorized Persons to Enter upon or Remain in School Building or Premises," 50 A.L.R.3d 340 (1991 and periodic supp.).

Without a narrowing construction, section 626.4 would suffer First Amendment overbreadth. For example, reasoned appeals for a student strike to protest the escalation of a war, or the firing of the football coach, might "disrupt" the "orderly operation" of a campus; so, too, might calls for the dismissal of the college president or for a cafeteria boycott to protest employment policies or the use of nonunion products. Yet neither the "content" of speech nor freedom of association can be restricted merely because such expression or association disrupts the tranquillity of a campus or offends the tastes of school administrators or the public. Protest may disrupt the placidity of the vacant mind just as a stone dropped in a still pool may disturb the tranquillity of the surface waters, but the courts have never held that such "disruption" falls outside the boundaries of the First Amendment. . . .

Without a narrowing construction, section 626.4 would also suffer overbreadth by unnecessarily restricting conduct enmeshed with First Amendment activities. Although conduct entwined with speech may be regulated if it is completely incompatible with the peaceful functioning of the campus, section 626.4 on its face fails to distinguish between protected activity such as peaceful picketing or assembly and unprotected conduct that is violent, physically obstructive, or otherwise coercive. . . .

In order to avoid the constitutional overbreadth that a literal construction of section 626.4 would entail, we interpret the statute to prohibit only incitement to violence or conduct physically incompatible with the peaceful functioning of the campus. We agree with the Attorney General in his statement: "The word 'disrupt' is commonly understood to mean a physical or forcible interference, interruption, or obstruction. In the campus context, disrupt means a *physical* or *forcible* interference with normal college activities."

The disruption must also constitute "a substantial and material threat" to the orderly operation of the campus or facility (*Tinker v. Des Moines School District*, 393 U.S. 503, 514 (1969)). The words "substantial and material" appear in the portion of the statute which authorizes reinstatement of permission to come onto the campus (Penal Code § 626.4(c)). Accordingly, we read those words as expressing the legislature's intent as to the whole function of the statute; we thus construe section 626.4 to permit exclusion from the campus only of one whose conduct or words are such as to constitute, or incite to, a substantial and material physical disruption incompatible with the peaceful functioning of the academic institution and of those upon its campus. Such a substantial and material disruption creates an emergency situation justifying the statute's provision for summary, but temporary, exclusion [514 P.2d at 701, 703–05].

The court then also rejected the vagueness claim:

Petitioners point out that even though the test of substantial and material physical disruption by acts of incitement of violence constitutes an acceptable constitutional standard for preventing overbroad applications of the statute in specific cases, the enactment still fails to provide the precision normally required in criminal legislation. Thus, for example, persons subject to summary banishment must guess at *what* must be disrupted (i.e., classes or the attendance lines for athletic events), and *how* the disruption must take place (by picketing or by a single zealous shout in a classroom or by a sustained sit-in barring use of a classroom for several days).

Our examination of the legislative history and purposes of section 626.4

reveals, however, that the Legislature intended to authorize the extraordinary remedy of summary banishment only when the person excluded has committed acts illegal under other statutes; since these statutes provide ascertainable standards for persons seeking to avoid the embrace of section 626.4, the instant enactment is not void for vagueness [514 P.2d at 705].

In *Kirstel v. State*, 284 A.2d 12 (Md. Ct. Spec. App. 1971), another court upheld a similar state statute against constitutional attack. This Maryland statute (since recodified as Md. Code Ann., Educ. § 26-102) authorized the "highest official or governing body" of each public college or university to deny campus access to individuals "who have no lawful business to pursue at the institution, or who are acting in a manner disruptive or disturbing to the normal educational functions of the institution." Like the litigants in *Braxton*, Kirstel argued that the statute was vague and overbroad, asserting in particular the vagueness of the "no lawful business" language in the statute. Also like *Braxton*, the court had to work hard to clarify and thus justify a statute that would not win any awards for precision. By equating the phrase "lawful business" with the similarly vague and technical phrase "constitutionally protected" activity, however, the *Kirstel* opinion adds little to an understanding of the Maryland statute.

One case that does strike down a trespass statute is *Grody v. State*, 278 N.E.2d 280 (Ind. 1972), where the law at issue provided:

> It shall be a misdemeanor for any person to refuse to leave the premises of any institution established for the purpose of the education of students enrolled therein when so requested, regardless of the reason, by the duly constituted officials of any such institution [Ind. Code Ann. § 10-4533].

The court held that the law was void on its face owing to vagueness and overbreadth in violation of the First and Fourteenth Amendments:

> This statute attempts to grant to some undefined school "official" the power to order cessation of *any* kind of activity whatsoever, by *any* person whatsoever, and the official does not need to have any special reason for the order. The official's power extends to teachers, employees, students, and visitors and is in no way confined to suppressing activities that are interfering with the orderly use of the premises. This statute empowers the official to order any person off the premises because he does not approve of his looks, his opinions, his behavior, no matter how peaceful, or *for no reason at all.* Since there are *no* limitations on the reason for such an order, the official can request a person to leave the premises solely because the person is engaging in expressive conduct even though that conduct may be clearly protected by the First Amendment. If the person chooses to continue the First Amendment activity, he can be prosecuted for a crime under § 10-4533. This statute is clearly overbroad [278 N.E.2d at 282–83].

Even if a regulation or statute is neither vague nor overbroad, it may be vulnerable to a procedural due process attack. There is authority for the proposition that notice and a hearing are sometimes required before a noncampus person can be excluded from a public campus. The court in the *Braxton* case, for example, having narrowly construed the California statute to avoid vagueness and overbreadth, then declared:

> We recognize, likewise, that the statute must be construed so as not to violate the precepts of procedural due process; hence, we interpret section 626.4 to require notice and a hearing on alleged misconduct before the issuance of any exclusion order unless the campus administrator reasonably finds that the situation is such an exigent one that the continued presence on the campus of the person from whom consent to remain is withdrawn constitutes a substantial and material threat of significant injury to persons or property (§ 626.4(c)). Even when an exclusion order issues without a hearing, a postexclusion hearing must be held as soon as reasonably possible not later than seven days following a request by the person excluded [514 P.2d at 700].

Similarly, in *Dunkel v. Elkins*, 325 F. Supp. 1235 (D. Md. 1971), the court construed the Maryland statute upheld in *Kirstel* to require that the institution provide notice and an opportunity for a hearing before excluding an outsider from campus. If a prior hearing is not feasible because of emergency conditions, then a prompt hearing must be held after the expulsion. The burden of proof is on the institution to establish that the person to be excluded fell within the terms of the statute.

A notice and a hearing were also required in *Watson v. Board of Regents of the University of Colorado*, 512 P.2d 1162 (Colo. 1973). The plaintiff was a consultant to the University of Colorado Black Student Alliance with substantial ties to the campus. The university had rejected his application for admission. Believing that a particular admissions committee member had made the decision to reject him, the plaintiff threatened his safety. The university president then notified the plaintiff in writing that he would no longer be allowed on campus. Nevertheless, the plaintiff returned to campus and was arrested for trespass. Relying on *Dunkel v. Elkins*, the court agreed that the exclusion violated procedural due process:

> Where students have been subjected to disciplinary action by university officials, courts have recognized that procedural due process requires—prior to imposition of the disciplinary action—adequate notice of the charges, reasonable opportunity to prepare to meet the charges, an orderly administrative hearing adapted to the nature of the case, and a fair and impartial decision. . . . The same protection must be afforded nonstudents who may be permanently denied access to university functions and facilities.
>
> As part of a valid Regent's regulation of this type, in addition to providing for a hearing, there should be a provision for the person or persons who will act as adjudicator(s).
>
> In the present posture of this matter we should not attempt to "spell out" all proper elements of such a regulation. This task should be undertaken first by the regents. We should say, however, that when a genuine emergency appears to exist and it is impractical for university officials to grant a prior hearing, the right of nonstudents to access to the university may be suspended without a prior hearing, so long as a hearing is thereafter provided with reasonable promptness [512 P.2d at 1165].[18]

[18]The *Watson* case, as well as *Braxton* and perhaps *Dunkel,* apparently assumes that nonstudents have liberty or property interests that the institution would infringe if it excluded

Most trespass litigation concerning postsecondary education, such as the cases above, has probed federal constitutional and state statutory limits on public institutions' authority. The debate has been extended to private institutions, however, by the litigation in *State v. Schmid*, 423 A.2d 615 (N.J. 1980), sometimes known as the *Princeton University* case.

Chris Schmid, a nonstudent and a member of the United States Labor Party, was arrested and convicted of trespass for attempting to distribute political materials on the campus of Princeton University. Princeton's regulations required nonstudents and non-university-affiliated organizations to obtain permission to distribute materials on campus. No such requirement applied to students or campus organizations. The regulations did not include any provisions indicating when permission would be granted or what times, manners, or places of expression were appropriate. Schmid claimed that the regulations violated his rights to freedom of expression under both the federal Constitution and the New Jersey state constitution.

First addressing the federal constitutional claim under the First Amendment, the court acknowledged that the "state action" requirement (this volume, Section 1.5.2), a predicate to the application of the First Amendment, "is not readily met in the case of a private educational institution." Reviewing the various theories on which state action has been grounded, the court extensively analyzed their applicability to the case but declined to hold that Princeton's exclusion of Schmid constituted state action under any of the theories.

Although, in the absence of a state action finding, the federal First Amendment could not apply to Schmid's claim, the court did not find itself similarly constrained in applying the state constitution. Addressing Schmid's state constitutional claim, the court determined that the state constitutional provisions protecting freedom of expression (even though similar to the First Amendment provision) could be construed more expansively than the First Amendment so as to reach Princeton's actions. The court reaffirmed that state constitutions are independent sources of individual rights; that state constitutional protections may surpass the protections of the federal Constitution; and that this greater expansiveness could exist even if the state provision is identical to the federal provision, because state constitutional rights are not intended to be simply mirror images of federal rights (see this volume, Section 1.3.1.1).

In determining whether the more expansive state constitutional protections did protect Schmid against the trespass claim, the court attempted to balance the "legitimate interests in private property with individual freedoms of speech and assembly":

> The state constitutional equipoise between expressional rights and property rights must be . . . gauged on a scale measuring the nature and extent of the public's use of such property. Thus, even as against the exercise of important rights of speech, assembly, petition, and the like, private property itself remains

---

a nonstudent from campus. *Watson* also analogizes the interests of the nonstudent to those of students. It is not clear that these premises would be sound in all respects under *Board of Regents v. Roth*, 408 U.S. 564 (1972) (this volume, Sections 3.6.2 and 3.6.2.1) and later U.S. Supreme Court case law on defining liberty and property interests (see, for example, Section 4.8.2). Administrators and counsel should thus be cautious in using *Watson* and the other 1970s cases on procedural due process rights accompanying exclusion from campus.

protected under due process standards from untoward interferences with or confiscatory restrictions upon its reasonable use. . . .

On the other hand, it is also clear that private property may be subjected by the state, within constitutional bounds, to reasonable restrictions upon its use in order to serve the public welfare. . . .

We are thus constrained to achieve the optimal balance between the protections to be accorded private property and those to be given to expressional freedoms exercised upon such property [423 A.2d at 629].

To strike the required balance, the court announced a "test" encompassing several "elements" and other "considerations":

We now hold that, under the state constitution, the test to be applied to ascertain the parameters of the rights of speech and assembly upon privately owned property and the extent to which such property reasonably can be restricted to accommodate these rights involves several elements. This standard must take into account (1) the nature, purposes, and primary use of such private property, generally, its "normal" use, (2) the extent and nature of the public's invitation to use that property, and (3) the purpose of the expressional activity undertaken upon such property in relation to both the private and public use of the property. This is a multifaceted test which must be applied to acertain whether in a given case owners of private property may be required to permit, subject to suitable restrictions, the reasonable exercise by individuals of the constitutional freedoms of speech and assembly.

Even when an owner of private property is constitutionally obligated under such a standard to honor speech and assembly rights of others, private property rights themselves must nonetheless be protected. The owner of such private property, therefore, is entitled to fashion reasonable rules to control the mode, opportunity, and site for the individual exercise of expressional rights upon his property. It is at this level of analysis—assessing the reasonableness of such restrictions—that weight may be given to whether there exist convenient and feasible alternative means to individuals to engage in substantially the same expressional activity. While the presence of such alternatives will not eliminate the constitutional duty, it may lighten the obligations upon the private property owner to accommodate the expressional rights of others and may also serve to condition the content of any regulations governing the time, place, and manner for the exercise of such expressional rights [423 A.2d at 630].

Applying each of the three elements in its test to the particular facts concerning Princeton's campus and Schmid's activity on it, the court concluded that Schmid did have state constitutional speech and assembly rights, which Princeton was obligated to honor:

The application of the appropriate standard in this case must commence with an examination of the primary use of the private property, namely, the campus and facilities of Princeton University. Princeton University itself has furnished the answer to this inquiry [in its university regulations] in expansively expressing its overriding educational goals, viz:

The central purposes of a university are the pursuit of truth, the discovery of new knowledge through scholarship and research, the teaching and general development of students, and the transmission of knowledge and learning to society at large. Free inquiry and free expression within the academic community are indispensable to the achievement of these goals. The freedom to teach and to learn depends upon the creation of appropriate conditions and opportunities on the campus as a whole as well as in classrooms and lecture halls. All members of the academic community share the responsibility for securing and sustaining the general conditions conducive to this freedom. . . .

Free speech and peaceable assembly are basic requirements of the university as a center for free inquiry and the search for knowledge and insight.

No one questions that Princeton University has honored this grand ideal and has in fact dedicated its facilities and property to achieve the educational goals expounded in this compelling statement.

In examining next the extent and nature of a public invitation to use its property, we note that a public presence within Princeton University is entirely consonant with the university's expressed educational mission. Princeton University, as a private institution of higher education, clearly seeks to encourage both a wide and continuous exchange of opinions and ideas and to foster a policy of openness and freedom with respect to the use of its facilities. The commitment of its property, facilities, and resources to educational purposes contemplates substantial public involvement and participation in the academic life of the university. The university itself has endorsed the educational value of an open campus and the full exposure of the college community to the "outside world"— that is, the public at large. Princeton University has indeed invited such public uses of its resources in fulfillment of its broader educational ideas and objectives.

The further question is whether the expressional activities undertaken by the defendant in this case are discordant in any sense with both the private and public uses of the campus and facilities of the university. There is nothing in the record to suggest that Schmid was evicted because the purpose of his activities, distributing political literature, offended the university's educational policies. The reasonable and normal inference thus to be extracted from the record in the instant case is that defendant's attempt to disseminate political material was not incompatible with either Princeton University's professed educational goals or the university's overall use of its property for educational purposes. Further, there is no indication that, even under the terms of the university's own regulations, Schmid's activities . . . directly or demonstrably "disrupt[ed] the regular and essential operations of the university" or that, in either the time, the place, or the manner of Schmid's distribution of the political materials, he "significantly infringed on the rights of others" or caused any interference or inconvenience with respect to the normal use of university property and the normal routine and activities of the college community [423 A.2d at 630–31].

Princeton, however, invoked the other considerations included in the court's test. It argued that, to protect its private property rights as an owner and its academic freedom as a higher education institution, it had to require that outsiders have permission to enter its campus and that its regulations reasonably implemented this necessary requirement. The court did not disagree with the first premise of Princeton's argument, but it did disagree that Princeton's regulations were a reasonable means of protecting its interests:

In addressing this argument, we must give substantial deference to the importance of institutional integrity and independence. Private educational institutions perform an essential social function and have a fundamental responsibility to assure the academic and general well-being of their communities of students, teachers, and related personnel. At a minimum, these needs, implicating academic freedom and development, justify an educational institution in controlling those who seek to enter its domain. The singular need to achieve essential educational goals and regulate activities that impact upon these efforts has been acknowledged even with respect to public educational institutions (see, for example, *Healy v. James*, 408 U.S. at 180 . . . ; *Tinker v. Des Moines Indep. Community School Dist.*, 393 U.S. 503, 513-14 . . . (1969)). Hence, private colleges and universities must be accorded a generous measure of autonomy and self-governance if they are to fulfill their paramount role as vehicles of education and enlightenment.

In this case, however, the university regulations that were applied to Schmid . . . contained no standards, aside from the requirement for invitation and permission, for governing the actual exercise of expressional freedom. Indeed, there were no standards extant regulating the granting or withholding of such authorization, nor did the regulations deal adequately with the time, place, or manner for individuals to exercise their rights of speech and assembly. Regulations thus devoid of reasonable standards designed to protect both the legitimate interests of the university as an institution of higher education and the individual exercise of expressional freedom cannot constitutionally be invoked to prohibit the otherwise noninjurious and reasonable exercise of such freedoms. . . .

In these circumstances, given the absence of adequate reasonable regulations, the required accommodation of Schmid's expressional and associational rights, otherwise reasonably exercised, would not constitute an unconstitutional abridgment of Princeton University's property rights. . . . It follows that, in the absence of a reasonable regulatory scheme, Princeton University did in fact violate defendant's state constitutional rights of expression in evicting him and securing his arrest for distributing political literature upon its campus [423 A.2d at 632-33].

The court thus reversed Schmid's conviction for trespass.

Princeton sought U.S. Supreme Court review of the New Jersey court's decision. The university argued that the court's interpretation of *state* constitutional law violated its rights under *federal* law. Specifically, it claimed a First Amendment right to institutional academic freedom (see this volume, Section 3.7.1)[19] and a Fifth Amendment right to protect its property from infringement by government (here the New Jersey court). In a per curiam opinion, the Supreme Court declined to address the merits of Princeton's arguments, declaring the appeal moot (see this volume, Section 1.4.2.3) because Princeton had changed its regulations since the time of Schmid's conviction (*Princeton University and State of New Jersey v. Schmid*, 455

---

[19]The arguments for and against the existence of an institutional academic freedom right are well developed in the briefs of the parties and the amici curiae. Lawyers facing this important issue may still want to consult these briefs and the resources they cite. See particularly the *Brief Amicus Curiae of the American Association of University Professors*, filed August 20, 1981, in *Princeton University and State of New Jersey v. Chris Schmid*, No. 80-1576, U.S. Supreme Court, Oct. Term 1980.

U.S. 100 (1982)). Although the Supreme Court therefore dismissed the appeal, the dismissal had no negative effect on the New Jersey court's opinion, which stands as authoritative law for that state.

The New Jersey Supreme Court's reasoning was subsequently approved and followed by the Pennsylvania Supreme Court in *Pennsylvania v. Tate,* 432 A.2d 1382 (Pa. 1981). The defendants had been arrested for trespassing at Muhlenberg College, a private institution, when they distributed leaflets on campus announcing a community-sponsored lecture by the then FBI director. The Pennsylvania court developed an analysis similar to the New Jersey court's and invoked the free expression guarantees of the Pennsylvania state constitution. The standardless nature of the college's regulations was again a crucial factor rendering the trespass conviction a violation of state constitutional rights.

State v. Schmid is a landmark case—the first to impose constitutional limitations on the authority of private institutions to exclude outsiders from their campuses. *Schmid* does not, however, create a new nationwide rule. The applicability of its analysis to private campuses in states other than New Jersey and Pennsylvania will vary, depending on the particular individual rights clauses in a state's constitution, the existing precedents construing their application to private entities, and the receptivity of a state's judges to the New Jersey court's view of the nature and use of private campuses. Even in New Jersey and Pennsylvania, the *Schmid* and *Tate* precedents do not create the same access rights to all private campuses; as *Schmid* emphasizes, the degree of access required depends on the primary use for which the institution dedicates its campus property and the scope of the public invitation to use that particular property. Administrators dealing with access of outsiders should consult counsel concerning their own state's law and their institution's status under it.

Nor does *Schmid* prohibit private institutions from regulating the activity of outsiders to whom they must permit entry. Institutions may still adopt regulatory standards that impose reasonable time, place, and manner restrictions on access. Indeed, the new regulations adopted by Princeton after Schmid's arrest were cited favorably by the New Jersey court. Although they were not at issue in the case, since they were not the basis of the trespass charge, the court noted that "these current amended regulations exemplify the approaches open to private educational entities seeking to protect their institutional integrity while at the same time recognizing individual rights of speech and assembly and accommodating the public whose presence nurtures academic inquiry and growth." The new Princeton regulations, which are set out in full in the court's opinion (423 A.2d at 617-18 n.2), thus provide substantial guidance for institutions that are subject to state law such as New Jersey's or that as a matter of educational policy desire to change their access regulations.

5.6.4. Soliciting and canvassing. The university campus may be an attractive marketplace not only for speakers, pamphleteers, and canvassers conveying social, political, or religious messages, but also for companies selling merchandise to college students (see C. Shea, "Businesses Cash In on a Wide-Open Bazaar of Frenzied Consumers: The College Campus," *Chron. Higher Educ.,* June 16, 1993, A33). Whether the enterprising outsider wishes to develop a market for ideas or for commodities, the public institution's authority to restrict contact with its students is limited by the First Amendment. As in other circumstances, because of the First Amendment's applicability, a public institution's authority to regulate soliciting and canvassing is more limited than that of a private institution.

Historically, litigation and discussion of free speech have focused on rights attending the communication of political or social thought. Although the U.S. Supreme Court's opinion in *Virginia State Board of Pharmacy v. Virginia Citizens Consumer Council*, 425 U.S. 748 (1976), made clear that the protection of the First Amendment likewise extends to purely "commercial speech," even when the communication is simply "I will sell you X at Y price," the degree of protection afforded commercial speech is less than that afforded noncommercial speech.

The Supreme Court has consistently approved time, place, and manner restrictions on speech where they (1) are not based on the speech's "content or subject matter," (2) "serve a significant governmental interest," and (3) "leave open ample alternative channels for communication of the information" (*Heffron v. International Society for Krishna Consciousness*, 452 U.S. 640 (1981); see also *Clark v. Community for Creative Non-Violence*, discussed in Section 4.9.2). Within these guidelines public institutions may subject both noncommercial and commercial speech to reasonable regulation of the time, place, and manner of delivery, although somewhat more flexible guidelines exist for commercial speech (see the *Central Hudson* case, below).[20] In addition, public institutions may regulate the content of commercial speech in ways that would not be permissible for other types of speech.

5.6.4.1. Commercial solicitation. Several court decisions involving American Future Systems, Inc., a corporation specializing in the sale of china and crystal, address the regulation of commercial speech by a public university. In *American Future Systems v. Pennsylvania State University*, 618 F.2d 252 (3d Cir. 1980) (*American Future Systems I*), the plaintiff corporation challenged the defendant university's regulations on commercial activities in campus residence halls. The regulations in question barred "the conducting of any business enterprise for profit" in student residence halls except where an individual student invites the salesperson to his or her room for the purpose of conducting business only with that student. No rules prevented businesses from placing advertisements in student newspapers or on student radio, or from making sales attempts by telephone or mail.

American Future Systems (AFS) scheduled a number of sales demonstrations in Penn State residence halls in the fall of 1977. When Penn State officials attempted to stop the sales demonstrations, AFS argued that such action violated its First Amendment "commercial speech" rights. At this point Penn State informed AFS "that it would be permitted to conduct the demonstration portion of its show if no attempts were made to sell merchandise to the students during the presentation" (618 F.2d at 254). Claiming that the sales transactions were essential to its presentation, AFS ceased its activity and commenced its lawsuit. AFS based its argument on the *Virginia State Board of Pharmacy* case (cited in Section 5.6.4):

> Plaintiff AFS is correct that in *Virginia Pharmacy Board* the Supreme
> Court ruled that commercial speech is entitled to some level of protection by the

[20]Cases are collected in Annot., "Validity of Regulation of College or University Denying or Restricting Right of Student to Receive Visitors in Dormitory," 78 A.L.R.3d 1109 (1977 and periodic supp.).

First Amendment (425 U.S. at 770 . . .). This holding, by itself, does not resolve the issue presented by this case, however. The statutory scheme discussed in *Virginia Pharmacy Board* effectively suppressed all dissemination of price information throughout the state. The case at hand presents a dramatically different fact situation, implicating many different concerns.

Penn State argues that it can restrict the use of its residence halls to purposes which further the educational function of the institution. It urges that transacting sales with groups of students in the dormitories does not further the educational goals of the university and, therefore, can be lawfully prohibited. It emphasizes that AFS seeks a ruling that its sales and demonstrations be permitted in the residence halls, areas which are not open to the general public. In light of all the facts of this case, we believe Penn State is correct [618 F.2d at 255].

In reaching its conclusion, the court inquired whether Penn State had established a "public forum" for free speech activity (see *Widmar v. Vincent*, this volume, Section 4.11.4) in the residence halls:

When the state restricts speech in some way, the court must look to the special interests of the government in regulating speech in the particular location. The focus of the court's inquiry must be whether there is a basic incompatibility between the communication and the primary activity of an area (*Grayned v. City of Rockford*, 408 U.S. 104, 116 . . . (1972)). . . .

As discussed above, members of the general public do not have unrestricted access to Penn State residence halls. "No Trespassing" signs are posted near the entrances to all the residence halls. Although nonresidents of the halls may enter the lobbies, they may not proceed freely to the private living areas. We believe that these facts demonstrate that the arena at issue here, the residence halls at Penn State, does not constitute a "public forum" under the First Amendment [618 F.2d at 256].

The court then inquired whether, despite the absence of a public forum, AFS could still claim First Amendment protection for solicitation and sales activities occurring in the residence halls. According to the court, such a claim depends on whether the activity impinges on the primary business for which the area in question is used:

We recognize that the absence of a "public forum" from this case does not end our inquiry, however. There are some "non-public-forum" areas where the communication does not significantly impinge upon the primary business carried on there. Penn State asserts that the AFS group sales do impinge significantly on the primary activities of a college dormitory. Penn State argues that its residence halls are "exclusively dedicated to providing a living environment which is conducive to activities associated with being a student and succeeding academically." It contends that group sales activities within the residence halls would disrupt the proper study atmosphere and the privacy of the students. It reiterates that there is no history of allowing group commercial transactions to take place in the dormitories. We conclude that Penn State has articulated legitimate interests which support its ban on group sales activity in the dormitories. We also conclude that these interests are furthered by the proscription against commercial transactions [618 F.2d at 256–57].

Completing its analysis, the court addressed and rejected a final argument made by AFS: that Penn State cannot distinguish between commercial and noncommercial speech in making rules for its residence halls and that, since Penn State permits political and other noncommercial group activities, it must permit commercial activities as well. The court replied:

> In a case decided two years after *Virginia Pharmacy Board*, the Supreme Court explicitly rejected plaintiff's view that commercial and noncommercial speech must be treated exactly alike.
>
>> We have not discarded the "commonsense" distinction between speech proposing a commercial transaction, which occurs in an area traditionally subject to government regulation, and other varieties of speech. . . . To require a parity of constitutional protection for commercial and noncommercial speech alike could invite dilution, simply by a leveling process, of the force of the amendment's guarantee with respect to the latter kind of speech. Rather than subject the First Amendment to such a devitalization, we instead have afforded commercial speech a limited measure of protection, commensurate with its subordinate position in the scale of First Amendment values, while allowing models of regulation that might be impermissible in the realm of noncommercial expression (*Ohralick v. Ohio State Bar Association*, 436 U.S. 447, 455–56 . . . (1978)). . . .
>
> Here Penn State has not totally suppressed the speech of plaintiff. It has restricted that speech somewhat, however. Although AFS sales representatives are allowed into the residence halls to present demonstrations to groups of students, they cannot consummate sales at these gatherings. Even that restriction is removed if the sales representative is invited to the hall by an individual student who decides to purchase the merchandise marketed by AFS.
>
> As noted above, Penn State has advanced reasonable objectives to support its ban on group commercial activity in the residence halls. Further, it has emphasized that traditionally there has been an absence of such activity in the halls. This places commercial speech in a quite different category from activities historically associated with college life, such as political meetings or football rallies. We cannot say that the record in this case reveals any arbitrary, capricious, or invidious distinction between commercial and noncommercial speech. We therefore conclude that AFS is incorrect in its assertion that the Penn State policy violates the First Amendment because it treats noncommercial speech differently from commercial speech [618 F.2d at 257–59].

Having determined that AFS's activities were commercial speech entitled to First Amendment protection, but that Penn State's regulations complied with First Amendment requirements applicable to such speech, the court in *American Future Systems I* upheld the regulations and affirmed the lower court's judgment for Penn State.

Soon, however, a second generation of litigation was born. In accordance with its understanding of the appellate court's opinion in the first lawsuit, AFS requested Penn State to allow group demonstrations that would not include consummation of sales and would take place only in residence hall common areas. AFS provided the university with a copy of its "script" for these demonstrations, a series of seventy-six cue cards. Penn State responded that AFS could use certain cue cards with information the university considered to have "educational value" but not cue cards with "price guarantee and payment plan information," which the university considered "an outright group commercial solicitation." AFS sued again, along with several Penn State students, arguing that Penn State's censorship of its cue cards violated its right to commercial speech and contradicted the court's opinion in *American Future Systems I*. After losing again in the trial court, AFS finally gained a victory when the appellate court ruled in its favor (*American Future Systems v. Pennsylvania State University*, 688 F.2d 907 (3d Cir. 1982) (*American Future Systems II*)).

The appellate court carefully distinguished this litigation from the prior litigation in *American Future Systems I* and identified the new issue presented:

> It is important at the outset to clarify which issues are not before us. Although AFS construes our decision in *American Future Systems I* as having established its constitutional free speech right to conduct demonstrations of a commercial product in common areas within the university's residence halls, we do not read that opinion so broadly. Penn State has not sought to bar all commercial activity from its residence halls. It has limited what ostensibly appears to be such a ban through its definition of "commercial," which excludes student contact with a peddler "if the contact was invited by the individual student involved." Therefore, we need not decide whether a state university may properly ban all commercial activity in its residence halls. Similarly, AFS does not challenge the distinction which the earlier opinion made between an actual consummation or completion of the "commercial transaction" and a group demonstration of AFS's products (618 F.2d at 258–59). Instead, it seeks only to conduct the demonstration in the common areas without censorship of the contents of that demonstration.
>
> Finally, although the university has conceded that portions of the demonstration may have some educational value, and it and the district court sought to draw the line between those portions of the demonstration which they deem educational and those portions which they deem commercial, it is unmistakable that the demonstration is geared to the sales of the products and represents commercial speech. Thus, the only issue is whether Penn State may censor the content of AFS's commercial speech conducted in the dormitory common rooms, where AFS has been permitted by the university to conduct its sales demonstration [688 F.2d at 912].

In resolving this issue, the court applied the test for ascertaining the validity of commercial speech regulations that the U.S. Supreme Court had established in *Central Hudson Gas & Electric Corp. v. Public Service Commission*, 447 U.S. 557 (1980):

> For commercial speech to come within [the First Amendment], it at least must concern lawful activity and not be misleading. Next, we ask whether the asserted governmental interest is substantial. If both inquiries yield positive answers, we must determine whether the regulation directly advances the government interest asserted and whether it is not more extensive than is necessary to serve that interest [688 F.2d at 913; quoting *Central Hudson* at 566].

Applying this test, the court determined that Penn State's prohibition of AFS's demonstration violated AFS's First Amendment rights:

In the instant situation, there has been no allegation that AFS's commercial speech activities are fraudulent, misleading, or otherwise unlawful. . . .

We, therefore, must first determine whether the university has advanced a substantial government interest to be achieved by the restrictions at issue. The only interest advanced by Penn State for precluding information on the price of the company's products and the nature of the contract it enters into with purchasers is that asserted in the prior action before this court—that is, its interest in maintaining the proper study atmosphere in its dormitories and in protecting the privacy of the students residing in those facilities. Restrictions on the contents of the demonstration as distinguished from the conduct of the demonstration cannot further these interests. The Supreme Court cases provide ample precedent for the proposition that price information has value. . . . The university does not contend that the mere act of convening a group in the common areas of the residence halls is inimical to the study atmosphere, since its policy permits such group activity. We conclude that Penn State has failed to show a substantial state interest, much less a plausible explanation, for its policy differentiating between the nature of the information contained in the AFS demonstration [688 F.2d at 913].

The court therefore reversed the lower court's entry of summary judgment for Penn State and remanded the case for trial.

Several students were also plaintiffs in *American Future Systems II*. They claimed that the university had violated their First Amendment rights to make purchases in group settings in the residence hall common areas and to host and participate in sales demonstrations in the private rooms of residence halls. The students argued that these rights are not aspects of commercial speech, as AFS's rights are, but are noncommercial speech, as well as freedom of association and due process, rights that deserve higher protection. The appellate court determined that the lower court's record was not sufficiently developed on these points and remanded the students' claims to the lower court for further consideration—thus leaving these arguments unresolved.

In further proceedings, after remand to the trial court, the plaintiff students and American Future Systems, Inc. obtained a preliminary injunction against Penn State's ban on group sales demonstrations in individual students' rooms (*American Future Systems v. Pennsylvania State University*, 553 F. Supp. 1268 (M.D. Pa. 1982)); and subsequently the court entered a permanent injunction against this policy (*American Future Systems v. Pennsylvania State University*, 568 F. Supp. 666 (M.D. Pa. 1983)). The court emphasized the students' own rights to receive information and, from that perspective, did not consider the speech at issue to be subject to the lower standards applicable to commercial speech. On appeal by the university, however, the U.S. Court of Appeals for the Third Circuit disagreed, considering the speech to be commercial and overruling the district court (*American Future Systems, Inc. v. Pennsylvania State University*, 752 F.2d 854 (3d Cir. 1985) (*American Future Systems III*)).

The appellate court decided that a state university's substantial interest as a property owner and educator in preserving dormitories for their intended study-oriented use, and in preventing them from becoming "rent-free merchandise marts," was sufficient to overcome both the commercial vendor's free speech rights to make group sales presentations in students' dormitory rooms and the students' free speech rights to join with others to hear and discuss this information. In applying the *Central Hudson* standards (above), the court found that, although the sales activities involved were lawful, the state university's substantial interests justified a narrowly drawn regulation prohibiting group demonstrations in students' dormitory rooms.

Subsequent to *American Future Systems III*, students on another campus brought a similar issue to court in another case involving American Future Systems' group demonstrations. The subject of this suit was the defendant's regulation prohibiting "private commercial enterprises" from operating on SUNY campuses or facilities. The defendant had used this resolution to bar AFS from holding group demonstrations in students' dormitory rooms. This case made it to the U.S. Supreme Court in *Board of Trustees of the State University of New York v. Fox*, 492 U.S. 469 (1989). The Court used the occasion to restate the last part of the *Central Hudson* test ("whether [the regulation] is not more extensive than necessary to serve [the government] interest"); as restated, it now requires only that the regulation be "narrowly tailored" to achieve the government's interest, or that there be a "reasonable fit" between the regulation and the government interest. This restatement makes the standard governing commercial speech more lenient, allowing courts to be more deferential to institutional interests when campus commercial activities are at issue. The Court remanded the case to the lower courts for reconsideration in accordance with this more deferential test. The Court also remanded the question whether the university's regulation was unconstitutionally overbroad on its face because it applied to and limited noncommercial speech (that is, more highly protected speech) as well as commercial speech.[21]

The three appellate court opinions in the complex *American Future Systems* litigation, supplemented by the Supreme Court's decision in the *Fox* case, yield considerable guidance for administrators concerned with commercial activity in public institutions. A public institution clearly has considerable authority to place restrictions on outsiders' access to its campus for such purposes. The institution may reasonably restrict the "time, place, and manner" of commercial activity—for instance, by limiting the places where group demonstrations may be held in residence halls, prohibiting the consummation of sales during group demonstrations, or prohibiting commercial solicitations in libraries or classrooms. The institution may also regulate the content of commercial activity to ensure that it is not fraudulent or misleading and does not propose illegal transactions. Other content restrictions—namely, restrictions that directly advance a substantial institutional interest and are narrowly tailored to achieve that interest—are also permissible.

Administrators cannot comfortably assume, however, that this authority is broad enough to validate every regulation of commercial activity. Regulations that censor or sharply curtail all dissemination of commercial information may infringe the First Amendment. *American Future Systems II* is a leading example. Similarly, a regulation prohibiting all in-person, one-on-one contacts with students, even when the representative does not attempt to close a deal or when the student has initiated

---

[21]On remand, the district court dismissed the case as moot (see the discussion of mootness in this volume, Section 1.4.2.3), since the plaintiff students were no longer residing in the dormitory or at the university and AFS had dropped out of the suit (764 F. Supp. 747 (N.D.N.Y. 1991)). The district court also refused to allow the plaintiffs to amend the complaint to add currently enrolled students (148 F.R.D. 474 (N.D.N.Y. 1993)).

the contact, may be invalid. In some locations, moreover, the institution's interest in regulating may be sufficiently weak that it cannot justify bans or sharp restrictions at these locations. Possible examples include orderly solicitations in the common areas of student unions or other less private or studious places on campus; solicitations of an individual student conducted in the student's own room by prior arrangement; and solicitations at the request of student organizations in locations customarily used by such organizations, when such solicitations involve no deceptive practices and propose no illegal or hazardous activity.

It is also clear from U.S. Supreme Court precedents (see, for example, *Consolidated Edison Co. v. Public Service Commission,* 447 U.S. 530 (1980)), that not all speech activity of commercial entrepreneurs is "commercial" speech. Activity whose purpose is not to propose or close a commercial transaction—for example, an educational seminar or a statement on political, economic, or other issues of public interest—may fall within First Amendment protections higher than those accorded commercial speech. Administrators should also be guided by this distinction when regulating, since their authority to limit access to campus and their authority to restrict the content of what is said will be narrower when entrepreneurs wish to engage in "public-interest" rather than "commercial" speech. While this distinction may become blurred when an entrepreneur combines both types of speech in the same activity, there are discussions in both *American Future Systems III* (752 F.2d at 862) and *Fox* (492 U.S. at 481) that will provide guidance in this circumstance.

5.6.4.2. Noncommercial canvassing. As discussed in Sections 5.6.4 and 5.6.4.1, noncommercial speech is afforded greater protection under the First Amendment than commercial speech. Consequently, a public institution's authority to regulate political canvassing, charitable solicitations, public opinion polling, and other types of noncommercial speech is more limited than its authority to regulate commercial sales and solicitations.

In *Brush v. Pennsylvania State University,* 414 A.2d 48 (Pa. 1980), students at Penn State challenged university restrictions on canvassing in residence halls. The regulations permitted canvassing (defined as "any attempt to influence student opinion, gain support, or promote a particular cause or interest") by registered individuals in the living areas of a dormitory if the residents of that building had voted in favor of open canvassing. A majority vote to ban canvassing precluded access to living areas by canvassers unless they were specifically invited in advance by a resident. All canvassers remained free, however, to reach students by mail or telephone and to contact residents in the dining halls, lobbies, and conference rooms of each dormitory.

The Supreme Court of Pennsylvania upheld these regulations. It determined that the university had substantial interests in protecting the privacy of its students, preventing breaches of security, and promoting quiet study conditions. The regulations reasonably restricted the time, place, and manner of speech in furtherance of these government interests. Additionally, insofar as the regulations did not eliminate effective alternatives to canvassing inside the living areas, the university had afforded canvassers ample opportunity to reach hall residents.

On the basis of *Brush*, public institutions can confidently exclude canvassers from the actual living quarters of student residence facilities when a majority of the residents have voted to preclude such access. Similar restrictions applied to dining halls, student unions, sidewalks, or other less private areas, however, may violate the First Amendment rights of the speakers and of the potential listeners who are not in favor of the restriction. No-canvassing rules imposed on student living areas with separate living units, such as married students' garden apartments or town houses, may also be unconstitutional; in such circumstances the institution's interests in security and study conditions may be weaker, and the students' (or student family's) interest in controlling their individual living space is greater. See generally *Schaumburg v. Citizens for Better Environment*, 444 U.S. 620 (1980).

Whether rules such as Penn State's would be valid if imposed directly by the administration and not decided by the student vote is not addressed in *Brush*. But given the strong institutional interests in security and in preserving conditions appropriate for study, it is likely that narrowly drawn no-canvassing rules limited to living areas of dormitories and other similar spaces would be constitutional even without approval by student vote. In *Chapman v. Thomas*, 743 F.2d 1056 (4th Cir. 1984), the court upheld such a restriction, calling the dormitory living area a "non-public forum" (see *Perry Education Assn. v. Perry Local Educators' Assn.*, 460 U.S. 37 (1983)), to which the institution may prohibit or selectively regulate access. For the same reason, no-canvassing rules would probably be constitutional, even without student vote, as applied to study halls, library stacks and reading rooms, laboratories, and similar restricted areas.

A later case, *Glover v. Cole*, 762 F.2d 1197 (4th Cir. 1985), provides further support for the validity of such content-neutral restrictions on noncommercial solicitation and also illustrates a different type of regulation that may be constitutionally employed to restrict such activity. The plaintiffs, members of a socialist political party, had sought to solicit donations and sell political publications on campus. The president of West Virginia State College (the defendant in the case) had prohibited this activity by invoking a systemwide policy prohibiting sales and fund-raising activities anywhere on campus by groups that were not sponsored by the students. The court determined that the plaintiffs' activities were "political advocacy" rather than commercial speech and thus highly protected by the First Amendment. Nevertheless, the regulation was valid because it was a content-neutral regulation of the *manner* of speech in a "limited public forum" and met the constitutional standards applicable to such regulations (see Section 4.9.2):

> There has been no direct infringement on Glover's and Measel's expressive activity, simply a prohibition against sales and fund raising on campus. Since the campus area is generally open for all debate and expressive conduct, we do not find that first amendment interests seriously are damaged by the administration's decision to limit the use of its property through uniform application of a sensible "manner" restriction. Plaintiffs' activities may be at the core of the first amendment, but the college has a right to preserve the campus for its intended purpose and to protect college students from the pressures of solicitation. In so ruling, we note that plaintiffs have more than ample alternative channels available to tap the student market for fund raising. The literature itself sets out in plain English requests for donations for the cause. Anyone interested enough to peruse the material learns that the preparation of the materials costs something and that the group is in need of financial (as well as moral and political) support. In addition, if the campus is plaintiffs' key market, they can organize a student group or obtain a student sponsor to raise funds on campus [762 F.2d at 1203].

The features noted by the court are important to the validity of all campus regulations of noncommercial solicitation. First of all, the regulation was narrow—limited to sales and fund-raising—and left other "more than ample" channels for on-campus expression open to outsiders such as the plaintiffs. In addition, the regulation applied neutrally and uniformly to all outside groups, without reference to the beliefs of the group or the viewpoints its members would express on campus.[22] Finally, the university could demonstrate that the regulation was tailored to the protection of significant institutional interests that would be impeded if outsiders could raise funds and sell items on campus. Campus regulation of noncommercial solicitation will not always be supported by such interests. In *Hays County Guardian v. Supple,* 969 F.2d 111 (5th Cir. 1992), for example, Southwest Texas State University had a regulation prohibiting the in-person distribution on campus of free newspapers containing advertisements. The plaintiffs—the publishers of a free newspaper distributed county-wide, joined by university students—challenged the regulation's application. The court invalidated the regulation because the university did not demonstrate any significant interest that the regulation was "narrowly tailored" to protect.

For discussion of the related topic of voter canvassing and registration, see Section 5.4.3.

Sec. 5.7. Community Activities of Faculty Members and Students

Besides being part of the academic community, faculty members and students are also private citizens, whose private lives may involve them in the broader local community. Thus, a postsecondary institution may be concerned not only with its authority over matters arising when the community comes onto the campus, as in Section 5.6, but also with its authority over matters arising when the campus goes out into the community.

Generally, an institution has much less authority over the activities of a student or a faculty member when those activities take place in the community rather than on the campus. The faculty-institution contract (Section 3.1) and the student-institution contract (Section 4.1.3) may have little or no application to the off-campus activities that faculty or students engage in as private citizens, or the contract may affirmatively protect faculty members or students from institutional interference in their private lives. In public institutions, faculty members (Section 3.7.5.1) and students (Section 4.5.2) have constitutional rights that protect them from undue institutional interference in their private lives.

In relation to First Amendment rights, a landmark teacher case, *Pickering v. Board of Education,* 391 U.S. 563 (1968) (see Section 3.7.1), created substantial protection for teachers against being disciplined for expressing themselves in the community on issues of public concern. A U.S. Court of Appeals case, *Pickings v. Bruce,* 430 F.2d 595 (8th Cir. 1970), establishes similar protections for students. The issue in

[22]In recent First Amendment free speech cases, the U.S. Supreme Court has increasingly relied on this principle of viewpoint neutrality to strike down government regulations that serve to discriminate against individuals or groups on the basis of viewpoint. *R.A.V. v. St. Paul,* discussed in Section 4.10, is one such case. The application of this viewpoint-neutrality principle to regulations limiting the access of outsiders to public education facilities is well illustrated by *Lamb's Chapel v. Center Moriches Union Free School District,* 113 S. Ct. 2141 (1993).

Pickings was that Southern State College had placed SURE (Students United for Rights and Equality), an officially recognized campus group, on probation for writing a letter to a local church criticizing its racial policies. SURE members claimed that the college's action deprived them of their First Amendment rights. In holding for the students, the court made this general statement concerning campus involvement in the community:

> Students and teachers retain their rights to freedom of speech, expression, and association while attending or teaching at a college or university. They have a right to express their views individually or collectively with respect to matters of concern to a college or to a larger community. They are [not] required to limit their expression of views to the campus or to confine their opinions to matters that affect the academic community only. It follows that here the administrators had no right to prohibit SURE from expressing its views on integration to the College View Baptist Church or to impose sanctions on its members or advisors for expressing these views. Such statements may well increase the tensions within the college and between the college and the community, but this fact cannot serve to restrict freedom of expression (*Tinker v. Des Moines Community School Dist.*, 393 U.S. at 508–09, 89 S. Ct. 733) [430 F.2d at 598].

For another case protecting the activities of students in the community, see *Thomas v. Granville Board of Education*, 607 F.2d 1043 (2d Cir. 1979), discussed in this volume, Section 4.5.2.[23] But if those activities are "detrimental to the interests of the institution," the college may have the authority to discipline students for off-campus misconduct "subject to the fundamental constitutional safeguards that apply to all disciplinary actions by educational officials" (74 *Opinions of the Attorney General* 147 (Maryland) (1989), Opinion No. 89-002).

Faculty members' activities, either in furtherance of their research or in their role as consultants, may result in tension with community members. In *Woodbridge Terrace Associates v. Lake,* a federal district court dismissed a defamation claim against a faculty member serving as a consultant to the Housing Coalition of Middlesex County, whose report on racial steering by an apartment complex resulted in litigation against the managers of the complex. The trial judge held that reports of expert witnesses are protected from defamation claims and dismissed those charges and additional charges that the professor interfered with the apartment complex's operations (R. Rudolph, "Judge Rejects Suit Against Prof Who Found Racial Bias in Apartment Rentals," *Newark Star Ledger,* Sept. 19, 1989, at 22).

In some instances a local government's authority over members of the campus community has been questioned. In *Little v. City of North Miami,* 805 F.2d 962 (11th Cir. 1986), a University of Florida law school professor challenged the city's actions against him. The professor had represented, on a pro bono basis, environmental groups in litigation against the state of Florida and the city of North Miami. The City Council of North Miami passed a resolution censuring the professor for "improper use of public funds to represent private parties in litigation against the State and

---

[23]For a discussion of the potential criminal liability of students engaging in off-campus protests, see Annot., "Participation of Student in Demonstration on or near Campus as Warranting Imposition of Criminal Liability for Breach of Peace, Disorderly Conduct, Trespass, Unlawful Assembly, or Similar Offense," 32 A.L.R.3d 551 (1970 and periodic supp.).

against the interests of the City of North Miami" (805 F.2d at 964). Copies of the resolution were sent to the president, regents, law school dean, Dade County legislators, and others, and an investigation of Little's activities ensued.

Little sued the city under Section 1983 (this volume, Section 2.3.3), claiming First Amendment and due process violations, and asserting that his reputation and his relationship with the university had been damaged and that he had suffered emotional distress. After the trial court dismissed all the constitutional claims, the appellate court reversed and held that the City Council's actions violated Little's First Amendment rights: "[A] municipality . . . may not retaliate against an individual because of that person's legitimate use of the courts" (805 F.2d at 968). The court also permitted Little's due process claim to go forward: "We see no reason why an attorney is not entitled to property or liberty interests in his or her business (professional) reputation/goodwill when the same rights have been extended to other businesses" (805 F.2d at 969).

State law or a college's own policies may limit certain outside activities of faculty and staff that may conflict with their duties and responsibilities to the college. Many colleges and some states, for example, have developed conflict-of-interest policies that may forbid a faculty member from holding a tenured position at two institutions of higher education. Depending on the state, it may not be permissible for a faculty member employed by a public college to serve concurrently in the state legislature (see, for example, *State ex rel. Spire v. Conway*, 472 N.W.2d 403 (Neb. 1991)), although this prohibition is not universal (see 26 *Opinions of the Attorney General* (Kansas) (Mar. 2, 1992), Opinion No. 92-31). Laws that prohibit state employees from serving as advocates before state agencies may also catch faculty or staff in their web, although a New Jersey court extricated a faculty member from the provisions of such a law (see *In re Determination of Executive Commission on Ethical Standards*, 561 A.2d 542 (N.J. 1989), discussed in Section 6.5 (intro.)).

On occasion, community members have sued a college because it restricted its constituents from interacting with the community in certain ways. For example, in *Pyeatte v. Board of Regents of the University of Oklahoma*, 102 F. Supp. 407 (W.D. Okla. 1951), *affirmed per curiam*, 342 U.S. 936 (1952), a group of boarding house owners in Norman, Oklahoma (site of the University of Oklahoma), sued the state board of regents when it promulgated a rule requiring all unmarried students to live in university dormitories if space was available. The plaintiffs asserted that the rule limited their right to contract with the university to provide student housing and thus violated the Fourteenth Amendment's Equal Protection Clause. The court viewed the rule as clearly within the regents' power to pass for the benefit of the university's students.

Selected Annotated Bibliography

Sec. 5.1 (General Principles)

Reynolds, Osborne M. *Handbook of Local Government Law* (West, 1982 plus periodic pocket part). A comprehensive, well-documented review of local government law. Divided into twenty-two chapters, including "Limits on State Control of Municipalities," "Relationship of Municipalities to Federal Government," "Powers of Municipalities," "Finances of Local Government," "Local Control of the Use of Property," and "Local Regulation of Trade, Business, and Other Enterprises."

Sec. 5.2 (Zoning and Land Use Regulation)

Hagman, Donald G., & Juergensmeyer, Julian C. *Urban Planning and Land Development Control Law* (2d ed., West, 1986). A thorough survey of land use law. Includes chapters on "Land-Use Planning," "Types of Zones and Uses," "Zoning Procedures," "Eminent Domain," "Urban Renewal," and other topics.

Johnston, Ronald. "Recent Cases in the Law on Intergovernmental Zoning Immunity: New Standards Designed to Maximize the Public Interests," 8 *Urban Lawyer* 327 (1976). A concise analysis of traditional zoning immunity concepts and trends in the case law.

Nelson, Robert H. *Zoning and Property Rights: An Analysis of the American System of Land Use Regulation* (MIT Press, 1977). A scholarly analysis of zoning theory and practice, discussing numerous public policy issues. Examines zoning history, land use planning, and federal regulation of land use and proposes a new regulatory model for land use.

Pearlman, Kenneth. "Zoning and the First Amendment," 16 *Urban Lawyer* 217 (1984). Examines the power of local government to zone land and reviews U.S. Supreme Court decisions on zoning, particularly with regard to commercial activity.

"Special Project: The Private Use of Public Power: The Private University and the Power of Eminent Domain," 27 *Vanderbilt L. Rev.* 681 (1974). A lengthy study of eminent domain as a land use planning technique to benefit private universities. Emphasis is on the use of eminent domain in conjunction with federal urban renewal programs. A case study involving Nashville, Tennessee, is included.

Tracy, JoAnn. "Comment: Single-Family Zoning Ordinances: The Constitutionality of Suburban Barriers Against Nontraditional Households," 31 *St. Louis U. L.J.* 1023 (1987). Reviews decisions of the Supreme Court and other courts on the definition of "family" for zoning purposes. Discusses Fourteenth Amendment implications of restrictions on relationships between residents, and suggests alternatives to marriage, blood, or adoption for limiting the number of occupants of single-family homes.

Sec. 5.3 (Local Government Taxation)

Ginsberg, William R. "The Real Property Tax Exemption of Nonprofit Organizations: A Perspective," 53 *Temple L.Q.* 291 (1980). An overview of the issues involved in granting tax-exempt status to nonprofit organizations. Discusses the judicial and statutory tests used to determine exempt status, the theoretical foundations for property tax exemption, and the problems unique to educational and religious uses of property. Includes numerous citations to state constitutional and statutory provisions on property tax exemption.

See Colombo entry in bibliography for Section 7.3.

Sec. 5.4 (Student Voting in the Community)

Reiff, Jonathan D. "Ohio Residency Law for Student Voters: Its Implications and a Proposal for More Effective Implementation of Residency Statutes," 28 *Cleveland*

State L. Rev. 449 (1979). An article written in the wake of an Ohio Supreme Court decision invalidating an Ohio statute that applied different voter eligibility standards to students and nonstudents. Author argues that this decision has created its own type of unfairness, allowing many temporary residents to influence local elections. Includes discussion of the concept of domicile, critique of arguments favoring student enfranchisement at the place of college residence, and review of the "judicial treatment of student voters" by courts across the nation.

Sec. 5.5 (Relations with Local Police)

Bickel, Robert. "The Relationship Between the University and Local Law Enforcement Agencies in Their Response to the Problem of Drug Abuse on the Campus," in D. Parker Young (ed.), *Higher Education: The Law and Campus Issues* (Institute of Higher Education, University of Georgia, 1973), 17–27. A practical discussion of the general principles of search and seizure, double jeopardy, and confidentiality in the campus drug abuse context; also discusses the necessity of administrators' having the advice of counsel.

Cowen, Lindsay. "The Campus and the Community: Problems of Dual Jurisdiction," in D. Parker Young (ed.), *Proceedings of a Conference on Higher Education: The Law and Student Protest* (Institute of Higher Education, University of Georgia, 1970), 28–32. A brief discussion of the policy considerations governing the division of authority between the institution and local law enforcement agencies.

Ferdico, John N. *Criminal Procedure for the Law Enforcement Officer* (2d ed., West, 1979). An introductory text on police and criminal court procedure, including arrest, search, admissions, investigation, and evidence.

Kalaidjian, Ed. "Problems of Dual Jurisdiction of Campus and Community," in G. Holmes (ed.), *Student Protest and the Law* (Institute of Continuing Legal Education, University of Michigan, 1969), 131–48. Addresses issues arising out of concurrent criminal and disciplinary proceedings and police entry onto campus.

Note, "Privacy Protection Act of 1980: Curbing Unrestricted Third-Party Searches in the Wake of *Zurcher v. Stanford Daily*," 14 *U. Mich. J. Law Reform* 519 (1981). Reviews the constitutional law implications of the *Zurcher* case and analyzes the various provisions of the Act passed by Congress in response to *Zurcher*.

Sec. 5.6 (Community Access to Institutional Property)

"Comment: The University and the Public: The Right of Access by Nonstudents to University Property," 54 *Cal. L. Rev.* 132 (1966). Discusses the appropriateness and constitutionality of using state trespass laws to limit the public's access to state university and college campuses. California's criminal trespass law designed for state colleges and universities (Cal. Penal Code § 602-7 (West 1965), since amended and recodified as Cal. Penal Code § 626.6 (West 1988)) is highlighted.

Finkin, Matthew. "On 'Institutional' Academic Freedom," 61 *Tex. L. Rev.* 817 (1983). Considers the collapse of the distinction between institutional autonomy and academic freedom and applies this discussion to *State v. Schmid*, the *Princeton University* case. Further described in Finkin entry in bibliography for Section 1.2.

VI

The College and
the State Government

◆ ◆ ◆

Sec. 6.1. General Background

Unlike the federal government (see Section 7.1) and local governments (Section 5.1), state governments have general rather than limited powers and can claim all power that is not denied them by the federal Constitution or their own state constitution, or that has not been preempted by federal law. Thus, the states have the greatest reservoir of legal authority over postsecondary education, although the extent to which this source is tapped varies greatly from state to state.

In states that do assert substantial authority over postsecondary education, questions may arise about the particular functions relegated to the legislative and the executive branches. In *Inter-Faculty Organization v. Carlson*, 478 N.W.2d 192 (Minn. 1991), for example, the Minnesota Supreme Court invalidated a governor's line-item vetoes of certain expenditure estimates in the legislature's higher education funding bill, because the action went beyond the governor's veto authority, which extended only to identifiable amounts dedicated to specific purposes. Similar questions may concern the division of authority among other state boards or officials that have functions regarding higher education (see Section 6.2 below).

Questions may also be raised about the state's legal authority, in relation to the federal government's, under federal spending or regulatory programs. In *Shapp v. Sloan*, 391 A.2d 595 (Pa. 1978), for instance, the specific questions were (1) whether, under Pennsylvania state law, the state legislature or the governor was legally entrusted with control over federal funds made available to the state; and (2) whether, under federal law, state legislative control of federal funds was consistent with the Supremacy Clause of the U.S. Constitution and the provisions of the funding statutes.

In a lengthy opinion addressing an array of legal complexities, the Pennsylvania Supreme Court held that the legislature had control of the federal funds under state law and that such control had not been exercised inconsistently with federal law.

The states' functions in matters concerning postsecondary education include regulating, funding, planning, and coordinating (including recent assessment and accountability initiatives; see, for example, P. Hutchings & T. Marchese, "Watching Assessment—Questions, Stories, Prospects," 22 *Change* 12 (Sept./Oct. 1990)). These functions are performed through myriad agencies, such as boards of regents; statewide planning or coordinating boards; departments of education or higher education; institutional licensure boards or commissions; and State Approval Agencies (SAAs), which operate under contract to the federal Veterans Administration to approve courses for which veterans' benefits may be expended. New agencies called State Postsecondary Review Entities (SPREs), created by the Higher Education Amendments of 1992 (106 Stat. 637 et seq., 20 U.S.C. § 1099a-3), monitor certain institutions that participate in Title IV student aid programs (see this volume, Section 8.3.3); states may create a new agency to be the SPRE, assign the SPRE function to an existing state agency, or form a consortium with other states. In addition, various professional and occupational licensure boards indirectly regulate postsecondary education by evaluating programs of study and establishing educational prerequisites for taking licensure examinations. Other state agencies whose primary function is not education (such as workers' compensation boards, labor boards, ethics boards, or environmental quality agencies) may also regulate postsecondary education as part of a broader class of covered institutions, corporations, or government agencies.

In addition, states exert authority over postsecondary institutions' own borrowing and financing activities. For instance, states may regulate the issuance of bonds and notes that institutions use to raise funds for projects such as building construction. States may also influence institutional financing by regulating charitable solicitations by institutions and their fund-raising firms (see generally New York University School of Law, Program on Philanthropy and the Law, "Fundraising into the 1990's: State Regulation of Charitable Solicitation After *Riley*," 24 *U. San Francisco L. Rev.* 571 (1990)). Moreover, a state can either encourage or deter various financial activities (and affect institutions' after-tax bottom line) through its system of taxation. Private institutions, or institutional property and activities, within the state usually are presumed subject to taxation under the state's various tax statutes unless a specific statutory or constitutional provision grants an exemption. *In re Middlebury College Sales and Use Tax*, 400 A.2d 965 (Vt. 1979), is illustrative. Although the Vermont statute granted general tax-exempt status to private institutions meeting federal standards for tax exemption under the Internal Revenue Code (see this volume, Section 7.3.1), the statute contained an exception for institutional "activities which are mainly commercial enterprises." Middlebury College operated a golf course and a skiing complex, the facilities of which were used for its physical education program and other college purposes. The facilities were also open to the public upon payment of rates comparable to those charged by commercial establishments. When the state sought to tax the college's purchases of equipment and supplies for the facilities, the college claimed that its purchases were tax exempt under the Vermont statute. The court rejected Middlebury's claim, holding that the college had failed to meet its burden of proving that the golfing and skiing activities were not "mainly commercial enterprises."

In addition to performing these planning, regulatory, and fiscal functions through its agencies and boards, the state is also the source of eminent domain (condemnation) powers by which private property may be taken for public use. The scope of these powers, and the extent of compensation required for particular takings, may be at issue either when the state seeks to take land owned by a private postsecondary institution or when a state institution or board seeks to take land owned by a private party. In *Curators of the University of Missouri v. Brown*, 809 S.W.2d 64 (Mo. Ct. App. 1991), for instance, the university successfully brought a condemnation action to obtain Brown's land to use as a parking lot for a "Scholars' Center" that operated as part of the university but was privately owned.

Moreover, the state, through its court system, is the source of the common law (see Section 1.3.1.4) that provides general legal context for most of the transactions and disputes in which institutions may become involved. For example, common law contract and tort principles may constrain an institution's freedom to terminate the employment of its personnel. That was not always the case. Under the traditional formulation of contract principles, called the "employment-at-will" doctrine, if the parties do not "fix the period of service and prescribe the conditions on which the contract may be terminated," then the "right of the employee to quit the service of the employer, for whatever reason, is the same as the right of the employer, for whatever reason, to dispense with the services of such employee" (*Adair v. United States*, 208 U.S. 161, 174–75 (1908)). These principles have often given institutions wide latitude in dealing with their administrators and support staffs. Courts in recent cases, however, have modified contract and tort law principles to create exceptions to the employment-at-will doctrine. In a leading example, *Monge v. Beebe Rubber Co.*, 316 A.2d 549 (N.H. 1974), the court held that an employee discharge made in bad faith is a breach of the employment contract; it then invalidated the discharge of an employee for refusing to date her foreman. And in *Fortune v. National Cash Register*, 364 N.E.2d 1251 (Mass. 1977), the court held that the employer's discharge of an employee to avoid paying him employee bonuses constituted a breach. Other courts have used tort law principles to limit the employment-at-will doctrine. In *Tameny v. Atlantic Richfield Co.*, 610 P.2d 1330 (Cal. 1980), for instance, the court recognized a "tort of wrongful discharge" applicable to situations where the reasons for the discharge violate state public policy.

Given the considerable, and growing, state involvement suggested by this discussion, postsecondary administrators have increasingly bumped against state agencies and legal requirements in the course of their daily institutional duties. Administrators should therefore stay abreast of state requirements and approval processes. Administrators should also encourage their legal counsel or their government relations office to monitor the growing body of state law and keep key institutional personnel apprised of developments and their potential impact on the institution. Legal counsel should be prepared to call upon special legal expertise to address certain complex matters of state law, such as the issuance of bonds.

Sec. 6.2. State Provision of Public Postsecondary Education

Public postsecondary education systems vary in type and organization from state to state. Such systems may be established by the state constitution, by legislative acts, or by a combination of the two, and may encompass a variety of institutions—from the large state university to smaller state colleges or teachers colleges, to community colleges, technical schools, and vocational schools.

Every state has at least one designated body that bears statewide responsibility for at least some aspects of its public postsecondary system.[1] These bodies are known by such titles as Board of Higher Education, Commission on Higher Education, Board of Regents, Regents, Board of Educational Finance, or Board of Governors. Most such boards are involved in some phase of planning, program review and approval, and budget development for the institutions under their control or within their sphere of influence. Other responsibilities—such as the development of databases and management information systems or the establishment of new degree-granting institutions—might also be imposed. Depending on their functions, boards are classifiable into two groups: governing and coordinating. Governing boards are legally responsible for the management and operation of the institutions under their control. Coordinating boards have the lesser responsibilities that their name implies. Most governing boards work directly with the institutions for which they are responsible. Coordinating boards may or may not do so. Although community colleges are closely tied to their locales, most come within the jurisdiction of some state board or agency.

The legal status of the institutions in the public postsecondary system varies from state to state and may vary as well from institution to institution within the same state. Typically, institutions established directly by a state constitution have more authority than institutions established by statute and, correspondingly, have more autonomy from the state governing board and the state legislature. In dealing with problems of legal authority, therefore, one must distinguish between "statutory" and "constitutional" institutions and, within these basic categories, carefully examine the terms of the provisions granting authority to each particular institution. (See V. L. Brown, "A Comparative Analysis of College Autonomy in Selected States," 60 *West's Educ. Law Rptr.* 299 (1990).)

State constitutional and statutory provisions may also grant certain authority over institutions to the state governing board or some other state agency or official. It is thus also important to examine the terms of any such provisions that are part of the law of the particular state. The relevant statutes and constitutional clauses do not always project clear answers, however, to the questions that may arise concerning the division of authority among the individual institution, the statewide governing or coordinating body, the legislature, the governor, and other state agencies (such as a civil service commission or a budget office) or officials (such as a commissioner of education). Because of the uncertainties, courts often have had to determine who holds the ultimate authority to make various critical decisions regarding public postsecondary education.

Disputes over the division of authority among the state, a statewide governing or coordinating body, the legislature, or other entities typically arise in one of two contexts: the creation or dissolution of an institution, and the management and control of the affairs of a public institution. Although public institutions created by a state constitution, such as the flagship universities of California and Michigan, can

---

[1]The information in this paragraph is drawn heavily from R. M. Millard, *State Boards of Higher Education,* ERIC Higher Education Research Report no. 4 (American Association for Higher Education, 1976).

be dissolved only by an amendment to the state constitution and are insulated from legislative control because of their constitutional status, public institutions created by legislative action (a statute) can also be dissolved by the legislature and are subject to legislative control. In some states, however, the allocation of authority is less clear. For example, in South Dakota the state constitution created the statewide governing board for public colleges and universities (the board of regents), but the state colleges and universities were created by statute. In *Kanaly v. State of South Dakota*, 368 N.W.2d 819 (S.D. 1985), taxpayers challenged the state legislature's decision to close the University of South Dakota–Springfield and transfer its campus and facilities to the state prison system. The state's Supreme Court ruled that the decision to change the use of these assets was clearly within the legislature's power. However, under the terms of a perpetual trust the legislature had established to fund state universities, the prison system had to reimburse the trust for the value of the land and buildings.

The court distinguished between the power to manage and control a state college (given by the state constitution to the board of regents) and the "power of the purse" (a legislative power). The state constitution, said the court, did not create the board of regents as "a fourth branch of government independent of any legislative policies." Previous decisions by the South Dakota Supreme Court had established that the board of regents did not have the power to change the character of an institution, to determine state educational policy, or to appropriate funding for the institutions (368 N.W.2d at 825). Said the court, "The legislature has the power to create schools, to fund them as it has the power of the purse, and to establish state educational policy and this necessarily includes the power to close a school if efficiency and economy so direct" (368 N.W.2d at 825). Transferring the property upon which the university was located to the state prison system was not the same, said the court, as transferring control of the institution itself from the regents to the prison system.

In situations where a state governing or coordinating board has the authority to establish or dissolve a college, a court's powers to review the criteria by which such a decision is made are limited. For example, a group of citizens formed a nonprofit corporation and asked the state of Missouri to approve the corporation's application to form a community college. In *State ex rel. Lake of the Ozarks Community College Steering Committee v. Coordinating Board for Higher Education*, 802 S.W.2d 533 (Mo. Ct. App. 1991), the steering committee of the corporation sued the state coordinating board for rejecting its application. The court dismissed the lawsuit as moot because the board had considered the petition and, having rejected it, had acted within its authority. The court noted that it was not proper in this instance for a court to define the standards by which the board evaluated the application.

Litigated issues related to the management and control of colleges and universities are numerous. They include:

Registration of doctoral programs (*Moore v. Board of Regents of the University of the State of New York*, 390 N.Y.S.2d 582 (N.Y. Sup. Ct. 1977), *affirmed*, 397 N.Y.S.2d 449 (N.Y. App. Div. 1977), *affirmed*, 407 N.Y.S.2d 452 (N.Y. 1978)).

Establishment of tuition rates (*Kowalski v. Board of Trustees of Macomb County Community College*, 240 N.W.2d 272 (Mich. Ct. App. 1976)).

Ability to make binding agreements with faculties (*Busboom v. Southeast Nebraska Technical Community College*, 232 N.W.2d 24 (Neb. 1975)).

Power to authorize expenditures by a constitutionally established university (*Regents of the University of Michigan v. State of Michigan*, 235 N.W.2d 1 (Mich. 1975); *Board of Regents of the University of Nebraska v. Exon*, 256 N.W.2d 330 (Neb. 1977); *State of New Mexico v. Kirkpatrick*, 524 P.2d 975 (N.M. 1974)).

Approval of budget amendments and appropriation of funds for the university system (*Board of Regents of Higher Education v. Judge*, 543 P.2d 1323 (Mont. 1975)).

Power to determine residency requirements for in-state tuition rates (*Schmidt v. Regents of the University of Michigan*, 233 N.W.2d 855 (Mich. Ct. App. 1975)).

Establishment of salary scales (*San Francisco Labor Council v. Regents of the University of California*, 608 P.2d 277 (Cal. 1980)).

Control of building design and construction (*State of Mississippi v. Board of Trustees of Institutions of Higher Learning*, 387 So. 2d 89 (Miss. 1980)).

Control over expenditure of "self-generated funds"—funds that the institution raises by and for itself through contracts with private entities and other means (*State of Mississippi* case above).

6.2.1. Statutorily based institutions. A public institution established by state statute is usually characterized, for legal purposes, by terms such as "state agency," "public corporation," or state "political subdivision." Such institutions—particularly institutions considered "state agencies"—are often subject to an array of state legislation applicable to state-created entities. A state agency, for example, is usually subject to the state's administrative procedure act and other requirements of state administrative law. State agencies, and sometimes other statutory institutions, may also be able to assert the legal defenses available to the state, such as sovereign immunity. In *Board of Trustees of Howard Community College v. John K. Ruff, Inc.*, 366 A.2d 360 (Md. 1976), for instance, the court's holding that the board of a regional community college was a state agency enabled the board to assert sovereign immunity as a defense against a suit for breach of contract.

The case of *Moore v. Board of Regents of the University of the State of New York*, 390 N.Y.S.2d 582 (N.Y. Sup. Ct. 1977), *affirmed*, 397 N.Y.S.2d 449 (N.Y. App. Div. 1977), *affirmed*, 407 N.Y.S.2d 452, (N.Y. 1978), illustrates the problem of dividing authority between a statutory institution and other entities claiming some authority over it. The trustees and chancellor of the State University of New York, together with several professors and doctoral students in the affected departments, sought a declaratory judgment that the university trustees were responsible under the law for providing the standards and regulations for the organization and operation of university programs, courses, and curricula in accordance with the state's master plan. The defendants were the state board of regents and the state commissioner of education. The case concerned the commissioner's deregistration of the doctoral programs in history and English at the State University of New York at Albany. In statements for the news media, each of the opposing litigants foresaw an ominous impact from a decision for the other side: if the commissioner and the state board won, the institution would continue to be subjected to "unprecedented intervention"; if the trustees won, the university would be placed beyond public accountability (*Chron. Higher Educ.*, Mar. 8, 1976, A3).

After analyzing the state's constitution, Education Law, and administrative regulations, the trial court concluded that the commissioner, acting for the board of regents, which was established by the state constitution, had the authority to make the decision:

> In support of this conclusion, the court points out that the board of regents is a constitutional body which was created in 1784 under the name of the Regents of the University of the State of New York (N.Y. Const. art. XI, § 2). The University of the State of New York (not to be confused with the State University of New York) is the name given to the entire educational community under the jurisdiction of the board of regents. It includes "all institutions of higher education which are now or may hereafter be incorporated in this state" (Laws of 1892, ch. 378; see Education Law, § 214).
>
> As of 1784, the regents were vested with full power and authority to make ordinances for the government of the colleges which should compose the university. In 1892, prior to the adoption of the 1894 constitution, the legislature granted broad powers to the regents; these powers included the power to charter institutions and colleges, and the legislation prohibited institutions not holding university or college degree-conferring powers from assuming the appellation of college or university or conferring degrees. These and other powers were, in effect, confirmed by the constitution of 1894 [references omitted].
>
> In its *amicus curiae* brief, the Commission on Independent Colleges and Universities notes that since 1787 the regents have registered programs and since 1910 they have conducted such registration through the commissioner. In construing the statute to allow the regents, through the commissioner, to register programs, the court relies not only on the historical grants of extensive power to the regents, but also on the rule that a long continued course of action by those administering a statute is entitled to great weight (see McKinney's *Cons. Laws of N.Y.*, Book 1, Statutes, § 129). Moreover, it would appear that the legislature has recognized the existence and exercise of this authority (Education Law, § 224, subd. 4). . . . The court also rejects plaintiffs' contention that, notwithstanding the existence of any power the regents and the commissioner may have to register programs in other institutions, they have no power to approve programs in the State University of New York. The State University of New York was created by the legislature on July 1, 1948 (Laws of 1948, ch. 695 [Education Law, § 352]), as a corporation within the State Education Department and the University of the State of New York. In 1961, chapter 388 of the Laws of 1961 gave the Board of Trustees of the State University of New York the authority to administer the internal affairs of the State University. Nothing contained in that statute, or in the legislative history leading to its passage, indicates that the State University was to become *sui generis* and not subject to the same requirements imposed by the regents and commissioner on private institutions of higher education in this state [390 N.Y.S.2d at 585–86].

This decision was affirmed by the Appellate Division of the New York Supreme Court (an intermediate appellate court) and subsequently by the New York Court of Appeals. In affirming, however, the New York Court of Appeals cautioned that the broad "policy-making" and "rule-making" power of the regents "is not unbridled and is not an all-encompassing power permitting the regents' intervention in the day-to-day operations of the institutions of higher education in New York."

In some states community colleges are operated and funded by state subdivisions, such as counties or municipalities. The relationship among the college, its related government entity (the city or county), and the state may raise issues of institutional autonomy versus control by either or both levels of government. For example, in *Atlantic Community College v. Civil Service Commission*, 279 A.2d 820 (N.J. 1971), the New Jersey Supreme Court was asked to determine whether nonprofessional and noninstructional employees of the county community college were to be treated as employees of the county (who were covered by the state civil service system) or whether the community college was autonomous for purposes of classification of its employees. The court, after reviewing the enabling legislation that authorized counties to establish colleges, determined that county colleges were not agents of county government but were "political subdivisions which serve a separate purpose and operate apart from the government bodies of the counties in which they are situated" (279 A.2d at 823). Since the colleges were governed by a board of trustees rather than by the elected leadership of the county, and since most of the colleges' funding came from the state rather than the county, the court found ample evidence of legislative intent that the colleges be autonomous from county government, and thus their employees were not part of the civil service system. The county colleges were, however, still subject to the rules and regulations of the state board of higher education.

Although state law defines the relationship between statutorily based institutions and relevant state agencies, clashes between these institutions and the state may also raise issues of federal law. Furthermore, third parties may also occasionally be able to use federal civil rights law to intervene in disputes between state boards and statutorily based institutions. For example, in *United States v. State of Alabama*, 791 F.2d 1450 (11th Cir. 1986), Alabama State University and several faculty, students, and citizens suing as individuals attempted to use Section 1983 (this volume, Section 2.3.3) and Title VI (Section 7.5.2) to reverse the state board of education's decertification of teacher education programs at that institution. The plaintiffs claimed that the state board's actions were in retaliation for the plaintiffs' involvement in desegregation litigation against the board. Although the appellate court ruled that the institution had no standing to sue the state board (because the university was a creation of the state), the individual plaintiffs could proceed against individual members of the board of education under federal civil rights law.

6.2.2. Constitutionally based institutions. A public institution established by the state's constitution is usually characterized, for legal purposes, as a "public trust," an "autonomous university," a "constitutional university," or a "constitutional body corporate." Such institutions enjoy considerable freedom from state legislative control and generally are not subject to state administrative law. Such institutions also may not be able to assert all the defenses to suit that the state may assert. If the institution is considered a public trust, its trustees must fulfill the special fiduciary duties of public trustees and administer the trust for the educational benefit of the public.

The case of *Regents of the University of Michigan v. State of Michigan*, 235 N.W.2d 1 (Mich. 1975), illustrates both the greater autonomy of constitutional (as opposed to statutory) institutions and the differing divisions of authority that are likely between the institution and other entities claiming authority over it. The University of Michigan, Michigan State University, and Wayne State University, all "constitutional" universities, challenged the constitutionality of various provisions in legislative appropriation acts that allegedly infringed on their autonomy. The court affirmed that, although the legislature could impose conditions on its appropriations to the institutions, it could not do so in a way that would "interfere with the management and control of those institutions." Thus, any particular condition in an appropriation act will be held unconstitutional if it constitutes an interference with institutional autonomy. Since most of the provisions challenged were no longer in effect and the controversy was therefore moot, the court refused to determine whether or not they constituted an interference. But the court did consider the challenge to a provision that prohibited the institutions from contracting for the construction of any "self-liquidating project" (a project that would ultimately pay for itself) without first submitting to the legislature schedules for liquidation of the debt incurred for construction and operation of the project. The court upheld this provision because it "is a mere reporting measure, without corollary of supervision or control on the part of the [legislative] committees receiving the information. . . . Universities may still enter into construction contracts for self-liquidating projects without prior legislative approval."

The institutions also challenged the State Board of Education's authority over higher education. The State Board of Education argued that it had the authority to approve program changes or new construction at the universities. Relying on the express terms of a constitutional provision setting out the board's powers and their relationship to powers of individual institutions, the court held that the State Board of Education's authority over the institutions was advisory only. The institutions were required only to inform the board of program changes, so that it could "knowledgeably carry out its advisory duties." Thus, although the state could impose some requirements on the plaintiff universities to accommodate the authority given other state agencies or branches of government, constitutionally created institutions retain exclusive authority to manage and control their own operations.

Similarly, in *San Francisco Labor Council v. Regents of the University of California*, 608 P.2d 277 (Cal. 1980), the court gave substantial protection to a constitutionally based institution's autonomy. The plaintiff labor council argued that the regents had failed to comply with a requirement set forth in the State Education Code—namely, that the board of regents, in setting salaries, must take account of prevailing minimum and maximum salaries in various localities. The board asserted that the state constitution exempted it from the Education Code's mandate. The California Supreme Court agreed with the board. The state constitutional provision at issue (as quoted by the court) reads:

> The University of California shall constitute a public trust, to be administered by the existing corporation known as "The Regents of the University of California," with full powers of organization and government, subject only to such legislative control as may be necessary to insure the security of its funds and compliance with the terms of the endowments of the university and such competitive bidding procedures as may be made applicable to the university by statute for the letting of construction contracts, sales of real property, and purchasing of materials, goods, and services [Cal. Const. Art. IX, § 9].

The court discussed the autonomy that the board enjoyed under this constitutional provision:

> Article IX, section 9, grants the regents broad powers to organize and govern the university and limits the legislature's power to regulate either the university or the regents. This contrasts with the comprehensive power of regulation the legislature possesses over other state agencies.
>
> The courts have also recognized the broad powers conferred upon the regents as well as the university's general immunity from legislative regulation. "The regents have the general rule-making power in regard to the university . . . and are . . . fully empowered with respect to the organization and government of the university. . . . The power of the regents to operate, control, and administer the university is virtually exclusive" (*Regents of University of California v. Superior Court* (1970), 3 Cal. 3d 529, 540; *California State Employees' Association v. Flournoy* (1973), 32 Cal. App. 3d 219, 233; *California State Employees' Association v. State of California* (1973), 32 Cal. App. 3d 103, 109; *Ishimatsu v. Regents of University of California* (1968), 266 Cal. App. 2d 854, 859–60; *California State Employees' Association v. Regents of University of California* (1968), 267 Cal. App. 2d 667, 671).
>
> We recently pointed out "the university is intended to operate as independently of the state as possible (see Cal. Const. art. IX, sec. 9)" (*Regents of University of California v. Superior Court* (1976), 17 Cal. 3d 533, 537). In that case we concluded the university is so autonomous that, unlike other state agencies, it is subject to the usury laws then applicable to private persons and private universities (17 Cal. 3d at 536–37) [608 P.2d at 278].

Nevertheless, the board of regents is not totally independent of state legislative control. The court outlined three areas where the legislature may regulate the board:

> It is true the university is not completely free from legislative regulation. In addition to the specific provisions set forth in article IX, section 9, there are three areas of legislative regulation. First, the legislature is vested with the power of appropriation, preventing the regents from compelling appropriations for salaries (*California State Employees' Association v. Flournoy*, supra, *California State Employees' Association v. State of California*, supra, at 109–10).
>
> Second, it is well settled that general police power regulations governing private persons and corporations may be applied to the university (*Regents of University of California v. Superior Court*, supra, at 536–37; *City Street IMP. Co. v. Regents* (1908), 153 Cal. 776, 778 et seq.; *Estate of Royer* (1899), 123 Cal. 614, 624). For example, workers' compensation laws applicable to the private sector may be made applicable to the university.
>
> Third, legislation regulating public agency activity not generally applicable to the public may be made applicable to the university when the legislation regulates matters of statewide concern not involving internal university affairs (*Tolman v. Underhill* (1952), 39 Cal. 2d 708, 712) [608 P.2d at 278, 279].

The court then held that the Education Code provision relied on by the plaintiff did not fit any of the three areas where the legislature could intervene and thus did not bind the board of regents.

Another case, *Board of Regents of the University of Oklahoma v. Baker*, 638 P.2d 464 (Okla. 1981), is similar to the *San Francisco Labor Council* case in both facts and outcome. The Oklahoma legislature had directed all state agencies, including the board of regents, to increase employee salaries by 6 percent. The board withheld the increase from certain university employees. The employees sued, arguing that the board had no authority to deny them raises authorized by the legislature. The Oklahoma Supreme Court rejected this argument, finding that "the determination of faculty salaries is clearly an integral part of the power to govern the university and a function essential in preserving the independence of the board." In reaching its conclusion, the court relied in part on the *San Francisco Labor Council* case.

In *Regents of the University of Michigan v. State*, 419 N.W.2d 773 (Mich. Ct. App. 1988), the University of Michigan was once again required to assert its constitutional autonomy against state attempts to regulate its operations. The Michigan legislature passed a law prohibiting any public educational institution from "making or maintaining . . . an investment in an organization operating in the Republic of South Africa." Although the University of Michigan had nearly completed its divestiture of South African–related assets, it challenged the law as violating its constitutional autonomy to make its own decisions about its resources. The state appellate court agreed, and the state appealed. The Michigan Supreme Court affirmed the lower courts (453 N.W.2d 656 (Mich. 1990)), despite the state's argument that the issue was moot because the university had divested its South African–related stocks voluntarily. For an analysis of the issues in the case, written by the university's counsel, see R. K. Daane, *"Regents of the University of Michigan v. State of Michigan:* South African Divestiture and Constitutional Autonomy," 15 *J. Coll. & Univ. Law* 313 (1989).

But statutes of general application that regulate the employment relationship between public employers and their employees have usually (but not always) been applied to constitutionally based institutions. For example, the University of Colorado asserted that its constitutional status exempted it from the application of the state's Civil Rights Act. In *Colorado Civil Rights Commission v. Regents of the University of Colorado*, 759 P.2d 726 (Colo. 1988), the university claimed that the state Civil Rights Commission lacked jurisdiction over a challenge to the university's decision to deny tenure to a Hispanic professor. Although the university argued that previous state Supreme Court decisions had required the legislature to "explicitly refer to the Regents in defining the term 'employer' for purposes of discriminatory employment practices" (759 P.2d at 733), the court found an implied legislative intent to include the regents within the term "employer" in the state's antidiscrimination statute.

The court noted that the Colorado constitution provided that colleges and universities "shall be subject to the control of the state, under the provisions of the constitution and such laws and regulations as the general assembly may provide" (Colo. Const. Art. VIII, § 5(1)). The constitution gives to the governing boards of the state colleges and universities, "whether established by constitution or by law," the power of general supervision over these institutions "unless otherwise provided by law" (Art. VIII, § 5(2)). This language, said the court, "clearly contemplates a limited power of 'general supervision' only" (759 P.2d 730). The enactment by the Colorado legislature of the nondiscrimination law, and its creation of a Civil Rights Commission to investigate discrimination claims against employers, constituted such a law that limited the authority of the university's governing board.

The court stated:

In the absence of some demonstrably countervailing constitutional or statutory rule, we know of no reason why the alleged denial of tenured status to a faculty member on the basis of a prohibited form of discrimination should not be subject to the enforcement procedures of a state statutory scheme clearly intended to redress such discriminatory practices at all levels of state and local government [759 P.2d at 730–31].

See also *Regents of the University of Michigan v. Michigan Employment Relations Commission*, 204 N.W.2d 218 (Mich. 1973), where the court held that the University of Michigan is a public employer and subject to the Public Employment Relations Act.

But a different result was reached in a Minnesota case in which the court was asked to determine whether the state's Veterans Preference Act applied to nonfaculty employment decisions of the University of Minnesota, a constitutionally based university. In *Winberg v. University of Minnesota*, 485 N.W.2d 325 (Minn. Ct. App. 1992), a state appellate court recognized the university's autonomy but ruled that limits could be placed on that autonomy by the legislature, given the university's acceptance of public funds. The Minnesota Supreme Court reversed (499 N.W.2d 799 (Minn. 1993)), holding that the Veterans Preference Act did not apply to the university's employment decisions because the university was not a "political subdivision" of the state. Only if the legislature had specifically referred to the university in the text of the law would it have bound the university, said the court. Having resolved the dispute through statutory interpretation, the court declined to address the constitutional issues raised by the university.

Sec. 6.3. State Chartering and Licensure of Private Postsecondary Institutions

6.3.1. Scope of state authority. The authority of states to regulate private postsecondary education is not as broad as their authority over their own public institutions (see Section 1.5.1). Nevertheless, under their police powers, states do have extensive regulatory authority that they have implemented through statutes and administrative regulations. This authority has frequently been upheld by the courts. In the leading case of *Shelton College v. State Board of Education*, 226 A.2d 612 (N.J. 1967), for instance, the court reviewed the authority of New Jersey to license degree-granting institutions and approve the basis and conditions on which they grant degrees. The State Board of Education had refused to approve the granting of degrees by the plaintiff college, and the college challenged the board's authority on a variety of grounds. In an informative opinion, the New Jersey Supreme Court rejected all the challenges and broadly upheld the board's decision and the validity of the statute under which the board had acted.

Similarly, in *Warder v. Board of Regents of the University of the State of New York*, 423 N.E.2d 352 (N.Y. 1981), the court rejected state administrative law and constitutional due process challenges to New York's authority to charter postsecondary institutions. The Unification Theological Seminary, a subdivision of the Unification Church (the church of Reverend Sun Myung Moon), sought to incorporate in New York and offer a master's degree in religious education. It applied for a provisional charter. In reviewing the application, the state education department subjected the seminary to an unprecedented lengthy and intensive investigation. The department had been concerned about charges of brainwashing and deceptive practices directed against the Unification Church. The department's investigation did not substantiate these charges but did uncover evidence suggesting other deficiencies. Ultimately, the department determined that the seminary had misrepresented itself as having degree-granting status, had refused to provide financial statements, and had not enforced its admissions policies.

The New York Court of Appeals held that, despite the singular treatment the seminary had received, the education department had a rational basis for its decision to deny the charter:

> Petitioners do not and cannot dispute that the board validly could deny a provisional charter to an institution that engaged in "brainwashing" and deception. That the broad investigation revealed no evidence of such practices does not mean that it was improperly undertaken in the first instance. The board cannot now be faulted because it discharged its responsibility for ensuring ethical educational programs of quality and in the process discovered serious deficiencies in the conduct of the academic program [423 N.E.2d at 357].

The seminary also charged that the legislature's grant of authority to the education department was vague and overbroad, and that the department had reviewed the seminary in a discriminatory and biased manner. Dispensing with the latter argument, the court found that the record did not contain evidence of discrimination or bias. Also rejecting the former argument, the court held that the New York statutes constituted a lawful delegation of authority to the state's board of regents:

> The board of regents is charged with broad policy-making responsibility for the state's educational system (Education Law § 207) and is specifically empowered to charter institutions of higher education (Education Law §§ 216, 217). In the meaningful discharge of those functions and to "encourage and promote education" (Education Law § 201), the regents ensure that acceptable academic standards are maintained in the programs offered (see *Moore v. Board of Regents of University of the State of New York,* . . . 378 N.E.2d 1022 [1978]). Thus, before an institution may be admitted to the academic community with degree-granting status, it must meet established standards (see 8 NYCRR [New York Code, Rules and Regulations] 3.21, 3.22, 52.1, 52.2); its purposes must be, "in whole or in part, of educational or cultural value deemed worthy of recognition and encouragement" (Education Law § 216). Given the broad responsibility of the board of regents for the quality of education provided in this state, it must be given wide latitude to investigate and evaluate institutions seeking to operate within the system [423 N.E.2d at 357].

Authority over private postsecondary institutions is exercised, in varying degrees depending on the state, in two basic ways. The first is incorporation or chartering, a function performed by all states. In some states postsecondary institutions are subject to the nonprofit corporation laws applicable to all nonprofit corporations; in others postsecondary institutions come under corporation statutes designed particularly for charitable institutions; and in a few states there are special statutes for incorporating educational institutions. Proprietary (profit-making) schools often fall under general business corporation laws. The states also have laws applicable to "foreign" corporations (that is, those chartered in another state), under which states may "register" or "qualify" out-of-state institutions that seek to do business in their jurisdiction.

The second method for regulating private postsecondary institutions is licensure. Imposed as a condition to offering education in the state or to granting degrees or using a collegiate name, licensure is a more substantial form of regulation than chartering. An overview of the kinds of provisions that are or can be included in state licensing systems, as well as some of the policy choices involved, can be found in *Model State Legislation: Report of the Task Force on Model State Legislation for Approval of Postsecondary Educational Institutions and Authorization to Grant Degrees*, Report no. 39 (Education Commission of the States, June 1973).

There are three different approaches to licensure:

> First, a state can license on the basis of *minimum standards*. The state may choose to specify, for example, that all degree-granting institutions have a board, administration, and faculty of certain characteristics, an organized curriculum with stipulated features, a library of given size, and facilities defined as adequate to the instruction offered. Among states pursuing this approach, the debate centers on what and in what detail the state should prescribe—some want higher levels of prescription to assure "quality," others want to allow room for "innovation."
>
> A second approach follows models developed in contemporary regional accreditation and stresses *realization of objectives*. Here the focus is less on a set of standards applicable to all than on encouragement for institutions to set their own goals and realize them as fully as possible. The role of the visiting team is not to inspect on the basis of predetermined criteria but to analyze the institution on its own terms and suggest new paths to improvement. This help-oriented model is especially strong in the eastern states with large numbers of well-established institutions; in some cases, a combined state-regional team will be formed to make a single visit and joint recommendation.
>
> A third model would take an *honest practice* approach. The essence of it is that one inspects to verify that an institution is run with integrity and fulfills basic claims made to the public. The honesty and probity of institutional officers, integrity of the faculty, solvency of the balance sheet, accuracy of the catalogue, adequacy of student records, equity of refund policies—these and related matters would be the subject of investigation. If an institution had an occupation-related program, employment records of graduates would be examined. It is unclear whether any state follows this model in its pure form, though it is increasingly advocated, and aspects of it do appear in state criteria. A claimed advantage is that, since it does not specify curricular components or assess their strengths and weaknesses (as the other two models might), an "honest practice" approach avoids undue state "control" of education [*Approaches to State Licensing of Private Degree-Granting Institutions* (Postsecondary Education Convening Authority, George Washington University, 1975), 17–19].

Almost all states have some form of licensing laws applicable to proprietary institutions, and the trend is toward increasingly stringent regulation of the proprietary sector (see, for example, M. C. Cage, "Plan Would Increase State Regulation of For-Profit Schools," *Chron. Higher Educ.*, Aug. 14, 1994, A17). Some states apply special requirements to non-degree-granting proprietary schools that are more extensive than the requirements for degree-granting institutions. In *New York Assn. of*

Career Schools v. State Education Department, 749 F. Supp. 1264 (S.D.N.Y. 1990), the court upheld the New York regulations on non-degree-granting schools as against an Equal Protection Clause attack.

In contrast, not all states have licensing laws for nonprofit postsecondary institutions. Among the states that do have laws, their strength and the effectiveness of their enforcement vary considerably. Often, by statutory mandate or the administrative practice of the licensing agency, regionally accredited institutions (see Section 8.3.1) are exempted from all or most licensing requirements for nonprofit schools.

State corporation laws ordinarily do not pose significant problems for postsecondary institutions, since their requirements can usually be met easily and routinely. Although licensing laws contain more substantial requirements, even in the more rigorous states these laws present few problems for established institutions, either because they are exempted by accreditation or because their established character makes compliance easy. For these institutions problems with licensing laws are most likely to arise if they establish new programs in other states and must therefore comply with the various licensing laws of those other states (see Section 6.4). The story is quite different for new institutions, especially if they have innovative (nontraditional) structures, programs, or delivery systems, or if they operate across state lines (Section 6.4). For these institutions licensing laws can be quite burdensome, because such laws may not be adapted to the particular characteristics of nontraditional education or receptive to out-of-state institutions.

When an institution does encounter problems with state licensing laws, administrators may have several possible legal arguments to raise, which generally stem from state administrative law or the due process clauses of state constitutions or the federal Constitution. Administrators should insist that the licensing agency proceed according to written standards and procedures, that it make them available to the institution, and that it scrupulously follow its own standards and procedures. If any standard or procedure appears to be outside the authority delegated to the licensing agency by state statute, it may be questioned before the licensing agency and challenged in court. Occasionally, even if standards and procedures are within the agency's delegated authority, the authorizing statute itself may be challenged as an unlawful delegation of legislative power. In *Packer Collegiate Institute v. University of the State of New York,* 81 N.E.2d 80 (N.Y. 1948), the court invalidated New York's licensing legislation because "the legislature has not only failed to set out standards or tests by which the qualifications of the schools might be measured, but has not specified, even in most general terms, what the subject matter of the regulations is to be." In *State v. Williams,* 117 S.E.2d 444 (N.C. 1960), the court used similar reasoning to invalidate a North Carolina law. However, a much more hospitable approach to legislative delegations of authority is found in more recent cases, such as *Shelton College* and *Warder,* both discussed earlier in this section, where the courts upheld state laws against charges that they were unlawful delegations of authority.

Perhaps the soundest legal argument for an institution involved with a state licensing agency is that the agency must follow the procedures in the state's administrative procedure act (where applicable) or the constitutional requirements of procedural due process. *Blackwell College of Business v. Attorney General,* 454 F.2d 928 (D.C. Cir. 1971), a case involving a federal agency function analogous to licensing, provides a good illustration. The case involved the withdrawal by the Immigration and Naturalization Service (INS) of Blackwell College's status as a school approved for attendance by nonimmigrant alien students under Section 1101(a)(15)(F) of the Immigration and Nationality Act. The INS had not afforded the college a hearing on the withdrawal of its approved status, but only an interview with agency officials and an opportunity to examine agency records concerning the withdrawal. The appellate court found that "the proceedings . . . were formless and uncharted" and did not meet the requirements of either the federal Administrative Procedure Act or constitutional due process. Invalidating the INS withdrawal of approval because of this lack of procedural due process, the court established guidelines for future government proceedings concerning the withdrawal of a school's license or approved status:

> The notice of intention to withdraw approval . . . should specify in reasonable detail the particular instances of failure to . . . [comply with agency requirements]. The documentary evidence the school is permitted to submit . . . can then be directed to the specific grounds alleged. In addition, if requested, the school should be granted a hearing before an official other than the one upon whose investigation the [agency] has relied for initiating its withdrawal proceedings. If the evidence against the school is based upon authentic records, findings may be based thereon, unless the purport of the evidence is denied, in which event the school may be required to support its denial by authentic records or live testimony. If, however, the data presented in support of noncompliance [are] hearsay evidence, the college, if it denies the truth of the evidence, shall have opportunity, if it so desires, to confront and cross-examine the person or persons who supplied the evidence, unless the particular hearsay evidence is appropriate for consideration under some accepted exception to the hearsay rule. In all the proceedings the school, of course, shall be entitled to representation and participation by counsel. The factual decision of the [agency] shall be based on a record thus compiled; and the record shall be preserved in a manner to enable review of the decision. . . . We should add that we do not mean that each and every procedural item discussed constitutes by itself a prerequisite of procedural due process. Rather our conclusion of unfairness relates to the totality of the procedure. . . . The ultimate requirement is a procedure that permits a meaningful opportunity to test and offer facts, present perspective, and invoke official discretion [454 F.2d at 936].

Although state incorporation and licensing laws are often sleeping dogs, they can sometimes bite hard. Institutional administrators—especially in new, expanding, or innovating institutions—should remain aware of the potential impact of these laws and the legal arguments available if problems arise.

6.3.2. Chartering and licensure of church-related institutions. In some respects, church-related institutions stand on the same footing as private secular institutions with respect to state chartering and licensure. In the *Warder* case (Section 6.3.1), for example, a religious seminary encountered the same kinds of problems that a secular institution might have encountered and raised the same kinds of legal issues that a secular institution might have raised. In other respects, however, the problems encountered and issues raised by church-related institutions may be unique to their religious mission and status. The predominant consideration in such situations is likely to be whether the church-related institution may invoke the freedom-of-religion guarantees in the federal Constitution or the state constitution—thus obtaining a shield against state regulation not available to secular institutions. The following two cases are illustrative.

In the first case, *New Jersey Board of Higher Education v. Shelton College*, 448 A.2d 988 (N.J. 1982), the New Jersey Supreme Court held that a state law requiring a license to grant degrees applied to religious as well as nonreligious private colleges. The court also held that application of the law to Shelton, a small fundamentalist Presbyterian college, did not violate either the Free Exercise Clause or the Establishment Clause of the First Amendment (see Section 1.6).[2] The college had begun offering instruction leading to the baccalaureate degree without first obtaining a state license. The state sought to enjoin Shelton from engaging in this activity within the state, and the New Jersey court granted the state's request.

While acknowledging that the state's licensing scheme imposed some burdens on Shelton's free exercise rights, the court found that the state had an overriding interest in regulating education and maintaining minimum academic standards. Given the strength of the state's interest in regulating and the absence of less restrictive means for fulfilling this interest, the state's interest outweighed the college's religious interests:

> Legislation that impedes the exercise of religion may be constitutional if there exists no less restrictive means of achieving some overriding state interest. . . .
> The legislation at issue here advances the state's interest in ensuring educational standards and maintaining the integrity of the baccalaureate degree. . . .
> That maintenance of minimum educational standards in all schools constitutes a substantial state interest is now beyond question. . . .
> [Moreover,] the First Amendment does not require the provision of religious exemptions where accommodation would significantly interfere with the attainment of an overriding state interest. . . .
> Here, accommodation of defendants' religious beliefs would entail a complete exemption from state regulation. . . . Such accommodation would cut to the heart of the legislation and severely impede the achievement of important state goals. Furthermore, if an exemption were created here, Shelton College would receive an advantage at the expense of those educational institutions that have submitted to state regulation. Such a development would undermine the integrity of the baccalaureate degree, erode respect for the state higher education scheme, and encourage others to seek exemptions. Thus, the uniform application of these licensing requirements is essential to the achievement of the state's interests. . . .
> In sum, although defendants' freedom of religion may suffer some indirect burden from this legislation, the constitutional balance nonetheless favors the state interest in uniform application of these higher education laws [448 A.2d at 995-97].

Nor did the state regulations result in any "excessive entanglement" with religion or otherwise infringe the Establishment Clause. Instead, the New Jersey law on its face created a religiously neutral regulatory scheme:

---

[2]The court referred to this litigation as *Shelton II* to distinguish it from *Shelton I* (*Shelton College v. State Board of Education*, discussed in Section 6.3.1).

The allegation of excessive entanglement rests on speculation about the manner in which these statutes and regulations might be applied. Although one could imagine an unconstitutional application of this regulatory scheme, we are confident that the board of higher education will pursue the least restrictive means to achieve the state's overriding concerns. Of course, should the board exercise its discretion in a manner that unnecessarily intrudes into Shelton's religious affairs, the college would then be free to challenge the constitutionality of such action [448 A.2d at 998].

In a similar case decided the same month as *Shelton College,* the Supreme Court of Tennessee upheld that state's authority to regulate degree granting by religious colleges. In *State ex rel. McLemore v. Clarksville School of Theology,* 636 S.W.2d 706 (Tenn. 1982), the school had also been offering instruction leading to a degree without obtaining a state license. When the state sought to enjoin it from offering degrees, the school argued that application of the state law would infringe its freedom of religion under the First Amendment.

The court agreed with the state's contention that the award of degrees is a purely secular activity and that the state's licensing requirement therefore did not interfere with the school's religious freedoms:

> The school is inhibited in no way by the Act as far as religion is concerned, the Act only proscribing the issuance of educational credentials by those institutions failing to meet the minimum requirements. The court holds, therefore, that applying the Act to defendant school does not violate the free exercise of religion clause of the Constitution, state or federal. . . .
>
> If the Act placed a burden upon the free exercise of religion by the defendants or posed a threat of entanglement between the affairs of the church and the state, the state would be required to show that "some compelling state interest" justified the burden and that there exists no less restrictive or entangling alternative (*Sherbert v. Verner,* 374 U.S. 398 . . . (1963); *Wisconsin v. Yoder,* 406 U.S. 205 . . . (1972)).
>
> We conclude, however, that this Act places neither a direct nor [an] indirect burden upon the free exercise of religion by the defendants nor threatens an entanglement between the affairs of church and state. . . .
>
> The Act does not regulate the beliefs, practices, or teachings of any institution; it merely sets forth minimum standards which must be met in order for an institution to be authorized to issue degrees. Moreover, the evidence shows that the granting of degrees is a purely secular activity. It is only this activity that brings the school under the regulation of the Act [636 S.W.2d at 708–09].

The court emphasized that the licensing statute did not interfere with the content of the school's teaching or with the act of teaching itself. But when the school sought to provide educational credentials as an end product of that teaching, it was properly subject to the state's authority to regulate a secular activity intimately related to the public welfare:

> The fact remains that the state is merely regulating the awarding of educational degrees. The supposed predicament of the school is not a result of the state's regulation of its religious function of training ministers but of its preem-

inent role of *awarding degrees*[,] which is, as conceded by its president and founder, a purely secular activity [636 S.W.2d at 711].

The Tennessee court thus rejected the school's First Amendment claims because the state regulation did not burden any religious activity of the school. In contrast, the New Jersey court recognized that the state regulation burdened Shelton College's religious activities; nonetheless, the court rejected the school's First Amendment claims because the state's educational interests were sufficiently strong to justify the burden.[3] By these varying paths, both cases broadly uphold state licensing authority over religiously affiliated degree-granting institutions. (For a dissenting view on the issues involved, see R. Kirk, "Shelton College and State Licensing of Religious Schools: An Educator's View of the Interface Between the Establishment and Free Exercise Clauses," 44 *Law & Contemporary Problems* 169 (1981).)

Sec. 6.4. State Regulation of Out-of-State Institutions

Postsecondary institutions have increasingly departed from the traditional mold of a campus-based organization existing at a fixed location within a single state. Nowadays both established and new institutions, public as well as private, are establishing branch campuses; off-campus programs; colleges without walls; TV, satellite, and similar media-based programs; and other innovative systems for delivering education to a wider audience (see K. P. Cross, J. R. Valley, & Associates, *Planning Non-Traditional Programs: An Analysis of the Issues for Postsecondary Education* (Jossey-Bass, 1974)). These developments have taken institutions into states other than the home states where they are incorporated, thus subjecting them to the regulatory jurisdiction of other (perhaps multiple) states.

For these multistate institutions, whether public or private, legal problems increase both in number and in complexity.[4] Not only must they meet the widely differing and possibly conflicting legal requirements of the various states, but they must also be prepared to contend with laws or administrative practices that may not be suited to or hospitable to either out-of-state or nontraditional programs. Institutional administrators contemplating the development of any program that will cross state lines should be sensitive to this added legal burden and to the legal arguments that may be used to lighten it.

A multistate institution may seek to apply the legal arguments in Section 6.3 to states that prohibit or limit the operation of the institution's programs within their boundaries; these legal arguments apply to all state regulation, whether it concerns out-of-state institutions or not. Out-of-state institutions may also raise particular questions concerning the state's authority over out-of-state, as opposed to in-state, institutions. Is the state licensing agency authorized under state law to license out-of-state schools that award degrees under the authority of their home states? Is the

---

[3]Later developments would now influence this line of analysis, in particular the *Smith* case and the Religious Freedom Restoration Act (see this volume, Section 1.6).

[4]Some of the background material in the first part of this section is drawn from prior work of one of the authors, included in Chapter Nine of *Nova University's Three National Doctoral Degree Programs* (Nova/N.Y.I.T. Press, 1977) and in Section 4.3 of *Legal and Other Constraints to the Development of External Degree Programs* (report under Grant NE-G-00-3-0208, National Institute of Education, Jan. 1975).

licensing agency authorized to apply standards to an out-of-state school which are higher than or different from the standards it applies to in-state schools? And, most intriguing, may the agency's authority be challenged under provisions of the federal or state constitution—in particular, the Commerce Clause or the First Amendment of the federal Constitution?

The Commerce Clause, in addition to being a rich lode of power for the federal government (see Section 7.1.3), also limits the authority of states to use their regulatory powers in ways that interfere with the free movement of goods and people across state lines. As the U.S. Supreme Court has emphasized, "the very purpose of the commerce clause was to create an area of free trade among the several states. . . . By its own force [the clause] created an area of trade free from interference by the states" (*Great A&P Tea Co. v. Cottrell*, 424 U.S. 366 (1976)). The term "commerce" has been very broadly construed by the courts. It includes both business and nonbusiness, profit and nonprofit activities. It encompasses the movement of goods or people, the communication of information or ideas, the provision of services that cross state lines, and all component parts of such transactions. As far back as 1910, in *International Textbook Co. v. Pigg*, 217 U.S. 91, the Supreme Court held that interstate educational activities were included in the category of commerce and that, therefore, an out-of-state correspondence school could not constitutionally be subjected to Kansas's foreign corporation requirements.[5]

What protection, then, might the Commerce Clause yield for multistate institutions? The zone of protection has been clearly identified in one circumstance: when the state subjects an out-of-state program to requirements that are different from and harsher than those applied to in-state (domestic) programs. Such differentiation is clearly unconstitutional. For one hundred years, it has been settled that states may not discriminate against interstate commerce, or goods or services from other states, in favor of their own intrastate commerce, goods, and services (see, for example, *Philadelphia v. New Jersey*, 437 U.S. 617 (1978)).

Beyond this principle of nondiscrimination or evenhandedness, the Commerce Clause's umbrella of protection against state regulation becomes more uncertain and more dependent on the facts of each particular case. Although a state may evenhandedly regulate the in-state or "localized" activities of out-of-state institutions, a potential Commerce Clause problem arises when the state regulation burdens the institution's ability to participate in interstate commerce. To resolve such problems, the courts engage in a delicate balancing process, attempting to preserve the authority of states to protect their governmental interests while protecting the principle of free trade and intercourse among the states. After a long period of feeling its way, the Supreme Court in 1970 finally agreed unanimously on this general approach:

> Where the statute regulates evenhandedly to effectuate a legitimate local public interest, and its effects on interstate commerce are only incidental, it will be upheld unless the burden imposed on such commerce is clearly excessive in

[5]Lawyers will want to compare the *Pigg* case with *Eli Lilly and Co. v. Sav-On Drugs*, 366 U.S. 276 (1961), where the Supreme Court distinguished between the intrastate and interstate activities of a foreign corporation engaged in interstate commerce and permitted the state to regulate the corporation's intrastate activities. See generally Annot., "Regulation and Licensing of Correspondence Schools and Their Canvassers or Solicitors," 92 A.L.R.2d 522 (1963 plus periodic supp.).

relation to the putative local benefits. If a legitimate local purpose is found, then the question becomes one of degree. And the extent of the burden that will be tolerated will, of course, depend on the nature of the local interest involved, and on whether it could be promoted as well with a lesser impact on interstate activities [*Pike v. Bruce Church*, 397 U.S. 137, 142 (1970)].

Under this test the state's interest must be "legitimate"—a label that courts have sometimes refused to apply to parochial or protectionist interests prompted by a state's design to isolate itself from the national economy. In one famous case, which arose after a state had refused to license an out-of-state business because the in-state market was already adequately served, the Court said that the state's decision was "imposed for the avowed purpose and with the practical effect of curtailing the volume of interstate commerce to aid local economic interests" and held that "the state may not promote its own economic advantages by curtailment or burdening of interstate commerce" (*H. P. Hood & Sons v. DuMond*, 336 U.S. 525 (1949)). On the other hand, under the *Pike* test, state interests in safety, fair dealing, accountability, or institutional competence would be legitimate interests to be accorded considerable weight. States clearly may regulate the localized activities of out-of-state institutions— along with those of in-state institutions—in order to promote such legitimate interests. In doing so, however, states must regulate sensitively, minimizing the impact on the institutions' interstate activities and ensuring that each regulation actually does further the interest asserted.

Commerce Clause issues, or other constitutional or statutory issues concerning state authority, are most likely to arise in situations where a state denies entry to an out-of-state program or places such burdensome restrictions on its entry that it is excluded in practical effect. A state might, for instance, deny entry to an out-of-state program by using academic standards higher than those applied to in-state programs. A state might impose a "need requirement" to which in-state programs are not subjected. Or a state might institute a need requirement that is applicable to both out-of-state and in-state programs but serves to freeze and preserve a market dominated by in-state schools. A state might also deny entry for lack of approval by a regional or statewide coordinating council dominated by in-state institutions. The relevant legal principles point to the possible vulnerability of state authority in each instance.

In *Nova University v. Board of Governors of the University of North Carolina*, 267 S.E.2d 596 (N.C. Ct. App. 1980), *affirmed*, 287 S.E.2d 872 (N.C. 1982), the North Carolina courts issued the first published court opinions exploring the legal questions raised in this section. By a 4-to-2 vote, the state's Supreme Court held that the state did not have the authority to regulate out-of-state institutions that operate educational programs in North Carolina but award degrees under the auspices of their home states. The plaintiff, Nova University, was licensed to award degrees under Florida law but organized small-group "cluster" programs in other states, including North Carolina. Successful participants received graduate degrees awarded in Florida. The board of governors of the University of North Carolina (pursuant to North Carolina General Statute 116-15, which authorized it to license degree-conferring institutions) claimed that Nova's curriculum was deficient and sought to deny the institution authority to operate its cluster programs in the state. The board claimed that the statute which authorized it to license degree conferrals included, by implication, the power to license teaching as well.

In rejecting the board's argument, the court acknowledged the important constitutional questions that the board's position would raise: "Were we . . . to interpret G.S. 116-15 as the Board suggests, serious constitutional questions arising under the First Amendment and the interstate commerce and Fourteenth Amendment due process clauses of the United States Constitution and the law of the land clause of the North Carolina constitution would arise." Looking to the language of General Statute 116-15, the court determined that it could reasonably be interpreted, and should be interpreted, to avoid these constitutional issues:

> All that Nova does in North Carolina is teach. Teaching and academic freedom are "special concern[s]" of the First Amendment to the United States Constitution (*Keyishian v. Board of Regents of New York*, 385 U.S. 589, 603 . . . (1967)); and the freedom to engage in teaching by individuals and private institutions comes within those liberties protected by the Fourteenth Amendment to the United States Constitution. . . .
>
> To say that it is conducting a "degree program" which is somehow different from or more than mere teaching, as the Board would have it, is nothing more than the Board's euphemization. Teaching is teaching and learning is learning, notwithstanding what reward might follow either process. The Board's argument that the power to license teaching is necessarily implied from the power to license degree conferrals simply fails to appreciate the large difference, in terms of the state's power to regulate, between the two kinds of activities. The Board accuses Nova of trying to accomplish an "end run" around the statute. In truth, the Board, if we adopted its position, would be guilty of an "end run" around the statutory limits on its licensing authority. . . .
>
> Here the legislature has clearly authorized the Board to license only degree conferrals, not teaching. Because of the statute's clear language limiting the Board's authority to license only degree conferrals and not separately to license the teaching which may lead to the conferral, the statute is simply not reasonably susceptible to a construction which would give the board the power to license such teaching [287 S.E.2d at 878, 881–82].

In a follow-up case, *Nova University v. Educational Institution Licensure Commission*, 483 A.2d 1172 (D.C. 1984), the same university challenged a District of Columbia statute that required all educational institutions seeking to operate in D.C. to obtain a license—even if they did not confer degrees in D.C. In upholding the statute, the court addressed the First Amendment issue outlined but not disposed of in the first *Nova* case. Nova argued that D.C.'s licensing was unconstitutional under the First Amendment, since it was a regulation of teaching and learning activities that were "pure speech." The court held that, even if Nova were engaged in free speech activities, the First Amendment does not immunize such institutions from all state regulation of business conduct determined to be adverse to the public interest. To determine whether the D.C. statute unduly restrained First Amendment activities, the court considered the purpose of the statute. Here the D.C. statute's sole purpose was to ensure that educational institutions in the District of Columbia meet minimal academic standards, regardless of the message being conveyed through their teaching. Since this important interest is content-neutral (see this volume, Section 4.9.2), and since Nova and other out-of-state schools were not being singled out (local schools being subject to the same regulation), the statute was constitutional.

Thus, the courts in the *Nova University* cases not only analyzed the state statutory issues but also outlined the sensitive constitutional issues that may loom on the horizon whenever state licensing authority is broadly construed. In contrast to other recent cases, which broadly construe state licensing authority over in-state institutions (see Section 6.3), the first *Nova* case more narrowly construes state authority over out-of-state schools. Moreover, although a more broadly and explicitly worded statute like that in D.C. could resolve the statutory issue in the first *Nova* case, such broader statutes may still be subjected to federal and state constitutional limitations such as those suggested by both *Nova* courts. Although the First Amendment argument in the second *Nova* case did not succeed, the result could be different for a statute that was not applied to out-of-state schools in a content-neutral and evenhanded fashion. Moreover, interstate commerce and other constitutional issues may arise, as the first *Nova* court indicated. The *Nova* cases therefore confirm that the legal principles in this section do provide substantial ammunition to out-of-state institutions, making it likely that they can hit the mark in some cases where state regulation stifles the development of legitimate interstate postsecondary programs.

Sec. 6.5. Other State Regulatory Laws Affecting Postsecondary Education Programs

Aside from the body of state law specifically designed to control the establishment and licensure of colleges and universities, discussed in Sections 6.2 and 6.3, public and private postsecondary institutions are subject to a variety of state statutes and regulations, most of which are not specifically tailored to educational operations. Many of these laws concern the institution's role either as employer or, in the case of public schools, as a government agency.

In some regulatory areas, especially with regard to private institutions, federal legislation has "preempted the field" (see Section 7.1), leaving little or no room for state law. Private-sector collective bargaining is a major example (see Section 7.2.3). In other areas, where there is little or no federal legislation, state legislation is primary. Major examples include collective bargaining laws covering public-sector employment;[6] workers' compensation laws; deceptive practices laws (for nonprofit entities); and open-meeting laws, administrative procedure acts, ethics codes, civil service laws, and contract and competitive bidding procedures for public agencies. In yet other areas, federal and state governments may share regulatory responsibilities, with some overlap and coordination of federal and state laws. Fair employment laws, occupational safety and health laws, environmental protection laws, unfair trade laws, unemployment compensation laws, and laws on solicitation of funds by charitable organizations are major examples. In this latter area, federal law will prevail over state law in case of conflict if the subject being regulated is within the federal government's constitutional powers.

As these examples suggest, state regulatory law may intrude on campus operations in many important respects. The cases in the sections below illustrate the kinds of legal disputes that may arise under the laws listed above. But many other state laws—ranging from state liquor-licensing laws (applicable to the campus

---

[6]Cases and authorities are collected in Annot., "Bargainable or Negotiable Issues in State Public Employment Labor Relations," 84 A.L.R.3d 242 (1978 and periodic supp.).

union) to landlord-tenant laws (sometimes applicable to residence halls) to toxic waste laws[7] (applicable to laboratories)—are also part of campus daily legal life.

In the past decade, states have enacted laws of general application that restrict the autonomy of public and, in many instances, private colleges and universities. For example, many states, including New York, have enacted legislation or issued executive orders that prohibit discrimination on the basis of sexual orientation. Although many colleges have established policies against such discrimination, those policies do not have the force of law in most states. However, in New York, the state's human rights agency ordered the law school of the State University of New York at Buffalo to bar military recruiters because of the military's policy of excluding individuals on the basis of their sexual orientation (G. Blumenstyk, "N.Y. Campus Ordered to Bar Military Recruiting Over Ban on Gays," *Chron. Higher Educ.*, Oct. 2, 1991, A29).

In addition, state common law and statutory developments concerning lawful grounds for discharge may affect the employment practices of both public and private institutions. Each state has its own nondiscrimination law, whose protections in some cases are broader than those of federal civil rights law.[8] Case law on sexual harassment may provide different standards than case law developed under federal legislation.[9] The treatment of common law wrongful-discharge claims differs by state and may influence personnel practices at colleges and universities. And in one state, a statute governs the conditions under which an employee may be discharged. Montana's Wrongful Discharge from Employment Act (Mont. Code Ann. § 39-2-901 et seq.) requires good cause for discharge and limits the remedies available to employees who successfully challenge a discharge under this statute. State whistleblower statutes, as well as common law in other states, prohibit retaliation against employees who "reasonably believe" that the college has violated a law or has tolerated an unsafe condition (see P. Burling & K. A. Matthews, *Responding to Whistleblowers: An Analysis of Whistleblower Protection Acts and Their Consequences* (National Association of College and University Attorneys, 1992); for an example of a university involved in a whistleblower case, see *McGill v. University of South Carolina*, 423 S.E.2d 109 (S.C. 1992)).

Other laws of general application include conflict-of-interest laws that restrict some activities of public employees. In *In re Determination of Executive Commission on Ethical Standards*, 561 A.2d 542 (N.J. 1989), the New Jersey Supreme Court was asked to determine whether the law (N.J. Stat. Ann. §§ 52:13D-12 to -27) applied to a Rutgers University law school professor in his conduct of a clinical program. The professor represented clients before the state's Council on Affordable Housing. The court ruled that the law's purpose was to prohibit state legislators from appearing before state agencies as advocates; the state legislature never intended the law to apply to the professor in this situation, the court said.

In addition to these laws of general application, state legislatures have enacted

[7]Cases and authorities are collected in Annot., "Validity, Construction, and Application of State Hazardous Waste Regulations," 86 A.L.R.4th 401 (1991 and periodic supp.).

[8]Cases and authorities are collected in Annot., "Application of State Law to Sex Discrimination in Employment," 87 A.L.R.3d 93 (1978 and periodic supp.). See also Annot., "Construction and Application of State Equal Rights Amendments Forbidding Determination of Rights Based on Sex," 90 A.L.R.3d 158 (1979 and periodic supp.).

[9]Cases and authorities are collected in Annot., "On-the-Job Sexual Harassment as Violation of State Civil Rights Law," 18 A.L.R.4th 328 (1982 and periodic supp.).

laws that deal directly with activities on college campuses. Several states, for example, have laws requiring fluency in English for all instructors, including teaching assistants (see Section 3.1.1). One such statute is Pennsylvania's English Fluency in Higher Education Act (24 Pa. Cons. Stat. Ann. §§ 6801–6806 (1993)). Some states have enacted legislation forbidding the sale of term papers or theses (see, for example, §§ 66400–66401 of the California Education Code and §§ 224(2) and (3) of the New York Education Law). For examples of litigation upholding convictions under these laws, see *State v. Saksniit*, 332 N.Y.S.2d 343 (N.Y. Sup. Ct. 1972), and *People v. Magee*, 423 N.Y.S.2d 417 (N.Y. Sup. Ct. 1979).

Twenty-six states have passed legislation criminalizing vandalism against research facilities that use animals (G. Blumenstyk, "State Laws Against Vandalism of Animal-Research Facilities Provoke Debate," *Chron. Higher Educ.*, Apr. 8, 1992, A26). A Texas law (§ 4.30(a) and (b)(2) of the Education Code) makes it a misdemeanor to engage in disruptive activity on a university campus (see *Arnold v. State*, 853 S.W.2d 543 (Tex. Ct. App. 1993), for a determination of the statute's constitutionality). Other state statutes impose certain reporting requirements on student athletes and their agents (see, for example, Fla. Stat. Ann. § 240.5337; Mich. Comp. Laws Ann. § 750.411e; and 18 Pa. Cons. Stat. Ann. § 7107). Some of these statutes impose criminal penalties (see, for example, S.C. Code Ann. § 59.102.30).

Other state laws require institutions to disclose campus crime statistics (see, for example, 24 Pa. Cons. Stat. Ann. § 2502-2; see also Wis. Stat. § 36.11(22)). New York and California have passed "truth-in-testing" laws that require disclosure of the questions and answers for standardized tests used to make admission decisions (see Section 7.2.10). And several states have passed antihazing laws (see Section 4.12.2).

Given the plethora of state laws that apply to colleges, either generally or specifically, administrators and counsel must monitor legislative and judicial developments in their state as well as at the federal level.

6.5.1. Open meetings and public disclosure. Open-meetings laws provide a particularly good illustration of the controversy and litigation that can be occasioned when a general state law is applied to the particular circumstances of postsecondary education. In an era of skepticism about public officials and institutions, public postsecondary administrators must be especially sensitive to laws whose purpose is to promote openness and accountability in government. As state entities, public postsecondary institutions are often subject to open-meetings laws and similar legislation, and the growing body of legal actions under such laws indicates that the public intends to make sure that public institutions comply.

Litigation to enforce or to clarify the effect of open-meetings laws on public institutions has been initiated by the media, faculty members, students, education associations, and members of the general public.[10] In *Arkansas Gazette Co. v. Pickens*, 522 S.W.2d 350 (Ark. 1975), for instance, a newspaper and one of its reporters argued that committees of the University of Arkansas board of trustees, and not just the full board itself, were subject to the Arkansas Freedom of Information Act. The reporter

---

[10]Cases and authorities are collected in Annot., "Validity, Construction, and Application of Statutes Making Public Proceedings Open to the Public," 38 A.L.R.3d 1070 (1971 and periodic supp.).

had been excluded from a committee meeting on a proposed rule change that would have allowed students of legal age to possess and consume intoxicating beverages in university-controlled facilities at the Fayetteville campus. The Arkansas Freedom of Information Act provided in part:

> It is vital in a democratic society that public business be performed in an open and public manner so that the electors shall be advised of the performance of public officials and of the decisions that are reached in public activity and in making public policy. Toward this end this Act is adopted, making it possible for them or their representatives to learn and to report fully the activities of the public officials [Ark. Code Ann. § 12-2802, now Ark. Code Ann. § 25-19-102].

The board of trustees contended, and the lower court agreed, that meetings of the board's committees were not "public meetings" within the meaning of the Act. The Arkansas Supreme Court reversed, reasoning that the "intent of the legislature, as so emphatically set forth in its statement of policy, [was] that public business be performed in an open and public manner" (522 S.W.2d at 353). The court could find no distinction between the board's business and that of its committees and thus applied the open-meetings requirement to both.

Wood v. Marston, 442 So. 2d 934 (Fla. 1983), concerned the application of Florida's open-meetings law to a University of Florida search-and-screen committee formed to recommend candidates for dean of the law school. The Florida statute stated that (with certain specified exceptions) "all meetings of any board or commission of any state agency . . . at which official acts are to be taken are declared to be public meetings open to the public at all times" (Fla. Stat. Ann. § 286.011). The plaintiffs, members of the local news media, sought to enjoin the search-and-screen committee from meeting in private session. Under existing Florida case law, committees that performed only advisory or "fact-gathering" functions, as distinguished from "decision-making" functions, did not perform "official acts" within the statute's meaning and thus were not covered by the statute. The defendants argued that, because the search-and-screen committee's decisions were subject to further review, the committee should be considered an advisory body exempted from the statute. The court rejected this claim:

> The search-and-screen committee had an admitted "fact-gathering" role in the solicitation and compilation of applications. It had an equally undisputed decision-making function in screening the applicants. In deciding which of the applicants to reject from further consideration, the committee performed a policy-based, decision-making function delegated to it by the president of the university through the faculty as a whole. Nor does the fact that the results were submitted to the faculty as a whole, which had the authority to review the work of the screening committee, render the committee's function any less policy based or decision making [442 So. 2d at 938–39].

Similarly, in *University of Alaska v. Geistauts,* 666 P.2d 424 (Alaska 1983), the Alaska Supreme Court applied the state's open-meetings law to the meetings of a university tenure committee. The statute provided in part that "all meetings of . . . subordinate units . . . of the state or of any of its political subdivisions are open to the public" (Alaska Stat. § 44.62.310(a)). The plaintiff, a disappointed tenure applicant, argued that the statute applied to the committee's deliberations on his tenure application. The university argued that the committee's deliberations fit into a statutory exception permitting closed sessions when the "subjects [to be discussed] tend to prejudice the reputation or character of any person," unless the affected individual requested that the session be open (Alaska Stat. § 44.62.310(c)(2)). The court held that the statutory exception applied. It then further held, however, that the tenure committee had failed to notify the plaintiff of the committee's meetings and that this failure deprived him of his statutory right to request that the meetings be open. The court therefore concluded that the committee's decision denying tenure was void and ordered that the plaintiff be reinstated for an additional year with the option to reapply for tenure and be considered by the then-current tenure committee. Left undiscussed by the Alaska court is the impact of the statute and decision on third parties whose opinions of the applicant may be sought, perhaps with a tacit or express understanding of confidentiality, in the course of the tenure review.

Not all cases, however, have been resolved in favor of openness. In *Donahue v. State*, 474 N.W.2d 537 (Iowa 1991), an associate professor denied promotion asserted that the meeting of the faculty appeals panel should have been open under Iowa's open-meetings law. The court ruled that the panel was an advisory board without policy-making power, and thus did not fit the statutory definition of "government body" contemplated by the statute. And in *Associated Students of the University of Colorado v. Regents of the University of Colorado*, 543 P.2d 59 (Colo. 1975), the plaintiffs sought to enjoin the regents from holding executive sessions barred to the public. After the trial court applied the state's open-meetings law to the board of regents and enjoined it from holding executive sessions except when matters covered by the attorney-client privilege would be discussed, the Colorado Supreme Court reversed. It held that the board was not subject to the open-meetings law because it was a constitutional body corporate (see Section 6.2.2) with broad powers under the state constitution and statutes to supervise its own affairs.[11] And in *The Missoulian v. Board of Regents of Higher Education*, 675 P.2d 962 (Mont. 1984), the court rejected a Montana newspaper's claim that the state's open-meetings law applied to the board of regents' periodic review of Montana state college presidents. Adopting a balancing test that weighed the individual's right to privacy against the public's right to know, the court held that the right to privacy prevailed under the particular facts of the case.

The legislative intent and clear meaning of the statutory language of open-meetings laws has great significance for the outcome of challenges under these laws. For example, the question of whether meetings of a university's animal use committees (see Section 7.2.9) are "public meetings" has been answered differently in several states. In *Animal Legal Defense Fund v. Institutional Animal Care and Use Committee of the University of Vermont*, 616 A.2d 224 (Vt. 1992), the Vermont Supreme Court determined that the animal use committee was a university committee and thus fell under the state law's ambit. But in *In re American Society for the Prevention of Cruelty to Animals, et al. v. Board of Trustees of the State University of New York*,

---

[11]The Colorado Supreme Court later criticized the outcome in *Associated Students* and declined to follow it in *Colorado Civil Rights Commission v. Regents of the University of Colorado* (discussed in Section 6.2.2). The Court noted that the Colorado legislature had amended the open-meetings law subsequent to the issuing of *Associated Students*, repudiating its holding.

568 N.Y.S.2d 631 (N.Y. App. Div. 1991), a New York appellate court ruled that the animal use committee was not a "public body" for purposes of the state law because the committee performed a federal function under federal law. The result was affirmed by the state's highest court (582 N.Y.S.2d 983 (N.Y. 1992)).

Georgia's highest court ruled that the proceedings of the student disciplinary board of the University of Georgia were subject to the state's open-meetings and open-records laws. In *Red and Black Publishing Co. v. Board of Regents*, 427 S.E.2d 257 (Ga. 1993), the university's student newspaper had sought access to the Student Organization Court's records and proceedings involving discipline for hazing charges against two fraternities. Although the law provided that meetings of the "governing body" of any state agency must be open to the public, the law also covered the meetings of committees created by the governing body at which official action is taken. The court found that the judicial board was a vehicle through which the university took official action in that it enforced the university's code of student conduct. Thus, the court ruled that the university must permit members of the public, including the media, to attend the disciplinary board's hearings.

State open-meetings laws have changed the way that boards and committees at some public institutions conduct their business. For a review of the interplay between these laws and the attorney-client privilege, see R. K. Daane, "Open Meetings Acts and the Attorney's 'Privilege' to Meet Privately with the School Board," 20 *Coll. Law Dig.* 193 (Mar. 1, 1990).

6.5.2. Open-records laws. As cousins of open-meetings laws, state public document acts and freedom-of-information laws also have had an important impact on postsecondary education.[12] In *Redding v. Brady*, 606 P.2d 1193 (Utah 1980), the editor of the student newspaper at Weber State College sued under the Utah Information Practices Act and the state's Public and Private Writings Act to compel the release of salary figures for all Weber State employees. When the court decided in Redding's favor,[13] the legislature responded by enacting the Publication of Higher Education Salary Data Act, which authorized limited disclosure of salaries of groups of employees but generally forbade the disclosure of "personally identifiable salary data." Redding then sued a second time, arguing that both the Utah state constitution and the federal Constitution's First Amendment created a public right of access to documents such as those he sought and that accordingly the legislation was unconstitutional.

In the second suit, *Redding v. Jacobsen*, 638 P.2d 503 (Utah 1981), the Utah Supreme Court agreed that there was an emerging right of access to government documents under recent First Amendment decisions of the U.S. Supreme Court. This

---

[12]Cases and authorities are collected in Annot., "What Constitutes Personal Matters Exempt from Disclosure by Invasion of Privacy Exemption Under State Freedom of Information Acts," 26 A.L.R.4th 666 (1983 and periodic supp.). For a related issue, see Annot., "What Constitutes Legitimate Research Justifying Inspection of State or Local Public Records Not Open to Inspection by General Public," 40 A.L.R.4th 333 (1985 and periodic supp.).

[13]For other examples of cases in which plaintiffs have succeeded in obtaining information, see *Carter v. Alaska Public Employees Assn.*, 663 P.2d 916 (Alaska 1983) (use of Public Records Disclosure Act to obtain a list of university employees and their job titles and locations); *Arkansas Gazette Co. v. Southern State College*, 620 S.W.2d 258 (Ark. 1981) (use of state Freedom of Information Act to obtain disclosure of the amounts of money that member schools of an athletic conference dispensed to student athletes).

emerging right, however, had to be balanced against employees' rights of privacy, which the state legislation sought to protect. Determining that the right to gather news should not prevail, in this particular instance, over a right to privacy which the legislature had deemed paramount, the court upheld the legislation's constitutionality.

Privacy may, however, take a back seat under some state open-records laws. In *Denver Publishing Co. v. University of Colorado*, 812 P.2d 682 (Colo. Ct. App. 1991), the court held that the state's open-records law required the university to disclose the settlement it had reached with a former chancellor. Although the court said that documents implicating the privacy of individuals would be protected from disclosure, the court did not view either the settlement agreement with the former chancellor, who had disputed his termination, or a letter agreement between another chancellor and the university as implicating protected privacy rights.

In *Red and Black Publishing Co. v. Board of Regents* (discussed in Section 6.5.1), the Georgia Supreme Court also ruled that the state's open-records law applied to the records of the student disciplinary board. Although the university argued that releasing the records would violate the Family Educational Rights and Privacy Act (FERPA), the state's high court disagreed. (The FERPA regulations have since been changed to permit the disclosure of disciplinary records to certain parties; see Section 4.16.1, this volume.) In contrast to the breadth of the Georgia court's interpretation of its open-records law, Connecticut's Supreme Court, in *University of Connecticut v. Freedom of Information Commission*, 585 A.2d 690 (Conn. 1991), ruled that Connecticut's open-records law did not require disclosure of names of students who worked for the university's police force.

Several courts have been asked to determine whether nonprofit foundations incorporated separately from a public college or university, but formed to raise funds for the institution, are subject to state open-records laws. In *State ex rel. Toledo Blade Co. v. University of Toledo Foundation*, 602 N.E.2d 1159 (Ohio 1992), Ohio's Supreme Court determined that the state's public records disclosure statute encompassed the foundation as a "public office." The newspaper had sought the names of donors to the foundation, and the court ruled that these names must be disclosed. Similarly, the Supreme Court of South Carolina held that the state's Freedom of Information Act compelled the Carolina Research and Development Foundation, which acquires and develops real estate for the University of South Carolina, to disclose its records. The court, in *Weston v. Carolina Research and Development Foundation*, 401 S.E.2d 161 (S.C. 1991), ruled that because the foundation received part of its funding from public monies, it met the definition of "public body" in the state FOIA.

An Illinois appellate court came to the opposite conclusion in a case involving a joint venture between Northwestern University (a private institution) and a development corporation owned by a public entity (the city of Evanston, Illinois). In *Hope v. Topcorp, Inc.*, 527 N.E.2d 1 (Ill. App. Ct. 1988), a taxpayers' group sought a preliminary injunction to force the development corporation and Northwestern to comply with the state's open-meetings law and its Freedom of Information Act. Although the corporation used public funds, the court ruled that the corporation was private because it was profit-making and because it was not performing a "governmental" function, and was thus exempt from the disclosure laws. And in *State ex rel. Guste v. Nicholls College Foundation*, 592 So. 2d 419 (La. Ct. App. 1991) (further discussed in Section 2.2.5), the court found that the foundation, a private nonprofit corporation linked to a state college, was not a public body, although it said that the state had the authority to inspect records of *public* funds received by the foundation.

Inquiries related to college athletics have spawned litigation over the application of state open-records laws. For example, in *University of Kentucky v. Courier-Journal*, 830 S.W.2d 373 (Ky. 1992), the University of Kentucky was required to disclose its response to an NCAA investigation of alleged rules violations. Although the university argued that appendices to the report, including documents and transcripts of interviews, came within the law's exception for "preliminary materials," the court disagreed, ruling that the entire report was a public document. In *Cremins v. Atlanta Journal*, 405 S.E.2d 675 (Ga. 1991), the *Atlanta Journal* succeeded in gaining information about outside income of some university coaches. And in *Milwaukee Journal v. Board of Regents of the University of Wisconsin System*, 472 N.W.2d 607 (Wis. Ct. App. 1991), the court ruled that the University of Wisconsin must disclose the names of applicants for the positions of football coach and athletic director.

In some states curriculum materials at a public institution may be considered a "public record" subject to inspection by the public. In *Russo v. Nassau County Community College*, 603 N.Y.S.2d 294 (N.Y. 1993), an individual filed a request under the state's Freedom of Information Act for class materials used in a college sex education course. Although a state appellate court denied the request, stating that the materials were not "records" under the law's definition, the state's high court reversed and granted access to the materials.

As these cases demonstrate, the general problem created by open-records statutes and similar laws is how to balance the public's right to know with an individual's right to privacy or an institution's need for confidentiality. Administrators must consider the complex interplay of all these interests. Sometimes the legislation provides guidelines or rules for striking this balance. Even in the absence of such provisions, some courts have narrowly construed open-records laws to avoid intrusion on compelling interests of privacy or confidentiality. The trend, however, appears to be in the direction of openness and public access, even when the institution considers the information sensitive or private.

6.5.3. State administrative procedure laws. State administrative law is another area of state law that has had an impact on the campus. Like the federal government, many states have statutes requiring that state agencies follow prescribed procedures when formulating binding rules. State boards and institutions of higher education may be considered state agencies subject to these rule-making statutes. In *Florida State University v. Dann*, 400 So. 2d 1304 (Fla. Dist. Ct. App. 1980), for instance, several faculty members challenged university procedures used to determine merit raises and other salary increases. The faculty members argued that the university had not conformed to the state rule-making statute when it created the salary increase procedures. The court agreed and invalidated the procedures.

Similarly, in *Board of Trustees v. Department of Administrative Services*, 429 N.E.2d 428 (Ohio 1981), laid-off employees of Ohio State University argued that they were entitled to reinstatement and other relief because their layoffs were executed under improperly issued rules. The court agreed. It considered the university's rules to be state agency rules subject to the state's Administrative Procedure Act. This Act required public notice of rule making, filing of rules with the executive and legislative branches of government, a public hearing on proposed rules, and notification of persons who would be especially affected by the rules. The university had failed to follow these procedures. Moreover, it had erroneously issued the rules under the aegis of its board of trustees. The applicable statutory provision grants such rule-making authority to the personnel departments of state universities, not the boards of trustees.

And in *McGrath v. University of Alaska,* 813 P.2d 1370 (Alaska 1991), the Alaska Supreme Court reviewed the claim of state university faculty that the state's Administrative Procedure Act applied to faculty grievance proceedings at the university. The university had promulgated its own policies regarding grievance proceedings; however, the court ruled that the APA superseded the university's policies.

The provisions of state administrative procedure acts, and their intended scope, vary considerably by state. For example, in *Jansen v. Atiyeh,* 743 P.2d 765 (Or. Ct. App. 1987), motel and hotel operators, taxi drivers, and caterers sought declaratory relief against the Oregon State Board of Higher Education, challenging its authority to provide housing and food to nonstudents attending a Shakespearean Festival at Southern Oregon State College. The court determined that the board's policy of permitting groups with an educational objective, even if they were not students, to use the college's facilities was within the board's authority over postsecondary education, and thus did not subject the board to the requirements of the state Administrative Procedure Act.

6.5.4. Unemployment compensation laws. Another active area of general law affecting the college campus is unemployment compensation. As developed in Section 7.3.3 of this volume, federal law requires most postsecondary institutions, public or private, to make contributions to a state unemployment insurance program. Participating institutions are treated the same as other employers in the state. In all instances an unemployment compensation scheme will cover only persons who have an "employment" relationship with the institution. *Vermont Institute of Community Development v. Department of Employment Security,* 436 A.2d 765 (Vt. 1981), for instance, concerned a loosely structured postsecondary institution that employed a small administrative staff, for whom it made unemployment contributions, and a faculty, primarily adjuncts, for whom it did not. Faculty members had written contracts with the school, under which they were paid according to the numbers of students enrolled in their classes. The institute approved the courses taught, but the faculty members selected the time and provided the place for the instruction.

The institute argued that this relationship with faculty members did not constitute "employment" under the Vermont unemployment compensation statute and that the institute therefore was not required to make unemployment contributions on behalf of its faculty members. The statute provided, however, that all services for wages are considered as employment except when:

(i) Such individual has been and will continue to be free from control or direction over the performance of such services, both under his contract of service and in fact; and

(ii) Such service is either outside the usual course of the business for which such service is performed, or . . . such service is performed outside of all the places of business of the enterprise for which such service is performed; and

(iii) Such individual is customarily engaged in an independently established trade, occupation, profession, or business [21 Vt. Stat. Ann. § 1301(6)(B)].

The court held that the institute's relationship with its employees did not fall within this exception. Such factors as the institute's setting a minimum number of hours of instruction and requiring end-of-course evaluations negated the institute's argument that it had satisfied condition (i). The institute also failed in its argument that it satisfied condition (iii) because its faculty members were all engaged primarily in nonteaching fields; the court held that "in order to satisfy the provision, the employees must be independently established, providing the same or similar services as they provide for the employer."

Courts even within the same state have disagreed about the eligibility of academic-year employees for unemployment compensation in the summer. In *Claims of Halperin,* 505 N.Y.S.2d 230 (N.Y. App. Div. 1986), the court ruled that, because the employment prospects of the academic-year employees for the forthcoming academic year were uncertain, they were entitled to unemployment benefits. But another New York court, addressing a similar issue, ruled that adjunct faculty who had taught on a regular basis had a reasonable expectation of continued employment for the next academic semester and thus were properly denied benefits during the summer (*Claim of Barton,* 510 N.Y.S.2d 38 (N.Y. App. Div. 1986)).

Individuals who leave work for personal reasons, or who refuse to perform certain required tasks, may be denied unemployment benefits in most states. The U.S. Supreme Court upheld a provision of Missouri's unemployment law that included a resignation because of pregnancy in a list of reasons for disqualifying voluntary separation from employment. In *Wimberly v. Labor and Industrial Commission of Missouri,* 479 U.S. 511 (1987), the Court rejected the plaintiff's argument that disqualification of persons who left because of pregnancy constituted sex discrimination. Although the state could not single out pregnancy for harsher treatment, the Court held, the state could characterize a resignation because of pregnancy as a "voluntary" separation. And in *Stepp v. Review Board of the Indiana Employment Security Division,* 521 N.E.2d 350 (Ind. Ct. App. 1988), the court ruled that a laboratory technician who refused to perform tests on AIDS-infected fluids could be denied unemployment benefits. The technician had refused to perform the tests on the grounds that AIDS was a "plague on men" and thus the tests were against God's will. Challenging her discharge for insubordination, the technician claimed that she had the right to refuse to perform unsafe work. The court disagreed, ruling that the laboratory's safety procedures were appropriate and did not justify her insubordination. She had not made a claim on the grounds of religious discrimination.

Many state laws exclude full-time college students from eligibility for unemployment compensation. In *Pima Community College v. Arizona Department of Economic Security,* 714 P.2d 472 (Ariz. Ct. App. 1986), the court was asked to determine whether a former student who had been employed by the college under the federal work-study program was a student or an employee for eligibility purposes. The court ruled that the individual was a student, and thus ineligible for unemployment compensation.

6.5.5. Workers' compensation laws. Workers' compensation law provides yet another illustration of general state law with substantial impact on the campus. Like unemployment compensation laws, workers' compensation laws cover postsecondary institutions much as they would any other employer. They provide compensation to the employee or the employee's family in cases where the employee has been injured or killed in the course of employment.

The concept of "employment" is again the key coverage issue (see A. Larson, *The Law of Workmen's Compensation*, vol. 1B, §§ 43–48 (Matthew Bender, 1993)). Several recent cases, for instance, have raised the question whether a varsity scholarship athlete has an employment relationship with his institution and is therefore covered by workers' compensation when he loses the scholarship because he is injured and unable to play.[14] In *Rensing v. Indiana State University Board of Trustees*, 444 N.E.2d 1170 (Ind. 1983), the Supreme Court of Indiana upheld the Industrial Board of Indiana's denial of workers' compensation to a scholarship athlete who was permanently disabled by an injury received in football practice. Indiana's intermediate appellate court had overruled the board's decision (437 N.E.2d 78 (Ind. Ct. App. 1982)). In reversing the appeals court and reinstating the board's decision, the state Supreme Court held that "there was no intent to enter into an employer-employee relationship" when the student and the university entered into the scholarship agreement. Since the plaintiff athlete was therefore not considered an "employee" under the Indiana Workmen's Compensation Act (Ind. Code § 22-3-6-1(b)), he was not eligible for benefits under the Act. In *Graczyk v. Workers' Compensation Appeals Board*, 229 Cal. Rptr. 494 (Cal. Ct. App. 1986), the court ruled that a student athlete who had received an athletic scholarship, and who was seriously injured during football practice, did not meet the statutory definition of "employee." In *Coleman v. Western Michigan University*, 336 N.W.2d 224 (Mich. Ct. App. 1983), the court ruled that although an athletic scholarship was "wages," the student was not an "employee" for purposes of the state's workers' compensation act. For critical commentary see A. Larson, *The Law of Workmen's Compensation*, vol. IA, § 22.21(c) (Matthew Bender, 1993); Note, "Workers' Compensation and College Athletes: Should Universities Be Responsible for Athletes Who Incur Serious Injuries?" 10 *J. Coll. & Univ. Law* 197 (1983–84), and Note, "Play for Pay: Should Scholarship Athletes Be Included Within State Workers' Compensation Systems?" 12 *Loyola of Los Angeles Entertainment Law J.* 441 (1992).

In another case illustrating the operation of workers' compensation statutes, *California State Polytechnic University–Pomona v. Workers' Compensation Appeals Board*, 179 Cal. Rptr. 605 (Cal. Ct. App. 1982), a claim had been filed on behalf of a former stenographer at the university who had been shot to death while working at her desk. A great deal of circumstantial evidence implicated a former boyfriend as the likely suspect. The boyfriend was never prosecuted for the shooting because of what the court termed "evidentiary problems." The deceased's family argued that she was killed in the course of employment. The university argued that she was killed out of "personal motives," a defense that would shield it from the workers' compensation claim. The court decided the case in favor of the university.

In another case the Vermont Supreme Court determined that student members of a volunteer fire department sponsored by Norwich University were not covered by

---

[14]Cases and authorities are collected in Annot., "Workers' Compensation: Student Athlete as 'Employee' of College or University Providing Scholarship or Similar Financial Assistance," 58 A.L.R.4th 1259 (1987 and periodic supp.).

the state's workers' compensation laws, leaving the university potentially exposed to negligence lawsuits as a result. In *Wolfe v. Yudichak*, 571 A.2d 592 (Vt. 1989), a student volunteer fire fighter injured when a fire truck skidded off the road sued the university for negligence. The court ruled that, under Vermont law, the fire brigade had the choice of whether or not it wished to participate in the workers' compensation system, and since the brigade had not done so, the university could not unilaterally decide that its members were covered by workers' compensation.

The compensability of stress-related injuries has received considerable judicial attention in recent years. For example, in *Decker v. Oklahoma State Technical University*, 766 P.2d 1371 (Okla. 1988), an instructor whose relationship with his supervisor was difficult and stressful successfully argued that his heart attack should be compensated as a work-related injury. For analysis of *Decker* and other workers' compensation issues related to college faculty, see K. N. Hasty, Note, "Workers' Compensation: Will College and University Professors Be Compensated for Mental Injuries Caused by Work-Related Stress?" 17 *J. Coll. & Univ. Law* 535 (1991).

On occasion, the "second job site" exception to the exclusion of injuries incurred on the way to or from one's place of work can result in workers' compensation benefits for faculty injured at home. This theory was not successful, however, in *Santa Rosa Junior College v. Workers' Compensation Appeals Board*, 708 P.2d 673 (Cal. 1985). The professor, who often graded papers and prepared for class at home because his office was noisy, was killed in an automobile accident on his way home from the college. The court denied benefits to his widow, ruling that the college did not require the professor to work at home and thus his home was not a second job site.

6.5.6. Laws regulating medical services and medical research. State laws regulating hospitals, clinics, and health care professionals are of particular concern to universities that have university-affiliated hospitals or health care clinical programs that utilize hospitals or clinics as training sites. The applicable restrictions may be in statutes, in administrative regulations, or in common law principles. All states have licensing laws for certain health care facilities and may also have certificate-of-need requirements for the construction of new health care facilities (see, for example, *Tulsa Area Hospital Council v. Oral Roberts University*, 626 P.2d 316 (Okla. 1981)). All states also have licensing laws for various health care practitioners, as well as unauthorized-practice laws. Informed-consent laws regarding medical treatment are another common example. More recent and controversial examples include laws regarding the disposal of medical and infectious waste (for example, Cal. Health & Safety Code § 7054.4); human medical experimentation (for example, Cal. Health & Safety Code, ch. 1.3); guardianship, living-will, and durable-power-of-attorney laws governing the acceptance or refusal of medical treatment by patients who are incompetent or otherwise incapable of expressing their wishes;[15] laws regarding a hospital's authority to decline to perform, or the extent to which it may regulate, certain procedures, such as abortion; laws regulating certain controversial research, such as genetic or fetal research; and laws regarding AIDS testing (for example, 35 Pa. Stat. Ann. § 7602 et seq., applied in *In re Milton S. Hershey Medical Center of the Pennsylvania State University*, 634 A.2d 159 (Pa. 1993)) and the obligation to treat AIDS patients

---

[15]*Federal* law (see 42 U.S.C. § 1396 (a)(w)(l) and 42 U.S.C. § 1395 cc(f)(1)) requires that Medicare and Medicaid providers inform patients of these state laws.

(for example, *State of Minnesota v. Clausen*, 491 N.W.2d 661 (Minn. Ct. App. 1992), applying the Minnesota Human Rights Act (Minn. Stat. Ann. § 363.01 et seq.)).

In *Cruzan v. Director, Missouri Department of Health*, 497 U.S. 261 (1990), for instance, Missouri law required that a comatose patient's desire to withdraw life-sustaining medical treatment be proved by clear and convincing evidence. Although the U.S. Supreme Court upheld the constitutionality of this requirement, it also recognized that the states' regulatory authority in this area is limited because, under the Fourteenth Amendment's Due Process Clause, persons have "a constitutionally protected liberty interest in refusing unwanted medical treatment." In *Webster v. Reproductive Health Services*, 492 U.S. 490 (1989), another Missouri law was at issue. The law prohibited state employees from performing abortions, banned the use of public hospitals and facilities for performing abortions, and required physicians to do viability testing before aborting after the twentieth week of pregnancy. The Court also upheld these restrictions. In *Planned Parenthood of Southeastern Pennsylvania v. Casey*, 112 S. Ct. 2791 (1992), the plaintiff challenged a Pennsylvania law that included informed-consent requirements for abortions, a husband notification requirement, and reporting requirements for facilities that perform abortions. The Court rejected arguments that these restrictions (except for the husband notification requirement) unduly burdened the right to choose abortion, and thus it upheld the constitutionality of all except the husband notification requirement. And in *St. Agnes Hospital v. Riddick*, 668 F. Supp. 478 (D. Md. 1987), the court interpreted and applied a Maryland law providing that a hospital may refuse to perform abortions or sterilization procedures (Md. Code Ann., Health—General § 20-214(b)).

Other recent cases illustrate problems with laws that restrict medical research. In *Lifchez v. Hartigan*, 735 F. Supp. 1361 (N.D. Ill. 1990), physicians challenged an Illinois statute providing that "No person shall sell or experiment upon a fetus produced by the fertilization of a human ovum by a human sperm unless such experimentation is therapeutic to the fetus thereby produced" (Ill. Rev. Stat. ch. 38, para. 81-26). The court held that the statute was unconstitutionally vague and that it invaded the woman's constitutional freedom to choose procedures such as embryo transfer. In *Moore v. Regents of the University of California*, 793 P.2d 479 (Cal. 1990), the plaintiff claimed that California property law accorded him ownership rights over the cells from his diseased spleen that researchers had used, and that he was therefore entitled to a share of the profits reaped from the research. Overruling an intermediate appellate court's decision, the California Supreme Court held that California law did not create such a property right for the plaintiff but did create fiduciary duties and informed-consent requirements that obligated the physician to inform the patient of any personal or economic interest that the physician might have in using the patient's tissue. And in *Brotherton v. Cleveland*, 923 F.2d 477 (6th Cir. 1991), the court held that a wife had a constitutionally protected property interest in her deceased husband's body, thus limiting the authority of state employees to use body parts for organ transplants or research without the wife's prior consent.

State tort law (see generally Section 2.3.1) is also very important in the health care context.[16] Malpractice law (regarding professional services of health care

---

[16]For a sampling of the many types of cases that may arise, see Annot., "Hospital's Liability for Injury Resulting from Failure to Have Sufficient Number of Nurses on Duty," 2 A.L.R.5th 286 (1992 and periodic supp.); Annot., "Application of Rule of Strict Liability in Tort to Person

workers), the law on releases and waivers (see Section 2.5.2.3), products liability (regarding drugs and medical equipment), and the tort of battery (covering physical, and sometimes emotional, harm from invasive medical procedures performed without informed consent) are all involved. In *Mink v. University of Chicago*, 460 F. Supp. 713 (N.D. Ill. 1978), for example, the court held that the women plaintiffs had a cause of action for battery against the university and the drug manufacturer for administering a drug as part of a medical experiment without their knowledge or consent; that the plaintiffs did not have a products liability claim against the manufacturer absent evidence of physical injury; and that the plaintiffs would have a claim for failure to notify of the drug's risks only if they had been physically injured. Liability issues may be especially complex in health care cases because of the numbers of parties potentially involved: the university; the medical center or hospital, which may be an entity separate from the university (see Section 2.2.5); physicians, who may or may not be employees or agents of the university; nurses, laboratory technicians, and other allied health personnel; and outside parties such as laboratories, drug and equipment manufacturers, and drug and equipment suppliers. See, for example, *Jaar v. University of Miami*, 474 So. 2d 239 (Fla. 1985).

Selected Annotated Bibliography

Sec. 6.1 (General Background)

Hustoles, Thomas. "Faculty and Staff Dismissals: Developing Contract and Tort Theories," 10 *J. Coll. & Univ. Law* 479 (1983–84). Reviews the employment-at-will doctrine and its decline, with special reference to higher education. Examines the contract and tort theories, recently devised by the courts, that have made it more difficult for institutions to dismiss employees serving under indefinite or "terminable-at-will" contracts. Article has greater application to administrative and staff positions than to regular faculty positions, which often are for a stated contract term or have the protection of tenure.

Schwartz, Bernard. *Administrative Law* (3d ed., Little, Brown, 1991). A comprehensive overview of the principles of administrative law. Although the book does not focus on education, its analyses can be applied to state postsecondary systems (to the extent that they are considered state agencies), to state agencies that charter or license private institutions, and to other state agencies whose regulatory authority extends to postsecondary institutions.

Sec. 6.2 (State Provision of Public Postsecondary Education)

Beckham, Joseph. "Reasonable Independence for Public Higher Education: Legal Implications of Constitutionally Autonomous Status," 7 *J. Law & Educ.* 177

---

or Entity Rendering Medical Services," 100 A.L.R.3d 1205 (1980 and periodic supp.); Annot., "Liability of Hospital or Medical Practitioner Under Doctrine of Strict Liability in Tort, or Breach of Warranty, for Harm Caused by Drug, Medical Instrument, or Similar Device Used in Treating Patient," 54 A.L.R.3d 258 (1973 and periodic supp.); Annot., "Validity and Construction of Contract Exempting Hospital or Doctor from Liability for Negligence to Patient," 6 A.L.R.3d 704 (1966 and periodic supp.).

(1978). Author argues for a constitutional grant of "limited autonomy" to "the state's higher education system" in order to "insure reasonable autonomy on selected issues of college and university governance."Article also discusses related issues, such as the constitutionality of legislative attempts to transfer power from an autonomous system, the effect "legislation relating to statewide concerns" has on an autonomous system, and the distinction between "appropriations and expenditures."

Crockett, Richard B. "Constitutional Autonomy and the North Dakota State Board of Higher Education," 54 *N.D. L. Rev.* 529 (1978). A study of the autonomy granted to North Dakota's public institutions of higher education by amendment to the state constitution. Examines judicial decisions both in North Dakota and in neighboring jurisdictions. Author concludes that "a grant of autonomy is significant and the constitutional authority of a governing board to control, manage, administer, or supervise the institutions under its jurisdiction may not be invoked or interfered with by a state legislature."

Feller, Irwin. *Universities and State Governments. A Study in Policy Analysis* (Praeger, 1986). Describes the role of universities in the shaping of public policy at the state level during the 1970s. The author—at various times a faculty member, member of a governor's staff, and researcher—discusses the ways in which policy research is used by lawmakers at the state level and the overall relationship of universities to state government.

Hines, Edward R. *Higher Education and State Governments: Renewed Partnership, Cooperation, or Competition?* ASHE-ERIC Higher Education Report no. 5 (Association for the Study of Higher Education, 1988). Examines state leadership in higher education (governing boards, coordinating boards, legislators, and lobbyists), state financial support for higher education in transition (including tuition pricing and student financial aid), current state/campus policy issues (such as academic program review and outcomes assessment), and the policy implications of state regulatory actions.

Horowitz, Harold W. "The Autonomy of the University of California Under the State Constitution," 25 *UCLA L. Rev.* 23 (1977). Discusses the state constitutional provisions that grant the University of California "constitutional" rather than "statutory" legal status. Analyzes judicial decisions interpreting the relative position of the board of regents under the state constitution vis-à-vis other branches of state government, and proposes a theory that would limit legislative interference with the governance of the university.

McGuinness, Aimes, & Paulson, Christine. *State Postsecondary Education Structures Handbook* (Education Commission of the States, 1991). Describes the structure, governance, and coordination of higher education in every state. Also includes recent trends and summaries of state boards and agencies.

Millard, Richard M. *State Boards of Higher Education*, ASHE-ERIC Higher Education Research Report no. 4 (American Association for Higher Education, 1976). Examines the history, structure, functions, and future directions of state governing and coordinating boards for higher education. Includes state-by-state tables and a bibliography.

Schaefer, Hugh. "The Legal Status of the Montana University System Under the New Montana Constitution," 35 *Mont. L. Rev.* 189 (1974). Compares and analyzes the new and old Montana constitutional provisions and discusses comparable provisions in other state constitutions. Considers the impact of such provisions on the state institution's relationships with other branches of state government.

Shekleton, James F. "The Road Not Taken: The Curious Jurisprudence Touching upon the Constitutional Status of the South Dakota Board of Regents," 39 *S.D. L. Rev.* 312 (1994). Reviews the constitutional powers given the state's governing board and analyzes the division of authority between that board and the state legislature to create, abolish, govern, and control the state's public colleges and universities.

Sec. 6.3 (State Chartering and Licensure of Private Postsecondary Institutions)

Dutile, Fernand, & Gaffney, Edward. *State and Campus: State Regulation of Religiously Affiliated Higher Education* (University of Notre Dame Press, 1984). Explores the relationship between state governments and church-related colleges and universities. Reviews the various types of state regulations and their validity under federal and state constitutions.

Hopkins, Bruce. *The Nonprofit Counsel* (Wiley). A monthly newsletter covering a range of legal matters pertinent to nonprofit corporations. Presents information and analysis on new legislation, administrative regulations, and current developments at both state and federal levels. Legal topics include taxation, tax exemption, regulation of fund-raising, charitable giving, and rules regarding private foundations.

Jung, Steven, et al. *The Final Technical Report: A Study of State Oversight in Postsecondary Education* (American Institutes for Research, 1977). An extensive report done by AIR under contract with the U.S. Office of Education. Compiles and assesses statutes and administrative regulations under which state agencies regulate postsecondary institutions. Includes studies of consumer protection incidents reported by state officials. Office (now Dept.) of Education reference: HEW, USOE, Contract No. 300-76-0377. AIR reference: AIR-59400-1277-FR.

Millard, Richard M. "Postsecondary Education and 'The Best Interests of the People of the States,'" 50 *J. Higher Educ.* 121 (1979). Discusses the status of licensing in the fifty states and other developments with respect to licensing.

Oleck, Howard. *Nonprofit Corporations, Organizations, and Associations* (6th ed., Prentice-Hall, 1994). A comprehensive survey of all types of nonprofit and tax-exempt institutions, foundations, and corporations. Has numerous chapters covering hundreds of subjects. Issues addressed include formation and dissolution of nonprofit entities, organization, tax exemptions, and lobbying. Also includes model forms.

O'Neill, Joseph P., & Barnett, Samuel. *Colleges and Corporate Change: Merger, Bankruptcy and Closure* (Conference of Small Colleges, 1981). A handbook primarily for trustees and administrators but also useful to attorneys. Chapters include "Indicators of Institutional Health," "Options for Collegiate Corporate Change," "Merger," and "Dissolution of the College Corporation." Discusses procedures for amending the college charter, disposition of assets, placement of faculty, and reorganization under federal bankruptcy law. Also includes state-by-state summary of laws and regulations governing collegiate corporate changes and state-by-state summary of regulations regarding institutional responsibility for student records.

Postsecondary Education Convening Authority. *Approaches to State Licensing of Private Degree-Granting Institutions,* Institute for Educational Leadership Report no. 8 (George Washington University, 1975). A report on the first conference of state officials who license private degree-granting institutions. Explores the concepts of chartering and licensing, the status of licensing in the fifty states, and the policy and legal problems facing licensing officials. Makes recommendations for the future.

Stewart, David, & Spille, Henry. *Diploma Mills: Degrees of Fraud* (American Council on Education/Macmillan, 1989). Addresses the problem of the sale of phony diplomas. Analyzes the businesses that engage in such activities, the lax state laws under which these businesses are licensed and allowed to sell the degrees, and the role of the federal government in alleviating the problem. Includes an appendix listing relevant state laws. Authors call for strengthening of the current laws that allow fraudulent degree-granting businesses to operate, and propose other steps to alleviate the problem.

Sec. 6.4 (State Regulation of Out-of-State Institutions)

Hughes, Earl, et al. *Nova University's Three National Doctoral Degree Programs* (Nova University, 1977). A Ford Foundation–funded case study on the development of multistate education programs. Chapter Nine (by Fred Nelson and William Kaplin) provides a discussion of "Legal and Political Constraints on Nova University's External Degree Programs."

Sec. 6.5 (Other State Regulatory Laws Affecting Postsecondary Education Programs)

Bakaly, Charles, & Grossman, Joel. *Modern Law of Employment Contracts: Formation, Operation and Remedies for Breach* (Harcourt Brace Jovanovich, 1983 and periodic supp.). A practical handbook on the legal relationship between employer and nonunionized employee. Topics include application of state contract law principles to employment contracts, issues regarding employee handbooks and employment manuals, wrongful discharge and the employment-at-will doctrine, and internal dispute-resolution mechanisms for employment disputes. Also includes appendices with state-by-state review of wrongful-discharge law, sample provisions for employee handbooks, and sample employment contract provisions.

Brown, Kimberly, Fishman, Phillip, & Jones, Nancy. *Legal and Policy Issues in the Language Proficiency Assessment of International Teaching Assistants* (Institute for Higher Education Law and Governance, University of Houston, 1990). Reviews the laws of eleven states that require English proficiency and discusses various legal theories that could be used to attack the application of these laws. An appendix includes the text of the laws.

Cleveland, Harlan. *The Costs and Benefits of Openness: Sunshine Laws and Higher Education* (Association of Governing Boards of Universities and Colleges, 1985). A research report that reviews state open-meeting laws and the court decisions and state attorney general opinions construing these laws. Compares the various state laws, using a list of twenty-three characteristics relating to openness. Author analyzes the costs and benefits of openness under these laws, concluding that the costs generally outweigh the benefits. Report includes an appendix of attorney general opinions and a bibliography. Reprinted in 12 *J. Coll & Univ. Law* 127 (1985).

Folsom, Ralph Haughwout. *State Antitrust Law and Practice* (Prentice-Hall Law and Business, 1988). A state-by-state analysis of antitrust laws and their enforcement. Updated annually.

Greer, Darryl G. *"Truth-in-Testing Legislation": An Analysis of Political and Legal Consequences, and Prospects* (Institute for Higher Education Law and Governance, University of Houston, 1983). Reviews the history and origins of testing legislation and discusses in depth two laws—those of California and New York—that mandate disclosure of standardized test questions and answers. An evaluation of the educational, legal, and political consequences of the laws is provided.

Hopkins, Bruce. *Charity Under Siege: Government Regulation of Fund Raising* (Wiley, 1980). Describes and analyzes the governmental scheme for regulating fundraising by nonprofit organizations. Presents state-by-state summary of laws on charitable solicitations; analyzes constitutional questions raised by government regulation of fund-raising; explores federal IRS oversight of tax-exempt organizations and the activities of private agencies as part of the overall regulatory scheme; and offers advice on how to comply with existing rules.

Madsen, Helen H. "New State Legislation on Informing Workers About Hazardous Substances in the Workplace: Will It Impact on University Teaching and Research?" 9 *J. Coll. & Univ. Law* 325 (1982–83). Reviews the legal situation in states that have enacted "laws giving employees the right to obtain basic information about hazardous substances with which they work." Provides an overview of some major issues involved in this area of regulation, contrasting different states' responses (or lack of response) to these issues. Also discusses factors that could improve state regulation of hazardous substances in the higher education context.

National Foundation for Unemployment Compensation and Workers' Compensation. *Highlights of State Unemployment Compensation Laws* (National Foundation, published annually). Provides an overview of coverage and state-by-state benefit payments, disqualifications, and appeal mechanisms. Much of the information is presented in tables; an appendix lists state administrators for both programs, changes in federal unemployment compensation laws, funding information, and a glossary of terms.

Rich, Ben A. "Malpractice Issues in the Academic Medical Center," 13 *J. Coll. & Univ. Law* 149 (1986). Considers the "standards of care applicable to health care practitioners," and the "special problems of patient care delivery" in academic medical centers, as well as the "special status of public academic medical centers and their employees." Gives special attention to problems of informed consent and to legal relations between universities and affiliated medical institutions.

See Bell & Majestic entry in bibliography for Section 7.2.

See Dutile & Gaffney entry for Section 6.3.

VII

The College and
the Federal Government

♦ ♦ ♦

Sec. 7.1. Federal Constitutional Powers over Education

The federal government is a government of limited powers; it has only those powers
that are expressly conferred by the U.S. Constitution or can reasonably be implied
from those conferred. The remaining powers are, under the Tenth Amendment, "reserved to the states respectively, or to the People." Although the Constitution does
not mention education, let alone delegate power over it to the federal government,
it does not follow that the Tenth Amendment reserves all authority over education
to the states or the people; see *Case v. Bowles*, 327 U.S. 92 (1946). Many federal
constitutional powers—particularly the spending power, the taxing power, the commerce power, and the civil rights enforcement powers—are broad enough to extend
to many matters concerning education. Whenever an activity falls within the scope
of one of these federal powers (for example, see Sections 7.2 to 7.5 below), the federal
government has authority over it.

   When Congress passes a law pursuant to its federal constitutional powers, that
law will "preempt" or supersede any state and local laws that impinge on the effectuation of Congress's powers (see generally *Hillsborough County v. Automated Medical Laboratories*, 471 U.S. 707, 712-713 (1985)). The application of this federal
"preemption doctrine" to postsecondary education is illustrated by *United States v.
City of Philadelphia*, 798 F.2d 81 (3d Cir. 1986) (discussed briefly in this volume,
Section 5.1), where the court held that military recruiting laws and policies, passed
pursuant to Congress's constitutional powers to raise and support armies, preempted
a local civil rights ordinance prohibiting discrimination against homosexuals. Moreover, when it passes federal laws pursuant to its constitutional powers, Congress

generally may abrogate the states' Eleventh Amendment immunity from suit and
enforce the law directly against the states; see *Pennsylvania v. Union Gas*, 491 U.S.
1 (1989).

7.1.1. Spending power. The current federal involvement in education stems primarily
from Congress's power (under Article I, Section 8, Clause 1) to spend its funds for
the "general welfare of the United States." (See generally A. Rosenthal, "Conditional
Federal Spending and the Constitution," 39 *Stanford L. Rev.* 1103 (1987).) The spending power is the basis of the federal aid-to-education programs discussed in Section
7.4 and the civil rights requirements discussed in Section 7.5. It is also the basis of
the student records (Buckley Amendment) requirements analyzed in Section 4.16.1.
The placement of conditions on grants for postsecondary education has been an
accepted practice at least since the Morrill Acts (see Section 7.4 (intro.), this volume,
and *Wyoming ex rel. Wyoming Agricultural College v. Irvin*, 206 U.S. 278 (1907)).
The constitutional validity of such conditions has also been clear at least since the
late 1930s, when the U.S. Supreme Court broadly construed the spending power in
the course of upholding innovative New Deal spending programs (see *Steward Machine Co. v. Davis*, 301 U.S. 548 (1937)). Thereafter, the courts have been willing to
uphold virtually any spending program that Congress believes will further the
general welfare (see, for example, *Helvering v. Davis*, 301 U.S. 619 (1937)) and any
condition on spending, whether imposed on governmental or private entities, that is
"germane" to or related to the activities and objectives for which the federal government is expending the funds (*South Dakota v. Dole*, 483 U.S. 203, 208 n.3 (majority
opinion) and 213–16 (dissenting opinion)). The spending power, however, does not
give the federal government a roving commission to regulate postsecondary education. What leverage the federal government exerts through the spending power arises
from its establishment of the purposes and conditions for its expenditure of funds.
Though fund recipients are subject to federal requirements, they can avoid the requirements by not accepting the funds.

In a 1981 case, *Pennhurst State School and Hospital v. Halderman*, 451 U.S.
1 (1981), the Court made its most important pronouncement on the spending power
since the New Deal cases of the 1930s. The plaintiff, a mentally retarded resident of
a special school and hospital operated by the state of Pennsylvania, claimed that she
had a right to "appropriate treatment"—a right derived in part from conditions that
the federal government had attached to certain grants received by the school. The
Court rejected the plaintiff's claim, asserting that Congress had not conditioned the
grants on the state's willingness to guarantee appropriate treatment and that the
language about treatment in the grant statute "represent[s] general statements of
federal policy, not newly created legal duties." In reaching its decision, the Court
adopted an interpretation of the spending power that emphasizes Congress's responsibility to speak clearly if it seeks to create "entitlements" or "rights" that state entities
(and perhaps private-sector grantees as well) must recognize as a condition to receiving federal money:

> [O]ur cases have long recognized that Congress may fix the terms on
> which it shall disburse federal money to the states. . . . However, legislation
> enacted pursuant to the spending power is much in the nature of a contract: in
> return for federal funds, the states agree to comply with federally imposed con-

ditions. The legitimacy of Congress's power to legislate under the spending power thus rests on whether the state voluntarily and knowingly accepts the terms of the "contract" (see *Steward Machine Co. v. Davis*, 301 U.S. 548, 585–98 . . . (1937)). There can, of course, be no knowing acceptance if a state is unaware of the conditions or is unable to ascertain what is expected of it. Accordingly, if Congress intends to impose a condition on the grant of federal moneys, it must do so unambiguously. . . . By insisting that Congress speak with a clear voice, we enable the states to exercise their choice knowingly, cognizant of the consequences of their participation [451 U.S. at 17].

Although this interpretation clearly benefits states in their dealings with the federal government, it does not create new substantive limits on the number or type of conditions that Congress may impose under the spending power. Instead, *Pennhurst* limits the circumstances in which courts may recognize, and federal agencies may enforce, grant conditions upon grantees. If Congress and the federal agencies fit within these circumstances by defining their conditions clearly before they award grants, they may impose such conditions to the same extent after *Pennhurst* as they could before.

7.1.2. Taxing power. The federal taxing power also comes from Article I, Section 8, Clause 1, which authorizes Congress "to lay and collect taxes" in order to raise the money it spends for the general welfare. The tax power is the basis for the laws discussed in Section 7.3. Though the purpose of the tax power is to raise revenue rather than to regulate as such, the power has been broadly construed to permit tax measures with substantial regulatory effects. The application of the tax power to postsecondary education was upheld in *Allen v. Regents of the University System of Georgia*, 304 U.S. 439 (1938), which concerned an admissions tax that the federal government had levied on state college football games. The tax power may be somewhat greater over private than over public institutions, since public institutions may enjoy a constitutional immunity from federal taxation of their sovereign functions (see Section 7.3.1), and the federal tax laws often treat public and private institutions differently.

7.1.3. Commerce power. The federal commerce power stems from Article I, Section 8, Clause 3 of the Constitution, which authorizes Congress "to regulate commerce with foreign nations, and among the several states." This is the primary regulatory power that has been applied to postsecondary education and is the basis for most of the laws discussed in Section 7.2. The commerce power has been broadly construed to permit the regulation of activities that are in or that "affect" interstate or foreign commerce. As the U.S. Supreme Court has often acknowledged, "Congress's power under the commerce clause is very broad. Even activity that is purely intrastate in character may be regulated by Congress, where the activity, combined with like conduct by others similarly situated, affects commerce among the states or with foreign nations" (*Fry v. United States*, 421 U.S. 542, 547 (1975)).

In a series of opinions in the late 1970s and early 1980s, the U.S. Supreme Court did attempt to limit Congress's use of the commerce power as a basis for regulating state and local governments. The key case was *National League of Cities v. Usery*, 426 U.S. 833 (1976). By a 5-to-4 vote, the Court relied on the Tenth Amend-

ment to invalidate federal wage-and-hour laws as applied to state and local government employees, reasoning that "their application will significantly alter or displace
the states' abilities to structure employer-employee relationships . . . in areas of traditional governmental functions." The Court premised this decision on a general
principle that "Congress may not exercise . . . [the commerce] power so as to force
directly upon the states its choices as to how essential decisions regarding the conduct
of integral governmental functions are to be made." In subsequent years, however,
lower courts and the Supreme Court itself struggled to understand and apply *National League*'s enigmatic distinctions between "traditional" and "nontraditional,"
and "integral" and "nonintegral," government functions. Finally, in *Garcia v. San
Antonio Metropolitan Transit Authority*, 469 U.S. 528 (1985), by a 5-to-4 vote, the
Court overruled *National League*:

> We therefore now reject, as unsound in principle and unworkable in
> practice, a rule of state immunity from federal regulation that turns on a judicial
> appraisal of whether a particular governmental function is "integral" or
> "traditional." . . .
>
> [T]he principal and basic limit on the federal commerce power is that in-
> herent in all congressional action—the built-in restraints that our system provides
> through state participation in federal governmental action. The political process
> ensures that laws that unduly burden the states will not be promulgated. . . .
>
> [T]he model of democratic decision making [that] the Court [identified
> in *National League*] underestimated, in our view, the solicitude of the national
> political process for the continued vitality of the states. Attempts by other courts
> since then to draw guidance from this model have proved it both impracticable
> and doctrinally barren. In sum, in *National League of Cities* the Court tried to
> repair what did not need repair [469 U.S. at 546–47, 556–57].

7.1.4. Civil rights enforcement powers. The civil rights enforcement powers are the
fourth major federal power source applicable to education. These powers derive from
the enforcement clauses of various constitutional amendments, particularly the Fourteenth Amendment (due process and equal protection), whose fifth section provides
that "the Congress shall have power to enforce, by appropriate legislation, the provisions of this article." In *Katzenbach v. Morgan*, 384 U.S. 641 (1966), the U.S. Supreme Court held that Section 5 of the Fourteenth Amendment empowers Congress
to "exercise its discretion in determining whether and what legislation is needed to
secure the [amendment's] guarantees," as long as the legislation is "adapted to carry
out the objects the . . . [amendment has] in view" and is not otherwise prohibited by
the Constitution.

The civil rights enforcement powers are the basis for some of the federal
employment discrimination laws (see Section 3.3). In *Fitzpatrick v. Bitzer*, 427 U.S.
445 (1976), for instance, the Court upheld the 1972 extension of Title VII to state and
local governments as an appropriate exercise of the Fourteenth Amendment enforcement power. These powers are also the basis for various civil rights regulatory statutes
that have some application to postsecondary education (for example, Section 1981,
discussed in Sections 3.3.2.4 and 4.2.4.1; and Section 1983, discussed in Sections 2.3.3
and 2.4.3). Some uncertainty remains about the scope of these powers (see *Oregon v.
Mitchell*, 400 U.S. 112 (1970)). There is also some uncertainty about the applicability
of these powers to the private sector, although the Thirteenth Amendment enforce-

ment power to eradicate "badges" and "incidents" of slavery clearly does extend to private institutions (see generally *Runyon v. McCrary*, 427 U.S. 160 (1976), discussed in Section 4.2.4.1).[1]

Sec. 7.2. Federal Regulation of Postsecondary Education

7.2.1. Overview. Despite the attempts of institutions and their national associations to limit the impact of federal regulations and federal funding conditions on postsecondary education, the federal presence on campus continues to increase. Although higher education has experienced some successes, particularly in the area of autonomy over "who may teach, what may be taught, how it shall be taught, and who may be admitted to study" (*Sweezy v. New Hampshire*, see Section 3.7.1), federal regulation affects even the academic core of a college or university. Although mandated self-regulation is still used in some areas of federal regulation, such as restrictions on the use of human subjects or research on animals, self-regulatory actions by institutions have been criticized as insufficient or self-serving (see Sections 3.7.7 and 7.4.4). And while the federal government has relied on the accrediting associations to ensure the integrity of certain federal programs, these agencies' standards and practices have been criticized by federal officials, and the federal government is shifting certain regulatory functions to state government (see Section 8.3.3).

In the following sections, the regulatory issues with the broadest application to postsecondary education have been selected for analysis. In addition to those discussed, other federal statutes may also become important in particular circumstances. The federal bankruptcy law (11 U.S.C. § 101 et seq.), for instance, is important when a student loan recipient declares bankruptcy (see Section 4.3.6.1) and when an institution encounters severe financial distress. The Export Administration Act (50 U.S.C. § 2401 et seq.) and the Arms Export Control Act (22 U.S.C. § 2778) can become important when the federal government seeks to restrict the flow of technical data to other countries (see *National Security Controls and University Research: Statutes, Regulations, and Policy Statements* (Assn. Amer. Univs., 1987 and periodic updates)). The Military Selective Service Act (50 U.S.C. § 451 et seq.) is important when the federal government seeks to prohibit nonregistrants from receiving federal student aid (see Section 4.3.2). The Communications Act of 1934, as amended (47 U.S.C. § 151 et seq.), is important when a postsecondary institution seeks or holds a Federal Communications Commission license to operate an instructional television channel or other broadcasting license. And the Medicare (42 U.S.C. § 1395 et seq.) and Medicaid

---

[1]For theoretical examinations of Congress's enforcement powers, see W. Cohen, "Congressional Power to Interpret Due Process and Equal Protection," 27 *Stanford L. Rev.* 603 (1975), and J. Choper, "Congressional Power to Expand Judicial Definitions of the Substantive Terms of the Civil War Amendments," 67 *Minn. L. Rev.* 299 (1982). For an extended analysis of congressional power to combat private discrimination, see Note, "Federal Power to Regulate Private Discrimination: The Revival of the Enforcement Clauses of the Reconstruction Era Amendments," 74 *Columbia L. Rev.* 449 (1974). For an analysis of congressional power under the Thirteenth Amendment and an argument that this power extends to enforcing affirmative action, see C. A. Baldwin, "The Thirteenth Amendment as an Effective Source of Constitutional Authority for Affirmative Action Legislation," 18 *Columbia J. Law & Social Problems* 77 (1983). For a review of enforcement issues under Section 1981 and the Thirteenth Amendment, see "Developments in the Law—Section 1981," 15 *Harvard Civil Rights-Civil Liberties L. Rev.* 29 (1981).

(42 U.S.C. § 1396 et seq.) statutes are important for institutions with teaching hospitals or other health programs delivering services for which the institution or staff members seek Medicare or Medicaid reimbursements (see C. Hitchner, "Medicare and Medicaid Reimbursement of Teaching Hospitals and Faculty Physicians," 10 *J. Coll. & Univ. Law* 79 (1983–84)). Even the federal election laws may affect campus activities, since the Federal Elections Commission has proposed a ban on campaigning on college campuses (J. B. Gould, " 'Rallying' to the Cause: Colleges, Politics and Where to Draw the Line," 83 *West's Educ. Law Rptr.* 529 (1993)).

Furthermore, many of the targets of federal regulation are also regulated by state law. Laws regarding worker safety and health, wages and hours, employment discrimination, and the environment exist at the state level in many states (see Section 6.5). The interplay between state and federal law can be complex and, occasionally, divisive. For example, public institutions in states that have banned discrimination on the basis of sexual orientation face a dilemma when military recruiters ask to conduct their activities on campus (see generally Comment, "Exclusion of Military Recruiters from Public School Campuses: The Case Against Federal Preemption," 39 *UCLA L. Rev.* 941 (1992)). The sections below can only hint at the scope and complexity of regulation in these areas; the assistance of expert counsel is recommended if issues arise in these or related areas.

7.2.2. Occupational Safety and Health Act.

7.2.2. Occupational Safety and Health Act. Private postsecondary institutions must conform to the federal Occupational Safety and Health Act of 1970 (OSHA) (29 U.S.C. § 651 et seq.). Under this Act a private institution must "furnish to each of [its] employees employment and a place of employment which are free from recognized hazards that are causing or are likely to cause death or serious physical harm" (29 U.S.C. § 654) (the General Duty Clause). Institutions must also comply with health and safety standards promulgated by the U.S. secretary of labor (§ 665). Violations may result in fines or imprisonment (§ 666).

Regulations of particular importance to higher education institutions include the Hazard Communication Standard (29 C.F.R. § 1910.1200), which requires employers to provide information and training to their workers about the hazards of the substances with which they are working. "Hazardous substances" are broadly defined, and OSHA standards also regulate the handling of blood and other body fluids (29 C.F.R. § 1910.1030) as well as chemicals. Research laboratories are required to develop a "chemical hygiene plan" and to specify work procedures and policies in writing (29 C.F.R. § 1910.1450). Employers are also required to maintain records of all "lost-time" injuries, and are subject to fines if records are incomplete (29 U.S.C. § 657(c)). In the higher education context, science laboratories, art rooms, hospitals, and maintenance shops are particular targets for enforcement of OSHA regulations.

OSHA prohibits retaliation against an employee for filing a complaint with the Occupational Safety and Health Administration regarding a potentially unsafe workplace.[2] The Act does not preempt an employee's right to pursue civil actions or other remedies under state laws (§ 653(b)(4)), although the Act preempts some over-

---

[2]Cases and authorities are collected in Annot., "Prohibition of Discrimination Against, or Discharge of, Employee Because of Exercise of Right Afforded by Occupational Safety and Health Act, under § 11(c)(1) of the Act (29 U.S.C.S. § 660(c)(1)," 66 A.L.R. Fed. 650 (1984 and periodic supp.).

lapping state laws. Many states have passed "right-to-know" laws that require employers to disclose the hazardous substances used at the workplace to employees, public-safety agencies (such as the local fire department), and the general public. If these laws overlap or conflict with OSHA, however, they are subject to preemption challenges. For example, in *New Jersey Chamber of Commerce v. Hughey*, 774 F.2d 587 (3d Cir. 1985), New Jersey's Right-to-Know Law was found to be preempted by OSHA, but only with regard to the regulation of safety in the workplace; the court allowed to stand the disclosure provisions to public-safety agencies and the general public.

OSHA does provide, however, that states with safety and enforcement plans approved by OSHA may assume responsiblity for workplace safety and health (29 U.S.C. § 667). But approval must precede a state's attempt to fashion its own occupational safety and health laws. For example, the U.S. Supreme Court struck portions of two Illinois laws that established training and examination requirements for workers at certain hazardous-waste facilities (*Gade v. National Solid Waste Management Assn.*, 112 S. Ct. 2374 (1992)). Illinois did not have an OSHA-aproved state plan, and the Court ruled that "a state law requirement that directly, substantially and specifically regulates occupational safety and health" is preempted by OSHA even if the state law has another nonoccupational purpose. Unless the state has an OSHA-approved state plan, the Court said, OSHA impliedly preempts any state regulation of an occupational safety and health issue where a federal standard has been established.

Public institutions of higher education are subject not to OSHA regulation but to state occupational safety and health laws.[3] For those states with OSHA-approved plans, state standards will be at or above the level of federal protection; for public institutions in states without OSHA-approved plans, the OSHA standard may be used to set tort standards of care. Institutions not subject to OSHA may therefore wish to adopt policies that conform to OSHA standards.

The Occupational Safety and Health Administration, which enforces OSHA, has been criticized for ineffective enforcement and for assessing fines too low to provide a disincentive to unsafe workplace practices. In response, Congress increased the penalties for OSHA violations (Omnibus Budget Reconciliation Act of 1990, Pub. L. No. 101-508, 104 Stat. 1388 (1990)). Furthermore, prosecutors in several states have filed criminal charges against corporations and their executives for manslaughter, murder, and assault; several of these cases have resulted in jury findings of guilt, although trial judges or appellate courts have reversed many of these jury verdicts on technical grounds (*Briggs v. Pymm Thermometer Corp.*, 537 N.Y.S.2d 553 (N.Y. App. Div. 1989); *People v. O'Neil*, 550 N.E.2d 1090 (Ill. App. Ct. 1990); see M. Bixby, "Workplace Homicide: Trends, Issues, and Policy," 70 *Or. L. Rev.* 333 (1991)). Commentators expect that the use of criminal statutes to attack unsafe workplace conditions will continue; an attempt to argue that OSHA preempted such criminal prosecutions failed (*Illinois v. Chicago Magnet Wire*, 534 N.E.2d 962 (Ill. 1989), *cert. denied sub nom Asta v. Illinois*, 493 U.S. 809 (1989)).

Several of the federal environmental laws make "knowing endangerment" of a

---

[3]Whether a state-related institution is covered by OSHA may be difficult to determine. For cases related to this issue, see Annot., "What Constitutes Political Subdivision of State, Under § 3(5) of Occupational Safety and Health Act (29 U.S.C.S. § 652(5)), so as to Be Excluded from Act's Definition of Employer," 94 A.L.R. Fed 851 (1989 and periodic supp.).

worker a felony (see Section 7.2.15). For further information, see R. Schwartz, Comment, "Criminalizing Occupational Safety Violations: The Use of 'Knowing Endangerment' Statutes to Punish Employers Who Maintain Toxic Working Conditions," 14 *Harvard Environmental Law Rev.* 487 (1990).

7.2.3. Labor-Management Relations Act. The Labor-Management Relations Act (29 U.S.C. § 141 et seq.) protects the employees of covered employers in "the exercise . . . of full freedom of association, self-organization, and designation of representatives of their own choosing, for the purpose of negotiating the terms and conditions of their employment or other mutual aid or protection" (29 U.S.C. § 151). Section 157 of the law permits employees to engage in "concerted activities for the purpose of . . . other mutual aid or protection," a right that applies whether or not the employees are represented by a union. The LMRA's application to faculty members is discussed in Section 3.2. Staff, administrators, and teaching assistants may also be covered by this law.

The Act defines "employee" to exclude "any individual employed as a supervisor" (29 U.S.C. § 152(3)); a "supervisor" is defined as "any individual having authority, in the interest of the employer, to hire, transfer, suspend, lay off, recall, promote, discharge, assign, reward, or discipline other employees, or responsibly to direct them, or to adjust their grievances, or effectively to recommend such action, if in connection with the foregoing the exercise of such authority is not of a merely routine or clerical nature, but requires the use of independent judgment" (§ 152(11)). The National Labor Relations Board, the federal agency that enforces the LMRA, has also excluded confidential and managerial employees from the Act's protections. The Act defines "employer" to exclude "any state or political subdivision thereof," thereby removing public employers, including public postsecondary institutions, from the Act's coverage (29 U.S.C. § 152(2)).[4] The LMRA thus applies only to private postsecondary institutions and, under current National Labor Relations Board rules, only to those with gross annual revenues of at least one million dollars (29 C.F.R. § 103.1).

Prior to 1974 acute care hospitals were exempt from coverage by the LMRA, out of concern for the serious public health consequences of labor stoppages. But in 1974 Congress amended the law, in the NLRA Amendments of 1974 (88 Stat. 395), and subjected all acute care hospitals to coverage by the LMRA. The congressional reports accompanying the amendments said that the National Labor Relations Board should give due consideration to "preventing proliferation of bargaining units in the health care industry" (S. Rep. No. 93-766, at 5; H.R. Rep. No. 93-1051, at 6-7 (1974), 93d Cong., 2d Sess., reprinted in 1974 *U.S. Code Cong. & Admin. News*, at 3946, 3950). After years of public hearings and consultation, the Board, in 1989, issued a rule defining appropriate bargaining units in the health care industry. The rule (codified at 29 C.F.R. § 103.30 (1990)) specifies that "except in extraordinary circumstances" or where there are existing nonconforming units, there will be no more than eight

---

[4]The determination of whether, for purposes of coverage by the LMRA, an institution is public or private is made by the National Labor Relations Board. One significant criterion is the percentage of an institution's budget supplied by state funds; in *University of Vermont and State Agricultural College*, 223 NLRB 423 (1976), the NLRB determined that the university, a state university, was subject to the LMRA because it received only 25 percent of its budget from state funds and because it was not a political subdivision of the state; the state legislature subsequently enacted a law making the university a political entity of the state (see Section 3.2.1).

bargaining units at acute care hospitals. The rule dictates the type of employee (physicians, nurses, skilled maintenance) for each of these units. Although the hospitals' trade association challenged the rule as unconstitutional and in violation of congressional intent regarding "undue proliferation," it was upheld by the U.S. Supreme Court in *American Hospital Assn. v. NLRB*, 111 S. Ct. 1539 (1991). For an example of the rule applied to a university hospital, see *Duke University*, 306 NLRB No. 101, 139 L.R.R.M. 1300 (1992).

Institutions that have attempted to use consultative decision-making practices for administrators and staff may wish to review the NLRB's recent decision in *Electromation Inc.*, 309 NLRB No. 163 (1992). In this case a union charged that the company's joint employee-employer "action committees," created to develop company policy on attendance, pay policies, and other issues, constituted an illegally dominated "labor organization" under 29 U.S.C. §§ 152(5) and 158(a)(2). The NLRB agreed with the union, citing the fact that the employer had created the committees unilaterally, specified their goals and responsibilities, appointed management representatives (employees volunteered for the committees), and permitted the committees to operate on paid time. The NLRB's ruling was affirmed by the U.S. Court of Appeals for the Seventh Circuit in *Electromation, Inc. v. NLRB*, 35 F.3d 1148 (7th Cir. 1994).

Public institutions, though not subject to the LMRA, are often subject to similar legislation at the state level (see Section 3.2.1). State collective bargaining laws often differ considerably from federal law; but in a decision that applies to public institutions in all states, the U.S. Supreme Court ruled that a state law requiring the University of California to permit union mail to be transported through its campus mail system violated federal Private Express Statutes (18 U.S.C. §§ 1693–1699, 39 U.S.C. §§ 601–606) that give the U.S. Postal Service a monopoly for mail delivery over postal routes (*Regents of the University of California v. Public Employee Relations Board*, 485 U.S. 589 (1988)).

7.2.4. *Fair Labor Standards Act.* The Fair Labor Standards Act (FLSA) (29 U.S.C. § 201 et seq.) establishes the minimum hourly wage and the piecework rates as well as overtime pay requirements for certain nonsupervisory employees. The law does not apply to independent contractors.[5] The law also requires that records be kept of the hours worked by nonexempt employees and the compensation paid therefor.

The FLSA is enforced by the Wage and Hour Division of the U.S. Department of Labor; no private right of action is available. The secretary of labor has two years from the date of the violation to file an enforcement action, but the statute provides that if the violation is "willful," the limitations period is extended to three years (29 U.S.C. § 255(a)). A violation is "willful" if the employer "knew or showed reckless disregard for the matter of whether its conduct was prohibited by the FLSA" (*McLaughlin v. Richland Shoe Co.*, 486 U.S. 128 (1988)).

In situations where an applicable state law establishes a minimum wage rate that conflicts with the federal standard, the higher rate must prevail (29 U.S.C. § 218).

----

[5]For analysis of how an individual's status as independent contractor or employee is determined under the FLSA, see Annot., "Determination of 'Independent Contractor' and 'Employee' Status for Purposes of § 3(e)(1) of the Fair Labor Standards Act (29 U.S.C.S. § 203(e)(1))," 51 A.L.R. Fed. 702 (1981 and periodic supp.).

The FLSA specifically exempts "any employee employed in a bona fide executive, administrative, or professional capacity" from the minimum wage and maximum hour requirements (29 U.S.C. § 213(a)(1)). The Department of Labor has promulgated regulations implementing this provision (29 C.F.R. Part 541). The regulations establish the conditions of employment that must exist before an employer may consider an employee to be an "executive," or an "administrative," or a "professional" employee. Of particular interest to higher education, the term "administrative" includes persons who perform "functions in the administration of [an] . . . educational establishment or institution, or of a department or subdivision thereof" (29 C.F.R. § 541.2(a)(2)) and meet the other conditions set by the regulations. Similarly, the term "professional" includes any person whose primary duty is "teaching, tutoring, instructing, or lecturing . . . and who [is] employed and engaged in this activity as a teacher in the . . . educational establishment or institution by which he is employed (29 C.F.R. § 541.3(a)(3)). Professionals also must meet the regulations' other conditions.

The DOL regulations were applied in *Prakash v. American University*, 727 F.2d 1174 (D.C. Cir. 1984), a case brought by a former physics professor seeking payment at the minimum wage rate for regular and overtime work previously performed. The university claimed that the professor was a professional exempted from the FLSA's coverage and thus not entitled to the statutory minimum wage. The appellate court remanded the case to the trial court for a determination of whether the university could prove that the professor's position had met all the conditions of professional capacity established in the DOL regulations.

Even more basic than whether one is a professional, executive, or administrative employee is the question whether one can be classified at all as an employee. In *Marshall v. Regis Educational Corp.*, 666 F.2d 1324 (10th Cir. 1981), the secretary of labor contended that the college's student residence-hall assistants (RAs) were "employees" within the meaning of the Act and therefore must be paid the prescribed minimum wage. The college argued that its RAs were not employees and that, even if they were, application of the Act to these RAs would violate the college's academic freedom protected by the First Amendment. Affirming the district court, the appellate court accepted the college's first argument and declined to consider the second. The court's opinion focuses on the unique circumstances of academic life:

> RAs resided in the dormitories where they assisted the residence directors and actively participated in the development and implementation of programs designed to enhance the quality of resident-hall living.
> Although RAs did not work a specified number of hours per day, they were generally available in the halls for an estimated twenty hours a week. In order to keep their status as RAs they were required to maintain a specified grade point average. In exchange for the performance of these duties, RAs received a reduced rate on their rooms, the use of a free telephone, and a $1,000 tuition credit. . . .
> The government contends that RAs were "employees" because they received compensation and the college enjoyed an immediate economic benefit from their services. The government emphasizes that RAs displaced employees whom Regis would otherwise have been required to hire. Regis counters that the primary purpose of the RA program was educational, that RAs at Regis were not "employees," but student recipients of financial aid. The college rejects the ar-

gument that RAs displace other employees, stressing that the peer counseling and educational aspects of the resident assistant program would be lost if it were operated without students. . . . In *Rutherford Food Corp. v. McComb*, 331 U.S. 722 (1947), . . . the Supreme Court declared that the determination of employment under the FLSA ought not depend on isolated factors but upon the "circumstances of the whole activity" (331 U.S. at 730). This test is controlling in the case at bar.

Our holding that RAs are not employees does not require the conclusion that no student working at the college would be within the scope of the FLSA. No such inference should be drawn. There are undoubtedly campus positions which can be filled by students and which require compliance with the FLSA. Students working in the bookstore selling books, working with maintenance, painting walls, etc., could arguably be "employees." . . .

The record shows that student athletes who receive tuition grants are required to maintain a specified academic average and to fulfill certain duties with respect to training programs and to participate in sports events on campus; student leaders in the student government associations are similarly situated. Selected student leaders have specified duties and responsibilities and receive tuition credits. . . .

We agree with the district court (considering the totality of the circumstances) in finding that RAs at Regis were legally indistinguishable from athletes and leaders in student government who received financial aid. We therefore hold that the RAs at Regis College were not "employees" within the meaning of the Act, but student recipients of financial aid [666 F.2d at 1326–28].

But in *Alabama A&M University v. King*, 1 Wage and Hour Cases 2d 1608 (Ala. Ct. Civ. App. 1994), the court not only held that residence hall counselors were employees but refused to apply the administrative exemption to them, making them eligible for overtime payments if they worked more than forty hours per week. In addition to the status of students under this law, the status of part-time instructors as employees or independent contractors also raises potential FLSA liability issues.

The FLSA has always applied to most private postsecondary institutions, but the Act's application to public postsecondary institutions has been the subject of historical turmoil. In 1966 Congress extended the Act's coverage to public hospitals and schools, including public postsecondary schools. Two years later the U.S. Supreme Court upheld this extension in *Maryland v. Wirtz*, 392 U.S. 183 (1968). But the Court expressly overruled its *Wirtz* opinion in *National League of Cities v. Usery*, 426 U.S. 833 (1976), thus prohibiting the federal government from enforcing the FLSA against public postsecondary institutions and other state and local government employers that Congress had brought under the Act's coverage in 1974. Then, completing the circle, the court overruled its *National League of Cities* opinion in *Garcia v. San Antonio Metropolitan Transit Authority*, 469 U.S. 528 (1985) (see Section 7.1.3).

Reacting to *Garcia*, Congress amended the FLSA to limit the application of its overtime requirements. State and local government employers, including public postsecondary institutions, may provide compensatory leave in lieu of overtime compensation (Pub. L. No. 99-150, codified at 29 U.S.C. §§ 207(o) and (p)). The amendments also discuss the treatment of volunteers who perform services for a public agency. Regulations implementing these amendments are found at 29 C.F.R. Part 553. The rules include a special limited exemption for public employees in executive, administrative, or professional jobs: these employees are exempted from the law's requirement that they be paid on a salary basis in order not to be eligible for the law's overtime provisions. This new rule was necessary to protect the exemption for public employees covered by public pay systems that reduce the pay of otherwise-exempt employees for partial day absences when paid leave is not used to cover such absences, and for deductions due to budget-required furloughs. The rule can be found at 29 C.F.R. Part 541.

The FLSA has no exemption for religiously affiliated institutions, so they must also comply with this law. The U.S. Supreme Court ruled in *Alamo Foundation v. Secretary of Labor*, 471 U.S. 290 (1985), that religious organizations engaged in commercial activities (such as selling books)—if those activities met the Act's "enterprise" and "economic reality" tests—were subject to minimum wage and overtime requirements. The Court ruled that neither the payment requirement nor the record-keeping provisions violated the Establishment Clause or the Free Exercise Clause; the record-keeping requirement applied only to the organization's business activities, not to its religious ones, and if individuals did not wish to receive wages, they could donate them back to the organization. The Fourth Circuit, following *Alamo*, ruled that a church-related elementary school was subject to the minimum wage and equal-pay provisions of the FLSA (*Dole v. Shenandoah Baptist Church*, 899 F.2d 1389 (4th Cir. 1990)). Thus, the secular activities of a religiously affiliated college or university are subject to FLSA requirements.

7.2.5. Employee Retirement Income Security Act. The Employee Retirement Income Security Act of 1974 (known as the Pension Reform Act or ERISA) establishes "standards of conduct, responsibility, and obligation for fiduciaries of employee benefit plans" (29 U.S.C. § 1001(b)). The terms "employee benefit plan" and "employee pension plan" are defined to encompass various health benefits, death benefits, disability benefits, unemployment benefits, retirement plans, and income deferral programs (29 U.S.C. § 1002(1) and (2)). The ERISA requirements for the creation and management of these plans are codified partly in the federal tax law (26 U.S.C. § 401 et seq.) and partly in the federal labor law (29 U.S.C. § 1001 et seq.). These requirements apply only to private postsecondary institutions. The plans of public institutions are excluded from coverage as "governmental plan(s)" under 29 U.S.C. § 1002(32) and 26 U.S.C. § 414(d).

The ERISA standards have been construed as minimum federal standards designed to curb the funding and disclosure abuses of employee pension and benefit plans (*Wadsworth v. Whaland*, 562 F.2d 70 (1st Cir. 1977), *cert. denied*, 435 U.S. 980 (1978)). Rules and regulations have been issued covering reporting and disclosure requirements, minimum standards of conduct, and fiduciary responsibilities (see 29 C.F.R. Parts 2510, 2520, 2530, and 2550). Interpretive bulletins explaining the Act have also been issued and reprinted at 29 C.F.R. Part 2509.

Some special rules apply to benefit plans for teachers and other employees of tax-exempt educational institutions. Under certain circumstances, for instance, such employees may delay their participation in a benefit plan until they reach the age of twenty-six (26 U.S.C. § 410(a)(1)(B)(ii); 29 U.S.C. § 1052(a)(1)(B)(ii)).

ERISA requirements are numerous and complex; a few are offered for purposes of illustration only. For example, the Consolidated Omnibus Budget Reconciliation Act of 1986 (Title X, Pub. L. No. 99-272, 100 Stat. 222 (1986)) amended

ERISA to require employers to permit employees who leave employment on good terms (for example, by retirement, voluntary resignations, or layoffs) to continue medical insurance coverage (at their own expense) at approximately the employer's group rate for eighteen months; their dependents have similar rights upon divorce or a child's emancipation. Other amendments to ERISA in the Retirement Equity Act of 1984 (98 Stat. 1426 et seq.) protect employees' pension benefits during periods of maternity or paternity leave (§ 102(e)); establish requirements for the provision, by pension plans, of joint and survivor annuities and preretirement survivor annuities for surviving spouses of employees (§ 103); and establish rules for the assignment of rights to pension benefits in divorce proceedings (§ 104).

A recently promulgated rule protects employers from lawsuits by workers who are dissatisfied with the return on their pension funds' investments. That rule, codified at 29 C.F.R. Part 2550, offers this protection if the employer fulfills the following conditions: the participant or beneficiary must have the opportunity under the plan (1) to choose from at least three investment alternatives; (2) to give investment instruction to the plan administrator on a frequent basis; (3) to diversify investments at least once every quarter; and (4) obtain information to make informed investment decisions.

With various listed exceptions, ERISA supersedes any and all state laws "insofar as they may now or hereinafter relate to any employee benefit plan" subject to the ERISA statute (29 U.S.C. § 1144(a)). The exceptions are for state laws regulating insurance, banking, or securities, and state criminal laws, none of which are superseded by ERISA (29 U.S.C. § 1144(b)). These provisions, and their relation to other provisions in the statute, have been the subject of varying interpretations by the courts, and it has often proved difficult in particular cases to determine when ERISA preempts state law. (See generally D. Gregory, "The Scope of ERISA Preemption of State Law: A Study in Effective Federalism," 48 *U. Pittsburgh L. Rev.* 427 (1987).)

Four U.S. Supreme Court cases address the ERISA preemption issue from different, but not contradictory, perspectives, and illustrate the wide reach of this law vis-à-vis state regulatory efforts. In *Alessi v. Raybestos-Manhattan,* 451 U.S. 504 (1981), the Court considered whether a state law prohibiting workers' compensation benefits from being used to offset pension benefits was preempted by ERISA. The Court held that the state statute was preempted: "ERISA makes clear that even indirect state action bearing on private pension plans may encroach upon the area of exclusive federal concern. . . . ERISA's authors clearly meant to preclude the states from avoiding through form the substance of the preemption provision." In *Shaw v. Delta Airlines,* 463 U.S. 85 (1983), an airline and other employers sought to have two New York State statutes preempted by ERISA insofar as they applied to employee benefit plans: the New York Human Rights Law, a comprehensive antidiscrimination statute prohibiting, among other actions, discrimination on the basis of pregnancy; and the New York Disability Benefits Law, which required employers (among other things) to pay sick-leave benefits to employees unable to work because of pregnancy. The Court determined that the ERISA preemption provision (§ 1144(a)) should be broadly construed and that both New York statutes "relate to" employee benefit plans within the meaning of that provision. The Court then proceeded to save both statutes from preemption (with some qualifications) by resorting to other ERISA provisions that limit the reach of the preemption clause.

A third Supreme Court opinion, *FMC Corp. v. Holliday,* 111 S. Ct. 403 (1990), ruled that ERISA preempted a Pennsylvania law that precluded reimbursement from a claimant's tort recovery for benefit payments from a benefit program. The Court distinguished between state regulation of self-funded employee benefit plans (which ERISA regulates, so that state regulation is thus preempted) and state regulation of insurance (which ERISA specifically exempts from preemption). The Court also ruled that self-funded employee health benefit plans are not subject to state insurance regulation, but health benefit plans covered by insurance can be regulated by the state. Other state laws, such as New Jersey's Family Leave Act, insofar as they dictate the continuation of medical benefits by the employer while the employee is using family leave, have also been nullified under ERISA (*New Jersey Business and Industry Assn. v. State of New Jersey*, 592 A.2d 660 (N.J. Super. Ct. App. Div. 1991).[6] In the fourth Supreme Court case, *Massachusetts v. Morash*, 490 U.S. 107 (1989), the Court refused to find that ERISA preempted a statute that required employers to pay discharged employees their full wages, including accrued vacation payments. According to the court, forty-seven other states have similar statutes.

The U.S. Supreme Court has also ruled that ERISA preempts common law contract or tort claims relating to employee benefits that are brought in state court, and that such claims may be removed to federal court and tried under ERISA (*Metropolitan Life Insurance v. Taylor*, 107 S. Ct. 1542 (1987)). Remedies for ERISA violations, if not specified in the statute, have been developed under federal common law (see S. H. Thomsen & W. M. Smith, "Developments in Common-Law Remedies Under ERISA," 27 *Tort and Insurance Law J.* 750 (1992)).

The relationship between ERISA and state and federal disability discrimination laws has yet to be resolved. In *McGann v. H&H Music Co.*, 946 F.2d 401 (5th Cir. 1992), the court ruled that ERISA did not limit an employer's right to change or terminate a group health insurance plan to exclude coverage of certain diseases (in this case, AIDS). Another federal appellate court ruled that insurance caps for HIV-related diseases did not violate ERISA (*Owens v. Storehouse*, 984 F.2d 394 (11th Cir. 1993)). However, refusal to include certain diseases within medical insurance coverage may violate the Americans with Disabilities Act (see Section 7.5.4 and W. F. Highberger, "The Impact of ERISA on Discrimination Claims of People with AIDS," 17 *Employment Relations Law J.* 449 (1992)); this issue will receive much judicial attention in the near future.

As a result of the evolving nature of the relationship between ERISA and related state laws, as well as the overall complexity of this law and its regulations and the pace of ERISA developments, assistance from experienced ERISA counsel is necessary.

7.2.6. Employment discrimination laws.

7.2.6. Employment discrimination laws. Aside from the nondiscrimination requirements that it imposes as conditions on federal spending (see Section 7.5), the federal government also directly regulates employment discrimination under several other statutes. Primary among them is Title VII of the Civil Rights Act of 1964 (42 U.S.C. § 2000e et seq.), amended by the Civil Rights Act of 1991. These statutes are set out

---

[6]The recently enacted federal Family and Medical Leave Act, 29 U.S.C. § 2601 et seq. (1993), requires employers to maintain employees' medical benefits while they are on leave. Because this is a federal law and it was enacted after ERISA, its provisions will not be preempted by ERISA.

and discussed in Section 3.3.2, which examines their particular applications to faculty members.

7.2.6.1. Application to administrators and staff. Courts have often been deferential to higher education institutions when considering employment discrimination claims brought against them. Usually, however, courts have displayed this deference in cases where the institution's refusal to hire, renew, or tenure a faculty member is alleged to be discriminatory. In such cases the reluctance of courts to intervene may stem from a recognition of the limits of their competence to second-guess decisions resulting from a peer review process that emphasizes subjective evaluation of scholarly work or teaching ability. Such considerations are usually absent in cases brought by administrators or staff personnel in positions without faculty status. Since the justifications for according deference to higher education institutions do not apply with the same force to these nonfaculty cases, courts may be more activist in applying federal nondiscrimination laws to them.

In addition to the differing degrees of deference, employment decisions regarding administrators and staff may raise different types of issues under federal nondiscrimination laws than do employment decisions regarding faculty. Two cases, both decided under the Age Discrimination in Employment Act (Section 3.3.2.5), illustrate two such issues. In *EEOC v. University of Texas Health Science Center,* 710 F.2d 1091 (5th Cir. 1983), the court considered the ADEA's application to a campus security force. The plaintiff had been refused employment because he exceeded the force's maximum hiring age of forty-five. The center argued that age was a bona fide occupational qualification (BFOQ) for the position of security officer, not subject to the Act's prohibition, because the job demanded an exceptional level of physical fitness. The court held in favor of the center—but only because it was able to present "consistent testimony at trial that physical strength, agility, and stamina are important to the training and performance of campus policemen. " In *EEOC v. Board of Trustees of Wayne County Community College,* 723 F.2d 509 (6th Cir. 1983), the court considered the applicability, to a community college president, of an ADEA provision excluding high-level public appointees in policy-making positions from the Act's protections. The EEOC argued that, because the college's board of trustees exercised broad policy-making powers, the president did not fall within the exclusion and was therefore protected by the Act. The court rejected this argument, reasoning that "shared, overlapping, and complementary authority [is] no less capable of being denominated policy making than is exclusive authority."

Federal law also prohibits discrimination against individuals on the basis of eligibility for military service and provides reemployment rights for individuals who must leave their jobs to serve on active duty in the military. The Veterans Readjustment Benefits Act (Pub. L. No. 89-358 (1966)), amended by the Vietnam Era Veterans' Readjustment Assistance Act of 1974 (Pub. L. No. 93-508, codified at 38 U.S.C. § 4212 et seq.), requires employers to restore individuals covered by these laws to their previous position or a similar one unless the employer can demonstrate that such restoration is impossible or unreasonable. Amendments added in 1991 (Pub. L. No. 102-25) require the employer to retrain returning veterans for their previous positions, if necessary; the amendments also regulate the provision of employer-offered health insurance for such individuals. In *King v. St. Vincent's Hospital,* 112 S. Ct. 570 (1991), the U.S. Supreme Court ruled unanimously that the Veterans' Readjustment Assistance Act does not limit the amount of time individuals may serve on active duty

before they lose the right to be restored to their former position; there is no requirement that the length of active duty be "reasonable," and reemployment rights
apparently do not expire as long as there is a position available for the veterans and
they are qualified or are able to become requalified.

Policies that prohibit women from working with substances that may harm
a fetus were ruled to be intentional sex discrimination in *United Automobile Workers
v. Johnson Controls, Inc.,* 111 S. Ct. 1196 (1991). The company had excluded all
women capable of bearing a child from jobs involving exposure to lead (which can
cause abnormal brain development in a fetus), in an effort to avoid the potential harm
to unborn children and the negligence litigation that might ensue. The Court, in a
unaminous opinion, ruled that such a policy constituted impermissible sex discrimination under Title VII, and that an employer who complied with OSHA regulations
(see Section 7.2.2) should not face increased negligence liability. This case has important implications for the employment of women in laboratory jobs or other positions
involving possible exposure to substances that could harm a fetus; EEOC Guidelines
on this issue should be consulted.

Sexual harassment (discussed in the context of faculty in Section 3.3.4.3) can
also pose a serious problem for nonfaculty employees and students (harassment of
students is discussed in Sections 4.6.3 and 7.5.3). Even if the harasser is not a university
employee, the university may face legal liability if the harassment can be linked to
the victim's job responsibilities (see, for example, L. McMillen, "Sexual Harassment
a Growing Problem as Some Donors Make Overtures to People Seeking Gifts from
Them," *Chron. Higher Educ.,* July 31, 1991, A19–A20). The development of the
"reasonable woman" standard (*Ellison v. Brady,* 924 F.2d 872 (9th Cir. 1991)) and the
remedies of compensatory and punitive damages now available under the Civil Rights
Act of 1991 make it more likely that charges of sexual harassment will be filed; the
right to a jury and recent judicial willingness to hold employers strictly accountable
for proven harassment suggest that institutions should educate their faculty and staff
about this issue and pursue complaints with the same attention they devote to other
allegedly illegal behavior.

7.2.6.2. Applicability to religious institutions. A major coverage issue under
federal employment discrimination statutes is their applicability to religious institutions. The issue parallels those that have arisen under federal collective bargaining
law (see the *Catholic Bishop* case in Section 3.2.1), unemployment compensation law
(see the *St. Martin's* case in Section 7.3.3), and federal tax law (see the *Bob Jones* case
in Section 7.3.1).

Section 702 of Title VII specifically exempts "a religious corporation, association, educational institution, or society" from its prohibition against religious discrimination "with respect to the employment of individuals of a particular religion"
if they are hired to perform "work connected with the carrying on by such corporation, association, educational institution, or society of its activities" (42 U.S.C.
§ 2000e-11). Not addressed in the statutory language was the meaning of "its activities"—did they have to be closely related to the organization's religious mission, or
would all activities of the organization be included within the exemption?

The U.S. Supreme Court addressed this issue, although not in the context of
higher education. In *Corporation of the Presiding Bishop of the Church of Jesus
Christ of Latter-Day Saints v. Amos,* 483 U.S. 327 (1987), the Court considered a

challenge to the Mormon Church's decision that all employees working for a gymnasium owned by the church but open to the public must be members of the Mormon Church. The plaintiffs argued that, although Title VII's religious exemption (Section 702) could properly be applied to religious activities of such an organization, the church should not be permitted to practice religious discrimination for jobs that had no relationship to religion. The issue facing the Court was whether Section 702's exemption for religious organizations extends to secular activities as well as religious ones, and, if so, whether such an interpretation violates the Establishment Clause of the First Amendment.

The Supreme Court refused to distinguish between secular and religious activities, saying that Section 702 could be applied to all activities of a religious organization without violating the Establishment Clause. Using the three-pronged test developed in *Lemon v. Kurtzman* (403 U.S. 602 (1971)) (see this volume, Section 1.6), the Court determined that Section 702 did not conflict with the Establishment Clause.

In examining whether Section 702 advanced religion (the second prong of the *Lemon* test), as the plaintiffs claimed, the Court said, "[I]t is a significant burden on a religious organization to require it, on pain of substantial liability, to predict which of its activities a secular court will consider religion" (483 U.S. at 336). The Court concluded that Section 702's purpose was to minimize governmental interference with the decisions of religious organizations, and that it neither advanced nor inhibited religion: "[A] law is not unconstitutional simply because it *allows* churches to advance religion, which is their very purpose" (483 U.S. at 337). Any such advancement in this case, according to the Court, could be attributed to the church, not the government. With regard to entanglement, the third prong of the *Lemon* test, the Court asserted: "It cannot be seriously contended that sec. 702 impermissibly entangles church and state; the statute effectuates a more complete separation of the two" (483 U.S. at 339).

Two pre-*Amos* appellate court opinions reached the same conclusion in the context of preferential hiring by religious universities. In *Pime v. Loyola University of Chicago*, 803 F.2d 351 (7th Cir. 1986), the court affirmed a lower court ruling (585 F. Supp. 435 (N.D. Ill. 1984)) that membership in a religious order can be a bona fide occupational qualification within the meaning of Title VII (see Section 3.3.2.1). The plaintiff, a Jew, had been a part-time lecturer in the university's philosophy department when it adopted a resolution that seven of the department's thirty-one tenure-track positions be reserved for Jesuit priests. The court, finding a historical relationship betwen members of the religious order and the university, concluded that the Jesuit "presence" was significant to the educational traditions and character of the university and important to its successful operation.

The same court also upheld the dismissal of another Title VII suit involving the theology department at another Catholic university, where half of the twenty-seven full-time faculty positions were held by Jesuits (*Maguire v. Marquette University*, 814 F.2d 1213 (7th Cir. 1987)). The plaintiff, who was rejected for a theology department position, claimed that the university's action constituted sex discrimination. The university asserted that its action fell within Title VII's Section 702 exemption allowing educational institutions controlled by religious groups to hire employees of a particular religion. Although the trial court dismissed the Title VII claim based on the exemption, the appellate court's affirmance rested on the narrower ground that the plaintiff had failed to establish a prima facie case of sex discrimination. The court also held that Section 702 should be read to allow the hiring committee of a theology department "broad latitude" when making decisions to hire employees of a particular religion.

But in *EEOC v. Kamehameha Schools*, 990 F.2d 458 (9th Cir. 1993), the federal court distinguished *Pime* and ruled that two private schools could not restrict their hiring to Protestants, even though the will that established the schools so required. In determining that the schools did not fit within the Section 702 exemption, the court examined the schools' ownership and affiliation, their purpose, the religious affiliations of the students, and the degree to which the education provided by the schools was religious in character. The court then concluded that being Protestant was not a bona fide occupational requirement for employment at the schools.

Although *Amos* apparently sanctions religious preferences in hiring for institutions qualifying for the Section 702 exemption, it does not exempt them from other Title VII prohibitions on race and sex discrimination (or from other nondiscrimination laws). Unless a religious institution can justify alleged sex or race discrimination as an exercise of its religious beliefs, it is still subject to review by enforcement agencies. In two cases decided in 1980 and 1981, the U.S. Court of Appeals for the Fifth Circuit thoroughly analyzed the extent to which religious schools are subject to these other prohibitions of Title VII, an issue not addressed by *Amos*. The cases also include useful analysis of how a religious college may respond to investigatory subpoenas and other information requests served on it by the Equal Employment Opportunity Commission (EEOC).

The first case, *EEOC v. Mississippi College*, 626 F.2d 477 (5th Cir. 1980), concerned a four-year coeducational school owned by the Mississippi Baptist Convention, an organization of Southern Baptist churches in Mississippi. The Baptist Convention's written policy stated a preference for employing active members of Baptist churches, and prohibited women from teaching courses concerning the Bible because no woman has been ordained as a minister in a Southern Baptist church. A female part-time faculty member, Dr. Summers, filed a charge with the EEOC when the college denied her application for a full-time faculty position. Summers alleged that the college's choice of a male constituted sex discrimination and that the college's employment policies discriminated against women and minorities as a class. When the EEOC attempted to investigate Summers' charge, the college refused to cooperate, and the EEOC sought court enforcement of a subpoena.

The college asserted that it had selected a male instead of Summers because he was a Baptist and she was not—thus making religion the grounds for its decision and exempting the decision from EEOC review under Title VII's exemption for religious institutions in Section 702. The court agreed in principle with the college but indicated the need for additional evidence on whether the college had accurately characterized its failure to hire Summers:

> If the district court determines on remand that the college applied its policy of preferring Baptists over non-Baptists in granting the faculty position to Bailey rather than Summers, then Section 702 exempts that decision from the application of Title VII and would preclude any investigation by the EEOC to determine whether the college used the preference policy as a guise to hide some other form of discrimination. On the other hand, should the evidence disclose

only that the college's preference policy could have been applied, but in fact it was not considered by the college in determining which applicant to hire, Section 702 does not bar the EEOC's investigation of Summers' individual sex discrimination claim [626 F.2d at 485–86].

The college also argued, in response to Summers' individual claim and her allegation of class discrimination against women and blacks, (1) that the employment relationship between a church-related school and its faculty is not within the purview of Title VII; and (2) that, if this relationship is within Title VII, its inclusion violates both the Establishment Clause and the Free Exercise Clause of the First Amendment.

The court easily rejected the first argument, reasoning that the relationship between a church-related school and its faculty is not comparable to the church-minister relationship, which is outside Title VII. The court spent more time on the second argument but rejected it as well.

Addressing the Establishment Clause issue first, the court relied on the *Lemon v. Kurtzman* line of cases to determine whether application of Title VII to the college would foster "excessive government entanglement with religion" (see Section 1.6). The court reasoned:

> The nature of the burden that might be imposed upon the college by the application of Title VII to it is largely hypothetical at this stage of the proceedings. The information requested by the EEOC's subpoena does not clearly implicate any religious practices of the college. . . . As noted previously, the exemption granted to religious institutions by Section 702 of Title VII must be construed broadly to exclude from the scope of the Act any employment decision made by a religious institution on the basis of religious discrimination. This construction of Section 702 largely allays the college's primary concern that it will be unable to continue its policy of preferring Baptists in hiring. The only practice brought to the attention of the district court that is clearly predicated upon religious beliefs that might not be protected by the exemption of Section 702 is the college's policy of hiring only men to teach courses in religion. The bare potential that Title VII would affect this practice does not warrant precluding the application of Title VII to the college. Before the EEOC could require the college to alter that practice, the college would have an opportunity to litigate in a federal forum whether Section 702 exempts or the First Amendment protects that particular practice. We thus determine that, in the factual context before us, the application of Title VII to the college could have only a minimal impact upon the college's religion-based practices.
>
> Although the college is a pervasively sectarian institution, the minimal burden imposed upon its religious practices by the application of Title VII and the limited nature of the resulting relationship between the federal government and the college cause us to find that application of the statute would not foster excessive government entanglement with religion. . . . We conclude that imposing the requirements of Title VII upon the college does not violate the establishment clause of the First Amendment [626 F.2d at 487–88].

The court then considered whether application of Title VII to the college would violate the Free Exercise Clause:

> In determining whether a statutory enactment violates the free exercise of a sincerely held religious belief, the Supreme Court has examined (1) the mag-

nitude of the statute's impact upon the exercise of the religious belief, (2) the existence of a compelling state interest justifying the burden imposed upon the exercise of the religious belief, and (3) the extent to which recognition of an exemption from the statute would impede the objectives sought to be advanced by the state. . . . As discussed previously, the impact of Title VII upon the exercise of the religious belief is limited in scope and degree. Section 702 excludes from the scope of Title VII those employment practices of the college that discriminate on the basis of religion. . . . However, the relevant inquiry is not the impact of the statute upon the institution, but the impact of the statute upon the institution's exercise of its sincerely held religious beliefs. The fact that those of the college's employment practices subject to Title VII do not embody religious beliefs or practices protects the college from any real threat of undermining its religious purpose of fulfilling the evangelical role of the Mississippi Baptist Convention, and allows us to conclude that the impact of Title VII on the free exercise of religious beliefs is minimal.

Second, the government has a compelling interest in eradicating discrimination in all forms. . . . Congress manifested that interest in the enactment of Title VII and the other sections of the Civil Rights Act of 1964. The proscription upon racial discrimination in particular is mandated not only by congressional enactments but also by the Thirteenth Amendment. We conclude that the government's compelling interest in eradicating discrimination is sufficient to justify the minimal burden imposed upon the college's free exercise of religious beliefs that results from the application of Title VII.

Moreover, we conclude that creating an exemption from the statutory enactment greater than that provided by Section 702 would seriously undermine the means chosen by Congress to combat discrimination and is not constitutionally required. If the environment in which [religious educational] institutions seek to achieve their religious and educational goals reflects unlawful discrimination, those discriminatory attitudes will be perpetuated with an influential segment of society, the detrimental effect of which cannot be estimated [626 F.2d at 488–89].

In *EEOC v. Southwestern Baptist Theological Seminary*, 651 F.2d 277 (5th Cir. 1981), *cert. denied*, 456 U.S. 905 (1982), the same court refined its *Mississippi College* analysis in the special context of religious seminaries. The defendant seminary is a nonprofit corporation owned, operated, supported, and controlled by the Southern Baptist Convention. This seminary offers degrees only in theology, religious education, and church music, and its purposes and character were described by the court as "wholly sectarian." The EEOC had asked the seminary to complete form EEO-6, a routine information report. When the seminary refused, the EEOC sued to compel compliance under 42 U.S.C. § 2000e-8(c), Title VII's record-keeping and reporting provision.

The court determined that the general principles set out in *Mississippi College* applied to this case but that the differing factual setting of this case required a result partly different from that in *Mississippi College*. In particular, the court held that "Title VII does not apply to the employment relationship between this seminary and its faculty." Reasoning that the Southwestern Baptist Seminary, unlike Mississippi College, was "entitled to the status of 'church'" and that its faculty "fit the definition of 'ministers,'" the court determined that Congress did not intend to include within

Title VII this ecclesiastical relationship, which is the special concern of the First Amendment. Using the same reasoning, the court also excluded from Title VII administrative positions that are "traditionally ecclesiastical or ministerial," citing as likely examples the "president and executive vice-president of the seminary, the chaplain, the dean of men and women, the academic deans, and those other personnel who equate to or supervise faculty." But the court refused to exclude other administrative and support staff from Title VII, even if the employees filling those positions are ordained ministers.

Having held "nonministerial" staff to be within Title VII, the court then considered whether the First Amendment would prohibit the EEOC from applying its reporting requirement to those employees. Again using the principles of *Mississippi College,* the court concluded that the First Amendment was not a bar and that the EEOC could require the seminary to provide the information requested in the EEO-6 form for its nonministerial employees. The court left open the question whether the First Amendment would prohibit the EEOC from obtaining further information on the seminary's nonministerial employees by use of the more intrusive investigatory subpoena, as was done in *Mississippi College.*

By attending at length to both statutory and constitutional issues, the opinions in the *Mississippi College* and *Southwestern Baptist Theological Seminary* cases clarify and validate Title VII's application to church-related colleges. The cases develop a balanced interpretation of the Section 702 exemption against the backdrop of First Amendment law. The exemption protects only employment decisions based on the religion of the applicant or employee. Once the college has shown that religion was the basis for its decision, the EEOC may not investigate further in search of evidence that religion was really a pretext for some other form of discrimination. Thus, according to this federal appellate court, in the narrow range covered by Section 702 the college is treated more favorably than in other Title VII contexts, where the EEOC may attempt to show pretext (see this volume, Section 3.3.2.1).

The U.S. Supreme Court appeared to afford even broader powers to a state civil rights agency, albeit in dicta, in *Dayton Christian Schools, Inc. v. Ohio Civil Rights Commission,* 766 F.2d 932 (6th Cir. 1985), *reversed,* 477 U.S. 619 (1986), a case brought under state civil rights law. A church-related school had discharged a pregnant teacher for filing a discrimination claim with the Ohio Civil Rights Commission (OCRC). The school asserted that a provision in its employment contract required teachers to adhere to the "Biblical chain of command" rather than taking disputes to external agencies. When the OCRC found probable cause to believe that sex discrimination had occurred and filed a complaint against the school for not responding to its conciliation agreement and consent order, the school filed a Section 1983 claim (see this volume, Section 2.3.3) to enjoin the pending administrative proceedings, claiming that OCRC review of its employment decisions violated both the Free Exercise Clause and the Establishment Clause of the First Amendment. Although the federal appeals court ruled that the First Amendment proscribes the application of Ohio's civil rights law to religious organizations, the U.S. Supreme Court reversed, stating that under *Younger v. Harris,* 401 U.S. 37 (1971), the lower courts should have abstained because state proceedings had been commenced and the school could raise its constitutional claims in that forum. The Court went on to say: "The Commission violates no constitutional rights by merely investigating the circumstances of Hoskinson's discharge in this case, if only to ascertain whether the ascribed religious-based reason was in fact the reason for the discharge" (477 U.S. at 628). Because the Court did not address fully the constitutional issues, the definitive answer to the struggle between nondiscrimination and the free exercise of religion by sectarian colleges has yet to be provided.

In most circumstances, however, the First Amendment does not appear to provide additional special treatment for the church-related college; Section 702 itself provides the full extent of protection the First Amendment requires. There is one exception recognized by the *Southwestern Baptist Theological Seminary* case: if the college is a seminary, the First Amendment may prohibit application of Title VII to "ministerial" employees and may limit the scope of the EEOC's investigation and enforcement activities regarding "nonministerial" employees. A second possible exception, not urged in either *Mississippi College* or *Southwestern Baptist Theological Seminary*, may be urged in other contexts: if an institution practices some form of discrimination prohibited by Title VII or other nondiscrimination laws, but can prove that its discrimination is based on religious belief, it may argue that the First Amendment protects such discrimination. The developing case law does not yet provide a definitive response to this argument. But the U.S. Supreme Court's opinion in the *Bob Jones* case (Section 7.3.1)—although addressing a tax benefit rather than a regulatory program such as Title VII—does suggest a general approach that courts may use in responding to the argument.

The ministerial exception has also been at issue in a claim brought under the Equal Pay Act (see Section 3.3.2.2). In *Dole v. Shenandoah Baptist Church*, 899 F.2d 1389 (4th Cir. 1991), a school run by the church had paid married male teachers a head-of-household salary supplement that it did not give to married female teachers. The court rejected the church's argument that the ministerial exemption should be applied to its teachers.

Several claims brought against religiously affiliated schools under the Age Discrimination in Employment Act (ADEA) (Section 3.3.2.6, this volume) have also met Establishment Clause defenses. In *DeMarco v. Holy Cross High School*, 797 F. Supp. 1142 (E.D.N.Y. 1992), *reversed*, 4 F.3d 166 (2d Cir. 1993), a federal appellate court reversed a trial judge's refusal to subject a Catholic high school to the ADEA. Although the plaintiff, a lay instructor, alleged that he was discharged because of his age, the school asserted that the discharge was based on the teacher's refusal to begin class with a prayer and on his failure to attend Mass with his students. Citing *NLRB v. Catholic Bishop* (Section 3.2.1) and asserting that "serious constitutional questions would be raised" if the school were required to defend its reason for discharging a lay instructor, the trial judge found no congressional intent to extend the ADEA to religious schools. The appellate court, however, held that the lower court had extended *Catholic Bishop* inappropriately, since an age discrimination claim requires a much more limited judicial inquiry than "the ongoing government supervision of all aspects of employment required under labor relations statutes like the NLRA" (4 F.3d at 169). In an age discrimination case, a court must consider not whether the decision maker's reason was "unwise or unreasonable" but whether the alleged reason for the discharge was the actual reason. Since these were factual issues, and not issues of religious doctrine, the Constitution was not implicated.

The court did, however, suggest that not all age discrimination claims would escape Establishment Clause concerns:

> There may be cases involving lay employees in which the relationship between employee and employer is so pervasively religious that it is impossible to engage in an age-discrimination inquiry without serious risk of offending the Establishment Clause. This is not such a case [4 F.3d at 172].

In conclusion, the court stated its belief that Congress intended religious organizations to be bound by the provisions of the ADEA.

7.2.7. Immigration laws. Many citizens of foreign countries come to the United States to study, teach, lecture, or do research at American higher education institutions. The conditions under which such foreign nationals may enter and remain in the United States are governed by a complex set of federal statutes codified in Title 8 of the *United States Code* and by regulations promulgated and administered primarily by the U.S. Department of State and the Immigration and Naturalization Service (INS) of the U.S. Department of Justice. The statutes and regulations establish numerous categories and subcategories for aliens entering the United States, with differing eligibility requirements and conditions of stay attaching to each.

Under the Immigration and Nationality Act and its various amendments (codified at 8 U.S.C. § 1101 et seq.), aliens may enter the United States either as immigrants or as nonimmigrants. Immigrants are admitted for permanent residence in the country (resident aliens). Nonimmigrants are admitted only for limited time periods to engage in narrowly defined types of activities (nonresident aliens). Eligibility for the immigrant class is subject to various numerical limitations and various priorities or preferences for certain categories of aliens (8 U.S.C. §§ 1151-1159). The nonimmigrant class is usually not limited numerically, but it is subdivided into eighteen specific categories (A through R), which define, and thus serve to limit, eligibility for nonimmigrant status. Of the two classes, the nonimmigrant is the greater source of problems for postsecondary institutions and is the focus for the remainder of this section.

Through a series of foreign policy crises—beginning with the Iranian crisis in 1979-80, when the federal government imposed new restrictions on foreign students from Iran—higher education institutions have been sensitized anew to immigration law's potential impact on the campuses. Aside from the need to adapt to such political crises, higher education institutions have a general interest in knowing the immigration status of each foreign national whom they enroll as a student, hire for a faculty or other position, or invite to the campus as a temporary guest, and in helping these foreign nationals adapt to this country and maintain their legal status for the term of their stay. (See generally D. Stewart, *Immigration and Education: The Crisis and the Opportunities* (Lexington Books, 1993).) In these situations administrators and counsel will need a sound grasp of the federal laws and regulations governing immigration. (See generally R. Hopper, "Immigration and Higher Education: Procedures and Strategies for Global Recruitment of Teachers and Scholars," *Immigration Briefings*, No. 93-9 (Sept. 1993).)

The immigration status of foreign students has been of increasing concern to higher education as the proportion of applicants and students from foreign countries has grown. In 1980 there were approximately 305,000 nonresident alien students on American campuses. Over the decade this figure grew steadily, reaching 397,000 nonresident alien students in 1990 (*Digest of Education Statistics* (U.S. National Center for Education Statistics, 1992), 174). (For further statistical data, see the Institute of

International Education's comprehensive annual census of foreign students, published under the title *Open Doors.*)

In recent years three new laws passed by Congress have extensively revised the Immigration and Nationality Act of 1952: the Immigration Reform and Control Act of 1986 (Pub. L. No. 99-603, 100 Stat. 3359 (1986)) (IRCA); the Immigration Act of 1990 (Pub. L. No. 101-649, 104 Stat. 4978 (1990)) (IMMACT '90); and the Miscellaneous and Technical Immigration and Naturalization Amendments of 1991 (Pub. L. No. 102-232, 105 Stat. 1733 (1991)) (MTINA). IRCA requires employers to verify that all individuals hired after November 6, 1982, are legally entitled to work in the United States. The law provides penalties for noncompliance and establishes an opportunity for all undocumented aliens who entered the United States before January 1, 1982, to apply for legalization without fear of deportation (8 U.S.C. §§ 1324a and 1324b). IRCA also includes important new protections against discrimination on the basis of alienage and national origin (see this volume, Section 3.3.3). The 1990 Act is the most comprehensive of the new laws. It amends the preference system for admission into the United States, revises the nonimmigrant categories, and repeals certain exclusions from admission. MTINA, as its name implies, further refines the changes made by the 1990 Act.

After the new legislation, nonimmigrant students continue to qualify for admission to the United States under one of three categories: "academic" student (8 U.S.C. § 1101(a)(15)(F)), "vocational" or "nonacademic" student (8 U.S.C. § 1101(a)(15)(M)), or "exchange visitor" (8 U.S.C. § 1101(a)(15)(J)).[7] In each category the statute provides that the "alien spouse and minor children" of the student may also qualify for admission "if accompanying him or following to join him."

The first of the three student categories is for aliens in the United States "temporarily and solely for the purpose of pursuing [a full] course of study at an established college, university, seminary, conservatory, . . . or other academic institution or in a language training program" (8 U.S.C. § 1101(a)(15)(F)(i)). The second category is for aliens in the United States "temporarily and solely for the purpose of pursuing a full course of study at an established vocational or other recognized nonacademic institution (other than a language training program)" (8 U.S.C. § 1101(a)(15)(M)(i)). The former category is called "F-1" and the included students are "F-1's"; the latter category is called "M-1" and the students are "M-1's." The spouses and children of these students are called "F-2's" and "M-2's," respectively. The third category, exchange visitor, is known as the "J" category. It includes any alien (and the family of any alien) "who is a bona fide student, scholar, trainee, teacher, professor, research assistant, specialist, or leader in a field of specialized knowledge or skill, or other person of similar description, who is coming temporarily to the United States as a participant in a program designated by the Director of the United States Information Agency, for the purpose of teaching, instructing or lecturing, studying,

---

[7]A fourth relevant category, for "trainees," is established by 8 U.S.C. § 1101(a)(15)(H)(iii). Regulations for this "H-3" category are at 7 C.F.R. § 214.2(h)(4) and 22 C.F.R. § 41.53(e). A fifth category into which some foreign students fall, the "G-4" category, was at issue in the *Elkins v. Moreno* litigation discussed in Section 4.3.5. This category, for employees of international treaty organizations and their immediate families, is established by 8 U.S.C. § 1101(a)(15)(G); long-term G-4's (in the country for more than sixteen years) may also become "N" visa holders (8 U.S.C. § 1101(a)(15)(N)). Pertinent regulations are in 8 C.F.R. § 214.2(g) and 22 C.F.R. § 41.21 et seq.

observing, conducting research, consulting, demonstrating special skills, or receiving training" (8 U.S.C. §1101(a)(15)(J)). Exchange visitors who will attend medical school, and the institutions they will attend, are subject to additional requirements under 8 U.S.C. §1182(j). Another provision of the statute, 8 U.S.C. §1182(e), establishes the conditions under which an alien who has been an exchange visitor may remain in or return to the United States, after returning to his or her country of nationality, for purposes of employment.[8]

The Department of State's role in regulating foreign students is shaped by its power to grant or deny visas to persons applying to enter the United States. Consular officials verify whether an applicant alien has met the requirements under one of the pertinent statutory categories and the corresponding requirements established by State Department regulations. The State Department's regulations for academic and nonacademic or vocational student visas are in 22 C.F.R. §41.61. Requirements for exchange visitor status are in 22 C.F.R. §41.62.

The Immigration and Naturalization Service has authority to approve the schools which foreign students may attend and for which they may obtain F-1 or M-1 visas from the State Department (8 C.F.R. §214.3). The INS is also responsible for ensuring that foreign students do not violate the conditions of their visas once they enter the United States. In particular, the INS must determine that holders of F-1 and M-1 student visas are making satisfactory progress toward the degree or other academic objective they are pursuing. The regulations under which the INS fulfills this responsibility are now located in 8 C.F.R. §214.2(f) for academic students and 8 C.F.R. §214.2(m) for vocational students. These regulations specify the periods of time for which foreign students may be admitted into the country and the circumstances that will constitute a "full course of study." In addition, the regulations establish the ground rules for on-campus employment of foreign students, off-campus employment (much more restricted than on-campus employment), transfers to another school, temporary absences from the country, and extensions of stay beyond the period of initial admission. Another regulation, 8 C.F.R. §248, establishes the ground rules for changing nonimmigrant status from a student category to a nonstudent category and vice versa. There are substantial differences in the regulatory provisions applicable to F-1 students and those applicable to M-1's.

A third federal government agency, the United States Information Agency, also has responsibilities regarding foreign students. It operates the exchange visitor program (see 22 C.F.R. §514.1 et seq.). This agency's regulations implementing the program are codified in 22 C.F.R. Part 514. Section 514.4(a) defines the status of "student" for purposes of these regulations. Sections 514.20 to 514.23 govern the roles of postsecondary institutions, professors, research scholars, trainees, and students that participate in exchange visitor programs.

In addition to its impact on enrollment of foreign students, immigration law also circumscribes the postsecondary institution's decisions on employing aliens in faculty or staff positions and inviting aliens to campus to lecture or otherwise par-

[8]The statute defines various categories of exchange visitors who must have returned to their homeland or last foreign residence, and been physically present there for at least two years after departing the United States, to be eligible for a visa or permanent residence. See Annot., "Foreign Residence Requirement for Educational (Exchange) Visitors Under §212(e) of Immigration and Nationality Act [8 U.S.C. §1182(e)]," 48 A.L.R. Fed. 509 (1991).

ticipate in campus life. Again, three nonimmigrant categories are particularly important: "exchange visitor" (8 U.S.C. §1101(a)(15)(J)), "temporary visitor" (8 U.S.C. §1101(a)(15)(B)), and "temporary worker" (8 U.S.C. §1101(a)(15)(H)). For the first and third, but not the second, of these categories, the statute also provides that the "alien spouse and minor children" of the alien may qualify for admission "if accompanying him or following to join him."

The first category, exchange visitor, is the "J" category already discussed with reference to students. The statutory definition, quoted above, is broad enough to include some types of employees as well. The second or "B" category is for aliens "visiting the United States temporarily for business or temporarily for pleasure," except those "coming for the purpose of study or of performing skilled or unskilled labor or as a representative of foreign press, radio, film, or other foreign information media coming to engage in such vocation" (8 U.S.C. §1101(a)(15)(B)). Visitors for business are B-1's, and visitors for pleasure are B-2's.

After IMMACT '90 and MTINA, the third, or "H," category includes three substantially revised subcategories of temporary alien workers: nurses, fashion models, and specialized workers (H-1's); other workers who will "perform temporary service or labor" when such services or labor are agricultural in nature or when "unemployed persons capable of performing such service or labor cannot be found in this country" (H-2's); and workers who will act as trainees (H-3's) (8 U.S.C. §1101(a)(15)(H)(i)–(iii)). For each subcategory the statute prescribes more limited rules for alien medical school graduates.

The Immigration Act of 1990 also created three new categories that are important to higher education institutions. The "O" visa is for nonimmigrant visitors who have extraordinary ability in the areas of arts, sciences, education, business, or athletics and are to be employed for a specific project or event such as an academic-year appointment or a lecture tour (8 U.S.C. §1101(a)(15)(O)). The "P" visa is for performing artists and (after 1991, when MTINA was enacted) athletes at an internationally recognized level of performance who seek to enter the United States as nonimmigrant visitors to perform, teach, or coach (8 U.S.C. §1101(a)(15)(P)). The "Q" visa is designated for international cultural exchange visitors "coming temporarily (for a period not to exceed fifteen months) to the United States as a participant in an international cultural exchange program approved by the Attorney General for the purpose of providing practical training, employment, and the sharing of the history, culture, and traditions of the country of the alien's nationality" (8 U.S.C. §1101(a)(15)(Q)).

The INS publishes a guide, entitled *Handbook for Employers* (INS Pub. No. M-274), that explains the law and regulations regarding visitors and foreign workers, and directs employers to the correct forms. See also R. Hopper, "College Hiring After the Immigration Act of 1990—Immigrant Employment Categories and Procedures," IHELG Monograph 91-9 (Institute for Higher Education Law and Governance, University of Houston, 1991).

The State Department and the INS have the same authority over these employment and visitor categories as they do over the foreign student categories. Pertinent State Department regulations are in 22 C.F.R. §41.31 (temporary visitors) and 22 C.F.R. §41.53 (temporary workers and trainees). Pertinent INS regulations are in 8 C.F.R. §214.2(b) (temporary visitors) and 8 C.F.R. §214.2(h) (temporary workers).

The U.S. Department of Labor issues "labor certifications" for aliens, indicating that their employment will not displace or adversely affect American workers (8

C.F.R. § 214.2(h)). Labor Department regulations on labor certification include "Labor Condition Applications and Requirements for Employers Using Aliens on H-1B Visas in Specialty Occupations and as Fashion Models" (Interim Final Rule, 58 Fed. Reg. 69226 (Dec. 31, 1993), to be codified at 20 C.F.R. § 655 and 29 C.F.R. § 507); "Attestations Filed by Employers Utilizing F-1 Students for Off-Campus Work" (29 C.F.R. § 508, with enforcement provisions located at 20 C.F.R. § 655); and "Temporary Employment of Aliens in the United States" under H-2 visas (20 C.F.R. § 655).

The federal government may exclude certain classes of aliens even though they fit within one of the immigrant or nonimmigrant categories. The Immigration Act of 1990 radically revised the classes of excludable aliens, most notably eliminating the exclusions based on publications, teachings, affiliations, and beliefs incompatible with our system of government. The exclusions based on sexual behavior and mental disabilities were also eliminated. The health, crime, and security-related grounds for exclusion were revised to reflect growing societal concerns such as AIDS, illicit drug use, and terrorist activities. The ideology-based exclusions were also amended. Although the statute still bars aliens who are members of communist or totalitarian parties, the attorney general may now grant exceptions when membership was involuntary or when membership was terminated a certain length of time prior to application for admission.

As amended by IMMACT '90, Section 1182 of Title 8 (8 U.S.C. § 1182) now codifies the classes of aliens subject to exclusion. Subsections (a)(1); (a)(3)(A), (C), and (D); and (a)(5)(B) have particular application to postsecondary education. Section 1182(a)(1) excludes certain aliens from admission into the United States on health-related grounds. Generally, an alien is inadmissible if his or her physical or mental health poses a threat to society or if he or she has a communicable disease of public health significance. In January 1991 the Department of Health and Human Services (HHS) proposed that infectious tuberculosis be the only disease on the list, thereby eliminating all sexually transmitted diseases (STDs), including acquired immune deficiency syndrome (AIDS) (Notice of Proposed Rulemaking, 56 Fed. Reg. 2486 (January 23, 1991)). After receiving over 40,000 comments about this notice, HHS stayed any changes to the list pending further review (Interim Final Rule, 58 Fed. Reg. 25000 (May 31, 1991)), thus leaving intact for the time being the list published at 42 C.F.R. § 34.2.

Section 1182(a)(3)(A) permits exclusion of aliens "who a consular officer or the Attorney General knows, or has reasonable ground to believe, seeks to enter the United States to engage solely, principally, or incidentally in . . . any unlawful activity." Section 1182(a)(5)(B) permits exclusion of an alien "who is a graduate of a medical school not accredited by a body or bodies approved for the purpose by the Secretary of Education and who is coming to the United States principally to perform services as a member of the medical profession." An exception exists, however, for graduate aliens who have passed parts I and II of the National Board of Medical Examiners Examination (or an equivalent approved by the U.S. secretary of health and human services) and have demonstrated competency in oral and written English. Section 1182(a)(3)(D) excludes aliens affiliated with a communist or totalitarian group unless the association was involuntary or has terminated (as discussed above). Section 1182(a)(3)(C) permits exclusion of aliens whom "the Secretary of State has reasonable ground to believe would have potentially serious adverse foreign policy consequences for the United States." There are, however, two important exceptions to this exclusion. One is for foreign officials (§ 1182(a)(3)(c)(ii)). The other is for aliens whose "past, current, or expected beliefs, statements, or associations" might otherwise raise foreign policy concerns but are "lawful within the United States" (§ 1182(a)(3)(c)(iii)). The second exception may be overridden "if the Secretary of State personally determines that the alien's admission would compromise a compelling United States foreign policy interest."

The ideology-based exclusions were the subject of a major U.S. Supreme Court case involving higher education. *Kleindienst v. Mandel,* 408 U.S. 753 (1976), concerned a Belgian citizen (Mandel) who was editor of a Belgian Left Socialist weekly and had authored a two-volume work entitled *Marxist Economic Theory.* In 1969 he applied for a nonimmigrant visa to enter the United States to give an address at Stanford University. When Mandel's planned visit became known, other higher education institutions invited him to address their groups. The theme of one conference was to be "Revolutionary Strategy in Imperialist Countries." The American Consulate in Brussels refused Mandel a visa because, among other reasons, his published views rendered him inadmissible under two provisions covering writings on communism and totalitarianism (8 U.S.C. §§ 1182(a)(28)(D) and 1182(a)(28)(G)(v), since repealed by IMMACT '90, as discussed above). Although the State Department subsequently did recommend that Mandel be admitted, the INS, acting on behalf of the attorney general, denied temporary admission. Mandel then brought suit along with eight other plaintiffs, all of whom were United States citizens and university professors in various social science fields. These plaintiffs asserted that their plans to participate with Mandel in various public forums had been disrupted by the visa denial. Thus, the plaintiffs argued, their First Amendment right to receive information had been abridged.

The Court held that Congress had plenary authority to enact legislation excluding aliens with certain political affiliations and beliefs; that the State Department and the attorney general's office acted within this authority in excluding Mandel; that Mandel, as an unadmitted and nonresident alien, had no constitutional right of entry to the United States, but that the remaining plaintiffs did possess First Amendment rights to receive information from Mandel; and that Congress's authority to exclude aliens and the Executive's discretion in exercising this authority prevailed over the First Amendment claims. Displaying extensive deference to congressional and Executive judgments regarding aliens, the Court stated:

> Plenary congressional power to make policies and rules for exclusion of aliens has long been firmly established. In the case of an alien excludable under Section 1182(a)(28), Congress has delegated conditional exercise of this power to the Executive. We hold that when the Executive exercises this power negatively on the basis of a facially legitimate and bona fide reason, the courts will neither look behind the exercise of that discretion, nor test it by balancing its justification against the First Amendment interests of those who seek personal communication with the applicant. What First Amendment or other grounds may be available for attacking exercise of discretion for which no justification whatsoever is advanced is a question we neither address [nor] decide in this case [408 U.S. at 769–70].

The *Mandel* case and other more recent controversies (see, for example, *Abourezk v. Reagan,* 785 F.2d 1043 (D.C. Cir. 1986), and J. Hook, "U.S. Denies Visas to

2 Marxist Cuban Professors Invited to Address Philosophy Meeting," *Chron. Higher Educ.,* Jan. 5, 1983, A8) underscore the practical impact of congressional power and Executive discretion to regulate the entry of foreign visitors. Administrators or faculty members who invite foreign scholars to their campuses or to their professional meetings should be sensitive to this power and discretion, under which the federal government may totally exclude certain scholars from visiting the United States or drastically curtail their activities when here. Administrators and faculty should also take careful note, however, of the new freedom-of-expression protections (8 U.S.C. § 1182(a)(3)(c)(iii)) created by IMMACT '90 that would now statutorily protect foreign scholars and journalists such as the plaintiff in *Kleindienst v. Mandel.*

Similarly, administrators should be aware that the federal government's treatment of visitors, as well as other foreign nationals within or seeking to enter the United States, may depend on contemporary trends in U.S. foreign policy. Two pieces of legislation in 1992 illustrate the use of immigration laws to effectuate current foreign policy goals. The Soviet Scientists Immigration Act of 1992 (Pub. L. No. 102-509, 106 Stat. 3316, codified at 8 U.S.C. § 1153) allows admission into the United States of highly specialized scientists of the independent states of the former Soviet Union and the Baltic States. Interim rules related to this law can be found at 58 Fed. Reg. 30699 (1993). The Chinese Student Protection Act of 1992 (Pub. L. No. 102-404, 106 Stat. 1969, codified at 8 U.S.C. § 1255), passed in response to the Tiananmen Square incident, allows Chinese nationals already admitted into this country to automatically adjust status under the immigration laws to lawful permanent resident status. Interim rules may be found at 58 Fed. Reg. 35832 (1993).

A case arising from the Iranian crisis also graphically illustrates the intertwining of foreign policy crises and immigration law. *Narenji v. Civiletti,* 617 F.2d 745 (D.C. Cir. 1979), arose as a challenge to presidential actions in the wake of the seizure of the United States Embassy in Iran. As part of the Executive's response to the crisis, the attorney general's office published a regulation governing nonimmigrant students from Iran residing in the United States. The regulation required all Iranian nonimmigrant postsecondary students to report to a local INS office or campus representative to "provide information as to residence and maintenance of nonimmigrant status" (617 F.2d at 746). Failure to comply with the regulation subjected the student to deportation proceedings. Iranian students challenged this regulation as both beyond the scope of the attorney general's authority and violative of the constitutional guarantee of equal protection. The trial court agreed in a lengthy opinion (481 F. Supp. 1132 (D.D.C. 1979)), but the U.S. Court of Appeals reversed, holding that the attorney general possessed statutory authority to act as he did. It also held that Congress and the Executive have broad discretion to draw distinctions on the basis of nationality when dealing with immigration matters, and courts will sustain these distinctions unless they are found to be totally irrational. Applying this "rational basis" test to the challenged regulation, the appellate court found that it was rationally related to the Executive's efforts to resolve the crisis generated by the embassy takeover.

As the foregoing discussion indicates, the immigration laws present a host of thorny problems for postsecondary administrators. Some of the questions that arise will be unforeseeable. Some will be dependent on the conduct of foreign affairs. Others will require detailed knowledge of the law's technicalities. Institutions that have been or expect to be confronted by a substantial number of immigration problems should consider having on staff an administrator or legal counsel (or both) knowledgeable about INS and State Department requirements and the paperwork necessary for handling this complex regulatory area.

7.2.8. Laws governing research on human subjects. Federal law regulates scientific and medical research, especially research on human subjects and genetic engineering. This body of law has been a focal point for the ongoing debate concerning the federal regulatory presence on the campuses. A number of interrelated policy issues have been implicated in the debate: the academic freedom of researchers, the burden and efficiency of federal "paperwork," the standards and methods for protecting safety and privacy of human subjects, and the interplay of legal and ethical standards.

Regulations on human subjects and related research are promulgated by various federal agencies. The Food and Drug Administration's regulations cover research on any product under its regulatory purview, whether or not that research is federally funded. Other federal agencies require that researchers receiving funds from their agencies follow certain guidelines with regard to the protection of human subjects. The regulations require institutions to set up review panels (institutional review boards, or IRBs) and to determine when informed consent must be obtained from the research subjects and what information must be provided to them.

The FDA regulations apply to clinical investigations regulated by the FDA under the Federal Food, Drug and Cosmetic Act (21 U.S.C. § 301 et seq.) and to clinical investigations that support applications for research or marketing permits regulated by the FDA. If an institution fails to comply with the FDA regulations, the agency may impose any of a number of sanctions. It may "(1) withhold approval of new studies . . . that are conducted at the institution" or reviewed by its institutional review board; "(2) direct that no new subjects be added to ongoing studies subject to [the FDA rules]; (3) terminate ongoing studies subject to [the FDA rules] where doing so would not endanger the subjects"; and "(4) when the apparent noncompliance creates a significant threat to the rights and welfare of human subjects," the agency may "notify the relevant State and Federal regulatory agencies and other parties with a direct interest" in the FDA's actions (21 C.F.R. § 56.120). If the institution's "IRB has refused or repeatedly failed to comply with" the FDA regulations and "the noncompliance adversely affects the rights or welfare of the subjects of a clinical investigation," the FDA commissioner may, when he deems it appropriate, disqualify the IRB or the parent institution from participation in FDA-governed research. Further, the FDA "will [refuse to] approve an application for a research permit for a clinical investigation that is to be under the review of a disqualified IRB or that is to be conducted at a disqualified institution, and it may refuse to consider in support of a marketing permit the data from a clinical investigation that was reviewed by a disqualified IRB [or] conducted at a disqualified institution" (21 C.F.R. § 56.121(d)). The commissioner may reinstate a disqualified IRB or institution upon its submission of a written plan for corrective action and adequate assurances that it will comply with FDA regulations (21 C.F.R. § 56.123).

The Department of Health and Human Services and several other federal agencies have issued common final rules regarding the protection of human subjects ("Federal Policy for the Protection of Human Subjects," 56 Fed. Reg. 28003 (June 18, 1991)), but each agency has retained control over the enforcement of these regulations for its own grantees. The FDA did not adopt the "Federal Policy," given its broader mandate to regulate all research involving human subjects.

The following federal agencies have adopted the joint final rules:

Department of Agriculture (7 C.F.R. Part 1c)
Department of Energy (10 C.F.R. Part 745)
National Aeronautics and Space Administration (14 C.F.R. Part 1230)
Department of Commerce (15 C.F.R. Part 27)
Consumer Product Safety Commission (16 C.F.R. Part 1028)
International Development Cooperation Agency, Agency for International Development (22 C.F.R. Part 225)
Department of Housing and Urban Development (24 C.F.R. Part 60)
Department of Justice (28 C.F.R. Part 46)
Department of Defense (32 C.F.R. Part 219)
Department of Education (34 C.F.R. Part 97)
Department of Veterans Affairs (38 C.F.R. Part 16)
Environmental Protection Agency (40 C.F.R. Part 26)
Department of Health and Human Services (45 C.F.R. Part 46)
National Science Foundation (45 C.F.R. Part 690)
Department of Transportation (49 C.F.R. Part 11)

Subsections of each agency's regulations are numbered identically for each provision (for example, the "Definitions" section under Department of Health and Human Services regulations is 45 C.F.R. § 46.102, and the same section under Department of Housing and Urban Development regulations is 24 C.F.R. § 60.102).

The joint regulations represent, in large part, a revised version of the Department of Health and Human Services (HHS) regulations governing research conducted on human subjects. The regulations, except for specifically enumerated exemptions set out below (or authorized by a department or agency head and published in the *Federal Register*), apply to all research involving human subjects conducted by these agencies or research funded in whole or part by a grant, contract, cooperative agreement, or fellowship from one of these agencies. Under Section __.103(b)[9] of the regulations, "Departments or agencies will conduct or support research covered by this policy only if the institution has an assurance approved as provided in this section, and only if the institution has certified to the department or agency head that the research has been reviewed and approved by an IRB [institutional review board] provided for in the assurance, and will be subject to continuing review by the IRB." The joint regulations do not provide elaborate sanctions for noncompliance, as do other agency regulations, but only general provisions on fund termination (§ __.122 and __.123).

[9]As noted in the previous paragraph, regulations pertaining to human subjects are identical for fifteen agencies. In this discussion of various subsections of the joint regulations, the chapter of the *Code of Federal Regulations* would correspond to the agency that provided the research funds, but the section number for each agency's human subjects regulations is identical. For the Department of Agriculture, for example, the section noted here would read "7 C.F.R. § 1c.103(b)."

As noted above, both the FDA and the joint federal agency regulations specify that an IRB must review research proposals involving the use of human subjects before the research is conducted. IRBs are fairly recent phenomena; until the early 1960s, only a small minority of research facilities had such committees. "In 1966, the Public Health Service (PHS) initiated the requirement that a committee of the investigator's 'institutional associates' review proposals for research involving human subjects as a condition for the receipt of a PHS grant." Following PHS's lead, other federal agencies began to require IRB monitoring of human subject research (See B. DuVal, "The Human Subjects Protection Committee: An Experiment in Decentralized Regulation," 1979 *American Bar Foundation Research J.* 571, especially 573–74 n.1). As now conceived by the federal agencies, the IRB is designed to ameliorate the tension that exists between institutional autonomy and federal supervision of research. Under these regulations the IRB must have at least five members with backgrounds sufficiently varied to supervise completely the common research activities conducted by the particular institution. Since the IRB must "ascertain the acceptability of proposed research in terms of institutional commitments and regulations, applicable law, and standards of professional conduct and practice" (§ __.107), the IRB must include members knowledgeable in these areas. No IRB may consist entirely of members of the same sex or the same profession. The IRB must also include at least one member whose primary expertise is nonscientific, such as an attorney, an ethicist, or a member of the clergy. Each IRB must have "at least one member who is not otherwise affiliated with the institution" and who is not a member of a family immediately affiliated with the institution (§ __.107).

The IRB has the duty, under the regulations, "to approve, require modifications in (to secure approval), or to disapprove" all research conducted under the regulations (§ __.109(a)). The IRB must also monitor the information provided subjects to ensure informed consent (§ __.109(b)). In addition, the IRB must conduct follow-up reviews of research it has approved "at intervals appropriate to the degree of risk, but not less than once per year" (§ __.109(e)). The institution may also review research already approved by an IRB and may either approve or disapprove such research, but an institution may not approve research disapproved by the IRB (§ __.112). If research is being conducted in violation of IRB requirements or if subjects have been seriously and unexpectedly harmed, the IRB may suspend or terminate the research (sec. __.113). The FDA regulations governing IRB responsibilities and functions are similar to the joint regulations on these points (see 21 C.F.R. §§ 56.108–56.112).

Informed consent, a doctrine arising from the law of torts, concerns the information that must be provided about the research to the human subject. The regulations are fairly typical in what they establish as the basic elements of informed consent:

(1) A statement that the study involves research, an explanation of the purposes of the research and the expected duration of the subject's participation, a description of the procedures to be followed, and identification of any procedures which are experimental;

(2) A description of any reasonably foreseeable risks or discomforts to the subject;

    (3) A description of any benefits to the subject or to others which may reasonably be expected from the research;

    (4) A disclosure of appropriate alternative procedures or courses of treatment, if any, that might be advantageous to the subject;

    (5) A statement describing the extent, if any, to which confidentiality of records identifying the subject will be maintained;

    (6) For research involving more than minimal risk, an explanation as to whether any compensation [will be given] and an explanation as to whether any medical treatments are available if injury occurs and, if so, what they consist of, or where further information may be obtained;

    (7) An explanation of whom to contact for answers to pertinent questions about the research and research subjects' rights, and whom to contact in the event of a research-related injury to the subject; and

    (8) A statement that participation is voluntary, refusal to participate will involve no penalty or loss of benefits to which the subject is otherwise entitled, and the subject may discontinue participation at any time without penalty or loss of benefits to which the subject is otherwise entitled [§__.116(a)(1)–(8)].

The regulations also require that, in "appropriate" circumstances (a concept the regulations do not define), additional elements of informed consent must be met, as outlined in §__.116(b)(1)-(6). The FDA regulations contain the same informed-consent requirements (21 C.F.R. §50.25(a) and (b)).

    The joint regulations also contain requirements for documenting informed consent. Unlike their FDA counterparts, the joint regulations set out several circumstances in which the IRB may either alter the elements of informed consent or waive the informed-consent requirement (see §__.116(c)(1) and (2) and compare 21 C.F.R. §50.25).

    The joint regulations contain several broad exemptions for specific areas of research (§__.101(b)(1)-(5)). The department or agency head has final authority to determine whether a particular activity is covered by the joint regulations (§__.101(c)). The department or agency head may also "require that specific research activities . . . conducted by [the department or agency], but not otherwise covered by this policy, comply with some or all of the requirements of this policy" (§__.101 (d)). And the department or agency head may "waive the applicability of this policy to specific research activities otherwise covered by this policy" (§__.101(i)).

    The Department of Health and Human Services has also issued several sets of more narrowly focused regulations. Final HHS regulations on research involving fetuses, pregnant women, and in vitro fertilization are codified in 45 C.F.R. §46.201 et seq. Final HHS regulations governing the protection of prisoner subjects of biomedical and behavioral research are codified in 45 C.F.R. §46.301 et seq. Final HHS regulations governing the use of children as research subjects are codified at 45 C.F.R. §46.401 et seq.

    Federally funded research using recombinant DNA is regulated differently from other federally funded research. Research projects are proposed to the NIH Recombinant DNA Advisory Committee. This committee recommends either approval or rejection, and the proposed action is published in the *Federal Register*. NIH "Guidelines on Recombinant DNA" (51 Fed. Reg. 16958) are revised several times a year, focusing on how such research may be conducted. Because of the volatility of this regulatory area, the only safe prediction is that frequent and substantial change can be expected, and that expert assistance is advisable.

Another research area subject to special regulation is the use of fetal tissue. Prior to 1973 there was no federal regulation of the use of fetal tissue in federally funded experiments or medical procedures. After a federal commission recomended that certain types of research on live fetuses were permissible if the IRB approved, the mother consented, and the father did not object, federal regulations were developed to regulate such research (45 C.F.R. §§ 46.201-46.211 (1988)). Regulations governing the use of tissue from dead fetuses in federally funded research were developed by the National Institutes of Health and are codified at 45 C.F.R. § 46.203(f) (1988), including a definition of "dead." The regulations indicate that the states will determine how fetal research and organ donations may be conducted. But some state laws forbidding the use of fetal tissue in research have been declared unconstitutional (see A. B. Bauer, "Bioethical and Legal Issues in Fetal Organ and Tissue Transplants," 26 *Houston L. Rev.* 955 (1989)).

In 1988 the assistant secretary for health placed a moratorium on federally funded fetal tissue research, believing that the use of fetuses in research or medical treatment encourages abortions. The ban halted the use of fetal tissue in the treatment of Parkinson's disease, and the NIH's Standing Advisory Committee recommended that it be lifted. However, it remained in effect for several years. In 1991 the U.S. House of Representatives voted to lift the ban as part of its reauthorization of the National Institutes of Health. In April of 1992, the U.S. Senate voted 87 to 10 to lift the ban as well. However, President Bush vetoed the legislation, and the House was unable to override the veto. The issue now appears to be resolved, since President Clinton signed an executive order ending the ban in January of 1993.

As reflected in the various regulatory actions discussed above, the law of human subject research is complex and rapidly evolving. The impact of this law on individual campuses will vary considerably, depending on their own research programs. Postsecondary administrators responsible for research will want to stay abreast of their institution's research emphases and issues of concern. In consultation with counsel, administrators should also keep abreast of changes in federal regulations and engage in a continuing process of extracting from the various sets of regulations the particular legal requirements applicable to their institution's research programs. Given the recent growth and volatility of legal developments and the sensitivity of some current areas of research emphasis, institutions that do not have a particular office or committee to oversee research may wish to reconsider their organizational structure.

7.2.9. Laws governing animal research. Although all states have statutes forbidding cruelty to animals, and antivivisection movements have been active in certain states for over a century, federal legislation to protect animals was not enacted until 1966. Recent activity by both scholars and animal rights activists has focused government, press, and scholarly attention on the issue of using animals in scientific research. Entire scholarly journals (for example, the *International Journal of the Study of Animal Problems*, founded in 1979) are devoted to this issue.

The Animal Welfare Act (AWA) (7 U.S.C. § 2131 et seq.) governs the treatment of animals used for research (whether or not it is federally funded) in or substantially affecting interstate or foreign commerce. The law "insure[s] that animals intended for use in research facilities or for exhibition purposes or for use as pets are provided humane care and treatment." Amended in 1970, 1976, and 1985, the law covers "any live or dead dog, cat, or monkey, guinea pig, hamster, or such warm-blooded animal as the Secretary may determine is being used, or is intended for use, for research, testing, experimentation, or exhibition purposes, or as a pet" (§2132(g)). Although the regulations promulgated under this law did not originally include rats, mice, and birds, a federal judge ruled that the exclusion of these animals was arbitrary and capricious (*Animal Legal Defense Fund v. Madigan*, 781 F. Supp. 797 (D.D.C. 1992)). A federal appellate court overturned this ruling on procedural grounds (23 F.3d 496 (D.C. Cir. 1994)).

The AWA is enforced by the Animal and Plant Health Inspection Service of the U.S. Department of Agriculture (whose regulations are codified at 9 C.F.R. ch. 1, subch. A, Parts 1, 2, and 3). The regulations, amended and substantially strengthened in 1991, require an institution, whether or not it receives federal funds, to appoint an Institutional Animal Care and Use Committee (IACUC), which operates in a manner similar to the IRBs that are used to review the use of human subjects in research. The IACUC must include at least one doctor of veterinary medicine, at least one member who is not affiliated (and who has no family members affiliated) with the institution, and no more than three members from the same administrative unit. The regulations are silent on whether, or how, a member of the IACUC may be removed.

The IACUC is required to "(1) Review, once every six months, the research facility's program for humane care and use of animals. . . . (2) Inspect, at least once every six months, all of the research facility's animal facilities, including animal study areas. . . . (3) Prepare reports of its evaluations conducted as required by paragraphs (1) and (2) of this section, and submit the reports to the Institutional Official of the research facility." The IACUC must also investigate public or employee complaints regarding the care and use of animals; it must review and approve, require modifications in, or withhold approval of proposed changes in the use or care of animals; and it may also suspend activity involving animals (9 C.F.R. §2.31(c)).

In order to conduct research using animals or to modify an approved research proposal, the researcher must submit the following information to the IACUC:

(1) Identification of the species and the approximate number of animals to be used;
(2) A rationale for involving animals, and for the appropriateness of the species and numbers of animals to be used;
(3) A complete description of the proposed use of the animals;
(4) A description of procedures designed to assure that discomfort and pain to animals will be limited to that which is unavoidable for the conduct of scientifically valuable research, including provision for the use of analgesic, anesthetic, and tranquilizing drugs where indicated and appropriate to minimize discomfort and pain to animals; and
(5) A description of any euthanasia method to be used [9 C.F.R. §2.31(e)].

In addition to the elements required to be present in the proposal, the regulations charge the IACUC with the responsibility of determining whether a research project meets the following requirements:

   (i) Procedures involving animals will avoid or minimize discomfort, distress,
       and pain to the animals;
  (ii) The principal investigator has considered alternatives to procedures that
       may cause more than momentary or slight pain or distress to the animals,
       and has provided a written narrative description of the methods and sources
       . . . used to determine that alternatives were not available;
 (iii) The principal investigator has provided written assurance that the activities
       do not unnecessarily duplicate previous experiments;
 (iv) Procedures that may cause more than momentary or slight pain or distress
       to the animals will:
       (A) Be performed with appropriate sedatives, analgesics or anesthetics, un-
           less withholding such agents is justified for scientific reasons, in writ-
           ing, by the principal investigator and will continue for only the
           necessary period of time;
       (B) Involve, in their planning, consultation with the attending veterinar-
           ian or his or her designee;
       (C) Not include the use of paralytics without anesthesia;
   (v) Animals that would otherwise experience severe or chronic pain or distress
       that cannot be relieved will be painlessly euthanized . . . ;
 (vi) The animal's living conditions will be appropriate to their species . . . and
       contribute to their health and comfort . . . ;
(vii) Medical care for animals will be available and provided as necessary by a
       qualified veterinarian;
(viii) Personnel conducting procedures on the species being maintained or stud-
       ied will be appropriately qualified and trained [9 C.F.R. § 2.31(d)].

The regulations also specify the procedures to be used if surgery is performed.

   The training of laboratory personnel is detailed in the regulations, as well as
the responsibilities of the attending veterinarian and record-keeping requirements.
The regulations further detail how handling, housing, exercise, transportation, and
socialization of the animals should be carried out. Institutions must develop written
plans for providing exercise for dogs and improving the psychological well-being of
primates (9 C.F.R. ch. 1, subch. A, Part 3). Penalties for violating the AWA include
civil and criminal sanctions, civil money penalties, imprisonment for not more than
one year, and/or a fine of $2,500 or less. Termination of federal funds, if relevant, is
also provided for.

   The Agriculture Department's regulations have been criticized by animal
rights activists as providing insufficient protection for laboratory animals and as
contrary to congressional intent. In early 1993 a federal trial judge agreed, ruling that
the regulations implementing the 1985 Animal Welfare Act were too lax and gave too
much authority to colleges and universities to regulate researchers' use and treatment
of animals (*Animal Legal Defense Fund v. Madigan*, 781 F. Supp. 797 (D.D.C. 1992),
vacated and remanded sub nom Animal Legal Defense Fund v. Espy, 23 F.3d 496 (D.C.
Cir. 1994)). This ruling was overturned in May 1994 because the appellate court ruled
that the Fund did not have the legal right to sue the government.

   The Public Health Service (PHS) policy governing the use and treatment of
animals in federally funded research has provisions similar to many of those in the
AWA. The PHS policy covers all vertebrates, including rats and mice, and requires
institutions to follow the guidelines in the NIH *Guide for the Care and Use of
Laboratory Animals* (1986). These guidelines require attention to the animal's com-

fort and consideration of the relevance of the experimental procedures to "human or animal health, the advancement of knowledge, or the good of society" ("U.S. Government Principles for the Utilization and Care of Vertebrate Animals Used in Testing, Research, and Training," in NIH *Guide,* at 38). A scholar of the animal rights and regulatory issues characterizes the present situation as a "thicket of unresolved issues" that undoubtedly will engender litigation and the scrutiny of federal funding agencies (R. Dresser, "Assessing Harm and Justification in Animal Research: Federal Policy Opens the Laboratory Door," 40 *Rutgers L. Rev.* 723 (1988)).

Animal rights activists have had little success in using the AWA to challenge the use or treatment of animals at particular research locations. For example, a federal appellate court held that the AWA does not provide a private right of action for individuals or organizations, nor does it authorize the court to name them guardians of certain animals taken from a medical research institute (*International Primate Protection League v. Institute for Behavioral Research, Inc.,* 799 F.2d 934 (4th Cir. 1988)). In *People for the Ethical Treatment of Animals (PETA) v. Institutional Animal Care and Use Committee,* (817 P.2d 1299 (Or. 1991), the Oregon Supreme Court ruled that the animal rights group lacked standing to seek judicial review of an IACUC's approval of a University of Oregon professor's research proposal involving the auditory systems of barn owls. The court said that the public's interest in the treatment of animals was represented by the IACUC, and that the plaintiffs had no personal stake in the outcome of the litigation.

Animal rights groups have also used state open-meetings laws (see Section 6.5.1) to seek access to the deliberations of IACUCs. In *Medlock v. Board of Trustees of the University of Massachusetts,* 580 N.E.2d 387 (Mass. App. Ct. 1991), plaintiffs argued that Massachusetts' open-meetings law required the IACUC to hold public meetings. The court ruled that the state law applied only to the university's board of trustees and that the IACUC did not "consider or discuss public policy matters in order to arrive at a decision on any public business" (580 N.E.2d at 392). A similar result, with different reasoning, occurred in *In re American Society for the Prevention of Cruelty to Animals, et al. v. Board of Trustees of the State University of New York,* 582 N.Y.S.2d 983 (N.Y. 1992), where the state's highest court ruled that the powers of the IACUC derived solely from federal law and thus that the committee was not a "public body" for purposes of New York's open-meetings law. But the Supreme Court of Vermont determined, in *Animal Legal Defense Fund v. Institutional Animal Care and Use Committee of the University of Vermont,* 616 A.2d 224 (Vt. 1992), that the university's IACUC was a public body under the state's open-meetings law, and was also subject to the state's Public Records Act. For an overview of the state of the law on access to IACUCs by an advocate of public access, see G. Francione, "Access to Animal Care Committees," 43 *Rutgers L. Rev.* 1 (1990).

Participants in the animal rights movement are attempting to secure more legislation that would further restrict the use of animals for research. The activists are seeking legislation to grant animal rights groups third-party standing to enforce the Animal Welfare Act. They also have sought to prohibit the pharmaceutical and cosmetics industries from using certain tests on animals, and they have lobbied for legislation that would place additional obligations on federal research proposals involving the use of animals.

Some laboratories that use animals and related research facilities have sustained damage, allegedly at the hands of animal rights activists. In 1992 Congress passed legislation that made destruction of or serious damage to animal research facilities a federal crime. The Animal Enterprise Protection Act of 1992 (Pub. L. No. 102-346, 106 Stat. 928) amends Title 18 of the *United States Code* by adding Section 43, directed at persons who cross state lines to disrupt or inflict serious damage on an animal enterprise. "Animal enterprise" is defined as a "commercial or academic enterprise that uses animals for food or fiber production, agriculture, research, or testing." "Serious damage" is defined as stealing, damaging, or causing property loss exceeding $10,000; causing serious bodily injury to another individual; or causing an individual's death. Penalties include fines, imprisonment, or both, and restitution is required.

7.2.10. Copyright laws

7.2.10.1. Overview. The basis for all copyright law is Article I, Section 8, Clause 8 of the U.S. Constitution, which authorizes Congress "to promote the progress of science and useful arts, by securing for limited times to authors and inventors the exclusive right to their respective writings and discoveries." In 1976, after many years of effort inside and outside government, Congress revised the federal copyright law. Effective as of January 1, 1978, the General Revision of the Copyright Law (17 U.S.C. § 101 et seq.) has particular relevance to educational institutions, because it specifies what kinds of copying of copyrighted materials may be done for teaching and scholarship. This question, previously governed by the judicially created "fair use" doctrine, is now governed by the codification of that doctrine in Section 107 of the Act. Another section that is particularly important to educational institutions, Section 108, deals with copying by libraries and archives. And a third pertinent section, Section 117 (added in 1980; 94 Stat. 3028), deals with copying of computer programs.

In 1990 Congress passed the Copyright Remedy Clarification Act (Pub. L. No. 101-553, 104 Stat. 2749), which allows copyright holders to collect damages from public colleges and universities. Prior to the amendment, several federal appellate courts had ruled that the Eleventh Amendment prohibited the application of the Copyright Act's damages provisions to state agencies.[10]

Another series of amendments to the copyright law also occurred in 1990. These amendments (the Visual Artists Rights Act of 1990 (104 Stat. 5128), the Architectural Works Copyright Protection Act of 1990 (104 Stat. 5133), and the Computer Software Rental Amendments Act of 1990 (104 Stat. 5134)) are part of the Judicial Improvements Act (Pub. L. No. 101-650). These Acts extend copyright protection to a wider array of works than were previously protected. The Visual Artists Rights Act amends Section 101 of 17 U.S.C. by adding visual art productions to the list of objects that receive copyright protection; it also lists objects excluded from the category of protected "visual arts." This law took effect on June 1, 1990. The Architectural Works Copyright Protection Act of 1990 adds architectural works as a category of protection under Section 101 of Title 17; it took effect on December 1, 1990. The Computer Software Rental Amendments Act of 1990 amends Section 109(b) of Title 17, and

---

[10]The implications of the amendment are discussed in R. Burgoyne, "The Copyright Remedy Clarification Act of 1990: State Educational Institutions Now Face Significant Monetary Exposure for Copyright Infringement," 18 *J. Coll. & Univ. Law* 367 (1992).

prohibits the owner of a record, tape, or software program from lending, selling, or renting these for direct or indirect commercial advantage; this law also took effect on December 1, 1990.

7.2.10.2. The fair use doctrine. Section 107 of the Act states that "the fair use of a copyrighted work . . . for purposes such as criticism, comment, news reporting, teaching (including multiple copies for classroom use), scholarship, or research is not an infringement of copyright." The section lists four factors that one must consider in determining whether a particular "use" is "fair": "(1) the purpose and character of the use, including whether such use is of a commercial nature or is for nonprofit educational purposes; (2) the nature of the copyrighted work; (3) the amount and substantiality of the portion used in relation to the copyrighted work as a whole; and (4) the effect of the use upon the potential market for or value of the copyrighted work."

Application of these rather vague standards to individual cases is left to the courts. Some guidance on their meaning may be found, however, in a document included in the legislative history of the revised Copyright Act: the "Agreement on Guidelines for Classroom Copying in Not-for-Profit Educational Institutions" (in H.R. Rep. No. 94-1476, 94th Cong., 2d Sess. (1976)). A second document in the legislative history, the "Guidelines for the Proviso of Subsection 108(g)(2)" (Conf. Rep. No. 94-1733, 94th Cong., 2d Sess. (1976)), provides comparable guidance on the provision within Section 108 dealing with copying for purposes of interlibrary loans. The "Guidelines for Classroom Copying" were adopted by thirty-eight educational organizations and the publishing industry to set minimum standards of educational fair use under Section 107 of the Act. Guidelines are established for "Single Copying for Teaching" (for example, a chapter from a book may be copied for the individual teacher's use in scholarly research, class preparation, or teaching) as well as for "Multiple Copies for Classroom Use" (for example, one copy per pupil in one course may be made, provided that the copying meets several tests; these tests, set out in the House Report, concern the brevity of the excerpt to be copied, the spontaneity of the use, and the cumulative effect of multiple copying in classes within the institution).

The guidelines were cited by a federal appeals court in *Marcus v. Rowley,* 695 F.2d 1171 (9th Cir. 1983). The case involved a public school teacher who reproduced approximately half of a copyrighted booklet and included it in course materials she distributed to her students at no charge. The court ruled that the teacher's use of the copyrighted material did not constitute fair use. The opinion emphasizes that a person need not have sold or profited from copying in order to violate the Copyright Act: "The first factor to be considered in determining the applicability of the doctrine of fair use is the purpose and character of the use, and specifically whether the use is of a commercial nature or is for a nonprofit educational purpose. . . . Nevertheless, a finding of a nonprofit educational purpose does not automatically compel a finding of fair use."

In another copyright case, *Addison-Wesley Publishing Co. v. New York University,* filed in December 1982 in federal district court (Civil Action No. 82 Civ. 8333, S.D.N.Y.), the Association of American Publishers coordinated a suit on behalf of nine publishing companies against NYU, nine of its faculty members, and a photocopying shop near the campus. The plaintiffs' complaint listed thirteen instances of alleged unlawful photocopying and sought a permanent injunction against further unlawful copying and an award of damages for the copyright owners. The suit was reportedly the first of its kind involving a university and its faculty members.

In April 1983 the parties reached an out-of-court settlement of the case. In return for the plaintiffs' withdrawal of their claims, NYU agreed to adopt and implement a copyright policy corresponding to the "Guidelines for Classroom Copying," publish its policy in the faculty handbook and publicize it to the faculty periodically by other means, post notices about its copyright policy at all campus copying facilities, and investigate alleged incidents of copyright violation and take appropriate action against faculty members "consistent with remedial and disciplinary actions taken in respect of violations of other university policies." The full texts of the settlement and of the NYU photocopying policy were published in 13 *Coll. Law Dig.* 258, printed in *West's Educ. Law Rptr.*, June 2, 1983 (Special NACUA Pamphlet). (See also D. Edwards, "University of North Carolina Copyright Guidelines on Photocopying," 14 *Coll. Law Dig.* 121, printed in *West's Educ. Law Rptr.*, Jan. 12, 1984 (Special NACUA Pamphlet), which critiques the NYU settlement and provides guidelines to help faculty and staff comply with the copyright law.)

The first higher education copyright case resulting in a judicial opinion is *Basic Books v. Kinko's Graphics Corp.*, 758 F. Supp. 1522 (S.D.N.Y. 1991). A group of publishers brought a copyright infringement action against a chain of copying shops for copying excerpts from their books without permission, compiling those excerpts into packets, and selling them to college students. Kinko's argued that its actions fit within the "fair use" doctrine of Section 107 of the Copyright Act. The trial judge wrote:

> The search for a coherent, predictable interpretation applicable to all cases remains elusive. This is so particularly because any common law interpretation proceeds on a case-by-case basis [758 F. Supp at 1530].

Using the four factors in the statute, as well as the "Agreement on Guidelines" promulgated as part of the NYU settlement, the court ruled that (1) Kinko's was merely repackaging the material for its own commercial purposes; (2) the material in the books was factual (which would suggest a lower level of protection under the fair use doctrine); (3) Kinko's had copied a substantial proportion of the work, and whether the book was out of print or not was irrelevant because copyright fees are the only "profits" available to the publisher once the book is unavailable. The court also found that even one chapter is a "substantial" portion if that chapter is meant to stand alone; and (4) Kinko's copying reduced the market for textbooks. Furthermore, the court ruled that, for an entire compilation to avoid violating the Act, *each* item in the compilation must pass the fair use test. The judge awarded the plaintiffs $510,000 in statutory damages plus legal fees. Kinko's decided not to appeal the decision, and settled the case in October 1991 for $1.875 million in combined damages and legal fees.

The Association of American Publishers "has mapped out a long-range program to monitor and seek compliance with the copyright law" ("Publishers Welcome Agreement Ending Kinko's Suit," reprinted in 22 *Coll. Law Dig.* 74 (Nov. 7, 1991). Given the potential cost of such litigation, seeking permission to copy or use copyrighted material is imperative. Individuals seeking permission may find useful the AAP's publication "How to Request Copyright Permissions" (reprinted in 22 *Coll.*

Law Dig. 75 (Nov. 7, 1991)), as well as "Use of Photocopied Anthologies for Courses Snarled by Delays and Costs of Copyright-Permission Process," *Chron. Higher Educ.*, Sept. 11, 1991, A19. The latter article describes the Copyright Clearance Center that will, for a modest fee, handle copyright requests for over 250 publishers.

The existence of the Copyright Clearance Center may make it difficult for defendants in copyright infringement cases to argue that making copies without paying a royalty was justified. In *American Geophysical Union v. Texaco, Inc.*, 802 F. Supp. 1 (S.D.N.Y. 1992), a federal trial judge found that Texaco had infringed the copyrights of several scientific journals by making multiple copies of scientific articles for its scientists and researchers to keep in their files. The judge noted that Texaco could have obtained a license that permits unlimited copying of the journals affiliated with the Copyright Clearance Center, and found that Texaco's actions violated three elements of the fair use test.

Copyright laws also apply to the authors of published works. Unless authors specifically retain the copyright, they must seek permission from the copyright holder (usually the publisher) to reproduce their own material. For a discussion of the fair use doctrine in the higher education context, see R. Kasunic, "Fair Use and the Educator's Right to Photocopy Copyrighted Material for Classroom Use," 19 *J. Coll. & Univ. Law* 271 (1993).

7.2.10.3. Use of unpublished material. The copyright laws cover unpublished as well as published material, a fact that many faculty (and administrators) are unaware of. And although the unauthorized use of unpublished material would ordinarily result in liability for the researcher rather than the institution, the college or university could face liability if the research were funded by an external grant made to the institution or if the faculty member argued that the institution shared liability for some other reason.

In a pair of cases, a federal appeals court ruled that unpublished material enjoys the same protection as published material and that the fair use doctrine applies to both types of material. In *New Era Publications International v. Henry Holt and Co.*, 873 F.2d 576 (2d Cir. 1989), the publishing company that owns the rights to the unpublished papers of L. Ron Hubbard, who founded the Church of Scientology, sued Henry Holt and Company, which was about to publish *Bare-Faced Messiah*, Russell Miller's biography of Hubbard. Miller had quoted from Hubbard's unpublished writings, and New Era alleged that doing so without its permission violated the Act. Although the court refused to stop publication of the book, the majority ruled that the Act had been infringed. The opinion says that the fair use doctrine bars virtually all use of unpublished sources without permission of the copyright holder.

Two years earlier, judges in the same circuit upheld a trial judge's ruling that Random House not publish a biography of J. D. Salinger until the author, Ian Hamilton, had removed all quotations from Salinger's unpublished letters (*Salinger v. Random House*, 811 F.2d 90 (2d Cir. 1987)). Hamilton had quoted from letters to Salinger's correspondents, which they had placed in university archives.

Legal scholars, including one of the Second Circuit judges, have criticized this pair of decisions, saying that privacy law provides an appropriate remedy if the authors of unpublished materials object to their publication, and that copyright law was not designed to protect material not intended for publication. Congress reacted to these cases by passing the Copyright Amendments Act in late 1992 (Pub. L. No. 102-492, 106 Stat. 3145). The law amends Section 107 of Title 17 (the fair use doctrine) by adding: "The fact that a work is unpublished shall not itself bar a finding of fair use if such finding is made upon consideration of all the above factors."

7.2.10.4. Other forms of copyright protection. An issue that may not have been contemplated by the drafters of the Copyright Act (and that certainly was not an issue for the framers of the Constitution) is the application of copyright protection to computer software. Unless it has been placed in the public domain, computer software is protected by copyright law (17 U.S.C. § 117), and duplication or distribution, even without charge, of copyrighted software violates the law. Both the content and the structure of the software program are protected (see *Whelan Associates, Inc. v. Jaslow Dental Laboratory, Inc.,* 797 F.2d 1222 (3d Cir. 1986). Institutions have entered license agreements with software companies, particularly where multiple copies of software are used or a computer network is in place. For an analysis of institutional liability for copyright violations involving software, see M. Gemignani, "A College's Liability for Unauthorized Copying of Microcomputer Software by Students," 15 *J. Law & Educ.* 421 (1986).

For a useful summary of the fair use doctrine and the application of copyright law to videotapes, software, performances and music, as well as written material, see T. Hemnes & A. Pyle, *A Guide to Copyright Issues in Higher Education* (National Association of College and University Attorneys, 1991). Faculty may wish to consult *Using Software: A Guide to the Ethical and Legal Use of Software for Members of the Academic Community* (1987) (available from EDUCOM Software Initiative, P.O. Box 364, Princeton, NJ 08540).

Advances in computer technology, and the spread of "electrocopying" through computerized databases, prompted Congress to enact amendments entitled "Criminal Penalties for Copyright Infringement" (Pub. L. No. 102-561, 106 Stat. 4233) in 1992. These amendments to the criminal code make certain types of copyright infringement a felony (18 U.S.C. § 2319(b)). They provide that violations of 18 U.S.C. § 2319(a) shall result in imprisonment for not more than five years or fines in the amount set forth in the criminal law, or both, if the offense consists of reproduction or distribution or both during any 180-day period of at least ten copies or records of one or more copyrighted works with a retail value of over $2,500. Stiffer penalties are prescribed for second and subsequent violations. The sharing of information gained from computerized databases through interlibrary loan, the circulation of copyrighted material on networked computers, and other dissemination of protected material have resulted in sometimes restrictive contracts between producers of information and institutional libraries or other users. They have also resulted in litigation.

Given the courts' strict interpretation of the fair use doctrine and the opportunities provided by computer networks and other technology for violation of the copyright laws, colleges and universities can expect publishers to pursue their rights aggressively. University counsel can expect more change in this area of copyright law as new technology makes information sharing easier and more difficult to detect through conventional means.

Copyright also applies to music. In 1988 several higher education associations entered an agreement with the American Society of Composers, Authors, and Publishers (ASCAP) and Broadcast Music, Inc. (BMI) on five-year music licenses. Institutions will pay blanket royalty fees for all copyrighted music in the ASCAP/BMI reportory that is publicly performed at their institutions. The agreement is reprinted in 18 *Coll. Law Dig.* 210 (Mar. 31, 1988).

In light of developments in copyright law, postsecondary institutions should thoroughly review their policies and practices on photocopying and other means of reproducing copyrighted works, with special attention to the copying of computer software. Institutions may wish to consider providing faculty and staff with explicit guidelines on the use of copyrighted material, particularly unpublished material, computer software, and music. The institution's copying policy should be published for staff and students as well as faculty members, and a notice apprising users of the policy's existence, and the places where it is published or available for distribution, should be posted at campus photocopying and computer facilities.

7.2.10.5. The "work made for hire" doctrine. Although the Copyright Act's "work made for hire" doctrine has seldom been applied in the higher education context, a Supreme Court decision clarifying the doctrine merits a brief discussion. The "work made for hire" doctrine is an exception to the Act's presumption that the author of a work also holds its copyright. In a "work made for hire," the employer is considered the "author" and owns the copyright unless the parties enter a written agreement that gives the copyright to the employee. A work is made "for hire" if (1) it is done by an employee within the scope of his or her employment, or (2) it is part of a larger work (such as a motion picture, a compilation, a text, or an atlas) and the parties agree in writing that it is made for hire.

In *Community for Creative Non-Violence v. Reid,* 490 U.S. 104 (1989), the Court was asked to decide who owned a statue commissioned by CCNV, an organization devoted to helping homeless people, for display at a Christmas pageant. Both Reid, the sculptor, and CCNV filed competing copyright registrations. The Court decided that the "work made for hire" doctrine did not apply to Reid because he was an independent contractor and not an employee of CCNV. The Court did rule, however, that CCNV might be a "coauthor" because of the suggestions that CCNV employees had made to the sculptor during the creation of the statue; it remanded that question to the trial court for such a determination.

The case is significant because it rejected approaches to the Act's interpretation used by federal appellate courts, which had ruled that a work was made for hire if an employer exercised control over its production (see, for example, *Siegel v. National Periodical Publications, Inc.,* 508 F.2d 909 (2d Cir. 1974)). The Court stated that the controlling issue is whether the author is an "employee," listing the factors relevant to such a determination. Because the Court found that Reid was an independent contractor, it did not define further the phrase "within the scope of employment." Thus, it is not clear whether an institution could, if it wished to, assert copyright ownership of a book, article, software program, or musical composition that was produced as the result of an agreement by the institution to give a faculty member a lighter teaching load (or a paid leave) in return for the production of that specific work.

The "work made for hire" doctrine also has potential relevance for copyright of materials prepared under the auspices of an external funding agent. Although some funding agreements specify whether the funding source will have superior rights to any inventions, discoveries, or other products of the research, other agreements are silent on this issue.

7.2.10.6. Copyright and coauthorship. On occasion coauthors (or former coauthors) become involved in copyright issues when portions of coauthored material are used by one author in a derivative work. In *Weismann v. Freeman,* 868 F.2d 1313

(2d Cir. 1989), *cert. denied*, 110 S. Ct. 219 (1989), a medical school professor was sued by his former research assistant, with whom he had researched and coauthored many scholarly works on nuclear medicine, when the professor put his name on a work written by the former assistant. Because the work (a syllabus reviewing the state of scientific knowledge on a medical issue) was based, in large part, on work the two had coauthored, the professor believed that he was a coauthor of the syllabus as well. He also claimed that his use of the material complied with the fair use doctrine.

The former assistant, now a professor herself, argued that the work in question contained some new material and was solely her work for copyright purposes. The appellate court ruled that joint authorship in prior existing works did not make the defendant a joint author in a derivative work: "[W]hen the work has been prepared in different versions, each version constitutes a separate work"; Section 103(b), according to the court, gives copyright protection to new portions of the derivative work but not to preexisting portions (868 F.2d at 1317). The court added: "The joint authorship of the underlying work does not confer any property right in the new work, save those rights which the co-author . . . of the previous works retains in the material used as part of the compilation of the derivative work" (868 F.2d at 1319), and "To support a copyright, a derivative work must be more than trivial, and the protection afforded a derivative work must reflect the degree to which the derivative work relies on preexisting material, without diminishing the scope of the latter's copyright protection" (868 F.2d at 1321). The court also rejected the defendant's fair use defense, noting that professional advancement in academe depends, in large part, on publication, and even if the plaintiff had no money damages, the defendant's appropriation of her work could "impair [her] scholarly recognition" (868 F.2d at 1325–26).

7.2.10.7. Copyright and standardized tests.

One further issue in copyright law of interest to colleges and universities, and most particularly to the testing agencies, is whether states can require disclosure of test questions, answers, and other copyrighted information under "truth-in-testing" laws. New York's Standardized Testing Act (N.Y. Educ. Law §§ 340–348) requires developers of standardized tests to disclose to test takers and to the public test questions, answers, answer sheets, and related research reports. In *Assn. of American Medical Colleges v. Carey*, 728 F. Supp. 873 (N.D.N.Y. 1990), the AAMC, which develops the Medical College Admissions Test, sought a declaratory judgment that the Copyright Act preempted such disclosure. A federal trial court issued a permanent injunction barring enforcement of Sections 341, 341(a), and 342 of the law. The state argued that two of the Copyright Act's exemptions permitted disclosure of the test materials (the "fair use" exemption and the "archives" exemption). The U.S. Court of Appeals for the Second Circuit vacated the permanent injunction and reversed and remanded the case for trial, stating that genuine issues of fact were unresolved concerning the effect of disclosure of test questions and answers on reuse of the test (the fourth, or "market impact," test under the fair use doctrine) (*Assn. of American Medical Colleges v. Cuomo*, 928 F.2d 519 (2d Cir. 1991)).

7.2.11. Patent laws.

The question of who owns a particular discovery, invention, or design is especially complicated in higher education institutions because of the faculty's academic freedom interests; the institution's interest in obtaining a return on its investment in researchers, facilities, and equipment; and the funding source's potential interest in the commercial application of the fruits of its investment. Furthermore, rapid advances in biotechnology have raised difficult questions of just what can be patented and whether patent law should be used to either encourage or discourage particular lines of research. Thus, legal and policy questions intertwine in any institution's approach to patent law.

The basis for all patent law (as well as copyright law) is Article I, Section 8, Clause 8 of the Constitution, which authorizes Congress "to promote the progress of science and useful arts, by securing for limited times to authors and inventors the exclusive right to their respective writings and discoveries." The current patent laws passed by Congress are contained in Title 35 of the *United States Code*. These laws are critical to the research mission of higher education, since they establish the means by which, and the extent to which, institutions or their faculty members, laboratory staffs, students, or external funding sources may protect the products of research.

Protection of research implicates basic patent law questions as well as related contract law questions about institutional arrangements for undertaking and utilizing research: What inventions or discoveries may be patented? Who may hold the patents? What arrangements have been made, or may be made, for licensing patent rights? Behind these legal issues lurk serious questions of policy: What degree and type of protection will allow researchers to share information without fear that their discoveries will be "stolen" by others? As between the institution and its faculty, staff, and students, who should hold the patents or license rights for patentable research products? As between the institution and government or industry sponsors of university research, who should hold the patents or license rights for patentable research products? Should commercial exploitation of university research be avoided; if so, how can it be avoided? The importance of both the legal and the policy questions is underscored by the complexity of new research in fields such as biological engineering and computer sciences, the growing research relationships between industry and academia, the presence of substantial government support for university research, and the development of university research consortia.

The core section of the federal patent statutes provides:

> Whoever invents or discovers any new and useful process, machine, manufacture, or composition of matter, or any new and useful improvement thereof, may obtain a patent therefor, subject to the conditions and requirements of this title [35 U.S.C. § 101].

Among the other requirements that the invention must meet are those of "novelty" (§ 102) and "nonobviousness" (§ 103). The holder of the patent has the exclusive right to the invention for seventeen years if the patent is registered with the U.S. Patent and Trademark Office and the invention or discovery is described in sufficient detail.

A patent owner may bring infringement proceedings against unauthorized use or manufacture of the patented item or use of a patented process. Remedies include (1) lost profits or a reasonable royalty, with interest and costs (35 U.S.C. § 284); (2) treble damages, if willful infringement is found; and (3) in exceptional cases, reasonable attorney's fees (35 U.S.C. § 285). Infringement proceedings are heard by the federal courts, with all appeals heard by the U.S. Court of Appeals for the Federal Circuit, a special court designed to create a uniform body of federal patent law.

The patent law was amended by the Process Patent Amendments Act of 1988, in Title IX of the Omnibus Trade and Competitiveness Act of 1988 (Pub. L. No. 100-418 §§ 9001–9101, 102 Stat. 1107, 1563 (1988), codifed in scattered sections of 35 U.S.C.). Prior to these amendments, a foreign manufacturer (or scientist) could use a patented process outside the United States without being liable for infringement proceedings; goods produced by U.S.-patented processes without authorization could be imported into the United States without penalty. The new law imposes liability for infringement on importers and entities that sell or use foreign goods made by a U.S.-patented process.

When two or more individuals share the ownership of a patent, each owner can grant a nonexclusive license in the product or sell his or her share of the patent without the consent of the other owners.

With regard to precisely what kinds of processes, inventions, or discoveries may be patented, the U.S. Supreme Court has explained the law's intent as follows:

> In choosing such expansive terms as "manufacture" and "composition of matter," modified by the comprehensive "any," Congress plainly contemplated that the patent laws would be given wide scope. . . .
> This is not to suggest that Section 101 has no limits or that it embraces every discovery. The laws of nature, physical phenomena, and abstract ideas have been held not patentable (see *Parker v. Flook*, 437 U.S. 584 (1978)). . . . Thus, a new mineral discovered in the earth or a new plant found in the wild is not patentable subject matter. Likewise, Einstein could not patent his celebrated law that $E = MC^2$; nor could Newton have patented the law of gravity. Such discoveries are "manifestations of . . . nature, free to all men and reserved exclusively to none" (*Funk Brothers Seed Co. v. Kalo Inoculant Co.*, 333 U.S. 127, 130) [*Diamond v. Chakrabarty*, 447 U.S. 303, 309 (1980)].

As increasing sophistication in biotechnology and genetics has increased our ability to alter both nonliving and living things, the scope of potentially patentable items has expanded geometrically. Two U.S. Supreme Court cases decided in 1980 and 1981 laid the foundation for current interpretations of what is patentable, and demonstrate the difficulty of determining what products of modern research are "patentable subject matter" under 35 U.S.C. § 101. The first of these cases, *Diamond v. Chakrabarty* (the source of the above quote), concerned a microbiologist with General Electric who sought to patent a strain of bacteria he had developed by genetic manipulation of a naturally occurring bacterium. The new organism is capable of breaking down multiple components of crude oil, a property possessed by no bacterium in its natural state, and is an important discovery in the control of oil spills. The patent examiner had rejected the application on the grounds that microorganisms are "products of nature" and, as living things, are not patentable subject matter. Chakrabarty, on the other hand, argued that his microorganism constituted a "manufacture" or "composition of matter" within 35 U.S.C. § 101.

In a 5-to-4 decision, the Court agreed with Chakrabarty, concluding that his microorganism was patentable because it was not a previously unknown natural phenomenon but a nonnaturally occurring manufacture—a product of human ingenuity. Rejecting the argument that patent law distinguishes between animate and inanimate things and encompasses only the latter, the Court found the relevant distinction to be between products of nature, whether living or not, and man-made inventions.

In the second case, *Diamond v. Diehr,* 450 U.S. 175 (1981), the Court also decided in favor of patentability by a narrow 5-to-4 margin. Diehr had sought a patent on a method for molding uncured synthetic rubber into cured products. A computer program developed as part of the process enables a computer to continuously recalculate the cure time and determine when the molding press should be opened to ensure a perfect cure. The Court's majority concluded that the invention qualified as a "process" under Section 101 rather than a "mathematical formula" and did not become unpatentable merely because the process involves a computer. The dissenters, in contrast, concluded that the invention made "no contribution to the art that is not entirely dependent upon the utilization of a computer in a familiar process" and was therefore unpatentable under *Gottschalk v. Benson,* 409 U.S. 63 (1971), and *Parker v. Flook,* 437 U.S. 584 (1978), which held that computer programs for solving mathematical problems are not patentable.

As the range of patentable entities broadens, so, too, does the debate about the propriety of issuing patents on certain discoveries. For example, the U.S. Patent and Trademark Office has issued patents on computer software (already protected by federal copyright law). The possibility of patent infringement proceedings for unauthorized copying of software is a much stronger disincentive than the remedies available under the Copyright Act. Experts in software design also worry that the ability to patent software will "slow the rate of development and limit opportunities for the individual and collaborative genius that created much of the best software in the past" (B. Kahin, "Software Patents: Franchising the Information Infrastructure," *Change,* May/June 1989, at 24).

Even more controversial is the decision of the Patent and Trademark Office to consider "non-naturally occurring, non-human multicellular organisms, including animals, to be patentable subject matter within the scope of 35 U.S.C. § 101." Although animal rights groups mounted both procedural and substantive challenges to this interpretive notice, the federal courts dismissed the case for lack of standing (*Animal Legal Defense Fund v. Quigg,* 710 F. Supp. 728 (N.D. Cal. 1989), *affirmed,* 932 F.2d 920 (Fed. Cir. 1991). The first animal patent was given in 1988 to the "inventor" of a genetically altered mouse that was given genes sensitive to cancer. Some commentators worry about broadening the interpretation of what is patentable and have suggested that a "research exemption" be added to the law. Such an exemption would permit scientists to extend their research in appropriate directions without having to fear patent infringement proceedings. The fact that many universities are placing severe restrictions on how patented cell material, processes, or genetically altered animals are used testifies to the high-stakes game that biotechnical research has become (K. Grassmuck, "Institutions' Limits on Sharing of Research Findings Prompt Debate; Chilling Effect on Science Predicted," *Chron. Higher Educ.,* Apr. 17, 1991, A31–A33). For an assessment of policy issues related to the new areas of patent, see R. Merges, "Intellectual Property in Higher Life Forms: The Patent System and Controversial Technologies," 47 *Md. L. Rev.* 1051 (1988).

Some scholars are predicting that patentability may eventually extend to humans, or at least to parts of humans. Discoveries made under the human genome project have been awarded patents; every element of that sophisticated gene-mapping program might eventually be patented, although experts doubt that patents would be extended to human beings because of constitutional limitations (see R. Eisenberg, "Patenting the Human Genome," 39 *Emory L.J.* 721 (1991)).

The level of patenting activity and the potential for high profits and even higher penalties make it essential that institutions, their employees, and funding sources clarify ownership and patent-filing rights. Fortunately, the patent law addresses these two issues for federally funded research. In 1980 Congress added important amendments (94 Stat. 3015) to the patent and trademark laws. (Federal trademark law is discussed in Section 7.2.12.) The amendments establish procedures for the federal Patent and Trademark Office and add a chapter to the patent laws, entitled "Patent Rights in Inventions Made with Federal Assistance." This chapter, codified in 35 U.S.C. §§ 200–211, contains several provisions directly applicable to colleges and universities (see A. Smith, "Implications of Uniform Patent Legislation to Colleges and Universities," 8 *J. Coll. & Univ. Law* 82 (1981–82)).

The chapter's stated goals are to "promote the utilization of inventions arising from federally supported research or development"; "promote collaboration between commercial concerns and nonprofit organizations, including universities"; and "ensure that inventions made by nonprofit organizations . . . are used in a manner to promote free competition and enterprise" (35 U.S.C. § 200). To achieve these goals, the Act establishes a uniform policy for disposition and licensing of rights to patentable inventions discovered in the course of federally funded research. This policy replaces the prior system, by which each federal agency decided for itself how and when its fund recipients could obtain patent rights to inventions resulting from agency funding. The new policy applies to any "contract, grant, or cooperative agreement" between a federal agency and a "nonprofit organization" (defined to include "universities and other institutions of higher education") or a "small business firm" (35 U.S.C. § 201).

Colleges and universities may elect to retain title to inventions made with the assistance of federal funding (35 U.S.C. § 202). There are three situations, however, in which the funding agency may refuse to extend this right to retain title:

> (i) when the funding agreement is for the operation of a government-owned research or production facility, (ii) in exceptional circumstances when it is determined by the agency that restriction or elimination of the right to retain title to any subject invention will better promote the policy and objectives of this chapter, or (iii) when it is determined by a government authority which is authorized by statute or executive order to conduct foreign intelligence or counterintelligence activities that the restriction or elimination of the right to retain title to any subject invention is necessary to protect the security of such activities [35 U.S.C. § 202(a)(i)–(iii)].

If the fund recipient elects to retain title, the Act provides that the federal funding agency shall receive a nonexclusive royalty-free license on behalf of the United States (35 U.S.C. § 202(c)(4)). In addition, the Act reserves "march-in" rights to federal agencies, similar to those reserved by individual agencies under the prior system, to ensure adequate utilization of inventions where the fund recipient has not fully exercised its right to use the patented invention (35 U.S.C. § 203). Other provisions of the Act deal with the assignment and licensing of patent rights by the fund recipient (35 U.S.C. § 202(c)(7) and (f) and the withholding of information about patentable inventions from third parties filing Freedom of Information Act requests (35 U.S.C. §§ 202(e)(5) and 205).

The Office of Federal Procurement Policy (OFPP) within the Office of Management and Budget (OMB) issued rules to implement the uniform patent policy in the 1980 amendments to the patent and trademark law. These rules are published in Circular No. A-124, 47 Fed. Reg. 7556, 7559–7566 (Feb. 19, 1982). Among other matters, the circular requires the use of a standard "patent rights clause" in funding agreements subject to the Act. The clause is contained in Attachment A to the circular. This clause, which may be modified in some respects by individual agencies, includes provisions on such matters as invention disclosure, elections to retain title, application to subcontractors, and march-in rights.

Ownership and licensing rights when research is privately funded are generally controlled by the funding agreement. Institutions vary in their willingness to agree to funding sources' preferences that research results not be disclosed until patents are secured (or at least applied for) or that funders be granted prepublication review of research results. For a survey of the patent and trade-secret protection policies of twenty-four major research universities and a discussion of the need to balance academic freedom with the profit-making needs of funding sources, see Note, "Patent and Trade Secret Protection in University-Industry Research Relationships in Biotechnology," 24 *Harvard Journal on Legislation* 191 (1987).

Ownership rights in a patented invention or discovery are governed by state property law, since a patent is considered personal property. Ownership of a patented (or patentable) discovery by an individual in the course of employment would be controlled by the factual circumstances surrounding the invention and the nature of the employment relationship. In the absence of language in an employment contract assigning ownership of any patentable discoveries to the employer, the employee generally would be declared the owner, but the employer might be awarded "shop rights" (the right to the royalty-free use of the patented invention or discovery for business purposes). Whether universities may claim ownership of patents, absent a knowing and voluntary waiver by the faculty inventor, is not clear. Although the Supreme Court of North Carolina ruled, in *Speck v. North Carolina Dairy Foundation,* 319 S.E.2d 139 (N.C. 1984), that the university owned the rights to a professor's invention because he used university resources (equipment, paid time) in making his discovery, one scholar argues that this result is an incorrect interpretation of *United States v. Dubilier Condenser Corp.,* 289 U.S. 178, amended, 289 U.S. 706 (1933). In *Dubilier* the Court ruled that unless the employee is hired to invent, and only to invent, the product, the invention belongs to the employee, not the employer. For a thorough discussion of this issue, see P. K. Chew, "Faculty Generated Inventions: Who Owns the Golden Egg?" 1992 *Wis. L. Rev.* 259 (1992).

7.2.12. Trademark laws. A trademark, trade name, or service mark is a symbol of a product (or, in the cases of colleges and universities, of an institution) that identifies that product, service, or institution to the general public. Princeton University's tiger, Yale's bulldog, and Wisconsin's badger are symbols of the institution (and, of course, its athletic teams). Trademark law confers a property right on the user of the symbol. Any other entity who uses a similar mark—if that mark could confuse the general public (or the consumer) about the entity the mark represents or about the maker of the product symbolized by the mark or name—may be subject to legal action for trademark infringement.

Trademark is governed by federal, state, and common law. The Trademark Act of 1946 (known as the Lanham Act), 15 U.S.C. §§ 1051–1127, as amended by the Trademark Revision Act of 1988, regulates the registration of trademarks and establishes the rights of the trademark holder and the remedies for infringement. Many states also have statutes similar to the Lanham Act, and the common law of unfair competition (discussed briefly in Section 7.2.13) is also used to challenge unauthorized use of trademarks.

The U.S. Department of Commerce's Office of Patent and Trademark records all federal registrations of trademarks, including those that have expired or been abandoned or canceled. Registration provides constructive notice on a national level to all potential infringers that this mark belongs to another. It also allows the mark to become "incontestable" after five years of continuous use, which confers the right to exclusive use of the trademark. Most state laws provide for registration of trademarks or service marks that are not used in interstate commerce, and thus would not qualify for Lanham Act protection.

Although the Lanham Act specifies how a trademark may be registered, and registration is generally recommended, it is not required in order to bring a trademark infringement action under the Lanham Act or state law. Infringement proceedings are usually brought in federal court, and the plaintiff seeks a preliminary injunction and temporary restraining order. Threshold issues include whether the mark is protectable and who has the superior right in the mark (who was first to use the mark). For example, the University of Pittsburgh lost a trademark infringement case against Champion Products because it could not demonstrate that it introduced the marks into commerce before Champion did (*University of Pittsburgh v. Champion Products, Inc.*, 566 F. Supp. 711 (W.D. Pa. 1983), *affirmed in part, reversed in part*, 686 F.2d 1040 (3d Cir. 1982)). The trademark holder generally must allege the likelihood of consumer confusion, deception, or mistake. Under similar state laws, the trademark holder may also state a cause of action for trademark dilution (the diminution in value of the "good will" attached to the trademark by unauthorized use and application to inferior products or services, or the blurring of the product's identity) or misappropriation (appropriation of another's time and/or economic investment and resulting injury to the trademark holder).

Remedies under both federal and state laws include injunctive relief and other equitable remedies, such as product recalls, destruction of the infringing materials, halting of advertising, or a requirement that the trademark infringer disclose the unauthorized trademark use in an advertisement. Monetary relief is available under federal law in the form of lost profits, royalties, or even treble damages. Attorney's fees are available in "exceptional cases" under Section 1117 of the Lanham Act. Punitive damages are not available under the Lanham Act, but may be available under some state laws.

Not all names or symbols may be registered with the U.S. Office of Patent and Trademark. L. E. Evans ("A Primer on Trademarks and Service Marks," 18 *St. Mary's L.J.* 137–62 (1986)) lists four categories, indicating degrees of protection:

1. Generic names, such as "aspirin," cannot be a trademark.
2. Descriptive marks are protected only if they have a secondary meaning (such as

Georgia Bulldog) and the public recognizes the mark as naming a specific product or entity.
3. Suggestive names, such as Coppertone and Sure, are protected if they suggest a characteristic of the product.
4. Distinctive names—fabricated words such as Exxon or words whose meaning has no direct connection to the product, such as Ivory soap or Apple computers—are protected.

Amendments to the Lanham Act by the Trademark Law Revision Act of 1988 resulted in extensive changes designed to bring U.S. trademark law closer to the law of other industrialized nations. Current law now permits registration of a trademark before it is actually used, as long as the trademark owner demonstrates a bona fide intent to use the trademark and then uses the trademark within six months to two years after registration. The term of trademark registration was reduced from twenty to ten years, and various definitions in the law were clarified and conformed to judicial precedent. Significant requirements for registration are also included in the law, and counsel inexperienced in trademark practice should seek expert advice before embarking on registration of licensing of trademarks. (See F. Hellwig, "The Trademark Law Revision Act of 1988: The 100th Congress Leaves Its Mark," 79 *Trademark Rptr.* 287 (1989), reprinted at 22 *Intellectual Property Law Rev.* 257 (1990).)

Another section of the Lanham Act may be of interest to administrators and counsel because it provides similar protection to trademark protection without requiring registration. Section 43(a) of the Lanham Act provides:

(a) Any person who, on or in connection with any goods or services, or any container for goods, uses in commerce any word, term, name, symbol, or device, or any combination thereof, or any false designation of origin, false or misleading description of fact, or false or misleading representation of fact, which—
(1) is likely to cause confusion, or to cause mistake, or to deceive as to the affiliation, connection, or association of such person with another person, or as to the origin, sponsorship, or approval of his or her goods, services, or commercial activities by another person, or
(2) in commercial advertising or promotion, misrepresents the nature, characteristics, qualities, or geographic origin of his or her or another person's goods, services, or commercial activities,
shall be liable in a civil action by any person who believes that he or she is or is likely to be damaged by such act.

Section 43(a) "evolved into something of a federal law of unfair competition, encompassing the infringement of unregistered marks, names, and trade dress" (R. S. Brown & R. C. Denicola, *Cases on Copyright: Unfair Competition and Related Topics* (5th ed., Foundation Press, 1990) at 531). Cases under Section 43(a) are brought in federal court. For an examination of the breadth of Section 43(a), see J. Bauer, "A Federal Law of Unfair Competition: What Should Be the Reach of Sec. 43(a) of the Lanham Act?" 31 *UCLA L. Rev.* 671 (1984).

Most trademark issues related to higher education involve the licensing of the college's symbols for clothing, souvenirs, and related items, for which the college receives a royalty.[11] Technically, these are "educational service marks" because the mark identifies a service—higher education—rather than a consumer product. Because the trademark laws provide protection to the trademark as a symbol of the product's integrity, a licensor must monitor the quality of the goods to which the trademark is attached in order to protect its rights in the mark. Other suggestions for developing a successful licensing program are contained in D. A. Anderson, "Licensing of College and University Trademarks," 8 *J. Coll. & Univ. Law* 97 (1981–82). But for some institutions, the symbol's significance lies in its ability to identify the institution. The University of Wyoming and Oklahoma State use the same marks—Pistol Pete, a cowboy on a bucking horse—as their institutional symbols. Oklahoma State holds a trademark on its symbol; the University of Wyoming has applied for trademark protection for its mark, which differs only in the colors of the cowboy's outfit (J. L. Nicklin, "Business Notes," *Chron. Higher Educ.,* Jan. 13, 1993, A28).

Counsel desiring further information on trademark practice may wish to consult D. Kane, *Trademark Law: A Practitioner's Guide* (2d ed., Practising Law Institute, 1991), which includes, in addition to basic information on trademark law, several chapters on litigation, evidentiary issues, Patent and Trademark Office proceedings, and licensing considerations.

7.2.13. Antitrust laws. There are three primary federal antitrust laws, each focusing on different types of anticompetitive conduct. The Sherman Act (15 U.S.C. § 1 et seq.), the basic antitrust statute, prohibits "every contract, combination . . . , or conspiracy, in restraint of trade or commerce." The Clayton Act, as amended by the Robinson-Patman Act (15 U.S.C. § 12 et seq.), supplements the Sherman Act with special provisions on price discrimination, exclusive dealing arrangements, and mergers. The Federal Trade Commission Act (15 U.S.C. § 41 et seq.), which is discussed separately in Section 7.2.14, prohibits "unfair methods of competition." These three statutes are enforceable by federal agencies: the Sherman and Clayton Acts by the Antitrust Division of the U.S. Department of Justice; the Clayton Act and the FTC Act by the Federal Trade Commission. The Sherman and Clayton Acts may also be enforced directly by private parties, who may bring "treble-damage" suits against alleged violators in federal court; if victorious, such private plaintiffs will be awarded three times the actual damages the violation caused them. Postsecondary institutions could thus find themselves defendants in antitrust suits brought by either government or private parties, as well as plaintiffs bringing their own treble-damage actions.

The constitutions of twenty states include antitrust provisions, and most states have statutes of general application that parallel, in most respects, the Sherman and Clayton Acts. Plaintiffs often combine state and federal claims in their federal court actions; the long history of common law remedies against monopolies and unfair business practices makes federal preemption of state antitrust laws unlikely. For an analysis of state antitrust law, see W. T. Lifland, *State Antitrust Law* (Law Journal Seminars Press, 1984 and annual updates).

In the past, it was thought that the antitrust laws had little, if any, application

[11]For analysis of cases relating to trademark protection for symbols or logos, see Annot., "Design of Recreational Object as Valid Trademark," 82 A.L.R. Fed. 9 (1987 and periodic supp.).

to colleges and universities. Being institutions whose mission was higher education, they were said to be engaged in the "liberal arts and learned professions" rather than in "trade or commerce" subject to antitrust liability (see generally *Atlantic Cleaners and Dyers v. United States*, 286 U.S. 427, 435–36 (1932)). Moreover, public institutions were considered immune from antitrust liability under the "state action" exemption developed in *Parker v. Brown*, 317 U.S. 341 (1943).[12] Postsecondary institutions, however, can no longer rest comfortably with this easy view of the law. Restrictions in the scope of both the "liberal arts and learned professions" exemption and the state action exemption have greatly increased the risk that particular institutions and institutional practices will be subjected to antitrust scrutiny.

The first chink in postsecondary education's armor was made in *Marjorie Webster Junior College v. Middle States Assn. of Colleges and Secondary Schools*, 432 F.2d 650 (D.C. Cir. 1970), discussed in Section 8.3.2.1. Although the court in that case affirmed the applicability of the "liberal arts and learned professions" exemption, it made clear that antitrust laws could nevertheless be applied to the "commercial aspects" of higher education and that educational institutions and associations could be subjected to antitrust liability if they acted with "a commercial motive." Then in 1975 the U.S. Supreme Court went beyond the *Marjorie Webster* reasoning in establishing that "the nature of an occupation, standing alone, does not provide sanctuary from the Sherman Act" (*Goldfarb v. Virginia State Bar*, 421 U.S. 773 (1975)). The *Goldfarb* opinion refuted the existence of any blanket "learned professions" or (apparently) "liberal arts" exemption. The Court did caution, however, in its often-quoted footnote 17 (421 U.S. at 788–89 n.17), that the "public service aspect" or other unique aspects of particular professional activities may require that they "be treated differently" than typical business activities. Finally, in *National Society of Professional Engineers v. United States*, 435 U.S. 679 (1978), the Supreme Court reaffirmed its rejection of a blanket "learned professions" exemption and emphasized that footnote 17 in *Goldfarb* should not be read as fashioning any broad new defense for professions. According to *Professional Engineers*, the learned professions (and presumably the liberal arts) cannot defend against antitrust claims by relying on an ethical position "that competition itself is unreasonable."

On the heels of these developments, the Supreme Court also decided two cases that refined and limited the state action exemption from antitrust liability. In these cases, *City of Lafayette v. Louisiana Power and Light Co.*, 435 U.S. 389 (1978), and *Community Communications Co. v. City of Boulder*, 455 U.S. 40 (1982), the specific problem was whether this exemption extended to political subdivisions of a state, such as cities. The Court concluded that an anticompetitive "state" action "cannot be exempt from antitrust scrutiny unless it constitutes the action of the [state] . . . itself in its sovereign capacity . . . or unless it constitutes municipal action in furtherance or implementation of clearly articulated and affirmatively expressed state policy" (*Boulder*, 455 U.S. at 52).

Under this formulation a public postsecondary institution would qualify for exemption if it is operated by "the state itself," so that its actions are those of "the

---

[12]This state action concept is a term of art with its own special meaning under the federal antitrust statutes and has no relation to the state action doctrine used in constitutional interpretation and discussed in Section 1.5.2.

state itself."[13] Some public institutions, however, particularly community colleges, may not fit this characterization (see Section 2.3.3). If an institution does not meet this "state itself" test, it may claim the state action exemption only for actions that further or implement "clearly articulated and affirmatively expressed state policy." It is clear from *Lafayette* and *Boulder* that many acts of state political subdivisions will not meet this requirement.[14]

Even if an institution is operated by the "state itself," courts may not consider that all its actions are taken by the state "in its sovereign capacity." A potential distinction between "proprietary enterprises" (nonsovereign) and "traditional governmental functions" (sovereign) has been raised in antitrust litigation but not accepted by a majority of the Supreme Court (see *Boulder*, 455 U.S. at 50 n.13 and 52 n.18). In *Jefferson County Pharmaceutical Assn. v. Abbott Laboratories*, 460 U.S. 150 (1983), the Court, in the special context of a Robinson-Patman Act price discrimination claim, held that the Act applies to a state university's purchases "for the purpose of competing against private enterprise in the retail market" but assumed, without deciding, that the Act would not apply to the state university's purchases "for consumption in traditional governmental functions."

Another Supreme Court case, decided shortly after *Boulder*, expands postsecondary education's exposure to antitrust liability in yet another way. In *American Society of Mechanical Engineers v. Hydrolevel Corp.*, 456 U.S. 556 (1982), the Court held that nonprofit organizations may be held liable under the antitrust laws not only for the actions of their officers and employees but also for the actions of unpaid volunteers with apparent authority (see Section 2.1) to act for the organization. As applied to postsecondary education, this decision could apparently subject institutions to antitrust liability for anticompetitive acts of volunteer groups—such as alumni councils, booster clubs, recruitment committees, and student organizations— if these acts are carried out with apparent authority.

But one area of intense effort by higher education organizations and the institutions they represent is, at least for the time being, immune from antitrust liability. The U.S. Supreme Court ruled in *Eastern Railroad Presidents Conference v. Noerr Motor Freight,* 365 U.S. 127 (1961), that an attempt to influence the passage of laws or decisions of the executive branch of the government does not violate the Sherman Act, even if the purpose is anticompetitive and would otherwise violate the Sherman Act. The Court reasoned that where the restraint is the result of valid governmental action, as opposed to private action, those urging the government action enjoy absolute immunity (under the First Amendment) from antitrust liability.

The *Noerr* doctrine was subsequently limited by the Supreme Court in *Allied Tube and Conduit Corp. v. Indian Head*, 486 U.S. 492 (1988). In that case the National Fire Protection Association, a private trade association, was developing product standards and fire protection codes that many states adopted. The manufacturers

---

[13]For cases analyzing the application of the "state action" doctrine under antitrust law, see Annot., "What Constitutes 'State Action' Under Rule Exempting State and Local Governmental Action from Antitrust Laws," 70 L. Ed. 2d 973 (1983 and periodic supp.).

[14]Another requirement—that the party seeking exemption must be subject to "active state supervision" of the actions for which it seeks exemption—apparently has no application to public postsecondary institutions. In *Town of Hallie v. City of Eau Claire*, 471 U.S. 34 (1985), the Supreme Court held that this additional requirement applies only to private parties claiming a state action exemption.

of steel conduit packed the association's annual meeting and were able to outvote the delegates who believed that plastic conduit was equally safe and could be included in the association's codes. The manufacturer of plastic conduit sued the metal conduit manufacturers, who cited *Noerr* as protecting their conduct. The Supreme Court disagreed, ruling that the private association had no official authority to set standards, and included members with horizontal and vertical business relationships and economic incentives to restrain competition. The fact that many states later adopted the association's codes did not transform its action into "government action," the basis for immunity under *Noerr*. Thus, lobbying efforts directed at legislative or executive branch members will enjoy *Noerr* immunity, but anticompetitive activities directed at private decision makers will not.

Two legislative developments (both in 1984) also bear on the potential liability of postsecondary institutions under federal antitrust laws. Unlike the case law developments, however, the new statutes narrow rather than expand liability. The first statute, the National Cooperative Research Act of 1984 (98 Stat. 1815), includes several provisions that may be used to limit the antitrust liability of joint research and development ventures. For a summary of this Act and a critique of issues it leaves unresolved, see D. Foster, G. Curtner, & E. Dell, "The National Cooperative Research Act of 1984 as a Shield from the Antitrust Laws," 5 *J. Law & Commerce* 347 (1985).

The second statute, the Local Government Antitrust Act of 1984 (98 Stat. 2750), provides partial relief for state political subdivisions that have become subject to antitrust liability as a result of the *Lafayette* and *Boulder* cases. This Act protects such political subdivisions and their officers and employees from paying monetary damages for antitrust violations they commit while acting "in an official capacity." They may still be sued for such violations, however, and subjected to court injunctions. The U.S. Supreme Court interpreted this legislation in *Fisher v. City of Berkeley*, 475 U.S. 260 (1986), in which a rent-control ordinance was found not to conflict with the Sherman Act, in part because it was imposed unilaterally by the municipality and no private interest or concerted action or conspiracy was involved. This legislation could be important for an institution in its capacity as a landlord or if the institution entered a joint venture with a municipality to build a mixed-use project that included student housing.

The most serious antitrust issue facing private higher education in recent years is the decision by the U.S. Department of Justice to investigate the practices of the "Overlap Group," a loose confederation of twenty-three northeastern colleges that, since 1956, have met annually to compare financial aid offers made to applicants. The members of the group adjusted their financial aid awards to students accepted at more than one of the colleges in the Overlap Group so that the cost to the student was approximately the same, no matter which institution the student attended. In addition to the Justice Department's investigation, a student from Wesleyan University initiated a class action antitrust lawsuit against the Ivy League members of the Overlap Group and two other institutions. The financial stakes were high in this case, for prevailing parties could be awarded treble damages. Eight Ivy League institutions entered a consent decree with the U.S. Department of Justice (*United States v. Brown University et al.*, Civil Action No. 91-CV-3274 (E.D. Pa., May 22, 1991)), in which they agreed to stop sharing financial aid information, but the Massachusetts Institute of Technology refused to sign the consent decree and chose to defend the Justice Department's antitrust action in court. In September 1992 a federal trial judge ruled that

MIT's participation in the Overlap Group violated federal antitrust law (*United States v. Brown University*, 805 F. Supp. 288 (E.D. Pa. 1992)). The judge conceded that some educational functions might be exempt from antitrust legislation, but he also held that any function that was "commercial in nature" was not exempt. To MIT's argument that providing financial aid was "charitable," rather than commercial, activity, the judge replied:

> M.I.T.'s attempt to disassociate the Overlap process from the commercial aspects of higher education is pure sophistry. . . . The court can conceive of few aspects of higher education that are more commercial than the price charged to students [805 F. Supp. at 289].

Although the judge believed that the Overlap process constituted price fixing per se, "in light of the Supreme Court's repeated counsel against presumptive invalidation of restraints involving professional associations," the judge evaluated the Overlap Group's conduct under the rule of reason.[15]

> No reasonable person could conclude that the Ivy Overlap Agreements did not supress competition. . . . [T]he member schools created a horizontal restraint which interfered with the natural functioning of the marketplace by eliminating students' ability to consider price differences when choosing a school and by depriving students of the ability to receive financial incentives which competition between those schools may have generated. Indeed, the member institutions formed the Ivy Overlap Group for the very purpose of eliminating economic competition for students. . . . [T]here was abundant and uncontroverted evidence that the fundamental objective of the Ivy Overlap Group was to eliminate price competition among the member institutions. . . . Not only did the effects of Overlap fall within the sphere of commerce, but its existence struck at the heart of the commercial relationship between school and student [805 F. Supp. at 302].

On appeal, the Third Circuit upheld the trial court's determination that tuition policies were not exempt from antitrust law, but it remanded the case for further consideration of the university's argument that the benefits of information sharing could be achieved only through the anticompetitive practices with which the Overlap Group was charged (*United States v. Brown University*, 5 F.3d 658 (3d Cir. 1993)). The court, in a 2-to-1 opinion, explained:

> Overlap affords MIT the benefit of an over-representation of high caliber students, with the concomitant institutional prestige, without forcing MIT to be responsive to market forces in terms of its tuition costs. By immunizing itself through the Overlap from competition for students based on a price/quality ratio, MIT achieves certain institutional benefits at a bargain. . . .
>
> We note the unfortunate fact that financial aid resources are limited even at the Ivy League schools. A trade-off may need to be made between providing

---

[15]Under the rule of reason, a court makes a factual determination of whether the restraint promotes competition through regulation or whether it suppresses competition. Relevant issues are the history of the restraint, the problem the restraint was designed to solve, the reason for selecting the remedy, and the purpose to be attained. (See *Chicago Board of Trade v. United States*, 246 U.S. 231 (1918).)

some financial aid to a large number of the most needy students or allowing the free market to bestow the limited financial aid on the very few most talented who may not need financial aid to attain their academic goals. Under such circumstances, if this trade-off is proven to be worthy in terms of obtaining a more diverse student body (or other legitimate institutional goals), the limitation on the choices of the most talented students might not be so egregious as to trigger [an antitrust violation] [5 F.3d at 677].

The dissenting judge questioned the propriety of applying federal antitrust law to the tuition-pricing decisions of private colleges: "It does seem ironic . . . that the Sherman Act, intended to prevent plundering by the 'robber barons,' is being advanced as a means to punish, not predations, but philanthropy" [5 F.3d at 685].

In December 1993 MIT and the U.S. Department of Justice announced a settlement of the case. The settlement permits MIT, and the other colleges that are members of the Overlap Group, to share applicants' financial data, through a computer network, on the assets, income, number of family members, and other relevant information for individuals accepted at more than one college in the Overlap Group. Although the amount of financial aid offered to these students may not be shared, the settlement permits the group to develop general guidelines for calculating financial aid awards, and will permit auditors to report imbalances in awards to other institutions. (W. Honan, "MIT Wins Right to Share Financial Aid Data in Antitrust Accord," *New York Times*, Dec. 23, 1993, A13.)

For an analysis of the application of antitrust law to tuition pricing, see D. Richmond, "Private Colleges and Tuition Price-Fixing: An Antitrust Primer," 17 *J. Coll. & Univ. Law* 271 (1991). For other issues related to financial aid and tuition packages, see Section 4.3.

Universities with hospitals may also face antitrust liability when peer review committees determine which doctors and other health care professionals may have hospital practice privileges. This is a complicated area of the law, and counsel to institutions with hospitals may wish to consult P. Proger, R. Busey, & T. Miller (eds.), *Developments in Antitrust Health Care Law* (American Bar Association, Section on Antitrust Law, 1990). The book includes an analysis of the application of the state action doctrine to antitrust actions against hospitals whose decisions on medical privileges are reviewed by a state official.

A final area of potential antitrust liability is the area of collegiate athletics. For a discussion of these issues, see Sections 4.15 and 8.4.

As a result of these various developments, administrators and counsel should accord antitrust considerations an important place in their legal planning.[16] Activities most likely to have antitrust implications, and therefore deserving special attention, include (1) broadcasting of college sports events (see *NCAA v. Board of Regents of the University of Oklahoma*, 468 U.S. 85 (1984) (athletic conference controls over televising intercollegiate football games)); (2) purchasing activities (see *Jefferson*

---

[16]In one situation nonprofit postsecondary institutions are still, by express statutory provision, excluded from antitrust liability for alleged price discrimination: "Nothing in [the Robinson-Patman Act] shall apply to purchases of their supplies for their own use by schools, colleges, universities, public libraries, churches, hospitals, and charitable institutions not operated for profit" (15 U.S.C. § 13c) (see this volume, Section 9.2). See also Section 7.2.14 regarding the limited application of the Federal Trade Commission Act to postsecondary institutions.

County Pharmaceutical Assn. v. Abbott Laboratories, 460 U.S. 150 (1983) (pharmaceutical purchases by, among others, two pharmacies at the University of Alabama's medical center)); (3) retail sales activities (see *Sunshine Books v. Temple University,* 697 F.2d 90 (3d Cir. 1982) (textbook sales by a university bookstore)); (4) health care planning and delivery by university medical centers (see generally G. Heitler, "Health Care and Antitrust," 14 *U. Toledo L. Rev.* 577 (1983)); and (5) relationships with accrediting agencies and professional organizations (see H. First, "Competition in the Legal Education Industry (II): An Antitrust Analysis," 54 *N.Y.U. L. Rev.* 1049 (1979)).

At the same time they plan to avoid antitrust liability, administrators and counsel should also consider the protections that antitrust law may provide them against the anticompetitive acts of others. In the *University of Oklahoma* case, for instance, two institutions used the antitrust laws to secure the right to negotiate their own deals for television broadcasting of their sports events. Antitrust law, then, has two sides to its coin; while one side may restrain the institution's policy choices, the other side may free it from restraints imposed by others.

7.2.14. Federal Trade Commission Act. The Federal Trade Commission Act (15 U.S.C. § 41 et seq.) prohibits covered entities from "using unfair methods of competition in or affecting commerce and unfair or deceptive acts or practices in or affecting commerce" (§ 45(a)(1)). The Act defines the entities it covers as "any company, trust, . . . or association, incorporated or unincorporated, which is organized to carry on business for its own profit or for that of its members" (15 U.S.C. § 44). This language clearly covers proprietary postsecondary institutions, thus subjecting them to the Act's prohibitions. Public institutions, on the other hand, are not covered. Nor, in most situations, could private nonprofit institutions be covered. In a leading precedent regarding nonprofit entities, *Community Blood Bank of Kansas City Area v. FTC,* 405 F.2d 1011 (8th Cir. 1969), the court refused to subject a blood bank to FTC jurisdiction, reasoning in part that the organization was "not organized for the profit of members or shareholders [and] [a]ny profit realized in [its] operations is devoted exclusively to the charitable purposes of the corporation."

Some courts have held, however, that the Act's definition of covered entities is broad enough to include a nonprofit entity if it is engaging in activities designed to benefit other, profit-making, entities economically. For instance, the courts have allowed the FTC to assert jurisdiction over the American Medical Association because "one of [the AMA's] objectives was to 'safeguard the material interests of the medical profession'" (*American Medical Assn. v. FTC,* 638 F.2d 443 (8th Cir. 1980), *affirmed by an equally divided court,* 455 U.S. 676 (1982)). In *FTC v. National Commission on Egg Nutrition,* 517 F.2d 485 (7th Cir. 1975), the court held that, because the Egg Nutrition Commission was "formed to promote 'the general interests of the egg industry,'" it was subject to the Act. And in the *Community Blood Bank* case, above, the court suggested that "trade associations" organized for the "pecuniary profits" of their members would be a classic example of a nonprofit entity covered by the Act. Although the principles of these cases would usually not apply to private, nonprofit postsecondary institutions, an institution's activities could apparently come within these principles if the institution entered into a profit-making business venture with another entity. A real estate syndicate, for example, or a research joint venture with industry might fall within the Act's definition, thus subjecting the institution's activities within that relationship to FTC jurisdiction.

The FTC's primary activity regarding proprietary postsecondary institutions has been its attempts to regulate certain practices of proprietary vocational and home-study schools. In late 1978 the FTC issued rules (16 C.F.R. Part 438) covering programs of instruction that "purport to prepare or qualify individuals or improve or upgrade the skills individuals need for employment in any specific occupation" (§ 438.1). Excluded, however, were programs of public institutions, programs of non-profit institutions, programs of two years' duration or longer that culminate in a standard college-level degree, and high school equivalency courses. These rules were scheduled to go into effect on January 4, 1980, but the effective date was stayed indefinitely as a result of the decision in *Katherine Gibbs School v. FTC*, 612 F.2d 658 (2d Cir. 1979), *rehearing en banc denied*, 628 F.2d 755 (2d Cir. 1979) (three judges dissenting). The court invalidated a number of the FTC rules because they were insufficiently specific and insufficiently justified. The court's opinion provides an extended and controversial analysis of FTC authority over proprietary schools. After the *Katherine Gibbs* decision, Part 438 was removed from 16 C.F.R.

But proprietary schools have been faced with another potential source of problems under the FTC Act. In some cases proprietary schools have recruited students, assisted them in obtaining federally guaranteed student loans, and then declared bankruptcy, leaving the students without an education but with a loan to repay. In several of these cases, the proprietary schools have had close relationships with one or more banks that provide federally guaranteed student loans to the proprietary schools' students. The FTC's "Holder Rule" allows the purchaser or borrower to hold a related lender responsible for the seller's misconduct (16 C.F.R. § 433.1(d)) and requires that such language appear in the loan document. Two federal courts have ruled that the Holder Rule does not provide a federal remedy for recipients of federally guaranteed student loans (*Jackson v. Culinary School of Washington*, 788 F. Supp. 1233 (D.D.C. 1992), *affirmed on other grounds*, 27 F.3d 573 (D.C. Cir. 1994); *Veal v. First American Savings Bank*, 914 F.2d 909 (7th Cir. 1990)). However, the FTC has issued a letter stating that the rule does apply (J. DeParle, "Indebted Students Gain in Battle on Fraudulent Trade Schools," *New York Times*, Aug. 4, 1991, at 32). If the Holder Rule does apply and the required language is not in loan documents, students whose loans have been obtained through the now defunct proprietary school may be able to avoid repaying the loan. For discussion of these issues, see C. Mansfield, "The Federal Trade Commission Holder Rule and Its Applicability to Student Loans—Reallocating the Risk of Proprietary School Failure," 26 *Wake Forest L. Rev.* 635 (1991).

7.2.15. Environmental laws. A complex web of federal and state laws regulates landowners and disposers of waste that may pollute water, soil, or air. Institutions of higher education fall into both of these categories and thus are subject to the strict regulation and the heavy civil and criminal penalties provided by these laws.[17]

---

[17]Pertinent summaries of case law on environmental regulation include "Validity and Construction of § 106(a) and (b)(1) of Comprehensive Environmental Response, Compensation, and Liability Act (42 U.S.C. § 9606(a) and (b)(1)), Authorizing Equitable Abatement Actions and Administrative Orders and Prescribing Fines for Noncompliance with Such Orders," 87 A.L.R. Fed. 217 (1988 and periodic supp.); "Governmental Recovery of Cost of Hazardous Waste Removal Under Comprehensive Environmental Response, Compensation, and Liability Act (42 U.S.C. § 9601 et seq.)," 70 A.L.R. Fed. 329 (1984 and periodic supp.); and "Liability Insurance Coverage for Violations of Antipollution Laws," 87 A.L.R.4th 444 (1991 and periodic supp.).

Most of the federal environmental protection laws are enforced by the Environmental Protection Agency. The two laws of major importance to institutions of higher education are the Resource Conservation and Recovery Act of 1976 (RCRA) and the Comprehensive Environmental Response, Compensation, and Liability Act of 1980 (CERCLA, also known as the Superfund Law). The Toxic Substances Control Act (TSCA) is also important to most colleges and universities, and most must also comply with the Clean Air Act and the Clean Water Act. The handling, storage, and disposal of radioactive materials is regulated by the Nuclear Regulatory Commission; the Occupational Safety and Health Administration (OSHA) regulates the communication of information about hazardous substances to workers (see Section 7.2.2). The Emergency Planning and Community Right-to-Know Act (EPCRA, 42 U.S.C. §§ 11001–11050, also known as Title III of the Superfund Amendments and Reauthorization Act (SARA)) requires institutions to disclose all chemicals that they use or store.

RCRA (42 U.S.C. § 6901 et seq.) regulates the generation, transportation, storage, and disposal of hazardous waste.[18] The law defines which "hazardous waste" is covered by the law, and excludes some substances, such as household products and specified industrial wastes. The law covers products intended to be recycled as well as those that are discarded, and specifies record-keeping requirements for tracking the waste from the time it is obtained until the time it is discarded. Generators, transporters, and owners of storage and disposal sites are covered by RCRA. Penalties include administrative compliance orders and revocation of RCRA permits; civil penalties of up to $25,000 per day per violation and criminal penalties of two to five years' imprisonment and fines of up to $50,000 per day per violation; and, for "knowing endangerment," imprisonment of up to fifteen years and fines of up to $250,000 for individuals and $1 million for corporations (42 U.S.C. § 6928). Under RCRA improper disposal of a hazardous substance by an employee or a student could result in criminal penalties. Other federal environmental laws, such as CERCLA and the Clean Water and Clean Air Acts, contain similar civil and criminal penalties. Furthermore, federal judges are interpreting the laws' *scienter* (knowledge) requirements for individual liability to permit juries to infer that a corporate officer, depending on his or her position in the organization, would know about the violation. For a discussion of these issues, see R. Marzulla & B. Kappel, "Nowhere to Run, Nowhere to Hide: Criminal Liability for Violations of Environmental Statutes in the 1990s," 16 *Columbia J. Environmental Law* 201 (1991). Most insurers do not include coverage for toxic-waste cleanup or liability in their directors' and officers' policies, potentially leaving corporations and their officers and directors personally liable. See Comment, "Whistling Past the Waste Site: Directors' and Officers' Personal Liability for Environmental Decisions and the Role of Liability Insurance Coverage," 140 *U. Pa. L. Rev.* 241 (1991), which, among other issues, discusses retroactive liability of officers and directors for disposal that was not unlawful prior to CERCLA.

CERCLA (42 U.S.C. § 9601 et seq.) and its amendments (Superfund Amendments and Reauthorization Act) govern the cleanup of hazardous-waste sites. Under CERCLA the generator of toxic material, the transporter of the material, and the

---

[18]Cases and authorities are collected in Annot., "Liability Under § 7003 of Resource Conservation and Recovery Act (RCRA) (42 U.S.C.S. § 6973) Pertaining to Imminent Danger from Solid or Hazardous Waste," 115 A.L.R. Fed. 191 (1993 and periodic supp.).

owner of the dump site have joint and several liability for cleanup costs. Some institutions are facing potential liability for the cleanup of hazardous-waste-disposal sites, even if they were not aware of the location of the site (D. Blum, "91 Colleges May Be Required to Help Pay for Cleanup of 2 Hazardous-Waste Sites," *Chron. Higher Educ.*, June 10, 1992, A25). One university became involved in litigation between the U.S. government and Alcan Aluminum Corporation when the corporation claimed that the university should share the cost of cleaning up a toxic-waste site. A federal trial court ruled that the university shared the liability and must share the cost (*United States v. Alcan Aluminum Corp.*, 755 F. Supp. 531 (N.D.N.Y. 1991).

Institutions also face potential liability under CERCLA when property that they own is contaminated, whether or not the institution generated the hazardous waste or even knew that it was on the site. The only way that a property owner may be able to avoid CERCLA liability is by establishing a "due diligence" defense: that it did not know, nor did it have reason to know, that the property was contaminated. To establish this defense, the purchaser of property must demonstrate that an investigation was made to determine whether the property was contaminated, and possibly that extensive testing was conducted. Such precautions are particularly important in cases where the property was formerly an industrial site. For an overview of this subject, see P. Marcotte, "Toxic Blackacre: Unprecedented Liability for Landowners," *American Bar Assn. J.*, Nov. 1, 1987, at 67–70. CERCLA contains provisions for actions against "potentially responsible parties" to recover cleanup costs, even if the cleanup is not mandated by a government agency (42 U.S.C. § 9607(a)(B)). Thus, institutions of higher education could take advantage of this provision if they purchase contaminated property, or they could be liable for contamination of property they no longer own, even if they did not cause the contamination. For a general overview of CERCLA and RCRA, see C. Chadd, T. Satinover, L. Bergeson, R. Neuman, & C. Bryant, *Avoiding Liability for Hazardous Waste: RCRA, CERCLA, and Related Corporate Law Issues* (Bureau of National Affairs, 1991).

Other federal laws that regulate the actions of most colleges and universities include the Clean Air Act (42 U.S.C. §§ 1857 et seq., 7551 et seq., and 7623), which regulates emissions of substances into the air. Emission sites on campuses may include laboratories, boilers, incinerators, and print shops. The Clean Water Act (33 U.S.C. § 1251 et seq.) prohibits the discharge of any pollutant into navigable waters, unless the EPA has issued a permit for such discharge. The law also prohibits the discharge of pollutants into storm sewers through such actions as landscape irrigation, air conditioning condensation, lawn watering, or swimming pool discharge. This law also regulates the treatment of wetlands. The Toxic Substances Control Act (15 U.S.C. § 2601 et seq.) regulates the use and disposal of "chemical substances which present an unreasonable risk of injury to health or the environment" (§ 2601(b)(2)), including PCBs (polycholorinated biphenyls) and asbestos; it also imposes recordkeeping and labeling requirements. Underground storage tanks and the land-based disposal of certain hazardous substances are regulated by the Hazardous and Solid Waste Amendments of 1984 (42 U.S.C. § 6924 et seq.).

Many states have passed environmental laws that are even more restrictive than federal law. Administrators and counsel should secure expert advice on compliance with both sets of laws, particularly in situations where they differ or cannot be complied with simultaneously.

Faced with the myriad of laws and the severe penalties they carry, colleges and universities should consider, if they have not already done so, adding one or more individuals with expertise in environmental regulation to their administrative staff. The regulation of hazardous substances in institutions of higher education is particularly difficult for two reasons: many of the generators of such substances are faculty and students, who may not be aware of the strict regulatory framework; and the locations where hazardous substances may be generated, stored, or disposed of are numerous, including not only science laboratories but art studios, maintenance shops, hospitals, buildings and grounds facilities, printing services, and supply storage facilities. Institutional counsel should consider the wisdom of an environmental compliance audit, both to ascertain the institution's compliance with these laws and to demonstrate the institution's good faith should a violation be alleged. For guidance on conducting such audits, see J. Moorman & L. Kirsch, "Environmental Compliance Assessments: Why Do Them, How to Do Them, and How Not to Do Them," 26 *Wake Forest L. Rev.* 97 (1991), as well as M. E. Kris & G. L. Vannelli, "Today's Criminal Environmental Enforcement Program: Why You May Be Vulnerable and Why You Should Guard Against Prosecution Through an Environmental Audit," 16 *Columbia J. Environmental Law* 227 (1991).

7.2.16. Americans with Disabilities Act. The Americans with Disabilities Act of 1990 (ADA) (Pub. L. No. 101-336, codified at 42 U.S.C. § 12101 et seq.) provides broad protections for individuals with disabilities in five areas: employment (see Section 3.3.2.5), public accommodations (see Section 4.2.4.3), state and local government services, transportation, and telecommunications. Similar in intent to Section 504 of the Rehabilitation Act (Section 7.5.4), the ADA provides broader protection, since a larger number of entities are subject to it (they need not be recipients of federal funds) and a larger number of activities are encompassed by it.

The law protects an "individual with a disability." Disability is defined as "a physical or mental impairment that substantially limits one or more major life activities" of the individual; "a record of such impairment; or being regarded as having such impairment" (42 U.S.C. § 12102). This definition, while covering current disabilities, also would prohibit discrimination against an individual based on a past disability that no longer exists, or a perceived disability that does not, in fact, exist. The definition of "impairment" includes contagious diseases, learning disabilities, HIV (whether symptomatic or asymptomatic), drug addiction, and alcoholism (36 C.F.R. § 104), although the employment provisions exclude current abusers of controlled substances from the law's protections (Section 3.3.2.5).

Title I of the ADA covers employment, and is discussed in Section 3.3.2.5. Title II requires nondiscrimination on the part of state and local government, a category that specifically includes state colleges and universities. Title II provides that "no qualified individual with a disability shall, by reason of such disability[,] be excluded from participation in or be denied the benefits of the services, programs, or activities of a public entity, or be subjected to discrimination by any such entity" (42 U.S.C. § 12132). For purposes of Title II, an individual with a disability is "qualified" when "with or without reasonable modification to rules, policies, or practices, the removal of architectural, communication, or transportation barriers, or the provision of auxiliary aids and services, [the individual] meets the essential eligibility requirements for the receipt of services or his participation in programs or activities provided by a public entity" (42 U.S.C. § 12131). Title II also incorporates the provisions of Titles

I and III (public accommodations), making them applicable to public institutions. The U.S. Department of Justice has the responsibility for providing technical assistance for, and for enforcing, Titles II and III of the ADA. Regulations interpreting Title II appear at 28 C.F.R. Part 35.

Title III extends the nondiscrimination provisions to places of public accommodation, whose definition includes colleges and universities, whether public or private, if they "affect commerce" (42 U.S.C. § 12181). Title III focuses on ten areas of institutional activity:

1. Eligibility criteria for the services provided by colleges and universities (28 C.F.R. § 36.301).
2. Modifications in policies, practices, or procedures (such as rules and regulations for parking or the policies of libraries) (28 C.F.R. § 36.302).
3. Auxiliary aids and services (such as interpreters or assistive technology) (28 C.F.R. § 36.303).
4. Removal of architectural barriers (28 C.F.R. § 36.304).
5. Alternatives to barrier removal (if removal is not readily achievable) (28 C.F.R. § 36.305).
6. Personal devices and services, which the law does not require the public accommodation to provide (28 C.F.R. § 36.306).
7. Conditions under which the public accommodation must provide accessible or special goods upon request (28 C.F.R. § 36.307).
8. Accessible seating in assembly areas (28 C.F.R. § 36.308).
9. Accessibility to and alternatives for examinations and courses that reflect the individual's ability rather than the individual's impairment (28 C.F.R. § 36.309).
10. Accessible transportation (28 C.F.R. § 36.310).

Title III imposes a wide range of requirements on colleges and universities, from admissions policies to residence hall and classroom accessibility to the actions of individual faculty (who may, for instance, be required to modify examinations or to use special technology in the classroom). The regulations also affect the college's planning for public performances, such as plays, concerts, or athletic events, and provide detailed guidelines for making buildings accessible during their renovation or construction. The implications of the ADA for a college's responsibility to provide auxiliary aids and services is discussed in Section 4.4. Public telephones must also be made accessible to individuals with disabilities, including those with hearing impairments. For an overview of some of the implications of the ADA for institutions of higher education, see F. Thrasher, "The Impact of Titles II and III of the Americans with Disabilities Act of 1990 on Academic and Student Services at Colleges, Universities, and Proprietary Schools," 22 *Coll. Law Dig.* 257 (June 18, 1992).

7.2.17. Family and Medical Leave Act. The Family and Medical Leave Act (FMLA) of 1993 (Pub. L. No. 103-3) applies to all organizations that have employed fifty or more employees, within a radius of seventy-five miles, for each working day during each of twenty or more weeks in the preceding year. Employees who qualify may take up to twelve weeks of unpaid leave in any twelve-month period for the following:

1.   The birth of a child and its care during the first year.
2.   The adoption of a child or placement in the employee's home of a foster child
     (not necessarily a newborn).
3.   The care of the employee's spouse, child, or parent with a serious health
     condition.
4.   The serious health condition of the employee.

Employees who take FMLA leave are entitled to reinstatement to an equivalent position upon their return to work, and the employer must maintain any health benefits to which the worker was entitled before taking FMLA leave.

The Department of Labor issued interim final rules interpreting the FMLA at 58 Fed. Reg. 31794, which will be codified at 29 C.F.R. Part 825. The regulations are lengthy and complicated; the following summary highlights only a few issues, and administrators should consult the full text of the regulations or employment counsel for assistance in applying the FMLA to the individual circumstances of employees.

Most institutions of higher education will easily meet the fifty-employee requirement for coverage. If an institution has a small satellite location more than seventy-five miles away that employs fewer than fifty employees (and those employees work exclusively at that location), it is not clear that those employees would be protected by the FMLA. Institutions facing this situation, however, should consider the appropriateness of excluding such employees from coverage when the majority of their employees have FMLA protection.

An employee who has worked for 1,250 hours during the previous twelve months (or, for a full-time salaried employee for whom records of hours worked are not kept, for twelve months in the past year) is entitled to twelve weeks of family and medical leave. The number of hours worked, according to the regulations, is to be calculated in conformance with Fair Labor Standards Act regulations (29 C.F.R. § 825.110(c)). Full-time faculty in institutions of higher education are deemed to have met the 1,250-hour test "in consideration of the time spent at home reviewing homework and tests" (29 C.F.R. § 825.110(c)).

The regulations specifically define the categories of "family member" (29 C.F.R. § 825.113). For example, "spouse" may include a common law spouse (if permitted by the law of the state in which the work site is located), but does not include an unmarried domestic partner. A "parent" is a biological parent or an individual who acted as the employee's parent when the employee was a child; this category does not include the parents of the employee's spouse. A "child" may be a biological, adopted, or foster child, stepchild, or a person for whom the employee is acting as a parent, if the child is either under age eighteen or is over eighteen but needs care because of a mental or physical disability.

The regulations expand upon the FMLA's definition of "serious health condition" and detail the employer's right to request medical certification of the employee's need for the leave, including consultation with second and third medical providers (29 C.F.R. §§ 825.114 and 825.305–307). The regulations also describe the employer's right to request certification of the employee's ability to return to work (29 C.F.R. § 825.310) and the meaning of an "equivalent position" (§ 825.215).

FMLA leave for medical reasons may be taken on an intermittent or part-time basis (called "reduced leave"), depending on the needs of the employee or the family member, but intermittent or reduced leave for the care of a newborn or an adopted child or a foster child may be taken only with the employer's agreement. If an employee takes intermittent or reduced leave, the employer may transfer that employee to a part-time position, as long as the pay and benefits remain equivalent (29 C.F.R. § 825.204).

The regulations also provide detailed information on the relationship between paid and unpaid leave, and the continuation of medical benefits. The law and regulations are silent on whether employers must continue or reinstate nonmedical benefits (such as tuition assistance or child-care benefit plans).

The law and regulations permit the employer to deny reinstatement (but not FMLA leave) to a "key employee," defined as a salaried employee who is among the highest-paid 10 percent of all employees within seventy-five miles of the work site. The employer must show that "substantial and grievous economic injury" to its operations will ensue if reinstatement is required (the economic impact of the employee's absence is not part of the test for substantial and grievous economic injury). The specificity of the showing that employers must make to justify refusal to reinstate a key employee (29 C.F.R. §§ 825.216–218) suggests that the exception will rarely be used.

The FMLA requires employers to post a notice detailing its provisions and instructing employees on how complaints may be filed. Employee handbooks must incorporate FMLA information; in the absence of a handbook, employers must provide written information about the FMLA to any employee who asks for FMLA leave. The regulations specify the type of information that employers must give those individuals who request such a leave (29 C.F.R. § 825.301), as well as the law's record-keeping requirements (§ 825.500).

Employees have two avenues for redressing alleged violations of the FMLA. They may file a complaint with the Department of Labor or a lawsuit in federal court. Damages include lost earnings, interest, liquidated damages (lost earnings and interest), reinstatement, and attorney's fees (29 C.F.R. §§ 825.400–404). For a description of the FMLA and a discussion of its application to colleges and universities, see T. Flygare, *The Family and Medical Leave Act of 1993: Applications in Higher Education* (National Association of College and University Attorneys, 1994).

Although the FMLA entitles employees to twelve weeks of unpaid leave for a serious medical condition, some employees may need additional time. The Americans with Disabilities Act (ADA, see this volume, Section 3.3.2.5) requires employers to provide "reasonable accommodation" for workers with disabilities. Such accommodations could include unpaid or paid leave (depending on the employer's policies) and part-time work. The FMLA and the ADA provide significant protections to employees with serious health conditions, and administrators should be aware that the ADA may be used to extend an employee's rights to leave for health-related reasons. For a discussion of the interplay between these two federal laws, see P. Mastroianni & D. K. Fram, "The Family and Medical Leave Act and the Americans with Disabilities Act: Areas of Contrast and Overlap," 9 *Labor Lawyer* 553 (1993).

Sec. 7.3. *Federal Taxation of Postsecondary Education*

Federal tax laws impose various filing, reporting, disclosure, withholding, and payment requirements on postsecondary institutions. This section briefly discusses the tax laws that have the most important applications to postsecondary education. These laws are based on Congress's taxing power (see Section 7.1.2). Federal tax law is highly technical and complex; to deal effectively with its many requirements, postsecondary institutions will need ready access to expert accounting and auditing services and the regular advice of counsel expert in taxation.

7.3.1. Income tax laws. Most postsecondary institutions, other than proprietary institutions, are eligible to attain tax-exempt status under the Internal Revenue Code. Depending on whether the institution is public or private, one of two different avenues to exemption may be chosen. If the institution is public, it must demonstrate that it is a political subdivision of a state under 26 U.S.C. Section 115 and related provisions or, alternatively, that it is immune from taxation under the constitutional doctrine of intergovernmental immunities (see G. Burke, "Federal Taxation of State Colleges and Universities: Recent Developments Call for Reconsideration of Theories of Exemption," 4 *J. Coll. & Univ. Law* 43 (1977)). If the institution is private, it must satisfy the statutory definition established by 26 U.S.C. Section 501(c)(3) by showing that it is

> organized and operated exclusively for religious, charitable . . . or educational purposes, . . . no part of the net earnings of which inures to the benefit of any private shareholder or individual, no substantial part of the activities of which is carrying on propaganda, or otherwise attempting, to influence legislation . . . and which does not participate in, . . . or intervene in, any political campaign on behalf of . . . any candidate for public office.

Through these requirements for tax exemption, the federal government influences the organizational structures and activities of educational institutions. The express language of the Internal Revenue Code, for example, limits an institution's lobbying efforts and political activities (26 U.S.C. §§ 501(c)(3), 501(h), and 4911; see also corresponding regulations in 26 C.F.R. § 1.501(c)(3)-1 and 26 C.F.R. § 1.501(h)-1 to (h)-3, which develop the definition of lobbying and the restrictions on institutional activities). The U.S. Department of Treasury promulgates regulations on many knotty questions concerning tax exemptions (see 26 C.F.R. § 1.501), such as what constitutes an educational purpose or organization within the meaning of Section 501(c)(3). The Treasury Department's Internal Revenue Service (IRS) also issues revenue rulings and revenue procedures, two devices by which it establishes and publicizes tax policies and procedures, as well as technical advice memoranda (TAMs) and private letter rulings.

The IRS has, for example, used revenue rulings and revenue procedures as a means of combating discrimination on the basis of race, color, and national or ethnic origin in private schools. Revenue Ruling 71-447, 1971-2 C.B. (*Cumulative Bulletin*) 230, announced the basic principle that "a private school that does not have a racially nondiscriminatory policy as to students does not qualify for exemption." The IRS predicated this ruling on its understanding that Congress's intention when it devised Section 501(c)(3) was to include only institutions that qualified as "common law charit[ies]," thus precluding exemptions for institutions operating "contrary to public policy" (1971-2 C.B. at 230). Subsequent IRS statements implemented this basic nondiscrimination principle. Revenue Procedure 72-54, 1972-2 C.B. 834, sets out rules requiring private schools to publicize their nondiscriminatory policies; Revenue Ruling 75-231, 1975-1 C.B. 158, provides illustrative examples regarding church-affiliated schools; and Revenue Procedure 75-50, 1975-2 C.B. 587 (superseding Revenue Procedure 72-54, above), establishes guidelines and record-keeping requirements for complying with the nondiscrimination principle.

The tax exemption and race discrimination problem, as well as the overall complexity of tax law and its impact on the campus, is illustrated by the celebrated case of *Bob Jones University v. United States*, 461 U.S. 574 (1983). The IRS had denied Bob Jones University and a second plaintiff, Goldsboro Christian Academy, tax-exempt status under Section 501(c)(3). Each school had racially discriminatory policies, Bob Jones prohibiting its students from interracial dating or marriage, Goldsboro denying admission to most blacks. The schools challenged the basic principle of Revenue Ruling 71-447 (above), arguing (1) that Section 501(c)(3) did not embrace the common law concept of charity and (2) that, even if it did, the schools' racial policies were mandated by sincerely held religious beliefs and thus protected by the Free Exercise Clause of the First Amendment (see this volume, Section 1.6). The case reached the U.S. Supreme Court embroiled in political controversy. The Reagan administration announced that Section 501(c)(3) did not give the IRS authority to deny tax-exempt status on the basis of race discrimination and attempted to overturn Revenue Ruling 71-447. Caught in a firestorm of adverse publicity, the administration then introduced legislation to amend Section 501(c)(3). Because the administration had compromised the federal government's position in the case, the Supreme Court took the extraordinary step of appointing special counsel to argue in favor of Revenue Ruling 71-447.

When the Court finally ruled on the merits, it upheld the longstanding IRS interpretation (and rejected the Reagan administration's reinterpretation) of Section 501(c)(3):

> In Revenue Ruling 71-447, the IRS formalized the policy, first announced in 1970, that Section 170 [the provision authorizing individuals to deduct amounts contributed to charity] and Section 501(c)(3) embrace the common-law "charity" concept. Under that view, to qualify for a tax exemption pursuant to Section 501(c)(3), an institution must show, first, that it falls within one of the . . . categories expressly set forth in that section, and second, that its activity is not contrary to settled public policy.
>
> . . .
>
> When the government grants exemptions or allows deductions all taxpayers are affected; the very fact of the exemption or deduction for the donor means that other taxpayers can be said to be indirect and vicarious "donors." Charitable exemptions are justified on the basis that the exempt entity confers a public benefit—a benefit which the society or the community may not itself choose or be able to provide, or which supplements and advances the work of public institutions already supported by tax revenues [461 U.S. at 585–91; footnote omitted].

The Court then considered whether racial discrimination is so contrary to settled public policy that institutions practicing it cannot be said to be charitable or to confer a public benefit:

[A] declaration that a given institution is not "charitable" should be made only where there can be no doubt that the activity involved is contrary to a fundamental public policy. But there can no longer be any doubt that racial discrimination in education violates deeply and widely accepted views of elementary justice. . . . Over the past quarter of a century, every pronouncement of this Court and myriad Acts of Congress and Executive Orders attest a firm national policy to prohibit racial segregation and discrimination in public education.
. . .

There can thus be no question that the interpretation of Section 170 and Section 501(c)(3) announced by the IRS in 1970 was correct. . . . Racially discriminatory educational institutions cannot be viewed as conferring a public benefit within the "charitable" concept discussed earlier, or within the congressional intent underlying . . . Section 501(c)(3) [461 U.S. at 592–96; footnote omitted].

Having concluded that Revenue Ruling 71-447 is consistent with Congress's intent concerning Section 501(c)(3) and a correct reading of public policy, the Court considered and rejected the plaintiffs' free exercise of religion claim:

Denial of tax benefits will inevitably have a substantial impact on the operation of private religious schools, but will not prevent those schools from observing their religious tenets.

The governmental interest at stake here is compelling. As discussed . . . , the Government has a fundamental, overriding interest in eradicating racial discrimination in education—discrimination that prevailed, with official approval, for the first 165 years of this Nation's constitutional history. That governmental interest substantially outweighs whatever burden denial of tax benefits places on petitioners' exercise of their religious beliefs. The interests asserted by petitioners cannot be accommodated with that compelling governmental interest . . . and no "less restrictive means" . . . are available to achieve the governmental interest [461 U.S. at 603–04; citations and footnote omitted].[19]

As *Bob Jones* suggests, the maintenance of tax-exempt status is a major concern of postsecondary institutions. Its loss can severely affect institutional financial resources. In addition to the obvious imposition of tax liability on institutional income, loss of a Section 501(c)(3) exemption would prevent donors from deducting their gifts as "charitable contributions" (26 U.S.C. § 170) on their own tax returns and might thus inhibit such giving. These financial repercussions create substantial inducement to comply with the standards established for tax exemption.

In addition to the provisions on exemption, other tax provisions also exert substantial influences on postsecondary institutions and their staffs and students. For instance, Section 117 of the Internal Revenue Code governs the taxability of scholarships, fellowships, assistantship awards, and other forms of financial aid. In general, if the recipient obtains financial aid in return for providing services that benefit the institution, the aid is considered to be compensation and is taxable to the student;

---

[19]The *Bob Jones* analysis may be affected by the later case of *Employment Division v. Smith*, 494 U.S. 872 (1990). Under the *Smith* analysis, it could be easier for the government to prevail in a case like *Bob Jones*. The *Smith* case, however, has been legislatively supplanted by the Religious Freedom Restoration Act of 1993 (Pub. L. No. 103-141, 107 Stat. 1488), which restores the law existing prior to *Smith*. See Section 1.6, this volume.

if no such "strings" are attached, the aid is treated as a gift and the recipient may exclude it from taxable income (see *Bingler v. Johnson*, 394 U.S. 741 (1969)). The distinction is important not only for the student receiving the aid but also for the institution—which must determine whether to withhold employment taxes from the student's award.

In the Tax Reform Act of 1986 (Pub. L. No. 99-514, 100 Stat. 2085), Congress amended Section 117 in three ways. First, only students who are degree candidates may exclude scholarships or fellowships from their gross income. Other students, such as postdoctoral students, must pay taxes on all such grants they receive. Second, the amount of any scholarships or fellowships is excludable from gross income only to the extent used for tuition, course-required fees, books, supplies, and equipment. Amounts used for expenses such as room and board are not excludable from income. Third, Congress explicitly affirmed that no portion of a scholarship or fellowship award that represents compensation for teaching, research, or other services is excludable from income. In 1988, in the Technical and Miscellaneous Revenue Act, Congress again amended Section 117 by adding a new paragraph, (d)(5), on tuition-reduction plans. This paragraph authorizes graduate students engaged in teaching and research to exclude from gross income a reduction in tuition that is not compensation for their teaching and research. The Treasury regulations implementing Section 117 are in 26 C.F.R. § 1. 117-1 et seq.

In addition to these Code provisions on taxation of scholarships and other financial aid, several other provisions are relevant to the financing of college educations. Section 135 provides that, for certain taxpayers and their dependents, the proceeds from redemption of U.S. Savings Bonds are not taxable if they are used for "qualified higher education expenses." Section 117(d) governs the tax status of qualified tuition-reduction plans for employees and their dependents. In general, this section excludes from gross income the amount of any tuition reduction for employees who are taking undergraduate courses either at the institution where they are employed or at another college or university that grants a tuition reduction to employees of that institution. To maintain this tax-free treatment, however, the institution must award tuition-reduction assistance in a way that does not discriminate in favor of highly compensated employees. Furthermore, various Code provisions (and IRS rulings), including Sections 115 and 501(c)(3), above, and Sections 61 and 451 on receipt of income, govern the tax status of the prepaid tuition programs adopted in recent years by a number of states (see generally M. Olivas (ed.), *Prepaid College Tuition Plans: Promise and Problems* (College Board Publications, 1993)), including Michigan.

In 1986 the state of Michigan established a prepayment tuition fund called the Michigan Education Trust (MET), into which parents could make payments for the benefit of their children. MET guaranteed full tuition payment for the beneficiaries at any Michigan state university or college, or an equivalent reimbursement if the student attended a private institution. MET's stated purpose was to encourage Michigan citizens to seek higher education at Michigan schools. Before MET went into effect, the IRS ruled that MET was not tax exempt under Section 501(c)(3) of the Internal Revenue Code. MET and the state filed a lawsuit seeking refund of taxes already paid to the federal government and a judicial declaration that MET is a tax-exempt educational organization. In *Michigan v. United States*, 802 F. Supp. 120

(W.D. Mich. 1992), the court rejected MET's and Michigan's statutory and constitutional arguments.

The court first found that MET is not a state entity, because it is funded by private participants, it has private beneficiaries, and the funds it holds may not be used for state purposes. Lacking status as an integral part of the state or an instrumentality of the state, MET could not be considered a state entity exempt from taxation under Section 115 of the Code. The court then analyzed whether MET is an exempt educational organization under Section 501(c)(3) or (c)(4). The court held that MET could not claim this status, because the "purpose of providing the tuition-guaranteeing service constitutes a substantial private purpose which destroys [MET's] exemption." Finally, MET could not make a constitutional claim to a tax-exempt status under "the doctrine that the states are constitutionally immune from federal taxation." Accordingly, the court granted the summary judgment motion of the United States. See generally J. Collins & L. Naoum, "Prepaid Tuition Agreements—Federal Tax Issues to Be Considered in Connection with Their Design and Implementation," 17 *Coll. Law Dig.* No. 7 (*West's Educ. Law Rptr.*, NACUA ed., Aug. 20, 1987).

Section 119 governs yet another matter of interest to postsecondary institutions: the taxability of meals or lodging furnished to an employee. Generally, if "the meals are furnished on the business premises of the employer" or "the employee is required to accept . . . lodging on the business premises of his employer as a condition of his employment" (26 U.S.C. § 119(a)(1)-(2)), the employee may exclude the value of the meals or lodging from income. Employees may also exclude the value of certain "qualified campus lodging" that the institution furnishes to them for an adequate rent (26 U.S.C. § 119(d)). See generally R. Wellen & H. Clemons, *Presidential Housing and Tax Reform: A Guide for Chief Executives* (American Association of State Colleges and Universities/National Association of College and University Attorneys, 1987).

One example of the types of problems that may arise under the lodging portion of Section 119 is *Winchell v. United States*, 564 F. Supp. 131 (D. Neb. 1983), *affirmed without opin.*, 725 F.2d 689 (8th Cir. 1984). The plaintiff was a college president who was provided free lodging in a house several miles from campus on land used by the college for athletic and other outdoor activities. The college's board of trustees had originally insisted that the president use the house as his personal residence. He was only "infrequently" required to use the house to carry out job-related duties (such as entertainment or meetings); his college office "ordinarily" sufficed to meet most of his administrative needs. To determine whether this lodging was "required . . . as a condition of employment" within the meaning of Section 119, the court considered various tests, one of which was that the taxpayer must "show that the free employer-provided housing is integrally related to the duties of the employee." Holding that the college president was unable to meet this test, the court determined that he was subject to taxation on the fair market rental value of the house, even though he had occupied it at the trustees' insistence.

Sections 511-513 of the Internal Revenue Code impose a tax on the "unrelated business income" of organizations that otherwise are exempt from taxation (26 U.S.C. § 511(a)(2)). Colleges and universities are expressly included within the types of organizations covered (26 U.S.C. § 511(a)(2)(B)). The tax applies to income generated by "any trade or business the conduct of which is not substantially related . . . to the exercise or performance by such organization of its charitable, educational, or other purpose or function" (26 U.S.C. §513(a)). The trade or business must be "regularly carried on" in order to be subject to the tax (26 U.S.C. §512(a)).[20] Even when these requirements (commonly known as the three requirements of (1) "trade or business," (2) "not substantially related," and (3) "regularly carried on") are met, there are various modifications (26 U.S.C. §512(b)(1)-(15)) and exceptions (26 U.S.C. §513(a)(1)-(3)) to the rule of tax liability. The "unrelated business income" tax (UBIT) will not apply, for instance, when "substantially all the work in carrying on [the] trade or business is performed for the organization without compensation" (26 U.S.C. §513(a)(1)); when the trade or business is conducted "by the organization primarily for the convenience of its members, students, . . . officers, or employees" (26 U.S.C. §513(a)(2)); and when the trade or business involves the "selling of merchandise substantially all of which has been received by the organization as gifts or contributions" (26 U.S.C. §513(a)(3)). Regulations elaborating the rules and exceptions on the unrelated business income tax are in 26 C.F.R. §§1.511-1 to 1.513-3. Other applications of these rules and exceptions are discussed in this volume, Sections 9.3.5.1 and 9.4.4.[21]

Other examples of Code provisions affecting higher education include the provisions applicable to the taxability of prizes and awards for scientific, educational, artistic, or literary achievements (26 U.S.C. §74); the tax exemptions for state and local bonds issued to finance higher education facilities (26 U.S.C. §§145 and 150); the availability of tax credits for sponsoring university research (26 U.S.C. §41); the deductibility of contributions made to higher education institutions for the purpose of receiving priority in obtaining athletic tickets (26 U.S.C. §170); the valuation and deductibility of gifts of appreciated property; the taxability of employer-provided educational benefits for employees and their spouses and dependents (26 U.S.C. §127); qualification requirements for employer-sponsored retirement or pension plans (see, for example, D. Gordon & D. Spuehler, "Questions and Answers Explaining the New Tax Rules Applicable to Tax-Sheltered Annuities," 17 *J. Coll. & Univ. Law* 435 (1991)); and the taxability of grants and fellowships awarded to foreign students and scholars (see generally D. Williams, "Foreign Students and Scholars and the United States Tax System," IHELG Monograph 91-2 (University of Houston Law Center, 1991)).

Besides taxability questions such as those discussed above, institutions also face questions regarding their obligations to withhold certain amounts from employees' paychecks and remit these amounts to IRS as tax payments credited to the employee. This withholding obligation is governed by Sections 3401-3406 of the

[20]The cases and rulings are collected in Annot., "When Will Income Received by Organization Exempt from Federal Income Tax Under §501 of Internal Revenue Code of 1954 (26 U.S.C.S. §501) Be Deemed Income from Unrelated Trade or Business Taxable Under §§511-513 of Code (26 U.S.C.S. §§511-513)," 70 A.L.R. Fed. 229 (1984 and periodic supp.).

[21]Helpful information on UBIT can be found in the outlines and papers presented at conferences and workshops sponsored by the National Association of College and University Attorneys and maintained in the files of NACUA's Legal Reference Service available to NACUA attorneys. At the 1992 annual conference, for example, a session on UBIT included these submissions: J. Burke, "Unrelated Business Income Tax Update"; M. Cerny, "UBIT from Tax Counsel's Point of View"; and T. Hopkins, "Unrelated Business Income Tax ('UBIT') Update: Overview; Nuts and Bolts."

Internal Revenue Code (26 U.S.C. §§ 3401–3406). Under Section 3401(a), only income considered to be "wages" is subject to withholding (see generally *Central Illinois Public Service Co. v. United States*, 435 U.S. 21 (1978)). In *Western Reserve Academy v. United States*, 619 F. Supp. 394 (W.D. Ohio 1985), *affirmed*, 801 F.2d 250 (6th Cir. 1986), the court relied on this distinction between income and wages to relieve the plaintiff from liability to withhold taxes on certain tuition-assistance payments to faculty because, at the time in question, the institution's legal obligation to treat such payments as wages was "speculative and imprecise."[22]

To deal with these myriad issues, institutions' legal counsel and tax advisers will need to be attentive to the Treasury regulations and the IRS revenue rulings, revenue procedures, technical advice memoranda, and private letter rulings (see above) and will need to monitor new developments closely. Counsel may on occasion need to obtain a private letter ruling for the institution; see H. Massler, "How to Get and Use IRS Private Letter Rulings," 33 *Practical Lawyer* 11 (1987). Administrators will also need to be aware of and ensure institutional compliance with the various filing requirements (see, for example, 26 U.S.C. § 6033(a)(1)) and public disclosure requirements (see, for example, 26 U.S.C. § 6104(e)) applicable to colleges and universities. In undertaking these functions, institutional personnel will want to consult the IRS's "Final Examination Guidelines Regarding Colleges and Universities" (Announcement 94-112, Aug. 1994). These guidelines, which provide the framework within which agents conduct audits, preview many IRS concerns, such as (1) employment tax and fringe benefit issues, (2) retirement or pension plans and other deferred-compensation arrangements, (3) income from research contracts, (4) scholarships and fellowships, (5) legislative and political activity expenses, and (6) income from college and university bookstores and other UBIT issues. (See, for example, B. Harding & E. McClellan, "Unreasonable Compensation: The Hidden Issue in the IRS College and University Examination Guidelines," 20 *J. Coll. & Univ. Law* 111 (1993).) The IRS guidelines are an excellent primer for colleges and universities on the various tax issues the IRS is likely to pursue in an audit and on the various document requests it is likely to make.

7.3.2. Social Security taxes. The laws establishing the Social Security system are found in two different titles of the *United States Code*. Title 42 (§ 401 et seq.) establishes the "Federal Old Age and Survivors Insurance Trust Fund and Federal Disability Insurance Trust Fund" and sets the requirements on eligibility for benefits. Title 26 (§ 3101 et seq.), the Federal Insurance Contributions Act (FICA), defines which employers and employees are subject to taxation and levies the appropriate tax (see J. H. Ditkoff, "Withholding and Employment Taxes: Practices, Penalties, and Questions of Policy," 37 *N.Y.U. Annual Institute on Federal Taxation*, Part 2, § 30.1 (1979)). The postsecondary education community's exposure to these laws was enhanced by the Social Security Amendments of 1983 (97 Stat. 65).

Passed in an effort to ensure the continued solvency of the Social Security system, these amendments affected the tax liability of postsecondary institutions in two ways. First, Section 102(b)(1)(C) of the amendments (97 Stat. 70) deleted the

---

[22]For cases on withholding, in this and other situations, see Annot., "What Constitutes Employer-Employee Relationship for Purpose of Federal Income Tax Withholdings," 51 A.L.R. Fed. 59 (1981 and periodic supp.).

language from 26 U.S.C. § 3121(b)(8)(B) that had previously provided an exemption from the system for "service performed in the employ of a religious, charitable, educational, or other organization" as defined in 26 U.S.C. § 501(c)(3). Thus, private institutions in that category can no longer claim such an exemption. Second, Section 103(a) of the amendments modified 42 U.S.C. § 418 et seq., which had allowed states voluntarily to enter into agreements with the U.S. secretary of health and human services for the coverage of state and local employees under the Social Security system. As amended, this provision forbids states that have entered such agreements from withdrawing from them, thus "locking" into the system states that are participating under voluntary agreements. The constitutionality of this provision was upheld in *Bowen v. Public Agencies Opposed to Social Security Entrapment*, 477 U.S. 41 (1986). Public postsecondary institutions covered by such an agreement thus have no option of dropping out.

Later, in the Omnibus Budget Reconciliation Act of 1990 (104 Stat. 1388), Congress again broadened the applicability of FICA to public postsecondary institutions and their employees. This Act added a new section (26 U.S.C. § 3121(b)(7)(F)) to the Code, which brought within FICA the employees of states and their political subdivisions and instrumentalities who are not members of a retirement system of their employer. Regulations implementing this provision are in 26 C.F.R. § 31.3121(b)(7).

Although the 1983 and 1990 Acts constricted the number of institutions and employees exempt from the Social Security tax, they left intact exemptions for several classes of employees common to postsecondary institutions.[23] Still exempt from coverage are (1) students "enrolled and regularly attending classes" who are also employees of the institution (see Revenue Ruling 78-17, 1978-1 C.B. 306), except for student employees at public institutions that are covered by, and include such students in, voluntary agreements between the state and the secretary of health and human services (26 U.S.C. § 3121(b)(10)); (2) students "enrolled and . . . regularly attending classes" who perform domestic services at college clubs, sororities, or fraternities (26 U.S.C. § 3121(b)(2)); (3) student nurses "enrolled and . . . regularly attending classes" at a state-approved nurses' training school who are employed at a "hospital or a nurses' training school" (26 U.S.C. § 3121(b)(13)); and (4) clergy whose services for the institution are performed in "the exercise of [their] ministry" or members of religious orders whose services for the institution are performed "in the exercise of duties required by such order" (26 U.S.C. § 3121(b)(8)). For the student categories, controversy has recently arisen over the meaning of the phrase "regularly attending classes" as it applies to part-time students; see S. Jaschik, "IRS Would Force More Students to Pay Social Security Taxes," *Chron. Higher Educ.*, June 1, 1994, A30.

The exemption for student nurses was at issue in *Johnson City Medical Center Hospital v. United States*, 999 F.2d 973 (6th Cir. 1993). Relying on the statutory exemption and the IRS regulation implementing it (26 C.F.R. § 31.3121(b)(13)-1), the hospital sought a refund of Federal Insurance Contribution Act (FICA) taxes paid

---

[23]The question of who is an "employee" for purposes of Social Security law is often difficult to answer. For relevant cases and authorities, see Annot., "Determination of Employer-Employee Relationship for Social Security Contribution and Unemployment Tax Purposes Under § 3121(d)(2) of Federal Insurance Contributions Act (26 U.S.C. § 3121(d)(2), § 3306(i) of Federal Unemployment Tax Act (26 U.S.C. § 3306(i)), and Implementing Regulations," 37 A.L.R. Fed. 95 (1978 and periodic supp.).

with respect to employees who were registered students at a nearby nursing school at East Tennessee State University. The United States relied on a revenue ruling interpreting the statutory exemption (Revenue Ruling 85-74, 1985-1 C.B. 331). That ruling set out three requirements the employer must meet to obtain the exemption: "(1) [t]he employment is substantially less than full time, (2) [t]he total amount of earnings is nominal, and (3) [t]he only services performed by the student nurse for the employer are incidental parts of the student nurse's training toward a [nursing] degree." The court determined that this ruling reflected Congress's intent for the exemption and upheld the ruling's validity. Then, applying the ruling to the facts of the case, the court held that the university did not meet two of the three requirements. It did meet the first requirement, because the student nurses worked no more than forty hours over a two-week period. However, because the student nurses earned the regular, and not a reduced, rate of pay for their services, their earnings were not nominal as provided in the second requirement; and because the work was not formally part of a nurses' training program, the hospital did not meet the third requirement. The employment of the student nurses therefore did not fall within the exemption, and the court denied the hospital's request for a refund.

As with the income tax laws (this volume, Section 7.3.1), institutions also have withholding obligations under the Social Security laws, specifically under the "FICA" provisions in 26 U.S.C. § 3101 et seq. Also as with the income tax laws, only income considered to be "wages" is subject to withholding (26 U.S.C. § 3121(a)). Using this distinction, the courts in the *Western Reserve Academy* case (cited in Section 7.3.1) relieved the academy of FICA withholding liability by the same reason it applied to income tax withholding liability. Other hotly debated questions arose in the 1980s concerning whether amounts transferred to retirement annuity contracts via salary reduction agreements were considered wages for FICA purposes. Congress also resolved that issue in the 1983 Social Security Amendments, adding a new section to the Code (26 U.S.C. § 3121(a)(5)(D)), which serves to include payments under salary-reduction agreements in the FICA wage base. See *Robert Morris College v. United States*, 11 Cl. Ct. 546 (U.S. Claims Ct. 1987).

The U.S. Department of Treasury regulations on FICA withholding include special provisions applicable to postsecondary institutions (26 C.F.R. § 31.3121(a)(18)-1 and 31.3121(b)(8)-2, (10)-2, and (13)-1). One special provision (arising from the 1983 amendments), for instance, allows universities that have hospitals affiliated with them to coordinate the Social Security withholding of university faculty members who also hold hospital staff positions (see 26 U.S.C. § 3121(s); 26 C.F.R. § 31.3121 (s)-1).

7.3.3. Unemployment compensation taxes.

7.3.3. *Unemployment compensation taxes.* The Federal Unemployment Tax Act (FUTA) (26 U.S.C. § 3301 et seq.) was originally passed in 1935 as a response to the unemployment of the Great Depression. Its purpose was and is to provide compensation to qualifying employees who are temporarily out of work. The federal government and the states share the responsibility for the Act's operation. Although ultimate responsibility for the tax rests with the federal government, states are permitted to implement their own unemployment plans. Where a state plan conforms to the requirements set out in the statute (26 U.S.C. §§ 3302–3305), the U.S. secretary of labor will annually certify the plan. This system allows the state to accept employers' contributions into a state unemployment fund and to be primarily responsible for administration of the compensation program funded from these contributions.

At one time FUTA exempted states and their political subdivisions from the unemployment compensation system. In 1976, however, Congress amended FUTA to bring states and their subdivisions within the statute and extend unemployment protection to their employees (26 U.S.C. § 3309(a)(1)(B)). Another 1976 amendment gave political subdivisions of a state the option of reimbursing the state for unemployment benefits paid to laid-off employees rather than making contributions in the same manner as private-sector employers (26 U.S.C. § 3309(a)(2)). The constitutionality of these amendments was upheld in *State of New Hampshire Department of Employment Security v. Marshall*, 616 F.2d 240 (1st Cir. 1980). In rejecting the state's argument that the amendments violated the Tenth Amendment of the Constitution (see this volume, Section 7.1.3), the court emphasized that states may decline to establish unemployment plans if they do not wish to obtain the benefits of the program, but that if they choose to participate, states must meet all the requirements set out in FUTA, including coverage of state employees. Thus, state colleges, universities, and community colleges, and their faculties and staffs, are clearly covered by the Act.

At one time most private postsecondary institutions (and private elementary and secondary schools) were also exempt from FUTA. In 1970 and 1976, however, Congress approved amendments that greatly narrowed this exemption. Private nonsectarian institutions were clearly subjected to the Act as a result of these amendments; there was some question, however, about church-related institutions. In *St. Martin Evangelical Lutheran Church v. South Dakota*, 451 U.S. 772 (1981), the plaintiffs challenged the applicability of the amendments to nonprofit church-related primary and secondary schools. The relevant exemption, as narrowed by the 1970 and 1976 amendments, provided that:

> This section shall not apply to service performed (1) in the employ of (A) a church or convention or association of churches, or (B) an organization which is operated primarily for religious purposes and which is operated, supervised, controlled, or principally supported by a church or convention or association of churches [26 U.S.C. § 3309(b)(1)].

The U.S. secretary of labor, relying on the legislative history of Section 3309, had ruled that church-related primary and secondary schools were not included within this language and were therefore subject to FUTA. The U.S. Supreme Court rejected the Labor Department's interpretation.

The Court's analysis in *St. Martin* of Section 3309's legislative history provides insight into FUTA's application to both elementary/secondary and postsecondary church-related schools:

> Section 3309 was added to FUTA in 1970. Although the legislative history directly discussing the intended coverage of its subsection (b)(1) is limited, the House Report had the following explanation:
>
>> This paragraph excludes services of persons where the employer is a church or convention or association of churches, but does not exclude certain services performed for an organization which may be religious in orientation unless it is operated primarily for religious purposes and is

operated, supervised, controlled, or principally supported by a church (or convention or association of churches). Thus, the services of the janitor of a church would be excluded, but services of a janitor for a separately incorporated college, although it may be church related, would be covered. A college devoted primarily to preparing students for the ministry would be exempt, as would a novitiate or a house of study training candidates to become members of religious orders. On the other hand, a church-related (separately incorporated) charitable organization (such as, for example, an orphanage or a home for the aged) would not be considered under this paragraph to be operated primarily for religious purposes (H.R. Rep. No. 91-612, p. 44 (1969)).

The Senate Report contained identical language (see S. Rep. No. 91-752, pp. 48–49 (1970)).

. . .

The above quotation from the 1969 House Report, and its Senate counterpart, however, are susceptible of a simpler and more reasonable explanation [than the explanation provided to the Court by the South Dakota Supreme Court and the U.S. secretary of labor] that corresponds directly with the language of the subsection. Congress drew a distinction between employees "of a church or convention or association of churches" (§ 3309(b)(1)(A)), on the one hand, and employees of "separately incorporated" organizations, on the other (see H.R. Rep. No. 91-612 at 44). The former uniformly would be excluded from coverage by § 3309(b)(1)(A), while the latter would be eligible for exclusion under § 3309-(b)(1)(B) only when the organization is "operated, supervised, controlled, or principally supported by a church or convention or association of churches." To hold, as respondent would have us do, that "organization" in subsection (b)(1)(B) also includes a church school that is not separately incorporated would make (b)(1)(A) and (b)(1)(B) redundant [451 U.S. at 781–83].

Apparently, under the *St. Martin* analysis, elementary and secondary schools are far more likely than postsecondary institutions to be exempt from FUTA. To be exempt under Section 3309(b)(1)(A), a college must be part of—not separately incorporated from—a "church or convention or association of churches." To be exempt under Section 3309(b)(1)(B), a college not only must have close ties to a sponsoring church but also must be "operated primarily for religious purposes." While such terms may be subject to considerable debate, apparently only a small proportion of church-related postsecondary institutions can qualify under these tests. The primary example, as the legislative history reveals, is the seminary.

FUTA has a number of provisions that take into account the special circumstances of higher education institutions. There are provisions, for instance, that exempt from coverage the services of regularly enrolled students who are employed by the institutions they attend (26 U.S.C. § 3306(c)(10)(B)), the services of certain students in cooperative work-study programs (26 U.S.C. § 3306(c)(10)(C)), and the services of certain student nurses and medical interns (26 U.S.C. § 3306(c)(13)). Another provision deals with the unique aspects of the academic calendar and details circumstances under which unemployment compensation is not payable to faculty, researchers, and administrators because of gaps in service attributable to customary vacation or recess periods or to periods between academic years or terms (26 U.S.C. § 3304(a)(6)(A)(i)).

Sec. 7.4. Federal Aid-to-Education Programs

The federal government's major function regarding postsecondary education is to establish national priorities and objectives for federal spending on education and to provide funds in accordance with those decisions. To implement its priorities and objectives, the federal government attaches a wide and varied range of conditions to the funds it makes available under its spending power (Section 7.1.1) and enforces these conditions against postsecondary institutions and other aid recipients. Some of these conditions are specific to the program for which funds are given. Others, called "cross-cutting" conditions, apply across a range of programs; they are discussed in Section 7.4.3 below. Cumulatively, these conditions exert a substantial influence on postsecondary institutions, often leading to institutional cries of economic coercion and federal control. In light of such criticisms, the federal role in funding postsecondary education has for many years been a major political and policy issue. The particular national goals to be achieved through funding and fund conditions, and the delivery and compliance mechanisms best suited to achieving these goals, will likely remain subjects of debate for the foreseeable future.

Federal spending for postsecondary education has a long history. Shortly after the founding of the United States, the federal government began endowing public higher education institutions with public lands. In 1862 Congress passed the first Morrill Act, providing grants of land or land scrip to the states for the support of agricultural and mechanical colleges, and later provided continuing appropriations for these colleges. The second Morrill Act, providing money grants for instruction in various branches of higher education, was passed in 1890. In 1944 Congress enacted the first GI Bill, which was followed in later years by successive programs providing funds to veterans to further their education. The National Defense Education Act, passed in 1958 after Congress was spurred by Russia's launching of *Sputnik,* included a large-scale program of low-interest loans for students in institutions of higher education. The Higher Education Facilities Act of 1963 authorized grants and low-interest loans to public and private nonprofit institutions of higher education for constructing and improving various educational facilities. Then, in 1965, Congress finally jumped broadly into supporting higher education with the passage of the Higher Education Act of 1965 (20 U.S.C. § 1001 et seq.). The Act's various titles authorized federal support for a range of postsecondary education activities, including community educational services; resources, training, and research for college libraries and personnel; strengthening of developing institutions; and student financial aid programs (see Section 4.3.2). The Act has been frequently amended since 1965 and continues to be the primary authorizing legislation for federal higher education spending.

7.4.1. Distinction between federal aid and federal procurement. Funds provided under the Higher Education Act and other aid programs should be sharply distinguished from funds provided under federal procurement programs. Many federal agencies, such as the U.S. Department of Defense, enter into procurement contracts with postsecondary institutions or consortia, the primary purpose of which is to obtain research or other services that meet the government's own needs. True aid-to-education programs, in contrast, directly serve the needs of institutions, their students and faculty, or the education community in general, rather than the government's own needs for goods or services. The two systems—assistance and procurement—operate independently of one another, with different statutory bases and different regulations, and often with different agency officials in charge. Guidelines for differentiating the two systems are set out in Chapter 63 of Subtitle V of 41 U.S.C.: "Using Procurement Contracts and Grant and Cooperative Agreements."

The bases of the federal procurement system are Title III of the Federal Property and Administrative Services Act of 1949 (41 U.S.C. § 251 et seq.); the Office of Federal Procurement Policy Act of 1974 (41 U.S.C. § 401 et seq.); the Armed Services Procurement Act (10 U.S.C. § 2301 et seq.); the Federal Acquisition Regulation (FAR) (48 C.F.R. ch. 1); and other miscellaneous public contract provisions (found particularly in 41 C.F.R. chs. 50–61). These sources establish uniform policies and procedures that individual agencies implement and supplement with regulations specific to their own procurement activities. The individual agency regulations are set out in 48 C.F.R. Chapters 2–49.

Federal procurement law permits federal agencies to exercise more substantial control over the details of procurement contracts than is typical with grants and other forms of federal aid; many standard clauses that must be used in procurement contracts are prescribed by federal regulations (see 48 C.F.R. §§ 16.1 to 16.7). Unlike assistance, moreover, procurement contracts "shall terminate . . . , whether for default or convenience, only when it is in the government's interest" (48 C.F.R. § 49.101(b) (1992)). Government contractors found guilty of fraud, embezzlement, antitrust violations, or other criminal or civil offenses impugning business integrity may be debarred or suspended for a specified time from obtaining other government contracts (48 C.F.R. §§ 3.104 to 3.111 (1992)). Contractors may appeal disputes concerning their government contracts to agency Boards of Contract Appeals, established pursuant to the Contract Disputes Act (41 U.S.C. § 601 et seq.), or may bypass this appeals process and bring an action directly in the U.S. Court of Federal Claims (41 U.S.C. § 609(a)(1)).

Other important federal laws also establish requirements applicable to the federal procurement system. Executive Orders 11246 and 11375 (Sections 3.3.2.8 and 3.4 of this volume), for instance, establish affirmative action requirements for federal government contractors. Similarly, the Davis-Bacon Act (40 U.S.C. § 276a et seq.), as implemented by Department of Labor regulations (29 C.F.R. Part 5), establishes rate-of-pay requirements for employees working under federal construction contracts. The Service Contract Labor Standards Act (41 U.S.C. § 351 et seq.) and its implementing regulations (29 C.F.R. Part 4) establish comparable requirements for employees working under federal service contracts.

Although laws such as these are designed for the procurement system rather than the federal aid system, they are often extended to federal aid recipients who enter procurement contracts as a means of accomplishing part of their work under a federal grant, loan, or cooperative agreement. (See, for example, 20 U.S.C. § 1232b (application of Davis-Bacon Act to procurement contracts of ED aid recipients); 48 C.F.R. § 22.300 et seq. (application of Davis-Bacon Act, Executive Orders 11246 and 11375, and Contract Work Hours and Safety Standards Act (40 U.S.C. § 327 et seq.), to procurement contracts of ED aid recipients); 29 C.F.R. § 5.2(h) and 41 C.F.R. § 60-1.1 (application of Davis-Bacon Act and Executive Order 11246 to procurement contracts of other federal aid recipients).)

7.4.2. Legal structure of aid programs. Federal aid for postsecondary education is disbursed by a number of federal agencies. The five most important are the U.S. Department of Education, the U.S. Department of Health and Human Services, the National Foundation of Arts and Humanities (comprised of the National Endowment for the Humanities, the National Endowment for the Arts, and the Institute of Museum Services), the National Science Foundation, and (at least with respect to student aid) the Department of Veterans Affairs. The U.S. Department of Education was created in 1979 by the Department of Education Organization Act (93 Stat. 668, 20 U.S.C. § 3401 et seq.). The Act transferred functions of the then U.S. Office of Education (a constituent unit of the then U.S. Department of Health, Education, and Welfare), the National Institute of Education, and several other federal agencies to the new department, which formally came into existence on May 4, 1980, in accordance with the Act and Executive Order 12212 (45 Fed. Reg. 29557 (May 2, 1980)).[24] The Act also redesignated the remainder of the then U.S. Department of Health, Education and Welfare (HEW) as the new U.S. Department of Health and Human Services (HHS). (The Public Health Service, previously a constituent agency of HEW and now of HHS, administers aid programs for students in medical, dental, pharmacy, nursing, and other health education programs (see 42 C.F.R. Part 57).)

The Department of Veterans Affairs administers the various veterans' educational benefits programs, authorized in 38 U.S.C. § 3011 et seq., 38 U.S.C. § 3451 et seq. and 10 U.S.C. § 2131 et seq. (See *Max Cleland, Administrator of VA v. National College of Business*, 435 U.S. 213 (1978), upholding various federal statutory requirements regarding veterans' use of VA benefits.) The DVA contracts with State Approving Agencies, which review courses and determine whether to approve them as courses for which veterans can expend veterans' benefits. The State Approving Agencies, and the institutions seeking approval for their courses, must follow criteria and procedures for such approvals that are set out in 38 U.S.C. § 3675 et seq. (see Section 4.3.2 of this volume). Regulations implementing the veterans' benefits programs are published in 38 C.F.R. Part 21.

Federal aid to postsecondary education is dispensed in a variety of ways. Depending on the program involved, federal agencies may award grants or make loans directly to individual students; guarantee loans made to individual students by third parties; award grants directly to faculty members; make grants or loans to postsecondary institutions; enter "cooperative agreements" (as opposed to procurement contracts) with postsecondary institutions; or award grants, make loans, or enter agreements with state agencies, which in turn provide aid to institutions or their students or faculty. Whether an institution is eligible to receive federal aid, either directly from the federal agency or a state agency or indirectly through its student recipients, depends on the requirements of the particular aid program. Typically, however, the institution must be accredited by a recognized accrediting agency or demonstrate compliance with one of the few statutorily prescribed substitutes for accreditation (see this volume, Section 8.3.1).

The "rules of the game" regarding eligibility, application procedures, the selection of recipients, allowable expenditures, conditions on spending, records and reports requirements, compliance reviews, and other federal aid requirements are set

[24]The House and Senate reports and congressional debates accompanying the legislation are found in 1979 *U.S. Code Cong. & Admin. News*, 96th Cong., 1st Sess., at 1514–1644.

out in a variety of sources. Postsecondary administrators will want to be familiar with these sources in order to maximize their institution's ability to obtain and effectively utilize federal money. Legal counsel will want to be familiar with these sources in order to protect their institution from challenges to its eligibility or to its compliance with applicable requirements.

The starting point is the statute that authorizes the particular federal aid program, along with the statute's legislative history. Occasionally, the appropriations legislation funding the program for a particular fiscal year will also contain requirements applicable to the expenditure of the appropriated funds. The next source, adding specificity to the statutory base, is the regulations for the program. These regulations, which are published in the *Federal Register* (Fed. Reg.) and then codified in the *Code of Federal Regulations* (C.F.R.), are the primary source of the administering agency's program requirements. Title 34 of the *Code of Federal Regulations* is the Education title, the location of the U.S. Department of Education's regulations.

Published regulations have the force of law and bind the government, the aid recipients, and all the outside parties. In addition, agencies may supplement their regulations with program manuals, program guidelines, policy guidance or memoranda, agency interpretations, and "dear colleague" letters. These materials generally do not have the status of law; although they may sometimes be binding on recipients who had actual notice of them before receiving federal funds, more often they are treated as agency suggestions that do not bind anyone (see 5 U.S.C. § 552(a)(1); 20 U.S.C. § 1232). Additional requirements or suggestions may be found in the grant award documents or agreements under which the agency dispenses the aid, or in agency grant and contract manuals that establish general agency policy.

Yet other rules of the game are in executive branch directives or congressional legislation applicable to a range of federal agencies or their contractors or grantees. The executive branch's Office of Management and Budget (OMB) circulars, for instance, set government-wide policy on matters such as allowable costs, indirect cost rates, and audit requirements. One of the most important of these circulars, OMB Circular A-21, "Cost Principles for Educational Institutions," was most recently revised in 1991 (56 Fed. Reg. 50224 (Oct. 3, 1991)). And the Single Audit Act of 1984 (98 Stat. 2327, codified at 31 U.S.C. § 7501(a)) "establish[es] uniform requirements for audits of federal financial assistance provided to State and Local governments."

Another example of legislation that sets general requirements is the Byrd Amendment (31 U.S.C. § 1352), which limits the use of federal funds for lobbying activities. This provision provides in part that:

(a)(1) None of the funds appropriated by any Act may be expended by the recipient of a Federal contract, grant, loan, or cooperative agreement to pay any person for influencing or attempting to influence an officer or employee of any agency, a Member of Congress, an officer or employee of Congress, or an employee of a Member of Congress in connection with any Federal action described in paragraph (2) of this subsection.

(2) The prohibition in paragraph (1) of this subsection applies with respect to the following Federal actions:

(A) The awarding of any Federal contract.

(B) The making of any Federal grant.

(C) The making of any Federal loan.

    (D) The entering into of any cooperative agreement.

    (E) The extension, continuation, renewal, amendment, or modification
          of any Federal contract, grant, loan, or cooperative agreement.

Applicants for federal assistance must certify that they are and will remain in compliance with this requirement, and they must also disclose certain lobbying activities paid for with nonfederal funds. The Office of Management and Budget promulgated Interim Final Guidance for implementing the Byrd Amendment in December 1989 (54 Fed. Reg. 52306–52311 (Dec. 20, 1989)). The OMB guidance required that the executive departments and agencies promulgate two sets of common rules to implement the amendment: one set for procurement contracts to appear in the Federal Acquisition Regulation; and one set for nonprocurement contracts, grants, loans, cooperative agreements, loan insurance commitments, and loan guarantee commitments. Both the Department of Defense and the Department of Education have issued final regulations implementing the Byrd Amendment (32 C.F.R. § 28.100 et seq. (1993) and 34 C.F.R. § 82.100 et seq. (1993)).

    There is also a federal statute, the General Education Provisions Act (20 U.S.C. § 1221 et seq.), that applies specifically and only to the U.S. Department of Education, placing additional restrictions on its rules of the game. The Act (GEPA) establishes numerous organizational, administrative, and other requirements applicable to ED spending programs. For instance, the Act establishes procedures that ED must follow when proposing program regulations (20 U.S.C. § 1232). The GEPA provisions on enforcement of conditions attached to federal funds do not apply, however, to Higher Education Act programs (20 U.S.C. § 1234i(2)). To supplement GEPA, the Department of Education has promulgated extensive general regulations published at 34 C.F.R. Parts 74–81. These "Education Department General Administrative Regulations" (EDGAR) establish uniform policies for all ED grant programs. The applicability of Part 74 of these regulations to higher education institutions is specified at 34 C.F.R. §§ 74.1(a), 74.4(b), and 81.2. Running to 150 pages in the *Code of Federal Regulations*, EDGAR tells you almost everything you wanted to know but were afraid to ask about the legal requirements for obtaining and administering ED grants.

    Other funding agencies also have general regulations that set certain conditions applicable to a range of their aid programs. The Public Health Service of HHS, for example, has published a final rule governing the investigation and reporting of scientific misconduct (codified at 42 C.F.R. Part 50, subpart A). The rule defines scientific misconduct and requires institutions receiving financial assistance to develop an administrative process for responding to a report of suspected misconduct. The institution must make an immediate inquiry to determine whether an investigation is needed; if so, the institution must advise the Office of Scientific Integrity (OSI) (now the Office of Research Integrity (ORI); see 57 Fed. Reg. 24262 (June 8, 1992)) that an investigation is warranted. The investigation must begin no later than thirty days after the inquiry has been completed. A full report on the progress and outcome of the investigation must be made to OSI. (The National Science Foundation has a similar scientific misconduct rule published at 45 C.F.R. Part 689.1 et seq.)

7.4.3. *"Cross-cutting" aid conditions.* In addition to the programmatic and fiscal requirements discussed in Section 7.4.2 above, various statutes and agency regulations establish requirements that are not specific to any particular aid program but, rather, implement broader federal policy objectives that "cut across" a range of programs or agencies. The civil rights statutes and regulations discussed in Section 7.5 are a prominent example. Others are the requirements concerning the privacy of student records (discussed in Section 4.16.1) and campus security (discussed in Section 4.17). Other leading examples are discussed in Sections 7.4.3.1 to 7.4.3.3 below. The growth and increasing variety of these "cross-cutting" requirements mark what is perhaps the most significant contemporary trend regarding federal involvement in postsecondary education.

     7.4.3.1. Drug-Free Workplace Act of 1988. The Drug-Free Workplace Act of 1988 (41 U.S.C. §§ 701–702) applies to institutions of higher education that contract with a federal agency to provide services or property worth at least $25,000 or that receive a grant from a federal agency for any amount.[25] To qualify for such a contract or grant, an applicant institution must certify to the contracting or granting agency that it will undertake various activities to provide a drug-free workplace. Grantees' activities must include:

(A) publishing a statement notifying employees that the unlawful manufacture, distribution, dispensation, possession, or use of a controlled substance is prohibited in the grantee's workplace and specifying the actions that will be taken against employees for violations of such prohibition;

(B) establishing a drug-free awareness program to inform employees about—
   (i) the dangers of drug abuse in the workplace;
   (ii) the grantee's policy of maintaining a drug-free workplace;
   (iii) any available drug counseling, rehabilitation, and employee assistance programs; and
   (iv) the penalties that may be imposed upon employees for drug abuse violations;

(C) making it a requirement that each employee to be engaged in the performance of such grant be given a copy of the statement required by subparagraph (A);

(D) notifying the employee in the statement required by subparagraph (A), that as a condition of employment on such grant, the employee will—
   (i) abide by the terms of the statement; and
   (ii) notify the employer of any criminal drug statute conviction for a violation occurring in the workplace no later than 5 days after such conviction;

(E) notifying the granting agency within 10 days after receiving notice of a conviction under subparagraph (D)(ii) from an employee or otherwise receiving actual notice of such conviction;

(F) imposing a sanction on, or requiring the satisfactory participation in a drug abuse assistance or rehabilitation program by, any employee who is so convicted, as required by section 7033 of this title; and

(G) making a good faith effort to continue to maintain a drug-free workplace through implementation of subparagraphs (A), (B), (C), (D), (E), and (F) [41 U.S.C. § 702(a)(1)].

---

[25]In addition to the requirements of the Drug-Free Workplace Act, some higher education institutions that contract with the Department of Defense will also be subject to that department's separate Drug-Free Workplace regulations (57 Fed. Reg. 32736, July 23, 1992) (Interim Final Rule); see also 57 Fed. Reg. 32769, July 23, 1992) (Notice of Proposed Rulemaking)).

The requirements for contractors, contained in Section 701(a)(1), are virtually identical. Section 706(2) of the Act defines "employee" as any employee of the grantee or contractor "directly engaged in the performance of work pursuant to the provisions of the grant or contract."

The Act also applies to individuals who receive a grant from a federal agency or who contract with a federal agency for any amount. Such individuals must certify that they "will not engage in the unlawful manufacture, distribution, dispensation, possession, or use of a controlled substance" in conducting grant activities or performing the contract (41 U.S.C. §§ 701(a)(2) and 702(a)(2)). Recipients of Pell grants (see Section 4.3.2, this volume) are not considered to be individual grantees for purposes of this section (20 U.S.C. § 1070a(i)).

Under Sections 701(b)(1) and 702(b)(1), contracts and grants (including contracts and grants to individuals) are "subject to suspension of payments . . . or termination . . . or both" and contractors and grantees are "subject to suspension or debarment" if they make a false certification, or violate their certification, or if so many of their employees have been convicted under criminal drug statutes for violations occurring in the workplace as to indicate the contractor's or grantee's failure to "make a good faith effort to provide a drug-free workplace."

The final regulations for grantees, entitled "Government-Wide Requirements for Drug-Free Workplace (Grants)" (55 Fed. Reg. 21681 (May 25, 1990)), are in the form of a common rule to be codified in various sections of the *Code of Federal Regulations* in the form adopted by each individual agency. The Department of Education regulations, for example, are codified in 34 C.F.R. Part 85. The regulations for contractors are in a separate final rule amending the Federal Acquisition Regulation, codified at 48 C.F.R. subparts 9.406-2(b)(2), 23.500, and 52.223-6 and 7.

The final grantee regulations include helpful advice in the form of public comments on the previous interim final rule, followed by the agencies' responses (55 Fed. Reg. at 21683–21688). The responses indicate, inter alia, that the Act does not require grantees to have alcohol and drug abuse programs, nor does the Act require drug testing (at 21684–21685). There are also responses prepared by the U.S. Department of Education that address several matters, including the certifications required under the various student financial aid programs (at 21688).

See generally L. White, *Complying with "Drug-Free Workplace" Laws on College and University Campuses* (National Association of College and University Attorneys, 1989).

7.4.3.2. Drug-Free Schools and Communities Act Amendments. The Drug-Free Schools and Communities Act Amendments of 1989 (103 Stat. 1928, 20 U.S.C. § 1145g) requires institutions receiving federal financial assistance to establish drug and alcohol programs for both students and employees. Specifically, the Act requires institutions to distribute the following materials annually to all students and employees:

(1)(A) standards of conduct that clearly prohibit, at a minimum, the unlawful possession, use, or distribution of illicit drugs and alcohol by students and employees on its property or as a part of any of its activities;

(B) a description of the applicable legal sanctions under local, State, or Federal law for the unlawful possession or distribution of illicit drugs and alcohol;

(C) a description of the health risks associated with the use of illicit drugs and the abuse of alcohol;

(D) a description of any drug or alcohol counseling, treatment, or rehabilitation or re-entry programs that are available to employees or students; and

(E) a clear statement that the institution will impose sanctions on students and employees (consistent with local, State, and Federal law), and a description of those sanctions, up to and including expulsion or termination of employment and referral for prosecution, for violations of the standards of conduct required by paragraph (1)(A) [20 U.S.C. § 1145g(a)(1)].

In addition, institutions must biennially review their programs to determine their effectiveness, to implement changes if needed, and to ensure that the required sanctions are being carried out. Upon request, institutions must provide to the secretary of education or to the public a copy of all materials they are required to distribute to students and employees and a copy of the report from the biennial review.

The statute does not require institutions to conduct drug tests or to identify students or employees who abuse alcohol. However, if an institution has notice that a student or an employee has violated one of the standards of conduct promulgated under the statute, it must enforce its published sanctions. The statute also does not require institutions to operate treatment programs; institutions must, however, notify students of counseling and treatment programs that are available to them.

In enforcing the standards of conduct and sanctions required by the statute, institutions should of course comply with the requirements of constitutional due process (this volume, Sections 3.6.2 and 4.8.2; see also Section 1.5.2) as well as the record-keeping requirements of the Buckley Amendment (this volume, Section 4.16.1).

Final regulations implementing the Drug-Free Schools and Communities Act Amendments were published in 55 Fed. Reg. 33580 (Aug. 16, 1990) and are codified in 34 C.F.R. Part 86.

7.4.3.3. Student Right-to-Know Act. The Student Right-to-Know Act (Title I of the Student-Right-to-Know and Campus Security Act) (104 Stat. 2381–2384 (1990)) amends Section 485 of the Higher Education Act (20 U.S.C. § 1092) to impose new information-sharing requirements on higher education institutions that participate in federal student aid programs. Section 103 (20 U.S.C. § 1092(a)(1)(L)) requires such institutions to compile and disclose "the completion or graduation rate of certificate-or-degree-seeking, full-time students" entering the institutions. Disclosure must be made both to current students and to prospective students. Section 104 of the Act (20 U.S.C. § 1092(e)) includes additional compilation and disclosure requirements applicable to those institutions that are "attended by students receiving athletically related student aid"; these requirements are discussed in Section 4.15.1 of this volume.

7.4.4. Enforcing compliance with aid conditions. The federal government has several methods for enforcing compliance with its various aid requirements. The responsible agency may periodically audit the institution's expenditures of federal money (see, for example, 20 U.S.C. § 1094(c)(1)(A)) and may take an "audit exception" for funds not spent in compliance with program requirements. The institution then owes the federal government the amount specified in the audit exception. In addition to audit exceptions, the agency may suspend or terminate the institution's funding under the program or programs in which noncompliance is found (see 34 C.F.R. §§ 74.113 to 74.115, and 34 C.F.R. §§ 75.901 and 75.903). Special provisions have been developed for the "limitation, suspension, or termination" of an institution's eligibility to participate in the Department of Education's major student aid programs (see 20 U.S.C. § 1094(c)(1)(D)). In addition, agencies are sometimes authorized to impose civil monetary penalties on institutions that fail to comply with program requirements (see, for example, 20 U.S.C. § 1094(c)(2)(B)).

Federal funding agencies also apparently have implied authority to sue institutions in court to obtain compliance with grant and contract conditions, although they seldom exercise this power. In *United States v. Frazer*, 297 F. Supp. 319 (M.D. Ala. 1968), a suit against the administrators of the Alabama state welfare system, the court held that the United States had standing to sue to enforce welfare grant requirements that personnel for federally financed programs be hired on a merit basis. In *United States v. Institute of Computer Technology*, 403 F. Supp. 922 (E.D. Mich. 1975), the court permitted the United States to sue a school that had allegedly breached a contract with the Office of Education, under which the school disbursed funds for the Basic Educational Opportunity Grant program. And in *United States v. Duffy*, 879 F.2d 192 (6th Cir. 1989), and similar cases, the federal government has sued recipients of health professions scholarships for breach of contract for failing to perform their required service commitments.

The federal government may also bring both civil suits and criminal prosecutions, under statutes such as the False Claims Act (31 U.S.C. § 3729), against institutions or institutional employees who have engaged in fraudulent activities relating to federal grant or contract funds (see S. D. Gordon, "The Liability of Colleges and Universities for Fraud, Waste, and Abuse in Federally Funded Grants and Projects," 75 *West's Educ. Law Rptr.* 13 (Aug. 13, 1992)). When such suits arise from allegations initially made by an employee of the institution that is the subject of the suit (or when an employee makes such allegations even if they are not followed by any lawsuit), the employee will often be protected from retaliation by a federal or state "whistleblower" statute (see P. Burling & K. A. Matthews, *Responding to Whistleblowers: An Analysis of Whistleblower Protection Acts and Their Consequences* (National Association of College and University Attorneys, 1992)).

In some circumstances private parties may also be able to sue institutions to enforce federal grant or contract conditions. For example, courts permit persons harmed by institutional noncompliance to bring a "private cause of action" to enforce the nondiscrimination requirements imposed on federal aid recipients under the civil rights spending statutes (this volume, Section 7.5.9). For other types of requirements, however, courts have been less willing to permit such implied causes of action. Student borrowers, for example, usually have not been able to sue their institutions to enforce aid conditions imposed upon the institution by the Higher Education Act (this volume, Section 4.3.2). See, for example, *L'ggrke v. Benkula*, 966 F.2d 1346 (10th Cir. 1992); but see *DeJesus Chavez v. LTV Aerospace Corp.*, 412 F. Supp. 4 (N.D. Tex. 1976), which did permit such a suit. In other circumstances statutes occasionally create express private causes of action whereby private parties can sue institutions in the name of the federal government to protect federal interests. Under the False Claims Act, for example, private individuals are expressly authorized to bring "qui tam" suits (suits by an individual "informer" on behalf of himself and the government) for monetary awards against federal fund recipients that have engaged in fraud (31 U.S.C. § 3730).

In addition to all these means of enforcement, Executive Order 12549 requires that departments and agencies in the executive branch participate in a government-wide system for debarment and suspension from eligibility for nonprocurement federal assistance. The Office of Management and Budget has promulgated debarment and suspension guidelines, as provided in Section 6 of the executive order, and individual agencies have promulgated their own agency regulations implementing the executive order and OMB guidelines. The Department of Education's regulations are published at 34 C.F.R. Part 85, subparts A–E. These regulations "apply to all persons who have participated, are currently participating or may reasonably be expected to participate in transactions under Federal nonprocurement programs" (§ 85.110(a)). Section 85.305 sets out the specific bases upon which ED may debar a person or entity from further participation in aid programs. Section 85.201 contains special provisions concerning the effect of debarment or suspension on an educational institution's participation in student aid programs under Title IV of the Higher Education Act.

7.4.5. Protecting institutional interests in disputes with funding agencies. Given the number and complexity of the conditions attached to federal spending programs, and the federal government's substantial enforcement powers, postsecondary institutions will want to keep attuned to all the procedural rights, legal arguments, and negotiating leverage they may utilize in case of disputes with federal funding agencies. The institution's legal position and negotiating strength will depend in large part on the applicable rules of the game and the institutional representative's knowledge of them. They will also depend on whether the institution is applying for aid or being threatened with a fund cutoff, since applicants typically have fewer procedural rights than recipients do.

Under the various statutes and regulations applicable to federal aid programs, fund recipients usually will be given notice and an opportunity for a hearing prior to any termination of funding (see, for example, 20 U.S.C. § 1094(c)(1)(D) and (c)(2)(A)). Hearings may also be provided before finalization of audit exceptions taken by federal auditors (see, for example, 20 U.S.C. § 1094(b)). If applicable statutes and regulations do not specify notice and hearing requirements prior to termination or suspension of federal funding, or prior to recoupment of funds by audit exception, the procedural due process protections of the Fifth Amendment may fill in at least a minimum of such requirements. The theory would be that the recipient of the funds (either an institution or an individual recipient) has a property interest in retention of the funds and benefits, and the funding agency cannot infringe this interest without first according appropriate procedural safeguards (see *Continental Training Services, Inc. v. Cavazos*, 893 F.2d 877, 892–894 (1990)).

Although such procedural protections are of vital concern, substantive issues—what the federal agencies are requiring institutions to do or refrain from doing—are sometimes even more important. (See generally P. Lacovara, "How Far Can the Federal Camel Slip Under the Academic Tent?" 4 *J. Coll. & Univ. Law* 223, 229–39 (1977).) In particular, institutions may seek to challenge the substantive validity of particular conditions that federal agencies attach to the expenditure of federal funds. Because the federal government's constitutional power to tax and spend is so broad (see Sections 7.1.1 and 7.1.2), such substantive challenges are difficult and speculative. The U.S. Supreme Court's decision in *Rust v. Sullivan*, 111 S. Ct. 1759 (1991), is illustrative.

The *Rust* case concerned the constitutionality of regulations promulgated by the U.S. Department of Health and Human Services to implement Title X of the Public Health Service Act, which provides federal funding for family-planning services. The Act states that "[n]one of the funds appropriated under this subchapter shall be used in programs where abortion is a method of family planning" (42 U.S.C. § 300a-6). The implementing regulations created three basic conditions that fund recipients must meet: (1) the funded project "may not provide counseling concerning the use of abortion as a method of family planning or provide referral for abortion as a method of family planning" (42 C.F.R. § 59.8(a)(1)); (2) the funded project may not engage in activities that "encourage, promote or advocate abortion as a method of family planning" (42 C.F.R. § 59.10(a)); and (3) the funded project must be "physically and financially separate" from any abortion-related activities that the fund recipient may engage in (42 C.F.R. § 59.9). Doctors from Title X clinics challenged the validity of the regulations on the ground that they violated their First Amendment free speech rights.

The doctors first argued that the regulations constituted a form of "viewpoint discrimination," because recipients who remained silent about or opposed abortion could retain their funding but recipients who advocated abortion could not. The Supreme Court rejected this argument:

> The Government can, without violating the Constitution, selectively fund a program to encourage certain activities it believes to be in the public interest, without at the same time funding an alternate program which seeks to deal with the problem in another way. In so doing, the Government has not discriminated on the basis of viewpoint; it has merely chosen to fund one activity to the exclusion of the other [111 S. Ct. at 1772].

The doctors also argued that the regulations unconstitutionally conditioned the receipt of a benefit (Title X funding) on the grantee's relinquishment of a constitutional right (freedom of speech regarding abortion-related matters). The Court rejected this argument as well and thus upheld the regulations:

> [H]ere the government is not denying a benefit to anyone, but is instead simply insisting that public funds be spent for the purposes for which they were authorized. The Secretary's regulations do not force the Title X grantee to give up abortion-related speech; they merely require that the grantee keep such activities separate and distinct from Title X activities. Title X expressly distinguishes between a Title X *grantee* and a Title X *project*. The grantee, which normally is a health care organization, may receive funds from a variety of sources for a variety of purposes. . . . The grantee receives Title X funds, however, for the specific and limited purpose of establishing and operating a Title X project. . . . The regulations govern the scope of the Title X *project's* activities, and leave the grantee unfettered in its other activities. The Title X *grantee* can continue to perform abortions, provide abortion-related services, and engage in abortion advocacy; it simply is required to conduct those activities through programs that are separate and independent from the project that receives Title X funds. . . .
> In contrast, our "unconstitutional conditions" cases involve situations in

which the government has placed a condition on the *recipient* of the subsidy rather than on a particular program or service, thus effectively prohibiting the recipient from engaging in the protected conduct outside the scope of the federally funded program [111 S. Ct. at 1774; citations omitted].

Despite the Court's strong statements in *Rust*, it is still possible in some circumstances to argue that particular aid conditions violate constitutional individual rights principles. *Rust* itself apparently establishes that the government's funding conditions may not substantially restrict the grantee's freedom of speech in a *nonproject* context. Furthermore, *Rust* contains cautionary language emphasizing that special sensitivities arise whenever funding conditions arguably restrict speech in an academic setting:

> This is not to suggest that funding by the Government, even when coupled with the freedom of the fund recipients to speak outside the scope of the Government-funded project, is invariably sufficient to justify government control over the content of expression. For example, this Court has . . . recognized that the university is a traditional sphere of free expression so fundamental to the functioning of our society that the Government's ability to control speech within that sphere by means of conditions attached to the expenditure of Government funds is restricted by the vagueness and overbreadth doctrines of the First Amendment [111 S. Ct. at 1776; citations omitted].

These limitations on the scope of *Rust* have been influential in several subsequent cases.

Board of Trustees of the Leland Stanford Junior University v. Sullivan, 773 F. Supp. 472 (D.D.C. 1991), directly presented questions concerning a federal funding agency's restrictions on speech in an academic context. The National Institutes of Health had issued a notice of its intention to award two contracts of $1.5 million each to universities to do research on an artificial heart device. Stanford submitted a proposal in response to this notice, in which it objected to a "Confidentiality of Information Clause" that NIH intended to insert into the contract (see Section 3.7.7.2 for further discussion of this clause and this case). Stanford and NIH entered a contract contingent on the resolution of this objection (and several others). When the parties could reach no resolution, NIH withdrew the contract from Stanford and awarded it to St. Louis University Medical Center.

Stanford sued, arguing that the confidentiality clause was an unconstitutional prior restraint (see generally Section 4.9.3) on the free speech of its researchers. The district court agreed with the university and ordered that the contract, minus the clause, be reawarded to Stanford. The court relied on *Rust* for the proposition that, although the government may place certain free speech restrictions upon project activities that receive federal funding, it may not so restrict other activities of the grantee. Distinguishing the situation before it from that in *Rust*, the court reasoned:

> The regulations at issue in the instant case broadly bind the grantee and not merely the artificial heart project. Dr. Oyer and the other individuals working for Stanford . . . on the project are prohibited by defendants' regulations from discussing preliminary findings of that project without permission. Unlike the health professionals in *Rust*, the Stanford researchers lack the option of speaking

regarding artificial heart research on their own time, or in circumstances where their speech is paid for by Stanford University or some other private donor, or not paid for by anyone at all. . . .

The regulation at issue here is not tailored to reach only the particular *program* that is in receipt of government funds; it broadly forbids the *recipients* of the funds from engaging in publishing activity related to artificial heart research at any time, under any auspices, and wholly apart from the particular program that is being aided [773 F. Supp. at 476; footnotes omitted].

The court was also favorably impressed by *Rust*'s language emphasizing the university's special role in society and the need for special care to avoid government conditions that are vague or overbroad (see generally Section 3.5.1). Relying on the language, the court concluded:

The regulations permit the contracting officer to prevent Stanford from issuing "preliminary invalidated findings" that "could create erroneous conclusions which might threaten public health or safety if acted upon," or that might have "adverse effects on . . . the Federal agency." 48 C.F.R. § 352.224-70. In the view of this Court, these standards are impermissibly vague. . . .

There is the related problem of the chilling effect of these vague and overbroad conditions. . . . [N]o prudent grantee is likely to publish that which the contracting officer has not cleared even if the reason for the refusal to clear appears to be wholly invalid. In sum, this case fits snugly in the "free expression at a university" category that *Rust* carved out of its general ruling [773 F. Supp. at 477-78].

Shortly after the *Stanford* decision, another federal district court in *Finley v. National Endowment for the Arts*, 795 F. Supp. 1457 (C.D. Cal. 1992), used similar overbreadth and vagueness reasoning to invalidate the National Endowment for the Arts' "decency clause." This congressionally mandated clause required that, in deciding whether to award an NEA grant, the NEA chairperson must ensure that "artistic excellence and artistic merit are the criteria by which applications are judged, taking into consideration general standards of decency and respect for the diverse beliefs and values of the American public" (20 U.S.C. § 954(d)). (For background on NEA funding controversies, as well as those regarding the National Endowment for the Humanities, see Note, "The National Endowment for the Humanities: Control of Funding Versus Academic Freedom," 45 *Vanderbilt L. Rev.* 455 (1992).) Even though the case involved art rather than higher education, and performance artists rather than universities or faculty members, the court nevertheless invoked the same language from *Rust* as the *Stanford* court had used:

[A]rtistic expression serves many of the same values central to a democratic society and underlying the First Amendment as does scholarly expression in other fields. . . . [G]overnment support has been critical to the health and well-being of the arts and humanities in American universities. . . .

[P]laintiffs analogize funding for the arts to funding of public universities. In both settings, limited public funds are allocated to support expressive activities, and some content-based decisions are unavoidable. Nonetheless, this fact does not permit the government to impose whatever restrictions it pleases on speech in a public university, nor should it provide such license in the arts funding context [795 F. Supp. at 1474, 1475].

(See also *Gay Men's Health Crisis v. Sullivan*, 792 F. Supp. 278, 292–304 (S.D.N.Y. 1992), another post-*Rust* case in which a court invalidated federal grant conditions— this time those of the Centers for Disease Control—on grounds of vagueness and overbreadth.)

When an aid condition is created by an agency rule or regulation rather than by the funding statute itself, an additional type of challenge may be available: that the rule or regulation is ultra vires—that is, beyond the bounds of the authority delegated to the agency under the funding statute.

In *Gay Men's Health Crisis*, for example, the plaintiff also challenged the CDC grant conditions on grounds that they went beyond the statutory authority under which CDC operated the grant program. This program provided grants for the development and use of AIDS educational materials. In the authorizing legislation, Congress had included a condition that "any informational materials used are not obscene" (42 U.S.C. § 300ee(d)). CDC's grant terms for the program, however, had prohibited the use of materials that are "offensive." In other words, although Congress had adopted an "obscenity" standard for judging materials used in grant projects, CDC had adopted a different "offensiveness" standard. CDC argued that Congress's standard was merely a floor or minimum and did not prevent CDC from adopting a higher standard. The court disagreed:

> Congress . . . addressed the precise issue addressed by the CDC grant terms, i.e., the funding of potentially "offensive" materials, and expressly limited the funding restriction to "obscene" materials. Thus, in enacting section 300ee Congress did not merely apply additional restrictions to supplement those promulgated by the CDC, but rather clearly articulated its own standard for limitations on the content of HIV prevention materials, which can only be plausibly construed as inconsistent with the [CDC's] "offensiveness" standard.
>
> Because Congress has directly spoken on the precise issue in question by enacting an "obscenity" standard, and has made its intent clear both in the language of the statute and in its legislative history, "that is the end of the matter." . . . Accordingly, the court finds that the CDC has exceeded its statutory authority, and the [CDC grant terms] are without effect [792 F. Supp. at 292; citations omitted].

Such substantive legal challenges, based on the federal Constitution, on state constitutions, or on administrative law considerations, provide an area ripe for creative activity by postsecondary institutions and their legal counsel.

Sec. 7.5. Civil Rights Compliance

7.5.1. General considerations. Postsecondary institutions receiving assistance under federal aid programs are obligated to follow not only the programmatic and technical requirements of each program under which aid is received (see Section 7.4) but also various civil rights requirements that apply generally to federal aid programs. These requirements are a major focus of federal spending policy, importing substantial social goals into education policy and making equality of educational opportunity a clear national priority in education. The implementation and enforcement of civil rights have often been steeped in controversy. Some argue that the federal role is too great, and some say that it is too small; some argue that the federal government proceeds too fast, and some insist that it is too slow; others argue that the compliance process is too cumbersome or costly for the affected institutions. Despite the controversy, it is clear that these federal civil rights efforts, over time, have provided a major force for social change in America.

As conditions on spending, the civil rights requirements represent an exercise of Congress's spending power (see Section 7.1.1) implemented through delegating authority to the various federal departments and agencies that administer federal aid programs. As nondiscrimination principles promoting equal opportunity, the civil rights requirements may also be justifiable as exercises of Congress's power to enforce the Fourteenth Amendment's Equal Protection Clause (see Section 7.1.4).

Four different federal statutes prohibit discrimination in educational programs receiving federal financial assistance. Title VI of the Civil Rights Act of 1964 prohibits discrimination on the basis of race, color, or national origin. Title IX of the Education Amendments of 1972 prohibits discrimination on the basis of sex. Section 504 of the Rehabilitation Act of 1973, as amended in 1974, prohibits discrimination against individuals with disabilities. The Age Discrimination Act of 1975 prohibits discrimination on the basis of age. Title IX is specifically limited to educational programs receiving federal financial assistance, while Title VI, Section 504, and the Age Discrimination Act apply to all programs receiving such assistance.

Each statute delegates enforcement responsibilities to each of the federal agencies disbursing federal financial assistance. Postsecondary institutions may thus be subject to the civil rights regulations of several federal agencies, the most important one being the Department of Education, created in 1979, which has assumed the functions of the former HEW Office for Civil Rights with respect to all educational programs transferred from HEW's Office of Education. ED has its own Office for Civil Rights under an assistant secretary for civil rights. The HEW civil rights regulations, formerly published in Volume 45 of the *Code of Federal Regulations* (C.F.R.), were redesignated as ED regulations and republished in 34 C.F.R. Parts 100–106.

Although the language of the four statutes is similar, each statute protects a different group of beneficiaries, and an act that constitutes discrimination against one group does not necessarily constitute discrimination if directed against another group. "Separate but equal" treatment of the sexes is sometimes permissible under Title IX, for instance, but such treatment of the races is never permissible under Title VI. Administrative regulations have considerably fleshed out the meaning of the statutes. Since 1978 HEW's (now ED's) Office for Civil Rights has also published policy interpretations of its regulations in the *Federal Register*. Judicial decisions contribute additional interpretive gloss on major points, but the administrative regulations remain the primary source for understanding the civil rights requirements.

Damages available under these four laws vary, in that Title VI, Title IX, and Section 504 of the Rehabilitation Act have been interpreted to permit compensatory damages, while the Age Discrimination Act has not. Equitable remedies and debarment from future federal contracts are available under all four laws.

7.5.2. *Title VI.* Title VI of the Civil Rights Act of 1964 (42 U.S.C. § 2000d) declares:

> No person in the United States shall, on the ground of race, color, or national origin, be excluded from participation in, be denied the benefits of, or

be subjected to discrimination under any program or activity receiving federal financial assistance.

Courts have generally held that Title VI incorporates the same standards for identifying unlawful racial discrimination as have been developed under the Fourteenth Amendment's Equal Protection Clause (see the discussion of the *Bakke* case in Section 4.2.5, and see generally Section 4.2.4.1). But courts have also held that the Department of Education and other federal agencies implementing Title VI may impose nondiscrimination requirements on recipients beyond those developed under the Equal Protection Clause (see *Guardians Assn. v. Civil Service Commission of the City of New York*, 463 U.S. 582 (1983), discussed in Section 7.5.7.2).

Section 100.3(b) of the Education Department's regulations provides the basic, and most specific, reference point for determining what actions are unlawful under Title VI and/or its implementing regulations:

(b) Specific discriminatory actions prohibited.
(1) A recipient under any program to which this part applies may not directly or through contractual or other arrangements, on ground of race, color, or national origin:
(i) Deny an individual any service, financial aid, or other benefit provided under the program;
(ii) Provide any service, financial aid, or other benefit to an individual which is different, or is provided in a different manner, from that provided to others under the program;
(iii) Subject an individual to segregation or separate treatment in any matter related to his receipt of any service, financial aid, or other benefit under the program;
(iv) Restrict an individual in any way in the enjoyment of any advantage or privilege enjoyed by others receiving any service, financial aid, or other benefit under the program;
(v) Treat an individual differently from others in determining whether he satisfies any admission, enrollment, quota, eligibility, membership, or other requirement or condition which individuals must meet in order to be provided any service, financial aid, or other benefit provided under the program;
(vi) Deny an individual an opportunity to participate in the program through the provision of services or otherwise or afford him an opportunity to do so which is different from that afforded others under the program (including the opportunity to participate in the program as an employee but only to the extent set forth in paragraph (c) of this section).
(vii) Deny a person the opportunity to participate as a member of a planning or advisory body which is an integral part of the program.
(2) A recipient, in determining the types of services, financial aid, or other benefits, or facilities which will be provided under any such program, or the class of individuals to whom, or the situations in which, such services, financial aid, other benefits, or facilities will be provided under any such program, or the class of individuals to be afforded an opportunity to participate in any such program, may not, directly or through contractual or other arrangements, utilize criteria or methods of administration which have the effect of subjecting individuals to discrimination because of their race, color,

or national origin, or have the effect of defeating or substantially impairing accomplishment of the objectives of the program as respect individuals of a particular race, color, or national origin.

(3) In determining the site or location of facilities, an applicant or recipient may not make selections with the effect of excluding individuals from, denying them the benefits of, or subjecting them to discrimination under any programs to which this regulation applies, on the ground of race, color, or national origin; or with the purpose or effect of defeating or substantially impairing the accomplishment of the objectives of the Act or this regulation [34 C.F.R. § 100.3(6)].

To supplement these regulations, the Department of Education has also developed criteria, as discussed below, that deal specifically with the problem of desegregating statewide systems of postsecondary education.

The dismantling of the formerly de jure segregated systems of higher education has given rise to considerable litigation over more than two decades. Although most of the litigation has attacked continued segregation in the higher education system of one state, the lengthiest lawsuit involved the alleged failure of the federal government to enforce Title VI in ten states. This litigation—begun in 1970 as *Adams v. Richardson*, continuing with various Education Department secretaries as defendant until it became *Adams v. Bell* in the 1980s, and culminating as *Women's Equity Action League v. Cavazos* in 1990—focused on the responsibilities of the Department of Health, Education and Welfare, and later the Education Department, to enforce Title VI, rather than examining the standards applicable to state higher education officials. The U.S. District Court ordered HEW to initiate enforcement proceedings against these states (*Adams v. Richardson*, 356 F. Supp. 92 (D.D.C. 1973)), and the U.S. Court of Appeals affirmed the decision (480 F.2d 1159 (D.C. Cir. 1973)). (See the further discussion of the case in Section 7.5.8.) In subsequent proceedings in the case, the district judge ordered HEW to revoke its acceptance of desegregation plans submitted by several states after the 1973 court opinions and to devise criteria for reviewing new desegregation plans to be submitted by the states that were the subject of the case (see *Adams v. Califano*, 430 F. Supp. 118 (D.D.C. 1977)). Finally, in 1990, the U.S. Court of Appeals for the D.C. Circuit ruled that no private right of action against government enforcement agencies existed under Title VI, and dismissed the case for lack of jurisdiction (*Women's Equity Action League v. Cavazos*, 906 F.2d 742 (D.C. Cir. 1990)).

After developing the criteria (42 Fed. Reg. 40780 (Aug. 11, 1977)), HEW revised and republished them (43 Fed. Reg. 6658 (Feb. 15, 1978)) as criteria applicable to all states having a history of de jure segregation in public higher education.[26] These "Revised Criteria Specifying the Ingredients of Acceptable Plans to Desegregate State Systems of Public Higher Education" require the affected states to take various affirmative steps, such as enhancing the quality of black state-supported colleges and universities, placing new "high-demand" programs on traditionally black campuses, eliminating unnecessary program duplication between black and white institutions, increasing the percentage of black academic employees in the system, and increasing

---

[26]Counsel concerned about the legal status of these criteria, and the extent to which they bind ED and the states, should consult *Adams v. Bell*, 711 F.2d 161, 165–66 (majority opinion), 206–07 (dissent) (D.C. Cir. 1983).

the enrollment of blacks at traditionally white public colleges. The revised criteria are analyzed in J. Godard, *Educational Factors Related to Federal Criteria for the Desegregation of Public Postsecondary Education* (Southern Regional Education Board, 1980).

Litigation alleging continued de jure segregation by state higher education officials has resulted in federal appellate court opinions in four states; the U.S. Supreme Court has ruled in one of these cases. Despite the amount of litigation, and the many years of litigation, settlement, or conciliation attempts, the standards imposed by the Equal Protection Clause of the Fourteenth Amendment and by Title VI are still unclear. These cases—brought by private plaintiffs, with the United States acting as intervenor—have been brought under both the Equal Protection Clause (by the private plaintiffs and the United States) and Title VI (by the United States); judicial analysis generally uses the Equal Protection Clause standard. Although the U.S. Supreme Court's opinion in *United States v. Fordice*, 112 S. Ct. 2727 (1992), is controlling, an examination of prior federal litigation is useful and establishes a context for analyzing *Fordice*.

Fordice and other recent federal court opinions must be read in the context of Supreme Court precedent in cases related to desegregating the public elementary and secondary schools. It is clear under the Fourteenth Amendment's Equal Protection Clause that, in the absence of a "compelling" state interest (see Section 4.2.5), no public institution may treat students differently on the basis of race. The leading case, of course, is *Brown v. Board of Education*, 347 U.S. 483 (1954). Though *Brown* concerned elementary and secondary schools, the precedent clearly applies to postsecondary education as well, as the Supreme Court affirmed in *Florida ex rel. Hawkins v. Board of Control*, 350 U.S. 413 (1956).

Cases involving postsecondary education have generally considered racial segregation within a state postsecondary system rather than within a single institution. One case, for instance, *Alabama State Teachers Assn. v. Alabama Public School and College Authority*, 289 F. Supp. 784 (D. Ala. 1968), *affirmed without majority opin.*, 393 U.S. 400 (1969), concerned the state's establishment of a branch of a predominantly white institution in a city already served by a predominantly black institution. The court rejected the plaintiff's argument that this action unconstitutionally perpetuated segregation in the state system, holding that states do not have an affirmative duty to dismantle segregated higher education (as opposed to elementary and secondary education). This interpretation of the Equal Protection Clause is clearly questionable after *Fordice*. Another case, *Norris v. State Council of Higher Education*, 327 F. Supp. 1368 (E.D. Va. 1971), *affirmed without opin.*, 404 U.S. 907 (1971), concerned a state plan to expand a predominantly white two-year institution into a four-year institution in an area where a predominantly black four-year institution already existed. In contrast to the Alabama case, the court overturned the action because it impeded desegregation in the state system.

The crux of the legal debate in the higher education desegregation cases has been whether the Equal Protection Clause and Title VI require the state to enact race-neutral policies (the "effort" test), or whether the state must go beyond race neutrality to ensure that any remaining vestige of the formerly segregated system (for example, racially identifiable institutions or concentrations of minority students in less prestigious or less well-funded institutions) is removed. Unlike elementary and secondary students, college students select the institution they wish to attend (assuming they meet the admission standards); and the remedies used in elementary and secondary school desegregation, such as busing and race-conscious assignment practices, are unavailable to colleges and universities. But just how the courts should weigh the "student choice" argument against the clear mandate of the Fourteenth Amendment was sharply debated by several federal courts prior to *Fordice.*

In *Geier v. University of Tennessee,* 597 F.2d 1056 (6th Cir. 1979), *cert. denied,* 444 U.S. 886 (1979), the court ordered the merger of two Tennessee universities, despite the state's claim that the racial imbalances at the schools were created by the students' exercise of free choice. The state had proposed expanding its programming at predominantly white University of Tennessee–Nashville; this action, the plaintiffs argued, would negatively affect the ability of Tennessee A&I State University, a predominantly black institution in Nashville, to desegregate its faculty and student body. Applying the reasoning of *Brown* and other elementary/secondary cases, the court ruled that the state's adoption of an "open-admissions" policy had not effectively dismantled the state's dual system of higher education, and ordered state officials to submit a plan for desegregating public higher education in Tennessee. In a separate decision, *Richardson v. Blanton,* 597 F.2d 1078 (6th Cir. 1979), the same court upheld the district court's approval of the state's desegregation plan.

In affirming the district court's decision in *Geier,* the appellate court noted that the merger order was based on a finding that the state's failure to "dismantle a statewide dual system, the 'heart' of which was an all-black TSU," was a continuing constitutional violation. The fact that the state had not been found guilty of practicing discrimination at the schools in the recent past was irrelevant. According to the court:

> The fundamental disagreement between the district court and the appellants concerns the duty of a state to remove the vestiges of state-imposed segregation. The appellants point to the obvious differences between elementary and secondary education on the one hand and higher education on the other. . . . The district court recognized these differences in the present case. Also, it agreed . . . that the "basic requirement" of the affirmative duty to dismantle a dual system of higher education was met when an open-admissions policy was adopted and good faith was exercised in dealing with admissions, faculty, and staff. However, the district court found that something beyond this basic requirement was needed to satisfy the constitutional imperative in the present case, where segregation was once required by state law and "egregious" conditions of segregation continued to exist in public higher education in the Nashville area. What was required, the court found, was affirmative action to remove these vestiges [597 F.2d at 1065].

The Sixth Circuit rejected the state's argument that elementary/secondary desegregation precedent, most specifically *Green v. County School Board,* 391 U.S. 430 (1968), did not apply to higher education. "We agree," said the court, "that the 'state's duty is as exacting' to eliminate the vestiges of state-imposed segregation in higher education as in elementary and secondary school systems; it is only the means of eliminating segregation which differ" (597 F.2d at 1065).

Seven years later the parties were back before the Sixth Circuit. The United States Department of Justice intervened in the case in order to object, on equal protection grounds, to a provision of the consent decree approved by the district court. The provision required the state to assist seventy-five black pre-professional students, through an affirmative action program, so that they could prepare for and be admitted to professional schools in Tennessee. Citing *Bazemore v. Friday*, 478 U.S. 385 (1986), the Justice Department argued that a race-specific remedy was inappropriate because of the voluntary nature of higher education. In *Bazemore* the Court had ruled that the state's affirmative attempts to desegregate North Carolina's 4-H clubs, and establish race-neutral admissions policies, constituted an adequate defense to a discrimination claim. When a voluntary activity, such as a 4-H club, was at issue, the Court had ruled, the state's efforts to disestablish a segregated dual system were the crux of the issue, regardless of whether those efforts were completely successful.

The Sixth Circuit, in *Geier v. Alexander*, 801 F.2d 799 (6th Cir. 1986) (*Geier II*), rejected the Department of Justice's interpretation of *Bazemore*, saying: "[I]t appears fallacious to extend *Bazemore* to any level of education" because, no matter how valuable the 4-H experience, "it cannot be compared to the value of an advanced education" (801 F.2d at 805). For a discussion of the court's analysis of the affirmative action provisions of the consent decree, see Section 4.2.5.

Geier was cited in subsequent higher education desegregation cases, sometimes with approval and sometimes with criticism. Desegregation cases brought in Mississippi and Louisiana, both within the jurisdiction of the U.S. Court of Appeals for the Fifth Circuit, show the complexities of these issues and the sharply differing interpretations of the Equal Protection Clause and Title VI. These cases proceeded through the judicial system at the same time; and, considered together, they illustrate the significance of the U.S. Supreme Court's pronouncements in *Fordice*.

The case that culminated in the Supreme Court's *Fordice* opinion began in 1975, when Jake Ayers and other private plaintiffs sued the governor of Mississippi and other state officials for maintaining the vestiges of a de jure segregated system. Although HEW had begun Title VI enforcement proceedings against Mississippi in 1969, it had rejected both desegregation plans submitted by the state, and this private litigation ensued. The United States intervened, and the parties attempted to conciliate the dispute for twelve years. They were unable to do so, and the trial ensued in 1987.

Mississippi had designated three categories of public higher education institutions: comprehensive universities (three historically white, none historically black); one urban institution (black); and four regional institutions (two white, two black). Admission standards differed both between categories and within categories, with the lowest admission standards at the historically black regional institutions. The plaintiffs argued, inter alia, that the state's admission standards, institutional classification and mission designations, duplication of programs, faculty and staff hiring and assignments, and funding perpetuated the prior segregated system of higher education; among other data, they cited the concentration of black students at the black institutions (over 95 percent of the students at each of the three black institutions were black, whereas blacks comprised less than 10 percent of the students at the three white universities and 13 percent at both white regional institutions). The state asserted that the existence of racially identifiable universities was permissible, since students could choose which institution to attend, and that the state's higher education policies and practices were race neutral in intent.

Although the district court acknowledged that the state had an affirmative duty to desegregate its higher education system, it rejected the *Green* precedent as inapplicable to higher education systems and followed the Court's ruling in *Bazemore*, described above. The district court said:

> [T]he affirmative duty to desegregate does not contemplate either restricting choice or the achievement of any degree of racial balance. . . . [W]hile student enrollment and faculty and staff hiring patterns are to be examined, greater emphasis should instead be placed on current state higher education policies and practices in order to insure that such policies and practices are racially neutral, developed and implemented in good faith, and do not substantially contribute to the continued racial identifiability of individual institutions [*Ayers v. Allain*, 674 F. Supp. 1523, 1553–54 (N.D. Miss. 1987)].

Applying this standard to the state's actions, and relying on the voluntariness of student choice under *Bazemore*, the court found no violation of law. It concluded that "current actions on the part of the defendants demonstrate conclusively that the defendants are fulfilling their affirmative duty to disestablish the former *de jure* segregated system of higher education" (674 F. Supp. at 1564).

A three-judge panel of the U.S. Court of Appeals for the Fifth Circuit initially did not view *Bazemore* as controlling, and overruled the district court. Because the plaintiffs in *Ayers* had alleged de jure segregation (*Bazemore* involved de facto segregation), the court ruled that the correct standard was that of *Geier v. Alexander* (discussed earlier in this section). The panel cited lower admission standards for predominantly black institutions, the small number of black faculty at white colleges, program duplication at nearby black and white institutions, and continued underfunding of black institutions as evidence of an illegal dual system (*Ayers v. Allain*, 893 F.2d 732 (5th Cir. 1990)). The state petitioned the Fifth Circuit for a rehearing *en banc*, which was granted. The *en banc* court reversed the panel, reinstating the decision of the district court (914 F.2d 676 (5th Cir. 1990)).

The *en banc* court relied on a case decided two decades earlier, *Alabama State Teachers Assn. v. Alabama Public School and College Authority*, 289 F. Supp. 784 (M.D. Ala. 1968), *affirmed per curiam*, 393 U.S. 400 (1969), which held that the scope of the state's duty to dismantle a racially dual system of higher education differed from, and was less strict than, its duty to desegregate public elementary and secondary school systems. The court noted that higher education is neither free nor compulsory (characteristics of public elementary and secondary education); that college students have a diversity of options generally unavailable to elementary and secondary school students; and that it was therefore inappropriate for a court to intervene in policy decisions, such as funding priorities and location of institutions, which were the province of the legislature.

The *en banc* court said that *Green* did not apply to the desegregation of higher education and that the standard articulated in *Bazemore* should have been applied in this case. Furthermore, it saw no conflict between *Green* and *Bazemore*, stating that *Green* had not outlawed all "freedom-of-choice" desegregation plans outside elementary and secondary education. The opinion in *Geier*, on which the earlier panel opinion had relied, received sharp criticism as an overreading of *Bazemore*. The court implied strongly that the remedies contemplated by the panel's decision would reduce freedom of choice for all students, including minorities, by imposing racial quotas for admission to segregated institutions. And it concluded that differences in funding, expenditures per student, admission standards, and program mix resulted from differences in institutional mission, not from racially motivated discrimination.

Despite its conclusion that the state's conduct did not violate the Equal Protection Clause (and, without specifically addressing it, Title VI), the court did find some present effects of the former de jure segregation. The majority wrote:

> The district court incorrectly concluded that the disparities among the institutions were not reminiscent of the former de jure segregated system. *Ayers I*, 674 F. Supp. at 1560. On the contrary, the disparities are very much reminiscent of the prior system. The inequalities among the institutions largely follow the mission designations, and the mission designations to some degree follow the historical racial assignments. But this does not mean the plaintiff class is denied equal educational opportunity or equal protection of law. The defendants have adopted good-faith, race-neutral policies and procedures and have fulfilled or exceeded their duty to open Mississippi universities to all citizens regardless of race. Their policies toward institutions are not racially motivated [914 F.2d at 692].

Clearly, the *en banc* majority interpreted the legal standard to require affirmative efforts, but not to mandate equivalent funding, admission standards, enrollment patterns, or program allocation. The plaintiffs appealed the *en banc* court's ruling to the U.S. Supreme Court.

At the same time, similar litigation was in progress in Louisiana. In 1974 the U.S. Department of Justice sued the state of Louisiana under both the Equal Protection Clause and Title VI, asserting that the state had established and maintained a racially segregated higher education system. The Justice Department cited duplicate programs at contiguous black and white institutions and the existence of three systems of public higher education as examples of continuing racial segregation. After seven years of pretrial conferences, the parties agreed to a consent decree, which was approved by a district court judge in 1981. Six years later, the United States charged that the state had not implemented the consent decree and that almost all of the state's institutions of higher education were still racially identifiable. The state argued that its good-faith efforts to desegregate higher education were sufficient.

In *United States v. Louisiana*, 692 F. Supp. 642 (E.D. La. 1988), a federal district judge granted summary judgment for the United States, agreeing that the state's actions had been insufficient to dismantle the segregated system. In later opinions (718 F. Supp. 499 (E.D. La. 1989), 718 F. Supp. 525 (E.D. La. 1989)), the judge ordered Louisiana to merge its three systems of public higher education, create a community college system, and reduce unwarranted duplicate programs, especially in legal education. Specifically, the court said, the law schools of Southern University and Louisiana State University, both of which are in Baton Rouge, should be merged. Appeals to the Supreme Court followed from all parties,[27] but the U.S. Supreme Court denied review for want of jurisdiction (*Louisiana, ex rel. Guste v. United States*, 110 S. Ct. 708 (1990)).

Despite the flurry of appeals, the district court continued to seek a remedy in

---

[27]For a description of the litigation history of this case, see Note, "Realizing the Dream: U.S. v. State of Louisiana," 50 *La. L. Rev.* 583 (1990).

this case. It adopted the report of a special master, which recommended that a single governing board be created, that the board classify each institution by mission, and that the graduate programs at the state's comprehensive institutions be evaluated for possible termination. The court also ordered the state to abolish its open-admissions policy and to use new admissions criteria consisting of a combination of high school grades, rank, courses, recommendations, extracurricular activities, and essays in addition to test scores (751 F. Supp. 621 (E.D. La. 1990)). After the Fifth Circuit's *en banc* opinion in *Ayers v. Allain* was issued, however, the district court judge vacated his earlier summary judgment, stating that although he disagreed with the Fifth Circuit's ruling, he had no choice but to follow it (*United States v. Louisiana*, 751 F. Supp. 606 (E.D. La. 1990)). The governor of Louisiana appealed this ruling, but the judge stayed both the appeal and the remedies he had ordered, pending the Supreme Court's opinion in *Ayers v. Allain,* now titled *United States v. Fordice.*[28]

The U.S. Supreme Court was faced with the issue addressed in *Geier:* which Supreme Court precedents control equal protection and Title VI jurisprudence in higher education desegregation—*Bazemore* or *Green?* In *United States v. Fordice,* 112 S. Ct. 2727 (1992), the Court reversed the decision of the Fifth Circuit's *en banc* majority, sharply criticizing the lower court's reasoning and the legal standard it had applied. First, the Court refused to choose between the two precedents. Justice White, writing for the eight-justice majority, rejected the Fifth Circuit's argument that *Bazemore* limited *Green* to segregation in elementary/secondary education:

> [*Bazemore*] neither requires nor justifies the conclusions reached by the two courts below. . . . *Bazemore* plainly does not excuse inquiry into whether Mississippi has left in place certain aspects of its prior dual system that perpetuate the racially segregated higher education system. If the State perpetuates policies and practices traceable to its prior system that continue to have segregative effects—whether by influencing student enrollment decisions or by fostering segregation in other facets of the university system—and such policies are without sound educational justification and can be practically eliminated, the State has not satisfied its burden of proving that it has dismantled its prior system. [112 S. Ct. at 2737].

The Court also criticized the lower courts for their interpretation of the *Alabama State Teachers Association* case: "Respondents are incorrect to suppose that *ASTA* validates policies traceable to the *de jure* system regardless of whether or not they are

---

[28]In proceedings subsequent to the Supreme Court's opinion in *Fordice,* the legal skirmishes in Louisiana continued. After *Fordice* was announced, the Fifth Circuit vacated the district court's summary judgment for the state and remanded the case for further proceedings in light of *Fordice.* The district court then ordered the parties to show cause why the 1988 liability determination and remedy should not be reinstated. It also reinstated its earlier liability finding and entered a new remedial order at 811 F. Supp. 1151 (E. D. La. 1993). By the end of 1993, the U.S. Court of Appeals for the Fifth Circuit had overturned a district court's order to create a single higher education system for the state's public colleges, to create new admissions criteria for state colleges, to create a community college system, and to eliminate duplicative programs in adjacent racially identifiable state institutions (*United States Louisiana,* 9 F.3d 1159 (5th Cir. 1993)). The case was remanded to the trial court for resolution of disputed facts and determination of whether program duplication violated *Fordice.*

educationally justifiable or can be practicably altered to reduce their segregative effects" (112 S. Ct. at 2737).

White's opinion articulated a standard that appears to be much closer to *Green* than to *Bazemore,* despite his insistence that *Bazemore* can be read to require the outcome in *Fordice.* White wrote:

> [W]e do not disagree with the Court of Appeals' observation that a state university system is quite different in very relevant respects from primary and secondary schools. [The Court then detailed several of the differences, including noncompulsory attendance, differing institutional missions, and the inappropriateness of desegregation remedies such as mandatory assignment of students or busing.] . . . We do not agree with the Court of Appeals or the District Court, however, that the adoption and implementation of race-neutral policies alone suffice to demonstrate that the State has completely abandoned its prior dual system. That college attendance is by choice and not by assignment does not mean that a race-neutral admissions policy cures the constitutional violation of a dual system. In a system based on choice, student attendance is determined not simply by admission policies, but also by many other factors. Although some of these factors clearly cannot be attributed to State policies, many can be. Thus, even after a State dismantles its segregative *admissions* policy, there may still be state action that is traceable to the State's prior *de jure* segregation and that continues to foster segregation. The Equal Protection Clause is offended by 'sophisticated as well as simple-minded modes of discrimination.' " *Lane v. Wilson,* 307 U.S. 268, 275 . . . (1939). If policies traceable to the *de jure* system are still in force and have discriminatory effects, those policies too must be reformed to the extent practicable and consistent with sound educational practices [112 S. Ct. at 2736].

The Court asserted that "there are several surviving aspects of Mississippi's prior dual system which are constitutionally suspect" (at 2738). Although it refused to list all these elements, it discussed four policies that, in particular, appeared to perpetuate the effects of prior de jure discrimination: admission policies (for discussion of this portion of the case, see Section 4.2.4.1), the duplication of programs at nearby white and black colleges, the state's "mission classification," and the fact that Mississippi operates eight public institutions. For each category the court noted the foundations of state policy in previous de jure segregation and a failure to alter that policy when de jure segregation officially ended. Furthermore, the Court took the lower courts to task for their failure to consider that state policies in each of these areas had influenced student access to higher education and had perpetuated segregation.

The Court emphasized that it was not calling for racial quotas; in its view, the fact "that an institution is predominantly white or black does not in itself make out a constitutional violation" (at 2743). It also refused the plaintiffs' invitation to order the state to provide equal funding for the three traditionally black institutions:

> If we understand private petitioners to press us to order the upgrading of Jackson State, Alcorn State, and Mississippi Valley *solely* so that they may be publicly financed, exclusively black enclaves by private choice, we reject that request. The State provides these facilities for *all* its citizens [112 S. Ct. at 2743].

The Court remanded the case so that the lower court could determine whether the state had "met its affirmative obligation to dismantle its prior dual system" under the standards of the Equal Protection Clause and Title VI.

Although they joined the Court's opinion, two justices provided concurring opinions, articulating concerns they believed were not adequately addressed in the majority opinion. Justice O'Connor reminded the Court that only in the most "narrow" of circumstances should a state be permitted to "maintain a policy or practice traceable to *de jure* segregation that has segregative effects" (at 2743). O'Connor wrote: "Where the State can accomplish legitimate educational objectives through less segregative means, the courts may infer lack of good faith." Even if the state could demonstrate that "maintenance of certain remnants of its prior system is essential to accomplish its legitimate goals," O'Connor added, "it still must prove that it has counteracted and minimized the segregative impact of such policies to the extent possible. Only by eliminating a remnant that unnecessarily continues to foster segregation or by negating insofar as possible its segregative impact can the State satisfy its constitutional obligation to dismantle the discriminatory system that should, by now, be only a distant memory" (112 S. Ct. at 2746). O'Connor's approach would appear to preclude a state from arguing that certain policies which had continued segregative impacts were justified by "sound educational policy."

Justice Thomas's concurrence articulates a concern expressed by many proponents of historically black colleges, who worry that the Court's opinion might result in the destruction of black colleges.[29] Because the black colleges could be considered "vestiges of a segregated system" and thus vulnerable under the Court's interpretation of the Equal Protection Clause and Title VI, Thomas wanted to stress that the *Fordice* ruling did *not* require the dismantling of traditionally black colleges. Thomas wrote:

> Today, we hold that "[i]f policies traceable to the *de jure* system are still in force and have discriminatory effects, those policies too must be reformed to the extent practicable and consistent with sound educational policies." . . . I agree that this statement defines the appropriate standard to apply in the higher-education context. I write separately to emphasize that this standard is far different from the one adopted to govern the grade-school context in *Green v. New Kent County*. . . . In particular, because it does not compel the elimination of all observed racial imbalance, it portends neither the destruction of historically black colleges nor the severing of those institutions from their distinctive histories and traditions [112 S. Ct. at 2744].

The majority opinion, Thomas noted, focused on the state's policies, not on the racial imbalances they had caused. He suggested that, as a result of the ruling in this case, district courts "will spend their time determining whether such policies have been adequately justified—a far narrower, more manageable task than that imposed under *Green*" (at 2745). Thomas emphasized the majority opinion's use of "sound educational practices" as a touchstone for determining whether a state's actions are justifiable:

---

[29]The unique issues facing historically black colleges with regard to desegregation are discussed later in this section.

Quite obviously, one compelling need to be considered is the *educational* need of the present and future *students* in the Mississippi university system, for whose benefit the remedies will be crafted.

In particular, we do not foreclose the possibility that there exists "sound educational justification" for maintaining historically black colleges *as such.* . . .

I think it indisputable that these institutions have succeeded in part because of their distinctive histories and traditions. . . . Obviously, a State cannot maintain such traditions by closing particular institutions, historically white or historically black, to particular racial groups. . . . Although I agree that a State is not constitutionally *required* to maintain its historically black institutions as such . . . I do not understand our opinion to hold that a State is *forbidden* from doing so. It would be ironic, to say the least, if the institutions that sustained blacks during segregation were themselves destroyed in an effort to combat its vestiges [112 S. Ct. at 2746–47; emphasis in original].

Thomas's concurrence articulates the concerns of some of the parties in the Louisiana and Mississippi cases—namely, that desegregation remedies would fundamentally change or even destroy the distinctive character of historically black colleges, instead of raising their funding to the level enjoyed by the public white institutions in those states (see P. Applebome, "Epilogue to Integration Fight at South's Public Universities," *New York Times,* May 29, 1992, A1, A21).

Justice Scalia wrote a blistering dissent, criticizing the "effectively unsustainable burden the Court imposes on Mississippi, and all States that formerly operated segregated universities" and stating unequivocally that *Green* "has no proper application in the context of higher education, provides no genuine guidance to States and lower courts, and is as likely to subvert as to promote the interests of those citizens on whose behalf the present suit was brought" (at 2746–47).

In Scalia's view, the Court's tests for ascertaining compliance with *Brown* were confusing and vague. He questioned how one would measure whether policies that perpetuate segregation have been eliminated to the extent "practicable" and consistent with "sound educational" practices (at 2747). Scalia also noted the differences in intensity of the words used by White to describe unlawful policies: those that "substantially restrict a person's choice of which institution to enter," "interfere" with a person's choice, "limit" choice, or "affect" choice: "If words have any meaning, in this last stage of decrepitude the requirement is so frail that almost anything will overcome it" (at 2747). Scalia asserted:

[O]ne must conclude that the Court is essentially applying to universities the amorphous standard adopted for primary and secondary schools in *Green.* . . . [T]oday's opinion requires state university administrators to prove that racially identifiable schools are *not* the consequence of any practice or practices . . . held over from the prior *de jure* regime. This will imperil virtually any practice or program plaintiffs decide to challenge—just as *Green* has—so long as racial imbalance remains. And just as under *Green,* so also under today's decision, the only practicable way of disproving that "existing racial identifiability is attributable to the State," *ante* at 2735, *is to eliminate extant segregation, i.e., to assure racial proportionality in the schools* [112 S. Ct. at 2748].

According to Scalia, "*Bazemore's* standard for dismantling a dual system ought to control here: discontinuation of discriminatory practices and adoption of a neutral admissions policy. . . . Only one aspect of an historically segregated university system need be eliminated: discriminatory admissions standards" (at 2750, 2751). In this regard, Scalia agreed with the majority opinion that the state's sole reliance on standardized admission tests appeared to have a racially exclusionary purpose and was not evidence of a neutral admissions process.

Scalia then argued that the majority opinion would harm traditionally black colleges, because it did not require equal funding of black and white institutions. Equal funding, he noted, would encourage students to attend their own-race institutions without "paying a penalty in the quality of education" (at 2752). "What the Court's test is designed to achieve is the elimination of predominantly black institutions. . . . There is nothing unconstitutional about a "black" school in the sense, not of a school that blacks *must* attend and that whites *cannot,* but of a school that, as a consequence of private choice in residence or in school selection, contains, and has long contained, a large black majority" (at 2752).

Scalia closed his dissent by reiterating his disdain for the "virtually standardless discretion conferred upon district judges" by the majority:

> What I do predict is a number of years of litigation-driven confusion and destabilization in the university systems of all the formerly *de jure* States, that will benefit neither blacks nor whites, neither predominantly black institutions nor predominantly white ones. Nothing good will come of this judicially ordained turmoil, except the public recognition that any Court that would knowingly impose it must hate segregation. We must find some other way of making that point [112 S. Ct. at 2753].

Despite Scalia's criticism, the opinion makes it clear that, although many elementary/secondary school desegregation remedies are unavailable to higher education, *Green* controls a district court judge's analysis of whether a state has eliminated the vestiges of a de jure segregated system of higher education.

The cases pending in Louisiana, as well as in Alabama, have already been influenced by *Fordice.* For example, in *United States v. Alabama,* 787 F. Supp. 1030 (N.D. Ala. 1991), a case that began in 1983, the plaintiffs, a group of black citizens that had joined the Justice Department's litigation, had argued that the state's allocation of "missions" to predominantly white and black public colleges perpetuated racial segregation because the black colleges received few funds for research or graduate education. They also argued that the white colleges' refusal to teach subjects related to race, such as black culture or history, had a discriminatory effect on black students.

A trial court had found, prior to *Fordice,* that the public system of higher education perpetuated earlier de jure segregation, but it had ruled against the plaintiffs on the curriculum issue. Both parties appealed. The state argued that its policies were race neutral and that public universities had a constitutionally protected right of academic freedom to determine what programs and courses would be offered to students, and the plaintiffs took issue with the academic freedom defense. A federal appellate court affirmed the trial court in part (14 F.3d 1534 (11th Cir. 1994)), and applied *Fordice's* teachings to the actions of the state. The court held that, simply because the state could demonstrate legitimate, race-neutral reasons for continuing its past practice of limiting the types of programs and degrees offered by historically black colleges, it was not excused from its obligation to redress the continuing segregative effects of such a policy. But the appellate court differed with the trial court on the curriculum issue, stating that the First Amendment did not limit the court's power to order white colleges and universities to modify their programs and curricula to redress the continuing effects of prior discrimination. The court remanded the case to the trial court to determine whether the state's allocation of research missions to predominantly white colleges perpetuates segregation, and, if so, to determine "whether such effects can be remedied in a manner that is practicable and educationally sound" (14 F.3d at 1556). The results in *Fordice* and in the Alabama litigation may prompt efforts in many southern and border states to reopen desegregation cases that have been closed for several years (see S. Jaschik, "High-Court Ruling Transforms Battles over Desegregation at Colleges in 19 States," *Chron. Higher Educ.*, July 8, 1992, A16).

    Fordice leaves many questions unanswered, however. Supporters of black colleges argue that the opinion could motivate state officials to merge black and white colleges or even to close the black colleges, limiting access for black students and reducing their educational choices. Historically black colleges, their supporters point out, provide a nurturing environment and more role models for black students than do predominantly white institutions, they have special services for underprepared students, and they have played and continue to play a critical role in the education of blacks. In its 1973 opinion in *Adams v. Richardson*, the U.S. Court of Appeals recognized the importance of traditionally black institutions in training black professionals:

> The problem of integrating higher education must be dealt with on a statewide rather than a school-by-school basis. Perhaps the most serious problem in this area is the lack of statewide planning to provide more and better-trained minority group doctors, lawyers, engineers, and other professionals. A predicate for minority access to quality postgraduate programs is a viable, coordinated statewide higher education policy that takes into account the special problems of minority students and of black colleges. . . . These black institutions currently fulfill a crucial need and will continue to play an important role in black higher education [480 F.2d at 1164–65].

Others argue, however, that single-race institutions, even historically black colleges, are contrary to the intent of the law and that segregating blacks in their own institutions disserves both blacks and whites.

    The *Fordice* opinion has been criticized by individuals of all races and political affiliations as insufficiently clear to provide appropriate guidance to states as they attempt to apply its outcome to desegregation of the still racially identifiable public institutions in many states. For a discussion of some of the unresolved issues, see S. Jaschik, "Whither Desegregation?" *Chron. Higher Educ.*, Jan. 26, 1991, A33.

    As the history of the last two decades of Title VI litigation makes clear, the desegregation of higher education is very much an unfinished business (see *The Black/White Colleges: Dismantling the Dual System of Higher Education* (U.S. Commission on Civil Rights, 1981)). Its completion poses knotty legal, policy, and administrative enforcement problems and requires a sensitive appreciation of the differing missions and histories of traditionally black and traditionally white institutions. The challenge is for lawyers, administrators, government officials, and the judiciary to work together to fashion solutions that will be consonant with the law's requirement to desegregate but will increase rather than limit the opportunities available to minority students and faculty.

For analyses of public policy issues and strategies regarding desegregation, see S. L. Myers (ed.), *Desegregation in Higher Education* (University Press of America, 1989), and J. Williams (ed.), *Desegregating America's Colleges and Universities: Title VI Regulation of Higher Education* (Teachers College Press, 1987). For a historical perspective and demonstration of history's continuing relevance to current concerns, see G. Kujovich, "Equal Opportunity in Higher Education and the Black Public College: The End of Separate but Equal," 72 *Minn. L. Rev.* 29 (1987), and L. Ware, "Will There Be a 'Different World' After *Fordice?*" 80 *Academe* 6 (May–June 1994).

7.5.3. *Title IX.* The central provision of Title IX of the Education Amendments of 1972 (20 U.S.C. § 1681 et seq.) declares:

> (a) No person in the United States shall, on the basis of sex, be excluded from participation in, be denied the benefits of, or be subjected to discrimination under any education program or activity receiving federal financial assistance, except that:
> (1) in regard to admissions to educational institutions, this section shall apply only to institutions of vocational education, professional education, and graduate higher education, and to public institutions of undergraduate higher education;
> (2) in regard to admissions to educational institutions, this section shall not apply (A) for one year from June 23, 1972, nor for six years after June 23, 1972, in the case of an educational institution which has begun the process of changing from being an institution which admits only students of one sex to being an institution which admits students of both sexes, but only if it is carrying out a plan for such a change which is approved by the secretary of education or (B) for seven years from the date an educational institution begins the process of changing from being an institution which admits only students of only one sex to being an institution which admits students of both sexes, but only if it is carrying out a plan for such a change which is approved by the secretary of education, whichever is the later;
> (3) this section shall not apply to an educational institution which is controlled by a religious organization if the application of this subsection would not be consistent with the religious tenets of such organization;
> (4) this section shall not apply to an educational institution whose primary purpose is the training of individuals for the military services of the United States, or the merchant marine;
> (5) in regard to admissions, this section shall not apply to any public institution of undergraduate higher education which is an institution that traditionally and continually from its establishment has had a policy of admitting only students of one sex.

Title IX also excludes from its coverage the membership practices of tax-exempt social fraternities and sororities (20 U.S.C. § 1681(a)(6)(A)); the membership practices of the YMCA, YWCA, Girl Scouts, Boy Scouts, Campfire Girls, and other tax-exempt, traditionally single-sex "youth service organizations" (20 U.S.C. § 1681(a)(6)(B)); American Legion, Boys State, Boys Nation, Girls State, and Girls Nation activities (20 U.S.C. § 1681(a)(7)); and father-son and mother-daughter activities if provided on a reasonably comparable basis for students of both sexes (20 U.S.C. § 1681(a)(8)).

The Department of Education's regulations implementing Title IX (34 C.F.R. Part 106) include provisions paralleling the language of the previously quoted Title VI regulations (see 34 C.F.R. § 106.31). Additional Title IX regulations specify in much greater detail the acts of discrimination prohibited in programs and activities receiving federal financial aid. Educational institutions may not discriminate on the basis of sex in admissions and recruitment (with certain exceptions) (see this volume, Section 4.2.4.2); in awarding financial assistance (Section 4.3.3); in athletic programs (Section 4.15.3); or in the employment of faculty and staff members (Section 3.3.2.3) or students (see 34 C.F.R. § 106.38). Section 106.32 of the regulations prohibits sex discrimination in housing accommodations with respect to fees, services, or benefits, but does not prohibit separate housing by sex (see this volume, Section 4.14.1). Section 106.33 requires that separate facilities for toilets, locker rooms, and shower rooms be comparable. Section 106.34 prohibits sex discrimination in student access to course offerings. Sections 106.36 and 106.38 require that counseling services and employment placement services be offered to students in such a way that there is no discrimination on the basis of sex. Section 106.39 prohibits sex discrimination in health and insurance benefits and services, including any medical, hospital, accident, or life insurance policy or plan that the recipient offers to its students. Under Section 106.40 an institution may not "apply any rule concerning a student's actual or potential parental, family, or marital status" that would have the effect of discrimination on the basis of sex, nor may the recipient discriminate against any student on the basis of pregnancy or childbirth.

Litigation brought under Title IX has addressed alleged sex discrimination in the funding of women's athletics (see Section 4.15.3), the employment of women faculty (see Section 3.3.4), and sexual harassment of women faculty and students. In *Franklin v. Gwinnett County Public Schools*, 112 S. Ct. 1028 (1992) (also discussed in Section 7.5.9), the Supreme Court ruled unanimously that plaintiffs suing under Title IX were not limited to equitable relief but could claim monetary damages as well. The case settled a conflict among the federal appellate courts: the lower court in *Franklin* had ruled that monetary damages were not available, whereas the U.S. Court of Appeals for the Third Circuit had ruled that they were (*Pfeiffer v. Marion Center Area School District*, 917 F.2d 779 (3d Cir. 1990)). As a result of this 1992 ruling, it is likely that an increasing number of both students and faculty will use Title IX to challenge alleged discrimination.

The type of damages available to plaintiffs under Title IX is particularly significant for students. Typical equitable remedies (back pay and orders requiring the school to refrain from future discriminatory behavior) are of little use to students, since they are usually due no back pay and are likely to have graduated or left school before the litigation has been completed.

In *Franklin* the plaintiff, a high school student at North Gwinnett High School in Gwinnett County, Georgia, sued her school board under Title IX and sought relief from both hostile environment and quid pro quo sexual harassment by a teacher. Her complaint alleged that the teacher, also a sports coach, had harassed her continually beginning in the fall of her sophomore year. Franklin accused the teacher of engaging her in sexually-oriented conversations, forcibly kissing her on the mouth on school property, telephoning her at home, and asking her to see him socially. She also alleged that during her junior year, the teacher went to Franklin's class, asked the teacher to excuse her, and then took her to a private office where he raped her. According to Franklin's complaint, school officials and teachers were aware of these occurrences. Although the school investigated them, it took no action to stop the harassment and agreed to let the teacher resign in return for dropping all harassment charges.

Franklin first filed a complaint with the U.S. Office of Civil Rights, which investigated her charges. OCR determined that the school district had violated Franklin's Title IX rights, and that verbal and physical sexual harassment had occurred. It also found that the district had interfered with her right to complain about the unlawful conduct. But, OCR concluded, because the teacher and the school principal had resigned and because the school had implemented a grievance procedure, the district was now in compliance with Title IX.

The U.S. Supreme Court ruled in Franklin's favor, but it did so on relatively narrow grounds. (The Court's reasoning and legal analysis are discussed in Section 7.5.9.) Franklin had alleged that the district, in failing to stop the harassment, had intentionally discriminated against her. The Court's discussion of the availability of damages in Title IX causes of action discusses only claims of intentional discrimination; the opinion does not discuss whether damages are available in claims of unintentional discrimination.[30]

Several important issues are left unresolved by the Court's *Franklin* opinion. First is the issue of when, and under what theories, the school or college will be found liable under Title IX for sexual harassment by a teacher or other employee. In *Franklin* the school administrators had actual knowledge of the teacher's misconduct. The Supreme Court did not address whether the school could be found liable because it had actual knowledge of the misconduct but failed to stop it, or whether the school could be liable even absent such knowledge because the teacher's or employee's intentional discrimination may be imputed to the school. (Under agency law, the employer may be held responsible for the unlawful conduct of its agent even if the employer does not have actual knowledge of the conduct; see Section 2.3.1.) If courts apply agency principles to Title IX sexual harassment claims, it may be easier to hold colleges liable for harassment by their employees because plaintiffs will not need to show intentional discrimination *on the part of the college*. In a case decided subsequent to *Franklin*, however, the trial judge stated that "liability of the [school district] is conditioned on both a finding of hostile environment and [the district's] knowing failure to act" (*Patricia H. v. Berkeley Unified School District*, 830 F. Supp. 1288, 1297 (N.D. Cal. 1993)). Since the district could not deny that it knew of the alleged harassment, the court did not address the issue of whether liability could have been predicated solely on agency principles.

The second unresolved issue is whether plaintiffs must always show that the discrimination (the sexual harassment) was intentional, or whether unintentional discrimination may also be actionable upon a showing of discriminatory *effect* (see

---

[30]In *Pennhurst State School and Hospital v. Halderman*, 451 U.S. 1 (1981), the Court stated that there was a rebuttable presumption that remedies were unavailable for lawsuits brought under statutes passed under Congress's spending powers when the violation was unintentional.

Section 7.5.7.2) or a showing that the employer was negligent. Although *Franklin* does not address this issue, federal district courts in cases subsequent to *Franklin* have required that plaintiffs demonstrate intentional discrimination. See, for example, *R.L.R. v. Prague Public School District I-103*, 838 F. Supp. 1526 (W.D. Okla. 1993). This issue is particularly important in cases where the alleged harasser is a student rather than the agent of the college; see G. Sorenson, "Peer Sexual Harassment: Remedies and Guidelines Under Federal Law," 92 *Ed. Law Rptr.* 1 (1994).

The *Franklin* opinion also does not resolve whether Title VII jurisprudence (which requires a showing of intent for disparate treatment claims but not for impact claims) applies to sexual harassment claims brought under Title IX. If Title VII precedents were to be transposed to Title IX, they would provide guidance on the issues discussed. For example, in a Title VII case, *Karibian v. Columbia University*, 14 F.3d 773 (2d Cir. 1994), a federal appellate court applied agency principles to hold the university liable for a supervisor's harassment of an employee. If the supervisor uses his actual or apparent authority to further the harassment, said the court, the university will be liable, whether or not the target of the harassment had notifed the university. If the harasser is not a supervisor, then liability will not attach unless the employer provided no reasonable complaint process or knew of the harassment but did nothing about it, according to the *Karibian* court. Thus, if *Karibian* were applied in Title IX cases, it would provide important guidance on issues—such as whether colleges should permit counselors, residence hall advisers, or other staff to promise individuals who report harassment in confidence that college officials will not be notified, particularly if the accused harasser is a faculty member or an administrator who could be regarded as a supervisor.

Despite these unanswered questions, *Franklin* has enormous significance for colleges and universities because it greatly increases the incentives for women students and faculty to challenge sex discrimination and sexual harassment in court. It also may persuade individuals considering litigation over alleged employment discrimination to use Title IX instead of Title VII because of the greater availability of money damages. For analysis of *Franklin v. Gwinett County*, and its implications for colleges and universities, see E. J. Vargyas, "*Franklin v. Gwinnett County Public Schools* and Its Impact on Title IX Enforcement," 19 *J. Coll. & Univ. Law* 373 (1993).

In the arena of sexual harassment of students, *Alexander v. Yale University*, 459 F. Supp. 1 (D. Conn. 1977), recognized a cause of action for sexual harassment under Title IX. This was the first application of the sexual harassment theory to college students outside of the employment relationship. Although the court dismissed the claims of five of the plaintiffs and ruled that the sixth did not prove the alleged harassment, the judge wrote:

> [I]t is perfectly reasonable to maintain that academic advancement conditioned upon submission to sexual demands constitutes sex discrimination in education, just as questions of job retention or promotion tied to sexual demands from supervisors have become increasingly recognized as potential violations of Title VII's ban against sex discrimination in employment [459 F. Supp. at 4].

Alexander was decided in the context of exchanging sexual favors for good grades (see Section 4.7.3), but the courts have been asked to address sexual harassment of students in other contexts as well. Where the student is an employee and the harassment occurs in that context, the student could seek remedies under either Title VII or similar state laws prohibiting sex discrimination (see Section 3.3.2.1) or Title IX. Although some courts have refused to permit employees to file claims of sex discrimination under Title IX (see, for example, *Storey v. Board of Regents of the University of Wisconsin System,* 600 F. Supp. 838 (W.D. Wis. 1985)) because of the availability of remedies under Title VII (see Section 3.3.2.1), a federal appeals court has made the distinctions between the two laws less significant. This court applied the standards for evaluating a sexual harassment case brought under Title VII to the same type of case brought under Title IX by a student employee.

In *Lipsett v. University of Puerto Rico,* 864 F.2d 881 (1st Cir. 1988), a medical resident who was dismissed from the medical school charged the school with hostile environment sexual harassment under Title IX, Section 1983, and the Fifth Amendment's Due Process Clause. Lipsett charged that her fellow students sexually harassed her verbally and that senior residents, her supervisors, refused to assign her appropriate responsibilities because of her sex. She also charged that her supervisors and professors refused to intervene in her behalf after she had notified them of the harassment. Under the deferential standard of review developed in *University of Michigan v. Ewing* (see Section 4.7.1), the trial court had awarded summary judgment for the university, because of alleged academic misconduct on the part of the plaintiff.

The First Circuit, however, applied the sexual harassment analysis developed under Title VII, referring in particular to the U.S. Supreme Court's decision in *Meritor Savings Bank v. Vinson* (see Section 3.3.4.3), which recognized a claim for hostile environment harassment under Title VII as well as quid pro quo harassment by a supervisor. Noting that the resident had a mixed status as both employee and student, the court ruled that the disparate treatment standard developed under Title VII, which requires the plaintiff to prove intentional discrimination, should also apply to Title IX sexual harassment claims filed by students who are also employees: "[O]ur present holding—that the Title VII standard for proving discriminatory treatment should apply to claims of sex discrimination arising under Title IX—is limited to the context of employment discrimination" (864 F.2d at 897).

Although the individuals accused of sexual harassment were student employees rather than faculty, the court ruled that the university could be held liable for their actions under Title VII precedent:

> We therefore hold, following *Meritor,* that in a Title IX case, an educational institution is liable upon a finding of hostile environment sexual harassment perpetrated by its supervisors upon employees *if* an official representing that institution knew, or in the exercise of reasonable care, should have known, of the harassment's occurrence, *unless* that official can show that he or she took appropriate steps to halt it. . . . We further hold that this standard also applies to situations in which the hostile environment harassment is perpetrated by the plaintiff's coworkers. . . . [For claims of quid pro quo harassment], an educational institution is absolutely liable for such acts "whether or not [it] knew, should have known, or approved of the supervisor's actions" [864 F.2d at 901].

The plaintiff also sued university officials under Section 1983 (see this volume, Section 2.3.3); the court held that "a state official, sued under section 1983 in his or her individual capacity, can be held liable for the behavior of his or her subordinates if (1) the behavior of such subordinates results in a constitutional violation and (2) the official's action or inaction was "affirmative[ly] link[ed]," *Oklahoma City v. Tuttle*, 471 U.S. 808 . . . (1985), to that behavior in the sense that it could be characterized as "supervisory encouragement, condonation, or acquiescence" *or* "gross negligence amounting to deliberate indifference" [864 F.2d at 902].

Since the plaintiff had discussed the harassment numerous times with the dean, the director of surgery, and the director of the surgical residency program, the court concluded that "supervisory encouragement" could be found and that liability could attach.

Although *Lipsett* places harassment of student employees within the *Meritor* framework, federal courts initially were unwilling to permit a student who was not also an employee to attack hostile environment sexual harassment under Title IX. In *Yale v. Alexander*, 631 F.2d 178 (2d Cir. 1980), the court affirmed the trial court's dismissal of all the plaintiffs' claims, because they had not proved that they had suffered a "distinct and palpable injury"; the mere presence of unwelcome sexual attention, according to the court, was insufficient to establish such an injury. (The U.S. Supreme Court subsequently declared that unwelcome sexual behavior was sexual harassment (under Title VII) whether or not the target could demonstrate actual injury (*Harris v. Forklift Systems;* see Section 3.3.4.4).) In *Alexander* the court used analogies from the employment context to justify its application of Title IX to sexual harassment.

Since *Alexander* was decided prior to the U.S. Supreme Court's opinion in *Meritor*, it might be misleading to suggest that *Alexander* precludes claims of hostile environment harassment by students. In a later case, a federal trial judge stated flatly that "Title IX simply does not permit a 'hostile environment' claim" (*Bougher v. University of Pittsburgh*, 713 F. Supp. 139 (W.D. Pa. 1989), *affirmed on other grounds*, 882 F.2d 74 (3d Cir. 1989)). But another trial court in the same federal circuit found that Title IX encompasses *both* forms of harassment (*Moire v. Temple University School of Medicine*, 613 F. Supp. 1360 (D. Pa. 1985), *affirmed without opin.*, 800 F.2d 1136 (3d Cir. 1986)). The trial judge wrote that "Temple might be liable under Title IX to the extent it condoned or ratified any individually discriminatory conduct of [the professors]" (613 F. Supp. at 1366). In a footnote the judge discussed both quid pro quo and hostile environment sexual harassment, noting that "the sexual harassment 'doctrine' has generally developed in the context of Title VII," but that "these guidelines seem equally applicable to Title IX" (613 F. Supp. at 1367, n.2). This approach has also been used in sexual harassment cases brought by children against public school systems; in a recent case, a trial court held that Title IX encompasses claims of hostile environment harassment (*Patricia H. v. Berkeley Unified School District*, 830 F. Supp. 1288 (N.D. Cal. 1993)).

The *Alexander, Bougher,* and *Moire* cases involved the alleged harassment of students by faculty members. Whether Title IX forbids hostile environment sexual harassment of a student by a fellow student (when the target is not an employee) is a more complicated issue, given the opinion of the U.S. Supreme Court in *R.A.V. v. City of St. Paul, Minn.*, 112 S. Ct. 2538 (1992), and the apparent invalidity of most campus codes prohibiting hate speech (see Section 4.10). In an opinion striking the

University of Wisconsin's rule against "hate speech" as violative of the First Amendment, a federal trial judge asserted that *Meritor* had no relevance for hostile environment harassment of one student by another. In *UWM Post v. Board of Regents, University of Wisconsin System,* 774 F. Supp. 1163 (E.D. Wis. 1991)), the judge offered three reasons for rejecting the university's claim that Title VII's hostile environment prohibitions should be applied to student speech. First, said the judge, Title VII concerns itself with employment, not education. Second, *Meritor* does not apply because students are not agents of the university, and liability in *Meritor* was based on agency theory. And third, Title VII is a statute, which cannot abrogate the protections of the Constitution (774 F. Supp. at 1177). Similarly, as one commentator has concluded, Title IX does not provide students with a remedy against the college or university for assaults or other sexually oriented misconduct committed by a fellow student unless that student was in a supervisory relationship with the student (for example, a graduate student supervising an undergraduate) or a co-worker, and the student victim was also an employee (see T. Steinberg, "Rape on College Campuses: Reform Through Title IX," 18 *J. Coll. & Univ. Law* 39, 58 (1991)).

In public institutions—and also in private colleges and universities in states whose constitutions contain free speech provisions that have been applied to conduct by private parties (see, for example, *State v. Schmid,* discussed in Sections 1.5.3 and 5.6.3)—administrators may find it difficult to discipline students for hostile environment sexual harassment of other students. Conversely, the Supreme Court's ruling in *Franklin* raises the financial stakes in Title IX litigation if the perpetrator of the sexual harassment, whether of the quid pro quo or the hostile environment variety, is a faculty member, an administrator, a fellow student in a supervisory role, or some other "agent" of the college or university.

Absent the student's ability to establish an agency relationship between the harasser and the institution, potential plaintiffs' remedies for peer sexual harassment may be limited.[31] The language of Title IX may provide some assistance in this regard, however, if plaintiffs argue that the harassment "denies them the benefits of . . . an education program" (20 U.S.C. § 1681(a)). For analysis of potential claims for peer sexual harassment, see J. Faber, "Expanding Title IX of the Education Amendments of 1972 to Prohibit Student to Student Sexual Harassment," 2 *UCLA Women's Law J.* 85 (1992).

Given the result in *Franklin,* colleges and universities may wish to review their policies on sexual harassment of students by faculty and other employees. And although consensual sexual relationships between faculty and students do not violate Title IX (as long as the student is beyond the statutory age of consent), some institutions have issued policies forbidding consensual sexual relationships between faculty and students, because of the conflict of interest and potential for abuse of the professor's power over the student's academic record. For a defense of such policies, see P. DeChiara, "The Need for Universities to Have Rules on Consensual Sexual Relationships Between Faculty Members and Students," 21 *Columbia J. Law & Social*

---

[31]In the elementary and secondary school context, jurisprudence is developing that may have relevance for Title IX hostile environment claims for peer harassment. In *Doe v. Petaluma City School District,* 830 F. Supp. 1560 (N.D. Cal. 1993), a trial court ruled that the school district could only be found liable for *peer* harassment if school officials knew of the harassment and took no remedial action.

Problems 137 (1988); for a criticism of such policies, see E. Keller, "Consensual Amorous Relationships Between Faculty and Students: The Constitutional Right to Privacy," 15 *J. Coll. & Univ. Law* 21 (1988). For a comprehensive collection of relevant articles, EEOC policy guidance on sexual harassment issues, and model institutional policies, see E. Cole (ed.), *Sexual Harassment on Campus: A Legal Compendium* (2d ed., National Association of College and University Attorneys, 1990).

7.5.4. Section 504. Section 504 of the Rehabilitation Act of 1973, as amended (29 U.S.C. § 794) states:

> No otherwise qualified individual with a disability in the United States . . . shall, solely by reason of his disability, be excluded from the participation in, be denied the benefits of, or be subjected to discrimination under any program or activity receiving federal financial assistance.

The Department of Education's regulations on Section 504 (34 C.F.R. Part 104) contain specific provisions that establish standards for postsecondary institutions to follow in their dealings with "qualified" students and applicants with disabilities; "qualified" employees and applicants for employment; and members of the public with disabilities who are seeking to take advantage of institutional programs and activities open to the public. A "qualified individual with a disability" is "any person who (i) has a physical or mental impairment which substantially limits one or more major life activities, (ii) has a record of such an impairment, or (iii) is regarded as having such an impairment" (34 C.F.R. § 104.3(j)). In the context of postsecondary and vocational education services, a "qualified" person with a disability is someone who "meets the academic and technical standards requisite to admission or participation in the recipient's education program or activity" (34 C.F.R. § 104.3(k)(3)). Whether an individual with a disability is "qualified" in other situations depends on different criteria. In the context of employment, a qualified individual with a disability is one who, "with reasonable accommodation, can perform the essential functions of the job in question" (34 C.F.R. § 104.3(k)(1)). With regard to other services, a qualified individual with a disability is someone who "meets the essential eligibility requirements for the receipt of such services" (34 C.F.R. § 104.3(k)(4)).[32]

Although the Section 504 regulations resemble those for Title VI and Title IX in the types of programs and activities considered, they differ in some of the means used for achieving nondiscrimination. The reason for these differences is that "different or special treatment of handicapped persons, because of their handicaps, may be necessary in a number of contexts in order to ensure equal opportunity" (42 Fed. Reg. 22676 (May 4, 1977)). Institutions receiving federal funds may not discriminate

---

[32]Cases and authorities are collected in Annot., "Who Is 'Individual with Handicaps' Under Rehabilitation Act of 1973 (29 U.S.C.S. §§ 701 et seq.)," 97 A.L.R. Fed. 694 (1990 and periodic supp.); Annot., "Who Is 'Qualified' Handicapped Person Protected from Employment Discrimination Under Rehabilitation Act of 1973 (29 U.S.C.S. §§ 701 et seq.) and Regulations Promulgated Thereunder," 80 A.L.R. Fed. 830 (1986 and periodic supp.); Annot., "Construction and Effect of § 504 of the Rehabilitation Act of 1973 (29 U.S.C.S. § 794) Prohibiting Discrimination Against Otherwise Qualified Handicapped Individuals in Specified Programs or Activities," 44 A.L.R. Fed. 148 (1979 and periodic supp.).

on the basis of disability in admission and recruitment of students (see this volume, Section 4.2.4.3); in providing financial assistance (Section 4.3.3); in athletic programs (Section 4.15.4); in housing accommodations (Section 4.14.1); or in the employment of faculty and staff members (Section 3.3.2.5) or students (see 34 C.F.R. § 104.46(c)). The regulations also prohibit discrimination on the basis of disability in a number of other programs and activities of postsecondary institutions.

Section 104.43 requires nondiscriminatory "treatment" of students in general. Besides prohibiting discrimination in the institution's own programs and activities, this section requires that, when an institution places students in an educational program or activity not wholly under its control, the institution "shall assure itself that the other education program or activity, as a whole, provides an equal opportunity for the participation of qualified handicapped persons." In a student-teaching program, for example, the "as a whole" concept allows the institution to make use of a particular external activity even though it discriminates, provided that the institution's entire student-teaching program, taken as a whole, offers student teachers with disabilities "the same range and quality of choice in student-teaching assignments afforded nonhandicapped students" (42 Fed. Reg. at 22692 (comment 30)). Furthermore, the institution must operate its programs and activities in "the most integrated setting appropriate"; that is, by integrating disabled persons with nondisabled persons to the maximum extent appropriate (34 C.F.R. § 104.43(d)).

The Education Department's regulations recognize that certain academic adjustment may be necessary to protect against discrimination on the basis of disability:

(a) *Academic requirements.* A recipient to which this subpart applies shall make such modifications to its academic requirements as are necessary to ensure that such requirements do not discriminate or have the effect of discriminating, on the basis of handicap, against a qualified handicapped applicant or student. Academic requirements that the recipient can demonstrate are essential to the program of instruction being pursued by such student or to any directly related licensing requirement will not be regarded as discriminatory within the meaning of this section. Modifications may include changes in the length of time permitted for the completion of degree requirements, substitution of specific courses required for the completion of degree requirements, and adaptation of the manner in which specific courses are conducted.

(b) *Other rules.* A recipient to which this subpart applies may not impose upon handicapped students other rules, such as the prohibition of tape recorders in classrooms or of dog guides in campus buildings, that have the effect of limiting the participation of handicapped students in the recipient's education program or activity.

(c) *Course examination.* In its course examinations or other procedures for evaluating students' academic achievement in its program, a recipient to which this subpart applies shall provide such methods for evaluating the achievement of students who have a handicap that impairs sensory, manual, or speaking skills as will best ensure that the results of the evaluation represent the student's achievement in the course, rather than reflecting the student's impaired sensory, manual, or speaking skills (except where such skills are the factors that the test purports to measure).

(d) *Auxiliary aids.* (1) A recipient to which this subpart applies shall take such steps as are necessary to ensure that no handicapped student is denied the benefits of, excluded from participation in, or otherwise subjected to discrimination under the education program or activity operated by the recipient because of the absence of educational auxiliary aids for students with impaired sensory, manual, or speaking skills. (2) Auxiliary aids may include taped texts, interpreters, or other effective methods of making orally delivered materials available to students with hearing impairments, readers in libraries for students with visual impairments, classroom equipment adapted for use by students with manual impairments, and other similar services and actions. Recipients need not provide attendants, individually prescribed devices, readers for personal use or study, or other devices or services of a personal nature [34 C.F.R. § 104.44].

Section 104.47(b) provides that counseling and placement services be offered on the same basis to disabled and nondisabled students. The institution is specifically charged with ensuring that job counseling is not more restrictive for disabled students. Under Section 104.47(c), an institution that supplies significant assistance to student social organizations must determine that these organizations do not discriminate against disabled students in their membership practices.

The institution's programs or activities—"when viewed in their entirety"—must be physically accessible to students with disabilities, and the institution's facilities must be usable by them. The regulations applicable to existing facilities differ from those applied to new construction:

(a) *Program accessibility.* A recipient shall operate each program or activity to which this part applies so that the program or activity, when viewed in its entirety, is readily accessible to handicapped persons. This paragraph does not require a recipient to make each of its existing facilities or every part of a facility accessible to and usable by handicapped persons.

(b) *Methods.* A recipient may comply with the requirements of paragraph (a) of this section through such means as redesign of equipment, reassignment of classes or other services to accessible buildings, assignment of aides to beneficiaries, home visits, delivery of health, welfare, or other social services at alternate accessible sites, alteration of existing facilities and construction of new facilities in conformance with the requirements of § 104.23, or any other methods that result in making its program or activity accessible to handicapped persons. A recipient is not required to make structural changes in existing facilities where other methods are effective in achieving compliance with paragraph (a) of this section. In choosing among available methods for meeting the requirement of paragraph (a) of this section, a recipient shall give priority to those methods that offer programs and activities to handicapped persons in the most integrated setting appropriate [34 C.F.R. § 104.22; see also policy interpretations of this regulation at 43 Fed. Reg. 36034 and 36035 (1978)].

If structural changes in existing facilities—that is, facilities existing in June 1977, when the regulations became effective—were necessary to make a program or an activity accessible, they must have been completed by June 1980. All new construction must be readily accessible when it is completed.[33]

---

[33]Institutions can comply with accessibility requirements by conforming to the *American National Standard Specifications for Making Buildings and Facilities Accessible to, and Usable by, the Physically Handicapped;* (published by the American National Standards Insti-

In *Southeastern Community College v. Davis*, 442 U.S. 397 (1979), set forth in Section 4.2.4.3 of this volume, the U.S. Supreme Court added some important interpretive gloss to the regulation on academic adjustments and assistance for disabled students (34 C.F.R. § 104.44). The Court quoted but did not question the validity of the regulation's requirement that an institution provide "auxiliary aids"—such as interpreters, taped texts, or braille materials—for students with sensory impairments. It made very clear, however, that the law does not require "major" or "substantial" modifications in an institution's curriculum or academic standards to accommodate disabled students. To require such modifications, the Court said, would be to read into Section 504 an "affirmative action obligation" not warranted by its "language, purpose, [or] history." Moreover, if the regulations were to be interpreted to impose such obligation, they would to that extent be invalid.

The Court acknowledged, however, that the line between discrimination and a lawful refusal to take affirmative action is not always clear. Thus, in some instances programmatic changes may be required where they would not fundamentally alter the program itself. In determining where this line is to be drawn, the Court would apparently extend considerable deference to postsecondary institutions' legitimate educational judgments respecting academic standards and course requirements. Davis had argued that Southeastern's insistence that its students be capable of performing all the functions of a professional nurse was discriminatory, since North Carolina law did not require as much from applicants for a license to practice. In a footnote to its opinion, the Court rejected this claim: "Respondent's argument misses the point. Southeastern's program, structured to train persons who will be able to perform all normal roles of a registered nurse, represents a legitimate academic policy, and is accepted by the state. In effect, it seeks to ensure that no graduate will pose a danger to the public in any professional role [that] he or she might be cast [in]. Even if the licensing requirements of North Carolina or some other state are less demanding, nothing in the Act requires an educational institution to lower its standards."

While *Davis* thus limits postsecondary institutions' legal obligation to modify their academic programs to accommodate disabled students, the opinion does not limit an institution's obligation to make its facilities physically accessible to qualified students with disabilities, as required by the regulations (34 C.F.R. § 104.22)—even when doing so involves major expense. In *Davis* the Court found that, because of her hearing disability, the plaintiff was not "otherwise qualified" for admission to the nursing program. When a person with a disability is qualified and has been admitted, however, Section 104.22 requires that facilities as a whole be "readily accessible" to that person.

The U.S. Supreme Court spoke a second time on the significance of Section 504—this time with regard to whether individuals with contagious diseases are pro-

---

tute, Inc., 1430 Broadway, New York, NY 10018) (34 C.F.R. § 104.32(c)). Under Section 2122 of the Tax Reform Act of 1976 [26 U.S.C. § 190], recipients that pay federal income tax are eligible to claim a tax deduction of up to $25,000 for architectural and transportation modifications made to improve accessibility for handicapped persons" (42 Fed. Reg. at 22689 (comment 20)). See also 42 U.S.C. § 4151 et seq. (Architectural Barriers Act of 1968) and 29 U.S.C. § 792 (the Act's federal Compliance Board) for further requirements applicable to buildings constructed, altered, or leased with federal aid funds.

tected by Section 504. In *School Board of Nassau County v. Arline*, 480 U.S. 273 (1987), the Court held that a teacher with tuberculosis was protected by Section 504 and that her employer was required to determine whether a reasonable accommodation could be made for her. Subsequent to *Arline*, Congress, in amendments to Section 504 (42 U.S.C. § 706 (8)(D)), and the EEOC, in regulations interpreting the employment provisions of the Americans with Disabilities Act (29 C.F.R. § 1630.2(r)), provided other statutory protections for students and staff with contagious diseases. For a discussion of the relevant legal principles under Section 504 in a case where a university dismissed a dental student suffering from AIDS, see *Doe v. Washington University*, 780 F. Supp. 628 (E.D. Mo. 1991).

The availability of compensatory damages under Section 504 was addressed in *Tanberg v. Weld County Sheriff*, 787 F. Supp. 970 (D. Colo. 1992). Citing *Franklin v. Gwinnett County Public Schools* (Section 7.5.9), the federal trial judge ruled that a plaintiff who proves intentional discrimination under Section 504 can be entitled to compensatory damages.

The significance of *Davis* may be limited for an additional reason, in that the Americans with Disabilities Act affords broader rights of access and accommodation to students, employees, and, in some cases, the general public than contemplated by *Davis*. The employment provisions of the Americans with Disabilities Act (ADA) are discussed in Section 3.3.2.5, while its public accommodations and other provisions are discussed in Section 7.2.16. Remedies are broader than those provided for by Section 504, and will now apply to all colleges and universities, whether or not they receive federal funds. For a comparison of Section 504 and the ADA with regard to access to colleges and universities for students with disabilities, see H. Kaufman, *Access to Institutions of Higher Education for Students with Disabilities* (National Association of College and University Attorneys, 1991). See also Note, "Americans with Disabilities Act of 1990: Significant Overlap with Section 504 for Colleges and Universities," 18 *J. Coll. & Univ. Law* 389 (1992).

7.5.5. Age Discrimination Act. The Age Discrimination Act of 1975 (42 U.S.C. § 6101 et seq.) contains a general prohibition on age discrimination in federally funded programs and activities. Under the Age Discrimination Act's original statement-of-purpose clause, the prohibition applied only to "unreasonable" discrimination—a limitation not found in the Title VI, Title IX, or Section 504 civil rights statutes (see Sections 7.5.2 to 7.5.4). Congress postponed the Act's effective date, however, and directed the U.S. Commission on Civil Rights to study age discrimination in federally assisted programs. After considering the commission's report, submitted in January 1978, Congress amended the Age Discrimination Act in October 1978 (Pub. L. No. 95-478) to strike the word "unreasonable" from the statement-of-purpose clause, thus removing a critical restriction on the Act's scope.

In 1979 the U.S. Department of Health, Education and Welfare issued final regulations under the Age Discrimination Act (44 Fed. Reg. 33768 (June 12, 1979)). These regulations, now codified in 45 C.F.R. Part 90, "state general, government-wide rules" for implementing this law (45 C.F.R. § 90.2(a)). Every federal agency administering federal aid programs must implement its own specific regulations consistent with HEW's (now HHS's) general regulations.

The general regulations, together with the extensive commentary that accompanies them (44 Fed. Reg. 33768–33775, 33780–33787), provide a detailed explanation of the Age Discrimination Act. The regulations are divided into several subparts. Subpart A explains the purpose and coverage of the Act and regulations and defines some of the regulatory terminology. The core of this subpart is Section 90.3:

Section 90.3 What programs and activities does the Age Discrimination Act of 1975 cover?

(a) The Age Discrimination Act of 1975 applies to any program or activity receiving federal financial assistance, including programs or activities receiving funds under the State and Local Fiscal Assistance Act of 1972 (31 U.S.C. § 1221 *et seq.*).

(b) The Age Discrimination Act of 1975 does not apply to:

(1) An age distinction contained in that part of a Federal, State, or local statute or ordinance adopted by an elected, general purpose legislative body which:

(i) Provides any benefits or assistance to persons based on age; or

(ii) Establishes criteria for participation in age-related terms; or

(iii) Describes intended beneficiaries or target groups in age-related terms.

(2) Any employment practice of any employer, employment agency, labor organization, or any labor-management joint apprenticeship training program, except for any program or activity receiving federal financial assistance for public service employment under the [Job Training Partnership Act] (29 U.S.C. § 1501 *et seq.*).

The commentary to the regulations explains this provision as follows:

The Act generally covers all programs and activities which receive federal financial assistance. However, the Act does not apply to any age distinction "established under authority of any law" [the statutory phrase] which provides benefits or establishes criteria for participation on the basis of age or in age-related terms. Thus, age distinctions which are "established under authority of any law" may continue in use. These regulations define "any law" to mean federal statutes, state statutes, or local statutes adopted by elected, general-purpose legislative bodies.

The Act also excludes from its coverage most employment practices, except for programs funded under the public service employment titles of the [Job Training Partnership Act]. These regulations do cover any program or activity which is both a program of federal financial assistance and provides employment such as the College Work-Study program [44 Fed. Reg. 33769].

Subpart B of the regulations explains the ADA's prohibition against age discrimination in programs covered by the Act. It also lists the exceptions to this prohibition. Section 90.12 sets out the prohibition as follows:

(a) *General rule:* No person in the United States shall, on the basis of age, be excluded from participation in, be denied the benefits of, or be subjected to discrimination under, any program or activity receiving federal financial assistance.

(b) *Specific rules:* A recipient may not, in any program or activity receiving federal financial assistance, directly or through contractual, licensing, or other

arrangements, use age distinctions or take any other actions which have the effect, on the basis of age, of:
(1) excluding individuals from, denying them the benefits of, or subjecting them to discrimination under, a program or activity receiving federal financial assistance, or
(2) denying or limiting individuals in their opportunity to participate in any program or activity receiving federal financial assistance.
(c) The specific forms of age discrimination listed in paragraph (b) of this section do not necessarily constitute a complete list.

The rest of subpart B sets out the exceptions to Section 90.12:

Section 90.13 Definitions of normal operation and statutory objective.
For purposes of Sections 90.14 and 90.15, the terms *normal operation* and *statutory objective* shall have the following meaning:
(a) *Normal operation* means the operation of a program or activity without significant changes that would impair its ability to meet its objectives.
(b) *Statutory objective* means any purpose of a program or activity expressly stated in any Federal statute, State statute, or local statute or ordinance adopted by an elected, general purpose legislative body.

Section 90.14 Exceptions to the rules against age discrimination. Normal operation or statutory objective of any program or activity.
A recipient is permitted to take an action otherwise prohibited by Section 90.12 if the action reasonably takes into account age as a factor necessary to the normal operation or the achievement of any statutory objective of a program or activity. An action reasonably takes into account age as a factor necessary to the normal operation or the achievement of any statutory objective of a program or activity, if:
(a) Age is used as a measure or approximation of one or more other characteristics; and
(b) The other characteristic(s) must be measured or approximated in order for the normal operation of the program or activity to continue, or to achieve any statutory objective of the program or activity; and
(c) The other characteristic(s) can be reasonably measured or approximated by the use of age; and
(d) The other characteristic(s) are impractical to measure directly on an individual basis.

Section 90.15 Exceptions to the rules against age discrimination. Reasonable factors other than age.
A recipient is permitted to take an action otherwise prohibited by Section 90.12 which is based on a factor other than age, even though that action may have a disproportionate effect on persons of different ages. An action may be based on a factor other than age only if the factor bears a direct and substantial relationship to the normal operation of the program or activity or to the achievement of a statutory objective.

Section 90.16 Burden of proof.
The burden of proving that an age distinction or other action falls within the exception outlined in Sections 90.14 and 90.15 is on the recipient of federal financial assistance.

Explanatory commentary accompanying the regulations makes it clear that recipients can never justify exceptions to the general prohibition on the basis of cost-benefit considerations alone, but only by meeting the specific tests in Sections 90.14 and 90.15 of the regulations (44 Fed. Reg. 33774, 33783).

Subpart C of the general regulations explains the responsibilities that each federal agency has in implementing the Act, including publication of its own regulations and review of any existing policies that employ age distinctions. Subpart D sets out requirements that each agency must follow in establishing compliance, investigation, conciliation, and enforcement procedures under the Act; and Subpart E provides for future review of the general regulations by HHS and future review of specific agency regulations by the agencies promulgating them.

Although the regulations and commentary add considerable particularity to the brief provisions of the Act, the full import of the Act for postsecondary institutions can be ascertained only by a study of the specific regulations that agencies have promulgated or will promulgate to fulfill the mandate of the general regulations. The HHS specific regulations, for example, are codified in 45 C.F.R. Part 91.

The Education Department published final rules to interpret the Age Discrimination Act as it applies to the department's financial assistance programs (most notably, the student financial assistance programs) at 34 C.F.R. Part 110 (56 Fed. Reg. 40194). The Education Department's regulations track the general regulations in many respects, and require institutions to provide the same type of assurance of compliance that they must provide under Titles IV and IX and Section 504. The regulations establish a procedure for filing a complaint with the department under the Age Discrimination Act (34 C.F.R. § 110.31); provide for mediation of disputes under the Act by the Federal Mediation and Conciliation Service (34 C.F.R. § 110.32); and describe the department's investigation process if mediation fails to resolve the complaint (34 C.F.R. § 110.33). Penalties for violations of the Act, including termination of funding or debarment from future funding, are contained at 34 C.F.R. § 110.35. A person filing a complaint under the Act must exhaust the administrative remedies provided by the regulations before filing a civil complaint in court (34 C.F.R. § 110.39).

Postsecondary administrators and counsel should consult both the specific and the general agency regulations, in conjunction with the Act itself, when reviewing institutional policies or practices that employ explicit or implicit age distinctions.

7.5.6. Affirmative action. Affirmative action poses a special problem under the federal civil rights statutes. The Department of Education's Title VI regulations both require and permit affirmative action under certain circumstances:

> (i) In administering a program regarding which the recipient has previously discriminated against persons on the ground of race, color, or national origin, the recipient must take affirmative action to overcome the effects of prior discrimination.
> (ii) Even in the absence of such prior discrimination, a recipient in administering a program may take affirmative action to overcome the effects of conditions which resulted in limiting participation by persons of a particular race, color, or national origin [34 C.F.R. § 100.3(b)(6)].

The Title IX regulations also permit affirmative action for voluntary correction of conditions that resulted in limited participation by the members of one sex in the institution's programs and activities (34 C.F.R. § 106.3(b)). However, both the Title IX and the Section 504 regulations require a recipient to engage in "remedial action" rather than "affirmative action" to overcome the effects of its own prior discrimination (34 C.F.R. § 106.3(a); 34 C.F.R. § 104.6(a)). In addition, the Section 504 regulations suggest that the recipient take only "voluntary action" rather than "affirmative action" to correct conditions that resulted in limited participation by the handicapped (34 C.F.R. § 104.6(b)). But none of the regulations define "affirmative action," "remedial action," or "voluntary action," or set out the limits of permissible action.

One federal district court has ruled that in a Title VI case some "affirmative action" may itself constitute a Title VI violation. In *Flanagan v. President and Directors of Georgetown College*, 417 F. Supp. 377 (D.D.C. 1976), the issue was that Georgetown Law Center had allocated 60 percent of its scholarship funds to minority students, who constituted only 11 percent of the class. The university claimed that the program was permissible under Section 100.3(b)(6)(ii) of the Title VI regulations. The court disagreed, holding that the scholarship program was not administered on a "racially neutral basis" and was "reverse discrimination on the basis of race, which cannot be justified by a claim of affirmative action." Subsequently, in *Regents of University of California v. Bakke*, 438 U.S. 265 (1978) (see Section 4.2.5), the first U.S. Supreme Court case on affirmative action under Title VI, a 5-to-4 majority of the Court agreed that Title VI did not require complete racial neutrality in affirmative action. But no majority of justices could agree on the extent to which Title VI and its regulations permit racial or ethnic preferences to be used as one part of an affirmative action program.

Like the Title VI, Title IX, and Section 504 regulations, the HHS general regulations under the Age Discrimination Act of 1975 (see Section 7.5.5) also include a provision on affirmative action:

> (a) Where a recipient is found to have discriminated on the basis of age, the recipient shall take any remedial action which the agency may require to overcome the effects of the discrimination. If another recipient exercises control over the recipient that has discriminated, both recipients may be required to take remedial action.
> (b) Even in the absence of a finding of discrimination, a recipient may take affirmative action to overcome the effects of conditions that resulted in limited participation in the recipient's program or activity on the basis of age.
> (c) If a recipient operating a program which serves the elderly or children, in addition to persons of other ages, provides special benefits to the elderly or to children, the provision of those benefits shall be presumed to be voluntary affirmative action provided that it does not have the effect of excluding otherwise eligible persons from participation in the program [45 C.F.R. § 90.49].

Paralleling the other civil rights regulations, this regulation distinguishes between required (subsection (a)) and permitted (subsection (b)) actions and, like Title IX and Section 504, uses the term "remedial action" to describe the former. Also like the Title IX and Section 504 regulations, this regulation specifies that "remedial action" is permitted only when the recipient has discriminated in the past against the class of persons whom the regulations protect. In addition, the Age Discrimination Act regulation contains a unique provision (subsection (c)), which, under certain circumstances, brings the provision of special benefits to two age groups—the elderly and children— under the protective umbrella of "voluntary affirmative action." The Act's regulations do not include explanatory commentary on Section 90.49. Nor, in common with the other civil rights regulations, do they define "remedial action" or "affirmative action" or (except for subsection (c)) the scope of permissible action.

Thus, the federal regulations give postsecondary administrators little guidance concerning the affirmative or remedial actions they must take to maintain compliance, or may take without jeopardizing compliance. Insufficient guidance, however, is not a justification for avoiding affirmative action when it is required by the regulations, nor should it deter administrators from taking voluntary action when it is their institution's policy to do so. Rather, administrators should proceed carefully, seeking the assistance of legal counsel and keeping abreast of the developing case law and agency policy interpretations on affirmative action. (See Sections 3.4 and 4.2.5.)

7.5.7. Scope and coverage problems. In recent years the scope and coverage of the civil rights statutes (this volume, Sections 7.5.2 to 7.5.5) have been the subject of intense debate, considerable litigation, and several congressional bills. The subsections below review the most complex and controversial of the scope and coverage issues.

The administrative regulations implementing the civil rights statutes (particularly the regulations of the Department of Education) provide the initial guidance on these issues. Courts have sometimes reviewed the regulations to determine whether they are authorized by the statute being implemented. Where there are gaps in the regulations or the statutes, courts have also stepped in to provide answers. And in one instance, after a controversial U.S. Supreme Court decision (in *Grove City College v. Bell*), Congress passed a law (the Civil Rights Restoration Act) that overturned a Court decision (see Section 7.5.7.4).

As the volume of litigation has increased, it has become apparent that the similarities of statutory language under the four civil rights statutes give rise to similar scope and coverage issues. Answers to an issue under one statute will thus provide guidance in answering comparable issues under another statute. There are some critical differences, however, in the statutory language and implementing regulations for each statute (for example, as explained in Section 7.5.7.1, Title VI and the Age Discrimination Act have provisions limiting their applicability to employment discrimination, whereas Title IX and Section 504 do not), and each statute has its own unique legislative history. Therefore, to gain a fine-tuned view of further developments, administrators and counsel should approach each statute and each scope and coverage issue separately, taking account of both their similarities to and their differences from the other statutes and other issues.

7.5.7.1. Coverage of employment discrimination. One question concerning scope and coverage is whether the civil rights statutes prohibit discrimination not only against students but also against employees. Both Title VI and the Age Discrimination Act contain provisions that permit coverage of discrimination against employees only when a "primary objective" of the federal aid is "to provide employment" (42 U.S.C. § 2000d-3; 42 U.S.C. § 6103(c)). Title IX and Section 504 do not contain any such express limitation. Consistent with the apparent open-endedness of the latter two statutes, both the Title IX and the Section 504 regulations have provisions comprehensively covering discrimination against employees (see Sections 3.3.2.3 and 3.3.2.5 of this volume), while the Title VI and the Age Discrimination Act regulations cover employment discrimination only in narrow circumstances (34 C.F.R. §§ 100.2 and 100.3(c); 45 C.F.R. § 90.3(b)(2)).

The first major U.S. Supreme Court case on scope and coverage—*North Haven Board of Education v. Bell,* 456 U.S. 512 (1982)—concerned employment. *North Haven* was a Title IX case. The plaintiffs, two school boards in Connecticut, challenged the validity of Subpart E of HEW's (now ED's) Title IX regulations, which prohibits recipients from discriminating against employees on the basis of sex. The Supreme Court considered two questions: (1) whether the Title IX statute applies to the employment practices of educational institutions; and (2) if it does, whether the scope and coverage of the Title IX employment regulations are consistent with the Title IX statute.

Looking to the wording of the statute, the statute's legislative history, and the statute's "postenactment history" in Congress and at HEW, the Court (with three dissenters) gave a clear, affirmative answer to the first question:

> Our starting point in determining the scope of Title IX is, of course, the statutory language. . . . Section 901(a)'s broad directive that "no person" may be discriminated against on the basis of gender appears, on its face, to include employees as well as students. Under that provision, employees, like other "persons," may not be "excluded from participation in," "denied the benefits of," or "subjected to discrimination under" education programs receiving federal financial support. . . . Because Section 901(a) neither expressly nor impliedly excludes employees from its reach, we should interpret the provision as covering and protecting these "persons" unless other considerations counsel to the contrary. After all, Congress easily could have substituted "student" or "beneficiary" for the word "person" if it had wished to restrict the scope of Section 901(a) [456 U.S. at 520–22].

After examining the legislative history of Title IX and its postenactment history, the Court concluded that Congress had intended to include employees within Title IX's protections.

Proceeding to the second question in *North Haven,* the Court then upheld the validity of the Title IX employment regulations. The major issue was whether the regulations are consistent with the statutory language applying Title IX's nondiscrimination prohibition to a "program or activity receiving federal financial assistance" and limiting the effect of a fund termination "to the particular program, or part thereof, in which . . . noncompliance has been . . . found." (This issue, which the Court characterized as an issue of the statute's "program specificity," is further discussed in Section 7.5.7.4.) After reviewing the provisions of the employment regulations and HEW's comments accompanying their publication, the Court concluded that the regulations are consistent with the statute's "program" focus and thus are valid.

The U.S. Supreme Court has also upheld Section 504's applicability to discrimination against employees. In *Consolidated Rail Corp. v. Darrone,* 465 U.S. 624 (1984), a locomotive engineer had been dismissed after having had his left hand and forearm amputated as a result of an accident. When the engineer claimed that he was fit for work and had been discriminated against because of his disability, the employer argued that Darrone was not protected by Section 504. That law, argued the railroad, applies to employment discrimination "only if the primary objective of the federal aid that [the employer] receives is to promote employment." In other words, unless the employee was paid with federal funds, the railroad argued (which he was not), Section 504 did not apply. The Court rejected this argument:

> It is clear that Section 504 itself contains no such limitation . . . ; rather, that section prohibits discrimination against the handicapped under "any program or activity receiving federal financial assistance." And it is unquestionable that the section was intended to reach employment discrimination. Indeed, enhancing employment of the handicapped was so much the focus of the 1973 legislation that Congress the next year felt it necessary to amend the statute to clarify whether Section 504 was intended to prohibit other types of discrimination as well (see § 111(a), Pub. L. 93-516, 88 Stat. 1617, 1619 (1974)). Thus, the language of Section 504 suggests that its bar on employment discrimination should not be limited to programs that receive federal aid the primary purpose of which is to promote employment.
>
> The legislative history, executive interpretation, and purpose of the 1973 enactment all are consistent with this construction [465 U.S. at 632-33].

7.5.7.2. Coverage of unintentional discriminatory acts. None of the four statutes explicitly state whether they prohibit actions whose effects are discriminatory (that is, actions that have a disproportionate or disparate impact on the class of persons protected) or whether such actions are prohibited only if taken with a discriminatory intent or motive. The regulations for Title VI and the Age Discrimination Act, however, contain provisions that apparently prohibit actions with discriminatory effects, even if those actions are not intentionally discriminatory (34 C.F.R. § 100.3(b)(2); 45 C.F.R. § 90.12), and the Section 504 regulations prohibit actions that have the effect of subjecting a qualified individual to discrimination on the basis of disability (34 C.F.R. § 104.4(b)(4) and (5)). Title IX's regulations prohibit testing or evaluation of skill that has a discriminatory effect on the basis of sex (34 C.F.R. §§ 106.21(b)(2) and 106.34), and also prohibit certain employment practices with discriminatory effects (34 C.F.R. § 106.51(a)(3)).

The leading U.S. Supreme Court case on the intent issue is *Guardians Assn. v. Civil Service Commission of the City of New York*, 463 U.S. 582 (1983). The justices issued six opinions in the case, none of which commanded a majority and which, according to Justice Powell, "further confuse rather than guide." The Court's basic difficulty was reconciling *Lau v. Nichols*, 414 U.S. 563 (1974), which held that Title VI and HEW's regulations prohibit actions with discriminatory effects, and *Regents of the University of California v. Bakke*, 438 U.S. 265 (1978), which indicated that Title VI reaches no further than the Fourteenth Amendment's Equal Protection Clause, which prohibits only intentional discrimination.

Although the Court could not agree on the import of these two cases, or on the analysis to adopt in the case before it, one can extract some meaning from *Guardians* by pooling the views expressed in the various opinions. A majority of the justices did hold that the intent standard is a necessary component of the Title VI statute. A different majority, however, held that, even though the statute embodies an intent test, the ED regulations that adopt an effects test are nevertheless valid. In his opinion Justice White tallied the differing views of the justices on these points (463 U.S. at 584 n.2, and 607 n.27). He then rationalized these seemingly contradictory conclusions by explaining that "the language of Title VI on its face is ambiguous; the word 'discrimination' is inherently so." The statute should therefore be amenable to a broader construction by ED, "at least to the extent of permitting, if not requiring, regulations that reach" discriminatory effects (463 U.S. at 592; see also 463 U.S. at 643–45 (opinion of Justice Stevens)).

The result of this confusing mélange of opinions is to validate the Education Department's regulations extending Title VI coverage to actions with discriminatory effects. At the same time, however, the *Guardians* opinions suggest that, if the department were to change its regulations so as to adopt an intent test, such a change would also be valid. Any such change, though, would in turn be subject to invalidation by Congress, which could amend the Title VI statute (or other statutes under which the issue arose) to replace its intent standard with an effects test. Such legislation would apparently be constitutional (see this volume, Sections 7.1.1 and 7.1.4; and see *City of Rome v. United States*, 446 U.S. 156 (1980)).

In *Alexander v. Choate*, 469 U.S. 287 (1985), the Court also considered the intent issue under Section 504. After reviewing the various opinions in the *Guardians* case on Title VI, the Court determined that that case does not control the intent issue under Section 504 because Section 504 raises considerations different from those raised by Title VI. In particular:

> Discrimination against the handicapped was perceived by Congress to be most often the product not of invidious animus, but rather of thoughtlessness and indifference—of benign neglect. . . . Federal agencies and commentators on the plight of the handicapped similarly have found that discrimination against the handicapped is primarily the result of apathetic attitudes rather than affirmative animus.
>
> In addition, much of the conduct that Congress sought to alter in passing the Rehabilitation Act would be difficult if not impossible to reach were the Act construed to proscribe only conduct fueled by a discriminatory intent. For example, elimination of architectural barriers was one of the central aims of the Act (see, for example, S. Rep. No. 93-318, p. 4 (1973), U.S. Code Cong. & Admin. News 1973, pp. 2076, 2080), yet such barriers were clearly not erected with the aim or intent of excluding the handicapped [469 U.S. at 295–97].

Although these considerations suggest that discriminatory intent need not be a requirement under Section 504, the Court also noted some countervailing considerations:

> At the same time, the position urged by respondents—that we interpret Section 504 to reach all action disparately affecting the handicapped—is also troubling. Because the handicapped typically are not similarly situated to the nonhandicapped, respondents' position would in essence require each recipient of federal funds first to evaluate the effects on the handicapped of every proposed action that might touch the interests of the handicapped, and then to consider alternatives for achieving the same objectives with less severe disadvantage to the handicapped. The formalization and policing of this process could lead to a wholly unwieldy administrative and adjudicative burden [469 U.S. at 298].

Faced with these difficulties, the Court declined to hold that one group of considerations would always have priority over the other: "While we reject the boundless notion that all disparate-impact showings constitute prima facie cases under Section 504, we assume without deciding that Section 504 reaches at least some conduct that has an unjustifiable disparate impact upon the handicapped." Thus "splitting the difference," the Court left for another day the specification of what types of Section 504 cases will not require evidence of a discriminatory intent.

A related, but different, issue involves the showing that plaintiffs must make to obtain compensatory damages under Title VI. In *Craft v. Board of Trustees of the University of Illinois,* 793 F.2d 140 (7th Cir. 1986), the court, reading together *Guardians* and *Alexander v. Choate,* held that the plaintiffs must show intentional discrimination to obtain *compensatory* damages under Title VI but need show only a disparate impact to obtain *equitable* (injunctive) relief. This distinction between compensatory and equitable relief had been suggested in both Justice White's and Justice Rehnquist's opinions in *Guardians.*

7.5.7.3. Scope of the phrase "receiving federal financial assistance." Each of the four civil rights statutes prohibits discrimination in (1) "a program or activity" that is (2) "receiving federal financial assistance." Uncertainty about the definitions of these two terms, and their interrelation, has created substantial questions about the scope of the civil rights statutes. The first term is discussed in Section 7.5.7.4; the second is discussed here. The major question regarding the second term is whether indirect or student-based aid, such as Pell Grants or veterans' education benefits, is "federal financial assistance," triggering the protections of the civil rights statutes.

The statutes do not define the phrase "federal financial assistance." But the Education Department's regulations for each statute contain a broad definition. Under Title IX, for instance:

"Federal financial assistance" means any of the following, when authorized or extended under a law administered by the department:

(1) A grant or loan of federal financial assistance, including funds made available for:
    (i) The acquisition, construction, renovation, restoration, or repair of a building or facility or any portion thereof; and
    (ii) Scholarships, loans, grants, wages, or other funds extended to any entity for payment to or on behalf of students admitted to that entity, or extended directly to such students for payment to that entity.

(2) A grant of federal real or personal property or any interest therein, including surplus property, and the proceeds of the sale or transfer of such property, if the federal share of the fair market value of the property is not, upon such sale or transfer, properly accounted for to the Federal government.

(3) Provision of the services of Federal personnel.

(4) Sale or lease of Federal property or any interest therein at nominal consideration, or at consideration reduced for the purpose of assisting the recipient or in recognition of public interest to be served thereby, or permission to use federal property or any interest therein without consideration.

(5) Any other contract, agreement, or arrangement which has as one of its purposes the provision of assistance to any education pro-

gram or activity, except a contract of insurance or guaranty [34 C.F.R. § 106.2(g)].

The definitions in the Title VI (34 C.F.R. § 100.13), Section 504 (34 C.F.R. § 104.3(h)-(i)), and ADA (45 C.F.R. § 90.4) regulations are similar.

The leading case addressing the definition of federal financial assistance is *Grove City College v. Bell*, 465 U.S. 555 (1984). The college, a private liberal arts institution, received no direct federal or state financial assistance. Many of the college's students, however, did receive Basic Educational Opportunity Grants (now Pell Grants), which they used to defray their educational costs at the college. The Education Department determined that Grove City was a recipient of "federal financial assistance" under 34 C.F.R. § 106.2(g)(1) and advised the college to execute an Assurance of Compliance (a form certifying that the college will comply with Title IX) as required by 34 C.F.R. § 106.4. The college refused, arguing that the indirect aid received by its students did not constitute federal financial assistance to the college.

The U.S. Supreme Court unanimously held that the student aid constituted aid to the college and that, if the college did not execute an Assurance of Compliance, the Education Department could terminate the student aid:

> [T]he language of Section 901(a) [of Title IX] contains no hint that Congress perceived a substantive difference between direct institutional assistance and aid received by a school through its students. The linchpin of Grove City's argument that none of its programs receives any federal assistance is a perceived distinction between direct and indirect aid, a distinction that finds no support in the text of Section 901(a). Nothing in Section 901(a) suggests that Congress elevated form over substance by making the application of the nondiscrimination principle dependent on the manner in which a program or activity receives federal assistance. There is no basis in the statute for the view that only institutions that themselves apply for federal aid or receive checks directly from the federal government are subject to regulation (*Bob Jones University v. Johnson*, 396 F. Supp. 597, 601–04 (D.S.C. 1974), *affirmed*, 529 F.2d 514 (4th Cir. 1975) [reaching a similar conclusion under Title VI regarding veterans' education benefits]). As the Court of Appeals observed, "by its all-inclusive terminology [Section 901(a)] appears to encompass *all* forms of federal aid to education, direct or indirect" (687 F.2d at 691 (emphasis in original)) [465 U.S. at 564].

7.5.7.4. Scope of the phrase "program or activity." The civil rights statutes proscribe discrimination in a "program or activity" that is "receiving" federal aid. Thus, besides determining that the aid involved fits the definition of "federal financial assistance" (Section 7.5.7.3), prior to 1988 it was not clear whether the entire institution or just those programs actually receiving funding from the federal government were subject to the dictates of these civil rights statutes. The Title VI regulations did contain a comprehensive definition of "program," however, that included within it the concept of "activity" (34 C.F.R. § 100.13(g)). The Title IX, Section 504, and Age Discrimination Act regulations had only sketchy references to these terms (34 C.F.R. § 106.31(a); 34 C.F.R. § 104.43(a); 45 C.F.R. § 90.3(a)).

Numerous questions about the "program or activity" concept arose in litigation prior to 1988. The most controversial was the question of how to apply this concept to indirect or student-based aid, such as Pell Grants or veterans' education benefits. Did all the institution's programs "receive" this aid, or was the institution itself the "program," thus binding the entire institution to the nondiscrimination requirement? Or was only the institution's financial aid office or some lesser portion of the institution bound? (Compare the majority opinion with the dissents in *Grove City College v. Bell*, discussed below.)

Another set of questions related to both indirect student-based aid and direct (or earmarked) institution-based aid, such as construction grants. If a program or an activity in an institution did not directly receive federal funds but benefited from the receipt of funds by other institutional programs or activities, was it subject to non-discrimination requirements? (See *Haffer v. Temple University*, 688 F.2d 14 (3d Cir. 1982), applying the "benefit theory" for extending the scope of a civil rights statute.) Or if a program or an activity did not directly receive federal funds but engaged in discriminatory practices that "infected" programs or activities which did directly receive funds, was it subject to nondiscrimination requirements? (See *Iron Arrow Honor Society v. Heckler*, 702 F.2d 549 (5th Cir. 1983), *vacated as moot*, 464 U.S. 67 (1983), adopting the "infection theory" for extending the scope of a civil rights stat-ute.) Although the passage of the Civil Rights Restoration Act of 1987 (which became effective in March 1988) has eliminated the uncertainty about these issues, a long road of litigation led to the Act's passage and is worthy of summary.

The U.S. Supreme Court first addressed the "program or activity" concept in *North Haven Board of Education v. Bell*, 456 U.S. 512 (1982), discussed in Section 7.5.7.1. In considering the validity of the Education Department's Title IX regulations on employment (Subpart E), the Court noted the " 'program-specific' nature of the [Title IX] statute" and indicated that, to be valid, the regulations must be "consistent with the Act's program specificity." To support this conclusion, the Court cited Section 901(a) of Title IX (20 U.S.C. § 1681(a)), prohibiting sex discrimination in a "program or activity" receiving federal funding; Section 902 (20 U.S.C. § 1682), au-thorizing federal agencies to implement regulations regarding any "program or ac-tivity" for which it provides funds; and another provision in Section 902—called the "pinpoint" provision—requiring that any fund termination by a federal agency "be limited in its effect to the particular program, or part thereof, in which . . . noncom-pliance has been . . . found."[34]

Although holding that Title IX is limited in its scope to particular programs and activities, the Court in *North Haven* declined to define "program," the key term giving life to the concept of program specificity. Two years later, however, the Court again confronted this definitional issue in *Grove City College v. Bell*, 465 U.S. 555 (1984), discussed in Section 7.5.7.3. Having unanimously agreed that the students' receipt of Basic Educational Opportunity Grants (BEOGs) constituted "federal finan-cial assistance" for the college, the justices then faced the problem of identifying the program or activity that received this assistance and was therefore subject to Title IX. With three of the justices dissenting, the Court held that the program or activity was

---

[34]Title VI also has a provision requiring the federal agency to "pinpoint" the particular program(s) subject to fund termination (42 U.S.C. § 2000d-1). Section 504 incorporates the "remedies, procedures, and rights" available under Title VI, thus apparently including the same pinpoint provision (29 U.S.C. § 794(a)(2)). The Age Discrimination Act's pinpoint provision (42 U.S.C. § 6104(b)), as developed in the general regulations (45 C.F.R. § 90.47(b)), is the most exacting of all, since it appears to prohibit the agency from using the infection theory to expand the scope of the fund cutoff.

not the entire institution (as the appellate court had determined) but only the college's financial aid program:

> Although Grove City does not itself disburse students' awards, BEOGs clearly augment the resources that the college itself devotes to financial aid. . . . However, the fact that federal funds eventually reach the college's general operating budget cannot subject Grove City to institution-wide coverage. . . . To the extent that the Court of Appeals' holding that BEOGs received by Grove City's students constitute aid to the entire institution rests on the possibility that federal funds received by one program or activity free up the college's own resources for use elsewhere, the Court of Appeals' reasoning is doubly flawed. First, there is no evidence that the federal aid received by Grove City's students results in the diversion of funds from the college's own financial aid program to other areas within the institution. Second, and more important, the Court of Appeals' assumption that Title IX applies to programs receiving a larger share of a school's own limited resources as a result of federal assistance earmarked for use elsewhere within the institution is inconsistent with the program-specific nature of the statute. Most federal educational assistance has economic ripple effects throughout the aided institution, and it would be difficult, if not impossible, to determine which programs or activities derive such indirect benefits. Under the Court of Appeals' theory, an entire school would be subject to Title IX merely because one of its students received a small BEOG or because one of its departments received an earmarked federal grant. This result cannot be squared with Congress's intent.
>
> The Court of Appeals' analogy between student financial aid received by an educational institution and nonearmarked direct grants provides a more plausible justification for its holding, but it too is faulty. Student financial aid programs, we believe, are *sui generis*. In neither purpose nor effect can BEOGs be fairly characterized as unrestricted grants that institutions may use for whatever purpose they desire. The BEOG program was designed not merely to increase the total resources available to educational institutions but to enable them to offer their services to students who had previously been unable to afford higher education. . . .
>
> We conclude that the receipt of BEOGs by some of Grove City's students does not trigger institution-wide coverage under Title IX. In purpose and effect, BEOGs represent federal financial assistance to the college's own financial aid program, and it is that program that may properly be regulated under Title IX [465 U.S. at 571–74].

The *Grove City* analysis of the "program or activity" issue proved to be highly controversial. Members of Congress criticized the analysis as being inconsistent with congressional intent. Civil rights groups and other interested parties criticized the decision's narrowing effect on federal enforcement of civil rights—not only under Title IX but also under the other three civil rights statutes using the same "program or activity" language, and not only for federal aid to education but for other types of federal assistance as well.

Between 1984 and 1987, several bills were introduced in Congress to overturn the *Grove City* decision, but none of them could muster sufficient support for passage. In 1987 the Civil Rights Restoration Act (CRRA) of 1987 (Pub. L. No. 100-259, 102 Stat. 28) was passed over the veto of President Reagan, and became effective on March

22, 1988. The CRRA amends the four civil rights laws (Title VI, Title IX, Section 504, and the Age Discrimination Act) by defining "program or activity" as:

> all the operations of . . . a college, university, or other postsecondary institution . . . any part of which is extended federal financial assistance [20 U.S.C.§ 1687].

This language clearly indicates that colleges will be covered in their entirety by these laws if any part of their operations is extended federal aid—although special language in Title IX, which does not appear in the other three laws, exempts religious organizations if the law's requirements are inconsistent with their religious tenets (20 U.S.C. § 1687). For analysis of the effect of the CRRA on colleges and universities, see R. Hendrickson, B. Lee, F. Loomis, & S. Olswang, "The Impact of the Civil Rights Restoration Act on Higher Education," 60 *West's Educ. Law Rptr.* 671 (1990).

Once the CRRA was passed, questions arose as to whether it could be applied retroactively. The courts have ruled in the affirmative; therefore, any claims that arose during the four years between the *Grove City* decision and the effective date of the CRRA would still be actionable. See *Lussier v. Dugger,* 904 F.2d 661 (11th Cir. 1990); see also *Ayers v. Allain,* 893 F.2d 732 (5th Cir. 1990), *reversed on other grounds,* 914 F.2d 676 (5th Cir. 1990).

7.5.8. Administrative enforcement. Compliance with each of the four civil rights statutes is enforced through a complex system of procedures and mechanisms administered by the federal agencies that provide financial assistance. Postsecondary administrators should develop a sound understanding of this enforcement process, so that they can satisfactorily pursue both the rights and the responsibilities of their institutions should compliance problems arise.

The Title VI statute delegates enforcement responsibility to the various federal funding agencies. Under Executive Order 12250, 45 Fed. Reg. 72995 (1980), the U.S. attorney general is responsible for coordinating agency enforcement efforts. The attorney general has implemented enforcement regulations (28 C.F.R. Part 42) as well as "Guidelines for the Enforcement of Title VI" (28 C.F.R. § 50.3), which impose various requirements on agencies responsible for enforcement. Each agency, for instance, must issue guidelines or regulations on Title VI for all programs under which it provides federal financial assistance (28 C.F.R. § 42.404). These regulations and guidelines must be available to the public (28 C.F.R. § 42.405). The Justice Department's regulations require the agencies to collect sufficient data, on such items as the racial composition of the population eligible for the program and the location of facilities, to determine compliance (28 C.F.R. § 42.406). All Title VI compliance decisions must be made by or be subject to the review of the agency's civil rights office. Programs found to be complying must be reviewed periodically to ensure continued compliance. A finding of probable noncompliance must be reported to the attorney general (28 C.F.R. § 42.407). Each agency must establish complaint procedures and publish them in its guidelines. All Title VI complaints must be logged in the agency records (28 C.F.R. § 42.408). If a finding of probable noncompliance is made, enforcement procedures shall be instituted after a "reasonable period" of negotiation. If negotiations continue for more than sixty days after the finding of noncompliance, the agency must notify the attorney general (28 C.F.R. § 42.411). If several agencies provide federal financial assistance to a substantial number of the same recipients for similar or related purposes, the agencies must coordinate Title VI enforcement efforts. The agencies shall designate one agency as the lead agency for Title VI compliance (28 C.F.R. § 42.413). Each agency must develop a written enforcement plan, specifying priorities, timetables, and procedures, which shall be available to the public (28 C.F.R. § 42.415).

Under the Department of Education's Title VI regulations, fund recipients must file assurances with ED that their programs comply with Title VI (34 C.F.R. § 100.4) and must submit "timely, complete, and accurate compliance reports at such times, and in such form and containing such information, as the responsible Department official or his designee may determine to be necessary to enable him to ascertain whether the recipient has complied or is complying" with Title VI (34 C.F.R. § 100.6(b)). ED may make periodic compliance reviews and must accept and respond to individual complaints from persons who believe that they are victims of discrimination (34 C.F.R. § 100.7). If an investigation reveals a violation that cannot be resolved by negotiation and voluntary compliance (34 C.F.R. § 100.7(d)), ED may refer the case to the Justice Department for prosecution (see this volume, Section 7.5.9) or commence administrative proceedings for fund termination (34 C.F.R. § 100.8). Any termination of funds must be "limited in its effect to the particular program, or part thereof, in which . . . noncompliance has been . . . found" (42 U.S.C. § 2000d-1; 34 C.F.R. § 100.8(c)). The regulations specify the procedural safeguards that must be observed in the fund termination proceedings: notice, the right to counsel, a written decision, an appeal to a reviewing authority, and a discretionary appeal to the secretary of education (34 C.F.R. §§ 100.9 and 100.10).

Like Title VI, Title IX enforcement is coordinated by the attorney general under Executive Order 12250. Title IX also includes the same limit as Title VI on the scope of fund termination (20 U.S.C. § 1682) and utilizes the same procedures for fund termination (34 C.F.R. § 106.71). An institution subject to Title IX must appoint at least one employee to coordinate its compliance efforts and must establish a grievance procedure for handling gender discrimination complaints within the institution (34 C.F.R. § 106.8).

Section 504 is also subject to Executive Order 12250, and funding agencies' enforcement efforts are thus also coordinated by the attorney general. The attorney general's coordination regulations, setting forth enforcement responsibilities of federal agencies for nondiscrimination on the basis of disability, are published in 28 C.F.R. Part 41. The Section 504 statute also establishes an Interagency Coordinating Council for Section 504 enforcement, the membership of which includes, among others, the attorney general and the secretary of education (29 U.S.C. § 794c). ED's Section 504 regulations for its own programs impose compliance responsibilities similar to those under Title IX. However, recipients with fewer than fifteen employees need not conform to certain requirements: (1) having a copy of the remedial plan available for inspection (34 C.F.R. § 104.6(c)(2)); (2) appointing an agency employee to coordinate the compliance effort (34 C.F.R. § 104.7(a)); and (3) establishing a grievance procedure for handling discrimination complaints (34 C.F.R. § 104.7(b)). Most postsecondary educational institutions are not excepted from these requirements, since most have more than the minimum number of employees. Section 504 also adopts the Title VI procedural regulations concerning fund terminations.

Under the Age Discrimination Act, federal funding agencies must propose implementing regulations and submit them to the secretary of health and human services for review; all such agency regulations must be consistent with HHS's "general regulations" (42 U.S.C. § 6103(a)(4); 45 C.F.R. § 90.31). Each agency must hold "compliance reviews" and other investigations to determine adherence to ADA requirements (45 C.F.R. § 90.44(a)). Each agency must also follow specified procedures when undertaking to terminate a recipient's funding (45 C.F.R. § 90.47). Termination of funds is limited to the "particular program or activity, or part of such program or activity, with respect to which [a] finding [of discrimination] has been made," and may not be based "in whole or in part on any finding with respect to any program or activity which does not receive Federal financial assistance" (42 U.S.C. § 6104(b)). The ADA contains a number of substantive exceptions to coverage, more expansive than the exceptions to the other civil rights statutes (see this volume, Section 7.5.5).

The federal courts exercise a limited review of federal agencies' enforcement efforts. If a federal agency terminates an institution's funding, the institution may appeal that decision to the courts once it has exhausted administrative review procedures within the agency.[35] In addition, if a federal agency abuses its enforcement authority during enforcement proceedings and before a final decision, an affected educational institution may also seek injunctive relief from such improper enforcement efforts. In *Mandel v. U.S. Department of Health, Education and Welfare*, 411 F. Supp. 542 (D. Md. 1976), the state of Maryland brought suit after HEW had commenced fund termination proceedings against the state, alleging Title VI violations in its system of higher education. The state sought judicial intervention, claiming that HEW had not in good faith sought voluntary compliance. Maryland complained that HEW delayed review of the state's original desegregation plan, prematurely cut off negotiations, did not provide guidelines on how to effect desegregation, and refused to rule either on the importance of statistics in assessing compliance or on the future of traditionally black educational institutions. The court found that HEW did not seek voluntary compliance in good faith. Maryland also complained that HEW failed to "pinpoint" which of the state's programs violated Title VI. The court held that HEW must pinpoint the offending programs before enforcement proceedings are begun:

> It is paradoxical to assume that a recipient of federal funding, such as a state or a large city, could rectify any discriminatory programs within its system without ever being informed which program was considered by HEW to be operating discriminatively. Consequently, a statewide or city-wide approach to enforcement of Title VI is, doubtless, not conducive to compliance by voluntary means and, in all likelihood, contrary to congressional nonvindictive intent.
>
> Other reasons come to the fore which, likewise, suggest that plaintiffs' reading of Title VI in this regard is a proper one. In . . . the state system . . . there are multitudinal programs receiving federal financing which, due to the nonpro-

---

[35]Such judicial review is expressly authorized by the Title VI and Title IX statutes (see 42 U.S.C. § 2000d-2; 20 U.S.C. § 1683). The Section 504 statute incorporates the remedies available under Title VI, thus apparently authorizing judicial review to the same extent authorized by Title VI (29 U.S.C. § 794(a)(c)). The Age Discrimination Act also specifically authorizes judicial review of administrative agency actions, but in terms somewhat different from those in Title VI and Title IX (42 U.S.C. § 6105).

grammatic approach assumed, are being condemned by defendants en masse. . . .
[In the state system] there is federal funding to programs within twenty-eight
institutions of higher education ranging from a unique cancer research center to
the student work-study program. To compel all of these programs, regardless of
whether or not each is discriminatory, to prepare a defense and endure protracted
enforcement proceedings is wasteful, counterproductive, and probably inimical
to the interests of the very persons Title VI was enacted to protect. It is far more
equitable, and more consistent with congressional intent, to require program
delineation prior to enforcement hearings than to include all programs in enforcement proceedings [411 F. Supp. at 558].

The U.S. Court of Appeals for the Fourth Circuit subsequently modified the
lower court's ruling to allow HEW to take a systemic approach if it first adopted
systemwide guidelines and gave Maryland time to comply voluntarily (562 F.2d 914
(4th Cir. 1977)). A rehearing was scheduled, however, because one judge had died
before the court's opinion was issued. On rehearing, three appellate judges voted to
affirm the lower court and three voted to reverse, and the equally divided vote had
the effect of automatically affirming the lower court (571 F.2d 1273 (4th Cir. 1978)).

Different questions are presented when judicial review of federal agency enforcement is sought not by postsecondary institutions but by the victims of the institutions' alleged discrimination. Such victims may seek judicial orders requiring a
federal agency to fulfill its statutory duty to enforce the civil rights statutes; or, on
a smaller scale, an alleged victim may challenge in court an agency's failure or refusal
to act on a complaint that he or she had filed with an agency responsible for enforcing
the civil rights statutes. The case law indicates that courts will not be receptive to such
requests for judicial intervention in administrative enforcement activities—at least
not unless Congress itself authorizes victims to seek such redress from the courts.

In *Adams v. Richardson*, 356 F. Supp. 92 (D.D.C. 1973), *affirmed*, 480 F.2d
1159 (D.C. Cir. 1973), some victims of unlawful discrimination sought judicial intervention to compel enforcement of Title VI. The plaintiffs accused HEW of failure
to enforce Title VI in the southern states. In the part of the case dealing with higher
education, HEW had found the higher education systems of ten states out of compliance with Title VI and had requested each state to submit a desegregation plan
within four months. Three years later, after the lawsuit had been filed and the court
was ready to rule, five states still had not submitted any plan and five had submitted
plans that did not remedy the violations. HEW had not commenced administrative
enforcement efforts or referred the cases to the Justice Department for prosecution.
The district court ordered HEW to commence enforcement proceedings:

> The time permitted by Title VI of the Civil Rights Act of 1964 to delay
> the commencement of enforcement proceedings against the ten states for the
> purpose of securing voluntary compliance has long since passed. The continua-
> tion of HEW financial assistance to the segregated systems of higher education
> in the ten states violates the rights of plaintiffs and others similarly situated
> protected by Title VI of the Civil Rights Act of 1964. Having once determined
> that a state system of higher education is in violation of Title VI, and having
> failed during a substantial period of time to achieve voluntary compliance, de-
> fendants have a duty to commence enforcement proceedings [356 F. Supp. at 94].

The appellate court agreed with the district court's conclusion but expressed more sympathy for HEW's enforcement problems:

> We agree with the district court's conclusion that HEW may not neglect this area of its responsibility. However, we are also mindful that desegregation problems in colleges and universities differ widely from those in elementary and secondary schools, and that HEW admittedly lacks experience in dealing with them. It has not yet formulated guidelines for desegregating statewide systems of higher learning, nor has it commented formally upon the desegregation plans of the five states which have submitted them. As regrettable as these revelations are, the stark truth of the matter is that HEW must carefully assess the significance of a variety of new factors as it moves into an unaccustomed area. None of these factors justifies a failure to comply with a congressional mandate; they may, however, warrant a more deliberate opportunity to identify and accommodate them [480 F.2d at 1164].

On this basis the appellate court modified the terms of the district court's injunction, so that HEW would be given more time to initiate enforcement proceedings.

After the appellate court's decision, the district court maintained jurisdiction over the case in order to supervise compliance with its injunction. The judge issued a number of other decisions after 1973, some of which were reviewed by the appellate court. In April 1977 the district court revoked HEW's approval of several states' higher education desegregation plans and ordered HEW to devise criteria (see this volume, Section 7.5.2) by which it would evaluate new plans to be submitted by these states. In March 1983 the court entered another order requiring HEW (by then ED) to obtain new plans from five states that had defaulted on plans previously accepted by HEW. This order established time limits by which ED was required to initiate formal enforcement proceedings against these states, and several others whose plans had never been approved, if they had not submitted new acceptable plans. The order also required ED to report systematically to the plaintiffs on enforcement activities regarding the states subject to the suit.

On the government's appeal of the district court's 1983 order, the appellate court remanded the case to the district court for a determination of whether the plaintiffs continued to have the legal "standing" (see Section 1.4.2) necessary to maintain the lawsuit and justify judicial enforcement of the order (*Women's Equity Action League v. Bell* and *Adams v. Bell*, 743 F.2d 42 (D.C. Cir. 1984)). In 1987 the district court dismissed the case, ruling that the plaintiffs lacked standing to pursue the litigation (*Adams v. Bennett*, 675 F. Supp. 668 (D.D.C. 1987)). The district judge reasoned that ED's Office for Civil Rights had not caused the segregation that the plaintiffs were subjected to, and that the degree to which ED's continued monitoring of state acts would redress this segregation was "speculative."

Although initially the appellate court reversed the district court, ordering additional hearings on what remedies should be granted to desegregate the dual systems, in 1990 it decided to dismiss the case, by then titled *Women's Equity Action League v. Cavazos* (906 F.2d 742 (D.C. Cir. 1990)). In the opinion, Judge Ruth Bader Ginsburg said that "Congress has not explicitly or implicitly authorized the grand scale action plaintiffs delineate" and called the plaintiffs' action an attempt to make the trial court a "nationwide overseer or pacer of procedures government agencies use to enforce civil rights prescriptions controlling educational institutions that receive federal funds" (906 F.2d at 744). If suits directly against a discriminating entity (for which a private right of action does exist under Title VI; see Section 7.5.9) are adequate to redress injuries, " 'federal courts will not oversee the overseer' " (906 F.2d at 748, quoting *Coker v. Sullivan*, 902 F.2d 84, 89 (D.C. Cir. 1990). The court further stated:

> Suits directly against the discriminating entities may be more arduous, and less effective in providing systemic relief, than continuing judicial oversight of federal government enforcement. But under our precedent, situation-specific litigation affords an adequate, even if imperfect, remedy. So far as we can tell, the suit targeting specific discriminatory acts of fund recipients is the only court remedy Congress has authorized for private parties, situated as plaintiffs currently are [906 F.2d at 751].

Only if Congress creates such a private right of action, said the court, may plaintiffs file claims directly against the government agency charged with enforcing the law.

Two other cases have reached similar results in situations where an individual victim has challenged an agency's enforcement activities. In *Marlow v. United States Department of Education*, 820 F.2d 581 (2d Cir. 1987), the court dismissed a lawsuit challenging ED's decision to take no action on an administrative complaint the plaintiff had filed under Section 504. The court held that there is no statutory or implied right of action against the federal funding agency for individual complainants who seek only judicial review of the agency's disposition of a particular complaint. Another federal appeals court reached the same conclusion in a similar suit, and held as well that an individual complainant cannot enjoin ED from continuing to fund the institution against which the complaint was made (*Salvador v. Bennett*, 800 F.2d 97 (7th Cir. 1986)).

7.5.9. Other enforcement remedies. Administrative negotiation and fund termination are not the only means federal agencies have for enforcing the civil rights statutes. In some cases the responsible federal agency may also go to court to enforce the civil rights obligations that educational institutions have assumed by accepting federal funds. Title VI authorizes agencies to enforce compliance not only by fund termination but also by "any other means authorized by law" (42 U.S.C. § 2000d-1). ED's Title VI regulations explain that "such other means may include, but are not limited to, (1) a reference to the Department of Justice with a recommendation that appropriate proceedings be brought to enforce any rights of the United States under any law of the United States (including other titles of the Act), or any assurance or other contractual undertaking, and (2) any applicable proceeding under state or local law" (34 C.F.R. § 100.9(a)). ED may not pursue these alternatives, however, "until (1) the responsible department official has determined that compliance cannot be secured by voluntary means, (2) the recipient or other person has been notified of its failure to comply and of the action to be taken to effect compliance, and (3) the expiration of at least ten days from the mailing of such notice to the recipient or other person" (34 C.F.R. § 100.9(d)). Similar enforcement alternatives and procedural limitations apply to enforcement of Title IX, Section 504, and the Age Discrimination Act.[36]

Besides administrative agency enforcement by fund termination or court suit, educational institutions may also be subject to private lawsuits brought by individuals who have allegedly been discriminated against in violation of the civil rights statutes or regulations. In legal terminology, the issue is whether the civil rights statutes afford these victims of discrimination a "private cause of action" against the institution that is allegedly discriminating.

The basic requisites for a private cause of action are outlined in *Cort v. Ash,* 422 U.S. 66 (1975): "In determining whether a private remedy is implicit in a statute not expressly providing one, several factors are relevant. First, is the plaintiff one of the class for whose *especial* benefit the statute was enacted—that is, does the statute create a federal right in favor of the plaintiff? Second, is there any indication of legislative intent, explicit or implicit, either to create such a remedy or to deny one? Third, is it consistent with the underlying purposes of the legislative scheme to imply such a remedy for the plaintiff? And finally, is the cause of action one traditionally relegated to state law, in an area basically the concern of the states, so that it would be inappropriate to infer a cause of action based solely on federal law?" (422 U.S. at 78; citations omitted).

If an individual can meet these requirements, three related issues may then arise: whether the individual must "exhaust" any available "administrative remedies" before bringing a private suit; whether the individual may obtain monetary damages, in addition to or instead of injunctive relief, if successful in the private suit; and whether the individual may obtain attorney's fees from the defendant if successful in the suit.

For many years courts and commentators disagreed on whether the civil rights statutes could be enforced by private causes of action. Developments since the late 1970s, however, have established a strong basis for acceptance of private causes of action under all four statutes. The 1979 case of *Cannon v. University of Chicago,* 441 U.S. 677 (1979), arising under Title IX, is illustrative.

The plaintiff in *Cannon* had been denied admission to the medical schools of the University of Chicago and Northwestern University. She sued both institutions, claiming that they had rejected her applications because of her sex and that such action violated Title IX. The U.S. Court of Appeals for the Seventh Circuit held that individuals cannot institute private suits to enforce Title IX. The U.S. Supreme Court reversed. While acknowledging that the statute does not expressly authorize a private cause of action, the Court held that one can be implied into the statute under the principles of *Cort v. Ash.* In applying the four considerations specified in that case, the Court in *Cannon* concluded: "Not only the words and history of Title IX, but

---

[36]ED's Title IX and Section 504 regulations incorporate the enforcement regulations for Title VI (see 34 C.F.R. § 106.71; 34 C.F.R. § 104.61). The Title IX statute also contains the same "other means authorized by law" language found in Title VI (see 20 U.S.C. § 1682), and the Section 504 statute incorporates the remedies and procedures available under Title VI (29 U.S.C. § 794a(a). The Age Discrimination Act has its own enforcement scheme, set out in the statute (42 U.S.C. § 6104) and the general regulations (45 C.F.R. §§ 90.41–90.50).

also its subject matter and underlying purposes, counsel application of a cause of action in favor of private victims of discrimination."

The discussion of the third consideration in *Cort*—whether a private cause of action would frustrate the statute's underlying purposes—is particularly illuminating. The Court identified two purposes of Title IX: to avoid the use of federal funds to support sex discrimination and to give individual citizens effective protection against such practices. While the first purpose is served by the statutory procedure for fund termination (see Section 7.5.8 of this chapter), the Court determined that a private remedy would be appropriate to effect a second purpose:

> [Termination] is . . . severe and often may not provide an appropriate means of accomplishing the second purpose if merely an isolated violation has occurred. In that situation, the violation might be remedied more efficiently by an order requiring an institution to accept an applicant who had been improperly excluded. Moreover, in that kind of situation it makes little sense to impose on an individual whose only interest is in obtaining a benefit for herself, or on HEW, the burden of demonstrating that an institution's practices are so pervasively discriminatory that a complete cutoff of federal funding is appropriate. The award of individual relief to a private litigant who has prosecuted her own suit is not only sensible but is also fully consistent with—and in some cases even necessary to—ordinary enforcement of the statute [441 U.S. at 705-06].

In a statement of particular interest to postsecondary administrators, the Court in *Cannon* also addressed and rejected the universities' argument that private suits would unduly interfere with their institutional autonomy:

> Respondents' principal argument against implying a cause of action under Title IX is that it is unwise to subject admissions decisions of universities to judicial scrutiny at the behest of disappointed applicants on a case-by-case basis. They argue that this kind of litigation is burdensome and inevitably will have an adverse effect on the independence of members of university committees.
>
> This argument is not original to this litigation. It was forcefully advanced in both 1964 and 1972 by the congressional opponents of Title VI and Title IX, and squarely rejected by the congressional majorities that passed the two statutes. In short, respondents' principal contention is not a legal argument at all; it addresses a policy issue that Congress has already resolved.
>
> History has borne out the judgment of Congress. Although victims of discrimination on the basis of race, religion, or national origin have had private Title VI remedies available at least since 1965, respondents have not come forward with any demonstration that Title VI litigation has been so costly or voluminous that either the academic community or the courts have been unduly burdened. Nothing but speculation supports the argument that university administrators will be so concerned about the risk of litigation that they will fail to discharge their important responsibilities in an independent and professional manner [441 U.S. at 709-10].

Subsequently, in the case of *Guardians Assn. v. Civil Service Commission of the City of New York*, 463 U.S. 582 (1983), the Supreme Court affirmed the availability of private causes of action under Title VI. The Court issued no majority opinion, however, so the case's teaching on the issue is limited and can be gleaned only from tallying the views of those justices who accepted private causes of action under Title VI. A year after *Guardians,* and relying in part on that case, the Supreme Court also finally held that individuals may bring private lawsuits to enforce Section 504 (*Consolidated Rail Corp. v. Darrone,* 465 U.S. 624 (1984)).[37]

Another development, illustrating legislative rather than judicial resolution of the "private cause of action" issue, occurred with passage of the 1978 amendments to the Age Discrimination Act. Congress added a new section to the Act, authorizing private suits by "any interested person" in federal district courts "to enjoin a violation of this Act by any program or activity receiving federal financial assistance" (42 U.S.C. § 6104(e)).

Courts permitting private enforcement suits under the civil rights statutes usually have not required the complainants to exhaust administrative remedies before filing suit. In its opinion in the *Cannon* case, for instance, the U.S. Supreme Court noted that it had "never withheld a private remedy where the statute explicitly confers a benefit on a class of persons . . . [but] does not assure those persons the ability to activate and participate in the administrative process contemplated by the statute." Title IX not only contains no such mechanism, according to the Court, but even HEW's (now ED's) procedures do not permit the complainant to participate in the administrative proceedings. Moreover, even if HEW finds the institution to be in violation of Title IX, the resulting compliance agreement need not necessarily include relief for the particular complainant. Accordingly, the Court concluded that individuals may institute suits to enforce Title IX without exhausting administrative remedies (see 441 U.S. at 706–08 n.41). Similarly, relying on *Cannon,* federal appeals courts have held that exhaustion is not required under Section 504 (see, for example, *Pushkin v. Regents of the University of Colorado,* 658 F.2d 1372, 1380–83 (10th Cir. 1981)). Case law under Title VI is more sparse, but there is some authority for not requiring exhaustion there also (see *Yakin v. University of Illinois, Chicago Circle,* 508 F. Supp. 848 (N.D. Ill. 1981)). The exception to this trend is the Age Discrimination Act, for which Congress itself has provided an exhaustion requirement. In the 1978 ADA amendments, the provision authorizing private suits also prohibits bringing such suits "if administrative remedies have not been exhausted" (42 U.S.C. § 6104(e)(2)(B)). Section 6104(f) of the amendments and the general ADA regulations (45 C.F.R. § 90.50) indicate when such exhaustion shall be deemed to have occurred.

Authorization of private causes of action, even when exhaustion has occurred or is not required, does not necessarily mean that a complainant may obtain every kind of remedy ordinarily available in civil lawsuits. *Cannon* did not itself resolve the remedies question, and in the wake of *Cannon,* a number of lower courts ruled that private causes of action under Title IX were limited to injunctive relief and that money damages were not available (see, for example, *Lieberman v. University of Chicago,* 660 F.2d 1185 (7th Cir. 1985)). In *Guardians,* however, a tally of the individual justices' views indicates that a majority would permit a damages remedy under Title VI if the plaintiff could prove that the defendant had discriminated *intentionally* (463 U.S. at 607 n.27; see also Section 7.5.7.2 of this chapter). And in *Darrone,* although the Court declined to determine "the extent to which money damages are

[37]Previously the Court had declined to decide this issue in *Southeastern Community College v. Davis* (442 U.S. at 404 n.5; see this volume, Section 4.2.4.3) and had bypassed it in *University of Texas v. Camenisch* (Section 4.4).

available" in a Section 504 case, it did authorize back-pay awards (a type of equitable relief) for victims of intentional discrimination.

In early 1992 the Supreme Court alleviated much of the uncertainty concerning remedies, and resolved some conflicts among lower courts, at least with respect to Title IX. In *Franklin v. Gwinnett County Public Schools*, 112 S. Ct. 1028 (1992), a student brought an action under Title IX seeking compensatory damages for alleged intentional sex discrimination—in particular, sexual harassment by a coach/teacher at her high school and the school administration's failure to protect her from this harassment despite having knowledge of it. The school district had agreed to close its investigation in return for the teacher's resignation. Although the U.S. Department of Education had investigated and determined that the school district violated the student's Title IX rights, the department terminated the investigation after the school and the school district came into compliance with Title IX. The student then filed her cause of action for damages, which was rejected by the lower courts.

Reversing, the Supreme Court stated three bases for holding that money damages is a permissible remedy under Title IX: first, the firmly established principle that, once a cause of action exists, the courts may use all appropriate remedies to enforce the plaintiff's rights unless Congress has expressly indicated otherwise; second, the *Cannon* Court's reliance on Congress's awareness that, in the decade immediately preceding enactment of Title IX, the Court had accepted implied rights of action in six cases and permitted damage remedies in three of them; and third, the enactment, subsequent to *Cannon,* of the Civil Rights Remedies Equalization Amendment of 1986 (42 U.S.C. § 2000d-7), discussed later in this section) and the Civil Rights Restoration Act of 1987 (see Section 7.5.7.4 in this chapter), which the Court regarded as implicit congressional acknowledgments that private remedies, including money damages, are available under Title IX. Although confessing that the multiple opinions in *Guardians Association* had made it difficult to determine the Court's viewpoint on damage remedies, the *Gwinnett* Court noted that "a clear majority [in *Guardians Association*] expressed the view that damages were available under Title VI in an action seeking remedies for an intentional violation, and no Justice challenged the traditional presumption in favor of a federal court's power to award appropriate relief in a cognizable cause of action." See generally E. Vargyas, "*Franklin v. Gwinnett County Public Schools* and Its Impact on Title IX Enforcement," 19 *J. Coll. & Univ. Law* 373 (1993).

The *Gwinnett* case, permitting compensatory damages under Title IX, also serves to reinforce the availability of such damages under Title VI—as the Court indicated by its reliance on the prior *Guardians Association* case. The *Gwinnett* reasoning will apparently apply to Section 504 as well; see, for example, *Wood v. President and Trustees of Spring Hill College*, 978 F.2d 1214 (11th Cir. 1992). The *Gwinnett* analysis does not extend to the Age Discrimination Act, however, since that statute expressly provides only for suits "to enjoin a violation of this Act" (42 U.S.C. § 6104(e)), thus indicating that injunctive relief (and not money damages) is the only permissible remedy.

While *Gwinnett*, read against the backdrop of *Guardians Association* and *Darrone*, thus settles many of the questions concerning remedies available in private causes of action, it is still unclear whether punitive damages (as opposed to compensatory damages) is an available remedy under Title IX, Title VI, or Section 504. It is also not clear that the Court would extend the availability of money damages under these statutes to cases where the plaintiff can prove only unintentional discrimination (see Section 7.5.7.2).

An additional complexity may arise when a private suit for money damages is brought against a state college or university. Such institutions may be considered arms of the state and, as such, may claim Eleventh Amendment immunity from suit in federal court (see Section 2.3.3). In *Atascadero State Hospital v. Scanlon*, 473 U.S. 234 (1985), the U.S. Supreme Court highlighted this point by holding that, in enacting Section 504, Congress did not abrogate the states' Eleventh Amendment immunity. Subsequently, however, Congress enacted the Civil Rights Remedies Equalization Amendment of 1986 (100 Stat. 1845, 42 U.S.C. § 2000d-7). This new statute specifically declares that states are not immune under the Eleventh Amendment from federal court suits alleging violations of Section 504, Title IX, Title VI, the Age Discrimination Act, or any other federal statute prohibiting discrimination by recipients of federal financial assistance.

The final issue regarding private causes of action concerns attorney's fees (see generally Section 1.4.5.3). When a plaintiff successfully invokes one of the civil rights statutes against an institution, the institution may be liable for the plaintiff's attorney's fees. Under the Civil Rights Attorney's Fees Awards Act of 1976 (42 U.S.C. §1988), courts have discretion to award "a reasonable attorney's fee" to "the prevailing party" in actions under Title IX, Title VI, and several other civil rights statutes.[38] Although this Act does not apply to Section 504 suits or ADA suits, the omission is inconsequential, because both Section 504 and the ADA have their own comparable provisions authorizing the award of attorney's fees (29 U.S.C. § 794a(b); 42 U.S.C. § 6104(e)(1)).

Sec. 7.6. Dealing with the Federal Government

7.6.1 Handling federal rule making and regulations. Administrative agencies write regulations both to implement legislation and to formalize their own housekeeping functions. To prepare such regulations, agencies typically engage in a process of rule making, which includes an opportunity for the public to comment on regulatory proposals. Information on particular agencies' rule-making activities is published in the *Federal Register*. Final regulations (along with summaries of public comment on proposed drafts) are also published in the *Federal Register*, and these regulations are then codified in the *Code of Federal Regulations*.

Postsecondary administrators have long complained that the multitude of federal regulations applying to the programs and practices of postsecondary institutions creates financial and administrative burdens for their institutions. These burdens can be decreased as postsecondary administrators and legal counsel take more active roles

---

[38]The cases are collected in Annot., "What Persons or Entities May Be Liable to Pay Attorney's Fees Awarded Under Civil Rights Attorney's Fees Awards Act of 1976 (42 U.S.C.S. § 1988)," 106 A.L.R. Fed. 636 (1992 plus periodic supp.); Annot., "What Persons or Entities May Be Liable to Pay Attorney's Fees Awarded Under Civil Rights Attorney's Fees Award Act of 1976 (42 U.S.C.S. § 1988)," 106 A.L.R. Fed. 636 (1993 plus periodic supp.); Annot., "Propriety of Amount of Attorney's Fees Awarded to Prevailing Parties Under Civil Rights Attorney's Fees Award Act of 1976 (42 U.S.C.S. § 1988)," 118 A.L.R. Fed. 1 (1994 plus periodic supp.).

in the process by which the federal government makes and enforces rules. The following suggestions outline a strategy for active involvement that an institution may undertake by itself, in conjunction with other similarly situated institutions, or through educational associations (see Section 8.1) to which it belongs. (See generally C. Saunders, "Regulating the Regulators," *Chron. Higher Educ.*, Mar. 22, 1976, A32, which includes suggestions similar to some of those below.)

1. Appoint someone to be responsible for monitoring the *Federal Register* and other publications for announcements and information on regulatory proposals and regulations that will affect postsecondary education. Each agency periodically prepares an agenda of all regulations it expects to propose, promulgate, or review in the near future, and publishes this agenda in the *Federal Register*. The *Federal Register* also publishes "Notice(s) of Intent" to publish rules (NOIs) (sometimes called "Advance Notice(s) of Proposed Rulemaking" (ANPRs)) and "Notice(s) of Proposed Rulemaking" (NPRMs), the latter of which are drafts of proposed regulations along with invitations for comments from interested parties. Notices of the establishment of a *committee* to negotiate rule making on a subject or proposed rule are also published in the *Federal Register*. If further information on a particular rule-making process or a particular regulatory proposal would be useful, have institutional personnel ask the agency for the pertinent information. Some agencies may have policies that make draft regulations or summaries available for review before the proposed form is published.

2. File comments and deliver testimony in response to NOIs and NPRMs when the rules would have a likely impact on institutional operations. Support these comments with specific explanations and data showing how the proposed regulations would have a negative impact on the institution. Have legal counsel review the proposed rules for legal and interpretive problems, and include legal questions or objections with your comments when appropriate. Consider filing comments in conjunction with other institutions that would be similarly affected by the proposed regulations. In addition, when negotiated rule making is provided, participate in the negotiation process if your institution is eligible to do so.

3. Keep federal agencies informed of your views on and experiences with particular federal regulations. Compile data concerning the regulations' impact on your institution and present these data to the responsible agency. Continue to communicate complaints and difficulties with final regulations to the responsible agency, even if the regulations were promulgated months or years ago. In addition, determine whether any federal advisory committee has been appointed for the agency or the issues that are of concern to your institution. (The Federal Advisory Committee Act, 5 U.S.C. App. §1, regulates the formation and operation of such committees.) If so, also keep the committee informed of your views and experience regarding particular regulations.

4. When the institution desires guidance concerning ambiguities or gaps in particular regulations, consider submitting questions to the administering agency. Make the questions specific and, if the institution has a particular viewpoint on how the ambiguity or gap should be resolved, forcefully argue that view. Legal counsel should be involved in this process. Once questions are submitted, press the agency for answers.

5. Be concerned not only with the substance of regulations but also with the

adequacy of the rule-making and rule-enforcing procedures. Be prepared to object whenever institutions are given insufficient notice of an agency's plans to make rules, too few opportunities to participate in rule making, or inadequate opportunities to criticize or receive guidance on already implemented regulations.

6. Develop an effective process for institutional self-regulation. With other institutions, develop criteria and data to use in determining the circumstances in which self-regulation is more effective than government regulation (see A. Blumrosen, "Six Conditions for Meaningful Self-Regulation," 69 *American Bar Assn. J.* 1264 (1983)). Use a record of institutional success at self-regulation, combined with developed rationales for self-regulation, to argue in selected situations that government regulation is unnecessary.

7. When an agency passes a particular regulation that your institution (and presumably others) believes will have an ill-advised impact on higher education interests, consider obtaining a review of the regulation's legality. Section 7.4.5 of this volume examines some of the legal defects that may exist. One of the most important considerations is whether the regulation is "ultra vires"—that is, whether, in promulgating the regulation, the agency has exceeded the scope of authority Congress has delegated to it. Such issues may be the basis for a court challenge of agency regulations. In *Bowen v. American Hospital Assn.*, 476 U.S. 610 (1986), for example, the U.S. Supreme Court invalidated Department of Health and Human Services regulations on the protection of disabled infants because they were beyond the agency's scope of authority under Section 504 of the Rehabilitation Act. Such legal issues may also be raised during the rule-making process itself, to bolster policy reasons for opposing particular regulations.

Several pieces of legislation enacted since the early 1980s provide new assistance for postsecondary institutions that do involve themselves in the federal regulatory process. One statute, the Regulatory Flexibility Act (5 U.S.C. § 601 et seq.), adds a new Chapter VI to the federal Administrative Procedure Act (see M. Stewart, "The New Regulatory Flexibility Act," 67 *American Bar Assn. J.* 66 (1981)). Another statute, the Negotiated Rulemaking Act of 1990 (5 U.S.C. §§ 561 et seq.), adds a new subchapter III to the Administrative Procedure Act. A third statute, the Equal Access to Justice Act (28 U.S.C. § 2412), amends Chapter V of the Administrative Procedure Act.

The Regulatory Flexibility Act benefits three types of "small entities," each of which is defined in Section 601: the "small business," the "small organization," and the "small governmental jurisdiction." The Act's purpose is "to establish as a principle of regulatory issuance that [federal administrative] agencies shall endeavor . . . to fit regulatory and informational requirements to the scale of the businesses, organizations, and governmental jurisdictions subject to regulation" (96 Stat. 1164 § 2(b)). To implement this principle, the Act provides that (1) in October and April of every year, agencies must publish a "regulatory flexibility agenda," which describes and explains any forthcoming regulations that are "likely to have a significant economic impact on a substantial number of small entities" (5 U.S.C. § 602); (2) agencies proposing new regulations must provide, for public comment, an "initial regulatory flexibility analysis" containing a description of "the impact of the proposed rule on small entities" and a description of "alternatives to the proposed rule" that would lessen its economic impact on small entities (§ 603); (3) agencies promulgating final regulations must issue a "final regulatory flexibility analysis" containing a summary of comments on the initial analysis and, where regulatory alternatives were rejected, an explanation of why they were rejected (§ 604); (4) for any regulation "which will have a significant economic impact on a substantial number of small entities," agencies must "assure that small entities have been given an opportunity to participate in the rulemaking" (§ 609); and (5) agencies must periodically review and, where appropriate, revise their regulations with an eye to reducing their economic impact on small entities (§ 610).

The key issue for postsecondary institutions under the Regulatory Flexibility Act is one of definition: to what extent will postsecondary institutions be considered to be within the definition for one of the three groups of "small entities" protected by the Act? The first definition, for the "small business" (§ 601(3)), is unlikely to apply, except to some proprietary institutions. The second definition, for the "small organization" (§ 601(4)), will apply to many, but not necessarily all, private nonprofit institutions. And the third definition, for the "small governmental jurisdiction" (§ 601(5)), will apparently apply to some, but relatively few, public institutions— primarily community colleges. Thus, not every postsecondary institution will be within the Act's protected classes.[39]

The second statute, the Negotiated Rulemaking Act of 1990 (104 Stat. 4969 (1990), codified at 5 U.S.C. §§ 561–570), was enacted to encourage agencies to use negotiations among interested parties as part of their rule-making process. Through an agency-established committee (5 U.S.C. § 565), agencies may informally negotiate a proposed rule that accommodates the varying interests of groups participating in the process and represents a consensus on the subject for which the committee was established. The rationale is that greater involvement and face-to-face discussion of opposing viewpoints will yield a proposed rule that may be formally adopted and enforced more quickly than would occur under more formal rule-making procedures (5 U.S.C. § 561 note).

The third new statute, the Equal Access to Justice Act, was originally promulgated in 1980 (Pub. L. No. 96-481, 94 Stat. 2321 (1980)), and then was amended and permanently renewed in 1985 (Pub. L. No. 99-80, 99 Stat. 183 (1985)). (See Comment, "Institutionalizing an Experiment: The Extension of the Equal Access to Justice Act—Questions Remaining, Questions Resolved," 14 *Fla. State L. Rev.* 925 (1987).) By authorizing courts to award attorney's fees and other expenses to certain parties that prevail in a civil action brought against or by a federal administrative agency, this Act assists institutions that must litigate with the federal government over procedural defects in rule making, substantive defects in regulations that were not resolved during the rule-making process, or interpretive issues regarding the application of regulations. If an institution prevails in such litigation, it may receive attorney's fees unless the agency shows that its position in the suit was "substantially justified" (28 U.S.C. § 2412(d)(1)(A)). Like the Regulatory Flexibility Act, this Act's application to postsecondary education is limited by its definitions: apparently, to be a "party" eligible for attorney's fees, a postsecondary institution must have no more than five hundred employees and, unless it is a 501(c)(3) organization (see this volume, Section 7.3.1), must have a net worth of not more than $7 million (28 U.S.C.

---

[39]Institutions falling outside the definitions in the Regulatory Flexibility Act, and covered institutions seeking additional leverage in the administrative process, will be aided by the rule-making protections in Executive Order 12866, discussed later in this section.

§ 2412(d)(2)(B)).[40] Moreover, state colleges and universities do not appear to be within the definition of "party," which includes a "unit of local government" but makes no reference to state-level agencies and entitites. Individual agencies must publish their own regulations implementing the Act; the Department of Education's regulations, for example, are in 34 C.F.R. Part 21.

Another recent development that will help postsecondary institutions cope with the federal regulatory process is Executive Order 12866, issued by President Clinton on September 30, 1993 (58 Fed. Reg. 51725). The executive order sets out twelve principles of regulation for federal administrative agencies, including the requirement that each agency "shall identify and assess available alternatives to direct regulation" (§ 1(b)(3)), "shall assess both the costs and the benefits of the intended regulation" (§ 1(b)(6)), and "shall seek views of appropriate state, local, and tribal officials before imposing regulatory requirements" on those entities (§ 1(b)(9)). The order also establishes a number of procedural requirements—for example, requiring each agency periodically to "prepare an agenda of all regulations under development or review" (§ 4(b) and (c)), periodically to "review its existing significant regulations to determine whether any such regulations should be modified or eliminated so as to make the agency's regulatory program more effective [and] less burdensome" (§ 5(a)), and to "provide the public with meaningful participation in the regulatory process" and "afford the public a meaningful opportunity to comment" on any proposed regulation (§ 6(a)(1)). In addition, the order addresses various structural matters. For example, it assigns to the Office of Information and Regulatory Affairs (OIRA) within the Office of Management and Budget (§ 2(b)) various responsibilities for monitoring the regulatory processes of each agency (see, for example, § 4(e)), and it requires that each agency appoint a regulatory policy officer "to foster the development of effective, innovative, and least burdensome regulations and to further the principles" in Section 1(b) of the order (§ 6(a)(2)).

7.6.2. Obtaining information. Information will often be an indispensable key to a postsecondary institution's ability to deal effectively with the federal government, in rule-making processes or otherwise. Critical information sometimes will be within the control of the institution—for example, information about its own operations and the effect of federal programs on these operations. At other times critical information will be under the government's control—for example, data collected by the government itself or information on competing policy considerations being weighed internally by an agency as it formulates regulatory proposals. When the latter type of information is needed, it may sometimes be obtained during the course of a rule-making proceeding (see Section 7.6.1 above). In addition, the following legislation may help institutional administrators and legal counsel: the Freedom of Information Act (FOIA) Amendments of 1974; the Privacy Act of 1974; the Government in the Sunshine Act of 1976; and the Government Printing Office Electronic Information Access Enhancement Act of 1993 (Pub. L. No. 103-40, 107 Stat. 112 (1993)), an Act facilitating electronic access to government data. Executive Orders 12866 and 12356 and successor government orders may also be of help.

[40]Cases are collected in Annot., "Who Is a Party Entitled to Recover Attorney's Fees Under Equal Access to Justice Act (28 U.S.C.S. § 2412(d))," 107 A.L.R. Fed. 827 (1992 and periodic supp.).

The Freedom of Information Act Amendments (5 U.S.C. § 552) afford the public access to information from federal government files that is not specifically exempted from disclosure by the legislation.[41] Nine categories of information are exempted from disclosure under Section 552(b), the most relevant to postsecondary institutions being national security information, federal agencies' internal personnel rules and practices, interagency or intra-agency memoranda or letters that would not be available except in litigation, and investigatory files compiled for law enforcement purposes.

The FOIA is useful when an institution believes that the government holds information that would be helpful in a certain situation but informal requests have not yielded the necessary materials. By making an FOIA request, an institution can obtain agency information that may help the institution understand agency policy initiatives; or document a claim, process a grievance, or prepare a lawsuit against the government or some third party; or determine what information the government has that it could use against the institution—for example, in a threatened fund termination proceeding. Specific procedures to follow in requesting such information are set out in the statute and in each agency's own policies on FOIA requests. Persons or institutions whose requests are denied by the agency may file a suit against the agency in a U.S. District Court. The burden of proof is on the agency to support its reasons for denial. (See A. Adler, *Using the Freedom of Information Act: A Step-by-Step Guide* (American Civil Liberties Union Foundation, 1990).)

The Privacy Act (codified in part at 5 U.S.C. § 552a) is discussed in Section 4.16.3 of this volume with regard to student records. The point to be made here is that someone who requests certain information under the FOIA may find an obstacle in the Privacy Act. The FOIA itself exempts "personnel and medical files and similar files the disclosure of which would constitute a clearly unwarranted invasion of personal privacy" (5 U.S.C. § 552(b)(6)). The Privacy Act provides an even broader protection for information whose release would infringe privacy interests. While the Act thus may foil someone who requests information, it may also protect a postsecondary institution and its employees and students when the federal government has information concerning them in its files. (For a discussion of the FOIA, the privacy exemption, and the Privacy Act, see Comment, "The Freedom of Information Act's Privacy Exemption and the Privacy Act of 1974," 11 *Harvard Civil Rights–Civil Liberties Law Rev.* 596 (1976), and M. Hulett, "Privacy and the Freedom of Information Act," 27 *Administrative Law Rev.* 275 (1975).) Individual agencies each publish their own regulations implementing the Privacy Act. The Department of Education's regulations are published in 34 C.F.R. § 5b.1 et seq.

The Government in the Sunshine Act (5 U.S.C. § 552b) assures the public that "meetings of multimember federal agencies shall be open with the exception of discussions of several narrowly defined areas" (H.R. Rep. No. 880, 94th Cong., 2d Sess. (1976), at 2, reprinted in 3 *U.S. Code Cong. & Admin. News* 2184 (1976)). Institutions can individually or collectively make use of this Act by sending a representative to observe and report on agency decision making that is expected to have a substantial impact on their operations.

---

[41]For analysis and discussion of when information may be considered to be "agency records" accessible under the Freedom of Information Act, see *Kissinger v. Reporters Committee for Freedom of the Press*, 445 U.S. 136 (1980), and *Forsham v. Harris*, 445 U.S. 169 (1980).

Executive Order 12866 (also discussed in Section 7.6.1 above) requires agencies to do various cost-benefit assessments of proposed regulations and to make this information available to the public after the regulations are published (§ 6(1)(3)(E)(i)). The order also provides that OIRA (see Section 7.6.1 above) will "maintain a publicly available log" containing information about the status of regulatory actions and the oral and written communications received from outsiders regarding regulatory matters (§ 6(b)(4)(C)).

Executive Order 12356 (47 Fed. Reg. 27836 (Apr. 6, 1982)) establishes the necessary procedures and the schedule for classifying and declassifying government documents related to national security. This order, signed by President Reagan in April 1982, revoked prior Executive Order 12065, which had been signed by President Carter in June 1978. Although this executive order is still in effect, President Clinton has convened a task force to propose changes to the classification system and draft a new executive order (58 Fed. Reg. 29480 (1993)).

The 1982 executive order has the same function as its predecessors, establishing standards and procedures for classifying and declassifying government documents related to national security. But the 1982 order appears more restrictive than the 1978 order, since it added additional materials to the list of what can be classified; broadened the concept of "national security"; switched, for borderline cases, from a presumption against to a presumption in favor of classification; and deleted procedures for declassification of material after a set number of years. It remains to be seen whether a new executive order by President Clinton will alter these aspects of the 1982 order.

Selected Annotated Bibliography

General

Gaffney, Edward M., & Moots, Philip R. *Government and Campus: Federal Regulation of Religiously Affiliated Higher Education* (University of Notre Dame Press, 1982). Analyzes various aspects of federal regulation of religiously affiliated colleges and universities. Chapters treat religious preference in employment; student admissions and discipline policies; restrictions on the use of federal funds; accommodation to the needs of disabled persons, including reformed alcoholics and drug abusers; tax problems; labor law problems; and sexual segregation of on- and off-campus student housing. Each chapter offers recommendations for regulatory changes that would reduce church-state tension. See also these authors' earlier work, *Church and Campus*, listed in the Chapter One bibliography for this volume (Section 1.6).

Sec. 7.1 (Federal Constitutional Powers over Education)

Nowak, John, Rotunda, Ronald, & Young, J. Nelson, *Constitutional Law* (4th ed., West, 1991). Provides, in Chapters 4-5, 9, and 15, a comprehensive overview of federal commerce power, taxing and spending powers, civil rights enforcement power, and the doctrine of federal preemption of state authority.

Sec. 7.2 (Federal Regulation of Postsecondary Education)

Albergo, Paul F., & Domone, Dana J. (eds.). *ERISA: The Law and the Code* (Bureau of National Affairs, 1994). Includes the text of the statute and all amendments, with cross-references, as well as a cross-referenced index and a section-by-section finding list for ERISA and the Internal Revenue Code.

Ansell, Edward O. (ed.). *Intellectual Property in Academe: A Legal Compendium* (National Association of College and University Attorneys, 1991). A collection of journal articles, conference outlines, and other materials on patent, trademark, and copyright law. Articles discuss the fair use doctrine and its implications for faculty research and teaching; the ownership and use of computer software; and expected future issues in the area of copyright, patent, and trademark law. An extensive selected bibliography is also included.

Bedrosian, Alex (ed.). *Advisor's Manual of Federal Regulations Affecting Foreign Students and Scholars* (rev. ed., National Association for Foreign Student Affairs, 1993). A practical guide covering all the federal regulations that are important to administrators and counsel who deal with foreign students, employees, or visitors. Discusses both nonimmigrant and immigrant status, with special emphasis on the F, M, H, and J nonimmigrant categories. Includes an appendix of sample forms.

Bell, Sheila, and Majestic, Martin. "Protection and Enforcement of College and University Trademarks," 10 *J. Coll. & Univ. Law* 63 (1983-84). Reviews issues of trademark law in the higher education setting. Describes and differentiates the trademark protection available under federal statutes, state statutes, and common law; explains the procedures to be followed in registering for state, federal, or international protection; and discusses the licensing of trademarks and the administrative and judicial remedies available for trademark violations.

Bender, David. *Computer Law: Software Protection and Litigation* (Matthew Bender, 1988). Applies traditional copyright law to the evolving area of the ownership and use of computer software. Practice aids and litigation suggestions are provided.

Blosser, Fred. *Primer on Occupational Safety and Health* (Bureau of National Affairs, 1992). Introduces the administrator to federal and state regulation of workplace safety and health. Included are regulations for mine, nuclear, and transportation workers as well as those in traditional workplaces. The standard-setting and regulatory processes are described, as well as employer responsibilities, record-keeping requirements, and nondiscrimination provisions.

Carter, Stephen L. "The Trouble with Trademark," 99 *Yale L.J.* 759 (1990). A critical analysis of contemporary trademark law as deviating from common law. Author argues that common law actions for unfair competition are more appropriate than laws that give the trademark holder nationwide exclusive use of the mark.

Chadd, Charles M., & Satinover, Terry. *Avoiding Liability for Hazardous Waste: RCRA, CERCLA, and Related Corporate Law Issues* (Bureau of National Affairs, 1991). An overview of federal laws and their interpretive regulations regarding the management of hazardous waste and the cleanup of contaminated sites. Also included are guidelines from the Environmental Protection Agency and a glossary.

Chase, Marcelle P. "Animal Rights: An Interdisciplinary, Selective Bibliography," 82 *Law Library J.* 359 (1990). An annotated comprehensive list of publications on animal rights and research.

Childress, James, et al. (eds.). *Biolaw: A Legal and Ethical Reporter on Medicine,*

Health Care, and Bioengineering (University Publications of America, 1986 and periodic supp.). A collection of chapters by eminent legal scholars on a variety of issues intersecting law and medicine. Topics discussed include the health care system, public health law, reproductive issues (including the effect of new technology in reproduction), genetic screening, mental health treatment, human experimentation, animal experimentation, death and dying, and artificial and transplanted organs.

Coleman, Barbara J. *Primer on ERISA* (4th ed., Bureau of National Affairs, 1993). A concise overview of the major provisions of the Employee Retirement Income Security Act, focusing on pension, health care, disability, and accident plans, and noting relevant sections of the Internal Revenue Code. Includes forms for disclosure, a calendar for reporting benefits, model statements of employee rights under ERISA, a checklist for summary plan descriptions, and other model statements.

Comegys, Walker B. *Antitrust Compliance Manual* (2d ed., Practising Law Institute, 1992). An introduction to the law of antitrust for lawyers and their corporate clients. Included are chapters on the background of antitrust legislation, the enforcement of antitrust laws (by the Justice Department, the Federal Trade Commission, and the states), antitrust audits, and antitrust compliance programs for organizations of various sizes. Also included are appendices with sample files and forms.

Crews, Kenneth D. *Copyright, Fair Use, and the Challenge for Universities: Promoting the Progress of Higher Education* (University of Chicago Press, 1993). Provides background on copyright law and discusses the fair use doctrine. Includes a survey of copyright policies at ninety-eight research universities and describes how universities have responded to legislation and litigation related to copyright. Guidelines for the development of institutional copyright policy are provided, and the *Basic Books v. Kinkos Graphics* case is discussed.

"Developments in the Law—Toxic Waste Litigation," 99 *Harvard L. Rev.* 1462 (1986). An overview of toxic-waste litigation and regulation through the mid-1980s.

Duston, Robert L., & Robbins, Scott. *A Practical Guide to Implementing the Family and Medical Leave Act* (College and University Personnel Association, 1993). Focuses on the implications of the Family and Medical Leave Act for colleges and universities. Topics include employee eligibility; calculation methods for determining entitlement to leave; restoration of benefits; and the interplay between the FMLA, the ADA, civil rights laws, state leave laws, and collective bargaining. Sample policies and forms and the Department of Labor regulations are also included.

DuVal, Benjamin S., Jr. "The Human Subjects Protection Committee: An Experiment in Decentralized Federal Regulation," 1979 *American Bar Foundation Research J.* 571 (1979). A review of the past performance of human subjects protection committees. Of particular interest to administrators is the section "Six Models of Review," which contains six case studies of human subject committees in six very different institutions.

Flygare, Thomas J. *The Family and Medical Leave Act of 1993: Applications in Higher Education* (National Association of College and University Attorneys, 1994). A comprehensive overview of the FMLA and its particular implications for higher education. Included are several hypothetical situations relevant to colleges and universities, and a discussion of how a college can determine whether the leave qualifies under the FMLA. A particularly helpful guide for supervisors, department chairs, and deans.

Ginsberg, Gilbert J., & Abrams, Daniel B. *Fair Labor Standards Handbook for States, Local Government and Schools* (Thompson Publishing Group, 1986). A loose-leaf service, updated monthly, that discusses the application of the FLSA to public employees. The sections covering exempt employees, overtime provisions, special rules for police and firefighters, record keeping, and enforcement are of particular significance for administrators at public colleges and universities. The statute, regulations, administrative rulings, and judicial interpretations are included in appendices.

Gordon, Charles, & Gordon, Ellen G. *Immigration and Nationality Law* (Matthew Bender, 1981 and periodic supp.). An abridgment, in loose-leaf form, of the eight-volume treatise *Immigration Law and Procedure*. Divided into two parts, the first on "Immigration" and the second on "Nationality and Citizenship." Of particular use to postsecondary administrators and counsel are Chapter 1, "General Survey"; Chapter 2, "What Aliens May Enter the United States"; and Chapter 3, "Procedure for Entering the United States."

Government Affairs Bulletin (National Association for Foreign Student Affairs). A periodic newsletter reporting on immigration and naturalization issues of current importance to institutions of higher education. Tracks legislation, regulations, and policy formulation in the legislative and executive branches. Also includes grant announcements and instructions for completing INS forms.

Greenwald, Robert A., Ryan, Mary Kay, & Mulvihill, James E. *Human Subjects Research: A Handbook for Institutional Review Boards* (Plenum Press, 1982). Provides guidelines for institutional review boards regarding informed consent, the protection of incompetent subjects, and other responsibilities of these federally mandated committees.

Henn, Harry G. *Copyright Law: A Practitioner's Guide* (2d ed., Practising Law Institute, 1988 plus periodic supp.). A practical analysis of issues of concern to attorneys involved in copyright litigation. Among the subjects discussed are litigation procedures, infringement actions, and the responsibilities of the Copyright Office. Forms, checklists, and other practice aids, as well as the text of relevant federal copyright legislation, are included.

Interpreter Releases and *Immigration Briefings* (Federal Publications, Inc.). Immigration law research resources published weekly and monthly, respectively. *Interpreter Releases* gives capsule summaries that track judicial and administrative decisions, legislation, and other actions and rulings of government agencies. Its sister publication, *Immigration Briefings,* gives an in-depth analysis of one particular area of immigration law of current importance.

Kane, Siegrun D. *Trademark Law: A Practitioner's Guide* (2d ed., Practising Law Institute, 1991). A thoroughly researched, cite-filled discussion of trademark for the nonexpert. Chapters include basic information on trademarks, selecting a trademark, searching a trademark, registering and using a trademark, protection against infringement, defenses to infringement, and numerous litigation issues. Appendices contain various forms, applications, renewal forms, declarations as to use, and a list of states with antidilution statutes.

Kaufman, Hattie. *Access to Institutions of Higher Education for Students with Disabilities* (National Association of College and University Attorneys, 1991). Discusses institutional responsibilities to provide access to and accommodation for disabled students under both the Rehabilitation Act and the Americans with Disabilities Act. Adjustments to academic programs, auxiliary aids, student housing, participation in athletic activities, transportation, and student activities are discussed. Portions of the regulations specific to colleges are included as an appendix.

Kirby, Wendy T. "Federal Antitrust Issues Affecting Institutions of Higher Education: An Overview," 11 *J. Coll. & Univ. Law* 345 (1984). A review of general antitrust law principles that apply to colleges and universities. Analyzes the potential antitrust liability of undergraduate institutions in the areas of commercial activities, athletics, accreditation, and joint ventures with private industry; and lists the "exemptions" or "immunities" that may be available to protect institutions threatened with antitrust liability. Includes a bibliography of secondary sources on antitrust law's application to higher education.

Kurzban, Ira. *Kurzban's Immigration Law Sourcebook* (4th ed., American Immigration Law Association, 1993). A reference tool detailing the statutory law, regulations, administrative decisions, and judicial precedents relating to immigration. These chapters will be particularly helpful to higher education administrators and counsel: Chapter 5 (Nonimmigrant Visas), Chapter 7 (Employment Based Immigration and Labor Certification), and Chapter 12 (Employer Sanctions, Unfair Immigration Related Employment Practices and Legalization). Includes discussion of the Immigration Act of 1990.

Lachs, Phyllis S. "University Patent Policy," 10 *J. Coll. & Univ. Law* 263 (1983–84). Reviews problems regarding university patents (including conflict-of-interest problems). Author argues that universities should assert patent rights over the results of scientific research by faculty and staff. An extensive model university patent policy, addressing the problems reviewed by the author, is included.

Lape, Laura G. "Ownership of Copyrightable Works of University Professors: The Interplay Between the Copyright Act and University Copyright Policies," 37 *Villanova L. Rev.* 223 (1992). Discusses attempts by universities to control the copyrightable works of professors. Analyzes cases about works made for hire, discusses the effectiveness of university copyright policies, and examines copyright policies at seventy research universities. Includes recommendations about how copyright ownership questions between professors and their institutions should be resolved.

Levine, Robert J. *Ethics and Regulation of Clinical Research* (2d ed., Yale University Press, 1986). Focuses on the ethics of research for administrators, members of institutional review boards, and researchers themselves. Discusses federal regulations, ethical analyses, and specific research projects that use humans as research subjects.

McCarthy, J. Thomas. *McCarthy's Desk Encyclopedia on Intellectual Property* (Bureau of National Affairs, 1991). A reference guide for lawyers and administrators who work regularly with intellectual property issues. Defines terms from patent, trademark, copyright, trade-secret, entertainment, and computer law. Entries are annotated with cases and statutes, regulations, treaties, and bibliographical citations.

Malone, Linda A. *Environmental Regulation of Land Use* (Clark Boardman Callaghan, 1991). A treatise that discusses every federal environmental and land use law, and the effect of the environment on land use. Topics covered include the management of coastal resources, water and air quality, soil conservation, ground-water purity, and noise control.

Moran, Robert D. *OSHA Handbook* (2d ed., Government Institutes, 1989). A practical and thorough manual on the Occupational Safety and Health Act. Included is an overview of the law, OSHA standards, the General Duty Clause, record-keeping requirements, inspections, citations and penalties, hearings and adjudication, and the Hazard Communication Standard. Appendices include forms, model policies and work rules, and litigation forms.

Moyer, Craig A., & Francis, Michael A. *Hazard Communication Handbook: A Right-to-Know Compliance Guide* (Clark Boardman Callaghan, 1993). A practical guide for laypersons written by a lawyer. Discusses the Hazard Communication Standard, reporting requirements and forms, emergency planning requirements, requirements for reporting an emergency release, chemical inventory reporting, reporting of toxic-chemical releases, trade-secrecy claims, and the Safe Drinking Water and Toxic Enforcement Act of 1986. Appendices include the SARA consolidated chemical list, relevant statutory and regulatory provisions, an EPA directory, and a glossary.

Patry, William F. *Latman's The Copyright Law* (7th ed., Bureau of National Affairs, 1993). A standard reference on copyright law. Thoroughly treats provisions of domestic copyright law, analyzing both the 1909 and the 1976 Copyright Acts. Includes appendices containing texts of the 1909 and 1976 Acts, Copyright Office regulations, and leading international conventions on copyrights.

President's Commission for the Study of Ethical Problems in Medicine and Biomedical and Behavioral Research. *First Biennial Report*, 47 Fed. Reg. 13272 (Mar. 29, 1982). A report prepared in response to two broad congressional mandates: "first, to review the federal rules and policies governing [human subject] research, and second, to determine how well those rules are being implemented or enforced." Chapter 2, dealing with "The Adequacy and Uniformity of the Regulations," uses the HHS regulations as a framework. Chapter 3, on "The Adequacy and Uniformity of the Regulations' Implementation," discusses the potential flaws inherent in the HHS and NIH compliance systems and those of other federal agencies. Report also evaluates the operation of IRBs and offers a series of recommendations for improving federal regulation of human subject research.

Proger, Phillip A., Busey, Roxane C., & Miller, Tina (eds.). *Developments in Antitrust Health Care Law* (Section of Antitrust Law, American Bar Association, 1990). Discusses the application of antitrust law to peer review evaluations and decisions to grant medical staff hospital privileges; to alternative health care delivery systems; to systems for reimbursing and providing health care networks; and to competition in markets for health care. The enforcement activities of the Federal Trade Commission are also discussed.

Richey, Charles R. *Manual on Employment Discrimination and Civil Rights Actions in the Federal Courts* (2d ed., Clark Boardman Callaghan, 1994). Discusses employment discrimination litigation under a variety of federal nondiscrimination laws, including Title VII, Section 1983, the Equal Pay Act, the Age Discrimination in Employment Act, the Rehabilitation Act of 1973, and the Equal Access to Justice Act. Also included is a state-by-state survey of the major nondiscrimination laws of each state. Common law claims often appended to discrimination claims are also reviewed.

Richmond, Douglas R. "Antitrust and Higher Education: An Overview," 61 *Mo. L. Rev.* 417 (1993). A review of antitrust theory, with special emphasis on the price-fixing charges against several Ivy League schools.

Rothstein, Laura F. *Disabilities and the Law* (Shepard's/McGraw-Hill, 1992). A reference guide designed for lawyers, educators, and medical professionals. Includes chapters on the Americans with Disabilities Act, the Rehabilitation Act, and federal and state laws related to disability discrimination, among others. The chapter on higher education discusses admissions, programs and services (including academic modifications and auxiliary services), athletics, health insurance, physical facilities, confidentiality requirements, learning-disabled students, and mentally impaired students. Updated annually.

Rothstein, Mark A. *Occupational Safety and Health Law* (3d ed., West, 1990). An overview of the federal Occupational Safety and Health Act (OSHA) and its relation to state law. Volume is divided into six parts: "The Scope of the Act," "Duties Under the Act," "Enforcement," "Contested Issues," "Adjudication," and "Extensions of the Act" (which examines the place of state law under OSHA). Appendices contain a table reviewing the "Status of State Plans," the "Commission Rules of Procedure," and the text of the Act.

Stever, Donald W. *Law of Chemical Regulation and Hazardous Waste* (Clark Boardman Callaghan, 1986 and periodic supp.). A three-volume guide to the regulation of chemicals under the Toxic Substances Control Act. Included are the regulation of storage, transportation, and disposal of hazardous waste; emergency and remedial responses to chemical-hazard situations; the regulation of toxic air emissions, wastewater effluents, and groundwater pollution; the regulation of chemicals in foods; and the regulation of workers' exposure to chemicals.

Wallach, Paul G., Davidson, Jeffery J., Atlas, Mark, & Meade, Kenneth R. *Environmental Requirements for Colleges and Universities* (American Council on Education, 1989). Summarizes eleven areas of federal environmental law, including RCRA, CERCLA, the Clean Water Act, the Hazard Communication Standard, the Toxic Substances Control Act, asbestos issues, underground storage tanks, the Clean Air Act, and the Safe Drinking Water Act.

Ware, David, Somers, Patricia, & Speake, Scott. "Immigration Law and Higher Education: Employment of International Employees," 20 *J. Coll. & Univ. Law* 51 (1993). Provides institutional administrators and novice counsel with an overview of immigration law, including definitions of the technical terms. Discusses the provisions applicable to the immigrant staff laborer, the immigrant highly skilled professor or researcher, the nonimmigrant visiting lecturer, and the nonimmigrant international student. Also outlines the labor certification and petitioning processes of the Department of Labor, employer sanctions for noncompliance, and tax issues facing institutions that hire aliens.

Yale-Loehr, Stephen (ed.). *Understanding the Immigration Act of 1990* (Federal Publications, 1991). A descriptive and analytical review of the 1990 legislation and its comprehensive overhaul of U.S. immigration law. Each of the thirteen chapters is aimed at a major aspect of the new law. Chapters 3 (employment-based immigrants), 5 (F-1 nonimmigrants), and 6 (H-1B nonimmigrants) will be particularly helpful to higher education institutions. Also includes the full text of the 1990 Act.

See Selected Annotated Bibliography for Chapter Three, Section 3.3, for references on federal employment discrimination legislation.

Sec. 7.3 (Federal Taxation of Postsecondary Education)

Ashford, Deborah, and Frank, Robert. *Lobbying and the Law: A Guide to Federal Tax Law Limitations on Legislative and Political Activities by Nonprofit Organizations* (2d ed., Hogan & Hartson/Frank & Company, 1990). Covers participation in political campaigns, direct and grass-roots lobbying, mass media communications, and activities excluded from the definition of lobbying. An appendix includes an overview of the lobbying laws of every state.

Bittker, Boris, and Rahdert, George K. "The Exemption of Nonprofit Organizations from Federal Income Taxation," 85 *Yale L.J.* 299 (1976). An overview of issues regarding the federal tax status of nonprofit entities. Discusses the unrelated business income tax, the taxation of capital gains and investment income of private foundations, and the tax status of organizations that engage in political activity. Also contains sections on the exemption of educational institutions and on appropriate methods by which to measure the income of nonprofit entities.

Colombo, John D. "Why Is Harvard Tax-Exempt? (and Other Mysteries of Tax Exemption for Private Educational Institutions)," 35 *Ariz. L. Rev.* 841 (1993). Examines federal and state exemptions for private educational institutions. Discusses the rationales presented to justify tax exemption for charitable institutions in general, including the donative theory that would limit exemption to those entities receiving a certain percentage of revenues from donations. Also discusses both the expansive definition of "education" and the manner in which the IRS and state taxing authorities circumscribe this definition. Includes five tables, setting out the total charitable donations received by various types of postsecondary institutions.

Harding, Bertrand, Jr., & Peterson, Norm. *U.S. Taxation of International Students and Scholars: A Manual for Advisers and Administrators* (rev. ed., National Association for Foreign Student Affairs, 1993). Practical advice on the taxability of scholarships, fellowships, living allowances, and travel grants for foreign students and scholars, as well as the withholding and reporting requirements imposed on their institutions. A related work by the same publisher—Deborah Vance, *U.S. Federal Income Tax Guide for International Students and Scholars* (rev. ed., National Association for Foreign Student Affairs, 1994)—provides a layperson's guide to U.S. taxation and filing requirements for foreign students and scholars.

Hopkins, Bruce. *The Law of Tax-Exempt Organizations* (6th ed., Wiley, 1992 and periodic supp.). A reference volume, for managers and administrators as well as counsel, that examines the pertinent federal law affecting the different types of nonprofit organizations, including colleges and universities. Emphasis is on how to obtain and maintain tax-exempt status. Contains citations to Internal Revenue Code provisions, Treasury Department revenue rulings, and court decisions.

Hopkins, Bruce. *The Nonprofit Counsel* (Wiley). A monthly newsletter that analyzes current developments in Congress, the Treasury Department, the IRS, and the courts regarding taxation of nonprofit organizations and related issues. See also entry in bibliography for Section 6.3.

Kaplan, Richard L. "Intercollegiate Athletics and the Unrelated Business Income Tax," 80 *Columbia L. Rev.* 1430 (1980). Reviews the unrelated business income tax as it affects the postsecondary institution's athletic program. Author argues that many schools' intercollegiate athletic programs have taken on the appearance of business activities unrelated to the institution's educational mission, and thus may be liable to taxation. Article also includes broader discussion of the unrelated business income tax in the higher education context.

Kelly, Marci. "Financing Higher Education: Federal Income-Tax Consequences," 17 *J. Coll. & Univ. L.* 307 (1991). Discusses federal tax law as it applies to the financing of education through scholarships, prizes, loans, and student employment. Provides guidance for administrators in counseling students, structuring new financial aid programs, and administering existing programs.

Symposium, "Federal Taxation and Charitable Organizations," 39 *Law & Contemporary Problems* 1–262 (1975). A sophisticated collection of articles on federal tax policy and law concerning charitable organizations. Includes J. H. Levi on "Financing Education and the Effects of the Tax Law," which discusses the impact of the Internal Revenue Code's charitable deduction provisions on postsecondary institutions; and J. F. Kirkwood and D. S. Mundel on "The Role of Tax Policy in Federal Support for Higher Education," which examines federal tax policy regarding higher education and compares tax programs with spending and regulatory programs.

Sec. 7.4 (*Federal Aid-to-Education Programs*)

Advisory Commission on Intergovernmental Relations. *The Evolution of a Problematic Partnership: The Feds and Higher Education* (Advisory Commission on Intergovernmental Relations, 1981). Examines the history and growth of the federal government's involvement in higher education. Chapters include "The Scope of Federal Involvement in Higher Education," "The Evolution of a Federal Role: 1787–1958," "Beginnings of a New Federal Role in Higher Education: The National Defense Education Act," "A Direct Federal Role Established: The Higher Education Acts of 1963 and 1965," "Equal Opportunity Preeminent: The 1972 Higher Education Amendments," and "A Growing Regulatory Presence." Contains various figures, graphs, and tables charting major developments in the relationship between the federal government and higher education.

Cappalli, Richard. *Rights and Remedies Under Federal Grants* (Bureau of National Affairs, 1979). A systematic treatment of the federal grants system. Contains sections on "The Theory and Structure of Grants," including analyses of types and purposes of federal grants and constitutional supports for the grant system; "Agency Enforcement of Grant Conditions"; "Expanding Bases of Judicial Intervention"; "Due Process and Federal Grants"; "Grantee Hearing Rights: Withholding of Entitlements"; "Termination of Competitive Grants"; "Grant Suspensions"; "Rights of Applicants for Federal Funds"; "Subgrantees"; "Guideposts for Reform"; and other topics. Author has also published a lengthier treatment of this topic and related topics in a three-volume treatise, *Federal Grants and Cooperative Agreements: Law, Policy, and Practice* (Clark Boardman Callaghan, 1982).

Federal Grants and Contracts Weekly (Capitol). A weekly newsletter. Lists new grant application opportunities, contains summaries and detailed explanations of new requests for proposals (RFPs), describes new grant programs, and analyzes the workings of the grant and contract processes.

Federal Grants Management Handbook (Grants Management Advisory Service, 1979 and periodic supp.). A guide particularly for administrators. Among the chapters are "Obtaining a Federal Grant"; "How to Organize for Receipt of Grant Funds"; "Financial Administration of Federal Grants"; "Reporting and Recordkeeping"; "How to Comply with 'Strings Attached' to Federal Grants"; and "Disputes, Appeals, and Remedies." Appendices include compilations of Office of Management and Budget and Department of Treasury circulars.

Green, Deirdre (ed.). *College and University Business Administration* (5th ed., National Association of College and University Business Officers, 1992). Includes two chapters of particular relevance to institutional administration of federal grants and contracts: Chapter 15 ("Auditing," by Warren Spruill), which includes discussion of both internal audits and external audits by federal government auditors; and Chapter 21 ("Research and Sponsored Programs" by Julie Norris), which discusses report and record-keeping requirements, allowability of costs, and certifications and assurances required by federal agencies (for example, Drug-Free Workplace, debarment and suspension, and lobbying certifications).

Lacovara, Philip, "How Far Can the Federal Camel Slip Under the Academic Tent?" 4 *J. Coll. & Univ. Law* 233 (1977). A constitutional analysis, in the postsecondary education context, of the federal government's spending power and potential First Amendment and due process limitations on that power. Outdated in its case law, but a good source for the foundational principles.

Olivas, Michael. *The Tribally Controlled Community College Assistance Act of 1978: The Failure of Federal Indian Higher Education Policy,* IHELG Monograph 82-1 (Institute for Higher Education Law and Governance, University of Houston, 1982). An analysis of the Act's design flaws, the bureaucratic delays in its implementation, and the impoverished condition of the tribal colleges that are the Act's intended beneficiaries. Includes recommendations for improving the Act and its administration. Another version of this paper is published in 9 *American Indian L. Rev.* 219 (1981).

O'Neil, Robert M. "God and Government at Yale: The Limits of Federal Regulation of Higher Education," 44 *U. Cincinnati L. Rev.* 525 (1975). An analysis of constitutional and nonconstitutional issues regarding the extent of federal authority to regulate higher education. Outdated in its case law, but another good source for the foundational principles.

O'Neil, Robert M. "Artists, Grants and Rights: The NEA Controversy Revisited," 9 *N.Y. Law School J. Human Rights* 85 (1991). Considers the viability of constitutional challenges to restrictions on the use of grant funds administered by the National Endowment for the Arts. Reviews the First Amendment's applicability to NEA grants, discusses the Helms amendment and congressional changes that followed, and analyzes recent cases challenging NEA grant restrictions on First Amendment grounds.

Palmer, Carolyn, & Gehring, Donald (eds.). *A Handbook for Complying with the Program & Review Requirements of the 1989 Amendments to the Drug-Free Schools and Communities Act* (College Administration Publications, 1992). A how-to manual for college administrators who are setting up or reviewing on-campus drug and alcohol programs in accordance with federal law. The handbook also provides a guide, supplemented by a comprehensive appendix, to federal and private funding sources, research and studies on the subject, organizations concerned with drug-free education, and model standards and guidelines.

Wallick, Robert D., & Chamblee, Daryl A. "Bridling the Trojan Horse: Rights and

Remedies of Colleges and Universities Under Federal Grant-Type Assistance Programs," 4 *J. Coll. & Univ. Law* 241 (1977). Discusses legal and policy aspects of federal assistance to postsecondary institutions. Suggests steps that legal counsel might take to protect the interests of institutions in grant programs.

Whitehead, Kenneth D. *Catholic Colleges and Federal Funding* (Ignatius Press, 1988). Examines the question whether religiously affiliated colleges and universities must safeguard "academic freedom" and have "institutional autonomy" in order to be eligible for federal aid. Discusses eligibility requirements (such as accreditation), accrediting agencies' policies, the current understanding of academic freedom and the role of the AAUP, and parallel issues regarding state (rather than federal) aid for religiously affiliated institutions. Written by the then deputy assistant secretary for higher education programs in the U.S. Deptartment of Education.

Sec. 7.5 (Civil Rights Compliance)

Baxter. Felix V. "The Affirmative Duty to Desegregate Institutions of Higher Education—Defining the Role of the Traditionally Black College," 11 *J. Law & Educ.* 1 (1982). Provides "an analytical framework to assess, in a consistent fashion, the role which [black] institutions should play in a unitary system." Reviews various legal strategies to deflect the "very real threat to black efforts to desegregate state systems of higher education."

Bell, Derrick A., Jr. "Black Colleges and the Desegregation Dilemma," 28 *Emory L.J.* 949 (1979). Reviews the development of desegregation law and its impact on black colleges. Author argues that black colleges continue to provide a special service to black Americans and that litigation and legislation should be tailored to accommodate and promote this service.

Campbell, Nancy Duff, et al. *Sex Discrimination in Education: Legal Rights and Remedies* (National Women's Law Center, 1983). A detailed, two-volume analysis of Title IX. Volume I examines such questions as Title IX's impact on admissions, campus health programs, and sexual harassment, and reviews litigation problems and strategies under Title IX. Volume II is a document sourcebook that includes the legislative history of Title IX, administrative regulations and guidelines, and various court and settlement documents.

Handicapped Requirements Handbook (Federal Programs Advisory Service, 1978 and periodic supp.). A comprehensive, practical guide to complying with Section 504 of the Rehabilitation Act of 1973. Includes Section 504 agency regulations and interpretations, summaries of court decisions, a self-evaluation questionnaire, and a glossary of terms.

Hunter, Howard O. "Federal Antibias Legislation and Academic Freedom: Some Problems with Enforcement Procedures," 27 *Emory L.J.* 609 (1978). Procedures used by federal agencies to enforce the statutes prohibiting discrimination by federal fund recipients, author argues, have a negative impact on academic freedom.

Preer, Jean. "Lawyers v. Educators: Changing Perceptions of Desegregation in Public Higher Education," 1 *N.C. Central L.J.* 74 (1979), reprinted in 53 *J. Higher Educ.* 119 (1982). Examines the tension between lawyers' and educators' perceptions of desegregation in public universities and colleges. Discusses three historical examples: the Morrill Act of 1890, "the reactions of civil rights lawyers and educators to the regional educational compact of the 1940s," and the "legal and educational

paradoxes" of *Adams v. Richardson* (see this chapter, Sections 7.5.2 and 7.5.8).
Author concludes that "both lawyers and educators need to expand their vision."
An extended version of these themes appears in Jean Preer, *Lawyers v. Educators:
Black Colleges and Desegregation in Public Higher Education* (Greenwood Press,
1982), especially rich in historical materials.

Shuck, Peter H. "The Graying of Civil Rights Law: The Age Discrimination Act of
1975," 89 *Yale L.J.* 27 (1979). A theoretical study of the Age Discrimination Act.
Article is divided into four parts: "The ADA and the Analogy to Title VI"; "The
Political Context and Legislative History of the ADA"; "Interpreting the ADA:
Reading Shadows on Walls" (which presents a detailed explication of the statute's
ambiguities and built-in exceptions); and "The Process, Substance, and Form of
Age Discrimination Policy." Author is critical of the ADA and furnishes a tren-
chant analysis of its inherent difficulties.

Wegner, Judith W. "The Antidiscrimination Model Reconsidered: Ensuring Equal
Opportunity Without Respect to Handicap Under Section 504 of the Rehabilitation Act of 1973," 69 *Cornell L. Rev.* 401 (1984). A comprehensive analysis of the
primary federal statute on discrimination against disabled persons. Author compares Section 504 to other antidiscrimination measures and "discusses the extent
to which traditional antidiscrimination principles . . . must be reshaped" to protect people with disabilities from discriminatory practices. Also discusses coverage
and enforcement issues and analyzes the elements of the plaintiff's prima facie case
and the defendant's defenses in situations where a disabled individual challenges
an exclusion from participation in a program, the denial of benefits of a program,
or unequal treatment within a program. Includes a section analyzing the U.S.
Supreme Court's decision in *Southeastern Community College v. Davis*.

Williams, John B., IV (ed.). *Desegregating America's Colleges and Universities: Title
VI Regulation of Higher Education* (Teachers College Press, 1987). Offers a range
of policy proposals aimed at increasing the proportion of blacks among college
students and faculty. Authors—including Barbara Newell, Larry Leslie, James
Blackwood, Charles Willie, and Edgar Epps—discuss trends in black enrollment
and degree attainment at the undergraduate and graduate levels, financial inequities in previously segregated systems of public postsecondary education, achievement of black and white students in predominantly white and predominantly
black institutions, and the future of Title VI enforcement. The book is intended
for administrators, faculty, policy makers. and researchers.

Wilson, Reginald (ed.). *Race and Equity in Higher Education* (American Council on
Education, 1983). Contains five essays produced by the American Council on Education–Aspen Institute Seminar on the Desegregation of Higher Education. Essays (by J. Egerton, J. E. Blackwell, J. L. Prestage, P. R. Dimond, and A. L.
Berrian) examine the history and politics of higher education desegregation, provide data on demographic changes in recent decades, analyze constitutional standards and remedies, evaluate desegregation plans of states involved in *Adams v.
Richardson* (see Sections 7.5.2 and 7.5.8) litigation, and propose new policies and
agendas.

Sec. 7.6 (Dealing with the Federal Government)

Adler, Allan R. (ed.). *Litigation Under the Federal Open Government Laws: The
Freedom of Information Act, the Privacy Act, the Government in the Sunshine Act,*

the Federal Advisory Committee Act (18th ed., American Civil Liberties Union Foundation, 1993). Provides analysis, practical advice, and trial strategies for obtaining information from federal government agencies. Updated annually.

Administrative Conference of the United States. *Federal Administrative Procedure Sourcebook: Statutes and Related Materials* (2d ed., Office of the Chairman, Administrative Conference, 1992). A handy guide that collects together materials on the Administrative Procedure Act, Equal Access to Justice Act, Federal Advisory Committee Act, Freedom of Information Act, Negotiated Rulemaking Act, Privacy Act, Regulatory Flexibility Act, and other legislation regarding the administrative process. Includes texts of the Acts, legislative histories, an overview of each Act, agency regulations and executive orders, citations and bibliographies, and materials on judicial review of federal agency decisions.

Bouchard, Robert F., & Franklin, Justin D. (eds.). *Guidebook to the Freedom of Information and Privacy Acts* (2d ed., Clark Boardman Callaghan, 1986). A compilation of materials that explain the FOIA and the Privacy Act and provide guidance on how to obtain information under them.

Brademus, John. *The Politics of Education* (University of Oklahoma Press, 1987). Discusses the federal role in education, the legislative process with reference to education, contemporary themes and concerns regarding education policy, and the relationship between education and democracy. Written "from a highly personal perspective" by a former congressman who became president of a large private university after leaving Congress.

Clune, William, III. *The Deregulation Critique of the Federal Role in Education*, Project Report no. 82-A11 (Institute for Research on Educational Finance and Governance, Stanford University, 1982). Analyzes the theoretical basis for deregulation, the criticisms of then current federal regulatory efforts, and the benefits and disadvantages of deregulation.

El-Khawas, Elaine. "Solving Problems Through Self-Regulation," 59 *Educ. Record* 323 (1978). Defines self-regulation as "voluntary actions to address problems that broadly affect the academic community." Acknowledges the difficulty of self-regulation and proposes "two kinds of initiatives: efforts to limit further government regulation and efforts to assure that existing regulations adequately come to terms with academic realities."

Lisman, Natasha. "Freedom of Scientific Research: A Frontier Issue in First Amendment Law," 35 *Boston Bar J.* 4 (Nov.–Dec. 1991). Author argues "that the development of scientific knowledge is among the vital interests protected by the First Amendment, and that the very nature of the process by which science creates and advances scientific knowledge dictates that the First Amendment protections apply not only to the scientific expression but also to scientific experimentation."

Mintz, Benjamin, & Miller, Nancy. *A Guide to Federal Agency Rulemaking* (2d ed., Office of the Chairman, Administrative Conference of the United States, 1991). Provides comprehensive explanation and analysis of federal agency rule-making processes, including judicial review of rule making. Includes discussion of the Administrative Flexibility Act, the Negotiated Rulemaking Act of 1990, and the Paperwork Reduction Act.

Rosenblum, Victor. "Dealing with Federal Regulatory Agencies," in Dennis H. Blumer (ed.), *Legal Issues for Postsecondary Education II* (American Association of

Community and Junior Colleges, 1976). Chapter 5 is a concise, practical, "how-to" guide written for administrators of postsecondary institutions.

Saunders, Charles B. "How to Keep Government from Playing the Featured Role," 59 *Educ. Record* 61 (1978). Author asserts that the federal presence on campus is permanent and proposes a strategy for coping with this presence. He suggests that both the government and postsecondary administrators adopt a "test of necessity" for determining when a new federal regulation may be needed, and that administrators commit themselves to "developing a system of self-regulation."

Steadman, John M., Schwartz, David, & Jacoby, Sidney B. *Litigation with the Federal Government* (3d ed. by Urban Lester and Michael Noone, American Law Institute/American Bar Association, 1994). An overview and analysis of how to sue the federal government and handle the problems encountered in such suits. Includes extensive discussion of the Federal Tort Claims Act, the Tucker Act (for certain claims based on a federal statute or regulation or on an express or implied contract), the Contract Disputes Act of 1978, and the Equal Access to Justice Act. Also discusses the process of settling cases against the federal government and the remnants of the sovereign immunity doctrine that still pose some barriers to suing the federal government.

See the Lacovara, O'Neil ("God and Government"), and Wallick & Chamblee entries for Section 7.4.

VIII

The College and
the Education
Associations

◆　◆　◆

Sec. 8.1. Overview of the Education Associations

The diversity of missions, structure, and program mix of American colleges and universities is captured when one considers the myriad of associations related, either wholly or in part, to postsecondary education. From the American Council on Education, which monitors and informs college presidents about a variety of issues affecting colleges and universities generally, to the League for Innovation in the Community Colleges, a small group that promotes new technology in community colleges, these associations perform numerous functions on behalf of all, some, or a few specialized institutions.

Many of these associations (such as the American Council on Education, the Association of American Colleges, and the Association of Governing Boards) have institutions as members; others (such as the American Association of University Professors, the American Association for Higher Education, and the National Association of Women Administrators, Deans and Counselors) have individuals as members. Although many of the associations are located in Washington, D.C., others are located in various cities throughout the United States. Education associations exist at the state level as well, particularly those whose members are institutions or boards of trustees.

Regardless of whether their members are institutions or individuals, most of these organizations fulfill multiple purposes. Many, particularly those located in the nation's capital, engage in lobbying activities, attempting to influence congressional action or the regulatory activities of executive-branch agencies. Their representatives may advise congressional staff in drafting legislation and ascertaining its impact on postsecondary education; they may also appear before congressional committees or assist congressional staff in inviting others to appear. They may also attend agency meetings and hearings on draft regulations, to make drafting suggestions and to explain the implications of these regulations for postsecondary education. The state-level equivalents of the education associations perform similar activities with regard to state legislation and regulations.

Many associations develop statements of policy on good professional practice and other matters for their constituencies. The statements promulgated by the American Association of University Professors, for instance, have had a substantial impact on the status of faculty on many campuses and on the judicial interpretation of "national custom and usage" in faculty employment relations (see Section 8.5).

Education and training, and information sharing, are significant activities of the education associations as well. Most have annual conferences, and many produce publications to inform and update their constituency. Many serve an important monitoring function for their members, particularly with regard to new legislative, administrative, and judicial developments.

Many associations have special interests or expertise regarding the legal issues in this book, and are excellent sources of legal information and law-related conferences and workshops. The American Council on Education, for example, prepares important analyses and alerts on current legal issues, especially those concerning congressional legislation and legislative proposals. The Association for Student Judicial Affairs has an annual national conference, regional gatherings, and a summer institute where legal issues of interest to personnel responsible for campus judicial affairs are discussed. And the National Association of College and University Attorneys provides a comprehensive array of services for member institutions and the attorneys who represent them, as well as for other "associate" members.

Some of the associations also act as amici curiae, or "friends of the court," in litigation affecting the interests of their members. When ongoing litigation affects the interests of postsecondary education generally, or a large group of institutions, many of the education organizations often will band together to submit an amicus brief, particularly if the case is before the U.S. Supreme Court. The associations have, on occasion, also provided expert witnesses to explain academic custom and practice, or to interpret the academic community's "general understanding" of important concepts such as tenure and academic freedom.

In addition, some associations perform the critical function of accrediting institutions or particular academic programs within institutions. The U.S. Department of Education relies on these private, nonprofit accrediting actions as a basis for certifying an institution's eligibility to participate in federal aid programs (see Section 8.3.3). The accrediting associations also play a significant role in the higher education community's self-regulation.

In their roles as quasi-regulators or as accreditors of higher education institutions, the education associations may make decisions that precipitate litigation against them by a college or university. For example, on many occasions a college or university has sued the National Collegiate Athletic Association (NCAA) over its regulation of college athletics (see Section 8.4). Institutions have also sued accrediting associations to challenge a withdrawal, threatened withdrawal, or denial of accreditation (see Section 8.3.2).

The education associations are a source of information, assistance, and practical advice for colleges and universities, and for members of the academic community, particularly with regard to federal regulation and with regard to professional and ethical practices. They provide services and expertise that few institutions have the resources to provide for themselves and a network of colleagues with similar interests and concerns.

Sec. 8.2. Applicable Legal Principles

The various education associations described in Section 8.1 are private rather than governmental entities. Being private, they are not created by and do not owe their existence directly to state and federal constitutions and authorizing legislation, as do federal, state, and local government agencies. Rather, they are created by the actions of private individuals or groups, and their legal status is shaped by state corporation law and the common law of "voluntary associations." These associations thus have whatever powers are set forth in their articles of incorporation or association and in the accompanying bylaws and rules. These powers are exercised through organizational structures and enforced through private sanctions, which are specified in the articles, bylaws, and rules. Some education associations are membership organizations that exercise power through their members (either institutions or individuals), or that extend particular prerogatives to and impose particular responsibilities on members. In such situations the articles, bylaws, and rules will also establish the qualifications for obtaining and maintaining membership.

Education associations may also develop various kinds of working relationships with one another. In such cases memoranda of understanding, consortium agreements, and other such documents may also become part of the basic governing law for the signatory associations.

State and federal law restricts the powers of private associations in a number of important ways. State corporation law may restrict the structures and procedures through which an association may operate. The common law of voluntary associations may superimpose upon the association's own standards and procedures a general obligation to act reasonably and fairly, especially toward its members, and may also require that the association follow its own rules; judicial review may be available to persons or organizations harmed by an association's failure to do so (see Sections 8.3.2.2 and 8.4.4 below).[1] Federal and state antitrust law may restrict associational activities that have anticompetitive or monopolistic effects (see Sections 8.3.2.4 and 8.4.3 below). Other statutes may occasionally impose special requirements on certain associations (see Sections 8.3.3 and 8.4.2 below). In the past, state and federal constitutional provisions protecting individual rights have also been applied to limit the authority of private associations; under current trends, however, these provisions will seldom apply to private education associations (see Sections 8.3.2.3 and 8.4.1 below; compare Section 1.5.2).

Many of the suits against education associations have been brought by institutions or individuals who were rejected or terminated as members or who were sanctioned by the association. These cases have been a testing ground for the development of legal restrictions on the powers of private associations. Such suits are

---

[1]For an extended analysis of common law principles and judicial review in an analogous area of concern, see W. Kaplin, "Professional Power and Judicial Review: The Health Professions," 44 *George Washington L. Rev.* 710, 716–50 (1976).

usually brought *by* institutions seeking to assert their rights as members or prospective members of the association (see, for example, the cases in Section 8.3.2). But suits are also occasionally brought *against* institutions when the institution sponsors a chapter of, or is otherwise affiliated with, an education association in which a student, faculty member, or staff member seeks to attain or maintain membership.

In *Blatt v. University of Southern California*, 85 Cal. Rptr. 601 (Cal. Ct. App. 1970), for instance, the plaintiff was a law student who was rejected for membership in his school's chapter of the Order of the Coif, a national legal honorary society. The student challenged his rejection on grounds that he had fulfilled all the prerequisites for membership in the society. He also asserted that the denial of membership would affect his financial and professional status—that is, his ability to obtain a higher-paying job and to attain the respect and prestige that membership affords. Holding that denial of membership in such an organization is not subject to judicial review unless the denial actually prevents the individual from attaining employment in a particular occupation or from practicing a specialty, the court rejected the plaintiff's request for an order compelling his admission:

> Membership in the Order does not give a member the right to practice the profession of law. It does not signify qualification for any specialized field of practice. It has no direct bearing on the number or type of clients that the attorney-member might have or on the income he will make in his professional practice. It does not affect his basic right to earn a living. We hold that in the absence of allegations of sufficient facts of arbitrary or discriminatory action, membership in the Order is an honor best determined by those in the academic field without judicial interference. Plaintiff's allegations of arbitrary or discriminatory action on the part of the election committee are insufficient to state a cause of action. No justiciable issue has been presented [85 Cal. Rptr. at 606].

The court also determined that, under the society's rules, the fulfillment of membership prerequisites does not entitle an individual to membership but only to a consideration of his or her application. According to the court, "[t]he complaint alleges that [the plaintiff's] name was on the eligible list and did receive consideration by the election committee under the general standards set forth in the Order's constitution. This is all that the individual defendants promised. The facts pleaded do not support the alleged conclusion that there was a breach of contract."

Sec. 8.3. The College and the Accrediting Agencies

8.3.1. Overview of accrediting agencies. Among the associations with which postsecondary administrators must cope, the ones most concerned with the educational missions of institutions and programs are the educational accrediting agencies. Educational accreditation, conducted by private associations rather than by a ministry of education or other government agency, is a development unique to the United States. As the system has evolved, the private accrediting agencies have assumed an important role in the development and maintenance of standards for postsecondary education and have gained considerable influence over individual institutions and programs seeking to obtain or preserve the accreditation that only these agencies can bestow. Over the years, however, their role has sometimes been controversial and sometimes misunderstood, and debate about accreditation involving college presidents, federal and state officials, Congress, accreditation officials, and officials of other associations has been almost continuous.

This debate peaked in the early 1990s. Much of it has concerned accrediting agencies' relationships with the federal government—especially, their monitoring of schools with high student default rates under federal student aid programs (see Section 8.3.3). Other recent debate has focused on various roles and responsibilities of accrediting agencies—specifically, in promulgating standards to promote cultural diversity at accredited institutions, in monitoring academic abuses on the part of student athletes, in overseeing programs that accredited institutions sponsor in foreign countries, and in monitoring nondiscrimination and academic freedom in religiously affiliated institutions. Also debated are the composition and functions of private umbrella groups (such as the former Council on Postsecondary Accreditation) that oversee the accreditation system.

There are two types of accreditation: institutional (or "regional") accreditation and program (or specialized) accreditation. Institutional accreditation applies to the entire institution and all its programs, departments, and schools; program accreditation applies to a particular school, department, or program within the institution, such as a school of medicine or law, a department of chemistry, or a program in medical technology. Program accreditation may also apply to an entire institution if it is a free-standing, specialized institution, such as a business school or technical school, whose curriculum is all in the same program area.

Institutional accreditation is granted by six regional agencies—membership associations composed of the accredited institutions in each region. Since each regional agency covers a separate, defined part of the country, each institution is subject to the jurisdiction of only one such agency. Program accreditation is granted by a multitude of proliferating "specialized" (or "professional" or "occupational") accrediting agencies, which may or may not be membership associations and are often sponsored by the particular profession or occupation whose educational programs are being accredited. The jurisdiction of these specialized agencies is nationwide.

From 1975 until 1993, a private organization, the Council on Postsecondary Accreditation (COPA), operated a nongovernmental recognition process for both regional and specialized agencies, and served as their representative at the national level. The organization disbanded effective December 31, 1993. In the wake of COPA's announcement of dissolution, various plans emerged within the higher education and accrediting communities for a national study of the accreditation system; for a successor organization to COPA; and for separate organizations for the regional agencies, the specialized agencies, and the agencies that accredit proprietary trade and technical schools.

Being private, accrediting agencies owe their existence and legal status to state corporation law and to the common law of "voluntary" (or private) associations (see Section 8.2). Their powers are enforced through private sanctions embodied in their articles, bylaws, and rules, the primary sanctions being the withdrawal and denial of accreditation. The force of these private sanctions is greatly enhanced, however, by the extensive public and private reliance on accrediting agencies' decisions.

The federal government relies in part on these agencies to identify the institutions and programs eligible for a wide range of aid-to-education programs, particularly those administered by the U.S. Department of Education (see Section 8.3.3).

The states demonstrate their reliance on the agencies' assessments when they exempt accredited institutions or programs from various licensing or other regulatory requirements (see Section 6.3). Some states also use accreditation to determine students' or institutions' eligibility under their own state funding programs (see, for example, Fla. Stat. Ann. §§ 240.4022 and 240.605); and the state approving agencies operating under contract with the Department of Veterans Affairs depend on accreditation in approving courses for veterans' programs (38 U.S.C. § 3675(a)(2)). State professional and occupational licensing boards rely on the accrediting agencies by making graduation from an accredited school or program a prerequisite to obtaining a license to practice in the state (see, for example, Cal. Bus. & Prof. Code § 1260)). Some states also rely on an institution's accredited status in granting tax exemptions (see, for example, Idaho Code § 63-3029A and Ind. Code § 6-3-3-5(d)).

Private professional societies may use professional accreditation in determining who is eligible for membership. Students, parents, and guidance counselors may employ accreditation as one criterion in choosing a school. And postsecondary institutions themselves often rely on accreditation in determining the acceptability of transfer credits, and in determining what academic credentials will qualify persons to apply for particular academic positions. In *Merwine v. Board of Trustees for State Institutions of Higher Learning*, 754 F.2d 631 (5th Cir. 1985), for example, the court upheld the defendant's requirement that applicants for certain faculty librarian positions must hold a master's degree from a program accredited by the American Library Association.

Because of this extensive public and private reliance on accrediting agencies, postsecondary administrators usually consider it necessary to maintain both institutional and program accreditation even if they disagree with an association's standards or requirements. Consequently, administrators and counsel should prepare to deal with the multitude of agencies by understanding the legal limits on their powers, the legal leverage an institution might apply if an agency threatens denial or withdrawal of accreditation, and the legal and practical consequences to the institution and its students if the institution or one of its programs loses (or voluntarily relinquishes) its accreditation.

Despite this focus on legal rights, institutions should not regard accrediting agencies as legal adversaries; accreditation usually depends on mutual help and cooperation, and the dynamic between institution and agency can be very constructive. Institutions and programs that are willing to cooperate and expend the necessary effort usually can obtain and keep accreditation without serious threat of loss. But serious differences can and do arise, particularly with institutions that are innovating with curricula, the use of resources, or delivery systems. Such institutions may not fit neatly into accrediting standards or may otherwise be difficult for accrediting agencies to evaluate. Similarly, institutions that establish branch campuses, operate in more than one state (see Section 6.4) or in foreign countries, contract for the delivery of educational services with nonaccredited outside organizations, or sponsor off-campus or "external" degree programs may pose particular problems for accrediting agencies.[2] So may institutions organized as proprietary entities, as illustrated by

---

[2]See generally E. Kuhns and S. V. Martorana, *Toward Academic Quality Off-Campus: Monitoring Requirements of Institutional Accrediting Bodies and the States for Off-Campus, Military Base, and Study Abroad Programs* (Council on Postsecondary Accreditation, 1983).

the *Marjorie Webster* case (Section 8.3.2.1), or institutions in financial crisis, as illustrated by the cases in Section 8.3.2.6. Controversies may also arise, as they prominently did in the early 1990s, over accrediting standards regarding cultural diversity of faculty and students. When these or other circumstances involve the institution in accreditation problems, they can be critical because of accreditation's importance to the institution. Administrators should then be prepared to deal, perhaps in an adversarial way at times, with the resulting conflicts between the institution and the agency.

8.3.2. Accreditation and the courts

8.3.2.1. Formative developments. The first reported case involving the powers of accrediting agencies arose in 1938, after the North Central Association of Colleges and Secondary Schools had threatened to withdraw the accreditation of North Dakota's State Agricultural College. The state's governor sought an injunction against North Central. Using traditional legal analysis, the court denied the governor's request, reasoning that "[i]n the absence of fraud, collusion, arbitrariness, or breach of contract, . . . the decisions of such voluntary associations must be accepted in litigation before the court as conclusive" (*North Dakota v. North Central Assn. of Colleges and Secondary Schools*, 23 F. Supp. 694 (E.D. Ill.), *affirmed*, 99 F.2d 697 (7th Cir. 1938)).[3]

Another case did not arise until 1967, when Parsons College sued the North Central Association. The association had placed the college on probation in 1963 and removed it in 1965 with the stipulation that the college's accreditation status be reviewed within three years. In 1967 the association conducted a two-day site visit of the college, after which the visiting team issued a report noting that "some improvements . . . had not been realized" and that "other deficiencies persisted." After a meeting at which the college made statements and answered questions, the executive board recommended that Parsons be dropped from membership, and the association's full membership voted to accept this recommendation. The college then appealed to the board of directors, which sustained the association's decision on the basis that the college was not "providing an adequate educational program for its students, especially those of limited ability."

When the college sought to enjoin the association from implementing its disaccreditation decision, the federal district court denied its request (*Parsons College v. North Central Assn. of Colleges and Secondary Schools*, 271 F. Supp. 65 (N.D. Ill. 1967)). Reflecting traditional judicial reluctance to examine the internal affairs of private associations, the court determined that the association was not bound by the federal Constitution's due process requirements, that the association had followed its

---

[3]Like the *North Central* case, the other cases in this subsection and the rest of Section 8.3.2 involve litigation between institutions and accrediting agencies. Litigation concerning accreditation can also arise between institutions and their *students* if the students consider themselves harmed by institutional actions or inactions that prompt a denial or withdrawal of accreditation. See *Behrend v. State*, 379 N.E.2d 617 (Ohio 1977), and compare *Lidecker v. Kendall College*, 550 N.E.2d 1121 (Ill. 1990)). Cases may also be brought by students who consider themselves harmed by an institution's alleged misrepresentation of its accreditation status. See *Malone v. Academy of Court Reporting*, 582 N.E.2d 54 (Ohio 1990), and compare *Lidecker v. Kendall College* (above).

own rules in withdrawing the college's accreditation, and that it had not acted arbitrarily or violated "rudimentary due process."

Shortly after *Parsons College*, another federal court tangled with accreditation issues in the *Marjorie Webster Junior College* case. The college, a proprietary (for-profit) institution, had applied to the Middle States Association for accreditation, and the association had refused to consider the application because the college was not a nonprofit organization. After a lengthy trial, the lower court held that the nonprofit criterion was invalid under the federal antitrust laws, the "developing common law regarding exclusion from membership in private associations," and the federal Constitution's Due Process Clause (*Marjorie Webster Junior College v. Middle States Assn. of Colleges and Secondary Schools*, 302 F. Supp. 459 (D.D.C. 1969)). The lower court ordered the association to consider the college's application and to accredit the college "if it should otherwise qualify for accreditation under Middle States' standards." The appellate court reversed, finding that in the circumstances of the case the association's reason for refusing to consider the application (the proprietary character of the college) was valid (432 F.2d 650 (D.C. Cir. 1970)).

A later case, the *Marlboro Corporation* case, concerned the Emery School, a private proprietary business school operated by the Marlboro Corporation. The litigation arose from the school's efforts to have its accreditation renewed by the Accrediting Commission of the Association of Independent Colleges and Schools. During the reapplication process, an inspection team visited the school and filed a substantially negative evaluation, to which the school responded in writing. The commission ordered a temporary extension of the school's accreditation and requested the school to submit evidence of compliance with association criteria in twelve specified areas of weakness. Rather than complying, the school submitted a progress report that admitted its deficiencies and indicated its plans to correct them. Refusing to accept a letter of intent as evidence of the correction of deficiencies, the commission denied accreditation. When the school appealed, the commission held a short hearing at which the school presented its case and responded to questions, after which the commission reaffirmed its refusal to renew Emery's accreditation.

The lower court denied the school's request for an injunction requiring the association to grant accreditation, and the appellate court affirmed (*Marlboro Corp. v. Assn. of Independent Colleges and Schools*, 556 F.2d 78 (1st Cir. 1977)). The school contended that the association had violated its rights to due process under the Constitution and under common law principles and that the denial of accreditation deprived it of rights protected by the rules and regulations of the U.S. commissioner of education (see Section 8.3.3). The appellate court held that none of the school's procedural rights had been violated, that the commission's decision was not "arbitrary and capricious," because "the irregularities in Emery's financial statement alone . . . justified the commission's decision," and that the rules of the Office of Education were not violated by the association's internal appeal procedure.[4]

---

[4]The procedures and standards of this same accrediting commission were also at issue in *Rockland Institute v. Assn. of Independent Colleges and Schools*, 412 F. Supp. 1015 (C.D. Cal. 1976). In relying on both *Parsons College* and *Marjorie Webster* to reject Rockland's challenge to its disaccreditation, the court ruled that the accrediting commision followed its own rules, that the rules provided sufficient procedural due process, and that the commission's evaluative standards were neither vague nor unreasonable.

The *Parsons College, Marjorie Webster,* and *Marlboro Corporation* cases form the core of contemporary law on judicial review of accrediting decisions. Together, the cases make clear that the courts will impose some constraints on accrediting agencies in their dealings with postsecondary institutions. Though the accrediting agencies ultimately won all three cases, each court opinion suggests some limits on the authority to deny or withdraw accreditation. It is equally clear, however, that the courts still view accrediting agencies with a restrained eye and do not subject them to the full panoply of controls that state and federal governments impose on their own agencies. Though the law on accreditation is too sparse to permit a precise description of all the rights postsecondary institutions have in dealing with accrediting agencies,[5] these cases, supplemented by later developments, do provide valuable guidelines, as discussed below. Another important and most recent guideline was included in the new Part H of Title IV created by the Higher Education Amendments of 1992 (see Section 8.3.3). Under this new part, in order for the secretary to recognize their accreditation, institutions must agree to submit disputes concerning denial, withdrawal, or termination of accreditation to arbitration before filing suit in court (20 U.S.C. § 1099b(e)); and such suits, if instituted, must be brought in the appropriate federal district court (20 U.S.C. § 1099b(f)).

8.3.2.2. Common law. At the very least, it is clear that courts will require an accrediting agency to follow its own rules in withdrawing accreditation (as in *Parsons College*) or refusing to renew accreditation (as in *Marlboro Corporation*). In *Parsons* the court decided that the "law applicable to determine the propriety of the expulsion of a member from a private association is the law which he agreed to when he voluntarily chose to join the association—that is, the rules of the association itself." The court then found that the college had neither charged nor proved that the association had violated these rules. It is less clear whether courts will require an agency to follow its own rules in considering an initial application for accreditation. There is no accreditation case on this point, and some judicial pronouncements in related areas suggest that the right to be judged by the rules accrues only after the applicant has been admitted to membership or otherwise approved by the association. The better view, however, is that an applicant can also require that the agency follow its own rules.

Beyond requiring that accrediting agencies follow their own rules, the courts may also hold agencies to a variously stated standard of fairness in their dealings with members and applicants. The old *North Central Association* case, for example, highlights "fraud" and "collusion" as circumstances that would invalidate agency actions. The *North Central* case and the *Parsons* case both highlight "arbitrariness," and *Parsons* also emphasizes the failure to provide "rudimentary due process." The *Marjorie Webster* case speaks of reasonableness, evenhandedness, and consistency with "public policy" as standards; the appellate court agreed with the lower court that, under a developing exception to the general rule of judicial nonintervention in private associations' affairs, an association possessing virtual monopolistic control in an area of public concern must exercise its power reasonably, "with an even hand, and not in conflict with the public policy of the jurisdiction."

[5]For an extended analysis of judicial review in a related area of the law, which can be used to predict available rights in accreditation, see W. Kaplin, "Professional Power and Judicial Review: The Health Professions," 44 *George Washington L. Rev.* 710, 716–50 (1976).

The primary "fairness" requirement seems to be that the agency must provide institutions with procedural due process before denying, withdrawing, or refusing to renew their accreditation. The institution appears to have a right to receive notice that its accreditation is being questioned, to know why, and to be heard on the question. *Parsons College* provides useful analysis of the extent of these protections.

In *Parsons* the college argued that the association's action should be invalidated, even though consistent with its own rules, if the action was "contrary to rudimentary due process or grounded in arbitrariness." Without admitting that such a legal standard applied to accrediting agencies, the court did analyze the association's action under this common law standard. The court defined rudimentary due process to include (1) an adequate opportunity to be heard, (2) a notice of the proceedings, (3) a notice of the specific charges, (4) sufficiently definite standards of evaluation, and (5) substantively adequate reasons for the decision. After reviewing the entire process by which the association reached its disaccreditation decision, the court concluded that "the college has failed to establish a violation of the commands of any of the several rules."

The court found that the college had been afforded the opportunity to speak and be heard at almost every stage of the proceedings and that the opportunity afforded was adequate for the type of proceeding involved:

> The nature of the hearing, if required by rudimentary due process, may properly be adjusted to the nature of the issue to be decided. In this case, the issue was not innocence but excellence. Procedures appropriate to decide whether a specific act of plain misconduct was committed are not suited to an expert evaluation of educational quality. . . .
>
> Here, no trial-type hearing, with confrontation, cross-examination, and assistance of counsel, would have been suited to the resolution of the issues to be decided. The question was not principally a matter of historical fact, but rather of the application of a standard of quality in a field of recognized expertise [271 F. Supp. at 72–73].

The court further found that the college had ample notice of the proceedings because "after a long history of questionable status, the visit of the examining team was adequate notice without more."

The requirement of specific charges was satisfied by the examining team's report given to the college. The court found that this report, "supplemented by the evidence produced by the college itself, contained all the information on which all subsequent decisions were made. No fuller disclosure could have been made."

The court also found the evaluative standards of the association to be sufficiently definite to inform the school of what was expected of it. Disagreeing with the college's claim that the standards were "so vague as to be unintelligible to men of ordinary intelligence," the court reasoned as follows:

> The standards of accreditation are not guides for the layman but for professionals in the field of education. Definiteness may prove, in another view, to be arbitrariness. The association was entitled to make a conscious choice in favor of flexible standards to accommodate variation in purpose and character among its constituent institutions, and to avoid forcing all into a rigid and uniform mold [271 F. Supp. at 73].

In contrast to the procedural aspects of accrediting activities, an agency's substantive decisions and standards will receive very limited review. Courts are familiar with problems of procedural fairness, and are well equipped to resolve them, but they do not have experience and expertise in evaluating educational quality. The *Parsons* court used this distinction in determining that the accrediting agency had not violated the last of the five due process rules set out above:

> In this field, the courts are traditionally even more hesitant to intervene. The public benefits of accreditation, dispensing information and exposing misrepresentation, would not be enhanced by judicial intrusion. Evaluation by the peers of the college, enabled by experience to make comparative judgments, will best serve the paramount interest in the highest practicable standards in higher education. The price for such benefits is inevitably some injury to those who do not meet the measure, and some risk of conservatism produced by appraisals against a standard of what has already proven valuable in education [271 F. Supp. at 74].

The *Marjorie Webster* appeals court also relied on the distinction between procedures and substantive decisions. To this court, the scope of judicial review depends on the amount of "deference" that courts should accord accrediting agencies, and this deference varies "both with the subject matter at issue and with the degree of harm resulting from the association's action." Since the issue in *Marjorie Webster* concerned the accrediting agency's "substantive standards," the appellate court accorded more deference to the agency than it would if the issue were "the fairness of the procedures by which the challenged determination was reached." Having thus weighed the "subject matter" and the "degree of harm," the court concluded that "substantial deference" should be accorded the association's judgment "regarding the ends that it serves and the means most appropriate to those ends."

The appellate court then considered the association's nonprofit criterion, which was based on the assumption that the profit motive is inconsistent with educational quality. The lower court had held that that assumption "is not supported by the evidence and is unwarranted." The appellate court "neither disregard[ed] nor disbelieve[d] the extensive testimony . . . regarding the values and benefits" of proprietary institutions. But in light of the substantial deference it accorded the association in setting its criteria for accreditation, the appellate court held that it had not "been shown to be unreasonable for [the association] to conclude that the desire for personal profit might influence educational goals in subtle ways difficult to detect but destructive, in the long run, of that atmosphere of academic inquiry which . . . [the association's] standards for accreditation seek to foster."

The recent case of *Wilfred Academy et al. v. Southern Assn. of Colleges and Schools*, 738 F. Supp. 200 (S.D. Tex. 1990), *reversed and vacated*, 957 F.2d 210 (5th Cir. 1992), illustrates the complexities that may arise when the common law concepts of fairness, developed in the above cases, are applied to accrediting agency decisions. Six cosmetology schools challenged a decision made by SACS, a regional accrediting agency, and COEI (Commission on Occupation Education Institutions), an independent branch of SACS, to withdraw their accreditation. The district court held that, although it would give "great deference to the expertise of the accrediting agency," such agencies nevertheless have an implied "duty of good faith and fair dealing" that arises from the "special relationship of trust and confidence" between an agency and its member schools. This special relationship "results from the tremendous disparity of bargaining power in favor of the accrediting agency and from the fact that loss of accreditation can deprive a school of the opportunity to participate in governmental programs, such as federal financial aid." The duty of good faith and fair dealing is breached whenever an accrediting agency violates fundamental "fairness," which in turn requires that accrediting decisions be "reasonable," not "arbitrary," and "supported by substantial evidence." Applying these standards, the district court determined that, in processing their charges against the plaintiff schools, the defendants utilized procedures that violated fundamental fairness in three ways:

> First, the Plaintiffs were faced with vague and general charges and were given no notice of the factual bases of the charges. Second, on several occasions COEI and SACS failed to communicate with the Schools through the appropriate channels. When COEI and SACS did provide information—often only when the Schools initiated the contact—that information was repeatedly confusing or contradictory. When the Schools admitted their understandable confusion, they were accused of feigning innocence and of refusal to cooperate with COEI. Third, the Plaintiffs were prevented by SACS from taking the corrective actions that SACS demanded by the charges, and SACS incorrectly interpreted the Schools' attempts to comply with SACS' rules and suggestions as attempts to circumvent SACS' authority [738 F. Supp. at 208].

In addition, the district court determined that the defendants failed to present "substantial evidence" that the plaintiffs had violated any of the defendants' accreditation standards. Therefore, the court enjoined the defendants from implementing their decision to withdraw the plaintiffs' accreditation.

On appeal in the *Wilfred Academy* case, the court reviewed the lower court's fact-findings and the degree of deference it had accorded the accrediting agency's judgments, concluding that its "findings wholly disregard the deference due to the association's accrediting decisions" and that "[s]ubstantial evidence supports COEI's decision to withdraw accreditation. . . ." Considering the judicial role in cases like this, and focusing primarily on judicial review of an agency's *substantive* judgments, the appellate court commented:

> Federal courts have consistently limited their review of decisions of accrediting associations to whether the decisions were "arbitrary and unreasonable" and whether they were supported by "substantial evidence." See, e.g., *Medical Institute of Minnesota v. National Ass'n of Trade and Technical Sch.*, 817 F.2d 1310, 1314 (8th Cir. 1987); *Rockland Inst. v. Association of Indep. Colleges and Sch.*, 412 F. Supp. 1015, 1016 (C.D. Cal. 1976). . . .
>
> In reviewing an accrediting association's decision to withdraw a member's accreditation, the courts have accorded the association's determination great deference. *Medical Inst. of Minnesota*, 817 F.2d at 1314; *Marjorie Webster Junior College, Inc. v. Middle States Ass'n of Colleges and Secondary Sch.*, 432 F.2d 650, 657 (D.C. Cir. 1970). Courts give accrediting associations such deference because of the professional judgment these associations must necessarily employ in making accreditation decisions. In considering the substance of accrediting agencies' rules, courts have recognized that "[t]he standards of accreditation are not guides for the layman but for professionals in the field of education." *Parsons College*

v. North Cent. Ass'n of Colleges and Secondary Sch., 271 F. Supp. 65, 73 (N.D. Ill. 1967). Consequently, courts are not free to conduct a *de novo* review or to substitute their judgment for the professional judgment of the educators involved in the accreditation process. *Medical Inst. of Minnesota,* 817 F.2d at 1315; *Rockland Inst.,* 412 F. Supp. at 1019. Instead, courts focus primarily on whether the accrediting body's internal rules provide a fair and impartial procedure and whether it has followed its rules in reaching its decision [957 F.2d at 214].

8.3.2.3. The U.S. Constitution. A number of cases have considered whether accrediting agency decisions are "state action" subject to the federal Constitution (see Section 1.5.2). The court in *Parsons College* rejected the college's claim that the association must comply with the due process requirements of the federal Constitution, reasoning that "the association stands on the same footing as any private corporation" and is not subject to "the constitutional limits applicable to government" (see Section 1.5). The lower court in the *Marlboro Corporation* case (416 F. Supp. 958, 959 (D. Mass. 1976)) also rejected the state action argument. On the other hand, the lower court in *Marjorie Webster* accepted the state action argument; and the appellate courts in *Marjorie Webster* and in *Marlboro Corporation* assumed, without deciding, that the accrediting agency was engaged in state action.

The appeals court in *Marjorie Webster,* in holding that the association's non-profit criterion was not unreasonable and therefore was valid, in fact engaged in a constitutional due process analysis. The lower court had found that the association's accreditation activities were "quasi-governmental" and thus could be considered "state action" subject to federal constitutional restraints. The appeals court then "assume[d] without deciding" that state action did exist. Thus, unlike the court in *Parsons College,* which specifically rejected the state action argument, the lower court in *Marjorie Webster* accepted the argument, and the appellate court left the question unanswered.

The appellate court in *Marlboro Corporation* considered whether the accrediting commission's procedures should be scrutinized under common law due process standards or under the more exacting standards of the U.S. Constitution's Due Process Clause. The lower court had held that the Constitution did not apply because the commission's action was not "state action." The court of appeals, however, found it unnecessary to decide this "close question," since, "even assuming that constitutional due process applies," none of the Emery School's procedural rights had been violated. To reach this conclusion, the appellate court did review the commission's procedures under the constitutional standard, stating that "under either constitutional or common law standards . . . procedural fairness is a flexible concept" to be considered case by case. The court held that "due process did not . . . require a full-blown adversary hearing in this context." It noted that the commission's inquiry concerned a routine reapplication for accreditation and was "broadly evaluative" rather than an accusatory inquiry with specific charges. "Emery was given ample opportunity to present its position by written submission and to argue it orally," and more formalized proceedings would have imposed too heavy a burden on the commission.

The court then considered Emery's claim that the decision to deny accreditation was tainted by bias because the chairman of the accrediting commission was the president of a school in direct competition with Emery. While it emphasized that a "decision by an impartial tribunal is an element of due process under any standard," the court found that the chairman took no part in the discussion or vote on Emery's application and in fact did not chair, or participate in, the December hearing. Recognizing the "local realities"—the prolonged evaluation process, the large number of people participating in the decision at various levels, and the commission's general practice of allowing interested commissioners to remain present without participating—the court viewed the question as "troublesome" but concluded that "Emery has [not] shown sufficient actual or apparent impropriety."

Although more recent cases continue to reflect a split in opinion, the weight of authority may be shifting against state action. In *Medical Institute of Minnesota v. National Assn. of Trade and Technical Schools*, 817 F.2d 1310 (8th Cir. 1987), for example, the court rejected the school's claim that the accrediting agency's decision denying reaccreditation was state (or federal) action subject to federal constitutional constraints. The school's argument relied heavily on the rationale of the district court in the *Marjorie Webster* case, but the *Medical Institute* court determined that this rationale has been undermined by two post–*Marjorie Webster* decisions of the U.S. Supreme Court: *Rendell-Baker v. Kohn* (Section 1.5.2) and *Blum v. Yaretsky*, 102 S. Ct. 2777 (1982). In *St. Agnes Hospital v. Riddick*, 668 F. Supp. 478 (D. Md. 1987), further proceedings in 748 F. Supp. 319 (D. Md. 1990), however, a federal district court distinguished the *Medical Institute* case and held that the Accreditation Council for Graduate Medical Education (ACGME) (of which defendant Riddick was chairman) had engaged in state action when it withdrew accreditation from the plaintiff's residency program in obstetrics and gynecology. The court relied on state regulations requiring that applicants for medical licensure must have at least one year of postgraduate clinical training in a program that meets "standards equivalent to those established by" ACGME. Under this regulatory scheme, according to the court, the state had delegated its authority to ACGME, and there was a direct nexus (see Section 1.5.2) between this delegation and the accreditation action challenged by the plaintiff.

In a similar case against ACGME, a different federal district court reached the same result, but the appellate court reversed (*McKeesport Hospital v. Accreditation Council for Graduate Medical Education*, 24 F.3d 519 (3d Cir. 1994)). Relying on the Supreme Court's decisions in *Rendell-Baker* and *Blum* and its later decision in the *Tarkanian* case (see Section 8.4.1), and following the *Medical Institute* case, the appellate court concluded that ACGME had not engaged in state action when it withdrew accreditation from the plaintiff's general surgery residency program. According to the two-judge majority:

> The district court concluded that the Board delegated its duties to the ACGME, thereby rendering the ACGME's actions fairly attributable to the state. We cannot agree. . . . [U]nder the [Pennsylvania Medical Practice] Act the state Board remains ultimately responsible for approving medical training facilities in Pennsylvania. Cf. *Tarkanian*, 488 U.S. at 195–98. . . . Merely because the state Board deems its obligation met by following the ACGME's accreditation decisions does not imbue the ACGME with the authority of the state nor does it shift the responsibility from the state Board to the ACGME. The Board remains the state actor. . . .
>
> The district court also found the connection between the state Board and the ACGME sufficient to turn the latter into a state actor. We must disagree. Sometimes, a state and an ostensibly private entity are so interdependent that state action will be found from their symbiotic relationship alone. . . . The ACGME's

relationship to the state is clearly distinguishable. The ACGME is self-governed and financed, and its standards are independently set; the state Board simply recognizes and relies upon its expertise.

Alternatively, a connection between the state and a specific decision of a private entity may render that decision chargeable to the state. . . . Under this approach, however, state action will be found only "when [the state] has exercised coercive power or has provided such significant encouragement, either overt or covert, that the [private decision] must in law be deemed that of the State"[;] "mere approval of or acquiesence in" the decision is not enough. *Blum*, 457 U.S. at 1004. . . . The required state coercion or encouragement of the ACGME's actions is not present here.

. . . The Board . . . does not control or regulate the ACGME's standard-setting or decision-making processes. Although it recognizes them, state law does not dictate or influence those actions. Rather, the ACGME's decisions are "judgments made by private parties according to . . . standards that are not established by the State." *Blum*, 457 U.S. at 1008 [24 F.3d at 524–25].

A third judge disagreed with the majority's reasoning but concurred in the result because, in his view, ACGME had provided the plaintiff all the due process that the federal Constitution would require. In a separate opinion—whose analysis appears to be more sound than the majority's—this judge distinguished the *Medical Institute* case and relied on *Riddick* in concluding that ACGME's action was state action (24 F.3d at 526–29; Becker, J., concurring).

Although Supreme Court cases such as *Rendell-Baker* have narrowed the state action concept, and although a trend against state action findings may be developing in the more recent accreditation cases, there still appears to be sound ground for judicial state action determinations in some delegation-of-authority cases, such as *McKeesport Hospital*. Moreover, a recent federal statutory development may tip the scales in favor of judicial findings of state action in some cases. In the Higher Education Amendments of 1992, Congress established new requirements that accrediting agencies must meet if they wish to obtain or retain recognition from the U.S. secretary of education (see Section 8.3.3). These requirements include specific and detailed responsibilities that accrediting agencies must undertake with respect to institutions' participation in Title IV student aid programs. (See 59 Fed. Reg. 22250–22251 (Apr. 29, 1994), which summarizes the new relationships between the secretary and the accrediting agencies.) In performing these responsibilities, accrediting agencies are obligated to accept and use default rate data, audit reports, program reviews, and other data that the secretary provides to them. These new responsibilities could strengthen state action arguments such as those used by the district court in *Marjorie Webster*, thus supporting claims that an accrediting agency recognized by the secretary of education is engaged in state (federal) action when it evaluates, and denies or revokes, the accreditation of an institution because of its failures in operating Title IV student aid programs.

8.3.2.4. Antitrust law. Federal or state antitrust law may sometimes also protect postsecondary institutions from certain accrediting actions that interfere with an institution's ability to compete with other institutions.

In responding to the plaintiff's antitrust claims in *Marjorie Webster*, the appellate court held that the "proscriptions of the Sherman Act were 'tailored for the business world' [*Eastern Railroad Presidents' Conference v. Noerr Motor Freight*, 365

U.S. 127, 141 (1961)], not for the noncommercial aspects of the liberal arts and the learned professions." The court also noted that, since the "process of accreditation is an activity distinct from the sphere of commerce," going "rather to the heart of the concept of education," an accreditation decision would violate the Act only if undertaken with "an intent or purpose to affect the commercial aspects of the profession." Since no such "commercial motive" had been shown, the association's action did not constitute a combination or conspiracy in restraint of the college's trade.

Subsequently, the antitrust approach was broadened and strengthened by the U.S. Supreme Court's decision in *Goldfarb v. Virginia State Bar*, 421 U.S. 773 (1975), the first case in which the Court clearly approved the applicability of federal antitrust law (Section 7.2.13) to professional associations. The application of these laws to accreditation was further strengthened by two Supreme Court cases following *Goldfarb*. In *National Society of Professional Engineers v. United States*, 435 U.S. 679 (1978), the Court reaffirmed its *Goldfarb* determination that the standard-setting activities of nonprofit professional associations are subject to scrutiny under antitrust laws. The Court then invalidated the society's ethical canon prohibiting members of the society from submitting competitive bids for engineering services. In *American Society of Mechanical Engineers v. Hydrolevel Corp.*, 102 S. Ct. 1935 (1982), the Court again subjected a nonprofit professional association to antitrust liability arising from its standard-setting activities. Going beyond *Goldfarb* and *National Society of Professional Engineers*, the Court held that a professional organization can be liable for the anticompetitive acts of its members and other agents, including unpaid volunteers, if the agents had "apparent authority" to act (see this volume, Section 2.1). The characteristics of the ASME that subjected it to antitrust liability are similar to those that could be attributed to accrediting agencies:

> ASME contends it should not bear the risk of loss for antitrust violations committed by its agents acting with apparent authority because it is a nonprofit organization, not a business seeking profit. But it is beyond debate that nonprofit organizations can be held liable under the antitrust laws.
>
> Although ASME may not operate for profit, it does derive benefits from its codes, including the fees the society receives for its code-related publications and services, the prestige the codes bring to the society, the influence they permit ASME to wield, and the aid the standards provide the profession of mechanical engineering. Since the antitrust violation in this case could not have occurred without ASME's codes and ASME's method of administering them, it is not unfitting that ASME will be liable for the damages arising from that violation (see W. Prosser, *Law of Torts* 459 (4th ed. 1971); W. Seavey, *Law of Agency* §83 (1964)). Furthermore, ASME is in the best position to take precautions that will prevent future antitrust violations. Thus, the fact that ASME is a nonprofit organization does not weaken the force of the antitrust and agency principles that indicate that ASME should be liable for Hydrolevel's antitrust injuries [102 S. Ct. at 1947–48].

See C. Chambers, "Implications of the *Hydrolevel* Decision for Postsecondary Accrediting Associations," 7 *Accreditation* no. 2 (Council on Postsecondary Accreditation, Summer 1982).

As these decisions clearly indicate, federal antitrust law can be a meaningful source of rights for postsecondary institutions, as well as their students and faculty, if they are harmed by accrediting activities that can be characterized as anticompetitive. Such rights may be asserted not only against decisions to deny, terminate, or condition an institution's accreditation, as in *Marjorie Webster,* but also against other activities undertaken by accrediting agencies or their agents in the process of fashioning and applying standards.

However, although antitrust laws clearly *apply* to such activities, that does not mean such activities, or any substantial portion of them, will *violate* antitrust laws. In *Zavaletta v. American Bar Assn.,* 721 F. Supp. 96 (E.D. Va. 1989), for example, students at an unaccredited law school sued the American Bar Association, claiming that its accrediting activities constituted an unreasonable restraint of trade under the Sherman Act (this volume, Section 7.2.13). The court did not dispute that the Act applied to the ABA's accrediting activities, but it nevertheless held that these "activities impose no restraint on trade, unreasonable or otherwise." Rather, according to the court, "the ABA merely expresses its educated opinion . . . about the quality of the school's program"—an expression protected by the First Amendment. Although the ABA communicates these opinions to state courts that control bar admissions, the resulting restraint on an unaccredited law school is caused by the independent actions of state courts in determining who may sit for the bar exam, not by the ABA's accreditation activities as such. (For a more recent controversy regarding ABA accreditation and the antitrust laws, see C. Leatherman, "Rebellion Brews in Tight-Knit World of Law Accreditation," *Chron. Higher Educ.,* June 1, 1994, A14.)

8.3.2.5. Defamation law. The first application of defamation law (Sections 2.3.1.2 and 4.13.4) to accrediting agencies and officials occurred in *Avins v. White,* 627 F.2d 637 (3d Cir. 1980). The plaintiff was a school official who alleged that he had been defamed by an accrediting official in the course of a site inspection. The case arose from the efforts of the Delaware Law School (DLS) to gain provisional American Bar Association accreditation. ABA accreditation is particularly important for law schools because in most states an individual must have graduated from an ABA-accredited school before he or she can take the state bar examination.

After a series of accreditation inspections of DLS, the then dean of DLS (Avins) sued the ABA consultant (White) who had participated in two of the inspections. The dean alleged three counts of defamation. The first two counts were based on statements in the reports of the inspection team; the third was based on remarks that the consultant had made to the dean at a luncheon meeting while they were in the presence of a third party (a Judge DiBona). The dean prevailed at a trial in federal district court, and the jury awarded him $50,000 in compensatory damages.

On appeal, the U.S. Court of Appeals for the Third Circuit considered each of the three defamation counts separately. Regarding the first two counts, the court held that the statements in the inspection team's reports could not be considered to have defamed the dean. The statements in the first report, according to the court, were not based on fact but were expressions of "pure opinion." Such expressions cannot be defamatory, because "ideas themselves," unlike their underlying facts, "cannot be false." The statements in the second report, according to the court, referred to the school rather than to the dean personally and therefore could not have defamed him. Thus, instead of submitting the first two counts to the jury, the district judge should have ruled the statements nondefamatory as a matter of law. The appellate court therefore reversed the district court's judgment on the first two counts.

The third count presented different problems. The appellate court ruled that the luncheon remarks cited in this count "may have been potentially defamatory." The consultant argued, however, that because of his role in the accreditation process, he possessed a "qualified privilege" to make the luncheon remarks, which addressed matters regarding the accreditation inspection. Neither the appellate court nor the dean disputed that the consultant could possess such a qualified privilege. The issue, rather, was whether the consultant had abused the privilege by making his remarks in the presence of the third party (Judge DiBona), who was not an official of the law school. The appellate court held that this issue was one for the jury, that the district judge had properly instructed the jury on when it could consider the qualified privilege to be abused, and that "the jury quite properly could have rejected the defense."

The appellate court could not determine whether the jury had actually found the luncheon remarks to be defamatory, however, since the district judge had submitted all three defamation counts to the jury as a package; it was "therefore impossible to determine whether the jury had based its verdict on all three allegedly defamatory statements or on only one or two of the incidents. Because of this technical complexity, the appellate court also reversed the district court's judgment on the third count and remanded the case to the district court for a new trial on that count only.

One critical issue then remained: the "standard of proof" the dean had to meet in order to sustain a defamation claim against the consultant. Although the issue applied to all three counts, the appellate court needed to address it only with respect to the third count, which it was remanding for a new trial. The consultant argued that the dean was a "public figure" for purposes of this lawsuit and therefore had to meet a higher standard of proof than that required for ordinary defamation claims. The district court had rejected this argument.

In a series of cases beginning with *New York Times v. Sullivan*, 376 U.S. 254 (1964), the U.S. Supreme Court formulated a "public-figure" doctrine in order to ensure that certain speakers' free speech rights would not be unduly chilled by the fear of defamation suits. To prevail on a defamation claim, a public figure must prove "actual malice" on the part of the defendant—that is, the plaintiff must prove that the defendant had made the statement with a knowledge of its falsity or with a reckless disregard for the truth. The appellate court determined that the dean was a public figure within the meaning of these Supreme Court precedents, thus overruling the district court's determination on the standard of proof to which the dean was subject:

> The [U.S. Supreme] Court in *Gertz* [*v. Robert Welch, Inc.*, 418 U.S. 323 (1974)] gave a description of who may be a public figure:
>
>> For the most part, those who attain [public-figure] status have assumed roles of especial prominence in the affairs of society. Some occupy positions of such persuasive power and influence that they are deemed public figures for all purposes. More commonly, those classed as public figures have thrust themselves to the forefront of particular controversies in order to influence the resolution of the issues involved. In either event, they invite attention and comment.
>
> The *Gertz* test envisions basically two types of public figures: (1) those who are public figures for *all* purposes; and (2) those who are public figures only in the context of a particular public controversy. . . .
>
> We have no difficulty in concluding that Avins is not a public figure for

all purposes, under the first part of the *Gertz* test. Although Avins was apparently well known in legal academic circles, we do not believe he possessed the fame and notoriety in the public eye necessary to make him a public figure for all purposes. This leaves the question whether Avins is a public figure in the limited context of the DLS accreditation struggle. We must accordingly consider whether (1) the DLS accreditation struggle was a public controversy and (2) if so, whether Avins voluntarily injected himself into that controversy.

Although DLS was formed and operated as a purely private law school, its success or failure was of importance to the Delaware State Bar as well as to any individual interested in attending an accredited law school in Delaware. It is the only law school in the State of Delaware. Accreditation of DLS would create a new source of attorneys who could qualify to take the Delaware Bar examinations and be admitted to practice in the state. Furthermore, a majority of DLS students were from out of state. Thus, DLS's accreditation would also affect the interests of students from a variety of locales and admission to state bars outside of Delaware.

Further, there is evidence in the record that mass meetings were held and that individuals from other states concerned about DLS visited the school. The local news media, as well as the Delaware Bar Association, publicized the events surrounding DLS's formation and struggle for accreditation. . . .

We therefore hold that DLS's accreditation was a legitimate public controversy within the meaning of *Gertz*. . . .

We have no difficulty in concluding that Avins voluntarily injected himself into the controversy surrounding DLS's accreditation. As creator, chief architect, and the first dean of DLS, Avins spearheaded its drive toward accreditation. Indeed, the first major hurdle which Avins had to surmount in behalf of DLS was accreditation. The record reveals that from the outset Avins, as dean, was actively involved in every facet of the accreditation struggle. He, in fact, invited the first three accreditation teams to inspect DLS, and he personally presented DLS's case before the Council and Accreditation Committee. . . .

It was Avins who, as dean of DLS, officially requested, invited, and affirmatively invoked the accreditation process of the American Bar Association. We therefore conclude that Avins played an affirmative and aggressive role in the accreditation process and that he was a public figure for that limited purpose [627 F.2d at 646-48].

The court justified this extension of the public-figure doctrine to the accreditation context by relying on the nature of the accreditation process itself:

We believe the importance of the accreditation process underscores the need for extension of the *New York Times* privilege to a private individual criticizing a public figure in the course of commenting on matters germane to accreditation. An accreditation evaluation by its nature is critical; the applicant school invites critical comments in seeking accreditation. In order to succeed, individuals involved in the accreditation process need to be assured that they may frankly and openly discuss accreditation matters. White, in criticizing Avins at the luncheon, was expressing a candid view of Avins' conduct during the accreditation process. To require an individual like White to insure the accuracy of his comments on accreditation matters would undoubtedly lead to self-censorship, which will jeopardize the efficacy and integrity of the accreditation process itself. Since the public is vitally affected by accreditation of educational institutions, we believe that self-censorship in the accreditation process would detrimentally affect an area of significant social importance [627 F.2d at 648–49].

Avins v. White thus provides additional insight into how courts view the accreditation process. The case affirms the societal importance of the process and underscores the need for courts to provide enough legal running room for accreditation to accomplish its societal purposes. More specifically, the case illustrates the steps administrators and counsel should take and the issues they will encounter in analyzing defamation claims in the accreditation context. The plaintiff's initial victory at trial suggests that defamation law can be a very real source of legal protection for institutions and their officials, and of legal liability for accrediting agencies and their officials. But the appellate court's reversal provides a mellowing effect: defamation law will not be applied so strictly that it discourages the candid criticism necessary to accreditation's success; and, when the institutional official allegedly defamed is a "public figure," defamation law will provide a remedy against accrediting agencies only in cases of malicious misconduct.

8.3.2.6. Bankruptcy law. On occasion, an accredited institution may file for bankruptcy. Such an action does not protect the institution from an accrediting agency seeking to withdraw the institution's accreditation. The federal Bankruptcy Code (see Section 4.3.7.1), as amended by the Omnibus Reconciliation Act of 1990 (104 Stat. 1388 (1991)), makes clear that the "accreditation status . . . of the debtor as an educational institution" is not considered to be property subject to the bankruptcy laws (11 U.S.C. § 541(b)(3)); and that the automatic stay provision, which prohibits others from obtaining possession or control of the debtor's property, does not apply to "any action by an accrediting agency regarding the accreditation status of the debtor as an educational institution" (11 U.S.C. § 362(b)).

These Bankruptcy Code amendments adopt and apply nationwide the holding in *In re Nasson College,* 80 Bankr. Rptr. 600 (D. Me. 1988), in which a college in bankruptcy sought an injunction ordering the New England Association of Schools and Colleges to restore its accreditation. The college had filed for bankruptcy and then ceased to offer educational programs, after which the accrediting agency had terminated the college's accreditation. The college argued that its accreditation was property included in the bankruptcy estate and that the agency's action therefore violated the Bankruptcy Code's automatic stay provision (11 U.S.C. § 362(a)(3)). The court rejected the college's argument, ruling that accreditation is not property but "[a] status . . . held in the nature of a trust for the [accrediting agency] and the public" (80 Bankr. Rptr. at 604).[6] See also, for a similar case, *In re Draughon Training Institute,* 119 Bankr. Rptr. 927 (W.D. La. 1990).

Given the thrust of the Bankruptcy Code amendments and the *In re Nasson College* case, it is apparently also clear that a debtor institution cannot resort to the "executory contract" provision of the Bankruptcy Code (11 U.S.C. § 365), which al-

---

[6]The college also argued that the termination of accreditation violated Section 525(a) of the Bankruptcy Code, which prohibits "governmental unit(s)" from discriminating against debtors in bankruptcy. The court rejected this argument as well, holding that the defendant was not a "governmental unit" for purposes of Section 525(a) and that the termination occurred because the college had ceased offering programs, not because it had become a debtor in bankruptcy.

lows debtors to continue performance under certain of its contracts, in order to protect its accreditation. *In re Statefield Oil Construction, Inc., d/b/a Golden State School,* 134 Bankr. Rptr. 399 (E.D. Cal. 1991), the bankruptcy court held that the bankruptcy amendments quoted above preclude a debtor from claiming that its accredited status constitutes an executory contract with the accrediting agency and an asset protected by 11 U.S.C. § 365. See M. Pelesh, "Accreditation and Bankruptcy: The Death of Executory Contract," 71 *West's Educ. Law Rptr.* 975 (Mar. 12, 1992). The *Golden State* litigation apparently closes the last possible door through which an accredited institution might have used bankruptcy laws as a shield to protect its accreditation during difficult financial times.

8.3.3. Accreditation and the U.S. Department of Education. The Department of Education (ED) plays an important and sometimes controversial role in the accrediting process. Various federal aid-to-education statutes specify accreditation "by a nationally recognized accrediting agency or association" as a prerequisite to eligibility for aid for the institution or its students (see, for example, the Higher Education Act of 1965, 20 U.S.C. § 1141(a)(5)). These provisions authorize or require the secretary of education to "publish a list of nationally recognized accrediting agencies or associations which he determines . . . to be reliable authority as to the quality of education or training offered." Most postsecondary institutions and programs attain eligibility for federal funds by obtaining accreditation from one of the accrediting bodies recognized by the secretary.

Major changes in the secretary's authority regarding accrediting agencies, and in the role that the agencies play in the determination of federal aid eligibility, were effected by the Higher Education Amendments of 1992 (Pub. L. No. 102-325, 106 Stat. 448 (1992), codified at 20 U.S.C. § 1101 et seq.), adding a new Part H to Title IV of the Higher Education Act (Pub. L. No. 102-325, § 499, 106 Stat. at 634, codified at 20 U.S.C. §§ 1099a to 1099-c-1). This new part, for the first time, establishes statutory standards that the secretary must follow in reviewing and "recognizing" accrediting agencies whose decisions the secretary will use in certifying institutions' eligibility to participate in the federal student aid programs authorized under Title IV of the Higher Education Act (see this volume, Section 4.3.2). Under these standards, the secretary must ensure that recognized agencies meet a number of specific eligibility criteria, undertake certain specific responsibilities, and employ certain operating procedures (106 Stat. 641, 20 U.S.C. § 1099b(a)).

Most specifically, these standards require that recognized agencies, when reviewing an institution's accreditation, must consider its default rates for Title IV student loan programs and its compliance with Title IV program responsibilities. In addition, the 1992 amendments require that agencies be autonomous of related trade associations or membership organizations (20 U.S.C. § 1099b(1)) and that individuals representing the general public serve on the governing boards of accrediting agencies (106 Stat. 644, 20 U.S.C. § 1099b(b)(2)) (one public member for every six board members). The 1992 amendments also require accrediting agencies to follow specified due process procedures in the accreditation process (106 Stat. 643, 20 U.S.C. § 1099b(a)(6)).

The 1992 amendments also establish a new role for the states, complementing that of the accrediting agencies (106 Stat. 637, 20 U.S.C. § 1099a-3). When the secretary has determined, pursuant to statutory criteria, that an institution has potential for misusing its Title IV funds, a state entity must review that institution, using yet another set of statutory criteria. State agencies performing this function, however, must contract with an "appropriate approved accrediting agency or association . . . or another peer review system" to review the quality of the institution's academic courses and programs (106 Stat. 640, 20 U.S.C. § 1099a-3(d)(15)).

Although accreditation by a recognized agency is the predominant means for obtaining eligibility to participate in federal aid programs, an alternative means for attaining eligibility is often provided. The primary one is a "preaccreditation status," under which an unaccredited institution or program may be eligible for funds if the secretary of education determines that there is "satisfactory assurance" or "reasonable assurance" that it will meet the accreditation standards of a nationally recognized agency within a reasonable time (see, for example, 20 U.S.C. § 1141(a)(5), 42 U.S.C. § 298b(6)). Approval by a recognized state agency is also an alternative available to public vocational education programs and to nursing programs under the student financial aid programs. Such alternatives generally are not available to proprietary institutions participating in federal student loan programs; these institutions must be accredited by a nationally recognized accrediting agency in order to be eligible. (See generally 34 C.F.R. §§ 600.4 to 600.6.)

The secretary of education periodically publishes in the *Federal Register* a list of nationally recognized accrediting agencies and associations; the secretary also publishes a list of recognized state agencies that approve public vocational education programs (see 20 U.S.C. § 1085(c)(4)) and a list of recognized state agencies for approval of nursing education (see 42 U.S.C. § 298b(6)). The secretary's criteria and procedures for recognition are also published in the *Federal Register* and codified in the *Code of Federal Regulations* at 34 C.F.R. Parts 602 and 603. The secretary amended the Part 602 regulations in 1988 (53 Fed. Reg. 25088 (July 1, 1988)) and amended them again in 1994 (59 Fed. Reg. 22250 (Apr. 29, 1994)) to implement the new statutory requirements set out in the Higher Education Amendments of 1992 (see above). The 1994 amendments to the regulations, like the earlier draft bills in Congress, were quite controversial and attracted widespread attention in the higher education community (see J. Zook, "Despite Changes, Accrediting Rules Still Trouble College Officials," *Chron. Higher Educ.*, May 25, 1994, A27).

Periodically, the secretary publishes a pamphlet containing a current list of recognized agencies, the criteria and procedures for listing, and background information on accreditation.[7] The listing process and other aspects of institutional eligibility for federal aid are administered within the Department of Education by the Accrediting Agency Evaluation Branch, part of the Higher Education Management Services Directorate of the Office of Postsecondary Education. A National Advisory Committee on Institutional Quality and Integrity assists the secretary in the recognition process.

To be included in the secretary's list of nationally recognized agencies, an agency must apply to the secretary for recognition and must meet the secretary's

---

[7]U.S. Department of Education, *Nationally Recognized Accrediting Agencies and Associations: Criteria and Procedures for Listing by the U.S. Secretary of Education and Current List* (periodic editions). The pamphlet may be obtained from the Accrediting Agency Evaluation Branch, Higher Education Management Services Directorate, Office of Postsecondary Education, U.S. Department of Education, Washington, DC 20202.

criteria for recognition. Agencies are reevaluated and their listings renewed or terminated at least once every five years (34 C.F.R. § 602.13(e)(2)). The criteria for recognition concern such matters as the agency's organization and membership, its administrative and fiscal capacities, its experience and its national acceptance by pertinent constituencies, its standards and procedures, its mechanisms for evaluation of institutions, and its operating processes (34 C.F.R. §§ 602.3 and 602.20 to 602.30). The criteria for recognition also cover matters concerning the agency's role in ensuring institutional compliance with the requirements governing Title IV student aid programs (34 C.F.R. §§ 602.26(b)(7), (b)(8), (b)(10), (b)(12), and 602.27(b)). Though these provisions give the secretary of education substantial influence over the accrediting process, he has no direct authority to regulate unwilling accrediting agencies. Agencies must apply for recognition before coming under the secretary's jurisdiction. Moreover, recognition only gives the secretary authority to ensure the agency's continued compliance with the criteria; it does not give him authority to overrule the agency's accrediting decisions on particular institutions or programs (see, however, 37 C.F.R. § 602.4(a), on agency obligations to notify the secretary, and 34 C.F.R. § 602.11(b)(1), on secretary review of complaints against an agency).

Postsecondary administrators who deal with accrediting agencies will find it beneficial to understand the relationship between the agencies and the Department of Education. The requirements in the secretary's criteria for recognition affect institutions in two ways: they are the source of additional standards that the agencies impose on institutions through the accreditation process, and they are a source of procedural and other protections that redound to the benefit of institutions and programs when an agency is investigating them or considering a denial or termination of accreditation. The criteria require, for example, that an accrediting agency follow specified processes in its accrediting activities (34 C.F.R. § 602.24); that an agency have "effective controls" against conflicts of interest (34 C.F.R. § 602.21(b)(5)) and inconsistent application of its standards (34 C.F.R. § 602.23(b)(3)); that an agency's policy- and decision-making bodies include public representatives (34 C.F.R. § 602.21(b)(4)); that an agency have effective processes for reviewing complaints against it (34 C.F.R. § 602.27(f)); and that all of an agency's procedures "satisfy due process requirements" (34 C.F.R. § 602.28). Because recognition is vitally important to an accrediting agency's influence and credibility in the postsecondary world, agencies will be disinclined to jeopardize their recognition by violating the secretary's criteria in their dealings with institutions. Institutional administrators therefore have considerable leverage to insist that accrediting agencies comply with these criteria.

Although an institution may complain to the secretary about an agency's violation of the recognition criteria (see 34 C.F.R. § 602.11(b)), it is unclear whether the secretary's criteria are enforceable in the courts upon suit by an individual institution. The prevailing judicial view is that government regulations are to be enforced by the government agency that promulgated them, unless a contrary intention appears from the regulations and the statute that authorized the regulations (see generally the "private cause of action" cases in Sections 7.5.8 and 7.5.9). Since there is no indication that the secretary's criteria are to be privately enforceable, the courts would likely leave problems concerning compliance with the criteria to the secretary. Thus, even though the *Marlboro* case (Section 8.3.2.1) suggests that courts may review an accrediting agency's actions for compliance with the secretary's criteria, institutional administrators should not assume that their institution could go to court and nullify any agency action not in compliance with these criteria. The likelihood that the criteria are not privately enforceable, however, does not mean they would be irrelevant in any suit by an institution against an accrediting agency. Since the judicial standards applying to accrediting agencies are not fully developed (see Section 8.3.2), courts may look to the secretary's criteria as evidence of accepted practice in accreditation or as a model to consult in formulating a remedy for an agency's violation of legal standards.

When the secretary applies the criteria to grant or deny recognition to a particular agency (see 34 C.F.R. §§ 602.10 to 602.15), a different question about the role of courts arises: On what grounds, and at whose request, may a court review the secretary's recognition decisions? The case of *Sherman College of Straight Chiropractic v. U.S. Commissioner of Education*, 493 F. Supp. 976 (D.D.C. 1980), is illustrative. The plaintiffs were two chiropractic schools that were not accredited by the Council on Chiropractic Education (CCE), the recognized professional accrediting agency for chiropractic schools. The plaintiffs espoused a chiropractic philosophy divergent from that represented by CCE and the schools it had accredited: the plaintiffs adhered to a limited view regarding diagnosis, called the "straight doctrine," whereas CCE took a broader view of diagnosis as an essential part of chiropractic practice. When the commissioner (now secretary) renewed CCE's status as a "nationally recognized" accrediting agency, the plaintiffs challenged his action in court.

Using federal administrative law principles, the court determined that the commissioner's renewal of CCE's recognition was a final agency action subject to judicial review. The court also determined that the plaintiffs, as parties aggrieved by the commissioner's action, had standing to challenge it. On the merits, however, the court rejected the plaintiffs' claim that the commissioner's decision was arbitrary and capricious, or an abuse of discretion:

> For four reasons, this court finds that the commissioner acted well "within the scope of his authority" (*Overton Park* [*v. Volpe*, 401 U.S. 402 (1971)]).
> First, *the commissioner correctly found that CCE satisfied the recognition criteria.* . . .
> Second, *plaintiffs have ready alternative routes to accreditation available to them.* There is no requirement that a given school be accredited by a particular agency, nor is there any limitation on the number of accrediting bodies that can be recognized in a given field. If dissatisfied with the existing agency in its field, plaintiffs are free to create and seek recognition for an agency which "represents them and that can coexist with CCE" (oral argument, July 15, 1980). . . .
> Third, *the commissioner has a limited statutory role in recognizing accrediting agencies.* Recognition of an agency or association clearly does not bestow monopoly jurisdiction over the field of program specialization as defined by the agency or association in its application for recognition (Boyer deposition, pp. 122-23). . . . Despite the manner in which an accrediting body such as CCE defines its "universe," recognition of that agency or association does not preclude the legitimate interests of those who do not believe they fall within that universe.
> Fourth, *the commissioner must not be required to arbitrate educational standards for the nation's professions.* The fundamental question underlying this action is how the commissioner should treat an intraprofessional doctrinal dis-

pute in deciding whether to grant or renew recognition to an accrediting agency that rejects the doctrine of a deviant splinter group. In this case, plaintiffs request the court to instruct the commissioner, among other things, that a chiropractic accrediting agency cannot require clinical diagnostic training. Such a precedent might ultimately require the commissioner to become "a specialist on the matter of educational philosophy" in every field and would make him a "referee in . . . intraprofessional combat" (Boyer deposition, pp. 36, 114). . . . Appropriately, therefore, the statutes do not call for the commissioner to pass upon the substantive standards of an accrediting agency, but only to determine that the agency is "reliable authority as to the quality of training offered." Surely, educational philosophies differ. However, the commissioner acted correctly in deciding the only issue [he] could legitimately determine: that CCE is a "reliable authority" under the statute [493 F. Supp. at 980–81].

The *Sherman College* case indicates that the secretary of education's decisions to grant or refuse recognition to petitioning accrediting agencies, or to renew or not renew such recognition, are reviewable in the federal courts (see also 34 C.F.R. § 602.15). A recognition decision may be challenged not only by the accrediting agency itself (as in a case of refusal or nonrenewal) but also by individual institutions that are injured by the decision. Students or faculty members may also be able to challenge recognition decisions whose effects injure them personally. The availability of judicial review, however, does not mean that courts are likely to overturn the secretary's decisions. As the *Sherman College* case illustrates, courts will accord the secretary considerable latitude in applying the recognition criteria and will not expect him to take sides in disputes over educational philosophies, professional doctrine, or other matters outside the scope of the recognition criteria.

8.3.4. Dealing with accrediting agencies. A postsecondary administrator dealing with an accrediting agency should obtain complete information from the agency about its organization and operation. Specifically, according to the secretary of education's criteria (Section 8.3.3), an accrediting agency recognized by the Department of Education must provide—in clearly written form—a definition of the scope of its activities (34 C.F.R. § 602.20); definitions of each level of accreditation status (34 C.F.R. § 602.27(c)(1)); and a description of its criteria and procedures for making accreditation decisions (34 C.F.R. § 602.27(c)(3)), procedures for appealing denials or withdrawals of accreditation (34 C.F.R. § 602.28(b)(5)), specified educational objectives (34 C.F.R. § 602.24(b)(1)(i)), and evaluative standards (34 C.F.R. § 602.26(b)(1)).

The accrediting agency also is required to make available the names and affiliations of the members of its policy- and decision-making bodies, and the names of its principal administrative personnel (34 C.F.R. § 602.27(c)(4)); and it must provide "advance public notice of proposed new or revised criteria" (34 C.F.R. § 602.27(e)). Most important for an administrator is the information on the agency's evaluative standards, procedures for making accrediting decisions, and procedures for appealing adverse decisions. An understanding of the standards and procedures can be critical to an effective presentation of the institution or program to the agency. Administrators should insist on receiving all this information and should also insist (as the court cases discussed in Section 8.3.2 make clear) that the agency follow its own rules in dealing with the institution (see generally Section 8.6).

Sec. 8.4. Athletic Associations and Conferences

Various associations and conferences have a hand in regulating intercollegiate athletics. Most institutions with intercollegiate programs are members of both a national association (for example, the National Collegiate Athletic Association (NCAA)) and a conference (for example, the Atlantic Coast Conference (ACC)).

The NCAA is the largest and most influential of the athletic associations. It is an unincorporated association composed of over nine hundred public and private colleges and universities. It has a constitution that sets forth the association's fundamental law, and it has enacted extensive bylaws that govern its operations. The constitution and bylaws are published in the *NCAA Manual,* which is updated periodically. To preserve the amateur nature of college athletics, and the fairness of competition, the NCAA includes in its bylaws a complex set of rules regarding recruiting, academic eligibility, and the like. Regarding eligibility, for instance, the NCAA has requirements on minimum grade point average and SAT or ACT scores for incoming freshman student athletes; requirements regarding satisfactory academic progress for student athletes; restrictions on transfers from one school to another; rules on "redshirting" and longevity as a player; limitations on financial aid, compensation, and employment; and limitations regarding professional contracts and players' agents (see generally G. Wong, *Essentials of Amateur Sports Law* (2d ed., Praeger, 1994), 239–284). (The NCAA has different rules for its different divisions, and the various conferences affiliated with the NCAA may also have rules on such matters, as long as they meet the minimum requirements of the NCAA.) To enforce these rules, the NCAA has an enforcement program that includes compliance audits, self-reporting, investigations, and official inquiries, culminating in a range of penalties that the NCAA can impose against its member institutions but not against the institutions' employees.

Legal issues often arise as a result of the rule-making and enforcement activities of these associations and conferences. Individual institutions have become involved in such legal issues in two ways. Coaches and student athletes penalized for violating conference or association rules have sued their institutions as well as the conference or association to contest the enforcement of these rules. And institutions themselves have sued conferences or associations over their rules, policies, or decisions. The majority of such disputes have involved the NCAA, since it is the primary regulator of intercollegiate athletics in the United States. The resulting litigation frequently presents a difficult threshold problem of determining what legal principles should apply to resolution of the dispute.

8.4.1. Federal constitutional constraints. In a series of cases, courts have considered whether the NCAA, as an institutional membership association for both public and private colleges and universities, is engaged in "state action" (see Section 1.5.2) and thus is subject to the constraints of the U.S. Constitution, such as due process and equal protection. In an early leading case, *Parish v. NCAA,* 506 F.2d 1028 (5th Cir. 1975), for example, several basketball players at Centenary College, later joined by the college, challenged the constitutionality of an NCAA academic requirement then known as the "1.600 rule." Using first the "government contacts" theory and then the "public function" theory (both are explained in Section 1.5.2), the court held that the NCAA was engaged in state action. It then proceeded to examine the NCAA's rule under constitutional due process and equal protection principles, holding the rule valid in both respects.

Subsequent to the decision in *Parish* and other similar decisions in NCAA cases, the U.S. Supreme Court issued several opinions that narrowed the circumstances under which courts will find state action (see especially *Rendell-Baker v. Kohn*, discussed in Section 1.5.2). In *Arlosoroff v. NCAA*, 746 F.2d 1019 (4th Cir. 1984), the court relied on these Supreme Court opinions to reach a result contrary to the *Parish* line of cases. The plaintiff was a varsity tennis player at Duke University (a private institution) whom the NCAA had declared ineligible for further competition because he had participated in amateur competition for several years before enrolling at Duke. He claimed that the bylaw under which the NCAA had acted was invalid under the Due Process and Equal Protection Clauses. Determining that the NCAA's promulgation and enforcement of the bylaw did not fit within either the government contacts or the public function theory, the court held that the NCAA was not engaged in state action and therefore was not subject to constitutional constraints.

In 1988 the United States Supreme Court came down on the *Arlosoroff* side of the debate in a 5-to-4 split decision in *NCAA v. Tarkanian*, 488 U.S. 179 (1988). The NCAA had opened an official inquiry into the basketball program at the University of Nevada, Las Vegas (UNLV). UNLV conducted its own investigation into the NCAA's allegations and reported its findings to the NCAA's Committee on Infractions. The committee then charged UNLV with thirty-eight infractions, including ten infractions concerning the alleged failure of its highly successful, towel-chewing basketball coach, Jerry Tarkanian, to cooperate with an NCAA investigation. As a result, the NCAA placed UNLV's basketball team on a two-year probation and ordered UNLV to show cause why further penalties should not be imposed "unless UNLV severed all ties during the probation between its intercollegiate program and Tarkanian." Reluctantly, after holding a hearing, UNLV suspended Tarkanian in 1977. Tarkanian sued both the university and the NCAA, alleging that they had deprived him of his property interest in the position of basketball coach without first affording him procedural due process protections. The trial court agreed and granted the coach injunctive relief and attorney's fees. The Nevada Supreme Court upheld the trial court's ruling, agreeing that Tarkanian's constitutional due process rights had been violated. This court regarded the NCAA's regulatory activities as state action because "many NCAA member institutions were either public or government-supported" and because the NCAA had participated in the dismissal of a public employee, traditionally a function reserved to the state (*Tarkanian v. NCAA*, 741 P.2d 1345 (Nev. 1987)).

The U.S. Supreme Court, analyzing the NCAA's role and its relationship with UNLV and the state, disagreed with the Nevada courts and held that the NCAA was not a state actor. The Court noted that UNLV, clearly a state actor, had actually suspended Tarkanian, and that the issue therefore was "whether UNLV's actions in compliance with the NCAA rules and recommendations turned the NCAA's conduct into state action." Defining state action as action engaged in by those "'who carry a badge of authority of a State and represent it in some capacity, whether they act in accordance with their authority or misuse it'" (488 U.S. at 191; quoting *Monroe v. Pape*, 365 U.S. 167, 172 (1961)), the Court concluded that "the source of the legislation adopted by the NCAA is not Nevada but the collective membership, speaking through an organization that is independent of any particular State." It further noted that the majority of the NCAA's membership consisted of private institutions (488 U.S. at 193 n.13).

The Court also rejected arguments that the NCAA was a state actor because UNLV had delegated its state power to the NCAA. While such a delegation of power could serve to transform a private party into a state actor, no such delegation had occurred. Tarkanian was suspended by UNLV, not by the NCAA; the NCAA could only enforce sanctions against the institution as a whole, not against specific employees. Moreover, UNLV could have taken other paths of action, albeit unpleasant ones, in lieu of suspending the coach: it could have withdrawn from the NCAA or accepted additional sanctions while still remaining a member. Further, although UNLV, as a representative of the state of Nevada, did contribute to the development of NCAA policy, in reality it was the full membership of the organization that promulgated the rules leading to Tarkanian's suspension, not the state of Nevada.

The Court also found that UNLV had not delegated state investigatory authority to the NCAA. Moreover, UNLV had not formed a partnership with the NCAA simply because it decided to adhere to the NCAA's recommendation regarding Tarkanian. The interests of UNLV and the NCAA were in fact hostile to one another:

> During the several years that the NCAA investigated the alleged violations, the NCAA and UNLV acted much more like adversaries than like partners engaged in a dispassionate search for the truth. The NCAA cannot be regarded as an agent of UNLV for purposes of that proceeding. It is more correctly characterized as an agent of its remaining members which, as competitors of UNLV, had an interest in the effective and evenhanded enforcement of the NCAA's recruitment standards [488 U.S. at 196].

Disagreeing with the U.S. Supreme court majority, the four dissenting justices argued that UNLV and the NCAA had acted jointly in disciplining Tarkanian; that the NCAA, which had no subpoena power and no direct power to sanction Tarkanian, could have acted only through the state; and that the NCAA was therefore engaged in state action.

The *Tarkanian* case does not foreclose all possibilities for finding that an athletic association or conference is engaged in state action. As the Supreme Court itself recognized, state action may be present "if the membership consist[s] entirely of institutions located within the same State, many of them public institutions created by [that State]" (488 U.S. at 193 n.13). Even if the member institutions were not all located in the same state, state action might exist if the conference were composed entirely of state institutions. For example, in *Stanley v. Big Eight Conference,* 463 F. Supp. 920 (D. Mo. 1978), a case preceding *Tarkanian,* the court applied the Fourteenth Amendment's Due Process Clause to the defendant conference because all its members were state universities. Even if a conference were like the NCAA, with both public and private members located in different states, courts might distinguish *Tarkanian* and find state action in a particular case where there was clear evidence that the conference and a state institution had genuinely mutual interests and were acting jointly to take adverse action against a particular student or coach. Finally, even if there were no basis for finding that a particular conference is engaged in state action, courts would still be able to find an individual *state institution* to be engaged in state action (see Section 1.5.2) when it directed the enforcement of conference rules, and suit could therefore be brought against the institution rather than the conference. In *Spath v. NCAA*, 728 F.2d 25 (1st Cir. 1984), for example, the court held that the University of Lowell, also a defendant, was a state actor even if the NCAA was not and therefore proceeded to the merits of the plaintiff's equal protection and due process claims. See also *Barbay v. NCAA and Louisiana State University*, 1987 Westlaw 5619 (E.D. La. 1987).

Moreover, even if federal state action arguments will not work and the federal Constitution therefore does not apply, athletic associations and conferences may occasionally be suable under state constitutions for violations of state constitutional rights (see generally Section 1.3.1.1). In *Hill v. NCAA*, 865 P.2d 633 (Cal. 1994) (this volume, Section 4.15.5), for example, the California Supreme Court held that the right-to-privacy guarantee of the California constitution could be applied to the NCAA even though it is a private organization.

8.4.2. State statutes regulating athletic associations' enforcement activities. Partially in response to the *Tarkanian* litigation and NCAA investigations in other states, and to protect in-state institutions as well as their athletic personnel and student athletes, a number of states have passed or considered "due process" statutes (see Fla. Stat. §§ 240.5339 to 240.5349 (1991); Ill. Ann. Stat., ch. 144, paras. 2901 to 2913 (1991); Nev. Rev. Stat. §§ 85-1202 to 85-1210 (1990); Nev. Rev. Stat. § 398.005 et seq.). Such statutes require national athletic associations to extend certain due process protections to those accused in any enforcement proceeding. The second Nevada statute referred to above, for example, requires that each accused be given the opportunity to confront all witnesses, that an impartial entity be empaneled to adjudicate the proceeding, and that all proceedings be made public (Nev. Rev. Stat. §§ 398.155 to 398.255). The state courts may issue injunctions against an association that violates the statute's requirements, and the persons harmed may also obtain damages under some of the statutes (for example, Nev. Rev. Stat. § 398.245). Many of the statutes' protections are not included in the NCAA's own enforcement regulations (see Comment, "Home Court Advantage: Florida Joins States Mandating Due Process in NCAA Proceedings," 20 *Fla. State L. Rev.* 871, 889–900 (1993)).

The NCAA challenged the Nevada statute in *NCAA v. Miller, Governor, State of Nevada*, 795 F. Supp. 1476 (D. Nev. 1992), *affirmed,* 10 F.3d 633 (9th Cir. 1993). The lower court held the statute unconstitutional as both an invalid restraint on interstate commerce and an invalid interference with the NCAA's contract with its members. First, the court found that the NCAA and its member institutions are heavily involved in interstate commerce through their athletic programs, and that the statute restrained that commerce by curtailing the NCAA's capacity to establish uniform rules for all of its members throughout the United States, thus violating the federal Constitution's Commerce Clause (Article I, Section 8, clause 3). Second, the court agreed that Nevada's statute "substantially impair[ed] existing contractual relations between itself and the Nevada member institutions[,] in violation of the Contracts Clause of Article I, Section 10 of the United States Constitution." Since the Nevada law would give Nevada schools an unfair advantage over other schools, it would undermine the basic purpose of the NCAA's agreement with its members and destroy the NCAA's goal of administering a uniform system for all its members.

In affirming, the appellate court focused only on the Commerce Clause problem (see generally Section 6.4, this volume, regarding the Commerce Clause). The court held that the statute directly regulated interstate commerce:

> It is clear that the Statute is directed at interstate commerce and only interstate commerce. By its terms, it regulates only interstate organizations, *i.e.*, national collegiate athletic associations which have member institutions in 40 or more states. Nev. Rev. Stat. 398.055. Moreover, courts have consistently held that the NCAA, which seems to be the only organization regulated by the Statute, is engaged in interstate commerce in numerous ways. It markets interstate intercollegiate athletic competition, . . . [it] schedules events that call for transportation of teams across state lines and it governs nationwide amateur athlete recruiting and controls bids for lucrative national and regional television broadcasting of college athletics [10 F.3d at 638].

According to the court, the statute would "have a profound effect" on the NCAA's interstate activities. Since the NCAA must apply its enforcement procedures "even-handedly and uniformly on a national basis" in order to maintain integrity in accomplishing its goals, it would have to apply Nevada's procedures in every other state as well. Thus, "the practical effect of [Nevada's] regulation is to control conduct beyond the boundaries of the State." Moreover, since other states had enacted or might enact procedural statutes that differed from Nevada's, the NCAA would be subjected to the potentially conflicting requirements of various states. In both respects, the Nevada statute created an unconstitutional restraint on interstate commerce.

The Nevada litigation should not be interpreted as casting doubt on all state statutes that regulate athletic associations and conferences. Not all statutes will have a substantial adverse effect on the association's activities in *other* states, and thus not all state statutes will work to restrain interstate commerce or to impair an association's contractual relations with its members. Various other types of regulatory statutes, and even some types of due process statutes, could be distinguishable from *Miller* in this respect. With such statutes, however, other legal issues may arise. In *Kneeland v. NCAA*, 850 F.2d 224 (5th Cir. 1988), for instance, the court refused to apply the Texas Open Records Act to the NCAA and the Southwest Athletic Conference, because they could not be considered governmental bodies subject to the Act.

8.4.3. Antitrust laws. Federal and state antitrust laws will apply to athletic associations and conferences in some circumstances. Such laws may be used to challenge the membership rules of the associations and conferences, their eligibility rules for student athletes, and other joint or concerted activities of the members that allegedly have anticompetitive or monopolistic effects. (See generally this volume, Section 7.2.13.) Most cases thus far have been brought against the NCAA, either by a member institution or by a student athlete. Member institutions could also become defendants in such lawsuits, however, since they are the parties that would be engaging in the joint or concerted activity under auspices of the conference or association.

The leading case, *NCAA v. Board of Regents of the University of Oklahoma*, 468 U.S. 85 (1984), concerned an NCAA plan for regulating the televising of college football games by its member institutions. The U.S. Supreme Court held that the NCAA's enforcement of the plan violated Section 1 of the Sherman Antitrust Act (15

U.S.C. § 1) and was therefore invalid. In its salient features, the challenged television plan was mandatory for all NCAA members; it limited the total number of games a member institution could have televised; it fixed prices at which each institution could sell the broadcast rights to its games; and it prohibited member institutions from selling the broadcast rights to their games unless those games were included in the NCAA's television package agreed upon with the networks. The plan was challenged by schools desiring to negotiate their own television contracts free from the set prices and output limitations imposed on them by the NCAA plan.

Although acknowledging from the outset that the NCAA plan was "perhaps the paradigm of an unreasonable restraint of trade," the Court held that it was not a per se violation of the Sherman Act. The Court reasoned that in the "industry" of college football such "restraints on competition are essential if the product is to be available at all" (468 U.S. at 99). In order to ensure the integrity of intercollegiate athletic competition, participating schools must act jointly through the NCAA. Through its regulatory activities in this field, the NCAA enables institutions to preserve "the character of college football" and thus "enables a product to be marketed which might otherwise be unavailable" (468 U.S. at 102). The Court thus found that, by maintaining the existence of college football in its traditional form, as opposed to allowing it to die out or become professionalized, the NCAA's actions as a whole "widen consumer choice—not only the choices available to sports fans but also those available to athletes—and hence can be viewed as procompetitive" (468 U.S. at 102).

Having rejected a rule of per se invalidity, the Court then analyzed the case under the "rule of reason," considering both the plan's anticompetitive impact and its procompetitive impact. In a lengthy discussion, the Court found that the NCAA television plan restricted individual institutions from negotiating their own television contracts and had a significant adverse impact on member institutions' ability to compete openly in the sports broadcasting market. The Court also found that the NCAA wields market power in this market. The Court then turned to the NCAA's alleged justifications for the plan, to determine whether they should take precedence over the plan's anticompetitive impact.

The NCAA argued that, if individual institutions were permitted to negotiate their own television contracts, the market could become saturated, and the prices that networks would pay for college football games would decrease as a result. The Court disagreed with this premise, noting that the NCAA's television plan was not "necessary to enable the NCAA to penetrate the market through an attractive package sale. Since broadcasting rights to college football constitute a unique product for which there is no ready substitute, there is no need for collective action in order to enable the product to compete against its nonexistent competitors" (468 U.S. at 115). The NCAA also argued that, if there was too much college football on television, fewer people would attend live games, thereby decreasing ticket sales, and its television plan was therefore needed to protect gate attendance. The Court rejected this argument as well, because such protection—through collective action—of what was presumed to be an inferior product was itself "inconsistent with the basic policy of the Sherman [Antitrust] Act" (468 U.S. at 116).

Under the rule of reason, therefore, the court held that the NCAA's enforcement of its television plan was a clear restraint of trade in violation of Section 1 of the Sherman Act.[8] See B. Gregory & J. C. Busey, "Alternative Broadcasting Arrangements After NCAA," 61 *Indiana L.J.* 65 (1985).

In a subsequent case, *McCormack v. NCAA*, 845 F.2d 1338 (5th Cir. 1988), the court considered the legality of the NCAA's eligibility rules, holding that they do not violate the Sherman Act. Alumni, football players, and cheerleaders of Southern Methodist University (SMU) sued the NCAA after it had suspended and imposed sanctions on the school's football program for violating the restrictions on compensation given to student athletes. Assuming without deciding that the football players had standing to sue, the court upheld the dismissal of the claim. It found that, under the rule of reason as used in the *University of Oklahoma* case, the NCAA's eligibility rules were a reasonable means of promoting the amateurism of college football. Unlike the regulations regarding the television plan in the *University of Oklahoma* case, the court found that "[i]t is reasonable to assume that most of the regulatory controls of the NCAA are justifiable means of fostering competition among amateur athletic teams and intercollegiate athletics" (845 F.2d at 1344).

More recently, two other important cases have also upheld NCAA eligibility regulations against antitrust challenges, each case employing different reasoning. In both cases a football player with one year of intercollegiate eligibility remaining entered himself in the professional football draft and used the services of an agent. Neither of the players was drafted, and each then attempted to rejoin his college— despite NCAA "no-draft" rules, which at that time prohibited players who had entered the draft or obtained an agent from returning to play. When the NCAA refused to let them play, each player sued the NCAA and their schools, challenging the no-draft rule as well as the no-agent rule under the Sherman Act.

In one of these cases, *Banks v. NCAA*, 746 F. Supp. 850 (N.D. Ind. 1990), *affirmed*, 977 F.2d 1081 (7th Cir. 1992)), the player filed suit under Section 1 of the Sherman Act (15 U.S.C. §1). Although acknowledging that the rule of reason was the appropriate standard for the case, the district court nevertheless rejected Banks's request for injunctive relief, because he had alleged no anticompetitive effect of the NCAA's rules even though there was clear evidence of a procompetitive effect of upholding the amateur nature of college football. The appellate court affirmed:

> Banks' allegation that the no-draft rule restrains trade is absurd. None of the NCAA rules affecting college football eligibility restrain trade in the market for college players because the NCAA does not exist as a minor league training ground for future NFL players but rather to provide an opportunity for competition among amateur students pursuing a collegiate education. . . . [T]he regulations of the NCAA are designed to preserve the honesty and integrity of intercollegiate athletics and foster fair competition among the participating amateur college students [977 F.2d at 1089–90; footnotes and citations omitted].

---

[8]Subsequent to the *University of Oklahoma* decision, the Federal Trade Commission challenged the television broadcasting arrangements of the College Football Association, whose members had been plaintiffs in the *University of Oklahoma* case. An FTC administrative law judge dismissed the FTC's antitrust case on jurisdictional grounds (*In re College Football Assn. and Capital Cities/ABC, Inc.*, Docket No. 9242 (July 29, 1991)). See generally this volume, Section 7.2.13.

In the other case, *Gaines v. NCAA,* 746 F. Supp. 738 (M.D. Tenn. 1990), the student football player filed suit under Section 2 of the Sherman Act (15 U.S.C. § 2) and sought an injunction against the NCAA and Vanderbilt University to reinstate his eligibility to play football. Unlike the court in *Banks,* the *Gaines* court accepted the NCAA's argument that its eligibility rules "are not subject to antitrust analysis because they are not designed to generate profits in a commercial activity but to preserve amateurism by assuring that the recruitment of student athletes does not become a commercial activity." The court distinguished the *University of Oklahoma* case by stressing that the rules involved there had commercial objectives (generation of broadcasting profits) whereas the no-draft and no-agent rules did not. The court also held that, even if the antitrust laws did apply to the NCAA's rules, these rules did not violate Section 2 of the Sherman Act, because the NCAA's no-agent and no-draft rules were justified by legitimate business reasons. (See generally Note, "An End Run Around the Sherman Act? *Banks v. NCAA* and *Gaines v. NCAA,*" 19 *J. Coll. & Univ. Law* 295 (1993).)

These antitrust cases beginning with *University of Oklahoma* clearly establish that the NCAA and other athletic associations and conferences are subject to antitrust laws, at least when their actions have some commercial purpose or impact. But their rules, even when they have anticompetitive effects, will generally not be considered per se violations of the Sherman Antitrust Act. They can be upheld under Section 1 if they are reasonable and if their procompetitive impact offsets their anticompetitive impact, and they can be upheld under Section 2 if they have legitimate business justifications.

8.4.4. Common law principles. Even if the courts refrain from applying the Constitution to most activities of athletic associations and conferences, and even if state statutes and antitrust laws have only a narrow range of applications, associations and conferences are still limited in an important way by another relevant body of legal principles: the common law of "voluntary private associations."[9] Primarily, these principles would require the NCAA and other conferences and associations to adhere to their own rules and procedures, fairly and in good faith, in their relations with their member institutions. *California State University, Hayward v. NCAA,* 121 Cal. Rptr. 85 (Cal. Ct. App. 1975), for instance, arose after the NCAA had declared the university's athletic teams indefinitely ineligible for postseason play. The university argued that the NCAA's decision was contrary to the NCAA's own constitution and bylaws. The appellate court affirmed the trial court's issuance of a preliminary injunction against the NCAA, holding the following principle applicable to the NCAA:

> Courts will intervene in the internal affairs of associations where the action by the association is in violation of its own bylaws or constitution. "It is true that courts will not interfere with the disciplining or expelling of members of such associations where the action is taken in good faith and in accordance

[9]This same body of common law also applies to private accrediting associations, as discussed in Section 8.3.2.2. Regarding the application of voluntary private association law to the NCAA, see Note, "Judicial Review of Disputes Between Athletes and the National Collegiate Athletic Association," 24 *Stanford L. Rev.* 903, 909–16 (1972).

its laws or rules, or it is not authorized by the bylaws of the association, a court may review the ruling of the board and direct the reinstatement of the member" [quoting another case] [121 Cal. Rptr. at 88, 89].

The case then went back to the lower court for a trial on the merits. The lower court again held in favor of the university and made its injunction against the NCAA permanent. In a second appeal, under the name *Trustees of State Colleges and Universities v. NCAA,* 147 Cal. Rptr. 187 (Cal. Ct. App. 1978), the appellate court again affirmed the lower court, holding that the NCAA had not complied with its constitution and bylaws in imposing a penalty on the institution. The appellate court also held that, even if the institution had violated NCAA rules, under the facts of the case the NCAA was estopped from imposing a penalty on the institution. (The *Hayward* case is extensively discussed in J. D. Dickerson & M. Chapman, "Contract Law, Due Process, and the NCAA," 5 *J. Coll. & Univ. Law* 197 (1978-79).)

As *Hayward* in particular demonstrates, postsecondary institutions do have legal weapons to use in disputes with the NCAA and other athletic associations or conferences. The common law clearly applies to such disputes. Antitrust law also has some applicability (see Section 8.4.3 above); some role may still be found for state regulatory statutes more narrowly crafted than the state of Nevada's; and the U.S. Constitution may also still have some application in a narrow range of cases. Administrators should be aware, however, that these weapons are two-edged: student athletes may also use them against the institution when the institution and the athletic association are jointly engaged in enforcing athletic rules against the student. In such circumstances the institution may be so aligned with the athletic association that it is subject to the same legal principles that bind the association. Moreover, if the institution is public, the U.S. Constitution may apply to the situation even if the courts do not consider the association itself to be engaged in state action.

Sec. 8.5. The American Association of University Professors

The American Association of University Professors (AAUP) is an organization of college and university faculty, librarians with faculty status, and graduate students. Administrators may be associate members but may not vote on AAUP policies. Since its inception in 1915, the AAUP has focused on developing "standards for sound academic practice" and affording faculty the protections of these standards. The organization was formed by a group of faculty, headed by John Dewey, in reaction to criticisms of the university from external and internal sources.[10] Early members were concerned about protecting academic freedom, developing a code of ethics, and creating agreed-upon standards for promotion through the faculty ranks. They also had a strong interest in strengthening and ensuring the faculty's role in institutional governance. Committees were established, most of which still exist today, on academic freedom and tenure (Committee A), appointment and promotion (Committee B), recruitment of faculty (Committee C), and a variety of other issues of concern to faculty, such as pensions and salaries.

The AAUP has led the movement to develop principles and standards that

---

[10]This discussion relies on W. P. Metzger's "Origins of the Association," 51 *AAUP Bulletin* 229 (1965).

The AAUP has led the movement to develop principles and standards that regulate faculty employment relationships. By the end of its founding year, 1915, the association issued a seminal declaration on academic freedom. In 1934 the AAUP and the Association of American Colleges (whose members were primarily liberal arts colleges) began developing what culminated in the 1940 "Statement of Principles on Academic Freedom and Tenure," which over 150 educational organizations have endorsed. Among the many other policy statements and committee reports developed since the 1940 statement are statements on procedural standards for the dismissal of faculty; recommended institutional regulations on academic freedom and tenure (including the standards for terminating faculty appointments on the grounds of financial exigency); and statements on discrimination, academic governance, and collective bargaining.

Committees deliberate about issues of significance to the academic community (such as the disclosure of confidential peer evaluations to candidates for promotion and tenure). The draft report circulates and then is presented to the membership for its comments. Administrators and other national organizations frequently provide comments as well. A revised version of the policy is then published and may be adopted by the association's governing body. Thus, by the time the policies and standards are published in final form, the academic community has been heavily involved in developing and refining them. The major policies, standards, and reports are collected in *AAUP Policy Documents and Reports* (AAUP, 1990), which is known as the "Red Book."

According to two scholars long involved in the work of the AAUP:

> The policy documents of the American Association of University Professors may be used in any of three ways. First, they offer guidance to all components of the academic community either for the development of institutional policy or for the resolution of concrete issues as they arise. Second, some documents, like the *Recommended Institutional Regulations on Academic Freedom and Tenure* (RIR), are fashioned in a form that is explicitly adaptable as official institutional policy, and they formalize particular advice the AAUP staff gives in recurring situations. . . . [Third,] parties to lawsuits—both administrators and faculty— have begun to invoke AAUP standards to buttress their cases, either because these standards express academic custom generally or because they serve as an aid to the interpretation of institutional regulations or policies that derive from AAUP sources [R. S. Brown, Jr., & M. W. Finkin, "The Usefulness of AAUP Policy Statements," 59 *Educ. Record* 30 (1978)].

Many colleges and universities have incorporated the 1940 statement into their policies and procedures, or into their collective bargaining agreements with faculty unions. Some institutions have incorporated other policy statements as well. If a college has explicitly incorporated an AAUP policy statement as institutional policy, the provisions of that statement are contractually binding on the institution. Even if the college has not formally incorporated the policy statement, it may have acted in conformance with its provisions over a long period of years; in such instances the policy statement may be regarded as binding under a theory of implied contract (see Section 3.1.1). Finally, in some cases (for instance, *Greene v. Howard University*, discussed in Section 3.1.1), courts have looked to AAUP policy statements as authoritative sources of academic custom and usage (see Section 1.3.2.3). Examples of the use of AAUP standards in litigation involving faculty status may be found in Sections 3.5.2 and 3.8.1. Thus, in various ways faculty members, institutions, and courts use AAUP standards and policies as guides to interpreting college policies, regulations, and faculty handbooks:

> The absence of detailed contracts, which are not common in the academic world, makes such documents the chief source of guidance toward the rights and duties of all parties. When regulations use terms customary in the academic world like "tenure," it is helpful to look to the academic community's understanding about what the term means, which to a large extent is found in the 1940 *Statement* and the commentary upon it [Introduction to *AAUP Policy Documents and Reports,* at xii].

Although its concerns are myriad, the AAUP historically has been most active in the area of the protection of faculty members' academic freedom and tenure rights. In fact, the AAUP's first investigation of academic freedom violations occurred in 1915, the year of its founding, when seventeen members of the University of Utah faculty resigned, protesting the discharge of several faculty members. As word of the new organization's existence spread, faculty at other institutions sought the AAUP's assistance, and thirteen cases of allegedly unjust dismissals were referred to the organization in the first year of its existence.[11] The organization reviews approximately 2,000 inquiries each year on specific problems related to AAUP standards (J. Kurland, "Implementing AAUP Standards," 66 *Academe* 414 (1980)).

Approximately half of these inquiries are resolved with a single response; the other half involve a formal complaint by a faculty member against one or more administrators or against faculty colleagues. In these cases the AAUP staff provide assistance in settling the dispute, and in some instances a group of AAUP members may investigate the complaint by visiting the institution and talking with the parties involved. Reports of the investigation of certain cases are published periodically in the AAUP's journal, *Academe.* If the membership believes that alleged violations of its principles of academic freedom or governance are sufficiently egregious and the institution is apparently not amenable to resolving these violations to the satisfaction of the membership, the membership may vote to sanction the institution's administration. As of late 1993, fifty colleges and universities were on the list of censured administrations, including five that have been on the list since the 1960s.

An area of AAUP activity that has created some controversy both outside and within the organization is its role in faculty collective bargaining. Discussions concerning a possible role for the AAUP in this regard began in the mid-1960s, when faculty at several large public colleges and universities began to organize into unions. Between that time and 1971, vigorous debates over the propriety of the association's serving as a bargaining agent occurred, and in 1971 the association's council adopted the following position:

> The Association will pursue collective bargaining as a major additional way of realizing the Association's goals in higher education, and will allocate

---

[11]For an account of the investigation of the University of Utah incidents and related historical information, see W. P. Metzger, "The First Investigation," 47 *AAUP Bulletin* 206 (1961).

such resources and staff as are necessary for the vigorous selective development of this activity beyond present levels ["Council Position on Collective Bargaining," 58 *AAUP Bulletin* 46 (1972)].

Local AAUP chapters thus joined local chapters of the National Education Association and the American Federation of Teachers in competing to represent the collective interests of faculty at various colleges and universities. The national association provides advice, assistance with contract negotiation if necessary, and other assistance to the local chapters, which act as the "union" for collective bargaining purposes. For discussion of the activities of these three associations in the early days of faculty bargaining, see J. W. Garbarino, *Faculty Bargaining: Change and Conflict* (McGraw-Hill, 1975).

In 1992 the AAUP represented the faculty on 85 campuses, the AFT was the agent for faculty on 302 campuses, and the NEA represented faculty on 377 campuses. A coalition of the AAUP and the AFT represented an additional 23 campuses, while a coalition of the AAUP and the NEA represented another 30 campuses. Independent associations represented faculty on 75 campuses (J. M. Douglas, *Directory of Faculty Contracts and Bargaining Agents in Institutions of Higher Education* (National Center for the Study of Collective Bargaining in Higher Education and the Professions, 1992).

A final area of AAUP activity is in the monitoring of legislation and litigation involving faculty status and academic freedom issues. The AAUP has provided amicus briefs in many significant cases, including *University of Pennsylvania v. EEOC* (discussed in Section 3.7.7.1); *Regents of the University of Michigan v. Ewing* (discussed in Section 4.7.1); and *Board of Regents v. Roth* and *Perry v. Sindermann* (discussed in Section 3.6.2.1). Although the association has a small Washington-based professional staff, much of its work depends on the talent and energy of its volunteer members, whose efforts have provided the academic community with significant guidance on standards and norms.

Sec. 8.6. Dealing with the Education Associations

Since educational associations can provide many benefits for institutions and their officers and personnel (see Section 8.1), postsecondary administrators should be knowledgeable about the various associations and their roles within academia. Armed with this knowledge, administrators should be able to make appropriate decisions about the institution's associational memberships and support of association goals, and about the institution's means for helping its personnel join and participate in associations that support their own job functions. In addition, each administrator should have particular familiarity with those associations whose work most closely parallels their own, and should reserve time for their own participation in these associations.

Administrators who need specific information about a particular association's organization and operation may find it in the association's bylaws, rules, standards, and official statements, as well as in charters or articles of incorporation or association. Associations may make such documents available upon request, at least for members. Administrators can insist that the association scrupulously follow the policies set out in these sources. The institution may have a legally enforceable claim against the association if it fails to do so, at least if the association is a membership association and the institution is a member. (See Sections 8.3.2.2 and 8.4.4 above.)

When an institution is in a potentially adverse relationship with an association, institutional administrators should secure copies of the association's evaluative standards or criteria, its explanation of the procedures it follows in making adverse decisions about an institution, and its statement of procedures that institutions can follow in appealing adverse decisions. An understanding of the standards and procedures can be critical to effective representation of the institution before the association. In particular, the administrator should take advantage of all procedural rights, such as notice and hearing, that association rules provide in situations where institutional interests are in jeopardy. If associational rules do not provide sufficient procedural safeguards, administrators should seek to have the association extend additional safeguards. The assistance of counsel should be obtained before any such initiatives are undertaken.

If the institution is subjected to an adverse association decision that appears to violate the association's own rules or the legal requirements developed in court cases, the first recourse is to exhaust all the association's internal appeals processes. Simultaneously, institutional administrators and counsel may want to negotiate with the association about ways that the institution can comply with the association's demands without undue burden to the institution. If negotiations and internal appeals fail to achieve a resolution satisfactory to the institution, outside recourse to the courts may be possible. But court actions should be a last resort, pursued only in exceptional circumstances and only when reasonable prospects for resolution within the association have ended (see generally Section 1.4.2).

Thus, the process for resolving disputes with education associations parallels the process for most other legal issues in this book. Courts may have a presence, but in the end it is usually in the best interests of academia for institutions and private educational associations to develop the capacity for constructive internal resolution of disputes. As long as affected parties have meaningful access to the internal process, and the process works fairly, courts and government agencies should allow it ample breathing space to permit educational expertise to operate. It should be a central goal of postsecondary institutions and educational associations to facilitate such constructive accommodations in the interests of all participants in the postsecondary community.

Selected Annotated Bibliography

Sec. 8.1 (Overview of the Education Associations)

Bloland, Harley. *Associations in Action: The Washington, D.C. Higher Education Community*, ASHE-ERIC Higher Education Report no. 2 (Association for the Study of Higher Education, 1985). Reviews the historical and political development of the associations that represent various higher education constituencies. Focuses on the activities and developing sophistication of the associations between 1960 and the mid-1980s.

Hawkins, Hugh. *Banding Together: The Rise of National Associations in American Higher Education, 1887–1950* (Johns Hopkins University Press, 1992). Traces the history of four national higher education associations: the Association of American Colleges, the Association of American Universities, the American Council on Education, and the National Association of State Universities and Land-Grant Colleges. Discusses their transformation from organizations of scholar-administrators to lobbyists and shapers of post–World War II American higher education.

Washington Information Directory (Congressional Quarterly, published biannually). A section on "Education and Culture" lists relevant associations located in the metropolitan Washington, D.C., area.

Sec. 8.2 (Applicable Legal Principles)

Developments in the Law, "Judicial Control of Actions of Private Associations," 76 *Harvard L. Rev.* 983 (1963). A classical and comprehensive treatment of the legal status of private voluntary associations, with extensive citation of American case law to 1963 and its British predecessors.

See Oleck entry in bibliography for Section 6.3.

Sec. 8.3 (The College and the Accrediting Agencies)

Finkin, Matthew. "Federal Reliance and Voluntary Accreditation: The Power to Recognize as the Power to Regulate," 2 *J. Law & Educ.* 339 (1973). An overview of the accreditation process and the role of the federal government in that process. Emphasizes the evolution—through the various federal aid-to-education statutes—of the relationship between private accrediting agencies and the U.S. Office of Education, the present status of the relationship, and the legal basis for the Office (now Department) of Education's recognition function. Author later published a sequel to this article (Federal Reliance on Educational Accreditation: The Scope of Administrative Discretion (Council on Postsecondary Accreditation, 1978)), in which he argues that portions of the secretary of education's recognition criteria exceed the scope of statutory authority. The sequel should be read in conjunction with a contrary article by Margaret Conway, listed in Symposium, "Accreditation," entry below.

Fisk, Robert S., & Duryea, E. D. *Academic Collective Bargaining and Regional Accreditation* (Council on Postsecondary Accreditation, 1977). A COPA Occasional Paper. Analyzes the potential impact of collective bargaining on regional accreditation and on the relationship between the institution and the agency that accredits it. Provides helpful perspective for administrators who must deal with accrediting agencies in circumstances where their faculty is unionized.

Heilbron, Louis H. *Confidentiality and Accreditation* (Council on Postsecondary Accreditation, 1976). Another COPA Occasional Paper. Examines various issues concerning the confidentiality of an accrediting agency's records and other agency information regarding individual institutions. Discusses the kinds of information the accrediting agency may collect, the institution's right to obtain such information, and the accrediting agency's right to maintain the confidentiality of such information by denying claims of federal or state agencies, courts, or other third parties seeking the disclosure.

Kaplin, William A. "Judicial Review of Accreditation: The *Parsons College* Case," 40 *J. Higher Educ.* 543 (1969). Analyzes the *Parsons College* case and evaluates its impact on accreditation and the courts.

Kaplin, William A. "The *Marjorie Webster* Decisions on Accreditation," 52 *Educ.*

Record 219 (1971). Analyzes the antitrust law, common law, and constitutional law aspects of the *Marjorie Webster* case and evaluates its impact on accreditation.

Kaplin, William A. *Respective Roles of Federal Government, State Governments, and Private Accrediting Agencies in the Governance of Postsecondary Education* (Council on Postsecondary Accreditation, 1975). Another COPA Occasional Paper. Examines the current and potential future roles of federal and state governments and the accrediting agencies, particularly with regard to determining eligibility for federal funding under U.S. Office (now Department) of Education programs. Useful background for understanding the Higher Education Amendments of 1992 as they affect accreditation.

Kaplin, William A. "Accrediting Agencies' Legal Responsibilities: In Pursuit of the Public Interest," 12 *J. Law & Educ.* 89 (1983). "Considers the evolution in the way courts have labeled or categorized accrediting agencies, and the legal and policy consequences of this evolution." Analyzes applicability of four labels to accrediting agencies—"governmental," "quasi-governmental," "quasi-public," and "private"—and selects "quasi-public" as most appropriate. Examines the "public-interest" concept, providing a discussion of legal standards, a definition of public interest, and guidance in "promoting the public interest." Also published as a COPA Occasional Paper (Council on Postsecondary Education, 1982).

Project on Nontraditional Education Final Reports (Council on Postsecondary Accreditation, 1978). Product of a project sponsored by COPA and funded by the W. K. Kellogg Foundation. Discusses problems encountered in accrediting innovative or nontraditional programs and institutions. The four-volume set includes a summary report by project director Grover Andrews (vol. 1) and nine individual reports (vols. 2-4), including the following: J. Harris, "Institutional Accreditation and Nontraditional Undergraduate Educational Institutions and Programs" (Rpt. no. 3); P. Dressel, "Problems and Principles in the Recognition or Accreditation of Graduate Education" (Rpt. no. 4); J. Harris, "Critical Characteristics of an Accreditable Institution, Basic Purposes of Accreditation, and Nontraditional Forms of Most Concern" (Rpt. no. 5); K. Anderson, "Regional Accreditation Standards" (Rpt. no. 9).

Selden, William K., & Porter, Harry V. *Accreditation: Its Purposes and Uses* (Council on Postsecondary Accreditation, 1977). Another COPA Occasional Paper. Explains the historical derivation of private accreditation, the purposes and uses of accreditation, and pressures on the accreditation system.

Symposium, "Accreditation," 50 *J. Higher Educ.*, issue 2 (Mar./Apr. 1979). Provides various perspectives on the accreditation system, its prospects, and its problems. Contains eleven articles, including Margaret Conway, "The Commissioner's Authority to List Accrediting Agencies and Associations: Necessity for an Eligibility Issue"; J. Hall, "Regional Accreditation and Nontraditional Colleges: A President's Point of View"; Jerry Miller & L. Boswell, "Accreditation, Assessment, and the Credentialing of Educational Accomplishment"; John Profit, "The Federal Connection for Accreditation"; W. Trout, "Regional Accreditation, Evaluative Criteria and Quality Assurance"; and Kenneth E. Young, "New Pressures on Accreditation."

Tayler, C. William, & Hylden, Thomas. "Judicial Review of Accrediting Agency Actions: *Marlboro Corporation d/b/a The Emery School v. The Association of Independent Colleges and Schools*," 4 *J. Coll. & Univ. Law* 199 (1978). Analyzes the *Emery School* case in the context of the developing law of educational accreditation. Discusses the scope of judicial review and the legal standards courts will apply in accreditation cases.

Young, Kenneth E., Chambers, Charles M., Kells, H. R., & Associates. *Understanding Accreditation: Contemporary Perspectives on Issues and Practices in Evaluating Educational Quality* (Jossey-Bass, 1983). A sourcebook on the history, purposes, problems, current status, and future prospects of postsecondary accreditation. Includes eighteen chapters by fourteen different authors, a substantial prologue and epilogue tying the chapters together, an appendix with various COPA documents, a glossary of terms, and an extensive bibliography.

Sec. 8.4 (Athletic Associations and Conferences)

Berry, Robert C., & Wong, Glenn M. *Law and Business of the Sports Industries: Common Issues in Amateur and Professional Sports* (see entry in bibliography for Section 4.15). Includes numerous sections on and discussions of the NCAA and other athletic associations, covering a range of topics.

Weistart, John C. "Antitrust Issues in the Regulation of College Sports," 5 *J. Coll. & Univ. Law* 77 (1979). A systematic treatment of antitrust law's particular applications to intercollegiate athletics. Reviews issues facing the NCAA regional conferences and particular schools.

Weistart, John C. "Legal Accountability and the NCAA," 10 *J. Coll. & Univ. Law* 167 (1983–84). An essay exploring the unique status and role of the NCAA in intercollegiate athletics. Reviews structural deficiencies, such as the NCAA's alleged failure to accommodate the interests of student athletes in its governance structure; and suggests that the NCAA should be considered to have a fiduciary relationship to its member institutions. Also examines the role of judicial supervision of NCAA activities and its effect on the NCAA's regulatory objectives.

Young, Sherry. "The NCAA Enforcement Program and Due Process: The Case for Internal Reform," 43 *Syracuse L. Rev.* 747 (1992). Outlines complaints about NCAA rules enforcement, traces case law challenging NCAA procedures, explains and critiques the current enforcement program, and calls for further amendment of the NCAA's enforcement procedures.

See Wong entry in bibliography for Section 4.15.

Sec. 8.5 (The American Association of University Professors)

American Association of University Professors. "Council Position on Collective Bargaining," 58 *AAUP Bulletin* 46 (1972). A report by the association's Collective Bargaining Council. Describes the rationale for the association's decision to act as a collective bargaining representative for college faculty, the issues addressed by the council in reaching this decision, and the supporting and dissenting opinions of AAUP leaders.

American Association of University Professors. "Seventy-Five Years: A Retrospective on the Occasion of the Seventy-Fifth Annual Meeting," 75 *Academe* 4 (1989). Special issue devoted to the history of the AAUP. Includes articles and reproductions of documents about the association's history and the development of its policies on academic freedom and tenure, as well as on collective bargaining and governance. Also examines the AAUP's work on the status of women, the economic status of the profession, the McCarthy era, and the association's activity in filling amicus briefs in cases of significance to higher education.

Metzger, Walter P. "Origins of the Association: An Anniversary Address," 51 *AAUP Bulletin* 229 (1965). Discusses the context for and development of the AAUP and describes early efforts of the association in the areas of academic freedom, tenure, institutional governance, and other issues of concern to faculty and administrators.

See *AAUP Policy Documents and Reports* ("Red Book") and Furniss entries in bibliography for Chapter Three (preceding Section 3.1).

IX

The College and
the Business/Industrial
Community

◆　◆　◆

Sec. 9.1. The Contract Context

Entry into the world of business and industry exposes higher education institutions to a substantial dose of commercial law. Since most commercial arrangements are embodied in contracts that define the core rights and responsibilities of the contracting parties, contract law is the foundation on which the institution's business relationships are built. This section discusses the basics of contract law as they apply to relationships between the institution and the business world. While the discussion is addressed primarily to nonlawyers, it includes numerous illustrations, citations, and reminders that should be of use to counsel; it also provides counsel with common ground on which to engage in business planning with administrators.

9.1.1. Types of contracts and contract terms. A contract is a promise, or a performance or forbearance, given in exchange for some type of compensation. The three basic elements of a contract are the offer; the acceptance; and the compensation, legally referred to as "consideration." A contract may involve goods, services, real estate, or any combination thereof. A contract may be either written or oral. Virtually all states have a "statute of frauds," however, providing that certain types of contracts (for example, contracts for the sale of real property) must be in writing in order to be enforceable. A written contract may be either a standard form contract or an instrument specifically designed to meet individual circumstances. While contracts typically are viewed as an exchange (for example, money for goods), they also can take the form of cooperative arrangements such as affiliation agreements or joint venture agreements.

The types of clauses contained in a contract depend on the purposes of the contract, the interests of the parties, and the scope and complexity of the transaction. Most commercial contracts include clauses specifying the scope and duration of the contract; price, payment, or profit-sharing arrangements; delivery, installation, or implementation requirements; and definitions of contract terms. Most commercial contracts also include general clauses containing representations of authority to contract and to perform; warranties of products or performance; limitations on liability (indemnification or hold-harmless clauses); provisions for termination, renewal, or amendment; definitions of breach or default; remedies for breach; dispute-resolution techniques (for example, arbitration); and a "choice of law," that is, a selection of a body of state law that will govern the transaction. Some contracts also may include special clauses containing representations that a party has complied with applicable law; has clear title to certain property; holds necessary licenses, bonds, or insurance coverages; or has certain copyright or patent rights. Overall, the parties can include any provisions they agree on that are not prohibited by state or federal law. They are, by a process of "private ordering," creating the private law that will govern their relationship.

Prior to 1954 state common law (see this volume, Section 1.3.1.4) governed all contracts. From 1954 to 1967, every state except Louisiana adopted some form of the Uniform Commercial Code (U.C.C.). The U.C.C. now governs contracts for the sale of goods, except for certain issues (for example, defenses) that the U.C.C. does not address. These issues are still governed by the common law (see U.C.C. § 1-103), as are domestic contracts that do not involve the sale of goods. For international transactions between parties in the United States and parties in certain other countries, the United Nations Convention on Contracts for the International Sale of Goods (15 U.S.C.A. Appendix (West Supp. 1993)) will govern the contract if the contract does not otherwise specify the applicable law.

For the most part, the U.C.C. is consistent with the common law of contract. Departures from the common law are contained primarily in Article 2, dealing with the sale of goods, and in Article 9, dealing with the assignment of contract rights. (See generally J. D. Calamari & J. M. Perillo, *The Law of Contracts* (3d ed., West, 1987).) When the U.C.C. does depart from the common law, the effect is that the rules applicable to the sale of goods will differ from those for the sale of labor, services, or land. Thus, it is important to know whether a particular contract is for the sale of goods, and thus subject to the U.C.C., or for the sale of services, labor, or land, and subject to the common law (see Section 9.2.2).

The starting point for making this distinction is the U.C.C.'s definition of "goods"—that is, "all things (including specifically manufactured goods) which are movable at the time of identification to the contract for sale" (U.C.C. § 2-105). This definition will sometimes be difficult to apply. In *Advent Systems Ltd. v. Unysis Corp.*, 925 F.2d 670 (3d Cir. 1991), for instance, a computer software producer sued a computer manufacturer for breach of contract. The plaintiff argued that the U.C.C. should not control the case because "the 'software' referred to in the agreement as a 'product' was not a 'good' but intellectual property outside the ambit of the [U.C.C.]." The court rejected the argument: "[A] computer program may be copyrightable as intellectual property [but this] does not alter the fact that once in the form of a floppy disc or other medium, the program is tangible, movable and available in the marketplace. The fact that some programs may be tailored for specific purposes need not alter their status as 'goods' because the code definition includes 'specifically manu-factured goods.'"

9.1.2. The offer and acceptance. An *offer* is the offeror's expression of a present intent to be bound to particular terms, subject to the offeree's acceptance of those terms in an appropriate manner. The offer sets out the basic terms of the contract, although the terms are subject to negotiation and those ultimately agreed on need not have been expressed in the initial offer. The scope of the offer is determined by an objective standard that focuses on what the offeree should reasonably have understood from the offeror's communication rather than on the subjective meaning the offeror or offeree may have attached to the communication. In *Board of Governors of Wayne State University v. Building Systems Housing Corp.*, 233 N.W.2d 195 (Mich. Ct. App. 1975), for example, university officers believed that they had accepted the defendant's bid (offer) and thus formed a contract. According to the court, however, the university had made a conditional acceptance that functioned as a counteroffer. The conditional nature of the acceptance was evidenced by the university's statement (in a letter) that formal documents would be drawn after the Department of Housing and Urban Development had approved the contract award and financing bonds had been sold. The court reasoned that this statement interjected additional terms that transformed the university's attempted acceptance into a counteroffer, since the defendant's bid did not contain any "promise to abide by the conditions of HUD approval and the sale of financing bonds."

 In general, an offer remains open for the time specified in the offer, and that time begins to run when the offer is received. An acceptance after the time specified becomes a new offer. If no time is specified, the offer will lapse in a reasonable time. In the case of option contracts not governed by the U.C.C., legally sufficient consideration usually must be given in exchange for any promise to keep an offer open for a certain period of time. See *Board of Control of Eastern Michigan University v. Burgess*, 206 N.W.2d 256 (Mich. Ct. App. 1973) (court refused to enforce an option contract, although agreement stated that consideration had been received, where one party had, in fact, received no such consideration). Under U.C.C. §2-205, however, consideration is not needed if a "merchant" offers to buy or sell goods and "gives assurance" that the offer is "open for a specified period." In *City University of New York v. Finalco, Inc.*, 514 N.Y.S.2d 244 (N.Y. App. Div. 1987), Finalco had stated in a bid to City University for a used IBM computer that "this offer is valid through the close of business, December 18, 1978." The court held that the offer was irrevocable, even with no consideration, and that Finalco was thus obligated to purchase the computer when the university accepted its bid on December 18.

 The offeror may specify the manner by which the offer is to be accepted. The parties are bound when the offeree has appropriately communicated its return promise to the offeror or begun performances in the manner specified. In *Finalco*, for instance, the parties became bound when the university sent the letter to Finalco accepting its bid. The parties were bound at this point, despite their "manifested . . . intention to adopt a formal written agreement," because the letter and Finalco's bid included sufficient evidence of mutual assent between the parties "prior to the execution of the writing."

 To be effective, an acceptance must be unequivocal, and under common law its terms must match the terms of the offer. As in the *Building Systems Housing* case, above, a proposed acceptance that conditions the offeree's consent to terms not in the original offer is a counteroffer; the original offeror then has the power to form the contract by accepting the counteroffer. Under the U.C.C., however, an acceptance may be effective despite some differences between its terms and those specified in the offer (U.C.C. § 2-207).

9.1.3. Consideration. Generally, consideration is the price to be paid or the benefit to be extended by one party for the other party's promise. Consideration transforms the arrangement into a type of bargained exchange. *St. Norbert College Foundation v. McCormick*, 260 N.W.2d 776 (Wis. 1978), illustrates the application of this concept. McCormick had initially approached the college, indicating that he wished to make two gifts for its benefit. To maximize his own tax advantages, McCormick proposed to make two stock transfers to, and to enter two buy-sell agreements with, the college. In the second of these agreements, McCormick agreed to transfer to the college seven thousand shares of Procter and Gamble stock, worth approximately $500,000, in return for an annual annuity of $5,000 for life. McCormick thereafter revoked this agreement, contending that it was not enforceable because it lacked adequate consideration. The court disagreed: "[T]he presence of consideration is clear from the document. Defendant agreed to sell the stock. Plaintiff agreed to pay the stipulated price—$5,000 per year for life to the defendant. It is not the amount of consideration that determines the validity of a contract. . . . '[I]nadequacy of consideration alone is not a fatal defect' (citing *Rust v. Fitzhugh*, 112 N.W. 508, 511 (Wis. 1907))."

Related to consideration, and a kind of modern alternative to it, is the doctrine of promissory estoppel. Under this doctrine, if (1) a promise or assurance is made that could reasonably be expected to induce some particular action by the person to whom the promise is addressed, (2) the person does take action in reliance on the promise or assurance, and (3) an injustice would otherwise occur, the courts will enforce the promise as a contract even though there was no consideration for it (see *Restatement (Second) of Contracts* § 90 (1979); see also § 87(2), recognizing judicial enforcement of some offers even without a promise). The trend is toward a low threshold for finding a promise and an emphasis on the "reliance interest" of the person addressed. In *Howard University v. Good Food Services, Inc.*, 608 A.2d 116 (D.C. 1992), for example, the university had contracted with an outside service (GFS) to provide meals campuswide. Although it was not required to do so by the contract, GFS listed the university as an additional insured on its insurance certificates each year for a four-year period, pursuant to the university's annual requests that it do so. Two years after GFS terminated this practice without notifying the university, a GFS employee was injured in a university kitchen and brought suit against the university. Among other defenses, the university asserted promissory estoppel against GFS for failing to maintain the university as an insured, a practice that the university claimed to have relied on to its detriment. In analyzing the university's defense, the court stated: "[T]o make out a claim of promissory estoppel, the following questions must be answered in the affirmative: First, was there a promise? Second, should the promisor have expected the promisee to rely on the promise? [Finally], did the promisee so rely to [its] detriment?" Although the court recognized that the university had grounds to assert promissory estoppel under this test, it nevertheless rejected the university's defense for procedural reasons.

9.1.4. Breach of contract. Either party may breach a contract by failing to perform as it has promised. In case of breach, and in the absence of a viable defense (see Section 2.3.2), a court may award damages as well as other remedies, as discussed in Section 9.1.5 below.

If the promise to perform is a conditional one, there can be no breach until all the conditions have been fulfilled or excused. In *Pioneer Roofing Co. v. Mardian Construction Co.*, 733 P.2d 652 (Ariz. Ct. App. 1986), the court considered a defendant's claim that contract conditions had been excused because of an emergency and because of a waiver by the other party. The case concerned the obligation of the Arizona board of regents to pay for unanticipated extra work performed and materials purchased by a subcontractor for a sports facility on the Northern Arizona University campus. According to the contract, no additional work that would increase the "Contract Sum" could be undertaken, except in an emergency, until the general contractor informed the architect about the additional work. The contract also required that the architect provide authorization "in advance and in writing" to the contractor before the extra work was initiated. Both conditions had to be met before the university would be obligated to pay claims for extra work. In defending itself against a claim for payment, the board of regents contended that neither condition had been met. The court rejected the board's defense. It held that the first condition did not apply, since the extra work, the reroofing of the structure, "was in response to an emergency that endangered the property"; and that the second condition had been waived by the architect's representative, who gave go-ahead instructions at a meeting where the emergency was discussed. (See also *Bellevue College v. Greater Omaha Realty Co.*, 348 N.W.2d 837 (Neb. 1984), where the plaintiff college successfully enforced a contract—despite an unfulfilled condition—because the failure to fulfill the condition was solely the fault of the defendant.)

Lack of performance also will not constitute a breach if there has been a rescission or release of the contract. When neither party has performed its promises, the parties may agree mutually to rescind their contract as long as no third party's rights are affected. If only one of the parties has performed its promise, a mutual rescission must be accompanied by some consideration (see Section 9.1.3) given by the nonperforming party to the party that has performed. Similarly, if one party releases the other from its contractual obligation to perform, some consideration from the nonperforming party may be required if the release is to be valid. The U.C.C. permits written release of an obligation without consideration, however, as do state statutes in some states.

Occasionally a court may also rescind a contract for good cause. In *Boise Junior College District v. Mattefs Construction Co.*, 450 P.2d 604 (Idaho 1969), for instance, the court determined that a construction contractor was "entitled to the equitable relief of rescission" because it had made a "material" mistake in failing to include the glass subcontractor's bid when compiling subcontractors' bids in order to calculate its own bid. The court indicated that, among pertinent considerations, "enforcement of a contract pursuant to the terms of the erroneous bid would be unconscionable; the mistake did not result from [the contractor's] violation of a positive legal duty or from culpable negligence; the [other] party . . . will not be prejudiced except by the loss of his bargain; and prompt notice of the error [was] given."

If a condition to performance has occurred or has been excused, *and* if the promise still has not been fulfilled or otherwise discharged, then a breach exists, for which a court will award damages, and perhaps other remedies as well, as discussed below.

9.1.5. Remedies. Because contracts are made in a bargained exchange, in which the parties presumably contemplate their resultant duties and liabilities, judicial remedies for breach of contract are limited to those that fulfill the reasonable expectations of the parties. American courts prefer money damages over "specific performance" (that is, an order to the breaching party to perform). Money damages may be "nominal" or "compensatory." Compensatory damages may be computed in one of three ways. "Expectation" damages are calculated to place the nonbreaching party as nearly as possible in the position it would have been in had the breaching party performed; "reliance" damages are calculated to return the nonbreaching party to its original position, as if it had never entered the contract; and "restitution" damages are calculated to return or restore to the nonbreaching party the dollar value of any benefit it had conferred on the breaching party. (See generally Calamari & Perillo, *The Law of Contracts,* (cited in Section 9.1.1), chs. 14–16.) The nonbreaching party may choose which type of calculation to use and has the burden of proving the existence of damages and calculating their amount with reasonable certainty. The nonbreaching party must also "mitigate" its damages and may not recover for loss that could have been avoided or mitigated with reasonable effort. The nonbreaching party also may not recover damages that were not foreseeable to the breaching party.

In order to avoid complicated court proceedings on proof of damages, the parties may insert a "liquidated damages" clause into the contract at formation. Liquidated damages represent an agreed-upon estimate of the actual damages that would likely be incurred in case of breach. The U.C.C., for instance, permits the enforcement of liquidated damages clauses when "the amount is reasonable in the light of anticipated or actual harm caused by the breach, the difficulties of proof of loss, and the inconvenience or infeasibility of otherwise obtaining an adequate remedy" (§ 2-718(1)).

9.1.6. Arbitration. Arbitration is a process by which contracting parties may resolve a dispute by asking a neutral third party to examine the claims and render a decision. The parties can agree in advance to have contract disputes resolved through arbitration by including an arbitration clause in the contract at formation. Without such a clause, the parties can still agree to arbitrate a particular dispute after it has arisen. In either case, the parties may specify whether the decision is binding on the parties or only advisory.

In comparison to protracted court litigation, arbitration (like mediation) offers a much quicker resolution at a much lower cost (see generally Section 1.4.6). Arbitration is an informal process that decreases the adversarial character of the dispute and increases the likelihood of a mutually beneficial outcome. The arbitrator is not bound by judicial precedents or rules of law and is thus free to resolve the dispute in an equitable manner. In addition, since the parties choose the arbitrator, they can ensure that he or she is familiar with the business context and proficient in the issues to be resolved.

Most states as well as the federal government have statutes that promote the use and enforceability of arbitration agreements.[1] The federal statute, the Federal Arbitration Act (FAA) (9 U.S.C. § 1 et seq.), applies to written arbitration agreements involving interstate commerce or maritime transactions and provides that such agreements are "valid, irrevocable, and enforceable." Federal and state courts, upon the request of a party, must stay any litigation on a covered transaction that is also the subject of pending arbitration. The federal district courts also are empowered to compel arbitration when a party fails, neglects, or refuses to submit a dispute to arbitration. The FAA also limits judicial review of arbitrators' decisions. Either party may petition a court to confirm an arbitrator's decision, and the court must confirm the decision unless there are demonstrated grounds for vacating or modifying it. A decision may be vacated only if it was influenced by fraud, corruption, or misconduct, and it may be modified only if it goes beyond the scope of the issues presented by the parties or contains a material miscalculation.

In *Volt Information Sciences v. Board of Trustees of Leland Stanford Junior University*, 489 U.S. 468 (1989), the U.S. Supreme Court considered the relationship between the Federal Arbitration Act and state law. Volt and Stanford had entered into a construction contract. The contract included an arbitration clause as well as a "choice-of-law" clause providing that the contract would be governed by California law. When a dispute arose over compensation for additional work done by Volt, Volt demanded arbitration while Stanford filed a breach-of-contract suit in California Superior Court against Volt and also sought indemnity from two other contractors not subject to the arbitration agreement.

Under the FAA, the court would have been required to compel enforcement of the private arbitration contract clause and to stay the litigation until the arbitration process was complete. However, a California statute—the California Arbitration Act—allows "a court to stay arbitration pending the resolution of related litigation," and Stanford invoked this statute because its suit included the indemnity claims against two other contractors. The Supreme Court held that the FAA does not preempt the California statute (see generally this volume, Section 7.1), and that, under the contract's choice-of-law clause, the California law should apply: "[T]he federal policy [under the Federal Arbitration Act] is simply to ensure the enforceability, according to their terms, of private agreements to arbitrate. . . . Where, as here, the parties have agreed to abide by state arbitration rules, enforcing those rules according to the terms of the agreement is fully consistent with the FAA's goals, even if the result is that arbitration is stayed when the Act would otherwise permit it to go forward."

University of Alaska v. Modern Construction, Inc., 522 P.2d 1132 (Alaska 1974), provides another perspective on arbitration. The university contracted with Modern to build a "Campus Activity Center." The contract provided that "[a]ll claims, disputes and other matters in question arising out of, or relating to, the Contract or the breach thereof" would be submitted to arbitration. The contract also contained elaborate procedures for approval of design changes and accompanying adjustments in the contract price (called "Change Orders"). After completing the project, Modern presented the university with a bill for "impact charges" attributable

[1]Most of the state statutes are based on the Uniform Arbitration Act (7 U.L.A. (*Uniform Laws Annotated*) 1 (Supp. 1991)). A number of states now also have statutes governing international arbitrations; see G. Walker, "Trends in State Legislation Governing International Arbitrations," 17 *N.C. J. International Law & Commercial Regulation* 419 (1992).

to several Change Orders. When the university refused to pay, Modern demanded arbitration. The university cooperated but recorded an objection that Modern's claims were beyond the scope of the contract and thus not arbitrable under the arbitration clause. The panel of arbitrators awarded Modern approximately 40 percent of its claim. Modern then asked the court to confirm the arbitration award, and the university simultaneously asked the court to vacate it. The court stated that, although the contract was ambiguous about whether the dispute was arbitrable, it would "allow ambiguous contract terms to be constructed in favor of arbitrability where such construction is not obviously contrary to the parties' intent, especially where, as here, the party contesting arbitrability drafted the contract." Thus, since "the arbitrators' decision on the arbitrability of Modern's claims for 'impact damages' due to delays was not based on an unreasonable interpretation of the contract," the Supreme Court of Alaska confirmed the arbitration award.

Sec. 9.2. The College as Purchaser

9.2.1. Purchase of goods. One of the most common commercial transactions of colleges and universities is the purchase of "goods"—that is, personal property generally categorizable as equipment, materials, or supplies. Computer equipment and software, for instance, would constitute goods whose acquisition commonly involves institutions in complex commercial transactions (see generally M. Bandman, "Balancing the Risks in Computer Contracts," 92 *Commercial Law J*. 384 (1987)). Purchases of goods are effectuated by means of contracts (see Section 9.1) providing for the transfer of title to (or a lease interest in) the goods from seller to purchaser in return for a monetary payment or other consideration. When payment is made over time, the parties may also execute and file documents giving the seller a security interest in the goods. Contracts for the sale of goods are typically governed by state contract and commercial law, in particular Article 2 (sales) and Article 9 (security interests) of the Uniform Commercial Code (see Section 9.1).

For public institutions the state's procurement law, embodied in statutory provisions and administrative regulations, usually will establish further requirements regarding purchasing, or a state higher education system may adopt procurement regulations of its own.[2] For example, public institutions may be required to purchase certain products or services from a "procurement list" (see, for example, Ohio Rev. Code Ann. § 4115.34) or to use competitive bidding for certain purchases (see, for example, Tex. Rev. Civ. Stat. Ann. art. 601b). Public institutions may also be subject to a variety of special provisions, in procurement laws or otherwise, that require or authorize "purchase preferences" for particular products or sellers that would benefit the state's own residents.[3] Some states, for instance, accord purchase preferences to

[2]Constitutionally based public institutions (Section 6.2.2) may be exempt from some or all state procurement statutes and may have authority to promulgate their own procurement rules and policies.

[3]The cases and authorities are collected in Annot., "Validity, Construction, and Effect of State and Local Laws Requiring Governmental Units to Give 'Purchase Preference' to Goods Manufactured or Services Rendered in the State," 84 A.L.R.4th 419 (1991 plus periodic supp.).

recycled paper products (for example, Cal. Pub. Cont. Code § 10860; Neb. Rev. Stat. § 81-15,159). Other states accord purchase preferences to designated small businesses (for example, Md. Code Ann., State Fin. & Proc. § 14-207(c); Minn. Stat. Ann. § 137.35). Iowa has a statute that requires state governing bodies (including state universities) to purchase coal "mined or produced within the state by producers who are, at the time such coal is purchased or produced, complying with all the workers' compensation and mining laws of the state" (Iowa Code Ann. § 73.6); and California has a statute that requires community colleges to give food purchase preferences to produce that is grown, or food that is processed, in the United States (Cal. Pub. Cont. Code § 3410).

In addition, some states have conflict-of-interest statutes that would apply to purchase transactions involving state higher education institutions and their suppliers (for example, La. Rev. Stat. Ann. §§ 42.1111C(2)(d), 1112B(2)&(3), and 1113B). In *In Re Beychok*, 495 So. 2d 1278 (La. 1986), the Supreme Court of Louisiana interpreted these statutes to prohibit Louisiana State University from entering purchase contracts with members of its governing board or their firms. The court held that Beychok, a member of the university's governing board and the CEO and majority stockholder of a baking company, had violated the statutes when his firm entered into a supply contract with the university. Beychok defended on the grounds that the university had awarded the contract through the use of sealed competitive bids. The court rejected the defense, however, because the statutes "protect against both actual and perceived conflicts of interest" and thus "do not require that there be actual corruption on the part of the public servant or actual loss by the state."

There is also some federal law that applies to institutional transactions for the sale of goods—in particular federal antitrust law (see Section 7.2.13). The Robinson-Patman Act (15 U.S.C. § 13 et seq.), for instance, prohibits sellers from engaging in certain types of discriminatory pricing practices and prohibits purchasers from knowingly inducing or receiving discriminatory prices arising from such prohibited pricing practices. In *Jefferson County Pharmaceutical Assn., Inc. v. Abbott Laboratories*, 460 U.S. 150 (1983), the U.S. Supreme Court considered the Act's applicability to purchases by public higher education institutions. The case concerned purchases of pharmaceutical products by two pharmacies at the University of Alabama's Medical Center. The plaintiff claimed that Abbott Laboratories and the university had violated the Act by entering transactions in which the pharmacies purchased products at lower prices than those charged to the plaintiff's member pharmacies. The university defended on the ground that the Act did not apply to purchases by state governmental entities. Because the university pharmacies had purchased the products at issue for *resale* in competition with private enterprises, the Court did not address the Act's application to state purchases "for *use* in traditional governmental functions"; the sole issue was whether the Act applied to purchases for resale. The Court answered this question affirmatively, since it could find no evidence that Congress intended to accord states the means to compete unfairly with commercial businesses by exempting them from the Act.

When the question concerns an institution's purchases for its own use, the Robinson-Patman Act expressly provides some protection for both public and private institutions. Section 13c (15 U.S.C. § 13c) exempts colleges, universities, and other listed entities from the Act with respect to "purchases of their supplies for their own use."[4] The exemption also extends to the sellers who enter into such transactions with colleges and universities. In *Logan Lanes v. Brunswick Corp.*, 378 F.2d 212 (9th Cir. 1967), the court broadly construed the scope of this exemption. At issue was the defendant's sale of bowling alleys and related equipment to a state board for use in the state university's student union. The alleys were used for a fee by the general public, as well as the university community, and were operated in competition with the plaintiff. The plaintiff complained that the defendant sold the alleys and equipment to the state board at a lower price than that charged the plaintiff. The court held that the transaction fell within the Section 13c exemption. The alleys and equipment were "supplies," within the meaning of Section 13c, because that term includes "anything needed to meet the institution's needs," including nonconsumable items that constitute capital expenditures. The alleys and equipment were also for the university's "own use" within the meaning of Section 13c, even though they were also used by the public, since "the primary purpose of the purchases . . . was to fulfill the needs of the university in providing bowling facilities for its students, faculty and staff."

To avoid legal challenges and liability arising from purchasing activities, and to meet the institution's ongoing needs for goods, institutional purchasing officers and legal counsel will need to be thoroughly familiar with Article 2 of the U.C.C. and to identify all other state and federal law potentially applicable to particular transactions. Careful negotiation and drafting of contract terms, and effective assertion of legal rights should the seller perform inadequately, are of course also critical. Among the most important protections for institutions are those available from warranties, which may be invoked to enforce the purchaser's interest in the quality and suitability of goods.

In most states Article 2 of the U.C.C. is the source of warranty law regarding the sale of goods. When a sales transaction involves both goods and services (for example, the purchase of carpet that the seller installs), U.C.C. warranty law will apply to the service as well as the goods provided by a particular supplier if the service is only incidental to the sale of the goods (see this volume, Section 9.2.2). Warranties may be either "express" or "implied." Section 2-313 of the U.C.C. governs express warranties. If a seller makes representations about product quality or performance by asserting facts, making promises, or providing a description, sample, or model of the goods, the goods must comply with these representations. In *Brooklyn Law School v. Raybon, Inc.*, 540 N.Y.S.2d 404 (N.Y. Sup. Ct. 1989), *reversed on other grounds*, 572 N.Y.S.2d 312 (N.Y. App. Div. 1991), for example, the school sued Raybon and twenty-six other defendants who had sold it asbestos products and installed them in the school facilities. The school alleged that the defendants made representations about the safety and fitness of the asbestos materials in advertisements directed at the general public, and that the school relied on these representations in purchasing the asbestos products. The trial court held that these allegations stated an express warranty claim, and it denied the defendant's motion to dismiss this claim. In dictum, the court suggested that any defendants whose primary function was to install the asbestos materials might not be subject to the express warranty claim, because the installation was a service incidental to the sale; but the court did not decide this

---

[4]The cases are collected in Annot., "Construction and Application of Provision in Robinson-Patman Act (15 U.S.C. § 13c) Exempting Nonprofit Institution from Price Discrimination Provisions of the Act," 3 A.L.R. Fed 996 (1970 and periodic supp.).

potential issue, since none of the defendants had alleged that they primarily provided a service.

Implied warranties are governed by Sections 2-314 and 2-315 of the U.C.C. Section 2-314 recognizes an implied warranty that goods are "merchantable"—that is, suitable for the ordinary purpose for which such goods are used—if the seller is a "merchant" who deals in goods of that kind. Section 2-315 recognizes an implied warranty of "fitness for a particular purpose" when the seller knows the purchaser's purpose for wanting the goods and the purchaser relies on the seller's expertise to provide goods suitable for the purpose. *Western Waterproofing Co., Inc. v. Lindenwood Colleges,* 662 S.W.2d 288 (Mo. Ct. App. 1983), concerned an alleged breach of implied warranty. Lindenwood had contracted with a waterproofing company (WWC) to install a soccer/football field in the college stadium. The field was used by Lindenwood's soccer team and was also leased to the St. Louis Cardinals football team for training camp. When the Cardinals used the field, parts of it "were torn up and holes and divots developed." In later use similar damage occurred, and pools of standing water formed on the field. Lindenwood claimed that WWC had "breached an implied warranty that the field was fit for its intended use." WWC argued that Lindenwood's implied warranty claim was barred, because Lindenwood was contributorily negligent for misusing the field by overwatering. The court rejected WWC's argument, holding that contributory negligence can be a defense to an implied warranty claim only if the purchaser's misuse is the "proximate cause of the alleged breach" of warranty. Thus, the court confirmed an arbitration award in Lindenwood's favor because the "principal cause of the field's deficiencies were in the design of the field itself and not Lindenwood's misuse of the field."

Sellers may disclaim (and thus avoid) warranties by inserting disclaimers into sales contracts. Purchasers may also disclaim (and thus lose) warranty protection in some circumstances by their own inaction. (Section 2-316(1) of the U.C.C. governs the disclaimer of express warranties; Section 2-316(2) governs the disclaimer of implied warranties.) When a warranty has not been disclaimed, there are nevertheless several defenses a seller may assert against a breach-of-warranty claim, including the complex "lack of privity" defense. To take full advantage of warranty law, administrators and purchasing officers will want to seek the assistance of counsel in dealing with these matters.

In addition to warranty and other breach-of-contract claims, institutions may also sometimes protect themselves by asserting claims for tortious performance of contract obligations. In *Board of Regents of the University of Washington v. Frederick & Nelson,* 579 P.2d 346 (Wash. 1978), for example, the university purchased furniture for a laboratory from F&N, the supplier. When the furniture did not meet the contract specifications, the manufacturer agreed to refinish the furniture on the university's premises. The university subsequently sustained fire damage at the site, apparently as a result of spontaneous combustion of oily rags that the manufacturer had left on the premises. The court held that, since F&N had allowed the manufacturer to perform F&N's contractual duty to bring the furniture up to specifications, F&N was liable to the university for the manufacturer's negligent performance of these duties, which resulted in the fire. See also *University Systems of New Hampshire v. United States Gypsum Co.,* 756 F. Supp. 640 (D.N.H. 1991) (asbestos case presenting numerous tort claims).

9.2.2. Purchase of services. Institutions commonly contract for the purchase of services as well as goods. Sometimes the same contract will cover both services and goods, as when the seller of equipment agrees to install, provide maintenance for, or train personnel in the use of the equipment. At other times the institution will contract with one party to purchase goods and contract with other parties for services related to the goods. The acquisition and operation of computer systems, for example, will customarily involve purchases of both goods (hardware and software) and services (installation of hardware, implementation of systems, periodic maintenance, and so forth).

Services may also be unrelated to and purchased independently of goods. Examples include accounting services, legal services, services of consultants, payroll services, and custodial services. Such services are often performed by corporations or individuals that have the legal status of "independent contractors" rather than (or in addition to) being performed by employees. Generally the activities of an independent contractor are not subject to the same level of control by the employer as are the activities of an employee; therefore, the independent contractor generally has more discretion regarding methods and equipment for the job, and may also work for many different employers during the same day or week. An independent contractor may or may not be an agent of the institution (see Section 2.3.2) in performing particular contractual duties. Since an institution could be liable in contract, and occasionally in tort, for the acts of a contractor acting as its agent, close attention must be given to contractual provisions that characterize the contractor's status and authority to act for the institution (see Section 2.3.2), and that allocate the risk of loss from any unlawful acts of the contractor (see Section 2.5.2).

The purchase of services, like the purchase of goods, is effectuated by contractual agreements governed by the contract law of the state. Unlike the purchase of goods, however, the purchase of services as such is not subject to Article 2 of the U.C.C. Even when the same transaction involves both goods and services—for example, a contract for the acquisition of a computer system—the U.C.C. will not apply to the service unless the goods are the dominant component of the transaction and the services are merely incidental to their sale. (See, for example, *Ames Contracting Co., Inc. v. City University of New York,* 466 N.Y.S.2d 182, 184-85 (N.Y. Ct. Cl. 1983), *reversed on other grounds,* 485 N.Y.S.2d 259 (N.Y. App. Div. 1985).)

Since Article 2 of the U.C.C. usually will not apply to the purchase of services, U.C.C. warranties (Section 9.2.1) usually will not protect the institution if the purchased services are unsatisfactory. Instead, the institution's legal recourse is a breach-of-contract claim (Section 9.1.4), supplemented by a tortious performance claim (Section 9.2.1) and, when professional services are involved, state malpractice law.

For public institutions state procurement law, purchase preference statutes, and conflict-of-interest statutes (Section 9.2.1) may apply to the purchase of services as well as goods. Moreover, "prevailing-wage" statutes may sometimes apply to the purchase of contractors' services. Such statutes require contractors working on certain public works projects (including those at state universities and colleges) to pay laborers the "prevailing wage" in the locality. Applicability of the statute typically depends on two factors: first, whether the project is considered a "public work"; second, whether the particular type of work to be performed falls into one of the statutorily defined categories (for example, construction, demolition, repair, alteration) for which the prevailing wage must be paid.[5] In *Sparkisian Bros., Inc. v. Hartnett*, 568 N.Y.S.2d 190 (N.Y. App. Div. 1991), the state commissioner of labor found that a contractor renovating a state university classroom building into a hotel/conference center had violated the state's prevailing-wage statute. The contractor appealed the commissioner's determination, arguing that the renovation was not a public work but, rather, a "private venture for profit." The court disagreed and upheld the commissioner's decision. To support its conclusion, the court cited a number of factors—including the reservation of 75 percent of the facility's space for the use of the state university system and its affiliates—that "tend to demonstrate the public use, public access, public ownership and public enjoyment characteristics of the project and [to] support [the commissioner's] determination, which is neither irrational nor unreasonable."

In addition, for certain tasks—such as accounting or payroll services, legal services, consulting services, food services, and janitorial or grounds-keeping work—state law may limit the authority of public institutions to purchase the services of outsiders. State civil service laws may expressly or implicitly require state agencies to use only civil service employees to perform such work, rather than contracting out to have it done, unless certain special circumstances exist (see, for example, Minn. Stat. § 16B.17 (1992); Cal. Govt. Code § 19130). Delegations of authority in the state constitution or state statutes may also impose such limits on state universities or colleges (see Cal. Const. art. IX, § 6; *California School Employees Assn. v. Sunnyvale Elementary School District of Santa Clara County*, 111 Cal. Rptr. 433 (Cal. Ct. App. 1973); and Cal. Govt. Code § 19130). Other state statutes or regulations, dealing specifically with contracts for special services, may also apply to and limit state educational institutions (see, for example, Cal. Govt. Code § 53060).

A series of cases concerning contracts for janitorial services illustrate how such "contracting-out" limits may affect public higher education institutions. In the first of these cases, *State ex rel. Sigall v. Aetna Cleaning Contractors of Cleveland, Inc.*, 345 N.E.2d 61 (Ohio 1976), the Ohio Supreme Court held that Kent State University could lawfully contract with an independent contractor to perform janitorial services that could also be performed by state civil service employees. The university had been unable to maintain a full complement of janitorial workers, despite regular recruiting from a state employment office, and had therefore contracted out for such services—admittedly at lower cost than the wages that civil service employees would have received for the same work. In the taxpayer's suit challenging this contract, the plaintiff alleged that Ohio's constitution and related state statutes required the school to use only civil service employees for such work. Determining that "no statutory provision exists which prohibits the contracting out of the custodial services at issue herein," and that the contracting out would not undermine the state's civil service system, the Ohio Supreme Court rejected the challenge:

> In the absence of proof of an intent to thwart the purposes of the civil service system, the board of trustees of a state university may lawfully contract

---

[5]The cases and statutes are collected in Annot., "What Projects Involve Work Subject to State Statutes Requiring Payment of Prevailing Wages on Public Works Projects," 10 A.L.R.5th 337 (1993 plus periodic supp.).

to have an independent contractor perform services which might also be performed by civil service employees [345 N.E.2d at 65].

In contrast, the court in *Washington Federation of State Employees, AFL-CIO Council 28 v. Spokane Community College*, 585 P.2d 474 (Wash. 1978), held that the college had violated the policy underlying the civil service system—that hiring be based on merit rather than politics—by contracting out for janitorial services. Although the contract would clearly have saved the college money, and although a separate statute permitted the state purchasing director to "purchase all materials, supplies, services, and equipment needed for . . . state institutions, colleges, community colleges and universities" (Wash. Rev. Code § 43.19.190), the Supreme Court of Washington voided the contract because "the College has no authority to enter into a contract for new services of a type which have regularly and historically been provided, and could continue to be provided, by civil service staff employees." Three judges strongly dissented, arguing that the majority had intruded upon the prerogative of the legislature in ruling that all state work had to be performed by state employees, even though no statute said so and one statute apparently stated the contrary (§ 43.19.190 above).

Similarly, in *Local 4501 Communications Workers of America v. Ohio State University*, 466 N.E.2d 912 (Ohio 1984), the Ohio Supreme Court (also over a vigorous dissent) held that the university could not contract out for janitorial services during a hiring freeze, while permitting the slow attrition of civil service workers. As in the Washington case, there was no state statute forbidding such a contract, but the court reasoned that the university was circumventing the civil service system; the contracts were thus void. In reaching this result, the court applied the rule from its earlier *Sigall* case, above, but determined that there was sufficient evidence that the university was attempting to thwart the civil service system.

Two years later, however, in *Local 4501 Communications Workers of America v. Ohio State University*, 494 N.E.2d 1082 (Ohio 1986), the same court severely limited its 1984 decision. Noting that the Ohio legislature had in the interim passed a statute permitting public employees to bargain collectively, the court held that civil service employees now had sufficient "protection" through the bargaining table and did not need the additional civil service protection provided by the court's 1984 decision. That decision was thus left to apply only in rare situations where a state agency had attempted to thwart the civil service system but the affected employees had no statutory right to bargain collectively.

As these cases illustrate, the authority of public institutions to "contract out" for services will depend on a variety of factors: the existence of a state statute that expressly permits or prohibits particular types of service contracts, the implications that courts may draw from the civil service laws, the impact that a particular contract would have on civil service employment, the presence or absence of collective bargaining in the employment field that would be affected by the service contract, and the provisions of collective bargaining contracts that the institution has entered with its employees. The weight to be given such factors, and the content of applicable statutes and regulations, will, of course, vary from state to state.

9.2.3. Purchase of real estate. While goods are personal property, land and buildings are real property. The U.C.C. is inapplicable to sales of real property; state real property law governs the bulk of the transaction. An institution's real property trans-actions may include the purchase of title to land and buildings, leasehold interests in land and buildings, and options to purchase or lease land or buildings, as well as easements, rights-of-way, and other interests in land. The title to property transfers only in the first of these types of transactions, and then only at settlement.

Real estate transactions are substantially different from transactions for the purchase of goods or services. The legal documents evidencing the transactions differ, as does the governing law. When an institution purchases land or buildings, for instance, there will be a sales contract with its own special provisions, one or more mortgages or deed-of-trust instruments creating the lender's security interest in the property, and the deed that transfers title to the property. Ancillary to the transaction, the institution may need to consider local zoning law and the property's zoning classification (see Section 5.2), as well as the real property tax status of the property under the institution's planned use(s) (see Sections 5.3 and 6.1). Because real estate purchases can be part of a broader entrepreneurial or academic endeavor, partnership or joint venture agreements may also be involved, as may other real estate transactions, such as purchase options, leases, or lease-backs.

9.2.4. The special case of design and construction contracts. One of the most complex purchasing situations an institution may encounter is that concerning design and construction contracts. Since there are usually more parties involved and more money at stake in these contracts than in other purchase contracts, both counsel and high-level administrators should be directly involved and keenly aware of the difficulties that may arise. See generally R. Rubin & L. Banick, "The Ten Commandments of Design and Construction Contracts," paper presented at the 32d Annual Conference of the National Association of College and University Attorneys, 1992.

9.2.4.1. General principles. Before an institution can develop the specifics of the contracts for a major construction project, it must first implement a financing plan. Then, as owner of the future building, the institution will typically contract with an architect or engineer, or both, to design and oversee the plans for construction. Next the institution will solicit bids from general contractors, select a contractor, and negotiate a construction contract. The general contractor will then hire subcontractors to do masonry work, electrical work, painting, plumbing, and so forth. Numerous suppliers will also be involved, as will insurance companies, bonding companies, and sometimes outside funding sources. Thus, in a standard design and construction arrangement, there are numerous parties that could be liable to the institution and to which the institution could be liable should difficulties arise.

The institution must determine what types of contracts it will seek to negotiate with the architect and general contractor. Construction contracts usually are fixed-price contracts resulting from competitive bidding. In such a contract, the entire project is planned from start to finish before any work is done. A price for the project is fixed, and the contractor begins work for that amount (with a possibility of adjustments for unexpected costs incurred during the work, if the contract so provides). A variation of this type of contract is the cost-plus contract, under which the contractor's profit margin is based on a set percentage of overall costs. This type of contract typically contains clauses under which the overall cost may exceed the base bid, taking into account labor and materials costs actually incurred during construction, but may not exceed a specified "guaranteed maximum cost." Yet another type of contract is the "fast-track design" contract, which an institution may use if the project must begin quickly. In such a contract, actual construction starts almost immediately, and details of cost and design are left to be resolved as the project develops—affording the obvious advantage of speed but also the obvious disadvantage of unresolved design issues and an incomplete, potentially escalating, budget for the project.

Various standard form contracts exist for both architectural and construction services. The American Institute of Architects and the National Construction Law Center, among others, offer standardized form contracts for various types of projects, especially private-sector projects. Some form contracts tend to favor the architect or contractor, and others the institution, so the institution should be careful in its selections. Moreover, the institution should consider adding terms or deleting particular clauses to make the contract fit the institution's particular purposes and concerns.

In negotiating and monitoring the contract, an institution must also anticipate and be wary of such problem areas as construction delays, compensation schemes, unsatisfactory work, insurance coverage, employment discrimination, and changes in design or materials. In addition, the contract should specify who may speak for and bind each of the parties and what dispute-resolution mechanisms will be used.

Although construction contracts may be more enmeshed in statutory law than other contracts are (see Section 9.2.4.2), the general contract principles discussed in Section 9.1 still apply. As indicated there, however, and as the court explained in *Ames Contracting Co., Inc. v. City University of New York* (cited in Section 9.2.2.), "Construction contracts are service contracts providing a combination of labor, skill and materials and are generally exempted from the operation of the Uniform Commercial Code." Making the same point in reference to a subcontractor, the court in *Manor Junior College v. Kaller's Inc.*, 507 A.2d 1245 (Pa. Super. Ct. 1986), noted that, "since . . . [the subcontractor] was hired by [the general contractor] to perform a service, specifically, to provide most of the labor for the installation of a roof, we must reject the assertion of appellant that the U.C.C. is applicable."

Kingery Construction Co. v. Board of Regents of the University of Nebraska, 203 N.W.2d 150 (Neb. 1973), illustrates how general contract principles apply to construction contracts. A general contractor brought an action for declaratory judgment to determine whether, under a contract with the University of Nebraska, it was required to paint exposed pipes in the building under construction. The general contractor's interpretation of the contract was that the mechanical contractor was solely responsible for completing the pipe painting. It did not, however, seek relief from the mechanical contractor; it sought only a declaration from the court that it was not under a contractual duty to the university to do the painting. Relying on basic principles of contract interpretation, the court held that, although "[q]uite possibly the contract, in part, duplicated requirements for painting as pertains to [the general contractor] and the mechanical contractor," the general contractor remained liable to the university to complete the disputed painting. (The court made no comment on possible liability of the mechanical contractor to the general contractor.)

9.2.4.2. Contract formation. Unlike a private contractor, a public college or university may be statutorily required to use a competitive-bidding process in deciding which general contractor to select. Competitive-bidding statutes come in many forms. California and New York have statutes pertaining specifically to state universities and construction contracts (Cal. Pub. Cont. Code § 10503; N.Y. Educ. Law § 376). Both statutes require institutions to engage in public bidding before awarding any major construction contract. Other states have more general statutes that apply to any building project the state undertakes (for example, S.H.A. 20 ILCS 3110/0.01 et seq. (1994); Tex. Rev. Civ. Stat. Ann. art. 601b). State statutes may also require that contractors or architects for public construction projects meet certain licensing requirements (for example, Fla. Stat. Ann. §§ 481.223 (architects) and 489.113 (contractors)).

Competitive bidding carries its own special baggage. An institution is required to accept the "lowest *responsible* bidder" to do the project. This phrase accords the institution some discretion to look behind the bid and assure itself that the lowest bidder is trustworthy and competent to do the work. Thus, an institution may reject the lowest bidder if that contractor is deemed to be nonresponsible, or it may reject all the bids if no responsible bid is received.

Requirements for advertising for bids can also create difficulties in the competitive-bidding process. In *Gibbs Construction Co., Inc. v. Board of Supervisors of Louisiana State University*, 447 So. 2d 90 (La. 1984), for instance, a general contractor sued the university after being denied a contract even though it was the lowest bidder. The contractor had not appeared at the pre-bid conference and thus was technically ineligible to submit a bid. The court upheld the lower court's dismissal of the suit because the contractor had not conformed to the advertised specifications that all eligible bidders were required to attend the pre-bid conference.

In addition to competitive-bidding and licensing statutes, public institutions in some states must also be concerned with minority set-aside statutes. Such statutes "set aside" a certain percentage of state construction work for minority contracting firms. In *City of Richmond v. J.A. Croson Co.*, 488 U.S. 469 (1989), the U.S. Supreme Court indicated that such programs may be constitutional but only if they meet a strict scrutiny standard of review (this volume, Section 3.4). Thus, if the state or a state university seeks to remedy past discrimination through a set-aside program, it will have a heavy burden of justification; a mere general assertion of past discrimination, without specific statistics identifying past discrimination in particular fields and a demonstration of how the set-aside ameliorates that discrimination, is not likely to suffice. Assuming that the statute is valid, the requirements it imposes on the institution will depend on the particular statutory provisions, which vary from state to state. In *Croson*, for example, the set-aside program required that 30 percent of the dollar amount of any contract be subcontracted to minority businesses. Other programs may only establish statewide goals or vest discretion in the institution or statewide system to set its own goals or take other actions favoring minority businesses. In California, for example, the regents of the University of California may consider whether a "substantially equal" bid is received from a "disadvantaged business enterprise" (Cal. Pub. Cont. Code § 10501); if so, the regents might favor that business over another business which submitted a lower bid. Moreover, under Cal. Pub. Cont. Code § 10500.5(a), the regents are encouraged to adopt measures such as set-aside "targets for utilization of small businesses, particularly disadvantaged business enterprises." The various state statutes include their own definitions of "minority" and may also encompass female-owned businesses (see S.H.A. 30 ILCS 575/1 et seq.).

9.2.4.3. Liability problems. Because of the number of parties involved and the complexities of the contract itself, numerous liability problems can arise with design and construction contracts. The following cases illustrate types of liabilities that may arise either for the institution or for other parties.

In *Broadway Maintenance Corp. v. Rutgers, The State University*, 447 A.2d 906 (N.J. 1982), the institution's potential liability to subcontractors was at issue. The subcontractors sued the university for damages suffered from delays caused when one subcontractor's work interfered with the timely completion of another's. They claimed that the university had failed to "synthesize" the work adequately, and thus was liable to the individual subcontractors for the costs of the additional time they had spent. The court held that, because the university had entrusted overall responsibility for supervision of the work to a general contractor, the university was not liable to the subcontractors for damages caused by the delays. This result obtained even though the university retained the power to terminate the general contract. Since the university had contracted with a general contractor to supervise the work, liability for failure to "synthesize" the work rested entirely on that general contractor. The court noted, however, that "if no one were designated to carry on the overall supervision, the reasonable implication would be that the owner [the university] would perform those duties." The court also pointed out that subcontractors "may have valid causes of action against each other for damages due to unjustifiable delay."

In *John Grace & Co. v. State University Construction Fund*, 472 N.Y.S.2d 757 (N.Y. App. Div. 1984), *affirmed as modified*, 475 N.E.2d 105 (N.Y. 1985), the defendant (Construction Fund) similarly escaped liability to a general contractor because it had fully entrusted the execution of the details of the construction contract to an engineer. The general contractor brought suit against the Construction Fund for the cost of repairs to a hot water distribution system the general contractor had installed. The contractor installed the system properly to the best of its knowledge, but the engineer hired by the Construction Fund had allowed improper components to be used in the installation, necessitating the repairs by the general contractor. As in *Broadway*, the court held that the Construction Fund had hired a third party (the engineer) to be responsible for the overall completion of the contract, and it was that third party who was ultimately liable to the general contractor for the cost of the repairs.

Davidson and Jones, Inc. v. North Carolina Department of Administration, 337 S.E.2d 463 (N.C. 1985), also involved a university's potential liability to a general contractor, but this time with unfavorable results for the university. The contractor had encountered unexpected amounts of rock to excavate. The contract with the university clearly stated that the university would pay $55 per cubic yard for any rock excavation in excess of 800 cubic yards. When there turned out to be a 400 percent overrun of excavation, causing a six-month delay, the contractor sued the university, demanding that it pay the agreed-upon $55 per cubic yard plus the additional costs the contractor incurred (such as the cost of keeping personnel at the job site) as a direct result of the delay. The state Supreme Court held that the university was liable for the additional, duration-related, costs, noting that "[t]he trial court found . . . that [duration-related costs] were customarily budgeted as a function of a project's expected duration and were included as such in a contractor's base bid [and] that it was not customary . . . to make any allowance for such costs in setting unit prices." Thus, because the contractor had no reasonable way of predicting 400 percent excavation overruns, the court awarded the contractor not only the $55 per cubic yard for the overruns but also over $110,000 for other on-site expenses associated with the extra time spent on the project.

In *Our Lady of Victory College and Academy v. Maxwell Steel Co.*, 278 S.W.2d 321 (Tex. Civ. App. 1955), the college sued a contractor for breach of implied warranty. A tower on which the contractor had installed a new steel water tank collapsed four months after the work was finished. The court held that the contractor was not liable to the university because the contractor had done exactly what the university had asked. The contractor was under no obligation to inspect the tower to determine whether it was capable of holding the heavier new tank; it was only under an obligation to complete the requested work competently. The university had accepted the completed project and made no complaint for four months, and there was no evidence that the contractor had been less than fully competent in installing the new tank. In short, the contractor could not be sued for successfully completing the task put to it by the university simply because completing that task was a poor idea on the university's part.

An institution may also seek to sue a general contractor because of a subcontractor's breach of contract. One such case is *United States Fidelity & Guaranty Co. v. Jacksonville State University*, 357 So. 2d 952 (Ala. 1978). The court used standard contract principles in deciding that the general contractor was liable to the university for the poor workmanship of the subcontractor. The general contractor was liable even though the architect for the project had specified which subcontractor to use. Although the contract contained conflicting terms regarding the general contractor's responsibility for the work of the subcontractors, the court accepted as controlling a clause stating that the general contractor would be responsible for all project work of the subcontractors. The contract also clearly stated that the subcontractors had no contractual relationship with the university and thus could not be directly liable to it for breach of contract. (Subcontractors would have a contractual relationship with the general contractor, however, who if sued might have the option of impleading the subcontractors, since they would ultimately be liable to the general contractor for their poor workmanship.)

These are but a few examples of the many liability issues that may arise from institutional construction contracts. Counsel will need to be heavily involved in the resolution of these problems if they arise, as well as in preventing such problems through careful contract drafting and construction planning.

Sec. 9.3. The College as Seller/Competitor

9.3.1. The growth of auxiliary enterprises. With increasing frequency and vigor, postsecondary institutions have expanded the scope of "auxiliary" enterprises or operations that involve the institution in the sale of goods, services, or leasehold (rental) interests in real estate.[6] In some situations such sales may be restricted to the members

---

[6]The phrases "auxiliary enterprises," "auxiliary operations," and "auxiliary activities," as used throughout Section 9.3, refer to a broad range of functions that are claimed to be "auxiliary" to the education and research that are the central mission of a higher education

of the campus community (students, faculty, staff); in other situations sales may also be made incidentally to the general public; and in yet other situations the general public or particular noncampus customers may be the primary sales target.

Examples include the sale of personal computers and software to students; child-care services provided for a fee at campus child-care centers; barbering and hairstyling services; travel services; computing services; graphics, printing, and copying services; credit card services; the sale of sundries, snack food, greeting cards, musical recordings, or trade paperbacks by campus bookstores or convenience stores; the sale of hearing aids at campus speech and hearing clinics; the sale of books by university presses; the sale of prescription drugs at university medical centers; summer sports camps on the campus; training programs for business and industry; entertainment and athletic events open to the public for an admission charge; hotel or dining facilities open to university guests or the public; rental of dormitory rooms to travelers or outside groups; rental of campus auditoriums, conference facilities, and athletic facilities; leasing of campus space to private businesses that operate on campus; conference management services; entrepreneurial uses of radio or television stations and related telecommunication facilities; and the sale of advertising space on athletic scoreboards or in university publications.

In addition, institutions may sell "rights" to other sellers, who then can market particular products or services on campus—for example, a sale of exclusive rights to a soft-drink company to market its soft drinks on campus. Similarly, institutions may sell other "rights" for a profit, such as broadcast rights for intercollegiate athletic contests or rights to use the institution's trademarks. The sale of rights (for example, patent rights), as well as the sale of goods and services (for example, medical services), also occurs with respect to research and development (see Section 9.4) and the operation of medical centers (see generally Section 6.5.6).

Institutions may engage in such activities for a variety of reasons. The goal may be to provide clinical-training opportunities for students (for example, speech and hearing clinics or hotel administration schools); to make campus life more convenient and self-contained, thus enhancing the quality of life (banks, fast-food restaurants, travel services, barber shops and hairstyling salons, convenience stores); to increase institutional visibility and good will with professional and corporate organizations or the general public (training programs, conference management services, rental of campus facilities); or to make productive use of underutilized space, especially in the summer (summer sports camps, rental of dormitory rooms and conference facilities). Increasingly, however, in addition to or in lieu of these goals, institutions may operate auxiliary enterprises in response to budgetary pressures or initiatives that necessitate the generation of new revenues or prompt particular institutional units to be self-supporting.

When auxiliary operations are for educational purposes and involve goods, services, or facilities not generally available from local businesses, few controversies

---

institution. To fall within this section, such functions must place the institution or one of its subsidiary or affiliated organizations (Section 2.2.5) in the position of seller and must be (or have the potential to be) income producing. These phrases, however, do not include investment activities generating dividends, interest, annuity income, or capital gains.

arise. Those that do usually involve tort and contract liability issues fitting within the scope of Sections 2.3 and 2.4 (this volume) or issues concerning government licenses and inspections (for example, for a campus food service). But when auxiliary operations arguably extend beyond educational purposes or put the institution in a competitive position, numerous new issues may arise. Critics may charge that the institution's activities are drawing customers away from local businesses; that the competition is unfair because of the institution's tax-exempt status, funding sources, and other advantages; that the institution's activities are inconsistent with its academic mission and are diverting institutional resources from academic to commercial concerns; or that the institution's activities expose it to substantial new risks that could result in monetary loss or loss of prestige from commercial contract and bill collection disputes (see generally Section 9.1) and tort liability claims (see generally Section 2.3.1). Problems may arise in the areas of public relations, government relations (especially with state legislatures), budgets and resources, and insurance and other risk management practices (see Section 2.5), in addition to the legal issues discussed below.

9.3.2. Institutional authority to operate auxiliary enterprises. The scope of an institution's authority under state law may be questioned whether or not the institution's activity puts it in competition with local businesses; but, as a practical matter, competitive activities are more likely to be controversial and to be challenged on authority grounds. Both public and private institutions may face such challenges, but they arise more frequently and with greater variety in the public sector.

9.3.2.1. Public institutions. For public institutions the general question is whether the constitutional and statutory provisions delegating authority to the institution (see generally Section 6.2, this volume) and the appropriations acts authorizing expenditures of public funds are broad enough to encompass the particular auxiliary operation at issue. Challenges may be made by business competitors, state taxpayers, or occasionally the state attorney general. Challenges may focus on the conduct of a particular activity or operation of a particular facility, on the construction of a particular facility, or on the financing arrangements (bond issues and otherwise) for construction or operation of a particular facility or activity.

Several important early cases from the 1920s to the 1940s illustrate the problem and lay the foundation for the more modern cases. One of the earliest (and, by today's standards, easiest) cases was *Long v. Board of Trustees*, 157 N.E. 395 (Ohio Ct. App. 1926)—a challenge to bookstore sales to students and faculty at Ohio State University. Noting that the sales were "practically upon a cost basis," the court upheld this activity because it was "reasonably incidental" to the operation of the university.

In another early case, *Batcheller v. Commonwealth ex rel. Rector and Visitors of the University of Virginia*, 10 S.E.2d 529 (Va. 1940), the issue was whether the university had authority to build and operate a commercial airport. The university offered a course in aeronautical engineering but, without an airport, had been unable to give its students flight instruction or to take advantage of flight instructors and related benefits that the Civil Aeronautics Authority offered at little or no cost. On the university's application, the State Corporation Commission issued it a permit to construct, maintain, and operate an airport for civil aircraft involved in commercial aviation. The plaintiffs, adjoining landowners, sought judicial review of the commission's decision, claiming that the commission had no authority to grant the permit because the university had no authority to operate such an airport. The court recognized that the university "has not only the powers expressly conferred upon it, but also the implied power to do whatever is reasonably necessary to effectuate the powers expressly granted." Quoting the commission, the court reasoned that:

> The University in making application for the permit in question was not asking for the right to engage in commercial aviation, but only for the right to operate and conduct an airport for the landing and departure of *civil aircraft engaged in commercial aviation*, upon which there could be given instruction in student flying so necessary and essential to its course in aeronautics. . . . [T]he University will be authorized by the permit to own and operate an airport upon which aircraft engaged in commercial aviation may land or take off, but this would not involve it in a purely commercial or industrial enterprise, but, as has been shown, in an enterprise necessary to and incidental to the full and complete instruction in the course in aeronautics which it has established [10 S.E.2d at 535; emphasis in original].

The airport thus fell into the category of "necessary but incidental enterprises," the operation of which is within the university's legal authority.

In *Turkovich v. Board of Trustees of the University of Illinois*, 143 N.E.2d 229 (Ill. 1957), taxpayers sought to enjoin the university from using state funds to construct, equip, and operate a television station. The plaintiffs claimed that (1) the university had no legal authority to operate a television station; and (2) there was no valid appropriation of funds for the purpose of building and maintaining a television station, either because the appropriation acts the university relied on were too general to encompass the challenged expenditures or because these acts violated the Illinois constitution's "itemization requirements" governing the legislative appropriation of state funds.

The university had obtained a permit from the FCC to construct and operate a noncommercial television station. The station was to be used to train and instruct students in the communications and broadcasting field, to facilitate the dissemination of research on a campuswide basis, to experiment in the planning and technique of television programming, and to educate the public. (It was not clear from the court's opinion whether the television station would operate in competition with local commercial stations.) Concerning the authority issue, the court determined that, under the statute creating the university, the board of trustees had "authority to do everything necessary in the management, operating and administration of the University, including any necessary or incidental powers in the furtherance of the corporate purposes." Since the challenged activity encompassed "research and experimentation," it was "well within the powers of the University without any additional statutory enactment upon the subject." Regarding the appropriation issues, the court held that "[t]he impracticability of detailing funds for the many activities and functions of the University in the Appropriation Act is readily apparent," and the legislature "cannot be expected to allocate funds to each of the myriad activities of the University and thereby practically substitute itself for the Board of Trustees in the management thereof." The court thus concluded that the board of trustees' expenditures for the television station were consistent with the relevant state appropriation acts and the constitutional mandates concerning appropriation of state monies.

The last of the leading early cases is *Villyard v. Regents of the University System of Georgia,* 50 S.E.2d 313 (Ga. 1948). The issue was whether the regents had the authority to operate a laundry and dry-cleaning business at one of the system's colleges, the Georgia State College for Women. The customers of the business were the college's students; faculty members, executive officers, staff, and their families; and, apparently, former employees and their families as well. The charges for the laundry and dry-cleaning services were lower than those of local commercial dry-cleaning and laundry businesses. The plaintiffs, operators of such businesses, sought to enjoin and restrict the college's enterprise. They claimed that it was unfair for the college "to use rent-free public property in the operation of said enterprise in competition with the private enterprises of petitioners" and that such activities represented a "capricious exercise of . . . power that thwarts the purpose of the legislature in establishing the University System." The court recognized that the regents' powers and duties under the Georgia Code "are untrammelled except by such restraints of law as are directly expressed, or necessarily implied. 'Under the powers granted, it becomes necessary . . . to look for limitations, rather than for authority to do specific acts.' *State v. Regents of the University System of Ga.,* 179 Ga. 210, 227, 175 S.E.2d 567, 576." Then, suggesting that the college's business was "reasonably related to the education, welfare, and health" of the student body, the court held that the business did not transgress any state constitutional or statutory limitations on the regents' authority. Further, "if the operation of the laundry and dry-cleaning service, at a price less than the commercial rate for the benefit of those connected with the school, is lawful, it matters not that such enterprise is competitive with the plaintiffs' business." In so deciding, the court apparently applied an expansive understanding of the college's educational purposes so as to encompass not only services to students but also services to faculty, staff, and others with connections to the college. The court did not specify the particular educational benefit that the students gained from the college's provision of services to this expansive group of customers.

The first of the leading modern cases is *Iowa Hotel Assn. v. State Board of Regents,* 114 N.W.2d 539 (Iowa 1962). The State University of Iowa had planned an addition to its Memorial Union, which would include guest rooms, food service facilities for guests, and banquet and conference rooms. The legislature had passed a statute authorizing the addition. The plaintiff hotel association, however, challenged the constitutionality of this statute and the university's financing and construction plans pursuant to the statute. The court rejected the challenge and upheld the university's authority to finance and construct the addition because it was "incident[al] to the main purpose and complete program of the university." In reaching this conclusion, the court noted that university representatives and organizations commonly invite individuals and groups to the campus; that "[f]ood, housing and entertainment are necessary incidents" of such visits; and that "the percentage of those who use [these services] without invitation is small." Although operation of the addition's facilities could put the university in competition with private enterprise, the university did not encourage sales to the general public and any resulting competition would be merely incidental. (In a later case, *Brack v. Mossman,* 170 N.W.2d 416 (Iowa 1969), the same court relied on its *Iowa Hotel* decision to uphold the

University of Iowa's authority to construct a multilevel parking garage on campus that would be used by campus visitors as well as students, faculty, and staff.)

Churchill v. Board of Trustees of the University of Alabama in Birmingham, 409 So. 2d 1382 (Ala. 1982), involved a quite different issue: Whether the university's speech and hearing clinic had authority to sell hearing aids to its patients. The plaintiffs were private hearing-aid dealers and a hearing-aid dealers association. They argued that the sale of hearing aids was a commercial rather than an educational activity and that neither the university nor other state agencies had authority to engage in commercial activities in competition with the private business sector. This argument rested on Section 35 of the Alabama constitution, which states that "the sole object and only legitimate end of government is to protect the citizen in the enjoyment of life, liberty, and property, and when the government assumes other functions it is usurpation and oppression."

The plaintiffs contended that the university's activity was a profit-making commercial venture that injures private enterprise. The university contended, however, that the sale of hearing aids in its own school clinics allowed students to reap the educational benefits of providing follow-up care to patients and receiving feedback from them—opportunities that would not arise if the clinics had to refer patients to private hearing-aid dealers. Reviewing the trial record, including expert testimony presented by both parties, the Alabama Supreme Court sided with the university:

> We believe the evidence before us . . . amply supports the conclusion that the dispensing of hearing aids, although in the broadest sense it is in competition with private enterprise, is a function which is reasonably related to and promotive of the educational, research, and service mission of a modern university [409 So. 2d at 1389].

The court agreed that "[t]he prohibition of Section 35 is not to be taken lightly" and that "each challenged activity [must] undergo careful scrutiny on a case by case basis to avoid the constitutional 'usurpation and oppression' admonition." Applied to this case, the court said, Section 35 would prohibit the university from engaging in the sale of hearing aids "solely for the purpose of raising revenues." On the other hand, under state statutes the university had clear authority to establish curriculum and provide education—activities that would not violate Section 35. Thus, the question was whether "the commercial aspect, rather than the instructional aspect, was the principal factor in the sale of the hearing aids"—a question the court answered in the negative.

Jansen v. Atiyeh, 743 P.2d 765 (Or. 1987), the most recent of the modern cases, involved the authority of the Oregon State Board of Higher Education, acting through Southern Oregon State College, to provide housing, food, and transportation services to groups of nonstudents attending the annual Oregon Shakespearean Festival. The plaintiffs were motel and hotel operators, taxi drivers, and caterers in the Ashland, Oregon, area. The festival, hosted by Ashland and operated by a nonprofit corporation unaffiliated with the college or the state board, offered a series of events running from spring through fall.

The college had devised and implemented a plan to increase revenues by opening college dormitory facilities to outside groups of more than fifteen persons who gather to pursue an educational objective. Certain groups attending the festival met this qualification and were provided housing and related services for a fee. To accommodate these groups, the college had to renovate some of its residence halls. The renovations were funded with the proceeds of revenue bonds issued pursuant to Article XI-F(1) of the Oregon constitution and Section 351.160(1) of the Oregon statutes. Article XI-F(1) authorized the board to issue revenue bonds "to finance the cost of buildings and other projects *for higher education,* and to construct, improve, repair, equip and furnish buildings and other structures for such purpose, and to purchase or improve sites therefor" (emphasis supplied). Section 351.160(1), which implements Article XI-F(1), authorized the board to use revenue bonds to "undertake the construction of any building or structure *for higher education . . .* and enter into contracts for the erection, improvement, repair, equipping and furnishing of buildings and structures for dormitories, housing, boarding, offstreet motor vehicle parking facilities and other *purposes for higher education*" (first emphasis supplied). The plaintiffs argued that the college's actions were inconsistent with these provisions because the use of the dormitories to house nonstudents did not satisfy the requirement that the constructed or improved buildings be used "for higher education."

The court recognized that "the crucial issue in this case is whether [the college's] policy of allowing the groups to use the facilities is within the definition of 'higher education.'" This term was not defined in the statute. But in light of the board's broad authority (under other statutory provisions) to supervise instruction and educational activities and to manage campus properties, the court concluded that "the legislature has delegated to the board the authority to interpret the term." The issue then became whether the board's interpretation "was within its discretion" and consistent "with the constitutional [and] statutory provisions." Concluding that it was, the court thereby rejected the plaintiffs' challenge:

> [T]he statutory scheme relating to higher education contemplates that the system may offer more than traditional formal degree programs. The Board may maintain "cultural development services," ORS 351.070(2)(c), as well as offer "extension" activities, ORS 351.070(2)(a), in its instructions. [The college] has decided that only groups having an educational mission may use its facilities. That use is within those contemplated by the legislative scheme [743 P.2d at 769].

Taken together, the early and modern cases illustrate the variety of approaches that courts may use in analyzing the authority of a public institution to engage in arguably commercial activities or to compete with private business enterprises. Common threads, however, run through these challenges and approaches. In general, courts would consider the particular functions and objectives of the enterprise; the relation of these functions and objectives to the institution's educational purposes (presumably including the creation of a wholesome and convenient residential life environment for students); the particular wording of the statutes or constitutional provisions delegating authority to the institution or limiting its powers; and judicial precedents in that state indicating how to construe the scope of delegated powers.[7]

---

[7]In some states there may be a narrow and specific statute that expressly authorizes the institution to engage in a particular entrepreneurial activity. See, for example, S.H.A. 110 ILCS 75/1 (1994) (sale of television broadcasting rights for intercollegiate athletic events). Such a statute would alleviate the need for the full analysis suggested here.

If a court were to find that an auxiliary enterprise serves an educational function or is related to the institution's educational purposes, it probably would conclude that the institution has the requisite authority to operate the enterprise, even if an incidental purpose or result is generation of profits or competition between the institution and private businesses. In contrast, the institution's authority would likely be held questionable or nonexistent if the competitive or profit-seeking aspects of its enterprise are not incidental to its educational aspects but instead are the primary or motivating force behind the institution's decision to operate the enterprise. It may be difficult, of course, to separate out, characterize, and weigh the institution's purposes, as all court opinions require. But if an institution carefully plans each auxiliary enterprise to further good-faith educational purposes, documents its purposes, and monitors the enterprise's operations to ensure that it adheres to its purposes, the courts are likely to construe the institution's authority broadly and defer to its expert educational judgments.

   9.3.2.2. Private institutions. For private institutions the basic question is whether the institution's corporate charter and bylaws, construed in light of state corporation law and educational licensing laws, authorize the institution to engage in the particular auxiliary activity at issue (see generally Sections 2.2.1 and 6.3.1). In *State ex rel. [a number of citizens] v. Southern Junior College*, 64 S.W.2d 9 (Tenn. 1933), the issue was whether the college had authority to operate a printing business. The state sued the college on behalf of various individuals who operated commercial printing businesses in the college's locale. The college was chartered as a nonprofit corporation and operated under the sponsorship of the Seventh-Day Adventist Church. In addition to academic education, the college offered training in various applied arts and occupations. It maintained the print shop and other enterprises (according to the court) in order to "instruct students in such lines of work, to give them practical experience, but also to make these different enterprises self-sustaining, and, if possible, to procure from such operations a profit for the general support of the school." Although the printing shop printed the college's catalogues and advertising matter, as well as religious literature for the Seventh-Day Adventist Church, the majority of the shop's receipts came from commercial printing, often in competition with local businesses, from which the college realized a profit.

   The court held that the operation of the print shop exceeded the college's authority under its charter. No authority could be implied from the charter's express grants of power, "since the carrying on of the business of commercial printing had no reasonable relation to the conduct of the school." Moreover, the printing shop ran afoul of a charter provision stating that "by no implication shall [the college] possess the power to . . . buy or sell products or engage in any kind of trading operation." Thus:

> Instead of being an incident, the commercial feature absorbed the greater part of the activities of this printing shop. Without doubt the defendant school was entitled to own a printer's outfit and to use that outfit in giving practical instructions to the students in this art. The institution, however, had no authority to employ this equipment commercially in the printing trade [64 S.W.2d at 10].

The court thereby recognized the private college's authority to operate auxiliary enterprises as long as they served a primary educational purpose, but it determined that the enterprise at issue went beyond the college's authority because its core purposes were more commercial than educational. In such circumstances the college's only recourse was to modify its operation so that educational purposes predominated or to obtain a charter amendment or other additional authority from the state legislature that permitted it to operate the enterprise in a commercial "profit-oriented" fashion.

As the *Southern Junior College* case illustrates, there are clear parallels between the issues facing private institutions and those facing public institutions. In each circumstance the all-important factors may be the primary function of the enterprise and the institution's primary purpose for operating it—a difficult inquiry without clear boundaries. Not all courts in all states will pursue this inquiry in the same way as the Tennessee court, according little deference to the institution's characterization of its purpose; and indeed the inquiry itself and the pertinent factors will differ depending on the particular wording of the institution's charter and the state's corporation laws. Other charters, for instance, may not have restrictive language about "trading" like that in Southern Junior College's charter. In general, it appears that nonprofit private institutions will have as much authority as public institutions to operate auxiliary enterprises, and perhaps more—and that private for-profit (proprietary) institutions may have even more authority than private nonprofit institutions.

9.3.3. State noncompetition statutes. Consistent with recent trends, several states now have statutes that prohibit institutions from engaging in certain types of competitive commercial transactions; and the number of such statutes is increasing. Virtually all these statutes focus on public institutions and do not cover private institutions.[8] Some statutes apply generally to state agencies and boards but include special provisions for state institutions of higher education; other statutes apply specifically and only to state higher education institutions. Some statutes apply broadly to sales of goods and services as well as to the commercial use of facilities, while others are limited to sales of goods. Yet others are even narrower, applying only to the sale of a particular type of goods or service—for example, hearing aids (Idaho Code § 54-2902(d)); uses of television or telecommunications facilities (Del. Code Ann. tit. 14, § 129(e)); or uses of other revenue-producing buildings and facilities (Iowa Code § 262.44). Some statutes set out specific prohibitions and rules; others delegate rule-making authority to the state board or the institutions. University medical centers and health care services often are exempted from these statutes.

An excellent example of the broader type of statute is a 1987 Arizona law on state competition with private enterprise (Ariz. Rev. Stat. Ann. § 41-2751 et seq.). The Arizona statute includes a specific section (41-2753) regulating state community colleges and universities; subsection (A)(1) of this section covers sales to "persons other than students, faculty, staff, and invited guests." It prohibits community colleges and universities from selling such persons "goods, services or facilities that are practically available from private enterprise." However, three important exceptions to this prohibition make it inapplicable (1) when the institution is "specifically authorized by statute" to provide a particular type of goods, service or facility; (2) when the "pro-

---

[8]One narrow exception apparently is Idaho Code § 54-2902(d), which prohibits both "state and local governmental entit[ies]" and "nonprofit organization[s]" from selling hearing aids for compensation.

vision of the goods, service or facility offers a valuable educational or research experience for students as part of their education or fulfills the public service mission" of the institution; and (3) when the institution is "sponsoring or providing facilities for recreational, cultural and athletic events or . . . facilities providing food services and sales."

In contrast to subsection A(1) of the Arizona statute, subsection A(3) covers sales to "students, faculty, staff, or invited guests." It prohibits community colleges and universities from providing such persons with "goods, services or facilities that are practically available from private enterprise *except as authorized by the state governing board*" (emphasis added), thus delegating responsibility and discretion regarding such matters to the board of regents and the board of directors for community colleges. Other subsections contain special provisions regarding competitive bidding (§ 41-2753(A)(2)) and special provisions regarding the institution's sale of "products and by-products which are an integral part of research or instruction" (§ 41-2753(B)). The entire section is implemented through rules adopted by the state governing board (§ 41-2753(C)) and is enforced through a complaint process administered by the governing board and through judicial review (§ 41-2753(D)).

Colorado has a statute similar to Arizona's, passed in 1988 (Colo. Rev. Stat. § 24-113-101 et seq.). Other states have different types of laws. The state of Washington law requires state higher education institutions, "in consultation with local business organizations and representatives of the small business community," to develop policies and mechanisms regarding the sale of goods and services that could be obtained from a commercial source (Wash. Rev. Code § 28B.63.010 et seq.). The Illinois University Retail Sales Act restricts sales by any "retail store carrying any line of general merchandise" that is operated by a state higher education institution or by a contractor or lessee located on the property of such an institution (S.H.A. 110 ILCS 115/1 (1994)). The Illinois statute also restricts credit sales by retail stores operated by state higher education institutions. And the Iowa statute (Iowa Code. ch. 23A) applies broadly to state agencies "engage[d] in the manufacturing, processing, sale, offering for sale, rental, leasing, delivery, dispensing, distributing, or advertising of goods or services to the public which are also offered by private enterprise," but it provides substantial exemptions for public higher education institutions (§§ 23 A.2(2) and 23 A.2(10)(K)).

Since most of these statutes are relatively new, and since not all of them permit enforcement by private lawsuits (see *Board of Governors of the University of North Carolina v. Helpingstine*, 714 F. Supp. 167, 175 (M.D.N.C. 1989)), there are few court opinions interpreting and applying the statutory provisions. A leading example thus far is *American Asbestos Training Center, Ltd. v. Eastern Iowa Community College*, 463 N.W.2d 56 (Iowa 1990), in which a private training center sought to enjoin a public community college from offering asbestos removal courses in competition with the center. The center relied on Chapter 23A of the Iowa Code (discussed above), arguing that the college's training programs were "services" that could not be offered in competition with private enterprise. The court disagreed. Construing the term "services," as applied to a community college, it held that "[t]eaching and training are distinct from, rather than included within, the meaning of 'services,'" and that the statute therefore was inapplicable to a community college's training programs. Alternatively, the court concluded that, even if training programs were considered "services," the statute still would not apply. The statute does not restrict services that are authorized specifically by some other statute, and other sections of the Iowa Code specifically do authorize community colleges to offer vocational and technical training.

In light of these statutory developments, business officers and legal counsel of public institutions will need to understand the scope of any noncompetition statute in effect in their state and to ensure that their institution's programs comply with any applicable statutory provisions. In addition, whether or not their state has a noncompetition statute, business officers, counsel, and governmental relations officers of public institutions should monitor state legislative activities regarding noncompetition issues and participate in the legislative process for any bill that is proposed. Some of the existing statutes are not well drafted, and it will behoove institutions faced with new proposals to avoid the weaknesses in some existing statutes. The state of Washington statute, discussed above, appears to embody the best approach and best drafting thus far available. And perhaps most important, both public and private institutions with substantial auxiliary enterprises—whether or not they are subject to a noncompetition statute—should maintain a system of self-study and self-regulation, including consultation with local business representatives, to help ensure that the institution's auxiliary operations serve the institutional mission and strike an appropriate balance between the institutional's interests and those of private enterprise.

9.3.4. Federal antitrust law. Whenever a postsecondary institution sells goods or services in competition with traditional businesses, as in the various situations described in Section 9.3.1 above, it becomes vulnerable to possible federal as well as state antitrust law challenges (see generally Section 7.2.13). Also, in certain circumstances, it might need to invoke the antitrust laws to protect itself from anticompetitive activities of others. In *NCAA v. Board of Regents of the University of Oklahoma,* 468 U.S. 85 (1984), for example, the university successfully invoked the Sherman Act to protect its competitive position in selling the rights to televise its football games (see Section 8.4.3, this volume). Antitrust claims against universities are illustrated by the two cases below (see also the *Jefferson County Pharmaceutical Assn.* case (discussed in Section 9.2.1), which is relevant to postsecondary institutions as sellers of goods as well as purchasers).

In *Sunshine Books, Ltd. v. Temple University,* 697 F.2d 90 (3d Cir. 1982), a sidewalk discount bookseller (Sunshine) brought suit alleging that the university had engaged in "predatory pricing" at its on-campus bookstore in order to monopolize the market for itself. At the beginning of the fall 1980 semester, Sunshine and the university bookstore engaged in an undergraduate textbook price war. To combat Sunshine's typical price of 10 percent below retail, the university lowered its prices by 15 percent to retain its students' patronage. In retaliation, Sunshine lowered its prices the extra 5 percent plus an additional twenty-five cents per book and then filed suit in federal district court. To prevail on its claim, according to the court, Sunshine had to show that the alleged predatory prices would not return a profit to the seller. For its proof Sunshine introduced accounting methods and calculations demonstrating that the university had sold the books below cost. In defense the university offered its own accounting methods and calculations, which differed materially from the plaintiff's and showed that the university had made a slight profit on its sale of the books. The district court adopted the university's version and granted summary judgment for the university. The appellate court reversed, holding that Sunshine's submissions on allocation of costs were sufficient to create genuine issues of material fact that precluded an order of summary judgment.

In *Ferguson v. Greater Pocatello Chamber of Commerce,* 848 F.2d 976 (9th Cir. 1988), Idaho State University had awarded an exclusive six-year lease to the local chamber of commerce and the *Idaho State Journal* to produce a spring trade show in the university's Minidome. The producers of a similar trade show that had previously been held at the Minidome brought suit against the university, the chamber of commerce, and the *Journal* for allegedly violating the Sherman Act. The federal district court granted summary judgment to the defendants, and the appellate court affirmed, because the plaintiffs were not able to show that the university's lease arrangement unreasonably restrained competition among producers of spring trade shows. The university had awarded the lease through a competitive-bidding process, and all producers—including the plaintiffs—"had an equal opportunity to bid on the lease." The university "did not destroy competition for the spring trade show; it merely forced competitors to bid against one another for the one show [it] was willing to house." Moreover, the Minidome could not be considered an "essential facility"— that is, a facility that was necessary to competition in the trade show market and thus had to be accessible to competitors. (For more on the "essential facilities" doctrine in antitrust law, see Section 9.4.5.) The university itself was not a competitor of the plaintiffs, nor had it excluded or refused to deal with the plaintiffs: "It has merely refused to house more than one trade show per spring, and it has decided that the show will be given to the producer who makes the best bid. The [plaintiffs] simply failed to outbid *their* competitors."

As in other antitrust contexts, state institutions involved in competitive activities may escape antitrust liability by asserting the state action exemption as a defense (see Section 7.2.13). An example is *Cowboy Book v. Board of Regents,* 728 F. Supp. 1518 (W.D. Okla. 1989), another case involving competition between a campus bookstore and a private bookseller. When the bookseller filed suit under the Sherman Act, the court held that the defendant, a state university, was immune from liability and dismissed the plaintiff's complaint. Similarly, in *Humana of Illinois, Inc. v. Board of Trustees of Southern Illinois University,* 1986-1 Trade Cas. (CCH) para. 67, 127, 1986 Westlaw 962 (C.D. Ill. 1986), a private for-profit hospital brought an antitrust action against a state university and a hospital affiliated with the university's medical school. The court held that the state action immunity covered both the university and the hospital affiliate; it therefore dismissed several parts of the suit challenging alleged anticompetitive effects of medical school policies. Such protection may not always be available to state institutions and their affiliates, however, since there are various limitations on the availability of the exemption, as discussed in 7.2.13.

9.3.5. Taxation of income from entrepreneurial activities. Both public and private institutions that engage in entrepreneurial activities may face various taxation issues arising under federal tax laws (see this volume, Section 7.3) as well as state and local tax laws (see Sections 5.3 and 6.1). These issues may arise both with respect to the institution's own activities and with respect to the activities of captive and affiliated organizations (see Rev. Rul. 58-194, 1958-1 C.B. 240, and see generally Section 2.2.5, this volume). The following discussion illustrates the problem and briefly surveys the applicable law.

9.3.5.1. Federal unrelated business income tax (UBIT). Under the Internal

Revenue Code and implementing regulations, an organization that is exempt from income taxation may nevertheless be subject to a tax on the income derived from entrepreneurial activities unrelated to the purposes for which the organization received its tax exemption (this volume, Section 7.3.1). Thus, despite their tax-exempt status, colleges and universities will need to consider this "UBI tax" or "UBIT" if they operate auxiliary enterprises or engage in other entrepreneurial activities that are or may become income-producing activities. The basic question is whether the entrepreneurial activity fits within the Internal Revenue Code's three-part statutory test for identifying unrelated business income (26 U.S.C. §§ 511 and 512; this volume, Section 7.3.1). The more difficult problems usually concern the third part—that the activity generating the income is not "substantially related" to the organization's exempt purposes.

In *Iowa State University of Science & Technology v. United States*, 500 F.2d 508 (Ct. Cl. 1974), for example, the court considered whether income from a university-owned commercial television station constituted unrelated business income to the university and was therefore subject to UBIT. The university operated the television station, WOI-TV, as an ABC network affiliate. The station's broadcasts were comprised of network programming (52 percent); recorded programming, such as feature films and syndicated shows (34 percent); and locally produced educational programming (14 percent). The university argued that its income from the television station was not taxable as unrelated business income because operation of the station was substantially related to the university's educational purpose.

The court acknowledged that "a profitable operation may be justified by factors which . . . show that the conduct of the business was substantially related to the exempt purpose of the institution." Nevertheless, the court rejected the university's argument that WOI-TV was an educational, not a commercial, enterprise because its purpose was to generate profits for the university's use in furthering its educational goals. Emphasizing that the source of the revenue, not its destination, determines whether the enterprise is sufficiently related to the educational goals of the university, the court determined that the source of the revenue at issue (television station operations) constituted a commercial enterprise indistinguishable from other commercial stations. It based its conclusion on the following findings: (1) the station was affiliated with a network; (2) the majority of the station's programming (75 percent) was commercially sponsored; (3) the station's programming policy was to maximize revenues, not to maximize educational programming; and (4) the local educational programming did not differ substantially, either in quantity or in subject matter, from that of stations whose admitted goal was profit maximization. (Educational programs produced by WOI-TV averaged eleven hours per week while the average educational TV station (with less funds than a commercial station) averaged nineteen hours per week.) The court thus concluded that the station's commercial attributes were so "overwhelming as to make it impossible for the operation of WOI-TV to be substantially related to the educational purposes of the University."

Other pertinent applications of the statutory definition of UBI can be found in the Treasury Department's Revenue Rulings and regulations. For example, Treasury has ruled in a "dual use" problem that the fees a university collected from the general public for use of the university ski slope were taxable as UBI, whereas income derived from students using the slope was not taxable, because student recreational use was substantially related to the university's educational purposes (Rev. Rul. 78-

98, 1978-1 C.B. 167). Treasury has also ruled that the sale of broadcasting rights to an annual intercollegiate athletic event was substantially related to exempt educational purposes, and income from the sale was thus not taxable (Rev. Rul. 80-296, 1980-2 C.B. 195). However, the leasing of a university stadium to a professional football team—with accompanying services such as utilities, ground maintenance, and security—was a trade or business unrelated to the university's educational purposes, making the lease income taxable (Rev. Rul. 80-298, 1980-2 C.B. 197). Similarly, Treasury regulations include examples indicating that a university's sponsorship of theater productions and symphony concerts open to the public is related to the educational purpose of the university, and the income generated is therefore tax exempt (26 C.F.R. § 1.513-1(d)(4)(iv)(Example 2)(1993)); and that the solicitation of paid advertising by the student staff of a campus newspaper is substantially related to exempt educational purposes, so that the advertising income is not taxable (26 C.F.R. § 1.513-1(d)(4)(iv)(Example 5)(1993)).

Even if a particular entrepreneurial activity fits the Internal Revenue Code's three-part test for an unrelated trade or business, the income may nevertheless be exempted from taxation under one of the various exceptions and modifications contained in the code (see this volume, Section 7.3.1). Under the exclusion for activities conducted "primarily for the convenience of . . . students, patients, officers, or employees" (26 U.S.C. § 513(a)(2)), for example, the income from sales at a campus bookstore or restaurant or at a university hospital's gift shop or cafeteria may escape taxation (see Treas. Reg. 1.513-1(e)(2); see also Rev. Rul. 58-194, 1958-1 C.B. 240).[9] The same result may pertain for income from the operation of vending machines or laundromats on campus (Treas. Reg. 1.513-1(e)(2); see also Rev. Rul. 81-19, 1981-3 C.B. 353). Also, under the modification for rents (26 U.S.C. § 512(b)(3)(A)(i) and (B)(i)), the income from renting campus sports facilities, auditoriums, or dormitories may escape taxation if the arrangement is structured carefully, so that substantial support or maintenance services are not provided along with the facility (see Treas. Reg. 1.512(b)-1(c)(5); and compare Rev. Rul. 80-298, 1980-2 C.B. 197, discussed above). (Other exemptions and modifications regarding entrepreneurial research are discussed in Section 9.4.4.)

When an exemption or modification does not apply, questions may nevertheless arise about the allocation of deductible expenses and computation of the tax. In the *Iowa State University* case (discussed above), for instance, the court considered the university's claim that it could offset its two radio stations' expenses against the taxable income generated by its television station. The university argued that such treatment was appropriate because the three stations constituted an integrated operation. The court disagreed, reasoning that (1) the two radio stations were noncommercial in nature, whereas the TV station was commercial; (2) unlike the television station, the radio stations' only source of funding was state appropriations; and (3) the income generated by the television station was not available for expenditure by the radio stations. Since the radio stations were not part of the same enterprise as the TV station, nor were they separate taxable businesses, the university could not use

---

[9]A bookstore selling items that fall within the "convenience doctrine," however, may still be subject to taxation on the sale of other items, either because they are not "convenience" items or because they are sold to the general public. See Priv. Ltr. Rul. 80-04-010 and 80-225-222.

their expenses to reduce the taxable income of the TV station. (The university could, however, pool the TV station's income and expenses together with those of other unrelated trades or businesses that it operated (500 F.2d at 522).)

A different type of allocation question was posed in *Rensselaer Polytechnic Institute v. Commissioner*, 732 F.2d 1058 (2d Cir. 1984), another "dual use" case (see generally Treas. Reg. 1.512(a)-1(c) and 1.513-1(d)(4)(iii)). RPI incurred expenses in operating its field house, which it used partly for exempt purposes (student uses) and partly for nonexempt purposes (commercial ice shows, public ice skating, and similar uses). The court allowed RPI to allocate a percentage of its expenses to the nonexempt use, the calculation to be based on the number of hours the field house was used for the nonexempt purposes compared to the total number of actual hours it was in use.[10]

As these examples suggest, the federal tax issues confronting institutions with auxiliary operations may be complex as well as numerous. In light of the increased attention on UBIT from Congress, the IRS, and the private business community, which has been evident since the mid-1980s, federal tax planning with the assistance of tax experts is a necessity. Institutions or their national education associations also should carefully monitor and become involved in, congressional and IRS developments.

9.3.5.2. State and local taxation. Even though an institution's property and activities generally are exempt from state and local taxation, particular auxiliary operations may nevertheless subject the institution to real estate taxes, personal property taxes, sales or use taxes, admission or entertainment taxes, and other such levies, depending on the purpose and character of the activity and the scope of available exemptions (see generally Section 5.3). In *In re Middlebury College Sales and Use Tax* (this volume, Section 6.1), for example, the college's purchases of equipment and supplies for its golf course and skiing complex were subject to state taxes because the golf and skiing operations were "mainly commercial enterprises."

Similarly, in *DePaul University v. Rosewell*, 531 N.E.2d 884 (Ill. App. Ct. 1988), the court held that university-owned tennis facilities leased to a private tennis club were subject to local real property taxation. An Illinois statute exempted real property owned by schools from taxation if the schools were located on the property or if the property was "used by such schools exclusively for school purposes, not leased by such schools or otherwise used with a view to profit" (Ill. Rev. Stat. ch. 120, para. 500.1, now S.H.A. 35 ILCS 200/15-35 (1994)). The lease agreement limited the university's use of the tennis facilities (for physical education classes and the tennis team's use) to a fixed number of total hours and to certain times of the day, and permitted additional university use only with the tennis club's permission and for a fee.

The university argued that it used the property "exclusively for school purposes," because the tennis club's use did not interfere with the university's own use of the facilities for university purposes; and that it did not lease the facility "with a view to profit," because the rents were used to support the university's tennis program, a legitimate school purpose. The court rejected both arguments. Regarding exclusive use, the court applied the "well-established principle that a property used for more than one purpose, to qualify for an exemption, must be used primarily for

---

[10]The IRS has expressed continuing disagreement with this judicial determination; see Priv. Ltr. Rul. 91-47-008 (Nov. 22, 1991).

an exempt purpose and only incidentally for a non-exempt purpose." Since the tennis club's use was primary, the university could not fit within this principle. Regarding profits, the court applied another established rule: that "the application of the revenues derived from [school-owned] property . . . to school purposes will not exempt the property producing the revenues from taxation unless the particular property itself is devoted exclusively to such purposes" (quoting an earlier case).

In other cases, however, institutions have been able to insulate particular auxiliary activities from taxation. In *City of Morgantown v. West Virginia Board of Regents* (this volume, Section 5.3.3), for example, ticket sales for university athletic and entertainment events were not subject to a local amusement tax because the revenues generated were "public moneys" and not "private profit." And in *In re University of North Carolina*, 268 S.E.2d 472 (N.C. 1980), the court rejected the attempts of two towns and a county to assess taxes on the property a university used for an airport, an inn, and off-campus electric and telephone systems. A state constitutional provision stated that "[p]roperty belonging to the State, counties and municipal corporations shall be exempt from taxation" (N.C. Const. art. V, § 2(3)). The local governments argued that the exemption did not apply because the property at issue was used for private purposes unrelated to educational activities, and exemption would give the university an unfair competitive advantage over like businesses in the area that are taxed. The court, however, held that state university property need not be used for wholly public purposes in order to qualify for the exemption; the only prerequisite under the constitution is ownership, not public or private use.

Such determinations on taxability will vary from jurisdiction to jurisdiction and statute to statute. Administrators and counsel must therefore key on the relevant state and local tax laws of their jurisdiction, the applicable exemptions, and the relative strictness with which courts of their state construe them. State institutions should also consider the availability of sovereign immunity as a shield against local government taxation (see *City of Boulder v. Regents of the University of Colorado*, this volume, Section 5.3.3). It is also important to distinguish between auxiliary enterprises that the institution operates itself and those operated by an affiliated organization (see Section 2.2.5), since the tax exemptions available in the two situations may differ (see *City of Ann Arbor v. University Cellar*, this volume, Section 5.3.2).

9.3.6. Administering auxiliary enterprises. As the discussion in Sections 9.3.1 to 9.3.5 suggests, decisions on establishing and operating auxiliary enterprises pose considerable challenges for public and private institutions alike, and involve considerations and judgments different from those that predominate in decision making on academic matters. Administrators should make sure that, through self-regulation and other means, questions about auxiliary enterprises receive high-level and continuing attention. Specifically, administrators should establish procedures and guidelines for reviewing and approving proposals for auxiliary enterprises, as well as processes for monitoring their operations; centralize decision making on major policy issues, to promote consistency in institutional objectives and to mobilize all institutional expertise; identify and resolve threshold questions about the institution's authority to operate and to fund particular enterprises (see Sections 9.3.2 and 9.3.3); and consult with representatives of local businesses as part of the review and approval process, in order to alleviate concerns of unfair competition.

Structural arrangements will also be important. An auxiliary enterprise may be operated by the institution itself, either through the central administration or by a school or an academic department. Alternatively, an enterprise may be operated by an outside entity with whom the institution negotiates a lease of land or facilities, a joint venture or partnership agreement, or other arrangement; or an institution may establish a subsidiary corporation or other affiliate, either profit or nonprofit (see Section 2.2.5), to operate an auxiliary enterprise. The various choices may have different consequences for institutional control, availability of business expertise, legal liability, and tax liability.

To attend to the mix of considerations, institutions will need to engage in substantial legal and business planning. Legal counsel, administrative policy makers, business managers, risk managers, and accountants will all need to work together. Lines of communication to the local business community will need to be opened and cooperative relationships cultivated. And involvement and oversight of high-ranking *academic* officers will need to be maintained, to ensure that auxiliary ventures are not inconsistent with and do not detract from the institution's academic mission. Probably the single most important factor for administrators to emphasize—if they seek to minimize legal authority problems and tax liabilities and to maximize good will with the campus community, the local business community, and local and state legislatures—is a correlative relationship between the objectives of the auxiliary enterprise and the academic mission of the institution.

Sec. 9.4. The College as Research Collaborator and Partner

It has become increasingly common for higher education institutions to align themselves with one another or with other outside entities in the pursuit of common objectives. The primary area of growth and concern is research collaboration involving institutions, individual faculty members, industrial sponsors, and government— the subject of Sections 9.4.1 to 9.4.7. The resulting structural arrangements, such as research consortia, joint ventures, and partnerships, are more complex and more cooperative than those for purchasing and selling transactions (discussed in Sections 9.2 and 9.3).

9.4.1. Potentials and problems. The potentials and problems arising from universities' and faculty members' research relationships with industry have garnered more attention than almost any other higher education development of the past twenty years. This attention is manifested in a wealth of recent books, journal and magazine articles, newspaper accounts, op-ed pieces, conference presentations, legislative hearings, and committee and association reports and policy statements. No single book, let alone a section of a book, can cover all the significant developments or all the significant legal and policy questions. The purpose of this section is to identify the major themes and issues; Sections 9.4.2 to 9.4.7 relate these themes and issues to legal problems that emerge from them and to leading statutory provisions, regulations, rulings, and cases.

Universities and faculty members undertake various types of research in collaboration with industry, but the primary focus is on biomedical and biotechnological research. The concerns escalate when such research moves from the pure science realm to the realm of technology transfer and product development, thus potentially placing entrepreneurial considerations in tension with academic considerations. (See generally M. Kenney, *Biotechnology: The University-Industrial Complex* (Yale University Press, 1986).) In this applied research context, questions about compliance with the government's environmental requirements (Section 7.2.15) and workplace safety requirements (Section 7.2.2) will often arise. Government also may become involved as a partial sponsor of university research done in affiliation with outside entities, thus raising legal questions about various government grant and contract requirements, such as the scientific misconduct prohibitions attached to research funding (see Section 7.4.2). Moreover, since biomedical and biotechnological research sometimes is conducted with human subjects, researchers will be expected to comply with federal requirements for such research (Section 7.2.8). When animals are used, other federal requirements concerning animal research (Section 7.2.9) must be followed. States also may place restrictions on medical research under both common law and statute (see Section 6.5.6). See generally H. Leskovac, *Research with Human Subjects: The Effects of Commercialization of University-Sponsored Research,* IHELG Monograph no. 89-4 (University of Houston Law Center, 1989).) Research collaborations with industry will also frequently involve the university in complex legal problems concerning contract and corporation law, patent ownership and patent licenses, antitrust laws, copyright and trademark laws, federal and state taxes, federal technology transfer incentives, and conflict-of-interest regulations, all of which are discussed below. Litigation raising these types of issues can present sensitive questions regarding the scope of judicial review; see D. Sacken, "Commercialization of Academic Knowledge and Judicial Deference," 19 *J. Coll. & Univ. Law* 1 (1992).

There are many reasons why universities seek to collaborate with business and industry. The financial benefits of such arrangements may be a major motivating factor, as institutions seek to enhance research budgets that are shrinking because of reductions in federal and state research funding and the transfer of research funds to ease other budgeting pressures caused by economic downturns. Clearly, however, research relationships can produce benefits other than the purely financial. An institution may seek to broaden the dialogue in which its researchers are engaged, especially to blend theory with practice; to open new avenues and perspectives to its students; to improve placement opportunities for its graduate students, thereby improving its competitive position in recruiting applicants to its various graduate programs; to enhance its ability to recruit new faculty members; or simply to gain access to new equipment and new or improved facilities for research. Institutions may also be motivated by a good-faith commitment to benefit society by putting academic research discoveries to practical use through transfer of technology.

Various competitive and budgetary pressures also may encourage individual faculty members or their research groups to form their own relationships with industry. Faculty salaries that do not keep pace with those in industry or with inflation may be one factor. Pressures to produce research results in order to meet the demands of promotion and tenure may also encourage faculty members to seek the funds, resources, and technical information available from industrial liaisons in order to boost their productivity. Some researchers may also need particular types of equipment or facilities, or access to particular technology, that cannot be made available within the institution because of their great expense or scarcity. Faculty members also face pressures to place their graduate students in desirable industrial positions and to have placement prospects that will help in recruiting other new graduate students. (See generally M. Davis, "University Research and the Wages of Commerce," 18 *J. Coll. & Univ. Law* 29, 31–36 (1991).)

In addition, federal and state governments have themselves encouraged university-industry collaboration. By placing new emphasis on economic vitality and technological competitiveness, they have created an increasingly hospitable governmental climate within which such collaborations can expand and flourish.

There are various structural and organizational arrangements by which universities or their faculties may engage in entrepreneurial research activities. The most traditional relationship is the grantor-grantee relationship, under which an industrial entity—the commercial sponsor—makes a grant to a particular university for the use of particular faculty members or departments in return for certain rights to use the research produced. Another traditional form is the purchase-of-services contract, under which the university provides training, consultant services, or equipment or facilities to an industrial entity for a fee. The most basic form, which is of great current importance, is the research agreement, especially the agreement for contracted research (see Section 9.4.2). Another basic form is the patent-licensing agreement (see Section 9.4.3). A different type of arrangement is the industrial affiliation, an ongoing, usually long-term, relationship between a particular university and a particular industrial entity, in which mutual benefits (such as access to each other's research facilities and experts) flow between the parties (see Kenney, *Biotechnology* (cited above), at 40–41).

More complicated structural arrangements include partnerships, limited partnerships, joint ventures (a business arrangement undertaken for a limited period of time or for a single purpose, thus differing from a partnership), and the creation (by the institution) of subsidiary corporations to engage in entrepreneurial research functions or to hold and license patent rights. The particular arrangements that may emerge from such structures or a combination of them include the research consortium, the research park, the specialized laboratory, and the patent-holding company. More than one university and more than one business corporation may be involved in such arrangements, and government funding and sponsorship may also play an important role. The legal and policy issues that may arise in such research relationships will depend, in part, on which particular structural arrangement is used. (See generally M. Goldstein, *Technology Transfer and Risk Management* (National Association of College and University Attorneys, 1990), at 16–22.)

Individual faculty members or research groups may form their own independent research relationships with industry. Faculty members may become part-time consultants or employees of a private research corporation; they may receive grants from industry and undertake particular research obligations under the grant; or they may enter contract research agreements of their own with industry. On another level, faculty members may become officers or directors of a private research corporation; they may become stockholders with an equity position in such a corporation; or they may establish their own private research corporations, in which they become partners or sole proprietors.

Virtually all such arrangements, involving either institutional or faculty relationships with industry, have the potential for creating complex combinations of legal, policy, and managerial issues. Perhaps most difficult are the potential conflict-of-interest issues (see Section 9.4.7) arising from arrangements that precipitate split loyalties, which could detract attention and drain resources from the academic enterprise. Research priorities might be subtly reshaped, for instance, to focus on areas where money is available from industry rather than on areas of greatest academic challenge or need (see Kenney, *Biotechnology*, at 111-13). Split loyalties may also encourage faculty to give more attention to research than to instruction, or to favor graduate education over undergraduate education. In addition, the university's traditional emphasis on open dialogue and the free flow of academic information may be undercut by university-industry arrangements that promote secrecy in order to serve industrial profit motives (see Kenney, *Biotechnology*, at 121-31). Disputes may also arise over the ownership and use of inventions and other products of research, as well as of equipment and facilities purchased for research purposes. The institution and its faculty may engage in contractual disputes over the faculty's obligations to the institution or freedom to engage in outside activities; the university and its research sponsors or partners may have similar disputes over interpretations of their research agreements. Products liability issues may arise if any persons are injured by the products that are moved to the market. And various other legal, financial, and political risks may be associated with university-industry relationships. (See generally Goldstein, *Technology Transfer* (cited above), at 6-10.)

Because of the heightened potential for problems and risks, university or faculty involvements in collaborative research ventures require the most careful attention. Before the institution enters any collaborative relationship, administrators and counsel should consider carefully all alternatives and options and weigh all possible benefits and risks. When they decide to enter new ventures, they should devise structural arrangements and draft the pertinent contracts with special care. The institution should consider appointing high-level officers to be in charge of sponsored research, technology transfer, and patent management; it might also consider appointing trustees with special sensitivities to the issues and forming a trustee committee to oversee the institution's outside research ventures. Institutions also should make sure that they are served by legal counsel with expertise in the complex problems of technology transfer and the structuring of commercial ventures, as well as by experienced risk managers familiar with commercial risks. Institutional policies should be adopted formally to deal with such matters as faculty conflicts of interest and patent ownership and licensing rights. And above all, administrators and institutional officers and trustees must maintain a keen appreciation for the institutional mission and the academic enterprise, so that they are not compromised or diluted by research collaborations with industry. (See generally R. Carboni, *Planning and Managing Industry-University Research Collaborations* (Quorum Books, 1992).)

9.4.2. The research agreement. The research agreement is typically the heart of the university-industry research relationship. It is a type of contract, interpreted and enforced in accordance with the contract law of the state whose law governs the transaction (see Section 9.1). This agreement may be the entire legal arrangement between the parties, as in contracted research, or it may be part of a broader collaboration that involves other legal documents or other agreements on activities other than research. One or more universities and one or more industrial sponsors are the parties to the contract. Particular faculty members (or departments or research groups) may be named in the agreement as principal investigators or may occasionally themselves be parties to the agreement. The research agreement may be either a short-term or a long-term agreement, or for a specific single project or a combination of projects. Depending on the type of project contemplated and the purposes of the arrangement, threshold questions may arise concerning the institution's authority to enter the agreement (see Section 9.3.2).

The complex process of negotiating and drafting a research agreement requires scientific and technical expertise as well as legal and administrative expertise. Like commercial contracts, the research agreement should include most of the types of provisions suggested in Section 9.1 above. In addition, there are numerous special concerns that will require the insertion of special provisions into the agreement (see generally D. Fowler, "University-Industry Research Relationships: The Research Agreement," 9 *J. Coll. & Univ. Law* 515 (1982-83)). Such special provisions should normally cover the following matters:

1. Research tasks and objectives—and whether and how the parties may modify them during the course of the project.
2. Supervision of the research—including the responsible researchers and officers within the university and the role, if any, for the corporate sponsor or particular members of the corporate team.
3. Participation in the project—particular members of the university faculty or research staff, or particular departments or research groups, that are obligated to participate in the research.
4. Funding cycles and payment schedules that the sponsor will adhere to and the nonfinancial contributions, if any, that the sponsor will make to the project or the university.
5. Type and frequency of progress reports and oral briefings that the university will provide to the sponsor.
6. Equipment for the research: who will provide it, and who will retain it when the project is concluded?
7. Inventions discovered during the project: who will own the patents, and who will have rights to licenses (exclusive or nonexclusive) and to royalty payments? (Similar questions would also arise regarding copyrights in projects that produce copyrightable materials.)
8. University obligations to disclose research results to the industrial sponsor.
9. Researchers' rights to publish their research results—and whether the sponsor may require a delay in publication for a period of time necessary to apply for patent protection.
10. University obligation to protect any trade secrets and proprietary information that the sponsor may release to university researchers or that may result from the project research.
11. Extent of access the sponsor's staff will have to university laboratories and facilities used for the project.
12. Rights of the sponsor to use the university's name, marks, and logos, or prohibitions on their use by the sponsor.
13. Indemnification, hold-harmless, or insurance requirements regarding special matters, such as environmental hazards and products liability.
14. Parties' obligations to protect university and faculty academic freedom and to protect against university or faculty conflicts of interest.

For helpful listings and discussion of suggested types of contract clauses and suggested language, see J. K. Wiltbank (ed.), *The Practical Aspects of Technology Transfer: A Legal Compendium* (National Association of College and University Attorneys, 1990), 119–246, 263–64.

If an industrial sponsor or university located in a foreign country is to be a party to the research agreement, the U.S. university will require additional expertise in laws governing foreign relations—for instance, the export control laws (see this volume, Section 7.2.1)—and in international and comparative law. The university also will need to understand and protect against its potential liabilities (including antitrust liability; products liability; and liability for patent, copyright, or trademark infringement) under the law of any foreign country in which project activities will take place or to which research products will be shipped. Equally, the university will need to understand and be ready to assert its rights under foreign law—for instance, rights to protection against patent, copyright, trademark, and trade-secret infringement by others. Taxation and tariff questions may also arise. The applicable law may be found not only in the codes and regulations of particular foreign countries but also in the provisions of treaties and conventions that may apply, such as the Berne Convention for the Protection of Literary and Artistic Works, the Paris Convention for the Protection of Industrial Property, the European Patent Convention, the Patent Cooperation Treaty, the Universal Copyright Convention, and the Beirut Agreement (the Agreement for Facilitating the International Circulation of Visual and Auditory Materials of an Educational, Scientific, and Cultural Character). See generally M. Leaffer (ed.), *International Treaties on Intellectual Property* (Bureau of National Affairs, 1990).

These concerns, among others, should be anticipated in the negotiation and drafting of international research agreements, and may lead to the inclusion of special provisions such as the following: (1) a choice-of-law clause specifying what role (if any) foreign law will have in the interpretation and application of the research agreement; (2) special indemnification, hold-harmless, or insurance clauses dealing with liabilities that arise under foreign or international law; (3) a special arbitration clause, or other dispute-resolution clause, adapted to the international context of the agreement (see the New York Convention on the Recognition and Enforcement of Foreign Arbitral Awards; see also *Mitsubishi v. Soler*, 473 U.S. 614 (1985), and note 1 in Section 9.1.6); (4) clauses regarding the parties' obligations to secure patent, trademark, or copyright protection under foreign or international law; (5) a clause establishing responsibilities for payment of taxes and tariffs imposed by foreign governments; (6) a clause providing for instruction for project staff in the language, culture, and business practices of foreign countries where project activities will be conducted; and (7) a clause allocating responsibility for paying particular foreign travel and shipping costs.

Whether the research agreement is domestic or international, problems of performance may arise that could result in contract interpretation disputes, claims of breach, or attempts to terminate the agreement (see generally Section 9.1). In the latter case, the terminating party may argue that it has terminated the agreement because of the breach of the other party. The other party may argue that the terminating party has breached the agreement. In either situation questions will arise concerning the rights and obligations of the parties upon termination. In general, the answers will depend on interpretation of the agreement's terms in accordance with the contract law of the state whose law governs the transactions. If the termination constitutes or was occasioned by a breach, the answers will also depend on the state law concerning money damages and other remedies for breach of contract (see Section 9.1.4 above).

The case of *Regents of the University of Colorado v. K.D.I. Precision Products, Inc.*, 488 F.2d 261 (10th Cir. 1973), illustrates the types of performance problems that can arise under a research agreement and, by implication, underscores the importance of a comprehensive and clear contract. The case addresses three questions that are likely to be asked when a research agreement is terminated: (1) What constitutes substantial performance under the contract? (2) Which party (or who else) has the rights to inventions developed or patents obtained under the contract? (3) Which party owns the equipment used in the project? The court looked to the express provisions of the agreement to resolve each of these issues. The University of Colorado, the plaintiff, had entered into a three-year research and development contract with K.D.I., the defendant, under which the university, for remuneration, was to help K.D.I. develop certain scientific devices. After the first year, K.D.I. terminated the contract. The university sued to recover payment for the work it had performed to the date of termination. K.D.I. defended on two grounds: first, that the university had failed to substantially perform its contract obligations and therefore was not entitled to recovery; second, that even if the university did substantially perform the contract, its recovery was subject to a set-off for the value of project equipment the university had allegedly "converted" to its use.

Regarding its first defense, K.D.I. made three arguments. First, it alleged that the university had failed to give it "exclusive" rights to the technical data developed under the research contract, including rights to all the original plans and designs. The court found that the university had specifically agreed to give K.D.I. "unlimited" (rather than "exclusive") rights to use, duplicate, or disclose the technical data and that the university had performed its obligations to extend such "unlimited" rights to K.D.I.

Second, K.D.I. alleged that the university did not substantially perform because it failed to complete a prior research contract whose work was continued in the current research contract. The court rejected this argument as well, because the current contract was "complete in itself as to the duties and obligations of the parties thereto. It comprises a separate research contract, and there is no intimation therein of the incorporation by reference to prior contracts."

Third, K.D.I. argued that the university did not substantially perform the research contract because it failed to disclose its development of a device called the Optical Communication Link (OCL). The court also rejected this argument, finding that the OCL was not developed under the research contract with K.D.I. Rather, it was developed by two of the university's professors, with the university's money and for use by the university; it was used for the university's own purposes; and it was not necessary to K.D.I.'s purposes. The university therefore had no obligation to disclose the development of the OCL.

Regarding its second defense, K.D.I. argued that certain equipment used by the university for the research project, and retained by the university at termination, was actually the property of K.D.I. The court found that, although K.D.I. had contributed a small amount toward the purchase of one piece of equipment and had made some attempts under the contract to correct problems with another piece, K.D.I. had no legal claim to the equipment. K.D.I. had not loaned or assigned the contested equipment to the university; it had been donated to the project by the university itself and other corporate donors. Moreover, "in the operative and dispositive portions of the contract, as it describes the research to be undertaken, there is no suggestion that title to the equipment was either in K.D.I. or was to vest therein." Since K.D.I. did not have legal rights to the equipment, the university could not have converted it; thus, there was no basis for set-off.

In rejecting K.D.I.'s second defense, the court compared the contract's treatment of equipment ownership (where the contract was silent) to the contract's treatment of patent rights—where the contract contained detailed clauses assigning patent rights to K.D.I. and requiring written disclosure by the university of each invention. K.D.I., therefore, did have patent rights under the contract, but not rights to equipment. No issue concerning patent rights arose in the case, however, because the university conceded K.D.I.'s rights in this realm, and K.D.I. did not allege that the university had attempted to assert patent rights belonging to K.D.I.

9.4.3. Patent law. Federal patent law (this volume, Section 7.2.11) is a primary consideration for universities contemplating a collaborative research relationship that could result in a patentable discovery.[11] Among the most important questions to consider are these: (1) What types of discoveries would be patentable? (2) Who would have the right to own the patents on patentable discoveries, and who would have what kinds of licenses to use the patented discoveries? (3) Would the academic researchers have the right to publish their research results prior to issuance of (or application for) patents on their discoveries, and would the industrial sponsor have any right to prepublication review? (4) What research designs or practices should be avoided because they could constitute infringement of *others'* patents? All these questions are discussed generally in Section 7.2.11. Questions 4 and 2 (in that order) are discussed further immediately below.

Universities and researchers engaged in collaborative research must avoid any use of another's invention, if a patent for that invention is in effect, unless they have obtained a license to use the invention from the holder of the patent rights. The use of a patented invention without a license may constitute patent infringement, to which substantial penalties attach. There is no general "research exemption," in either the federal patent statutes or the judge-made law, that excuses one from infringement liability if the patented invention was used for research purposes. Although the courts have created an "experimental use exemption," it has been construed narrowly to apply only to purely academic research. It thus would not likely apply to research done in collaboration with an outside sponsor that has a commercial interest in the outcome, or to research from which the university or its researchers may profit by discovering and patenting inventions with potential com-

---

[11]Other federal law protecting intellectual property rights, of course, also may be important. Federal copyright law, for example, may protect computer software and other works used or developed in collaborative research ventures (see Section 7.2.10); and the Semiconductor Chip Protection Act of 1984 (17 U.S.C. §§ 901–914) provides similar protection for the architecture of semiconductor chips (see "Reverse Engineering Under Semiconductor Chip Protection Act of 1984," 113 A.L.R. Fed. 381 (1993 and periodic supp.)). State law may also provide some protections—in particular, protection for research that can be considered a "trade secret"; see P. Shockley, "The Availability of 'Trade Secret' Protection for University Research," 20 *J. Coll. & Univ. Law* 309 (1994).

mercial applications. (See generally R. Eisenberg, "Patents and the Progress of Science: Exclusive Rights and Experimental Use," 56 *U. Chicago L. Rev.* 1017 (1989).)

The questions about ownership of patent rights are probably the ones most likely to arise and to be controversial in collaborative research, and they also are the ones most amenable to resolution by careful advance planning. The most basic ownership questions concern the respective interests of the university and its faculty and staff researchers—questions that will arise even when there is no outside sponsorship. The questions become more complex when the institution, or a faculty or staff member, has commercial sponsorship for the research, thus interposing a third party with proprietary interests in the research. The problems are further compounded if government is also a sponsor of the research, although questions regarding federal sponsorship have been clarified by the Patent and Trademark Amendments of 1980, which allow universities to obtain patent rights to inventions developed in the course of federally funded research (see this volume, Section 7.2.11).

The case of *University Patents, Inc. v. Kligman*, 762 F. Supp. 1212 (E.D. Pa. 1991), illustrates the basic elements of the problem and underscores a pitfall that all parties should avoid. The University of Pennsylvania sued Dr. Kligman, an emeritus professor of dermatology who had made major medical advances in the treatment of acne and other skin conditions, and Johnson and Johnson Baby Products Co., to which Dr. Kligman had licensed the patent rights to his most recent discovery. University Patents, Inc., had an agreement with the university to manage its patent rights and joined as a plaintiff in the suit because it was allegedly a beneficiary of the university's arrangement with Dr. Kligman. The plaintiffs claimed that Dr. Kligman had breached his employment contract, and in particular an implied agreement arising from the university's patent policy, when he assigned his rights to Johnson and Johnson rather than the university and did not assign royalties to the university.

Dr. Kligman and the university had never signed a formal agreement regarding patent rights and royalties arising from the professor's research. Thus, the university had no express contract on which to base its claim. The university did, however, have a policy that any patentable discoveries made by employees with the use of university equipment, time, and staff were the property of the university. This policy was delineated in a number of handbooks published by the university and received by Dr. Kligman. Although the handbooks also included the actual patent agreement forms to be executed by faculty members involved in research, there was no evidence that the professor had signed such an agreement or been requested to do so. In lieu of a written agreement, the university relied on the professor's knowledge of the patent policy, and his continued employment with the university after the policy's promulgation, to imply that he had acquiesced in assigning to the university the patent rights he might acquire. The university also relied on the fact that twenty-three years earlier, the professor had assigned royalties to the university from his patent on a drug marketed as Retin-A. The university claimed that letters written at the time of that assignment, and the assignment itself, were evidence that the professor knew of and accepted that patent policy.

The federal district court was not impressed by the university's argument regarding the Retin-A royalties. Noting that Dr. Kligman apparently had developed Retin-A on his own time, with his own resources, and without the use of university facilities, the court determined that Dr. Kligman's assignment of millions of dollars in royalties to the university was gratuitous on his part and not pursuant to any agreement with the school. Nevertheless, focusing on general rules of contract formation (see Section 9.1.1) along with specialized principles regarding employee handbooks as well as the assignment of patent rights, the district court somewhat reluctantly denied the professor's motion for summary judgment:

> This is a close case, particularly in view of the manner in which the University conveyed its Patent Policy and its lax enforcement thereof. On the current record, however, the court cannot conclude that no jury reasonably could find that an implied contract to assign the patent in question was formed between Dr. Kligman and the University. There is evidence, however scant, from which one could find that Dr. Kligman was aware of the Patent Policy since August 1967 and manifested an intent to be bound by it [762 F. Supp. at 1228].

Although allowing the university's case to proceed, the district judge emphasized that courts should be most reluctant to recognize implied contracts to assign patent rights. The court cited the U.S. Supreme Court's own explanation for such hesitancy:

> "The reluctance of courts to imply or infer an agreement by the employee to assign his patent is due to a recognition of the peculiar nature of the act of invention, which consists neither in finding out the laws of nature, nor in fruitful research as to the operation of natural laws, but in discovering how those laws may be utilized or applied for some beneficial purpose, by a process, a device, or a machine. It is the result of an inventive act, the birth of an idea and its reduction to practice; the product of original thought; a concept demonstrated to be true by practical application or embodiment in tangible form" [762 F. Supp. at 1221; quoting *United States v. Dubilier*, 289 U.S. 178, 188 (1933)].

In light of this understanding, the court gave great weight to "the general rule[s] . . . that an individual owns the patent rights in the subject matter of which he is an inventor even though he conceived of the subject matter or reduced it to practice during the course of employment" and that "[t]he 'mere existence of an employer-employee relationship does not of itself entitle the employer to an assignment of any inventions which the employee devises during the employment' (*Aetna-Standard Engineering Co. v. Rowland*, 493 A.2d 1375, 1378 (Pa. 1985)) even where the employee uses the time and facilities of the employer."

Given the courts' reluctance to imply an assignment of patent rights, and the courts' particular respect for the "inventive act," universities engaged in collaborative research should be especially careful to develop and implement express patent agreements with faculty and staff and with all outside sponsors of research. Carefully drawn and widely distributed internal policies, and carefully drafted employment contracts (see Section 3.1.1) and research contracts (see Section 9.4.2), are the safest methods of clarifying rights, effecting assignments in appropriate circumstances, and balancing the rights and interests of all parties. All such arrangements should be spelled out explicitly and clearly in writing, to ensure that courts will recognize them in the event of disputes.

9.4.4. Federal tax exemptions for research. Like auxiliary enterprises (Section 9.3.5), income-producing research activities may precipitate numerous federal tax issues.

The most common issues concern the applicability of the unrelated business income tax (UBIT) (this volume, Section 7.3.1) to the income generated from collaborative research arrangements. Fortunately for higher education institutions, most of their research-related income can be insulated from UBIT if they engage in careful tax planning that is sensitive to the structure and characteristics of each proposed research activity.

First, any research activity that is "substantially related" to the institution's exempt purposes (that is, the educational, scientific, or charitable purposes providing the basis for the institution's tax exemption) does not fit the definition of an unrelated business, and the income will escape UBIT for that reason alone. Second, even if a particular institutional research activity is not "substantially related" (or its character is unclear in this respect), generated income may nevertheless be insulated from UBIT under a statutory "modification" of the Internal Revenue Code, which provides that "[i]n the case of a college, university, or hospital, there shall be excluded all income derived by research performed by any person" (26 U.S.C. §512(b)(8)). Another statutory modification excludes research undertaken for the U.S. government or a state government (26 U.S.C. §512(b)(7)). The problem with these two modifications is that the statute does not define the key term "research," thus making the scope of the provisions uncertain. The Treasury regulations (Treas. Reg. §1.501(c)(3)-1(d)(5)(ii)) help by making clear that both theoretical and applied research may qualify but that activities "of a type ordinarily carried on as an incident to commercial or industrial operations . . . [such as] ordinary testing or inspection of materials or products" do not qualify as research. Further guidance is available from a smattering of Revenue Rulings, Tax Court decisions, and federal court decisions, especially *Midwest Research Institute v. United States*, 554 F. Supp. 1379, 1385–89 (W.D. Mo. 1983), *affirmed per curiam*, 744 F.2d 635 (8th Cir. 1984). In this case the court clarified the distinction between "research" and "testing or inspection" and stated, among other things, that research may qualify for the exclusion even if it is conducted for a fee for a private sponsor that receives a private benefit, and even if the research arrangement puts the exempt entity in competition with other taxpaying businesses (see also *IIT Research Institute v. United States*, 9 Cl. Ct. 13 (1985)).

Other UBIT modifications may also apply to research-related activities and provide further assistance in insulating the university from UBIT. Under 26 U.S.C. §512(b)(2), for instance, royalty income—that is, payments from third parties for the use of some valuable right, such as a copyright, trademark, or patent—is excludable from taxation.[12] Thus, when a university owns patents and licenses its patent rights to third parties in return for license fees, the resulting income is excludable as royalty income (see Rev. Rul. 76-297, 1976-2 C.B. 178). Similarly, income from the rental of real property is excludable (26 U.S.C. §512(b)(3)(A)(i)). Thus, if a university rents laboratory space, for example, to a corporate organization, the rental income would generally not be taxable under UBIT. Dividends from investments are also excludable from UBIT (26 U.S.C. §512(b)(1)), as are capital gains (26 U.S.C. §512(b)(5)), thus

---

[12]For assistance in defining the term "royalty" and understanding the attributes that render royalties nontaxable under UBIT, see, for example, *Fraternal Order of Police v. Commissioner*, 87 T.C. (Tax Court) 747 (1986), *affirmed*, 833 F.2d 717 (7th Cir. 1987); *Disabled American Veterans v. United States*, 650 F.2d 1178 (Cl. Ct. 1981).

excluding certain passive income a university might receive if it held an equity position in a for-profit research corporation.

There are a number of important limitations, however, on these avenues of tax avoidance. The exclusion of royalty income or rental income will be jeopardized if personal services are provided along with the rights licensed or property rented (see Rev. Rul. 76-297, 1976-2 C.B. 178; Rev. Rul. 81-178, 1981-2 C.B. 135; and this volume, Section 9.3.5.1). The income from rental of *personal* property is generally not excludable (26 U.S.C. §512(b)(1)(A)(ii)). Thus, for example, a university could not deduct income from rental of computer time on a computer having excess capacity (see *Midwest Research Institute,* above, 554 F. Supp. at 1388). And the above exclusions will not apply to royalty or rental income, dividends, or capital gains derived from debt-financed property (property the institution has acquired with borrowed funds) (26 U.S.C. §512(b)(2) and (3)).

Whenever an institution moves beyond basic structural arrangements, such as sponsored-research agreements and patent-licensing agreements, to more complex arrangements, such as joint ventures and subsidiary corporations, additional considerations may affect UBIT's application to the income generated. If a university contracts with or creates a separate corporation for patent management, this arrangement would make it more difficult to determine whether and to whom the royalty exclusion applies (see Rev. Rul. 73-193, 1973-1 C.B. 262). Or if a university establishes a taxable subsidiary corporation to engage in certain product development functions, this arrangement would raise additional questions concerning the taxability of royalties, rent, or dividend income the university received from its subsidiary (see 26 U.S.C. §512(b)(13)). Moreover, such other research arrangements as the establishment of a subsidiary corporation or joint venturing with another separately established corporation may raise questions about whether the subsidiary or other corporation qualifies for tax-exempt status under 26 U.S.C. §501(c)(3) (see this volume, Section 7.3.1).

In *Washington Research Foundation v. Commissioner,* 50 T.C. (Tax Court) *mem.* 1457, 1985 Westlaw 15192 (1985), for example, the court affirmed the IRS's denial of WRF's application for recognition as a tax-exempt organization under Section 501(c)(3). To obtain an exemption under this section, an organization must show that it is "operated exclusively for exempt purposes." To meet this "operational test," an organization must be operated primarily for scientific, educational, or charitable purposes (exempt purposes), and it must not be engaged in any substantial nonexempt purpose (Treas. Reg. §1.501(c)(3)-1(c)(1)). WRF's stated purposes were "(1) [t]o financ[e] . . . scientific research at . . . universities . . . ; (2) to increase the rate of technology transfer from research departments of universities . . . to industry . . . ; and (3) to strengthen and diversify the economy of Washington State." WRF argued that these were scientific, educational, and charitable purposes. The court examined and rejected each of WRF's characterizations of its purposes. First, although WRF matched universities' research activities with industry's needs and contributed its net income to universities, these activities were not "scientific." Second, WRF's publication of scientific newsletters and scientific advances was intended to benefit commercial entities, rather than the academic community or the general public, and therefore was not "educational." Third, WRF's activities were not charitable, because they primarily benefited private industry rather than the community at large. In contrast, according to the court, WRF was operated for a substantial commercial purpose, because its primary function was to develop patents to make them available to private industry, it competed with other commercial firms, and it planned its activities so as to maximize profits.

Besides raising questions about the tax status of a subsidiary or separate corporation, some research arrangements could involve the university so deeply in commercial, profit-making activities that its own tax-exempt status would be questioned. Joint ventures and partnerships are the arrangements most likely to raise such concerns and thus to require especially careful tax planning (see C. Kertz & J. Hasson, "University Research and Development Activities: The Federal Income Tax Consequences of Research Contracts, Research Subsidiaries and Joint Ventures," 13 *J. Coll. & Univ. Law* 109, 124–45 (1986)).

9.4.5. Antitrust law. Federal antitrust laws (see this volume, Section 7.2.13) apply to and create potential liabilities for universities or their separate research entities when they engage in certain types of collaborative research activities. As with other applications of antitrust law to the campus, the predicate to liability is the existence of concerted research activities that have anticompetitive or monopolistic effects on the market. The risks of such effects are probably greater with applied than with basic research because of the potential competitive market uses for the products of applied research.

Particular activities within or adjunct to an overall research collaboration (joint venture, consortium, or other concerted activity) may make the collaboration vulnerable to antitrust challenges. Such challenges might be made, for example, when patent-licensing and enforcement activities, taken together, allow a research venture to control a certain market or access to a certain technology needed to compete in the market (see generally *SCM Corp. v. Xerox Corp.*, 463 F. Supp. 983 (D. Conn. 1978), *certified question answered*, 645 F.2d 1195 (2d Cir. 1981)); or when the joint operation of a common facility, such as a laboratory or medical treatment facility involving expensive specialized equipment, puts the collaborators in a competitive position in the market and they exclude potential competitors from use of the facility (see generally *MCI Communications Corp. v. American Telephone and Telegraph Co.*, 708 F.2d 1081 (7th Cir. 1983)); or when a computer network is operated under similar circumstances as part of a research collaboration.

Fortunately for higher education institutions, a 1984 law considerably eases these antitrust concerns. The National Cooperative Research Act of 1984 (15 U.S.C. §§ 4301–4305) limits the federal and state antitrust liability of "joint research and development ventures," as defined in Section 4301(a)(6) and (b) of the Act. Section 4302 stipulates that, in antitrust actions against such ventures, the "rule of reason" rather than the "per se rule" applies. Section 4303 exempts research and development ventures from treble-damages liability under 15 U.S.C. § 15 by limiting any recoveries against them in civil suits to actual damages, interest, and costs of suit, including attorney's fees. To claim the protection of Section 4303, the joint venture previously must have filed a written notification with the U.S. attorney general and the Federal Trade Commission, as provided in Section 4305(a) (see generally D. Foster, G. Curtner, & E. Dell, "The National Cooperative Research Act of 1984 as a Shield from the Antitrust Laws," 5 *J. Law & Commerce* 347 (1985)).

9.4.6. Federal government incentives for research collaboration. The federal government provides numerous types of incentives for technology transfer and university-industry research collaboration. Knowledge of such incentives, and how to obtain and deploy their benefits, will be important for higher education institutions contemplating or participating in collaborative activities.

One type of incentive involves the creation of exemptions from or modifications of federal regulatory requirements. The Patent and Trademark Amendments of 1980 (94 Stat. 3015, discussed in this volume, Section 7.2.11), for example, modified federal patent law to facilitate technology transfer and university-industry collaborations involving inventions discovered during federally funded research projects. The National Cooperative Research Act of 1984 (discussed in Section 9.4.5) provides special protections against antitrust liability for "joint research and development ventures." And amendments to export control laws and regulations have been implemented to ease their impact on university research collaborations with foreign scientists (M. Lam, "Restrictions on Technology Transfer Among Academic Researchers: Will Recent Changes in the Export Control System Make a Difference?" 13 *J. Coll. & Univ. Law* 311 (1986)).

Congress may also build incentives for research collaboration into the federal tax laws. The statutory modifications to UBIT that exclude certain research income and royalty income (this volume, Section 9.4.4) are examples. In addition, special tax treatment for investors in certain research and development ventures may facilitate university participation in such ventures (see J. Bartlett & J. Siena, "Research and Development Limited Partnerships as a Device to Exploit University Owned Technology," 10 *J. Coll. & Univ. Law* 435 (1983–84)). At various times and in various ways, Congress has provided other tax credits, charitable deductions, expense deductions, accelerated depreciation formulas, and similar devices that encourage involvement of sponsors in university research. Section 231 of the Tax Reform Act of 1986 (Pub. L. No. 99-514), for example, authorizes certain tax credits for sponsors of research at universities (26 U.S.C. § 41). Such incentives, combined with the lenient treatment of income from research-related activities, have created a highly favorable tax environment for universities to exploit their expertise in new technologies.

Government also provides direct monetary incentives for biotechnology and biomedical research that may involve or lead to university-industry collaborations. Many National Science Foundation and National Institutes of Health grant programs, for instance, would fall into this category. Government agencies also may provide funds for technology risk assessment projects. The U.S. Department of Agriculture, for example, has awarded grants under its Biotechnology Risk Assessment Research Grants Program (see 57 Fed. Reg. 14308 (Apr. 17, 1992)).

Other legislation and executive orders have created yet other types of incentives. The Stevenson-Wydler Technology Innovation Act of 1980 (94 Stat. 2311, 15 U.S.C. § 3701 et seq.), as amended, is a primary example. The Act constituted a first step toward development of a comprehensive national policy on technology and acknowledged the role of academia in scientific discoveries and advances. One of its stated purposes is to "encourag[e] the exchange of scientific personnel among academia, industry, and Federal laboratories" (15 U.S.C. § 3702(5)). Another purpose—added by a later amendment, the National Competitiveness Technology Transfer Act of 1989— is to stimulate "collaboration between universities, the private sector, and government-owned, contractor-operated laboratories in order to foster the development of technologies in areas of significant economic potential" (15 U.S.C. § 3701).

The 1980 Stevenson-Wydler Act established Centers for Industrial Technology to be operated by universities or other nonprofit organizations for the purpose of collecting and disseminating "scientific, engineering, and technical information among universities and industry" (15 U.S.C. § 3705(a)(4)). These centers were developed under the auspices of the Department of Commerce and the National Science Foundation, which provided nonrenewable planning grants for their creation. In 1988 Congress reorganized these centers into the National Technical Information Service and authorized the secretary of commerce to carry out the functions of the service (National Technical Information Act, 102 Stat. 2594, codified at 15 U.S.C. § 3704(b)). These functions include the collection and dissemination of nonclassified scientific information gathered from parties with which the information service has contracted.

The Federal Technology Transfer Act of 1986 (100 Stat. 1795, codified at 15 U.S.C. §§ 3710a–3710d) added important new provisions to assist in the transfer of commercially useful technology from federal laboratories to the private sector. Under this 1986 Act, federally operated laboratories were authorized to enter into cooperative research and development agreements and intellectual property–licensing agreements with state and local government agencies, nonprofit organizations (including universities), corporations, partnerships, and foundations (15 U.S.C. § 3710a). The Act also governs the distribution of royalties received from the licensing of inventions under such agreements; an inventor who has assigned his or her right in the invention to the government receives 15 percent of the royalties from the invention, and the government laboratory receives the remaining 85 percent.

In 1988 Congress further amended the Stevenson-Wydler Act in the Technology Competitiveness Act (102 Stat. 1107, 1426, codified at 15 U.S.C. § 3704a). The Act established a clearinghouse to serve as a "central repository of information" with the objective of enhancing the competitiveness of American business. Under this Act the secretary of commerce, through the National Institute of Standards and Technology, may establish relationships with universities and other entities to collect and disseminate information.

Another similar example of a federal incentive is the Omnibus Trade and Competitiveness Act (102 Stat. 1107, 1514, codified at 20 U.S.C. § 1145), amending the Higher Education Act of 1965. This Act authorized the appropriation of millions of dollars to fund regional technology transfer centers throughout the United States. Each region contains a center operated by a designated higher education institution within the region to facilitate the transfer of technology from the federal government to academia and the private sector. The specific goal of each regional center is to have a positive economic impact on its region.

9.4.7. Conflicts of interest. The growth of university-industry research collaborations, with the resultant potential for financial gains and split loyalties (Section 9.4.1), has created an enhanced awareness of ethical issues in research and technology transfer. Increased attention to scientific misconduct (see Sections 3.5.2 and 7.4.2) is one manifestation. Another, and perhaps most prominent, manifestation is the spotlight now being cast on conflict-of-interest issues. (See generally H. Leskovac, Comment, "Ties That Bind: Conflicts of Interest in University-Industry Links," 17 *U. Cal. Davis L. Rev.* 895 (1984).)

The concept of conflict of interest, as applied to higher education, has several important variables. In the traditional conflict-of-interest situation, an employee or officer of an institution—motivated by an outside financial interest or the prospect of personal financial gain—exerts inappropriate influence on the institution's business judgments or contracting decisions. A newer and more subtle conflict situation is the "conflict of commitment," in which outside commitments (or the search for outside commitments) lead an institutional employee or officer to lessen or subvert commitment to the institution. In either situation the conflict may be an actual conflict or merely a potential conflict or appearance of conflict; the institution must be concerned about both. Furthermore, conflicts may be occasioned either by an individual employee acting on his own behalf rather than on behalf of the university, or by the university itself acting for itself through its officers and employees. Thus, the university itself may have a conflict, and may need to monitor its own activities as well as the outside activities of its employees if it is to escape the debilitating effects of conflicts of interest.

The potential debilitating effects are numerous. As one author has described:

> Among the manifestations of these conflicts are the use of students and university equipment for private gain, the division of working time in such a way as to slight the university, the shifting of research to accommodate corporate sponsors, the transfer of patentable inventions from the university to private laboratories, and the suppressing of research results [M. Kenney, *Biotechnology: The University-Industrial Complex* (Yale University Press, 1986), at 113].

Another commentator, focusing especially on conflicts of commitment, has noted three sets of concerns:

> (1) the concern that the industrial sponsor will attempt to *improperly control the scientific or technical approach* to the work funded by the sponsor, thereby invading and diminishing the objectivity and independence of the scientific investigator; (2) the problem that faculty investigators, induced by proprietary concerns on the part of the industrial sponsor, may become *improperly secretive about their work*, not only to the detriment of free and open dissemination of any scientific and technological developments, but also to the detriment of interaction with and among their students; and (3) the concern that the industrial sponsor will *improperly attempt to influence or control the choice of, or approach to, future research* in the same or related areas. These problems are generally regarded as particularly acute if the faculty investigators involved (or the university itself) have, or will have, *an equity or some other on-going financial interest in the industrial sponsor* [D. Fowler, "Conflicts of Interest: A Working Paper" (presented at conference of National Association of College and University Attorneys, Mar. 11-12, 1983, at 1-2)].

And yet another commentator focuses on other types of conflicts, called "intellectual conflicts," which may "be less obvious" than conflicts of commitment but nevertheless strike "at the heart of the academic enterprise." Such conflicts may create "[c]ognitive dissonance—the subtle shifting of one's ideas toward those positions favoring personal interests" (R. H. Linnell, "Professional Activities for Additional Income: Benefits and Problems," in R. H. Linnell (ed.), *Dollars and Scholars* (University of Southern California Press, 1982), 43-70, at 62).

Both the legislative and the executive branches of the federal government and of state governments have become increasingly concerned with conflicts of interest in university-industry research relationships, especially for research supported with government funding. In such circumstances, yet another variation on conflict of interest may occur: the "risk of conflict between the private interests of individuals, or of the companies with which they are involved, and the public interest that [government] funding should serve" (Investigator Financial Disclosure Policy, 59 Fed. Reg. 33308 (National Science Foundation, June 28, 1994)). Though persistent, such legislative and executive concerns have not yet resulted in substantial government regulation of conflicts of interest in research. There are, however, some important developments.

At the federal level, some older and more general conflict-of-interest statutes, such as the Anti-Kickback Act (41 U.S.C. §§ 51 and 54), could apply to research activities. More recently, narrow conflict-of-interest provisions have appeared in appropriations acts, OMB circulars, departmental contracting regulations, and agency grant policies or terms and conditions. Examples include Section 8107 of the Fiscal Year 1992 Department of Defense Appropriations Act (Pub. L. No. 102-172), which contains a conflict-of-interest provision applicable to Federally Funded Research and Development Centers (105 Stat. 1150, 1199 (102d Cong., 1st Sess. (1991)); Department of Defense Federal Acquisition Regulations (48 C.F.R. § 235.017(a)(2) and 48 C.F.R. Part 203: "Improper Business Practice and Personal Conflicts of Interest"); and Department of Energy Acquisition Regulations (48 C.F.R. subpart 909.5: "Organizational Conflicts of Interest"). The most recent example, several years in development, is the National Science Foundation's "Investigator Financial Disclosure Policy," 59 Fed. Reg. 33308 (June 28, 1994).

At the state level, a number of states have ethics-in-government statutes or administrative regulations that would have some application to research activities at state colleges and universities. Under the Illinois Governmental Ethics Act (S.H.A. 5 ILCS 420/1-101 et seq. (1994)), for example, state government employees who earn more than $35,000 annually must file a statement of economic interest. Members of the board of regents and trustees and employees of the state colleges and universities are expressly covered, but there is a potentially large exception for "those primarily employed by the State in teaching as distinguished from administrative duties" (§ 604A-101(f)). The statement must be filed annually and must list income, honoraria, gifts, and capital assets and identify the source thereof, and must also list any other association, aside from the employment, that the employee has with Illinois state agencies and institutions. Additionally, faculty members are subject to the following conflict-of-interest statute:

> No full time member of the faculty of any State-supported institution of higher learning may undertake, contract for or accept anything of value in return for research or consulting services for any person other than that institution on whose faculty he serves unless (a) he has the prior written approval of the President of that institution, or a designee of such President, to perform the outside research or consulting services, such request to contain an estimate of the amount of time which will be involved, and (b) he submits to the President of that institution or such designee, annually, a statement of the amount of actual time he has spent on such outside research or consulting services [S.H.A. 110 ILCS 100/1 (1994)].

Under the Georgia statutes (tit. 45, ch. 10, art. 2 of the Official Code of Georgia: "Conflicts of Interest"), state employees are prohibited from entering business transactions with the agency that employs them (Ga. Code Ann. § 45-10-23). There is a small exception, however, for employees of the board of regents of the University System of Georgia (§ 45-10-23), which allows them to serve "as members of the governing boards of private, nonprofit, educational, athletic, or research related foundations and associations which are organized for the purpose of supporting institutions of higher education in [Georgia]," even though these organizations may transact business with the employees' institution. Another exception allows state employees to lease laboratory and research facilities owned by the board of regents for certain private business purposes when the facilities are not otherwise in use (§ 45-10-25(a)(16)). Another provision prohibits members of the board of regents and trustees and officials of higher education institutions from entering or profiting from certain transactions and contracts with their institutions (§ 45-10-40).

Virginia has a statute (Va. Code Ann. §§ 2.1-639.1 to 2.1-639.24), entitled the State and Local Government Conflicts of Interest Act. Its provisions apply to all state and local government employees, prohibiting them from accepting anything of value from sources other than the agency that employs them and from having a personal interest in any contract of the agency that employs them. There is a specific exception, however, for authors of textbooks who are affiliated with higher education institutions that have contracted with a publisher to sell the author's book (§ 2.1-639.6.C.4). Violation of the Act is a misdemeanor; and if the employee is convicted, a judge may order him or her to vacate the position.

Institutions that engage in sponsored research activities, or whose faculty and staff engage in them, will of course need to track the continuing debate and developments at all levels and branches of government and in the national educational and professional organizations. The key to success in managing conflicts of interest, however, is effective institutional policies and enforcement mechanisms—whether or not government may require them. Such policies may range from disclosure requirements and confidentiality requirements to prohibitions of certain types of transactions and limitations on outside employment. If sensitively constructed and clearly drafted, such policies are likely to be constitutional. In *Adamsons v. Wharton*, 771 F.2d 41 (2d Cir. 1985), for example, a state medical school enacted a rule limiting the amount of a faculty member's income from private practice. The plaintiff challenged the constitutionality of the regulation on three grounds: that it deprived him of his "property" without due process of law; that, in exempting part-time professors, the regulation discriminated against him in violation of equal protection; and that the regulation violated his First Amendment freedom of association. The court rejected all three claims, calling them "farfetched at best" and noting that the regulation was supported by the medical school's "legitimate interest in promoting devotion to teaching."

Numerous resources are available to guide institutions that are devising or reviewing conflict-of-interest policies. Among the most helpful are the reports and statements of various national associations. See, for example, the Association of American Universities' February 1985 report on university-industry relations (Burke entry in the bibliography for Section 9.4, at the end of this chapter); the 1965 joint statement of the AAUP and the American Council on Education, "On Preventing Conflicts of Interest in Government-Sponsored Research at Universities," reprinted in *AAUP Policy Documents and Reports* (AAUP, 1990), 83–85; *Guidelines for Dealing with Faculty Conflicts of Commitment and Conflicts of Interest in Research* (Association of American Medical Colleges, 1990); and AHC Task Force on Science Policy, *Conflicts of Interest in Academic Health Centers* (Association of Academic Health Centers, 1990).

Selected Annotated Bibliography

General

Greene, Deirdre (ed.). *College and University Business Administration* (5th ed., National Association of College and University Business Officers, 1992). A three-volume overview of management and accounting principles designed specifically for use by higher education administrators, especially business officers. The first volume is devoted to "institutionwide systems" and includes a chapter on legal issues (by Marcus Mills). Volume 2 covers "fiscal functions" and deals with such topics as taxation, endowment management, risk management and insurance, and auditing. Volume 3 covers "institutional functions" such as facilities management, research and sponsored programs, and auxiliary enterprises. All chapters end with a bibliographical list of resources and a list of names and addresses of government and professional organizations that work on matters discussed in the chapter.

Sec. 9.1 (The Contract Context)

Calamari, John D., and Perillo, Joseph M. *The Law of Contracts* (3d ed., West, 1987). A comprehensive discussion of the principles of the law of contracts. Individual chapters are devoted to such subjects as offer and acceptance, consideration, promissory estoppel, breach, and damages.

Sec. 9.2 (The College as Purchaser)

Cole, Elsa Kircher, and Goldblatt, Steven M. "Award of Construction Contracts: Public Institutions' Authority to Select the Lowest Responsible Bidder," 16 *J. Coll. & Univ. Law* 177 (1989). A review of the statutes and case law on when and how institutions may reject an apparent low bidder as nonresponsible. Includes helpful suggestions on factors and processes to be used in making such a decision.
Special Project, "Article Two Warranties in Commercial Transactions: An Update," 72 *Cornell L. Rev.* 1159 (1987). A comprehensive analysis of express and implied warranties applicable to the sale of goods under the Uniform Commercial Code.
Sweet, Justin. *Sweet on Construction Industry Contracts: Major AIA Documents* (2d ed., Wiley Law Pubs., 1992 plus annual supp.). A thorough and practical analysis of the American Institute of Architects forms used in construction contracting, with advice on selecting forms, drafting contracts, and handling contract disputes.
Weltzenbach, Lanora (ed.). *Contracting for Services* (National Association of College and University Business Officers, 1982). An overview of the various phases of the contracting process as it relates to services. Provides practical assistance in managing each phase. Includes case studies; analysis of particular contract clauses; sample contracts for nine service areas (cleaning and custodial, food, bookstore,

vending, security, professional, consultant, construction, and equipment maintenance); and technical discussions applying contracting principles to four specific
types of services (food, professional design, risk management consultant, and billing and collection).

See Bookman entry in bibliography for Section 2.3.

Sec. 9.3 (The College as Seller/Competitor)

Niccolls, Carol S., Nave, Margaret E., & Olswang, Steven G. "Unrelated Business
Income Tax and Unfair Competition: Current Status of the Law," 15 *J. Coll. &
Univ. Law* 249 (1989). A discussion of the current and emerging legal issues regarding the unrelated business income tax and its application to colleges and
universities. The authors cite numerous IRS and court decisions to illustrate the
various income-producing enterprises undertaken by colleges and universities and
their treatment by the IRS and the courts.

Toohey, Daniel, & Gray, Todd. "Doing Business in the New Technology: Problems
for College and University Counsel," 10 *J. Coll. & Univ. Law* 455 (1983–84).
Explores legal problems that may arise when higher education institutions operate
radio or television stations and related auxiliary facilities. Covers FCC rules regarding "remunerative uses" of telecommunication facilities, state statutory restraints
on telecommunications competition, and tax consequences under UBIT. Primarily for legal counsel.

See Bookman entry in bibliography for Section 2.3 and Kirby entry and Proger, Busey,
& Miller entry in bibliography for Section 7.2.

Sec. 9.4 (The College as Research Collaborator and Partner)

Bartlett, Joseph W., & Siena, James V. "Research and Development Limited Partnerships as a Device to Exploit University Owned Technology," 10 *J. Coll. & Univ.
Law* 435 (1983–84). Describes Research and Development Limited Partnerships
and encourages universities to use these partnerships to reduce their tax exposure
while exploring the potential for commercial returns from technology developed
at the institution.

Braxton, John M. (ed.). Symposium, "Perspectives on Research Misconduct," 35 *J.
Higher Educ.* 239 (1994). A special issue (May/June) that includes these articles:
Melissa Anderson, Karen Louis, & Jason Earle, "Disciplinary and Department
Effects on Observations of Faculty and Graduate Student Misconduct"; John Brax-
ton & Alan Bayer, "Perceptions of Research Misconduct and an Analysis of Their
Correlates"; Mary Fox, "Scientific Misconduct and Editorial and Peer Review
Processes"; Mary Fox & John Braxton, "Misconduct and Social Control in Science:
Issues, Problems, Solutions"; Edward Hackett, "A Social Control Perspective on
Scientific Misconduct"; Karen Herman, Philip Sunshine, Montgomery Fisher,
James Zwolenik and Charles Herz, "Investigating Misconduct in Science: The
National Science Foundation Model"; Marcel LaFollette, "The Politics of Re-
search Misconduct: Congressional Oversight, Universities, and Science"; Alan
Price, "Definitions and Boundaries of Research Misconduct: Perspectives from a
Federal Government Viewpoint"; and Nicholas Steneck, "Research Universities
and Scientific Misconduct: History, Policies, and the Future."

Burke, April. "University Policies on Conflict of Interest and Delay of Publication: Report of the Clearinghouse on University-Industry Relations, Association of American Universities, February 1985," reprinted in 12 *J. Coll. & Univ. Law* 175 (1985). A survey of university policies on conflicts of interest and delays in publication of sponsored research. Offered as guidance for university administrators in formulating or reviewing policies of their own.

Eisenberg, Rebecca S. "Academic Freedom and Academic Values in Sponsored Research," 66 *Tex. L. Rev.* 1363 (1988). Examines the tripartite relationship among researchers, universities, and research sponsors. Identifies contemporary threats to academic values stemming from sponsored research and suggests that the "traditional American conception of academic freedom . . . is ill-adapted to the task of protecting academic values in sponsored research within universities." See also David M. Rabban, "Does Academic Freedom Limit Faculty Autonomy?" 66 *Tex. L. Rev.* 1405 (1988), responding to the Eisenberg article and disagreeing that there is any actual conflict between academic freedom and the academic values it was designed to advance.

Fairweather, James S. *Entrepreneurship and Higher Education: Lessons for Colleges, Universities, and Industry,* ERIC/Higher Education Research Report no. 6 (Association for the Study of Higher Education, 1988). Discusses economic and academic motivations of institutions competing for government- and corporate-sponsored research projects and the potential ramifications on academic freedom, property rights, facilities use, and recruitment of faculty and students. Provides a cost-benefit framework for use by institutions to determine whether to enter into sponsored-research contracts.

Fowler, Donald R. "University-Industry Research Relationships: The Research Agreement," 9 *J. Coll. & Univ. Law* 515 (1982-83). Identifies and suggests solutions to fifteen potential problems encountered in drafting research contracts between universities and industry. Agreement provisions discussed include the scope of the research project, control over the conduct of the contracted research, funding, receipt of sponsor's proprietary information, intellectual property rights, indemnification and hold-harmless clauses, and potential conflicts of interest.

Goldstein, Michael B. *Technology Transfer and Risk Management* (National Association of College and University Attorneys, 1990). A pamphlet full of practical advice on identifying and controlling legal and other risks an institution may face when involving itself in the transfer of technology to the marketplace. Includes checklists for risk management and a review of various structural models for institutional involvement in technology transfer.

Greene, Deirdre (ed.). *College and University Business Administration* (5th ed., National Association of College and University Business Officers, 1992), listed and described in the "General" section at the beginning of this chapter's bibliography. Includes an extensive chapter on "Research and Sponsored Programs" by Julie T. Norris (vol. 3, ch. 21), which explores ethical, financial, and contractual considerations and legal requirements for institutions engaging in sponsored research. Includes discussion of intellectual property and technology transfer as well as federal government certification requirements for matters such as use of animal and human subjects, biohazards, and lobbying activities.

Kertz, Consuela Lauda, & Hasson, James K. "University Research and Development Activities: The Federal Income Tax Consequences of Research Contracts, Research

Subsidiaries and Joint Ventures," 13 *J. Coll. & Univ. Law* 109 (1986). Analyzes tax considerations attaching to each of the structural arrangements through which colleges and universities may engage in income-generating research. Includes discussion of the several bases for exempting research income from the federal unrelated business income tax. Also discusses the problem of protecting the institution's (or subsidiary's) tax-exempt status.

Korn, Davie E. Note, "Patent and Trade Secret Protection in University-Industry Research Relationships in Biotechnology," 24 *Harvard J. on Legislation* 191 (1987). Balances the competitive interests of industry against the university's need for openness in research. Examines the university's options for retaining title to and licensing inventions, and the implications of each option for access to research data. Also discusses policies on publication delay to protect patent rights and policies on prior review of publications by research sponsors.

Maatz, Claire T. "Comment: University Physician-Researcher Conflicts of Interest: The Inadequacy of Current Controls and Proposed Reform," 7 *High Technology Law J.* 137 (1992). Examines the potential conflicts of interest of "physician-researchers" involved in industry-sponsored research projects, and the effects of such conflicts not only on the university's academic integrity but also on the rights, and sometimes health, of the physician's patients. Calls for universities and funding sources to adopt conflict-of-interest guidelines for the ultimate protection of the institution and human subjects used in the research. Discusses the inadequacies of legal remedies for patients injured in the research setting and proposes that universities institute full-disclosure requirements for researchers and establish mechanisms to monitor the research from beginning to end. Includes numerous footnote sources.

Rosenblum, Jerald E., and Fields, Kathy A. "Product Liability Risks of University Research Licensing and How They Affect Commercialization—Is It Time for a Legislative Solution?" 73 *J. Patent & Trademark Office Society* 514 (1991). Examines the effect of the Patent and Trademark Amendments of 1980, under which universities may own the patent on federally funded research results, on the exposure of universities to products liability lawsuits.

Shockley, Pat. "Availability of 'Trade Secret' Protection for University Research," 20 *J. Coll. & Univ. Law* 309 (1994). Analyzes the potential use of trade-secret jurisprudence to protect university-generated research. Discusses the effect of Freedom of Information Act requests on the secrecy of research and reviews state laws regarding protection of trade secrets.

Symposium, "Focus on Secrecy and University Research," 19 *J. Coll. & Univ. Law* 197 (1993). Includes the following articles: Peter M. Brody, "The First Amendment, Governmental Censorship, and Sponsored Research"; John Shattuck, "Secrecy on Campus"; Wade L. Robison & John T. Sanders, "The Myths of Academia: Open Inquiry and Funded Research"; and R. Robert Kreiser, "AAUP Perspectives on Academic Freedom and United States Intelligence Agencies." Topics include First Amendment rights of researchers and institutions, problems associated with accepting projects funded by intelligence agencies, and researchers' duties of loyalty in today's economically driven sponsored-research market. For other articles on the same types of concerns, developed from papers presented at the same conference, see Tom L. Beauchamp, "Ethical Issues in Funding and Monitoring University Research," 11 *Business & Professional Ethics J.* 5 (1992); Nicholas H. Steneck,

"Whose Academic Freedom Needs to Be Protected? The Case of Classified Research," 11 *Business & Professional Ethics J.* 17 (1992); and John T. Sanders & Wade L. Robison, "Research Funding and the Value-Dependence of Science," 11 *Business & Professional Ethics J.* 33 (1992).

Wiltbank, J. Kelly (ed.). *The Practical Aspects of Technology Transfer: A Legal Compendium* (National Association of College and University Attorneys, 1990). As the foreword states, this book gives a "sampling of the subject, from a philosophical overview to nuts-and-bolts ideas." Includes reprints of leading articles, conference papers, sample agreements, a summary of relevant statutes and regulations, and a selected bibliography of sources.

See Lachs entry in bibliography for Section 7.2.

Statute Index

◆ ◆ ◆

NOTE: All statutes are federal statutes unless otherwise indicated by designation of a state.

Case Index

◆ ◆ ◆

Subject Index

◆ ◆ ◆